Collins
French
Dictionary

HarperCollins Publishers
Westerhill Road
Bishopbriggs
Glasgow
G64 2QT
Great Britain

First Edition 2005

© HarperCollins Publishers 2005

ISBN 0-00-720320-9

Collins® and Bank of English® are
registered trademarks of
HarperCollins Publishers Limited

www.collins.co.uk

A catalogue record for this book is
available from the British Library

HarperCollins Publishers, Inc.
10 East 53rd Street, New York,
NY 10022

ISBN 0-06-074914-8

Library of Congress Cataloging-in-
Publication Data has been applied for

www.harpercollins.com

HarperCollins books may be
purchased for educational, business,
or sales promotional use. For
information, please write to:
Special Markets Department,
HarperCollins Publishers Inc., 10 East
53rd Street, New York, NY 10022

Typeset by Morton Word Processing
Ltd, Scarborough

Printed in Italy by Amadeus S.r.l.

Acknowledgements
We would like to thank those authors
and publishers who kindly gave
permission for copyright material to
be used in the Collins Word Web. We
would also like to thank Times
Newspapers Ltd for providing
valuable data.

editors/rédaction
Pierre-Henri Cousin • Lorna Sinclair Knight
Catherine E. Love • Jean-François Allain • Claude Nimmo
Bob Grossmith • Jean-Benoit Ormal-Grenon
Cécile Aubinière-Robb • Claire Calder • Christine Penman

editorial staff/secrétariat de rédaction
Val McNulty • John Podbielski

series editor/collection dirigée par
Lorna Sinclair Knight

William Collins' dream of knowledge for all began with the publication of his first book in 1819. A self-educated mill worker, he not only enriched millions of lives, but also founded a flourishing publishing house. Today, staying true to this spirit, Collins books are packed with inspiration, innovation, and practical expertise. They place you at the centre of a world of possibility and give you exactly what you need to explore it.

Language is the key to this exploration, and at the heart of Collins Dictionaries, is language as it is really used. New words, phrases, and meanings spring up every day, and all of them are captured and analysed by the Collins Word Web. Constantly updated, and with over 2.5 billion entries, this living language resource is unique to our dictionaries.

Words are tools for life. And a Collins Dictionary makes them work for you.

Collins. Do more.

INTRODUCTION

We are delighted that you have decided to buy this Collins French Dictionary, and hope you will enjoy and benefit from using it at home, at school, on holiday or at work.

The innovative use of colour guides you quickly and efficiently to the word you want, and the comprehensive wordlist provides a wealth of modern and idiomatic phrases not normally found in a dictionary this size.

In addition, the supplement provides you with guidance on using the dictionary, along with entertaining ways of improving your dictionary skills.

We hope that you will enjoy using it and that it will significantly enhance your language studies.

Note on trademarks

COMMENT UTILISER VOTRE ROBERT & COLLINS MINI

Les informations contenues dans ce dictionnaire sont présentées à l'aide de plusieurs polices de caractères, de symboles, abréviations, parenthèses et crochets. Les conventions et symboles utilisés sont expliqués dans les sections qui suivent.

Entrées

Les mots que vous cherchez dans le dictionnaire (les 'entrées') sont classés par ordre alphabétique. Ils sont imprimés en couleur pour pouvoir être repérés rapidement. Les deux entrées figurant en haut de page indiquent le premier et le dernier mot qui apparaissent sur la page en question.

Des informations sur l'emploi ou sur la forme de certaines entrées sont données entre parenthèses, après la transcription phonétique. Ces indications apparaissent sous forme abrégée et en italique (ex: (*fam*), (*COMM*)).

Plusieurs mots appartenant à la même famille peuvent être regroupés dans un même article. Dans la partie anglais-français et pour les préfixes de la partie français-anglais, la graphie de l'entrée principale est reprise par un tilde: ~ dans les sous-entrées (ex: **accept, ~ance**). Les sous-entrées apparaissent en caractères rouges, légèrement plus petits que ceux de l'entrée.

Les expressions courantes dans lesquelles apparaît l'entrée sont indiquées par des caractères romains gras (ex **avoir du retard**).

Transcription phonétique

La transcription phonétique symbolisant la prononciation de chaque entrée est indiquée entre crochets immédiatement après l'entrée (ex **fumer** [fyme]; **knead** [niːd]). La liste des symboles phonétiques figure aux pages xiii et xiv.

Traductions

Les traductions interchangeables sont séparées par une virgule; lorsque plusieurs sens coexistent, ces traductions sont séparées par un point-virgule. Vous trouverez souvent entre parenthèses d'autres mots en italique qui précèdent les traductions. Ces mots fournissent certains des contextes dans lesquels l'entrée est susceptible d'être utilisée (ex **rough** (*voice*) ou (*weather*)) ou offrent des synonymes (ex **rough** (*violent*)).

'Mots-clés'

Une importance particulière est accordée à certains mots français et anglais qui sont considérés comme des "mots-clés" dans chacune des langues. Cela peut être dû à leur utilisation très fréquente ou au fait qu'ils ont divers types d'usages (ex **vouloir, plus; get, that**). Une combinaison de losanges et de chiffres vous aident à distinguer différentes catégories grammaticales et différents sens. D'autres renseignements utiles apparaissent en italique et entre parenthèses dans la langue de l'utilisateur.

Données grammaticales

Les catégories grammaticales sont données sous forme abrégée et en italique après la transcription phonétique des entrées (ex *vt, adv, conj*).

Le genre des noms français est indiqué de la manière suivante: *nm* pour un nom masculin et *nf* pour un nom féminin. Le féminin et le pluriel irréguliers sont également indiqués (**directeur, trice; cheval, aux**).

Le masculin et le féminin des adjectifs sont mentionnés lorsque ces deux formes sont différentes (ex **noir, e**). Lorsque l'adjectif a un féminin ou un pluriel irrégulier, ces formes sont clairement indiquées (ex **net, nette**). Les pluriels irréguliers des noms et les formes irrégulières des verbes anglais sont indiqués entre parenthèses, avant la catégorie grammaticale (ex **man** ... (*pl* **men**) *n*; **give** (*pt* **gave**, *pp* **given**) *vt*).

USING YOUR COLLINS FRENCH DICTIONARY

A wealth of information is presented in the dictionary, using various typefaces, sizes of type, symbols, abbreviations and brackets. The conventions and symbols used are explained in the following sections.

Headwords

The words you look up in a dictionary — "headwords" — are listed alphabetically. They are printed in colour for rapid identification. The two headwords appearing at the top of each page indicate the first and last word dealt with on the page in question.

Information about the usage or form of certain headwords is given in brackets after the phonetic spelling. This usually appears in abbreviated form and in italics (e.g. *(fam)*, *(COMM)*).
Where appropriate, words related to headwords are grouped in the same entry (ronger, rongeur; accept, acceptance) in a slightly smaller coloured type than the headword.

Common expressions in which the headword appears are shown in black bold roman type (e.g. **avoir du retard**).

Phonetic spellings

The phonetic spelling of each headword (indicating its pronunciation) is given in square brackets immediately after the headword (e.g. fumer [fyme]; knead [ni:d]). A list of the phonetic symbols is given on pages xiii and xiv.

Translations

Headword translations are given in ordinary type and, where more than one meaning or usage exists, these are separated by a semi-colon. You will often find other words in italics in brackets before the translations. These offer suggested contexts in which the headword might appear (e.g. rough *(voice)* or *(weather)*) or provide synonyms (e.g. rough *(violent)*).

"Key" words

Special status is given to certain French and English words which are considered as "key" words in each language. They may, for example, occur very frequently or have several types of usage (e.g. vouloir, plus; get, that). A combination of lozenges and numbers helps you to distinguish different parts of speech and different meanings. Further helpful information is provided in brackets and in italics in the relevant language for the user.

Grammatical information

Parts of speech are given in abbreviated form in italics after the phonetic spellings of headwords (e.g. *vt, adv, conj*).

Genders of French nouns are indicated as follows: *nm* for a masculine and *nf* for a feminine noun. Feminine and irregular plural forms of nouns are also shown (**directeur, trice; cheval, aux**).

Adjectives are given in both masculine and feminine forms where these forms are different (e.g. **noir, e**). Clear information is provided where adjectives have an irregular feminine or plural form (e.g. **net, nette**).

adjectif, locution adjective	adj	adjective, adjectival phrase
abréviation	ab(b)r	abbreviation
adverbe, locution adverbiale	adv	adverb, adverbial phrase
administration	ADMIN	administration
agriculture	AGR	agriculture
anatomie	ANAT	anatomy
architecture	ARCHIT	architecture
article défini	art déf	definite article
article indéfini	art indéf	indefinite article
attribut	attrib	predicative
l'automobile	AUT(O)	the motor car and motoring
auxiliaire	aux	auxiliary
aviation, voyages aériens	AVIAT	flying, air travel
biologie	BIO(L)	biology
botanique	BOT	botany
anglais de Grande-Bretagne	BRIT	British English
commerce, finance, banque	COMM	commerce, finance, banking
comparatif	compar	comparative
informatique	COMPUT	computing
conditionnel	cond	conditional
chimie	CHEM	chemistry
conjonction	conj	conjunction
construction	CONSTR	building
nom utilisé comme adjectif, ne peut s'employer ni comme attribut, ni après le nom qualifié	cpd	compound element: used as an adjective and which cannot follow the noun it qualifies
cuisine, art culinaire	CULIN	cookery
article défini	def art	definite article
déterminant: article démonstratif ou indéfini etc	dét	determiner: article, demonstrative etc
diminutif	dimin	diminutive
économie	ECON	economics
électricité, électronique	ELEC	electricity, electronics
exclamation, interjection	excl	exclamation, interjection
féminin	f	feminine
langue familière (! emploi vulgaire)	fam(!)	informal usage (! very offensive)
emploi figuré	fig	figurative use
(verbe anglais) dont la particule est inséparable du verbe dans la plupart des sens	fus	(phrasal verb) where the particle cannot be separated from main verb in most or all senses
généralement	gén, gen	generally
géographie, géologie	GEO	geography, geology
géométrie	GEOM	geometry
impersonnel	impers	impersonal
article indéfini	indef art	indefinite article
langue familière (! emploi vulgaire)	inf(!)	informal usage (! particularly offensive)
infinitif	infin	infinitive
informatique	INFORM	computing

ABRÉVIATIONS ABBREVIATIONS

invariable	inv	invariable
irrégulier	irreg	irregular
domaine juridique	JUR	law
grammaire, linguistique	LING	grammar, linguistics
masculin	m	masculine
mathématiques, algèbre	MATH	mathematics, calculus
médecine	MÉD, MED	medical term, medicine
masculin ou féminin, suivant le sexe	m/f	either masculine or feminine depending on sex
domaine militaire, armée	MIL	military matters
musique	MUS	music
nom	n	noun
navigation, nautisme	NAVIG, NAUT	sailing, navigation
nom ou adjectif numéral	num	numeral adjective or noun
	o.s.	oneself
péjoratif	péj, pej	derogatory, pejorative
photographie	PHOT(O)	photography
physiologie	PHYSIOL	physiology
pluriel	pl	plural
politique	POL	politics
participe passé	pp	past participle
préposition	prép, prep	preposition
pronom	pron	pronoun
psychologie, psychiatrie	PSYCH	psychology, psychiatry
temps du passé	pt	past tense
quelque chose	qch	
quelqu'un	qn	
religions, domaine ecclésiastique	REL	religions, church service
	sb	somebody
enseignement, système scolaire et universitaire	SCOL	schooling, schools and universities
singulier	sg	singular
	sth	something
subjonctif	sub	subjunctive
sujet (grammatical)	su(b)j	(grammatical) subject
superlatif	superl	superlative
techniques, technologie	TECH	technical term, technology
télécommunications	TEL	telecommunications
télévision	TV	television
typographie	TYP(O)	typography, printing
anglais des USA	US	American English
verbe	vb	verb
verbe ou groupe verbal à fonction intransitive	vi	verb or phrasal verb used intransitively
verbe ou groupe verbal à fonction transitive	vt	verb or phrasal verb used transitively
zoologie	ZOOL	zoology
marque déposée	®	registered trademark
indique une équivalence culturelle	≈	introduces a cultural equivalent

TRANSCRIPTION PHONÉTIQUE

CONSONNES

CONSONANTS

NB. **p, b, t, d, k, g** sont suivis
d'une aspiration en anglais.

NB. **p, b, t, d, k, g** are not
aspirated in French.

pou*p*ée	p	*pu*ppy
*b*om*b*e	b	*b*a*b*y
*t*en*t*e *t*hermal	t	*t*en*t*
*d*in*d*e	d	*d*a*dd*y
*c*o*q* *qu*i *k*épi	k	*c*ork *k*iss *ch*ord
*g*a*g* ba*gu*e	g	*g*ag *gu*ess
*s*ale *c*e na*t*ion	s	*s*o ri*c*e ki*ss*
*z*éro ro*s*e	z	cou*s*in bu*zz*
ta*ch*e *ch*at	ʃ	*sh*eep *s*ugar
*g*ilet *j*uge	ʒ	plea*s*ure bei*g*e
	tʃ	*ch*urch
	dʒ	*j*udge *g*eneral
*f*er *ph*are	f	*f*arm ra*ff*le
*v*al*v*e	v	*v*ery re*v*
	θ	*th*in ma*th*s
	ð	*th*at o*th*er
*l*ent sa*ll*e	l	*l*ittle ba*ll*
*r*are *r*ent*r*er	R	
	r	*r*at ra*r*e
*m*a*m*an fe*mm*e	m	*m*u*mm*y co*m*b
*n*on *n*o*nn*e	n	*n*o ra*n*
a*gn*eau vi*gn*e	ɲ	
	ŋ	si*ng*ing ba*n*k
*h*op!	h	*h*at re*h*eat
*y*eux pa*ill*e p*i*ed	j	*y*et
n*ou*er *ou*i	w	*w*all be*w*ail
*h*uile l*u*i	ɥ	
	x	lo*ch*

DIVERS

MISCELLANEOUS

pour l'anglais: le r final se
prononce en liaison devant
une voyelle

ˈ

in English transcription:
final r can be pronounced
before a vowel

pour l'anglais: précède la
syllabe accentuée

ˌ

in French wordlist and
transcription: no liaison

PHONETIC TRANSCRIPTION

Voyelles

NB. La mise en équivalence de certains sons n'indique qu'une ressemblance approximative.

ici v*ie* l*y*re	i i:	
	ɪ	
jou*er* ét*é*	e	
l*ai*t jou*e*t merci	ɛ	
pl*a*t *a*mour	a	
b*a*s p*â*te	ɑ ɑ:	
	ʌ	
l*e* pr*e*mier	ə	
b*eu*rre p*eu*r	œ	
p*eu* d*eu*x	ø ɜ:	
*o*r h*o*mme	ɒ	
m*o*t *eau* g*au*che	o ɔ:	
gen*ou* r*ou*e	u ʊ	
	u:	
r*ue* *u*rne	y	

Diphtongues

ɪə	
ɛə	
eɪ	
aɪ	
aʊ	
əʊ	
ɔɪ	
ʊə	

Nasales

mat*in* pl*ein*	ɛ̃
br*un*	œ̃
s*ang* *an* d*ans*	ɑ̃
n*on* p*on*t	ɔ̃

Vowels

NB. The pairing of some vowel sounds only indicates approximate equivalence.

h*ee*l b*ea*d	
h*i*t p*i*ty	
s*e*t t*e*nt	
b*a*t *a*pple	
*a*fter c*a*r c*a*lm	
f*u*n c*ou*sin	
*o*ver *a*bove	
*u*rn f*e*rn w*o*rk	
w*a*sh p*o*t	
b*o*rn c*o*rk	
f*u*ll s*oo*t	
b*oo*n l*ew*d	

Diphthongs

b*ee*r t*ie*r
t*ea*r f*ai*r th*e*re
d*a*te pl*ai*ce d*ay*
l*i*fe b*uy* c*ry*
*ow*l f*ou*l n*ow*
l*ow* n*o*
b*oi*l b*oy* *oi*ly
p*oo*r t*ou*r

Nasal Vowels

xiv

A, a

a [a] *vb voir* **avoir**

MOT-CLÉ

à [a] (*à* + *le* = **au**, *à* + *les* = **aux**) *prép* **1**
(*endroit, situation*) at, in; **être à Paris/au
Portugal** to be in Paris/Portugal; **être à la
maison/à l'école** to be at home/at
school; **à la campagne** in the country;
c'est à 10 km/20 minutes (d'ici) it's
10 km/20 minutes away

2 (*direction*) to; **aller à Paris/au Portugal**
to go to Paris/Portugal; **aller à la
maison/à l'école** to go home/to school;
à la campagne to the country

3 (*temps*): **à 3 heures/minuit** at 3
o'clock/midnight; **au printemps/mois de
juin** in the spring/the month of June

4 (*attribution, appartenance*) to; **le livre est
à Paul/à lui/à nous** this book is Paul's/
his/ours; **donner qch à qn** to give sth to
sb

5 (*moyen*) with; **se chauffer au gaz** to
have gas heating; **à bicyclette** on a *ou* by
bicycle; **à la main/machine** by hand/
machine

6 (*provenance*) from; **boire à la bouteille**
to drink from the bottle

7 (*caractérisation, manière*): **l'homme aux
yeux bleus** the man with the blue eyes;
à la russe the Russian way

8 (*but, destination*): **tasse à café** coffee
cup; **maison à vendre** house for sale

9 (*rapport, évaluation, distribution*): **100
km/unités à l'heure** 100 km/units per
ou an hour; **payé à l'heure** paid by the
hour; **cinq à six** five to six

---

abaisser [abese] *vt* to lower, bring down;
(*manette*) to pull down; **s'~** *vi* to go
down; (*fig*) to demean o.s.

abandon [abɑ̃dɔ̃] *nm* abandoning; giving
up; withdrawal; **être à l'~** to be in a state
of neglect

abandonner [abɑ̃dɔne] *vt* (*personne*) to
abandon; (*projet, activité*) to abandon,
give up; (*SPORT*) to retire *ou* withdraw
from; (*céder*) to surrender; **s'~ à** (*paresse,
plaisirs*) to give o.s. up to

abasourdir [abazuʀdiʀ] *vt* to stun, stagger

abat-jour [abaʒuʀ] *nm inv* lampshade

abats [aba] *nmpl* (*de bœuf, porc*) offal *sg*;
(*de volaille*) giblets

abattement [abatmɑ̃] *nm*: **~ fiscal** ≈ tax
allowance

abattoir [abatwaʀ] *nm* slaughterhouse

abattre [abatʀ] *vt* (*arbre*) to cut down, fell;
(*mur, maison*) to pull down; (*avion, personne*) to shoot down; (*animal*) to shoot,
kill; (*fig*) to wear out, tire out; to demoral-
ize; **s'~** *vi* to crash down; **ne pas se
laisser ~** to keep one's spirits up, not to
let things get one down; **s'~ sur** to beat
down on; (*fig*) to rain down on

abbaye [abei] *nf* abbey

abbé [abe] *nm* priest; (*d'une abbaye*) abbot

abcès [apsɛ] *nm* abscess

abdiquer [abdike] *vi* to abdicate

abdominaux [abdɔmino] *nmpl*: **faire des
~** to do exercises for one's abdominals,
do one's abdominals

abeille [abɛj] *nf* bee

aberrant, e [abeʀɑ̃, ɑ̃t] *adj* absurd

aberration [abeʀasjɔ̃] *nf* aberration

abêtir [abetiʀ] *vt* to make morons of (*ou* a
moron of)

abîme [abim] *nm* abyss, gulf

abîmer [abime] *vt* to spoil, damage; **s'~**

vi to get spoilt *ou* damaged

ablation [ablasjɔ̃] *nf* removal

aboiement [abwamɑ̃] *nm* bark, barking

abois [abwa] *nmpl*: **aux ~** at bay

abolir [abɔliʀ] *vt* to abolish

abominable [abɔminabl] *adj* abominable

abondance [abɔ̃dɑ̃s] *nf* abundance

abondant, e [abɔ̃dɑ̃, ɑ̃t] *adj* plentiful, abundant, copious; **abonder** *vi* to abound, be plentiful; **abonder dans le sens de qn** to concur with sb

abonné, e [abɔne] *nm/f* subscriber; season ticket holder

abonnement [abɔnmɑ̃] *nm* subscription; (*transports, concerts*) season ticket

abonner [abɔne] *vt*: **s'~ à** to subscribe to, take out a subscription to

abord [abɔʀ] *nm*: **au premier ~** at first sight, initially; **~s** *nmpl* (*environs*) surroundings; **d'~** first

abordable [abɔʀdabl] *adj* (*prix*) reasonable; (*personne*) approachable

aborder [abɔʀde] *vi* to land ♦ *vt* (*sujet, difficulté*) to tackle; (*personne*) to approach; (*rivage etc*) to reach

aboutir [abutiʀ] *vi* (*négociations etc*) to succeed; **~ à** to end up at; **n'~ à rien** to come to nothing

aboyer [abwaje] *vi* to bark

abréger [abʀeʒe] *vt* to shorten

abreuver [abʀœve]: **s'~** *vi* to drink; **abreuvoir** *nm* watering place

abréviation [abʀevjasjɔ̃] *nf* abbreviation

abri [abʀi] *nm* shelter; **être à l'~** to be under cover; **se mettre à l'~** to shelter

abricot [abʀiko] *nm* apricot

abriter [abʀite] *vt* to shelter; **s'~** *vt* to shelter, take cover

abrupt, e [abʀypt] *adj* sheer, steep; (*ton*) abrupt

abruti, e [abʀyti] *adj* stunned, dazed ♦ *nm/f* (*fam*) idiot, moron; **~ de travail** overworked

absence [apsɑ̃s] *nf* absence; (*MÉD*) blackout; **avoir des ~s** to have mental blanks

absent, e [apsɑ̃, ɑ̃t] *adj* absent ♦ *nm/f* absentee; **absenter: s'absenter** *vi* to take time off work; (*sortir*) to leave, go out

absolu, e [apsɔly] *adj* absolute; **absolument** *adv* absolutely

absorbant, e [apsɔʀbɑ̃, ɑ̃t] *adj* absorbent

absorber [apsɔʀbe] *vt* to absorb; (*gén MÉD: manger, boire*) to take

abstenir [apstəniʀ] *vb*: **s'~ de qch/de faire** to refrain from sth/from doing

abstraction [apstʀaksjɔ̃] *nf* abstraction

abstrait, e [apstʀɛ, ɛt] *adj* abstract

absurde [apsyʀd] *adj* absurd

abus [aby] *nm* abuse; **~ de confiance** breach of trust; **abuser** *vi* to go too far, overstep the mark; **abuser de** (*duper*) to take advantage of; **abusif, -ive** *adj* exorbitant; (*punition*) excessive

acabit [akabi] *nm*: **de cet ~** of that type

académie [akademi] *nf* academy; (*SCOL: circonscription*) ≈ regional education authority

---

Académie française

ⓘ The **Académie française** was founded by Cardinal Richelieu in 1635 during the reign of Louis XIII. It consists of forty elected scholars and writers who are known as "les Quarante" or "les Immortels". One of the Académie's functions is to regulate the development of the French language and its recommendations are frequently the subject of lively public debate. It has produced several editions of its famous dictionary and awards various literary prizes.

---

acajou [akaʒu] *nm* mahogany

acariâtre [akaʀjatʀ] *adj* cantankerous

accablant, e [akablɑ̃, ɑ̃t] *adj* (*chaleur*) oppressive; (*témoignage, preuve*) overwhelming

accablement [akabləmɑ̃] *nm* despondency

accabler [akable] *vt* to overwhelm, overcome; **~ qn d'injures** to heap *ou* shower abuse on sb

accalmie [akalmi] *nf* lull

accaparer [akapaʀe] *vt* to monopolize; (*suj: travail etc*) to take up (all) the time *ou* attention of

accéder [aksede]: **~ à** *vt* (*lieu*) to reach; (*accorder: requête*) to grant, accede to

accélérateur [akseleʀatœʀ] *nm* accelerator

accélération [akseleʀasjɔ̃] *nf* acceleration

accélérer [akseleʀe] *vt* to speed up ♦ *vi* to accelerate

accent [aksɑ̃] *nm* accent; (*PHONÉTIQUE, fig*) stress; **mettre l'~ sur** (*fig*) to stress; **~ aigu/grave/circonflexe** acute/grave/circumflex accent; **accentuer** *vt* (*LING*) to accent; (*fig*) to accentuate, emphasize; **s'accentuer** *vi* to become more marked *ou* pronounced

acceptation [akseptasjɔ̃] *nf* acceptance

accepter [aksepte] *vt* to accept; **~ de faire** to agree to do

accès [akse] *nm* (*à un lieu*) access; (*MÉD: de toux*) fit; (*de fièvre*) bout; **d'~ facile** easily accessible; **facile d'~** easy to get to; **~ de colère** fit of anger; **accessible** *adj* accessible; (*livre, sujet*): **accessible à qn** within the reach of sb

accessoire [akseswaʀ] *adj* secondary; incidental ♦ *nm* accessory; (*THÉÂTRE*) prop

accident [aksidɑ̃] *nm* accident; **par ~** by chance; **~ de la route** road accident; **~ du travail** industrial injury *ou* accident; **accidenté, e** *adj* damaged; injured; (*relief, terrain*) uneven; hilly; **accidentel, le** *adj* accidental

acclamations [aklamasjɔ̃] *nfpl* cheers

acclamer [aklame] *vt* to cheer, acclaim

acclimater [aklimate]: **s'~** *vi* (*personne*) to adapt (o.s.)

accolade [akɔlad] *nf* (*amicale*) embrace; (*signe*) brace

accommodant, e [akɔmɔdɑ̃, ɑ̃t] *adj* accommodating, easy-going

accommoder [akɔmɔde] *vt* (*CULIN*) to prepare; **s'~ de** *vt* to put up with; (*se contenter de*) to make do with

accompagnateur, -trice [akɔ̃paɲatœʀ, tʀis] *nm/f* (*MUS*) accompanist; (*de voyage: guide*) guide; (*de voyage organisé*) courier

accompagner [akɔ̃paɲe] *vt* to accompany, be *ou* go *ou* come with; (*MUS*) to accompany

accompli, e [akɔ̃pli] *adj* accomplished

accomplir [akɔ̃pliʀ] *vt* (*tâche, projet*) to carry out; (*souhait*) to fulfil; **s'~** *vi* to be fulfilled

accord [akɔʀ] *nm* agreement; (*entre des styles, tons etc*) harmony; (*MUS*) chord; **d'~!** OK!; **se mettre d'~** to come to an agreement; **être d'~ (pour faire qch)** to agree (to do sth)

accordéon [akɔʀdeɔ̃] *nm* (*MUS*) accordion

accorder [akɔʀde] *vt* (*faveur, délai*) to grant; (*harmoniser*) to match; (*MUS*) to tune; **s'~** *vt* to get on together; to agree

accoster [akɔste] *vt* (*NAVIG*) to draw alongside ♦ *vi* to berth

accotement [akɔtmɑ̃] *nm* verge (*BRIT*), shoulder

accouchement [akuʃmɑ̃] *nm* delivery, (child)birth; labour

accoucher [akuʃe] *vi* to give birth, have a baby; **~ d'un garçon** to give birth to a boy; **accoucheur** *nm:* (**médecin**) **accoucheur** obstetrician

accouder [akude]: **s'~** *vi* to rest one's elbows on/against; **accoudoir** *nm* armrest

accoupler [akuple] *vt* to couple; (*pour la reproduction*) to mate; **s'~** *vt* to mate

accourir [akuʀiʀ] *vi* to rush *ou* run up

accoutrement [akutʀəmɑ̃] (*péj*) *nm* (*tenue*) outfit

accoutumance [akutymɑ̃s] *nf* (*gén*) adaptation; (*MÉD*) addiction

accoutumé, e [akutyme] *adj* (*habituel*) customary, usual

accoutumer [akutyme] *vt:* **s'~ à** to get accustomed *ou* used to

accréditer [akʀedite] *vt* (*nouvelle*) to substantiate

accroc [akʀo] *nm* (*déchirure*) tear; (*fig*) hitch, snag

accrochage [akrɔʃaʒ] *nm* (*AUTO*) collision; (*dispute*) clash, brush

accrocher [akrɔʃe] *vt* (*fig*) to catch, attract; **s'~** (*se disputer*) to have a clash *ou* brush; **~ qch à** (*suspendre*) to hang sth (up) on; (*attacher: remorque*) to hitch sth (up) to; **~ qch à** (*déchirer*) to catch sth (on); **~ un passant** (*heurter*) to hit a pedestrian; **s'~ à** (*rester pris à*) to catch on; (*agripper, fig*) to hang on *ou* cling to

accroissement [akrwasmã] *nm* increase

accroître [akrwatr] *vt*: **s'~** *vi* to increase

accroupir [akrupiʀ]: **s'~** *vi* to squat, crouch (down)

accru, e [akry] *pp de* **accroître**

accueil [akœj] *nm* welcome; **comité d'~** reception committee; **accueillir** *vt* to welcome; (*aller chercher*) to meet, collect

acculer [akyle] *vt*: **~ qn à** *ou* **contre** to drive sb back against

accumuler [akymyle] *vt* to accumulate, amass; **s'~** *vi* to accumulate; to pile up

accusation [akyzasjɔ̃] *nf* (*gén*) accusation; (*JUR*) charge; (*partie*): **l'~** the prosecution

accusé, e [akyze] *nm/f* accused; defendant; **~ de réception** acknowledgement of receipt

accuser [akyze] *vt* to accuse; (*fig*) to emphasize, bring out; to show; **~ qn de** to accuse sb of; (*JUR*) to charge sb with; **~ réception de** to acknowledge receipt of

acerbe [asɛʀb] *adj* caustic, acid

acéré, e [asere] *adj* sharp

acharné, e [aʃaʀne] *adj* (*efforts*) relentless; (*lutte, adversaire*) fierce, bitter

acharner [aʃaʀne] *vb*: **s'~ contre** to set o.s. against; (*suj: malchance*) to dog; **s'~ à faire** to try doggedly to do; (*persister*) to persist in doing

achat [aʃa] *nm* purchase; **faire des ~s** to do some shopping; **faire l'~ de qch** to purchase sth

acheminer [aʃ(ə)mine] *vt* (*courrier*) to forward, dispatch; **s'~ vers** to head for

acheter [aʃ(ə)te] *vt* to buy, purchase; (*soudoyer*) to buy; **~ qch à** (*marchand*) to buy *ou* purchase sth from; (*ami etc: offrir*) to buy sth for; **acheteur, -euse** *nm/f* buyer; shopper; (*COMM*) buyer

achever [aʃ(ə)ve] *vt* to complete, finish; (*blessé*) to finish off; **s'~** *vi* to end

acide [asid] *adj* sour, sharp; (*CHIMIE*) acid(ic) ♦ *nm* (*CHIMIE*) acid; **acidulé, e** *adj* slightly acid

acier [asje] *nm* steel; **aciérie** *nf* steelworks *sg*

acné [akne] *nf* acne

acolyte [akɔlit] (*péj*) *nm* associate

acompte [akɔ̃t] *nm* deposit

à-côté [akote] *nm* side-issue; (*argent*) extra

à-coup [aku] *nm*: **par ~~s** by fits and starts

acoustique [akustik] *nf* (*d'une salle*) acoustics *pl*

acquéreur [akerœr] *nm* buyer, purchaser

acquérir [akeriʀ] *vt* to acquire

acquis, e [aki, iz] *pp de* **acquérir** ♦ *nm* (accumulated) experience; **son aide nous est ~e** we can count on her help

acquit [aki] *vb voir* **acquérir** ♦ *nm* (*quittance*) receipt; **par ~ de conscience** to set one's mind at rest

acquitter [akite] *vt* (*JUR*) to acquit; (*facture*) to pay, settle; **s'~ de** *vt* (*devoir*) to discharge; (*promesse*) to fulfil

âcre [akr] *adj* acrid, pungent

acrobate [akrɔbat] *nm/f* acrobat; **acrobatie** *nf* acrobatics *sg*

acte [akt] *nm* act, action; (*THÉÂTRE*) act; **prendre ~ de** to note, take note of; **faire ~ de candidature** to apply; **faire ~ de présence** to put in an appearance; **~ de naissance** birth certificate

acteur [aktœr] *nm* actor

actif, -ive [aktif, iv] *adj* active ♦ *nm* (*COMM*) assets *pl*; (*fig*): **avoir à son ~** to have to one's credit; **population active** working population

action [aksjɔ̃] *nf* (*gén*) action; (*COMM*) share; **une bonne ~** a good deed; **actionnaire** *nm/f* shareholder; **actionner** *vt* (*mécanisme*) to activate; (*machine*) to operate

activer [aktive] *vt* to speed up; **s'~** *vi* to bustle about; to hurry up

activité [aktivite] *nf* activity; **en ~** (*volcan*) active; (*fonctionnaire*) in active life

actrice [aktʀis] *nf* actress

actualiser [aktɥalize] *vt* to bring up to date

actualité [aktɥalite] *nf* (*d'un problème*) topicality; (*événements*) **l'~** current events; **les ~s** *nfpl* (*CINÉMA, TV*) the news; **d'~** topical

actuel, le [aktɥɛl] *adj* (*présent*) present; (*d'actualité*) topical; **à l'heure ~le** at the present time; **actuellement** *adv* at present, at the present time

acuité [akɥite] *nf* acuteness

acuponcteur [akypɔ̃ktœʀ] *nm* acupuncturist

acuponcture [akypɔ̃ktyʀ] *nf* acupuncture

adaptateur [adaptatœʀ] *nm* (*ÉLEC*) adapter

adapter [adapte] *vt* to adapt; **s'~ (à)** (*suj: personne*) to adapt (to); **~ qch à** (*approprier*) to adapt sth to (fit); **~ qch sur/dans/à** (*fixer*) to fit sth on/into/to

additif [aditif] *nm* additive

addition [adisjɔ̃] *nf* addition; (*au café*) bill; **additionner** *vt* to add (up)

adepte [adɛpt] *nm/f* follower

adéquat, e [adekwa(t), at] *adj* appropriate, suitable

adhérent, e [adeʀɑ̃, ɑ̃t] *nm/f* member

adhérer [adeʀe]: **~ à** *vt* (*coller*) to adhere *ou* stick to; (*se rallier à*) to join; **adhésif, -ive** *adj* adhesive, sticky; **ruban adhésif** sticky *ou* adhesive tape; **adhésion** *nf* joining; (*fait d'être membre*) membership; (*accord*) support

adieu, x [adjø] *excl* goodbye ♦ *nm* farewell

adjectif [adʒɛktif] *nm* adjective

adjoindre [adʒwɛ̃dʀ] *vt*: **~ qch à** to attach sth to; (*ajouter*) to add sth to; **s'~** *vt* (*collaborateur etc*) to take on, appoint; **adjoint, e** *nm/f* assistant; **adjoint au maire** deputy mayor; **directeur adjoint** assistant

manager

adjudant [adʒydɑ̃] *nm* (*MIL*) warrant officer

adjuger [adʒyʒe] *vt* (*prix, récompense*) to award; (*lors d'une vente*) to auction (off); **s'~** *vt* to take for o.s.

adjurer [adʒyʀe] *vt*: **~ qn de faire** to implore *ou* beg sb to do

admettre [admɛtʀ] *vt* (*laisser entrer*) to admit; (*candidat: SCOL*) to pass; (*tolérer*) to allow, accept; (*reconnaître*) to admit, acknowledge

administrateur, -trice [administratœʀ, tʀis] *nm/f* (*COMM*) director; (*ADMIN*) administrator

administration [administʀasjɔ̃] *nf* administration; **l'A~** ≈ the Civil Service

administrer [administʀe] *vt* (*firme*) to manage, run; (*biens, remède, sacrement etc*) to administer

admirable [admiʀabl] *adj* admirable, wonderful

admirateur, -trice [admiʀatœʀ, tʀis] *nm/f* admirer

admiration [admiʀasjɔ̃] *nf* admiration

admirer [admiʀe] *vt* to admire

admis, e [admi, iz] *pp de* **admettre**

admissible [admisibl] *adj* (*candidat*) eligible; (*comportement*) admissible, acceptable

admission [admisjɔ̃] *nf* admission; acknowledgement; **demande d'~** application for membership

ADN *sigle m* (= *acide désoxyribonucléique*) DNA

adolescence [adɔlesɑ̃s] *nf* adolescence

adolescent, e [adɔlesɑ̃, ɑ̃t] *nm/f* adolescent, teenager

adonner [adɔne]: **s'~ à** *vt* (*sport*) to devote o.s. to; (*boisson*) to give o.s. over to

adopter [adɔpte] *vt* to adopt; **adoptif, -ive** *adj* (*parents*) adoptive; (*fils, patrie*) adopted

adorable [adɔʀabl] *adj* delightful, adorable

adorer [adɔʀe] *vt* to adore; (*REL*) to worship

adosser [adose] *vt*: **~ qch à** *ou* **contre** to stand sth against; **s'~ à** *ou* **contre** to lean with one's back against

adoucir [adusir] *vt* (*goût, température*) to make milder; (*avec du sucre*) to sweeten; (*peau, voix*) to soften; (*caractère*) to mellow

adresse [adres] *nf* (*domicile*) address; (*dextérité*) skill, dexterity; **~ électronique** email address

adresser [adrese] *vt* (*lettre: expédier*) to send; (: *écrire l'adresse sur*) to address; (*injure, compliments*) to address; **s'~ à** (*parler à*) to speak to, address; (*s'informer auprès de*) to go and see; (: *bureau*) to enquire at; (*suj: livre, conseil*) to be aimed at; **~ la parole à** to speak to, address

adroit, e [adrwa, wat] *adj* skilful, skilled

adulte [adylt] *nm/f* adult, grown-up ♦ *adj* (*chien, arbre*) fully-grown, mature; (*attitude*) adult, grown-up

adultère [adylter] *nm* (*acte*) adultery

advenir [advənir] *vi* to happen

adverbe [adverb] *nm* adverb

adversaire [adverser] *nm/f* (SPORT, *gén*) opponent, adversary

adverse [advers] *adj* opposing

aération [aerasjɔ̃] *nf* airing; (*circulation de l'air*) ventilation

aérer [aere] *vt* to air; (*fig*) to lighten; **s'~** *vi* to get some (fresh) air

aérien, ne [aerjɛ̃, jɛn] *adj* (AVIAT) air *cpd*, aerial; (*câble, métro*) overhead; (*fig*) light; **compagnie ~ne** airline

aéro... [aero] *préfixe*: **aérobic** *nm* aerobics *sg*; **aérogare** *nf* airport (buildings); (*en ville*) air terminal; **aéroglisseur** *nm* hovercraft; **Aéronavale** *nf* ≈ Fleet Air Arm (BRIT), ≈ Naval Air Force (US); **aérophagie** *nf* (MÉD) wind, aerophagia (MÉD); **aéroport** *nm* airport; **aéroporté, e** *adj* airborne, airlifted; **aérosol** *nm* aerosol

affable [afabl] *adj* affable

affaiblir [afeblir] *vt*: **s'~** *vi* to weaken

affaire [afer] *nf* (*problème, question*) matter; (*criminelle, judiciaire*) case; (*scandaleuse etc*)

affair; (*entreprise*) business; (*marché, transaction*) deal; business *no pl*; (*occasion intéressante*) bargain; **~s** *nfpl* (*intérêts publics et privés*) affairs; (*activité commerciale*) business *sg*; (*effets personnels*) things, belongings; **ce sont mes ~s** (*cela me concerne*) that's my business; **ça fera l'~** that will do (nicely); **se tirer d'~** to sort it *ou* things out for o.s.; **avoir ~ à** (*être en contact*) to be dealing with; **les A~s étrangères** Foreign Affairs; **affairer: s'affairer** *vi* to busy o.s., bustle about

affaisser [afese]: **s'~** *vi* (*terrain, immeuble*) to subside, sink; (*personne*) to collapse

affaler [afale] *vb*: **s'~ (dans/sur)** to collapse *ou* slump (into/onto)

affamé, e [afame] *adj* starving

affectation [afektasjɔ̃] *nf* (*nomination*) appointment; (*manque de naturel*) affectation

affecter [afekte] *vt* to affect; **~ qch à** to allocate *ou* allot sth to; **~ qn à** to appoint sb to; (*diplomate*) to post sb to

affectif, -ive [afektif, iv] *adj* emotional

affection [afeksjɔ̃] *nf* affection; (*mal*) ailment; **affectionner** *vt* to be fond of; **affectueux, -euse** *adj* affectionate

affermir [afermir] *vt* to consolidate, strengthen; (*muscles*) to tone up

affichage [afiʃaʒ] *nm* billposting; (*électronique*) display

affiche [afiʃ] *nf* poster; (*officielle*) notice; (THÉÂTRE) bill

afficher [afiʃe] *vt* (*affiche*) to put up; (*réunion*) to put up a notice about; (*électroniquement*) to display; (*fig*) to exhibit, display; **"défense d'~"** "stick no bills"

affilée [afile]: **d'~** *adv* at a stretch

affiler [afile] *vt* to sharpen

affilier [afilje]: **s'~ à** *vt* (*club, société*) to join

affiner [afine] *vt* to refine

affirmatif, -ive [afirmatif, iv] *adj* affirmative

affirmation [afirmasjɔ̃] *nf* assertion

affirmer [afirme] *vt* to assert

affligé, e [afliʒe] *adj* distressed, grieved; **~**

de (*maladie, tare*) afflicted with
affliger [aflize] *vt* (*peiner*) to distress, grieve
affluence [aflyɑ̃s] *nf* crowds *pl*; **heures d'~** rush hours; **jours d'~** busiest days
affluent [aflyɑ̃] *nm* tributary
affluer [aflye] *vi* (*secours, biens*) to flood in, pour in; (*sang*) to rush, flow
affolant, e [afɔlɑ̃, ɑ̃t] *adj* frightening
affolement [afɔlmɑ̃] *nm* panic
affoler [afɔle] *vt* to throw into a panic; **s'~** *vi* to panic
affranchir [afRɑ̃ʃiR] *vt* to put a stamp *ou* stamps on, (*à la machine*) to frank (*BRIT*), meter (*US*); (*fig*) to free, liberate; **affranchissement** *nm* postage
affréter [afRete] *vt* to charter
affreux, -euse [afRø, øz] *adj* dreadful, awful
affront [afRɔ̃] *nm* affront; **affrontement** *nm* clash, confrontation
affronter [afRɔ̃te] *vt* to confront, face
affubler [afyble] (*péj*) *vt*: **~ qn de** to rig *ou* deck sb out in
affût [afy] *nm*: **à l'~ (de)** (*gibier*) lying in wait (for); (*fig*) on the look-out (for)
affûter [afyte] *vt* to sharpen, grind
afin [afɛ̃]: **~ que** *conj* so that, in order that; **~ de faire** in order to do, so as to do
africain, e [afRikɛ̃, ɛn] *adj*, *nm/f* African
Afrique [afRik] *nf*: **l'~** Africa; **l'~ du Sud** South Africa
agacer [agase] *vt* to irritate
âge [aʒ] *nm* age; **quel ~ as-tu?** how old are you?; **prendre de l'~** to be getting on (in years); **âgé, e** *adj* old, elderly; **âgé de 10 ans** 10 years old
agence [aʒɑ̃s] *nf* agency, office; (*succursale*) branch; **~ de voyages** travel agency; **~ immobilière** estate (*BRIT*) *ou* real estate (*US*) agent's (office)
agencer [aʒɑ̃se] *vt* to put together; (*local*) to arrange, lay out
agenda [aʒɛ̃da] *nm* diary
agenouiller [aʒ(ə)nuje]: **s'~** *vi* to kneel (down)

agent [aʒɑ̃] *nm* (*aussi*: **~ de police**) policeman; (*ADMIN*) official, officer; **~ d'assurances** insurance broker
agglomération [aglɔmeRasjɔ̃] *nf* town; built-up area; **l'~ parisienne** the urban area of Paris
aggloméré [aglɔmeRe] *nm* (*bois*) chipboard
aggraver [agRave]: **s'~** *vi* to worsen
agile [aʒil] *adj* agile, nimble
agir [aʒiR] *vi* to act; **il s'agit de** (*ça traite de*) it is about; (*il est important de*) it's a matter *ou* question of
agitation [aʒitasjɔ̃] *nf* (hustle and) bustle; (*trouble*) agitation, excitement; (*politique*) unrest, agitation
agité, e [aʒite] *adj* fidgety, restless; (*troublé*) agitated, perturbed; (*mer*) rough
agiter [aʒite] *vt* (*bouteille, chiffon*) to shake; (*bras, mains*) to wave; (*préoccuper, exciter*) to perturb; **s'~** *vi* (*enfant, élève*) to fidget
agneau, x [aɲo] *nm* lamb
agonie [agɔni] *nf* mortal agony, death pangs *pl*; (*fig*) death throes *pl*
agrafe [agRaf] *nf* (*de vêtement*) hook, fastener; (*de bureau*) staple; **agrafer** *vt* to fasten; to staple; **agrafeuse** *nf* stapler
agrandir [agRɑ̃diR] *vt* to enlarge; **s'~** *vi* (*ville, famille*) to grow, expand; (*trou, écart*) to get bigger; **agrandissement** *nm* (*PHOTO*) enlargement
agréable [agReabl] *adj* pleasant, nice
agréé, e [agRee] *adj*: **concessionnaire ~** registered dealer
agréer [agRee] *vt* (*requête*) to accept; **~ à** to please, suit; **veuillez ~ ...** (*formule épistolaire*) yours faithfully
agrégation [agRegasjɔ̃] *nf* highest teaching diploma in France; **agrégé, e** *nm/f* holder of the *agrégation*
agrément [agRemɑ̃] *nm* (*accord*) consent, approval; **agrémenter** *vt* to embellish, adorn
agresser [agRese] *vt* to attack; **agresseur** *nm* aggressor, attacker; (*POL, MIL*) aggressor; **agressif, -ive** *adj* aggressive

agricole [agʀikɔl] *adj* agricultural; **agri-culteur** *nm* farmer; **agriculture** *nf* agri-culture, farming

agripper [agʀipe] *vt* to grab, clutch; **s'~ à** to cling (on) to, clutch, grip

agroalimentaire [agʀoalimɑ̃tɛʀ] *nm* farm-produce industry

agrumes [agʀym] *nmpl* citrus fruit(s)

aguerrir [ageʀiʀ] *vt* to harden

aguets [age] *nmpl*: **être aux ~** to be on the look out

aguicher [agiʃe] *vt* to entice

ahuri, e [ayʀi] *adj* (*stupéfait*) flabbergasted

ai [e] *vb voir* **avoir**

aide [ed] *nm/f* assistant; carer ♦ *nf* assis-tance, help; (*secours financier*) aid; **à l'~ de** (*avec*) with the help *ou* aid of; **appeler (qn) à l'~** to call for help (from sb); **~ fa-miliale** home help, mother's help; **~ judi-ciaire** ♦ *nf* legal aid; **~ sociale** ♦ *nf* (*assis-tance*) state aid; **aide-mémoire** *nm inv* memoranda pages *pl*; (*key facts*) hand-book; **aide-soignant, e** *nm/f* auxiliary nurse

aider [ede] *vt* to help; **s'~ de** (*se servir de*) to use, make use of

aie *etc* [e] *vb voir* **avoir**

aïe [aj] *excl* ouch!

aïeul, e [ajœl] *nm/f* grandparent, grandfather(-mother)

aïeux [ajø] *nmpl* grandparents; (*ancêtres*) forebears, forefathers

aigle [egl] *nm* eagle

aigre [egʀ] *adj* sour, sharp; (*fig*) sharp, cut-ting; **aigre-doux, -ce** *adj* (*sauce*) sweet and sour; **aigreur** *nf* sourness; sharpness; **aigreurs d'estomac** heartburn *sg*; **aigrir** *vt* (*personne*) to embitter; (*caractère*) to sour

aigu, ë [egy] *adj* (*objet, douleur*) sharp; (*son, voix*) high-pitched, shrill; (*note*) high(-pitched)

aiguille [eguij] *nf* needle; (*de montre*) hand; **~ à tricoter** knitting needle

aiguiller [eguije] *vt* (*orienter*) to direct; **ai-guilleur du ciel** *nm* air-traffic controller

aiguillon [eguijɔ̃] *nm* (*d'abeille*) sting; **aiguillonner** *vt* to spur *ou* goad on

aiguiser [egize] *vt* to sharpen; (*fig*) to stimulate; (: *sens*) to excite

ail [aj, o] *nm* garlic

aile [ɛl] *nf* wing; **aileron** *nm* (*de requin*) fin; **ailier** *nm* winger

aille *etc* [aj] *vb voir* **aller**

ailleurs [ajœʀ] *adv* elsewhere, somewhere else; **partout/nulle part ~** everywhere/ nowhere else; **d'~** (*du reste*) moreover, besides; **par ~** (*d'autre part*) moreover, furthermore

aimable [ɛmabl] *adj* kind, nice

aimant [ɛmɑ̃] *nm* magnet

aimer [eme] *vt* to love; (*d'amitié, affection, par goût*) to like; · (*souhait*): **j'~ais ...** I would like ...; **bien ~ qn/qch** to like sb/ sth; **j'~ais mieux faire** I'd much rather do

aine [ɛn] *nf* groin

aîné, e [ene] *adj* elder, older; (*le plus âgé*) eldest, oldest ♦ *nm/f* oldest child *ou* one, oldest boy *ou* son/girl *ou* daughter

ainsi [ɛ̃si] *adv* (*de cette façon*) like this, in this way, thus; (*ce faisant*) thus ♦ *conj* thus, so; **~ que** (*comme*) (just) as; (*et aus-si*) as well as; **pour ~ dire** so to speak; **et ~ de suite** and so on

aïoli [ajɔli] *nm* garlic mayonnaise

air [ɛʀ] *nm* air; (*mélodie*) tune; (*expression*) look, air; **prendre l'~** to get some (fresh) air; **avoir l'~** (*sembler*) to look, appear; **avoir l'~ de** to look like; **avoir l'~ de fai-re** to look as though one is doing, appear to be doing; **en l'~** (*promesses*) empty

aisance [ɛzɑ̃s] *nf* ease; (*richesse*) affluence

aise [ɛz] *nf* comfort; **être à l'~** *ou* **à son ~** to be comfortable; (*pas embarrassé*) to be at ease; (*financièrement*) to be comfortably off; **se mettre à l'~** to make o.s. com-fortable; **être mal à l'~** to be uncomfort-able; (*gêné*) to be ill at ease; **en faire à son ~** to do as one likes; **aisé, e** *adj* easy; (*assez riche*) well-to-do, well-off

aisselle [ɛsɛl] *nf* armpit

ait [ɛ] *vb voir* **avoir**

ajonc [aʒɔ̃] *nm* gorse *no pl*

ajourner [aʒuʀne] *vt* (*réunion*) to adjourn; (*décision*) to defer, postpone

ajouter [aʒute] *vt* to add

ajusté, e [aʒyste] *adj*: **bien ~** (*robe etc*) close-fitting

ajuster [aʒyste] *vt* (*régler*) to adjust; (*vêtement*) to alter; (*coup de fusil*) to aim; (*cible*) to aim at; (*TECH, gén: adapter*): **~ qch à** to fit sth to

alarme [alaʀm] *nf* alarm; **donner l'~** to give *ou* raise the alarm; **alarmer** *vt* to alarm; **s'alarmer** *vi* to become alarmed; **alarmiste** *adj, nm/f* alarmist

album [albɔm] *nm* album

albumine [albymin] *nf* albumin; **avoir de l'~** to suffer from albuminuria

alcool [alkɔl] *nm*: **l'~** alcohol; **un ~** a spirit, a brandy; **bière sans ~** non-alcoholic *ou* alcohol-free beer; **~ à brûler** methylated spirits (*BRIT*), wood alcohol (*US*); **~ à 90°** surgical spirit; **alcoolique** *adj, nm/f* alcoholic; **alcoolisé, e** *adj* alcoholic; **une boisson non alcoolisée** a soft drink; **alcoolisme** *nm* alcoholism; **alcootest** ® *nm* Breathalyser ®; (*test*) breath-test

aléas [alea] *nmpl* hazards; **aléatoire** *adj* uncertain; (*INFORM*) random

alentour [alãtuʀ] *adv* around, round about; **~s** *nmpl* (*environs*) surroundings; **aux ~s de** in the vicinity *ou* neighbourhood of, round about; (*temps*) round about

alerte [alɛʀt] *adj* agile, nimble; brisk, lively ♦ *nf* alert; warning; **~ à la bombe** bomb scare; **alerter** *vt* to alert

algèbre [alʒɛbʀ] *nf* algebra

Alger [alʒe] *n* Algiers

Algérie [alʒeʀi] *nf*: **l'~** Algeria; **algérien, ne** *adj* Algerian ♦ *nm/f*: **Algérien, ne** Algerian

algue [alg] *nf* (*gén*) seaweed *no pl*; (*BOT*) alga

alibi [alibi] *nm* alibi

aliéné, e [aljene] *nm/f* insane person, lunatic (*péj*)

aligner [aliɲe] *vt* to align, line up; (*idées, chiffres*) to string together; (*adapter*): **~ qch sur** to bring sth into alignment with; **s'~** (*soldats etc*) to line up; **s'~ sur** (*POL*) to align o.s. on

aliment [alimã] *nm* food; **alimentaire** *adj*: **denrées alimentaires** foodstuffs; **alimentation** *nf* (*commerce*) food trade; (*magasin*) grocery store; (*régime*) diet; (*en eau etc, de moteur*) supplying; (*INFORM*) feed; **alimenter** *vt* to feed; (*TECH*): **alimenter (en)** to supply (with); to feed (with); (*fig*) to sustain, keep going

alinéa [alinea] *nm* paragraph

aliter [alite]: **s'~** *vi* to take to one's bed

allaiter [alete] *vt* to (breast-)feed, nurse; (*suj: animal*) to suckle

allant [alã] *nm* drive, go

alléchant, e [aleʃã, ãt] *adj* (*odeur*) mouth-watering; (*offre*) enticing

allécher [aleʃe] *vt*: **~ qn** to make sb's mouth water; to tempt *ou* entice sb

allée [ale] *nf* (*de jardin*) path; (*en ville*) avenue, drive; **~s et venues** comings and goings

allégé, e [aleʒe] *adj* (*yaourt etc*) low-fat

alléger [aleʒe] *vt* (*voiture*) to make lighter; (*chargement*) to lighten; (*souffrance*) to alleviate, soothe

allègre [a(l)lɛgʀ] *adj* lively, cheerful

alléguer [a(l)lege] *vt* to put forward (as proof *ou* an excuse)

Allemagne [alman] *nf*: **l'~** Germany; **allemand, e** *adj* German ♦ *nm/f*: **Allemand, e** German ♦ *nm* (*LING*) German

aller [ale] *nm* (*trajet*) outward journey; (*billet: aussi*: **~ simple**) single (*BRIT*) *ou* one-way (*US*) ticket ♦ *vi* (*gén*) to go; **~ à** (*convenir*) to suit; (*suj: forme, pointure etc*) to fit; **~ (bien) avec** (*couleurs, style etc*) to go (well) with; **je vais y ~/me fâcher** I'm going to go/to get angry; **~ voir** to go and see, go to see; **allez!** come on!; **allons!** come now!; **comment allez-vous?**

how are you?; **comment ça va?** how are you?; (*affaires etc*) how are things?; **il va bien/mal** he's well/not well, he's fine/ill; **ça va bien/mal** (*affaires etc*) it's going well/not going well; ~ **mieux** to be better; **s'en ~** (*partir*) to be off, go, leave; (*disparaître*) to go away; ~ **retour** return journey (*BRIT*), round trip; (*billet*) return (ticket) (*BRIT*), round trip ticket (*US*)

allergique [alɛʀʒik] *adj*: ~ **à** allergic to

alliage [aljaʒ] *nm* alloy

alliance [aljɑ̃s] *nf* (*MIL, POL*) alliance; (*bague*) wedding ring

allier [alje] *vt* (*POL, gén*) to ally; (*fig*) to combine; **s'~** to become allies; to combine

allô [alo] *excl* hullo, hallo

allocation [alɔkasjɔ̃] *nf* allowance; ~ **(de) chômage** unemployment benefit; ~**s familiales** ≃ child benefit

allocution [a(l)lɔkysjɔ̃] *nf* short speech

allonger [alɔ̃ʒe] *vt* to lengthen, make longer; (*étendre: bras, jambe*) to stretch (out); **s'~** *vi* to get longer; (*se coucher*) to lie down, stretch out; ~ **le pas** to hasten one's step(s)

allouer [alwe] *vt* to allocate, allot

allumage [alymaʒ] *nm* (*AUTO*) ignition

allume-cigare [alymsigaʀ] *nm inv* cigar lighter

allumer [alyme] *vt* (*lampe, phare, radio*) to put *ou* switch on; (*pièce*) to put *ou* switch the light(s) on in; (*feu*) to light; **s'~** *vi* (*lumière, lampe*) to come *ou* go on

allumette [alymɛt] *nf* match

allure [alyʀ] *nf* (*vitesse*) speed, pace; (*démarche*) walk; (*aspect, air*) look; **avoir de l'~** to have style; **à toute ~** at top speed

allusion [a(l)lyzjɔ̃] *nf* allusion; (*sousentendu*) hint; **faire ~ à** to allude *ou* refer to; to hint at

---

MOT-CLÉ

alors [alɔʀ] *adv* **1** (*à ce moment-là*) then, at that time; **il habitait alors à Paris** he lived in Paris at that time

2 (*par conséquent*) then; **tu as fini? alors je m'en vais** have you finished? I'm going then; **et alors?** so what?; **alors que** *conj* **1** (*au moment où*) when, as; **il est arrivé alors que je partais** he arrived as I was leaving

2 (*pendant que*) while, when; **alors qu'il était à Paris, il a visité ...** while *ou* when he was in Paris, he visited ...

3 (*tandis que*) whereas, while; **alors que son frère travaillait dur, lui se reposait** while his brother was working hard, HE would rest

---

alouette [alwɛt] *nf* (sky)lark

alourdir [aluʀdiʀ] *vt* to weigh down, make heavy

aloyau [alwajo] *nm* sirloin

Alpes [alp] *nfpl*: **les ~** the Alps

alphabet [alfabɛ] *nm* alphabet; (*livre*) ABC (book); **alphabétique** *adj* alphabetical; **alphabétiser** *vt* to teach to read and write; (*pays*) to eliminate illiteracy in

alpinisme [alpinism] *nm* mountaineering, climbing; **alpiniste** *nm/f* mountaineer, climber

Alsace [alzas] *nf* Alsace; **alsacien, ne** *adj* Alsatian ♦ *nm/f*: **Alsacien, ne** Alsatian

altérer [alteʀe] *vt* (*vérité*) to distort; **s'~** *vi* to deteriorate

alternateur [altɛʀnatœʀ] *nm* alternator

alternatif, -ive [altɛʀnatif, iv] *adj* alternating; **alternative** *nf* (*choix*) alternative; **alternativement** *adv* alternately; **alterner** *vi* to alternate

Altesse [altɛs] *nf* Highness

altitude [altityd] *nf* altitude, height

alto [alto] *nm* (*instrument*) viola

aluminium [alyminjɔm] *nm* aluminium (*BRIT*), aluminum (*US*)

amabilité [amabilite] *nf* kindness

amadouer [amadwe] *vt* to mollify, soothe

amaigrir [amegʀiʀ] *vt* to make thin(ner); **amaigrissant, e** *adj* (*régime*) slimming

amalgame [amalgam] (*péj*) *nm* (strange) mixture

amande [amɑ̃d] *nf* (*de l'amandier*) almond; **amandier** *nm* almond (tree)

amant [amɑ̃] *nm* lover

amarrer [amaʀe] *vt* (NAVIG) to moor; (*gén*) to make fast

amas [amɑ] *nm* heap, pile; **amasser** *vt* to amass; **s'amasser** *vi* (*foule*) to gather

amateur [amatœʀ] *nm* amateur; **en ~** (*péj*) amateurishly; **~ de musique/sport** *etc* music/sport lover

amazone [amazon] *nf*: **en ~** sidesaddle

ambassade [ɑ̃basad] *nf* embassy; **l'~ de France** the French Embassy; **ambassadeur, -drice** *nm/f* ambassador(-dress)

ambiance [ɑ̃bjɑ̃s] *nf* atmosphere

ambiant, e [ɑ̃bjɑ̃, jɑ̃t] *adj* (*air, milieu*) surrounding; (*température*) ambient

ambigu, ë [ɑ̃bigy] *adj* ambiguous

ambitieux, -euse [ɑ̃bisjø, jøz] *adj* ambitious

ambition [ɑ̃bisjɔ̃] *nf* ambition

ambulance [ɑ̃bylɑ̃s] *nf* ambulance; **ambulancier, -ière** *nm/f* ambulance man/woman (BRIT), paramedic (US)

ambulant, e [ɑ̃bylɑ̃, ɑ̃t] *adj* travelling, itinerant

âme [ɑm] *nf* soul

amélioration [ameljɔʀasjɔ̃] *nf* improvement

améliorer [ameljɔʀe] *vt* to improve; **s'~** *vi* to improve, get better

aménager [amenaʒe] *vt* (*agencer, transformer*) to fit out; to lay out; (: *quartier, territoire*) to develop; (*installer*) to fix up, put in; **ferme aménagée** converted farmhouse

amende [amɑ̃d] *nf* fine; **faire ~ honorable** to make amends

amener [am(ə)ne] *vt* to bring; (*causer*) to bring about; **s'~** *vi* to show up (*fam*), turn up

amenuiser [amənɥize]: **s'~** *vi* (*chances*) to grow slimmer, lessen

amer, amère [amɛʀ] *adj* bitter

américain, e [ameʀikɛ̃, ɛn] *adj* American ♦ *nm/f*: **A~, e** American

Amérique [ameʀik] *nf*: **l'~** America; **l'~ centrale/latine** Central/Latin America; **l'~ du Nord/du Sud** North/South America

amertume [amɛʀtym] *nf* bitterness

ameublement [amœblamɑ̃] *nm* furnishing; (*meubles*) furniture

ameuter [amøte] *vt* (*peuple*) to rouse

ami, e [ami] *nm/f* friend; (*amant/maîtresse*) boyfriend/girlfriend ♦ *adj*: **pays/groupe ~** friendly country/group

amiable [amjabl]: **à l'~** *adv* (JUR) out of court; (*gén*) amicably

amiante [amjɑ̃t] *nm* asbestos

amical, e, -aux [amikal, o] *adj* friendly; **amicalement** *adv* in a friendly way; (*formule épistolaire*) regards

amidon [amidɔ̃] *nm* starch

amincir [amɛ̃siʀ] *vt*: **~ qn** to make sb thinner *ou* slimmer; (*suj: vêtement*) to make sb look slimmer

amincissant, e [amɛ̃sisɑ̃, ɑ̃t] *adj*: **régime ~** (slimming) diet; **crème ~e** slimming cream

amiral, -aux [amiʀal, o] *nm* admiral

amitié [amitje] *nf* friendship; **prendre en ~** to befriend; **~s, Christèle** best wishes, Christèle; **présenter ses ~s à qn** to send sb one's best wishes

ammoniaque [amɔnjak] *nf* ammonia (water)

amnistie [amnisti] *nf* amnesty

amoindrir [amwɛ̃dʀiʀ] *vt* to reduce

amollir [amɔliʀ] *vt* to soften

amonceler [amɔ̃s(ə)le] *vt* to pile *ou* heap up; **s'~** *vi* to pile *ou* heap up; (*fig*) to accumulate

amont [amɔ̃]: **en ~** *adv* upstream

amorce [amɔʀs] *nf* (*sur un hameçon*) bait; (*explosif*) cap; primer; priming; (*fig: début*) beginning(s), start; **amorcer** *vt* to start

amorphe [amɔʀf] *adj* passive, lifeless

amortir [amɔʀtiʀ] *vt* (*atténuer: choc*) to absorb, cushion; (*bruit, douleur*) to deaden; (COMM: *dette*) to pay off; **~ un achat** to make a purchase pay for itself; **amortisseur** *nm* shock absorber

amour [amuʀ] _nm_ love; **faire l'~** to make love; **amouracher: s'amouracher de** (_péj_) _vt_ to become infatuated with; **amoureux, -euse** _adj_ (_regard, tempéra-ment_) amorous; (_vie, problèmes_) love _cpd_; (_personne_): **amoureux (de qn)** in love (with sb) ♦ _nmpl_ courting couple(s); **amour-propre** _nm_ self-esteem, pride

amovible [amɔvibl] _adj_ removable, de-tachable

ampère [ɑ̃pɛʀ] _nm_ amp(ere)

amphithéâtre [ɑ̃fiteɑtʀ] _nm_ am-phitheatre; (_d'université_) lecture hall _ou_ theatre

ample [ɑ̃pl] _adj_ (_vêtement_) roomy, ample; (_gestes, mouvement_) broad; (_ressources_) ample; **amplement** _adv_: **c'est ample-ment suffisant** that's more than enough; **ampleur** _nf_ (_de dégâts, problème_) extent

amplificateur [ɑ̃plifikatœʀ] _nm_ amplifier

amplifier [ɑ̃plifje] _vt_ (_fig_) to expand, in-crease

ampoule [ɑ̃pul] _nf_ (_électrique_) bulb; (_de médicament_) phial; (_aux mains, pieds_) blis-ter; **ampoulé, e** (_péj_) _adj_ pompous, bombastic

amputer [ɑ̃pyte] _vt_ (_MÉD_) to amputate; (_fig_) to cut _ou_ reduce drastically

amusant, e [amyzɑ̃, ɑ̃t] _adj_ (_divertissant, spirituel_) entertaining, amusing; (_comique_) funny, amusing

amuse-gueule [amyzgœl] _nm inv_ appe-tizer, snack

amusement [amyzmɑ̃] _nm_ (_divertissement_) amusement; (_jeu etc_) pastime, diversion

amuser [amyze] _vt_ (_divertir_) to entertain, amuse; (_égayer, faire rire_) to amuse; **s'~** _vi_ (_jouer_) to play; (_se divertir_) to enjoy o.s., have fun; (_fig_) to mess around

amygdale [amidal] _nf_ tonsil

an [ɑ̃] _nm_ year; **avoir quinze ~s** to be fifteen (years old); **le jour de l'~, le pre-mier de l'~, le nouvel ~** New Year's Day

analogique [analɔʒik] _adj_ (_INFORM, montre_) analog

analogue [analɔg] _adj_: **~ (à)** analogous

(to), similar (to)

analphabète [analfabɛt] _nm/f_ illiterate

analyse [analiz] _nf_ analysis; (_MÉD_) test; **analyser** _vt_ to analyse; to test

ananas [anana(s)] _nm_ pineapple

anarchie [anaʀʃi] _nf_ anarchy

anatomie [anatɔmi] _nf_ anatomy

ancêtre [ɑ̃sɛtʀ] _nm/f_ ancestor

anchois [ɑ̃ʃwa] _nm_ anchovy

ancien, ne [ɑ̃sjɛ̃, jɛn] _adj_ old; (_de jadis, de l'antiquité_) ancient; (_précédent, ex-_) former, old; (_par l'expérience_) senior ♦ _nm/f_ (_dans une tribu_) elder; **~-combattant** ♦ _nm_ war veteran; **anciennement** _adv_ formerly; **ancienneté** _nf_ (_ADMIN_) (length of) ser-vice; (_privilèges obtenus_) seniority

ancre [ɑ̃kʀ] _nf_ anchor; **jeter/lever l'~** to cast/weigh anchor; **ancrer** _vt_ (_CONSTR: câble etc_) to anchor; (_fig_) to fix firmly

Andorre [ɑ̃dɔʀ] _nf_ Andorra

andouille [ɑ̃duj] _nf_ (_CULIN_) sausage made of chitterlings; (_fam_) clot, nit

âne [ɑn] _nm_ donkey, ass; (_péj_) dunce

anéantir [aneɑ̃tiʀ] _vt_ to annihilate, wipe out; (_fig_) to obliterate, destroy

anémie [anemi] _nf_ anaemia; **anémique** _adj_ anaemic

ânerie [ɑnʀi] _nf_ stupidity; (_parole etc_) stu-pid _ou_ idiotic comment _etc_

anesthésie [anɛstezi] _nf_ anaesthesia; **faire une ~ locale/générale à qn** to give sb a local/general anaesthetic

ange [ɑ̃ʒ] _nm_ angel; **être aux ~s** to be over the moon

angélus [ɑ̃ʒelys] _nm_ angelus; (_cloches_) evening bells _pl_

angine [ɑ̃ʒin] _nf_ throat infection; **~ de poitrine** angina

anglais, e [ɑ̃glɛ, ɛz] _adj_ English ♦ _nm/f:_ **A~, e** Englishman(-woman) ♦ _nm_ (_LING_) English; **les A~** the English; **filer à l'~e** to take French leave

angle [ɑ̃gl] _nm_ angle; (_coin_) corner; **~ droit** right angle

Angleterre [ɑ̃glətɛʀ] _nf:_ **l'~** England

anglo... [ɑ̃glɔ] _préfixe_ Anglo-, anglo(-);

anglophone *adj* English-speaking

angoisse [ɑ̃gwas] *nf* anguish, distress; **angoissé, e** *adj* (*personne*) distressed; **angoisser** *vt* to harrow, cause anguish to ♦ *vi* to worry, fret

anguille [ɑ̃gij] *nf* eel

anicroche [anikʀɔʃ] *nf* hitch, snag

animal, e, -aux [animal, o] *adj, nm* animal

animateur, -trice [animatœʀ, tʀis] *nm/f* (*de télévision*) host; (*de groupe*) leader, organizer

animation [animasjɔ̃] *nf* (*voir animé*) busyness; liveliness; (*CINÉMA: technique*) animation; **~s culturelles** cultural activities

animé, e [anime] *adj* (*lieu*) busy, lively; (*conversation, réunion*) lively, animated

animer [anime] *vt* (*ville, soirée*) to liven up; (*mener*) to lead; **s'~** *vi* to liven up

anis [ani(s)] *nm* (*CULIN*) aniseed; (*BOT*) anise

ankyloser [ɑ̃kiloze] : **s'~** *vi* to get stiff

anneau, x [ano] *nm* (*de rideau, bague*) ring; (*de chaîne*) link

année [ane] *nf* year

annexe [anɛks] *adj* (*problème*) related; (*document*) appended; (*salle*) adjoining ♦ *nf* (*bâtiment*) annex(e); (*jointe à une lettre*) enclosure

anniversaire [anivɛʀsɛʀ] *nm* birthday; (*d'un événement, bâtiment*) anniversary

annonce [anɔ̃s] *nf* announcement; (*signe, indice*) sign; (*aussi*: **~ publicitaire**) advertisement; **les petites ~s** the classified advertisements, the small ads

annoncer [anɔ̃se] *vt* to announce; (*être le signe de*) to herald; **s'~ bien/difficile** to look promising/difficult; **annonceur, -euse** *nm/f* (*publicitaire*) advertiser; (*TV, RADIO: speaker*) announcer

annuaire [anɥɛʀ] *nm* yearbook, annual; **~ téléphonique** (telephone) directory, phone book

annuel, le [anɥɛl] *adj* annual, yearly

annuité [anɥite] *nf* annual instalment

annulation [anylasjɔ̃] *nf* cancellation

annuler [anyle] *vt* (*rendez-vous, voyage*) to cancel, call off; (*jugement*) to quash (*BRIT*), repeal (*US*); (*MATH, PHYSIQUE*) to cancel out

anodin, e [anɔdɛ̃, in] *adj* (*blessure*) harmless; (*détail*) insignificant, trivial

anonymat [anɔnima] *nm* anonymity

anonyme [anɔnim] *adj* anonymous; (*fig*) impersonal

ANPE *sigle f* (= *Agence nationale pour l'emploi*) national employment agency

anorexie [anɔʀɛksi] *nf* anorexia

anormal, e, -aux [anɔʀmal, o] *adj* abnormal

anse [ɑ̃s] *nf* (*de panier, tasse*) handle

antan [ɑ̃tɑ̃]: **d'~** *adj* of long ago

antarctique [ɑ̃taʀktik] *adj* Antarctic ♦ *nm*: **l'A~** the Antarctic

antécédents [ɑ̃tesedɑ̃] *nmpl* (*MÉD etc*) past history *sg*

antenne [ɑ̃tɛn] *nf* (*de radio*) aerial; (*d'insecte*) antenna, feeler; (*poste avancé*) outpost; (*petite succursale*) sub-branch; **passer à l'~** to go on the air

antérieur, e [ɑ̃teʀjœʀ] *adj* (*d'avant*) previous, earlier; (*de devant*) front

anti... [ɑ̃ti] *préfixe* anti...; **antialcoolique** *adj* anti-alcohol; **antiatomique** *adj*: **abri antiatomique** fallout shelter; **antibiotique** *nm* antibiotic; **antibrouillard** *adj*: **phare antibrouillard** fog lamp (*BRIT*) *ou* light (*US*)

anticipation [ɑ̃tisipasjɔ̃] *nf*: **livre/film d'~** science fiction book/film

anticipé, e [ɑ̃tisipe] *adj*: **avec mes remerciements ~s** thanking you in advance *ou* anticipation

anticiper [ɑ̃tisipe] *vt* (*événement, coup*) to anticipate, foresee

anti...: anticonceptionnel, le *adj* contraceptive; **anticorps** *nm* antibody; **antidépresseur** *nm* antidepressant; **antidote** *nm* antidote; **antigel** *nm* antifreeze; **antihistaminique** *nm* antihistamine

antillais, e [ɑ̃tijɛ, ɛz] *adj* West Indian, Caribbean ♦ *nm/f*: **A~, e** West Indian, Caribbean

Antilles [ɑ̃tij] *nfpl*: **les ~** the West Indies

antilope [ɑ̃tilɔp] *nf* antelope
anti...: **antimite(s)** *adj*, *nm*: **(produit) antimite(s)** mothproofer; moth repellent; **antipathique** *adj* unpleasant, disagreeable; **antipelliculaire** *adj* anti-dandruff
antipodes [ɑ̃tipɔd] *nmpl* (*fig*): **être aux ~ de** to be the opposite extreme of
antiquaire [ɑ̃tikɛʀ] *nm/f* antique dealer
antique [ɑ̃tik] *adj* antique; (*très vieux*) ancient, antiquated; **antiquité** *nf* (*objet*) antique; **l'Antiquité** Antiquity; **magasin d'antiquités** antique shop
anti...: **antirabique** *adj* rabies *cpd*; **antirouille** *adj inv* anti-rust *cpd*; **antisémite** *adj* anti-Semitic; **antiseptique** *adj*, *nm* antiseptic; **antivol** *adj*, *nm*: **(dispositif) antivol** anti-theft device
antre [ɑ̃tʀ] *nm* den, lair
anxiété [ɑ̃ksjete] *nf* anxiety
anxieux, -euse [ɑ̃ksjø, jøz] *adj* anxious, worried
AOC *sigle f* (= *appellation d'origine contrôlée*) label guaranteeing the quality of wine

┌─────────────────────┐
│   **AOC**   │
└─────────────────────┘

i AOC *is the highest French wine classification. It indicates that the wine meets strict requirements concerning the vineyard of origin, the type of vine grown, the method of production, and the volume of alcohol present.*

août [u(t)] *nm* August
apaiser [apeze] *vt* (*colère, douleur*) to soothe; (*personne*) to calm (down), pacify; **s'~** *vi* (*tempête, bruit*) to die down, subside; (*personne*) to calm down
apanage [apanaʒ] *nm*: **être l'~ de** to be the privilege *ou* prerogative of
aparté [aparte] *nm* (*entretien*) private conversation; **en ~** in an aside
apathique [apatik] *adj* apathetic
apatride [apatʀid] *nm/f* stateless person
apercevoir [apɛʀsəvwaʀ] *vt* to see; **s'~ de** *vt* to notice; **s'~ que** to notice that
aperçu [apɛʀsy] *nm* (*vue d'ensemble*) general survey

apéritif [aperitif] *nm* (*boisson*) aperitif; (*réunion*) drinks *pl*
à-peu-près [apøpʀɛ] (*péj*) *nm inv* vague approximation
apeuré, e [apœʀe] *adj* frightened, scared
aphte [aft] *nm* mouth ulcer
apiculture [apikyltyʀ] *nf* beekeeping, apiculture
apitoyer [apitwaje] *vt* to move to pity; **s'~ (sur)** to feel pity (for)
aplanir [aplaniʀ] *vt* to level; (*fig*) to smooth away, iron out
aplatir [aplatiʀ] *vt* to flatten; **s'~** *vi* to become flatter; (*écrasé*) to be flattened; **s'~ devant qn** (*fig*: *s'humilier*) to crawl to sb
aplomb [aplɔ̃] *nm* (*équilibre*) balance, equilibrium; (*fig*) self-assurance; nerve; **d'~** steady
apogée [apɔʒe] *nm* (*fig*) peak, apogee
apologie [apɔlɔʒi] *nf* vindication, praise
a posteriori [apɔsteʀjɔʀi] *adv* after the event
apostrophe [apɔstʀɔf] *nf* (*signe*) apostrophe
apostropher [apɔstʀɔfe] *vt* (*interpeller*) to shout at, address sharply
apothéose [apɔteoz] *nf* pinnacle (of achievement); (*MUS*) grand finale
apôtre [apotʀ] *nm* apostle
apparaître [apaʀɛtʀ] *vi* to appear
apparat [apaʀa] *nm*: **tenue d'~** ceremonial dress
appareil [apaʀɛj] *nm* (*outil, machine*) piece of apparatus, device; (*électrique, ménager*) appliance; (*avion*) (aero)plane, aircraft *inv*; (*téléphonique*) phone; (*dentier*) brace (*BRIT*), braces (*US*); **"qui est à l'~?"** "who's speaking?"; **dans le plus simple ~** in one's birthday suit; **appareiller** *vi* (*NAVIG*) to cast off, get under way ♦ *vt* (*assortir*) to match up; **appareil(-photo)** *nm* camera
apparemment [apaʀamɑ̃] *adv* apparently
apparence [apaʀɑ̃s] *nf* appearance; **en ~** apparently

apparent, e [apaʀã, ãt] *adj* visible; (*évident*) obvious; (*superficiel*) apparent

apparenté, e [apaʀãte] *adj*: ~ **à** related to; (*fig*) similar to

apparition [apaʀisjɔ̃] *nf* appearance; (*surnaturelle*) apparition

appartement [apaʀtəmã] *nm* flat (*BRIT*), apartment (*US*)

appartenir [apaʀtəniʀ]: ~ **à** *vt* to belong to; **il lui appartient de** it is his duty to

apparu, e [apaʀy] *pp de* **apparaître**

appât [apa] *nm* (*PÊCHE*) bait; (*fig*) lure, bait; **appâter** *vt* to lure

appauvrir [apovʀiʀ] *vt* to impoverish

appel [apɛl] *nm* call; (*nominal*) roll call; (: *SCOL*) register; (*MIL: recrutement*) call-up; **faire ~ à** (*invoquer*) to appeal to; (*avoir recours à*) to call on; (*nécessiter*) to call for, require; **faire ~** (*JUR*) to appeal; **faire l'~** to call the roll; to call the register; **sans ~** (*fig*) final, irrevocable; ~ **d'offres** (*COMM*) invitation to tender; **faire un ~ de phares** to flash one's headlights; ~ **(téléphonique)** (tele)phone call

appelé [ap(ə)le] *nm* (*MIL*) conscript

appeler [ap(ə)le] *vt* to call; (*faire venir: médecin etc*) to call, send for; **s'~** *vi*: **elle s'appelle Gabrielle** her name is Gabrielle, she's called Gabrielle; **comment ça s'appelle?** what is it called?; **être appelé à** (*fig*) to be destined to

appendice [apẽdis] *nm* appendix; **appendicite** *nf* appendicitis

appentis [apãti] *nm* lean-to

appesantir [apəzãtiʀ]: **s'~** *vi* to grow heavier; **s'~ sur** (*fig*) to dwell on

appétissant, e [apetisã, ãt] *adj* appetizing, mouth-watering

appétit [apeti] *nm* appetite; **bon ~!** enjoy your meal!

applaudir [aplodiʀ] *vt* to applaud ♦ *vi* to applaud, clap; **applaudissements** *nmpl* applause *sg*, clapping *sg*

application [aplikasjɔ̃] *nf* application

applique [aplik] *nf* wall lamp

appliquer [aplike] *vt* to apply; (*loi*) to enforce; **s'~** *vi* (*élève etc*) to apply o.s.; **s'~ à** to apply to

appoint [apwɛ̃] *nm* (*extra*) contribution *ou* help; **chauffage d'~** extra heating

appointements [apwɛ̃tmã] *nmpl* salary *sg*

apport [apɔʀ] *nm* (*approvisionnement*) supply; (*contribution*) contribution

apporter [apɔʀte] *vt* to bring

apposer [apoze] *vt* (*signature*) to affix

appréciable [apʀesjabl] *adj* appreciable

apprécier [apʀesje] *vt* to appreciate; (*évaluer*) to estimate, assess

appréhender [apʀeãde] *vt* (*craindre*) to dread; (*arrêter*) to apprehend; **appréhension** *nf* apprehension, anxiety

apprendre [apʀãdʀ] *vt* to learn; (*événement, résultats*) to learn of, hear of; ~ **qch à qn** (*informer*) to tell sb (of) sth; (*enseigner*) to teach sb sth; ~ **à faire qch** to learn to do sth; ~ **à qn à faire qch** to teach sb to do sth; **apprenti, e** *nm/f* apprentice; **apprentissage** *nm* learning; (*COMM, SCOL: période*) apprenticeship

apprêté, e [apʀete] *adj* (*fig*) affected

apprêter [apʀete] *vt*: **s'~ à faire qch** to get ready to do sth

appris, e [apʀi, iz] *pp de* **apprendre**

apprivoiser [apʀivwaze] *vt* to tame

approbation [apʀɔbasjɔ̃] *nf* approval

approchant, e [apʀɔʃã, ãt] *adj* similar; **quelque chose d'~** something like that

approche [apʀɔʃ] *nf* approach

approcher [apʀɔʃe] *vi* to approach, come near ♦ *vt* to approach; (*rapprocher*): ~ **qch (de qch)** to bring *ou* put sth near (to sth); **s'~** *vi* to approach, go *ou* come near to; ~ **de** (*lieu, but*) to draw near to; (*quantité, moment*) to approach

approfondir [apʀɔfɔ̃diʀ] *vt* to deepen; (*question*) to go further into

approprié, e [apʀɔpʀije] *adj*: ~ **(à)** appropriate (to), suited to

approprier [apʀɔpʀije]: **s'~** *vt* to appropriate, take over

approuver [apʀuve] *vt* to agree with;

(*trouver louable*) to approve of

approvisionner [apʀovizjɔne] *vt* to supply; (*compte bancaire*) to pay funds into; **s'~ en** to stock up with

approximatif, -ive [apʀɔksimatif, iv] *adj* approximate, rough; (*termes*) vague

appt *abr* = **appartement**

appui [apɥi] *nm* support; **prendre ~ sur** to lean on; (*objet*) to rest on; **l'~ de la fenêtre** the windowsill, the window ledge; **appui(e)-tête** *nm inv* headrest

appuyer [apɥije] *vt* (*poser*): **~ qch sur/contre** to lean *ou* rest sth on/against; (*soutenir: personne, demande*) to support, back (up) ♦ *vi*: **~ sur** (*bouton, frein*) to press, push; (*mot, détail*) to stress, emphasize; **s'~ sur** to lean on; (*fig: compter sur*) to rely on

âpre [ɑpʀ] *adj* acrid, pungent; **~ au gain** grasping

après [apʀɛ] *prép* after ♦ *adv* afterwards; **2 heures ~** 2 hours later; **~ qu'il est** *ou* **soit parti** after he left; **~ avoir fait** after having done; **d'~** (*selon*) according to; **~ coup** after the event, afterwards; **~ tout** (*au fond*) after all; **et (puis) ~?** so what?; **après-demain** *adv* the day after tomorrow; **après-guerre** *nm* post-war years *pl*; **après-midi** *nm ou nf inv* afternoon; **après-rasage** *nm inv* aftershave; **après-shampooing** *nm inv* conditioner; **après-ski** *nm inv* snow boot

à-propos [apʀɔpo] *nm* (*d'une remarque*) aptness; **faire preuve d'~** to show presence of mind

apte [apt] *adj* capable; (*MIL*) fit

aquarelle [akwaʀɛl] *nf* watercolour

aquarium [akwaʀjɔm] *nm* aquarium

arabe [aʀab] *adj* Arabic; (*désert, cheval*) Arabian; (*nation, peuple*) Arab ♦ *nm/f*: **A~** Arab ♦ *nm* (*LING*) Arabic

Arabie [aʀabi] *nf*: **l'~ (Saoudite)** Saudi Arabia

arachide [aʀaʃid] *nf* (*plante*) groundnut (plant); (*graine*) peanut, groundnut

araignée [aʀeɲe] *nf* spider

arbitraire [aʀbitʀɛʀ] *adj* arbitrary

arbitre [aʀbitʀ] *nm* (*SPORT*) referee; (: *TENNIS, CRICKET*) umpire; (*fig*) arbiter, judge; (*JUR*) arbitrator; **arbitrer** *vt* to referee; to umpire; to arbitrate

arborer [aʀbɔʀe] *vt* to bear, display

arbre [aʀbʀ] *nm* tree; (*TECH*) shaft; **~ généalogique** family tree

arbuste [aʀbyst] *nm* small shrub

arc [aʀk] *nm* (*arme*) bow; (*GÉOM*) arc; (*ARCHIT*) arch; **en ~ de cercle** semi-circular

arcade [aʀkad] *nf* arch(way); **~s** *nfpl* (*série*) arcade *sg*, arches

arcanes [aʀkan] *nmpl* mysteries

arc-boutant [aʀkbutɑ̃] *nm* flying buttress

arceau, x [aʀso] *nm* (*métallique etc*) hoop

arc-en-ciel [aʀkɑ̃sjɛl] *nm* rainbow

arche [aʀʃ] *nf* arch; **~ de Noé** Noah's Ark

archéologie [aʀkeɔlɔʒi] *nf* arch(a)eology; **archéologue** *nm/f* arch(a)eologist

archet [aʀʃɛ] *nm* bow

archevêque [aʀʃəvɛk] *nm* archbishop .

archi... [aʀʃi] (*fam*) *préfixe* tremendously; **archicomble** (*fam*) *adj* chock-a-block; **archiconnu, e** (*fam*) *adj* enormously well-known

archipel [aʀʃipɛl] *nm* archipelago

architecte [aʀʃitɛkt] *nm* architect

architecture [aʀʃitɛktyʀ] *nf* architecture

archives [aʀʃiv] *nfpl* (*collection*) archives

arctique [aʀktik] *adj* Arctic ♦ *nm*: **l'A~** the Arctic

ardemment [aʀdamɑ̃] *adv* ardently, fervently

ardent, e [aʀdɑ̃, ɑ̃t] *adj* (*soleil*) blazing; (*amour*) ardent, passionate; (*prière*) fervent

ardeur [aʀdœʀ] *nf* ardour (*BRIT*), ardor (*US*); (*du soleil*) heat

ardoise [aʀdwaz] *nf* slate

ardu, e [aʀdy] *adj* (*travail*) arduous; (*problème*) difficult

arène [aʀɛn] *nf* arena; **~s** *nfpl* (*amphithéâtre*) bull-ring *sg*

arête [aʀɛt] *nf* (*de poisson*) bone; (*d'une montagne*) ridge

argent [aʀʒɑ̃] *nm* (*métal*) silver; (*monnaie*)

money; **~ de poche** pocket money; **~ liquide** ready money, (ready) cash; **argenté, e** *adj* (*couleur*) silver, silvery; **en métal argenté** silver-plated; **argenterie** *nf* silverware

argentin, e [aʀʒɑ̃tɛ̃, in] *adj* Argentinian, Argentine

Argentine [aʀʒɑ̃tin] *nf*: **l'~** Argentina, the Argentine

argile [aʀʒil] *nf* clay

argot [aʀgo] *nm* slang; **argotique** *adj* slang *cpd*; (*très familier*) slangy

argument [aʀgymɑ̃] *nm* argument

argumentaire [aʀgymɑ̃tɛʀ] *nm* sales leaflet

argumenter [aʀgymɑ̃te] *vi* to argue

argus [aʀgys] *nm* guide to second-hand car etc prices

aride [aʀid] *adj* arid

aristocratie [aʀistɔkʀasi] *nf* aristocracy; **aristocratique** *adj* aristocratic

arithmétique [aʀitmetik] *adj* arithmetic(al) ♦ *nf* arithmetic

armateur [aʀmatœʀ] *nm* shipowner

armature [aʀmatyʀ] *nf* framework; (*de tente etc*) frame; **soutien-gorge à/sans ~** underwired/unwired bra

arme [aʀm] *nf* weapon; **~s** *nfpl* (*~ment*) weapons, arms; (*blason*) (coat of) arms; **~ à feu** firearm

armée [aʀme] *nf* army; **~ de l'air** Air Force; **~ de terre** Army

armement [aʀməmɑ̃] *nm* (*matériel*) arms *pl*, weapons *pl*

armer [aʀme] *vt* to arm; (*arme à feu*) to cock; (*appareil-photo*) to wind on; **~ qch de** to reinforce sth with; **s'~ de** to arm o.s. with

armistice [aʀmistis] *nm* armistice; **l'A~** ≈ Remembrance (*BRIT*) *ou* Veterans (*US*) Day

armoire [aʀmwaʀ] *nf* (tall) cupboard; (*penderie*) wardrobe (*BRIT*), closet (*US*)

armoiries [aʀmwaʀi] *nfpl* coat *sg* of arms

armure [aʀmyʀ] *nf* armour *no pl*, suit of armour; **armurier** *nm* gunsmith

arnaque [aʀnak] (*fam*) *nf* swindling; **c'est**

de l'~ it's a rip-off; **arnaquer** (*fam*) *vt* to swindle

aromates [aʀɔmat] *nmpl* seasoning *sg*, herbs (and spices)

aromathérapie [aʀɔmateʀapi] *nf* aromatherapy

aromatisé, e [aʀɔmatize] *adj* flavoured

arôme [aʀom] *nm* aroma

arpenter [aʀpɑ̃te] *vt* (*salle, couloir*) to pace up and down

arpenteur [aʀpɑ̃tœʀ] *nm* surveyor

arqué, e [aʀke] *adj* arched; (*jambes*) bandy

arrache-pied [aʀaʃpje]: **d'~-~** *adv* relentlessly

arracher [aʀaʃe] *vt* to pull out; (*page etc*) to tear off, tear out; (*légumes, herbe*) to pull up; (*bras etc*) to tear off; **s'~** *vt* (*article recherché*) to fight over; **~ qch à qn** to snatch sth from sb; (*fig*) to wring sth out of sb

arraisonner [aʀezɔne] *vt* (*bateau*) to board and search

arrangeant, e [aʀɑ̃ʒɑ̃, ɑ̃t] *adj* accommodating, obliging

arrangement [aʀɑ̃ʒmɑ̃] *nm* agreement, arrangement

arranger [aʀɑ̃ʒe] *vt* (*gén*) to arrange; (*réparer*) to fix, put right; (*régler: différend*) to settle, sort out; (*convenir à*) to suit, be convenient for; **s'~** *vi* (*se mettre d'accord*) to come to an agreement; **je vais m'~** I'll manage; **ça va s'~** it'll sort itself out

arrestation [aʀestasjɔ̃] *nf* arrest

arrêt [aʀe] *nm* stopping; (*de bus etc*) stop; (*JUR*) judgment, decision; **à l'~** stationary; **tomber en ~ devant** to stop short in front of; **sans ~** (*sans interruption*) nonstop; (*très fréquemment*) continually; **~ de travail** stoppage (of work); **~ maladie** sick leave

arrêté [aʀete] *nm* order, decree

arrêter [aʀete] *vt* to stop; (*chauffage etc*) to turn off, switch off; (*fixer: date etc*) to appoint, decide on; (*criminel, suspect*) to arrest; **s'~** *vi* to stop; **~ de faire** to stop

doing
arrhes [aʀ] *nfpl* deposit *sg*
arrière [aʀjɛʀ] *nm* back; (*SPORT*) fullback
♦ *adj inv:* **siège/roue ~** back *ou* rear
seat/wheel; **à l'~** behind, at the back; **en
~** behind; (*regarder*) back, behind; (*tomber, aller*) backwards; **arriéré, e** *adj* (*péj*)
backward ♦ *nm* (*d'argent*) arrears *pl*;
arrière-goût *nm* aftertaste; **arrière-
grand-mère** *nf* great-grandmother;
arrière-grand-père *nm* great-grand-
father; **arrière-pays** *nm inv* hinterland;
arrière-pensée *nf* ulterior motive; mental reservation; **arrière-plan** *nm* background; **arrière-saison** *nf* late autumn;
arrière-train *nm* hindquarters *pl*
arrimer [aʀime] *vt* to secure; (*cargaison*) to
stow
arrivage [aʀivaʒ] *nm* consignment
arrivée [aʀive] *nf* arrival; (*ligne d'~*) finish
arriver [aʀive] *vi* to arrive; (*survenir*) to
happen, occur; **il arrive à Paris à 8h** he
gets to *ou* arrives in Paris at 8; **~ à** (*atteindre*) to reach; **~ à faire qch** to succeed
in doing sth; **en ~ à** (*finir par*) to come to;
il arrive que it happens that; **il lui arrive
de faire** he sometimes does; **arriviste**
nm/f go-getter
arrobase [aʀɔbaz] *nf* (*INFORM*) @, 'at' sign
arrogance [aʀɔgɑ̃s] *nf* arrogance
arrogant, e [aʀɔgɑ̃, ɑ̃t] *adj* arrogant
arrondir [aʀɔ̃diʀ] *vt* (*forme, objet*) to
round; (*somme*) to round off
arrondissement [aʀɔ̃dismɑ̃] *nm* (*ADMIN*)
≈ district
arroser [aʀoze] *vt* to water; (*victoire*) to celebrate (over a drink); (*CULIN*) to baste;
arrosoir *nm* watering can
arsenal, -aux [aʀsənal, o] *nm* (*NAVIG*) naval dockyard; (*MIL*) arsenal; (*fig*) gear
art [aʀ] *nm* art
artère [aʀtɛʀ] *nf* (*ANAT*) artery; (*rue*) main
road
arthrite [aʀtʀit] *nf* arthritis
artichaut [aʀtiʃo] *nm* artichoke
article [aʀtikl] *nm* article; (*COMM*) item, ar-

ticle; **à l'~ de la mort** at the point of
death; **~s de luxe** luxury goods
articulation [aʀtikylasjɔ̃] *nf* articulation;
(*ANAT*) joint
articuler [aʀtikyle] *vt* to articulate
artifice [aʀtifis] *nm* device, trick
artificiel, le [aʀtifisjɛl] *adj* artificial
artisan [aʀtizɑ̃] *nm* artisan, (self-employed)
craftsman; **artisanal, e, -aux** *adj* of *ou*
made by craftsmen; (*péj*) cottage industry
cpd; **de fabrication artisanale** homemade; **artisanat** *nm* arts and crafts *pl*
artiste [aʀtist] *nm/f* artist; (*de variétés*) entertainer; (*musicien etc*) performer; **artistique** *adj* artistic
as[1] [a] *vb voir* **avoir**
as[2] [ɑs] *nm* ace
ascendance [asɑ̃dɑ̃s] *nf* (*origine*) ancestry
ascendant, e [asɑ̃dɑ̃, ɑ̃t] *adj* upward
♦ *nm* influence
ascenseur [asɑ̃sœʀ] *nm* lift (*BRIT*), elevator
(*US*)
ascension [asɑ̃sjɔ̃] *nf* ascent; (*de montagne*) climb; **l'A~** (*REL*) the Ascension

---

Ascension

i La fête de l'Ascension *is a French
public holiday, usually in May. As it
falls on a Thursday, many people take Friday off work and enjoy a long weekend;
see also faire le* **pont**.

---

aseptisé, e (*péj*) *adj* sanitized
aseptiser [asɛptize] *vt* (*ustensile*) to sterilize; (*plaie*) to disinfect
asiatique [azjatik] *adj* Asiatic, Asian
♦ *nm/f:* **A~** Asian
Asie [azi] *nf:* **l'~** Asia
asile [azil] *nm* (*refuge*) refuge, sanctuary;
(*POL*): **droit d'~** (political) asylum; **~ (de
vieillards)** old people's home
aspect [aspɛ] *nm* appearance, look; (*fig*)
aspect, side; **à l'~ de** at the sight of
asperge [aspɛʀʒ] *nf* asparagus *no pl*
asperger [aspɛʀʒe] *vt* to spray, sprinkle
aspérité [asperite] *nf* bump, protruding

bit (of rock *etc*)

asphalte [asfalt] *nm* asphalt

asphyxier [asfiksje] *vt* to suffocate, asphyxiate; (*fig*) to stifle

aspirateur [aspiratœʀ] *nm* vacuum cleaner; **passer l'~** to vacuum

aspirer [aspiʀe] *vt* (*air*) to inhale; (*liquide*) to suck (up); (*suj: appareil*) to suck up; **~ à** to aspire to

aspirine [aspiʀin] *nf* aspirin

assagir [asaʒiʀ]: **s'~** *vi* to quieten down, settle down

assaillir [asajiʀ] *vt* to assail, attack

assainir [aseniʀ] *vt* (*logements*) to clean up; (*eau, air*) to purify

assaisonnement [asezɔnmã] *nm* seasoning

assaisonner [asezɔne] *vt* to season

assassin [asasɛ̃] *nm* murderer; assassin; **assassiner** *vt* to murder; (*esp POL*) to assassinate

assaut [aso] *nm* assault, attack; **prendre d'~** to storm, assault; **donner l'~** to attack

assécher [asefe] *vt* to drain

assemblage [asãblaʒ] *nm* (*action*) assembling; (*de couleurs, choses*) collection

assemblée [asãble] *nf* (*réunion*) meeting; (*assistance*) gathering; (*POL*) assembly

assembler [asãble] *vt* (*joindre, monter*) to assemble, put together; (*amasser*) to gather (together), collect (together); **s'~** *vi* to gather

assener, asséner [asene] *vt*: **~ un coup à qn** to deal sb a blow

assentiment [asãtimã] *nm* assent, consent

asseoir [aswaʀ] *vt* (*malade, bébé*) to sit up; (*personne debout*) to sit down; (*autorité, réputation*) to establish; **s'~** *vi* to sit (o.s.) down

assermenté, e [asɛʀmãte] *adj* sworn, on oath

asservir [asɛʀviʀ] *vt* to subjugate, enslave

assez [ase] *adv* (*suffisamment*) enough, sufficiently; (*passablement*) rather, quite,

fairly; **~ de pain/livres** enough *ou* sufficient bread/books; **vous en avez ~?** have you got enough?; **j'en ai ~!** I've had enough!

assidu, e [asidy] *adj* (*appliqué*) assiduous, painstaking; (*ponctuel*) regular

assied *etc* [asje] *vb voir* **asseoir**

assiéger [asjeʒe] *vt* to besiege

assiérai *etc* [asjeʀe] *vb voir* **asseoir**

assiette [asjɛt] *nf* plate; (*contenu*) plate(ful); **il n'est pas dans son ~** he's not feeling quite himself; **~ à dessert** dessert plate; **~ anglaise** assorted cold meats; **~ creuse** (soup) dish, soup plate; **~ plate** (dinner) plate

assigner [asiɲe] *vt*: **~ qch à** (*poste, part, travail*) to assign sth to

assimiler [asimile] *vt* to assimilate, absorb; (*comparer*): **~ qch/qn à** to liken *ou* compare sth/sb to

assis, e [asi, iz] *pp de* **asseoir** ♦ *adj* sitting (down), seated; **assise** *nf* (*fig*) basis, foundation; **assises** *nfpl* (*JUR*) assizes

assistance [asistãs] *nf* (*public*) audience; (*aide*) assistance; **enfant de l'A~ publique** child in care

assistant, e [asistã, ãt] *nm/f* assistant; (*d'université*) probationary lecturer; **~(e) social(e)** social worker

assisté, e [asiste] *adj* (*AUTO*) power assisted; **~ par ordinateur** computer-assisted

assister [asiste] *vt* (*aider*) to assist; **~ à** (*scène, événement*) to witness; (*conférence, séminaire*) to attend, be at; (*spectacle, match*) to be at, see

association [asɔsjasjɔ̃] *nf* association

associé, e [asɔsje] *nm/f* associate; (*COMM*) partner

associer [asɔsje] *vt* to associate; **s'~** *vi* to join together; **s'~ à qn pour faire** to join (forces) with sb to do; **s'~ à** (*couleurs, qualités*) to be combined with; (*opinions, joie de qn*) to share in; **~ qn à** (*profits*) to give sb a share of; (*affaire*) to make sb a partner in; (*joie, triomphe*) to include sb in;

~ qch à (*allier à*) to combine sth with
assoiffé, e [aswafe] *adj* thirsty
assombrir [asɔ̃bʀiʀ] *vt* to darken; (*fig*) to fill with gloom
assommer [asɔme] *vt* (*étourdir, abrutir*) to knock out, stun
Assomption [asɔ̃psjɔ̃] *nf*: **l'~** the Assumption

Assomption

i La fête de l'Assomption *on August 15 is a French national holiday. Traditionally, large numbers of holidaymakers set out on this date, frequently causing chaos on the roads; see also* faire le **pont**.

---

assorti, e [asɔʀti] *adj* matched, matching; (*varié*) assorted; **~ à** matching; **assortiment** *nm* assortment, selection
assortir [asɔʀtiʀ] *vt* to match; **~ qch à** to match sth with; **~ qch de** to accompany sth with
assoupi, e [asupi] *adj* dozing, sleeping
assoupir [asupiʀ]: **s'~** *vi* to doze off
assouplir [asupliʀ] *vt* to make supple; (*fig*) to relax; **assouplissant** *nm* (fabric) softener
assourdir [asuʀdiʀ] *vt* (*bruit*) to deaden, muffle; (*suj: bruit*) to deafen
assouvir [asuviʀ] *vt* to satisfy, appease
assujettir [asyʒetiʀ] *vt* to subject
assumer [asyme] *vt* (*fonction, emploi*) to assume, take on
assurance [asyʀɑ̃s] *nf* (*certitude*) assurance; (*confiance en soi*) (self-)confidence; (*contrat*) insurance (policy); (*secteur commercial*) insurance; **~ maladie** health insurance; **~ tous risques** (*AUTO*) comprehensive insurance; **~s sociales** ≃ National Insurance (*BRIT*), ≃ Social Security (*US*); **assurance-vie** *nf* life assurance *ou* insurance
assuré, e [asyʀe] *adj* (*certain: réussite, échec*) certain, sure; (*air*) assured; (*pas*) steady ♦ *nm/f* insured (person); **assurément** *adv* assuredly, most certainly

assurer [asyʀe] *vt* (*FIN*) to insure; (*victoire etc*) to ensure; (*frontières, pouvoir*) to make secure; (*service*) to provide, operate; **s'~ (contre)** (*COMM*) to insure o.s. (against); **s'~ de/que** (*vérifier*) to make sure of/that; **s'~ (de)** (*aide de qn*) to secure; **~ à qn que** to assure sb that; **~ qn de** to assure sb of; **assureur** *nm* insurer
asthmatique [asmatik] *adj, nm/f* asthmatic
asthme [asm] *nm* asthma
asticot [astiko] *nm* maggot
astiquer [astike] *vt* to polish, shine
astre [astʀ] *nm* star
astreignant, e [astʀeɲɑ̃, ɑ̃t] *adj* demanding
astreindre [astʀɛ̃dʀ] *vt*: **~ qn à faire** to compel *ou* force sb to do; **s'~** *vi*: **s'~ à faire** to force o.s. to do
astrologie [astʀɔlɔʒi] *nf* astrology
astronaute [astʀonot] *nm/f* astronaut
astronomie [astʀɔnɔmi] *nf* astronomy
astuce [astys] *nf* shrewdness, astuteness; (*truc*) trick, clever way; **astucieux, -euse** *adj* clever
atelier [atəlje] *nm* workshop; (*de peintre*) studio
athée [ate] *adj* atheistic ♦ *nm/f* atheist
Athènes [atɛn] *n* Athens
athlète [atlɛt] *nm/f* (*SPORT*) athlete; **athlétisme** *nm* athletics *sg*
atlantique [atlɑ̃tik] *adj* Atlantic ♦ *nm*: **l'(océan) A~** the Atlantic (Ocean)
atlas [atlas] *nm* atlas
atmosphère [atmɔsfɛʀ] *nf* atmosphere
atome [atom] *nm* atom; **atomique** *adj* atomic, nuclear
atomiseur [atɔmizœʀ] *nm* atomizer
atout [atu] *nm* trump; (*fig*) asset
âtre [ɑtʀ] *nm* hearth
atroce [atʀɔs] *adj* atrocious
attabler [atable]: **s'~** *vi* to sit down at (the) table
attachant, e [ataʃɑ̃, ɑ̃t] *adj* engaging, lovable, likeable
attache [ataʃ] *nf* clip, fastener; (*fig*) tie

attacher [ataʃe] *vt* to tie up; (*étiquette*) to attach, tie on; (*ceinture*) to fasten ♦ *vi* (*poêle, riz*) to stick; **s'~ à** (*par affection*) to become attached to; **s'~ à faire** to endeavour to do; **~ qch à** to tie *ou* attach sth to

attaque [atak] *nf* attack; (*cérébrale*) stroke; (*d'épilepsie*) fit; **~ à main armée** armed attack

attaquer [atake] *vt* to attack; (*en justice*) to bring an action against, sue ♦ *vi* to attack; **s'~ à** ♦ *vt* (*personne*) to attack; (*problème*) to tackle

attardé, e [ataʀde] *adj* (*enfant*) backward; (*passants*) late

attarder [ataʀde]: **s'~** *vi* to linger

atteindre [atɛ̃dʀ] *vt* to reach; (*blesser*) to hit; (*émouvoir*) to affect; **atteint, e** *adj* (*MÉD*): **être atteint de** to be suffering from; **atteinte** *nf*: **hors d'atteinte** out of reach; **porter atteinte à** to strike a blow at

atteler [at(ə)le] *vt* (*cheval, bœufs*) to hitch up; **s'~ à** (*travail*) to buckle down to

attelle [atɛl] *nf* splint

attenant, e [at(ə)nɑ̃, ɑ̃t] *adj*: **~ (à)** adjoining

attendant [atɑ̃dɑ̃] *adv*: **en ~** meanwhile, in the meantime

attendre [atɑ̃dʀ] *vt* (*gén*) to wait for; (*être destiné ou réservé à*) to await, be in store for ♦ *vi* to wait; **s'~ à (ce que)** to expect (that); **~ un enfant** to be expecting a baby; **~ de faire/d'être** to wait until one does/is; **attendez qu'il vienne** wait until he comes; **~ qch de** to expect sth of

attendrir [atɑ̃dʀiʀ] *vt* to move (to pity); (*viande*) to tenderize; **attendrissant, e** *adj* moving, touching

attendu, e [atɑ̃dy] *adj* (*visiteur*) expected; (*événement*) long-awaited; **~ que** considering that, since

attentat [atɑ̃ta] *nm* assassination attempt; **~ à la bombe** bomb attack; **~ à la pudeur** indecent assault *no pl*

attente [atɑ̃t] *nf* wait; (*espérance*) expectation

attenter [atɑ̃te]: **~ à** *vt* (*liberté*) to violate; **~ à la vie de qn** to make an attempt on sb's life

attentif, -ive [atɑ̃tif, iv] *adj* (*auditeur*) attentive; (*examen*) careful; **~ à** careful to

attention [atɑ̃sjɔ̃] *nf* attention; (*prévenance*) attention, thoughtfulness *no pl*; **à l'~ de** for the attention of; **faire ~ (à)** to be careful (of); **faire ~ (à ce) que** to be *ou* make sure that; **~!** careful!, watch out!; **attentionné, e** *adj* thoughtful, considerate

atténuer [atenɥe] *vt* (*douleur*) to alleviate, ease; (*couleurs*) to soften

atterrer [ateʀe] *vt* to dismay, appal

atterrir [ateʀiʀ] *vi* to land; **atterrissage** *nm* landing

attestation [atɛstasjɔ̃] *nf* certificate

attester [atɛste] *vt* to testify to

attirail [atiʀaj] (*fam*) *nm* gear; (*péj*) paraphernalia

attirant, e [atiʀɑ̃, ɑ̃t] *adj* attractive, appealing

attirer [atiʀe] *vt* to attract; (*appâter*) to lure, entice; **~ qn dans un coin** to draw sb into a corner; **~ l'attention de qn** to attract sb's attention; **~ l'attention de qn sur** to draw sb's attention to; **s'~ des ennuis** to bring trouble upon o.s., get into trouble

attiser [atize] *vt* (*feu*) to poke (up)

attitré, e [atitʀe] *adj* (*habituel*) regular, usual; (*agréé*) accredited

attitude [atityd] *nf* attitude; (*position du corps*) bearing

attouchements [atuʃmɑ̃] *nmpl* (*sexuels*) fondling *sg*

attraction [atʀaksjɔ̃] *nf* (*gén*) attraction; (*de cabaret, cirque*) number

attrait [atʀɛ] *nm* appeal, attraction

attrape-nigaud [atʀapnigo] (*fam*) *nm* con

attraper [atʀape] *vt* (*gén*) to catch; (*habitude, amende*) to get, pick up; (*fam: duper*) to con; **se faire ~** (*fam*) to be told off

attrayant, e [atʀɛjɑ̃, ɑ̃t] *adj* attractive

attribuer [atʀibɥe] *vt* (*prix*) to award; (*rôle*, *tâche*) to allocate, assign; (*imputer*): **~ qch à** to attribute sth to; **s'~** *vt* (*s'approprier*) to claim for o.s.; **attribut** *nm* attribute

attrister [atʀiste] *vt* to sadden

attroupement [atʀupmɑ̃] *nm* crowd

attrouper [atʀupe]: **s'~** *vi* to gather

au [o] *prép* +*dét* = **à +le**

aubaine [obɛn] *nf* godsend

aube [ob] *nf* dawn, daybreak; **à l'~** at dawn *ou* daybreak

aubépine [obepin] *nf* hawthorn

auberge [obɛʀʒ] *nf* inn; **~ de jeunesse** youth hostel

aubergine [obɛʀʒin] *nf* aubergine

aubergiste [obɛʀʒist] *nm/f* inn-keeper, hotel-keeper

aucun, e [okœ̃, yn] *dét* no, *tournure négative* +any; (*positif*) any ♦ *pron* none, *tournure négative* +any; any(one); **sans ~ doute** without any doubt; **plus qu'~ autre** more than any other; **~ des deux** neither of the two; **~ d'entre eux** none of them; **aucunement** *adv* in no way, not in the least

audace [odas] *nf* daring, boldness; (*péj*) audacity; **audacieux, -euse** *adj* daring, bold

au-delà [od(ə)la] *adv* beyond ♦ *nm*: **l'~** the hereafter; **~-~ de** beyond

au-dessous [odsu] *adv* underneath; below; **~-~ de** under(neath), below; (*limite*, *somme etc*) below, under; (*dignité*, *condition*) below

au-dessus [odsy] *adv* above; **~-~ de** above

au-devant [od(ə)vɑ̃]: **~-~ de** *prép*: **aller ~-~ de** (*personne*, *danger*) to go (out) and meet; (*souhaits de qn*) to anticipate

audience [odjɑ̃s] *nf* audience; (*JUR*: *séance*) hearing

audimat ® [odimat] *nm* (*taux d'écoute*) ratings *pl*

audio-visuel, le [odjovizɥɛl] *adj* audio-visual

auditeur, -trice [oditœʀ, tʀis] *nm/f* lis-

tener

audition [odisjɔ̃] *nf* (*ouïe*, *écoute*) hearing; (*JUR*: *de témoins*) examination; (*MUS*, *THÉÂTRE*: *épreuve*) audition

auditoire [oditwaʀ] *nm* audience

auge [oʒ] *nf* trough

augmentation [ɔgmɑ̃tasjɔ̃] *nf* increase; **~ (de salaire)** rise (in salary) (*BRIT*), (pay) raise (*US*)

augmenter [ɔgmɑ̃te] *vt* (*gén*) to increase; (*salaire*, *prix*) to increase, raise, put up; (*employé*) to increase the salary of ♦ *vi* to increase

augure [ogyʀ] *nm*: **de bon/mauvais ~** of good/ill omen; **augurer** *vt*: **augurer bien de** to augur well for

aujourd'hui [oʒuʀdɥi] *adv* today

aumône [omon] *nf inv* alms *sg*; **aumônier** *nm* chaplain

auparavant [opaʀavɑ̃] *adv* before(hand)

auprès [opʀɛ]: **~ de** *prép* next to, close to; (*recourir*, *s'adresser*) to; (*en comparaison de*) compared with

auquel [okɛl] *prép* +*pron* = **à +lequel**

aurai *etc* [oʀe] *vb voir* **avoir**

auréole [oʀeɔl] *nf* halo; (*tache*) ring

aurons *etc* [oʀɔ̃] *vb voir* **avoir**

aurore [oʀɔʀ] *nf* dawn, daybreak

ausculter [ɔskylte] *vt* to sound (the chest of)

aussi [osi] *adv* (*également*) also, too; (*de comparaison*) as ♦ *conj* therefore, consequently; **~ fort que** as strong as; **moi ~** me too

aussitôt [osito] *adv* straight away, immediately; **~ que** as soon as

austère [ostɛʀ] *adj* austere

austral, e [ostʀal] *adj* southern

Australie [ostʀali] *nf*: **l'~** Australia; **australien, ne** *adj* Australian ♦ *nm/f*: **Australien, ne** Australian

autant [otɑ̃] *adv* so much; (*comparatif*): **~ (que)** as much (as); (*nombre*) as many (as); **~ (de)** so much (*ou* many); as much (*ou* many); **~ partir** we (*ou* you *etc*) may as well leave; **~ dire que ...** one might as well say that ...; **pour ~** for all that; **d'~ plus/mieux (que)** all the more/the better (since)

autel [otɛl] *nm* altar

auteur [otœʀ] *nm* author

authenticité [otɑ̃tisite] *nf* authenticity

authentique [otɑ̃tik] *adj* authentic, genuine

auto [oto] *nf* car

auto...: **autobiographie** *nf* autobiography; **autobronzant** *nm* self-tanning cream (*or* lotion *etc*); **autobus** *nm* bus; **autocar** *nm* coach

autochtone [otɔktɔn] *nm/f* native

auto...: **autocollant, e** *adj* self-adhesive; (*enveloppe*) self-seal ♦ *nm* sticker; **auto-couchettes** *adj*: **train auto-couchettes** car sleeper train; **autocuiseur** *nm* pressure cooker; **autodéfense** *nf* self-defence; **autodidacte** *nm/f* self-taught person; **auto-école** *nf* driving school; **autographe** *nm* autograph

automate [ɔtɔmat] *nm* (*machine*) (automatic) machine

automatique [ɔtɔmatik] *adj* automatic ♦ *nm*: **l'~** direct dialling; **automatiquement** *adv* automatically; **automatiser** *vt* to automate

automne [ɔtɔn] *nm* autumn (*BRIT*), fall (*US*)

automobile [ɔtɔmɔbil] *adj* motor *cpd* ♦ *nf* (motor) car; **automobiliste** *nm/f* motorist

autonome [ɔtɔnɔm] *adj* autonomous; **autonomie** *nf* autonomy; (*POL*) self-government, autonomy

autopsie [ɔtɔpsi] *nf* post-mortem (examination), autopsy

autoradio [otoʀadjo] *nm* car radio

autorisation [ɔtɔʀizasjɔ̃] *nf* permission, authorization; (*papiers*) permit

autorisé, e [ɔtɔʀize] *adj* (*opinion, sources*) authoritative

autoriser [ɔtɔʀize] *vt* to give permission for, authorize; (*fig*) to allow (of)

autoritaire [ɔtɔʀitɛʀ] *adj* authoritarian

autorité [ɔtɔʀite] *nf* authority; **faire ~** to be authoritative

autoroute [otoʀut] *nf* motorway (*BRIT*), highway (*US*); **~ de l'information** (*INFORM*) information superhighway

auto-stop [otostɔp] *nm*: **faire de l'~-~** to hitch-hike; **prendre qn en ~-~** to give sb a lift; **auto-stoppeur, -euse** *nm/f* hitch-hiker

autour [otuʀ] *adv* around; **~ de** around; **tout ~** all around

---
MOT-CLÉ
---

autre [otʀ] *adj* **1** (*différent*) other, different; **je préférerais un autre verre** I'd prefer another *ou* a different glass

2 (*supplémentaire*) other; **je voudrais un autre verre d'eau** I'd like another glass of water

3: **autre chose** something else; **autre part** somewhere else; **d'autre part** on the other hand

♦ *pron*: **un autre** another (one); **nous/vous autres** us/you; **d'autres** others; **l'autre** the other (one); **les autres** the others; (*autrui*) others; **l'un et l'autre** both of them; **se détester l'un l'autre/les uns les autres** to hate each other *ou* one another; **d'une semaine à l'autre** from one week to the next; (*incessamment*) any week now; **entre autres** among other things

---

autrefois [otʀəfwa] *adv* in the past

autrement [otʀəmɑ̃] *adv* differently; (*d'une manière différente*) in another way; (*sinon*) otherwise; **~ dit** in other words

Autriche [otʀiʃ] *nf*: **l'~** Austria; **autrichien, ne** *adj* Austrian ♦ *nm/f*: **Autrichien, ne** Austrian

autruche [otʀyʃ] *nf* ostrich

autrui [otʀɥi] *pron* others

auvent [ovɑ̃] *nm* canopy

aux [o] *prép* +*dét* = **à +les**

auxiliaire [ɔksiljɛʀ] *adj, nm/f* auxiliary

auxquelles [okɛl] *prép* +*pron* = **à +lesquelles**

auxquels [okɛl] *prép* +*pron* = **à** +**lesquels**

avachi, e [avaʃi] *adj* limp, flabby

aval [aval] *nm*: **en ~** downstream, downriver

avalanche [avalɑ̃ʃ] *nf* avalanche

avaler [avale] *vt* to swallow

avance [avɑ̃s] *nf* (*de troupes etc*) advance; progress; (*d'argent*) advance; (*sur un concurrent*) lead; **~s** *nfpl* (*amoureuses*) advances; **(être) en ~** (to be) early; (*sur un programme*) (to be) ahead of schedule; **à l'~, d'~** in advance

avancé, e [avɑ̃se] *adj* advanced; (*travail*) well on, well under way

avancement [avɑ̃smɑ̃] *nm* (*professionnel*) promotion

avancer [avɑ̃se] *vi* to move forward, advance; (*projet, travail*) to make progress; (*montre, réveil*) to be fast; to gain ♦ *vt* to move forward, advance; (*argent*) to advance; (*montre, pendule*) to put forward; **s'~** *vi* to move forward, advance; (*fig*) to commit o.s.

avant [avɑ̃] *prép, adv* before ♦ *adj inv*: **siège/roue ~** front seat/wheel ♦ *nm* (*d'un véhicule, bâtiment*) front; (*SPORT: joueur*) forward; **~ qu'il (ne) fasse/de faire** before he does/doing; **~ tout** (*surtout*) above all; **à l'~** (*dans un véhicule*) in (the) front; **en ~** forward(s); **en ~ de** in front of

avantage [avɑ̃taʒ] *nm* advantage; **~s sociaux** fringe benefits; **avantager** *vt* (*favoriser*) to favour; (*embellir*) to flatter; **avantageux, -euse** *adj* (*prix*) attractive

avant...: **avant-bras** *nm inv* forearm; **avantcoureur** *adj inv*: **signe avantcoureur** advance indication *ou* sign; **avant-dernier, -ière** *adj, nm/f* next to last, last but one; **avant-goût** *nm* foretaste; **avant-guerre** *nm* pre-war years; **avant-hier** *adv* the day before yesterday; **avant-première** *nf* (*de film*) preview; **avant-projet** *nm* (preliminary) draft; **avant-propos** *nm* foreword; **avant-veille** *nf*: **l'avant-veille** two days before

avare [avaʀ] *adj* miserly, avaricious ♦ *nm/f* miser; **~ de** (*compliments etc*) sparing of

avarié, e [avaʀje] *adj* (*aliment*) rotting

avaries [avaʀi] *nfpl* (*NAVIG*) damage *sg*

avec [avɛk] *prép* with; (*à l'égard de*) to(wards), with; **et ~ ça?** (*dans magasin*) anything else?

avenant, e [av(ə)nɑ̃, ɑ̃t] *adj* pleasant; **à l'~** in keeping

avènement [avɛnmɑ̃] *nm* (*d'un changement*) advent, coming

avenir [avniʀ] *nm* future; **à l'~** in future; **politicien d'~** politician with prospects *ou* a future

aventure [avɑ̃tyʀ] *nf* adventure; (*amoureuse*) affair; **aventurer: s'aventurer** *vi* to venture; **aventureux, -euse** *adj* adventurous, venturesome; (*projet*) risky, chancy

avenue [avny] *nf* avenue

avérer [aveʀe]: **s'~** *vb* +*attrib* to prove (to be)

averse [avɛʀs] *nf* shower

averti, e [avɛʀti] *adj* (well-)informed

avertir [avɛʀtiʀ] *vt*: **~ qn (de qch/que)** to warn sb (of sth/that); (*renseigner*) to inform sb (of sth/that); **avertissement** *nm* warning; **avertisseur** *nm* horn, siren

aveu, x [avø] *nm* confession

aveugle [avœgl] *adj* blind ♦ *nm/f* blind man/woman; **aveuglément** *adv* blindly; **aveugler** *vt* to blind

aviateur, -trice [avjatœʀ, tʀis] *nm/f* aviator, pilot

aviation [avjasjɔ̃] *nf* aviation; (*sport*) flying; (*MIL*) air force

avide [avid] *adj* eager; (*péj*) greedy, grasping

avilir [aviliʀ] *vt* to debase

avion [avjɔ̃] *nm* (aero)plane (*BRIT*), (air)plane (*US*); **aller (quelque part) en ~** to go (somewhere) by plane, fly (somewhere); **par ~** by airmail; **~ à réaction** jet (plane)

aviron [aviʀɔ̃] *nm* oar; (*sport*): **l'~** rowing

avis [avi] *nm* opinion; (*notification*) notice; **à mon ~** in my opinion; **changer d'~** to change one's mind; **jusqu'à nouvel ~** until further notice

avisé, e [avize] *adj* sensible, wise; **bien/mal ~ de** well-/ill-advised to

aviser [avize] *vt* (*informer*): **~ qn de/que** to advise *ou* inform sb of/that ♦ *vi* to think about things, assess the situation; **nous ~ons sur place** we'll work something out once we're there; **s'~ de qch/que** to become suddenly aware of sth/that; **s'~ de faire** to take it into one's head to do

avocat, e [avɔka, at] *nm/f* (*JUR*) barrister (*BRIT*), lawyer ♦ *nm* (*CULIN*) avocado (pear); **~ de la défense** counsel for the defence; **~ général** assistant public prosecutor

avoine [avwan] *nf* oats *pl*

MOT-CLÉ

avoir [avwaʀ] *nm* assets *pl*, resources *pl*; (*COMM*) credit

♦ *vt* 1 (*posséder*) to have; **elle a 2 enfants/une belle maison** she has (got) 2 children/a lovely house; **il a les yeux bleus** he has (got) blue eyes

2 (*âge, dimensions*) to be; **il a 3 ans** he is 3 (years old); **le mur a 3 mètres de haut** the wall is 3 metres high; *voir aussi* **faim; peur** *etc*

3 (*fam: duper*) to do, have; **on vous a eu!** you've been done *ou* had!

4: **en avoir contre qn** to have a grudge against sb; **en avoir assez** to be fed up; **j'en ai pour une demi-heure** it'll take me half an hour

♦ *vb aux* 1 to have; **avoir mangé/dormi** to have eaten/slept

2 (*avoir +à +infinitif*): **avoir à faire qch** to have to do sth; **vous n'avez qu'à lui demander** you only have to ask him

♦ *vb impers* 1: **il y a** (+ *singulier*) there is; (+ *pluriel*) there are; **qu'y-a-t-il?, qu'est-ce qu'il y a?** what's the matter?, what is it?; **il doit y avoir une explication** there must be an explanation; **il n'y a qu'à ...** we (*ou* you *etc*) will just have to ...

2 (*temporel*): **il y a 10 ans** 10 years ago; **il y a 10 ans/longtemps que je le sais** I've known it for 10 years/a long time; **il y a 10 ans qu'il est arrivé** it's 10 years since he arrived

---

avoisiner [avwazine] *vt* to be near *ou* close to; (*fig*) to border *ou* verge on

avortement [avɔʀtəmɑ̃] *nm* abortion

avorter [avɔʀte] *vi* (*MÉD*) to have an abortion; (*fig*) to fail

avoué, e [avwe] *adj* avowed ♦ *nm* (*JUR*) ≃ solicitor

avouer [avwe] *vt* (*crime, défaut*) to confess (to); **~ avoir fait/que** to admit *ou* confess to having done/that

avril [avʀil] *nm* April

---

poisson d'avril

ⓘ *The traditional prank on April 1 in France is to stick a cut-out paper fish, known as a* **poisson d'avril**, *to someone's back without being caught.*

---

axe [aks] *nm* axis; (*de roue etc*) axle; (*fig*) main line; **axer** *vt*: **axer qch sur** to centre sth on

ayons *etc* [ɛjɔ̃] *vb voir* **avoir**

azote [azɔt] *nm* nitrogen

B, b

baba [baba] *nm*: **~ au rhum** rum baba

babines [babin] *nfpl* chops

babiole [babjɔl] *nf* (*bibelot*) trinket; (*vétille*) trifle

bâbord [babɔʀ] *nm*: **à ~** to port, on the port side

baby-foot [babifut] *nm* table football

baby-sitting [babisitiŋ] *nm*: **faire du ~-~** to baby-sit

bac [bak] *abr m* = **baccalauréat** ♦ *nm* (*récipient*) tub

baccalauréat [bakalɔʀea] *nm* high school

diploma

baccalauréat

i *In France the* **baccalauréat** *or* **bac** *is the school-leaving certificate taken at a* lycée *at the age of seventeen or eighteen, enabling entry to university. Different subject combinations are available from the broad subject range studied.*

bâche [baʃ] *nf* tarpaulin

bachelier, -ière [baʃəlje, jɛʀ] *nm/f* holder of the baccalauréat

bâcler [bɑkle] *vt* to botch (up)

badaud, e [bado, od] *nm/f* idle onlooker, stroller

badigeonner [badiʒɔne] *vt* (*barbouiller*) to daub

badiner [badine] *vi*: ~ **avec qch** to treat sth lightly

baffe [baf] (*fam*) *nf* slap, clout

baffle [bafl] *nm* speaker

bafouer [bafwe] *vt* to deride, ridicule

bafouiller [bafuje] *vi, vt* to stammer

bâfrer [bɑfʀe] (*fam*) *vi* to guzzle

bagages [bagaʒ] *nmpl* luggage *sg*; ~ **à main** hand-luggage

bagarre [bagaʀ] *nf* fight, brawl; **bagarrer: se bagarrer** *vi* to have a fight *ou* scuffle, fight

bagatelle [bagatɛl] *nf* trifle

bagne [baɲ] *nm* penal colony

bagnole [baɲɔl] (*fam*) *nf* car

bagout [bagu] *nm*: **avoir du ~** to have the gift of the gab

bague [bag] *nf* ring; ~ **de fiançailles** engagement ring

baguette [bagɛt] *nf* stick; (*cuisine chinoise*) chopstick; (*de chef d'orchestre*) baton; (*pain*) stick of (French) bread; ~ **magique** magic wand

baie [bɛ] *nf* (*GÉO*) bay; (*fruit*) berry; ~ **(vitrée)** picture window

baignade [bɛɲad] *nf* bathing; **"~ interdite"** "no bathing"

baigner [beɲe] *vt* (*bébé*) to bath; **se ~** *vi* to have a swim, go swimming *ou* bathing

baignoire [bɛɲwaʀ] *nf* bath(tub)

bail [baj, bo] (*pl* **baux**) *nm* lease

bâillement [bɑjmɑ̃] *nm* yawn

bâiller [bɑje] *vi* to yawn; (*être ouvert*) to gape

bâillonner [bɑjɔne] *vt* to gag

bain [bɛ̃] *nm* bath; **prendre un ~** to have a bath; **se mettre dans le ~** (*fig*) to get into it *ou* things; ~ **de soleil: prendre un ~ de soleil** to sunbathe; ~**s de mer** sea bathing *sg*; **bain-marie** *nm*: **faire chauffer au bain-marie** (*boîte etc*) to immerse in boiling water

baiser [beze] *nm* kiss ♦ *vt* (*main, front*) to kiss; (*fam!*) to screw (!)

baisse [bɛs] *nf* fall, drop; **être en ~** to be falling, be declining

baisser [bese] *vt* to lower; (*radio, chauffage*) to turn down ♦ *vi* to fall, drop, go down; (*vue, santé*) to fail, dwindle; **se ~** *vi* to bend down

bal [bal] *nm* dance; (*grande soirée*) ball; ~ **costumé** fancy-dress ball

balade [balad] *nf* (*à pied*) walk, stroll; (*en voiture*) drive; **balader** (*fam*): **se balader** *vi* to go for a walk *ou* stroll; to go for a drive; **baladeur** *nm* personal stereo, Walkman ®

balafre [balafʀ] *nf* (*cicatrice*) scar

balai [balɛ] *nm* broom, brush; **balai-brosse** *nm* (long-handled) scrubbing brush

balance [balɑ̃s] *nf* scales *pl*; (*signe*): **la B~** Libra

balancer [balɑ̃se] *vt* to swing; (*fam: lancer*) to fling, chuck; (: *jeter*) to chuck out; **se ~** *vi* to swing, rock; **se ~ de** (*fam*) not to care about

balançoire [balɑ̃swaʀ] *nf* swing; (*sur pivot*) seesaw

balayer [baleje] *vt* (*feuilles etc*) to sweep up, brush up; (*pièce*) to sweep; (*objections*) to sweep aside; (*suj: radar*) to scan; **balayeur, -euse** *nm/f* roadsweeper

balbutier [balbysje] *vi, vt* to stammer

balcon [balkɔ̃] *nm* balcony; (*THÉÂTRE*) dress circle

baleine [balɛn] *nf* whale

balise [baliz] *nf* (*NAVIG*) beacon; (marker) buoy; (*AVIAT*) runway light, beacon; (*AUTO, SKI*) sign, marker; **baliser** *vt* to mark out (with lights *etc*)

balivernes [balivɛRn] *nfpl* nonsense *sg*

ballant, e [balɑ̃, ɑ̃t] *adj* dangling

balle [bal] *nf* (*de fusil*) bullet; (*de sport*) ball; (*fam: franc*) franc

ballerine [bal(ə)Rin] *nf* (*danseuse*) ballet dancer; (*chaussure*) ballet shoe

ballet [balɛ] *nm* ballet

ballon [balɔ̃] *nm* (*de sport*) ball; (*jouet, AVIAT*) balloon; **~ de football** football

ballot [balo] *nm* bundle; (*péj*) nitwit

ballottage [balɔtaʒ] *nm* (*POL*) second ballot

ballotter [balɔte] *vt*: **être ballotté** to be thrown about

balnéaire [balneɛR] *adj* seaside *cpd*; **station ~** seaside resort

balourd, e [baluR, uRd] *adj* clumsy

balustrade [balystRad] *nf* railings *pl*, handrail

bambin [bɑ̃bɛ̃] *nm* little child

bambou [bɑ̃bu] *nm* bamboo

ban [bɑ̃] *nm*: **mettre au ~ de** to outlaw from; **~s** *nmpl* (*de mariage*) banns

banal, e [banal] *adj* banal, commonplace; (*péj*) trite; **banalité** *nf* banality

banane [banan] *nf* banana; (*sac*) waist-bag, bum-bag

banc [bɑ̃] *nm* seat, bench; (*de poissons*) shoal; **~ d'essai** (*fig*) testing ground

bancaire [bɑ̃kɛR] *adj* banking; (*chèque, carte*) bank *cpd*

bancal, e [bɑ̃kal] *adj* wobbly

bandage [bɑ̃daʒ] *nm* bandage

bande [bɑ̃d] *nf* (*de tissu etc*) strip; (*MÉD*) bandage; (*motif*) stripe; (*magnétique etc*) tape; (*groupe*) band; (: *péj*) bunch; **faire ~ à part** to keep to o.s.; **~ dessinée** comic strip; **~ sonore** sound track

---

bande dessinée

i   *The* **bande dessinée** *or* **BD** *enjoys a huge following in France amongst adults as well as children. An international show takes place every year at Angoulême in January every year. Astérix, Tintin, Lucky Luke and Gaston Lagaffe are among the most famous cartoon characters.*

---

bandeau, x [bɑ̃do] *nm* headband; (*sur les yeux*) blindfold

bander [bɑ̃de] *vt* (*blessure*) to bandage; **~ les yeux à qn** to blindfold sb

banderole [bɑ̃dRɔl] *nf* banner, streamer

bandit [bɑ̃di] *nm* bandit; **banditisme** *nm* violent crime, armed robberies *pl*

bandoulière [bɑ̃duljɛR] *nf*: **en ~** (slung *ou* worn) across the shoulder

banlieue [bɑ̃ljø] *nf* suburbs *pl*; **lignes/ quartiers de ~** suburban lines/areas; **trains de ~** commuter trains

banlieusard, e [bɑ̃ljøzaR] *nm/f* (suburban) commuter

bannière [banjɛR] *nf* banner

bannir [baniR] *vt* to banish

banque [bɑ̃k] *nf* bank; (*activités*) banking; **~ d'affaires** merchant bank; **banque-route** *nf* bankruptcy

banquet [bɑ̃kɛ] *nm* dinner; (*d'apparat*) banquet

banquette [bɑ̃kɛt] *nf* seat

banquier [bɑ̃kje] *nm* banker

banquise [bɑ̃kiz] *nf* ice field

baptême [batɛm] *nm* christening; baptism; **~ de l'air** first flight

baptiser [batize] *vt* to baptize, christen

baquet [bakɛ] *nm* tub, bucket

bar [baR] *nm* bar

baraque [baRak] *nf* shed; (*fam*) house; **baraqué, e** (*fam*) *adj* well-built, hefty; **baraquements** *nmpl* (*provisoires*) huts

baratin [baRatɛ̃] (*fam*) *nm* smooth talk, patter; **baratiner** *vt* to chat up

barbare [baRbaR] *adj* barbaric; **barbarie** *nf* barbarity

barbe [baʀb] *nf* beard; **la ~!** (*fam*) damn it!; **quelle ~!** (*fam*) what a drag *ou* bore!; **à la ~ de qn** under sb's nose; **~ à papa** candy-floss (*BRIT*), cotton candy (*US*)

barbelé [baʀbəle] *adj, nm*: **(fil de fer) ~** barbed wire *no pl*

barber [baʀbe] (*fam*) *vt* to bore stiff

barbiturique [baʀbityʀik] *nm* barbiturate

barboter [baʀbɔte] *vi* (*enfant*) to paddle

barbouiller [baʀbuje] *vt* to daub; **avoir l'estomac barbouillé** to feel queasy

barbu, e [baʀby] *adj* bearded

barda [baʀda] (*fam*) *nm* kit, gear

barder [baʀde] *vi*: **ça va ~** sparks will fly, things are going to get hot

barème [baʀɛm] *nm* (*SCOL*) scale; (*table de référence*) table

baril [baʀi(l)] *nm* barrel; (*poudre*) keg

bariolé, e [baʀjɔle] *adj* gaudily-coloured

baromètre [baʀɔmɛtʀ] *nm* barometer

baron, ne [baʀɔ̃] *nm/f* baron(ess)

baroque [baʀɔk] *adj* (*ART*) baroque; (*fig*) weird

barque [baʀk] *nf* small boat

barquette [baʀkɛt] *nf* (*pour repas*) tray; (*pour fruits*) punnet

barrage [baʀaʒ] *nm* dam; (*sur route*) road-block, barricade

barre [baʀ] *nf* bar; (*NAVIG*) helm; (*écrite*) line, stroke

barreau, x [baʀo] *nm* bar; (*JUR*): **le ~** the Bar

barrer [baʀe] *vt* (*route etc*) to block; (*mot*) to cross out; (*chèque*) to cross (*BRIT*); (*NAVIG*) to steer; **se ~** (*fam*) *vi* to clear off

barrette [baʀɛt] *nf* (*pour cheveux*) (hair) slide (*BRIT*) *ou* clip (*US*)

barricader [baʀikade]: **se ~** *vi* to barricade o.s.

barrière [baʀjɛʀ] *nf* fence; (*obstacle*) barrier; (*porte*) gate

barrique [baʀik] *nf* barrel, cask

bar-tabac [baʀtaba] *nm* bar (which sells tobacco and stamps)

bas, basse [bɑ, bɑs] *adj* low ♦ *nm* bottom, lower part; (*vêtement*) stocking ♦ *adv* low; (*parler*) softly; **au ~ mot** at the lowest estimate; **en ~** down below; (*d'une liste, d'un mur etc*) at/to the bottom; (*dans une maison*) downstairs; **en ~ de** at the bottom of; **un enfant en ~ âge** a young child; **~ ...!** down with ...!; **~ morceaux** *nmpl* (*viande*) cheap cuts

basané, e [bazane] *adj* tanned

bas-côté [bɑkote] *nm* (*de route*) verge (*BRIT*), shoulder (*US*)

bascule [baskyl] *nf*: **(jeu de) ~** seesaw; **(balance à) ~** scales *pl*; **fauteuil à ~** rocking chair

basculer [baskyle] *vi* to fall over, topple (over); (*benne*) to tip up ♦ *vt* (*contenu*) to tip out; (*benne*) to tip up

base [bɑz] *nf* base; (*POL*) rank and file; (*fondement, principe*) basis; **de ~** basic; **à ~ de café** *etc* coffee *etc* -based; **~ de données** database; **baser** *vt* to base; **se baser sur** *vt* (*preuves*) to base one's argument on

bas-fond [bɑfɔ̃] *nm* (*NAVIG*) shallow; **~-~s** *nmpl* (*fig*) dregs

basilic [bazilik] *nm* (*CULIN*) basil

basket [baskɛt] *nm* trainer (*BRIT*), sneaker (*US*); (*aussi*: **~-ball**) basketball

basque [bask] *adj, nm/f* Basque

basse [bɑs] *adj voir* **bas** ♦ *nf* (*MUS*) bass; **basse-cour** *nf* farmyard

bassin [basɛ̃] *nm* (*pièce d'eau*) pond, pool; (*de fontaine, GÉO*) basin; (*ANAT*) pelvis; (*portuaire*) dock

bassine [basin] *nf* (*ustensile*) basin; (*contenu*) bowl(ful)

basson [basɔ̃] *nm* bassoon

bas-ventre [bavɑ̃tʀ] *nm* (lower part of the) stomach

bat [ba] *vb voir* **battre**

bataille [batɑj] *nf* (*MIL*) battle; (*rixe*) fight; **batailler** *vi* to fight

bâtard, e [bɑtaʀ, aʀd] *nm/f* illegitimate child, bastard (*péj*)

bateau, x [bato] *nm* boat, ship; **bateau-mouche** *nm* passenger pleasure boat (on the Seine)

bâti, e [bati] *adj*: **bien ~** well-built
batifoler [batifɔle] *vi* to frolic about
bâtiment [batimɑ̃] *nm* building; (*NAVIG*) ship, vessel; (*industrie*) building trade
bâtir [batir] *vt* to build
bâtisse [batis] *nf* building
bâton [batɔ̃] *nm* stick; **à ~s rompus** informally
bats [ba] *vb voir* **battre**
battage [bataʒ] *nm* (*publicité*) (hard) plugging
battant [batɑ̃, ɑ̃t] *nm*: **porte à double ~** double door
battement [batmɑ̃] *nm* (*de cœur*) beat; (*intervalle*) interval (*between classes, trains*); **10 minutes de ~** 10 minutes to spare
batterie [batri] *nf* (*MIL, ÉLEC*) battery; (*MUS*) drums *pl*, drum kit; **~ de cuisine** pots and pans *pl*, kitchen utensils *pl*
batteur [batœr] *nm* (*MUS*) drummer; (*appareil*) whisk
battre [batr] *vt* to beat; (*blé*) to thresh; (*passer au peigne fin*) to scour; (*cartes*) to shuffle ♦ *vi* (*cœur*) to beat; (*volets etc*) to bang, rattle; **se ~** *vi* to fight; **~ la mesure** to beat time; **~ son plein** to be at its height, be going full swing; **~ des mains** to clap one's hands
battue [baty] *nf* (*chasse*) beat; (*policière etc*) search, hunt
baume [bom] *nm* balm
baux [bo] *nmpl de* **bail**
bavard, e [bavar, ard] *adj* (very) talkative, gossipy; **bavarder** *vi* to chatter; (*commérer*) to gossip; (*divulguer un secret*) to blab
bave [bav] *nf* dribble; (*de chien etc*) slobber; (*d'escargot*) slime; **baver** *vi* to dribble; (*chien*) to slobber; **en baver** (*fam*) to have a hard time (of it); **baveux, -euse** *adj* (*omelette*) runny; **bavoir** *nm* bib
bavure [bavyr] *nf* smudge; (*fig*) hitch; (*policière etc*) blunder
bayer [baje] *vi*: **~ aux corneilles** to stand gaping
bazar [bazar] *nm* general store; (*fam*) jumble; **bazarder** (*fam*) *vt* to chuck out

BCBG *sigle adj* (= *bon chic bon genre*) preppy, smart and trendy
BCE *sigle f* (= *Banque centrale européenne*) ECB
BD *sigle f* = **bande dessinée**
bd *abr* = **boulevard**
béant, e [beɑ̃, ɑ̃t] *adj* gaping
béat, e [bea, at] *adj*: **~ d'admiration** struck dumb with admiration; **béatitude** *nf* bliss
beau (bel), belle [bo, bɛl] (*mpl* **beaux**) *adj* beautiful, lovely; (*homme*) handsome; (*femme*) beautiful ♦ *adv*: **il fait beau** the weather's fine; **un ~jour** one (fine) day; **de plus belle** more than ever, even more; **on a ~essayer** however hard we try; **bel et bien** well and truly

---
MOT-CLÉ
---

beaucoup [boku] *adv* **1** a lot; **il boit beaucoup** he drinks a lot; **il ne boit pas beaucoup** he doesn't drink much *ou* a lot
2 (*suivi de plus, trop etc*) much, a lot, far; **il est beaucoup plus grand** he is much *ou* a lot *ou* far taller
3: **beaucoup de** (*nombre*) many, a lot of; (*quantité*) a lot of; **beaucoup d'étudiants/de touristes** a lot of *ou* many students/tourists; **beaucoup de courage** a lot of courage; **il n'a pas beaucoup d'argent** he hasn't got much *ou* at lot of money
4: **de beaucoup** by far

---

beau...: **beau-fils** *nm* son-in-law; (*remariage*) stepson; **beau-frère** *nm* brother-in-law; **beau-père** *nm* father-in-law; (*remariage*) stepfather
beauté [bote] *nf* beauty; **de toute ~** beautiful; **finir qch en ~** to complete sth brilliantly
beaux-arts [bozar] *nmpl* fine arts
beaux-parents [boparɑ̃] *nmpl* wife's/husband's family, in-laws
bébé [bebe] *nm* baby
bec [bɛk] *nm* beak, bill; (*de théière*) spout; (*de casserole*) lip; (*fam*) mouth; **~ de gaz** (street) gaslamp; **~ verseur** pouring lip

bécane [bekan] (*fam*) *nf* bike

bec-de-lièvre [bɛkdəljɛvʀ] *nm* harelip

bêche [bɛʃ] *nf* spade; **bêcher** *vt* to dig

bécoter [bekɔte]: **se ~** *vi* to smooch

becqueter [bɛkte] (*fam*) *vt* to eat

bedaine [bədɛn] *nf* paunch

bedonnant, e [bədɔnɑ̃, ɑ̃t] *adj* potbellied

bée [be] *adj*: **bouche ~** gaping

beffroi [befʀwa] *nm* belfry

bégayer [begeje] *vt*, *vi* to stammer

bègue [bɛg] *nm/f*: **être ~** to have a stammer

beige [bɛʒ] *adj* beige

beignet [bɛɲɛ] *nm* fritter

bel [bɛl] *adj voir* **beau**

bêler [bele] *vi* to bleat

belette [bəlɛt] *nf* weasel

belge [bɛlʒ] *adj* Belgian ♦ *nm/f*: **B~** Belgian

Belgique [bɛlʒik] *nf*: **la ~** Belgium

bélier [belje] *nm* ram; (*signe*): **le B~** Aries

belle [bɛl] *adj voir* **beau** ♦ *nf* (*SPORT*) decider; **belle-fille** *nf* daughter-in-law; (*remariage*) stepdaughter; **belle-mère** *nf* mother-in-law; stepmother; **belle-sœur** *nf* sister-in-law

belliqueux, -euse [belikø, øz] *adj* aggressive, warlike

belvédère [bɛlvedɛʀ] *nm* panoramic viewpoint (*or small building there*)

bémol [bemɔl] *nm* (*MUS*) flat

bénédiction [benediksjɔ̃] *nf* blessing

bénéfice [benefis] *nm* (*COMM*) profit; (*avantage*) benefit; **bénéficier: bénéficier de** *vt* to enjoy; (*situation*) to benefit by *ou* from; **bénéfique** *adj* beneficial

bénévole [benevɔl] *adj* voluntary, unpaid

bénin, -igne [benɛ̃, iɲ] *adj* minor, mild; (*tumeur*) benign

bénir [beniʀ] *vt* to bless; **bénit, e** *adj* consecrated; **eau bénite** holy water

benjamin, e [bɛ̃ʒamɛ̃, in] *nm/f* youngest child

benne [bɛn] *nf* skip; (*de téléphérique*) (*cable*) car; **~ basculante** tipper (*BRIT*), dump truck (*US*)

BEP *sigle m* (= *brevet d'études professionnelles*) technical school certificate

béquille [bekij] *nf* crutch; (*de bicyclette*) stand

berceau, x [bɛʀso] *nm* cradle, crib

bercer [bɛʀse] *vt* to rock, cradle; (*suj: musique etc*) to lull; **~ qn de** (*promesses etc*) to delude sb with; **berceuse** *nf* lullaby

béret (basque) [beʀɛ (bask(ə))] *nm* beret

berge [bɛʀʒ] *nf* bank

berger, -ère [bɛʀʒe, ɛʀ] *nm/f* shepherd(-ess); **~ allemand** alsatian (*BRIT*), German shepherd

berlingot [bɛʀlɛ̃go] *nm* (*bonbon*) boiled sweet, humbug (*BRIT*)

berlue [bɛʀly] *nf*: **j'ai la ~** I must be seeing things

berner [bɛʀne] *vt* to fool

besogne [bəzɔɲ] *nf* work *no pl*, job

besoin [bəzwɛ̃] *nm* need; **avoir ~ de qch/faire qch** to need sth/to do sth; **au ~** if need be; **le ~** (*pauvreté*) need, want; **être dans le ~** to be in need *ou* want; **faire ses ~s** to relieve o.s.

bestiaux [bɛstjo] *nmpl* cattle

bestiole [bɛstjɔl] *nf* (*tiny*) creature

bétail [betaj] *nm* livestock, cattle *pl*

bête [bɛt] *nf* animal; (*bestiole*) insect, creature ♦ *adj* stupid, silly; **il cherche la petite ~** he's being pernickety *ou* overfussy; **~ noire** pet hate

bêtement [bɛtmɑ̃] *adv* stupidly

bêtise [betiz] *nf* stupidity; (*action*) stupid thing (to say *ou* do)

béton [betɔ̃] *nm* concrete; (**en**) **~** (*alibi, argument*) cast iron; **~ armé** reinforced concrete; **bétonnière** *nf* cement mixer

betterave [bɛtʀav] *nf* beetroot (*BRIT*), beet (*US*); **~ sucrière** sugar beet

beugler [bøgle] *vi* to low; (*radio etc*) to blare ♦ *vt* (*chanson*) to bawl out

Beur [bœʀ] *nm/f* person of North African origin living in France

beurre [bœʀ] *nm* butter; **beurrer** *vt* to butter; **beurrier** *nm* butter dish

beuverie [bøvʀi] *nf* drinking session

bévue [bevy] *nf* blunder

Beyrouth [berut] *n* Beirut

bi... [bi] *préfixe* bi..., two-

biais [bjɛ] *nm* (*moyen*) device, expedient; (*aspect*) angle; **en ~, de ~** (*obliquement*) at an angle; **par le ~ de** by means of; **biaiser** *vi* (*fig*) to sidestep the issue

bibelot [biblo] *nm* trinket, curio

biberon [bibʀɔ̃] *nm* (feeding) bottle; **nourrir au ~** to bottle-feed

bible [bibl] *nf* bible

biblio... [bibl] *préfixe*: **bibliobus** *nm* mobile library van; **bibliographie** *nf* bibliography; **bibliothécaire** *nm/f* librarian; **bibliothèque** *nf* library; (*meuble*) bookcase

bic ® [bik] *nm* Biro ®

bicarbonate [bikaʀbɔnat] *nm*: **~ (de soude)** bicarbonate of soda

biceps [bisɛps] *nm* biceps

biche [biʃ] *nf* doe

bichonner [biʃɔne] *vt* to pamper

bicolore [bikɔlɔʀ] *adj* two-coloured

bicoque [bikɔk] (*péj*) *nf* shack

bicyclette [bisiklɛt] *nf* bicycle

bide [bid] (*fam*) *nm* (*ventre*) belly; (*THÉÂTRE*) flop

bidet [bidɛ] *nm* bidet

bidon [bidɔ̃] *nm* can ♦ *adj inv* (*fam*) phoney

bidonville [bidɔ̃vil] *nm* shanty town

bidule [bidyl] (*fam*) *nm* thingumajig

MOT-CLÉ

---

bien [bjɛ̃] *nm* **1** (*avantage, profit*): **faire du bien à qn** to do sb good; **dire du bien de** to speak well of; **c'est pour son bien** it's for his own good

2 (*possession, patrimoine*) possession, property; **son bien le plus précieux** his most treasured possession; **avoir du bien** to have property; **biens** (**de consommation** *etc*) (consumer *etc*) goods

3 (*moral*): **le bien** good; **distinguer le bien du mal** to tell good from evil

♦ *adv* **1** (*de façon satisfaisante*) well; **elle travaille/mange bien** she works/eats well; **croyant bien faire, je/il ...** thinking I/he was doing the right thing, I/he ...; **c'est bien fait!** it serves him (*ou* her *etc*) right!

2 (*valeur intensive*) quite; **bien jeune** quite young; **bien assez** quite enough; **bien mieux** (very) much better; **j'espère bien y aller** I do hope to go; **je veux bien le faire** (*concession*) I'm quite willing to do it; **il faut bien le faire** it has to be done

3: **bien du temps/des gens** quite a time/a number of people

♦ *adj inv* **1** (*en bonne forme, à l'aise*): **je me sens bien** I feel fine; **je ne me sens pas bien** I don't feel well; **on est bien dans ce fauteuil** this chair is very comfortable

2 (*joli, beau*) good-looking; **tu es bien dans cette robe** you look good in that dress

3 (*satisfaisant*) good; **elle est bien, cette maison/secrétaire** it's a good house/she's a good secretary

4 (*moralement*) right; (: *personne*) good, nice; (*respectable*) respectable; **ce n'est pas bien de ...** it's not right to ...; **elle est bien, cette femme** she's a nice woman, she's a good sort; **des gens biens** respectable people

5 (*en bons termes*): **être bien avec qn** to be on good terms with sb

♦ *préfixe*: **bien-aimé, e** *adj, nm/f* beloved; **bien-être** *nm* well-being; **bienfaisance** *nf* charity; **bienfaisant, e** *adj* (*chose*) beneficial; **bienfait** *nm* act of generosity, benefaction; (*de la science etc*) benefit; **bienfaiteur, -trice** *nm/f* benefactor/benefactress; **bien-fondé** *nm* soundness; **bien-fonds** *nm* property; **bienheureux, -euse** *adj* happy; (*REL*) blessed, blest; **bien que** *conj* (al)though; **bien sûr** *adv* certainly

---

bienséant, e [bjɛ̃seã, ãt] *adj* seemly

bientôt [bjɛ̃to] *adv* soon; **à ~** see you

soon

bienveillant, e [bjɛ̃vɛjɑ̃, ɑ̃t] *adj* kindly

bienvenu, e [bjɛ̃vny] *adj* welcome; **bienvenue** *nf*: **souhaiter la bienvenue à** to welcome; **bienvenue à** welcome to

bière [bjɛʀ] *nf* (*boisson*) beer; (*cercueil*) bier; **~ (à la) pression** draught beer; **~ blonde** lager; **~ brune** brown ale

biffer [bife] *vt* to cross out

bifteck [biftɛk] *nm* steak

bifurquer [bifyʀke] *vi* (*route*) to fork; (*véhicule*) to turn off

bigarré, e [bigaʀe] *adj* multicoloured; (*disparate*) motley

bigorneau, x [bigɔʀno] *nm* winkle

bigot, e [bigo, ɔt] (*péj*) *adj* bigoted

bigoudi [bigudi] *nm* curler

bijou, x [biʒu] *nm* jewel; **bijouterie** *nf* jeweller's (shop); **bijoutier, -ière** *nm/f* jeweller

bikini [bikini] *nm* bikini

bilan [bilɑ̃] *nm* (*fig*) (net) outcome; (*: de victimes*) toll; (*COMM*) balance sheet(s); **un ~ de santé** a (medical) checkup; **faire le ~ de** to assess, review; **déposer son ~** to file a bankruptcy statement

bile [bil] *nf* bile; **se faire de la ~** (*fam*) to worry o.s. sick

bilieux, -euse [biljø, øz] *adj* bilious; (*fig: colérique*) testy

bilingue [bilɛ̃g] *adj* bilingual

billard [bijaʀ] *nm* (*jeu*) billiards *sg*; (*table*) billiard table; **~ américain** pool

bille [bij] *nf* (*gén*) ball; (*du jeu de ~s*) marble

billet [bije] *nm* (*aussi:* **~ de banque**) (bank)note; (*de cinéma, de bus etc*) ticket; (*courte lettre*) note; **~ Bige** cheap rail ticket for under-26s; **billetterie** *nf* ticket office; (*distributeur*) ticket machine; (*BANQUE*) cash dispenser

billion [biljɔ̃] *nm* billion (*BRIT*), trillion (*US*)

billot [bijo] *nm* block

bimensuel, le [bimɑ̃sɥɛl] *adj* bimonthly

binette [binɛt] *nf* hoe

bio... [bjɔ] *préfixe* bio...; **biochimie** *nf* biochemistry; **biodiversité** *nf* biodiversity; **bioéthique** *nf* bioethics *sg*; **biographie** *nf* biography; **biologie** *nf* biology; **biologique** *adj* biological; (*produits, aliments*) organic; **biologiste** *nm/f* biologist

Birmanie [biʀmani] *nf* Burma

bis [bis] *adv*: **12 ~** 12a *ou* A ♦ *excl, nm* encore

bisannuel, le [bizanɥɛl] *adj* biennial

biscornu, e [biskɔʀny] *adj* twisted

biscotte [biskɔt] *nf* toasted bread (*sold in packets*)

biscuit [biskɥi] *nm* biscuit; **~ de savoie** sponge cake

bise [biz] *nf* (*fam: baiser*) kiss; (*vent*) North wind; **grosses ~s (de)** (*sur lettre*) love and kisses (from)

bisou [bizu] (*fam*) *nm* kiss

bissextile [bisɛkstil] *adj*: **année ~** leap year

bistouri [bisturi] *nm* lancet

bistro(t) [bistro] *nm* bistro, café

bitume [bitym] *nm* asphalt

bizarre [bizaʀ] *adj* strange, odd

blafard, e [blafaʀ, aʀd] *adj* wan

blague [blag] *nf* (*propos*) joke; (*farce*) trick; **sans ~!** no kidding!; **blaguer** *vi* to joke

blaireau, x [blɛʀo] *nm* (*ZOOL*) badger; (*brosse*) shaving brush

blairer [blere] (*fam*) *vt*: **je ne peux pas le ~** I can't bear *ou* stand him

blâme [blɑm] *nm* blame; (*sanction*) reprimand; **blâmer** *vt* to blame

blanc, blanche [blɑ̃, blɑ̃ʃ] *adj* white; (*non imprimé*) blank ♦ *nm/f* white, white man(-woman) ♦ *nm* (*couleur*) white; (*espace non écrit*) blank; (*aussi:* **~ d'œuf**) (egg-)white; (*aussi:* **~ de poulet**) breast, white meat; (*aussi:* **vin ~**) white wine; **~ cassé** off-white; **chèque en ~** blank cheque; **à ~** (*chauffer*) white-hot; (*tirer, charger*) with blanks; **blanc-bec** *nm* greenhorn; **blanche** *nf* (*MUS*) minim (*BRIT*), half-note (*US*); **blancheur** *nf* whiteness

blanchir [blɑ̃ʃiʀ] *vt* (*gén*) to whiten; (*linge*) to launder; (*CULIN*) to blanch; (*fig: discul-*

per) to clear ♦ *vi* to grow white; (*cheveux*) to go white; **blanchisserie** *nf* laundry
blason [blazɔ̃] *nm* coat of arms
blasphème [blasfɛm] *nm* blasphemy
blazer [blazɛʀ] *nm* blazer
blé [ble] *nm* wheat; **~ noir** buckwheat
bled [blɛd] (*péj*) *nm* hole
blême [blɛm] *adj* pale
blessant, e [blesɑ̃, ɑ̃t] *adj* (*offensant*) hurtful
blessé, e [blese] *adj* injured ♦ *nm/f* injured person, casualty
blesser [blese] *vt* to injure; (*délibérément*: *MIL etc*) to wound; (*offenser*) to hurt; **se ~** to injure o.s.; **se ~ au pied** *etc* to injure one's foot *etc*; **blessure** *nf* (*accidentelle*) injury; (*intentionnelle*) wound
bleu, e [blø] *adj* blue; (*bifteck*) very rare ♦ *nm* (*couleur*) blue; (*contusion*) bruise; (*vêtement*: *aussi*: **~s**) overalls *pl*; **~ marine** navy blue; **bleuet** *nm* cornflower; **bleuté, e** *adj* blue-shaded
blinder [blɛ̃de] *vt* to armour; (*fig*) to harden
bloc [blɔk] *nm* (*de pierre etc*) block; (*de papier à lettres*) pad; (*ensemble*) group, block; **serré à ~** tightened right down; **en ~** as a whole; **~ opératoire** operating *ou* theatre block; **~ sanitaire** toilet block; **blocage** *nm* (*des prix*) freezing; (*PSYCH*) hang-up; **bloc-notes** *nm* note pad
blocus [blɔkys] *nm* blockade
blond, e [blɔ̃, blɔ̃d] *adj* fair, blond; (*sable, blés*) golden; **~ cendré** ash blond; **blonde** *nf* (*femme*) blonde; (*bière*) lager; (*cigarette*) Virginia cigarette
bloquer [blɔke] *vt* (*passage*) to block; (*pièce mobile*) to jam; (*crédits, compte*) to freeze; **se ~** to jam; (*PSYCH*) to have a mental block
blottir [blɔtiʀ]: **se ~** *vi* to huddle up
blouse [bluz] *nf* overall
blouson [bluzɔ̃] *nm* blouson jacket; **~ noir** (*fig*) ≃ rocker
blue-jean [bludʒin] *nm* (pair of) jeans
bluff [blœf] *nm* bluff; **bluffer** *vi* to bluff
bobard [bɔbaʀ] (*fam*) *nm* tall story
bobine [bɔbin] *nf* reel; (*ÉLEC*) coil

bocal, -aux [bɔkal, o] *nm* jar
bock [bɔk] *nm* glass of beer
body [bɔdi] *nm* body(suit); (*SPORT*) leotard
bœuf [bœf] *nm* ox; (*CULIN*) beef
bof! [bɔf] (*fam*) *excl* don't care!; (*pas terrible*) nothing special
bogue [bɔg] *nm*: **le ~ de l'an 2000** the millennium bug
bohème [bɔɛm] *adj* happy-go-lucky, unconventional; **bohémien, ne** *nm/f* gipsy
boire [bwaʀ] *vt* to drink; (*s'imprégner de*) to soak up; **~ un coup** (*fam*) to have a drink
bois [bwa] *nm* wood; **de ~, en ~** wooden; **boisé, e** *adj* woody, wooded
boisson [bwasɔ̃] *nf* drink
boîte [bwat] *nf* box; (*fam*: *entreprise*) firm; **aliments en ~** canned *ou* tinned (*BRIT*) foods; **~ aux lettres** letter box; **~ d'allumettes** box of matches; (*vide*) matchbox; **~ (de conserve)** can *ou* tin (*BRIT*) (of food); **~ de nuit** night club; **~ de vitesses** gear box; **~ postale** PO Box; **~ vocale** (*TEL*) voice mail
boiter [bwate] *vi* to limp; (*fig: raisonnement*) to be shaky
boîtier [bwatje] *nm* case
boive *etc* [bwav] *vb voir* **boire**
bol [bɔl] *nm* bowl; **un ~ d'air** a breath of fresh air; **j'en ai ras le ~** (*fam*) I'm fed up with this; **avoir du ~** (*fam*) to be lucky
bolide [bɔlid] *nm* racing car; **comme un ~** at top speed, like a rocket
bombardement [bɔ̃baʀdəmɑ̃] *nm* bombing
bombarder [bɔ̃baʀde] *vt* to bomb; **~ qn de** (*cailloux, lettres*) to bombard sb with
bombe [bɔ̃b] *nf* bomb; (*atomiseur*) (aerosol) spray; **bombé, e** *adj* (*forme*) rounded; **bomber** *vt*: **bomber le torse** to swell out one's chest

MOT-CLÉ

bon, bonne [bɔ̃, bɔn] *adj* 1 (*agréable, satisfaisant*) good; **un bon repas/restaurant** a good meal/restaurant; **être bon en maths** to be good at maths

2 (*charitable*): **être bon (envers)** to be good (to)

3 (*correct*) right; **le bon numéro/moment** the right number/moment

4 (*souhaits*): **bon anniversaire** happy birthday; **bon voyage** have a good trip; **bonne chance** good luck; **bonne année** happy New Year; **bonne nuit** good night

5 (*approprié, apte*): **bon à/pour** fit to/for

6: **bon enfant** *adj inv* accommodating, easy-going; **bonne femme** (*péj*) woman; **de bonne heure** early; **bon marché** *adj inv* cheap ♦ *adv* cheap; **bon mot** witticism; **bon sens** common sense; **bon vivant** jovial chap; **bonnes œuvres** charitable works, charities

♦ *nm* **1** (*billet*) voucher; (*aussi*: **bon cadeau**) gift voucher; **bon d'essence** petrol coupon; **bon du Trésor** Treasury bond

2: **avoir du bon** to have its good points; **pour de bon** for good

♦ *adv*: **il fait bon** it's *ou* the weather is fine; **sentir bon** to smell good; **tenir bon** to stand firm

♦ *excl* good!; **ah bon?** really?; *voir aussi* **bonne**

---

bonbon [bɔ̃bɔ̃] *nm* (boiled) sweet

bonbonne [bɔ̃bɔn] *nf* demijohn

bond [bɔ̃] *nm* leap; **faire un ~** to leap in the air

bondé, e [bɔ̃de] *adj* packed (full)

bondir [bɔ̃diʀ] *vi* to leap

bonheur [bɔnœʀ] *nm* happiness; **porter ~ (à qn)** to bring (sb) luck; **au petit ~** haphazardly; **par ~** fortunately

bonhomie [bɔnɔmi] *nf* goodnaturedness

bonhomme [bɔnɔm] (*pl* **bonshommes**) *nm* fellow; **~ de neige** snowman

bonifier [bɔnifje] *vt* to improve

boniment [bɔnimɑ̃] *nm* patter *no pl*

bonjour [bɔ̃ʒuʀ] *excl, nm* hello; (*selon l'heure*) good morning/afternoon; **c'est simple comme ~!** it's easy as pie!

bonne [bɔn] *adj voir* **bon** ♦ *nf* (*domestique*) maid; **bonnement** *adv*: **tout bonnement** quite simply

bonnet [bɔnɛ] *nm* hat; (*de soutien-gorge*) cup; **~ de bain** bathing cap

bonshommes [bɔ̃zɔm] *nmpl de* **bonhomme**

bonsoir [bɔ̃swaʀ] *excl* good evening

bonté [bɔ̃te] *nf* kindness *no pl*

bonus [bɔnys] *nm* no-claims bonus

bord [bɔʀ] *nm* (*de table, verre, falaise*) edge; (*de rivière, lac*) bank; (*de route*) side; **(monter) à ~** (to go) on board; **jeter par-dessus ~** to throw overboard; **le commandant de/les hommes du ~** the ship's master/crew; **au ~ de la mer** at the seaside; **être au ~ des larmes** to be on the verge of tears

bordeaux [bɔʀdo] *nm* Bordeaux (wine) ♦ *adj inv* maroon

bordel [bɔʀdɛl] *nm* brothel; (*fam!*) bloody mess (*!*)

bordelais, e [bɔʀdəlɛ, ɛz] *adj* of *ou* from Bordeaux

border [bɔʀde] *vt* (*être le long de*) to line; (*qn dans son lit*) to tuck up; (*garnir*): **~ qch de** to edge sth with

bordereau, x [bɔʀdəro] *nm* (*formulaire*) slip

bordure [bɔʀdyʀ] *nf* border; **en ~ de** on the edge of

borgne [bɔʀɲ] *adj* one-eyed

borne [bɔʀn] *nf* boundary stone; (*aussi*: **~ kilométrique**) kilometre-marker; ≈ milestone; **~s** *nfpl* (*fig*) limits; **dépasser les ~s** to go too far

borné, e [bɔʀne] *adj* (*personne*) narrow-minded

borner [bɔʀne] *vt*: **se ~ à faire** (*se contenter de*) to content o.s. with doing; (*se limiter à*) to limit o.s. to doing

bosquet [bɔskɛ] *nm* grove

bosse [bɔs] *nf* (*de terrain etc*) bump; (*enflure*) lump; (*du bossu, du chameau*) hump; **avoir la ~ des maths** *etc* (*fam*) to have a gift for maths *etc*; **il a roulé sa ~** (*fam*) he's been around

bosser [bɔse] (*fam*) *vi* (*travailler*) to work; (*travailler dur*) to slave (away)

bossu, e [bɔsy] *nm/f* hunchback

botanique [bɔtanik] *nf* botany ♦ *adj* botanic(al)

botte [bɔt] *nf* (*soulier*) (high) boot; (*gerbe*): ~ **de paille** bundle of straw; ~ **de radis** bunch of radishes; ~**s de caoutchouc** wellington boots; **botter** *vt*: **ça me botte** (*fam*) I fancy that

bottin [bɔtɛ̃] *nm* directory

bottine [bɔtin] *nf* ankle boot

bouc [buk] *nm* goat; (*barbe*) goatee; ~ **émissaire** scapegoat

boucan [bukɑ̃] (*fam*) *nm* din, racket

bouche [buʃ] *nf* mouth; **rester ~ bée** to stand open-mouthed; **le ~ à ~** the kiss of life; ~ **d'égout** manhole; ~ **d'incendie** fire hydrant; ~ **de métro** métro entrance

bouché, e [buʃe] *adj* (*temps, ciel*) overcast; **c'est ~** there's no future in it

bouchée [buʃe] *nf* mouthful; ~**s à la reine** chicken vol-au-vents

boucher, -ère [buʃe] *nm/f* butcher ♦ *vt* (*trou*) to fill up; (*obstruer*) to block (up); **se ~** *vi* (*tuyau etc*) to block up, get blocked up; **j'ai le nez bouché** my nose is blocked; **se ~ le nez** to hold one's nose; **boucherie** *nf* butcher's (shop); (*fig*) slaughter

bouche-trou [buʃtʀu] *nm* (*fig*) stop-gap

bouchon [buʃɔ̃] *nm* stopper; (*de tube*) top; (*en liège*) cork; (*fig: embouteillage*) holdup; (*PÊCHE*) float

boucle [bukl] *nf* (*forme, figure*) loop; (*objet*) buckle; ~ **de cheveux** curl; ~ **d'oreille** earring

bouclé, e [bukle] *adj* (*cheveux*) curly

boucler [bukle] *vt* (*fermer: ceinture etc*) to fasten; (*terminer*) to finish off; (*fam: enfermer*) to shut away; (*quartier*) to seal off ♦ *vi* to curl

bouclier [buklije] *nm* shield

bouddhiste [budist] *nm/f* Buddhist

bouder [bude] *vi* to sulk ♦ *vt* to stay away from

boudin [budɛ̃] *nm*: ~ **(noir)** black pudding; ~ **blanc** white pudding

boue [bu] *nf* mud

bouée [bwe] *nf* buoy; ~ **(de sauvetage)** lifebuoy

boueux, -euse [bwø, øz] *adj* muddy

bouffe [buf] (*fam*) *nf* grub (*fam*), food

bouffée [bufe] *nf* (*de cigarette*) puff; **une ~ d'air pur** a breath of fresh air

bouffer [bufe] (*fam*) *vi* to eat

bouffi, e [bufi] *adj* swollen

bougeoir [buʒwaʀ] *nm* candlestick

bougeotte [buʒɔt] *nf*: **avoir la ~** (*fam*) to have the fidgets

bouger [buʒe] *vi* to move; (*dent etc*) to be loose; (*s'activer*) to get moving ♦ *vt* to move; **les prix/les couleurs n'ont pas bougé** prices/colours haven't changed

bougie [buʒi] *nf* candle; (*AUTO*) spark(ing) plug

bougon, ne [buɡɔ̃, ɔn] *adj* grumpy

bougonner [buɡɔne] *vi, vt* to grumble

bouillabaisse [bujabɛs] *nf* type of fish soup

bouillant, e [bujɑ̃, ɑ̃t] *adj* (*qui bout*) boiling; (*très chaud*) boiling (hot)

bouillie [buji] *nf* (*de bébé*) cereal; **en ~** (*fig*) crushed

bouillir [bujiʀ] *vi, vt* to boil; ~ **d'impatience** to seethe with impatience

bouilloire [bujwaʀ] *nf* kettle

bouillon [bujɔ̃] *nm* (*CULIN*) stock *no pl*; **bouillonner** *vi* to bubble; (*fig: idées*) to bubble up

bouillotte [bujɔt] *nf* hot-water bottle

boulanger, -ère [bulɑ̃ʒe, ɛʀ] *nm/f* baker; **boulangerie** *nf* bakery; **boulangerie-pâtisserie** *nf* baker's and confectioner's (shop)

boule [bul] *nf* (*gén*) ball; ~**s** *nfpl* (*jeu*) bowls; **se mettre en ~** (*fig: fam*) to fly off the handle, to blow one's top; **jouer aux** ~**s** to play bowls; ~ **de neige** snowball

bouleau, x [bulo] *nm* (silver) birch

bouledogue [buldɔg] *nm* bulldog

boulet [bulɛ] *nm* (*aussi*: ~ **de canon**) can-

nonball
boulette [bulɛt] *nf* (*de viande*) meatball
boulevard [bulvaʀ] *nm* boulevard
bouleversant, e [bulvɛʀsɑ̃, ɑ̃t] *adj* (*scène, récit*) deeply moving
bouleversement [bulvɛʀsəmɑ̃] *nm* upheaval
bouleverser [bulvɛʀse] *vt* (*émouvoir*) to overwhelm; (*causer du chagrin*) to distress; (*pays, vie*) to disrupt; (*papiers, objets*) to turn upside down
boulon [bulɔ̃] *nm* bolt
boulot, te [bulo, ɔt] *adj* plump, tubby ♦ *nm* (*fam: travail*) work
boum [bum] *nm* bang ♦ *nf* (*fam*) party
bouquet [bukɛ] *nm* (*de fleurs*) bunch (of flowers), bouquet; (*de persil etc*) bunch; **c'est le ~!** (*fam*) that takes the biscuit!
bouquin [bukɛ̃] (*fam*) *nm* book; **bouquiner** (*fam*) *vi* to read; **bouquiniste** *nm/f* bookseller
bourbeux, -euse [buʀbø, øz] *adj* muddy
bourbier [buʀbje] *nm* (quag)mire
bourde [buʀd] (*fam*) *nf* (*erreur*) howler; (*gaffe*) blunder
bourdon [buʀdɔ̃] *nm* bumblebee; **bourdonner** *vi* to buzz
bourg [buʀ] *nm* small market town
bourgeois, e [buʀʒwa, waz] (*péj*) *adj* ≈ (upper) middle class; **bourgeoisie** *nf* ≈ upper middle classes *pl*
bourgeon [buʀʒɔ̃] *nm* bud
Bourgogne [buʀgɔɲ] *nf*: **la ~** Burgundy ♦ *nm*: **b~** burgundy (wine)
bourguignon, ne [buʀgiɲɔ̃, ɔn] *adj* of *ou* from Burgundy, Burgundian
bourlinguer [buʀlɛ̃ge] (*fam*) *vi* to knock about a lot, get around a lot
bourrade [buʀad] *nf* shove, thump
bourrage [buʀaʒ] *nm*: **~ de crâne** brainwashing; (*SCOL*) cramming
bourrasque [buʀask] *nf* squall
bourratif, -ive [buʀatif, iv] (*fam*) *adj* filling, stodgy (*pej*)
bourré, e [buʀe] *adj* (*fam: ivre*) plastered, tanked up (*BRIT*); (*rempli*): **~ de** crammed

full of
bourreau, x [buʀo] *nm* executioner; (*fig*) torturer; **~ de travail** workaholic
bourrelet [buʀlɛ] *nm* fold *ou* roll (of flesh)
bourrer [buʀe] *vt* (*pipe*) to fill; (*poêle*) to pack; (*valise*) to cram (full)
bourrique [buʀik] *nf* (*âne*) ass
bourru, e [buʀy] *adj* surly, gruff
bourse [buʀs] *nf* (*subvention*) grant; (*porte-monnaie*) purse; **la B~** the Stock Exchange
boursier, -ière [buʀsje, jɛʀ] *nm/f* (*étudiant*) grant holder
boursoufler [buʀsufle]: **se ~** *vi* to swell (up)
bous [bu] *vb voir* **bouillir**
bousculade [buskylad] *nf* (*hâte*) rush; (*cohue*) crush; **bousculer** *vt* (*heurter*) to knock into; (*fig*) to push, rush
bouse [buz] *nf* dung *no pl*
bousiller [buzije] (*fam*) *vt* (*appareil*) to wreck
boussole [busɔl] *nf* compass
bout [bu] *vb voir* **bouillir** ♦ *nm* bit; (*d'un bâton etc*) tip; (*d'une ficelle, table, rue, période*) end; **au ~ de** at the end of, after; **pousser qn à ~** to push sb to the limit; **venir à ~ de** to manage to finish
boutade [butad] *nf* quip, sally
boute-en-train [butɑ̃tʀɛ̃] *nm inv* (*fig*) live wire
bouteille [butɛj] *nf* bottle; (*de gaz butane*) cylinder
boutique [butik] *nf* shop
bouton [butɔ̃] *nm* button; (*sur la peau*) spot; (*BOT*) bud; **~ d'or** buttercup; **boutonner** *vt* to button up; **boutonnière** *nf* buttonhole; **bouton-pression** *nm* press stud
bouture [butyʀ] *nf* cutting
bovins [bɔvɛ̃] *nmpl* cattle *pl*
bowling [bulin] *nm* (tenpin) bowling; (*salle*) bowling alley
box [bɔks] *nm* (*d'écurie*) loose-box; (*JUR*): **~ des accusés** dock
boxe [bɔks] *nf* boxing; **boxeur** *nm* boxer

boyaux [bwajo] *nmpl (viscères)* entrails, guts

BP *abr* = **boîte postale**

bracelet [braslε] *nm* bracelet

braconnier [brakɔnje] *nm* poacher

brader [brade] *vt* to sell off; **braderie** *nf* cut-price shop/stall

braguette [bragεt] *nf* fly *ou* flies *pl (BRIT)*, zipper *(US)*

brailler [braje] *vi* to bawl, yell

braire [brεR] *vi* to bray

braise [brεz] *nf* embers *pl*

brancard [brãkaR] *nm (civière)* stretcher; **brancardier** *nm* stretcher-bearer

branchages [brãʃaʒ] *nmpl* boughs

branche [brãʃ] *nf* branch

branché, e [brãʃe] *(fam) adj* trendy

brancher [brãʃe] *vt* to connect (up); *(en mettant la prise)* to plug in

brandir [brãdiR] *vt* to brandish

branle [brãl] *nm*: **mettre en ~** to set in motion; **branle-bas** *nm inv* commotion

braquer [brake] *vi (AUTO)* to turn (the wheel) ♦ *vt (revolver etc)*: **~ qch sur** to aim sth at, point sth at; *(mettre en colère)*: **~ qn** to put sb's back up

bras [bra] *nm* arm; **~ dessus, ~ dessous** arm in arm; **se retrouver avec qch sur les ~** *(fam)* to be landed with sth; **~ droit** *(fig)* right hand man; **~ de fer** arm wrestling

brasier [braзje] *nm* blaze, inferno

bras-le-corps [bralkɔR] *adv*: **à ~-~-~** (a)round the waist

brassard [brasaR] *nm* armband

brasse [bras] *nf (nage)* breast-stroke

brassée [brase] *nf* armful

brasser [brase] *vt* to mix; **~ l'argent/les affaires** to handle a lot of money/business

brasserie [brasRi] *nf (restaurant)* café-restaurant; *(usine)* brewery

brave [brav] *adj (courageux)* brave; *(bon, gentil)* good, kind

braver [brave] *vt* to defy

bravo [bravo] *excl* bravo ♦ *nm* cheer

bravoure [bravuR] *nf* bravery

break [brεk] *nm (AUTO)* estate car

brebis [brəbi] *nf* ewe; **~ galeuse** black sheep

brèche [brεʃ] *nf* breach, gap; **être toujours sur la ~** *(fig)* to be always on the go

bredouille [brəduj] *adj* empty-handed

bredouiller [brəduje] *vi, vt* to mumble, stammer

bref, brève [brεf, εv] *adj* short, brief ♦ *adv* in short; **d'un ton ~** sharply, curtly; **en ~** in short, in brief

Brésil [brezil] *nm* Brazil; **brésilien, -ne** *adj* Brazilian ♦ *nm/f*: **Brésilien, ne** Brazilian

Bretagne [brətaɲ] *nf* Brittany

bretelle [brətεl] *nf (de vêtement, de sac)* strap; *(d'autoroute)* slip road *(BRIT)*, entrance/exit ramp *(US)*; **~s** *nfpl (pour pantalon)* braces *(BRIT)*, suspenders *(US)*

breton, ne [brətɔ̃, ɔn] *adj* Breton ♦ *nm/f*: **B~, ne** Breton

breuvage [brœvaʒ] *nm* beverage, drink

brève [brεv] *adj voir* **bref**

brevet [brəvε] *nm* diploma, certificate; **~ (d'invention)** patent; **breveté, e** *adj* patented

bribes [brib] *nfpl (de conversation)* snatches; **par ~** piecemeal

bricolage [brikɔlaʒ] *nm*: **le ~** do-it-yourself

bricole [brikɔl] *nf (babiole)* trifle

bricoler [brikɔle] *vi (petits travaux)* to do DIY jobs; *(passe-temps)* to potter about ♦ *vt (réparer)* to fix up; **bricoleur, -euse** *nm/f* handyman(-woman), DIY enthusiast

bride [brid] *nf* bridle; **tenir qn en ~** to keep a tight rein on sb

bridé, e [bride] *adj*: **yeux ~s** slit eyes

bridge [bridʒ] *nm (CARTES)* bridge

brièvement [brijεvmã] *adv* briefly

brigade [brigad] *nf (POLICE)* squad; *(MIL)* brigade; **brigadier** *nm* sergeant

brigandage [brigãdaʒ] *nm* robbery

briguer [brige] *vt* to aspire to

brillamment [bʀijamɑ̃] *adv* brilliantly

brillant, e [bʀijɑ̃, ɑ̃t] *adj* (*remarquable*) bright; (*luisant*) shiny, shining

briller [bʀije] *vi* to shine

brimer [bʀime] *vt* to bully

brin [bʀɛ̃] *nm* (*de laine, ficelle etc*) strand; (*fig*): **un ~ de** a bit of; **~ d'herbe** blade of grass; **~ de muguet** sprig of lily of the valley

brindille [bʀɛ̃dij] *nf* twig

brio [bʀijo] *nm*: **avec ~** with panache

brioche [bʀijoʃ] *nf* brioche (bun); (*fam: ventre*) paunch

brique [bʀik] *nf* brick; (*de lait*) carton

briquer [bʀike] *vt* to polish up

briquet [bʀikɛ] *nm* (cigarette) lighter

brise [bʀiz] *nf* breeze

briser [bʀize] *vt* to break; **se ~** *vi* to break

britannique [bʀitanik] *adj* British ♦ *nm/f*: **B~** British person, Briton; **les B~s** the British

brocante [bʀokɑ̃t] *nf* junk, second-hand goods *pl*; **brocanteur, -euse** *nm/f* junk-shop owner; junk dealer

broche [bʀoʃ] *nf* brooch; (*CULIN*) spit; (*MÉD*) pin; **à la ~** spit-roasted

broché, e [bʀoʃe] *adj* (*livre*) paper-backed

brochet [bʀoʃɛ] *nm* pike *inv*

brochette [bʀoʃɛt] *nf* (*ustensile*) skewer; (*plat*) kebab

brochure [bʀoʃyʀ] *nf* pamphlet, brochure, booklet

broder [bʀode] *vt* to embroider ♦ *vi* to embroider the facts; **broderie** *nf* embroidery

broncher [bʀɔ̃ʃe] *vi*: **sans ~** without flinching, without turning a hair

bronches [bʀɔ̃ʃ] *nfpl* bronchial tubes; **bronchite** *nf* bronchitis

bronze [bʀɔ̃z] *nm* bronze

bronzer [bʀɔ̃ze] *vi* to get a tan; **se ~** to sunbathe

brosse [bʀos] *nf* brush; **coiffé en ~** with a crewcut; **~ à cheveux** hairbrush; **~ à dents** toothbrush; **~ à habits** clothes-brush; **brosser** *vt* (*nettoyer*) to brush; (*fig:*

tableau etc) to paint; **se brosser les dents** to brush one's teeth

brouette [bʀuɛt] *nf* wheelbarrow

brouhaha [bʀuaa] *nm* hubbub

brouillard [bʀujaʀ] *nm* fog

brouille [bʀuj] *nf* quarrel

brouiller [bʀuje] *vt* (*œufs, message*) to scramble; (*idées*) to mix up; (*rendre trouble*) to cloud; (*désunir: amis*) to set at odds; **se ~** *vi* (*vue*) to cloud over; (*gens*) to fall out

brouillon, ne [bʀujɔ̃, ɔn] *adj* (*sans soin*) untidy; (*qui manque d'organisation*) disorganized ♦ *nm* draft; **(papier) ~** rough paper

broussailles [bʀusaj] *nfpl* undergrowth *sg*; **broussailleux, -euse** *adj* bushy

brousse [bʀus] *nf*: **la ~** the bush

brouter [bʀute] *vi* to graze

broutille [bʀutij] *nf* trifle

broyer [bʀwaje] *vt* to crush; **~ du noir** to be down in the dumps

bru [bʀy] *nf* daughter-in-law

brugnon [bʀyɲɔ̃] *nm* (*BOT*) nectarine

bruiner [bʀɥine] *vb impers*: **il bruine** it's drizzling, there's a drizzle

bruire [bʀɥiʀ] *vi* (*feuilles*) to rustle

bruit [bʀɥi] *nm*: **un ~** a noise, a sound; (*fig: rumeur*) a rumour; **le ~** noise; **sans ~** without a sound, noiselessly; **~ de fond** background noise; **bruitage** *nm* sound effects *pl*

brûlant, e [bʀylɑ̃, ɑ̃t] *adj* burning; (*liquide*) boiling (hot)

brûlé, e [bʀyle] *adj* (*fig: démasqué*) blown ♦ *nm*: **odeur de ~** smell of burning

brûle-pourpoint [bʀylpuʀpwɛ̃]: **à ~-~** *adv* point-blank

brûler [bʀyle] *vt* to burn; (*suj: eau bouillante*) to scald; (*consommer: électricité, essence*) to use; (*feu rouge, signal*) to go through ♦ *vi* to burn; (*jeu*): **tu brûles!** you're getting hot!; **se ~** to burn o.s.; (*s'ébouillanter*) to scald o.s.

brûlure [bʀylyʀ] *nf* (*lésion*) burn; **~s d'estomac** heartburn *sg*

brume [bʀym] *nf* mist; **brumisateur** *nm* atomizer

brun, e [bʀœ̃, bʀyn] *adj* (*gén, bière*) brown; (*cheveux, tabac*) dark; **elle est ~e** she's got dark hair

brunch [bʀœntʃ] *nm* brunch

brunir [bʀyniʀ] *vi* to get a tan

brushing [bʀœʃiŋ] *nm* blow-dry

brusque [bʀysk] *adj* abrupt; **brusquer** *vt* to rush

brut, e [bʀyt] *adj* (*minerai, soie*) raw; (*diamant*) rough; (*COMM*) gross; **(pétrole) ~** crude (oil)

brutal, e, -aux [bʀytal, o] *adj* brutal; **brutaliser** *vt* to handle roughly, manhandle

Bruxelles [bʀysɛl] *n* Brussels

bruyamment [bʀyjamã] *adv* noisily

bruyant, e [bʀyjã, ãt] *adj* noisy

bruyère [bʀyjɛʀ] *nf* heather

BTS *sigle m* (= *brevet de technicien supérieur*) vocational training certificate taken at the end of a higher education course

bu, e [by] *pp de* **boire**

buccal, e, -aux [bykal, o] *adj*: **par voie ~e** orally

bûche [byʃ] *nf* log; **prendre une ~** (*fig*) to come a cropper; **~ de Noël** Yule log

bûcher [byʃe] *nm* (*funéraire*) pyre; (*supplice*) stake ♦ *vi* (*fam*) to swot (*BRIT*), slave (away) ♦ *vt* (*fam*) to swot up (*BRIT*), slave away at; **bûcheron** *nm* woodcutter; **bûcheur, -euse** (*fam*) *adj* hard-working

budget [bydʒɛ] *nm* budget

buée [bɥe] *nf* (*sur une vitre*) mist

buffet [byfɛ] *nm* (*meuble*) sideboard; (*de réception*) buffet; **~ (de gare)** (station) buffet, snack bar

buffle [byfl] *nm* buffalo

buis [bɥi] *nm* box tree; (*bois*) box(wood)

buisson [bɥisɔ̃] *nm* bush

buissonnière [bɥisɔnjɛʀ] *adj*: **faire l'école ~** to skip school

bulbe [bylb] *nm* (*BOT, ANAT*) bulb

Bulgarie [bylgaʀi] *nf* Bulgaria

bulle [byl] *nf* bubble

bulletin [byltɛ̃] *nm* (*communiqué, journal*) bulletin; (*SCOL*) report; **~ d'informations** news bulletin; **~ de salaire** pay-slip; **~ (de vote)** ballot paper; **~ météorologique** weather report

bureau, x [byʀo] *nm* (*meuble*) desk; (*pièce, service*) office; **~ de change** (foreign) exchange office *ou* bureau; **~ de poste** post office; **~ de tabac** tobacconist's (shop); **~ de vote** polling station; **bureaucratie** [byʀokʀasi] *nf* bureaucracy

burin [byʀɛ̃] *nm* cold chisel; (*ART*) burin

burlesque [byʀlɛsk] *adj* ridiculous; (*LITTÉRATURE*) burlesque

bus¹ [by] *vb voir* **boire**

bus² [bys] *nm* bus

busqué, e [byske] *adj* (*nez*) hook(ed)

buste [byst] *nm* (*torse*) chest; (*seins*) bust

but¹ [by] *vb voir* **boire**

but² [by(t)] *nm* (*cible*) target; (*fig*) goal, aim; (*FOOTBALL etc*) goal; **de ~ en blanc** point-blank; **avoir pour ~ de faire** to aim to do; **dans le ~ de** with the intention of

butane [bytan] *nm* (*camping*) butane; (*usage domestique*) Calor gas ®

buté, e [byte] *adj* stubborn, obstinate

buter [byte] *vi*: **~ contre** (*cogner*) to bump into; (*trébucher*) to stumble against; **se ~** *vi* to get obstinate, dig in one's heels; **~ contre une difficulté** (*fig*) to hit a snag

butin [bytɛ̃] *nm* booty, spoils *pl*; (*d'un vol*) loot

butiner [bytine] *vi* (*abeilles*) to gather nectar

butte [byt] *nf* mound, hillock; **être en ~ à** to be exposed to

buvais *etc* [byvɛ] *vb voir* **boire**

buvard [byvaʀ] *nm* blotter

buvette [byvɛt] *nf* bar

buveur, -euse [byvœʀ, øz] *nm/f* drinker

C, c

c' [s] *dét voir* **ce**

CA *sigle m* = **chiffre d'affaires**

ça [sa] *pron* (*pour désigner*) this; (: *plus loin*) that; (*comme sujet indéfini*) it; **comment ~ va?** how are you?; **~ va?** (*d'accord?*) OK?, all right?; **où ~?** where's that?; **pourquoi ~?** why's that?; **qui ~?** who's that?; **~ alors!** well really!; **~ fait 10 ans (que)** it's 10 years (since); **c'est ~** that's right; **~ y est** that's it

çà [sa] *adv*: **~ et là** here and there

cabane [kaban] *nf* hut, cabin

cabaret [kabaʀɛ] *nm* night club

cabas [kabɑ] *nm* shopping bag

cabillaud [kabijo] *nm* cod *inv*

cabine [kabin] *nf* (*de bateau*) cabin; (*de piscine etc*) cubicle; (*de camion, train*) cab; (*d'avion*) cockpit; **~ d'essayage** fitting room; **~ (téléphonique)** call *ou* (tele)phone box

cabinet [kabinɛ] *nm* (*petite pièce*) closet; (*de médecin*) surgery (BRIT), office (US); (*de notaire etc*) office; (: *clientèle*) practice; (POL) Cabinet; **~s** *nmpl* (w.-c.) toilet *sg*; **~ d'affaires** business consultancy; **~ de toilette** toilet

câble [kɑbl] *nm* cable

cabosser [kabɔse] *vt* to dent

cabrer [kabʀe]: **se ~** *vi* (*cheval*) to rear up

cabriole [kabʀijɔl] *nf*: **faire des ~s** to caper about

cacahuète [kakaɥɛt] *nf* peanut

cacao [kakao] *nm* cocoa

cache [kaʃ] *nm* mask, card (for masking)

cache-cache [kaʃkaʃ] *nm*: **jouer à ~-~** to play hide-and-seek

cachemire [kaʃmiʀ] *nm* cashmere

cache-nez [kaʃne] *nm inv* scarf, muffler

cacher [kaʃe] *vt* to hide, conceal; **se ~** *vi* (*volontairement*) to hide; (*être caché*) to be hidden *ou* concealed; **~ qch à qn** to hide *ou* conceal sth from sb

cachet [kaʃɛ] *nm* (*comprimé*) tablet; (*de la poste*) postmark; (*rétribution*) fee; (*fig*) style, character; **cacheter** *vt* to seal

cachette [kaʃɛt] *nf* hiding place; **en ~** on the sly, secretly

cachot [kaʃo] *nm* dungeon

cachotterie [kaʃɔtʀi] *nf*: **faire des ~s** to be secretive

cactus [kaktys] *nm* cactus

cadavre [kadɑvʀ] *nm* corpse, (dead) body

Caddie ®, **caddy** [kadi] *nm* (*supermarket*) trolley

cadeau, x [kado] *nm* present, gift; **faire un ~ à qn** to give sb a present *ou* gift; **faire ~ de qch à qn** to make a present of sth to sb, give sb sth as a present

cadenas [kadnɑ] *nm* padlock

cadence [kadɑ̃s] *nf* (*tempo*) rhythm; (*de travail etc*) rate; **en ~** rhythmically

cadet, te [kadɛ, ɛt] *adj* younger; (*le plus jeune*) youngest ♦ *nm/f* youngest child *ou* one

cadran [kadʀɑ̃] *nm* dial; **~ solaire** sundial

cadre [kɑdʀ] *nm* frame; (*environnement*) surroundings *pl* ♦ *nm/f* (ADMIN) managerial employee, executive; **dans le ~ de** (*fig*) within the framework *ou* context of

cadrer [kɑdʀe] *vi*: **~ avec** to tally *ou* correspond with ♦ *vt* to centre

cafard [kafaʀ] *nm* cockroach; **avoir le ~** (*fam*) to be down in the dumps

café [kafe] *nm* coffee; (*bistro*) café ♦ *adj inv* coffee(-coloured); **~ au lait** white coffee; **~ noir** black coffee; **~ tabac** *tobacconist's or newsagent's serving coffee and spirits*; **cafetière** *nf* (*pot*) coffee-pot

cafouiller [kafuje] (*fam*) *vi* to get into a shambles

cage [kaʒ] *nf* cage; **~ d'escalier** (stair)well; **~ thoracique** rib cage

cageot [kaʒo] *nm* crate

cagibi [kaʒibi] (*fam*) *nm* (*débarras*) box-room

cagnotte [kaɲɔt] *nf* kitty

cagoule [kagul] *nf* (*passe-montagne*) balaclava

cahier [kaje] *nm* notebook; **~ de brouillons** roughbook, jotter; **~ d'exercices** exercise book

cahot [kao] *nm* jolt, bump

caïd [kaid] *nm* big chief, boss

caille [kaj] *nf* quail

cailler [kaje] *vi* (*lait*) to curdle; **ça caille** (*fam*) it's freezing; **caillot** *nm* (blood) clot

caillou, x [kaju] *nm* (little) stone; **cailloteux, -euse** *adj* (*route*) stony

Caire [kɛʀ] *nm*: **le ~** Cairo

caisse [kɛs] *nf* box; (*tiroir où l'on met la recette*) till; (*où l'on paye*) cash desk (*BRIT*), check-out; (*de banque*) cashier's desk; **~ d'épargne** savings bank; **~ de retraite** pension fund; **~ enregistreuse** cash register; **caissier, -ière** *nm/f* cashier

cajoler [kaʒɔle] *vt* (*câliner*) to cuddle; (*amadouer*) to wheedle, coax

cake [kɛk] *nm* fruit cake

calandre [kalɑ̃dʀ] *nf* radiator grill

calanque [kalɑ̃k] *nf* rocky inlet

calcaire [kalkɛʀ] *nm* limestone ♦ *adj* (*eau*) hard; (*GÉO*) limestone *cpd*

calciné, e [kalsine] *adj* burnt to ashes

calcul [kalkyl] *nm* calculation; **le ~** arithmetic; **~ (biliaire)** (gall)stone; **calculatrice** *nf* calculator; **calculer** *vt* to calculate, work out; **calculette** *nf* pocket calculator

cale [kal] *nf* (*de bateau*) hold; (*en bois*) wedge; **~ sèche** dry dock

calé, e [kale] (*fam*) *adj* clever, bright

caleçon [kalsɔ̃] *nm* (*d'homme*) boxer shorts; (*de femme*) leggings

calembour [kalɑ̃buʀ] *nm* pun

calendrier [kalɑ̃dʀije] *nm* calendar; (*fig*) timetable

calepin [kalpɛ̃] *nm* notebook

caler [kale] *vt* to wedge ♦ *vi* (*moteur, véhicule*) to stall

calfeutrer [kalføtʀe] *vt* to (make) draughtproof; **se ~** *vi* to make o.s. snug and comfortable

calibre [kalibʀ] *nm* calibre

califourchon [kalifuʀʃɔ̃]: **à ~** *adv* astride

câlin, e [kɑlɛ̃, in] *adj* cuddly, cuddlesome; (*regard, voix*) tender; **câliner** *vt* to cuddle

calmant [kalmɑ̃] *nm* tranquillizer, sedative; (*pour la douleur*) painkiller

calme [kalm] *adj* calm, quiet ♦ *nm* calm(ness), quietness; **calmer** *vt* to calm (down); (*douleur, inquiétude*) to ease, soothe; **se calmer** *vi* to calm down

calomnie [kalɔmni] *nf* slander; (*écrite*) libel; **calomnier** *vt* to slander; to libel

calorie [kalɔʀi] *nf* calorie

calotte [kalɔt] *nf* (*coiffure*) skullcap; (*fam: gifle*) slap; **~ glaciaire** (*GÉO*) icecap

calquer [kalke] *vt* to trace; (*fig*) to copy exactly

calvaire [kalvɛʀ] *nm* (*croix*) wayside cross, calvary; (*souffrances*) suffering

calvitie [kalvisi] *nf* baldness

camarade [kamaʀad] *nm/f* friend, pal; (*POL*) comrade; **camaraderie** *nf* friendship

cambouis [kɑ̃bwi] *nm* dirty oil *ou* grease

cambrer [kɑ̃bʀe]: **se ~** *vi* to arch one's back

cambriolage [kɑ̃bʀijɔlaʒ] *nm* burglary; **cambrioler** *vt* to burgle (*BRIT*), burglarize (*US*); **cambrioleur, -euse** *nm/f* burglar

camelote [kamlɔt] (*fam*) *nf* rubbish, trash, junk

caméra [kameʀa] *nf* (*CINÉMA, TV*) camera; (*d'amateur*) cine-camera

caméscope ® [kameskɔp] *nm* camcorder ®

camion [kamjɔ̃] *nm* lorry (*BRIT*), truck; **~ de dépannage** breakdown (*BRIT*) *ou* tow (*US*) truck; **camion-citerne** *nm* tanker; **camionnette** *nf* (small) van; **camionneur** *nm* (*chauffeur*) lorry (*BRIT*) *ou* truck driver; (*entrepreneur*) haulage contractor (*BRIT*), trucker (*US*)

camisole [kamizɔl] *nf*: **~ (de force)** straitjacket

camomille [kamɔmij] *nf* camomile; (*boisson*) camomile tea

camoufler [kamufle] *vt* to camouflage; (*fig*) to conceal, cover up

camp [kɑ̃] *nm* camp; *(fig)* side; **~ de vacances** children's holiday camp *(BRIT)*, summer camp *(US)*

campagnard, e [kɑ̃paɲaʀ, aʀd] *adj* country *cpd*

campagne [kɑ̃paɲ] *nf* country, countryside; *(MIL, POL, COMM)* campaign; **à la ~** in the country

camper [kɑ̃pe] *vi* to camp ♦ *vt* to sketch; **se ~ devant** to plant o.s. in front of; **campeur, -euse** *nm/f* camper

camping [kɑ̃piŋ] *nm* camping; **(terrain de) ~** campsite, camping site; **faire du ~** to go camping; **camping-car** *nm* camper, motorhome *(US)*; **camping-gaz** ® *nm inv* camp(ing) stove

Canada [kanada] *nm*: **le ~** Canada; **canadien, ne** *adj* Canadian ♦ *nm/f*: **Canadien, ne** Canadian; **canadienne** *nf (veste)* fur-lined jacket

canaille [kanɑj] *(péj) nf* scoundrel

canal, -aux [kanal, o] *nm* canal; *(naturel)* channel; **canalisation** *nf (tuyau)* pipe; **canaliser** *vt* to canalize; *(fig)* to channel

canapé [kanape] *nm* settee, sofa

canard [kanaʀ] *nm* duck; *(fam: journal)* rag

canari [kanaʀi] *nm* canary

cancans [kɑ̃kɑ̃] *nmpl (malicious)* gossip *sg*

cancer [kɑ̃seʀ] *nm* cancer; *(signe)*: **le C~** Cancer; **~ de la peau** skin cancer

cancre [kɑ̃kʀ] *nm* dunce

candeur [kɑ̃dœʀ] *nf* ingenuousness, guilelessness

candidat, e [kɑ̃dida, at] *nm/f* candidate; *(à un poste)* applicant, candidate; **candidature** *nf (POL)* candidature; *(à poste)* application; **poser sa candidature à un poste** to apply for a job

candide [kɑ̃did] *adj* ingenuous, guileless

cane [kan] *nf (female)* duck

caneton [kantɔ̃] *nm* duckling

canette [kanɛt] *nf (de bière)* (flip-top) bottle

canevas [kanva] *nm (COUTURE)* canvas

caniche [kaniʃ] *nm* poodle

canicule [kanikyl] *nf* scorching heat

canif [kanif] *nm* penknife, pocket knife

canine [kanin] *nf* canine (tooth)

caniveau, x [kanivo] *nm* gutter

canne [kan] *nf* (walking) stick; **~ à pêche** fishing rod; **~ à sucre** sugar cane

cannelle [kanɛl] *nf* cinnamon

canoë [kanɔe] *nm* canoe; *(sport)* canoeing

canon [kanɔ̃] *nm (arme)* gun; *(HISTOIRE)* cannon; *(d'une arme: tube)* barrel; *(fig: norme)* model; *(MUS)* canon

canot [kano] *nm* ding(h)y; **~ de sauvetage** lifeboat; **~ pneumatique** inflatable ding(h)y; **canotier** *nm* boater

cantatrice [kɑ̃tatʀis] *nf* (opera) singer

cantine [kɑ̃tin] *nf* canteen

cantique [kɑ̃tik] *nm* hymn

canton [kɑ̃tɔ̃] *nm* district consisting of several communes; *(en Suisse)* canton

cantonade [kɑ̃tɔnad]: **à la ~** *adv* to everyone in general

cantonner [kɑ̃tɔne]: **se ~ à** *vt* to confine o.s. to

cantonnier [kɑ̃tɔnje] *nm* roadmender

canular [kanylaʀ] *nm* hoax

caoutchouc [kautʃu] *nm* rubber

cap [kap] *nm (GÉO)* cape; *(promontoire)* headland; *(fig: tournant)* watershed; *(NAVIG)*: **changer de ~** to change course; **mettre le ~ sur** to head *ou* steer for

CAP *sigle m* (= *Certificat d'aptitude professionnelle*) *vocational training certificate taken at secondary school*

capable [kapabl] *adj* able, capable; **~ de qch/faire** capable of sth/doing

capacité [kapasite] *nf (compétence)* ability; *(JUR, contenance)* capacity

cape [kap] *nf* cape, cloak; **rire sous ~** to laugh up one's sleeve

CAPES [kapɛs] *sigle m* (= *Certificat d'aptitude pédagogique à l'enseignement secondaire*) *teaching diploma*

capillaire [kapileʀ] *adj (soins, lotion)* hair *cpd*; *(vaisseau etc)* capillary

capitaine [kapitɛn] *nm* captain

capital, e, -aux [kapital, o] *adj (œuvre)* major; *(question, rôle)* fundamental ♦ *nm* capital; (*fig*) stock; **d'une importance ~e** of capital importance; *voir aussi* **capitaux**; **~ (social)** authorized capital; **capitale** *nf* (*ville*) capital; (*lettre*) capital (letter); **capitalisme** *nm* capitalism; **capitaliste** *adj, nm/f* capitalist; **capitaux** *nmpl* (*fonds*) capital *sg*

capitonné, e [kapitɔne] *adj* padded

caporal, -aux [kapɔral, o] *nm* lance corporal

capot [kapo] *nm* (AUTO) bonnet (BRIT), hood (US)

capote [kapɔt] *nf* (*de voiture*) hood (BRIT), top (US); (*fam*) condom

capoter [kapɔte] *vi* (*négociations*) to founder

câpre [kɑpʀ] *nf* caper

caprice [kapʀis] *nm* whim, caprice; **faire des ~s** to make a fuss; **capricieux, -euse** *adj* (*fantasque*) capricious, whimsical; (*enfant*) awkward

Capricorne [kapʀikɔʀn] *nm*: **le ~** Capricorn

capsule [kapsyl] *nf* (*de bouteille*) cap; (BOT *etc, spatiale*) capsule

capter [kapte] *vt* (*ondes radio*) to pick up; (*fig*) to win, capture

captivant, e [kaptivɑ̃, ɑ̃t] *adj* captivating

captivité [kaptivite] *nf* captivity

capturer [kaptyʀe] *vt* to capture

capuche [kapyʃ] *nf* hood

capuchon [kapyʃɔ̃] *nm* hood; (*de stylo*) cap, top

capucine [kapysin] *nf* (BOT) nasturtium

caquet [kakɛ] *nm*: **rabattre le ~ à qn** (*fam*) to bring sb down a peg or two

caqueter [kakte] *vi* to cackle

car [kaʀ] *nm* coach ♦ *conj* because, for

carabine [kaʀabin] *nf* rifle

caractère [kaʀaktɛʀ] *nm* (*gén*) character; **avoir bon/mauvais ~** to be good-/ill-natured; **en ~s gras** in bold type; **en petits ~s** in small print; **~s d'imprimerie** (block) capitals; **caractériel, le** *adj* (*traits*) (of) character; (*enfant*) emotionally disturbed

caractérisé, e [kaʀakteʀize] *adj* sheer, downright

caractériser [kaʀakteʀize] *vt* to be characteristic of

caractéristique [kaʀakteʀistik] *adj, nf* characteristic

carafe [kaʀaf] *nf* (*pour eau, vin ordinaire*) carafe

caraïbe [kaʀaib] *adj* Caribbean ♦ *n*: **les C~s** the Caribbean (Islands)

carambolage [kaʀɑ̃bɔlaʒ] *nm* multiple crash, pileup

caramel [kaʀamɛl] *nm* (*bonbon*) caramel, toffee; (*substance*) caramel

carapace [kaʀapas] *nf* shell

caravane [kaʀavan] *nf* caravan; **caravaning** *nm* caravanning

carbone [kaʀbɔn] *nm* carbon; (*double*) carbon (copy); **carbonique** *adj*: **gaz carbonique** carbon dioxide; **neige carbonique** dry ice; **carbonisé, e** *adj* charred

carburant [kaʀbyʀɑ̃] *nm* (motor) fuel

carburateur [kaʀbyʀatœʀ] *nm* carburettor

carcan [kaʀkɑ̃] *nm* (*fig*) yoke, shackles *pl*

carcasse [kaʀkas] *nf* carcass; (*de véhicule etc*) shell

cardiaque [kaʀdjak] *adj* cardiac, heart *cpd* ♦ *nm/f* heart patient; **être ~** to have heart trouble

cardigan [kaʀdigɑ̃] *nm* cardigan

cardiologue [kaʀdjɔlɔg] *nm/f* cardiologist, heart specialist

carême [kaʀɛm] *nm*: **le C~** Lent

carence [kaʀɑ̃s] *nf* (*manque*) deficiency

caresse [kaʀɛs] *nf* caress

caresser [kaʀese] *vt* to caress; (*animal*) to stroke

cargaison [kaʀgɛzɔ̃] *nf* cargo, freight

cargo [kaʀgo] *nm* cargo boat, freighter

caricature [kaʀikatyʀ] *nf* caricature

carie [kaʀi] *nf*: **la ~ (dentaire)** tooth decay; **une ~** a bad tooth

carillon [kaʀijɔ̃] *nm* (*air, de pendule*) chimes *pl*

caritatif, -ive [kaʀitatif, iv] *adj*: **organisation caritative** charity

carnassier, -ière [karnasje, jɛr] *adj* carnivorous

carnaval [karnaval] *nm* carnival

carnet [karnɛ] *nm* (*calepin*) notebook; (*de tickets, timbres etc*) book; **~ de chèques** cheque book; **~ de notes** school report

carotte [karɔt] *nf* carrot

carpette [karpɛt] *nf* rug

carré, e [kare] *adj* square; (*fig: franc*) straightforward ♦ *nm* (*MATH*) square; **mètre/kilomètre ~** square metre/ kilometre

carreau, x [karo] *nm* (*par terre*) (floor) tile; (*au mur*) (wall) tile; (*de fenêtre*) (window) pane; (*motif*) check, square; (*CARTES: couleur*) diamonds *pl*; **tissu à ~x** checked fabric

carrefour [karfur] *nm* crossroads *sg*

carrelage [karlaʒ] *nm* (*sol*) (tiled) floor

carrelet [karlɛ] *nm* (*poisson*) plaice

carrément [karemɑ̃] *adv* (*franchement*) straight out, bluntly; (*sans hésiter*) straight; (*intensif*) completely; **c'est ~ impossible** it's completely impossible

carrière [karjɛr] *nf* (*métier*) career; (*de roches*) quarry; **militaire de ~** professional soldier

carrossable [karɔsabl] *adj* suitable for (motor) vehicles

carrosse [karɔs] *nm* (horse-drawn) coach

carrosserie [karɔsri] *nf* body, coachwork *no pl*

carrure [karyr] *nf* build; (*fig*) stature, calibre

cartable [kartabl] *nm* satchel, (school)bag

carte [kart] *nf* (*de géographie*) map; (*marine, du ciel*) chart; (*d'abonnement, à jouer*) card; (*au restaurant*) menu; (*aussi:* **~ de visite**) (visiting) card; **à la ~** (*au restaurant*) à la carte; **donner ~ blanche à qn** to give sb a free rein; **~ bancaire** cash card; **~ de crédit** credit card; **~ de fidélité** loyalty card; **~ d'identité** identity card; **~ de séjour** residence permit; **~ grise** (*AUTO*) ≈ (car) registration book, logbook; **~ postale** postcard; **~ routière** road map; **~ té-**

léphonique phonecard

carter [kartɛr] *nm* sump

carton [kartɔ̃] *nm* (*matériau*) cardboard; (*boîte*) (cardboard) box; **faire un ~** (*fam*) to score a hit; **~ (à dessin)** portfolio; **carton-pâte** *nm* pasteboard

cartouche [kartuʃ] *nf* cartridge; (*de cigarettes*) carton

cas [kɑ] *nm* case; **ne faire aucun ~ de** to take no notice of; **en aucun ~** on no account; **au ~ où** in case; **en ~ de** in case of, in the event of; **en ~ de besoin** if need be; **en tout ~** in any case, at any rate; **~ de conscience** matter of conscience

casanier, -ière [kazanje, jɛr] *adj* stay-at-home

cascade [kaskad] *nf* waterfall, cascade; (*fig*) stream, torrent; **cascadeur, -euse** *nm/f* stuntman(-girl)

case [kɑz] *nf* (*hutte*) hut; (*compartiment*) compartment; (*sur un formulaire, de mots croisés etc*) box

caser [kɑze] (*fam*) *vt* (*placer*) to put (away); (*loger*) to put up; **se ~** *vi* (*se marier*) to settle down; (*trouver un emploi*) to find a (steady) job

caserne [kazɛrn] *nf* barracks *pl*

cash [kaʃ] *adv*: **payer ~** to pay cash down

casier [kazje] *nm* (*pour courrier*) pigeonhole; (*compartiment*) compartment; (*à clef*) locker; **~ judiciaire** police record

casino [kazino] *nm* casino

casque [kask] *nm* helmet; (*chez le coiffeur*) (hair-)drier; (*pour audition*) (head-)phones *pl*, headset

casquette [kaskɛt] *nf* cap

cassant, e [kasɑ̃, ɑ̃t] *adj* brittle; (*fig: ton*) curt, abrupt

cassation [kasasjɔ̃] *nf*: **cour de ~** final court of appeal

casse [kɑs] (*fam*) *nf* (*pour voitures*): **mettre à la ~** to scrap; (*dégâts*): **il y a eu de la ~** there were a lot of breakages; **casse-cou** *adj inv* daredevil, reckless; **casse-croûte** *nm inv* snack; **casse-noix** *nm in-*

inv nutcrackers *pl*; **casse-pieds** (*fam*) *adj inv*: **il est casse-pieds** he's a pain in the neck

casser [kɑse] *vt* to break; (*JUR*) to quash; **se ~** *vi* to break; **~ les pieds à qn** (*fam*: *irriter*) to get on sb's nerves; **se ~ la tête** (*fam*) to go to a lot of trouble

casserole [kɑsʀɔl] *nf* saucepan

casse-tête [kɑstɛt] *nm inv* (*difficultés*) headache (*fig*)

cassette [kɑsɛt] *nf* (*bande magnétique*) cassette; (*coffret*) casket

casseur [kɑsœʀ] *nm* hooligan

cassis [kasis] *nm* blackcurrant

cassoulet [kasulɛ] *nm* bean and sausage hot-pot

cassure [kɑsyʀ] *nf* break, crack

castor [kastɔʀ] *nm* beaver

castrer [kastʀe] *vt* (*mâle*) to castrate; (: *cheval*) to geld; (*femelle*) to spay

catalogue [katalɔg] *nm* catalogue

cataloguer [katalɔge] *vt* to catalogue, to list; (*péj*) to put a label on

catalyseur [katalizœʀ] *nm* catalyst; **catalytique** *adj*: **pot catalytique** catalytic convertor

catastrophe [katastʀɔf] *nf* catastrophe, disaster; **catastrophé, e** (*fam*) *adj* stunned

catch [katʃ] *nm* (all-in) wrestling

catéchisme [kateʃism] *nm* catechism

catégorie [kategɔʀi] *nf* category; **catégorique** *adj* categorical

cathédrale [katedʀal] *nf* cathedral

catholique [katɔlik] *adj*, *nm/f* (Roman) Catholic; **pas très ~** a bit shady *ou* fishy

catimini [katimini]: **en ~** *adv* on the sly

cauchemar [koʃmaʀ] *nm* nightmare

cause [koz] *nf* cause; (*JUR*) lawsuit, case; **à ~ de** because of, owing to; **pour ~ de** on account of; **(et) pour ~** and for (a very) good reason; **être en ~** (*intérêts*) to be at stake; **remettre en ~** to challenge; **causer** *vt* to cause ♦ *vi* to chat, talk; **causerie** *nf* (*conférence*) talk; **causette** *nf*: **faire la causette** to have a chat

caution [kosjɔ̃] *nf* guarantee, security; (*JUR*) bail (bond); (*fig*) backing, support; **libéré sous ~** released on bail; **cautionner** *vt* (*répondre de*) to guarantee; (*soutenir*) to support

cavalcade [kavalkad] *nf* (*fig*) stampede

cavalier, -ière [kavalje, jɛʀ] *adj* (*désinvolte*) offhand ♦ *nm/f* rider; (*au bal*) partner ♦ *nm* (*ÉCHECS*) knight

cave [kav] *nf* cellar

caveau, x [kavo] *nm* vault

caverne [kavɛʀn] *nf* cave

CCP *sigle m* = **compte chèques postaux**

CD *sigle m* (= *compact disc*) CD

CD-ROM [sedeʀɔm] *sigle m* CD-ROM

CE *n abr* (= *Communauté Européenne*) EC

MOT-CLÉ
---

ce, cette [sə, sɛt] (*devant nm* **cet** + *voyelle ou h aspiré; pl* **ces**) *dét* (*proximité*) this; these *pl*; (*non-proximité*) that; those *pl*; **cette maison(-ci/là)** this/that house; **cette nuit** (*qui vient*) tonight; (*passée*) last night

♦ *pron* 1: **c'est** it's *ou* it is; **c'est un peintre** he's *ou* he is a painter; **ce sont des peintres** they're *ou* they are painters; **c'est le facteur** (*à la porte*) it's the postman; **qui est-ce?** who is it?; (*en désignant*) who is he/she?; **qu'est-ce?** what is it?

2 **ce qui, ce que** what; (*chose qui*): **il est bête, ce qui me chagrine** he's stupid, which saddens me; **tout ce qui bouge** everything that *ou* which moves; **tout ce que je sais** all I know; **ce dont j'ai parlé** what I talked about; **ce que c'est grand!** it's so big!; *voir aussi* **-ci**; **est-ce que**; **n'est-ce pas**; **c'est-à-dire**

---

ceci [səsi] *pron* this

cécité [sesite] *nf* blindness

céder [sede] *vt* (*donner*) to give up ♦ *vi* (*chaise, barrage*) to give way; (*personne*) to give in; **~ à** to yield to, give in to

CEDEX [sedɛks] *sigle m* (= *courrier*

d'entreprise à distribution exceptionnelle) postal service for bulk users

cédille [sedij] *nf* cedilla

cèdre [sɛdʀ] *nm* cedar

CEI *abr m* (= *Communauté des États Indépendants*) CIS

ceinture [sɛ̃tyʀ] *nf* belt; (*taille*) waist; **~ de sécurité** safety *ou* seat belt

cela [s(ə)la] *pron* that; (*comme sujet indéfini*) it; **quand/où ~?** when/where (was that?)

célèbre [selɛbʀ] *adj* famous; **célébrer** *vt* to celebrate

céleri [sɛlʀi] *nm*: **~(-rave)** celeriac; **~ (en branche)** celery

célibat [seliba] *nm* (*homme*) bachelorhood; (*femme*) spinsterhood; (*prêtre*) celibacy; **célibataire** *adj* single, unmarried ♦ *nm* bachelor ♦ *nf* unmarried woman

celle(s) [sɛl] *pron voir* **celui**

cellier [selje] *nm* storeroom (*for wine*)

cellule [selyl] *nf* (*gén*) cell

cellulite [selylit] *nf* excess fat, cellulite

MOT-CLÉ

celui, celle [səlɥi, sɛl] (*mpl* **ceux**, *fpl* **celles**) *pron* 1: **celui-ci/là, celle-ci/là** this one/that one; **ceux-ci, celles-ci** these (ones); **ceux-là, celles-là** those (ones); **celui de mon frère** my brother's; **celui du salon/du bas** the one in (*ou* from) the lounge/below
2: **celui qui bouge** the one which *ou* that moves; (*personne*) the one who moves; **celui que je vois** the one (which *ou* that) I see; the one (whom) I see; **celui dont je parle** the one I'm talking about
3 (*valeur indéfinie*): **celui qui veut** whoever wants

---

cendre [sɑ̃dʀ] *nf* ash; **~s** *nfpl* (*d'un défunt*) ashes; **sous la ~** (*CULIN*) in (the) embers; **cendrier** *nm* ashtray

cène [sɛn] *nf*: **la ~** (Holy) Communion

censé, e [sɑ̃se] *adj*: **être ~ faire** to be supposed to do

censeur [sɑ̃sœʀ] *nm* (*SCOL*) deputy-head

(*BRIT*), vice-principal (*US*); (*CINÉMA, POL*) censor

censure [sɑ̃syʀ] *nf* censorship; **censurer** *vt* (*CINÉMA, PRESSE*) to censor; (*POL*) to censure

cent [sɑ̃] *num* a hundred, one hundred; **centaine** *nf*: **une centaine (de)** about a hundred, a hundred or so; **des centaines (de)** hundreds (of); **centenaire** *adj* hundred-year-old ♦ *nm* (*anniversaire*) centenary; (*monnaie*) cent **centième** *num* hundredth; **centigrade** *nm* centigrade; **centilitre** *nm* centilitre; **centime** *nm* centime; **centimètre** *nm* centimetre; (*ruban*) tape measure, measuring tape

central, e, -aux [sɑ̃tʀal, o] *adj* central ♦ *nm*: **~ (téléphonique)** (telephone) exchange; **centrale** *nf* power station

centre [sɑ̃tʀ] *nm* centre; **~ commercial** shopping centre; **centre-ville** *nm* town centre, downtown (area) (*US*)

centuple [sɑ̃typl] *nm*: **le ~ de qch** a hundred times sth; **au ~** a hundredfold

cep [sɛp] *nm* (vine) stock

cèpe [sɛp] *nm* (edible) boletus

cependant [s(ə)pɑ̃dɑ̃] *adv* however

céramique [seʀamik] *nf* ceramics *sg*

cercle [sɛʀkl] *nm* circle; **~ vicieux** vicious circle

cercueil [sɛʀkœj] *nm* coffin

céréale [seʀeal] *nf* cereal; **~s** *nfpl* breakfast cereal

cérémonie [seʀemɔni] *nf* ceremony; **sans ~** informally

cerf [sɛʀ] *nm* stag

cerfeuil [sɛʀfœj] *nm* chervil

cerf-volant [sɛʀvɔlɑ̃] *nm* kite

cerise [s(ə)ʀiz] *nf* cherry; **cerisier** *nm* cherry (tree)

cerne [sɛʀn] *nm*: **avoir des ~s** to have shadows *ou* dark rings under one's eyes

cerner [sɛʀne] *vt* (*MIL etc*) to surround; (*fig: problème*) to delimit, define

certain, e [sɛʀtɛ̃, ɛn] *adj* certain ♦ *dét* certain; **d'un ~ âge** past one's prime, not so young; **un ~ temps** (quite) some time; **~s**

♦ *pron* some; **certainement** *adv* (*probablement*) most probably *ou* likely; (*bien sûr*) certainly, of course

certes [sɛʀt] *adv* (*sans doute*) admittedly; (*bien sûr*) of course

certificat [sɛʀtifika] *nm* certificate

certifier [sɛʀtifje] *vt*: ~ **qch à qn** to assure sb of sth; **copie certifiée conforme (à l'original)** certified copy of the original

certitude [sɛʀtityd] *nf* certainty

cerveau, x [sɛʀvo] *nm* brain

cervelas [sɛʀvəla] *nm* saveloy

cervelle [sɛʀvɛl] *nf* (*ANAT*) brain; (*CULIN*) brains

ces [se] *dét voir* **ce**

CES *sigle m* (= *Collège d'enseignement secondaire*) ≈ (junior) secondary school (*BRIT*)

cesse [sɛs]: **sans** ~ *adv* (*tout le temps*) continually, constantly; (*sans interruption*) continuously; **il n'a eu de** ~ **que** he did not rest until; **cesser** *vt* to stop ♦ *vi* to stop, cease; **cesser de faire** to stop doing; **cessez-le-feu** *nm inv* ceasefire

c'est-à-dire [sɛtadiʀ] *adv* that is (to say)

cet, cette [sɛt] *dét voir* **ce**

ceux [sø] *pron voir* **celui**

CFC *abr* (= *chlorofluorocarbon*) CFC

CFDT *sigle f* (= *Confédération française démocratique du travail*) French trade union

CGT *sigle f* (= *Confédération générale du travail*) French trade union

chacun, e [ʃakœ̃, yn] *pron* each; (*indéfini*) everyone, everybody

chagrin [ʃagʀɛ̃] *nm* grief, sorrow; **avoir du** ~ to be grieved; **chagriner** *vt* to grieve

chahut [ʃay] *nm* uproar; **chahuter** *vt* to rag, bait ♦ *vi* to make an uproar

chaîne [ʃɛn] *nf* chain; (*RADIO, TV*: *stations*) channel; ~**s** *nfpl* (*AUTO*) (snow) chains; **travail à la** ~ production line work; ~ **(de montage)** production *ou* assembly line; ~ **de montagnes** mountain range; **(hi-fi)** hi-fi system; ~ **laser** CD player; ~ **(stéréo)** stereo (system); **chaînette** *nf* (small) chain

chair [ʃɛʀ] *nf* flesh; **avoir la** ~ **de poule** to

have goosepimples *ou* gooseflesh; **bien en** ~ plump, well-padded; **en** ~ **et en os** in the flesh; ~ **à saucisse** sausage meat

chaire [ʃɛʀ] *nf* (*d'église*) pulpit; (*d'université*) chair

chaise [ʃɛz] *nf* chair; ~ **longue** deckchair

châle [ʃɑl] *nm* shawl

chaleur [ʃalœʀ] *nf* heat; (*fig: accueil*) warmth; **chaleureux, -euse** *adj* warm

chaloupe [ʃalup] *nf* launch; (*de sauvetage*) lifeboat

chalumeau, x [ʃalymo] *nm* blowlamp, blowtorch

chalutier [ʃalytje] *nm* trawler

chamailler [ʃamaje]: **se** ~ *vi* to squabble, bicker

chambouler [ʃɑ̃bule] (*fam*) *vt* to disrupt, turn upside down

chambre [ʃɑ̃bʀ] *nf* bedroom; (*POL, COMM*) chamber; **faire** ~ **à part** to sleep in separate rooms; ~ **à air** (*de pneu*) (inner) tube; ~ **à coucher** bedroom; ~ **à un lit/deux lits** (*à l'hôtel*) single-/twin-bedded room; ~ **d'amis** spare *ou* guest room; ~ **noire** (*PHOTO*) dark room; **chambrer** *vt* (*vin*) to bring to room temperature

chameau, x [ʃamo] *nm* camel

chamois [ʃamwa] *nm* chamois

champ [ʃɑ̃] *nm* field; ~ **de bataille** battlefield; ~ **de courses** racecourse; ~ **de tir** rifle range

champagne [ʃɑ̃paɲ] *nm* champagne

champêtre [ʃɑ̃pɛtʀ] *adj* country *cpd*, rural

champignon [ʃɑ̃piɲɔ̃] *nm* mushroom; (*terme générique*) fungus; ~ **de Paris** button mushroom

champion, ne [ʃɑ̃pjɔ̃, jɔn] *adj, nm/f* champion; **championnat** *nm* championship

chance [ʃɑ̃s] *nf*: **la** ~ luck; ~**s** *nfpl* (*probabilités*) chances; **avoir de la** ~ to be lucky; **il a des** ~ **de réussir** he's got a good chance of passing

chanceler [ʃɑ̃s(ə)le] *vi* to totter

chancelier [ʃɑ̃səlje] *nm* (*allemand*) chancellor

chanceux, -euse [ʃɑ̃sø, øz] *adj* lucky

chandail [ʃɑ̃daj] *nm* (thick) sweater

Chandeleur [ʃɑ̃dlœʀ] *nf*: **la ~** Candlemas

chandelier [ʃɑ̃dəlje] *nm* candlestick

chandelle [ʃɑ̃dɛl] *nf* (tallow) candle; **dîner aux ~s** candlelight dinner

change [ʃɑ̃ʒ] *nm* (*devises*) exchange

changement [ʃɑ̃ʒmɑ̃] *nm* change; **~ de vitesses** gears *pl*

changer [ʃɑ̃ʒe] *vt* (*modifier*) to change, alter; (*remplacer*, COMM) to change ♦ *vi* to change, alter; **se ~** *vi* to change (o.s.); **~ de** (*remplacer*: *adresse, nom, voiture etc*) to change one's; (*échanger*: *place, train etc*) to change; **~ d'avis** to change one's mind; **~ de vitesse** to change gear

chanson [ʃɑ̃sɔ̃] *nf* song

chant [ʃɑ̃] *nm* song; (*art vocal*) singing; (*d'église*) hymn

chantage [ʃɑ̃taʒ] *nm* blackmail; **faire du ~** to use blackmail

chanter [ʃɑ̃te] *vt, vi* to sing; **si cela lui chante** (*fam*) if he feels like it; **chanteur, -euse** *nm/f* singer

chantier [ʃɑ̃tje] *nm* (building) site; (*sur une route*) roadworks *pl*; **mettre en ~** to put in hand; **~ naval** shipyard

chantilly [ʃɑ̃tiji] *nf voir* **crème**

chantonner [ʃɑ̃tɔne] *vi, vt* to sing to oneself, hum

chanvre [ʃɑ̃vʀ] *nm* hemp

chaparder [ʃapaʀde] (*fam*) *vt* to pinch

chapeau, x [ʃapo] *nm* hat; **~!** well done!

chapelet [ʃaplɛ] *nm* (REL) rosary

chapelle [ʃapɛl] *nf* chapel

chapelure [ʃaplyʀ] *nf* (dried) breadcrumbs *pl*

chapiteau, x [ʃapito] *nm* (*de cirque*) marquee, big top

chapitre [ʃapitʀ] *nm* chapter

chaque [ʃak] *dét* each, every; (*indéfini*) every

char [ʃaʀ] *nm* (MIL): **~ (d'assaut)** tank; **~ à voile** sand yacht

charabia [ʃaʀabja] (*péj*) *nm* gibberish

charade [ʃaʀad] *nf* riddle; (*mimée*) charade

charbon [ʃaʀbɔ̃] *nm* coal; **~ de bois** charcoal

charcuterie [ʃaʀkytʀi] *nf* (*magasin*) pork butcher's shop and delicatessen; (*produits*) cooked pork meats *pl*; **charcutier, -ière** *nm/f* pork butcher

chardon [ʃaʀdɔ̃] *nm* thistle

charge [ʃaʀʒ] *nf* (*fardeau*) load, burden; (*explosif*, ÉLEC, MIL, JUR) charge; (*rôle, mission*) responsibility; **~s** *nfpl* (*du loyer*) service charges; **à la ~ de** (*dépendant de*) dependent upon; (*aux frais de*) chargeable to; **prendre en ~** to take charge of; (*suj: véhicule*) to take on; (*dépenses*) to take care of; **~s sociales** social security contributions

chargé, e [ʃaʀʒe] *adj* (*emploi du temps, journée*) full, heavy

chargement [ʃaʀʒmɑ̃] *nm* (*objets*) load

charger [ʃaʀʒe] *vt* (*voiture, fusil, caméra*) to load; (*batterie*) to charge ♦ *vi* (MIL *etc*) to charge; **se ~ de** *vt* to see to; **~ qn de (faire) qch** to put sb in charge of (doing) sth

chariot [ʃaʀjo] *nm* trolley; (*charrette*) waggon

charité [ʃaʀite] *nf* charity

charmant, e [ʃaʀmɑ̃, ɑ̃t] *adj* charming

charme [ʃaʀm] *nm* charm; **charmer** *vt* to charm

charnel, le [ʃaʀnɛl] *adj* carnal

charnière [ʃaʀnjɛʀ] *nf* hinge; (*fig*) turning-point

charnu, e [ʃaʀny] *adj* fleshy

charpente [ʃaʀpɑ̃t] *nf* frame(work); **charpentier** *nm* carpenter

charpie [ʃaʀpi] *nf*: **en ~** (*fig*) in shreds *ou* ribbons

charrette [ʃaʀɛt] *nf* cart

charrier [ʃaʀje] *vt* (*entraîner: fleuve*) to carry (along); (*transporter*) to carry, carry

charrue [ʃaʀy] *nf* plough (BRIT), plow (US)

charter [ʃaʀtɛʀ] *nm* (*vol*) charter flight

chasse [ʃas] *nf* hunting; (*au fusil*) shooting; (*poursuite*) chase; (*aussi:* **~ d'eau**) flush; **~ gardée** private hunting grounds *pl;* **prendre en ~** to give chase to; **tirer la ~ (d'eau)** to flush the toilet, pull the chain; **~ à courre** hunting; **chasse-neige** *nm inv* snowplough (*BRIT*), snowplow (*US*); **chasser** *vt* to hunt; (*expulser*) to chase away *ou* out, drive away *ou* out; **chasseur, -euse** *nm/f* hunter ♦ *nm* (*avion*) fighter

châssis [ʃasi] *nm* (*AUTO*) chassis; (*cadre*) frame

chat [ʃa] *nm* cat

châtaigne [ʃatɛɲ] *nf* chestnut; **châtaignier** *nm* chestnut (tree)

châtain [ʃatɛ̃] *adj inv* (*cheveux*) chestnut (brown); (*personne*) chestnut-haired

château, x [ʃato] *nm* (*forteresse*) castle; (*résidence royale*) palace; (*manoir*) mansion; **~ d'eau** water tower; **~ fort** stronghold, fortified castle

châtier [ʃatje] *vt* to punish; **châtiment** *nm* punishment

chaton [ʃatɔ̃] *nm* (*ZOOL*) kitten

chatouiller [ʃatuje] *vt* to tickle; **chatouilleux, -euse** *adj* ticklish; (*fig*) touchy, over-sensitive

chatoyer [ʃatwaje] *vi* to shimmer

châtrer [ʃatʀe] *vt* (*mâle*) to castrate; (: *cheval*) to geld; (*femelle*) to spay

chatte [ʃat] *nf* (she-)cat

chaud, e [ʃo, ʃod] *adj* (*gén*) warm; (*très ~*) hot; **il fait ~** it's warm; it's hot; **avoir ~** to be warm; to be hot; **ça me tient ~** it keeps me warm; **rester au ~** to stay in the warm

chaudière [ʃodjɛʀ] *nf* boiler

chaudron [ʃodʀɔ̃] *nm* cauldron

chauffage [ʃofaʒ] *nm* heating; **~ central** central heating

chauffard [ʃofaʀ] *nm* (*péj*) reckless driver

chauffe-eau [ʃofo] *nm inv* water-heater

chauffer [ʃofe] *vt* to heat ♦ *vi* to heat up, warm up; (*trop ~: moteur*) to overheat; **se ~** *vi* (*au soleil*) to warm o.s.

chauffeur [ʃofœʀ] *nm* driver; (*privé*) chauffeur

chaume [ʃom] *nm* (*du toit*) thatch; **chau-**

mière *nf* (thatched) cottage

chaussée [ʃose] *nf* road(way)

chausse-pied [ʃospje] *nm* shoe-horn

chausser [ʃose] *vt* (*bottes, skis*) to put on; (*enfant*) to put shoes on; **~ du 38/42** to take size 38/42

chaussette [ʃosɛt] *nf* sock

chausson [ʃosɔ̃] *nm* slipper; (*de bébé*) bootee; **~ (aux pommes)** (apple) turn-over

chaussure [ʃosyʀ] *nf* shoe; **~s à talon** high-heeled shoes; **~s de marche** walking shoes/boots; **~s de ski** ski boots

chauve [ʃov] *adj* bald; **chauve-souris** *nf* bat

chauvin, e [ʃovɛ̃, in] *adj* chauvinistic

chaux [ʃo] *nf* lime; **blanchi à la ~** white-washed

chavirer [ʃaviʀe] *vi* to capsize

chef [ʃɛf] *nm* head, leader; (*de cuisine*) chef; **~ d'accusation** charge; **~ d'entreprise** company head; **~ d'état** head of state; **~ de famille** head of the family; **~ de gare** station master; **~ d'orchestre** conductor; **~ de service** department head; **chef-d'œuvre** *nm* masterpiece; **chef-lieu** *nm* county town

chemin [ʃ(ə)mɛ̃] *nm* path; (*itinéraire, direction, trajet*) way; **en ~** on the way; **~ de fer** railway (*BRIT*), railroad (*US*); **par ~ de fer** by rail

cheminée [ʃ(ə)mine] *nf* chimney; (*à l'intérieur*) chimney piece, fireplace; (*de bateau*) funnel

cheminement [ʃ(ə)minmɑ̃] *nm* progress

cheminot [ʃ(ə)mino] *nm* railwayman

chemise [ʃ(ə)miz] *nf* shirt; (*dossier*) folder; **~ de nuit** nightdress

chemisier [ʃ(ə)mizje, jɛʀ] *nm* blouse

chenal, -aux [ʃənal, o] *nm* channel

chêne [ʃɛn] *nm* oak (tree); (*bois*) oak

chenil [ʃ(ə)nil] *nm* kennels *pl*

chenille [ʃ(ə)nij] *nf* (*ZOOL*) caterpillar

chèque [ʃɛk] *nm* cheque (*BRIT*), check (*US*); **~ sans provision** bad cheque; **~ de**

voyage traveller's cheque; **chéquier** [ʃekje] *nm* cheque book

cher, -ère [ʃɛʀ] *adj* (*aimé*) dear; (*coûteux*) expensive, dear ♦ *adv*: **ça coûte ~** it's expensive

chercher [ʃɛʀʃe] *vt* to look for; (*gloire etc*) to seek; **aller ~** to go for, go and fetch; **~ à faire** to try to do; **chercheur, -euse** *nm/f* researcher, research worker

chère [ʃɛʀ] *adj voir* **cher**

chéri, e [ʃeʀi] *adj* beloved, dear; **(mon) ~** darling

chérir [ʃeʀiʀ] *vt* to cherish

cherté [ʃɛʀte] *nf*: **la ~ de la vie** the high cost of living

chétif, -ive [ʃetif, iv] *adj* (*enfant*) puny

cheval, -aux [ʃ(ə)val, o] *nm* horse; (*AUTO*): **~ (vapeur)** horsepower *no pl*; **faire du ~** to ride; **à ~** on horseback; **à ~ sur** astride; (*fig*) overlapping; **~ de course** racehorse

chevalet [ʃ(ə)valɛ] *nm* easel

chevalier [ʃ(ə)valje] *nm* knight

chevalière [ʃ(ə)valjɛʀ] *nf* signet ring

chevalin, e [ʃ(ə)valɛ̃, in] *adj*: **boucherie ~e** horse-meat butcher's

chevaucher [ʃ(ə)voʃe] *vi* (*aussi*: **se ~**) to overlap (each other) ♦ *vt* to be astride, straddle

chevaux [ʃəvo] *nmpl de* **cheval**

chevelu, e [ʃəv(ə)ly] (*péj*) *adj* long-haired

chevelure [ʃəv(ə)lyʀ] *nf* hair *no pl*

chevet [ʃ(ə)vɛ] *nm*: **au ~ de qn** at sb's bedside; **lampe de ~** bedside lamp

cheveu, x [ʃ(ə)vø] *nm* hair; **~x** *nmpl* (*chevelure*) hair *sg*; **avoir les ~x courts** to have short hair

cheville [ʃ(ə)vij] *nf* (*ANAT*) ankle; (*de bois*) peg; (*pour une vis*) plug

chèvre [ʃɛvʀ] *nf* (she-)goat

chevreau, x [ʃəvʀo] *nm* kid

chèvrefeuille [ʃevʀəfœj] *nm* honey-suckle

chevreuil [ʃəvʀœj] *nm* roe deer *inv*; (*CULIN*) venison

chevronné, e [ʃəvʀɔne] *adj* seasoned

chez [ʃe] *prép* 1 (*à la demeure de*) at; (: *direction*) to; **chez qn** at/to sb's house *ou* place; **chez moi** at home; (*direction*) home

2 (+*profession*) at; (: *direction*) to; **chez le boulanger/dentiste** at *ou* to the baker's/dentist's

3 (*dans le caractère, l'œuvre de*) in; **chez les renards/Racine** in foxes/Racine

chez-soi [ʃeswa] *nm inv* home

chic [ʃik] *adj inv* chic, smart; (*fam: généreux*) nice, decent ♦ *nm* stylishness; **~ (alors)!** (*fam*) great!; **avoir le ~ de** to have the knack of

chicane [ʃikan] *nf* (*querelle*) squabble; **chicaner** *vi* (*ergoter*): **chicaner sur** to quibble about

chiche [ʃiʃ] *adj* niggardly, mean ♦ *excl* (*à un défi*) you're on!

chichis [ʃiʃi] (*fam*) *nmpl* fuss *sg*

chicorée [ʃikɔʀe] *nf* (*café*) chicory; (*salade*) endive

chien [ʃjɛ̃] *nm* dog; **~ de garde** guard dog; **chien-loup** *nm* wolfhound

chiendent [ʃjɛ̃dɑ̃] *nm* couch grass

chienne [ʃjɛn] *nf* dog, bitch

chier [ʃje] (*fam!*) *vi* to crap (!)

chiffon [ʃifɔ̃] *nm* (piece of) rag; **chiffonner** *vt* to crumple; (*fam: tracasser*) to concern

chiffre [ʃifʀ] *nm* (*représentant un nombre*) figure, numeral; (*montant, total*) total, sum; **en ~s ronds** in round figures; **~ d'affaires** turnover; **chiffrer** *vt* (*dépense*) to put a figure to, assess; (*message*) to (en)code, cipher; **se chiffrer à** to add up to, amount to

chignon [ʃiɲɔ̃] *nm* chignon, bun

Chili [ʃili] *nm*: **le ~** Chile; **chilien, ne** *adj* Chilean ♦ *nm/f*: **Chilien, ne** Chilean

chimie [ʃimi] *nf* chemistry; **chimique** *adj* chemical; **produits chimiques** chemicals

chimpanzé [ʃɛ̃pɑ̃ze] *nm* chimpanzee

Chine [ʃin] nf: **la ~** China; **chinois, e** adj Chinese ♦ nm/f: **Chinois, e** Chinese ♦ nm (LING) Chinese

chiot [ʃjo] nm pup(py)

chiper [ʃipe] (fam) vt to pinch

chipoter [ʃipɔte] (fam) vi (ergoter) to quibble

chips [ʃips] nfpl crisps (BRIT), (potato) chips (US)

chiquenaude [ʃiknod] nf flick, flip

chirurgical, e, -aux [ʃiryrʒikal, o] adj surgical

chirurgie [ʃiryrʒi] nf surgery; **~ esthétique** plastic surgery; **chirurgien, ne** nm/f surgeon

chlore [klɔr] nm chlorine

choc [ʃɔk] nm (heurt) impact, shock; (collision) crash; (moral) shock; (affrontement) clash

chocolat [ʃɔkɔla] nm chocolate; **~ au lait** milk chocolate; **~ (chaud)** hot chocolate

chœur [kœr] nm (chorale) choir; (OPÉRA, THÉÂTRE) chorus; **en ~** in chorus

choisir [ʃwazir] vt to choose, select

choix [ʃwa] nm choice, selection; **avoir le ~** to have the choice; **premier ~** (COMM) class one; **de ~** choice, selected; **au ~** as you wish

chômage [ʃomaʒ] nm unemployment; **mettre au ~** to make redundant, put out of work; **être au ~** to be unemployed ou out of work; **chômeur, -euse** nm/f unemployed person

chope [ʃɔp] nf tankard

choper [ʃɔpe] (fam) vt (objet, maladie) to catch

choquer [ʃɔke] vt (offenser) to shock; (deuil) to shake

chorale [kɔral] nf choir

choriste [kɔrist] nm/f choir member; (OPÉRA) chorus member

chose [ʃoz] nf thing; **c'est peu de ~** it's nothing (really)

chou, x [ʃu] nm cabbage; **mon petit ~** (my) sweetheart; **~ à la crème** choux bun; **~x de Bruxelles** Brussels sprouts;

chouchou, te (fam) nm/f darling; (SCOL) teacher's pet; **choucroute** nf sauerkraut

chouette [ʃwet] nf owl ♦ adj (fam) great, smashing

chou-fleur [ʃuflœr] nm cauliflower

choyer [ʃwaje] vt (dorloter) to cherish; (: excessivement) to pamper

chrétien, ne [kretjɛ̃, jɛn] adj, nm/f Christian

Christ [krist] nm: **le ~** Christ; **christianisme** nm Christianity

chrome [krom] nm chromium; **chromé, e** adj chromium-plated

chronique [krɔnik] adj chronic ♦ nf (de journal) column, page; (historique) chronicle; (RADIO, TV): **la ~ sportive** the sports review

chronologique [krɔnɔlɔʒik] adj chronological

chronomètre [krɔnɔmetr] nm stopwatch; **chronométrer** vt to time

chrysanthème [krizɑ̃tɛm] nm chrysanthemum

chuchotement [ʃyʃɔtmɑ̃] nm whisper

chuchoter [ʃyʃɔte] vt, vi to whisper

chut [ʃyt] excl sh!

chute [ʃyt] nf fall; (déchet) scrap; **faire une ~ (de 10 m)** to fall (10 m); **~ (d'eau)** waterfall; **la ~ des cheveux** hair loss; **~ libre** free fall; **~s de pluie/neige** rain/snowfalls

Chypre [ʃipr] nm/f Cyprus

-ci [si] adv voir **par** ♦ dét: **ce garçon-~/-là** this/that boy; **ces femmes-~/-là** these/those women

cible [sibl] nf target

ciboulette [sibulet] nf (small) chive

cicatrice [sikatris] nf scar; **cicatriser** vt to heal

ci-contre [sikɔ̃tr] adv opposite

ci-dessous [sidəsu] adv below

ci-dessus [sidəsy] adv above

cidre [sidr] nm cider

Cie abr (= compagnie) Co.

ciel [sjɛl] nm sky; (REL) heaven; **cieux** nmpl (REL) heaven sg; **à ~ ouvert** open-air; (mine) open-cast

cierge [sjɛrʒ] *nm* candle

cieux [sjø] *nmpl de* **ciel**

cigale [sigal] *nf* cicada

cigare [sigar] *nm* cigar

cigarette [sigaret] *nf* cigarette

ci-gît [siʒi] *adv* +*vb* here lies

cigogne [sigɔɲ] *nf* stork

ci-inclus, e [siɛ̃kly, yz] *adj, adv* enclosed

ci-joint, e [siʒwɛ̃, ɛ̃t] *adj, adv* enclosed

cil [sil] *nm* (eye)lash

cime [sim] *nf* top; (*montagne*) peak

ciment [simã] *nm* cement

cimetière [simtjɛr] *nm* cemetery; (*d'église*) churchyard

cinéaste [sineast] *nm/f* film-maker

cinéma [sinema] *nm* cinema; **cinématographique** *adj* film *cpd*, cinema *cpd*

cinglant, e [sɛ̃glã, ãt] *adj* (*remarque*) biting

cinglé, e [sɛ̃gle] (*fam*) *adj* crazy

cinq [sɛ̃k] *num* five; **cinquantaine** *nf*: **une cinquantaine (de)** about fifty; **avoir la cinquantaine** (*âge*) to be around fifty; **cinquante** *num* fifty; **cinquantenaire** *adj, nm/f* fifty-year-old; **cinquième** *num* fifth

cintre [sɛ̃tr] *nm* coat-hanger

cintré, e [sɛ̃tre] *adj* (*chemise*) fitted

cirage [siraʒ] *nm* (shoe) polish

circonflexe [sirkɔ̃flɛks] *adj*: **accent ~** circumflex accent

circonscription [sirkɔ̃skripsjɔ̃] *nf* district; **~ électorale** (*d'un député*) constituency

circonscrire [sirkɔ̃skrir] *vt* (*sujet*) to define, delimit; (*incendie*) to contain

circonstance [sirkɔ̃stãs] *nf* circumstance; (*occasion*) occasion; **~s atténuantes** mitigating circumstances

circuit [sirkɥi] *nm* (*ÉLEC, TECH*) circuit; (*trajet*) tour, (round) trip

circulaire [sirkylɛr] *adj, nf* circular

circulation [sirkylasjɔ̃] *nf* circulation; (*AUTO*): **la ~** (the) traffic

circuler [sirkyle] *vi* (*sang, devises*) to circulate; (*véhicules*) to drive (along); (*passants*) to walk along; (*train, bus*) to run; **faire ~** (*nouvelle*) to spread (about), circulate; (*badauds*) to move on

cire [sir] *nf* wax; **ciré** *nm* oilskin; **cirer** *vt* to wax, polish

cirque [sirk] *nm* circus; (*fig*) chaos, bedlam; **quel ~!** what a carry-on!

cisaille(s) [sizaj] *nf(pl)* (gardening) shears *pl*

ciseau, x [sizo] *nm*: **~ (à bois)** chisel; **~x** *nmpl* (*paire of*) scissors

ciseler [siz(ə)le] *vt* to chisel, carve

citadin, e [sitadɛ̃, in] *nm/f* city dweller

citation [sitasjɔ̃] *nf* (*d'auteur*) quotation; (*JUR*) summons *sg*

cité [site] *nf* town; (*plus grande*) city; **~ universitaire** students' residences *pl*

citer [site] *vt* (*un auteur*) to quote (from); (*nommer*) to name; (*JUR*) to summon

citerne [sitɛrn] *nf* tank

citoyen, ne [sitwajɛ̃, jɛn] *nm/f* citizen

citron [sitrɔ̃] *nm* lemon; **~ vert** lime; **citronnade** *nf* still lemonade

citrouille [sitruj] *nf* pumpkin

civet [sivɛ] *nm*: **~ de lapin** rabbit stew

civière [sivjɛr] *nf* stretcher

civil, e [sivil] *adj* (*mariage, poli*) civil; (*non militaire*) civilian; **en ~** in civilian clothes; **dans le ~** in civilian life

civilisation [sivilizasjɔ̃] *nf* civilization

clair, e [klɛr] *adj* light; (*pièce*) light, bright; (*eau, son, fig*) clear ♦ *adv*: **voir ~** to see clearly; **tirer qch au ~** to clear sth up, clarify sth; **mettre au ~** (*notes etc*) to tidy up; **~ de lune** ♦ *nm* moonlight; **clairement** *adv* clearly

clairière [klɛrjɛr] *nf* clearing

clairon [klɛrɔ̃] *nm* bugle; **claironner** *vt* (*fig*) to trumpet, shout from the rooftops

clairsemé, e [klɛrsəme] *adj* sparse

clairvoyant, e [klɛrvwajã, ãt] *adj* perceptive, clear-sighted

clandestin, e [klãdɛstɛ̃, in] *adj* clandestine, secret; (*mouvement*) underground; (*travailleur*) illegal; **passager ~** stowaway

clapier [klapje] *nm* (rabbit) hutch

clapoter [klapɔte] *vi* to lap

claque [klak] *nf* (*gifle*) slap; **claquer** *vi* (*porte*) to bang, slam; (*fam: mourir*) to snuff it ♦ *vt* (*porte*) to slam, bang; (*doigts*) to snap; (*fam: dépenser*) to blow; **il claquait des dents** his teeth were chattering; **être claqué** (*fam*) to be dead tired; **se claquer un muscle** to pull *ou* strain a muscle; **claquettes** *nfpl* tap-dancing *sg*

clarinette [klaʀinɛt] *nf* clarinet

clarté [klaʀte] *nf* (*luminosité*) brightness; (*d'un son, de l'eau*) clearness; (*d'une explication*) clarity

classe [klɑs] *nf* class; (SCOL: *local*) class(room); (: *leçon, élèves*) class; **aller en ~** to go to school; **classement** *nm* (*rang: SCOL*) place; (: *SPORT*) placing; (*liste: SCOL*) class list (in order of merit); (: *SPORT*) placings *pl*

classer [klɑse] *vt* (*idées, livres*) to classify; (*papiers*) to file; (*candidat*) to grade; (JUR: *affaire*) to close; **se ~ premier/dernier** to come first/last; (*SPORT*) to finish first/last; **classeur** *nm* (*cahier*) file

classique [klɑsik] *adj* classical; (*sobre: coupe etc*) classic(al); (*habituel*) classic

clause [kloz] *nf* clause

clavecin [klav(ə)sɛ̃] *nm* harpsichord

clavicule [klavikyl] *nf* collarbone

clavier [klavje] *nm* keyboard

clé [kle] *nf* key; (MUS) clef; (*de mécanicien*) spanner (BRIT), wrench (US); **prix ~s en main** (*d'une voiture*) on-the-road price; **~ anglaise** (monkey) wrench; **~ de contact** ignition key

clef [kle] *nf* = **clé**

clément, e [klemɑ̃, ɑ̃t] *adj* (*temps*) mild; (*indulgent*) lenient

clerc [klɛʀ] *nm:* **~ de notaire** solicitor's clerk

clergé [klɛʀʒe] *nm* clergy

cliché [kliʃe] *nm* (*fig*) cliché; (*négatif*) negative; (*photo*) print

client, e [klijɑ̃, klijɑ̃t] *nm/f* (*acheteur*) customer, client; (*d'hôtel*) guest, patron; (*du docteur*) patient; (*de l'avocat*) client; **clientèle** *nf* (*du magasin*) customers *pl*, clien-

tèle; (*du docteur, de l'avocat*) practice

cligner [kliɲe] *vi:* **~ des yeux** to blink (one's eyes); **~ de l'œil** to wink; **clignotant** *nm* (AUTO) indicator; **clignoter** *vi* (*étoiles etc*) to twinkle; (*lumière*) to flicker

climat [klima] *nm* climate

climatisation [klimatizasjɔ̃] *nf* air conditioning; **climatisé, e** *adj* air-conditioned

clin d'œil [klɛ̃dœj] *nm* wink; **en un ~** in a flash

clinique [klinik] *nf* private hospital

clinquant, e [klɛ̃kɑ̃, ɑ̃t] *adj* flashy

clip [klip] *nm* (*boucle d'oreille*) clip-on; **(vidéo) ~** (pop) video

cliquer [klike] *vt:* **~ sur** to click on

cliqueter [klik(ə)te] *vi* (*ferraille*) to jangle; (*clés*) to jingle

clochard, e [klɔʃaʀ, aʀd] *nm/f* tramp

cloche [klɔʃ] *nf* (*d'église*) bell; (*fam*) clot; **cloche-pied: à cloche-pied** *adv* on one leg, hopping (along); **clocher** *nm* church tower; (*en pointe*) steeple ♦ *vi* (*fam*) to be *ou* go wrong; **de clocher** (*péj*) parochial

cloison [klwazɔ̃] *nf* partition (wall)

cloître [klwatʀ] *nm* cloister; **cloîtrer** *vt:* **se cloîtrer** to shut o.s. up *ou* away

clone [klɔn] *nm* clone ♦ *vt* cloner

cloque [klɔk] *nf* blister

clore [klɔʀ] *vt* to close; **clos, e** *adj* *voir* **maison; huis**

clôture [klotyʀ] *nf* closure; (*barrière*) enclosure

clou [klu] *nm* nail; **~s** *nmpl* (*passage ~té*) pedestrian crossing; **pneus à ~s** studded tyres; **le ~ du spectacle** the highlight of the show; **~ de girofle** clove; **clouer** *vt* to nail down *ou* up; **clouer le bec à qn** (*fam*) to shut sb up

clown [klun] *nm* clown

club [klœb] *nm* club

CMU *nf* (= *couverture maladie universelle*) system of free health care for those on low incomes

CNRS *sigle m* (= *Centre nationale de la recherche scientifique*) ≈ SERC (BRIT), ≈ NSF (US)

coaguler [kɔagyle] *vt, vi* (*aussi:* **se ~:**

sang) to coagulate

coasser [kɔase] *vi* to croak

cobaye [kɔbaj] *nm* guinea-pig

coca [kɔka] *nm* Coke ®

cocaïne [kɔkain] *nf* cocaine

cocasse [kɔkas] *adj* comical, funny

coccinelle [kɔksinɛl] *nf* ladybird (*BRIT*), ladybug (*US*)

cocher [kɔʃe] *vt* to tick off

cochère [kɔʃɛʀ] *adj f*: **porte ~** carriage entrance

cochon, ne [kɔʃɔ̃, ɔn] *nm* pig ♦ *adj* (*fam*) dirty, smutty; **~ d'Inde** guinea pig; **cochonnerie** (*fam*) *nf* (*saleté*) filth; (*marchandise*) rubbish, trash

cocktail [kɔktɛl] *nm* cocktail; (*réception*) cocktail party

coco [kɔko] *nm voir* **noix**

cocorico [kɔkɔʀiko] *excl, nm* cock-a-doodle-do

cocotier [kɔkɔtje] *nm* coconut palm

cocotte [kɔkɔt] *nf* (*en fonte*) casserole; **~ (minute)** pressure cooker; **ma ~** (*fam*) sweetie (pie)

cocu [kɔky] (*fam*) *nm* cuckold

code [kɔd] *nm* code ♦ *adj*: **phares ~s** dipped lights; **se mettre en ~(s)** to dip one's (head)lights; **~ à barres** bar code; **~ civil** Common Law; **~ de la route** highway code; **~ pénal** penal code; **~ postal** (*numéro*) post (*BRIT*) *ou* zip (*US*) code

cœur [kœʀ] *nm* heart; (*CARTES: couleur*) hearts *pl*; (: *carte*) heart; **avoir bon ~** to be kind-hearted; **avoir mal au ~** to feel sick; **en avoir le ~ net** to be clear in one's own mind (about it); **par ~** by heart; **de bon ~** willingly; **cela lui tient à ~** that's (very) close to his heart

coffre [kɔfʀ] *nm* (*meuble*) chest; (*d'auto*) boot (*BRIT*), trunk (*US*); **coffre(-fort)** *nm* safe; **coffret** *nm* casket

cognac [kɔɲak] *nm* brandy, cognac

cogner [kɔɲe] *vi* to knock; **se ~ la tête** to bang one's head

cohérent, e [kɔeʀɑ̃, ɑ̃t] *adj* coherent, consistent

cohorte [kɔɔʀt] *nf* troop

cohue [kɔy] *nf* crowd

coi, coite [kwa, kwat] *adj*: **rester ~** to remain silent

coiffe [kwaf] *nf* headdress

coiffé, e [kwafe] *adj*: **bien/mal ~** with tidy/untidy hair

coiffer [kwafe] *vt* (*fig: surmonter*) to cover, top; **se ~** to do one's hair; **~ qn** to do sb's hair; **coiffeur, -euse** *nm/f* hairdresser; **coiffeuse** *nf* (*table*) dressing table; **coiffure** *nf* (*cheveux*) hairstyle, hairdo; (*art*): **la coiffure** hairdressing

coin [kwɛ̃] *nm* corner; (*pour ~cer*) wedge; **l'épicerie du ~** the local grocer; **dans le ~** (*aux alentours*) in the area, around about; (*habiter*) locally; **je ne suis pas du ~** I'm not from here; **au ~ du feu** by the fireside; **regard en ~** sideways glance

coincé, e [kwɛ̃se] *adj* stuck, jammed; (*fig: inhibé*) inhibited, hung up (*fam*)

coincer [kwɛ̃se] *vt* to jam; (*fam: attraper*) to pinch

coïncidence [kɔɛ̃sidɑ̃s] *nf* coincidence

coïncider [kɔɛ̃side] *vi* to coincide

coing [kwɛ̃] *nm* quince

col [kɔl] *nm* (*de chemise*) collar; (*encolure, cou*) neck; (*de montagne*) pass; **~ de l'utérus** cervix; **~ roulé** polo-neck

colère [kɔlɛʀ] *nf* anger; **une ~** a fit of anger; **(se mettre) en ~** (to get) angry; **coléreux, -euse** *adj*, **colérique** *adj* quick-tempered, irascible

colifichet [kɔlifiʃɛ] *nm* trinket

colimaçon [kɔlimasɔ̃] *nm*: **escalier en ~** spiral staircase

colin [kɔlɛ̃] *nm* hake

colique [kɔlik] *nf* diarrhoea

colis [kɔli] *nm* parcel

collaborateur, -trice [kɔ(l)labɔʀatœʀ, tʀis] *nm/f* (*aussi POL*) collaborator; (*d'une revue*) contributor

collaborer [kɔ(l)labɔʀe] *vi* to collaborate; **~ à** to collaborate on; (*revue*) to contribute to

collant, e [kɔlɑ̃, ɑ̃t] *adj* sticky; (*robe etc*)

clinging, skintight; (*péj*) clinging ♦ *nm* (*bas*) tights *pl*; (*de danseur*) leotard

collation [kɔlasjɔ̃] *nf* light meal

colle [kɔl] *nf* glue; (*à papiers peints*) (wallpaper) paste; (*fam: devinette*) teaser, riddle; (*SCOL: fam*) detention

collecte [kɔlɛkt] *nf* collection; **collectif, -ive** *adj* collective; (*visite, billet*) group *cpd*

collection [kɔlɛksjɔ̃] *nf* collection; (*ÉDITION*) series; **collectionner** *vt* to collect; **collectionneur, -euse** *nm/f* collector

collectivité [kɔlɛktivite] *nf* group; **~s locales** (*ADMIN*) local authorities

collège [kɔlɛʒ] *nm* (*école*) (secondary) school; (*assemblée*) body; **collégien** *nm* schoolboy; **collégienne** *nf* schoolgirl

---
collège

ⓘ The **collège** is a state secondary school for children aged between eleven and fifteen. Pupils follow a nationally prescribed curriculum consisting of a common core and various options. Schools are free to arrange their own timetable and choose their own teaching methods. Before leaving the collège, pupils are assessed by examination and course work for their **brevet des collèges**.

---

collègue [kɔl(l)ɛg] *nm/f* colleague

coller [kɔle] *vt* (*papier, timbre*) to stick (on); (*affiche*) to stick up; (*enveloppe*) to stick down; (*morceaux*) to stick *ou* glue together; (*fam: mettre, fourrer*) to stick, shove; (*SCOL: fam*) to keep in ♦ *vi* (*être collant*) to be sticky; (*adhérer*) to stick; **~ à** to stick to; **être collé à un examen** (*fam*) to fail an exam

collet [kɔlɛ] *nm* (*piège*) snare, noose; (*cou*): **prendre qn au ~** to grab sb by the throat

collier [kɔlje] *nm* (*bijou*) necklace; (*de chien, TECH*) collar

collimateur [kɔlimatœʀ] *nm*: **avoir qn/ qch dans le ~** (*fig*) to have sb/sth in one's sights

colline [kɔlin] *nf* hill

collision [kɔlizjɔ̃] *nf* collision, crash; **entrer en ~ (avec)** to collide (with)

colloque [kɔ(l)lɔk] *nm* symposium

collyre [kɔliʀ] *nm* eye drops

colmater [kɔlmate] *vt* (*fuite*) to seal off; (*brèche*) to plug, fill in

colombe [kɔlɔ̃b] *nf* dove

Colombie [kɔlɔ̃bi] *nf*: **la ~** Colombia

colon [kɔlɔ̃] *nm* settler

colonel [kɔlɔnɛl] *nm* colonel

colonie [kɔlɔni] *nf* colony; **~ (de vacances)** holiday camp (*for children*)

colonne [kɔlɔn] *nf* column; **se mettre en ~ par deux** to get into twos; **~ (vertébrale)** spine, spinal column

colorant [kɔlɔʀɑ̃, ɑ̃t] *nm* colouring

colorer [kɔlɔʀe] *vt* to colour

colorier [kɔlɔʀje] *vt* to colour (in)

coloris [kɔlɔʀi] *nm* colour, shade

colporter [kɔlpɔʀte] *vt* to hawk, peddle

colza [kɔlza] *nm* rape(seed)

coma [kɔma] *nm* coma; **être dans le ~** to be in a coma

combat [kɔ̃ba] *nm* fight, fighting *no pl*; **~ de boxe** boxing match; **combattant** *nm*: **ancien combattant** war veteran; **combattre** *vt* to fight; (*épidémie, ignorance*) to combat, fight against

combien [kɔ̃bjɛ̃] *adv* (*quantité*) how much; (*nombre*) how many; **~ de** (*quantité*) how much; (*nombre*) how many; **~ de temps** how long; **~ ça coûte/pèse?** how much does it cost/weigh?; **on est le ~ aujourd'hui?** (*fam*) what's the date today?

combinaison [kɔ̃binɛzɔ̃] *nf* combination; (*astuce*) device, scheme; (*de femme*) slip; (*de plongée*) wetsuit; (*bleu de travail*) boiler suit (*BRIT*), coveralls *pl* (*US*)

combine [kɔ̃bin] *nf* trick; (*péj*) scheme, fiddle (*BRIT*)

combiné [kɔ̃bine] *nm* (*aussi: ~ téléphonique*) receiver

combiner [kɔ̃bine] *vt* (*grouper*) to combine; (*plan, horaire*) to work out, devise

comble [kɔ̃bl] *adj* (*salle*) packed (full)
♦ *nm* (*du bonheur, plaisir*) height; **~s** *nmpl*
(CONSTR) attic *sg*, loft *sg*; **c'est le ~!** that
beats everything!
combler [kɔ̃ble] *vt* (*trou*) to fill in; (*besoin,
lacune*) to fill; (*déficit*) to make good; (*satisfaire*) to fulfil
combustible [kɔ̃bystibl] *nm* fuel
comédie [kɔmedi] *nf* comedy; (*fig*) playacting *no pl*; **faire la ~** (*fam*) to make a
fuss; **~ musicale** musical; **comédien, ne**
nm/f actor(-tress)

Comédie française
---

i Founded in 1680 by Louis XIV, the
Comédie française is the French na-
tional theatre. Subsidized by the state, the
company performs mainly in the Palais
Royal in Paris and stages mainly classical
French plays.

---

comestible [kɔmestibl] *adj* edible
comique [kɔmik] *adj* (*drôle*) comical;
(THÉÂTRE) comic ♦ *nm* (*artiste*) comic, comedian
comité [kɔmite] *nm* committee; **~ d'entreprise** works council
commandant [kɔmɑ̃dɑ̃] *nm* (*gén*) commander, commandant; (NAVIG, AVIAT) captain
commande [kɔmɑ̃d] *nf* (COMM) order; **~s**
nfpl (AVIAT *etc*) controls; **sur ~** to order;
commandement *nm* command; (REL)
commandment; **commander** *vt* (COMM)
to order; (*diriger, ordonner*) to command;
commander à qn de faire to command
ou order sb to do
commando [kɔmɑ̃do] *nm* commando
(squad)

MOT-CLÉ
---

comme [kɔm] *prép* 1 (*comparaison*) like;
tout comme son père just like his father;
fort comme un bœuf as strong as an ox;
joli comme tout ever so pretty
2 (*manière*) like; **faites-le comme ça** do it

like this, do it this way; **comme ci,
comme ça** so-so, middling
3 (*en tant que*) as a; **donner comme prix**
to give as a prize; **travailler comme secrétaire** to work as a secretary
♦ *conj* 1 (*ainsi que*) as; **elle écrit comme
elle parle** she writes as she talks; **comme
si** as if
2 (*au moment où, alors que*) as; **il est parti
comme j'arrivais** he left as I arrived
3 (*parce que, puisque*) as; **comme il était
en retard, il ...** as he was late, he ...
♦ *adv*: **comme il est fort/c'est bon!** he's
so strong/it's so good!

---

commémorer [kɔmemɔre] *vt* to commemorate
commencement [kɔmɑ̃smɑ̃] *nm* beginning, start
commencer [kɔmɑ̃se] *vt, vi* to begin,
start; **~ à** *ou* **de faire** to begin *ou* start
doing
comment [kɔmɑ̃] *adv* how; **~?** (*que dites-
vous*) pardon?
commentaire [kɔmɑ̃tɛr] *nm* (*remarque*)
comment, remark; (*exposé*) commentary
commenter [kɔmɑ̃te] *vt* (*jugement, événement*) to comment (up)on; (RADIO, TV:
match, manifestation) to cover
commérages [kɔmeraʒ] *nmpl* gossip *sg*
commerçant, e [kɔmɛrsɑ̃, ɑ̃t] *nm/f* shopkeeper, trader
commerce [kɔmɛrs] *nm* (*activité*) trade,
commerce; (*boutique*) business; **~ électronique** e-commerce; **commercial, e,
-aux** *adj* commercial, trading; (*péj*) commercial; **les commerciaux** the sales
people; **commercialiser** *vt* to market
commère [kɔmɛr] *nf* gossip
commettre [kɔmɛtr] *vt* to commit
commis [kɔmi] *nm* (*de magasin*) (shop) assistant; (*de banque*) clerk
commissaire [kɔmisɛr] *nm* (*de police*) ≃
(police) superintendent; **commissaire-
priseur** *nm* auctioneer; **commissariat**
nm police station

commission [kɔmisjɔ̃] nf (comité, pourcentage) commission; (message) message; (course) errand; **~s** nfpl (achats) shopping sg

commode [kɔmɔd] adj (pratique) convenient, handy; (facile) easy; (personne): **pas ~** awkward (to deal with) ♦ nf chest of drawers; **commodité** nf convenience

commotion [kɔmosjɔ̃] nf: **~ (cérébrale)** concussion; **commotionné, e** adj shocked, shaken

commun, e [kɔmœ̃, yn] adj common; (pièce) communal, shared; (effort) joint; **ça sort du ~** it's out of the ordinary; **le ~ des mortels** the common run of people; **en ~** (faire) jointly; **mettre en ~** to pool, share; voir aussi **communs**

communauté [kɔmynote] nf community

commune [kɔmyn] nf (ADMIN) commune, ≈ district; (: urbaine) ≈ borough

communicatif, -ive [kɔmynikatif, iv] adj (rire) infectious; (personne) communicative

communication [kɔmynikasjɔ̃] nf communication; **~ (téléphonique)** (telephone) call

communier [kɔmynje] vi (REL) to receive communion

communion [kɔmynjɔ̃] nf communion

communiquer [kɔmynike] vt (nouvelle, dossier) to pass on, convey; (peur etc) to communicate ♦ vi to communicate; **se ~ à** (se propager) to spread to

communisme [kɔmynism] nm communism; **communiste** adj, nm/f communist

communs [kɔmœ̃] nmpl (bâtiments) outbuildings

commutateur [kɔmytatœʀ] nm (ÉLEC) (change-over) switch, commutator

compact, e [kɔpakt] adj (dense) dense; (appareil) compact

compagne [kɔpaɲ] nf companion

compagnie [kɔpaɲi] nf (firme, MIL) company; **tenir ~ à qn** to keep sb company; **fausser ~ à qn** to give sb the slip, slip ou sneak away from sb; **~ aérienne** airline (company)

compagnon [kɔpaɲɔ̃] nm companion

comparable [kɔpaʀabl] adj: **~ (à)** comparable (to)

comparaison [kɔpaʀezɔ̃] nf comparison

comparaître [kɔpaʀɛtʀ] vi: **~ (devant)** to appear (before)

comparer [kɔpaʀe] vt to compare; **~ qch/qn à** ou **et** (pour choisir) to compare sth/sb with ou and; (pour établir une similitude) to compare sth/sb to

compartiment [kɔpaʀtimɑ̃] nm compartment

comparution [kɔpaʀysjɔ̃] nf (JUR) appearance

compas [kɔpa] nm (GÉOM) (pair of) compasses pl; (NAVIG) compass

compatible [kɔpatibl] adj compatible

compatir [kɔpatiʀ] vi to sympathize

compatriote [kɔpatʀijɔt] nm/f compatriot

compensation [kɔpɑ̃sasjɔ̃] nf compensation

compenser [kɔpɑ̃se] vt to compensate for, make up for

compère [kɔpɛʀ] nm accomplice

compétence [kɔpetɑ̃s] nf competence

compétent, e [kɔpetɑ̃, ɑ̃t] adj (apte) competent, capable

compétition [kɔpetisjɔ̃] nf (gén) competition; (SPORT: épreuve) event; **la ~ automobile** motor racing

complainte [kɔplɛ̃t] nf lament

complaire [kɔplɛʀ]: **se ~** vi: **se ~ dans** to take pleasure in

complaisance [kɔplɛzɑ̃s] nf kindness; **pavillon de ~** flag of convenience

complaisant, e [kɔplɛzɑ̃, ɑ̃t] adj (aimable) kind, obliging

complément [kɔplemɑ̃] nm complement; (reste) remainder; **~ d'information** (ADMIN) supplementary ou further information; **complémentaire** adj complementary; (additionnel) supplementary

complet, -ète [kɔplɛ, ɛt] adj complete; (plein: hôtel etc) full ♦ nm (aussi: **~veston**) suit; **pain ~** wholemeal bread; **complètement** adv completely;

compléter vt (*porter à la quantité voulue*) to complete; (*augmenter: connaissances, études*) to complement, supplement; (: *garde-robe*) to add to; **se compléter** (*caractères*) to complement one another

complexe [kɔ̃plɛks] *adj*, *nm* complex; **complexé, e** *adj* mixed-up, hung-up

complication [kɔ̃plikasjɔ̃] *nf* complexity, intricacy; (*difficulté, ennui*) complication

complice [kɔ̃plis] *nm* accomplice; **complicité** *nf* complicity

compliment [kɔ̃plimɑ̃] *nm* (*louange*) compliment; **~s** *nmpl* (*félicitations*) congratulations

compliqué, e [kɔ̃plike] *adj* complicated, complex; (*personne*) complicated

compliquer [kɔ̃plike] vt to complicate; **se ~** to become complicated

complot [kɔ̃plo] *nm* plot

comportement [kɔ̃pɔrtəmɑ̃] *nm* behaviour

comporter [kɔ̃pɔrte] vt (*consister en*) to consist of, comprise; (*inclure*) to have; **se ~** vi to behave

composant [kɔ̃pozɑ̃] *nm*, **composante** [kɔ̃pozɑ̃t] *nf* component

composé [kɔ̃poze] *nm* compound

composer [kɔ̃poze] vt (*musique, texte*) to compose; (*mélange, équipe*) to make up; (*numéro*) to dial; (*constituer*) to make up, form ♦ vi (*transiger*) to come to terms; **se ~ de** to be composed of, be made up of; **compositeur, -trice** *nm/f* (*MUS*) composer; **composition** *nf* composition; (*SCOL*) test

composter [kɔ̃pɔste] vt (*billet*) to punch

compote [kɔ̃pɔt] *nf* stewed fruit *no pl*; **~ de pommes** stewed apples

compréhensible [kɔ̃preɑ̃sibl] *adj* comprehensible; (*attitude*) understandable

compréhensif, -ive [kɔ̃preɑ̃sif, iv] *adj* understanding

comprendre [kɔ̃prɑ̃dr] vt to understand; (*se composer de*) to comprise, consist of

compresse [kɔ̃prɛs] *nf* compress

compression [kɔ̃presjɔ̃] *nf* compression;

(*de personnes*) reduction

comprimé [kɔ̃prime] *nm* tablet

comprimer [kɔ̃prime] vt to compress; (*fig: crédit etc*) to reduce, cut down

compris, e [kɔ̃pri, iz] *pp de* **comprendre** ♦ *adj* (*inclus*) included; **~ entre** (*situé*) contained between; **l'électricité ~e/non ~e, y/non ~ l'électricité** including/excluding electricity; **10 euros tout ~** 10 euros all inclusive *ou* all-in

compromettre [kɔ̃prɔmɛtr] vt to compromise; **compromis** *nm* compromise

comptabilité [kɔ̃tabilite] *nf* (*activité*) accounting, accountancy; (*comptes*) accounts *pl*, books *pl*; (*service*) accounts office

comptable [kɔ̃tabl] *nm/f* accountant

comptant [kɔ̃tɑ̃] *adv*: **payer ~** to pay cash; **acheter ~** to buy for cash

compte [kɔ̃t] *nm* count; (*total, montant*) count, (right) number; (*bancaire, facture*) account; **~s** *nmpl* (*FINANCE*) accounts, books; (*fig*) explanation *sg*; **en fin de ~** all things considered; **s'en tirer à bon ~** to get off lightly; **pour le ~ de** on behalf of; **pour son propre ~** for one's own benefit; **tenir ~ de** to take account of; **travailler à son ~** to work for oneself; **rendre ~ (à qn) de qch** to give (sb) an account of sth; *voir aussi* **rendre** ♦ **~ à rebours** countdown; **~: chèques postaux** Post Office account; **~ courant** current account; **~ rendu** account, report; (*de film, livre*) review; **compte-gouttes** *nm inv* dropper

compter [kɔ̃te] vt to count; (*facturer*) to charge for; (*avoir à son actif, comporter*) to have; (*prévoir*) to allow, reckon; (*penser, espérer*): **~ réussir** to expect to succeed ♦ vi to count; (*être économe*) to economize; (*figurer*): **~ parmi** to be *ou* rank among; **~ sur** to count (up)on; **~ avec qch/qn** to reckon with *ou* take account of sth/sb; **sans ~ que** besides which

compteur [kɔ̃tœr] *nm* meter; **~ de vitesse** speedometer

comptine [kɔ̃tin] *nf* nursery rhyme

comptoir [kɔ̃twaʀ] *nm* (*de magasin*) counter; (*bar*) bar

compulser [kɔ̃pylse] *vt* to consult

comte [kɔ̃t] *nm* count; **comtesse** *nf* countess

con, ne [kɔ̃, kɔn] (*fam!*) *adj* damned *ou* bloody (*BRIT*) stupid (*!*)

concéder [kɔ̃sede] *vt* to grant; (*défaite, point*) to concede

concentré, e [kɔ̃sɑ̃tre] *adj* (*lait*) condensed ♦ *nm*: **~ de tomates** tomato purée

concentrer [kɔ̃sɑ̃tre] *vt* to concentrate; **se ~** *vi* to concentrate

concept [kɔ̃sɛpt] *nm* concept

conception [kɔ̃sɛpsjɔ̃] *nf* conception; (*d'une machine etc*) design; (*d'un problème, de la vie*) approach

concerner [kɔ̃sɛʀne] *vt* to concern; **en ce qui me concerne** as far as I am concerned

concert [kɔ̃sɛʀ] *nm* concert; **de ~** (*décider*) unanimously; **concerter: se concerter** *vi* to put their *etc* heads together

concession [kɔ̃sesjɔ̃] *nf* concession; **concessionnaire** *nm/f* agent, dealer

concevoir [kɔ̃s(ə)vwaʀ] *vt* (*idée, projet*) to conceive (of); (*comprendre*) to understand; (*enfant*) to conceive; **bien/mal conçu** well-/badly-designed

concierge [kɔ̃sjɛʀʒ] *nm/f* caretaker

conciliabules [kɔ̃siljabyl] *nmpl* (private) discussions, confabulations

concilier [kɔ̃silje] *vt* to reconcile; **se ~** *vt* to win over

concis, e [kɔ̃si, iz] *adj* concise

concitoyen, ne [kɔ̃sitwajɛ̃, jɛn] *nm/f* fellow citizen

concluant, e [kɔ̃klyɑ̃, ɑ̃t] *adj* conclusive

conclure [kɔ̃klyʀ] *vt* to conclude; **conclusion** *nf* conclusion

conçois *etc* [kɔ̃swa] *vb voir* **concevoir**

concombre [kɔ̃kɔ̃bʀ] *nm* cucumber

concorder [kɔ̃kɔʀde] *vi* to tally, agree

concourir [kɔ̃kuʀiʀ] *vi* (*SPORT*) to com-

pete; **~ à** (*effet etc*) to work towards

concours [kɔ̃kuʀ] *nm* competition; (*SCOL*) competitive examination; (*assistance*) aid, help; **~ de circonstances** combination of circumstances; **~ hippique** horse show

concret, -ète [kɔ̃kʀɛ, ɛt] *adj* concrete

concrétiser [kɔ̃kʀetize]: **se ~** *vi* to materialize

conçu, e [kɔ̃sy] *pp de* **concevoir**

concubinage [kɔ̃kybinaʒ] *nm* (*JUR*) cohabitation

concurrence [kɔ̃kyʀɑ̃s] *nf* competition; **faire ~ à** to be in competition with; **jusqu'à ~ de** up to

concurrent, e [kɔ̃kyʀɑ̃, ɑ̃t] *nm/f* (*SPORT, ÉCON etc*) competitor; (*SCOL*) candidate

condamner [kɔ̃dane] *vt* (*blâmer*) to condemn; (*JUR*) to sentence; (*porte, ouverture*) to fill in, block up; **~ qn à 2 ans de prison** to sentence sb to 2 years' imprisonment

condensation [kɔ̃dɑ̃sasjɔ̃] *nf* condensation

condenser [kɔ̃dɑ̃se] *vt* to condense; **se ~** *vi* to condense

condisciple [kɔ̃disipl] *nm/f* fellow student

condition [kɔ̃disjɔ̃] *nf* condition; **~s** *nfpl* (*tarif, prix*) terms; (*circonstances*) conditions; **à ~ de ou que** provided that; **conditionnel, le** *nm* conditional (tense)

conditionnement [kɔ̃disjɔnmɑ̃] *nm* (*emballage*) packaging

conditionner [kɔ̃disjɔne] *vt* (*déterminer*) to determine; (*COMM: produit*) to package; **air conditionné** air conditioning

condoléances [kɔ̃dɔleɑ̃s] *nfpl* condolences

conducteur, -trice [kɔ̃dyktœʀ, tʀis] *nm/f* driver ♦ *nm* (*ÉLEC etc*) conductor

conduire [kɔ̃dyiʀ] *vt* to drive; (*délégation, troupeau*) to lead; **se ~** *vi* to behave; **~ à** to lead to; **~ qn quelque part** to take sb somewhere; to drive sb somewhere

conduite [kɔ̃dyit] *nf* (*comportement*) behaviour; (*d'eau, de gaz*) pipe; **sous la ~ de** led by; **~ à gauche** left-hand drive

cône [kon] *nm* cone

confection [kɔ̃fɛksjɔ̃] *nf* (*fabrication*) making; (*COUTURE*): **la ~** the clothing industry

confectionner [kɔ̃fɛksjɔne] *vt* to make

conférence [kɔ̃feʀɑ̃s] *nf* conference; (*exposé*) lecture; **~ de presse** press conference; **conférencier, -ière** *nm/f* speaker, lecturer

confesser [kɔ̃fese] *vt* to confess; **se ~** *vi* (*REL*) to go to confession; **confession** *nf* confession; (*culte: catholique etc*) denomination

confiance [kɔ̃fjɑ̃s] *nf* (*en l'honnêteté de qn*) confidence, trust; (*en la valeur de qch*) faith; **avoir ~ en** to have confidence *ou* faith in, trust; **faire ~ à qn** to trust sb; **mettre qn en ~** to win sb's trust; **~ en soi** self-confidence

confiant, e [kɔ̃fjɑ̃, jɑ̃t] *adj* confident; trusting

confidence [kɔ̃fidɑ̃s] *nf* confidence; **confidentiel, le** *adj* confidential

confier [kɔ̃fje] *vt*: **~ à qn** (*objet, travail*) to entrust to sb; (*secret, pensée*) to confide to sb; **se ~ à qn** to confide in sb

confins [kɔ̃fɛ̃] *nmpl*: **aux ~ de** on the borders of

confirmation [kɔ̃fiʀmasjɔ̃] *nf* confirmation

confirmer [kɔ̃fiʀme] *vt* to confirm

confiserie [kɔ̃fizʀi] *nf* (*magasin*) confectioner's *ou* sweet shop; **~s** *nfpl* (*bonbons*) confectionery *sg*

confisquer [kɔ̃fiske] *vt* to confiscate

confit, e [kɔ̃fi, it] *adj*: **fruits ~s** crystallized fruits ♦ *nm*: **~ d'oie** conserve of goose

confiture [kɔ̃fityʀ] *nf* jam; **~ d'oranges** (orange) marmalade

conflit [kɔ̃fli] *nm* conflict

confondre [kɔ̃fɔ̃dʀ] *vt* (*jumeaux, faits*) to confuse, mix up; (*témoin, menteur*) to confound; **se ~** *vi* to merge; **se ~ en excuses** to apologize profusely; **confondu, e** *adj* (*stupéfait*) speechless, overcome

conforme [kɔ̃fɔʀm] *adj*: **~ à** (*loi, règle*) in accordance with; **conformément** *adv*: **conformément à** in accordance with;

conformer *vt*: **se conformer à** to conform to

confort [kɔ̃fɔʀ] *nm* comfort; **tout ~** (*COMM*) with all modern conveniences; **confortable** *adj* comfortable

confrère [kɔ̃fʀɛʀ] *nm* colleague

confronter [kɔ̃fʀɔ̃te] *vt* to confront

confus, e [kɔ̃fy, yz] *adj* (*vague*) confused; (*embarrassé*) embarrassed; **confusion** *nf* (*voir confus*) confusion; embarrassment; (*voir confondre*) confusion, mixing up

congé [kɔ̃ʒe] *nm* (*vacances*) holiday; **en ~** on holiday; **semaine de ~** week off; **prendre ~ de qn** to take one's leave of sb; **donner son ~ à** to give in one's notice to; **~ de maladie** sick leave; **~ de maternité** maternity leave; **~s payés** paid holiday

congédier [kɔ̃ʒedje] *vt* to dismiss

congélateur [kɔ̃ʒelatœʀ] *nm* freezer

congeler [kɔ̃ʒ(ə)le] *vt* to freeze; **les produits congelés** frozen foods

congestion [kɔ̃ʒɛstjɔ̃] *nf* congestion; **~ cérébrale** stroke; **congestionner** *vt* (*rue*) to congest; (*visage*) to flush

congrès [kɔ̃gʀɛ] *nm* congress

conifère [kɔnifɛʀ] *nm* conifer

conjecture [kɔ̃ʒɛktyʀ] *nf* conjecture

conjoint, e [kɔ̃ʒwɛ̃, wɛ̃t] *adj* joint ♦ *nm/f* spouse

conjonction [kɔ̃ʒɔ̃ksjɔ̃] *nf* (*LING*) conjunction

conjonctivite [kɔ̃ʒɔ̃ktivit] *nf* conjunctivitis

conjoncture [kɔ̃ʒɔ̃ktyʀ] *nf* circumstances *pl*; **la ~ actuelle** the present (economic) situation

conjugaison [kɔ̃ʒygɛzɔ̃] *nf* (*LING*) conjugation

conjuguer [kɔ̃ʒyge] *vt* (*LING*) to conjugate; (*efforts etc*) to combine

conjuration [kɔ̃ʒyʀasjɔ̃] *nf* conspiracy

conjurer [kɔ̃ʒyʀe] *vt* (*sort, maladie*) to avert; (*implorer*) to beseech, entreat

connaissance [kɔnɛsɑ̃s] *nf* (*savoir*) knowledge *no pl*; (*personne connue*) acquaintance; **être sans ~** to be unconscious;

perdre/reprendre ~ to lose/regain consciousness; **à ma ~** to (the best of) my knowledge; **faire la ~ de qn** to meet sb
connaisseur [kɔnɛsœʀ, øz] *nm* connoisseur
connaître [kɔnɛtʀ] *vt* to know; (*éprouver*) to experience; (*avoir: succès*) to have, enjoy; **~ de nom/vue** to know by name/sight; **ils se sont connus à Genève** they (first) met in Geneva; **s'y ~ en qch** to know a lot about sth
connecter [kɔnɛkte] *vt* to connect; **se ~** (*INFORM*) to log on
connerie [kɔnʀi] (*fam!*) *nf* stupid thing (to do/say)
connu, e [kɔny] *adj* (*célèbre*) well-known
conquérir [kɔkeʀiʀ] *vt* to conquer
consacrer [kɔsakʀe] *vt* (*employer*) to devote, dedicate; (*REL*) to consecrate
conscience [kɔsjɑs] *nf* conscience; **avoir/prendre ~ de** to be/become aware of; **perdre ~** to lose consciousness; **avoir mauvaise ~** to have a guilty conscience; **consciencieux, -euse** *adj* conscientious; **conscient, e** *adj* conscious
conscrit [kɔskʀi] *nm* conscript
consécutif, -ive [kɔsekytif, iv] *adj* consecutive; **~ à** following upon
conseil [kɔsɛj] *nm* (*avis*) piece of advice; (*assemblée*) council; **des ~s** advice; **prendre ~ (auprès de qn)** to take advice (from sb); **~ d'administration** board (of directors); **le ~ des ministres** ≃ the Cabinet; **~ municipal** town council
conseiller, -ère [kɔseje, ɛʀ] *nm/f* adviser ♦ *vt* (*personne*) to advise; (*méthode, action*) to recommend, advise; **~ à qn de** to advise sb to; **~ municipal** town councillor
consentement [kɔsɑtmɑ] *nm* consent
consentir [kɔsɑtiʀ] *vt* to agree, consent
conséquence [kɔsekɑs] *nf* consequence; **en ~** (*donc*) consequently; (*de façon appropriée*) accordingly; **conséquent, e** *adj* logical, rational; (*fam: important*) substantial; **par conséquent** consequently
conservateur, -trice [kɔsɛʀvatœʀ, tʀis]

nm/f (*POL*) conservative; (*de musée*) curator ♦ *nm* (*pour aliments*) preservative
conservatoire [kɔsɛʀvatwaʀ] *nm* academy
conserve [kɔsɛʀv] *nf* (*gén pl*) canned *ou* tinned (*BRIT*) food; **en ~** canned, tinned (*BRIT*)
conserver [kɔsɛʀve] *vt* (*faculté*) to retain, keep; (*amis, livres*) to keep; (*préserver, aussi CULIN*) to preserve
considérable [kɔsideʀabl] *adj* considerable, significant, extensive
considération [kɔsideʀasjɔ] *nf* consideration; (*estime*) esteem
considérer [kɔsideʀe] *vt* to consider; **~ qch comme** to regard sth as
consigne [kɔsiɲ] *nf* (*de gare*) left luggage (office) (*BRIT*), checkroom (*US*); (*ordre, instruction*) instructions *pl*; **~ (automatique)** left-luggage locker; **consigner** *vt* (*note, pensée*) to record; (*punir: élève*) to put in detention; (*COMM*) to put a deposit on
consistant, e [kɔsistɑ, ɑt] *adj* (*mélange*) thick; (*repas*) solid
consister [kɔsiste] *vi*: **~ en/à faire** to consist of/in doing
consœur [kɔsœʀ] *nf* (lady) colleague
console [kɔsɔl] *nf*: **~ de jeux** games console
consoler [kɔsɔle] *vt* to console
consolider [kɔsɔlide] *vt* to strengthen; (*fig*) to consolidate
consommateur, -trice [kɔsɔmatœʀ, tʀis] *nm/f* (*ÉCON*) consumer; (*dans un café*) customer
consommation [kɔsɔmasjɔ] *nf* (*boisson*) drink; (*ÉCON*) consumption
consommer [kɔsɔme] *vt* (*suj: personne*) to eat *ou* drink, consume; (: *voiture, machine*) to use, consume; (*mariage*) to consummate ♦ *vi* (*dans un café*) to (have a) drink
consonne [kɔsɔn] *nf* consonant
conspirer [kɔspiʀe] *vi* to conspire
constamment [kɔstamɑ] *adv* constantly
constant, e [kɔstɑ, ɑt] *adj* constant; (*personne*) steadfast

constat [kɔ̃sta] *nm* (*de police, d'accident*) report; **~ (à l')amiable** *jointly-agreed statement for insurance purposes*; **~ d'échec** acknowledgement of failure

constatation [kɔ̃statasjɔ̃] *nf* (*observation*) (observed) fact, observation

constater [kɔ̃state] *vt* (*remarquer*) to note; (*ADMIN, JUR: attester*) to certify

consterner [kɔ̃stɛʀne] *vt* to dismay

constipé, e [kɔ̃stipe] *adj* constipated

constitué, e [kɔ̃stitɥe] *adj*: **~ de** made up *ou* composed of

constituer [kɔ̃stitɥe] *vt* (*équipe*) to set up; (*dossier, collection*) to put together; (*suj: éléments: composer*) to make up, constitute; (*représenter, être*) to constitute; **se ~ prisonnier** to give o.s. up; **constitution** *nf* (*composition*) composition, make-up; (*santé, POL*) constitution

constructeur [kɔ̃stʀyktœʀ] *nm* manufacturer, builder

constructif, -ive [kɔ̃stʀyktif, iv] *adj* constructive

construction [kɔ̃stʀyksjɔ̃] *nf* construction, building

construire [kɔ̃stʀɥiʀ] *vt* to build, construct

consul [kɔ̃syl] *nm* consul; **consulat** *nm* consulate

consultant, e [kɔ̃syltɑ̃, ɑ̃t] *adj, nm* consultant

consultation [kɔ̃syltasjɔ̃] *nf* consultation; **~s** *nfpl* (*POL*) talks; **heures de ~** (*MÉD*) surgery (*BRIT*) *ou* office (*US*) hours

consulter [kɔ̃sylte] *vt* to consult ♦ *vi* (*médecin*) to hold surgery (*BRIT*), be in (the office) (*US*); **se ~** *vi* to confer

consumer [kɔ̃syme] *vt* to consume; **se ~** *vi* to burn

contact [kɔ̃takt] *nm* contact; **au ~ de** (*air, peau*) on contact with; (*gens*) through contact with; **mettre/couper le ~** (*AUTO*) to switch on/off the ignition; **entrer en** *ou* **prendre ~ avec** to get in touch *ou* contact with; **contacter** *vt* to contact, get in touch with

contagieux, -euse [kɔ̃taʒjø, jøz] *adj* infectious; (*par le contact*) contagious

contaminer [kɔ̃tamine] *vt* to contaminate

conte [kɔ̃t] *nm* tale; **~ de fées** fairy tale

contempler [kɔ̃tɑ̃ple] *vt* to contemplate, gaze at

contemporain, e [kɔ̃tɑ̃pɔʀɛ̃, ɛn] *adj, nm/f* contemporary

contenance [kɔ̃t(ə)nɑ̃s] *nf* (*d'un récipient*) capacity; (*attitude*) bearing, attitude; **perdre ~** to lose one's composure

conteneur [kɔ̃t(ə)nœʀ] *nm* container

contenir [kɔ̃t(ə)niʀ] *vt* to contain; (*avoir une capacité de*) to hold; **se ~** *vi* to contain o.s.

content, e [kɔ̃tɑ̃, ɑ̃t] *adj* pleased, glad; **~ de** pleased with; **contenter** *vt* to satisfy, please; **se contenter de** to content o.s. with

contentieux [kɔ̃tɑ̃sjø] *nm* (*COMM*) litigation; (*service*) litigation department

contenu [kɔ̃t(ə)ny] *nm* (*d'un récipient*) contents *pl*; (*d'un texte*) content

conter [kɔ̃te] *vt* to recount, relate

contestable [kɔ̃tɛstabl] *adj* questionable

contestation [kɔ̃tɛstasjɔ̃] *nf* (*POL*) protest

conteste [kɔ̃tɛst]: **sans ~** *adv* unquestionably, indisputably; **contester** *vt* to question, contest ♦ *vi* (*POL, gén*) to protest, rebel (against established authority)

contexte [kɔ̃tɛkst] *nm* context

contigu, ë [kɔ̃tigy] *adj*: **~ (à)** adjacent (to)

continent [kɔ̃tinɑ̃] *nm* continent

continu, e [kɔ̃tiny] *adj* continuous; **faire la journée ~e** to work without taking a full lunch break; **(courant) ~** direct current, DC

continuel, le [kɔ̃tinɥɛl] *adj* (*qui se répète*) constant, continual; (*continu*) continuous

continuer [kɔ̃tinɥe] *vt* (*travail, voyage etc*) to continue (with), carry on (with), go on (with); (*prolonger: alignement, rue*) to continue ♦ *vi* (*vie, bruit*) to continue, go on; **~ à** *ou* **de faire** to go on *ou* continue doing

contorsionner [kɔ̃tɔʀsjɔne]: **se ~** *vi* to

contort o.s., writhe about

contour [kɔ̃tuʀ] *nm* outline, contour; **contourner** *vt* to go round; (*difficulté*) to get round

contraceptif, -ive [kɔ̃tʀaseptif, iv] *adj, nm* contraceptive; **contraception** *nf* contraception

contracté, e [kɔ̃tʀakte] *adj* tense

contracter [kɔ̃tʀakte] *vt* (*muscle etc*) to tense, contract; (*maladie, dette*) to contract; (*assurance*) to take out; **se ~** *vi* (*muscles*) to contract

contractuel, le [kɔ̃tʀaktɥel] *nm/f* (*agent*) traffic warden

contradiction [kɔ̃tʀadiksjɔ̃] *nf* contradiction; **contradictoire** *adj* contradictory, conflicting

contraignant, e [kɔ̃tʀɛɲɑ̃, ɑ̃t] *adj* restricting

contraindre [kɔ̃tʀɛ̃dʀ] *vt*: **~ qn à faire** to compel sb to do; **contrainte** *nf* constraint

contraire [kɔ̃tʀɛʀ] *adj, nm* opposite; **~ à** contrary to; **au ~** on the contrary

contrarier [kɔ̃tʀaʀje] *vt* (*personne: irriter*) to annoy; (*fig: projets*) to thwart, frustrate; **contrariété** *nf* annoyance

contraste [kɔ̃tʀast] *nm* contrast

contrat [kɔ̃tʀa] *nm* contract; **~ de travail** employment contract

contravention [kɔ̃tʀavɑ̃sjɔ̃] *nf* parking ticket

contre [kɔ̃tʀ] *prép* against; (*en échange*) (in exchange) for; **par ~** on the other hand

contrebande [kɔ̃tʀəbɑ̃d] *nf* (*trafic*) contraband, smuggling; (*marchandise*) contraband, smuggled goods *pl*; **faire la ~ de** to smuggle; **contrebandier, -ière** *nm/f* smuggler

contrebas [kɔ̃tʀəba]: **en ~** *adv* (down) below

contrebasse [kɔ̃tʀəbas] *nf* (double) bass

contre...: **contrecarrer** *vt* to thwart; **contrecœur**: **à contrecœur** *adv* (be)grudgingly, reluctantly; **contrecoup** *nm* repercussions *pl*; **contredire** *vt* (*per-*

sonne) to contradict; (*faits*) to refute

contrée [kɔ̃tʀe] *nf* (*région*) region; (*pays*) land

contrefaçon [kɔ̃tʀəfasɔ̃] *nf* forgery

contrefaire [kɔ̃tʀəfɛʀ] *vt* (*document, signature*) to forge, counterfeit

contre...: **contre-indication** (*pl* **contre-indications**) *nf* (*MÉD*) contraindication; **"contre-indication en cas d'eczéma"** "should not be used by people with eczema"; **contre-indiqué, e** *adj* (*MÉD*) contraindicated; (*déconseillé*) unadvisable, ill-advised; **contre-jour**: **à contre-jour** *adv* against the sunlight

contremaître [kɔ̃tʀəmɛtʀ] *nm* foreman

contrepartie [kɔ̃tʀəpaʀti] *nf*: **en ~** in return

contre-pied [kɔ̃tʀəpje] *nm*: **prendre le ~~ de** (*opinion*) to take the opposing view of; (*action*) to take the opposite course to

contre-plaqué [kɔ̃tʀəplake] *nm* plywood

contrepoids [kɔ̃tʀəpwa] *nm* counterweight, counterbalance

contrepoison [kɔ̃tʀəpwazɔ̃] *nm* antidote

contrer [kɔ̃tʀe] *vt* to counter

contresens [kɔ̃tʀəsɑ̃s] *nm* (*erreur*) misinterpretation; (*de traduction*) mistranslation; **à ~** the wrong way

contretemps [kɔ̃tʀətɑ̃] *nm* hitch; **à ~** (*fig*) at an inopportune moment

contrevenir [kɔ̃tʀəv(ə)niʀ]: **~ à** *vt* to contravene

contribuable [kɔ̃tʀibɥabl] *nm/f* taxpayer

contribuer [kɔ̃tʀibɥe]: **~ à** *vt* to contribute towards; **contribution** *nf* contribution; **contributions directes/indirectes** direct/ indirect taxation; **mettre à contribution** to call upon

contrôle [kɔ̃tʀol] *nm* checking *no pl*, check; (*des prix*) monitoring, control; (*test*) test, examination; **perdre le ~ de** (*véhicule*) to lose control of; **~ continu** (*SCOL*) continuous assessment; **~ d'identité** identity check

contrôler [kɔ̃tʀole] *vt* (*vérifier*) to check;

(*surveiller: opérations*) to supervise; (: *prix*) to monitor, control; (*maîtriser*, COMM: *firme*) to control; **se ~** *vi* to control o.s.; **contrôleur, -euse** *nm/f* (*de train*) (ticket) inspector; (*de bus*) (bus) conductor(-tress)

contrordre [kɔ̃trɔrdr] *nm*: **sauf ~** unless otherwise directed

controversé, e [kɔ̃trɔverse] *adj* (*personnage, question*) controversial

contusion [kɔ̃tyzjɔ̃] *nf* bruise, contusion

convaincre [kɔ̃vɛ̃kr] *vt*: **~ qn (de qch)** to convince sb (of sth); **~ qn (de faire)** to persuade sb (to do)

convalescence [kɔ̃valesɑ̃s] *nf* convalescence

convenable [kɔ̃vnabl] *adj* suitable; (*assez bon, respectable*) decent

convenance [kɔ̃vnɑ̃s] *nf*: **à ma/votre ~** to my/your liking; **~s** *nfpl* (*normes sociales*) proprieties

convenir [kɔ̃vnir] *vi* to be suitable; **~ à** to suit; **~ de** (*bien-fondé de qch*) to admit (to), acknowledge; (*date, somme etc*) to agree upon; **~ que** (*admettre*) to admit that; **~ de faire** to agree to do

convention [kɔ̃vɑ̃sjɔ̃] *nf* convention; **~s** *nfpl* (*convenances*) convention *sg*; **~ collective** (*ÉCON*) collective agreement; **conventionné, e** *adj* (*ADMIN*) applying charges laid down by the state

convenu, e [kɔ̃vny] *pp de* **convenir ♦** *adj* agreed

conversation [kɔ̃vɛrsasjɔ̃] *nf* conversation

convertir [kɔ̃vertir] *vt*: **~ qn (à)** to convert sb (to); **se ~ (à)** to be converted (to); **~ qch en** to convert sth into

conviction [kɔ̃viksjɔ̃] *nf* conviction

convienne *etc* [kɔ̃vjɛn] *vb voir* **convenir**

convier [kɔ̃vje] *vt*: **~ qn à** (*dîner etc*) to (cordially) invite sb to

convive [kɔ̃viv] *nm/f* guest (*at table*)

convivial, e, -aux [kɔ̃vivjal, jo] *adj* (*INFORM*) user-friendly

convocation [kɔ̃vɔkasjɔ̃] *nf* (*document*) notification to attend; (: *JUR*) summons *sg*

convoi [kɔ̃vwa] *nm* convoy; (*train*) train

convoiter [kɔ̃vwate] *vt* to covet

convoquer [kɔ̃vɔke] *vt* (*assemblée*) to convene; (*subordonné*) to summon; (*candidat*) to ask to attend

convoyeur [kɔ̃vwajœr] *nm*: **~ de fonds** security guard

coopération [kɔɔperasjɔ̃] *nf* co-operation; (*ADMIN*): **la C~** ≈ Voluntary Service Overseas (*BRIT*), ≈ Peace Corps (*US*)

coopérer [kɔɔpere] *vi*: **~ (à)** to co-operate (in)

coordonnées [kɔɔrdɔne] *nfpl*: **donnez-moi vos ~** (*fam*) can I have your details please?

coordonner [kɔɔrdɔne] *vt* to coordinate

copain [kɔpɛ̃] (*fam*) *nm* mate, pal; (*petit ami*) boyfriend

copeau, x [kɔpo] *nm* shaving

copie [kɔpi] *nf* copy; (*SCOL*) script, paper; **copier** *vt, vi* to copy; **copier sur** to copy from; **copieur** *nm* (photo)copier

copieux, -euse [kɔpjø, jøz] *adj* copious

copine [kɔpin] (*fam*) *nf* mate, pal; (*petite amie*) girlfriend

copropriété [kɔprɔprijete] *nf* co-ownership, joint ownership

coq [kɔk] *nm* cock, rooster; **coq-à-l'âne** *nm inv* abrupt change of subject

coque [kɔk] *nf* (*de noix, mollusque*) shell; (*de bateau*) hull; **à la ~** (*CULIN*) (soft-) boiled

coquelicot [kɔkliko] *nm* poppy

coqueluche [kɔklyʃ] *nf* whooping-cough

coquet, te [kɔkɛ, ɛt] *adj* appearance-conscious; (*logement*) smart, charming

coquetier [kɔk(ə)tje] *nm* egg-cup

coquillage [kɔkijaʒ] *nm* (*mollusque*) shellfish *inv*; (*coquille*) shell

coquille [kɔkij] *nf* shell; (*TYPO*) misprint; **~ St Jacques** scallop

coquin, e [kɔkɛ̃, in] *adj* mischievous, roguish; (*polisson*) naughty

cor [kɔr] *nm* (*MUS*) horn; (*MÉD*): **~ (au pied)** corn

corail, -aux [kɔraj, o] *nm* coral *no pl*

Coran [kɔrɑ̃] *nm*: **le ~** the Koran

corbeau, x [kɔrbo] *nm* crow

corbeille [kɔrbɛj] *nf* basket; **~ à papier** waste paper basket *ou* bin

corbillard [kɔrbijar] *nm* hearse

corde [kɔrd] *nf* rope; (*de violon, raquette*) string; **usé jusqu'à la ~** threadbare; **~ à linge** washing *ou* clothes line; **~ à sauter** skipping rope; **~s vocales** vocal cords

cordée *nf* (*d'alpinistes*) rope, roped party

cordialement [kɔrdjalmɑ̃] *adv* (*formule épistolaire*) (kind) regards

cordon [kɔrdɔ̃] *nm* cord, string; **~ ombilical** umbilical cord; **~ sanitaire/de police** sanitary/police cordon

cordonnerie [kɔrdɔnri] *nf* shoe repairer's (shop); **cordonnier** *nm* shoe repairer

Corée [kɔre] *nf*: **la ~ du Sud/du Nord** South/North Korea

coriace [kɔrjas] *adj* tough

corne [kɔrn] *nf* horn; (*de cerf*) antler

cornée [kɔrne] *nf* cornea

corneille [kɔrnɛj] *nf* crow

cornemuse [kɔrnəmyz] *nf* bagpipes *pl*

cornet [kɔrnɛ] *nm* (*paper*) cone; (*de glace*) cornet, cone

corniche [kɔrniʃ] *nf* (*route*) coast road

cornichon [kɔrniʃɔ̃] *nm* gherkin

Cornouailles [kɔrnwaj] *nf* Cornwall

corporation [kɔrpɔrasjɔ̃] *nf* corporate body

corporel, le [kɔrpɔrɛl] *adj* bodily; (*punition*) corporal

corps [kɔr] *nm* body; **à ~ perdu** headlong; **prendre ~** to take shape; **~ à ~** *adv* hand-to-hand *♦ nm* clinch; **le ~ électoral** the electorate; **le ~ enseignant** the teaching profession

corpulent, e [kɔrpylɑ̃, ɑ̃t] *adj* stout

correct, e [kɔrɛkt] *adj* correct; (*fam: acceptable: salaire, hôtel*) reasonable, decent; **correcteur, -trice** *nm/f* (*SCOL*) examiner; **correction** *nf* (*voir corriger*) correction; (*voir correct*) correctness; (*coups*) thrashing; **correctionnel, le** *adj* (*JUR*): **tribunal correctionnel** ≈ criminal court

correspondance [kɔrɛspɔ̃dɑ̃s] *nf* correspondence; (*de train, d'avion*) connection; **cours par ~** correspondence course; **vente par ~** mail-order business

correspondant, e [kɔrɛspɔ̃dɑ̃, ɑ̃t] *nm/f* correspondent; (*TÉL*) person phoning (*ou* being phoned)

correspondre [kɔrɛspɔ̃dr] *vi* to correspond, tally; **~ à** to correspond to; **~ avec qn** to correspond with sb

corrida [kɔrida] *nf* bullfight

corridor [kɔridɔr] *nm* corridor

corrigé [kɔriʒe] *nm* (*SCOL: d'exercise*) correct version

corriger [kɔriʒe] *vt* (*devoir*) to correct; (*punir*) to thrash; **~ qn de** (*défaut*) to cure sb of

corroborer [kɔrɔbɔre] *vt* to corroborate

corrompre [kɔrɔ̃pr] *vt* to corrupt; (*acheter: témoin etc*) to bribe

corruption [kɔrypsjɔ̃] *nf* corruption; (*de témoins*) bribery

corsage [kɔrsaʒ] *nm* bodice; (*chemisier*) blouse

corsaire [kɔrsɛr] *nm* pirate

corse [kɔrs] *adj, nm/f* Corsican *♦ nf*: **la C~** Corsica

corsé, e [kɔrse] *adj* (*café*) full-flavoured; (*sauce*) spicy; (*problème*) tough

corset [kɔrsɛ] *nm* corset

cortège [kɔrtɛʒ] *nm* procession

cortisone [kɔrtizɔn] *nf* cortisone

corvée [kɔrve] *nf* chore, drudgery *no pl*

cosmétique [kɔsmetik] *nm* beauty care product

cosmopolite [kɔsmɔpɔlit] *adj* cosmopolitan

cossu, e [kɔsy] *adj* (*maison*) opulent(-looking)

costaud, e [kɔsto, od] (*fam*) *adj* strong, sturdy

costume [kɔstym] *nm* (*d'homme*) suit; (*de théâtre*) costume; **costumé, e** *adj* dressed up; **bal costumé** fancy dress ball

cote [kɔt] *nf* (*en Bourse*) quotation; **~ d'alerte** danger *ou* flood level

côte [kot] *nf* (*rivage*) coast(line); (*pente*)

hill; (ANAT) rib; (d'un tricot, tissu) rib, rib-bing no pl; ~ **à** ~ side by side; **la C~ (d'Azur)** the (French) Riviera

coté, e [kɔte] adj: **être bien** ~ to be highly rated

côté [kote] nm (gén) side; (direction) way, direction; **de chaque** ~ **(de)** on each side (of); **de tous les** ~**s** from all directions; **de quel** ~ **est-il parti?** which way did he go?; **de ce/de l'autre** ~ this/the other way; **du** ~ **de** (provenance) from; (direction) towards; (proximité) near; **de** ~ (regarder) sideways; (mettre) aside; **mettre de l'argent de** ~ to save some money; **à** ~ (right) nearby; (voisins) next door; **à** ~ **de** beside, next to; (en comparaison) compared to; **être aux** ~**s de** to be by the side of

coteau, x [kɔto] nm hill

côtelette [kotlɛt] nf chop

côtier, -ière [kotje, jɛʀ] adj coastal

cotisation [kɔtizasjɔ̃] nf subscription, dues pl; (pour une pension) contributions pl

cotiser [kɔtize] vi: ~ **(à)** to pay contributions (to); **se** ~ to club together

coton [kɔtɔ̃] nm cotton; ~ **hydrophile** cotton wool (BRIT), absorbent cotton (US); **Coton-Tige** ® nm cotton bud

côtoyer [kotwaje] vt (fréquenter) to rub shoulders with

cou [ku] nm neck

couchant [kuʃɑ̃] adj: **soleil** ~ setting sun

couche [kuʃ] nf layer; (de peinture, vernis) coat; (de bébé) nappy (BRIT), diaper (US); ~ **d'ozone** ozone layer; ~**s sociales** social levels ou strata

couché, e [kuʃe] adj lying down; (au lit) in bed

coucher [kuʃe] nm (du soleil) setting ♦ vt (personne) to put to bed; (: loger) to put up; (objet) to lay on its side ♦ vi to sleep; **se** ~ vi (pour dormir) to go to bed; (pour se reposer) to lie down; (soleil) to set; ~ **de soleil** sunset

couchette [kuʃɛt] nf couchette; (pour voyageur, sur bateau) berth

coucou [kuku] nm cuckoo

coude [kud] nm (ANAT) elbow; (de tuyau, de la route) bend; ~ **à** ~ shoulder to shoulder, side by side

coudre [kudʀ] vt (bouton) to sew on ♦ vi to sew

couenne [kwan] nf (de lard) rind

couette [kwɛt] nf duvet, quilt; ~**s** nfpl (cheveux) bunches

couffin [kufɛ̃] nm Moses basket

couler [kule] vi to flow, run; (fuir: stylo, récipient) to leak; (nez) to run; (sombrer: bateau) to sink ♦ vt (cloche, sculpture) to cast; (bateau) to sink; (faire échouer: personne) to bring down

couleur [kulœʀ] nf colour (BRIT), color (US); (CARTES) suit; **film/télévision en** ~**s** colo(u)r film/television

couleuvre [kulœvʀ] nf grass snake

coulisse [kulis] nf: ~**s** nfpl (THÉÂTRE) wings; (fig): **dans les** ~**s** behind the scenes; **coulisser** vi to slide, run

couloir [kulwaʀ] nm corridor, passage; (d'avion) aisle; (de bus) gangway; ~ **aérien/de navigation** air/shipping lane

coup [ku] nm (heurt, choc) knock; (affectif) blow, shock; (agressif) blow; (avec arme à feu) shot; (de l'horloge) stroke; (tennis, golf) stroke; (boxe) blow; (fam: fois) time; ~ **de coude** nudge (with the elbow); ~ **de tonnerre** clap of thunder; ~ **de sonnette** ring of the bell; **donner un** ~ **de balai** to give the floor a sweep; **boire un** ~ (fam) to have a drink; **être dans le** ~ to be in on it; **du** ~ **...** as a result; **d'un seul** ~ (subitement) suddenly; (à la fois) at one go; **du premier** ~ first time; **du même** ~ at the same time; **à tous les** ~**s** (fam) every time; **tenir le** ~ to hold out; **après** ~ afterwards; **à** ~ **sûr** definitely, without fail; ~ **sur** ~ in quick succession; **sur le** ~ outright; **sous le** ~ **de** (surprise etc) under the influence of; **en** ~ **de vent** in a tearing hurry; ~ **de chance** stroke of luck; ~ **de couteau** stab (of a knife); ~ **d'État** coup; ~ **de feu** shot; ~ **de fil** (fam) phone call; **~ de frein** (sharp) braking *no pl*; **~ de main**: **donner un ~ de main à qn** to give sb a (helping) hand; **~ d'œil** glance; **~ de pied** kick; **~ de poing** punch; **~ de soleil** sunburn *no pl*; **~ de téléphone** phone call; **~ de tête** (*fig*) (sudden) impulse

coupable [kupabl] *adj* guilty ♦ *nm/f* (*gén*) culprit; (*JUR*) guilty party

coupe [kup] *nf* (*verre*) goblet; (*à fruits*) dish; (*SPORT*) cup; (*de cheveux, de vêtement*) cut; (*graphique, plan*) (cross) section

coupe-papier [kuppapje] *nm inv* paper knife

couper [kupe] *vt* to cut; (*retrancher*) to cut (out); (*route, courant*) to cut off; (*appétit*) to take away; (*vin à table*) to dilute ♦ *vi* to cut; (*prendre un raccourci*) to take a short-cut; **se ~** *vi* (*se blesser*) to cut o.s.; **~ la parole à qn** to cut sb short

couple [kupl] *nm* couple

couplet [kuplɛ] *nm* verse

coupole [kupɔl] *nf* dome

coupon [kupɔ̃] *nm* (*ticket*) coupon; (*reste de tissu*) remnant; **coupon-réponse** *nm* reply coupon

coupure [kupyʀ] *nf* cut; (*billet de banque*) note; (*de journal*) cutting; **~ de courant** power cut

cour [kuʀ] *nf* (*de ferme, jardin*) (court)yard; (*d'immeuble*) back yard; (*JUR, royale*) court; **faire la ~ à qn** to court sb; **~ d'assises** court of assizes; **~ de récréation** play-ground; **~ martiale** court-martial

courage [kuʀaʒ] *nm* courage, bravery; **courageux, -euse** *adj* brave, coura-geous

couramment [kuʀamɑ̃] *adv* commonly; (*parler*) fluently

courant, e [kuʀɑ̃, ɑ̃t] *adj* (*fréquent*) com-mon; (*COMM, gén: normal*) standard; (*en cours*) current ♦ *nm* current; (*fig*) move-ment; (: *d'opinion*) trend; **être au ~ (de)** (*fait, nouvelle*) to know (about); **mettre qn au ~ (de)** to tell sb (about); (*nouveau tra-vail etc*) to teach sb the basics (of); **se te-**

nir au ~ (de) (*techniques etc*) to keep o.s. up-to-date (on); **dans le ~ de** (*pendant*) in the course of; **le 10 ~** (*COMM*) the 10th inst.; **~ d'air** draught; **~ électrique** (electric) current, power

courbature [kuʀbatyʀ] *nf* ache

courbe [kuʀb] *adj* curved ♦ *nf* curve; **courber** *vt* to bend; **se courber** *vi* (*per-sonne*) to bend (down), stoop

coureur, -euse [kuʀœʀ, øz] *nm/f* (*SPORT*) runner (*ou* driver); (*péj*) womanizer; man-hunter; **~ automobile** racing driver

courge [kuʀʒ] *nf* (*CULIN*) marrow; **cour-gette** *nf* courgette (*BRIT*), zucchini (*US*)

courir [kuʀiʀ] *vi* to run ♦ *vt* (*SPORT*: *épreuve*) to compete in; (*risque*) to run; (*danger*) to face; **~ les magasins** to go round the shops; **le bruit court que** the rumour is going round that

couronne [kuʀɔn] *nf* crown; (*de fleurs*) wreath, circlet

courons *etc* [kuʀɔ̃] *vb voir* **courir**

courrier [kuʀje] *nm* mail, post; (*lettres à écrire*) letters *pl*; **~ électronique** E-mail

courroie [kuʀwa] *nf* strap; (*TECH*) belt

courrons *etc* [kuʀɔ̃] *vb voir* **courir**

cours [kuʀ] *nm* (*leçon*) class; (: *particulier*) lesson; (*série de leçons, cheminement*) course; (*écoulement*) flow; (*COMM*: *de de-vises*) rate; (: *de denrées*) price; **donner li-bre ~ à** to give free expression to; **avoir ~** (*SCOL*) to have a class *ou* lecture; **en ~** (*année*) current; (*travaux*) in progress; **en ~ de route** on the way; **au ~ de** in the course of, during; **~ d'eau** waterway; **~ du soir** night school; **~ intensif** crash course

course [kuʀs] *nf* running; (*SPORT*: *épreuve*) race; (*d'un taxi*) journey, trip; (*commission*) errand; **~s** *nfpl* (*achats*) shopping *sg*; **faire des ~s** to do some shopping

court, e [kuʀ, kuʀt(ə)] *adj* short ♦ *adv* short ♦ *nm*: **~ (de tennis)** (tennis) court; **à ~ de** short of; **prendre qn de ~** to catch sb unawares; **court-circuit** *nm* short-circuit

courtier, -ère [kuʀtje, jɛʀ] *nm/f* broker
courtiser [kuʀtize] *vt* to court, woo
courtois, e [kuʀtwa, waz] *adj* courteous; **courtoisie** *nf* courtesy
couru, e [kuʀy] *pp de* **courir**
cousais *etc* [kuze] *vb voir* **coudre**
couscous [kuskus] *nm* couscous
cousin, e [kuzɛ̃, in] *nm/f* cousin
coussin [kusɛ̃] *nm* cushion
cousu, e [kuzy] *pp de* **coudre**
coût [ku] *nm* cost; **le ~ de la vie** the cost of living; **coûtant** *adj m*: **au prix coûtant** at cost price
couteau, x [kuto] *nm* knife
coûter [kute] *vt, vi* to cost; **combien ça coûte?** how much is it?, what does it cost?; **coûte que coûte** at all costs; **coûteux, -euse** *adj* costly, expensive
coutume [kutym] *nf* custom
couture [kutyʀ] *nf* sewing; (*profession*) dressmaking; (*points*) seam; **couturier** *nm* fashion designer; **couturière** *nf* dressmaker
couvée [kuve] *nf* brood, clutch
couvent [kuvã] *nm* (*de sœurs*) convent; (*de frères*) monastery
couver [kuve] *vt* to hatch; (*maladie*) to be coming down with ♦ *vi* (*feu*) to smoulder; (*révolte*) to be brewing
couvercle [kuvɛʀkl] *nm* lid; (*de bombe aérosol etc, qui se visse*) cap, top
couvert, e [kuvɛʀ, ɛʀt] *pp de* **couvrir** ♦ *adj* (*ciel*) overcast ♦ *nm* place setting; (*place à table*) place; **~s** *nmpl* (*ustensiles*) cutlery *sg*; **~ de** covered with *ou* in; **mettre le ~** to lay the table
couverture [kuvɛʀtyʀ] *nf* blanket; (*de livre, assurance, fig*) cover; (*presse*) coverage; **~ chauffante** electric blanket
couveuse [kuvøz] *nf* (*de maternité*) incubator
couvre-feu [kuvʀəfø] *nm* curfew
couvre-lit [kuvʀəli] *nm* bedspread
couvreur [kuvʀœʀ] *nm* roofer
couvrir [kuvʀiʀ] *vt* to cover; **se ~** *vi* (*s'habiller*) to cover up; (*se coiffer*) to put

on one's hat; (*ciel*) to cloud over
cow-boy [kɔbɔj] *nm* cowboy
crabe [kʀab] *nm* crab
cracher [kʀaʃe] *vi, vt* to spit
crachin [kʀaʃɛ̃] *nm* drizzle
crack [kʀak] *nm* (*fam: as*) ace
craie [kʀɛ] *nf* chalk
craindre [kʀɛ̃dʀ] *vt* to fear, be afraid of; (*être sensible à: chaleur, froid*) to be easily damaged by
crainte [kʀɛ̃t] *nf* fear; **de ~ de/que** for fear of/that; **craintif, -ive** *adj* timid
cramoisi, e [kʀamwazi] *adj* crimson
crampe [kʀɑ̃p] *nf* cramp
crampon [kʀɑ̃pɔ̃] *nm* (*de chaussure de football*) stud; (*de chaussure de course*) spike; (*d'alpinisme*) crampon; **cramponner** *vb*: **se cramponner (à)** to hang *ou* cling on (to)
cran [kʀɑ̃] *nm* (*entaille*) notch; (*de courroie*) hole; (*fam: courage*) guts *pl*; **~ d'arrêt** safety catch
crâne [kʀɑn] *nm* skull
crâner [kʀɑne] (*fam*) *vi* to show off
crapaud [kʀapo] *nm* toad
crapule [kʀapyl] *nf* villain
craquement [kʀakmã] *nm* crack, snap; (*du plancher*) creak, creaking *no pl*
craquer [kʀake] *vi* (*bois, plancher*) to creak; (*fil, branche*) to snap; (*couture*) to come apart; (*fig: accusé*) to break down; (*: fam*) to crack up ♦ *vt* (*allumette*) to strike; **j'ai craqué** (*fam*) I couldn't resist it
crasse [kʀas] *nf* grime, filth; **crasseux, -euse** *adj* grimy, filthy
cravache [kʀavaʃ] *nf* (*riding*) crop
cravate [kʀavat] *nf* tie
crawl [kʀol] *nm* crawl; **dos ~é** backstroke
crayon [kʀɛjɔ̃] *nm* pencil; **~ à bille** ballpoint pen; **~ de couleur** crayon, colouring pencil; **crayon-feutre** (*pl* **crayons-feutres**) *nm* felt(-tip) pen
créancier, -ière [kʀeãsje, jɛʀ] *nm/f* creditor
création [kʀeasjɔ̃] *nf* creation
créature [kʀeatyʀ] *nf* creature

crèche [kʀɛʃ] *nf* (*de Noël*) crib; (*garderie*) crèche, day nursery

crédit [kʀedi] *nm* (*gén*) credit; **~s** *nmpl* (*fonds*) funds; **payer/acheter à ~** to pay/buy on credit *ou* on easy terms; **faire ~ à qn** to give sb credit; **créditer** *vt*: **créditer un compte (de)** to credit an account (with)

crédule [kʀedyl] *adj* credulous, gullible

créer [kʀee] *vt* to create

crémaillère [kʀemajɛʀ] *nf*: **pendre la ~** to have a house-warming party

crématoire [kʀematwaʀ] *adj*: **four ~** crematorium

crème [kʀɛm] *nf* cream; (*entremets*) cream dessert ♦ *adj inv* cream(-coloured); **un (café) ~** ≃ a white coffee; **~ anglaise** (egg) custard; **~ chantilly** whipped cream; **~ fouettée = crème chantilly**; **crémerie** *nf* dairy; **crémeux, -euse** *adj* creamy

créneau, x [kʀeno] *nm* (*de fortification*) crenel(le); (*dans marché*) gap, niche; (*AUTO*): **faire un ~** to reverse into a parking space (*between two cars alongside the kerb*)

crêpe [kʀɛp] *nf* (*galette*) pancake ♦ *nm* (*tissu*) crêpe; **crêpé, e** *adj* (*cheveux*) backcombed; **crêperie** *nf* pancake shop *ou* restaurant

crépiter [kʀepite] *vi* (*friture*) to sputter, splutter; (*fire*) to crackle

crépu, e [kʀepy] *adj* frizzy, fuzzy

crépuscule [kʀepyskyl] *nm* twilight, dusk

cresson [kʀesɔ̃] *nm* watercress

crête [kʀɛt] *nf* (*de coq*) comb; (*de vague, montagne*) crest

creuser [kʀøze] *vt* (*trou, tunnel*) to dig; (*sol*) to dig a hole in; (*fig*) to go (deeply) into; **ça creuse** that gives you a real appetite; **se ~ la cervelle** (*fam*) to rack one's brains

creux, -euse [kʀø, kʀøz] *adj* hollow ♦ *nm* hollow; **heures creuses** slack periods; (*électricité, téléphone*) off-peak periods; **avoir un ~** (*fam*) to be hungry

crevaison [kʀəvɛzɔ̃] *nf* puncture

crevasse [kʀəvas] *nf* (*dans le sol, la peau*) crack; (*de glacier*) crevasse

crevé, e [kʀəve] (*fam*) *adj* (*fatigué*) all in, exhausted

crever [kʀəve] *vt* (*ballon*) to burst ♦ *vi* (*pneu*) to burst; (*automobiliste*) to have a puncture (*BRIT*) *ou* a flat (tire) (*US*); (*fam*) to die

crevette [kʀəvɛt] *nf*: **~ (rose)** prawn; **~ grise** shrimp

cri [kʀi] *nm* cry, shout; (*d'animal: spécifique*) cry, call; **c'est le dernier ~** (*fig*) it's the latest fashion

criant, e [kʀijɑ̃, kʀijɑ̃t] *adj* (*injustice*) glaring

criard, e [kʀijaʀ, kʀijaʀd] *adj* (*couleur*) garish, loud; (*voix*) yelling

crible [kʀibl] *nm* riddle; **passer qch au ~** (*fig*) to go over sth with a fine-tooth comb; **criblé, e** *adj*: **criblé de** riddled with; (*de dettes*) crippled with

cric [kʀik] *nm* (*AUTO*) jack

crier [kʀije] *vi* (*pour appeler*) to shout, cry (out); (*de douleur etc*) to scream, yell ♦ *vt* (*injure*) to shout (out), yell (out)

crime [kʀim] *nm* crime; (*meurtre*) murder; **criminel, le** *nm/f* criminal; (*assassin*) murderer

crin [kʀɛ̃] *nm* (*de cheval*) hair *no pl*

crinière [kʀinjɛʀ] *nf* mane

crique [kʀik] *nf* creek, inlet

criquet [kʀikɛ] *nm* grasshopper

crise [kʀiz] *nf* crisis; (*MÉD*) attack; (: *d'épilepsie*) fit; **piquer une ~ de nerfs** to go hysterical; **~ cardiaque** heart attack; **~ de foie** bilious attack

crisper [kʀispe] *vt* (*poings*) to clench; **se ~** *vi* (*visage*) to tense; (*personne*) to get tense

crisser [kʀise] *vi* (*neige*) to crunch; (*pneu*) to screech

cristal, -aux [kʀistal, o] *nm* crystal; **cristallin, e** *adj* crystal-clear

critère [kʀitɛʀ] *nm* criterion

critiquable [kʀitikabl] *adj* open to criticism

critique [kʀitik] *adj* critical ♦ *nm/f* (*de théâtre, musique*) critic ♦ *nf* criticism; (*THÉÂTRE etc: article*) review

critiquer [kʀitike] *vt* (*dénigrer*) to criticize; (*évaluer*) to assess, examine (critically)

croasser [kʀɔase] *vi* to caw

Croatie [kʀɔasi] *nf* Croatia

croc [kʀo] *nm* (*dent*) fang; (*de boucher*) hook; **croc-en-jambe** *nm*: **faire un croc-en-jambe à qn** to trip sb up

croche [kʀɔʃ] *nf* (*MUS*) quaver (*BRIT*), eighth note (*US*); **croche-pied** *nm* = **croc-en-jambe**

crochet [kʀɔʃɛ] *nm* hook; (*détour*) detour; (*TRICOT: aiguille*) crochet hook; (*: technique*) crochet; **vivre aux ~s de qn** to live *ou* sponge off sb

crochu, e [kʀɔʃy] *adj* (*nez*) hooked; (*doigts*) claw-like

crocodile [kʀɔkɔdil] *nm* crocodile

croire [kʀwaʀ] *vt* to believe; **se ~ fort** to think one is strong; **~ que** to believe *ou* think that; **~ à, ~ en** to believe in

crois [kʀwa] *vb voir* **croître**

croisade [kʀwazad] *nf* crusade

croisé, e [kʀwaze] *adj* (*veste*) double-breasted

croisement [kʀwazmɑ̃] *nm* (*carrefour*) crossroads *sg*; (*BIO*) crossing; (*: résultat*) crossbreed

croiser [kʀwaze] *vt* (*personne, voiture*) to pass; (*route*) to cross, cut across; (*BIO*) to cross ♦ *vi* (*personnes, véhicules*) to pass each other; (*routes, lettres*) to cross; (*regards*) to meet; **~ les jambes/bras** to cross one's legs/fold one's arms

croisière [kʀwazjɛʀ] *nf* cruise

croissance [kʀwasɑ̃s] *nf* growth

croissant [kʀwasɑ̃] *nm* (*à manger*) croissant; (*motif*) crescent

croître [kʀwatʀ] *vi* to grow

croix [kʀwa] *nf* cross; **~ gammée** swastika; **la C~ Rouge** the Red Cross

croque-monsieur [kʀɔkməsjø] *nm inv* toasted ham and cheese sandwich

croquer [kʀɔke] *vt* (*manger*) to crunch; (*: fruit*) to munch; (*dessiner*) to sketch; **chocolat à ~** plain dessert chocolate

croquis [kʀɔki] *nm* sketch

cross [kʀɔs] *nm*: **faire du ~ (à pied)** to do cross-country running

crosse [kʀɔs] *nf* (*de fusil*) butt; (*de revolver*) grip

crotte [kʀɔt] *nf* droppings *pl*; **crotté, e** *adj* muddy, mucky; **crottin** *nm* dung, manure; (*fromage*) (small round) cheese (*made of goat's milk*)

crouler [kʀule] *vi* (*s'effondrer*) to collapse; (*être délabré*) to be crumbling

croupe [kʀup] *nf* rump; **en ~** pillion

croupir [kʀupiʀ] *vi* to stagnate

croustillant, e [kʀustijɑ̃, ɑ̃t] *adj* crisp

croûte [kʀut] *nf* crust; (*du fromage*) rind; (*MÉD*) scab; **en ~** (*CULIN*) in pastry

croûton [kʀutɔ̃] *nm* (*CULIN*) crouton; (*bout du pain*) crust, heel

croyable [kʀwajabl] *adj* credible

croyant, e [kʀwajɑ̃, ɑ̃t] *nm/f* believer

CRS *sigle fpl* (= *Compagnies républicaines de sécurité*) state security police force ♦ *sigle m* member of the CRS

cru, e [kʀy] *pp de* **croire** ♦ *adj* (*non cuit*) raw; (*lumière, couleur*) harsh; (*paroles*) crude ♦ *nm* (*vignoble*) vineyard; (*vin*) wine; **un grand ~** a great vintage; **jambon ~** Parma ham

crû [kʀy] *pp de* **croître**

cruauté [kʀyote] *nf* cruelty

cruche [kʀyʃ] *nf* pitcher, jug

crucifix [kʀysifi] *nm* crucifix; **crucifixion** *nf* crucifixion

crudités [kʀydite] *nfpl* (*CULIN*) salads

crue [kʀy] *nf* (*inondation*) flood

cruel, le [kʀyɛl] *adj* cruel

crus *etc* [kʀy] *vb voir* **croire**; **croître**

crûs *etc* [kʀy] *vb voir* **croître**

crustacés [kʀystase] *nmpl* shellfish

Cuba [kyba] *nf* Cuba; **cubain, e** *adj* Cuban ♦ *nm/f*: **Cubain, e** Cuban

cube [kyb] *nm* cube; (*jouet*) brick; **mètre ~** cubic metre; **2 au ~** 2 cubed

cueillette [kœjɛt] *nf* picking; (*quantité*) crop, harvest

cueillir [kœjiʀ] *vt* (*fruits, fleurs*) to pick, gather; (*fig*) to catch

cuiller [kɥijɛʀ], **cuillère** [kɥijɛʀ] *nf* spoon; ~ **à café** coffee spoon; (*CULIN*) teaspoonful; ~ **à soupe** soup-spoon; (*CULIN*) tablespoonful; **cuillerée** *nf* spoonful

cuir [kɥiʀ] *nm* leather; ~ **chevelu** scalp

cuire [kɥiʀ] *vt* (*aliments*) to cook; (*au four*) to bake ♦ *vi* to cook; **bien cuit** (*viande*) well done; **trop cuit** overdone

cuisant, e [kɥizɑ̃, ɑ̃t] *adj* (*douleur*) stinging; (*fig: souvenir, échec*) bitter

cuisine [kɥizin] *nf* (*pièce*) kitchen; (*art culinaire*) cookery, cooking; (*nourriture*) cooking, food; **faire la ~** to cook; **cuisiné, e** *adj*: **plat cuisiné** ready-made meal *ou* dish; **cuisiner** *vt* to cook; (*fam*) to grill ♦ *vi* to cook; **cuisinier, -ière** *nm/f* cook; **cuisinière** *nf* (*poêle*) cooker

cuisse [kɥis] *nf* thigh; (*CULIN*) leg

cuisson [kɥisɔ̃] *nf* cooking

cuit, e [kɥi, kɥit] *pp de* **cuire**

cuivre [kɥivʀ] *nm* copper; **les ~s** (*MUS*) the brass

cul [ky] (*fam!*) *nm* arse (!)

culbute [kylbyt] *nf* somersault; (*accidentelle*) tumble, fall

culminant, e [kylminɑ̃, ɑ̃t] *adj*: **point ~** highest point

culminer [kylmine] *vi* to reach its highest point

culot [kylo] (*fam*) *nm* (*effronterie*) cheek

culotte [kylɔt] *nf* (*de femme*) knickers *pl* (*BRIT*), panties *pl*

culpabilité [kylpabilite] *nf* guilt

culte [kylt] *nm* (*religion*) religion; (*hommage, vénération*) worship; (*protestant*) service

cultivateur, -trice [kyltivatœʀ, tʀis] *nm/f* farmer

cultivé, e [kyltive] *adj* (*personne*) cultured, cultivated

cultiver [kyltive] *vt* to cultivate; (*légumes*) to grow, cultivate

culture [kyltyʀ] *nf* cultivation; (*connaissances etc*) culture; **les ~s intensives** intensive farming; ~ **physique** physical training; **culturel, le** *adj* cultural; **culturisme** *nm* body-building

cumin [kymɛ̃] *nm* cumin

cumuler [kymyle] *vt* (*emplois*) to hold concurrently; (*salaires*) to draw concurrently

cupide [kypid] *adj* greedy, grasping

cure [kyʀ] *nf* (*MÉD*) course of treatment

curé [kyʀe] *nm* parish priest

cure-dent [kyʀdɑ̃] *nm* toothpick

cure-pipe [kyʀpip] *nm* pipe cleaner

curer [kyʀe] *vt* to clean out

curieusement [kyʀjøzmɑ̃] *adv* curiously

curieux, -euse [kyʀjø, jøz] *adj* (*indiscret*) curious, inquisitive; (*étrange*) strange, curious ♦ *nmpl* (*badauds*) onlookers; **curiosité** *nf* curiosity; (*site*) unusual feature

curriculum vitae [kyʀikylɔmvite] *nm inv* curriculum vitae

curseur [kyʀsœʀ] *nm* (*INFORM*) cursor

cutané, e [kytane] *adj* skin

cuti-réaction [kytiʀeaksjɔ̃] *nf* (*MÉD*) skintest

cuve [kyv] *nf* vat; (*à mazout etc*) tank

cuvée [kyve] *nf* vintage

cuvette [kyvɛt] *nf* (*récipient*) bowl, basin; (*GÉO*) basin

CV *sigle m* (*AUTO*) = **cheval vapeur**; (*COMM*) = **curriculum vitae**

cyanure [sjanyʀ] *nm* cyanide

cybercafé [sibɛʀkafe] *nm* cybercafé

cyclable [siklabl] *adj*: **piste ~** cycle track

cyclable [siklabl] *adj*: **piste ~** cycle track

cycle [sikl] *nm* cycle; **cyclisme** *nm* cycling; **cycliste** *nm/f* cyclist ♦ *adj* cycle *cpd*; **coureur cycliste** racing cyclist

cyclomoteur [siklomɔtœʀ] *nm* moped

cyclone [siklon] *nm* hurricane

cygne [siɲ] *nm* swan

cylindre [silɛ̃dʀ] *nm* cylinder; **cylindrée** *nf* (*AUTO*) (cubic) capacity

cymbale [sɛ̃bal] *nf* cymbal

cynique [sinik] *adj* cynical

cystite [sistit] *nf* cystitis

D, d

d' [d] *prép voir* **de**

dactylo [daktilo] *nf* (*aussi:* ~**graphe**) typist; (*aussi:* ~**graphie**) typing; **dactylographier** *vt* to type (out)

dada [dada] *nm* hobby-horse

daigner [deɲe] *vt* to deign

daim [dɛ̃] *nm* (fallow) deer *inv*; (*cuir suédé*) suede

dalle [dal] *nf* paving stone, slab

daltonien, ne [daltɔnjɛ̃, jɛn] *adj* colour-blind

dam [dɑ̃] *nm*: **au grand ~ de** much to the detriment (*ou* annoyance) of

dame [dam] *nf* lady; (*CARTES, ÉCHECS*) queen; ~**s** *nfpl* (*jeu*) draughts *sg* (*BRIT*), checkers *sg* (*US*)

damner [dɑne] *vt* to damn

dancing [dɑ̃siŋ] *nm* dance hall

Danemark [danmaRk] *nm* Denmark

danger [dɑ̃ʒe] *nm* danger; **dangereux, -euse** *adj* dangerous

danois, e [danwa, waz] *adj* Danish ♦ *nm/f*: **D~, e** Dane ♦ *nm* (*LING*) Danish

---
MOT-CLÉ
---

dans [dɑ̃] *prép* **1** (*position*) in; (*à l'intérieur de*) inside; **c'est dans le tiroir/le salon** it's in the drawer/lounge; **dans la boîte** in *ou* inside the box; **marcher dans la ville** to walk about the town

2 (*direction*) into; **elle a couru dans le salon** she ran into the lounge

3 (*provenance*) out of, from; **je l'ai pris dans le tiroir/salon** I took it out of *ou* from the drawer/lounge; **boire dans un verre** to drink out of *ou* from a glass

4 (*temps*) in; **dans 2 mois** in 2 months, in 2 months' time

5 (*approximation*) about; **dans les 20 F** about 20F

danse [dɑ̃s] *nf*: **la ~** dancing; **une ~** a

dance; **la ~ classique** ballet; **danser** *vi, vt* to dance; **danseur, -euse** *nm/f* ballet dancer; (*au bal etc*) dancer; (: *cavalier*) partner

dard [daR] *nm* (*d'animal*) sting

date [dat] *nf* date; **de longue ~** long-standing; **~ de naissance** date of birth; **~ de péremption** expiry date; **~ limite** deadline; **dater** *vt, vi* to date; **dater de** to date from; **à dater de** (as) from

datte [dat] *nf* date

dauphin [dofɛ̃] *nm* (*ZOOL*) dolphin

davantage [davɑ̃taʒ] *adv* more; (*plus longtemps*) longer; **~ de** more

---
MOT-CLÉ
---

de, d' [də] (*de + le* = **du**, *de + les* = **des**) *prép* **1** (*appartenance*) of; **le toit de la maison** the roof of the house; **la voiture d'Elisabeth/de mes parents** Elizabeth's/my parents' car

2 (*provenance*) from; **il vient de Londres** he comes from London; **elle est sortie du cinéma** she came out of the cinema

3 (*caractérisation, mesure*): **un mur de brique/bureau d'acajou** a brick wall/mahogany desk; **un billet de 50 F** a 50F note; **une pièce de 2 m de large** *ou* **large de 2 m** a room 2m wide, a 2m-wide room; **un bébé de 10 mois** a 10-month-old baby; **12 mois de crédit/travail** 12 months' credit/work; **augmenter de 10 F** to increase by 10F; **de 14 à 18** from 14 to 18

♦ *dét* **1** (*phrases affirmatives*) some (*souvent omis*); **du vin, de l'eau, des pommes** (some) wine, (some) water, (some) apples; **des enfants sont venus** some children came; **pendant des mois** for months

2 (*phrases interrogatives et négatives*) any; **a-t-il du vin?** has he got any wine?; **il n'a pas de pommes/d'enfants** he hasn't (got) any apples/children, he has no apples/children

dé |de| *nm* (à jouer) die *ou* dice; (aussi: ~ **à coudre**) thimble

dealer |dilœʀ| (fam) *nm* (drug) pusher

déambuler |deɑ̃byle| *vi* to stroll about

débâcle |debɑkl| *nf* rout

déballer |debale| *vt* to unpack

débandade |debɑ̃dad| *nf* (dispersion) scattering

débarbouiller |debaʀbuje| *vt* to wash; **se ~** *vi* to wash (one's face)

débarcadère |debaʀkadɛʀ| *nm* wharf

débardeur |debaʀdœʀ| *nm* (maillot) tank top

débarquer |debaʀke| *vt* to unload, land ♦ *vi* to disembark; (fig: fam) to turn up

débarras |debaʀɑ| *nm* (pièce) lumber room; (placard) junk cupboard; **bon ~!** good riddance!; **débarrasser** *vt* to clear; **se débarrasser de** *vt* to get rid of; **débarrasser qn de** (vêtements, paquets) to relieve sb of

débat |deba| *nm* discussion, debate; **débattre** *vt* to discuss, debate; **se débattre** *vi* to struggle

débaucher |debɔʃe| *vt* (licencier) to lay off, dismiss; (entraîner) to lead astray, debauch

débile |debil| (fam) *adj* (idiot) dim-witted

débit |debi| *nm* (d'un liquide, fleuve) flow; (d'un magasin) turnover (of goods); (élocution) delivery; (bancaire) debit; **~ de boissons** drinking establishment; **~ de tabac** tobacconist's; **haut ~** (Internet) ≈ broadband; **débiter** *vt* (compte) to debit; (couper: bois, viande) to cut up; (péj: dire) to churn out; **débiteur, -trice** *nm/f* debtor ♦ *adj* in debit; (compte) debit *cpd*

déblayer |debleje| *vt* to clear

débloquer |deblɔke| *vt* (prix, crédits) to free

déboires |debwaʀ| *nmpl* setbacks

déboiser |debwaze| *vt* to deforest

déboîter |debwate| *vt* (AUTO) to pull out; **se ~ le genou** *etc* to dislocate one's knee *etc*

débonnaire |debɔnɛʀ| *adj* easy-going, good-natured

débordé, e |debɔʀde| *adj*: **être ~ (de)** (travail, demandes) to be snowed under (with)

déborder |debɔʀde| *vi* to overflow; (lait etc) to boil over; **~ (de) qch** (dépasser) to extend beyond sth

débouché |debuʃe| *nm* (pour vendre) outlet; (perspective d'emploi) opening

déboucher |debuʃe| *vt* (évier, tuyau etc) to unblock; (bouteille) to open ♦ *vi*: **~ de** to emerge from; **~ sur** (études) to lead on to

débourser |debuʀse| *vt* to pay out

déboussolé, e |debusɔle| (fam) *adj* disorientated

debout |d(ə)bu| *adv*: **être ~** (personne) to be standing, stand; (: levé, éveillé) to be up; **se mettre ~** to stand up; **se tenir ~** to stand; **~!** stand up!; (du lit) get up!; **cette histoire ne tient pas ~** this story doesn't hold water

déboutonner |debutɔne| *vt* to undo, unbutton

débraillé, e |debʀaje| *adj* slovenly, untidy

débrancher |debʀɑ̃ʃe| *vt* to disconnect; (appareil électrique) to unplug

débrayage |debʀejaʒ| *nm* (AUTO) clutch; **débrayer** *vi* (AUTO) to declutch; (cesser le travail) to stop work

débris |debʀi| *nmpl* fragments

débrouillard, e |debʀujaʀ, aʀd| (fam) *adj* smart, resourceful

débrouiller |debʀuje| *vt* to disentangle, untangle; **se ~** *vi* to manage; **débrouillez-vous** you'll have to sort things out yourself

début |deby| *nm* beginning, start; **~s** *nmpl* (de carrière) début *sg*; **~ juin** in early June; **débutant, e** *nm/f* beginner, novice; **débuter** *vi* to begin, start; (faire ses débuts) to start out

deçà |dəsa|: **en ~ de** *prép* this side of

décadence |dekadɑ̃s| *nf* decline

décaféiné, e |dekafeine| *adj* decaffeinated

décalage |dekalaʒ| *nm* gap; **~ horaire** time difference

décaler [dekale] *vt* to shift

décalquer [dekalke] *vt* to trace

décamper [dekɑ̃pe] (*fam*) *vi* to clear out *ou* off

décaper [dekape] *vt* (*surface peinte*) to strip

décapiter [dekapite] *vt* to behead; (*par accident*) to decapitate

décapotable [dekapɔtabl] *adj* convertible

décapsuleur [dekapsylœR] *nm* bottle-opener

décarcasser [dekaRkase]: **se ~** (*fam*) *vi* to flog o.s. to death

décédé, e [desede] *adj* deceased

décéder [desede] *vi* to die

déceler [des(ə)le] *vt* (*trouver*) to discover, detect

décembre [desɑ̃bR] *nm* December

décemment [desamɑ̃] *adv* decently

décennie [deseni] *nf* decade

décent, e [desɑ̃, ɑ̃t] *adj* decent

déception [desɛpsjɔ̃] *nf* disappointment

décerner [desɛRne] *vt* to award

décès [desɛ] *nm* death

décevant, e [des(ə)vɑ̃, ɑ̃t] *adj* disappointing

décevoir [des(ə)vwaR] *vt* to disappoint

déchaîner [deʃene] *vt* (*violence*) to unleash; (*enthousiasme*) to arouse; **se ~** (*tempête*) to rage; (*personne*) to fly into a rage

déchanter [deʃɑ̃te] *vi* to become disillusioned

décharge [deʃaRʒ] *nf* (*dépôt d'ordures*) rubbish tip *ou* dump; (*électrique*) electrical discharge; **décharger** *vt* (*marchandise, véhicule*) to unload; (*tirer*) to discharge; **se décharger** *vi* (*batterie*) to go flat; **décharger qn de** (*responsabilité*) to release sb from

décharné, e [deʃaRne] *adj* emaciated

déchausser [deʃose] *vt* (*skis*) to take off; **se ~** *vi* to take off one's shoes; (*dent*) to come *ou* work loose

déchéance [deʃeɑ̃s] *nf* (*physique*) degeneration; (*morale*) decay

déchet [deʃɛ] *nm* (*reste*) scrap; **~s** *nmpl* (*ordures*) refuse *sg*, rubbish *sg*; **~s nucléaires** nuclear waste

déchiffrer [deʃifRe] *vt* to decipher

déchiqueter [deʃik(ə)te] *vt* to tear *ou* pull to pieces

déchirant, e [deʃiRɑ̃, ɑ̃t] *adj* heart-rending

déchirement [deʃiRmɑ̃] *nm* (*chagrin*) wrench, heartbreak; (*gén pl: conflit*) rift, split

déchirer [deʃiRe] *vt* to tear; (*en morceaux*) to tear up; (*arracher*) to tear out; (*fig: conflit*) to tear (apart); **se ~** *vi* to tear, rip; **se ~ un muscle** to tear a muscle

déchirure [deʃiRyR] *nf* (*accroc*) tear, rip; **~ musculaire** torn muscle

déchoir [deʃwaR] *vi* (*personne*) to lower o.s., demean o.s.

déchu, e [deʃy] *adj* (*roi*) deposed

décidé, e [deside] *adj* (*personne, air*) determined; **c'est ~** it's decided; **décidément** *adv* really

décider [deside] *vt*: **~ qch** to decide on sth; **se ~ (à faire)** to decide (to do), make up one's mind (to do); **se ~ pour** to decide on *ou* in favour of; **~ de faire/que** to decide to do/that; **~ qn (à faire qch)** to persuade sb (to do sth)

décimal, e, -aux [desimal, o] *adj* decimal; **décimale** *nf* decimal

décimètre [desimɛtR] *nm* decimetre

décisif, -ive [desizif, iv] *adj* decisive

décision [desizjɔ̃] *nf* decision

déclaration [deklaRasjɔ̃] *nf* declaration; (*discours: POL etc*) statement; **~ (d'impôts)** ≈ tax return

déclarer [deklaRe] *vt* to declare; (*décès, naissance*) to register; **se ~** *vi* (*feu*) to break out

déclencher [deklɑ̃ʃe] *vt* (*mécanisme etc*) to release; (*sonnerie*) to set off; (*attaque, grève*) to launch; (*provoquer*) to trigger off; **se ~** *vi* (*sonnerie*) to go off

déclic [deklik] *nm* (*bruit*) click

décliner [dekline] *vi* to decline ♦ *vt* (*invitation*) to decline; (*nom, adresse*) to state

décocher [dekɔʃe] vt (coup de poing) to throw; (flèche, regard) to shoot

décoiffer [dekwafe] vt: ~ **qn** to mess up sb's hair; **je suis toute décoiffée** my hair is in a real mess

déçois etc [deswa] vb voir **décevoir**

décollage [dekɔlaʒ] nm (AVIAT) takeoff

décoller [dekɔle] vt to unstick ♦ vi (avion) to take off; **se ~** vi to come unstick

décolleté, e [dekɔlte] adj low-cut ♦ nm low neck(line); (plongeant) cleavage

décolorer [dekɔlɔʀe]: **se ~** vi to fade; **se faire ~ les cheveux** to have one's hair bleached

décombres [dekɔbʀ] nmpl rubble sg, debris sg

décommander [dekɔmɑde] vt to cancel; **se ~** vi to cry off

décomposé, e [dekɔpoze] adj (pourri) decomposed; (visage) haggard, distorted

décompte [dekɔt] nm deduction; (facture) detailed account

déconcerter [dekɔsɛʀte] vt to disconcert, confound

déconfit, e [dekɔfi, it] adj crestfallen

décongeler [dekɔʒ(ə)le] vt to thaw

déconner [dekɔne] (fam) vi to talk rubbish

déconseiller [dekɔseje] vt: ~ **qch (à qn)** to advise (sb) against sth; **c'est déconseillé** it's not recommended

décontracté, e [dekɔtʀakte] adj relaxed, laid-back (fam)

décontracter [dekɔtʀakte]: **se ~** vi to relax

déconvenue [dekɔv(ə)ny] nf disappointment

décor [dekɔʀ] nm décor; (paysage) scenery; **~s** nmpl (THÉÂTRE) scenery sg, décor sg; (CINÉMA) set sg; **décorateur** nm (interior) decorator; **décoration** nf decoration; **décorer** vt to decorate

décortiquer [dekɔʀtike] vt to shell; (fig: texte) to dissect

découcher [dekuʃe] vi to spend the night away from home

découdre [dekudʀ]: **se ~** vi to come unstitched

découler [dekule] vi: ~ **de** to ensue ou follow from

découper [dekupe] vt (papier, tissu etc) to cut up; (viande) to carve; (article) to cut out; **se ~ sur** to stand out against

décourager [dekuʀaʒe] vt to discourage; **se ~** vi to lose heart, become discouraged

décousu, e [dekuzy] adj unstitched; (fig) disjointed, disconnected

découvert, e [dekuvɛʀ, ɛʀt] adj (tête) bare, uncovered; (lieu) open, exposed ♦ nm (bancaire) overdraft; **découverte** nf discovery; **faire la découverte de** to discover

découvrir [dekuvʀiʀ] vt to discover; (enlever ce qui couvre) to uncover; (dévoiler) to reveal; **se ~** vi (chapeau) to take off one's hat; (vêtement) to take something off; (ciel) to clear

décret [dekʀɛ] nm decree; **décréter** vt to decree

décrié, e [dekʀije] adj disparaged

décrire [dekʀiʀ] vt to describe

décrocher [dekʀɔʃe] vt (détacher) to take down; (téléphone) to take off the hook; (: pour répondre) to lift the receiver; (fam: contrat etc) to get, land ♦ vi (fam: abandonner) to drop out; (: cesser d'écouter) to switch off

décroître [dekʀwatʀ] vi to decrease, decline

décrypter [dekʀipte] vt to decipher

déçu, e [desy] pp de **décevoir**

décupler [dekyple] vt, vi to increase tenfold

dédaigner [dedɛɲe] vt to despise, scorn; (négliger) to disregard, spurn; **dédaigneux, -euse** adj scornful, disdainful; **dédain** nm scorn, disdain

dédale [dedal] nm maze

dedans [dədɑ] adv inside; (pas en plein air) indoors, inside ♦ nm inside; **au ~** inside

dédicacer [dedikase] vt: ~ **(à qn)** to sign (for sb), autograph (for sb)

dédier [dedje] *vt* to dedicate

dédire [dediʀ]: **se ~** *vi* to go back on one's word, retract

dédommagement [dedɔmaʒmɑ̃] *nm* compensation

dédommager [dedɔmaʒe] *vt*: **~ qn (de)** to compensate sb (for)

dédouaner [dedwane] *vt* to clear through customs

dédoubler [deduble] *vt* (*classe, effectifs*) to split (into two)

déduire [dedɥiʀ] *vt*: **~ qch (de)** (*ôter*) to deduct sth (from); (*conclure*) to deduce *ou* infer sth (from)

déesse [dees] *nf* goddess

défaillance [defajɑ̃s] *nf* (*syncope*) blackout; (*fatigue*) (sudden) weakness *no pl*; (*technique*) fault, failure; **~ cardiaque** heart failure

défaillir [defajiʀ] *vi* to feel faint; (*mémoire etc*) to fail

défaire [defɛʀ] *vt* to undo; (*installation*) to take down, dismantle; **se ~** *vi* to come undone; **se ~ de** to get rid of

défait, e [defɛ, ɛt] *adj* (*visage*) haggard, ravaged; **défaite** *nf* defeat

défalquer [defalke] *vt* to deduct

défaut [defo] *nm* (*moral*) fault, failing, defect; (*tissus*) fault, flaw; (*manque, carence*): **~ de** shortage of; **prendre qn en ~** to catch sb out; **faire ~** (*manquer*) to be lacking; **à ~ de** for lack *ou* want of

défavorable [defavɔʀabl] *adj* unfavourable (*BRIT*), unfavorable (*US*)

défavoriser [defavɔʀize] *vt* to put at a disadvantage

défection [defeksjɔ̃] *nf* defection, failure to give support

défectueux, -euse [defɛktɥø, øz] *adj* faulty, defective

défendre [defɑ̃dʀ] *vt* to defend; (*interdire*) to forbid; **se ~** *vi* to defend o.s.; **~ à qn qch/de faire** to forbid sb sth/to do; **il se défend** (*fam: se débrouille*) he can hold his own; **se ~ de/contre** (*se protéger*) to protect o.s. from/against; **se ~ de** (*se garder*

de) to refrain from

défense [defɑ̃s] *nf* defence; (*d'éléphant etc*) tusk; **"~ de fumer"** "no smoking"

déférer [defeʀe] *vt* (*JUR*) to refer; **~ à** (*requête, décision*) to defer to

déferler [defɛʀle] *vi* (*vagues*) to break; (*fig: foule*) to surge

défi [defi] *nm* challenge; **lancer un ~ à qn** to challenge sb; **sur un ton de ~** defiantly

déficit [defisit] *nm* (*COMM*) deficit; **déficitaire** *adj* in deficit

défier [defje] *vt* (*provoquer*) to challenge; (*mort, autorité*) to defy

défigurer [defigyʀe] *vt* to disfigure

défilé [defile] *nm* (*GÉO*) (narrow) gorge *ou* pass; (*soldats*) parade; (*manifestants*) procession, march; **~ de mode** fashion parade

défiler [defile] *vi* (*troupes*) to march past; (*sportifs*) to parade; (*manifestants*) to march; (*visiteurs*) to pour, stream; **se ~** *vi*: **il s'est défilé** (*fam*) he wriggled out of it

définir [definiʀ] *vt* to define

définitif, -ive [definitif, iv] *adj* (*final*) final, definitive; (*pour longtemps*) permanent, definitive; (*refus*) definite; **définitive** *nf*: **en définitive** eventually; (*somme toute*) in fact; **définitivement** *adv* (*partir, s'installer*) for good

défoncer [defɔ̃se] *vt* (*porte*) to smash in *ou* down; **se ~** (*fam*) *vi* (*travailler*) to work like a dog; (*drogué*) to get high

déformer [defɔʀme] *vt* to put out of shape; (*pensée, fait*) to distort; **se ~** *vi* to lose its shape

défouler [defule]: **se ~** *vi* to unwind, let off steam

défraîchir [defʀeʃiʀ]: **se ~** *vi* to fade

défricher [defʀiʃe] *vt* to clear (for cultivation)

défunt, e [defœ̃, œ̃t] *nm/f* deceased

dégagé, e [degaʒe] *adj* (*route, ciel*) clear; **sur un ton ~** casually

dégagement [degaʒmɑ̃] *nm*: **voie de ~**

slip road

dégager [degaʒe] *vt* (*exhaler*) to give off; (*délivrer*) to free, extricate; (*désencombrer*) to clear; (*isoler: idée, aspect*) to bring out; **se ~** *vi* (*passage, ciel*) to clear

dégarnir [degaʀniʀ] *vt* (*vider*) to empty, clear; **se ~** *vi* (*tempes, crâne*) to go bald

dégâts [dega] *nmpl* damage *sg*

dégel [deʒɛl] *nm* thaw; **dégeler** *vt* to thaw (out)

dégénérer [deʒenere] *vi* to degenerate

dégingandé, e [deʒɛ̃gɑ̃de] *adj* gangling

dégivrer [deʒivʀe] *vt* (*frigo*) to defrost; (*vitres*) to de-ice

dégonflé, e [degɔ̃fle] *adj* (*pneu*) flat

dégonfler [degɔ̃fle] *vt* (*pneu, ballon*) to let down, deflate; **se ~** *vi* (*fam*) to chicken out

dégouliner [deguline] *vi* to trickle, drip

dégourdi, e [deguʀdi] *adj* smart, resourceful

dégourdir [deguʀdiʀ] *vt*: **se ~ les jambes** to stretch one's legs (*fig*)

dégoût [degu] *nm* disgust, distaste; **dégoûtant, e** *adj* disgusting; **dégoûté, e** *adj* disgusted; **dégoûté de** sick of; **dégoûter** *vt* to disgust; **dégoûter qn de qch** to put sb off sth

dégrader [degrade] *vt* (*MIL: officier*) to degrade; (*abîmer*) to damage, deface; **se ~** *vi* (*relations, situation*) to deteriorate

dégrafer [degrafe] *vt* to unclip, unhook

degré [dǝgʀe] *nm* degree

dégressif, -ive [degʀesif, iv] *adj* on a decreasing scale

dégringoler [degʀɛ̃gɔle] *vi* to tumble (down)

dégrossir [degʀosiʀ] *vt* (*fig: projet*) to work out roughly

déguenillé, e [deg(ǝ)nije] *adj* ragged, tattered

déguerpir [degɛʀpiʀ] *vi* to clear off

dégueulasse [degœlas] (*fam*) *adj* disgusting

dégueuler [degœle] (*fam*) *vi* to throw up

déguisement [degizmɑ̃] *nm* (*pour s'amuser*) fancy dress

déguiser [degize]: **se ~** *vi* (*se costumer*) to dress up; (*pour tromper*) to disguise o.s.

dégustation [degystasjɔ̃] *nf* (*de fromages etc*) sampling; **~ de vins** wine-tasting session

déguster [degyste] *vt* (*vins*) to taste; (*fromages etc*) to sample; (*savourer*) to enjoy, savour

dehors [dǝɔʀ] *adv* outside; (*en plein air*) outdoors ♦ *nm* outside ♦ *nmpl* (*apparences*) appearances; **mettre** *ou* **jeter ~** (*expulser*) to throw out; **au ~** outside; **au ~ de** outside; **en ~** (*hormis*) apart from

déjà [deʒa] *adv* already; (*auparavant*) before, already

déjeuner [deʒœne] *vi* to (have) lunch; (*le matin*) to have breakfast ♦ *nm* lunch

déjouer [deʒwe] *vt* (*complot*) to foil

delà [dǝla] *adv*: **en ~ (de), au ~ (de)** beyond

délabrer [delabre]: **se ~** *vi* to fall into decay, become dilapidated

délacer [delase] *vt* (*chaussures*) to undo

délai [delɛ] *nm* (*attente*) waiting period; (*sursis*) extension of time; (*temps accordé*) time limit; **sans ~** without any delay; **dans les ~s** within the time limit

délaisser [delese] *vt* to abandon, desert

délasser [delase] *vt* to relax; **se ~** *vi* to relax

délavé, e [delave] *adj* faded

délayer [deleje] *vt* (*CULIN*) to mix (with water *etc*); (*peinture*) to thin down

delco [dɛlko] *nm* (*AUTO*) distributor

délecter [delɛkte]: **se ~** *vi* to revel *ou* delight in

délégué, e [delege] *nm/f* representative

déléguer [delege] *vt* to delegate

délibéré, e [delibere] *adj* (*conscient*) deliberate

délibérer [delibere] *vi* to deliberate

délicat, e [delika, at] *adj* delicate; (*plein de tact*) tactful; (*attention*) thoughtful; **délicatement** *adv* delicately; (*avec douceur*) gently

délice [delis] *nm* delight

délicieux, -euse [delisjø, jøz] *adj (au goût)* delicious; *(sensation)* delightful

délimiter [delimite] *vt (terrain)* to delimit, demarcate

délinquance [delɛ̃kɑ̃s] *nf* criminality

délirant, e [deliʀɑ̃, ɑ̃t] *(fam) adj* wild

délirer [deliʀe] *vi* to be delirious; **tu délires!** *(fam)* you're crazy!

délit [deli] *nm* (criminal) offence

délivrer [delivʀe] *vt (prisonnier)* to (set) free, release; *(passeport)* to issue

déloger [delɔʒe] *vt (objet coincé)* to dislodge

déloyal, e, -aux [delwajal, o] *adj (ami)* disloyal; *(procédé)* unfair

deltaplane [dɛltaplan] *nm* hang-glider

déluge [delyʒ] *nm (pluie)* downpour; *(biblique)* Flood

déluré, e [delyʀe] *(péj) adj* forward, pert

demain [d(ə)mɛ̃] *adv* tomorrow

demande [d(ə)mɑ̃d] *nf (requête)* request; *(revendication)* demand; *(d'emploi)* application; *(ÉCON):* **la ~** demand; **"~s d'emploi"** *(annonces)* "situations wanted"; **~ en mariage** proposal (of marriage)

demandé, e [d(ə)mɑ̃de] *adj (article etc):* **très ~** (very) much in demand

demander [d(ə)mɑ̃de] *vt* to ask for; *(chemin, heure etc)* to ask; *(nécessiter)* to require, demand; **se ~ si/pourquoi** *etc* to wonder whether/why *etc;* **~ qch à qn** to ask sb for sth; **~ un service à qn** to ask sb a favour; **~ à qn de faire** to ask sb to do; **demandeur, -euse** *nm/f:* **demandeur d'emploi** job-seeker; **~ d'asile** asylum-seeker

démangeaison [demɑ̃ʒɛzɔ̃] *nf* itching; **avoir des ~s** to be itching

démanger [demɑ̃ʒe] *vi* to itch

démanteler [demɑ̃t(ə)le] *vt* to break up

démaquillant [demakijɑ̃] *nm* make-up remover

démaquiller [demakije] *vt:* **se ~** to remove one's make-up

démarche [demaʀʃ] *nf (allure)* gait, walk; *(intervention)* step; *(fig: intellectuelle)* thought processes *pl;* **faire les ~s nécessaires (pour obtenir qch)** to take the necessary steps (to obtain sth)

démarcheur, -euse [demaʀʃœʀ, øz] *nm/f (COMM)* door-to-door salesman(-woman)

démarque [demaʀk] *nf (article)* markdown

démarrage [demaʀaʒ] *nm* start

démarrer [demaʀe] *vi (conducteur)* to start (up); *(véhicule)* to move off; *(travaux)* to get moving; **démarreur** *nm (AUTO)* starter

démêlant [demelɑ̃] *nm* conditioner

démêler [demele] *vt* to untangle; **démêlés** *nmpl* problems

déménagement [demenaʒmɑ̃] *nm* move; **camion de ~** removal van

déménager [demenaʒe] *vt (meubles)* to (re)move ♦ *vi* to move (house); **déménageur** *nm* removal man

démener [dem(ə)ne]: **se ~** *vi (se dépenser)* to exert o.s.; *(pour obtenir qch)* to go to great lengths

dément, e [demɑ̃, ɑ̃t] *adj (fou)* mad, crazy; *(fam)* brilliant, fantastic

démentiel, le [demɑ̃sjɛl] *adj* insane

démentir [demɑ̃tiʀ] *vt* to refute; **~ que** to deny that

démerder [demɛʀde] *(fam):* **se ~** *vi* to sort things out for o.s.

démesuré, e [dem(ə)zyʀe] *adj* immoderate

démettre [demɛtʀ] *vt:* **~ qn de** *(fonction, poste)* to dismiss sb from; **se ~ l'épaule** *etc* to dislocate one's shoulder *etc*

demeurant [d(ə)mœʀɑ̃]: **au ~** *adv* for all that

demeure [d(ə)mœʀ] *nf* residence; **demeurer** *vi (habiter)* to live; *(rester)* to remain

demi, e [dəmi] *adj* half ♦ *nm (bière)* ≃ half-pint *(0,25 litres)* ♦ *préfixe:* **~...** half-, semi..., demi-; **trois heures/bouteilles et ~es** three and a half hours/bottles, three hours/bottles and a half; **il est 2 heures**

et ~e/midi et ~ it's half past 2/half past 12; **à ~** half-; **à la ~e** (*heure*) on the half-hour; **demi-cercle** *nm* semicircle; **en demi-cercle ♦** *adj* semicircular ♦ *adv* in a half circle; **demi-douzaine** *nf* half-dozen, half a dozen; **demi-finale** *nf* semifinal; **demi-frère** *nm* half-brother; **demi-heure** *nf* half-hour, half an hour; **demi-journée** *nf* half-day, half a day; **demi-litre** *nm* half-litre, half a litre; **demi-livre** *nf* half-pound, half a pound; **demi-mot** *adv*: **à demi-mot** without having to spell things out; **demi-pension** *nf* (*à l'hôtel*) half-board; **demi-pensionnaire** *nm/f*: **être demi-pensionnaire** to take school lunches; **demi-place** *nf* half-fare

démis, e [demi, iz] *adj* (*épaule etc*) dislocated

demi-sel [dəmisɛl] *adj inv* (*beurre, fromage*) slightly salted

demi-sœur [dəmisœʀ] *nf* half-sister

démission [demisjɔ̃] *nf* resignation; **donner sa ~** to give *ou* hand in one's notice; **démissionner** *vi* to resign

demi-tarif [dəmitaʀif] *nm* half-price; **voyager à ~-~** to travel half-fare

demi-tour [dəmituʀ] *nm* about-turn; **faire ~-~** to turn (and go) back

démocratie [demɔkʀasi] *nf* democracy; **démocratique** *adj* democratic

démodé, e [demɔde] *adj* old-fashioned

demoiselle [d(ə)mwazɛl] *nf* (*jeune fille*) young lady; (*célibataire*) single lady, maiden lady; **~ d'honneur** bridesmaid

démolir [demɔliʀ] *vt* to demolish

démon [demɔ̃] *nm* (*enfant turbulent*) devil, demon; **le D~** the Devil

démonstration [demɔ̃stʀasjɔ̃] *nf* demonstration

démonté, e [demɔ̃te] *adj* (*mer*) raging, wild

démonter [demɔ̃te] *vt* (*machine etc*) to take down, dismantle

démontrer [demɔ̃tʀe] *vt* to demonstrate

démordre [demɔʀdʀ] *vi*: **ne pas ~ de** to refuse to give up, stick to

démouler [demule] *vt* to turn out

démuni, e [demyni] *adj* (*sans argent*) impoverished; **~ de** without

démunir [demyniʀ] *vt*: **~ qn de** to deprive sb of; **se ~ de** to part with, give up

dénaturer [denatyʀe] *vt* (*goût*) to alter; (*pensée, fait*) to distort

dénicher [deniʃe] (*fam*) *vt* (*objet*) to unearth; (*restaurant etc*) to discover

dénier [denje] *vt* to deny

dénigrer [denigʀe] *vt* to denigrate, run down

dénivellation [denivelasjɔ̃] *nf* (*pente*) slope

dénombrer [denɔ̃bʀe] *vt* to count

dénomination [denɔminasjɔ̃] *nf* designation, appellation

dénommé, e [denɔme] *adj*: **un ~ Dupont** a certain Mr Dupont

dénoncer [denɔ̃se] *vt* to denounce

dénouement [denumɑ̃] *nm* outcome

dénouer [denwe] *vt* to unknot, undo; **se ~** *vi* (*nœud*) to come undone

dénoyauter [denwajote] *vt* to stone

denrée [dɑ̃ʀe] *nf*: **~s (alimentaires)** foodstuffs

dense [dɑ̃s] *adj* dense; **densité** *nf* density

dent [dɑ̃] *nf* tooth; **~ de lait/sagesse** milk/wisdom tooth; **dentaire** *adj* dental

dentelé, e [dɑ̃t(ə)le] *adj* jagged, indented

dentelle [dɑ̃tɛl] *nf* lace *no pl*

dentier [dɑ̃tje] *nm* denture

dentifrice [dɑ̃tifʀis] *nm* toothpaste

dentiste [dɑ̃tist] *nm/f* dentist

dentition [dɑ̃tisjɔ̃] *nf* teeth

dénuder [denyde] *vt* to bare

dénué, e [denɥe] *adj*: **~ de** devoid of; **dénuement** *nm* destitution

déodorant [deɔdɔʀɑ̃] *nm* deodorant

déontologie [deɔtɔlɔʒi] *nf* code of practice

dépannage [depanaʒ] *nm*: **service de ~** (*AUTO*) breakdown service

dépanner [depane] *vt* (*voiture, télévision*) to fix, repair; (*fig*) to bail out, help out; **dépanneuse** *nf* breakdown lorry (*BRIT*), tow truck (*US*)

dépareillé, e [depareje] *adj* (*collection, service*) incomplete; (*objet*) odd

départ [depar] *nm* departure; (*SPORT*) start; **au ~** at the start; **la veille de son ~** the day before he leaves/left

départager [departaʒe] *vt* to decide between

département [departəmɑ̃] *nm* department

---
département

i France is divided into 96 administrative units called **départements**. These local government divisions are headed by a state-appointed **préfet**, and administered by an elected **Conseil général**. *Départements* are usually named after prominent geographical features such as rivers or mountain ranges; see also **DOM-TOM**.

---

dépassé, e [depase] *adj* superseded, outmoded; **il est complètement ~** he's completely out of his depth, he can't cope

dépasser [depase] *vt* (*véhicule, concurrent*) to overtake; (*endroit*) to pass, go past; (*somme, limite*) to exceed; (*fig: en beauté etc*) to surpass, outshine ♦ *vi* (*jupon etc*) to show

dépaysé, e [depeize] *adj* disoriented

dépaysement [depeizmɑ̃] *nm* (*changement*) change of scenery

dépecer [depəse] *vt* to joint, cut up

dépêche [depɛʃ] *nf* dispatch

dépêcher [depeʃe]: **se ~** *vi* to hurry

dépeindre [depɛ̃dʀ] *vt* to depict

dépendance [depɑ̃dɑ̃s] *nf* dependence; (*bâtiment*) outbuilding

dépendre [depɑ̃dʀ]: **~ de** *vt* to depend on; (*financièrement etc*) to be dependent on

dépens [depɑ̃] *nmpl*: **aux ~ de** at the expense of

dépense [depɑ̃s] *nf* spending *no pl*, expense, expenditure *no pl*; **dépenser** *vt* to spend; (*énergie*) to expend, use up; **se dépenser** *vi* to exert o.s.; **dépensier, -ière** *adj*: **il est dépensier** he's a spendthrift

dépérir [deperir] *vi* (*personne*) to waste away; (*plante*) to wither

dépêtrer [depetre] *vt*: **se ~ de** to extricate o.s. from

dépeupler [depœple]: **se ~** *vi* to become depopulated

dépilatoire [depilatwar] *adj* depilatory, hair-removing

dépister [depiste] *vt* to detect; (*voleur*) to track down

dépit [depi] *nm* vexation, frustration; **en ~ de** in spite of; **en ~ du bon sens** contrary to all good sense; **dépité, e** *adj* vexed, frustrated

déplacé, e [deplase] *adj* (*propos*) out of place, uncalled-for

déplacement [deplasmɑ̃] *nm* (*voyage*) trip, travelling *no pl*

déplacer [deplase] *vt* (*table, voiture*) to move, shift; **se ~** *vi* to move; (*voyager*) to travel; **se ~ une vertèbre** to slip a disc

déplaire [deplɛr] *vt*: **ça me déplaît** I don't like this, I dislike this; **se ~** to be unhappy; **déplaisant, e** *adj* disagreeable

dépliant [deplijɑ̃] *nm* leaflet

déplier [deplije] *vt* to unfold

déplorer [deplɔre] *vt* to deplore

déployer [deplwaje] *vt* (*carte*) to open out; (*ailes*) to spread; (*troupes*) to deploy

déporter [depɔrte] *vt* (*exiler*) to deport; (*dévier*) to carry off course

déposer [depoze] *vt* (*gén: mettre, poser*) to lay *ou* put down; (*à la banque, à la consigne*) to deposit; (*passager*) to drop (off), set down; (*roi*) to depose; (*plainte*) to lodge; (*marque*) to register; **se ~** *vi* to settle; **dépositaire** *nm/f* (*COMM*) agent; **déposition** *nf* statement

dépôt [depo] *nm* (*à la banque, sédiment*) deposit; (*entrepôt*) warehouse, store

dépotoir [depɔtwar] *nm* dumping ground, rubbish dump

dépouiller [depuje] *vt* (*documents*) to go through, peruse; ~ **qn/qch de** to strip sb/sth of; ~ **le scrutin** to count the votes

dépourvu, e [depuʀvy] *adj*: ~ **de** lacking in, without; **prendre qn au** ~ to catch sb unprepared

déprécier [depʀesje]: **se** ~ *vi* to depreciate

dépression [depʀesjɔ̃] *nf* depression; ~ **(nerveuse)** (nervous) breakdown

déprimant, e [depʀimɑ̃, ɑ̃t] *adj* depressing

déprimer [depʀime] *vi* to be/get depressed

MOT-CLÉ

depuis [dəpɥi] *prép* **1** (*point de départ dans le temps*) since; **il habite Paris depuis 1983/l'an dernier** he has been living in Paris since 1983/last year; **depuis quand le connaissez-vous?** how long have you known him?

2 (*temps écoulé*) for; **il habite Paris depuis 5 ans** he has been living in Paris for 5 years; **je le connais depuis 3 ans** I've known him for 3 years

3 (*lieu*): **il a plu depuis Metz** it's been raining since Metz; **elle a téléphoné depuis Valence** she rang from Valence

4 (*quantité, rang*) from; **depuis les plus petits jusqu'aux plus grands** from the youngest to the oldest

♦ *adv* (*temps*) since (then); **je ne lui ai pas parlé depuis** I haven't spoken to him since (then)

depuis que *conj* (ever) since; **depuis qu'il m'a dit ça** (ever) since he said that to me

---

député, e [depyte] *nm/f* (*POL*) ≃ Member of Parliament (*BRIT*), ≃ Member of Congress (*US*)

députer [depyte] *vt* to delegate

déraciner [deʀasine] *vt* to uproot

dérailler [deʀaje] *vi* (*train*) to be derailed; **faire** ~ to derail

déraisonner [deʀezɔne] *vi* to talk nonsense, rave

dérangement [deʀɑ̃ʒmɑ̃] *nm* (*gêne*) trouble; (*gastrique etc*) disorder; **en** ~ (*téléphone, machine*) out of order

déranger [deʀɑ̃ʒe] *vt* (*personne*) to trouble, bother; (*projets*) to disrupt, upset; (*objets, vêtements*) to disarrange; **se** ~ *vi*: **surtout ne vous dérangez pas pour moi** please don't put yourself out on my account; **est-ce que cela vous dérange si ...?** do you mind if ...?

déraper [deʀape] *vi* (*voiture*) to skid; (*personne, semelles*) to slip

dérégler [deʀegle] *vt* (*mécanisme*) to put out of order; (*estomac*) to upset

dérider [deʀide]: **se** ~ *vi* to brighten up

dérision [deʀizjɔ̃] *nf*: **tourner en** ~ to deride; **dérisoire** *adj* derisory

dérive [deʀiv] *nf*: **aller à la** ~ (*NAVIG, fig*) to drift

dérivé, e [deʀive] *nm* (*TECH*) by-product

dériver [deʀive] *vt* (*MATH*) to derive; (*cours d'eau etc*) to divert ♦ *vi* (*bateau*) to drift; ~ **de** to derive from

dermatologue [dɛʀmatɔlɔg] *nm/f* dermatologist

dernier, -ière [dɛʀnje, jɛʀ] *adj* last; (*le plus récent*) latest, last; **lundi/le mois** ~ last Monday/month; **c'est le** ~ **cri** it's the very latest thing; **en** ~ last; **ce** ~ the latter; **dernièrement** *adv* recently

dérobé, e [deʀɔbe] *adj*: **à la** ~**e** surreptitiously

dérober [deʀɔbe] *vt* to steal; **se** ~ *vi* (*s'esquiver*) to slip away; **se** ~ **à** (*justice, regards*) to hide from; (*obligation*) to shirk

dérogation [deʀɔgasjɔ̃] *nf* (special) dispensation

déroger [deʀɔʒe]: ~ **à** *vt* to go against, depart from

dérouiller [deʀuje] *vt*: **se** ~ **les jambes** to stretch one's legs

déroulement [deʀulmɑ̃] *nm* (*d'une opération etc*) progress

dérouler [deʀule] *vt* (*ficelle*) to unwind; **se**

~ *vi* (*avoir lieu*) to take place; (*se passer*) to go (off); **tout s'est déroulé comme prévu** everything went as planned

dérouter [deʀute] *vt* (*avion, train*) to reroute, divert; (*étonner*) to disconcert, throw (out)

derrière [dɛʀjɛʀ] *adv, prép* behind ♦ *nm* (*d'une maison*) back; (*postérieur*) behind, bottom; **les pattes de ~** the back *ou* hind legs; **par ~** from behind; (*fig*) behind one's back

des [de] *dét voir* **de** ♦ *prép* +*dét* = **de** +**les**

dès [dɛ] *prép* from; **~ que** as soon as; **~ son retour** as soon as he was (*ou* is) back

désabusé, e [dezabyze] *adj* disillusioned

désaccord [dezakɔʀ] *nm* disagreement; **désaccordé, e** *adj* (*MUS*) out of tune

désaffecté, e [dezafɛkte] *adj* disused

désagréable [dezagʀeabl] *adj* unpleasant

désagréger [dezagʀeʒe]: **se ~** *vi* to disintegrate, break up

désagrément [dezagʀemɑ̃] *nm* annoyance, trouble *no pl*

désaltérer [dezaltere] *vt*: **se ~** to quench one's thirst

désapprobateur, -trice [dezapʀɔbatœʀ, tʀis] *adj* disapproving

désapprouver [dezapʀuve] *vt* to disapprove of

désarmant, e [dezaʀmɑ̃, ɑ̃t] *adj* disarming

désarroi [dezaʀwa] *nm* disarray

désastre [dezastʀ] *nm* disaster; **désastreux, -euse** *adj* disastrous

désavantage [dezavɑ̃taʒ] *nm* disadvantage; **désavantager** *vt* to put at a disadvantage

descendre [desɑ̃dʀ] *vt* (*escalier, montagne*) to go (*ou* come) down; (*valise, paquet*) to take *ou* get down; (*étagère etc*) to lower; (*fam: abattre*) to shoot down ♦ *vi* to go (*ou* come) down; (*passager: s'arrêter*) to get out, alight; **~ à pied/en voiture** to walk/drive down; **~ du train** to get out of *ou* get off the train; **~ de cheval** to dismount; **~ à l'hôtel** to stay at a hotel

descente [desɑ̃t] *nf* descent, going down; (*chemin*) way down; (*SKI*) downhill (race); **~ de lit** bedside rug; **~ (de police)** (police) raid

description [dɛskʀipsjɔ̃] *nf* description

désemparé, e [dezɑ̃paʀe] *adj* bewildered, distraught

désemplir [dezɑ̃pliʀ] *vi*: **ne pas ~** to be always full

déséquilibre [dezekilibʀ] *nm* (*position*): **en ~** unsteady; (*fig: des forces, du budget*) imbalance; **déséquilibré, e** *nm/f* (*PSYCH*) unbalanced person; **déséquilibrer** *vt* to throw off balance

désert, e [dezɛʀ, ɛʀt] *adj* deserted ♦ *nm* desert; **déserter** *vi, vt* to desert; **désertique** *adj* desert *cpd*

désespéré, e [dezɛspeʀe] *adj* desperate

désespérer [dezɛspeʀe] *vi*: **~ (de)** to despair (of); **désespoir** *nm* despair; **en désespoir de cause** in desperation

déshabiller [dezabije] *vt* to undress; **se ~** *vi* to undress (o.s.)

déshériter [dezeʀite] *vt* to disinherit; **déshérités** *nmpl*: **les déshérités** the underprivileged

déshonneur [dezɔnœʀ] *nm* dishonour

déshydraté, e [dezidʀate] *adj* dehydrated

desiderata [deziderata] *nmpl* requirements

désigner [deziɲe] *vt* (*montrer*) to point out, indicate; (*dénommer*) to denote; (*candidat etc*) to name

désinfectant, e [dezɛ̃fɛktɑ̃, ɑ̃t] *adj, nm* disinfectant

désinfecter [dezɛ̃fɛkte] *vt* to disinfect

désintégrer [dezɛ̃tegʀe]: **se ~** *vi* to disintegrate

désintéressé, e [dezɛ̃teʀese] *adj* disinterested, unselfish

désintéresser [dezɛ̃teʀese] *vt*: **se ~ (de)** to lose interest (in)

désintoxication [dezɛ̃tɔksikasjɔ̃] *nf*: **faire une cure de ~** to undergo treatment for alcoholism (*ou* drug addiction)

désinvolte [dezɛ̃vɔlt] *adj* casual, off-hand; **désinvolture** *nf* casualness

désir [deziʀ] *nm* wish; (*sensuel*) desire; **désirer** *vt* to want, wish for; (*sexuellement*) to desire; **je désire ...** (*formule de politesse*) I would like ...

désister [deziste]: **se ~** *vi* to stand down, withdraw

désobéir [dezɔbeiʀ] *vi*: **~ (à qn/qch)** to disobey (sb/sth); **désobéissant, e** *adj* disobedient

désobligeant, e [dezɔbliʒɑ̃, ɑ̃t] *adj* disagreeable

désodorisant [dezɔdɔʀizɑ̃] *nm* air freshener, deodorizer

désœuvré, e [dezœvʀe] *adj* idle

désolé, e [dezɔle] *adj* (*paysage*) desolate; **je suis ~** I'm sorry

désoler [dezɔle] *vt* to distress, grieve

désopilant, e [dezɔpilɑ̃, ɑ̃t] *adj* hilarious

désordonné, e [dezɔʀdɔne] *adj* untidy

désordre [dezɔʀdʀ] *nm* disorder(liness), untidiness; (*anarchie*) disorder; **en ~** in a mess, untidy

désorienté, e [dezɔʀjɑ̃te] *adj* disorientated

désormais [dezɔʀmɛ] *adv* from now on

désossé, e [dezɔse] *adj* (*viande*) boned

desquelles [dekɛl] *prép +pron* = **de +lesquelles**

desquels [dekɛl] *prép +pron* = **de +lesquels**

desséché, e [deseʃe] *adj* dried up

dessécher [deseʃe]: **se ~** *vi* to dry out

dessein [desɛ̃] *nm*: **à ~** intentionally, deliberately

desserrer [deseʀe] *vt* to loosen; (*frein*) to release

dessert [desɛʀ] *nm* dessert, pudding

desserte [desɛʀt] *nf* (*table*) side table; (*transport*): **la ~ du village est assurée par autocar** there is a coach service to the village

desservir [desɛʀviʀ] *vt* (*ville, quartier*) to serve; (*débarrasser*): **~ (la table)** to clear the table

dessin [desɛ̃] *nm* (*œuvre, art*) drawing; (*motif*) pattern, design; **~ animé** cartoon (film); **~ humoristique** cartoon; **dessinateur, -trice** *nm/f* drawer; (*de bandes dessinées*) cartoonist; (*industriel*) draughtsman(-woman) (*BRIT*), draftsman(-woman) (*US*); **dessiner** *vt* to draw; (*concevoir*) to design

dessous [d(ə)su] *adv* underneath, beneath ♦ *nm* underside ♦ *nmpl* (*sous-vêtements*) underwear *sg*; **en ~, par ~** underneath; **au-~ (de)** below; (*peu digne de*) beneath; **avoir le ~** to get the worst of it; **les voisins du ~** the downstairs neighbours; **dessous-de-plat** *nm inv* tablemat

dessus [d(ə)sy] *adv* on top; (*collé, écrit*) on it ♦ *nm* top; **en ~** above; **par ~** ♦ *adv* over it ♦ *prép* over; **au-~ (de)** above; **avoir le ~** to get the upper hand; **dessus-de-lit** *nm inv* bedspread

destin [destɛ̃] *nm* fate; (*avenir*) destiny

destinataire [destinatɛʀ] *nm/f* (*POSTES*) addressee; (*d'un colis*) consignee

destination [destinasjɔ̃] *nf* (*lieu*) destination; (*usage*) purpose; **à ~ de** bound for, travelling to

destinée [destine] *nf* fate; (*existence, avenir*) destiny

destiner [destine] *vt*: **~ qch à qn** (*envisager de donner*) to intend sb to have sth; (*adresser*) to intend sth for sb; **être destiné à** (*usage*) to be meant for

désuet, -ète [dezɥɛ, ɛt] *adj* outdated, outmoded

détachant [detaʃɑ̃] *nm* stain remover

détachement [detaʃmɑ̃] *nm* detachment

détacher [detaʃe] *vt* (*enlever*) to detach, remove; (*délier*) to untie; (*ADMIN*): **~ qn (auprès de** *ou* **à)** to post sb (to); **se ~** *vi* (*se séparer*) to come off; (:*page*) to come out; (*se défaire*) to come undone; **se ~ sur** to stand out against; **se ~ de** (*se désintéresser*) to grow away from

détail [detaj] *nm* detail; (*COMM*): **le ~** retail; **en ~** in detail; **au ~** (*COMM*) retail; **détaillant** *nm* retailer; **détaillé, e** *adj* (*plan, explications*) detailed; (*facture*) itemized; **détailler** *vt* (*expliquer*) to explain in detail

détaler [detale] (*fam*) *vi* (*personne*) to take off

détartrant [detartrɑ̃] *nm* scale remover

détaxé, e [detakse] *adj*: **produits ~s** tax-free goods

détecter [detɛkte] *vt* to detect

détective [detɛktiv] *nm*: ~ (**privé**) private detective

déteindre [detɛ̃dʀ] *vi* (*au lavage*) to run, lose its colour

détendre [detɑ̃dʀ] *vt* (*corps, esprit*) to relax; **se ~** *vi* (*ressort*) to lose its tension; (*personne*) to relax

détenir [det(ə)niʀ] *vt* (*record, pouvoir, secret*) to hold; (*prisonnier*) to detain, hold

détente [detɑ̃t] *nf* relaxation

détention [detɑ̃sjɔ̃] *nf* (*d'armes*) possession; (*captivité*) detention; ~ **préventive** custody

détenu, e [det(ə)ny] *nm/f* prisoner

détergent [detɛʀʒɑ̃] *nm* detergent

détériorer [deteʀjɔʀe] *vt* to damage; **se ~** *vi* to deteriorate

déterminé, e [detɛʀmine] *adj* (*résolu*) determined; (*précis*) specific, definite

déterminer [detɛʀmine] *vt* (*fixer*) to determine; **se ~ à faire qch** to make up one's mind to do sth

déterrer [detɛʀe] *vt* to dig up

détestable [detɛstabl] *adj* foul, detestable

détester [detɛste] *vt* to hate, detest

détonner [detɔne] *vi* (*fig*) to clash

détour [detuʀ] *nm* detour; (*tournant*) bend, curve; **ça vaut le ~** it's worth the trip; **sans ~** (*fig*) plainly

détourné, e [detuʀne] *adj* (*moyen*) roundabout

détournement [detuʀnəmɑ̃] *nm*: ~ **d'avion** hijacking

détourner [detuʀne] *vt* to divert; (*par la force*) to hijack; (*yeux, tête*) to turn away; (*de l'argent*) to embezzle; **se ~** *vi* to turn away

détracteur, -trice [detʀaktœʀ, tʀis] *nm/f* disparager, critic

détraquer [detʀake] *vt* to put out of order; (*estomac*) to upset; **se ~** *vi* (*machine*) to go wrong

détrempé, e [detʀɑ̃pe] *adj* (*sol*) sodden, waterlogged

détresse [detʀɛs] *nf* distress

détriment [detʀimɑ̃] *nm*: **au ~ de** to the detriment of

détritus [detʀity(s)] *nmpl* rubbish *sg*, refuse *sg*

détroit [detʀwa] *nm* strait

détromper [detʀɔ̃pe] *vt* to disabuse

détruire [detʀɥiʀ] *vt* to destroy

dette [dɛt] *nf* debt

DEUG *sigle m* (= *diplôme d'études universitaires générales*) *diploma taken after 2 years at university*

deuil [dœj] *nm* (*perte*) bereavement; (*période*) mourning; **être en ~** to be in mourning

deux [dø] *num* two; **tous les ~** both; **ses ~ mains** both his hands, his two hands; ~ **fois** twice; **deuxième** *num* second; **deuxièmement** *adv* secondly; **deux-pièces** *nm inv* (*tailleur*) two-piece suit; (*de bain*) two-piece (swimsuit); (*appartement*) two-roomed flat (*BRIT*) *ou* apartment (*US*); **deux-points** *nm inv* colon *sg*; **deux-roues** *nm inv* two-wheeled vehicle

devais *etc* [dəvɛ] *vb voir* **devoir**

dévaler [devale] *vt* to hurtle down

dévaliser [devalize] *vt* to rob, burgle

dévaloriser [devalɔʀize] *vt* to depreciate; **se ~** *vi* to depreciate

dévaluation [devalɥasjɔ̃] *nf* devaluation

devancer [d(ə)vɑ̃se] *vt* (*coureur, rival*) to get ahead of; (*arriver*) to arrive before; (*prévenir: questions, désirs*) to anticipate

devant [d(ə)vɑ̃] *adv* in front; (*à distance: en avant*) ahead ♦ *prép* in front of; (*en avant*) ahead of; (*avec mouvement: passer*) past; (*en présence de*) before, in front of; (*étant donné*) in view of ♦ *nm* front; **prendre les ~s** to make the first move; **les pattes de**

~ the front legs, the forelegs; **par ~** (*boutonner*) at the front; (*entrer*) the front way; **aller au~ de qn** to go out to meet sb; **aller au~ de** (*désirs de qn*) to anticipate

devanture [d(ə)vãtyʀ] *nf* (*étalage*) display; (*vitrine*) (shop) window

déveine [devɛn] (*fam*) *nf* rotten luck *no pl*

développement [dev(ə)lɔpmã] *nm* development; **pays en voie de ~** developing countries

développer [dev(ə)lɔpe] *vt* to develop; **se ~** *vi* to develop

devenir [dəv(ə)niʀ] *vb* +*attrib* to become; **que sont-ils devenus?** what has become of them?

dévergondé, e [devɛʀgɔ̃de] *adj* wild, shameless

déverser [devɛʀse] *vt* (*liquide*) to pour (out); (*ordures*) to tip (out); **se ~ dans** (*fleuve*) to flow into

dévêtir [devetiʀ]: **se ~** *vi* to undress

devez *etc* [dəve] *vb voir* **devoir**

déviation [devjasjɔ̃] *nf* (AUTO) diversion (BRIT), detour (US)

devienne *etc* [dəvjɛn] *vb voir* **devenir**

dévier [devje] *vt* (*fleuve, circulation*) to divert; (*coup*) to deflect ♦ *vi* to veer (off course)

devin [dəvɛ̃] *nm* soothsayer, seer

deviner [d(ə)vine] *vt* to guess; (*apercevoir*) to distinguish; **devinette** *nf* riddle

devins *etc* [dəvɛ̃] *vb voir* **devenir**

devis [d(ə)vi] *nm* estimate, quotation

dévisager [deviʒaʒe] *vt* to stare at

devise [dəviz] *nf* (*formule*) motto, watchword; **~s** *nfpl* (*argent*) currency *sg*

deviser [dəvize] *vi* to converse

dévisser [devise] *vt* to unscrew, undo

dévoiler [devwale] *vt* to unveil

devoir [d(ə)vwaʀ] *nm* duty; (SCOL) homework *no pl*; (: *en classe*) exercise ♦ *vt* (*argent, respect*): **~ qch (à qn)** to owe (sb) sth; (+*infin: obligation*): **il doit le faire** he has to do it, he must do it; (: *intention*): **le nouveau centre commercial doit**

ouvrir en mai the new shopping centre is due to open in May; (: *probabilité*): **il doit être tard** it must be late

dévolu [devɔly] *nm*: **jeter son ~ sur** to fix one's choice on

dévorer [devɔʀe] *vt* to devour

dévot, e [devo, ɔt] *adj* devout, pious; **dévotion** *nf* devoutness

dévoué, e [devwe] *adj* devoted

dévouement [devumã] *nm* devotion

dévouer [devwe]: **se ~** *vi* (*se sacrifier*): **se ~ (pour)** to sacrifice o.s. (for); (*se consacrer*): **se ~ à** to devote *ou* dedicate o.s. to

dévoyé, e [devwaje] *adj* delinquent

devrai *etc* [dəvʀe] *vb voir* **devoir**

diabète [djabɛt] *nm* diabetes *sg*; **diabétique** *nm/f* diabetic

diable [djabl] *nm* devil

diabolo [djabɔlo] *nm* (*boisson*) lemonade with fruit cordial

diagnostic [djagnɔstik] *nm* diagnosis *sg*; **diagnostiquer** *vt* to diagnose

diagonal, e, -aux [djagɔnal, o] *adj* diagonal; **diagonale** *nf* diagonal; **en diagonale** diagonally

diagramme [djagʀam] *nm* chart, graph

dialecte [djalɛkt] *nm* dialect

dialogue [djalɔg] *nm* dialogue

diamant [djamã] *nm* diamond

diamètre [djamɛtʀ] *nm* diameter

diapason [djapazɔ̃] *nm* tuning fork

diaphragme [djafʀagm] *nm* diaphragm

diapo [djapo] (*fam*) *nf* slide

diapositive [djapozitiv] *nf* transparency, slide

diarrhée [djaʀe] *nf* diarrhoea

dictateur [diktatœʀ] *nm* dictator; **dictature** *nf* dictatorship

dictée [dikte] *nf* dictation

dicter [dikte] *vt* to dictate

dictionnaire [diksjɔnɛʀ] *nm* dictionary

dicton [diktɔ̃] *nm* saying, dictum

dièse [djɛz] *nm* sharp

diesel [djezɛl] *nm* diesel ♦ *adj inv* diesel

diète [djɛt] *nf* (*jeûne*) starvation diet; (*régime*) diet; **diététique** *adj*: **magasin dié-**

tétique health food shop

dieu, x [djø] *nm* god; **D~** God; **mon D~!** good heavens!

diffamation [difamasjɔ̃] *nf* slander; (*écrite*) libel

différé [difere] *nm* (*TV*): **en ~** (pre-) recorded

différemment [diferamɑ̃] *adv* differently

différence [diferɑ̃s] *nf* difference; **à la ~ de** unlike; **différencier** *vt* to differentiate; **différend** *nm* difference (of opinion), disagreement

différent, e [diferɑ̃, ɑ̃t] *adj* (*dissemblable*) different; **~ de** different from; (*divers*) different, various

différer [difere] *vt* to postpone, put off ♦ *vi*: **~ (de)** to differ (from)

difficile [difisil] *adj* difficult; (*exigeant*) hard to please; **difficilement** *adv* with difficulty

difficulté [difikylte] *nf* difficulty; **en ~** (*bateau, alpiniste*) in difficulties

difforme [difɔrm] *adj* deformed, misshapen

diffuser [difyze] *vt* (*chaleur*) to diffuse; (*émission, musique*) to broadcast; (*nouvelle*) to circulate; (*COMM*) to distribute

digérer [diʒere] *vt* to digest; (*fam: accepter*) to stomach, put up with; **digestif** *nm* (after-dinner) liqueur; **digestion** *nf* digestion

digne [diɲ] *adj* dignified; **~ de** worthy of; **~ de foi** trustworthy; **dignité** *nf* dignity

digue [dig] *nf* dike, dyke

dilapider [dilapide] *vt* to squander

dilemme [dilɛm] *nm* dilemma

dilettante [diletɑ̃t] *nm/f*: **faire qch en ~** to dabble in sth

diligence [diliʒɑ̃s] *nf* stagecoach

diluer [dilɥe] *vt* to dilute

diluvien, ne [dilyvjɛ̃, jɛn] *adj*: **pluie ~ne** torrential rain

dimanche [dimɑ̃ʃ] *nm* Sunday

dimension [dimɑ̃sjɔ̃] *nf* (*grandeur*) size; (~s) dimensions

diminué, e [diminɥe] *adj*: **il est très ~**

depuis son accident he's not at all the man he was since his accident

diminuer [diminɥe] *vt* to reduce, decrease; (*ardeur etc*) to lessen; (*dénigrer*) to belittle ♦ *vi* to decrease, diminish; **diminutif** *nm* (*surnom*) pet name; **diminution** *nf* decreasing, diminishing

dinde [dɛ̃d] *nf* turkey

dindon [dɛ̃dɔ̃] *nm* turkey

dîner [dine] *nm* dinner ♦ *vi* to have dinner

dingue [dɛ̃g] (*fam*) *adj* crazy

dinosaure [dinɔzɔr] *nm* dinosaur

diplomate [diplɔmat] *adj* diplomatic ♦ *nm* diplomat; (*fig*) diplomatist; **diplomatie** *nf* diplomacy

diplôme [diplom] *nm* diploma; **avoir des ~s** to have qualifications; **diplômé, e** *adj* qualified

dire [dir] *nm*: **au ~ de** according to ♦ *vt* to say; (*secret, mensonge, heure*) to tell; **~ qch à qn** to tell sb sth; **~ à qn qu'il fasse** *ou* **de faire** to tell sb to do; **on dit que** they say that; **ceci dit** that being said; **si cela lui dit** (*plaire*) if he fancies it; **que dites-vous de** (*penser*) what do you think of; **on dirait que** it looks (*ou* sounds *etc*) as if; **dis/dites (donc)!** I say!

direct, e [dirɛkt] *adj* direct ♦ *nm* (*TV*): **en ~** live; **directement** *adv* directly

directeur, -trice [dirɛktœr, tris] *nm/f* (*d'entreprise*) director; (*de service*) manager(-eress); (*d'école*) head(teacher) (*BRIT*), principal (*US*)

direction [dirɛksjɔ̃] *nf* (*sens*) direction; (*d'entreprise*) management; (*AUTO*) steering; **"toutes ~s"** "all routes"

dirent [dir] *vb voir* **dire**

dirigeant, e [diriʒɑ̃, ɑ̃t] *adj* (*classe*) ruling ♦ *nm/f* (*d'un parti etc*) leader

diriger [diriʒe] *vt* (*entreprise*) to manage, run; (*véhicule*) to steer; (*orchestre*) to conduct; (*recherches, travaux*) to supervise; **se ~** *vi* (*s'orienter*) to find one's way; **se ~ vers** *ou* **sur** to make *ou* head for

dis *etc* [di] *vb voir* **dire**

discernement [disɛrnəmɑ̃] *nm* (*bon sens*)

discernment, judgement

discerner [diseʀne] *vt* to discern, make out

discipline [disiplin] *nf* discipline; **discipliner** *vt* to discipline

discontinu, e [diskɔ̃tiny] *adj* intermittent

discontinuer [diskɔ̃tinɥe] *vi*: **sans ~** without stopping, without a break

discordant, e [diskɔʀdɑ̃, ɑ̃t] *adj* discordant

discothèque [diskɔtɛk] *nf* (*boîte de nuit*) disco(thèque)

discours [diskuʀ] *nm* speech

discret, -ète [diskʀɛ, ɛt] *adj* discreet; (*parfum, maquillage*) unobtrusive; **discrétion** *nf* discretion; **à discrétion** as much as one wants

discrimination [diskʀiminasjɔ̃] *nf* discrimination; **sans ~** indiscriminately

disculper [diskylpe] *vt* to exonerate

discussion [diskysjɔ̃] *nf* discussion

discutable [diskytabl] *adj* debatable

discuté, e [diskyte] *adj* controversial

discuter [diskyte] *vt* (*débattre*) to discuss; (*contester*) to question, dispute ♦ *vi* to talk; (*protester*) to argue; **~ de** to discuss

dise *etc* [diz] *vb voir* **dire**

diseuse [dizøz] *nf*: **~ de bonne aventure** fortuneteller

disgracieux, -euse [disgʀasjø, jøz] *adj* ungainly, awkward

disjoindre [disʒwɛ̃dʀ] *vt* to take apart; **se ~** *vi* to come apart

disjoncteur [disʒɔ̃ktœʀ] *nm* (*ÉLEC*) circuit breaker

disloquer [dislɔke]: **se ~** *vi* (*parti, empire*) to break up

disons [dizɔ̃] *vb voir* **dire**

disparaître [dispaʀɛtʀ] *vi* to disappear; (*se perdre: traditions etc*) to die out; **faire ~** (*tache*) to remove; (*douleur*) to get rid of

disparition [dispaʀisjɔ̃] *nf* disappearance; **espèce en voie de ~** endangered species

disparu, e [dispaʀy] *nm/f* missing person ♦ *adj*: **être porté ~** to be reported missing

dispensaire [dispɑ̃sɛʀ] *nm* community clinic

dispenser [dispɑ̃se] *vt*: **~ qn de** to exempt sb from; **se ~ de** *vt* (*corvée*) to get out of

disperser [dispɛʀse] *vt* to scatter; **se ~** *vi* to break up

disponibilité [dispɔnibilite] *nf* availability; **disponible** *adj* available

dispos [dispo] *adj m*: **(frais et) ~** fresh (as a daisy)

disposé, e [dispoze] *adj*: **bien/mal ~** (*humeur*) in a good/bad mood; **~ à** (*prêt à*) willing *ou* prepared to

disposer [dispoze] *vt* to arrange ♦ *vi*: **vous pouvez ~** you may leave; **~ de** to have (at one's disposal); **se ~ à faire** to prepare to do, be about to do

dispositif [dispozitif] *nm* device; (*fig*) system, plan of action

disposition [dispozisjɔ̃] *nf* (*arrangement*) arrangement, layout; (*humeur*) mood; **prendre ses ~s** to make arrangements; **avoir des ~s pour la musique** *etc* to have a special aptitude for music *etc*; **à la ~ de qn** at sb's disposal; **je suis à votre ~** I am at your service

disproportionné, e [dispʀopɔʀsjɔne] *adj* disproportionate, out of all proportion

dispute [dispyt] *nf* quarrel, argument; **disputer** *vt* (*match*) to play; (*combat*) to fight; **se disputer** *vi* to quarrel

disquaire [diskɛʀ] *nm/f* record dealer

disqualifier [diskalifje] *vt* to disqualify

disque [disk] *nm* (*MUS*) record; (*forme, pièce*) disc; (*SPORT*) discus; **~ compact** compact disc; **~ dur** hard disk; **disquette** *nf* floppy disk, diskette

disséminer [disemine] *vt* to scatter

disséquer [diseke] *vt* to dissect

dissertation [disɛʀtasjɔ̃] *nf* (*SCOL*) essay

dissimuler [disimyle] *vt* to conceal

dissipé, e [disipe] *adj* (*élève*) undisciplined, unruly

dissiper [disipe] *vt* to dissipate; (*fortune*)

to squander; **se ~** *vi* (*brouillard*) to clear, disperse

dissolvant [disɔlvã] *nm* nail polish remover

dissonant, e [disɔnã, ãt] *adj* discordant

dissoudre [disudʀ] *vt* to dissolve; **se ~** *vi* to dissolve

dissuader [disɥade] *vt*: **~ qn de faire** to dissuade sb from doing; **dissuasion** *nf*: **force de dissuasion** deterrent power

distance [distãs] *nf* distance; (*fig*: *écart*) gap; **à ~** at *ou* from a distance; **distancer** *vt* to outdistance

distant, e [distã, ãt] *adj* (*réservé*) distant; **~ de** (*lieu*) far away from

distendre [distãdʀ]: **se ~** *vi* to distend

distillerie [distilʀi] *nf* distillery

distinct, e [distɛ̃(kt), ɛ̃kt] *adj* distinct; **distinctement** *adv* distinctly, clearly; **distinctif, -ive** *adj* distinctive

distingué, e [distɛ̃ge] *adj* distinguished

distinguer [distɛ̃ge] *vt* to distinguish

distraction [distʀaksjɔ̃] *nf* (*inattention*) absent-mindedness; (*passe-temps*) distraction, entertainment

distraire [distʀɛʀ] *vt* (*divertir*) to entertain, divert; (*déranger*) to distract; **se ~** *vi* to amuse *ou* enjoy o.s.; **distrait, e** *adj* absent-minded

distrayant, e [distʀɛjã, ãt] *adj* entertaining

distribuer [distʀibɥe] *vt* to distribute, hand out; (*CARTES*) to deal (out); (*courrier*) to deliver; **distributeur** *nm* (*COMM*) distributor; (*automatique*) (vending) machine; (: *de billets*) (cash) dispenser; **distribution** *nf* distribution; (*postale*) delivery; (*choix d'acteurs*) casting, cast

dit, e [di, dit] *pp de* **dire** ♦ *adj* (*fixé*): **le jour ~** the arranged day; (*surnommé*): **X, ~ Pierrot** X, known as Pierrot

dites [dit] *vb voir* **dire**

divaguer [divage] *vi* to ramble; (*fam*) to rave

divan [divã] *nm* divan

diverger [divɛʀʒe] *vi* to diverge

divers, e [divɛʀ, ɛʀs] *adj* (*varié*) diverse, varied; (*différent*) different, various; **~es personnes** various *ou* several people

diversifier [divɛʀsifje] *vt* to vary

diversité [divɛʀsite] *nf* (*variété*) diversity

divertir [divɛʀtiʀ]: **se ~** *vi* to amuse *ou* enjoy o.s.; **divertissement** *nm* distraction, entertainment

divin, e [divɛ̃, in] *adj* divine

diviser [divize] *vt* to divide; **division** *nf* division

divorce [divɔʀs] *nm* divorce; **divorcé, e** *nm/f* divorcee; **divorcer** *vi* to get a divorce, get divorced

divulguer [divylge] *vt* to divulge, disclose

dix [dis] *num* ten; **dixième** *num* tenth

dizaine [dizen] *nf*: **une ~ (de)** about ten, ten or so

do [do] *nm* (*note*) C; (*en chantant la gamme*) do(h)

docile [dɔsil] *adj* docile

dock [dɔk] *nm* dock; **docker** *nm* docker

docteur [dɔktœʀ] *nm* doctor; **doctorat** *nm* doctorate; **doctoresse** *nf* lady doctor

doctrine [dɔktʀin] *nf* doctrine

document [dɔkymã] *nm* document; **documentaire** *adj, nm* documentary; **documentaliste** *nm/f* (*SCOL*) librarian; **documentation** *nf* documentation, literature; **documenter** *vt*: **se documenter (sur)** to gather information (on)

dodo [dɔdo] *nm* (*langage enfantin*): **aller faire ~** to go to beddy-byes

dodu, e [dɔdy] *adj* plump

dogue [dɔg] *nm* mastiff

doigt [dwa] *nm* finger; **à deux ~s de** within an inch of; **~ de pied** toe; **doigté** *nm* (*MUS*) fingering; (*fig*: *habileté*) diplomacy, tact

doit *etc* [dwa] *vb voir* **devoir**

doléances [dɔleãs] *nfpl* grievances

dollar [dɔlaʀ] *nm* dollar

domaine [dɔmen] *nm* estate, property; (*fig*) domain, field

domestique [dɔmestik] *adj* domestic

♦ *nm/f* servant, domestic; **domestiquer**
vt to domesticate

domicile [dɔmisil] *nm* home, place of residence; **à ~** at home; **livrer à ~** to deliver; **domicilié, e** *adj*: **"domicilié à ..."**
"address ..."

dominant, e [dɔminɑ̃, ɑ̃t] *adj* (*opinion*)
predominant

dominer [dɔmine] *vt* to dominate; (*sujet*)
to master; (*surpasser*) to outclass, surpass;
(*surplomber*) to tower above, dominate
♦ *vi* to be in the dominant position; **se ~**
vi to control o.s.

domino [dɔmino] *nm* domino

dommage [dɔmaʒ] *nm*: **~s** (*dégâts*) damage *no pl*; **c'est ~!** what a shame!; **c'est
~ que** it's a shame *ou* pity that;
dommages-intérêts *nmpl* damages

dompter [dɔ̃(p)te] *vt* to tame; **dompteur,
-euse** *nm/f* trainer

DOM-TOM [dɔmtɔm] *sigle m* (= *départements et territoires d'outre-mer*) French overseas departments and territories

don [dɔ̃] *nm* gift; (*charité*) donation; **avoir
des ~s pour** to have a gift *ou* talent for;
elle a le ~ de m'énerver she's got a
knack of getting on my nerves

donc [dɔ̃k] *conj* therefore, so; (*après une digression*) so, then

donjon [dɔ̃ʒɔ̃] *nm* keep

donné, e [dɔne] *adj* (*convenu: lieu, heure*)
given; (*pas cher: fam*): **c'est ~** it's a gift;
étant ~ ... given ...; **données** *nfpl* data

donner [dɔne] *vt* to give; (*vieux habits etc*)
to give away; (*spectacle*) to put on; **~ qch
à qn** to give sb sth, give sth to sb; **~ sur**
(*suj: fenêtre, chambre*) to look (out) onto;
ça donne soif/faim it makes you (feel)
thirsty/hungry; **se ~ à fond** to give one's
all; **se ~ du mal** to take (great) trouble;
s'en ~ à cœur joie (*fam*) to have a great
time

MOT-CLÉ

dont [dɔ̃] *pron relatif* **1** (*appartenance: objets*) whose, of which; (*appartenance: êtres*

animés) whose; **la maison dont le toit est
rouge** the house the roof of which is red,
the house whose roof is red; **l'homme
dont je connais la sœur** the man whose
sister I know

2 (*parmi lesquel(le)s*): **2 livres, dont l'un
est ...** 2 books, one of which is ...; **il y
avait plusieurs personnes, dont Gabrielle** there were several people, among
them Gabrielle; **10 blessés, dont 2
grièvement** 10 injured, 2 of them seriously

3 (*complément d'adjectif, de verbe*): **le fils
dont il est si fier** the son he's so proud
of; **ce dont je parle** what I'm talking
about

doré, e [dɔre] *adj* golden; (*avec dorure*)
gilt, gilded

dorénavant [dɔrenavɑ̃] *adv* henceforth

dorer [dɔre] *vt* to gild; **(faire) ~** (*CULIN*) to
brown

dorloter [dɔrlɔte] *vt* to pamper

dormir [dɔrmir] *vi* to sleep; (*être endormi*)
to be asleep

dortoir [dɔrtwar] *nm* dormitory

dorure [dɔryr] *nf* gilding

dos [do] *nm* back; (*de livre*) spine; **"voir au
~"** "see over"; **de ~** from the back

dosage [dozaʒ] *nm* mixture

dose [doz] *nf* dose; **doser** *vt* to measure
out; **il faut savoir doser ses efforts** you
have to be able to pace yourself

dossard [dosar] *nm* number (*worn by
competitor*)

dossier [dosje] *nm* (*documents*) file; (*de
chaise*) back; (*PRESSE*) feature; **un ~ scolaire** a school report

dot [dɔt] *nf* dowry

doter [dɔte] *vt*: **~ de** to equip with

douane [dwan] *nf* customs *pl*; **(droits de)
~** (customs) duty; **douanier, -ière** *adj*
customs *cpd* ♦ *nm* customs officer

double [dubl] *adj, adv* double ♦ *nm* (*2 fois
plus*): **le ~ (de)** twice as much (*ou* many)
(as); (*autre exemplaire*) duplicate, copy;

(*sosie*) double; (*TENNIS*) doubles *sg*; **en ~ (exemplaire)** in duplicate; **faire ~ emploi** to be redundant

double-cliquer [dublklike] *vi* (*INFORM*) to double-click

doubler [duble] *vt* (*multiplier par 2*) to double; (*vêtement*) to line; (*dépasser*) to overtake, pass; (*film*) to dub; (*acteur*) to stand in for ♦ *vi* to double

doublure [dublyʀ] *nf* lining; (*CINÉMA*) stand-in

douce [dus] *adj voir* **doux**; **douceâtre** *adj* sickly sweet; **doucement** *adv* gently; (*lentement*) slowly; **doucereux, -euse** (*péj*) *adj* sugary; **douceur** *nf* softness; (*de quelqu'un*) gentleness; (*de climat*) mildness

douche [duʃ] *nf* shower; **doucher: se doucher** *vi* take *ou* take a shower

doudoune [dudun] *nf* padded jacket

doué, e [dwe] *adj* gifted, talented; **être ~ pour** to have a gift for

douille [duj] *nf* (*ÉLEC*) socket

douillet, te [dujɛ, ɛt] *adj* cosy; (*péj: à la douleur*) soft

douleur [dulœʀ] *nf* pain; (*chagrin*) grief, distress; **douloureux, -euse** *adj* painful

doute [dut] *nm* doubt; **sans ~** no doubt; (*probablement*) probably; **sans aucun ~** without a doubt; **douter** *vt* to doubt; **douter de** (*sincérité de qn*) to have (one's) doubts about; (*réussite*) to be doubtful of; **se douter de qch/que** to suspect sth/that; **je m'en doutais** I suspected as much; **douteux, -euse** *adj* (*incertain*) doubtful; (*péj*) dubious-looking

Douvres [duvʀ] *n* Dover

doux, douce [du, dus] *adj* soft; (*sucré*) sweet; (*peu fort*: moutarde, clément: climat) mild; (*pas brusque*) gentle

douzaine [duzɛn] *nf* (*12*) dozen; (*environ 12*): **une ~ (de)** a dozen or so

douze [duz] *num* twelve; **douzième** *num* twelfth

doyen, ne [dwajɛ̃, jɛn] *nm/f* (*en âge*) most senior member; (*de faculté*) dean

dragée [dʀaʒe] *nf* sugared almond

draguer [dʀage] *vt* (*rivière*) to dredge; (*fam*) to try to pick up

dramatique [dʀamatik] *adj* dramatic; (*tragique*) tragic ♦ *nf* (*TV*) (television) drama

dramaturge [dʀamatyʀʒ] *nm* dramatist, playwright

drame [dʀam] *nm* drama

drap [dʀa] *nm* (*de lit*) sheet; (*tissu*) woollen fabric

drapeau, x [dʀapo] *nm* flag

drap-housse [dʀaus] *nm* fitted sheet

dresser [dʀese] *vt* (*mettre vertical, monter*) to put up, erect; (*liste*) to draw up; (*animal*) to train; **se ~** *vi* (*obstacle*) to stand; (*personne*) to draw o.s. up; **~ qn contre qn** to set sb against sb; **~ l'oreille** to prick up one's ears

drogue [dʀɔg] *nf* drug; **la ~** drugs *pl*; **drogué, e** *nm/f* drug addict; **droguer** *vt* (*victime*) to drug; **se droguer** *vi* (*aux stupéfiants*) to take drugs; (*péj: de médicaments*) to dose o.s. up; **droguerie** *nf* hardware shop; **droguiste** *nm* keeper/owner of a hardware shop

droit, e [dʀwa, dʀwat] *adj* (*non courbe*) straight; (*vertical*) upright, straight; (*fig: loyal*) upright, straight(forward); (*opposé à gauche*) right, right-hand ♦ *adv* straight ♦ *nm* (*prérogative*) right; (*taxe*) duty, tax; (: *d'inscription*) fee; (*JUR*): **le ~** law; **avoir le ~ de** to be allowed to; **avoir ~ à** to be entitled to; **être dans son ~** to be within one's rights; **à ~e** on the right; (*direction*) (to the) right; **~s d'auteur** royalties; **~s de l'homme** human rights; **~s d'inscription** enrolment fee; **droite** *nf* (*POL*): **la droite** the right (wing); **droitier, -ière** *nm/f* right-handed person; **droiture** *nf* uprightness, straightness

drôle [dʀol] *adj* funny; **une ~ d'idée** a funny idea; **drôlement** (*fam*) *adv* (*très*) terribly, awfully

dromadaire [dʀɔmadɛʀ] *nm* dromedary

dru, e [dʀy] *adj* (*cheveux*) thick, bushy; (*pluie*) heavy

du [dy] *dét voir* **de** ♦ *prép* +dét = **de + le**

dû, due [dy] *vb voir* **devoir** ♦ *adj (somme)* owing, owed; *(causé par)*: **~ à** due to ♦ *nm* due

duc [dyk] *nm* duke; **duchesse** *nf* duchess

dûment [dymɑ̃] *adv* duly

dune [dyn] *nf* dune

Dunkerque [dœ̃kɛʀk] *n* Dunkirk

duo [dɥo] *nm (MUS)* duet

dupe [dyp] *nf* dupe ♦ *adj*: **(ne pas) être ~ de** (not) to be taken in by

duplex [dyplɛks] *nm (appartement)* split-level apartment, duplex

duplicata [dyplikata] *nm* duplicate

duquel [dykɛl] *prép +pron* = **de +lequel**

dur, e [dyʀ] *adj (pierre, siège, travail, problème)* hard; *(voix, climat)* harsh; *(sévère)* hard, harsh; *(cruel)* hard(-hearted); *(porte, col)* stiff; *(viande)* tough ♦ *adv* hard ♦ *nm (fam: meneur)* tough nut; **~ d'oreille** hard of hearing

durant [dyʀɑ̃] *prép (au cours de)* during; *(pendant)* for; **des mois ~** for months

durcir [dyʀsiʀ] *vt, vi* to harden; **se ~** *vi* to harden

durée [dyʀe] *nf* length; *(d'une pile etc)* life; **de courte ~** *(séjour)* short

durement [dyʀmɑ̃] *adv* harshly

durer [dyʀe] *vi* to last

dureté [dyʀte] *nf* hardness; harshness; stiffness; toughness

durit ® [dyʀit] *nf* (car radiator) hose

dus *etc* [dy] *vb voir* **devoir**

duvet [dyvɛ] *nm* down; *(sac de couchage)* down-filled sleeping bag

DVD *sigle m* (= *digital versatile disc*) DVD

dynamique [dinamik] *adj* dynamic; **dynamisme** *nm* dynamism

dynamite [dinamit] *nf* dynamite

dynamo [dinamo] *nf* dynamo

dysenterie [disɑ̃tʀi] *nf* dysentery

dyslexie [dislɛksi] *nf* dyslexia, word-blindness

E, e

eau, x [o] *nf* water; **~x** *nfpl (MÉD)* waters; **prendre l'~** to leak, let in water; **tomber à l'~** *(fig)* to fall through; **~ courante** running water; **~ de Javel** bleach; **~ de toilette** toilet water; **~ douce** fresh water; **~ gazeuse** sparkling (mineral) water; **~ minérale** mineral water; **~ plate** still water; **~ potable** drinking water; **eau-de-vie** *nf* brandy; **eau-forte** *nf* etching

ébahi, e [ebai] *adj* dumbfounded

ébattre [ebatʀ]: **s'~** *vi* to frolic

ébaucher [eboʃe] *vt* to sketch out, outline; **s'~** *vi* to take shape

ébène [ebɛn] *nf* ebony; **ébéniste** *nm* cabinetmaker

éberlué, e [ebɛʀlɥe] *adj* astounded

éblouir [ebluiʀ] *vt* to dazzle

éborgner [ebɔʀɲe] *vt* to blind in one eye

éboueur [ebwœʀ] *nm* dustman *(BRIT)*, garbageman *(US)*

ébouillanter [ebujɑ̃te] *vt* to scald; *(CULIN)* to blanch

éboulement [ebulmɑ̃] *nm* rock fall

ébouler [ebule]: **s'~** *vi* to crumble, collapse; **éboulis** *nmpl* fallen rocks

ébouriffé, e [eburife] *adj* tousled

ébranler [ebrɑ̃le] *vt* to shake; *(affaiblir)* to weaken; **s'~** *vi (partir)* to move off

ébrécher [ebreʃe] *vt* to chip

ébriété [ebrijete] *nf*: **en état d'~** in a state of intoxication

ébrouer [ebrue]: **s'~** *vi* to shake o.s.

ébruiter [ebrɥite] *vt* to spread, disclose

ébullition [ebylisjɔ̃] *nf* boiling point

écaille [ekaj] *nf (de poisson)* scale; *(matière)* tortoiseshell; **écailler** *vt (poisson)* to scale; **s'écailler** *vi* to flake *ou* peel (off)

écarlate [ekaʀlat] *adj* scarlet

écarquiller [ekaʀkije] *vt*: **~ les yeux** to stare wide-eyed

écart [ekaʀ] *nm* gap; **à l'~** out of the way; **à l'~ de** away from; **faire un ~** *(voi-*

ture) to swerve; **~ de conduite** misdemeanour

écarté, e [ekaʀte] *adj* (*lieu*) out-of-the-way, remote; (*ouvert*): **les jambes ~es** legs apart; **les bras ~s** arms outstretched

écarter [ekaʀte] *vt* (*séparer*) to move apart, separate; (*éloigner*) to push back, move away; (*ouvrir: bras, jambes*) to spread, open; (: *rideau*) to draw (back); (*éliminer: candidat, possibilité*) to dismiss; **s'~** *vi* to part; (*s'éloigner*) to move away; **s'~ de** to wander from

écervelé, e [esɛʀvəle] *adj* scatterbrained, featherbrained

échafaud [eʃafo] *nm* scaffold

échafaudage [eʃafodaʒ] *nm* scaffolding

échafauder [eʃafode] *vt* (*plan*) to construct

échalote [eʃalɔt] *nf* shallot

échancrure [eʃɑ̃kʀyʀ] *nf* (*de robe*) scoop neckline

échange [eʃɑ̃ʒ] *nm* exchange; **en ~ de** in exchange *ou* return for; **échanger** *vt*: **échanger qch (contre)** to exchange sth (for); **échangeur** *nm* (*AUTO*) interchange

échantillon [eʃɑ̃tijɔ̃] *nm* sample

échappement [eʃapmɑ̃] *nm* (*AUTO*) exhaust

échapper [eʃape]: **~ à** *vt* (*gardien*) to escape (from); (*punition, péril*) to escape; **s'~** *vi* to escape; **~ à qn** (*détail, sens*) to escape sb; (*objet qu'on tient*) to slip out of sb's hands; **laisser ~** (*cri etc*) to let out; **l'~ belle** to have a narrow escape

écharde [eʃaʀd] *nf* splinter (of wood)

écharpe [eʃaʀp] *nf* scarf; **avoir le bras en ~** to have one's arm in a sling

échasse [eʃas] *nf* stilt

échassier [eʃasje] *nm* wader

échauffer [eʃofe] *vt* (*moteur*) to overheat; **s'~** *vi* (*SPORT*) to warm up; (*dans la discussion*) to become heated

échéance [eʃeɑ̃s] *nf* (*d'un paiement: date*) settlement date; (*fig*) deadline; **à brève ~** in the short term; **à longue ~** in the long run

échéant [eʃeɑ̃]: **le cas ~** *adv* if the case arises

échec [eʃɛk] *nm* failure; (*ÉCHECS*): **~ et mat/au roi** checkmate/check; **~s** *nmpl* (*jeu*) chess *sg*; **tenir en ~** to hold in check

échelle [eʃɛl] *nf* ladder; (*fig, d'une carte*) scale

échelon [eʃ(ə)lɔ̃] *nm* (*d'échelle*) rung; (*ADMIN*) grade; **échelonner** *vt* to space out

échevelé, e [eʃəv(ə)le] *adj* tousled, dishevelled

échine [eʃin] *nf* backbone, spine

échiquier [eʃikje] *nm* chessboard

écho [eko] *nm* echo; **échographie** *nf*: **passer une échographie** to have a scan

échoir [eʃwaʀ] *vi* (*dette*) to fall due; (*délais*) to expire; **~ à** to fall to

échouer [eʃwe] *vi* to fail; **s'~** *vi* to run aground

échu, e [eʃy] *pp de* **échoir**

éclabousser [eklabuse] *vt* to splash

éclair [eklɛʀ] *nm* (*d'orage*) flash of lightning, lightning *no pl*; (*gâteau*) éclair

éclairage [eklɛʀaʒ] *nm* lighting

éclaircie [eklɛʀsi] *nf* bright interval

éclaircir [eklɛʀsiʀ] *vt* to lighten; (*fig: mystère*) to clear up; (: *point*) to clarify; **s'~** *vi* (*ciel*) to clear; **s'~ la voix** to clear one's throat; **éclaircissement** *nm* (*sur un point*) clarification

éclairer [eklere] *vt* (*lieu*) to light (up); (*personne: avec une lampe etc*) to light the way for; (*fig: problème*) to shed light on ♦ *vi*: **~ mal/bien** to give a poor/good light; **s'~ à la bougie** to use candlelight

éclaireur, -euse [eklerœʀ, øz] *nm/f* (*scout*) (boy) scout/(girl) guide ♦ *nm* (*MIL*) scout

éclat [ekla] *nm* (*de bombe, de verre*) fragment; (*du soleil, d'une couleur etc*) brightness, brilliance; (*d'une cérémonie*) splendour; (*scandale*): **faire un ~** to cause a commotion; **~s de voix** shouts; **~ de rire** roar of laughter

éclatant, e [eklatɑ̃, ɑ̃t] *adj* brilliant

éclater [eklate] *vi* (*pneu*) to burst; (*bombe*) to explode; (*guerre*) to break out; (*groupe*, *parti*) to break up; **~ en sanglots/de rire** to burst out sobbing/laughing

éclipser [eklipse]: **s'~** *vi* to slip away

éclore [eklɔR] *vi* (*œuf*) to hatch; (*fleur*) to open (out)

écluse [eklyz] *nf* lock

écœurant, e [ekœRã, ãt] *adj* (*gâteau etc*) sickly; (*fig*) sickening

écœurer [ekœRe] *vt*: **~ qn** (*nourriture*) to make sb feel sick; (*conduite*, *personne*) to disgust sb

école [ekɔl] *nf* school; **aller à l'~** to go to school; **~ maternelle/primaire** nursery/primary school; **~ publique** state school; **écolier, -ière** *nm/f* schoolboy(-girl)

école maternelle
---

i *Nursery school* (*l'école maternelle*) *is publicly funded in France and, though not compulsory, is attended by most children between the ages of two and six. Statutory education begins with primary school* (*l'école primaire*) *from the age of six to ten or eleven.*

écologie [ekɔlɔʒi] *nf* ecology; **écologique** *adj* environment-friendly; **écologiste** *nm/f* ecologist

éconduire [ekɔ̃dɥiR] *vt* to dismiss

économe [ekɔnɔm] *adj* thrifty ♦ *nm/f* (*de lycée etc*) bursar (*BRIT*), treasurer (*US*)

économie [ekɔnɔmi] *nf* economy; (*gain: d'argent, de temps etc*) saving; (*science*) economics *sg*; **~s** *nfpl* (*pécule*) savings; **économique** *adj* (*avantageux*) economical; (*ÉCON*) economic; **économiser** *vt*, *vi* to save; **économiseur** *nm* (*INFORM*): **~ d'écran** screensaver

écoper [ekɔpe] *vi* to bale out; **~ de 3 ans de prison** (*fig: fam*) to get sentenced to 3 years

écorce [ekɔRs] *nf* bark; (*de fruit*) peel

écorcher [ekɔRʃe] *vt*: **s'~ le genou/la main** to graze one's knee/one's hand;

écorchure *nf* graze

écossais, e [ekɔse, ɛz] *adj* Scottish ♦ *nm/f*: **É~, e** Scot

Écosse [ekɔs] *nf*: **l'~** Scotland

écosser [ekɔse] *vt* to shell

écoulement [ekulmã] *nm* (*d'eau*) flow

écouler [ekule] *vt* (*objet*) to sell; **s'~** *vi* (*eau*) to flow (out); (*temps*) to pass (by)

écourter [ekuRte] *vt* to curtail, cut short

écoute [ekut] *nf* (*RADIO, TV*): **temps/heure d'~** listening (*ou* viewing) time/hour; **rester à l'~ (de)** to stay tuned in (to); **~s téléphoniques** phone tapping *sg*

écouter [ekute] *vt* to listen to; **écouteur** *nm* (*TÉL*) receiver; (*RADIO*) headphones *pl*, headset

écoutille [ekutij] *nf* hatch

écran [ekRã] *nm* screen; **petit ~** television; **~ total** sunblock

écrasant, e [ekRazã, ãt] *adj* overwhelming

écraser [ekRaze] *vt* to crush; (*piéton*) to run over; **s'~** *vi* to crash; **s'~ contre** to crash into

écrémé, e [ekReme] *adj* (*lait*) skimmed

écrevisse [ekRəvis] *nf* crayfish *inv*

écrier [ekRije]: **s'~** *vi* to exclaim

écrin [ekRɛ̃] *nm* case, box

écrire [ekRiR] *vt* to write; **s'~** to write to each other; **ça s'écrit comment?** how is it spelt?; **écrit** *nm* (*examen*) written paper; **par écrit** in writing

écriteau, x [ekRito] *nm* notice, sign

écriture [ekRityR] *nf* writing; **l'É~, les É~s** the Scriptures

écrivain [ekRivɛ̃] *nm* writer

écrou [ekRu] *nm* nut

écrouer [ekRue] *vt* to imprison

écrouler [ekRule]: **s'~** *vi* to collapse

écru, e [ekRy] *adj* (*couleur*) off-white, écru

ECU [eky] *sigle m* ECU

écueil [ekœj] *nm* reef; (*fig*) pitfall

éculé, e [ekyle] *adj* (*chaussure*) down-at-heel; (*fig: péj*) hackneyed

écume [ekym] *nf* foam; **écumer** *vt* (*CULIN*) to skim; **écumoire** *nf* skimmer

écureuil [ekyʀœj] *nm* squirrel

écurie [ekyʀi] *nf* stable

écusson [ekysɔ̃] *nm* badge

écuyer, -ère [ekɥije, jɛʀ] *nm/f* rider

eczéma [ɛgzema] *nm* eczema

édenté, e [edɑ̃te] *adj* toothless

EDF *sigle f* (= *Électricité de France*) *national electricity company*

édifice [edifis] *nm* edifice, building

édifier [edifje] *vt* to build, erect; (*fig*) to edify

Édimbourg [edɛ̃buʀ] *n* Edinburgh

éditer [edite] *vt* (*publier*) to publish; (*annoter*) to edit; **éditeur, -trice** *nm/f* publisher; **édition** *nf* edition; (*industrie du livre*) publishing

édredon [edʀədɔ̃] *nm* eiderdown

éducateur, -trice [edykatœʀ, tʀis] *nm/f* teacher; (*in special school*) instructor

éducatif, -ive [edykatif, iv] *adj* educational

éducation [edykasjɔ̃] *nf* education; (*familiale*) upbringing; (*manières*) (good) manners *pl*; **~ physique** physical education

édulcorant [edylkɔʀɑ̃] *nm* sweetener

éduquer [edyke] *vt* to educate; (*élever*) to bring up

effacé, e [efase] *adj* unassuming

effacer [efase] *vt* to erase, rub out; **s'~** *vi* (*inscription etc*) to wear off; (*pour laisser passer*) to step aside

effarant, e [efaʀɑ̃, ɑ̃t] *adj* alarming

effarer [efaʀe] *vt* to alarm

effaroucher [efaʀuʃe] *vt* to frighten *ou* scare away

effectif, -ive [efɛktif, iv] *adj* real ♦ *nm* (*SCOL*) (*pupil*) numbers *pl*; (*entreprise*) staff, workforce; **effectivement** *adv* (*réellement*) actually, really; (*en effet*) indeed

effectuer [efɛktɥe] *vt* (*opération*) to carry out; (*trajet*) to make

efféminé, e [efemine] *adj* effeminate

effervescent, e [efɛʀvesɑ̃, ɑ̃t] *adj* effervescent

effet [efe] *nm* effect; (*impression*) impression; **~s** *nmpl* (*vêtements etc*) things; **faire ~** (*médicament*) to take effect; **faire bon/mauvais ~ sur qn** to make a good/bad impression on sb; **en ~** indeed; **~ de serre** greenhouse effect

efficace [efikas] *adj* (*personne*) efficient; (*action, médicament*) effective; **efficacité** *nf* efficiency; effectiveness

effilocher [efilɔʃe]: **s'~** *vi* to fray

efflanqué, e [eflɑ̃ke] *adj* emaciated

effleurer [eflœʀe] *vt* to brush (against); (*sujet*) to touch upon; (*suj: idée, pensée*): **ça ne m'a pas effleuré** it didn't cross my mind

effluves [eflyv] *nmpl* exhalation(s)

effondrer [efɔ̃dʀe]: **s'~** *vi* to collapse

efforcer [efɔʀse]: **s'~ de** *vt*: **s'~ de faire** to try hard to do

effort [efɔʀ] *nm* effort

effraction [efʀaksjɔ̃] *nf*: **s'introduire par ~ dans** to break into

effrayant, e [efʀejɑ̃, ɑ̃t] *adj* frightening

effrayer [efʀeje] *vt* to frighten, scare

effréné, e [efʀene] *adj* wild

effriter [efʀite]: **s'~** *vi* to crumble

effroi [efʀwa] *nm* terror, dread *no pl*

effronté, e [efʀɔ̃te] *adj* cheeky

effroyable [efʀwajabl] *adj* horrifying, appalling

effusion [efyzjɔ̃] *nf* effusion; **sans ~ de sang** without bloodshed

égal, e, -aux [egal, o] *adj* equal; (*constant: vitesse*) steady ♦ *nm/f* equal; **être ~ à** (*prix, nombre*) to be equal to; **ça lui est ~** it's all the same to him, he doesn't mind; **sans ~** matchless, unequalled; **d'~ à ~** as equals; **également** *adv* equally; (*aussi*) too, as well; **égaler** *vt* to equal; **égaliser** *vt* (*sol, salaires*) to level (out); (*chances*) to equalize ♦ *vi* (*SPORT*) to equalize; **égalité** *nf* equality; **être à égalité** to be level

égard [egaʀ] *nm*: **~s** consideration *sg*; **à cet ~** in this respect; **par ~ pour** out of consideration for; **à l'~ de** towards

égarement [egaʀmɑ̃] *nm* distraction

égarer [egaʀe] *vt* to mislay; **s'~** *vi* to get

lost, lose one's way; (*objet*) to go astray

égayer [egeje] vt to cheer up; (*pièce*) to brighten up

églantine [eglɑ̃tin] nf wild *ou* dog rose

églefin [egləfɛ̃] nm haddock

église [egliz] nf church; **aller à l'~** to go to church

égoïsme [egɔism] nm selfishness; **égoïste** adj selfish

égorger [egɔRʒe] vt to cut the throat of

égosiller [egozije]: **s'~** vi to shout o.s. hoarse·

égout [egu] nm sewer

égoutter [egute] vi to drip; **s'~** vi to drip; **égouttoir** nm draining board; (*mobile*) draining rack

égratigner [egRatiɲe] vt to scratch; **égratignure** nf scratch

Égypte [eʒipt] nf: **l'~** Egypt; **égyptien, ne** adj ·Egyptian ♦ nm/f: **Égyptien, ne** Egyptian

eh [e] excl hey!; **~ bien** well

éhonté, e [eɔ̃te] adj shameless, brazen

éjecter [eʒɛkte] vt (*TECH*) to eject; (*fam*) to kick *ou* chuck out

élaborer [elabɔRe] vt to elaborate; (*projet, stratégie*) to work out; (*rapport*) to draft

élan [elɑ̃] nm (*ZOOL*) elk, moose; (*SPORT*) run up; (*fig: de tendresse etc*) surge; **prendre de l'~** to gather speed

élancé, e [elɑ̃se] adj slender

élancement [elɑ̃smɑ̃] nm shooting pain

élancer [elɑ̃se]: **s'~** vi to dash, hurl o.s.

élargir [elaRʒiR] vt to widen; **s'~** vi to widen; (*vêtement*) to stretch

élastique [elastik] adj elastic ♦ nm (*de bureau*) rubber band; (*pour la couture*) elastic *no pl*

électeur, -trice [elɛktœR, tRis] nm/f elector, voter

élection [elɛksjɔ̃] nf election

électorat [elɛktɔRa] nm electorate

électricien, ne [elɛktRisjɛ̃, jɛn] nm/f electrician

électricité [elɛktRisite] nf electricity; **allumer/éteindre l'~** to put on/off the light

électrique [elɛktRik] adj electric(al)

électrocuter [elɛktRɔkyte] vt to electrocute

électroménager [elɛktRomenaʒe] adj, nm: **appareils ~s, l'~** domestic (electrical) appliances

électronique [elɛktRɔnik] adj electronic ♦ nf electronics *sg*

électrophone [elɛktRɔfɔn] nm record player

élégance [elegɑ̃s] nf elegance

élégant, e [elegɑ̃, ɑ̃t] adj elegant

élément [elemɑ̃] nm element; (*pièce*) component, part; **~s de cuisine** kitchen units; **élémentaire** adj elementary

éléphant [elefɑ̃] nm elephant

élevage [el(ə)vaʒ] nm breeding; (*de bovins*) cattle rearing; **truite d'~** farmed trout

élévation [elevasjɔ̃] nf (*hausse*) rise

élevé, e [el(ə)ve] adj high; **bien/mal ~** well-/ill-mannered

élève [elɛv] nm/f pupil

élever [el(ə)ve] vt (*enfant*) to bring up, raise; (*animaux*) to breed; (*hausser: taux, niveau*) to raise; (*édifier: monument*) to put up, erect; **s'~** vi (*avion*) to go up; (*niveau, température*) to rise; **s'~ à** (*suj: frais, dégâts*) to amount to, add up to; **s'~ contre qch** to rise up against sth; **~ la voix** to raise one's voice; **éleveur, -euse** nm/f breeder

élimé, e [elime] adj threadbare

éliminatoire [eliminatwaR] nf (*SPORT*) heat

éliminer [elimine] vt to eliminate

élire [eliR] vt to elect

elle [ɛl] pron (*sujet*) she; (: *chose*) it; (*complément*) her; it; **~s** (*sujet*) they; (*complément*) them; **~-même** herself; itself; **~s-mêmes** themselves; *voir aussi* **il**

élocution [elɔkysjɔ̃] nf delivery; **défaut d'~** speech impediment

éloge [elɔʒ] nm (*gén no pl*) praise; **faire l'~ de** to praise; **élogieux, -euse** adj laudatory, full of praise

éloigné, e [elwaɲe] adj distant, far-off;

(*parent*) distant; **éloignement** *nm* (*distance, aussi fig*) distance

éloigner [elwaɲe] *vt* (*échéance*) to put off, postpone; (*soupçons, danger*) to ward off; (*objet*): ~ **qch (de)** to move *ou* take sth away (from); (*personne*): ~ **qn (de)** to take sb away *ou* remove sb (from); **s'~ (de)** (*personne*) to go away (from); (*véhicule*) to move away (from); (*affectivement*) to become estranged (from); **ne vous éloignez pas!** don't go far away!

élu, e [ely] *pp de* **élire** ♦ *nm/f* (POL) elected representative

éluder [elyde] *vt* to evade

Élysée [elize] *nm*: **(le palais de) l'~** the Élysée Palace (*the French president's residence*)

émacié, e [emasje] *adj* emaciated

émail, -aux [emaj, o] *nm* enamel

émaillé, e [emaje] *adj* (*fig*): ~ **de** dotted with

émanciper [emãsipe] *vt*: **s'~** *vi* (*fig*) to become emancipated *ou* liberated

émaner [emane]: ~ **de** *vt* to come from

emballage [ãbalaʒ] *nm* (*papier*) wrapping; (*boîte*) packaging

emballer [ãbale] *vt* to wrap (up); (*dans un carton*) to pack (up); (*fig: fam*) to thrill (to bits); **s'~** *vi* (*moteur*) to race; (*cheval*) to bolt; (*fig: personne*) to get carried away

embarcadère [ãbaʀkadeʀ] *nm* wharf, pier

embarcation [ãbaʀkasjɔ̃] *nf* (small) boat, (small) craft *inv*

embardée [ãbaʀde] *nf*: **faire une ~** to swerve

embarquement [ãbaʀkəmã] *nm* (*de passagers*) boarding; (*de marchandises*) loading

embarquer [ãbaʀke] *vt* (*personne*) to embark; (*marchandise*) to load; (*fam*) to cart off ♦ *vi* (*passager*) to board; **s'~** *vi* to board; **s'~ dans** (*affaire, aventure*) to embark upon

embarras [ãbaʀa] *nm* (*gêne*) embarrassment; **mettre qn dans l'~** to put sb in

an awkward position; **vous n'avez que l'~ du choix** the only problem is choosing

embarrassant, e [ãbaʀasã, ãt] *adj* embarrassing

embarrasser [ãbaʀase] *vt* (*encombrer*) to clutter (up); (*gêner*) to hinder, hamper; ~ **qn** to put sb in an awkward position; **s'~ de** to burden o.s. with

embauche [ãboʃ] *nf* hiring; **embaucher** *vt* to take on, hire

embaumer [ãbome] *vt*: ~ **la lavande** *etc* to be fragrant with (the scent of) lavender *etc*

embellie [ãbeli] *nf* brighter period

embellir [ãbeliʀ] *vt* to make more attractive; (*une histoire*) to embellish ♦ *vi* to grow lovelier *ou* more attractive

embêtements [ãbetmã] *nmpl* trouble *sg*

embêter [ãbete] *vt* to bother; **s'~** *vi* (*s'ennuyer*) to be bored

emblée [ãble]: **d'~** *adv* straightaway

embobiner [ãbɔbine] *vt* (*fam*) to get round

emboîter [ãbwate] *vt* to fit together; **s'~ (dans)** to fit (into); ~ **le pas à qn** to follow in sb's footsteps

embonpoint [ãbɔ̃pwɛ̃] *nm* stoutness

embouchure [ãbuʃyʀ] *nf* (GÉO) mouth

embourber [ãbuʀbe]: **s'~** *vi* to get stuck in the mud

embourgeoiser [ãbuʀʒwaze]: **s'~** *vi* to become middle-class

embouteillage [ãbutejaʒ] *nm* traffic jam

emboutir [ãbutiʀ] *vt* (*heurter*) to crash into, ram

embranchement [ãbʀãʃmã] *nm* (*routier*) junction

embraser [ãbʀaze]: **s'~** *vi* to flare up

embrassades [ãbʀasad] *nfpl* hugging and kissing

embrasser [ãbʀase] *vt* to kiss; (*sujet, période*) to embrace, encompass; **s'~** to kiss (each other)

embrasure [ãbʀazyʀ] *nf*: **dans l'~ de la porte** in the door(way)

embrayage [ɑ̃bʀejaʒ] nm clutch

embrayer [ɑ̃bʀeje] vi (AUTO) to let in the clutch

embrocher [ɑ̃bʀɔʃe] vt to put on a spit

embrouiller [ɑ̃bʀuje] vt to muddle up; (fils) to tangle (up); s'~ vi (personne) to get in a muddle

embruns [ɑ̃bʀœ̃] nmpl sea spray sg

embryon [ɑ̃bʀijɔ̃] nm embryo

embûches [ɑ̃byʃ] nfpl pitfalls, traps

embué, e [ɑ̃bɥe] adj misted up

embuscade [ɑ̃byskad] nf ambush

éméché, e [emeʃe] adj tipsy, merry

émeraude [em(ə)ʀod] nf emerald

émerger [emɛʀʒe] vi to emerge; (faire saillie, aussi fig) to stand out

émeri [em(ə)ʀi] nm: **toile** ou **papier ~** emery paper

émerveillement [emɛʀvejmɑ̃] nm wonder

émerveiller [emɛʀveje] vt to fill with wonder; s'~ **de** to marvel at

émettre [emɛtʀ] vt (son, lumière) to give out, emit; (message etc: RADIO) to transmit; (billet, timbre, emprunt) to issue; (hypothèse, avis) to voice, put forward ♦ vi to broadcast

émeus etc [emø] vb voir **émouvoir**

émeute [emøt] nf riot

émietter [emjete] vt to crumble

émigrer [emigʀe] vi to emigrate

émincer [emɛ̃se] vt to cut into thin slices

éminent, e [eminɑ̃, ɑ̃t] adj distinguished

émission [emisjɔ̃] nf (RADIO, TV) programme, broadcast; (d'un message) transmission; (de timbre) issue

emmagasiner [ɑ̃magazine] vt (amasser) to store up

emmanchure [ɑ̃mɑ̃ʃyʀ] nf armhole

emmêler [ɑ̃mele] vt to tangle (up); (fig) to muddle up; s'~ vi to get in a tangle

emménager [ɑ̃menaʒe] vi to move in; ~ **dans** to move into

emmener [ɑ̃m(ə)ne] vt to take (with one); (comme otage, capture) to take away; ~ **qn au cinéma** to take sb to the cinema

emmerder [ɑ̃mɛʀde] (fam!) vt to bug, bother; s'~ vi to be bored stiff

emmitoufler [ɑ̃mitufle] s'~ vi to wrap up (warmly)

émoi [emwa] nm commotion

émotif, -ive [emɔtif, iv] adj emotional

émotion [emosjɔ̃] nf emotion

émousser [emuse] vt to blunt; (fig) to dull

émouvoir [emuvwaʀ] vt to move; s'~ vi to be moved; (s'indigner) to be roused

empailler [ɑ̃paje] vt to stuff

empaqueter [ɑ̃pakte] vt to parcel up

emparer [ɑ̃paʀe]: s'~ **de** vt (objet) to seize, grab; (comme otage, MIL) to seize; (suj: peur etc) to take hold of

empâter [ɑ̃pate]: s'~ vi to thicken out

empêchement [ɑ̃pɛʃmɑ̃] nm (unexpected) obstacle, hitch

empêcher [ɑ̃peʃe] vt to prevent; ~ **qn de faire** to prevent ou stop sb (from) doing; **il n'empêche que** nevertheless; **il n'a pas pu s'~ de rire** he couldn't help laughing

empereur [ɑ̃pʀœʀ] nm emperor

empester [ɑ̃peste] vi to stink, reek

empêtrer [ɑ̃petʀe] vt: s'~ **dans** (fils etc) to get tangled up in

emphase [ɑ̃faz] nf pomposity, bombast

empiéter [ɑ̃pjete] vi: ~ **sur** to encroach upon

empiffrer [ɑ̃pifʀe]: s'~ (fam) vi to stuff o.s.

empiler [ɑ̃pile] vt to pile (up)

empire [ɑ̃piʀ] nm empire; (fig) influence

empirer [ɑ̃piʀe] vi to worsen, deteriorate

emplacement [ɑ̃plasmɑ̃] nm site

emplettes [ɑ̃plɛt] nfpl shopping sg

emplir [ɑ̃pliʀ] vt to fill; s'~ **(de)** to fill (with)

emploi [ɑ̃plwa] nm use; (COMM, ÉCON) employment; (poste) job, situation; **mode d'~** directions for use; ~ **du temps** timetable, schedule

employé, e [ɑ̃plwaje] nm/f employee; ~ **de bureau** office employee ou clerk

employer [ɑ̃plwaje] *vt* to use; (*ouvrier, main-d'œuvre*) to employ; **s'~ à faire** to apply *ou* devote o.s. to doing; **employeur, -euse** *nm/f* employer

empocher [ɑ̃pɔʃe] *vt* to pocket

empoigner [ɑ̃pwaɲe] *vt* to grab

empoisonner [ɑ̃pwazɔne] *vt* to poison; (*empester: air, pièce*) to stink out; (*fam*): **~ qn** to drive sb mad

emporté, e [ɑ̃pɔʀte] *adj* quick-tempered

emporter [ɑ̃pɔʀte] *vt* to take (with one); (*en dérobant ou enlevant, emmener: blessés, voyageurs*) to take away; (*entraîner*) to carry away; **s'~** *vi* (*de colère*) to lose one's temper; **l'~ (sur)** to get the upper hand (of); **plats à ~** take-away meals

empreint, e [ɑ̃pʀɛ̃, ɛ̃t] *adj*: **~ de** (*regret, jalousie*) marked with; **empreinte** *nf*: **empreinte (de pas)** footprint; **empreinte (digitale)** fingerprint

empressé, e [ɑ̃pʀese] *adj* attentive

empressement [ɑ̃pʀesmɑ̃] *nm* (*hâte*) eagerness

empresser [ɑ̃pʀese]: **s'~** *vi*: **s'~ auprès de qn** to surround sb with attentions; **s'~ de faire** (*se hâter*) to hasten to do

emprise [ɑ̃pʀiz] *nf* hold, ascendancy

emprisonnement [ɑ̃pʀizɔnmɑ̃] *nm* imprisonment

emprisonner [ɑ̃pʀizɔne] *vt* to imprison

emprunt [ɑ̃pʀœ̃] *nm* loan

emprunté, e [ɑ̃pʀœ̃te] *adj* (*fig*) ill-at-ease, awkward

emprunter [ɑ̃pʀœ̃te] *vt* to borrow; (*itinéraire*) to take, follow

ému, e [emy] *pp de* **émouvoir ♦** *adj* (*gratitude*) touched; (*compassion*) moved

---
| *MOT-CLÉ* |
---

en [ɑ̃] *prép* **1** (*endroit, pays*) in; (*direction*) to; **habiter en France/ville** to live in France/town; **aller en France/ville** to go to France/town

2 (*moment, temps*) in; **en été/juin** in summer/June

3 (*moyen*) by; **en avion/taxi** by plane/taxi

4 (*composition*) made of; **c'est en verre** it's (made of) glass; **un collier en argent** a silver necklace

5 (*description, état*): **une femme (habillée) en rouge** a woman (dressed) in red; **peindre qch en rouge** to paint sth red; **en T/étoile** T/star-shaped; **en chemise/chaussettes** in one's shirt-sleeves/socks; **en soldat** as a soldier; **cassé en plusieurs morceaux** broken into several pieces; **en réparation** being repaired, under repair; **en vacances** on holiday; **en deuil** in mourning; **le même en plus grand** the same but *ou* only bigger

6 (*avec gérondif*) while, on, by; **en dormant** while sleeping, as one sleeps; **en sortant** on going out, as he *etc* went out; **sortir en courant** to run out

♦ *pron* **1** (*indéfini*): **j'en ai/veux** I have/want some; **en as-tu?** have you got any?; **je n'en veux pas** I don't want any; **j'en ai 2** I've got 2; **combien y en a-t-il?** how many (of them) are there?; **j'en ai assez** I've got enough (of it *ou* them); (*j'en ai marre*) I've had enough

2 (*provenance*) from there; **j'en viens** I've come from there

3 (*cause*): **il en est malade/perd le sommeil** he is ill/can't sleep because of it

4 (*complément de nom, d'adjectif, de verbe*): **j'en connais les dangers** I know its *ou* the dangers; **j'en suis fier/ai besoin** I am proud of it/need it

---

ENA *sigle f* (= *École Nationale d'Administration*) *one of the Grandes Écoles*

encadrement [ɑ̃kadʀəmɑ̃] *nm* (*cadres*) managerial staff

encadrer [ɑ̃kadʀe] *vt* (*tableau, image*) to frame; (*fig: entourer*) to surround; (*personnel, soldats etc*) to train

encaissé, e [ɑ̃kese] *adj* (*vallée*) steep-sided; (*rivière*) with steep banks

encaisser [ɑ̃kese] *vt* (*chèque*) to cash; (*argent*) to collect; (*fam: coup, défaite*) to take

encart [ɑ̃kaʀ] *nm* insert

en-cas [ɑ̃kɑ] *nm* snack

encastré, e [ɑ̃kastʀe] *adj*: **four ~** built-in oven

enceinte [ɑ̃sɛ̃t] *adj f*: **~ (de 6 mois)** (6 months) pregnant ♦ *nf* (*mur*) wall; (*espace*) enclosure; (*aussi*: **~ acoustique**) (loud)speaker

encens [ɑ̃sɑ̃] *nm* incense

encercler [ɑ̃sɛʀkle] *vt* to surround

enchaîner [ɑ̃ʃene] *vt* to chain up; (*mouvements, séquences*) to link (together) ♦ *vi* to carry on

enchanté, e [ɑ̃ʃɑ̃te] *adj* (*ravi*) delighted; (*magique*) enchanted; **~ (de faire votre connaissance)** pleased to meet you

enchantement [ɑ̃ʃɑ̃tmɑ̃] *nm* delight; (*magie*) enchantment

enchère [ɑ̃ʃɛʀ] *nf* bid; **mettre/vendre aux ~s** to put up for (sale by)/sell by auction

enchevêtrer [ɑ̃ʃ(ə)vetʀe]: **s'~** *vi* to get in a tangle

enclencher [ɑ̃klɑ̃ʃe] *vt* (*mécanisme*) to engage; **s'~** *vi* to engage

enclin, e [ɑ̃klɛ̃, in] *adj*: **~ à** inclined *ou* prone to

enclos [ɑ̃klo] *nm* enclosure

enclume [ɑ̃klym] *nf* anvil

encoche [ɑ̃kɔʃ] *nf* notch

encoignure [ɑ̃kɔɲyʀ] *nf* corner

encolure [ɑ̃kɔlyʀ] *nf* (*cou*) neck

encombrant, e [ɑ̃kɔ̃bʀɑ̃, ɑ̃t] *adj* cumbersome, bulky

encombre [ɑ̃kɔ̃bʀ]: **sans ~** *adv* without mishap *ou* incident; **encombrement** *nm*: **être pris dans un encombrement** to be stuck in a traffic jam

encombrer [ɑ̃kɔ̃bʀe] *vt* to clutter (up); (*gêner*) to hamper; **s'~ de** (*bagages etc*) to load *ou* burden o.s. with

encontre [ɑ̃kɔ̃tʀ]: **à l'~ de** *prép* against, counter to

MOT-CLÉ

encore [ɑ̃kɔʀ] *adv* **1** (*continuation*) still; **il y travaille encore** he's still working on it;

pas encore not yet

2 (*de nouveau*) again; **j'irai encore demain** I'll go again tomorrow; **encore une fois** (once) again; **encore deux jours** two more days

3 (*intensif*) even, still; **encore plus fort/mieux** even louder/better, louder/better still

4 (*restriction*) even so *ou* then, only; **encore pourrais-je le faire si ...** even so, I might be able to do it if ...; **si encore** if only **encore que** *conj* although

---

encouragement [ɑ̃kuʀaʒmɑ̃] *nm* encouragement

encourager [ɑ̃kuʀaʒe] *vt* to encourage

encourir [ɑ̃kuʀiʀ] *vt* to incur

encrasser [ɑ̃kʀase] *vt* to make filthy

encre [ɑ̃kʀ] *nf* ink; **encrier** *nm* inkwell

encroûter [ɑ̃kʀute]: **s'~** (*fam*) *vi* (*fig*) to get into a rut, get set in one's ways

encyclopédie [ɑ̃siklɔpedi] *nf* encyclopaedia

endetter [ɑ̃dete]: **s'~** *vi* to get into debt

endiablé, e [ɑ̃djable] *adj* (*danse*) furious

endimanché, e [ɑ̃dimɑ̃ʃe] *adj* in one's Sunday best

endive [ɑ̃div] *nf* chicory *no pl*

endoctriner [ɑ̃dɔktʀine] *vt* to indoctrinate

endommager [ɑ̃dɔmaʒe] *vt* to damage

endormi, e [ɑ̃dɔʀmi] *adj* asleep

endormir [ɑ̃dɔʀmiʀ] *vt* to put to sleep; (*suj: chaleur etc*) to send to sleep; (*MÉD: dent, nerf*) to anaesthetize; (*fig: soupçons*) to allay; **s'~** *vi* to fall asleep, go to sleep

endosser [ɑ̃dose] *vt* (*responsabilité*) to take, shoulder; (*chèque*) to endorse; (*uniforme, tenue*) to put on, don

endroit [ɑ̃dʀwa] *nm* place; (*opposé à l'envers*) right side; **à l'~** (*vêtement*) the right way out; (*objet posé*) the right way round

enduire [ɑ̃dɥiʀ] *vt* to coat

enduit [ɑ̃dɥi] *nm* coating

endurance [ɑ̃dyʀɑ̃s] *nf* endurance

endurant, e [ɑ̃dyʀɑ̃, ɑ̃t] *adj* tough, hardy

endurcir [ādyRsiR]: **s'~** *vi* (*physiquement*) to become tougher; (*moralement*) to become hardened

endurer [ādyRe] *vt* to endure, bear

énergétique [eneRʒetik] *adj* (*aliment*) energy-giving

énergie [eneRʒi] *nf* (*PHYSIQUE*) energy; (*TECH*) power; (*morale*) vigour, spirit; **énergique** *adj* energetic, vigorous; (*mesures*) drastic, stringent

énervant, e [eneRvā, āt] *adj* irritating, annoying

énerver [eneRve] *vt* to irritate, annoy; **s'~** *vi* to get excited, get worked up

enfance [āfās] *nf* childhood

enfant [āfā] *nm/f* child; **~ de chœur** *nm* (*REL*) altar boy; **enfantillage** (*péj*) *nm* childish behaviour *no pl*; **enfantin, e** *adj* (*puéril*) childlike; (*langage, jeu etc*) children's *cpd*

enfer [āfeR] *nm* hell

enfermer [āfeRme] *vt* to shut up; (*à clef, interner*) to lock up

enfiévré, e [āfjevRe] *adj* feverish

enfiler [āfile] *vt* (*vêtement*) to slip on, slip into; (*perles*) to string; (*aiguille*) to thread

enfin [āfē] *adv* at last; (*en énumérant*) lastly; (*toutefois*) still; (*pour conclure*) in a word; (*somme toute*) after all

enflammer [āflame]: **s'~** *vi* to catch fire; (*MÉD*) to become inflamed

enflé, e [āfle] *adj* swollen

enfler [āfle] *vi* to swell (up)

enfoncer [āfɔ̃se] *vt* (*clou*) to drive in; (*faire pénétrer*): **~ qch dans** to push (*ou* drive) sth into; (*forcer: porte*) to break open; **s'~** *vi* to sink; **s'~ dans** to sink into; (*forêt, ville*) to disappear into

enfouir [āfwiR] *vt* (*dans le sol*) to bury; (*dans un tiroir etc*) to tuck away

enfourcher [āfuRʃe] *vt* to mount

enfreindre [āfRɛ̃dR] *vt* to infringe, break

enfuir [āfɥiR]: **s'~** *vi* to run away *ou* off

enfumer [āfyme] *vt* (*pièce*) to fill with smoke

engageant, e [āgaʒā, āt] *adj* attractive, appealing

engagement [āgaʒmā] *nm* commitment

engager [āgaʒe] *vt* (*embaucher*) to take on; (: *artiste*) to engage; (*commencer*) to start; (*lier*) to bind, commit; (*impliquer*) to involve; (*investir*) to invest, lay out; (*inciter*) to urge; (*introduire: clé*) to insert; **s'~** *vi* (*promettre*) to commit o.s.; (*MIL*) to enlist; (*débuter: conversation etc*) to start (up); **s'~ à faire** to undertake to do; **s'~ dans** (*rue, passage*) to turn into; (*fig: affaire, discussion*) to enter into, embark on

engelures [āʒlyR] *nfpl* chilblains

engendrer [āʒādRe] *vt* to breed, create

engin [āʒē] *nm* machine; (*outil*) instrument; (*AUT*) vehicle; (*AVIAT*) aircraft *inv*

englober [āglɔbe] *vt* to include

engloutir [āglutiR] *vt* to swallow up

engoncé, e [āgɔ̃se] *adj*: **~ dans** cramped in

engorger [āgɔRʒe] *vt* to obstruct, block

engouement [āgumā] *nm* (sudden) passion

engouffrer [āgufRe] *vt* to swallow up, devour; **s'~ dans** to rush into

engourdir [āguRdiR] *vt* to numb; (*fig*) to dull, blunt; **s'~** *vi* to go numb

engrais [āgRe] *nm* manure; **~ (chimique)** (chemical) fertilizer

engraisser [āgRese] *vt* to fatten (up)

engrenage [āgRənaʒ] *nm* gears *pl*, gearing; (*fig*) chain

engueuler [āgœle] (*fam*) *vt* to bawl at

enhardir [āaRdiR]: **s'~** *vi* to grow bolder

énigme [enigm] *nf* riddle

enivrer [ānivRe] *vt*: **s'~** to get drunk

enjambée [āʒābe] *nf* stride

enjamber [āʒābe] *vt* to stride over

enjeu, x [āʒø] *nm* stakes *pl*

enjôler [āʒole] *vt* to coax, wheedle

enjoliver [āʒɔlive] *vt* to embellish; **enjoliveur** *nm* (*AUTO*) hub cap

enjoué, e [āʒwe] *adj* playful

enlacer [ālase] *vt* (*étreindre*) to embrace, hug

enlaidir [ālediR] *vt* to make ugly ♦ *vi* to

become ugly

enlèvement [ālevmā] *nm* (*rapt*) abduction, kidnapping

enlever [āl(ə)ve] *vt* (*ôter: gén*) to remove; (*: vêtement, lunettes*) to take off; (*emporter: ordures etc*) to take away; (*kidnapper*) to abduct, kidnap; (*obtenir: prix, contrat*) to win; (*prendre*): ~ **qch à qn** to take sth (away) from sb

enliser [ālize]: **s'~** *vi* to sink, get stuck

enneigé, e [āneʒe] *adj* (*route, maison*) snowed-up; (*paysage*) snowy

ennemi, e [ɛnmi] *adj* hostile; (*MIL*) enemy *cpd ♦ nm/f* enemy

ennui [ānɥi] *nm* (*lassitude*) boredom; (*difficulté*) trouble *no pl*; **avoir des ~s** to have problems; **ennuyer** *vt* to bother; (*lasser*) to bore; **s'ennuyer** *vi* to be bored; **ennuyeux, -euse** *adj* boring, tedious; (*embêtant*) annoying

énoncé [enɔ̃se] *nm* (*de problème*) terms *pl*

énoncer [enɔ̃se] *vt* (*faits*) to set out, state

enorgueillir [ānɔrgœjir]: **s'~ de** *vt* to pride o.s. on

énorme [enɔrm] *adj* enormous, huge; **énormément** *adv* enormously; **énormément de neige/gens** an enormous amount of snow/number of people; **énormité** *nf* (*propos*) outrageous remark

enquérir [ākerir]: **s'~ de** *vt* to inquire about

enquête [āket] *nf* (*de journaliste, de police*) investigation; (*judiciaire, administrative*) inquiry; (*sondage d'opinion*) survey; **enquêter** *vi* to investigate

enquiers *etc* [ākje] *vb voir* **enquérir**

enquiquiner [ākikine] (*fam*) *vt* to annoy, irritate, bother

enraciné, e [ārasine] *adj* deep-rooted

enragé, e [āraʒe] *adj* (*MÉD*) rabid, with rabies; (*fig*) fanatical

enrageant, e [āraʒā, āt] *adj* infuriating

enrager [āraʒe] *vi* to be in a rage

enrayer [āreje] *vt* to check, stop

enregistrement [ār(ə)ʒistrəmā] *nm* recording; ~ **des bagages** (*à l'aéroport*) baggage check-in

enregistrer [ār(ə)ʒistre] *vt* (*MUS etc*) to record; (*fig: mémoriser*) to make a mental note of; (*bagages: à l'aéroport*) to check in

enrhumer [āryme] *vt*: **s'~, être enrhumé** to catch a cold

enrichir [āriʃir] *vt* to make rich(er); (*fig*) to enrich; **s'~** *vi* to get rich(er)

enrober [ārɔbe] *vt*: ~ **qch de** to coat sth with

enrôler [ārole] *vt* to enlist; **s'~ (dans)** to enlist (in)

enrouer [ārwe]: **s'~** *vi* to go hoarse

enrouler [ārule] *vt* (*fil, corde*) to wind (up)

ensanglanté, e [āsāglāte] *adj* covered with blood

enseignant, e [āsɛɲā, āt] *nm/f* teacher

enseigne [āsɛɲ] *nf* sign; ~ **lumineuse** neon sign

enseignement [āsɛɲ(ə)mā] *nm* teaching; (*ADMIN*) education

enseigner [āsɛɲe] *vt, vi* to teach; ~ **qch à qn** to teach sb sth

ensemble [āsābl] *adv* together ♦ *nm* (*groupement*) set; (*vêtements*) outfit; (*totalité*): **l'~ du/de la** the whole ou entire; (*unité, harmonie*) unity; **impression/idée d'~** overall ou general impression/idea; **dans l'~** (*en gros*) on the whole

ensemencer [ās(ə)māse] *vt* to sow

ensevelir [āsəv(ə)lir] *vt* to bury

ensoleillé, e [āsɔleje] *adj* sunny

ensommeillé, e [āsɔmeje] *adj* drowsy

ensorceler [āsɔrsəle] *vt* to enchant, bewitch

ensuite [āsɥit] *adv* then, next; (*plus tard*) afterwards, later

ensuivre [āsɥivr]: **s'~** *vi* to follow, ensue; **et tout ce qui s'ensuit** and all that goes with it

entaille [ātaj] *nf* cut; (*sur un objet*) notch

entamer [ātame] *vt* (*pain, bouteille*) to start; (*hostilités, pourparlers*) to open

entasser [ātase] *vt* (*empiler*) to pile up, heap up; **s'~** *vi* (*s'amonceler*) to pile up; **s'~ dans** (*personnes*) to cram into

entendre [ɑ̃tɑ̃dʀ] *vt* to hear; (*comprendre*) to understand; (*vouloir dire*) to mean; **s'~** *vi* (*sympathiser*) to get on; (*se mettre d'accord*) to agree; **j'ai entendu dire que** I've heard (it said) that

entendu, e [ɑ̃tɑ̃dy] *adj* (*réglé*) agreed; (*au courant: air*) knowing; **(c'est)** ~ all right, agreed; **bien** ~ of course

entente [ɑ̃tɑ̃t] *nf* understanding; (*accord, traité*) agreement; **à double** ~ (*sens*) with a double meaning

entériner [ɑ̃teʀine] *vt* to ratify, confirm

enterrement [ɑ̃tɛʀmɑ̃] *nm* (*cérémonie*) funeral, burial

enterrer [ɑ̃teʀe] *vt* to bury

entêtant, e [ɑ̃tɛtɑ̃, ɑ̃t] *adj* heady

entêté, e [ɑ̃tete] *adj* stubborn

en-tête [ɑ̃tɛt] *nm* heading; **papier à ~-~** headed notepaper

entêter [ɑ̃tete]: **s'~** *vi*: **s'~ (à faire)** to persist (in doing)

enthousiasme [ɑ̃tuzjasm] *nm* enthusiasm; **enthousiasmer** *vt* to fill with enthusiasm; **s'enthousiasmer (pour qch)** to get enthusiastic (about sth); **enthousiaste** *adj* enthusiastic

enticher [ɑ̃tiʃe]: **s'~ de** *vt* to become infatuated with

entier, -ère [ɑ̃tje, jɛʀ] *adj* whole; (*total: satisfaction etc*) complete; (*fig: caractère*) unbending ♦ *nm* (MATH) whole; **en** ~ totally, wholly; **lait** ~ full-cream milk; **entièrement** *adv* entirely, wholly

entonner [ɑ̃tɔne] *vt* (*chanson*) to strike up

entonnoir [ɑ̃tɔnwaʀ] *nm* funnel

entorse [ɑ̃tɔʀs] *nf* (MÉD) sprain; (*fig*): ~ **au règlement** infringement of the rule

entortiller [ɑ̃tɔʀtije] *vt* (*enrouler*) to twist, wind; (*fam: cajoler*) to get round

entourage [ɑ̃tuʀaʒ] *nm* circle; (*famille*) circle of family/friends; (*ce qui enclôt*) surround

entourer [ɑ̃tuʀe] *vt* to surround; (*apporter son soutien à*) to rally round; ~ **de** to surround with

entracte [ɑ̃tʀakt] *nm* interval

entraide [ɑ̃tʀɛd] *nf* mutual aid; **s'~r** *vi* to help each other

entrain [ɑ̃tʀɛ̃] *nm* spirit; **avec/sans** ~ spiritedly/half-heartedly

entraînement [ɑ̃tʀɛnmɑ̃] *nm* training

entraîner [ɑ̃tʀene] *vt* (*charrier*) to carry *ou* drag along; (TECH) to drive; (*emmener: personne*) to take (off); (*influencer*) to lead; (SPORT) to train; (*impliquer*) to entail; **s'~** *vi* (SPORT) to train; **s'~ à qch/à faire** to train o.s. for sth/to do; ~ **qn à faire** (*inciter*) to lead sb to do; **entraîneur, -euse** *nm/f* (SPORT) coach, trainer ♦ *nm* (HIPPISME) trainer

entraver [ɑ̃tʀave] *vt* (*action, progrès*) to hinder

entre [ɑ̃tʀ] *prép* between; (*parmi*) among(st); **l'un d'~ eux/nous** one of them/us; ~ **eux** among(st) themselves; **entrebâillé, e** *adj* half-open, ajar; **entrechoquer: s'entrechoquer** *vi* to knock *ou* bang together; **entrecôte** *nf* entrecôte *ou* rib steak; **entrecouper** *vt*: **entrecouper qch de** to intersperse sth with; **entrecroiser: s'entrecroiser** *vi* to intertwine

entrée [ɑ̃tʀe] *nf* entrance; (*accès: au cinéma etc*) admission; (*billet*) (admission) ticket; (CULIN) first course

entre...: entrefaites: sur ces entrefaites *adv* at this juncture; **entrefilet** *nm* paragraph (*short article*); **entrejambes** *nm* crotch; **entrelacer** *vt* to intertwine; **entremêler: s'entremêler** *vi* to become entangled; **entremets** *nm* (*cream*) dessert; **entremise** *nf* intervention; **par l'entremise de** through

entreposer [ɑ̃tʀəpoze] *vt* to store, put into storage

entrepôt [ɑ̃tʀəpo] *nm* warehouse

entreprenant, e [ɑ̃tʀəpʀənɑ̃, ɑ̃t] *adj* (*actif*) enterprising; (*trop galant*) forward

entreprendre [ɑ̃tʀəpʀɑ̃dʀ] *vt* (*se lancer dans*) to undertake; (*commencer*) to begin *ou* start (upon)

entrepreneur [ɑ̃tʀəpʀənœʀ, øz] *nm*: ~

(en bâtiment) (building) contractor

entreprise [ɑ̃trəpriz] *nf* (*société*) firm, concern; (*action*) undertaking, venture

entrer [ɑ̃tre] *vi* to go (*ou* come) in, enter ♦ *vt* (*INFORM*) to enter, input; **(faire) ~ qch dans** to get sth into; **~ dans** (*gén*) to enter; (*pièce*) to enter; (*club*) to join; (*heurter*) to run into; **~ à l'hôpital** to go into hospital; **faire ~** (*visiteur*) to show in

entresol [ɑ̃trəsɔl] *nm* mezzanine

entre-temps [ɑ̃trətɑ̃] *adv* meanwhile

entretenir [ɑ̃trət(ə)nir] *vt* to maintain; (*famille, maîtresse*) to support, keep; **~ qn (de)** to speak to sb (about)

entretien [ɑ̃trətjɛ̃] *nm* maintenance; (*discussion*) discussion, talk; (*pour un emploi*) interview

entrevoir [ɑ̃trəvwar] *vt* (*à peine*) to make out; (*brièvement*) to catch a glimpse of

entrevue [ɑ̃trəvy] *nf* (*audience*) interview

entrouvert, e [ɑ̃truver, ɛrt] *adj* half-open

énumérer [enymere] *vt* to list, enumerate

envahir [ɑ̃vair] *vt* to invade; (*suj: inquiétude, peur*) to come over; **envahissant, e** (*péj*) *adj* (*personne*) interfering, intrusive

enveloppe [ɑ̃v(ə)lɔp] *nf* (*de lettre*) envelope; (*crédits*) budget; **envelopper** *vt* to wrap; (*fig*) to envelop, shroud

envenimer [ɑ̃v(ə)nime] *vt* to aggravate

envergure [ɑ̃vergyr] *nf* (*fig*) scope; (*personne*) calibre

enverrai *etc* [ɑ̃vere] *vb voir* **envoyer**

envers [ɑ̃ver] *prép* towards, to ♦ *nm* other side; (*d'une étoffe*) wrong side; **à l'~** (*verticalement*) upside down; (*pull*) back to front; (*chaussettes*) inside out

envie [ɑ̃vi] *nf* (*sentiment*) envy; (*souhait*) desire, wish; **avoir ~ de (faire)** to feel like (doing); (*plus fort*) to want (to do); **avoir ~ que** to wish that; **cette glace me fait ~** I fancy some of that ice cream; **envier** *vt* to envy; **envieux, -euse** *adj* envious

environ [ɑ̃virɔ̃] *adv*: **~ 3 h/2 km** (around) about 3 o'clock/2 km; *voir aussi* **environs**

environnant, e [ɑ̃virɔnɑ̃, ɑ̃t] *adj* surrounding

environnement [ɑ̃virɔnmɑ̃] *nm* environment

environs [ɑ̃virɔ̃] *nmpl* surroundings; **aux ~ de** (round) about

envisager [ɑ̃vizaʒe] *vt* to contemplate, envisage; **~ de faire** to consider doing

envoi [ɑ̃vwa] *nm* (*paquet*) parcel, consignment; **coup d'~** (*SPORT*) kick-off

envoler [ɑ̃vɔle]: **s'~** *vi* (*oiseau*) to fly away; (*avion*) to take off; (*papier, feuille*) to blow away; (*fig*) to vanish (into thin air)

envoûter [ɑ̃vute] *vt* to bewitch

envoyé, e [ɑ̃vwaje] *nm/f* (*POL*) envoy; (*PRESSE*) correspondent

envoyer [ɑ̃vwaje] *vt* to send; (*lancer*) to hurl, throw; **~ chercher** to send for; **~ promener qn** (*fam*) to send sb packing

Éole [eɔl] *sigle m* (= *est-ouest-liaison-express*) *Paris high-speed, east-west subway service*

épagneul, e [epaɲœl] *nm/f* spaniel

épais, se [epe, ɛs] *adj* thick; **épaisseur** *nf* thickness

épancher [epɑ̃ʃe]: **s'~** *vi* to open one's heart

épanouir [epanwir]: **s'~** *vi* (*fleur*) to bloom, open out; (*visage*) to light up; (*personne*) to blossom

épargne [eparɲ] *nf* saving

épargner [eparɲe] *vt* to save; (*ne pas tuer ou endommager*) to spare ♦ *vi* to save; **~ qch à qn** to spare sb sth

éparpiller [eparpije] *vt* to scatter; **s'~** *vi* to scatter; (*fig*) to dissipate one's efforts

épars, e [epar, ars] *adj* scattered

épatant, e [epatɑ̃, ɑ̃t] (*fam*) *adj* super

épater [epate] (*fam*) *vt* (*étonner*) to amaze; (*impressionner*) to impress

épaule [epol] *nf* shoulder

épauler [epole] *vt* (*aider*) to back up, support; (*arme*) to raise (to one's shoulder) ♦ *vi* to (take) aim

épaulette [epolɛt] *nf* (*MIL*) epaulette; (*rembourrage*) shoulder pad

épave [epav] *nf* wreck

épée [epe] *nf* sword

épeler [ep(ə)le] *vt* to spell

éperdu, e [epɛʀdy] *adj* distraught, overcome; (*amour*) passionate

éperon [epʀɔ̃] *nm* spur

épervier [epɛʀvje] *nm* sparrowhawk

épi [epi] *nm* (*de blé, d'orge*) ear; (*de maïs*) cob

épice [epis] *nf* spice

épicé, e [epise] *adj* spicy

épicer [epise] *vt* to spice

épicerie [episʀi] *nf* grocer's shop; (*denrées*) groceries *pl*; ~ **fine** delicatessen; **épicier, -ière** *nm/f* grocer

épidémie [epidemi] *nf* epidemic

épiderme [epidɛʀm] *nm* skin

épier [epje] *vt* to spy on, watch closely

épilepsie [epilɛpsi] *nf* epilepsy

épiler [epile] *vt* (*jambes*) to remove the hair from; (*sourcils*) to pluck

épilogue [epilɔg] *nm* (*fig*) conclusion, dénouement; **épiloguer** *vi*: **épiloguer sur** to hold forth on

épinards [epinaʀ] *nmpl* spinach *sg*

épine [epin] *nf* thorn, prickle; (*d'oursin etc*) spine; ~ **dorsale** backbone; **épineux, -euse** *adj* thorny

épingle [epɛ̃gl] *nf* pin; ~ **à cheveux** hairpin; ~ **de nourrice** *ou* **de sûreté** safety pin; **épingler** *vt* (*badge, décoration*): **épingler qch sur** to pin sth on(to); (*fam*) to catch, nick

épique [epik] *adj* epic

épisode [epizɔd] *nm* episode; **film/roman à ~s** serial; **épisodique** *adj* occasional

éploré, e [eplɔʀe] *adj* tearful

épluche-légumes [eplyʃlegym] *nm inv* (potato) peeler

éplucher [eplyʃe] *vt* (*fruit, légumes*) to peel; (*fig*) to go over with a fine-tooth comb; **épluchures** *nfpl* peelings

éponge [epɔ̃ʒ] *nf* sponge; **éponger** *vt* (*liquide*) to mop up; (*surface*) to sponge; (*fig: déficit*) to soak up

épopée [epɔpe] *nf* epic

époque [epɔk] *nf* (*de l'histoire*) age, era; (*de l'année, la vie*) time; **d'~** (*meuble*) period *cpd*

époumoner [epumɔne]: **s'~** *vi* to shout o.s. hoarse

épouse [epuz] *nf* wife; **épouser** *vt* to marry

épousseter [epuste] *vt* to dust

époustouflant, e [epustuflɑ̃, ɑ̃t] (*fam*) *adj* staggering, mind-boggling

épouvantable [epuvɑ̃tabl] *adj* appalling, dreadful

épouvantail [epuvɑ̃taj] *nm* scarecrow

épouvante [epuvɑ̃t] *nf* terror; **film d'~** horror film; **épouvanter** *vt* to terrify

époux [epu] *nm* husband ♦ *nmpl* (married) couple

éprendre [epʀɑ̃dʀ]: **s'~ de** *vt* to fall in love with

épreuve [epʀœv] *nf* (*d'examen*) test; (*malheur, difficulté*) trial, ordeal; (*PHOTO*) proof; (*TYPO*) proof; (*SPORT*) event; **à toute ~** unfailing; **mettre à l'~** to put to the test

épris, e [epʀi, iz] *pp de* **éprendre**

éprouvant, e [epʀuvɑ̃, ɑ̃t] *adj* trying, testing

éprouver [epʀuve] *vt* (*tester*) to test; (*marquer, faire souffrir*) to afflict, distress; (*ressentir*) to experience

éprouvette [epʀuvɛt] *nf* test tube

épuisé, e [epɥize] *adj* exhausted; (*livre*) out of print; **épuisement** *nm* exhaustion

épuiser [epɥize] *vt* (*fatiguer*) to exhaust, wear *ou* tire out; (*stock, sujet*) to exhaust; **s'~** *vi* to wear *ou* tire o.s. out, exhaust o.s.

épuisette [epɥizɛt] *nf* shrimping net

épurer [epyʀe] *vt* (*liquide*) to purify; (*parti etc*) to purge

équateur [ekwatœʀ] *nm* equator; (**la république de**) **l'É~** Ecuador

équation [ekwasjɔ̃] *nf* equation

équerre [ekɛʀ] *nf* (*à dessin*) (set) square

équilibre [ekilibʀ] *nm* balance; **garder/perdre l'~** to keep/lose one's balance; **être en ~** to be balanced; **équilibré, e** *adj* well-balanced; **équilibrer** *vt* to balance; **s'équilibrer** *vi* (*poids*) to balance; (*fig: défauts etc*) to balance each other out

équipage [ekipaʒ] nm crew

équipe [ekip] nf team

équipé, e [ekipe] adj: **bien/mal ~** well-/poorly-equipped; **équipée** nf escapade

équipement [ekipmã] nm equipment; **~s** nmpl (installations) amenities, facilities

équiper [ekipe] vt to equip; **~ qn/qch de** to equip sb/sth with

équipier, -ière [ekipje, jɛʀ] nm/f team member

équitable [ekitabl] adj fair

équitation [ekitasjɔ̃] nf (horse-)riding; **faire de l'~** to go riding

équivalent, e [ekivalɑ̃, ɑ̃t] adj, nm equivalent

équivaloir [ekivalwaʀ]: **~ à** vt to be equivalent to

équivoque [ekivɔk] adj equivocal, ambiguous; (louche) dubious ♦ nf (incertitude) doubt

érable [eʀabl] nm maple

érafler [eʀafle] vt to scratch; **éraflure** nf scratch

éraillé, e [eʀaje] adj (voix) rasping

ère [ɛʀ] nf era; **en l'an 1050 de notre ~** in the year 1050 A.D.

érection [eʀɛksjɔ̃] nf erection

éreinter [eʀɛ̃te] vt to exhaust, wear out; (critiquer) to pull to pieces

ériger [eʀiʒe] vt (monument) to erect

ermite [ɛʀmit] nm hermit

éroder [eʀɔde] vt to erode

érotique [eʀɔtik] adj erotic

errer [eʀe] vi to wander

erreur [eʀœʀ] nf mistake, error; **faire ~** to be mistaken; **par ~** by mistake; **~ judiciaire** miscarriage of justice

érudit, e [eʀydi, it] adj erudite, learned

éruption [eʀypsjɔ̃] nf eruption; (MÉD) rash

es [ɛ] vb voir **être**

ès [ɛs] prép: **licencié ~ lettres/sciences** ≃ Bachelor of Arts/Science

escabeau, x [ɛskabo] nm (tabouret) stool; (échelle) stepladder

escadron [ɛskadʀɔ̃] nm squadron

escalade [ɛskalad] nf climbing no pl; (POL etc) escalation; **escalader** vt to climb

escale [ɛskal] nf (NAVIG: durée) call; (endroit) port of call; (AVIAT) stop(over); **faire ~ à** (NAVIG) to put in at; (AVIAT) to stop over at; **vol sans ~** nonstop flight

escalier [ɛskalje] nm stairs pl; **dans l'~** on the stairs; **~ roulant** escalator

escamoter [ɛskamɔte] vt (esquiver) to get round, evade; (faire disparaître) to conjure away

escapade [ɛskapad] nf: **faire une ~** to go on a jaunt; (s'enfuir) to run away ou off

escargot [ɛskaʀgo] nm snail

escarpé, e [ɛskaʀpe] adj steep

escarpin [ɛskaʀpɛ̃] nm low-fronted shoe, court shoe (BRIT)

escient [ɛsjɑ̃] nm: **à bon ~** advisedly

esclaffer [ɛsklafe]: **s'~** vi to guffaw

esclandre [ɛsklɑ̃dʀ] nm scene, fracas

esclavage [ɛsklavaʒ] nm slavery

esclave [ɛsklav] nm/f slave

escompte [ɛskɔ̃t] nm discount; **escompter** vt (fig) to expect

escorte [ɛskɔʀt] nf escort; **escorter** vt to escort

escrime [ɛskʀim] nf fencing

escrimer [ɛskʀime]: **s'~** vi: **s'~ à faire** to wear o.s. out doing

escroc [ɛskʀo] nm swindler, conman; **escroquer** [ɛskʀɔke] vt: **escroquer qch (à qn)** to swindle sth (out of sb); **escroquerie** nf swindle

espace [ɛspas] nm space

espacer [ɛspase] vt to space out; **s'~** vi (visites etc) to become less frequent

espadon [ɛspadɔ̃] nm swordfish inv

espadrille [ɛspadʀij] nf rope-soled sandal

Espagne [ɛspaɲ] nf: **l'~** Spain; **espagnol, e** adj Spanish ♦ nm/f: **Espagnol, e** Spaniard ♦ nm (LING) Spanish

escouade [ɛskwad] nf squad

espèce [ɛspɛs] nf (BIO, BOT, ZOOL) species inv; (gén: sorte) sort, kind, type; (péj): **~ de maladroit!** you clumsy oaf!; **~s** nfpl (COMM) cash sg; **en ~** in cash

espérance [ɛspeʀɑ̃s] nf hope; **~ de vie**

life expectancy

espérer [espere] *vt* to hope for; **j'espère (bien)** I hope so; **~ que/faire** to hope that/to do

espiègle [εspjεgl] *adj* mischievous

espion, ne [εspjɔ̃, jɔn] *nm/f* spy; **espionnage** *nm* espionage, spying; **espionner** *vt* to spy (up)on

esplanade [εsplanad] *nf* esplanade

espoir [εspwaʀ] *nm* hope

esprit [εspʀi] *nm* (*intellect*) mind; (*humour*) wit; (*mentalité, d'une loi etc, fantôme etc*) spirit; **faire de l'~** to try to be witty; **reprendre ses ~s** to come to; **perdre l'~** to lose one's mind

esquimau, de, x [εskimo, od] *adj* Eskimo ♦ *nm/f*: **E~, de** Eskimo ♦ *nm*: **E~** ® ice lolly (*BRIT*), popsicle (*US*)

esquinter [εskɛ̃te] (*fam*) *vt* to mess up

esquisse [εskis] *nf* sketch; **esquisser** *vt* to sketch; **esquisser un sourire** to give a vague smile

esquiver [εskive] *vt* to dodge; **s'~** *vi* to slip away

essai [εsε] *nm* (*tentative*) attempt, try; (*de produit*) testing; (*RUGBY*) try; (*LITTÉRATURE*) essay; **~s** *nmpl* (*AUTO*) trials; **~ gratuit** (*COMM*) free trial; **à l'~** on a trial basis

essaim [εsɛ̃] *nm* swarm

essayer [eseje] *vt* to try; (*vêtement, chaussures*) to try (on); (*méthode, voiture*) to try (out) ♦ *vi* to try; **~ de faire** to try *ou* attempt to do

essence [esɑ̃s] *nf* (*de voiture*) petrol (*BRIT*), gas(oline) (*US*); (*extrait de plante*) essence; (*espèce: d'arbre*) species *inv*

essentiel, le [esɑ̃sjεl] *adj* essential; **c'est l'~** (*ce qui importe*) that's the main thing; **l'~ de** the main part of

essieu, x [esjø] *nm* axle

essor [esɔʀ] *nm* (*de l'économie etc*) rapid expansion

essorer [esɔʀe] *vt* (*en tordant*) to wring (out); (*par la force centrifuge*) to spin-dry; **essoreuse** *nf* spin-dryer

essouffler [esufle]: **s'~** *vi* to get out of breath

essuie-glace [εsɥiglas] *nm inv* windscreen (*BRIT*) *ou* windshield (*US*) wiper

essuyer [esɥije] *vt* to wipe; (*fig: échec*) to suffer; **s'~** *vi* (*après le bain*) to dry o.s.; **~ la vaisselle** to dry up

est¹ [ε] *vb voir* **être**

est² [εst] *nm* east ♦ *adj inv* east; (*région*) east(ern); **à l'~** in the east; (*direction*) to the east, east(wards); **à l'~ de** (to the) east of

estampe [εstɑ̃p] *nf* print, engraving

est-ce que [εskə] *adv*: **~ c'est cher/c'était bon?** is it expensive/was it good?; **quand est-ce qu'il part?** when does he leave?, when is he leaving?; *voir aussi* **que**

esthéticienne [εstetisjεn] *nf* beautician

esthétique [εstetik] *adj* attractive

estimation [εstimasjɔ̃] *nf* valuation, (*chiffre*) estimate

estime [εstim] *nf* esteem, regard; **estimer** *vt* (*respecter*) to esteem; (*expertiser: bijou etc*) to value; (*évaluer: coût etc*) to assess, estimate; (*penser*): **estimer que/être** to consider that/o.s. to be

estival, e, -aux [εstival, o] *adj* summer *cpd*

estivant, e [εstivɑ̃, ɑ̃t] *nm/f* (summer) holiday-maker

estomac [εstɔma] *nm* stomach

estomaqué, e [εstɔmake] (*fam*) *adj* flabbergasted

estomper [εstɔ̃pe]: **s'~** *vi* (*sentiments*) to soften; (*contour*) to become blurred

estrade [εstʀad] *nf* platform, rostrum

estragon [εstʀagɔ̃] *nm* tarragon

estuaire [εstɥεʀ] *nm* estuary

et [e] *conj* and; **~ lui?** what about him?; **~ alors!** so what!

étable [etabl] *nf* cowshed

établi [etabli] *nm* (work)bench

établir [etabliʀ] *vt* (*papiers d'identité, facture*) to make out; (*liste, programme*) to draw up; (*entreprise*) to set up; (*réputation, usage, fait, culpabilité*) to establish; **s'~** *vi* to be established; **s'~ (à son compte)** to set up in business; **s'~ à/près de** to settle in/near

tablissement [etablismɑ̃] nm (entreprise, institution) establishment; **~ scolaire** school, educational establishment

tage [etaʒ] nm (d'immeuble) storey, floor; **à l'~** upstairs; **au 2ème ~** on the 2nd (BRIT) ou 3rd (US) floor

tagère [etaʒɛʀ] nf (rayon) shelf; (meuble) shelves pl

tai [etɛ] nm stay, prop

tain [etɛ̃] nm pewter no pl

tais etc [etɛ] vb voir **être**

tal [etal] nm stall

talage [etalaʒ] nm display; (devanture) display window; **faire ~ de** to show off, parade

taler [etale] vt (carte, nappe) to spread (out); (peinture) to spread; (échelonner: paiements, vacances) to spread, stagger; (marchandises) to display; (connaissances) to parade; **s'~** vi (liquide) to spread out; (fam) to fall flat on one's face; **s'~ sur** (suj: paiements etc) to be spread out over

talon [etalɔ̃] nm (cheval) stallion

tanche [etɑ̃ʃ] adj (récipient) watertight; (montre, vêtement) waterproof; **étancher** vt: **étancher sa soif** to quench one's thirst

tang [etɑ̃] nm pond

tant [etɑ̃] vb voir **être**; **donné**

tape [etap] nf stage; (lieu d'arrivée) stopping place; (: CYCLISME) staging point

tat [eta] nm (POL, condition) state; **en mauvais ~** in poor condition; **en ~ (de marche)** in (working) order; **remettre en ~** to repair; **hors d'~** out of order; **être en ~/hors d'~ de faire** to be in a/in no fit state to do; **être dans tous ses ~s** to be in a state; **faire ~ de** (alléguer) to put forward; **l'É~** the State; **~ civil** civil status; **~ des lieux** inventory of fixtures; **étatiser** vt to bring under state control; **état-major** nm (MIL) staff; **États-Unis** nmpl: **les États-Unis** the United States

tau, x [eto] nm vice (BRIT), vise (US)

étayer [eteje] vt to prop ou shore up

etc. [ɛtseteʀa] adv etc

et c(a)etera [ɛtseteʀa] adv et cetera, and so on

été [ete] pp de **être** ♦ nm summer

éteindre [etɛ̃dʀ] vt (lampe, lumière, radio) to turn ou switch off; (cigarette, feu) to put out, extinguish; **s'~** vi (feu, lumière) to go out; (mourir) to pass away; **éteint, e** adj (fig) lacklustre, dull; (volcan) extinct

étendard [etɑ̃daʀ] nm standard

étendre [etɑ̃dʀ] vt (pâte, liquide) to spread; (carte etc) to spread out; (linge) to hang up; (bras, jambes) to stretch out; (fig: agrandir) to extend; **s'~** vi (augmenter, se propager) to spread; (terrain, forêt etc) to stretch; (s'allonger) to stretch out; (se coucher) to lie down; (fig: expliquer) to elaborate

étendu, e [etɑ̃dy] adj extensive; **étendue** nf (d'eau, de sable) stretch, expanse; (importance) extent

éternel, le [etɛʀnɛl] adj eternal

éterniser [etɛʀnize]: **s'~** vi to last for ages; (visiteur) to stay for ages

éternité [etɛʀnite] nf eternity; **ça a duré une ~** it lasted for ages

éternuement [etɛʀnymɑ̃] nm sneeze

éternuer [etɛʀnɥe] vi to sneeze

êtes [ɛt(z)] vb voir **être**

éthique [etik] adj ethical

ethnie [ɛtni] nf ethnic group

éthylisme [etilism] nm alcoholism

étiez [etje] vb voir **être**

étinceler [etɛ̃s(ə)le] vi to sparkle

étincelle [etɛ̃sɛl] nf spark

étiqueter [etik(ə)te] vt to label

étiquette [etikɛt] nf label; (protocole): **l'~** etiquette

étirer [etiʀe]: **s'~** vi (personne) to stretch; (convoi, route): **s'~ sur** to stretch out over

étoffe [etɔf] nf material, fabric

étoffer [etɔfe] vt to fill out; **s'~** vi to fill out

étoile [etwal] nf star; **à la belle ~** in the open; **~ de mer** starfish; **~ filante** shoot-

ing star; **étoilé, e** *adj* starry
étonnant, e [etɔnɑ̃, ɑ̃t] *adj* amazing
étonnement [etɔnmɑ̃] *nm* surprise, amazement
étonner [etɔne] *vt* to surprise, amaze; **s'~ que/de** to be amazed that/at; **cela m'~ait (que)** (*j'en doute*) I'd be very surprised (if)
étouffant, e [etufɑ̃, ɑ̃t] *adj* stifling
étouffée [etufe]: **à l'~** *adv* (CULIN: *légumes*) steamed; (: *viande*) braised
étouffer [etufe] *vt* to suffocate; (*bruit*) to muffle; (*scandale*) to hush up ♦ *vi* to suffocate; **s'~** *vi* (*en mangeant etc*) to choke; **on étouffe** it's stifling
étourderie [eturdəri] *nf* (*caractère*) absent-mindedness *no pl*; (*faute*) thoughtless blunder
étourdi, e [eturdi] *adj* (*distrait*) scatterbrained, heedless
étourdir [eturdir] *vt* (*assommer*) to stun, daze; (*griser*) to make dizzy *ou* giddy; **étourdissement** *nm* dizzy spell
étourneau, x [eturno] *nm* starling
étrange [etrɑ̃ʒ] *adj* strange
étranger, -ère [etrɑ̃ʒe, ɛr] *adj* foreign; (*pas de la famille, non familier*) strange ♦ *nm/f* foreigner; stranger ♦ *nm*: **à l'~** abroad
étrangler [etrɑ̃gle] *vt* to strangle; **s'~** *vi* (*en mangeant etc*) to choke

---

MOT-CLÉ

être [etr] *nm* being; **être humain** human being
♦ *vb +attrib* **1** (*état, description*) to be; **il est instituteur** he is *ou* he's a teacher; **vous êtes grand/intelligent/fatigué** you are *ou* you're tall/clever/tired
2 (*+à: appartenir*) to be; **le livre est à Paul** the book is Paul's *ou* belongs to Paul; **c'est à moi/eux** it is *ou* it's mine/theirs
3 (*+de: provenance*): **il est de Paris** he is from Paris; (: *appartenance*): **il est des nôtres** he is one of us

4 (*date*): **nous sommes le 10 janvier** it' the 10th of January (today)
♦ *vi* to be; **je ne serai pas ici demain** won't be here tomorrow
♦ *vb aux* **1** to have; to be; **être arrivé. allé** to have arrived/gone; **il est parti** h has left, he has gone
2 (*forme passive*) to be; **être fait par** to b made by; **il a été promu** he has bee promoted
3 (*+à: obligation*): **c'est à réparer** it need repairing; **c'est à essayer** it should b tried
♦ *vb impers* **1**: **il est +adjectif** it is *+adjec tive*; **il est impossible de le faire** it's im possible to do it
2 (*heure, date*): **il est 10 heures, c'est 1** **heures** it is *ou* it's 10 o'clock
3 (*emphatique*): **c'est moi** it's me; **c'est** **lui de le faire** it's up to him to do it

---

étreindre [etrɛ̃dr] *vt* to clutch, grip (*amoureusement, amicalement*) to embrace **s'~** *vi* to embrace
étrenner [etrene] *vt* to use (*ou* wear) fo the first time; **étrennes** *nfpl* Christma box *sg*
étrier [etrije] *nm* stirrup
étriqué, e [etrike] *adj* skimpy
étroit, e [etrwa, wat] *adj* narrow (*vêtement*) tight; (*fig: liens, collaboration*) close; **à l'~** cramped; **~ d'esprit** narrow minded
étude [etyd] *nf* studying; (*ouvrage, rappor* study; (SCOL: *salle de travail*) study room **~s** *nfpl* (SCOL) studies; **être à l'~** (*proje etc*) to be under consideration; **faire de ~s (de droit/médecine)** to study (law medicine)
étudiant, e [etydjɑ̃, ɑ̃t] *nm/f* student
étudier [etydje] *vt, vi* to study
étui [etyi] *nm* case
étuve [etyv] *nf* steamroom
étuvée [etyve]: **à l'~** *adv* braised
eu, eue [y] *pp de* **avoir**
euh [ø] *excl* er

uro [øʀo] *nm* euro

Euroland [øʀɔlɑ̃d] *nm* Euroland

Europe [øʀɔp] *nf*: **l'~** Europe; **européen, ne** *adj* European ♦ *nm/f*: **Européen, ne** European

eus *etc* [y] *vb voir* **avoir**

eux [ø] *pron* (*sujet*) they; (*objet*) them

évacuer [evakɥe] *vt* to evacuate

évader [evade]: **s'~** *vi* to escape

évaluer [evalɥe] *vt* (*expertiser*) to appraise, evaluate; (*juger approximativement*) to estimate

évangile [evɑ̃ʒil] *nm* gospel

évanouir [evanwiʀ]: **s'~** *vi* to faint; (*disparaître*) to vanish, disappear; **évanouissement** *nm* (*syncope*) fainting fit

évaporer [evapɔʀe]: **s'~** *vi* to evaporate

évasé, e [evaze] *adj* (*manches, jupe*) flared

évasif, -ive [evazif, iv] *adj* evasive

évasion [evazjɔ̃] *nf* escape

évêché [eveʃe] *nm* bishop's palace

éveil [evɛj] *nm* awakening; **être en ~** to be alert; **éveillé, e** *adj* awake; (*vif*) alert, sharp; **éveiller** *vt* to (a)waken; (*soupçons etc*) to arouse; **s'éveiller** *vi* to (a)waken; (*fig*) to be aroused

événement [evenmɑ̃] *nm* event

éventail [evɑ̃taj] *nm* fan; (*choix*) range

éventaire [evɑ̃tɛʀ] *nm* stall, stand

éventer [evɑ̃te] *vt* (*secret*) to uncover; **s'~** *vi* (*parfum*) to go stale

éventualité [evɑ̃tɥalite] *nf* eventuality; possibility; **dans l'~ de** in the event of

éventuel, le [evɑ̃tɥɛl] *adj* possible; **éventuellement** *adv* possibly

évêque [evɛk] *nm* bishop

évertuer [evɛʀtɥe]: **s'~** *vi*: **s'~ à faire** to try very hard to do

éviction [eviksjɔ̃] *nf* (*de locataire*) eviction

évidemment [evidamɑ̃] *adv* (*bien sûr*) of course; (*certainement*) obviously

évidence [evidɑ̃s] *nf* obviousness; (*fait*) obvious fact; **de toute ~** quite obviously *ou* evidently; **être en ~** to be clearly visible; **mettre en ~** (*fait*) to highlight; **évident, e** *adj* obvious, evident; **ce n'est**

pas évident! (*fam*) it's not that easy!

évider [evide] *vt* to scoop out

évier [evje] *nm* (kitchen) sink

évincer [evɛ̃se] *vt* to oust

éviter [evite] *vt* to avoid; **~ de faire** to avoid doing; **~ qch à qn** to spare sb sth

évolué, e [evɔlɥe] *adj* advanced

évoluer [evɔlɥe] *vi* (*enfant, maladie*) to develop; (*situation, moralement*) to evolve, develop; (*aller et venir*) to move about; **évolution** *nf* development, evolution

évoquer [evɔke] *vt* to call to mind, evoke; (*mentionner*) to mention

ex... [ɛks] *préfixe* ex-

exact, e [ɛgza(kt), ɛgzakt] *adj* exact; (*correct*) correct; (*ponctuel*) punctual; **l'heure ~e** the right *ou* exact time; **exactement** *adv* exactly

ex aequo [ɛgzeko] *adj* equally placed; **arriver ~** to finish neck and neck

exagéré, e [ɛgzaʒeʀe] *adj* (*prix etc*) excessive

exagérer [ɛgzaʒeʀe] *vt* to exaggerate ♦ *vi* to exaggerate; (*abuser*) to go too far

exalter [ɛgzalte] *vt* (*enthousiasmer*) to excite, elate

examen [ɛgzamɛ̃] *nm* examination; (*SCOL*) exam(ination); **à l'~** under consideration

examinateur, -trice [ɛgzaminatœʀ, tʀis] *nm/f* examiner

examiner [ɛgzamine] *vt* to examine

exaspérant, e [ɛgzaspeʀɑ̃, ɑ̃t] *adj* exasperating

exaspérer [ɛgzaspeʀe] *vt* to exasperate

exaucer [ɛgzose] *vt* (*vœu*) to grant

excédent [ɛksedɑ̃] *nm* surplus; **en ~** surplus; **~ de bagages** excess luggage

excéder [ɛksede] *vt* (*dépasser*) to exceed; (*agacer*) to exasperate

excellent, e [ɛkselɑ̃, ɑ̃t] *adj* excellent

excentrique [ɛksɑ̃tʀik] *adj* eccentric

excepté, e [ɛksɛpte] *adj, prép*: **les élèves ~s, ~ les élèves** except for the pupils

exception [ɛksɛpsjɔ̃] *nf* exception; **à l'~ de** except for, with the exception of; **d'~** (*mesure, loi*) special, exceptional; **excep-**

tionnel, le *adj* exceptional; **exception-nellement** *adv* exceptionally

excès [ɛksɛ] *nm* surplus ♦ *nmpl* excesses; **faire des ~** to overindulge; **~ de vitesse** speeding *no pl*; **excessif, -ive** *adj* excessive

excitant, e [ɛksitɑ̃, ɑ̃t] *adj* exciting ♦ *nm* stimulant; **excitation** *nf* (*état*) excitement

exciter [ɛksite] *vt* to excite; (*suj: café etc*) to stimulate; **s'~** *vi* to get excited

exclamation [ɛksklamasjɔ̃] *nf* exclamation

exclamer [ɛksklame]: **s'~** *vi* to exclaim

exclure [ɛksklyʀ] *vt* (*faire sortir*) to expel; (*ne pas compter*) to exclude, leave out; (*rendre impossible*) to exclude, rule out; **il est exclu que** it's out of the question that ...; **il n'est pas exclu que ...** it's not impossible that ...; **exclusif, -ive** *adj* exclusive; **exclusion** *nf* exclusion; **à l'exclusion de** with the exclusion *ou* exception of; **exclusivité** *nf* (*COMM*) exclusive rights *pl*; **film passant en exclusivité à** film showing only at

excursion [ɛkskyʀsjɔ̃] *nf* (*en autocar*) excursion, trip; (*à pied*) walk, hike

excuse [ɛkskyz] *nf* excuse; **~s** *nfpl* (*regret*) apology *sg*, apologies; **excuser** *vt* to excuse; **s'excuser (de)** to apologize (for); **"excusez-moi"** "I'm sorry"; (*pour attirer l'attention*) "excuse me"

exécrable [ɛgzekʀabl] *adj* atrocious

exécuter [ɛgzekyte] *vt* (*tuer*) to execute; (*tâche etc*) to execute, carry out; (*MUS: jouer*) to perform, execute; **s'~** *vi* to comply; **exécutif, -ive** *adj, nm* (*POL*) executive; **exécution** *nf* execution; **mettre à exécution** to carry out

exemplaire [ɛgzɑ̃plɛʀ] *nm* copy

exemple [ɛgzɑ̃pl] *nm* example; **par ~** for instance, for example; **donner l'~** to set an example

exempt, e [ɛgzɑ̃, ɑ̃(p)t] *adj*: **~ de** (*dispensé de*) exempt from; (*sans*) free from

exercer [ɛgzɛʀse] *vt* (*pratiquer*) to exercise, practise; (*influence, contrôle*) to exert; (*former*) to exercise, train; **s'~** *vi* (*sportif, mu-*

sicien) to practise

exercice [ɛgzɛʀsis] *nm* exercise

exhaustif, -ive [ɛgzostif, iv] *adj* exhaustive

exhiber [ɛgzibe] *vt* (*montrer: papiers, certificat*) to present, produce; (*péj*) to display, flaunt; **s'~** *vi* to parade; (*suj: exhibitionniste*) to expose o.s.; **exhibitionniste** [ɛgzibisjɔnist] *nm/f* flasher

exhorter [ɛgzɔʀte] *vt* to urge

exigeant, e [ɛgziʒɑ̃, ɑ̃t] *adj* demanding (*péj*) hard to please

exigence [ɛgziʒɑ̃s] *nf* demand, requirement

exiger [ɛgziʒe] *vt* to demand, require

exigu, ë [ɛgzigy] *adj* cramped, tiny

exil [ɛgzil] *nm* exile; **exiler** *vt* to exile; **s'exiler** *vi* to go into exile

existence [ɛgzistɑ̃s] *nf* existence

exister [ɛgziste] *vi* to exist; **il existe un/des** there is a/are (some)

exonérer [ɛgzɔneʀe] *vt*: **~ de** to exempt from

exorbitant, e [ɛgzɔʀbitɑ̃, ɑ̃t] *adj* exorbitant

exorbité, e [ɛgzɔʀbite] *adj*: **yeux ~s** bulging eyes

exotique [ɛgzɔtik] *adj* exotic; **yaourt au fruits ~s** tropical fruit yoghurt

expatrier [ɛkspatʀije] *vt*: **s'~** to leave one's country

expectative [ɛkspɛktativ] *nf*: **être dans l'~** to be still waiting

expédient [ɛkspedjɑ̃, jɑ̃t] (*péj*) *nm*: **vivre d'~s** to live by one's wits

expédier [ɛkspedje] *vt* (*lettre, paquet*) to send; (*troupes*) to dispatch; (*fam: travail etc*) to dispose of, dispatch; **expéditeur, -trice** *nm/f* sender; **expédition** *nf* sending; (*scientifique, sportive, MIL*) expedition

expérience [ɛkspeʀjɑ̃s] *nf* (*de la vie*) experience; (*scientifique*) experiment

expérimenté, e [ɛkspeʀimɑ̃te] *adj* experienced

expérimenter [ɛkspeʀimɑ̃te] *vt* to test out, experiment with

expert, e [ɛkspɛʀ, ɛʀt] *adj, nm* expert; **expert-comptable** *nm* ≃ chartered accountant (BRIT), ≃ certified public accountant (US)

expertise [ɛkspɛʀtiz] *nf* (évaluation) expert evaluation

expertiser [ɛkspɛʀtize] *vt* (objet de valeur) to value; (voiture accidentée etc) to assess damage to

expier [ɛkspje] *vt* to expiate, atone for

expirer [ɛkspiʀe] *vi* (prendre fin, mourir) to expire; (respirer) to breathe out

explicatif, -ive [ɛksplikatif, iv] *adj* explanatory

explication [ɛksplikasjɔ̃] *nf* explanation; (discussion) discussion; (dispute) argument; **~ de texte** (SCOL) critical analysis

explicite [ɛksplisit] *adj* explicit

expliquer [ɛksplike] *vt* to explain; **s'~** to explain (o.s.); **s'~ avec qn** (discuter) to explain o.s. to sb; **son erreur s'explique** one can understand his mistake

exploit [ɛksplwa] *nm* exploit, feat; **exploitant, e** *nm/f*: **exploitant (agricole)** farmer

exploitation *nf* exploitation; (d'une entreprise) running; **~ agricole** farming concern; **exploiter** *vt* (personne, don) to exploit; (entreprise, ferme) to run, operate; (mine) to exploit, work

explorer [ɛksplɔʀe] *vt* to explore

exploser [ɛksploze] *vi* to explode, blow up; (engin explosif) to go off; (personne: de colère) to flare up; **explosif, -ive** *adj, nm* explosive; **explosion** *nf* explosion

exportateur, -trice [ɛkspɔʀtatœʀ, tʀis] *adj* export *cpd*, exporting ♦ *nm* exporter

exportation [ɛkspɔʀtasjɔ̃] *nf* (action) exportation; (produit) export

exporter [ɛkspɔʀte] *vt* to export

exposant [ɛkspozɑ̃] *nm* exhibitor

exposé, e [ɛkspoze] *nm* talk ♦ *adj*: **~ au sud** facing south

exposer [ɛkspoze] *vt* (marchandise) to display; (peinture) to exhibit, show; (parler de) to explain, set out; (mettre en danger,

orienter, PHOTO) to expose; **exposition** *nf* (manifestation) exhibition; (PHOTO) exposure

exprès¹ [ɛkspʀɛ] *adv* (délibérément) on purpose; (spécialement) specially

exprès², -esse [ɛkspʀɛs] *adj* (ordre, défense) express, formal ♦ *adj inv* (PTT) express ♦ *adv* express

express [ɛkspʀɛs] *adj, nm*: **(café) ~** espresso (coffee); **(train) ~** fast train

expressément [ɛkspʀesemɑ̃] *adv* (spécialement) specifically

expressif, -ive [ɛkspʀesif, iv] *adj* expressive

expression [ɛkspʀesjɔ̃] *nf* expression

exprimer [ɛkspʀime] *vt* (sentiment, idée) to express; (jus, liquide) to press out; **s'~** *vi* (personne) to express o.s

exproprier [ɛkspʀɔpʀije] *vt* to buy up by compulsory purchase, expropriate

expulser [ɛkspylse] *vt* to expel; (locataire) to evict; (SPORT) to send off

exquis, e [ɛkski, iz] *adj* exquisite

extase [ɛkstaz] *nf* ecstasy; **extasier: s'extasier sur** *vt* to go into raptures over

extension [ɛkstɑ̃sjɔ̃] *nf* (fig) extension

exténuer [ɛkstenɥe] *vt* to exhaust

extérieur, e [ɛksteʀjœʀ] *adj* (porte, mur etc) outer, outside; (au dehors: escalier, w.-c.) outside; (commerce) foreign; (influences) external; (apparent: calme, gaieté etc) surface *cpd* ♦ *nm* (d'une maison, d'un récipient etc) outside, exterior; (apparence) exterior; **à l'~** outside; (à l'étranger) abroad; **extérieurement** *adv* on the outside; (en apparence) on the surface

exterminer [ɛkstɛʀmine] *vt* to exterminate, wipe out

externat [ɛkstɛʀna] *nm* day school

externe [ɛkstɛʀn] *adj* external, outer ♦ *nm/f* (MÉD) non-resident medical student (BRIT), extern (US); (SCOL) day pupil

extincteur [ɛkstɛ̃ktœʀ] *nm* (fire) extinguisher

extinction [ɛkstɛ̃ksjɔ̃] *nf*: **~ de voix** loss of voice

extorquer [ɛkstɔʀke] *vt* to extort
extra [ɛkstʀa] *adj inv* first-rate; (*fam*) fantastic ♦ *nm inv* extra help
extrader [ɛkstʀade] *vt* to extradite
extraire [ɛkstʀɛʀ] *vt* to extract; **extrait** *nm* extract
extraordinaire [ɛkstʀaɔʀdinɛʀ] *adj* extraordinary; (*POL: mesures etc*) special
extravagant, e [ɛkstʀavagɑ̃, ɑ̃t] *adj* extravagant
extraverti, e [ɛkstʀavɛʀti] *adj* extrovert
extrême [ɛkstʀɛm] *adj, nm* extreme; **extrêmement** *adv* extremely; **extrême-onction** *nf* last rites *pl*; **Extrême-Orient** *nm* Far East
extrémité [ɛkstʀemite] *nf* end; (*situation*) straits *pl*, plight; (*geste désespéré*) extreme action; **~s** *nfpl* (*pieds et mains*) extremities
exubérant, e [ɛgzybeʀɑ̃, ɑ̃t] *adj* exuberant
exutoire [ɛgzytwaʀ] *nm* outlet, release

F, f

F *abr* = **franc**
fa [fa] *nm inv* (*MUS*) F; (*en chantant la gamme*) fa
fable [fabl] *nf* fable
fabricant [fabʀikɑ̃, ɑ̃t] *nm* manufacturer
fabrication [fabʀikasjɔ̃] *nf* manufacture
fabrique [fabʀik] *nf* factory; **fabriquer** *vt* to make; (*industriellement*) to manufacture; (*fig*): **qu'est-ce qu'il fabrique?** (*fam*) what is he doing?
fabulation [fabylasjɔ̃] *nf* fantasizing
fac [fak] (*fam*) *abr f* (*SCOL*) = **faculté**
façade [fasad] *nf* front, façade
face [fas] *nf* face; (*fig: aspect*) side ♦ *adj*: **le côté ~** heads; **en ~ de** opposite; (*fig*) in front of; **de ~** (*voir*) face on; **~ à** facing; (*fig*) faced with, in the face of; **faire ~ à** to face; **~ à ~** *adv* facing each other ♦ *nm inv* encounter
fâché, e [faʃe] *adj* angry; (*désolé*) sorry
fâcher [faʃe] *vt* to anger; **se ~** *vi* to get angry; **se ~ avec** (*se brouiller*) to fall out with
fâcheux, -euse [faʃø, øz] *adj* unfortunate, regrettable
facile [fasil] *adj* easy; (*caractère*) easygoing; **facilement** *adv* easily
facilité *nf* easiness; (*disposition, don*) aptitude; **facilités de paiement** easy terms; **faciliter** *vt* to make easier
façon [fasɔ̃] *nf* (*manière*) way; (*d'une robe etc*) making-up, cut; **~s** *nfpl* (*péj*) fuss *sg*; **de ~ à/à ce que** so as to/that; **de toute ~** anyway, in any case
façonner [fasɔne] *vt* (*travailler: matière*) to shape, fashion
facteur, -trice [faktœʀ] *nm/f* postman(-woman) (*BRIT*), mailman(-woman) (*US*) ♦ *nm* (*MATH: fig: élément*) factor
factice [faktis] *adj* artificial
faction [faksjɔ̃] *nf* faction; **être de ~** to be on guard (duty)
facture [faktyʀ] *nf* (*à payer: gén*) bill; invoice
facturer [faktyʀe] *vt* to invoice
facultatif, -ive [fakyltatif, iv] *adj* optional
faculté [fakylte] *nf* (*intellectuelle, d'université*) faculty; (*pouvoir, possibilité*) power
fade [fad] *adj* insipid
fagot [fago] *nm* bundle of sticks
faible [fɛbl] *adj* weak; (*voix, lumière, vent*) faint; (*rendement, revenu*) low ♦ *nm* (*pour quelqu'un*) weakness, soft spot; **faiblesse** *nf* weakness; **faiblir** *vi* to weaken; (*lumière*) to dim; (*vent*) to drop
faïence [fajɑ̃s] *nf* earthenware *no pl*
faignant, e [fɛɲɑ̃, ɑ̃t] *nm/f* = **fainéant, e**
faille [faj] *vb voir* **falloir** ♦ *nf* (*GÉO*) fault; (*fig*) flaw, weakness
faillir [fajiʀ] *vi*: **j'ai failli tomber** I almost *ou* very nearly fell
faillite [fajit] *nf* bankruptcy
faim [fɛ̃] *nf* hunger; **avoir ~** to be hungry; **rester sur sa ~** (*aussi fig*) to be left wanting more
fainéant, e [fɛneɑ̃, ɑ̃t] *nm/f* idler, loafer

MOT-CLÉ
---

faire [fɛʀ] *vt* **1** (*fabriquer, être l'auteur de*) to make; **faire du vin/une offre/un film** to make wine/an offer/a film; **faire du bruit** to make a noise

2 (*effectuer: travail, opération*) to do; **que faites-vous?** (*quel métier etc*) what do you do?; (*quelle activité: au moment de la question*) what are you doing?; **faire la lessive** to do the washing

3 (*études*) to do; (*sport, musique*) to play; **faire du droit/du français** to do law/French; **faire du rugby/piano** to play rugby/the piano

4 (*simuler*): **faire le malade/l'ignorant** to act the invalid/the fool

5 (*transformer, avoir un effet sur*): **faire de qn un frustré/avocat** to make sb frustrated/a lawyer; **ça ne me fait rien** (*m'est égal*) I don't care *ou* mind; (*me laisse froid*) it has no effect on me; **ça ne fait rien** it doesn't matter; **faire que** (*impliquer*) to mean that

6 (*calculs, prix, mesures*): **2 et 2 font 4** 2 and 2 are *ou* make 4; **ça fait 10 m/15 F** it's 10 m/15F; **je vous le fais 10 F** I'll let you have it for 10F

7: **qu'a-t-il fait de sa valise?** what has he done with his case?

8: **ne faire que: il ne fait que critiquer** (*sans cesse*) all he (ever) does is criticize; (*seulement*) he's only criticizing

9 (*dire*) to say; **"vraiment?" fit-il** "really?" he said

10 (*maladie*) to have; **faire du diabète** to have diabetes *sg*

♦ *vi* **1** (*agir, s'y prendre*) to act, do; **il faut faire vite** (*ou* you *etc*) must act quickly; **comment a-t-il fait pour?** how did he manage to?; **faites comme chez vous** make yourself at home

2 (*paraître*) to look; **faire vieux/démodé** to look old/old-fashioned; **ça fait bien** it looks good

♦ *vb substitut* to do; **ne le casse pas**

comme je l'ai fait don't break it as I did; **je peux le voir? - faites!** can I see it? - please do!

♦ *vb impers* **1**: **il fait beau** *etc* the weather is fine *etc*; *voir aussi* **jour**; **froid** *etc*

2 (*temps écoulé, durée*): **ça fait 2 ans qu'il est parti** it's 2 years since he left; **ça fait 2 ans qu'il y est** he's been there for 2 years

♦ *vb semi-aux* **1**: **faire** +*infinitif* (*action directe*) to make; **faire tomber/bouger qch** to make sth fall/move; **faire démarrer un moteur/chauffer de l'eau** to start up an engine/heat some water; **cela fait dormir** it makes you sleep; **faire travailler les enfants** to make the children work *ou* get the children to work

2 (*indirectement, par un intermédiaire*): **faire réparer qch** to get *ou* have sth repaired; **faire punir les enfants** to have the children punished

se faire *vi* **1** (*vin, fromage*) to mature

2: **cela se fait beaucoup/ne se fait pas** it's done a lot/not done

3: **se faire** +*nom ou pron*: **se faire une jupe** to make o.s. a skirt; **se faire des amis** to make friends; **se faire du souci** to worry; **il ne s'en fait pas** he doesn't worry

4: **se faire** +*adj* (*devenir*): **se faire vieux** to be getting old; (*délibérément*): **se faire beau** to do o.s. up

5: **se faire à** (*s'habituer*) to get used to; **je n'arrive pas à me faire à la nourriture/au climat** I can't get used to the food/climate

6: **se faire** +*infinitif*: **se faire examiner la vue/opérer** to have one's eyes tested/to have an operation; **se faire couper les cheveux** to get one's hair cut; **il va se faire tuer/punir** he's going to get himself killed/get (himself) punished; **il s'est fait aider** he got somebody to help him; **il s'est fait aider par Simon** he got Simon to help him; **se faire faire un vêtement** to get a garment made for o.s.

7 (*impersonnel*): **comment se fait-il/faisait-il que?** how is it/was it that?

faire-part [fɛʀpaʀ] *nm inv* announcement (*of birth, marriage etc*)

faisable [fəzabl] *adj* feasible

faisan, e [fəzɑ̃, an] *nm/f* pheasant; **faisandé, e** *adj* high (*bad*)

faisceau, x [fɛso] *nm* (*de lumière etc*) beam

faisons [fəzɔ̃] *vb voir* **faire**

fait, e [fɛ, fɛt] *adj* (*mûr: fromage, melon*) ripe ♦ *nm* (*événement*) event, occurrence; (*réalité, donnée*) fact; **être au ~ (de)** to be informed (of); **au ~** (*à propos*) by the way; **en venir au ~** to get to the point; **du ~ de ceci/qu'il a menti** because of *ou* on account of this/his having lied; **de ce ~** for this reason; **en ~** in fact; **prendre qn sur le ~** to catch sb in the act; **~ divers** news item

faîte [fɛt] *nm* top; (*fig*) pinnacle, height

faites [fɛt] *vb voir* **faire**

faitout [fɛtu] *nm*, **fait-tout** [fɛtu] *nm inv* stewpot

falaise [falɛz] *nf* cliff

falloir [falwaʀ] *vb impers*: **il faut qu'il parte/a fallu qu'il parte** (*obligation*) he has to *ou* must leave/had to leave; **il a fallu le faire** it had to be done; **il faut faire attention** you have to be careful; **il me faudrait 100 F** I would need 100 F; **il vous faut tourner à gauche après l'église** you have to turn left past the church; **nous avons ce qu'il (nous) faut** we have what we need; **s'en ~: il s'en est fallu de 100 F/5 minutes** we/they *etc* were 100 F short/5 minutes late (*ou* early); **il s'en faut de beaucoup qu'il soit** he is far from being; **il s'en est fallu de peu que cela n'arrive** it very nearly happened

falsifier [falsifje] *vt* to falsify, doctor

famé, e [fame] *adj*: **mal ~** disreputable, of ill repute

famélique [famelik] *adj* half-starved

fameux, -euse [famø, øz] *adj* (*illustre*) famous; (*bon: repas, plat etc*) first-rate, first-class; (*valeur intensive*) real, downright

familial, e, -aux [familjal, jo] *adj* family *cpd*

familiarité [familjaʀite] *nf* familiarity; **~s** *nfpl* (*privautés*) familiarities

familier, -ère [familje, jɛʀ] *adj* (*connu*) familiar; (*atmosphère*) informal, friendly; (*LING*) informal, colloquial ♦ *nm* regular (*visitor*)

famille [famij] *nf* family; **il a de la ~ à Paris** he has relatives in Paris

famine [famin] *nf* famine

fanatique [fanatik] *adj* fanatical ♦ *nm/f* fanatic; **fanatisme** *nm* fanaticism

faner [fane]: **se ~** *vi* to fade

fanfare [fɑ̃faʀ] *nf* (*orchestre*) brass band; (*musique*) fanfare

fanfaron, ne [fɑ̃faʀɔ̃, ɔn] *nm/f* braggart

fantaisie [fɑ̃tezi] *nf* (*spontanéité*) fancy, imagination; (*caprice*) whim ♦ *adj*: **bijou ~** costume jewellery; **fantaisiste** (*péj*) *adj* unorthodox, eccentric

fantasme [fɑ̃tasm] *nm* fantasy

fantasque [fɑ̃task] *adj* whimsical, capricious

fantastique [fɑ̃tastik] *adj* fantastic

fantôme [fɑ̃tom] *nm* ghost, phantom

faon [fɑ̃] *nm* fawn

farce [faʀs] *nf* (*viande*) stuffing; (*blague*) (practical) joke; (*THÉÂTRE*) farce; **farcir** *vt* (*viande*) to stuff

fardeau, x [faʀdo] *nm* burden

farder [faʀde]: **se ~** *vi* to make (o.s.) up

farfelu, e [faʀfəly] *adj* hare-brained

farine [faʀin] *nf* flour; **farineux, -euse** *adj* (*sauce, pomme*) floury

farouche [faʀuʃ] *adj* (*timide*) shy, timid

fart [faʀt] *nm* (ski) wax

fascicule [fasikyl] *nm* volume

fascination [fasinasjɔ̃] *nf* fascination

fasciner [fasine] *vt* to fascinate

fascisme [faʃism] *nm* fascism

fasse *etc* [fas] *vb voir* **faire**

faste [fast] *nm* splendour

fastidieux, -euse [fastidjø, jøz] *adj* tedious, tiresome

fastueux, -euse [fastyø, øz] *adj* sumptuous, luxurious

fatal, e [fatal] *adj* fatal; (*inévitable*) inevitable; **fatalité** *nf* (*destin*) fate; (*coïncidence*) fateful coincidence

fatidique [fatidik] *adj* fateful

fatigant, e [fatigã, ãt] *adj* tiring; (*agaçant*) tiresome

fatigue [fatig] *nf* tiredness, fatigue; **fatigué, e** *adj* tired; **fatiguer** *vt* to tire, make tired; (*fig: agacer*) to annoy ♦ *vi* (*moteur*) to labour, strain; **se fatiguer** to get tired

fatras [fatra] *nm* jumble, hotchpotch

faubourg [fobuR] *nm* suburb

fauché, e [foʃe] (*fam*) *adj* broke

faucher [foʃe] *vt* (*herbe*) to cut; (*champs, blés*) to reap; (*fig: véhicule*) to mow down; (*fam: voler*) to pinch

faucille [fosij] *nf* sickle

faucon [fokɔ̃] *nm* falcon, hawk

faudra [fodra] *vb voir* **falloir**

faufiler [fofile]: **se ~** *vi*: **se ~ dans** to edge one's way into; **se ~ parmi/entre** to thread one's way among/between

faune [fon] *nf* (*ZOOL*) wildlife, fauna

faussaire [foseR] *nm* forger

fausse [fos] *adj voir* **faux**; **faussement** *adv* (*accuser*) wrongly, wrongfully; (*croire*) falsely

fausser [fose] *vt* (*objet*) to bend, buckle; (*fig*) to distort; **~ compagnie à qn** to give sb the slip

faut [fo] *vb voir* **falloir**

faute [fot] *nf* (*erreur*) mistake, error; (*mauvaise action*) misdemeanour; (*FOOTBALL etc*) offence; (*TENNIS*) fault; **c'est de sa/ma ~** it's his/my fault; **être en ~** to be in the wrong; **~ de** (*temps, argent*) for *ou* through lack of; **sans ~** without fail; **~ de frappe** typing error; **~ de goût** error of taste; **~ professionnelle** professional misconduct *no pl*

fauteuil [fotœj] *nm* armchair; **~ roulant** wheelchair

fauteur [fotœR] *nm*: **~ de troubles** trouble-maker

fautif, -ive [fotif, iv] *adj* (*responsable*) at fault, in the wrong; (*incorrect*) incorrect, inaccurate; **il se sentait ~** he felt guilty

fauve [fov] *nm* wildcat ♦ *adj* (*couleur*) fawn

faux¹ [fo] *nf* scythe

faux², fausse [fo, fos] *adj* (*inexact*) wrong; (*voix*) out of tune; (*billet*) fake, forged; (*sournois, postiche*) false ♦ *adv* (*MUS*) out of tune ♦ *nm* (*copie*) fake, forgery; (*opposé au vrai*): **le ~** falsehood; **faire ~ bond à qn** to stand sb up; **fausse alerte** false alarm; **fausse couche** miscarriage; **~ frais** ♦ *nmpl* extras, incidental expenses; **~ pas** tripping *no pl*; (*fig*) faux pas; **~ témoignage** (*délit*) perjury; **faux-filet** *nm* sirloin; **faux-monnayeur** *nm* counterfeiter, forger

faveur [favœR] *nf* favour; **traitement de ~** preferential treatment; **en ~ de** in favour of

favorable [favɔRabl] *adj* favourable

favori, te [favɔRi, it] *adj, nm/f* favourite

favoriser [favɔRize] *vt* to favour

fax [faks] *nm* fax; **faxer** *vt* to fax

FB *abr* (= *franc belge*) BF

fébrile [febRil] *adj* feverish, febrile

fécond, e [fekɔ̃, ɔ̃d] *adj* fertile; **féconder** *vt* to fertilize; **fécondité** *nf* fertility

fécule [fekyl] *nf* potato flour; **féculent** *nm* starchy food

fédéral, e, -aux [federal, o] *adj* federal

fée [fe] *nf* fairy; **féerique** *adj* magical, fairytale *cpd*

feignant, e [fɛɲã, ãt] *nm/f* = **fainéant, e**

feindre [fɛ̃dR] *vt* to feign; **~ de faire** to pretend to do

feinte [fɛ̃t] *nf* (*SPORT*) dummy

fêler [fele] *vt* to crack

félicitations [felisitasjɔ̃] *nfpl* congratulations

féliciter [felisite] *vt*: **~ qn (de)** to congratulate sb (on)

félin, e [felɛ̃, in] *nm* (big) cat

fêlure [felyʀ] *nf* crack

femelle [fəmɛl] *adj, nf* female

féminin, e [feminɛ̃, in] *adj* feminine; (*sexe*) female; (*équipe, vêtements etc*) women's ♦ *nm* (LING) feminine; **féministe** [feminist] *adj* feminist

femme [fam] *nf* woman; (*épouse*) wife; **~ au foyer** housewife; **~ de chambre** chambermaid; **~ de ménage** cleaning lady

fémur [femyʀ] *nm* femur, thighbone

fendre [fɑ̃dʀ] *vt* (*couper en deux*) to split; (*fissurer*) to crack; (*traverser: foule, air*) to cleave through; **se ~** *vi* to crack

fenêtre [f(ə)nɛtʀ] *nf* window

fenouil [fənuj] *nm* fennel

fente [fɑ̃t] *nf* (*fissure*) crack; (*de boîte à lettres etc*) slit

féodal, e, -aux [feɔdal, o] *adj* feudal

fer [fɛʀ] *nm* iron; **~ à cheval** horseshoe; **~ (à repasser)** iron; **~ forgé** wrought iron

ferai *etc* [fəʀe] *vb voir* **faire**

fer-blanc [fɛʀblɑ̃] *nm* tin(plate)

férié, e [feʀje] *adj*: **jour ~** public holiday

ferions *etc* [fəʀjɔ̃] *vb voir* **faire**

ferme [fɛʀm] *adj* firm ♦ *adv* (*travailler etc*) hard ♦ *nf* (*exploitation*) farm; (*maison*) farmhouse

fermé, e [fɛʀme] *adj* closed, shut; (*gaz, eau etc*) off; (*fig: milieu*) exclusive

fermenter [fɛʀmɑ̃te] *vi* to ferment

fermer [fɛʀme] *vt* to close, shut; (*cesser l'exploitation de*) to close down, shut down; (*eau, électricité, robinet*) to put off, turn off; (*aéroport, route*) to close ♦ *vi* to close, shut; (*magasin: definitivement*) to close down, shut down; **se ~** *vi* to close, shut

fermeté [fɛʀməte] *nf* firmness

fermeture [fɛʀmətyʀ] *nf* closing; (*dispositif*) catch; **heures de ~** closing times; **~ éclair** ® zip (fastener) (BRIT), zipper (US)

fermier [fɛʀmje, jɛʀ] *nm* farmer; **fermière** *nf* woman farmer; (*épouse*) farmer's wife

fermoir [fɛʀmwaʀ] *nm* clasp

féroce [feʀɔs] *adj* ferocious, fierce

ferons [fəʀɔ̃] *vb voir* **faire**

ferraille [feʀaj] *nf* scrap iron; **mettre à la ~** to scrap

ferrer [feʀe] *vt* (*cheval*) to shoe

ferronnerie [feʀɔnʀi] *nf* ironwork

ferroviaire [feʀɔvjɛʀ] *adj* rail(way) *cpd* (BRIT), rail(road) *cpd* (US)

ferry(boat) [feʀe(bot)] *nm* ferry

fertile [fɛʀtil] *adj* fertile; **~ en incidents** eventful, packed with incidents

féru, e [feʀy] *adj*: **~ de** with a keen interest in

fervent, e [fɛʀvɑ̃, ɑ̃t] *adj* fervent

fesse [fɛs] *nf* buttock; **fessée** *nf* spanking

festin [festɛ̃] *nm* feast

festival [festival] *nm* festival

festivités [festivite] *nfpl* festivities

festoyer [festwaje] *vi* to feast

fêtard [fetaʀ, aʀd] (*fam*) *nm* high liver, merry-maker

fête [fɛt] *nf* (*religieuse*) feast; (*publique*) holiday; (*réception*) party; (*kermesse*) fête, fair; (*du nom*) feast day, name day; **faire la ~** to live it up; **faire ~ à qn** to give sb a warm welcome; **les ~s (de fin d'année)** the festive season; **la salle des ~s** the village hall; **~ foraine** (fun) fair; **fêter** *vt* to celebrate; (*personne*) to have a celebration for

feu, x [fø] *nm* (*gén*) fire; (*signal lumineux*) light; (*de cuisinière*) ring; **~x** *nmpl* (AUTO) (traffic) lights; **au ~!** (*incendie*) fire!; **à ~ doux/vif** over a slow/brisk heat; **à petit ~** (CULIN) over a gentle heat; (*fig*) slowly; **faire ~** to fire; **prendre ~** to catch fire; **mettre le ~ à** to set fire to; **faire du ~** to make a fire; **avez-vous du ~?** (*pour cigarette*) have you (got) a light?; **~ arrière** rear light; **~ d'artifice** (*spectacle*) fireworks *pl*; **~ de joie** bonfire; **~ rouge/vert/orange** red/green/amber (BRIT) *ou* yellow (US) light; **~x de brouillard** fog-lamps; **~x de croisement** dipped (BRIT) *ou* dimmed (US) headlights; **~x de position** sidelights; **~x de route** headlights

feuillage [fœjaʒ] *nm* foliage, leaves *pl*

feuille [fœj] nf (d'arbre) leaf; (de papier) sheet; ~ **de maladie** medical expenses claim form; ~ **de paie** pay slip

feuillet [fœje] nm leaf

feuilleté, e [fœjte] adj: **pâte** ~ flaky pastry

feuilleter [fœjte] vt (livre) to leaf through

feuilleton [fœjtɔ̃] nm serial

feutre [føtR] nm felt; (chapeau) felt hat; (aussi: **stylo-~**) felt-tip pen; **feutré, e** adj (atmosphère) muffled

fève [fɛv] nf broad bean

février [fevRije] nm February

FF abr (= franc français) FF

fiable [fjabl] adj reliable

fiançailles [fjɑ̃saj] nfpl engagement sg

fiancé, e [fjɑ̃se] nm/f fiancé(e) ♦ adj: **être** ~ **(à)** to be engaged (to)

fiancer [fjɑ̃se]: **se** ~ vi to become engaged

fibre [fibR] nf fibre; ~ **de verre** fibreglass, glass fibre

ficeler [fis(ə)le] vt to tie up

ficelle [fisɛl] nf string no pl; (morceau) piece ou length of string

fiche [fiʃ] nf (pour fichier) (index) card; (formulaire) form; (ÉLEC) plug

ficher [fiʃe] vt (dans un fichier) to file; (PO-LICE) to put on file; (fam: faire) to do; (: donner) to give; (: mettre) to stick ou shove; **se** ~ **de** (fam: se gausser) to make fun of; **fiche-(moi) le camp** (fam) clear off; **fiche-moi la paix** (fam) leave me alone; **je m'en fiche!** (fam) I don't care!

fichier [fiʃje] nm file

fichu, e [fiʃy] pp de **ficher** (fam) ♦ adj (fam: fini, inutilisable) bust, done for; (: intensif) wretched, darned ♦ nm (foulard) (head)scarf; **mal** ~ (fam) feeling lousy

fictif, -ive [fiktif, iv] adj fictitious

fiction [fiksjɔ̃] nf fiction; (fait imaginé) invention

fidèle [fidɛl] adj faithful ♦ nm/f (REL): **les** ~**s** (à l'église) the congregation sg; **fidélité** nf fidelity

fier¹ [fje]: **se** ~ **à** vt to trust

fier², fière [fjɛR] adj proud; **fierté** nf pride

fièvre [fjɛvR] nf fever; **avoir de la** ~**/39 de** ~ to have a high temperature/a temperature of 39ºC; **fiévreux, -euse** adj feverish

figé, e [fiʒe] adj (manières) stiff; (société) rigid; (sourire) set

figer [fiʒe]: **se** ~ vi (huile) to congeal; (personne) to freeze

fignoler [fiɲɔle] (fam) vt to polish up

figue [fig] nf fig; **figuier** nm fig tree

figurant, e [figyRɑ̃, ɑ̃t] nm/f (THÉÂTRE) walk-on; (CINÉMA) extra

figure [figyR] nf (visage) face; (forme, personnage) figure; (illustration) picture, diagram

figuré, e [figyRe] adj (sens) figurative

figurer [figyRe] vi to appear ♦ vt to represent; **se** ~ **que** to imagine that

fil [fil] nm (brin, fig: d'une histoire) thread; (électrique) wire; (d'un couteau) edge; **au** ~ **des années** with the passing of the years; **au** ~ **de l'eau** with the stream ou current; **coup de** ~ (fam) phone call; ~ **à coudre** (sewing) thread; ~ **de fer** wire; ~ **de fer barbelé** barbed wire

filament [filamɑ̃] nm (ÉLEC) filament

filandreux, -euse [filɑ̃dRø, øz] adj stringy

filature [filatyR] nf (fabrique) mill; (policière) shadowing no pl, tailing no pl

file [fil] nf line; (AUTO) lane; **en** ~ **indienne** in single file; **à la** ~ (d'affilée) in succession; ~ **(d'attente)** queue (BRIT), line (US)

filer [file] vt (tissu, toile) to spin; (prendre en filature) to shadow, tail; (fam: donner): ~ **qch à qn** to slip sb sth ♦ vi (bas) to run; (aller vite) to fly past; (fam: partir) to make ou be off; ~ **doux** to toe the line

filet [filɛ] nm net; (CULIN) fillet; (d'eau, de sang) trickle; ~ **(à provisions)** string bag

filiale [filjal] nf (COMM) subsidiary

filière [filjɛR] nf (carrière) path; **suivre la** ~ (dans sa carrière) to work one's way up (through the hierarchy)

filiforme [filifɔRm] *adj* spindly

filigrane [filigRan] *nm* (*d'un billet, timbre*) watermark

fille [fij] *nf* girl; (*opposé à* fils) daughter; **vieille ~** old maid; **fillette** *nf* (little) girl

filleul, e [fijœl] *nm/f* godchild, godson/ daughter

film [film] *nm* (*pour photo*) (roll of) film; (*œuvre*) film, picture, movie; **~ d'épouvante** horror film; **~ policier** thriller

filon [filɔ̃] *nm* vein, lode; (*fig*) lucrative line, money spinner

fils [fis] *nm* son; **~ à papa** daddy's boy

filtre [filtR] *nm* filter; **filtrer** *vt* to filter; (*fig: candidats, visiteurs*) to screen

fin[1] [fɛ̃] *nf* end; **~s** *nfpl* (*but*) ends; **prendre ~** to come to an end; **mettre ~ à** to put an end to; **à la ~** in the end, eventually; **en ~ de compte** in the end; **sans ~** endless; **~ juin** at the end of June

fin[2], **e** [fɛ̃, fin] *adj* (*papier, couche, fil*) thin; (*cheveux, visage*) fine; (*taille*) neat, slim; (*esprit, remarque*) subtle ♦ *adv* (*couper*) finely; **~ prêt** quite ready; **~es herbes** mixed herbs

final, e [final, o] *adj* final ♦ *nm* (*MUS*) finale; **finale** *nf* final; **quarts de finale** quarter finals; **finalement** *adv* finally, in the end; (*après tout*) after all

finance [finɑ̃s]: **~s** *nfpl* (*situation*) finances; (*activités*) finance *sg*; **moyennant ~** for a fee; **financer** *vt* to finance; **financier, -ière** *adj* financial

finaud, e [fino, od] *adj* wily

finesse [fines] *nf* thinness; (*raffinement*) fineness; (*subtilité*) subtlety

fini, e [fini] *adj* finished; (*MATH*) finite ♦ *nm* (*d'un objet manufacturé*) finish

finir [finiR] *vt* to finish ♦ *vi* to finish, end; **~ par faire** to end up *ou* finish up doing; **~ de faire** to finish doing; (*cesser*) to stop doing; **il finit par m'agacer** he's beginning to get on my nerves; **en ~ avec** to be *ou* have done with; **il va mal ~** he will come to a bad end

finition [finisjɔ̃] *nf* (*résultat*) finish

finlandais, e [fɛ̃lɑ̃dɛ, ɛz] *adj* Finnish ♦ *nm/f*: **F~, e** Finn

Finlande [fɛ̃lɑ̃d] *nf*: **la ~** Finland

fiole [fjɔl] *nf* phial

firme [fiRm] *nf* firm

fis [fi] *vb voir* **faire**

fisc [fisk] *nm* tax authorities *pl*; **fiscal, e, -aux** *adj* tax *cpd*, fiscal; **fiscalité** *nf* tax system

fissure [fisyR] *nf* crack; **fissurer** *vt* to crack; **se fissurer** *vi* to crack

fiston [fistɔ̃] (*fam*) *nm* son, lad

fit [fi] *vb voir* **faire**

fixation [fiksasjɔ̃] *nf* (*attache*) fastening; (*PSYCH*) fixation

fixe [fiks] *adj* fixed; (*emploi*) steady, regular ♦ *nm* (*salaire*) basic salary; **à heure ~** at a set time; **menu à prix ~** set menu

fixé, e [fikse] *adj*: **être ~ (sur)** (*savoir à quoi s'en tenir*) to have made up one's mind (about)

fixer [fikse] *vt* (*attacher*): **~ qch (à/sur)** to fix *ou* fasten sth (to/onto); (*déterminer*) to fix, set; (*regarder*) to stare at; **se ~** *vi* (*s'établir*) to settle down; **se ~ sur** (*suj: attention*) to focus on

flacon [flakɔ̃] *nm* bottle

flageoler [flaʒɔle] *vi* (*jambes*) to sag

flageolet [flaʒɔlɛ] *nm* (*CULIN*) dwarf kidney bean

flagrant, e [flagRɑ̃, ɑ̃t] *adj* flagrant, blatant; **en ~ délit** in the act

flair [flɛR] *nm* sense of smell; (*fig*) intuition; **flairer** *vt* (*humer*) to sniff (at); (*détecter*) to scent

flamand, e [flamɑ̃, ɑ̃d] *adj* Flemish ♦ *nm* (*LING*) Flemish ♦ *nm/f*: **F~, e** Fleming; **les F~s** the Flemish

flamant [flamɑ̃] *nm* flamingo

flambant [flɑ̃bɑ̃, ɑ̃t] *adv*: **~ neuf** brand new

flambé, e [flɑ̃be] *adj* (*CULIN*) flambé

flambeau, x [flɑ̃bo] *nm* (flaming) torch

flambée [flɑ̃be] *nf* blaze; (*fig: des prix*) explosion

flamber [flɑ̃be] *vi* to blaze (up)

flamboyer [flɑ̃bwaje] *vi* to blaze (up)

flamme [flɑm] *nf* flame; (*fig*) fire, fervour; **en ~s** on fire, ablaze

flan [flɑ̃] *nm* (*CULIN*) custard tart *ou* pie

flanc [flɑ̃] *nm* side; (*MIL*) flank

flancher [flɑ̃ʃe] (*fam*) *vi* to fail, pack up

flanelle [flanɛl] *nf* flannel

flâner [flɑne] *vi* to stroll; **flânerie** *nf* stroll

flanquer [flɑ̃ke] *vt* to flank; (*fam: mettre*) to chuck, shove; (: *jeter*): **~ par terre/à la porte** to fling to the ground/chuck out

flaque [flak] *nf* (*d'eau*) puddle; (*d'huile, de sang etc*) pool

flash [flaʃ] (*pl* **es**) *nm* (*PHOTO*) flash; **~ (d'information)** newsflash

flasque [flask] *adj* flabby

flatter [flate] *vt* to flatter; **se ~ de qch** to pride o.s. on sth; **flatterie** *nf* flattery *no pl*; **flatteur, -euse** *adj* flattering

fléau, x [fleo] *nm* scourge

flèche [flɛʃ] *nf* arrow; (*de clocher*) spire; **monter en ~** (*fig*) to soar, rocket; **partir en ~** to be off like a shot; **fléchette** *nf* dart

fléchir [fleʃiʀ] *vt* (*corps, genou*) to bend; (*fig*) to sway, weaken ♦ *vi* (*fig*) to weaken, flag

flemmard, e [flemaʀ, aʀd] (*fam*) *nm/f* lazybones *sg*, loafer

flemme [flɛm] *nf* (*fam*) laziness; **j'ai la ~ de le faire** I can't be bothered doing it

flétrir [fletʀiʀ]: **se ~** *vi* to wither

fleur [flœʀ] *nf* flower; (*d'un arbre*) blossom; **en ~** (*arbre*) in blossom; **à ~s** flowery

fleuri, e [flœʀi] *adj* (*jardin*) in flower *ou* bloom; (*tissu, papier*) flowery

fleurir [flœʀiʀ] *vi* (*rose*) to flower; (*arbre*) to blossom; (*fig*) to flourish ♦ *vt* (*tombe*) to put flowers on; (*chambre*) to decorate with flowers

fleuriste [flœʀist] *nm/f* florist

fleuve [flœv] *nm* river

flexible [flɛksibl] *adj* flexible

flic [flik] (*fam: péj*) *nm* cop

flipper [flipœʀ] *nm* pinball (machine)

flirter [flœʀte] *vi* to flirt

flocon [flɔkɔ̃] *nm* flake

flopée [flɔpe] (*fam*) *nf*: **une ~ de** loads of, masses of

floraison [flɔʀɛzɔ̃] *nf* flowering

flore [flɔʀ] *nf* flora

florissant, e [flɔʀisɑ̃, ɑ̃t] *adj* (*économie*) flourishing

flot [flo] *nm* flood, stream; **~s** *nmpl* (*de la mer*) waves; **être à ~** (*NAVIG*) to be afloat; **entrer à ~s** to stream *ou* pour in

flottant, e [flɔtɑ̃, ɑ̃t] *adj* (*vêtement*) loose

flotte [flɔt] *nf* (*NAVIG*) fleet; (*fam: eau*) water; (: *pluie*) rain.

flottement [flɔtmɑ̃] *nm* (*fig*) wavering, hesitation

flotter [flɔte] *vi* to float; (*nuage, odeur*) to drift; (*drapeau*) to fly; (*vêtements*) to hang loose; (*fam: pleuvoir*) to rain; **faire ~** to float; **flotteur** *nm* float

flou, e [flu] *adj* fuzzy, blurred; (*fig*) woolly, vague

fluctuation [flyktɥasjɔ̃] *nf* fluctuation

fluet, te [flyɛ, ɛt] *adj* thin, slight

fluide [flɥid] *adj* fluid; (*circulation etc*) flowing freely ♦ *nm* fluid

fluor [flyɔʀ] *nm*: **dentifrice au ~** fluoride toothpaste

fluorescent, e [flyɔʀesɑ̃, ɑ̃t] *adj* fluorescent

flûte [flyt] *nf* flute; (*verre*) flute glass; (*pain*) long loaf; **~!** drat it!; **~ à bec** recorder

flux [fly] *nm* incoming tide; (*écoulement*) flow; **le ~ et le reflux** the ebb and flow

FM *sigle f* (= *fréquence modulée*) FM

foc [fɔk] *nm* jib

foi [fwa] *nf* faith; **digne de ~** reliable; **être de bonne/mauvaise ~** to be sincere/insincere; **ma ~ ...** well ...

foie [fwa] *nm* liver; **crise de ~** stomach upset

foin [fwɛ̃] *nm* hay; **faire du ~** (*fig: fam*) to kick up a row

foire [fwaʀ] *nf* fair; (*fête foraine*) (fun) fair; **faire la ~** (*fig: fam*) to whoop it up; **~ (exposition)** trade fair

fois [fwa] *nf* time; **une/deux ~** once/

twice; **2 ~ 2** 2 times 2; **une ~** (*passé*) once; (*futur*) sometime; **une ~ pour toutes** once and for all; **une ~ que** once; **des ~** (*parfois*) sometimes; **à la ~** (*ensemble*) at once

foison [fwazɔ̃] *nf*: **à ~** in plenty; **foisonner** *vi* to abound

fol [fɔl] *adj voir* **fou**

folie [fɔli] *nf* (*d'une décision, d'un acte*) madness, folly; (*état*) madness, insanity; **la ~ des grandeurs** delusions of grandeur; **faire des ~s** (*en dépenses*) to be extravagant

folklorique [fɔlklɔʀik] *adj* folk *cpd*; (*fam*) weird

folle [fɔl] *adj, nf voir* **fou**; **follement** *adv* (*très*) madly, wildly

foncé, e [fɔ̃se] *adj* dark

foncer [fɔ̃se] *vi* to go darker; (*fam: aller vite*) to tear *ou* belt along; **~ sur** to charge at

foncier, -ère [fɔ̃sje, jɛʀ] *adj* (*honnêteté etc*) basic, fundamental; (*COMM*) real estate *cpd*

fonction [fɔ̃ksjɔ̃] *nf* function; (*emploi, poste*) post, position; **~s** *nfpl* (*professionnelles*) duties; **voiture de ~** company car; **en ~ de** (*par rapport à*) according to; **faire ~ de** to serve as; **la ~ publique** the state *ou* civil (*BRIT*) service; **fonctionnaire** *nm/f* state employee, local authority employee; (*dans l'administration*) ≃ civil servant; **fonctionner** *vi* to work, function

fond [fɔ̃] *nm* (*d'un récipient, trou*) bottom; (*d'une salle, scène*) back; (*d'un tableau, décor*) background; (*opposé à la forme*) content; (*SPORT*) long distance (running); **au ~ de** at the bottom of; at the back of; **à ~** (*connaître, soutenir*) thoroughly; (*appuyer, visser*) right down *ou* home; **à ~ (de train)** full tilt; **dans le ~, au ~** (*en somme*) basically, really; **de ~ en comble** from top to bottom; *voir aussi* **fonds**; **~ de teint** foundation (cream)

fondamental, e, -aux [fɔ̃damãtal, o] *adj* fundamental

fondant, e [fɔ̃dã, ãt] *adj* (*neige*) melting; (*poire*) that melts in the mouth

fondateur, -trice [fɔ̃datœʀ, tʀis] *nm/f* founder

fondation [fɔ̃dasjɔ̃] *nf* founding; (*établissement*) foundation; **~s** *nfpl* (*d'une maison*) foundations

fondé, e [fɔ̃de] *adj* (*accusation etc*) well-founded; **être ~ à** to have grounds for *ou* good reason to

fondement [fɔ̃dmã] *nm*: **sans ~** (*rumeur etc*) groundless, unfounded

fonder [fɔ̃de] *vt* to found; (*fig*) to base; **se ~ sur** (*suj: personne*) to base o.s. on

fonderie [fɔ̃dʀi] *nf* smelting works *sg*

fondre [fɔ̃dʀ] *vt* (*aussi:* **faire ~**) to melt; (*dans l'eau*) to dissolve; (*fig: mélanger*) to merge, blend ♦ *vi* (*à la chaleur*) to melt; (*dans l'eau*) to dissolve; (*fig*) to melt away; (*se précipiter*): **~ sur** to swoop down on; **~ en larmes** to burst into tears

fonds [fɔ̃] *nm* (*COMM*): **~ (de commerce)** business ♦ *nmpl* (*argent*) funds

fondu, e [fɔ̃dy] *adj* (*beurre, neige*) melted; (*métal*) molten; **fondue** *nf* (*CULIN*) fondue

font [fɔ̃] *vb voir* **faire**

fontaine [fɔ̃tɛn] *nf* fountain; (*source*) spring

fonte [fɔ̃t] *nf* melting; (*métal*) cast iron; **la ~ des neiges** the (spring) thaw

foot [fut] (*fam*) *nm* football

football [futbol] *nm* football, soccer; **footballeur** *nm* footballer

footing [futiŋ] *nm* jogging; **faire du ~** to go jogging

for [fɔʀ] *nm*: **dans son ~ intérieur** in one's heart of hearts

forain, e [fɔʀɛ̃, ɛn] *adj* fairground *cpd* ♦ *nm* (*marchand*) stallholder; (*acteur*) fairground entertainer

forçat [fɔʀsa] *nm* convict

force [fɔʀs] *nf* strength; (*PHYSIQUE, MÉCANIQUE*) force; **~s** *nfpl* (*physiques*) strength *sg*; (*MIL*) forces; **à ~ d'insister** by dint of insisting; as he (*ou* I *etc*) kept on insisting; **de ~** forcibly, by force; **les ~s de l'ordre** the police

forcé, e [fɔʀse] *adj* forced; **c'est ~** *(fam)* it's inevitable; **forcément** *adv* inevitably; **pas forcément** not necessarily

forcené, e [fɔʀsəne] *nm/f* maniac

forcer [fɔʀse] *vt* to force; *(voix)* to strain ♦ *vi (SPORT)* to overtax o.s.; **~ la dose** *(fam)* to overdo it; **se ~ (à faire)** to force o.s. (to do)

forcir [fɔʀsiʀ] *vi (grossir)* to broaden out

forer [fɔʀe] *vt* to drill, bore

forestier, -ère [fɔʀestje, jeʀ] *adj* forest *cpd*

forêt [fɔʀe] *nf* forest

forfait [fɔʀfe] *nm (COMM)* all-in deal *ou* price; **forfaitaire** *adj* inclusive

forge [fɔʀʒ] *nf* forge, smithy; **forger** *vt* to forge; *(fig: prétexte)* to contrive, make up; **forgeron** *nm* (black)smith

formaliser [fɔʀmalize]: **se ~** *vi*: **se ~ (de)** to take offence (at)

formalité [fɔʀmalite] *nf* formality; **simple ~** mere formality

format [fɔʀma] *nm* size; **formater** *vt (disque)* to format

formation [fɔʀmasjɔ̃] *nf (développement)* forming; *(apprentissage)* training; **~ permanente** continuing education; **~ professionnelle** vocational training

forme [fɔʀm] *nf (gén)* form; *(d'un objet)* shape, form; **~s** *nfpl (bonnes manières)* proprieties; *(d'une femme)* figure *sg*; **être en ~** *(SPORT etc)* to be on form; **en bonne et due ~** in due form

formel, le [fɔʀmel] *adj (catégorique)* definite, positive; **formellement** *adv (absolument)* positively; **formellement interdit** strictly forbidden

former [fɔʀme] *vt* to form; *(éduquer)* to train; **se ~** *vi* to form

formidable [fɔʀmidabl] *adj* tremendous

formulaire [fɔʀmyleʀ] *nm* form

formule [fɔʀmyl] *nf (gén)* formula; *(expression)* phrase; **~ de politesse** polite phrase; *(en fin de lettre)* letter ending; **for-**

muler *vt (émettre: désir)* to formulate

fort, e [fɔʀ, fɔʀt] *adj* strong; *(intensité, rendement)* high, great; *(corpulent)* stout; *(doué)* good, able ♦ *adv (serrer, frapper)* hard; *(parler)* loud(ly); *(beaucoup)* greatly, very much; *(très)* very ♦ *nm (édifice)* fort; *(point ~)* strong point, forte; **~e tête** rebel; **forteresse** *nf* stronghold

fortifiant [fɔʀtifjɑ̃, jɑ̃t] *nm* tonic

fortifier [fɔʀtifje] *vt* to strengthen, fortify

fortiori [fɔʀsjɔʀi]: **à ~** *adv* all the more so

fortuit, e [fɔʀtɥi, it] *adj* fortuitous, chance *cpd*

fortune [fɔʀtyn] *nf* fortune; **faire ~** to make one's fortune; **de ~** makeshift; **fortuné, e** *adj* wealthy

fosse [fos] *nf (grand trou)* pit; *(tombe)* grave

fossé [fose] *nm* ditch; *(fig)* gulf, gap

fossette [foset] *nf* dimple

fossile [fosil] *nm* fossil

fossoyeur [foswajœʀ] *nm* gravedigger

fou (fol), folle [fu, fɔl] *adj* mad; *(déréglé etc)* wild, erratic; *(fam: extrême, très grand)* terrific, tremendous ♦ *nm/f* madman(-woman) ♦ *nm (du roi)* jester; **être ~ de** to be mad *ou* crazy about; **avoir le ~rire** to have the giggles

foudre [fudʀ] *nf*: **la ~** lightning

foudroyant, e [fudʀwajɑ̃, ɑ̃t] *adj (progrès)* lightning *cpd*; *(succès)* stunning; *(maladie, poison)* violent

foudroyer [fudʀwaje] *vt* to strike down; **être foudroyé** to be struck by lightning; **~ qn du regard** to glare at sb

fouet [fwe] *nm* whip; *(CULIN)* whisk; **de plein ~** *(se heurter)* head on; **fouetter** *vt* to whip; *(crème)* to whisk

fougère [fuʒeʀ] *nf* fern

fougue [fug] *nf* ardour, spirit; **fougueux, -euse** *adj* fiery

fouille [fuj] *nf* search; **~s** *nfpl (archéologiques)* excavations; **fouiller** *vt* to search; *(creuser)* to dig ♦ *vi* to rummage; **fouillis** *nm* jumble, muddle

fouiner [fwine] *(péj)* *vi*: **~ dans** to nose

around *ou* about in

foulard [fulaʀ] *nm* scarf

foule [ful] *nf* crowd; **la ~** crowds *pl*; **une ~ de** masses of

foulée [fule] *nf* stride

fouler [fule] *vt* to press; (*sol*) to tread upon; **se ~ la cheville** to sprain one's ankle; **ne pas se ~** not to overexert o.s.; **il ne se foule pas** he doesn't put himself out; **foulure** *nf* sprain

four [fuʀ] *nm* oven; (*de potier*) kiln; (*THÉÂTRE: échec*) flop

fourbe [fuʀb] *adj* deceitful

fourbu, e [fuʀby] *adj* exhausted

fourche [fuʀʃ] *nf* pitchfork

fourchette [fuʀʃɛt] *nf* fork; (*STATISTIQUE*) bracket, margin

fourgon [fuʀgɔ̃] *nm* van; (*RAIL*) wag(g)on; **fourgonnette** *nf* (small) van

fourmi [fuʀmi] *nf* ant; **~s** *nfpl* (*fig*) pins and needles; **fourmilière** *nf* ant-hill; **fourmiller** *vi* to swarm

fournaise [fuʀnɛz] *nf* blaze; (*fig*) furnace, oven

fourneau, x [fuʀno] *nm* stove

fournée [fuʀne] *nf* batch

fourni, e [fuʀni] *adj* (*barbe, cheveux*) thick; (*magasin*): **bien ~ (en)** well stocked (with)

fournir [fuʀniʀ] *vt* to supply; (*preuve, exemple*) to provide, supply; (*effort*) to put in; **fournisseur, -euse** *nm/f* supplier; **fournisseur** *m* **d'accès** service provider; **fourniture** *nf* supply(ing); **fournitures scolaires** school stationery

fourrage [fuʀaʒ] *nm* fodder

fourré, e [fuʀe] *adj* (*bonbon etc*) filled; (*manteau etc*) fur-lined ♦ *nm* thicket

fourrer [fuʀe] (*fam!*) *vt* to stick, shove; **se ~ dans/sous** to get into/under; **fourre-tout** *nm inv* (*sac*) holdall; (*fig*) rag-bag

fourrière [fuʀjɛʀ] *nf* pound

fourrure [fuʀyʀ] *nf* fur; (*sur l'animal*) coat

fourvoyer [fuʀvwaje]: **se ~** *vi* to go astray, stray

foutre [futʀ] (*fam!*) *vt* = **ficher**; **foutu, e** (*fam!*) *adj* = **fichu, e**

foyer [fwaje] *nm* (*maison*) home; (*famille*) family; (*de cheminée*) hearth; (*de jeunes etc*) (social) club; (*résidence*) hostel; (*salon*) foyer; **lunettes à double ~** bi-focals

fracas [fʀaka] *nm* (*d'objet qui tombe*) crash; **fracassant, e** *adj* (*succès*) thundering; **fracasser** *vt* to smash

fraction [fʀaksjɔ̃] *nf* fraction; **fractionner** *vt* to divide (up), split (up)

fracture [fʀaktyʀ] *nf* fracture; **~ du crâne** fractured skull; **fracturer** *vt* (*coffre, serrure*) to break open; (*os, membre*) to fracture

fragile [fʀaʒil] *adj* fragile, delicate; (*fig*) frail; **fragilité** *nf* fragility

fragment [fʀagmɑ̃] *nm* (*d'un objet*) fragment, piece

fraîche [fʀɛʃ] *adj voir* **frais**; **fraîcheur** *nf* coolness; (*d'un aliment*) freshness; **fraîchir** *vi* to get cooler; (*vent*) to freshen

frais, fraîche [fʀɛ, fʀɛʃ] *adj* fresh; (*froid*) cool ♦ *adv* (*récemment*) newly, fresh(ly) ♦ *nm*: **mettre au ~** to put in a cool place ♦ *nmpl* (*gén*) expenses; (*COMM*) costs; **il fait ~** it's cool; **servir ~** serve chilled; **prendre le ~** to take a breath of cool air; **faire des ~** to go to a lot of expense; **~ de scolarité** school fees (*BRIT*), tuition (*US*); **~ généraux** overheads

fraise [fʀɛz] *nf* strawberry; **~ des bois** wild strawberry

framboise [fʀɑ̃bwaz] *nf* raspberry

franc, franche [fʀɑ̃, fʀɑ̃ʃ] *adj* (*personne*) frank, straightforward; (*visage*) open; (*net: refus*) clear; (*: coupure*) clean; (*intensif*) downright ♦ *nm* (*HIST*) franc

français, e [fʀɑ̃sɛ, ɛz] *adj* French ♦ *nm/f*: **F~, e** Frenchman(-woman) ♦ *nm* (*LING*) French; **les F~** the French

France [fʀɑ̃s] *nf*: **la ~** France

franche [fʀɑ̃ʃ] *adj voir* **franc**; **franchement** *adv* frankly; (*nettement*) definitely; (*tout à fait: mauvais etc*) downright

franchir [fʀɑ̃ʃiʀ] *vt* (*obstacle*) to clear, get over; (*seuil, ligne, rivière*) to cross; (*distance*) to cover

franchise [fʀɑ̃ʃiz] *nf* frankness; (*douanière*) exemption; (*ASSURANCES*) excess

franc-maçon [fʀɑ̃masɔ̃] *nm* freemason

franco [fʀɑ̃ko] *adv* (*COMM*): **~ (de port)** postage paid

francophone [fʀɑ̃kɔfɔn] *adj* French-speaking

franc-parler [fʀɑ̃paʀle] *nm inv* outspokenness; **avoir son ~-~** to speak one's mind

frange [fʀɑ̃ʒ] *nf* fringe

frangipane [fʀɑ̃ʒipan] *nf* almond paste

franquette [fʀɑ̃kɛt]: **à la bonne ~** *adv* without any fuss

frappant, e [fʀapɑ̃, ɑ̃t] *adj* striking

frappé, e [fʀape] *adj* iced

frapper [fʀape] *vt* to hit, strike; (*étonner*) to strike; **~ dans ses mains** to clap one's hands; **frappé de stupeur** dumbfounded

frasques [fʀask] *nfpl* escapades

fraternel, le [fʀatɛʀnɛl] *adj* brotherly, fraternal; **fraternité** *nf* brotherhood

fraude [fʀod] *nf* fraud; (*SCOL*) cheating; **passer qch en ~** to smuggle sth in (*ou* out); **~ fiscale** tax evasion; **frauder** *vi, vt* to cheat; **frauduleux, -euse** *adj* fraudulent

frayer [fʀeje] *vt* to open up, clear ♦ *vi* to spawn; **se ~ un chemin dans la foule** to force one's way through the crowd

frayeur [fʀejœʀ] *nf* fright

fredonner [fʀədɔne] *vt* to hum

freezer [fʀizœʀ] *nm* freezing compartment

frein [fʀɛ̃] *nm* brake; **mettre un ~ à** (*fig*) to curb, check; **~ à main** handbrake; **freiner** *vi* to brake ♦ *vt* (*progrès etc*) to check

frêle [fʀɛl] *adj* frail, fragile

frelon [fʀəlɔ̃] *nm* hornet

frémir [fʀemiʀ] *vi* (*de peur, d'horreur*) to shudder; (*de colère*) to shake; (*feuillage*) to quiver

frêne [fʀɛn] *nm* ash

frénétique [fʀenetik] *adj* frenzied, frenetic

fréquemment [fʀekamɑ̃] *adv* frequently

fréquent, e [fʀekɑ̃, ɑ̃t] *adj* frequent

fréquentation [fʀekɑ̃tasjɔ̃] *nf* frequenting;

~s *nfpl* (*relations*) company *sg*

fréquenté, e [fʀekɑ̃te] *adj*: **très ~** (very) busy; **mal ~** patronized by disreputable elements

fréquenter [fʀekɑ̃te] *vt* (*lieu*) to frequent; (*personne*) to see; **se ~** to see each other

frère [fʀɛʀ] *nm* brother

fresque [fʀɛsk] *nf* (*ART*) fresco

fret [fʀɛ(t)] *nm* freight

frétiller [fʀetije] *vi* (*poisson*) to wriggle

fretin [fʀətɛ̃] *nm*: **menu ~** small fry

friable [fʀijabl] *adj* crumbly

friand, e [fʀijɑ̃, fʀijɑ̃d] *adj*: **~ de** very fond of ♦ *nm*: **~ au fromage** cheese puff

friandise [fʀijɑ̃diz] *nf* sweet

fric [fʀik] (*fam*) *nm* cash, bread

friche [fʀiʃ]: **en ~** *adj, adv* (lying) fallow

friction [fʀiksjɔ̃] *nf* (*massage*) rub, rubdown; (*TECH, fig*) friction; **frictionner** *vt* to rub (down)

frigidaire ® [fʀiʒidɛʀ] *nm* refrigerator

frigide [fʀiʒid] *adj* frigid

frigo [fʀigo] (*fam*) *nm* fridge

frigorifié, e [fʀigɔʀifje] (*fam*) *adj*: **être ~** to be frozen stiff

frigorifique [fʀigɔʀifik] *adj* refrigerating

frileux, -euse [fʀilø, øz] *adj* sensitive to (the) cold

frime [fʀim] (*fam*) *nf*: **c'est de la ~** it's a lot of eyewash, it's all put on; **frimer** (*fam*) *vi* to show off

frimousse [fʀimus] *nf* (sweet) little face

fringale [fʀɛ̃gal] (*fam*) *nf*: **avoir la ~** to be ravenous

fringant, e [fʀɛ̃gɑ̃, ɑ̃t] *adj* dashing

fringues [fʀɛ̃g] (*fam*) *nfpl* clothes

fripé, e [fʀipe] *adj* crumpled

fripon, ne [fʀipɔ̃, ɔn] *adj* roguish, mischievous ♦ *nm/f* rascal, rogue

fripouille [fʀipuj] *nf* scoundrel

frire [fʀiʀ] *vt, vi*: **faire ~** to fry

frisé, e [fʀize] *adj* (*cheveux*) curly; (*personne*) curly-haired

frisson [fʀisɔ̃] *nm* (*de froid*) shiver; (*de peur*) shudder; **frissonner** *vi* (*de fièvre, froid*) to shiver; (*d'horreur*) to shudder

frit, e [fʀi, fʀit] *pp de* **frire**; **frite** *nf*: **(pommes) frites** chips (*BRIT*), French fries; **friteuse** *nf* chip pan; **friture** *nf* (*huile*) (deep) fat; (*plat*): **friture (de poissons)** fried fish

frivole [fʀivɔl] *adj* frivolous

froid, e [fʀwa, fʀwad] *adj, nm* cold; **il fait ~** it's cold; **avoir/prendre ~** to be/catch cold; **être en ~ avec** to be on bad terms with; **froidement** *adv* (*accueillir*) coldly; (*décider*) coolly

froideur [fʀwadœʀ] *nf* coldness

froisser [fʀwase] *vt* to crumple (up), crease; (*fig*) to hurt, offend; **se ~** *vi* to crumple, crease; (*personne*) to take offence; **se ~ un muscle** to strain a muscle

frôler [fʀole] *vt* to brush against; (*suj: projectile*) to skim past; (*fig*) to come very close to

fromage [fʀɔmaʒ] *nm* cheese; **~ blanc** soft white cheese

froment [fʀɔmɑ̃] *nm* wheat

froncer [fʀɔ̃se] *vt* to gather; **~ les sourcils** to frown

frondaisons [fʀɔ̃dezɔ̃] *nfpl* foliage *sg*

front [fʀɔ̃] *nm* forehead, brow; (*MIL*) front; **de ~** (*se heurter*) head-on; (*rouler*) together (*i.e. 2 or 3 abreast*); (*simultanément*) at once; **faire ~ à** to face up to

frontalier, -ère [fʀɔ̃talje, jɛʀ] *adj* border *cpd*, frontier *cpd*

frontière [fʀɔ̃tjɛʀ] *nf* frontier, border

frotter [fʀɔte] *vi* to rub, scrape ♦ *vt* to rub; (*pommes de terre, plancher*) to scrub; **~ une allumette** to strike a match

fructifier [fʀyktifje] *vi* to yield a profit

fructueux, -euse [fʀyktɥø, øz] *adj* fruitful

frugal, e, -aux [fʀygal, o] *adj* frugal

fruit [fʀɥi] *nm* fruit *gen no pl*; **~ de la passion** passion fruit; **~s de mer** seafood(s); **~s secs** dried fruit *sg*; **fruité, e** *adj* fruity; **fruitier, -ère** *adj*: **arbre fruitier** fruit tree

fruste [fʀyst] *adj* unpolished, uncultivated

frustrer [fʀystʀe] *vt* to frustrate

FS *abr* (= franc suisse) SF

fuel(-oil) [fjul(ɔjl)] *nm* fuel oil; (*domestique*) heating oil

fugace [fygas] *adj* fleeting

fugitif, -ive [fyʒitif, iv] *adj* (*fugace*) fleeting ♦ *nm/f* fugitive

fugue [fyg] *nf*: **faire une ~** to run away, abscond

fuir [fɥiʀ] *vt* to flee from; (*éviter*) to shun ♦ *vi* to run away; (*gaz, robinet*) to leak

fuite [fɥit] *nf* flight; (*écoulement, divulgation*) leak; **être en ~** to be on the run; **mettre en ~** to put to flight

fulgurant, e [fylgyʀɑ̃, ɑ̃t] *adj* lightning *cpd*, dazzling

fulminer [fylmine] *vi* to thunder forth

fumé, e [fyme] *adj* (*CULIN*) smoked; (*verre*) tinted; **fumée** *nf* smoke

fumer [fyme] *vi* to smoke; (*soupe*) to steam ♦ *vt* to smoke

fûmes *etc* [fym] *vb voir* **être**

fumet [fyme] *nm* aroma

fumeur, -euse [fymœʀ, øz] *nm/f* smoker

fumeux, -euse [fymø, øz] (*péj*) *adj* woolly, hazy

fumier [fymje] *nm* manure

fumiste [fymist] *nm/f* (*péj: paresseux*) shirker

funèbre [fynɛbʀ] *adj* funeral *cpd*; (*fig: atmosphère*) gloomy

funérailles [fyneʀaj] *nfpl* funeral *sg*

funeste [fynɛst] *adj* (*erreur*) disastrous

fur [fyʀ]: **au ~ et à mesure** *adv* as one goes along; **au ~ et à mesure que** as

furet [fyʀe] *nm* ferret

fureter [fyʀ(ə)te] (*péj*) *vi* to nose about

fureur [fyʀœʀ] *nf* fury; **être en ~** to be infuriated; **faire ~** to be all the rage

furibond, e [fyʀibɔ̃, ɔ̃d] *adj* furious

furie [fyʀi] *nf* fury; (*femme*) shrew, vixen; **en ~** (*mer*) raging; **furieux, -euse** *adj* furious

furoncle [fyʀɔ̃kl] *nm* boil

furtif, -ive [fyʀtif, iv] *adj* furtive

fus [fy] *vb voir* **être**

fusain [fyzɛ̃] *nm* (*ART*) charcoal

fuseau, x [fyzo] *nm* (*pour filer*) spindle;

(*pantalon*) (ski) pants; ~ **horaire** time zone
fusée [fyze] *nf* rocket; ~ **éclairante** flare
fuser [fyze] *vi* (*rires etc*) to burst forth
fusible [fyzibl] *nm* (ÉLEC: *fil*) fuse wire;
(: *fiche*) fuse
fusil [fyzi] *nm* (*de guerre, à canon rayé*) rifle,
gun; (*de chasse, à canon lisse*) shotgun,
gun; **fusillade** *nf* gunfire *no pl*, shooting
no pl; **fusiller** *vt* to shoot; **fusil-
mitrailleur** *nm* machine gun
fusionner [fyzjɔne] *vi* to merge.
fut [fy] *vb voir* **être**
fût [fy] *vb voir* **être** ♦ *nm* (*tonneau*) barrel,
cask
futé, e [fyte] *adj* crafty; **Bison** ~ ® *TV
and radio traffic monitoring service*
futile [fytil] *adj* futile; frivolous
futur, e [fytyr] *adj, nm* future '
fuyant, e [fɥijã, ãt] *vb voir* **fuir** ♦ *adj* (*regard etc*) evasive; (*lignes etc*) receding
fuyard, e [fɥijar, ard] *nm/f* runaway

G, g

gâcher [ɡaʃe] *vt* (*gâter*) to spoil; (*gaspiller*)
to waste; **gâchis** *nm* waste *no pl*
gadoue [ɡadu] *nf* sludge
gaffe [ɡaf] *nf* blunder; **faire** ~ (*fam*) to be
careful
gage [ɡaʒ] *nm* (*dans un jeu*) forfeit; (*fig: de
fidélité, d'amour*) token
gageure [ɡaʒyr] *nf*: **c'est une** ~ it's attempting the impossible
gagnant, e [ɡaɲɑ̃, ãt] *nm/f* winner
gagne-pain [ɡaɲpɛ̃] *nm inv* job
gagner [ɡaɲe] *vt* to win; (*somme d'argent,
revenu*) to earn; (*aller vers, atteindre*) to
reach; (*envahir: sommeil, peur*) to overcome; (: *mal*) to spread to ♦ *vi* to win;
(*fig*) to gain; ~ **du temps/de la place** to
gain time/save space; ~ **sa vie** to earn
one's living
gai, e [ɡe] *adj* cheerful; (*un peu ivre*) merry; **gaiement** *adv* cheerfully; **gaieté** *nf*
cheerfulness; **de gaieté de cœur** with a

light heart
gaillard [ɡajar, ard] *nm* (*strapping*) fellow
gain [ɡɛ̃] *nm* (*revenu*) earnings *pl*; (*bénéfice:
gén pl*) profits *pl*
gaine [ɡɛn] *nf* (*corset*) girdle; (*fourreau*)
sheath
gala [ɡala] *nm* official reception; **de** ~
(*soirée etc*) gala
galant, e [ɡalɑ̃, ãt] *adj* (*courtois*) courteous, gentlemanly; (*entreprenant*) flirta-
tious, gallant; (*scène, rendez-vous*) romantic
galère [ɡaler] *nf* galley; **quelle ~!** (*fam*) it's
a real grind!; **galérer** (*fam*) *vi* to slog
away, work hard; (*rencontrer les difficultés*)
to have a hassle
galerie [ɡalri] *nf* gallery; (THÉÂTRE) circle;
(*de voiture*) roof rack; (*fig: spectateurs*)
audience; ~ **de peinture** (private) art gallery; ~ **marchande** shopping arcade
galet [ɡalɛ] *nm* pebble
galette [ɡalɛt] *nf* flat cake; ~ **des Rois**
cake eaten on Twelfth Night
galipette [ɡalipɛt] *nf* somersault
Galles [ɡal] *nfpl*: **le pays de** ~ Wales;
gallois, e *adj* Welsh ♦ *nm/f*: **Gallois, e**
Welshman(-woman) ♦ *nm* (LING) Welsh
galon [ɡalɔ̃] *nm* (MIL) stripe; (*décoratif*)
piece of braid
galop [ɡalo] *nm* gallop; **galoper** *vi* to gallop
galopin [ɡalɔpɛ̃] *nm* urchin, ragamuffin
gambader [ɡɑ̃bade] *vi* (*animal, enfant*) to
leap about
gambas [ɡɑ̃bas] *nfpl* Mediterranean
prawns
gamin, e [ɡamɛ̃, in] *nm/f* kid ♦ *adj* childish
gamme [ɡam] *nf* (MUS) scale; (*fig*) range
gammé, e [ɡame] *adj*: **croix ~e** swastika
gang [ɡɑ̃ɡ] *nm* (*de criminels*) gang
gant [ɡɑ̃] *nm* glove; ~ **de toilette** face flannel (BRIT), face cloth
garage [ɡaraʒ] *nm* garage; **garagiste**
nm/f garage owner; (*employé*) garage
mechanic
garantie [ɡarɑ̃ti] *nf* guarantee; **(bon de)** ~

guarantee *ou* warranty slip

garantir [garɑ̃tir] *vt* to guarantee

garce [gars] (*fam*) *nf* bitch

garçon [garsɔ̃] *nm* boy; (*célibataire*): **vieux ~** bachelor; (*serveur*): **~ (de café)** waiter; **~ de courses** messenger; **~ d'honneur** best man; **garçonnière** *nf* bachelor flat

garde [gard(ə)] *nm* (*de prisonnier*) guard; (*de domaine etc*) warden; (*soldat, sentinelle*) guardsman ♦ *nf* (*soldats*) guard; **de ~** on duty; **monter la ~** to stand guard; **mettre en ~** to warn; **prendre ~ (à)** to be careful (of); **~ champêtre** ♦ *nm* rural policeman; **~ du corps** ♦ *nm* bodyguard; **~ des enfants** ♦ *nf* (*après divorce*) custody of the children; **~ à vue** ♦ *nf* (*JUR*) ≈ police custody; **garde-à-vous** *nm*: **être/se mettre au garde-à-vous** to be at/stand to attention; **garde-barrière** *nm/f* level-crossing keeper; **garde-boue** *nm inv* mudguard; **garde-chasse** *nm* gamekeeper; **garde-malade** *nf* home nurse; **garde-manger** *nm inv* (*armoire*) meat safe; (*pièce*) pantry, larder

garder [garde] *vt* (*conserver*) to keep; (*surveiller: enfants*) to look after; (: *immeuble, lieu, prisonnier*) to guard; **se ~** *vi* (*aliment: se conserver*) to keep; **se ~ de faire** to be careful not to do; **~ le lit/la chambre** to stay in bed/indoors; **pêche/chasse gardée** private fishing/hunting (ground)

garderie [gardəri] *nf* day nursery, crèche

garde-robe [gardərɔb] *nf* wardrobe

gardien, ne [gardjɛ̃, jɛn] *nm/f* (*garde*) guard; (*de prison*) warder; (*de domaine, réserve*) warden; (*de musée etc*) attendant; (*de phare, cimetière*) keeper; (*d'immeuble*) caretaker; (*fig*) guardian; **~ de but** goalkeeper; **~ de la paix** policeman; **~ de nuit** night watchman

gare [gar] *nf* station; **~ routière** bus station

garer [gare] *vt* to park; **se ~** *vi* to park

gargariser [gargarize]: **se ~** *vi* to gargle

gargote [gargɔt] *nf* cheap restaurant

gargouille [garguj] *nf* gargoyle

gargouiller [garguje] *vi* to gurgle

garnement [garnəmɑ̃] *nm* rascal, scallywag

garni, e [garni] *adj* (*plat*) served with vegetables (*and chips or rice etc*)

garnison [garnizɔ̃] *nf* garrison

garniture [garnityr] *nf* (*CULIN*) vegetables *pl*; **~ de frein** brake lining

gars [ga] (*fam*) *nm* guy

Gascogne [gaskɔɲ] *nf* Gascony; **le golfe de ~** the Bay of Biscay

gas-oil [gazɔjl] *nm* diesel (oil)

gaspiller [gaspije] *vt* to waste

gastronome [gastronɔm] *nm/f* gourmet; **gastronomie** *nf* gastronomy; **gastronomique** *adj* gastronomic

gâteau, x [gɑto] *nm* cake; **~ sec** biscuit

gâter [gɑte] *vt* to spoil; **se ~** *vi* (*dent, fruit*) to go bad; (*temps, situation*) to change for the worse

gâterie [gɑtri] *nf* little treat

gâteux, -euse [gɑtø, øz] *adj* senile

gauche [goʃ] *adj* left, left-hand; (*maladroit*) awkward, clumsy ♦ *nf* (*POL*) left (wing); **le bras ~** the left arm; **le côté ~** the left-hand side; **à ~** on the left; (*direction*) (to the) left; **gaucher, -ère** *adj* left-handed; **gauchiste** *nm/f* leftist

gaufre [gofr] *nf* waffle

gaufrette [gofrɛt] *nf* wafer

gaulois, e [golwa, waz] *adj* Gallic ♦ *nm/f*: **G~, e** Gaul

gaver [gave] *vt* to force-feed; **se ~ de** to stuff o.s. with

gaz [gaz] *nm inv* gas

gaze [gaz] *nf* gauze

gazer [gaze] (*fam*) *vi*: **ça gaze?** how's things?

gazette [gazɛt] *nf* news sheet

gazeux, -euse [gazø, øz] *adj* (*boisson*) fizzy; (*eau*) sparkling

gazoduc [gazodyk] *nm* gas pipeline

gazon [gazɔ̃] *nm* (*herbe*) grass; (*pelouse*) lawn

gazouiller [gazuje] *vi* to chirp; (*enfant*) to babble

geai [ʒɛ] *nm* jay

géant, e [ʒeɑ̃, ɑ̃t] *adj* gigantic; (COMM) giant-size ♦ *nm/f* giant

geindre [ʒɛ̃dR] *vi* to groan, moan

gel [ʒɛl] *nm* frost

gélatine [ʒelatin] *nf* gelatine

gelée [ʒ(ə)le] *nf* jelly; (gel) frost

geler [ʒ(ə)le] *vt, vi* to freeze; **il gèle** it's freezing

gélule [ʒelyl] *nf* (MÉD) capsule

gelures [ʒəlyR] *nfpl* frostbite *sg*

Gémeaux [ʒemo] *nmpl*: **les ~** Gemini

gémir [ʒemiR] *vi* to groan, moan

gênant, e [ʒenɑ̃, ɑ̃t] *adj* (irritant) annoying; (embarrassant) embarrassing

gencive [ʒɑ̃siv] *nf* gum

gendarme [ʒɑ̃daRm] *nm* gendarme; **gendarmerie** *nf* military police force in countryside and small towns; their police station or barracks

gendre [ʒɑ̃dR] *nm* son-in-law

gêné, e [ʒene] *adj* embarrassed

gêner [ʒene] *vt* (incommoder) to bother; (encombrer) to be in the way; (embarrasser): **~ qn** to make sb feel ill-at-ease

général, e, -aux [ʒeneral, o] *adj, nm* general; **en ~** usually, in general; **générale** *nf*: **(répétition) générale** final dress rehearsal; **généralement** *adv* generally; **généraliser** *vt, vi* to generalize; **se généraliser** *vi* to become widespread; **généraliste** *nm/f* general practitioner, G.P.

génération [ʒeneRasjɔ̃] *nf* generation

généreux, -euse [ʒeneRø, øz] *adj* generous

générique [ʒeneRik] *nm* (CINÉMA) credits *pl*

générosité [ʒeneRozite] *nf* generosity

genêt [ʒ(ə)nɛ] *nm* broom *no pl* (shrub)

génétique [ʒenetik] *adj* genetic; **génétiquement** *adv*: **génétiquement modifié** genetically-modified

Genève [ʒ(ə)nɛv] *n* Geneva

génial, e, -aux [ʒenjal, jo] *adj* of genius; (fam: formidable) fantastic, brilliant

génie [ʒeni] *nm* genius; (MIL): **le ~** the En-gineers *pl*; **~ civil** civil engineering

genièvre [ʒənjɛvR] *nm* juniper

génisse [ʒenis] *nf* heifer

génital, e, -aux [ʒenital, o] *adj* genital; **les parties ~es** the genitals

génoise [ʒenwaz] *nf* sponge cake

genou, x [ʒ(ə)nu] *nm* knee; **à ~x** on one's knees; **se mettre à ~x** to kneel down

genre [ʒɑ̃R] *nm* kind, type, sort; (LING) gender; **avoir bon ~** to look a nice sort; **avoir mauvais ~** to be coarse-looking; **ce n'est pas son ~** it's not like him

gens [ʒɑ̃] *nmpl* (f in some phrases) people *pl*

gentil, le [ʒɑ̃ti, ij] *adj* kind; (enfant: sage) good; (endroit etc) nice; **gentillesse** *nf* kindness; **gentiment** *adv* kindly

géographie [ʒeɔgRafi] *nf* geography

geôlier [ʒolje, jɛR] *nm* jailer

géologie [ʒeɔlɔʒi] *nf* geology

géomètre [ʒeɔmɛtR] *nm/f* (arpenteur) (land) surveyor

géométrie [ʒeɔmetRi] *nf* geometry; **géométrique** *adj* geometric

géranium [ʒeRanjɔm] *nm* geranium

gérant, e [ʒeRɑ̃, ɑ̃t] *nm/f* manager(-eress)

gerbe [ʒɛRb] *nf* (de fleurs) spray; (de blé) sheaf

gercé, e [ʒɛRse] *adj* chapped

gerçure [ʒɛRsyR] *nf* crack

gérer [ʒeRe] *vt* to manage

germain, e [ʒɛRmɛ̃, ɛn] *adj*: **cousin ~** first cousin

germe [ʒɛRm] *nm* germ; **germer** *vi* to sprout; (semence) to germinate

geste [ʒɛst] *nm* gesture

gestion [ʒɛstjɔ̃] *nf* management

gibier [ʒibje] *nm* (animaux) game

giboulée [ʒibule] *nf* sudden shower

gicler [ʒikle] *vi* to spurt, squirt

gifle [ʒifl] *nf* slap (in the face); **gifler** *vt* to slap (in the face)

gigantesque [ʒigɑ̃tɛsk] *adj* gigantic

gigogne [ʒigɔɲ] *adj*: **lits ~s** truckle (BRIT) *ou* trundle beds

gigot [ʒigo] *nm* leg (of mutton *ou* lamb)

gigoter [ʒiɡɔte] *vi* to wriggle (about)

gilet [ʒile] *nm* waistcoat; (*pull*) cardigan; ~ **de sauvetage** life jacket

gin [dʒin] *nm* gin; **~-tonic** gin and tonic

gingembre [ʒɛ̃ʒɑ̃bʀ] *nm* ginger

girafe [ʒiʀaf] *nf* giraffe

giratoire [ʒiʀatwaʀ] *adj*: **sens ~** roundabout

girofle [ʒiʀɔfl] *nf*: **clou de ~** clove

girouette [ʒiʀwɛt] *nf* weather vane *ou* cock

gitan, e [ʒitɑ̃, an] *nm/f* gipsy

gîte [ʒit] *nm* (*maison*) home; (*abri*) shelter; ~ **(rural)** holiday cottage *ou* apartment

givre [ʒivʀ] *nm* (hoar) frost; **givré, e** *adj* covered in frost; (*fam: fou*) nuts; **orange givrée** orange sorbet (*served in peel*)

glace [ɡlas] *nf* ice; (*crème glacée*) ice cream; (*miroir*) mirror; (*de voiture*) window

glacé, e [ɡlase] *adj* (*mains, vent, pluie*) freezing; (*lac*) frozen; (*boisson*) iced

glacer [ɡlase] *vt* to freeze; (*gâteau*) to ice; (*fig*): ~ **qn** (*intimider*) to chill sb; (*paralyser*) to make sb's blood run cold

glacial, e [ɡlasjal, jo] *adj* icy

glacier [ɡlasje] *nm* (*GÉO*) glacier; (*marchand*) ice-cream maker

glacière [ɡlasjɛʀ] *nf* icebox

glaçon [ɡlasɔ̃] *nm* icicle; (*pour boisson*) ice cube

glaïeul [ɡlajœl] *nm* gladiolus

glaise [ɡlɛz] *nf* clay

gland [ɡlɑ̃] *nm* acorn; (*décoration*) tassel

glande [ɡlɑ̃d] *nf* gland

glander [ɡlɑ̃de] (*fam*) *vi* to fart around (!)

glauque [ɡlok] *adj* dull blue-green

glissade [ɡlisad] *nf* (*par jeu*) slide; (*chute*) slip; **faire des ~s sur la glace** to slide on the ice

glissant, e [ɡlisɑ̃, ɑ̃t] *adj* slippery

glissement [ɡlismɑ̃] *nm*: ~ **de terrain** landslide

glisser [ɡlise] *vi* (*avancer*) to glide *ou* slide along; (*coulisser, tomber*) to slide; (*déraper*) to slip; (*être glissant*) to be slippery ♦ *vt* to slip; **se ~ dans** to slip into

global, e, -aux [ɡlɔbal, o] *adj* overall

globe [ɡlɔb] *nm* globe

globule [ɡlɔbyl] *nm* (*du sang*) corpuscle

globuleux, -euse [ɡlɔbylø, øz] *adj*: **yeux ~** protruding eyes

gloire [ɡlwaʀ] *nf* glory; **glorieux, -euse** *adj* glorious

glousser [ɡluse] *vi* to cluck; (*rire*) to chuckle; **gloussement** *nm* cluck; chuckle

glouton, ne [ɡlutɔ̃, ɔn] *adj* gluttonous

gluant, e [ɡlyɑ̃, ɑ̃t] *adj* sticky, gummy

glucose [ɡlykoz] *nm* glucose

glycine [ɡlisin] *nf* wisteria

goal [ɡol] *nm* goalkeeper

GO *sigle* (= grandes ondes) LW

gobelet [ɡɔblɛ] *nm* (*en étain, verre, argent*) tumbler; (*d'enfant, de pique-nique*) beaker; (*à dés*) cup

gober [ɡɔbe] *vt* to swallow (whole)

godasse [ɡɔdas] (*fam*) *nf* shoe

godet [ɡɔdɛ] *nm* pot

goéland [ɡɔelɑ̃] *nm* (sea)gull

goélette [ɡɔelɛt] *nf* schooner

gogo [ɡɔɡo]: **à ~** *adv* galore

goguenard, e [ɡɔɡ(ə)naʀ, aʀd] *adj* mocking

goinfre [ɡwɛ̃fʀ] *nm* glutton

golf [ɡɔlf] *nm* golf; (*terrain*) golf course

golfe [ɡɔlf] *nm* gulf; (*petit*) bay

gomme [ɡɔm] *nf* (*à effacer*) rubber (*BRIT*), eraser; **gommer** *vt* to rub out (*BRIT*), erase

gond [ɡɔ̃] *nm* hinge; **sortir de ses ~s** (*fig*) to fly off the handle

gondoler [ɡɔ̃dɔle]: **se ~** *vi* (*planche*) to warp; (*métal*) to buckle

gonflé, e [ɡɔ̃fle] *adj* swollen; **il est ~** (*fam: courageux*) he's got some nerve; (*impertinent*) he's got a nerve

gonfler [ɡɔ̃fle] *vt* (*pneu, ballon: en soufflant*) to blow up; (: *avec une pompe*) to pump up; (*nombre, importance*) to inflate ♦ *vi* to swell (up); (*CULIN: pâte*) to rise; **gonfleur** *nm* pump

gonzesse [ɡɔ̃zɛs] (*fam*) *nf* chick, bird (*BRIT*)

goret [gɔʀɛ] *nm* piglet

gorge [gɔʀʒ] *nf* (ANAT) throat; (*vallée*) gorge

gorgé, e [gɔʀʒe] *adj*: **~ de** filled with; (*eau*) saturated with; **gorgée** *nf* (*petite*) sip; (*grande*) gulp

gorille [gɔʀij] *nm* gorilla; (*fam*) bodyguard

gosier [gozje] *nm* throat

gosse [gɔs] (*fam*) *nm/f* kid

goudron [gudʀɔ̃] *nm* tar; **goudronner** *vt* to tar(mac) (BRIT), asphalt (US)

gouffre [gufʀ] *nm* abyss, gulf

goujat [guʒa] *nm* boor

goulot [gulo] *nm* neck; **boire au ~** to drink from the bottle

goulu, e [guly] *adj* greedy

gourd, e [guʀ, guʀd] *adj* numb (with cold)

gourde [guʀd] *nf* (*récipient*) flask; (*fam*) (*clumsy*) clot *ou* oaf ♦ *adj* oafish

gourdin [guʀdɛ̃] *nm* club, bludgeon

gourer [guʀe] (*fam*): **se ~** to boob

gourmand, e [guʀmɑ̃, ɑ̃d] *adj* greedy; **gourmandise** [guʀmɑ̃diz] *nf* greed; (*bonbon*) sweet

gourmet [guʀmɛ] *nm* gourmet

gourmette [guʀmɛt] *nf* chain bracelet

gousse [gus] *nf*: **~ d'ail** clove of garlic

goût [gu] *nm* taste; **avoir bon ~** to taste good; **de bon ~** tasteful; **de mauvais ~** tasteless; **prendre ~ à** to develop a taste *ou* a liking for

goûter [gute] *vt* (*essayer*) to taste; (*apprécier*) to enjoy ♦ *vi* to have (afternoon) tea ♦ *nm* (afternoon) tea

goutte [gut] *nf* drop; (MÉD) gout; (*alcool*) brandy; **tomber ~ à ~** to drip; **goutte-à-goutte** *nm* (MÉD) drip

gouttelette [gut(ə)lɛt] *nf* droplet

gouttière [gutjɛʀ] *nf* gutter

gouvernail [guvɛʀnaj] *nm* rudder; (*barre*) helm, tiller

gouvernante [guvɛʀnɑ̃t] *nf* governess

gouvernement [guvɛʀnəmɑ̃] *nm* government

gouverner [guvɛʀne] *vt* to govern

grabuge [gʀabyʒ] (*fam*) *nm* mayhem

grâce [gʀɑs] *nf* (*charme*) grace; (*faveur*) favour; (JUR) pardon; **~s** *nfpl* (REL) grace *sg*; **faire ~ à qn de qch** to spare sb sth; **rendre ~(s) à** to give thanks to; **demander ~** to beg for mercy; **~ à** thanks to; **gracier** *vt* to pardon; **gracieux, -euse** *adj* graceful

grade [gʀad] *nm* rank; **monter en ~** to be promoted

gradin [gʀadɛ̃] *nm* tier; step; **~s** *nmpl* (*de stade*) terracing *sg*

gradué, e [gʀadɥe] *adj*: **verre ~** measuring jug

graduel, le [gʀadɥɛl] *adj* gradual

graduer [gʀadɥe] *vt* (*effort etc*) to increase gradually; (*règle, verre*) to graduate

graffiti [gʀafiti] *nmpl* graffiti

grain [gʀɛ̃] *nm* (*gén*) grain; (NAVIG) squall; **~ de beauté** beauty spot; **~ de café** coffee bean; **~ de poivre** peppercorn; **~ de poussière** speck of dust; **~ de raisin** grape

graine [gʀɛn] *nf* seed

graissage [gʀɛsaʒ] *nm* lubrication, greasing

graisse [gʀɛs] *nf* fat; (*lubrifiant*) grease; **graisser** *vt* to lubricate, grease; (*tacher*) to make greasy; **graisseux, -euse** *adj* greasy

grammaire [gʀa(m)mɛʀ] *nf* grammar; **grammatical, e, -aux** *adj* grammatical

gramme [gʀam] *nm* gramme

grand, e [gʀɑ̃, gʀɑ̃d] *adj* (*haut*) tall; (*gros, vaste, large*) big, large; (*long*) long; (*plus âgé*) big; (*adulte*) grown-up; (*sens abstraits*) great ♦ *adv*: **~ ouvert** wide open; **au ~ air** in the open (air); **les ~s blessés** the severely injured; **~ ensemble** housing scheme; **~ magasin** department store; **~e personne** grown-up; **~e surface** hypermarket; **~es écoles** prestige schools of *university level*; **~es lignes** (RAIL) main lines; **~es vacances** summer holidays; **grand-chose** [gʀɑ̃ʃoz] *nm/f inv*: **pas grand-chose** not much; **Grande-**

Bretagne *nf* (Great) Britain; **grandeur** *nf* (*dimension*) size; **grandeur nature** life-size; **grandiose** *adj* imposing; **grandir** *vi* to grow ♦ *vt*: **grandir qn** (*suj: vêtement, chaussure*) to make sb look taller; **grand-mère** *nf* grandmother; **grand-messe** *nf* high mass; **grand-peine**: **à grand-peine** *adv* with difficulty; **grand-père** *nm* grandfather; **grand-route** *nf* main road; **grands-parents** *nmpl* grandparents

grange [gʀɑ̃ʒ] *nf* barn

granit(e) [gʀanit] *nm* granite

graphique [gʀafik] *adj* graphic ♦ *nm* graph

grappe [gʀap] *nf* cluster; **~ de raisin** bunch of grapes

gras, se [gʀɑ, gʀɑs] *adj* (*viande, soupe*) fatty; (*personne*) fat; (*surface, main*) greasy; (*plaisanterie*) coarse; (*TYPO*) bold ♦ *nm* (*CULIN*) fat; **faire la ~se matinée** to have a lie-in (*BRIT*), sleep late (*US*); **grassement** *adv*: **grassement payé** handsomely paid; **grassouillet, te** *adj* podgy, plump

gratifiant, e [gʀatifjɑ̃, jɑ̃t] *adj* gratifying

gratin [gʀatɛ̃] *nm* (*plat*) cheese-topped dish; (*croûte*) cheese topping; **gratiné, e** *adj* (*CULIN*) au gratin

gratis [gʀatis] *adv* free

gratitude [gʀatityd] *nf* gratitude

gratte-ciel [gʀatsjɛl] *nm inv* skyscraper

gratte-papier [gʀatpapje] (*péj*) *nm inv* penpusher

gratter [gʀate] *vt* (*avec un outil*) to scrape; (*enlever: avec un outil*) to scrape off; (: *avec un ongle*) to scratch; (*enlever avec un ongle*) to scratch off ♦ *vi* (*irriter*) to be scratchy; (*démanger*) to itch; **se ~** to scratch (o.s.)

gratuit, e [gʀatɥi, ɥit] *adj* (*entrée, billet*) free; (*fig*) gratuitous

gravats [gʀava] *nmpl* rubble *sg*

grave [gʀav] *adj* (*maladie, accident*) serious, bad; (*sujet, problème*) serious, grave; (*air*) grave, solemn; (*voix, son*) deep, low-pitched; **gravement** *adv* seriously; (*parler, regarder*) gravely

graver [gʀave] *vt* to engrave

graveur [gʀavœʀ] *nm*: **~ de CD/DVD** CD/DVD burner

gravier [gʀavje] *nm* gravel *no pl*; **gravillons** *nmpl* loose chippings *ou* gravel *sg*

gravir [gʀaviʀ] *vt* to climb (up)

gravité [gʀavite] *nf* (*de maladie, d'accident*) seriousness; (*de sujet, problème*) gravity

graviter [gʀavite] *vi* to revolve

gravure [gʀavyʀ] *nf* engraving; (*reproduction*) print

gré [gʀe] *nm*: **de bon ~** willingly; **contre le ~ de qn** against sb's will; **de son (plein) ~** of one's own free will; **bon ~ mal ~** like it or not; **de ~ ou de force** whether one likes it or not; **savoir ~ à qn de qch** to be grateful to sb for sth

grec, grecque [gʀɛk] *adj* Greek; (*classique: vase etc*) Grecian ♦ *nm/f*: **G~, Grecque** Greek ♦ *nm* (*LING*) Greek

Grèce [gʀɛs] *nf*: **la ~** Greece

greffe [gʀɛf] *nf* (*BOT, MÉD: de tissu*) graft; (*MÉD: d'organe*) transplant; **greffer** *vt* (*BOT, MÉD: tissu*) to graft; (*MÉD: organe*) to transplant

greffier [gʀefje, jeʀ] *nm* clerk of the court

grêle [gʀɛl] *adj* (very) thin ♦ *nf* hail; **grêler** *vb impers*: **il grêle** it's hailing; **grêlon** *nm* hailstone

grelot [gʀəlo] *nm* little bell

grelotter [gʀələte] *vi* to shiver

grenade [gʀənad] *nf* (*explosive*) grenade; (*BOT*) pomegranate

grenat [gʀəna] *adj inv* dark red

grenier [gʀənje] *nm* attic; (*de ferme*) loft

grenouille [gʀənuj] *nf* frog

grès [gʀɛ] *nm* sandstone; (*poterie*) stoneware

grésiller [gʀezije] *vi* to sizzle; (*RADIO*) to crackle

grève [gʀɛv] *nf* (*d'ouvriers*) strike; (*plage*) shore; **se mettre en/faire ~** to go on/be on strike; **~ de la faim** hunger strike; **~ du zèle** work-to-rule (*BRIT*), slowdown (*US*); **~ sauvage** wildcat strike

gréviste [gʀevist] *nm/f* striker

gribouiller [gʀibuje] *vt* to scribble, scrawl

grièvement [gʀijɛvmɑ̃] adv seriously

griffe [gʀif] nf claw; (de couturier) label; **griffer** vt to scratch

griffonner [gʀifɔne] vt to scribble

grignoter [gʀiɲɔte] vt (personne) to nibble at; (souris) to gnaw at ♦ vi to nibble

gril [gʀil] nm steak ou grill pan; **faire cuire au ~** to grill; **grillade** nf (viande etc) grill

grillage [gʀijaʒ] nm (treillis) wire netting; (clôture) wire fencing

grille [gʀij] nf (clôture) wire fence; (portail) (metal) gate; (d'égout) (metal) grate; (fig) grid

grille-pain [gʀijpɛ̃] nm inv toaster

griller [gʀije] vt (pain) to toast; (viande) to grill; (fig: ampoule etc) to blow; **faire ~** to toast; to grill; (châtaignes) to roast; **~ un feu rouge** to jump the lights

grillon [gʀijɔ̃] nm cricket

grimace [gʀimas] nf grimace; (pour faire rire): **faire des ~s** to pull ou make faces

grimper [gʀɛ̃pe] vi, vt to climb

grincer [gʀɛ̃se] vi (objet métallique) to grate; (plancher, porte) to creak; **~ des dents** to grind one's teeth

grincheux, -euse [gʀɛ̃ʃø, øz] adj grumpy

grippe [gʀip] nf flu, influenza; **grippé, e** adj: **être grippé** to have flu

gris, e [gʀi, gʀiz] adj grey; (ivre) tipsy

grisaille [gʀizaj] nf greyness, dullness

griser [gʀize] vt to intoxicate

grisonner [gʀizɔne] vi to be going grey

grisou [gʀizu] nm firedamp

grive [gʀiv] nf thrush

grivois, e [gʀivwa, waz] adj saucy

Groenland [gʀɔɛnlɑ̃d] nm Greenland

grogner [gʀɔɲe] vi to growl; (fig) to grumble; **grognon, ne** adj grumpy

groin [gʀwɛ̃] nm snout

grommeler [gʀɔm(ə)le] vi to mutter to o.s.

gronder [gʀɔ̃de] vi to rumble; (fig: révolte) to be brewing ♦ vt to scold; **se faire ~** to get a telling-off

groom [gʀum] nm bellboy

gros, se [gʀo, gʀos] adj big, large; (obèse)

fat; (travaux, dégâts) extensive; (épais) thick; (rhume, averse) heavy ♦ adv: **risquer/gagner ~** to risk/win a lot ♦ nm/f fat man/woman ♦ nm (COMM): **le ~** the wholesale business; **prix de ~** wholesale price; **par ~ temps/grosse mer** in rough weather/heavy seas; **en ~** roughly; (COMM) wholesale; **~ lot** jackpot; **~ mot** coarse word; **~ plan** (PHOTO) close-up; **~ sel** cooking salt; **~ titre** headline; **~se caisse** big drum

groseille [gʀozɛj] nf: **~ (rouge/blanche)** red/white currant; **~ à maquereau** gooseberry

grosse [gʀos] adj voir **gros**; **grossesse** nf pregnancy; **grosseur** nf size; (tumeur) lump

grossier, -ière [gʀosje, jɛʀ] adj coarse; (insolent) rude; (dessin) rough; (travail) roughly done; (imitation, instrument) crude; (évident: erreur) gross; **grossièrement** adv (sommairement) roughly; (vulgairement) coarsely; **grossièretés** nfpl: **dire des grossièretés** to use coarse language

grossir [gʀosiʀ] vi (personne) to put on weight ♦ vt (exagérer) to exaggerate; (au microscope) to magnify; (suj: vêtement): **~ qn** to make sb look fatter

grossiste [gʀosist] nm/f wholesaler

grosso modo [gʀosomɔdo] adv roughly

grotesque [gʀɔtɛsk] adj (extravagant) grotesque; (ridicule) ludicrous

grotte [gʀɔt] nf cave

grouiller [gʀuje] vi: **~ de** to be swarming with; **se ~** (fam) ♦ vi to get a move on; **grouillant, e** adj swarming

groupe [gʀup] nm group; **le ~ des 7** Group of 7; **~ sanguin** blood group; **groupement** nm (action) grouping; (groupe) group; **grouper** vt to group; **se grouper** vi to gather

grue [gʀy] nf crane

grumeaux [gʀymo] nmpl lumps

guenilles [gənij] nfpl rags

guenon [gənɔ̃] nf female monkey

guépard [gepaʀ] nm cheetah

guêpe [gɛp] *nf* wasp

guêpier [gepje] *nm* (*fig*) trap

guère [gɛʀ] *adv* (*avec adjectif, adverbe*): **ne ... ~** hardly; (*avec verbe*): **ne ... ~** (*pas beaucoup*) *tournure négative +much*; (*pas souvent*) hardly ever; (*pas longtemps*) *tournure négative +(very) long*; **il n'y a ~ que/de** there's hardly anybody (*ou* anything) but/hardly any; **ce n'est ~ difficile** it's hardly difficult; **nous n'avons ~ de temps** we have hardly any time

guéridon [geʀidɔ̃] *nm* pedestal table

guérilla [geʀija] *nf* guerrilla warfare

guérillero [geʀijeʀo] *nm* guerrilla

guérir [geʀiʀ] *vt* (*personne, maladie*) to cure; (*membre, plaie*) to heal ♦ *vi* (*malade, maladie*) to be cured; (*blessure*) to heal; **guérison** *nf* (*de maladie*) curing; (*de membre, plaie*) healing; (*de malade*) recovery; **guérisseur, -euse** *nm/f* healer

guerre [gɛʀ] *nf* war; **~ civile** civil war; **en ~** at war; **faire la ~ à** to wage war against; **guerrier, -ière** *adj* warlike ♦ *nm/f* warrior

guet [gɛ] *nm*: **faire le ~** to be on the watch *ou* look-out; **guet-apens** [getapɑ̃] *nm* ambush; **guetter** *vt* (*épier*) to watch (intently); (*attendre*) to watch (out) for; (*hostilement*) to be lying in wait for

gueule [gœl] *nf* (*d'animal*) mouth; (*fam: figure*) face; (: *bouche*) mouth; **ta ~!** (*fam*) shut up!; **~ de bois** (*fam*) hangover; **gueuler** (*fam*) *vi* to bawl; **gueuleton** (*fam*) *nm* blow-out

gui [gi] *nm* mistletoe

guichet [giʃɛ] *nm* (*de bureau, banque*) counter; **les ~s** (*à la gare, au théâtre*) the ticket office *sg*; **~ automatique** cash dispenser (*BRIT*), automatic telling machine (*US*)

guide [gid] *nm* guide ♦ *nf* (*éclaireuse*) girl guide; **guider** *vt* to guide

guidon [gidɔ̃] *nm* handlebars *pl*

guignol [giɲɔl] *nm* ≈ Punch and Judy show; (*fig*) clown

guillemets [gijmɛ] *nmpl*: **entre ~** in inverted commas

guillotiner [gijɔtine] *vt* to guillotine

guindé, e [gɛ̃de] *adj* (*personne, air*) stiff, starchy; (*style*) stilted

guirlande [giʀlɑ̃d] *nf* (*fleurs*) garland; **~ de Noël** tinsel garland; **~ lumineuse** string of fairy lights; **~ de papier** paper chain

guise [giz] *nf*: **à votre ~** as you wish *ou* please; **en ~ de** by way of

guitare [gitaʀ] *nf* guitar

gym [ʒim] *nf* (*exercices*) gym; **gymnase** *nm* gym(nasium); **gymnaste** *nm/f* gymnast; **gymnastique** *nf* gymnastics *sg*; (*au réveil etc*) keep-fit exercises *pl*

gynécologie [ʒinekɔlɔʒi] *nf* gynaecology; **gynécologique** *adj* gynaecological; **gynécologue** *nm/f* gynaecologist

H, h

habile [abil] *adj* skilful; (*malin*) clever; **habileté** [abilte] *nf* skill, skilfulness; cleverness

habillé, e [abije] *adj* dressed; (*chic*) dressy

habillement [abijmɑ̃] *nm* clothes *pl*

habiller [abije] *vt* to dress; (*fournir en vêtements*) to clothe; **s'~** *vi* to dress (o.s.); (*se déguiser, mettre des vêtements chic*) to dress up

habit [abi] *nm* outfit; **~s** *nmpl* (*vêtements*) clothes; **~ (de soirée)** evening dress; (*pour homme*) tails *pl*

habitant, e [abitɑ̃, ɑ̃t] *nm/f* inhabitant; (*d'une maison*) occupant; **loger chez l'~** to stay with the locals

habitation [abitasjɔ̃] *nf* house; **~s à loyer modéré** (block of) council flats

habiter [abite] *vt* to live in ♦ *vi*: **~ à/dans** to live in

habitude [abityd] *nf* habit; **avoir l'~ de faire** to be in the habit of doing; (*expérience*) to be used to doing; **d'~** usually; **comme d'~** as usual

habitué, e [abitɥe] *nm/f* (*de maison*) regular visitor; (*de café*) regular (customer)

habituel, le [abityɛl] *adj* usual

habituer [abitɥe] *vt*: ~ **qn à** to get sb used to; **s'~ à** to get used to

'hache [aʃ] *nf* axe

'hacher [aʃe] *vt* (*viande*) to mince; (*persil*) to chop; **'hachis** nm mince *no pl*; **hachis Parmentier** ≃ shepherd's pie

'hachisch [aʃiʃ] *nm* hashish

'hachoir [aʃwaʀ] *nm* (*couteau*) chopper; (*appareil*) (meat) mincer; (*planche*) chopping board

'hagard, e [agaʀ, aʀd] *adj* wild, distraught

'haie [ɛ] *nf* hedge; (*SPORT*) hurdle

'haillons [ajɔ̃] *nmpl* rags

'haine [ɛn] *nf* hatred

'haïr [aiʀ] *vt* to detest, hate

'hâlé, e [ɑle] *adj* (sun)tanned, sunburnt

haleine [alɛn] *nf* breath; **hors d'~** out of breath; **tenir en ~** (*attention*) to hold spellbound; (*incertitude*) to keep in suspense; **de longue ~** long-term

'haleter [alte] *vt* to pant

'hall [ol] *nm* hall

'halle [al] *nf* (covered) market; **~s** *nfpl* (*d'une grande ville*) central food market *sg*

hallucinant, e [alysinɑ̃, ɑ̃t] *adj* staggering

hallucination [alysinasjɔ̃] *nf* hallucination

'halte [alt] *nf* stop, break; (*endroit*) stopping place ♦ *excl* stop!; **faire ~** to stop

haltère [altɛʀ] *nm* dumbbell, barbell; **~s** *nmpl*: **(poids et) ~s** (*activité*) weightlifting *sg*; **haltérophilie** *nf* weightlifting

'hamac [amak] *nm* hammock

'hamburger [ɑ̃buʀɡœʀ] *nm* hamburger

'hameau, x [amo] *nm* hamlet

hameçon [amsɔ̃] *nm* (fish) hook

'hanche [ɑ̃ʃ] *nf* hip

'hand-ball [ɑ̃dbal] *nm* handball

'handicapé, e [ɑ̃dikape] *nm/f* physically (*ou* mentally) handicapped person; **~ moteur** spastic

hangar [ɑ̃ɡaʀ] *nm* shed; (*AVIAT*) hangar

'hanneton [antɔ̃] *nm* cockchafer

'hanter [ɑ̃te] *vt* to haunt

'hantise [ɑ̃tiz] *nf* obsessive fear

'happer [ape] *vt* to snatch; (*suj: train etc*) to hit

'haras [aʀa] *nm* stud farm

'harassant, e [aʀasɑ̃, ɑ̃t] *adj* exhausting

'harcèlement [aʀsɛlmɑ̃] *nm* harassment; **~ sexuel** sexual harassment

'harceler [aʀsəle] *vt* to harass; **~ qn de questions** to plague sb with questions

'hardi, e [aʀdi] *adj* bold, daring

'hareng [aʀɑ̃] *nm* herring

'hargne [aʀɲ] *nf* aggressiveness; **'hargneux, -euse** *adj* aggressive

'haricot [aʀiko] *nm* bean; **~ blanc** haricot bean; **~ vert** green bean; **~ rouge** kidney bean

harmonica [aʀmɔnika] *nm* mouth organ

harmonie [aʀmɔni] *nf* harmony; **harmonieux, -euse** *adj* harmonious; (*couleurs, couple*) well-matched

'harnacher [aʀnaʃe] *vt* to harness

'harnais [aʀnɛ] *nm* harness

'harpe [aʀp] *nf* harp

'harponner [aʀpɔne] *vt* to harpoon; (*fam*) to collar

'hasard [azaʀ] *nm*: **le ~** chance, fate; **un ~** a coincidence; **au ~** (*aller*) aimlessly; (*choisir*) at random; **par ~** by chance; **à tout ~** (*en cas de besoin*) just in case; (*en espérant trouver ce qu'on cherche*) on the off chance (*BRIT*); **'hasarder** *vt* (*mot*) to venture; **se hasarder à faire** to risk doing

'hâte [ɑt] *nf* haste; **à la ~** hurriedly, hastily; **en ~** posthaste, with all possible speed; **avoir ~ de** to be eager *ou* anxious to; **'hâter** *vt* to hasten; **se hâter** *vi* to hurry; **'hâtif, -ive** *adj* (*travail*) hurried; (*décision, jugement*) hasty

'hausse [os] *nf* rise, increase; **être en ~** to be going up; **'hausser** *vt* to raise; **hausser les épaules** to shrug (one's shoulders)

'haut, e [o, ot] *adj* high; (*grand*) tall ♦ *adv* high ♦ *nm* top (part); **de 3 m de ~** 3 m high, 3 m in height; **des ~s et des bas** ups and downs; **en ~ lieu** in high places; **à ~e voix, (tout) ~** aloud, out loud; **du ~ de** from the top of; **de ~ en bas** from top to bottom; **plus ~** higher up, further up; (*dans un texte*) above; (*parler*) louder; **en ~** (*être/aller*) at/to the top; (*dans une maison*) upstairs; **en ~ de** at the top of

'**hautain, e** [ˈotɛ̃, ɛn] *adj* haughty

'**hautbois** [ˈobwa] *nm* oboe

'**haut-de-forme** [ˈodfɔʀm] *nm* top hat

'**hauteur** [ˈotœʀ] *nf* height; **à la ~ de** (*accident*) near; (*fig: tâche, situation*) equal to; **à la ~** (*fig*) up to it

'**haut...:** '**haut-fourneau** *nm* blast *ou* smelting furnace; '**haut-le-cœur** *nm inv* retch, heave; '**haut-parleur** *nm* (loud)speaker

'**havre** [ˈavʀ] *nm* haven

'**Haye** [ˈɛ] *n*: **la ~** the Hague

'**hayon** [ˈɛjɔ̃] *nm* hatchback

hebdo [ebdo] (*fam*) *nm* weekly

hebdomadaire [ebdɔmadɛʀ] *adj, nm* weekly

hébergement [ebɛʀʒəmɑ̃] *nm* accommodation

héberger [ebɛʀʒe] *vt* (*touristes*) to accommodate, lodge; (*amis*) to put up; (*réfugiés*) to take in

hébété, e [ebete] *adj* dazed

hébreu, x [ebʀø] *adj m, nm* Hebrew

hécatombe [ekatɔ̃b] *nf* slaughter

hectare [ɛktaʀ] *nm* hectare

'**hein** [ˈɛ̃] *excl* eh?

'**hélas** [ˈelɑs] *excl* alas! ♦ *adv* unfortunately

'**héler** [ˈele] *vt* to hail

hélice [elis] *nf* propeller

hélicoptère [elikɔptɛʀ] *nm* helicopter

helvétique [ɛlvetik] *adj* Swiss

hématome [ematɔm] *nm* nasty bruise

hémicycle [emisikl] *nm* (*POL*): **l'~** ≃ the benches (of the Commons) (*BRIT*), ≃ the floor (of the House of Representatives) (*US*)

hémisphère [emisfɛʀ] *nm*: **l'~ nord/sud** the northern/southern hemisphere

hémorragie [emɔʀaʒi] *nf* bleeding *no pl*, haemorrhage

hémorroïdes [emɔʀɔid] *nfpl* piles, haemorrhoids

'**hennir** [ˈeniʀ] *vi* to neigh, whinny; '**hennissement** *nm* neigh, whinny

hépatite [epatit] *nf* hepatitis

herbe [ɛʀb] *nf* grass; (*CULIN, MÉD*) herb; **~s de Provence** mixed herbs; **en ~** unripe; (*fig*) budding; **herbicide** *nm* weed-killer; **herboriste** *nm/f* herbalist

'**hère** [ˈɛʀ] *nm*: **pauvre ~** poor wretch

héréditaire [eʀeditɛʀ] *adj* hereditary

'**hérisser** [ˈeʀise] *vt*: **~ qn** (*fig*) to ruffle sb; **se ~** *vi* to bristle, bristle up; '**hérisson** *nm* hedgehog

héritage [eʀitaʒ] *nm* inheritance; (*coutumes, système*) heritage, legacy

hériter [eʀite] *vi*: **~ de qch (de qn)** to inherit sth (from sb); **héritier, -ière** [eʀitje, jɛʀ] *nm/f* heir(-ess)

hermétique [ɛʀmetik] *adj* airtight; watertight; (*fig: obscur*) abstruse; (: *impénétrable*) impenetrable

hermine [ɛʀmin] *nf* ermine

'**hernie** [ˈɛʀni] *nf* hernia

héroïne [eʀɔin] *nf* heroine; (*drogue*) heroin

héroïque [eʀɔik] *adj* heroic

'**héron** [ˈeʀɔ̃] *nm* heron

'**héros** [ˈeʀo] *nm* hero

hésitant [ezitɑ̃, ɑ̃t] *adj* hesitant

hésitation [ezitasjɔ̃] *nf* hesitation

hésiter [ezite] *vi*: **~ (à faire)** to hesitate (to do)

hétéroclite [eteʀɔklit] *adj* heterogeneous; (*objets*) sundry

hétérogène [eteʀɔʒɛn] *adj* heterogeneous

hétérosexuel, le [eteʀɔsɛkɥɛl] *adj* heterosexual

'**hêtre** [ˈɛtʀ] *nm* beech

heure [œʀ] *nf* hour; (*SCOL*) period; (*moment*) time; **c'est l'~** it's time; **quelle ~ est-il?** what time is it?; **2 ~s (du matin)** 2 o'clock (in the morning); **être à l'~** to be on time; (*montre*) to be right; **mettre à l'~** to set right; **à une ~ avancée (de la nuit)** at a late hour of the night; **à toute ~** at any time; **24 ~s sur 24** round the clock, 24 hours a day; **à l'~ qu'il est** at this time (of day); by now; **sur l'~** at once; **~ de pointe** rush hour; (*téléphone*) peak period; **~ d'affluence** rush hour; **~s creuses** slack periods; (*pour électricité, téléphone etc*) off-peak periods; **~s supplémentaires** overtime *sg*

heureusement [œʀøzmɑ̃] *adv* (*par bonheur*) fortunately, luckily

heureux, -euse [œʀø, øz] *adj* happy; (*chanceux*) lucky, fortunate

'**heurter** ['œʀte] *vt* (*mur*) to strike, hit; (*personne*) to collide with; **se ~ à** *vt* (*fig*) to come up against

'**heurts** ['œʀ] *nmpl* (*fig*) clashes

hexagone [ɛgzagɔn] *nm* hexagon; (*la France*) France (*because of its shape*)

hiberner [ibɛʀne] *vi* to hibernate

'**hibou, x** ['ibu] *nm* owl

'**hideux, -euse** ['idø, øz] *adj* hideous

hier [jɛʀ] *adv* yesterday; **~ soir** last night, yesterday evening; **toute la journée d'~** all day yesterday; **toute la matinée d'~** all yesterday morning

'**hiérarchie** ['jeʀaʀʃi] *nf* hierarchy

'**hi-fi** ['ifi] *adj inv* hi-fi ♦ *nf* hi-fi

hilare [ilaʀ] *adj* mirthful

hindou, e [ɛ̃du] *adj* Hindu ♦ *nm/f*: **H~, e** Hindu

hippique [ipik] *adj* equestrian, horse *cpd*; **un club ~** a riding centre; **un concours ~** a horse show; **hippisme** *nm* (horse)riding

hippodrome [ipɔdʀom] *nm* racecourse

hippopotame [ipɔpɔtam] *nm* hippopotamus

hirondelle [iʀɔ̃dɛl] *nf* swallow

hirsute [iʀsyt] *adj* (*personne*) shaggy-haired; (*barbe*) shaggy; (*tête*) tousled

'**hisser** ['ise] *vt* to hoist, haul up; **se ~** *vi* to heave o.s. up

histoire [istwaʀ] *nf* (*science, événements*) history; (*anecdote, récit, mensonge*) story; (*affaire*) business *no pl*; **~s** *nfpl* (*chichis*) fuss *no pl*; (*ennuis*) trouble *sg*; **historique** *adj* historical; (*important*) historic

'**hit-parade** ['itpaʀad] *nm*: **le ~-~** the charts

hiver [ivɛʀ] *nm* winter; **hivernal, e, -aux** *adj* winter *cpd*; (*glacial*) wintry; **hiverner** *vi* to winter

HLM *nm ou f* (= *habitation à loyer modéré*) council flat; **des HLM** council housing

'**hobby** ['ɔbi] *nm* hobby

'**hocher** ['ɔʃe] *vt*: **~ la tête** to nod; (*signe négatif ou dubitatif*) to shake one's head

'**hochet** ['ɔʃe] *nm* rattle

'**hockey** ['ɔkɛ] *nm*: **~ (sur glace/gazon)** (ice/field) hockey

'**hold-up** ['ɔldœp] *nm inv* hold-up

'**hollandais, e** ['ɔlɑ̃dɛ, ɛz] *adj* Dutch ♦ *nm* (*LING*) Dutch ♦ *nm/f*: **H~, e** Dutchman(-woman); **les H~** the Dutch

'**Hollande** ['ɔlɑ̃d] *nf*: **la ~** Holland

'**homard** ['ɔmaʀ] *nm* lobster

homéopathique [ɔmeɔpatik] *adj* homoeopathic

homicide [ɔmisid] *nm* murder; **~ involontaire** manslaughter

hommage [ɔmaʒ] *nm* tribute; **~s** *nmpl*: **présenter ses ~s** to pay one's respects; **rendre ~ à** to pay tribute *ou* homage to

homme [ɔm] *nm* man; **~ d'affaires** businessman; **~ d'État** statesman; **~ de main** hired man; **~ de paille** stooge; **~ politique** politician; **homme-grenouille** *nm* frogman

homo...: **homogène** *adj* homogeneous; **homologue** *nm/f* counterpart; **homologué, e** *adj* (*SPORT*) ratified; (*tarif*) authorized; **homonyme** *nm* (*LING*) homonym; (*d'une personne*) namesake; **homosexuel, le** *adj* homosexual

'**Hongrie** ['ɔ̃gʀi] *nf*: **la ~** Hungary; '**hongrois, e** *adj* Hungarian ♦ *nm/f*: **Hongrois, e** Hungarian ♦ *nm* (*LING*) Hungarian

honnête [ɔnɛt] *adj* (*intègre*) honest; (*juste, satisfaisant*) fair; **honnêtement** *adv* honestly; **honnêteté** *nf* honesty

honneur [ɔnœʀ] *nm* honour; (*mérite*) credit; **en l'~ de** in honour of; (*événement*) on the occasion of; **faire ~ à** (*engagements*) to honour; (*famille*) to be a credit to; (*fig*: *repas etc*) to do justice to

honorable [ɔnɔrabl] *adj* worthy, honourable; (*suffisant*) decent

honoraire [ɔnɔrɛr] *adj* honorary; **professeur ~** professor emeritus; **honoraires** [ɔnɔrɛr] *nmpl* fees *pl*

honorer [ɔnɔre] *vt* to honour; (*estimer*) to hold in high regard; (*faire honneur à*) to do credit to; **honorifique** [ɔnɔrifik] *adj* honorary

'**honte** ['ɔ̃t] *nf* shame; **avoir ~ de** to be ashamed of; **faire ~ à qn** to make sb (feel) ashamed; '**honteux, -euse** *adj* ashamed; (*conduite, acte*) shameful

hôpital, -aux [ɔpital, o] *nm* hospital

'**hoquet** ['ɔkɛ] *nm*: **avoir le ~** to have (the) hiccoughs; '**hoqueter** *vi* to hiccough

horaire [ɔrɛr] *adj* hourly ♦ *nm* timetable, schedule; **~s** *nmpl* (*d'employé*) hours; **~ souple** flexitime

horizon [ɔrizɔ̃] *nm* horizon

horizontal, e, -aux [ɔrizɔ̃tal, o] *adj* horizontal

horloge [ɔrlɔ̃ʒ] *nf* clock; **l'~ parlante** the speaking clock; **horloger, -ère** *nm/f* watchmaker; clockmaker

'**hormis** ['ɔrmi] *prép* save

horoscope [ɔrɔskɔp] *nm* horoscope

horreur [ɔrœr] *nf* horror; **quelle ~!** how awful!; **avoir ~ de** to loathe *ou* detest; **horrible** *adj* horrible; **horrifier** *vt* to horrify

horripiler [ɔripile] *vt* to exasperate

'**hors** ['ɔr] *prép*: **~ de** out of; **~ pair** outstanding; **~ de propos** inopportune; **être ~ de soi** to be beside o.s.; **~ d'usage** out of service; '**hors-bord** *nm inv* speedboat (*with outboard motor*); '**hors-d'œuvre** *nm inv* hors d'œuvre; '**hors-jeu** *nm inv* offside; '**hors-la-loi** *nm inv* outlaw; '**hors-taxe** *adj* (*boutique, articles*) duty-free

hortensia [ɔrtɑ̃sja] *nm* hydrangea

hospice [ɔspis] *nm* (*de vieillards*) home

hospitalier, -ière [ɔspitalje, jɛr] *adj* (*accueillant*) hospitable; (*MÉD*: *service, centre*) hospital *cpd*

hospitaliser [ɔspitalize] *vt* to take/send to hospital, hospitalize

hospitalité [ɔspitalite] *nf* hospitality

hostie [ɔsti] *nf* host (*REL*)

hostile [ɔstil] *adj* hostile; **hostilité** *nf* hostility

hosto [ɔsto] (*fam*) *nm* hospital

hôte [ot] *nm* (*maître de maison*) host; (*invité*) guest

hôtel [otɛl] *nm* hotel; **aller à l'~** to stay in a hotel; **~ de ville** town hall; **~ (particulier)** (*private*) mansion; **hôtelier, -ière** *adj* hotel *cpd* ♦ *nm/f* hotelier; **hôtellerie** *nf* hotel business

hôtesse [otɛs] *nf* hostess; **~ de l'air** air stewardess; **~ (d'accueil)** receptionist

'**hotte** ['ɔt] *nf* (*panier*) basket (*carried on the back*); **~ aspirante** cooker hood

houblon [ublɔ̃] *nm* (*BOT*) hop; (*pour la bière*) hops *pl*

'**houille** ['uj] *nf* coal; **~ blanche** hydroelectric power

'**houle** ['ul] *nf* swell; '**houleux, -euse** *adj* stormy

'**houligan** ['uligɑ̃] *nm* hooligan

'**hourra** ['ura] *excl* hurrah!

'**houspiller** ['uspije] *vt* to scold

'**housse** ['us] *nf* cover

'**houx** ['u] *nm* holly

HTML *sigle m* HTML

'**hublot** ['yblo] *nm* porthole

'**huche** ['yʃ] *nf*: **~ à pain** bread bin

'**huer** ['ɥe] *vt* to boo

huile [ɥil] *nf* oil; **~ solaire** suntan oil; **huiler** *vt* to oil; **huileux, -euse** *adj* oily

huis [ɥi] *nm*: **à ~ clos** in camera

huissier [ɥisje] *nm* usher; (*JUR*) ≃ bailiff

'**huit** ['ɥi(t)] *num* eight; **samedi en ~** a week on Saturday; **dans ~ jours** in a week; '**huitaine** *nf*: **une huitaine (de jours)** a week or so; '**huitième** *num* eighth

huître [ɥitr] *nf* oyster

humain, e [ymɛ̃, ɛn] *adj* human; *(compatissant)* humane ♦ *nm* human (being); **humanitaire** *adj* humanitarian; **humanité** *nf* humanity

humble [œ̃bl] *adj* humble

humecter [ymɛkte] *vt* to dampen

'humer ['yme] *vt (plat)* to smell; *(parfum)* to inhale

humeur [ymœʀ] *nf* mood; **de bonne/mauvaise ~** in a good/bad mood

humide [ymid] *adj* damp; *(main, yeux)* moist; *(climat, chaleur)* humid; *(saison, route)* wet

humilier [ymilje] *vt* to humiliate

humilité [ymilite] *nf* humility, humbleness

humoristique [ymɔʀistik] *adj* humorous

humour [ymuʀ] *nm* humour; **avoir de l'~** to have a sense of humour; **~ noir** black humour

'huppé, e ['ype] *(fam) adj* posh

'hurlement ['yʀləmɑ̃] *nm* howling *no pl*, howl, yelling *no pl*, yell

'hurler ['yʀle] *vi* to howl, yell

hurluberlu [yʀlybɛʀly] *(péj) nm* crank

'hutte ['yt] *nf* hut

hybride [ibʀid] *adj, nm* hybrid

hydratant, e [idʀatɑ̃, ɑ̃t] *adj (crème)* moisturizing

hydraulique [idʀolik] *adj* hydraulic

hydravion [idʀavjɔ̃] *nm* seaplane

hydrogène [idʀɔʒɛn] *nm* hydrogen

hydroglisseur [idʀɔglisœʀ] *nm* hydroplane

hyène [jɛn] *nf* hyena

hygiénique [iʒenik] *adj* hygienic

hymne [imn] *nm* hymn; **~ national** national anthem

hypermarché [ipɛʀmaʀʃe] *nm* hypermarket

hypermétrope [ipɛʀmetʀɔp] *adj* long-sighted

hypertension [ipɛʀtɑ̃sjɔ̃] *nf* high blood pressure

hypnose [ipnoz] *nf* hypnosis; **hypnotiser** *vt* to hypnotize; **hypnotiseur** *nm* hypnotist

hypocrisie [ipɔkʀizi] *nf* hypocrisy; **hypocrite** *adj* hypocritical

hypothèque [ipɔtɛk] *nf* mortgage

hypothèse [ipɔtɛz] *nf* hypothesis

hystérique [isteʀik] *adj* hysterical

I, i

iceberg [ajsbɛʀg] *nm* iceberg

ici [isi] *adv* here; **jusqu'~** as far as this; *(temps)* so far; **d'~ demain** by tomorrow; **d'~ là** by then, in the meantime; **d'~ peu** before long

icône [ikon] *nf* icon

idéal, e, -aux [ideal, o] *adj* ideal ♦ *nm* ideal; **idéaliste** *adj* idealistic ♦ *nm/f* idealist

idée [ide] *nf* idea; **avoir dans l'~ que** to have an idea that; **~ fixe** obsession; **~ reçue** generally accepted idea; **~s noires** black *ou* dark thoughts

identifier [idɑ̃tifje] *vt* to identify; **s'~ à** *(héros etc)* to identify with

identique [idɑ̃tik] *adj*: **~ (à)** identical (to)

identité [idɑ̃tite] *nf* identity

idiot, e [idjo, idjɔt] *adj* idiotic ♦ *nm/f* idiot; **idiotie** *nf* idiotic thing

idole [idɔl] *nf* idol

if [if] *nm* yew

igloo [iglu] *nm* igloo

ignare [iɲaʀ] *adj* ignorant

ignifugé, e [iɲifyʒe] *adj* fireproof

ignoble [iɲɔbl] *adj* vile

ignorant, e [iɲɔʀɑ̃, ɑ̃t] *adj* ignorant

ignorer [iɲɔʀe] *vt* not to know; *(personne)* to ignore

il [il] *pron* he; *(animal, chose, en tournure impersonnelle)* it; **~s** they; *voir aussi* **avoir**

île [il] *nf* island; **l'~ Maurice** Mauritius; **les ~s anglo-normandes** the Channel Islands; **les ~s Britanniques** the British Isles

illégal, e, -aux [i(l)legal, o] *adj* illegal

illégitime [i(l)leʒitim] *adj* illegitimate

illettré, e [i(l)letʀe] *adj, nm/f* illiterate

illimité, e [i(l)limite] *adj* unlimited

illisible [i(l)lizibl] *adj* illegible; (*roman*) unreadable

illogique [i(l)lɔʒik] *adj* illogical

illumination [i(l)lyminasjɔ̃] *nf* illumination; (*idée*) flash of inspiration

illuminer [i(l)lymine] *vt* to light up; (*monument, rue: pour une fête*) to illuminate; (*: au moyen de projecteurs*) to floodlight

illusion [i(l)lyzjɔ̃] *nf* illusion; **se faire des ~s** to delude o.s.; **faire ~** to delude *ou* fool people; **illusionniste** *nm/f* conjuror

illustration [i(l)lystrasjɔ̃] *nf* illustration

illustre [i(l)lystr] *adj* illustrious

illustré, e [i(l)lystre] *adj* illustrated ♦ *nm* comic

illustrer [i(l)lystre] *vt* to illustrate; **s'~** to become famous, win fame

îlot [ilo] *nm* small island, islet

ils [il] *pron voir* **il**

image [imaʒ] *nf* (*gén*) picture; (*métaphore*) image; **~ de marque** brand image; (*fig*) public image; **imagé, e** *adj* (*texte*) full of imagery; (*langage*) colourful

imaginaire [imaʒinɛr] *adj* imaginary

imagination [imaʒinasjɔ̃] *nf* imagination; **avoir de l'~** to be imaginative

imaginer [imaʒine] *vt* to imagine; (*inventer: expédient*) to devise, think up; **s'~** *vt* (*se figurer: scène etc*) to imagine, picture; **s'~ que** to imagine that

imbattable [ɛ̃batabl] *adj* unbeatable

imbécile [ɛ̃besil] *adj* idiotic ♦ *nm/f* idiot; **imbécillité** *nf* idiocy; (*action*) idiotic thing; (*film, livre, propos*) rubbish

imbiber [ɛ̃bibe] *vt* to soak; **s'~ de** to become saturated with

imbu, e [ɛ̃by] *adj*: **~ de** full of

imbuvable [ɛ̃byvabl] *adj* undrinkable; (*personne: fam*) unbearable

imitateur, -trice [imitatœr, tris] *nm/f* (*gén*) imitator; (*MUSIC-HALL*) impersonator

imitation [imitasjɔ̃] *nf* imitation; (*de personnalité*) impersonation

imiter [imite] *vt* to imitate; (*contrefaire*) to forge; (*ressembler à*) to look like

immaculé, e [imakyle] *adj* (*linge, surface, réputation*) spotless; (*blancheur*) immaculate

immangeable [ɛ̃mɑ̃ʒabl] *adj* inedible

immatriculation [imatrikylasjɔ̃] *nf* registration

immatriculer [imatrikyle] *vt* to register; **faire/se faire ~** to register

immédiat, e [imedja, jat] *adj* immediate ♦ *nm*: **dans l'~** for the time being; **immédiatement** *adv* immediately

immense [i(m)mɑ̃s] *adj* immense

immerger [imɛrʒe] *vt* to immerse, submerge

immeuble [imœbl] *nm* building; (*à usage d'habitation*) block of flats

immigration [imigrasjɔ̃] *nf* immigration

immigré, e [imigre] *nm/f* immigrant

imminent, e [iminɑ̃, ɑ̃t] *adj* imminent

immiscer [imise]: **s'~** *vi*: **s'~ dans** to interfere in *ou* with

immobile [i(m)mɔbil] *adj* still, motionless

immobilier, -ière [imɔbilje, jɛr] *adj* property *cpd* ♦ *nm*: **l'~** the property business

immobiliser [imɔbilize] *vt* (*gén*) to immobilize; (*circulation, véhicule, affaires*) to bring to a standstill; **s'~** (*personne*) to stand still; (*machine, véhicule*) to come to a halt

immonde [i(m)mɔ̃d] *adj* foul

immoral, e, -aux [i(m)mɔral, o] *adj* immoral

immortel, le [imɔrtɛl] *adj* immortal

immuable [imɥabl] *adj* unchanging

immunisé, e [im(m)ynize] *adj*: **~ contre** immune to

immunité [imynite] *nf* immunity

impact [ɛ̃pakt] *nm* impact

impair, e [ɛ̃pɛr] *adj* odd ♦ *nm* faux pas, blunder

impardonnable [ɛ̃pardɔnabl] *adj* unpardonable, unforgivable

imparfait, e [ɛ̃parfɛ, ɛt] *adj* imperfect

impartial, e, -aux [ɛ̃parsjal, jo] *adj* impartial, unbiased

impasse [ɛ̃pɑs] *nf* dead end, cul-de-sac;

(fig) deadlock

impassible [ɛpasibl] *adj* impassive

impatience [ɛpasjɑ̃s] *nf* impatience

impatient, e [ɛpasjɑ̃, jɑ̃t] *adj* impatient; **impatienter: s'impatienter** *vi* to get impatient

impeccable [ɛpekabl] *adj (parfait)* perfect; *(propre)* impeccable; *(fam)* smashing

impensable [ɛpɑ̃sabl] *adj (événement hypothétique)* unthinkable; *(événement qui a eu lieu)* unbelievable

imper [ɛpɛR] *(fam) nm* raincoat

impératif, -ive [ɛperatif, iv] *adj* imperative ♦ *nm (LING)* imperative; **~s** *nmpl (exigences: d'une fonction, d'une charge)* requirements; *(: de la mode)* demands

impératrice [ɛperatris] *nf* empress

imperceptible [ɛpɛRsɛptibl] *adj* imperceptible

impérial, e, -aux [ɛperjal, jo] *adj* imperial; **impériale** *nf* top deck

impérieux, -euse [ɛperjø, jøz] *adj (caractère, ton)* imperious; *(obligation, besoin)* pressing, urgent

impérissable [ɛperisabl] *adj* undying

imperméable [ɛpɛRmeabl] *adj* waterproof; *(fig):* **~ à** impervious to ♦ *nm* raincoat

impertinent, e [ɛpɛRtinɑ̃, ɑ̃t] *adj* impertinent

imperturbable [ɛpɛRtyRbabl] *adj (personne, caractère)* unperturbable; *(sang-froid, gaieté, sérieux)* unshakeable

impétueux, -euse [ɛpetɥø, øz] *adj* impetuous

impitoyable [ɛpitwajabl] *adj* pitiless, merciless

implanter [ɛplɑ̃te]: **s'~** *vi* to be set up

impliquer [ɛplike] *vt* to imply; **~ qn (dans)** to implicate sb (in)

impoli, e [ɛpɔli] *adj* impolite, rude

impopulaire [ɛpɔpylɛR] *adj* unpopular

importance [ɛpɔRtɑ̃s] *nf* importance; **sans ~** unimportant

important, e [ɛpɔRtɑ̃, ɑ̃t] *adj* important; *(en quantité: somme, retard)* considerable,
sizeable; *(: dégâts)* extensive; *(péj: airs, ton)* self-important ♦ *nm:* **l'~** the important thing

importateur, -trice [ɛpɔRtatœR, tris] *nm/f* importer

importation [ɛpɔRtasjɔ̃] *nf* importation; *(produit)* import

importer [ɛpɔRte] *vt (COMM)* to import; *(maladies, plantes)* to introduce ♦ *vi (être important)* to matter; **il importe qu'il fasse** it is important that he should do; **peu m'importe** *(je n'ai pas de préférence)* I don't mind; *(je m'en moque)* I don't care; **peu importe (que)** it doesn't matter (if); *voir aussi* **n'importe**

importun, e [ɛpɔRtœ̃, yn] *adj* irksome, importunate; *(arrivée, visite)* inopportune, illtimed ♦ *nm* intruder; **importuner** *vt* to bother

imposable [ɛpozabl] *adj* taxable

imposant, e [ɛpozɑ̃, ɑ̃t] *adj* imposing

imposer [ɛpoze] *vt (taxer)* to tax; **s'~** *(être nécessaire)* to be imperative; **~ qch à qn** to impose sth on sb; **en ~ à** to impress; **s'~ comme** to emerge as; **s'~ par** to win recognition through

impossibilité [ɛpɔsibilite] *nf* impossibility; **être dans l'~ de faire qch** to be unable to do sth

impossible [ɛpɔsibl] *adj* impossible; **il m'est ~ de le faire** it is impossible for me to do it, I can't possibly do it; **faire l'~** to do one's utmost

imposteur [ɛpɔstœR] *nm* impostor

impôt [ɛpo] *nm* tax; **~s** *nmpl (contributions)* (income) tax *sg;* **payer 100 euros d'~s** to pay 100 euros in tax; **~ foncier** land tax; **~ sur le chiffre d'affaires** corporation *(BRIT) ou* corporate *(US)* tax; **~ sur le revenu** income tax

impotent, e [ɛpotɑ̃, ɑ̃t] *adj* disabled

impraticable [ɛpRatikabl] *adj (projet)* impracticable, unworkable; *(piste)* impassable

imprécis, e [ɛpResi, iz] *adj* imprecise

imprégner [ɛpReɲe] *vt (tissu)* to impregnate; *(lieu, air)* to fill; **s'~ de** *(fig)* to absorb

imprenable [ɛpʀənabl] *adj* (*forteresse*) impregnable; **vue ~** unimpeded outlook

imprésario [ɛpʀesaʀjo] *nm* manager

impression [ɛpʀesjɔ̃] *nf* impression; (*d'un ouvrage, tissu*) printing; **faire bonne ~** to make a good impression; **impressionnant, e** *adj* (*imposant*) impressive; (*bouleversant*) upsetting; **impressionner** *vt* (*frapper*) to impress; (*bouleverser*) to upset

imprévisible [ɛpʀevizibl] *adj* unforeseeable

imprévoyant, e [ɛpʀevwajɑ̃, ɑ̃t] *adj* lacking in foresight; (*en matière d'argent*) improvident

imprévu, e [ɛpʀevy] *adj* unforeseen, unexpected ♦ *nm* (*incident*) unexpected incident; **des vacances pleines d'~** holidays full of surprises; **en cas d'~** if anything unexpected happens; **sauf ~** unless anything unexpected crops up

imprimante [ɛpʀimɑ̃t] *nf* printer

imprimé [ɛpʀime] *nm* (*formulaire*) printed form; (*POSTES*) printed matter *no pl*; (*tissu*) printed fabric; **~ à fleur** floral print

imprimer [ɛpʀime] *vt* to print; (*publier*) to publish; **imprimerie** *nf* printing; (*établissement*) printing works *sg*; **imprimeur** *nm* printer

impromptu, e [ɛpʀɔ̃pty] *adj* (*repas, discours*) impromptu; (*départ*) sudden; (*visite*) surprise

impropre [ɛpʀɔpʀ] *adj* inappropriate; **~ à** unfit for

improviser [ɛpʀɔvize] *vt, vi* to improvise

improviste [ɛpʀɔvist]: **à l'~** *adv* unexpectedly, without warning

imprudence [ɛpʀydɑ̃s] *nf* (*d'une personne, d'une action*) carelessness *no pl*; (*d'une remarque*) imprudence *no pl*; **commettre une ~** to do something foolish

imprudent, e [ɛpʀydɑ̃, ɑ̃t] *adj* (*conducteur, geste, action*) careless; (*remarque*) unwise, imprudent; (*projet*) foolhardy

impudent, e [ɛpydɑ̃, ɑ̃t] *adj* impudent

impudique [ɛpydik] *adj* shameless

impuissant, e [ɛpɥisɑ̃, ɑ̃t] *adj* helpless; (*sans effet*) ineffectual; (*sexuellement*) impotent

impulsif, -ive [ɛpylsif, iv] *adj* impulsive

impulsion [ɛpylsjɔ̃] *nf* (*ÉLEC, instinct*) impulse; (*élan, influence*) impetus

impunément [ɛpynemɑ̃] *adv* with impunity

inabordable [inabɔʀdabl] *adj* (*cher*) prohibitive

inacceptable [inaksɛptabl] *adj* unacceptable

inaccessible [inaksesibl] *adj* inaccessible

inachevé, e [inaʃve] *adj* unfinished

inactif, -ive [inaktif, iv] *adj* inactive; (*remède*) ineffective; (*BOURSE: marché*) slack ♦ *nm*: **les ~s** the non-working population

inadapté, e [inadapte] *adj* (*gén*): **~ à** not adapted to, unsuited to; (*PSYCH*) maladjusted

inadéquat, e [inadekwa(t), kwat] *adj* inadequate

inadmissible [inadmisibl] *adj* inadmissible

inadvertance [inadvɛʀtɑ̃s]: **par ~** *adv* inadvertently

inaltérable [inalteʀabl] *adj* (*matière*) stable; (*fig*) unfailing; **~ à** unaffected by

inanimé, e [inanime] *adj* (*matière*) inanimate; (*évanoui*) unconscious; (*sans vie*) lifeless

inanition [inanisjɔ̃] *nf*: **tomber d'~** to faint with hunger (and exhaustion)

inaperçu, e [inapɛʀsy] *adj*: **passer ~** to go unnoticed

inapte [inapt] *adj*: **~ à** incapable of; (*MIL*) unfit for

inattaquable [inatakabl] *adj* (*texte, preuve*) irrefutable

inattendu, e [inatɑ̃dy] *adj* unexpected

inattentif, -ive [inatɑ̃tif, iv] *adj* inattentive; **~ à** (*dangers, détails*) heedless of; **inattention** *nf*: **faute d'inattention** careless mistake

inauguration [inogyʀasjɔ̃] *nf* inauguration

inaugurer [inogyʀe] *vt* (*monument*) to unveil; *(exposition, usine)* to open; *(fig)* to inaugurate

inavouable [inavwabl] *adj* shameful; *(bénéfices)* undisclosable

incalculable [ɛ̃kalkylabl] *adj* incalculable

incandescence [ɛ̃kɑ̃desɑ̃s] *nf*: **porter à ~** to heat white-hot

incapable [ɛ̃kapabl] *adj* incapable; **~ de faire** incapable of doing; *(empêché)* unable to do

incapacité [ɛ̃kapasite] *nf* (incompétence) incapability; *(impossibilité)* incapacity; **dans l'~ de faire** unable to do

incarcérer [ɛ̃karsere] *vt* to incarcerate, imprison

incarné, e [ɛ̃karne] *adj* (ongle) ingrown

incarner [ɛ̃karne] *vt* to embody, personify; *(THÉÂTRE)* to play

incassable [ɛ̃kasabl] *adj* unbreakable

incendiaire [ɛ̃sɑ̃djɛr] *adj* incendiary; *(fig: discours)* inflammatory

incendie [ɛ̃sɑ̃di] *nm* fire; **~ criminel** arson *no pl*; **~ de forêt** forest fire; **incendier** *vt* *(mettre le feu à)* to set fire to, set alight; *(brûler complètement)* to burn down; **se faire incendier** *(fam)* to get a rocket

incertain, e [ɛ̃sɛrtɛ̃, ɛn] *adj* uncertain; *(temps)* unsettled; *(imprécis: contours)* indistinct, blurred; **incertitude** *nf* uncertainty

incessamment [ɛ̃sesamɑ̃] *adv* very shortly

incident [ɛ̃sidɑ̃, ɑ̃t] *nm* incident; **~ de parcours** minor hitch *ou* setback; **~ technique** technical difficulties *pl*

incinérer [ɛ̃sinere] *vt* (ordures) to incinerate; *(mort)* to cremate

incisive [ɛ̃siziv] *nf* incisor

inciter [ɛ̃site] *vt*: **~ qn à (faire) qch** to encourage sb to do sth; *(à la révolte etc)* to incite sb to do sth

inclinable [ɛ̃klinabl] *adj*: **siège à dossier ~** reclining seat

inclinaison [ɛ̃klinɛzɔ̃] *nf* (déclivité: d'une route etc) incline; (: d'un toit) slope; *(état penché)* tilt

inclination [ɛ̃klinasjɔ̃] *nf* (penchant) inclination; **~ de (la) tête** nod (of the head); **~ (de buste)** bow

incliner [ɛ̃kline] *vt* (pencher) to tilt ♦ *vi*: **~ à qch/à faire** to incline towards sth/doing; **s'~ (devant)** to bow (before); *(céder)* to give in *ou* yield (to); **~ la tête** to give a slight bow

inclure [ɛ̃klyr] *vt* to include; *(joindre à un envoi)* to enclose; **jusqu'au 10 mars inclus** until 10th March inclusive

incognito [ɛ̃kɔɲito] *adv* incognito ♦ *nm*: **garder l'~** to remain incognito

incohérent, e [ɛ̃kɔerɑ̃, ɑ̃t] *adj* (comportement) inconsistent; *(geste, langage, texte)* incoherent

incollable [ɛ̃kɔlabl] *adj* (riz) non-stick; **il est ~** *(fam)* he's got all the answers

incolore [ɛ̃kɔlɔr] *adj* colourless

incommoder [ɛ̃kɔmɔde] *vt* (chaleur, odeur): **~ qn** to bother sb

incomparable [ɛ̃kɔ̃parabl] *adj* incomparable

incompatible [ɛ̃kɔ̃patibl] *adj* incompatible

incompétent, e [ɛ̃kɔ̃petɑ̃, ɑ̃t] *adj* incompetent

incomplet, -ète [ɛ̃kɔ̃plɛ, ɛt] *adj* incomplete

incompréhensible [ɛ̃kɔ̃preɑ̃sibl] *adj* incomprehensible

incompris, e [ɛ̃kɔ̃pri, iz] *adj* misunderstood

inconcevable [ɛ̃kɔ̃s(ə)vabl] *adj* inconceivable

inconciliable [ɛ̃kɔ̃siljabl] *adj* irreconcilable

inconditionnel, le [ɛ̃kɔ̃disjɔnɛl] *adj* unconditional; *(partisan)* unquestioning ♦ *nm/f* (d'un homme politique) ardent supporter; *(d'un écrivain, d'un chanteur)* ardent admirer; *(d'une activité)* fanatic

inconfort [ɛ̃kɔ̃fɔr] *nm* discomfort; **inconfortable** *adj* uncomfortable

incongru, e [ɛ̃kɔ̃gry] *adj* unseemly

inconnu, e [ɛ̃kɔny] *adj* unknown ♦ *nm/f* stranger ♦ *nm*: **l'~** the unknown; **inconnue** *nf* unknown factor

inconsciemment [ɛ̃kɔ̃sjamɑ̃] *adv* unconsciously

inconscient, e [ɛ̃kɔ̃sjɑ̃, jɑ̃t] _adj_ unconscious; _(irréfléchi)_ thoughtless, reckless; _(sentiment)_ subconscious ♦ _nm_ (PSYCH): **l'~** the unconscious; **~ de** unaware of

inconsidéré, e [ɛ̃kɔ̃sideʀe] _adj_ ill-considered

inconsistant, e [ɛ̃kɔ̃sistɑ̃, ɑ̃t] _adj_ _(fig)_ flimsy, weak

inconsolable [ɛ̃kɔ̃sɔlabl] _adj_ inconsolable

incontestable [ɛ̃kɔ̃tɛstabl] _adj_ indisputable

incontinent, e [ɛ̃kɔ̃tinɑ̃, ɑ̃t] _adj_ incontinent

incontournable [ɛ̃kɔ̃tuʀnabl] _adj_ unavoidable

incontrôlable [ɛ̃kɔ̃tʀolabl] _adj_ unverifiable; _(irrépressible)_ uncontrollable

inconvenant, e [ɛ̃kɔ̃v(ə)nɑ̃, ɑ̃t] _adj_ unseemly, improper

inconvénient [ɛ̃kɔ̃venjɑ̃] _nm_ disadvantage, drawback; **si vous n'y voyez pas d'~** if you have no objections

incorporer [ɛ̃kɔʀpɔʀe] _vt_: **~ (à)** to mix in (with); **~ (dans)** _(paragraphe etc)_ to incorporate (in); (MIL: _appeler_) to recruit (into); **il a très bien su s'~ à notre groupe** he was very easily incorporated into our group

incorrect, e [ɛ̃kɔʀɛkt] _adj_ _(impropre, inconvenant)_ improper; _(défectueux)_ faulty; _(inexact)_ incorrect; _(impoli)_ impolite; _(déloyal)_ underhand

incorrigible [ɛ̃kɔʀiʒibl] _adj_ incorrigible

incrédule [ɛ̃kʀedyl] _adj_ incredulous; (REL) unbelieving

increvable [ɛ̃kʀəvabl] _(fam)_ _adj_ tireless

incriminer [ɛ̃kʀimine] _vt_ _(personne)_ to incriminate; _(action, conduite)_ to bring under attack; _(bonne foi, honnêteté)_ to call into question

incroyable [ɛ̃kʀwajabl] _adj_ incredible

incruster [ɛ̃kʀyste] _vt_ (ART) to inlay; **s'~** _vi_ _(invité)_ to take root

inculpé, e [ɛ̃kylpe] _nm/f_ accused

inculper [ɛ̃kylpe] _vt_: **~ (de)** to charge (with)

inculquer [ɛ̃kylke] _vt_: **~ qch à** to inculcate sth in _ou_ instil sth into

inculte [ɛ̃kylt] _adj_ uncultivated; _(esprit, peuple)_ uncultured

Inde [ɛ̃d] _nf_: **l'~** India

indécent, e [ɛ̃desɑ̃, ɑ̃t] _adj_ indecent

indéchiffrable [ɛ̃deʃifʀabl] _adj_ indecipherable

indécis, e [ɛ̃desi, iz] _adj_ _(par nature)_ indecisive; _(temporairement)_ undecided

indéfendable [ɛ̃defɑ̃dabl] _adj_ indefensible

indéfini, e [ɛ̃defini] _adj_ _(imprécis, incertain)_ undefined; _(illimité,_ LING) indefinite; **indéfiniment** _adv_ indefinitely; **indéfinissable** _adj_ indefinable

indélébile [ɛ̃delebil] _adj_ indelible

indélicat, e [ɛ̃delika, at] _adj_ tactless

indemne [ɛ̃dɛmn] _adj_ unharmed; **indemniser** _vt_: **indemniser qn (de)** to compensate sb (for)

indemnité [ɛ̃dɛmnite] _nf_ _(dédommagement)_ compensation _no pl_; _(allocation)_ allowance; **indemnité de licenciement** redundancy payment

indépendamment [ɛ̃depɑ̃damɑ̃] _adv_ independently; **~ de** _(abstraction faite de)_ irrespective of; _(en plus de)_ over and above

indépendance [ɛ̃depɑ̃dɑ̃s] _nf_ independence

indépendant, e [ɛ̃depɑ̃dɑ̃, ɑ̃t] _adj_ independent; **~ de** independent of

indescriptible [ɛ̃dɛskʀiptibl] _adj_ indescribable

indésirable [ɛ̃deziʀabl] _adj_ undesirable

indestructible [ɛ̃dɛstʀyktibl] _adj_ indestructible

indétermination [ɛ̃detɛʀminasjɔ̃] _nf_ _(irrésolution: chronique)_ indecision; (: _temporaire)_ indecisiveness

indéterminé, e [ɛ̃detɛʀmine] _adj_ _(date, cause, nature)_ unspecified; _(forme, longueur, quantité)_ indeterminate

index [ɛ̃dɛks] _nm_ _(doigt)_ index finger; _(d'un livre etc)_ index; **mettre à l'~** to blacklist; **indexé, e** _adj_ (ÉCON): **indexé (sur)**

index-linked (to)

indic [ɛ̃dik] (fam) nm (POLICE) grass

indicateur [ɛ̃dikatœʀ] nm (POLICE) informer; (TECH) gauge, indicator

indicatif, -ive [ɛ̃dikatif, iv] adj: **à titre ~** for (your) information ♦ nm (LING) indicative; (RADIO) theme ou signature tune; (TÉL) dialling code

indication [ɛ̃dikasjɔ̃] nf indication; (renseignement) information no pl; **~s** nfpl (directives) instructions

indice [ɛ̃dis] nm (marque, signe) indication, sign; (POLICE: lors d'une enquête) clue; (JUR: présomption) piece of evidence; (SCIENCE, ÉCON, TECH) index

indicible [ɛ̃disibl] adj inexpressible

indien, ne [ɛ̃djɛ̃, jɛn] adj Indian ♦ nm/f: **I~, ne** Indian

indifféremment [ɛ̃diferamɑ̃] adv (sans distinction) equally (well)

indifférence [ɛ̃diferɑ̃s] nf indifference

indifférent, e [ɛ̃diferɑ̃, ɑ̃t] adj (peu intéressé) indifferent; **ça m'est ~** it doesn't matter to me; **elle m'est ~e** I am indifferent to her

indigence [ɛ̃diʒɑ̃s] nf poverty

indigène [ɛ̃diʒɛn] adj native, indigenous; (des gens du pays) local ♦ nm/f native

indigeste [ɛ̃diʒɛst] adj indigestible

indigestion [ɛ̃diʒɛstjɔ̃] nf indigestion no pl

indigne [ɛ̃diɲ] adj unworthy

indigner [ɛ̃diɲe] vt: **s'~ (de ou contre)** to get indignant (at)

indiqué, e [ɛ̃dike] adj (date, lieu) agreed; (traitement) appropriate; (conseillé) advisable

indiquer [ɛ̃dike] vt (suj: pendule, aiguille) to show; (: étiquette, panneau) to show, indicate; (renseigner sur) to point out, tell; (déterminer: date, lieu) to give, state; (signaler, dénoter) to indicate, point to; **~ qch/qn à qn** (montrer du doigt) to point sth/sb out to sb; (faire connaître: médecin, restaurant) to tell sb of sth/sb

indirect, e [ɛ̃diʀɛkt] adj indirect

indiscipliné, e [ɛ̃disipline] adj undisciplined

indiscret, -ète [ɛ̃diskʀɛ, ɛt] adj indiscreet

indiscutable [ɛ̃diskytabl] adj indisputable

indispensable [ɛ̃dispɑ̃sabl] adj indispensable, essential

indisposé, e [ɛ̃dispoze] adj indisposed

indisposer [ɛ̃dispoze] vt (incommoder) to upset; (déplaire à) to antagonize; (énerver) to irritate

indistinct, e [ɛ̃distɛ̃(kt), ɛ̃kt] adj indistinct; **indistinctement** adv (voir, prononcer) indistinctly; (sans distinction) indiscriminately

individu [ɛ̃dividy] nm individual; **individuel, le** adj (gén) individual; (responsabilité, propriété, liberté) personal; **chambre individuelle** single room; **maison individuelle** detached house

indolore [ɛ̃dɔlɔʀ] adj painless

indomptable [ɛ̃dɔ̃(p)tabl] adj untameable; (fig) invincible

Indonésie [ɛ̃dɔnezi] nf Indonesia

indu, e [ɛ̃dy] adj: **à une heure ~e** at some ungodly hour

induire [ɛ̃dɥiʀ] vt: **~ qn en erreur** to lead sb astray, mislead sb

indulgent, e [ɛ̃dylʒɑ̃, ɑ̃t] adj (parent, regard) indulgent; (juge, examinateur) lenient

industrialisé, e [ɛ̃dystʀijalize] adj industrialized

industrie [ɛ̃dystʀi] nf industry; **industriel, le** adj industrial ♦ nm industrialist

inébranlable [inebʀɑ̃labl] adj (masse, colonne) solid; (personne, certitude, foi) unshakeable

inédit, e [inedi, it] adj (correspondance, livre) hitherto unpublished; (spectacle, moyen) novel, original; (film) unreleased

ineffaçable [inefasabl] adj indelible

inefficace [inefikas] adj (remède, moyen) ineffective; (machine, employé) inefficient

inégal, e, -aux [inegal, o] adj unequal; (irrégulier) uneven; **inégalable** adj matchless; **inégalé, e** adj (record) unequalled; (beauté) unrivalled; **inégalité** nf inequality

inépuisable [inepɥizabl] adj inexhaustible

inerte [inɛʀt] *adj* (*immobile*) lifeless; (*sans réaction*) passive

inespéré, e [inɛspeʀe] *adj* unexpected, unhoped-for

inestimable [inɛstimabl] *adj* priceless; (*fig: bienfait*) invaluable

inévitable [inevitabl] *adj* unavoidable; (*fatal, habituel*) inevitable

inexact, e [inɛgza(kt), akt] *adj* inaccurate

inexcusable [inɛkskyzabl] *adj* unforgivable

inexplicable [inɛksplikabl] *adj* inexplicable

in extremis [inɛkstʀemis] *adv* at the last minute ♦ *adj* last-minute

infaillible [ɛ̃fajibl] *adj* infallible

infâme [ɛ̃fɑm] *adj* vile

infarctus [ɛ̃faʀktys] *nm*: ~ **(du myocarde)** coronary (thrombosis)

infatigable [ɛ̃fatigabl] *adj* tireless

infect, e [ɛ̃fɛkt] *adj* revolting; (*personne*) obnoxious; (*temps*) foul

infecter [ɛ̃fɛkte] *vt* (*atmosphère, eau*) to contaminate; (*MÉD*) to infect; **s'~** to become infected *ou* septic; **infection** *nf* infection; (*puanteur*) stench

inférieur, e [ɛ̃feʀjœʀ] *adj* lower; (*en qualité, intelligence*) inferior; ~ **à** (*somme, quantité*) less *ou* smaller than; (*moins bon que*) inferior to

infernal, e, -aux [ɛ̃fɛʀnal, o] *adj* (*insupportable: chaleur, rythme*) infernal; (: *enfant*) horrid; (*satanique, effrayant*) diabolical

infidèle [ɛ̃fidɛl] *adj* unfaithful

infiltrer [ɛ̃filtʀe] *vb*: **s'~ dans** to get into; (*liquide*) to seep through; (*fig: groupe, ennemi*) to infiltrate

infime [ɛ̃fim] *adj* minute, tiny

infini, e [ɛ̃fini] *adj* infinite ♦ *nm* infinity; **à l'~** endlessly; **infiniment** *adv* infinitely; **infinité** *nf*: **une infinité de** an infinite number of

infinitif [ɛ̃finitif, iv] *nm* infinitive

infirme [ɛ̃fiʀm] *adj* disabled ♦ *nm/f* disabled person

infirmerie [ɛ̃fiʀməʀi] *nf* medical room

infirmier, -ière [ɛ̃fiʀmje] *nm/f* nurse; **infirmière chef** sister

infirmité [ɛ̃fiʀmite] *nf* disability

inflammable [ɛ̃flamabl] *adj* (in)flammable

inflation [ɛ̃flasjɔ̃] *nf* inflation

infliger [ɛ̃fliʒe] *vt*: ~ **qch (à qn)** to inflict sth (on sb); (*amende, sanction*) to impose sth (on sb)

influençable [ɛ̃flyɑ̃sabl] *adj* easily influenced

influence [ɛ̃flyɑ̃s] *nf* influence; **influencer** *vt* to influence; **influent, e** *adj* influential

informateur, -trice [ɛ̃fɔʀmatœʀ, tʀis] *nm/f* (*POLICE*) informer

informaticien, ne [ɛ̃fɔʀmatisjɛ̃, jɛn] *nm/f* computer scientist

information [ɛ̃fɔʀmasjɔ̃] *nf* (*renseignement*) piece of information; (*PRESSE, TV: nouvelle*) item of news; (*diffusion de renseignements, INFORM*) information; (*JUR*) inquiry, investigation; **~s** *nfpl* (*TV*) news *sg*

informatique [ɛ̃fɔʀmatik] *nf* (*technique*) data processing; (*science*) computer science ♦ *adj* computer *cpd*; **informatiser** *vt* to computerize

informe [ɛ̃fɔʀm] *adj* shapeless

informer [ɛ̃fɔʀme] *vt*: ~ **qn (de)** to inform sb (of); **s'~ (de/si)** to inquire *ou* find out (about/whether *ou* if)

infos [ɛ̃fo] *nfpl*: **les ~** the news *sg*

infraction [ɛ̃fʀaksjɔ̃] *nf* offence; ~ **à** violation *ou* breach of; **être en ~** to be in breach of the law

infranchissable [ɛ̃fʀɑ̃ʃisabl] *adj* impassable; (*fig*) insuperable

infrarouge [ɛ̃fʀaʀuʒ] *adj* infrared

infrastructure [ɛ̃fʀastʀyktyʀ] *nf* (*AVIAT, MIL*) ground installations *pl*; (*ÉCON: touristique etc*) infrastructure

infuser [ɛ̃fyze] *vt, vi* (*thé*) to brew; (*tisane*) to infuse; **infusion** *nf* (*tisane*) herb tea

ingénier [ɛ̃ʒenje]: **s'~** *vi*: **s'~ à faire** to strive to do

ingénierie [ɛ̃ʒeniʀi] *nf* engineering; ~ **génétique** genetic engineering

ingénieur [ɛ̃ʒenjœʀ] *nm* engineer; **ingénieur du son** sound engineer

ingénieux, -euse [ɛ̃ʒenjø, jøz] *adj* ingenious, clever

ingénu, e [ɛ̃ʒeny] *adj* ingenuous, artless

ingérer, e [ɛ̃ʒeʀe] *vb*: **s'~ dans**

ingrat, e [ɛ̃gʀa, at] *adj (personne)* ungrateful; *(travail, sujet)* thankless; *(visage)* unprepossessing

ingrédient [ɛ̃gʀedjɑ̃] *nm* ingredient

ingurgiter [ɛ̃gyʀʒite] *vt* to swallow

inhabitable [inabitabl] *adj* uninhabitable

inhabité, e [inabite] *adj* uninhabited

inhabituel, le [inabitɥɛl] *adj* unusual

inhibition [inibisjɔ̃] *nf* inhibition

inhumain, e [inymɛ̃, ɛn] *adj* inhuman

inhumation [inymasjɔ̃] *nf* burial

inhumer [inyme] *vt* to inter, bury

inimaginable [inimaʒinabl] *adj* unimaginable

ininterrompu, e [inɛ̃teʀɔ̃py] *adj (file, série)* unbroken; *(flot, vacarme)* uninterrupted, non-stop; *(effort)* unremitting, continuous; *(suite, ligne)* unbroken

initial, e, -aux [inisjal, jo] *adj* initial; **initiale** *nf* initial; **initialiser** *vt* to initialize

initiation [inisjasjɔ̃] *nf*: **~ à** introduction to

initiative [inisjativ] *nf* initiative

initier [inisje] *vt*: **~ qn à** to initiate sb into; *(faire découvrir: art, jeu)* to introduce sb to

injecté, e [ɛ̃ʒekte] *adj*: **yeux ~s de sang** bloodshot eyes

injecter [ɛ̃ʒekte] *vt* to inject; **injection** *nf* injection; **à injection** *(AUTO)* fuel injection *cpd*

injure [ɛ̃ʒyʀ] *nf* insult, abuse *no pl*; **injurier** *vt* to insult, abuse; **injurieux, -euse** *adj* abusive, insulting

injuste [ɛ̃ʒyst] *adj* unjust, unfair; **injustice** *nf* injustice

inlassable [ɛ̃lɑsabl] *adj* tireless

inné, e [i(n)ne] *adj* innate, inborn

innocent, e [inɔsɑ̃, ɑ̃t] *adj* innocent; **innocenter** *vt* to clear, prove innocent

innombrable [i(n)nɔ̃bʀabl] *adj* innumerable

innommable [i(n)nɔmabl] *adj* unspeakable

innover [inɔve] *vi* to break new ground

inoccupé, e [inɔkype] *adj* unoccupied

inodore [inɔdɔʀ] *adj (gaz)* odourless; *(fleur)* scentless

inoffensif, -ive [inɔfɑ̃sif, iv] *adj* harmless, innocuous

inondation [inɔ̃dasjɔ̃] *nf* flood

inonder [inɔ̃de] *vt* to flood; **~ de** to flood with

inopiné, e [inɔpine] *adj* unexpected; *(mort)* sudden

inopportun, e [inɔpɔʀtœ̃, yn] *adj* illtimed, untimely

inoubliable [inublijabl] *adj* unforgettable

inouï, e [inwi] *adj* unheard-of, extraordinary

inox [inɔks] *nm* stainless steel

inqualifiable [ɛ̃kalifjabl] *adj* unspeakable

inquiet, -ète [ɛ̃kjɛ, ɛ̃kjɛt] *adj* anxious; inquiétant, e *adj* worrying, disturbing; inquiéter *vt* to worry; **s'inquiéter** to worry; **s'inquiéter de** to worry about; *(s'enquérir de)* to inquire about; **inquiétude** *nf* anxiety

insaisissable [ɛ̃sezisabl] *adj (fugitif, ennemi)* elusive; *(différence, nuance)* imperceptible

insalubre [ɛ̃salybʀ] *adj* insalubrious

insatisfaisant, e [ɛ̃satisfəzɑ̃, ɑ̃t] *adj* unsatisfactory

insatisfait, e [ɛ̃satisfɛ, ɛt] *adj (non comblé)* unsatisfied; *(mécontent)* dissatisfied

inscription [ɛ̃skʀipsjɔ̃] *nf* inscription; *(immatriculation)* enrolment

inscrire [ɛ̃skʀiʀ] *vt (marquer: sur son calepin etc)* to note *ou* write down; *(: sur un mur, une affiche etc)* to write; *(: dans la pierre, le métal)* to inscribe; *(mettre: sur une liste, un budget etc)* to put down; **s'~** *(pour une excursion etc)* to put one's name down; **s'~ (à)** *(club, parti)* to join; *(université)* to register *ou* enrol (at); *(examen, concours)* to register (for); **~ qn à** *(club, parti)* to enrol sb at

insecte [ɛ̃sɛkt] nm insect; insecticide nm insecticide

insensé, e [ɛ̃sɑ̃se] adj mad

insensibiliser [ɛ̃sɑ̃sibilize] vt to anaesthetize

insensible [ɛ̃sɑ̃sibl] adj (nerf, membre) numb; (dur, indifférent) insensitive

inséparable [ɛ̃separabl] adj inseparable ♦ nm: **~s** (oiseaux) lovebirds

insigne [ɛ̃siɲ] nm (d'un parti, club) badge; (d'une fonction) insignia ♦ adj distinguished

insignifiant, e [ɛ̃siɲifjɑ̃, jɑ̃t] adj insignificant; trivial

insinuer [ɛ̃sinɥe] vt to insinuate; **s'~ dans** (fig) to worm one's way into

insipide [ɛ̃sipid] adj insipid

insister [ɛ̃siste] vi to insist; (continuer à sonner) to keep on trying; **~ sur** (détail, sujet) to lay stress on

insolation [ɛ̃sɔlasjɔ̃] nf (MÉD) sunstroke no pl

insolent, e [ɛ̃sɔlɑ̃, ɑ̃t] adj insolent

insolite [ɛ̃sɔlit] adj strange, unusual

insomnie [ɛ̃sɔmni] nf insomnia no pl

insonoriser [ɛ̃sɔnɔrize] vt to soundproof

insouciant, e [ɛ̃susjɑ̃, jɑ̃t] adj carefree; **~ du danger** heedless of (the) danger

insoumis, e [ɛ̃sumi, iz] adj (caractère, enfant) rebellious, refractory; (contrée, tribu) unsubdued

insoupçonnable [ɛ̃supsɔnabl] adj unsuspected; (personne) above suspicion

insoupçonné, e [ɛ̃supsɔne] adj unsuspected

insoutenable [ɛ̃sut(ə)nabl] adj (argument) untenable; (chaleur) unbearable

inspecter [ɛ̃spɛkte] vt to inspect; inspecteur, -trice nm/f inspector; **inspecteur d'Académie** (regional) director of education; **inspecteur des finances** ≃ tax inspector (BRIT), ≃ Internal Revenue Service agent (US); inspection nf inspection

inspirer [ɛ̃spire] vt (gén) to inspire ♦ vi (aspirer) to breathe in; **s'~ de** (suj: artiste) to draw one's inspiration from

instable [ɛ̃stabl] adj unstable; (meuble, équilibre) unsteady; (temps) unsettled

installation [ɛ̃stalasjɔ̃] nf installation; **~s** nfpl facilities

installer [ɛ̃stale] vt (loger, placer) to put; (meuble, gaz, électricité) to put in; (rideau, étagère, tente) to put up; (appartement) to fit out; **s'~** (s'établir: artisan, dentiste etc) to set o.s. up; (se loger) to settle; (emménager) to settle in; (sur un siège, à un emplacement) to settle (down); (fig: maladie, grève) to take a firm hold

instance [ɛ̃stɑ̃s] nf (ADMIN: autorité) authority; **affaire en ~** matter pending; **être en ~ de divorce** to be awaiting a divorce

instant [ɛ̃stɑ̃] nm moment, instant; **dans un ~** in a moment; **à l'~** this instant; **pour l'~** for the moment, for the time being

instantané, e [ɛ̃stɑ̃tane] adj (lait, café) instant; (explosion, mort) instantaneous ♦ nm snapshot

instar [ɛ̃star]: **à l'~ de** prép following the example of, like

instaurer [ɛ̃stɔre] vt to institute; (couvre-feu) to impose

instinct [ɛ̃stɛ̃] nm instinct; **instinctivement** adv instinctively

instit [ɛ̃stit] (fam) nm/f (primary school) teacher

instituer [ɛ̃stitɥe] vt to establish

institut [ɛ̃stity] nm institute; **~ de beauté** beauty salon; **Institut universitaire de technologie** ≃ polytechnic

instituteur, -trice [ɛ̃stitytœr, tris] nm/f (primary school) teacher

institution [ɛ̃stitysjɔ̃] nf institution; (collège) private school

instructif, -ive [ɛ̃stryktif, iv] adj instructive

instruction [ɛ̃stryksjɔ̃] nf (enseignement, savoir) education; (JUR) (preliminary) investigation and hearing; **~s** nfpl (ordres, mode d'emploi) instructions; **~ civique** civics sg

instruire [ɛ̃stʀɥiʀ] *vt* (*élèves*) to teach; (*recrues*) to train; (*JUR: affaire*) to conduct the investigation for; **s'~** to educate o.s.; **instruit, e** *adj* educated

instrument [ɛ̃stʀymɑ̃] *nm* instrument; **~ à cordes/vent** stringed/wind instrument; **~ de mesure** measuring instrument; **~ de musique** musical instrument; **~ de travail** (working) tool

insu [ɛ̃sy] *nm*: **à l'~ de qn** without sb knowing (it)

insubmersible [ɛ̃sybmɛʀsibl] *adj* unsinkable

insuffisant, e [ɛ̃syfizɑ̃, ɑ̃t] *adj* (*en quantité*) insufficient; (*en qualité*) inadequate; (*sur une copie*) poor

insulaire [ɛ̃sylɛʀ] *adj* island *cpd*; (*attitude*) insular

insuline [ɛ̃sylin] *nf* insulin

insulte [ɛ̃sylt] *nf* insult; **insulter** *vt* to insult

insupportable [ɛ̃sypɔʀtabl] *adj* unbearable

insurger [ɛ̃syʀʒe] *vb*: **s'~ (contre)** to rise up *ou* rebel (against)

insurmontable [ɛ̃syʀmɔ̃tabl] *adj* (*difficulté*) insuperable; (*aversion*) unconquerable

insurrection [ɛ̃syʀɛksjɔ̃] *nf* insurrection

intact, e [ɛ̃takt] *adj* intact

intangible [ɛ̃tɑ̃ʒibl] *adj* intangible; (*principe*) inviolable

intarissable [ɛ̃taʀisabl] *adj* inexhaustible

intégral, e, -aux [ɛ̃tegʀal, o] *adj* complete; **texte ~** unabridged version; **bronzage ~** all-over suntan; **intégralement** *adv* in full; **intégralité** *nf* whole; **dans son intégralité** in full; **intégrant, e** *adj*: **faire partie intégrante de** to be an integral part of

intègre [ɛ̃tegʀ] *adj* upright

intégrer [ɛ̃tegʀe] *vt*: **bien s'~** to integrate well

intégrisme [ɛ̃tegʀism] *nm* fundamentalism

intellectuel, le [ɛ̃telɛktɥɛl] *adj* intellectual

♦ *nm/f* intellectual; (*péj*) highbrow

intelligence [ɛ̃teliʒɑ̃s] *nf* intelligence; (*compréhension*): **l'~ de** the understanding of; (*complicité*): **regard d'~** glance of complicity; (*accord*): **vivre en bonne ~ avec qn** to be on good terms with sb

intelligent, e [ɛ̃teliʒɑ̃, ɑ̃t] *adj* intelligent

intelligible [ɛ̃teliʒibl] *adj* intelligible

intempéries [ɛ̃tɑ̃peʀi] *nfpl* bad weather *sg*

intempestif, -ive [ɛ̃tɑ̃pestif, iv] *adj* untimely

intenable [ɛ̃t(ə)nabl] *adj* (*chaleur*) unbearable

intendant, e [ɛ̃tɑ̃dɑ̃] *nm/f* (*MIL*) quartermaster; (*SCOL*) bursar

intense [ɛ̃tɑ̃s] *adj* intense; **intensif, -ive** *adj* intensive; **un cours intensif** a crash course

intenter [ɛ̃tɑ̃te] *vt*: **~ un procès contre** *ou* **à** to start proceedings against

intention [ɛ̃tɑ̃sjɔ̃] *nf* intention; (*JUR*) intent; **avoir l'~ de faire** to intend to do; **à l'~ de** for; (*renseignement*) for the benefit of; (*film, ouvrage*) aimed at; **à cette ~** with this aim in view; **intentionné, e** *adj*: **bien intentionné** well-meaning *ou* -intentioned; **mal intentionné** ill-intentioned

interactif, -ive [ɛ̃teʀaktif, iv] *adj* (*COMPUT*) interactive

intercalaire [ɛ̃teʀkalɛʀ] *nm* divider

intercaler [ɛ̃teʀkale] *vt* to insert

intercepter [ɛ̃teʀsepte] *vt* to intercept; (*lumière, chaleur*) to cut off

interchangeable [ɛ̃teʀʃɑ̃ʒabl] *adj* interchangeable

interclasse [ɛ̃teʀklɑs] *nm* (*SCOL*) break (between classes)

interdiction [ɛ̃teʀdiksjɔ̃] *nf* ban; **~ de stationner** no parking; **~ de fumer** no smoking

interdire [ɛ̃teʀdiʀ] *vt* to forbid; (*ADMIN*) to ban, prohibit; (: *journal, livre*) to ban; **~ à qn de faire** to forbid sb to do; (*suj: empêchement*) to prevent sb from doing

interdit, e [ɛ̃tɛʀdi, it] *adj* (*stupéfait*) taken aback

intéressant, e [ɛ̃teʀesɑ̃, ɑ̃t] *adj* interesting; (*avantageux*) attractive

intéressé, e [ɛ̃teʀese] *adj* (*parties*) involved, concerned; (*amitié, motifs*) self-interested

intéresser [ɛ̃teʀese] *vt* (*captiver*) to interest; (*toucher*) to be of interest to; (*ADMIN: concerner*) to affect, concern; **s'~ à** to be interested in

intérêt [ɛ̃teʀɛ] *nm* interest; (*égoïsme*) self-interest; **tu as ~ à accepter** it's in your interest to accept; **tu as ~ à te dépêcher** you'd better hurry

intérieur, e [ɛ̃teʀjœʀ] *adj* (*mur, escalier, poche*) inside; (*commerce, politique*) domestic; (*cour, calme, vie*) inner; (*navigation*) inland ♦ *nm* (*d'une maison, d'un récipient etc*) inside; (*d'un pays, aussi décor, mobilier*) interior; **à l'~ (de)** inside; **intérieurement** *adv* inwardly

intérim [ɛ̃teʀim] *nm* interim period; **faire de l'~** to temp; **assurer l'~ (de)** to deputize for; **par ~** interim

intérimaire [ɛ̃teʀimɛʀ] *adj* (*directeur, ministre*) acting; (*secrétaire, personnel*) temporary ♦ *nm/f* (*secrétaire*) temporary secretary, temp (*BRIT*)

interlocuteur, -trice [ɛ̃tɛʀlɔkytœʀ, tʀis] *nm/f* speaker; **son ~** the person he was speaking to

interloquer [ɛ̃tɛʀlɔke] *vt* to take aback

intermède [ɛ̃tɛʀmɛd] *nm* interlude

intermédiaire [ɛ̃tɛʀmedjɛʀ] *adj* intermediate; (*solution*) temporary ♦ *nm/f* intermediary; (*COMM*) middleman; **sans ~** directly; **par l'~ de** through

interminable [ɛ̃tɛʀminabl] *adj* endless

intermittence [ɛ̃tɛʀmitɑ̃s] *nf*: **par ~** sporadically, intermittently

internat [ɛ̃tɛʀna] *nm* (*SCOL*) boarding school

international, e, -aux [ɛ̃tɛʀnasjɔnal, o] *adj, nm/f* international

interne [ɛ̃tɛʀn] *adj* internal ♦ *nm/f* (*SCOL*) boarder; (*MÉD*) houseman

interner [ɛ̃tɛʀne] *vt* (*POL*) to intern; (*MÉD*) to confine to a mental institution

Internet [ɛ̃tɛʀnɛt] *nm* Internet

interpeller [ɛ̃tɛʀpəle] *vt* (*appeler*) to call out to; (*apostropher*) to shout at; (*POLICE, POL*) to question; (*concerner*) to concern

interphone [ɛ̃tɛʀfɔn] *nm* intercom; (*d'immeuble*) entry phone

interposer [ɛ̃tɛʀpoze] *vt*: **s'~** to intervene; **par personnes interposées** through a third party

interprétation [ɛ̃tɛʀpʀetasjɔ̃] *nf* interpretation

interprète [ɛ̃tɛʀpʀɛt] *nm/f* interpreter; (*porte-parole*) spokesperson

interpréter [ɛ̃tɛʀpʀete] *vt* to interpret; (*jouer*) to play; (*chanter*) to sing

interrogateur, -trice [ɛ̃teʀɔgatœʀ, tʀis] *adj* questioning, inquiring

interrogatif, -ive [ɛ̃teʀɔgatif, iv] *adj* (*LING*) interrogative

interrogation [ɛ̃teʀɔgasjɔ̃] *nf* question; (*action*) questioning; (*SCOL*) (written *ou* oral) test

interrogatoire [ɛ̃teʀɔgatwaʀ] *nm* (*POLICE*) questioning *no pl*; (*JUR, aussi fig*) cross-examination

interroger [ɛ̃teʀɔʒe] *vt* to question; (*INFORM*) to consult; (*SCOL*) to test

interrompre [ɛ̃teʀɔ̃pʀ] *vt* (*gén*) to interrupt; (*négociations*) to break off; (*match*) to stop; **s'~** to break off; **interrupteur** *nm* switch; **interruption** *nf* interruption; (*pause*) break; **sans interruption** without stopping

intersection [ɛ̃tɛʀsɛksjɔ̃] *nf* intersection

interstice [ɛ̃tɛʀstis] *nm* crack; (*de volet*) slit

interurbain, e [ɛ̃tɛʀyʀbɛ̃, ɛn] *adj* (*TÉL*) long-distance

intervalle [ɛ̃tɛʀval] *nm* (*espace*) space; (*de temps*) interval; **à deux jours d'~** two days apart

intervenir [ɛ̃tɛʀvəniʀ] *vi* (*gén*) to intervene; **~ auprès de qn** to intervene with sb

intervention [ɛ̃tɛRvɑ̃sjɔ̃] *nf* intervention; (*discours*) speech; ~ **chirurgicale** (surgical) operation

intervertir [ɛ̃tɛRvɛRtiR] *vt* to invert (the order of), reverse

interview [ɛ̃tɛRvju] *nf* interview

intestin [ɛ̃tɛstɛ̃, in] *nm* intestine

intime [ɛ̃tim] *adj* intimate; (*vie*) private; (*conviction*) inmost; (*dîner, cérémonie*) quiet ♦ *nm/f* close friend; **un journal** ~ a diary

intimider [ɛ̃timide] *vt* to intimidate

intimité [ɛ̃timite] *nf*: **dans l'**~ in private; (*sans formalités*) with only a few friends, quietly

intitulé, e [ɛ̃tityle] *adj* entitled

intolérable [ɛ̃tɔleRabl] *adj* intolerable

intox [ɛ̃tɔks] (*fam*) *nf* brainwashing

intoxication [ɛ̃tɔksikasjɔ̃] *nf*: ~ **alimentaire** food poisoning

intoxiquer [ɛ̃tɔksike] *vt* to poison; (*fig*) to brainwash

intraduisible [ɛ̃tRadɥizibl] *adj* untranslatable; (*fig*) inexpressible

intraitable [ɛ̃tRɛtabl] *adj* inflexible, uncompromising

intranet [ɛ̃tRanɛt] *nm* intranet

intransigeant, e [ɛ̃tRɑ̃ziʒɑ̃, ɑ̃t] *adj* intransigent

intransitif, -ive [ɛ̃tRɑ̃zitif, iv] *adj* (*LING*) intransitive

intrépide [ɛ̃tRepid] *adj* dauntless

intrigue [ɛ̃tRig] *nf* (*scénario*) plot; **intriguer** *vt* to puzzle, intrigue

intrinsèque [ɛ̃tRɛ̃sɛk] *adj* intrinsic

introduction [ɛ̃tRɔdyksjɔ̃] *nf* introduction

introduire [ɛ̃tRɔdɥiR] *vt* to introduce; (*visiteur*) to show in; (*aiguille, clef*): ~ **qch dans** to insert *ou* introduce sth into; **s'**~ **(dans)** to get in(to); (*dans un groupe*) to get o.s. accepted (into)

introuvable [ɛ̃tRuvabl] *adj* which cannot be found; (*COMM*) unobtainable

introverti, e [ɛ̃tRɔvɛRti] *nm/f* introvert

intrus, e [ɛ̃tRy, yz] *nm/f* intruder

intrusion [ɛ̃tRyzjɔ̃] *nf* intrusion

intuition [ɛ̃tɥisjɔ̃] *nf* intuition

inusable [inyzabl] *adj* hard-wearing

inusité, e [inyzite] *adj* rarely used

inutile [inytil] *adj* useless; (*superflu*) unnecessary; **inutilement** *adv* unnecessarily; **inutilisable** *adj* unusable

invalide [ɛ̃valid] *adj* disabled ♦ *nm*: ~ **de guerre** disabled ex-serviceman

invasion [ɛ̃vazjɔ̃] *nf* invasion

invectiver [ɛ̃vɛktive] *vt* to hurl abuse at

invendable [ɛ̃vɑ̃dabl] *adj* unsaleable; (*COMM*) unmarketable; **invendus** *nmpl* unsold goods

inventaire [ɛ̃vɑ̃tɛR] *nm* inventory; (*COMM: liste*) stocklist; (: *opération*) stocktaking *no pl*

inventer [ɛ̃vɑ̃te] *vt* to invent; (*subterfuge*) to devise, invent; (*histoire, excuse*) to make up, invent; **inventeur** *nm* inventor; **inventif, -ive** *adj* inventive; **invention** *nf* invention

inverse [ɛ̃vɛRs] *adj* opposite ♦ *nm* opposite; **dans l'ordre** ~ in the reverse order; **en sens** ~ in (*ou* from) the opposite direction; **dans le sens** ~ **des aiguilles d'une montre** anticlockwise; **tu t'es trompé, c'est l'**~ you've got it wrong, it's the other way round; **inversement** *adv* conversely; **inverser** *vt* to invert, reverse; (*ÉLEC*) to reverse

investigation [ɛ̃vɛstigasjɔ̃] *nf* investigation

investir [ɛ̃vɛstiR] *vt* to invest; **investissement** *nm* investment; **investiture** *nf* nomination

invétéré, e [ɛ̃vetere] *adj* inveterate

invisible [ɛ̃vizibl] *adj* invisible

invitation [ɛ̃vitasjɔ̃] *nf* invitation

invité, e [ɛ̃vite] *nm/f* guest

inviter [ɛ̃vite] *vt* to invite

invivable [ɛ̃vivabl] *adj* unbearable

involontaire [ɛ̃vɔlɔ̃tɛR] *adj* (*mouvement*) involuntary; (*insulte*) unintentional; (*complice*) unwitting

invoquer [ɛ̃vɔke] *vt* (*Dieu, muse*) to call upon, invoke; (*prétexte*) to put forward (as an excuse); (*loi, texte*) to refer to

invraisemblable [ɛ̃vRɛsɑ̃blabl] *adj* (*fait,*

nouvelle) unlikely, improbable; *(insolence, habit)* incredible

iode [jɔd] *nm* iodine

irai *etc* [iʀe] *vb voir* **aller**

Irak [iʀak] *nm* Iraq; **irakien, ne** *adj* Iraqi ♦ *nm/f*: **Irakien, ne** Iraqi

Iran [iʀɑ̃] *nm* Iran; **iranien, ne** *adj* Iranian ♦ *nm/f*: **Iranien, ne** Iranian

irascible [iʀasibl] *adj* short-tempered

irions *etc* [iʀjɔ̃] *vb voir* **aller**

iris [iʀis] *nm* iris

irlandais, e [iʀlɑ̃dɛ, ɛz] *adj* Irish ♦ *nm/f*: **Irlandais, e** Irishman(-woman); **les Irlandais** the Irish

Irlande [iʀlɑ̃d] *nf* Ireland; **~ du Nord** Northern Ireland; **la République d'~** the Irish Republic

ironie [iʀɔni] *nf* irony; **ironique** *adj* ironical; **ironiser** *vi* to be ironical

irons *etc* [iʀɔ̃] *vb voir* **aller**

irradier [iʀadje] *vt* to irradiate

irraisonné, e [iʀɛzɔne] *adj* irrational

irrationnel, le [iʀasjɔnɛl] *adj* irrational

irréalisable [iʀealizabl] *adj* unrealizable; *(projet)* impracticable

irrécupérable [iʀekypeʀabl] *adj* beyond repair; *(personne)* beyond redemption

irréductible [iʀedyktibl] *adj (volonté)* indomitable; *(ennemi)* implacable

irréel, le [iʀeɛl] *adj* unreal

irréfléchi, e [iʀefleʃi] *adj* thoughtless

irrégularité [iʀegylaʀite] *nf* irregularity; *(de travail, d'effort, de qualité)* unevenness *no pl*

irrégulier, -ière [iʀegylje, jɛʀ] *adj* irregular; *(travail, effort, qualité)* uneven; *(élève, athlète)* erratic

irrémédiable [iʀemedjabl] *adj* irreparable

irremplaçable [iʀɑ̃plasabl] *adj* irreplaceable

irréparable [iʀepaʀabl] *adj (objet)* beyond repair; *(dommage etc)* irreparable

irréprochable [iʀepʀɔʃabl] *adj* irreproachable, beyond reproach; *(tenue)* impeccable

irrésistible [iʀezistibl] *adj* irresistible; *(be-*

soin, désir, preuve, logique) compelling; *(amusant)* hilarious

irrésolu, e [iʀezɔly] *adj (personne)* irresolute; *(problème)* unresolved

irrespectueux, -euse [iʀɛspɛktɥø, øz] *adj* disrespectful

irrespirable [iʀɛspiʀabl] *adj* unbreathable; *(fig)* oppressive

irresponsable [iʀɛspɔ̃sabl] *adj* irresponsible

irriguer [iʀige] *vt* to irrigate

irritable [iʀitabl] *adj* irritable

irriter [iʀite] *vt* to irritate

irruption [iʀypsjɔ̃] *nf*: **faire ~ (chez qn)** to burst in (on sb)

Islam [islam] *nm* Islam; **islamique** *adj* Islamic; **islamiste** *adj (militant)* Islamic; *(mouvement)* Islamic fundamentalist ♦ *nm/f* Islamic fundamentalist

Islande [islɑ̃d] *nf* Iceland

isolant, e [izɔlɑ̃, ɑ̃t] *adj* insulating; *(insonorisant)* soundproofing

isolation [izɔlasjɔ̃] *nf* insulation

isolé, e [izɔle] *adj* isolated; *(contre le froid)* insulated

isoler [izɔle] *vt* to isolate; *(prisonnier)* to put in solitary confinement; *(ville)* to cut off, isolate; *(contre le froid)* to insulate; **s'~** *vi* to isolate o.s.; **isoloir** [izɔlwaʀ] *nm* polling booth

Israël [isʀaɛl] *nm* Israel; **israélien, ne** *adj* Israeli ♦ *nm/f*: **Israélien, ne** Israeli; **israélite** *adj* Jewish ♦ *nm/f*: **Israélite** Jew (Jewess)

issu, e [isy] *adj*: **~ de** *(né de)* descended from; *(résultant de)* stemming from; **issue** *nf (ouverture, sortie)* exit; *(solution)* way out, solution; *(dénouement)* outcome; **à l'issue de** at the conclusion *ou* close of; **voie sans issue** dead end; **issue de secours** emergency exit

Italie [itali] *nf* Italy; **italien, ne** *adj* Italian ♦ *nm/f*: **Italien, ne** Italian ♦ *nm (LING)* Italian

italique [italik] *nm*: **en ~** in italics

itinéraire [itineʀeʀ] *nm* itinerary, route; **~**

bis diversion

IUT *sigle m* = **Institut universitaire de technologie**

IVG *sigle f* (= *interruption volontaire de grossesse*) abortion

ivoire [ivwaʀ] *nm* ivory

ivre [ivʀ] *adj* drunk; **~ de** (*colère, bonheur*) wild with; **ivresse** *nf* drunkenness; **ivrogne** *nm/f* drunkard

J, j

j' [ʒ] *pron voir* **je**

jacasser [ʒakase] *vi* to chatter

jacinthe [ʒasɛ̃t] *nf* hyacinth

jadis [ʒadis] *adv* long ago

jaillir [ʒajiʀ] *vi* (*liquide*) to spurt out; (*cris, responses*) to burst forth

jais [ʒɛ] *nm* jet; **(d'un noir) de ~** jet-black

jalousie [ʒaluzi] *nf* jealousy; (*store*) slatted blind

jaloux, -ouse [ʒalu, uz] *adj* jealous

jamais [ʒamɛ] *adv* never; (*sans négation*) ever; **ne ... ~** never; **à ~** for ever

jambe [ʒɑ̃b] *nf* leg

jambon [ʒɑ̃bɔ̃] *nm* ham; **~ blanc** boiled *ou* cooked ham; **jambonneau, x** *nm* knuckle of ham

jante [ʒɑ̃t] *nf* (*wheel*) rim

janvier [ʒɑ̃vje] *nm* January

Japon [ʒapɔ̃] *nm* Japan; **japonais, e** *adj* Japanese ♦ *nm/f*: **Japonais, e** Japanese ♦ *nm* (*LING*) Japanese

japper [ʒape] *vi* to yap, yelp

jaquette [ʒakɛt] *nf* (*de cérémonie*) morning coat

jardin [ʒaʀdɛ̃] *nm* garden; **~ d'enfants** nursery school; **jardinage** *nm* gardening; **jardiner** *vi* to do some gardening; **jardinier, -ière** *nm/f* gardener; **jardinière** *nf* planter; (*de fenêtre*) window box; **jardinière de légumes** mixed vegetables

jargon [ʒaʀgɔ̃] *nm* (*baragouin*) gibberish; (*langue professionnelle*) jargon

jarret [ʒaʀɛ] *nm* back of knee; (*CULIN*) knuckle, shin

jarretelle [ʒaʀtɛl] *nf* suspender (*BRIT*), garter (*US*)

jarretière [ʒaʀtjɛʀ] *nf* garter

jaser [ʒaze] *vi* (*médire*) to gossip

jatte [ʒat] *nf* basin, bowl

jauge [ʒoʒ] *nf* (*instrument*) gauge; **~ d'essence** petrol gauge; **~ d'huile** (oil) dipstick

jaune [ʒon] *adj, nm* yellow ♦ *adv* (*fam*): **rire ~** to laugh on the other side of one's face; **~ d'œuf** (egg) yolk; **jaunir** *vi, vt* to turn yellow; **jaunisse** *nf* jaundice

Javel [ʒavɛl] *nf voir* **eau**

javelot [ʒavlo] *nm* javelin

J.-C. *abr* = **Jésus-Christ**

je, j' [ʒə] *pron* I

jean [dʒin] *nm* jeans *pl*

Jésus-Christ [ʒezykʀi(st)] *n* Jesus Christ; **600 avant/après ~-~** *ou* **J.-C.** 600 B.C./ A.D.

jet[1] [ʒɛ] *nm* (*lancer: action*) throwing *no pl*; (: *résultat*) throw; (*jaillissement: d'eaux*) jet; (: *de sang*) spurt; **~ d'eau** spray

jet[2] [dʒɛt] *nm* (*avion*) jet

jetable [ʒ(ə)tabl] *adj* disposable

jetée [ʒəte] *nf* jetty; (*grande*) pier

jeter [ʒ(ə)te] *vt* (*gén*) to throw; (*se défaire de*) to throw away *ou* out; **se ~ dans** to flow into; **~ qch à qn** to throw sth to sb; (*de façon agressive*) to throw sth at sb; **~ un coup d'œil (à)** to take a look (at); **~ un sort à qn** to cast a spell on sb; **se ~ sur qn** to rush at sb

jeton [ʒ(ə)tɔ̃] *nm* (*au jeu*) counter; (*de téléphone*) token

jette *etc* [ʒɛt] *vb voir* **jeter**

jeu, x [ʒø] *nm* (*divertissement, TECH: d'une pièce*) play; (*TENNIS: partie, FOOTBALL etc: façon de jouer*) game; (*THÉÂTRE etc*) acting; (*série d'objets, jouet*) set; (*CARTES*) hand; (*au casino*): **le ~** gambling; **être en ~** to be at stake; **entrer/mettre en ~** to come to/ bring into play; **~ de cartes** pack of cards; **~ d'échecs** chess set; **~ de hasard** game of chance; **~ de mots** pun; **~ de**

société parlour game; **~ télévisé** television quiz; **~ vidéo** video game

jeudi [ʒødi] *nm* Thursday

jeun [ʒœ̃]: **à ~** *adv* on an empty stomach; **être à ~** to have eaten nothing; **rester à ~** not to eat anything

jeune [ʒœn] *adj* young; **les ~s** young people; **~ fille** girl; **~ homme** young man; **~s mariés** newly-weds

jeûne [ʒøn] *nm* fast

jeunesse [ʒœnɛs] *nf* youth; (*aspect*) youthfulness

joaillerie [ʒɔajʀi] *nf* jewellery; (*magasin*) jeweller's; **joaillier, -ière** *nm/f* jeweller

jogging [dʒɔgin] *nm* jogging; (*survêtement*) tracksuit; **faire du ~** to go jogging

joie [ʒwa] *nf* joy

joindre [ʒwɛ̃dʀ] *vt* to join; (*à une lettre*): **~ qch à** to enclose sth with; (*contacter*) to contact, get in touch with; **se ~ à** to join; **~ les mains** to put one's hands together

joint, e [ʒwɛ̃, ɛ̃t] *adj*: **pièce ~e** enclosure ♦ *nm* joint; (*ligne*) join; **~ de culasse** cylinder head gasket; **~ de robinet** washer

joli, e [ʒɔli] *adj* pretty, attractive; **c'est du ~!** (*ironique*) that's very nice!; **c'est bien ~, mais ...** that's all very well but ...

jonc [ʒɔ̃] *nm* (bul)rush

jonction [ʒɔ̃ksjɔ̃] *nf* junction

jongleur, -euse [ʒɔ̃glœʀ, øz] *nm/f* juggler

jonquille [ʒɔ̃kij] *nf* daffodil

Jordanie [ʒɔʀdani] *nf*: **la ~** Jordan

joue [ʒu] *nf* cheek

jouer [ʒwe] *vt* to play; (*somme d'argent, réputation*) to stake, wager; (*simuler: sentiment*) to affect, feign ♦ *vi* to play; (*THÉÂTRE, CINÉMA*) to act; (*au casino*) to gamble; (*bois, porte: se voiler*) to warp; (*clef, pièce: avoir du jeu*) to be loose; **~ sur** (*miser*) to gamble on; **~ de** (*MUS*) to play; **~ à** (*jeu, sport, roulette*) to play; **~ un tour à qn** to play a trick on sb; **~ serré** to play a close game; **~ la comédie** to put on an act; **bien joué!** well done!; **on joue Hamlet au théâtre X** Hamlet is on at the X theatre

jouet [ʒwɛ] *nm* toy; **être le ~ de** (*illusion etc*) to be the victim of

joueur, -euse [ʒwœʀ, øz] *nm/f* player; **être beau ~** to be a good loser

joufflu, e [ʒufly] *adj* chubby-cheeked

joug [ʒu] *nm* yoke

jouir [ʒwiʀ] *vi* (*sexe: fam*) to come ♦ *vt*: **~ de** to enjoy; **jouissance** *nf* pleasure; (*JUR*) use

joujou [ʒuʒu] (*fam*) *nm* toy

jour [ʒuʀ] *nm* day; (*opposé à la nuit*) day, daytime; (*clarté*) daylight; (*fig: aspect*) light; (*ouverture*) gap; **au ~ le ~** from day to day; **de nos ~s** these days; **du ~ au lendemain** overnight; **il fait ~** it's daylight; **au grand ~** (*fig*) in the open; **mettre au ~** to disclose; **mettre à ~** to update; **donner le ~ à** to give birth to; **voir le ~** to be born; **~ férié** public holiday; **~ de fête** holiday; **~ ouvrable** week-day, working day

journal, -aux [ʒuʀnal, o] *nm* (news)paper; (*spécialisé*) journal; (*intime*) diary; **~ de bord** log; **~ télévisé** television news *sg*

journalier, -ière [ʒuʀnalje, jɛʀ] *adj* daily; (*banal*) everyday

journalisme [ʒuʀnalism] *nm* journalism; **journaliste** *nm/f* journalist

journée [ʒuʀne] *nf* day; **faire la ~ continue** to work over lunch

journellement [ʒuʀnɛlmã] *adv* daily

joyau, x [ʒwajo] *nm* gem, jewel

joyeux, -euse [ʒwajø, øz] *adj* joyful, merry; **~ Noël!** merry Christmas!; **~ anniversaire!** happy birthday!

jubiler [ʒybile] *vi* to be jubilant, exult

jucher [ʒyʃe] *vt, vi* to perch

judas [ʒyda] *nm* (*trou*) spy-hole

judiciaire [ʒydisjɛʀ] *adj* judicial

judicieux, -euse [ʒydisjø, jøz] *adj* judicious

judo [ʒydo] *nm* judo

juge [ʒyʒ] *nm* judge; **~ d'instruction** examining (*BRIT*) *ou* committing (*US*) magistrate; **~ de paix** justice of the peace; **~ de touche** linesman

jugé [ʒyʒe]: **au ~** adv by guesswork

jugement [ʒyʒmɑ̃] nm judgment; (JUR: au pénal) sentence; (: au civil) decision

jugeote [ʒyʒɔt] (fam) nf commonsense

juger [ʒyʒe] vt to judge; (estimer) to consider; **~ qn/qch satisfaisant** to consider sb/sth (to be) satisfactory; **~ bon de faire** to see fit to do; **~ de** to appreciate

juif, -ive [ʒɥif, ʒɥiv] adj Jewish ♦ nm/f: **J~, ive** Jew (Jewess)

juillet [ʒɥije] nm July

---

14 juillet

i In France, **le 14 juillet** is a national holiday commemorating the storming of the Bastille during the French Revolution, celebrated by parades, music, dancing and firework displays. In Paris, there is a military parade along the Champs-Élysées, attended by the President.

---

juin [ʒɥɛ̃] nm June

jumeau, -elle, x [ʒymo, ɛl] adj, nm/f twin

jumeler [ʒym(ə)le] vt to twin

jumelle [ʒymɛl] adj, nf voir **jumeau**; **~s** nfpl (appareil) binoculars

jument [ʒymɑ̃] nf mare

jungle [ʒœ̃gl] nf jungle

jupe [ʒyp] nf skirt

jupon [ʒypɔ̃] nm waist slip

juré, e [ʒyʁe] nm/f juror

jurer [ʒyʁe] vt (obéissance etc) to swear, vow ♦ vi (dire des jurons) to swear, curse; (dissoner): **~ (avec)** to clash (with); **~ de faire/que** to swear to do/that; **~ de qch** (s'en porter garant) to swear to sth

juridique [ʒyʁidik] adj legal

juron [ʒyʁɔ̃] nm curse, swearword

jury [ʒyʁi] nm jury; (ART, SPORT) panel of judges; (SCOL) board of examiners

jus [ʒy] nm juice; (de viande) gravy, (meat) juice; **~ de fruit** fruit juice

jusque [ʒysk]: **jusqu'à** prép (endroit) as far

as, (up) to; (moment) until, till; (limite) up to; **~ sur/dans** up to; (y compris) even on/in; **jusqu'à ce que** until; **jusqu'à présent** so far; **jusqu'où?** how far?

justaucorps [ʒystokɔʁ] nm leotard

juste [ʒyst] adj (équitable) just, fair; (légitime) just; (exact) right; (pertinent) apt; (étroit) tight; (insuffisant) on the short side ♦ adv rightly, correctly; (chanter) in tune; (exactement, seulement) just; **~ assez/au-dessus** just enough/above; **au ~** exactly; **le ~ milieu** the happy medium; **c'était ~** it was a close thing; **justement** adv justly; (précisément) just, precisely; **justesse** nf (précision) accuracy; (d'une remarque) aptness; (d'une opinion) soundness; **de justesse** only just

justice [ʒystis] nf (équité) fairness, justice; (ADMIN) justice; **rendre ~ à qn** to do sb justice; **justicier, -ière** nm/f righter of wrongs

justificatif, -ive [ʒystifikatif, iv] adj (document) supporting; **pièce justificative** written proof

justifier [ʒystifje] vt to justify; **~ de** to prove

juteux, -euse [ʒytø, øz] adj juicy

juvénile [ʒyvenil] adj youthful

K, k

K [ka] nm (INFORM) K

kaki [kaki] adj inv khaki

kangourou [kɑ̃guʁu] nm kangaroo

karaté [kaʁate] nm karate

karting [kaʁtiŋ] nm go-carting, karting

kascher [kaʃɛʁ] adj kosher

kayak [kajak] nm canoe, kayak; **faire du ~** to go canoeing

képi [kepi] nm kepi

kermesse [kɛʁmɛs] nf fair; (fête de charité) bazaar, (charity) fête

kidnapper [kidnape] vt to kidnap

kilo [kilo] nm = **kilogramme**

kilo...: **kilogramme** nm kilogramme; **ki-**

lométrage *nm* number of kilometres travelled, ≃ mileage; **kilomètre** *nm* kilometre; **kilométrique** *adj* (*distance*) in kilometres

kinésithérapeute [kinezitɛʀapøt] *nm/f* physiotherapist

kiosque [kjɔsk] *nm* kiosk, stall; **~ à musique** bandstand

kir [kiʀ] *nm* kir (*white wine with blackcurrant liqueur*)

kit [kit] *nm*: **en ~** in kit form

klaxon [klaksɔn] *nm* horn; **klaxonner** *vi*, *vt* to hoot (*BRIT*), honk (*US*)

km *abr* = **kilomètre**

km/h *abr* (= *kilomètres/heure*) ≃ mph

K.-O. (*fam*) *adj inv* shattered, knackered

Kosovo [kɔsovo] *nm* Kosovo

k-way ® [kawɛ] *nm* (*lightweight nylon*) cagoule

kyste [kist] *nm* cyst

L, l

l' [l] *art déf voir* **le**

la [la] *art déf voir* **le** ♦ *nm* (*MUS*) A; (*en chantant la gamme*) la

là [la] *adv* there; (*ici*) here; (*dans le temps*) then; **elle n'est pas ~** she isn't here; **c'est ~ que** this is where; **~ où** where; **de ~** (*fig*) hence; **par ~** (*fig*) by that; *voir aussi* **-ci; ce; celui; là-bas** *adv* there

label [label] *nm* stamp, seal

labeur [labœʀ] *nm* toil *no pl*, toiling *no pl*

labo [labo] (*fam*) *nm* (= *laboratoire*) lab

laboratoire [labɔʀatwaʀ] *nm* laboratory; **~ de langues** language laboratory

laborieux, -euse [labɔʀjø, jøz] *adj* (*tâche*) laborious

labour [labuʀ] *nm* ploughing *no pl*; **~s** *nmpl* (*champs*) ploughed fields; **cheval de ~** plough- *ou* cart-horse; **labourer** *vt* to plough

labyrinthe [labiʀɛ̃t] *nm* labyrinth, maze

lac [lak] *nm* lake

lacer [lase] *vt* to lace *ou* do up

lacérer [laseʀe] *vt* to tear to shreds

lacet [lasɛ] *nm* (*de chaussure*) lace; (*de route*) sharp bend; (*piège*) snare

lâche [lɑʃ] *adj* (*poltron*) cowardly; (*desserré*) loose, slack ♦ *nm/f* coward

lâcher [lɑʃe] *vt* to let go of; (*ce qui tombe, abandonner*) to drop; (*oiseau, animal: libérer*) to release, set free; (*fig: mot, remarque*) to let slip, come out with ♦ *vi* (*freins*) to fail; **~ les amarres** (*NAVIG*) to cast off (the moorings); **~ prise** to let go

lâcheté [lɑʃte] *nf* cowardice

lacrymogène [lakʀimɔʒɛn] *adj*: **gaz ~** teargas

lacté, e [lakte] *adj* (*produit, régime*) milk *cpd*

lacune [lakyn] *nf* gap

là-dedans [ladədɑ̃] *adv* inside (there), in it; (*fig*) in that

là-dessous [ladsu] *adv* underneath, under there; (*fig*) behind that

là-dessus [ladsy] *adv* on there; (*fig: sur ces mots*) at that point; (: *à ce sujet*) about that

ladite [ladit] *dét voir* **ledit**

lagune [lagyn] *nf* lagoon

là-haut [lao] *adv* up there

laïc [laik] *adj, nm/f* = **laïque**

laid, e [lɛ, lɛd] *adj* ugly; **laideur** *nf* ugliness *no pl*

lainage [lɛnaʒ] *nm* (*vêtement*) woollen garment; (*étoffe*) woollen material

laine [lɛn] *nf* wool

laïque [laik] *adj* lay, civil; (*SCOL*) state *cpd* ♦ *nm/f* layman(-woman)

laisse [lɛs] *nf* (*de chien*) lead, leash; **tenir en ~** to keep on a lead *ou* leash

laisser [lese] *vt* to leave ♦ *vb aux*: **~ qn faire** to let sb do; **se ~ aller** to let o.s. go; **laisse-toi faire** let me (*ou* him *etc*) do it; **laisser-aller** *nm* carelessness, slovenliness; **laissez-passer** *nm inv* pass

lait [lɛ] *nm* milk; **frère/sœur de ~** foster brother/sister; **~ condensé/concentré** evaporated/condensed milk; **~ démaquillant** cleansing milk; **laitage** *nm* dairy product; **laiterie** *nf* dairy; **laitier, -ière** *adj* dairy *cpd* ♦ *nm/f* milkman (dairywoman)

laiton [lɛtɔ̃] *nm* brass

laitue [lety] *nf* lettuce

laïus [lajys] (*péj*) *nm* spiel

lambeau, x [lɑ̃bo] *nm* scrap; **en ~x** in tatters, tattered

lambris [lɑ̃bri] *nm* panelling *no pl*

lame [lam] *nf* blade; (*vague*) wave; (*lamelle*) strip; **~ de fond** ground swell *no pl*; **~ de rasoir** razor blade; **lamelle** *nf* thin strip *ou* blade

lamentable [lamɑ̃tabl] *adj* appalling

lamenter [lamɑ̃te] *vb*: **se ~ (sur)** to moan (over)

lampadaire [lɑ̃padɛʀ] *nm* (*de salon*) standard lamp; (*dans la rue*) street lamp

lampe [lɑ̃p] *nf* lamp; (*TECH*) valve; **~ à souder** blowlamp; **~ de chevet** bedside lamp; **~ de poche** torch (*BRIT*), flashlight (*US*)

lampion [lɑ̃pjɔ̃] *nm* Chinese lantern

lance [lɑ̃s] *nf* spear; **~ d'incendie** fire hose

lancée [lɑ̃se] *nf*: **être/continuer sur sa ~** to be under way/keep going

lancement [lɑ̃smɑ̃] *nm* launching

lance-pierres [lɑ̃spjɛʀ] *nm inv* catapult

lancer [lɑ̃se] *nm* (*SPORT*) throwing *no pl*, throw ♦ *vt* to throw; (*émettre, projeter*) to throw out, send out; (*produit, fusée, bateau, artiste*) to launch; (*injure*) to hurl, fling; **se ~** *vi* (*prendre de l'élan*) to build up speed; (*se précipiter*): **se ~ sur** *ou* **contre** to rush at; **se ~ dans** (*discussion*) to launch into; (*aventure*) to embark on; **~ qch à qn** to throw sth to sb; (*de façon agressive*) to throw sth at sb; **~ du poids** putting the shot

lancinant, e [lɑ̃sinɑ̃, ɑ̃t] *adj* (*douleur*) shooting

landau [lɑ̃do] *nm* pram (*BRIT*), baby carriage (*US*)

lande [lɑ̃d] *nf* moor

langage [lɑ̃gaʒ] *nm* language

langouste [lɑ̃gust] *nf* crayfish *inv*; **langoustine** *nf* Dublin Bay prawn

langue [lɑ̃g] *nf* (*ANAT, CULIN*) tongue; (*LING*) language; **tirer la ~ (à)** to stick out one's tongue (at); **de ~ française** French-speaking; **~ maternelle** native language, mother tongue; **~ vivante/étrangère** modern/foreign language

langueur [lɑ̃gœʀ] *nf* languidness

languir [lɑ̃giʀ] *vi* to languish; (*conversation*) to flag; **faire ~ qn** to keep sb waiting

lanière [lanjɛʀ] *nf* (*de fouet*) lash; (*de sac, bretelle*) strap

lanterne [lɑ̃tɛʀn] *nf* (*portable*) lantern; (*électrique*) light, lamp; (*de voiture*) (side)light

laper [lape] *vt* to lap up

lapidaire [lapidɛʀ] *adj* (*fig*) terse

lapin [lapɛ̃] *nm* rabbit; (*peau*) rabbitskin; (*fourrure*) cony; **poser un ~ à qn** (*fam*) to stand sb up

Laponie [lapɔni] *nf* Lapland

laps [laps] *nm*: **~ de temps** space of time, time *no pl*

laque [lak] *nf* (*vernis*) lacquer; (*pour cheveux*) hair spray

laquelle [lakɛl] *pron voir* **lequel**

larcin [larsɛ̃] *nm* theft

lard [laʀ] *nm* (*bacon*) (streaky) bacon; (*graisse*) fat

lardon [lardɔ̃] *nm*: **~s** chopped bacon

large [larʒ] *adj* wide, broad; (*fig*) generous ♦ *adv*: **calculer/voir ~** to allow extra/think big ♦ *nm* (*largeur*): **5 m de ~** 5 m wide *ou* in width; (*mer*): **le ~** the open sea; **au ~ de** off; **~ d'esprit** broadminded; **largement** *adv* widely; (*de loin*) greatly; (*au moins*) easily; (*généreusement*) generously; **c'est largement suffisant** that's ample; **largesse** *nf* generosity; **largesses** *nfpl* (*dons*) liberalities; **largeur** *nf* (*qu'on mesure*) width; (*impression visuelle*) wideness, width; (*d'esprit*) broadness

larguer [large] *vt* to drop; **~ les amarres** to cast off (the moorings)

larme [larm] *nf* tear; (*fam: goutte*) drop; **en ~s** in tears; **larmoyer** *vi* (*yeux*) to water; (*se plaindre*) to whimper

larvé, e [laʀve] *adj* (*fig*) latent

laryngite [laʀɛ̃ʒit] *nf* laryngitis

las, lasse [lɑ, lɑs] *adj* weary

laser [lazeʀ] *nm*: **(rayon) ~** laser (beam); **chaîne ~** compact disc (player); **disque ~** compact disc

lasse [lɑs] *adj voir* **las**

lasser [lɑse] *vt* to weary, tire; **se ~ de** *vt* to grow weary *ou* tired of

latéral, e, -aux [lateʀal, o] *adj* side *cpd*, lateral

latin, e [latɛ̃, in] *adj* Latin ♦ *nm/f*: **L~, e** Latin ♦ *nm* (*LING*) Latin

latitude [latityd] *nf* latitude

latte [lat] *nf* lath, slat; (*de plancher*) board

lauréat, e [lɔʀea, at] *nm/f* winner

laurier [lɔʀje] *nm* (*BOT*) laurel; (*CULIN*) bay leaves *pl*

lavable [lavabl] *adj* washable

lavabo [lavabo] *nm* washbasin; **~s** *nmpl* (*toilettes*) toilet *sg*

lavage [lavaʒ] *nm* washing *no pl*, wash; **~ de cerveau** brainwashing *no pl*

lavande [lavɑ̃d] *nf* lavender

lave [lav] *nf* lava *no pl*

lave-linge [lavlɛ̃ʒ] *nm inv* washing machine

laver [lave] *vt* to wash; (*tache*) to wash off; **se ~** *vi* to have a wash, wash; **se ~ les mains/dents** to wash one's hands/clean one's teeth; **~ qn de** (*accusation*) to clear sb of; **laverie** *nf*: **laverie (automatique)** launderette; **lavette** *nf* dish cloth; (*fam*) drip; **laveur, -euse** *nm/f* cleaner; **lave-vaisselle** *nm inv* dishwasher; **lavoir** *nm* wash house; (*évier*) sink

laxatif, -ive [laksatif, iv] *adj*, *nm* laxative

layette [lɛjɛt] *nf* baby clothes

┌─────────────┐
│ *MOT-CLÉ* │
└─────────────┘

le [lə], **la**, **l'** (*pl* **les**) *art déf* **1** the; **le livre/la pomme/l'arbre** the book/the apple/the tree; **les étudiants** the students

2 (*noms abstraits*): **le courage/l'amour/la jeunesse** courage/love/youth

3 (*indiquant la possession*): **se casser la jambe** *etc* to break one's leg *etc*; **levez la main** put your hand up; **avoir les yeux gris/le nez rouge** to have grey eyes/a red nose

4 (*temps*): **le matin/soir** in the morning/evening; mornings/evenings; **le jeudi** *etc* (*d'habitude*) on Thursdays *etc*; (*ce jeudi-là* *etc*) on (the) Thursday

5 (*distribution, évaluation*) a, an; **10 F le mètre/kilo** 10F a *ou* per metre/kilo; **le tiers/quart de** a third/quarter of

♦ *pron* **1** (*personne: mâle*) him; (*personne: femelle*) her; (: *pluriel*) them; **je le/la/les vois** I can see him/her/them

2 (*animal, chose: singulier*) it; (: *pluriel*) them; **je le** (*ou* **la**) **vois** I can see it; **je les vois** I can see them

3 (*remplaçant une phrase*): **je ne le savais pas** I didn't know (about it); **il était riche et ne l'est plus** he was once rich but no longer is

---

lécher [leʃe] *vt* to lick; (*laper: lait, eau*) to lick *ou* lap up; **lèche-vitrines** *nm*: **faire du lèche-vitrines** to go window-shopping

leçon [l(ə)sɔ̃] *nf* lesson; **faire la ~ à** (*fig*) to give a lecture to; **~s de conduite** driving lessons

lecteur, -trice [lektœʀ, tʀis] *nm/f* reader; (*d'université*) foreign language assistant ♦ *nm* (*TECH*): **~ de cassettes/CD** cassette/CD player; **~ de disquette** disk drive

lecture [lektyʀ] *nf* reading

ledit [lədi], **ladite** (*mpl* **lesdits**, *fpl* **lesdites**) *dét* the aforesaid

légal, e, -aux [legal, o] *adj* legal; **légaliser** *vt* to legalize; **légalité** *nf* law

légendaire [leʒɑ̃dɛʀ] *adj* legendary

légende [leʒɑ̃d] *nf* (*mythe*) legend; (*de carte, plan*) key; (*de dessin*) caption

léger, -ère [leʒe, ɛʀ] *adj* light; (*bruit, retard*) slight; (*personne: superficiel*) thoughtless; (: *volage*) free and easy; **à la légère** (*parler, agir*) rashly, thoughtlessly; **lé-**

gèrement adv (s'habiller, bouger) lightly; (un peu) slightly; **manger légèrement** to eat a light meal; **légèreté** nf lightness; (d'une remarque) flippancy

Légion d'honneur

i Created by Napoleon in 1802 to reward service to the state, **la Légion d'honneur** is a prestigious French order headed by the President of the Republic, the Grand Maître. Members receive an annual tax-free payment.

législatif, -ive [leʒislatif, iv] adj legislative; **législatives** nfpl general election sg

légitime [leʒitim] adj (JUR) lawful, legitimate; (fig) rightful, legitimate; **en état de ~ défense** in self-defence

legs [lɛg] nm legacy

léguer [lege] vt: **~ qch à qn** (JUR) to bequeath sth to sb

légume [legym] nm vegetable

lendemain [lɑ̃dmɛ̃] nm: **le ~** the next ou following day; **le ~ matin/soir** the next ou following morning/evening; **le ~ de** the day after

lent, e [lɑ̃, lɑ̃t] adj slow; **lentement** adv slowly; **lenteur** nf slowness no pl

lentille [lɑ̃tij] nf (OPTIQUE) lens sg; (CULIN) lentil

léopard [leɔpaʀ] nm leopard

lèpre [lɛpʀ] nf leprosy

MOT-CLÉ

lequel, laquelle [ləkɛl, lakɛl] (mpl **lesquels**, fpl **lesquelles**) (à + lequel = **auquel**, de + lequel = **duquel** etc) pron 1 (interrogatif) which, which one

2 (relatif: personne: sujet) who; (: objet, après préposition) whom; (: chose) which

♦ adj: **auquel cas** in which case

les [le] dét voir **le**

lesbienne [lɛsbjɛn] nf lesbian

lesdites [ledit], **lesdits** [ledi] dét pl voir **ledit**

léser [leze] vt to wrong

lésiner [lezine] vi: **ne pas ~ sur les moyens** (pour mariage etc) to push the boat out

lésion [lezjɔ̃] nf lesion, damage no pl

lesquelles, lesquels [lekɛl] pron pl voir **lequel**

lessive [lesiv] nf (poudre) washing powder; (linge) washing no pl, wash; **lessiver** vt to wash; (fam: fatiguer) to tire out, exhaust

lest [lɛst] nm ballast

leste [lɛst] adj sprightly, nimble

lettre [lɛtʀ] nf letter; **~s** nfpl (littérature) literature sg; (SCOL) arts (subjects); **à la ~** literally; **en toutes ~s** in full

leucémie [løsemi] nf leukaemia

MOT-CLÉ

leur [lœʀ] adj possessif their; **leur maison** their house; **leurs amis** their friends

♦ pron 1 (objet indirect) (to) them; **je leur ai dit la vérité** I told them the truth; **je le leur ai donné** I gave it to them, I gave them it

2 (possessif): **le(la) leur, les leurs** theirs

leurre [lœʀ] nm (fig: illusion) delusion; (: duperie) deception; **leurrer** vt to delude, deceive

leurs [lœʀ] adj voir **leur**

levain [ləvɛ̃] nm leaven

levé, e [ləve] adj: **être ~** to be up; **levée** nf (POSTES) collection

lever [l(ə)ve] vt (vitre, bras etc) to raise; (soulever de terre, supprimer: interdiction, siège) to lift; (impôts, armée) to levy ♦ vi to rise ♦ nm: **au ~** on getting up; **se ~** vi to get up; (soleil) to rise; (jour) to break; (brouillard) to lift; **~ de soleil** sunrise; **~ du jour** daybreak

levier [ləvje] nm lever

lèvre [lɛvʀ] nf lip

lévrier [levʀije] nm greyhound

levure [l(ə)vyʀ] nf yeast; **~ chimique** baking powder

lexique [lɛksik] *nm* vocabulary; (*glossaire*) lexicon

lézard [lezaʀ] *nm* lizard

lézarde [lezaʀd] *nf* crack

liaison [ljɛzɔ̃] *nf* (*rapport*) connection; (*transport*) link; (*amoureuse*) affair; (*PHONÉTIQUE*) liaison; **entrer/être en ~ avec** to get/be in contact with

liane [ljan] *nf* creeper

liant, e [ljɑ̃, ljɑ̃t] *adj* sociable

liasse [ljas] *nf* wad, bundle

Liban [libɑ̃] *nm*: **le ~** (the) Lebanon; **libanais, e** *adj* Lebanese ♦ *nm/f*: **Libanais, e** Lebanese

libeller [libele] *vt* (*chèque, mandat*): **~ (au nom de)** to make out (to); (*lettre*) to word

libellule [libelyl] *nf* dragonfly

libéral, e, -aux [libeʀal, o] *adj, nm/f* liberal; **profession ~e** (liberal) profession

libérer [libeʀe] *vt* (*délivrer*) to free, liberate; (*relâcher: prisonnier*) to discharge, release; (: *d'inhibitions*) to liberate; (*gaz*) to release; **se ~** *vi* (*de rendez-vous*) to get out of previous engagements

liberté [libɛʀte] *nf* freedom; (*loisir*) free time; **~s** *nfpl* (*privautés*) liberties; **mettre/être en ~** to set/be free; **en ~ provisoire/surveillée/conditionnelle** on bail/probation/parole

libraire [libʀɛʀ] *nm/f* bookseller

librairie [libʀeʀi] *nf* bookshop

libre [libʀ] *adj* free; (*route, voie*) clear; (*place, salle*) free; (*ligne*) not engaged; (*SCOL*) non-state; **~ de qch/de faire** free from sth/to do; **~ arbitre** free will; **libre-échange** *nm* free trade; **libre-service** *nm* self-service store

Libye [libi] *nf*: **la ~** Libya

licence [lisɑ̃s] *nf* (*permis*) permit; (*diplôme*) degree; (*liberté*) liberty; **licencié, e** *nm/f* (*SCOL*): **licencié ès lettres/en droit** ≈ Bachelor of Arts/Law

licenciement [lisɑ̃simɑ̃] *nm* redundancy

licencier [lisɑ̃sje] *vt* (*débaucher*) to make redundant, lay off; (*renvoyer*) to dismiss

licite [lisit] *adj* lawful

lie [li] *nf* dregs *pl*, sediment

lié, e [lje] *adj*: **très ~ avec** very friendly with *ou* close to

liège [ljɛʒ] *nm* cork

lien [ljɛ̃] *nm* (*corde, fig: affectif*) bond; (*rapport*) link, connection; **~ de parenté** family tie

lier [lje] *vt* (*attacher*) to tie up; (*joindre*) to link up; (*fig: unir, engager*) to bind; **se ~ avec** to make friends with; **~ qch à** to tie *ou* link sth to; **~ conversation avec** to strike up a conversation with

lierre [ljɛʀ] *nm* ivy

liesse [ljɛs] *nf*: **être en ~** to be celebrating *ou* jubilant

lieu, x [ljø] *nm* place; (*endroit: d'un accident etc*) scene *sg*; **en ~ sûr** in a safe place; **en premier ~** in the first place; **en dernier ~** lastly; **avoir ~** to take place; **tenir ~ de** to serve as; **donner ~ à** to give rise to; **au ~ de** instead of; **lieu-dit** (*pl* **lieux-dits**) *nm* locality

lieutenant [ljøt(ə)nɑ̃] *nm* lieutenant

lièvre [ljɛvʀ] *nm* hare

ligament [ligamɑ̃] *nm* ligament

ligne [liɲ] *nf* (*gén*) line; (*TRANSPORTS: liaison*) service; (: *trajet*) route; (*silhouette*) figure; **entrer en ~ de compte** to come into it

lignée [liɲe] *nf* line, lineage

ligoter [ligɔte] *vt* to tie up

ligue [lig] *nf* league; **liguer** *vt*: **se liguer contre** (*fig*) to combine against

lilas [lila] *nm* lilac

limace [limas] *nf* slug

limande [limɑ̃d] *nf* dab

lime [lim] *nf* file; **~ à ongles** nail file; **limer** *vt* to file

limier [limje] *nm* bloodhound; (*détective*) sleuth

limitation [limitasjɔ̃] *nf*: **~ de vitesse** speed limit

limite [limit] *nf* (*de terrain*) boundary; (*partie ou point extrême*) limit; **vitesse/charge**

~ maximum speed/load; **cas** ~ borderline case; **date** ~ deadline; **limiter** *vt* (*restreindre*) to limit, restrict; (*délimiter*) to border; **limitrophe** *adj* border *cpd*

limoger [limɔʒe] *vt* to dismiss

limon [limɔ̃] *nm* silt

limonade [limɔnad] *nf* lemonade

lin [lɛ̃] *nm* (*tissu*) linen

linceul [lɛ̃sœl] *nm* shroud

linge [lɛ̃ʒ] *nm* (*serviettes etc*) linen; (*lessive*) washing; (*aussi*: ~ **de corps**) underwear; **lingerie** *nf* lingerie, underwear

lingot [lɛ̃go] *nm* ingot

linguistique [lɛ̃gɥistik] *adj* linguistic ♦ *nf* linguistics *sg*

lion, ne [ljɔ̃, ljɔn] *nm/f* lion (lioness); (*signe*): **le L~** Leo; **lionceau, x** *nm* lion cub

liqueur [likœʀ] *nf* liqueur

liquidation [likidasjɔ̃] *nf* (*vente*) sale

liquide [likid] *adj* liquid ♦ *nm* liquid; (*COMM*): **en** ~ in ready money *ou* cash; **liquider** *vt* to liquidate; (*COMM*: *articles*) to clear, sell off; **liquidités** *nfpl* (*COMM*) liquid assets

lire [liʀ] *nf* (*monnaie*) lira ♦ *vt*, *vi* to read

lis [lis] *nm* = **lys**

lisible [lizibl] *adj* legible

lisière [lizjɛʀ] *nf* (*de forêt*) edge

lisons [lizɔ̃] *vb voir* **lire**

lisse [lis] *adj* smooth

liste [list] *nf* list; **faire la** ~ **de** to list; ~ **électorale** electoral roll; **listing** *nm* (*INFORM*) printout

lit [li] *nm* bed; **petit** ~, **lit à une place** single bed; **grand** ~, **lit à deux places** double bed; **faire son** ~ to make one's bed; **aller/se mettre au** ~ to go to/get into bed; ~ **de camp** campbed; ~ **d'enfant** cot (*BRIT*), crib (*US*)

literie [litʀi] *nf* bedding, bedclothes *pl*

litière [litjɛʀ] *nf* litter

litige [litiʒ] *nm* dispute

litre [litʀ] *nm* litre

littéraire [liteʀɛʀ] *adj* literary ♦ *nm/f* arts student; **elle est très** ~ (*she's very literary*)

littéral, e, -aux [literal, o] *adj* literal

littérature [literatyʀ] *nf* literature

littoral, -aux [litɔʀal, o] *nm* coast

liturgie [lityʀʒi] *nf* liturgy

livide [livid] *adj* livid, pallid

livraison [livʀɛzɔ̃] *nf* delivery

livre [livʀ] *nm* book ♦ *nf* (*poids, monnaie*) pound; ~ **de bord** logbook; ~ **de poche** paperback

livré, e [livʀe] *adj*: ~ **à soi-même** left to o.s. *ou* one's own devices; **livrée** *nf* livery

livrer [livʀe] *vt* (*COMM*) to deliver; (*otage, coupable*) to hand over; (*secret, information*) to give away; **se** ~ **à** (*se confier*) to confide in; (*se rendre, s'abandonner*) to give o.s. up to; (*faire: pratiques, actes*) to indulge in; (*enquête*) to carry out

livret [livʀe] *nm* booklet; (*d'opéra*) libretto; ~ **de caisse d'épargne** (savings) bankbook; ~ **de famille** (official) family record book; ~ **scolaire** (school) report book

livreur, -euse [livʀœʀ, øz] *nm/f* delivery boy *ou* man/girl *ou* woman

local, e, -aux [lɔkal, o] *adj* local ♦ *nm* (*salle*) premises *pl*; *voir aussi* **locaux**; **localiser** *vt* (*repérer*) to locate, place; (*limiter*) to confine; **localité** *nf* locality

locataire [lɔkatɛʀ] *nm/f* tenant; (*de chambre*) lodger

location [lɔkasjɔ̃] *nf* (*par le locataire, le loueur*) renting; (*par le propriétaire*) renting out, letting; (*THÉÂTRE*) booking office; "~ **de voitures**" "car rental"; **habiter en** ~ to live in rented accommodation; **prendre une** ~ (**pour les vacances**) to rent a house *etc* (for the holidays)

locaux [lɔko] *nmpl* premises

locomotive [lɔkɔmɔtiv] *nf* locomotive, engine

locution [lɔkysjɔ̃] *nf* phrase

loge [lɔʒ] *nf* (*THÉÂTRE: d'artiste*) dressing room; (: *de spectateurs*) box; (*de concierge, franc-maçon*) lodge

logement [lɔʒmɑ̃] *nm* accommodation *no pl* (*BRIT*), accommodations *pl* (*US*); (*appartement*) flat (*BRIT*), apartment (*US*); (*héber-*

gement) housing *no pl*

loger [lɔʒe] *vt* to accommodate ♦ *vi* to live; **se ~ dans** *(suj: balle, flèche)* to lodge itself in; **trouver à se ~** to find accommodation; **logeur, -euse** *nm/f* landlord(-lady)

logiciel [lɔʒisjɛl] *nm* software

logique [lɔʒik] *adj* logical ♦ *nf* logic

logis [lɔʒi] *nm* abode, dwelling

logo [lɔgo] *nm* logo

loi [lwa] *nf* law; **faire la ~** to lay down the law

loin [lwɛ̃] *adv* far; *(dans le temps: futur)* a long way off; *(: passé)* a long time ago; **plus ~** further; **~ de** far from; **au ~** far off; **de ~** from a distance; *(fig: de beaucoup)* by far

lointain, e [lwɛ̃tɛ̃, ɛn] *adj* faraway, distant; *(dans le futur, passé)* distant; *(cause, parent)* remote, distant ♦ *nm*: **dans le ~** in the distance

loir [lwaʀ] *nm* dormouse

loisir [lwaziʀ] *nm*: **heures de ~** spare time; **~s** *nmpl (temps libre)* leisure *sg*; *(activités)* leisure activities; **avoir le ~ de faire** to have the time *ou* opportunity to do; **à ~** at leisure

londonien, ne [lɔ̃dɔnjɛ̃, jɛn] *adj* London *cpd*, of London ♦ *nm/f*: **L~, ne** Londoner

Londres [lɔ̃dʀ] *n* London

long, longue [lɔ̃, lɔ̃g] *adj* long ♦ *adv*: **en savoir ~** to know a great deal ♦ *nm*: **de 3 m de ~** 3 m long, 3 m in length; **ne pas faire ~ feu** not to last long; **(tout) le ~ de** (all) along; **tout au ~ de** *(année, vie)* throughout; **de ~ en large** *(marcher)* to and fro, up and down; *voir aussi* **longue**

longer [lɔ̃ʒe] *vt* to go *(ou* walk *ou* drive) along(side); *(suj: mur, route)* to border

longiligne [lɔ̃ʒiliɲ] *adj* long-limbed

longitude [lɔ̃ʒityd] *nf* longitude

longtemps [lɔ̃tɑ̃] *adv* (for) a long time, (for) long; **avant ~** before long; **pour** *ou* **pendant ~** for a long time; **mettre ~ à faire** to take a long time to do

longue [lɔ̃g] *adj voir* **long** ♦ *nf*: **à la ~** in

the end; **longuement** *adv (longtemps)* for a long time; *(en détail)* at length

longueur [lɔ̃gœʀ] *nf* length; **~s** *nfpl (fig: d'un film etc)* tedious parts; **en ~** lengthwise; **tirer en ~** to drag on; **à ~ de journée** all day long; **~ d'onde** wavelength

longue-vue [lɔ̃gvy] *nf* telescope

look [luk] *(fam) nm* look, image

lopin [lɔpɛ̃] *nm*: **~ de terre** patch of land

loque [lɔk] *nf (personne)* wreck; **~s** *nfpl (habits)* rags

loquet [lɔkɛ] *nm* latch

lorgner [lɔʀɲe] *vt* to eye; *(fig)* to have one's eye on

lors [lɔʀ]: **~ de** *prép* at the time of; during

lorsque [lɔʀsk] *conj* when, as

losange [lɔzɑ̃ʒ] *nm* diamond

lot [lo] *nm (part)* share; *(de ~erie)* prize; *(fig: destin)* fate, lot; *(COMM, INFORM)* batch; **le gros ~** the jackpot

loterie [lɔtʀi] *nf* lottery

loti, e [lɔti] *adj*: **bien/mal ~** well-/badly off

lotion [losjɔ̃] *nf* lotion

lotissement [lɔtismɑ̃] *nm* housing development; *(parcelle)* plot, lot

loto [lɔto] *nm* lotto

Loto

i   **Le Loto** *is a state-run national lottery with large cash prizes. Participants select 7 numbers out of 49. The more correct numbers, the greater the prize. The draw is televised twice weekly.*

---

lotte [lɔt] *nf* monkfish

louable [lwabl] *adj* commendable

louanges [lwɑ̃ʒ] *nfpl* praise *sg*

loubard [lubaʀ] *(fam) nm* lout

louche [luʃ] *adj* shady, fishy, dubious ♦ *nf* ladle; **loucher** *vi* to squint

louer [lwe] *vt (maison: suj: propriétaire)* to let, rent (out); *(: locataire)* to rent; *(voiture etc: entreprise)* to hire out *(BRIT)*, rent (out); *(: locataire)* to hire, rent; *(réserver)* to book; *(faire l'éloge de)* to praise; **"à ~"**

"to let" (*BRIT*), "for rent" (*US*)
loup [lu] *nm* wolf
loupe [lup] *nf* magnifying glass
louper [lupe] (*fam*) *vt* (*manquer*) to miss; (*examen*) to flunk
lourd, e [luʀ, luʀd] *adj, adv* heavy; **~ de** (*conséquences, menaces*) charged with; **il fait ~** the weather is close, it's sultry; **lourdaud, e** (*péj*) *adj* clumsy; **lourdement** *adv* heavily; **lourdeur** *nf* weight; **lourdeurs d'estomac** indigestion
loutre [lutʀ] *nf* otter
louveteau, x [luv(ə)to] *nm* wolf-cub; (*scout*) cub (scout)
louvoyer [luvwaje] *vi* (*fig*) to hedge, evade the issue
loyal, e, -aux [lwajal, o] *adj* (*fidèle*) loyal, faithful; (*fair-play*) fair; **loyauté** *nf* loyalty, faithfulness; fairness
loyer [lwaje] *nm* rent
lu, e [ly] *pp de* **lire**
lubie [lybi] *nf* whim, craze
lubrifiant [lybʀifjɑ̃, jɑ̃t] *nm* lubricant
lubrifier [lybʀifje] *vt* to lubricate
lubrique [lybʀik] *adj* lecherous
lucarne [lykaʀn] *nf* skylight
lucide [lysid] *adj* lucid; (*accidenté*) conscious
lucratif, -ive [lykʀatif, iv] *adj* lucrative, profitable; **à but non ~** non profit-making
lueur [lɥœʀ] *nf* (*pâle*) (faint) light; (*chatoyante*) glimmer *no pl*; (*fig*) glimmer; gleam
luge [lyʒ] *nf* sledge (*BRIT*), sled (*US*)
lugubre [lygybʀ] *adj* gloomy, dismal

| MOT-CLÉ |

lui [lɥi] *pron* **1** (*objet indirect: mâle*) (to) him; (: *femelle*) (to) her; (: *chose, animal*) (to) it; **je lui ai parlé** I have spoken to him (*ou* to her); **il lui a offert un cadeau** he gave him (*ou* her) a present
2 (*après préposition, comparatif: personne*) him; (: *chose, animal*) it; **elle est contente de lui** she is pleased with him; **je la**

connais mieux que lui I know her better than he does; I know her better than him
3 (*sujet, forme emphatique*) he; **lui, il est à Paris** HE is in Paris
4: lui-même himself; itself

---

luire [lɥiʀ] *vi* to shine; (*en rougeoyant*) to glow
lumière [lymjɛʀ] *nf* light; **mettre en ~** (*fig*) to highlight; **~ du jour** daylight
luminaire [lyminɛʀ] *nm* lamp, light
lumineux, -euse [lyminø, øz] *adj* luminous; (*éclairé*) illuminated; (*ciel, couleur*) bright; (*rayon*) of light, light *cpd*; (*fig: regard*) radiant
lunatique [lynatik] *adj* whimsical, temperamental
lundi [lœ̃di] *nm* Monday; **~ de Pâques** Easter Monday
lune [lyn] *nf* moon; **~ de miel** honeymoon
lunette [lynɛt] *nf:* **~s ♦** *nfpl* glasses, spectacles; (*protectrices*) goggles; **~ arrière** (*AUTO*) rear window; **~s de soleil** sunglasses
lus *etc* [ly] *vb voir* **lire**
lustre [lystʀ] *nm* (*de plafond*) chandelier; (*fig: éclat*) lustre; **lustrer** *vt* to shine
lut [ly] *vb voir* **lire**
luth [lyt] *nm* lute
lutin [lytɛ̃] *nm* imp, goblin
lutte [lyt] *nf* (*conflit*) struggle; (*sport*) wrestling; **lutter** *vi* to fight, struggle
luxe [lyks] *nm* luxury; **de ~** luxury *cpd*
Luxembourg [lyksɑ̃buʀ] *nm:* **le ~** Luxembourg
luxer [lykse] *vt:* **se ~ l'épaule** to dislocate one's shoulder
luxueux, -euse [lyksɥø, øz] *adj* luxurious
luxure [lyksyʀ] *nf* lust
luxuriant, e [lyksyʀjɑ̃, jɑ̃t] *adj* luxuriant
lycée [lise] *nm* secondary school; **lycéen, ne** *nm/f* secondary school pupil
lyophilisé, e [ljɔfilize] *adj* (*café*) freeze-dried
lyrique [liʀik] *adj* lyrical; (*OPÉRA*) lyric; **artiste ~** opera singer

lys [lis] *nm* lily

M, m

M *abr* = **Monsieur**

m' [m] *pron voir* **me**

ma [ma] *adj voir* **mon**

macaron [makaʀɔ̃] *nm* (*gâteau*) macaroon; (*insigne*) (round) badge

macaronis [makaʀɔni] *nmpl* macaroni *sg*

macédoine [masedwan] *nf*: ~ **de fruits** fruit salad; ~ **de légumes** mixed vegetables

macérer [maseʀe] *vi, vt* to macerate; (*dans du vinaigre*) to pickle

mâcher [mɑʃe] *vt* to chew; **ne pas ~ ses mots** not to mince one's words

machin [maʃɛ̃] (*fam*) *nm* thing(umajig)

machinal, e, -aux [maʃinal, o] *adj* mechanical, automatic; **machinalement** *adv* mechanically, automatically

machination [maʃinasjɔ̃] *nf* frame-up

machine [maʃin] *nf* machine; (*locomotive*) engine; ~ **à écrire** typewriter; ~ **à laver/coudre** washing/sewing machine; ~ **à sous** fruit machine

macho [matʃo] (*fam*) *nm* male chauvinist

mâchoire [mɑʃwaʀ] *nf* jaw

mâchonner [mɑʃɔne] *vt* to chew (at)

maçon [masɔ̃] *nm* builder; (*poseur de briques*) bricklayer; **maçonnerie** *nf* (*murs*) brickwork; (*pierres*) masonry, stonework

maculer [makyle] *vt* to stain

Madame [madam] (*pl* **Mesdames**) *nf*: ~ **X** Mrs X; **occupez-vous de ~/Monsieur/Mademoiselle** please serve this lady/gentleman/(young) lady; **bonjour ~/Monsieur/Mademoiselle** good morning; (*ton déférent*) good morning Madam/Sir/Madam; (*le nom est connu*) good morning Mrs/Mr/Miss X; **~/Monsieur/Mademoiselle!** (*pour appeler*) Madam/Sir/Miss!; **~/Monsieur/Mademoiselle** (*sur lettre*) Dear Madam/Sir/Madam; **chère ~/cher Monsieur/chère**

Mademoiselle Dear Mrs/Mr/Miss X; **Mesdames** Ladies

madeleine [madlɛn] *nf* madeleine; *small sponge cake*

Mademoiselle [madmwazɛl] (*pl* **Mesdemoiselles**) *nf* Miss; *voir aussi* **Madame**

madère [madɛʀ] *nm* Madeira (wine)

magasin [magazɛ̃] *nm* (*boutique*) shop; (*entrepôt*) warehouse; **en ~** (*COMM*) in stock

magazine [magazin] *nm* magazine

Maghreb [magʀɛb] *nm*: **le ~** North Africa; **maghrébin, e** *adj* North African ♦ *nm/f*: **Maghrébin, e** North African

magicien, ne [maʒisjɛ̃, jɛn] *nm/f* magician

magie [maʒi] *nf* magic; **magique** *adj* magic; (*enchanteur*) magical

magistral, e, -aux [maʒistʀal, o] *adj* (*œuvre, adresse*) masterly; (*ton*) authoritative; **cours ~** lecture

magistrat [maʒistʀa] *nm* magistrate

magnat [magna] *nm* tycoon

magnétique [maɲetik] *adj* magnetic

magnétiser [maɲetize] *vt* to magnetize; (*fig*) to mesmerize, hypnotize

magnétophone [maɲetɔfɔn] *nm* tape recorder; ~ **à cassettes** cassette recorder

magnétoscope [maɲetɔskɔp] *nm* videotape recorder

magnifique [maɲifik] *adj* magnificent

magot [mago] (*fam*) *nm* (*argent*) pile (of money); (*économies*) nest egg

magouille [maguj] (*fam*) *nf* scheming; **magouiller** (*fam*) *vi* to scheme

magret [magʀɛ] *nm*: ~ **de canard** duck steaklet

mai [mɛ] *nm* May

---
mai
---

i Le premier mai *is a public holiday in France marking union demonstrations in the United States in 1886 to secure the eight-hour working day. It is traditional to exchange and wear sprigs of lily of the valley.* Le 8 mai *is a public holiday in*

France commemorating the surrender of the German army to Eisenhower on May 7, 1945. There are parades of ex-servicemen in most towns. The social upheavals of May and June 1968, marked by student demonstrations, strikes and rioting, are generally referred to as "les événements de **mai 68"**. *De Gaulle's government survived, but reforms in education and a move towards decentralization ensued.*

maigre [mɛgʀ] *adj* (very) thin, skinny; (*viande*) lean; (*fromage*) low-fat; (*végétation*) thin, sparse; (*fig*) poor, meagre, skimpy; **jours ~s** days of abstinence, fish days; **maigreur** *nf* thinness; **maigrir** *vi* to get thinner, lose weight; **maigrir de 2 kilos** to lose 2 kilos

maille [maj] *nf* stitch; **avoir ~ à partir avec qn** to have a brush with sb; **~ à l'endroit/à l'envers** plain/purl stitch

maillet [majɛ] *nm* mallet

maillon [majɔ̃] *nm* link

maillot [majo] *nm* (*aussi:* **~ de corps**) vest; (*de sportif*) jersey; **~ de bain** swimsuit; (*d'homme*) bathing trunks *pl*

main [mɛ̃] *nf* hand; **à la ~** in one's hand; **se donner la ~** to hold hands; **donner** *ou* **tendre la ~ à qn** to hold out one's hand to sb; **serrer la ~ à qn** to shake hands with sb; **sous la ~** to *ou* at hand; **à remettre en ~s propres** to be delivered personally; **mettre la dernière ~ à** to put the finishing touches to; **se faire/perdre la ~** to get one's hand in/lose one's touch; **avoir qch bien en ~** to have (got) the hang of sth; **main-d'œuvre** *nf* manpower, labour; **main-forte** *nf*: **prêter main-forte à qn** to come to sb's assistance; **mainmise** *nf* (*fig*): **mainmise sur** complete hold on

maint, e [mɛ̃, mɛ̃t] *adj* many a; **~s** many; **à ~es reprises** time and (time) again

maintenant [mɛ̃t(ə)nɑ̃] *adv* now; (*actuellement*) nowadays

maintenir [mɛ̃t(ə)niʀ] *vt* (*retenir, soutenir*) to support; (*contenir: foule etc*) to hold back; (*conserver, affirmer*) to maintain; **se ~** *vi* (*prix*) to keep steady; (*amélioration*) to persist

maintien [mɛ̃tjɛ̃] *nm* (*sauvegarde*) maintenance; (*attitude*) bearing

maire [mɛʀ] *nm* mayor; **mairie** *nf* (*bâtiment*) town hall; (*administration*) town council

mais [mɛ] *conj* but; **~ non!** of course not!; **~ enfin** but after all; (*indignation*) look here!

maïs [mais] *nm* maize (BRIT), corn (US)

maison [mɛzɔ̃] *nf* house; (*chez-soi*) home; (*COMM*) firm ♦ *adj inv* (*CULIN*) homemade; (*fig*) in-house, own; **à la ~** at home; (*direction*) home; **~ close** *ou* **de passe** brothel; **~ de repos** convalescent home; **~ de santé** mental home; **~ des jeunes** ≈ youth club; **~ mère** parent company; **maisonnée** *nf* household, family; **maisonnette** *nf* small house, cottage

┌─────────────────────────────────────┐
│ maisons des jeunes et de la culture │
└─────────────────────────────────────┘

i **Maisons des jeunes et de la culture** *are centres for young people which organize a wide range of sporting and cultural activities, and are also engaged in welfare work. The centres are, in part, publicly financed.*

maître, -esse [mɛtʀ, mɛtʀɛs] *nm/f* master (mistress); (*SCOL*) teacher, schoolmaster(-mistress) ♦ *nm* (*peintre etc*) master; (*titre*): **M~** Maître, *term of address gen for a barrister* ♦ *adj* (*principal, essentiel*) main; **être ~ de** (*soi, situation*) to be in control of; **une maîtresse femme** a managing woman; **~ chanteur** blackmailer; **~ d'école** schoolmaster; **~ d'hôtel** (*domestique*) butler; (*d'hôtel*) head waiter; **~ nageur** lifeguard; **maîtresse** *nf* (*amante*) mistress; **maîtresse (d'école)** teacher, (school)mistress; **maîtresse de maison**

hostess; (*ménagère*) housewife

maîtrise [metʀiz] *nf* (*aussi*: ~ **de soi**) self-control, self-possession; (*habileté*) skill, mastery; (*suprématie*) mastery, command; (*diplôme*) ≃ master's degree; **maîtriser** *vt* (*cheval, incendie*) to (bring under) control; (*sujet*) to master; (*émotion*) to control, master; **se maîtriser** to control o.s.

maïzena ® [maizena] *nf* cornflour

majestueux, -euse [maʒɛstɥø, øz] *adj* majestic

majeur, e [maʒœʀ] *adj* (*important*) major; (*JUR*) of age ♦ *nm* (*doigt*) middle finger; **en ~e partie** for the most part; **la ~e partie de** most of

majoration [maʒɔʀasjɔ̃] *nf* rise, increase

majorer [maʒɔʀe] *vt* to increase

majoritaire [maʒɔʀitɛʀ] *adj* majority *cpd*

majorité [maʒɔʀite] *nf* (*gén*) majority; (*parti*) party in power; **en ~** mainly

majuscule [maʒyskyl] *adj, nf*: (**lettre**) ~ capital (letter)

mal [mal, mo] (*pl* **maux**) *nm* (*opposé au bien*) evil; (*tort, dommage*) harm; (*douleur physique*) pain, ache; (*~adie*) illness, sickness *no pl* ♦ *adv* badly ♦ *adj* bad, wrong; **être ~ à l'aise** to be uncomfortable; **être ~ avec qn** to be on bad terms with sb; **il a ~ compris** he misunderstood; **dire/penser du ~ de** to speak/think ill of; **ne voir aucun ~ à** to see no harm in, see nothing wrong in; **faire ~ à qn** to hurt sb; **se faire ~** to hurt o.s.; **se donner du ~ pour faire qch** to go to a lot of trouble to do sth; **ça fait ~** it hurts; **j'ai ~ au dos** my back hurts; **avoir ~ à la tête/à la gorge/aux dents** to have a headache/a sore throat/toothache; **avoir le ~ du pays** to be homesick; *voir aussi* **cœur**; **maux**; ~ **de mer** seasickness; ~ **en point** in a bad state

malade [malad] *adj* ill, sick; (*poitrine, jambe*) bad; (*plante*) diseased ♦ *nm/f* invalid, sick person; (*à l'hôpital etc*) patient; **tomber ~** to fall ill; **être ~ du cœur** to have heart trouble *ou* a bad heart; ~

mental mentally sick *ou* ill person; **maladie** *nf* (*spécifique*) disease, illness; (*mauvaise santé*) illness, sickness; **maladif, -ive** *adj* sickly; (*curiosité, besoin*) pathological

maladresse [maladʀɛs] *nf* clumsiness *no pl*; (*gaffe*) blunder

maladroit, e [maladʀwa, wat] *adj* clumsy

malaise [malɛz] *nm* (*MÉD*) feeling of faintness; (*fig*) uneasiness, malaise; **avoir un ~** to feel faint

malaisé, e [maleze] *adj* difficult

malaria [malaʀja] *nf* malaria

malaxer [malakse] *vt* (*pétrir*) to knead; (*mélanger*) to mix

malchance [malʃɑ̃s] *nf* misfortune, ill luck *no pl*; **par ~** unfortunately; **malchanceux, -euse** *adj* unlucky

mâle [mɑl] *adj* (*aussi ÉLEC, TECH*) male; (*viril: voix, traits*) manly ♦ *nm* male

malédiction [malediksjɔ̃] *nf* curse

mal...: **malencontreux, -euse** *adj* unfortunate, untoward; **mal-en-point** *adj inv* in a sorry state; **malentendant, e** *nm/f*: **les malentendants** the hard of hearing; **malentendu** *nm* misunderstanding; **malfaçon** *nf* fault; **malfaisant, e** *adj* evil, harmful; **malfaiteur** *nm* lawbreaker, criminal; (*voleur*) burglar, thief; **malfamé, e** *adj* disreputable

malgache [malgaʃ] *adj* Madagascan, Malagasy ♦ *nm/f*: **M~** Madagascan, Malagasy ♦ *nm* (*LING*) Malagasy

malgré [malgʀe] *prép* in spite of, despite; ~ **tout** all the same

malhabile [malabil] *adj* clumsy, awkward

malheur [malœʀ] *nm* (*situation*) adversity, misfortune; (*événement*) misfortune; (*: très grave*) disaster, tragedy; **faire un ~** to be a smash hit; **malheureusement** *adv* unfortunately; **malheureux, -euse** *adj* (*triste*) unhappy, miserable; (*infortuné, regrettable*) unfortunate; (*malchanceux*) unlucky; (*insignifiant*) wretched ♦ *nm/f* poor soul; **les malheureux** the destitute

malhonnête [malɔnɛt] *adj* dishonest; **malhonnêteté** *nf* dishonesty

malice [malis] nf mischievousness; (*méchanceté*): **par ~** out of malice ou spite; **sans ~** guileless; **malicieux, -euse** adj mischievous

malin, -igne [malɛ̃, maliɲ] adj (*futé: f gén: maline*) smart, shrewd; (*MÉD*) malignant

malingre [malɛ̃gʀ] adj puny

malle [mal] nf trunk; **mallette** nf (small) suitcase; (*porte-documents*) attaché case

malmener [malməne] vt to manhandle; (*fig*) to give a rough handling to

malodorant, e [malɔdɔʀã, ãt] adj foul- ou ill-smelling

malotru [malɔtʀy] nm lout, boor

malpoli, e [malpɔli] adj impolite

malpropre [malpʀɔpʀ] adj dirty

malsain, e [malsɛ̃, ɛn] adj unhealthy

malt [malt] nm malt

Malte [malt] nf Malta

maltraiter [maltʀete] vt to manhandle, ill-treat

malveillance [malvejãs] nf (*animosité*) ill will; (*intention de nuire*) malevolence

malversation [malvɛʀsasjɔ̃] nf embezzlement

maman [mamã] nf mum(my), mother

mamelle [mamɛl] nf teat

mamelon [mam(ə)lɔ̃] nm (*ANAT*) nipple

mamie [mami] nf (*fam*) granny

mammifère [mamifɛʀ] nm mammal

mammouth [mamut] nm mammoth

manche [mãʃ] nf (*de vêtement*) sleeve; (*d'un jeu, tournoi*) round; (*GÉO*): **la M~** the Channel ♦ nm (*d'outil, casserole*) handle; (*de pelle, pioche etc*) shaft; **à ~s courtes/longues** short-/long-sleeved

manchette [mãʃet] nf (*de chemise*) cuff; (*coup*) forearm blow; (*titre*) headline

manchot [mãʃo, ɔt] nm one-armed man; armless man; (*ZOOL*) penguin

mandarine [mãdaʀin] nf mandarin (orange), tangerine

mandat [mãda] nm (*postal*) postal ou money order; (*d'un député etc*) mandate; (*procuration*) power of attorney, proxy; (*POLICE*) warrant; **~ d'arrêt** warrant for arrest; **mandataire** nm/f (*représentant*) representative; (*JUR*) proxy

manège [manɛʒ] nm riding school; (*à la foire*) roundabout, merry-go-round; (*fig*) game, ploy

manette [manɛt] nf lever, tap; **~ de jeu** joystick

mangeable [mãʒabl] adj edible, eatable

mangeoire [mãʒwaʀ] nf trough, manger

manger [mãʒe] vt to eat; (*ronger: suj: rouille etc*) to eat into ou away ♦ vi to eat; **donner à ~ à** (*enfant*) to feed; **mangeur, -euse** nm/f eater; **gros mangeur** big eater

mangue [mãg] nf mango

maniable [manjabl] adj (*outil*) handy; (*voiture, voilier*) easy to handle

maniaque [manjak] adj finicky, fussy ♦ nm/f (*méticuleux*) fusspot; (*fou*) maniac

manie [mani] nf (*tic*) odd habit; (*obsession*) mania; **avoir la ~ de** to be obsessive about

manier [manje] vt to handle

manière [manjɛʀ] nf (*façon*) way, manner; **~s** nfpl (*attitude*) manners; (*chichis*) fuss sg; **de ~ à** so as to; **de cette ~** in this way ou manner; **d'une certaine ~** in a way; **de toute ~** in any case

maniéré, e [manjere] adj affected

manif [manif] (*fam*) nf demo

manifestant, e [manifestã, ãt] nm/f demonstrator

manifestation [manifestasjɔ̃] nf (*de joie, mécontentement*) expression, demonstration; (*symptôme*) outward sign; (*culturelle etc*) event; (*POL*) demonstration

manifeste [manifest] adj obvious, evident ♦ nm manifesto; **manifester** vt (*volonté, intentions*) to show, indicate; (*joie, peur*) to express, show ♦ vi to demonstrate; **se manifester** vi (*émotion*) to show ou express itself; (*difficultés*) to arise; (*symptômes*) to appear

manigance [manigãs] nf scheme; **manigancer** vt to plot

manipulation [manipylasjɔ̃] nf handling;

(*POL, génétique*) manipulation

manipuler [manipyle] *vt* to handle; (*fig*) to manipulate

manivelle [manivɛl] *nf* crank

mannequin [mankɛ̃] *nm* (*COUTURE*) dummy; (*MODE*) model

manœuvre [manœvʀ] *nf* (*gén*) manœuvre (*BRIT*), maneuver (*US*) ♦ *nm* labourer; **manœuvrer** *vt* to manœuvre (*BRIT*), maneuver (*US*); (*levier, machine*) to operate ♦ *vi* to manœuvre

manoir [manwaʀ] *nm* manor *ou* country house

manque [mãk] *nm* (*insuffisance*): ~ **de** lack of; (*vide*) emptiness, gap; (*MÉD*) withdrawal; **être en état de** ~ to suffer withdrawal symptoms

manqué, e [mãke] *adj* failed; **garçon** ~ tomboy

manquer [mãke] *vi* (*faire défaut*) to be lacking; (*être absent*) to be missing; (*échouer*) to fail ♦ *vt* to miss ♦ *vb impers*: **il (nous) manque encore 10 euros** we are still 10 euros short; **il manque des pages (au livre)** there are some pages missing (from the book); **il/cela me manque** I miss him/this; ~ **à** (*règles etc*) to be in breach of, fail to observe; ~ **de** to lack; **je ne ~ai pas de le lui dire** I'll be sure to tell him; **il a manqué (de) se tuer** he very nearly got killed

mansarde [mãsaʀd] *nf* attic; **mansardé, e** *adj*: **chambre mansardée** attic room

manteau, x [mãto] *nm* coat

manucure [manykyʀ] *nf* manicurist

manuel, le [manɥɛl] *adj* manual ♦ *nm* (*ouvrage*) manual, handbook

manufacture [manyfaktyʀ] *nf* factory; **manufacturé, e** *adj* manufactured

manuscrit, e [manyskʀi, it] *adj* handwritten ♦ *nm* manuscript

manutention [manytãsjɔ̃] *nf* (*COMM*) handling

mappemonde [mapmɔ̃d] *nf* (*plane*) map of the world; (*sphère*) globe

maquereau, x [makʀo] *nm* (*ZOOL*) mackerel *inv*; (*fam*) pimp

maquette [makɛt] *nf* (*à échelle réduite*) (scale) model; (*d'une page illustrée*) paste-up

maquillage [makijaʒ] *nm* making up; (*crème etc*) make-up

maquiller [makije] *vt* (*personne, visage*) to make up; (*truquer: passeport, statistique*) to fake; (: *voiture volée*) to do over (*respray etc*); **se** ~ *vi* to make up (one's face)

maquis [maki] *nm* (*GÉO*) scrub; (*MIL*) maquis, underground fighting *no pl*

maraîcher, -ère [maʀeʃe, ɛʀ] *adj*: **cultures maraîchères** market gardening *sg* ♦ *nm/f* market gardener

marais [maʀɛ] *nm* marsh, swamp

marasme [maʀasm] *nm* stagnation, slump

marathon [maʀatɔ̃] *nm* marathon

maraudeur [maʀodœʀ, øz] *nm* prowler

marbre [maʀbʀ] *nm* marble

marc [maʀ] *nm* (*de raisin, pommes*) marc; ~ **de café** coffee grounds *pl ou* dregs *pl*

marchand, e [maʀʃã, ãd] *nm/f* shopkeeper, tradesman(-woman); (*au marché*) stallholder; (*de vins, charbon*) merchant ♦ *adj*: **prix/valeur** ~(**e**) market price/value; ~(**e**) **de fruits** fruiterer (*BRIT*), fruit seller (*US*); ~(**e**) **de journaux** newsagent; ~(**e**) **de légumes** greengrocer (*BRIT*), produce dealer (*US*); ~(**e**) **de poissons** fishmonger; **marchander** *vi* to bargain, haggle; **marchandise** *nf* goods *pl*, merchandise *no pl*

marche [maʀʃ] *nf* (*d'escalier*) step; (*activité*) walking; (*promenade, trajet, allure*) walk; (*démarche*) walk, gait; (*MIL etc*) march; (*fonctionnement*) running; (*des événements*) course; **dans le sens de la** ~ (*RAIL*) facing the engine; **en** ~ (*monter etc*) while the vehicle is moving *ou* in motion; **mettre en** ~ to start; **se mettre en** ~ (*personne*) to get moving; (*machine*) to start; **être en état de** ~ to be in working order; ~ **à suivre** (correct) procedure; ~ **arrière** reverse (gear); **faire** ~ **arrière** to reverse; (*fig*) to backtrack, back-pedal

marché [maʀʃe] *nm* market; *(transaction)* bargain, deal; **faire du ~ noir** to buy and sell on the black market; **~ aux puces** flea market; **M~ commun** Common Market

marchepied [maʀʃəpje] *nm* (RAIL) step

marcher [maʀʃe] *vi* to walk; (MIL) to march; *(aller: voiture, train, affaires)* to go; *(prospérer)* to go well; *(fonctionner)* to work, run; *(fam: consentir)* to go along, agree; *(: croire naïvement)* to be taken in; **faire ~ qn** *(taquiner)* to pull sb's leg; *(tromper)* to lead sb up the garden path; **marcheur, -euse** *nm/f* walker

mardi [maʀdi] *nm* Tuesday; **M~ gras** Shrove Tuesday

mare [maʀ] *nf* pond; *(flaque)* pool

marécage [maʀekaʒ] *nm* marsh, swamp; **marécageux, -euse** *adj* marshy

maréchal, -aux [maʀeʃal, o] *nm* marshal; **maréchal-ferrant** [maʀeʃalferɑ̃, maʀeʃo-] *(pl* **maréchaux-ferrants)** *nm* blacksmith, farrier

marée [maʀe] *nf* tide; *(poissons)* fresh (sea) fish; **~ haute/basse** high/low tide; **~ montante/descendante** rising/ebb tide; **~ noire** oil slick

marelle [maʀɛl] *nf* hopscotch

margarine [maʀɡaʀin] *nf* margarine

marge [maʀʒ] *nf* margin; **en ~ de** (fig) on the fringe of; **~ bénéficiaire** profit margin

marginal, e, -aux [maʀʒinal, o] *nm/f (original)* eccentric; *(déshérité)* dropout

marguerite [maʀɡəʀit] *nf* . marguerite, (oxeye) daisy; *(d'imprimante)* daisy-wheel

mari [maʀi] *nm* husband

mariage [maʀjaʒ] *nm* marriage; *(noce)* wedding; **~ civil/religieux** registry office (BRIT) *ou* civil/church wedding

marié, e [maʀje] *adj* married ♦ *nm* (bride)groom; **les ~s** the bride and groom; **les (jeunes) ~s** the newly-weds; **mariée** *nf* bride

marier [maʀje] *vt* to marry; *(fig)* to blend; **se ~** *vr* to get married; **se ~ (avec)** to marry

marin, e [maʀɛ̃, in] *adj* sea *cpd*, marine ♦ *nm* sailor

marine [maʀin] *adj voir* **marin** ♦ *adj inv* navy (blue) ♦ *nm* (MIL) marine ♦ *nf* navy; **~ de guerre** navy; **~ marchande** merchant navy

mariner [maʀine] *vt:* **faire ~** to marinade

marionnette [maʀjɔnɛt] *nf* puppet

maritalement [maʀitalmɑ̃] *adv:* **vivre ~** to live as husband and wife

maritime [maʀitim] *adj* sea *cpd*, maritime

mark [maʀk] *nm* mark

marmelade [maʀməlad] *nf* stewed fruit, compote; **~ d'oranges** marmalade

marmite [maʀmit] *nf* (cooking-)pot

marmonner [maʀmɔne] *vt, vi* to mumble, mutter

marmot [maʀmo] *(fam) nm* kid

marmotter [maʀmɔte] *vt* to mumble

Maroc [maʀɔk] *nm:* **le ~** Morocco; **marocain, e** [maʀɔkɛ̃, ɛn] *adj* Moroccan ♦ *nm/f:* **Marocain, e** Moroccan

maroquinerie [maʀɔkinʀi] *nf (articles)* fine leather goods *pl;* *(boutique)* shop selling fine leather goods

marquant, e [maʀkɑ̃, ɑ̃t] *adj* outstanding

marque [maʀk] *nf* mark; *(COMM: de nourriture)* brand; *(: de voiture, produits manufacturés)* make; *(de disques)* label; **de ~** *(produits)* high-class; *(visiteur etc)* distinguished, well-known; **une grande ~ de vin** a well-known brand of wine; **~ de fabrique** trademark; **~ déposée** registered trademark

marquer [maʀke] *vt* to mark; *(inscrire)* to write down; *(bétail)* to brand; (SPORT: *but etc)* to score; *(: joueur)* to mark; *(accentuer: taille etc)* to emphasize; *(manifester: refus, intérêt)* to show ♦ *vi (événement)* to stand out, be outstanding; (SPORT) to score

marqueterie [maʀkɛtʀi] *nf* inlaid work, marquetry

marquis [maʀki] *nm* marquis, marquess; **marquise** *nf* marchioness; *(auvent)* glass canopy *ou* awning

marraine [maʀɛn] *nf* godmother

marrant, e [maʀɑ̃, ɑ̃t] *(fam) adj* funny
marre [maʀ] *(fam) adv*: **en avoir ~ de** to be fed up with
marrer [maʀe]: **se ~** *(fam) vi* to have a (good) laugh
marron [maʀɔ̃] *nm (fruit)* chestnut ♦ *adj inv* brown; **~s glacés** candied chestnuts; **marronnier** *nm* chestnut (tree)
mars [maʀs] *nm* March
Marseille [maʀsɛj] *n* Marseilles

Marseillaise

i La Marseillaise *has been France's national anthem since 1879. The words of the "Chant de guerre de l'armée du Rhin", as the song was originally called, were written to an anonymous tune by the army captain Rouget de Lisle in 1792. Adopted as a marching song by the battalion of Marseilles, it was finally popularized as the* Marseillaise.

---
marsouin [maʀswɛ̃] *nm* porpoise
marteau, x [maʀto] *nm* hammer; **être ~** *(fam)* to be nuts; **marteau-piqueur** *nm* pneumatic drill
marteler [maʀtəle] *vt* to hammer
martien, ne [maʀsjɛ̃, jɛn] *adj* Martian, of *ou* from Mars
martyr, e [maʀtiʀ] *nm/f* martyr; **martyre** *nm* martyrdom; *(fig: sens affaibli)* agony, torture; **martyriser** *vt (REL)* to martyr; *(fig)* to bully; *(enfant)* to batter, beat
marxiste [maʀksist] *adj, nm/f* Marxist
mascara [maskaʀa] *nm* mascara
masculin, e [maskylɛ̃, in] *adj* masculine; *(sexe, population)* male; *(équipe, vêtements)* men's; *(viril)* manly ♦ *nm* masculine; **masculinité** *nf* masculinity
masochiste [mazɔʃist] *adj* masochistic
masque [mask] *nm* mask; **masquer** *vt (cacher: paysage, porte)* to hide, conceal; *(dissimuler: vérité, projet)* to mask, obscure
massacre [masakʀ] *nm* massacre, slaughter; **massacrer** *vt* to massacre, slaughter; *(fam: texte etc)* to murder

massage [masaʒ] *nm* massage
masse [mas] *nf* mass; *(ÉLEC)* earth; *(maillet)* sledgehammer; *(péj)*: **la ~** 'the masses *pl*; **une ~ de** *(fam)* masses *ou* loads of; **en ~** ♦ *adv (acheter)* in bulk; *(en foule)* en masse ♦ *adj (exécutions, production)* mass *cpd*
masser [mase] *vt (assembler: gens)* to gather; *(pétrir)* to massage; **se ~** *vi (foule)* to gather; **masseur, -euse** *nm/f* masseur(-euse)
massif, -ive [masif, iv] *adj (porte)* solid, massive; *(visage)* heavy, large; *(bois, or)* solid; *(dose)* massive; *(déportations etc)* mass *cpd* ♦ *nm (montagneux)* massif; *(de fleurs)* clump, bank
massue [masy] *nf* club, bludgeon
mastic [mastik] *nm (pour vitres)* putty; *(pour fentes)* filler
mastiquer [mastike] *vt (aliment)* to chew, masticate
mat, e [mat] *adj (couleur, métal)* mat(t); *(bruit, son)* dull ♦ *adj inv (ÉCHECS)*: **être ~** to be checkmate
mât [mɑ] *nm (NAVIG)* mast; *(poteau)* pole, post
match [matʃ] *nm* match; **faire ~ nul** to draw; **~ aller** first leg; **~ retour** second leg, return match
matelas [mat(ə)la] *nm* mattress; **~ pneumatique** air bed *ou* mattress; **matelassé, e** *adj (vêtement)* padded; *(tissu)* quilted
matelot [mat(ə)lo] *nm* sailor, seaman
mater [mate] *vt (personne)* to bring to heel, subdue; *(révolte)* to put down
matérialiser [mateʀjalize]: **se ~** *vi* to materialize
matérialiste [mateʀjalist] *adj* materialistic
matériaux [mateʀjo] *nmpl* material(s)
matériel, le [mateʀjɛl] *adj* material ♦ *nm* equipment *no pl*; *(de camping etc)* gear *no pl*; *(INFORM)* hardware
maternel, le [mateʀnɛl] *adj (amour, geste)* motherly, maternal; *(grand-père, oncle)* maternal; **maternelle** *nf (aussi:* **école maternelle)** (state) nursery school

maternité [matɛʀnite] *nf* (*établissement*) maternity hospital; (*état de mère*) motherhood, maternity; (*grossesse*) pregnancy; **congé de ~** maternity leave

mathématique [matematik] *adj* mathematical; **mathématiques** *nfpl* (*science*) mathematics *sg*

maths [mat] (*fam*) *nfpl* maths

matière [matjɛʀ] *nf* matter; (*COMM, TECH*) material, matter *no pl*; (*fig: d'un livre etc*) subject matter, material; (*SCOL*) subject; **en ~ de** as regards; **~s grasses** fat content *sg*; **~s premières** raw materials

hôtel Matignon

i L'**hôtel Matignon** *is the Paris office and residence of the French Prime Minister. By extension, the term "Matignon" is often used to refer to the Prime Minister or his staff.*

matin [matɛ̃] *nm, adv* morning; **du ~ au soir** from morning till night; **de bon** *ou* **grand ~** early in the morning; **matinal, e, -aux** *adj* (*toilette, gymnastique*) morning *cpd*; **être matinal** (*personne*) to be up early; to be an early riser; **matinée** *nf* morning; (*spectacle*) matinée

matou [matu] *nm* tom(cat)

matraque [matʀak] *nf* (*de policier*) truncheon (*BRIT*), billy (*US*)

matricule [matʀikyl] *nm* (*MIL*) regimental number; (*ADMIN*) reference number

matrimonial, e, -aux [matʀimɔnjal, jo] *adj* marital, marriage *cpd*

maudire [modiʀ] *vt* to curse; **maudit, e** (*fam*) *adj* (*satané*) blasted, confounded

maugréer [mogʀee] *vi* to grumble

maussade [mosad] *adj* sullen; (*temps*) gloomy

mauvais, e [mɔvɛ, ɛz] *adj* bad; (*faux*): **le ~ numéro/moment** the wrong number/ moment; (*méchant, malveillant*) malicious, spiteful; **il fait ~** the weather is bad; **la mer est ~e** the sea is rough; **~ plaisant** hoaxer; **~e herbe** weed; **~e langue** gossip, scandalmonger (*BRIT*); **~e passe** bad patch

mauve [mov] *adj* mauve

maux [mo] *nmpl de* **mal**; **~ de ventre** stomachache *sg*

maximum [maksimɔm] *adj, nm* maximum; **au ~** (*le plus possible*) as much as one can; (*tout au plus*) at the (very) most *ou* maximum; **faire le ~** to do one's level best

mayonnaise [majɔnɛz] *nf* mayonnaise

mazout [mazut] *nm* (fuel) oil

Me *abr* = **Maître**

me, m' [m(ə)] *pron* (*direct: téléphoner, attendre etc*) me; (*indirect: parler, donner etc*) (to) me; (*réfléchi*) myself

mec [mɛk] (*fam*) *nm* bloke, guy

mécanicien, ne [mekanisjɛ̃, jɛn] *nm/f* mechanic; (*RAIL*) (train *ou* engine) driver

mécanique [mekanik] *adj* mechanical ♦ *nf* (*science*) mechanics *sg*; (*mécanisme*) mechanism; **ennui ~** engine trouble *no pl*

mécanisme [mekanism] *nm* mechanism

méchamment [meʃamɑ̃] *adv* nastily, maliciously, spitefully

méchanceté [meʃɑ̃ste] *nf* nastiness, maliciousness; **dire des ~s à qn** to say spiteful things to sb

méchant, e [meʃɑ̃, ɑ̃t] *adj* nasty, malicious, spiteful; (*enfant: pas sage*) naughty; (*animal*) vicious

mèche [mɛʃ] *nf* (*de cheveux*) lock; (*de lampe, bougie*) wick; (*d'un explosif*) fuse; **de ~ avec** in league with

méchoui [meʃwi] *nm* barbecue of a whole roast sheep

méconnaissable [mekɔnɛsabl] *adj* unrecognizable

méconnaître [mekɔnɛtʀ] *vt* (*ignorer*) to be unaware of; (*mésestimer*) to misjudge

mécontent, e [mekɔ̃tɑ̃, ɑ̃t] *adj*: **~ (de)** discontented *ou* dissatisfied *ou* displeased (with); (*contrarié*) annoyed (at); **mécontentement** *nm* dissatisfaction, discontent, displeasure; (*irritation*) annoyance

médaille [medaj] *nf* medal

médaillon [medajɔ̃] *nm* (*bijou*) locket

médecin [med(ə)sɛ̃] *nm* doctor; **~ légiste** forensic surgeon

médecine [med(ə)sin] *nf* medicine

média [medja] *nmpl*: **les ~** the media; **médiatique** *adj* media *cpd*; **médiatisé, e** *adj* reported in the media; **ce procès a été très médiatisé** (*péj*) this trial was turned into a media event

médical, e, -aux [medikal, o] *adj* medical; **passer une visite ~e** to have a medical

médicament [medikamɑ̃] *nm* medicine, drug

médiéval, e, -aux [medjeval, o] *adj* medieval

médiocre [medjɔkʀ] *adj* mediocre, poor

médire [mediʀ] *vi*: **~ de** to speak ill of; **médisance** *nf* scandalmongering (*BRIT*)

méditer [medite] *vi* to meditate

Méditerranée [mediteʀane] *nf*: **la (mer) ~** the Mediterranean (Sea); **méditerranéen, ne** *adj* Mediterranean ♦ *nm/f*: **Méditerranéen, ne** native *ou* inhabitant of a Mediterranean country

méduse [medyz] *nf* jellyfish

meeting [mitiŋ] *nm* (*POL, SPORT*) rally

méfait [mefɛ] *nm* (*faute*) misdemeanour, wrongdoing; **~s** *nmpl* (*ravages*) ravages, damage *sg*

méfiance [mefjɑ̃s] *nf* mistrust, distrust

méfiant, e [mefjɑ̃, jɑ̃t] *adj* mistrustful, distrustful

méfier [mefje]: **se ~** *vi* to be wary; to be careful; **se ~ de** to mistrust, distrust, be wary of

mégarde [megaʀd] *nf*: **par ~** (*accidentellement*) accidentally; (*par erreur*) by mistake

mégère [meʒɛʀ] *nf* shrew

mégot [mego] (*fam*) *nm* cigarette end

meilleur, e [mejœʀ] *adj, adv* better ♦ *nm*: **le ~** the best; **le ~ des deux** the better of the two; **~ marché** (*inv*) cheaper; **meilleure** *nf*: **la meilleure** the best (one)

mélancolie [melɑ̃kɔli] *nf* melancholy, gloom; **mélancolique** *adj* melancholic, melancholy

mélange [melɑ̃ʒ] *nm* mixture; **mélanger** *vt* to mix; (*vins, couleurs*) to blend; (*mettre en désordre*) to mix up, muddle (up)

mélasse [melas] *nf* treacle, molasses *sg*

mêlée [mele] *nf* mêlée, scramble; (*RUGBY*) scrum(mage)

mêler [mele] *vt* (*unir*) to mix; (*embrouiller*) to muddle (up), mix up; **se ~** *vi* to mix, mingle; **se ~ à** (*personne: se joindre*) to join; (: *s'associer à*) to mix with; **se ~ de** (*suj: personne*) to meddle with, interfere in; **mêle-toi de ce qui te regarde!** mind your own business!

mélodie [melɔdi] *nf* melody; **mélodieux, -euse** *adj* melodious

melon [m(ə)lɔ̃] *nm* (*BOT*) (honeydew) melon; (*aussi:* **chapeau ~**) bowler (hat)

membre [mɑ̃bʀ] *nm* (*ANAT*) limb; (*personne, pays, élément*) member ♦ *adj* member *cpd*

mémé [meme] (*fam*) *nf* granny

MOT-CLÉ
---

même [mɛm] *adj* 1 (*avant le nom*) same; **en même temps** at the same time

2 (*après le nom: renforcement*): **il est la loyauté même** he is loyalty itself; **ce sont ses paroles/celles-là mêmes** they are his very words/the very ones

♦ *pron*: **le(la) même** the same one

♦ *adv* 1 (*renforcement*): **il n'a même pas pleuré** he didn't even cry; **même lui l'a dit** even HE said it; **ici même** at this very place

2: **à même: à même la bouteille** straight from the bottle; **à même la peau** next to the skin; **être à même de faire** to be in a position to do, be able to do

3: **de même: faire de même** to do likewise; **lui de même** so does (*ou* did *ou* is) he; **de même que** just as; **il en va de même pour** the same goes for

mémo [memo] *(fam)* nm memo

mémoire [memwaʀ] nf memory ♦ nm *(SCOL)* dissertation, paper; **~s** nmpl *(souvenirs)* memoirs; **à la ~ de** to the *ou* in memory of; **de ~** from memory; **~ morte/vive** *(INFORM)* ROM/RAM

mémorable [memɔʀabl] adj memorable, unforgettable

menace [mənas] nf threat; **menacer** vt to threaten

ménage [menaʒ] nm *(travail)* housekeeping, housework; *(couple)* (married) couple; *(famille, ADMIN)* household; **faire le ~** to do the housework; **ménagement** nm care and attention; **ménager, -ère** adj household cpd, domestic ♦ vt *(traiter: personne)* to handle with tact; *(utiliser)* to use sparingly; *(prendre soin de)* to take (great) care of, look after; *(organiser)* to arrange; **ménager qch à qn** *(réserver)* to have sth in store for sb; **ménagère** nf housewife

mendiant, e [mɑ̃djɑ̃, jɑ̃t] nm/f beggar

mendier [mɑ̃dje] vi to beg ♦ vt to beg (for)

mener [m(ə)ne] vt to lead; *(enquête)* to conduct; *(affaires)* to manage ♦ vi: **~ à/ dans** *(emmener)* to take to/into; **~ qch à bien** to see sth through (to a successful conclusion), complete sth successfully

meneur, -euse [mənœʀ, øz] nm/f leader; *(péj)* agitator

méningite [menɛ̃ʒit] nf meningitis no pl

ménopause [menopoz] nf menopause

menottes [mənɔt] nfpl handcuffs

mensonge [mɑ̃sɔ̃ʒ] nm lie; *(action)* lying no pl; **mensonger, -ère** adj false

mensualité [mɑ̃sɥalite] nf *(traite)* monthly payment

mensuel, le [mɑ̃sɥɛl] adj monthly

mensurations [mɑ̃syʀasjɔ̃] nfpl measurements

mental, e, -aux [mɑ̃tal, o] adj mental; **mentalité** nf mentality

menteur, -euse [mɑ̃tœʀ, øz] nm/f liar

menthe [mɑ̃t] nf mint

mention [mɑ̃sjɔ̃] nf *(annotation)* note, comment; *(SCOL)* grade; **~ bien** *etc* ≃ grade B *etc* *(ou* upper 2nd class *etc)* pass *(BRIT)*, ≃ pass with (high) honors *(US)*; *(ADMIN)*: **"rayer les ~s inutiles"** "delete as appropriate"; **mentionner** vt to mention

mentir [mɑ̃tiʀ] vi to lie

menton [mɑ̃tɔ̃] nm chin

menu, e [məny] adj *(personne)* slim, slight; *(frais, difficulté)* minor ♦ adv *(couper, hacher)* very fine ♦ nm menu; **~ touristique/gastronomique** economy/ gourmet's menu

menuiserie [mənɥizʀi] nf *(métier)* joinery, carpentry; *(passe-temps)* woodwork; **menuisier** nm joiner, carpenter

méprendre [mepʀɑ̃dʀ]: **se ~** vi: **se ~ sur** to be mistaken (about)

mépris [mepʀi] nm *(dédain)* contempt, scorn; **au ~ de** regardless of, in defiance of; **méprisable** adj contemptible, despicable; **méprisant, e** adj scornful; **méprise** nf mistake, error; **mépriser** vt to scorn, despise; *(gloire, danger)* to scorn, spurn

mer [mɛʀ] nf sea; *(marée)* tide; **en ~** at sea; **en haute** *ou* **pleine ~** off shore, on the open sea; **la ~ du Nord/Rouge** the North/Red Sea

mercenaire [mɛʀsənɛʀ] nm mercenary, hired soldier

mercerie [mɛʀsəʀi] nf *(boutique)* haberdasher's shop *(BRIT)*, notions store *(US)*

merci [mɛʀsi] excl thank you ♦ nf: **à la ~ de qn/qch** at sb's mercy/the mercy of sth; **~ beaucoup** thank you very much; **~ de** thank you for; **sans ~** merciless(ly)

mercredi [mɛʀkʀədi] nm Wednesday

mercure [mɛʀkyʀ] nm mercury

merde [mɛʀd] *(fam!)* nf shit (!) ♦ excl (bloody) hell (!)

mère [mɛʀ] nf mother; **~ célibataire** unmarried mother

merguez [mɛʀɡez] nf merguez sausage *(type of spicy sausage from N Africa)*

méridional, e, -aux [meʀidjɔnal, o] adj

southern ♦ *nm/f* Southerner

meringue [məʀɛ̃g] *nf* meringue

mérite [meʀit] *nm* merit; **avoir du ~ (à faire qch)** to deserve credit (for doing sth); **mériter** *vt* to deserve

merlan [mɛʀlɑ̃] *nm* whiting

merle [mɛʀl] *nm* blackbird

merveille [mɛʀvɛj] *nf* marvel, wonder; **faire ~** to work wonders; **à ~** perfectly, wonderfully; **merveilleux, -euse** *adj* marvellous, wonderful

mes [me] *adj voir* **mon**

mésange [mezɑ̃ʒ] *nf* tit(mouse)

mésaventure [mezavɑ̃tyʀ] *nf* misadventure, misfortune

Mesdames [medam] *nfpl de* **Madame**

Mesdemoiselles [medmwazɛl] *nfpl de* **Mademoiselle**

mesquin, e [mɛskɛ̃, in] *adj* mean, petty; **mesquinerie** *nf* meanness; (*procédé*) mean trick

message [mesaʒ] *nm* message; **messager, -ère** *nm/f* messenger; **messagerie** *nf* (*INTERNET*): **messagerie électronique** bulletin board

messe [mɛs] *nf* mass

Messieurs [mesjø] *nmpl de* **Monsieur**

mesure [m(ə)zyʀ] *nf* (*évaluation, dimension*) measurement; (*récipient*) measure; (*MUS: cadence*) time, tempo; (*: division*) bar; (*retenue*) moderation; (*disposition*) measure, step; **sur ~** (*costume*) made-to-measure; **dans la ~ où** insofar as, inasmuch as; **à ~ que** as; **être en ~ de** to be in a position to; **dans une certaine ~** to a certain extent

mesurer [məzyʀe] *vt* to measure; (*juger*) to weigh up, assess; (*modérer: ses paroles etc*) to moderate; **se ~ avec** to have a confrontation with; **il mesure 1 m 80** he's 1 m 80 tall

met [me] *vb voir* **mettre**

métal, -aux [metal, o] *nm* metal; **métallique** *adj* metallic

météo [meteo] *nf* (*bulletin*) weather report

météorologie [meteɔʀɔlɔʒi] *nf* meteorology

méthode [metɔd] *nf* method; (*livre, ouvrage*) manual, tutor

méticuleux, -euse [metikylø, øz] *adj* meticulous

métier [metje] *nm* (*profession: gén*) job; (*: manuel*) trade; (*artisanal*) craft; (*technique, expérience*) (acquired) skill *ou* technique; (*aussi:* ~ **à tisser**) (weaving) loom; **avoir du ~** to have practical experience

métis, se [metis] *adj, nm/f* half-caste, half-breed

métrage [metʀaʒ] *nm*: **long/moyen/court** ~ full-length/medium-length/short film

mètre [mɛtʀ] *nm* metre; (*règle*) (metre) rule; (*ruban*) tape measure; **métrique** *adj* metric

métro [metʀo] *nm* underground (*BRIT*), subway

métropole [metʀɔpɔl] *nf* (*capitale*) metropolis; (*pays*) home country

mets [me] *nm* dish

metteur [metœʀ] *nm*: ~ **en scène** (*THÉÂTRE*) producer; (*CINÉMA*) director

---

MOT-CLÉ

---

mettre [mɛtʀ] *vt* **1** (*placer*) to put; **mettre en bouteille/en sac** to bottle/put in bags *ou* sacks; **mettre en charge (pour)** to charge (with), indict (for)

2 (*vêtements: revêtir*) to put on; (*: porter*) to wear; **mets ton gilet** put your cardigan on; **je ne mets plus mon manteau** I no longer wear my coat

3 (*faire fonctionner: chauffage, électricité*) to put on; (*: reveil, minuteur*) to set; (*installer: gaz, eau*) to put in, lay on; **mettre en marche** to start up

4 (*consacrer*): **mettre du temps à faire qch** to take time to do sth *ou* over sth

5 (*noter, écrire*) to say, put (down); **qu'est-ce qu'il a mis sur la carte?** what did he say *ou* write on the card?; **mettez au pluriel ...** put ... into the plural

6 (*supposer*): **mettons que ...** let's suppose *ou* say that ...

7: y mettre du sien to pull one's weight

se mettre *vi* 1 (*se placer*): **vous pouvez vous mettre là** you can sit (*ou* stand) there; **où ça se met?** where does it go?; **se mettre au lit** to get into bed; **se mettre au piano** to sit down at the piano; **se mettre de l'encre sur les doigts** to get ink on one's fingers

2 (*s'habiller*): **se mettre en maillot de bain** to get into *ou* put on a swimsuit; **n'avoir rien à se mettre** to have nothing to wear

3: **se mettre à** to begin, start; **se mettre à faire** to begin *ou* start doing *ou* to do; **se mettre au piano** to start learning the piano; **se mettre au travail/à l'étude** to get down to work/one's studies

meuble [mœbl] *nm* piece of furniture; **des ~s** furniture; **meublé** *nm* furnished flatlet (*BRIT*) *ou* room; **meubler** *vt* to furnish

meugler [møgle] *vi* to low, moo

meule [møl] *nf* (*de foin, blé*) stack; (*de fromage*) round; (*à broyer*) millstone

meunier [mønje, jɛʀ] *nm* miller; **meunière** *nf* miller's wife

meure *etc* [mœʀ] *vb voir* **mourir**

meurtre [mœʀtʀ] *nm* murder; **meurtrier, -ière** *adj* (*arme etc*) deadly; (*fureur, instincts*) murderous ♦ *nm/f* murderer(-eress)

meurtrir [mœʀtʀiʀ] *vt* to bruise; (*fig*) to wound; **meurtrissure** *nf* bruise

meus *etc* [mœ] *vb voir* **mouvoir**

meute [møt] *nf* pack

mexicain, e [mɛksikɛ̃, ɛn] *adj* Mexican ♦ *nm/f*: **M~, e** Mexican

Mexico [mɛksiko] *n* Mexico City

Mexique [mɛksik] *nm*: **le ~** Mexico

Mgr *abr* = **Monseigneur**

mi [mi] *nm* (*MUS*) E; (*en chantant la gamme*) mi ♦ *préfixe*: **~...** half(-); mid-; **à la ~-janvier** in mid-January; **à ~-hauteur** halfway up; **mi-bas** *nm inv* knee sock

miauler [mjole] *vi* to mew

miche [miʃ] *nf* round *ou* cob loaf

mi-chemin [miʃmɛ̃]: **à ~-~** *adv* halfway, midway

mi-clos, e [miklo, kloz] *adj* half-closed

micro [mikʀo] *nm* mike, microphone; (*IN-FORM*) micro

microbe [mikʀɔb] *nm* germ, microbe

micro...: **micro-onde** *nf*: **four à micro-ondes** microwave oven; **micro-ordinateur** *nm* microcomputer; **microscope** *nm* microscope; **microscopique** *adj* microscopic

midi [midi] *nm* midday, noon; (*moment du déjeuner*) lunchtime; (*sud*) south; **à ~** at 12 (o'clock) *ou* midday *ou* noon; **le M~** the South (of France), the Midi

mie [mi] *nf* crumb (of the loaf)

miel [mjɛl] *nm* honey; **mielleux, -euse** *adj* (*personne*) unctuous, syrupy

mien, ne [mjɛ̃, mjɛn] *pron*: **le(la) ~(ne), les ~(ne)s** mine; **les ~s** my family

miette [mjɛt] *nf* (*de pain, gâteau*) crumb; (*fig: de la conversation etc*) scrap; **en ~s** in pieces *ou* bits

---

MOT-CLÉ

---

mieux [mjø] *adv* 1 (*d'une meilleure façon*): **mieux (que)** better (than); **elle travaille/mange mieux** she works/eats better; **elle va mieux** she is better

2 (*de la meilleure façon*) best; **ce que je sais le mieux** what I know best; **les livres les mieux faits** the best made books

3: **de mieux en mieux** better and better

♦ *adj* 1 (*plus à l'aise, en meilleure forme*) better; **se sentir mieux** to feel better

2 (*plus satisfaisant*) better; **c'est mieux ainsi** it's better like this; **c'est le mieux des deux** it's the better of the two; **le(la) mieux, les mieux** the best; **demandez-lui, c'est le mieux** ask him, it's the best thing

3 (*plus joli*) better-looking

4: **au mieux** at best; **au mieux avec** on the best of terms with; **pour le mieux** for the best

♦ *nm* 1 (*progrès*) improvement

2: de mon/ton mieux as best I/you can
(*ou* could); **faire de son mieux** to do
one's best

---

mièvre [mjɛvʀ] *adj* mawkish (*BRIT*), sickly
sentimental
mignon, ne [miɲɔ̃, ɔn] *adj* sweet, cute
migraine [migʀɛn] *nf* headache; (*MÉD*) migraine
mijoter [miʒɔte] *vt* to simmer; (*préparer
avec soin*) to cook lovingly; (*fam: tramer*)
to plot, cook up ♦ *vi* to simmer
mil [mil] *num* = **mille**
milieu, x [miljø] *nm* (*centre*) middle; (*BIO,
GÉO*) environment; (*entourage social*) milieu; (*provenance*) background; (*pègre*): **le
~** the underworld; **au ~ de** in the middle
of; **au beau** *ou* **en plein ~ (de)** right in
the middle (of); **un juste ~** a happy
medium
militaire [militɛʀ] *adj* military, army *cpd*
♦ *nm* serviceman
militant, e [militɑ̃, ɑ̃t] *adj, nm/f* militant
militer [milite] *vi* to be a militant
mille [mil] *num* a *ou* one thousand ♦ *nm*
(*mesure*): **~ (marin)** nautical mile; **mettre
dans le ~** (*fig*) to be bang on target;
millefeuille *nm* cream *ou* vanilla slice;
millénaire *nm* millennium ♦ *adj*
thousand-year-old; (*fig*) ancient; **mille-
pattes** *nm inv* centipede
millésimé, e [milezime] *adj* vintage *cpd*
millet [mijɛ] *nm* millet
milliard [miljaʀ] *nm* milliard, thousand
million (*BRIT*), billion (*US*); **milliardaire**
nm/f multimillionaire (*BRIT*), billionaire (*US*)
millier [milje] *nm* thousand; **un ~ (de)** a
thousand or so, about a thousand; **par ~s**
in (their) thousands, by the thousand
milligramme [miligʀam] *nm* milligramme
millimètre [milimɛtʀ] *nm* millimetre
million [miljɔ̃] *nm* million; **deux ~s de**
two million; **millionnaire** *nm/f* million-
aire
mime [mim] *nm/f* (*acteur*) mime(r) ♦ *nm*
(*art*) mime, miming; **mimer** *vt* to mime;

(*singer*) to mimic, take off
mimique [mimik] *nf* (*grimace*) (funny)
face; (*signes*) gesticulations *pl*, sign language *no pl*
minable [minabl] *adj* (*décrépit*) shabby(-
looking); (*médiocre*) pathetic
mince [mɛ̃s] *adj* thin; (*personne, taille*) slim,
slender; (*fig: profit, connaissances*) slight,
small, weak ♦ *excl*: **~ alors!** drat it!, darn
it! (*US*); **minceur** *nf* thinness; (*d'une personne*) slimness, slenderness; **mincir** *vi* to
get slimmer
mine [min] *nf* (*physionomie*) expression,
look; (*allure*) exterior, appearance; (*de
crayon*) lead; (*gisement, explosif, fig: source*)
mine; **avoir bonne ~** (*personne*) to look
well; (*ironique*) to look an utter idiot;
avoir mauvaise ~ to look unwell *ou*
poorly; **faire ~ de faire** to make a pretence of doing; **~ de rien** although you
wouldn't think so
miner [mine] *vt* (*saper*) to undermine,
erode; (*MIL*) to mine
minerai [minʀɛ] *nm* ore
minéral, e, -aux [mineʀal, o] *adj, nm*
mineral
minéralogique [mineʀalɔʒik] *adj*: **numéro ~** registration number
minet, te [minɛ, ɛt] *nm/f* (*chat*) pussy-cat;
(*péj*) young trendy
mineur, e [minœʀ] *adj* minor ♦ *nm/f* (*JUR*)
minor, person under age ♦ *nm* (*travailleur*)
miner
miniature [minjatyʀ] *adj, nf* miniature
minibus [minibys] *nm* minibus
mini-cassette [minikasɛt] *nf* cassette (recorder)
minier, -ière [minje, jɛʀ] *adj* mining
mini-jupe [miniʒyp] *nf* mini-skirt
minime [minim] *adj* minor, minimal
minimiser [minimize] *vt* to minimize; (*fig*)
to play down
minimum [minimɔm] *adj, nm* minimum;
au ~ (*au moins*) at the very least
ministère [ministɛʀ] *nm* (*aussi REL*) ministry; (*cabinet*) government

ministre [ministʀ] nm (aussi REL) minister

Minitel ® [minitel] nm videotext terminal and service

Minitel

ℹ️ **Minitel** is a personal computer terminal supplied free of change by France-Télécom to telephone subscribers. It serves as a computerized telephone directory as well as giving access to various services, including information on train timetables, the stock market and situations vacant. Services are accessed by phoning the relevant number and charged to the subscriber's phone bill.

---

minoritaire [minɔʀitɛʀ] adj minority

minorité [minɔʀite] nf minority; **être en ~** to be in the ou a minority

minuit [minɥi] nm midnight

minuscule [minyskyl] adj minute, tiny ♦ nf: **(lettre) ~** small letter

minute [minyt] nf minute; **à la ~** (just) this instant; (faire) there and then; **minuter** vt to time; **minuterie** nf time switch

minutieux, -euse [minysjø, jøz] adj (personne) meticulous; (travail) minutely detailed

mirabelle [miʀabɛl] nf (cherry) plum

miracle [miʀakl] nm miracle

mirage [miʀaʒ] nm mirage

mire [miʀ] nf: **point de ~** (fig) focal point

miroir [miʀwaʀ] nm mirror

miroiter [miʀwate] vi to sparkle, shimmer; **faire ~ qch à qn** to paint sth in glowing colours for sb, dangle sth in front of sb's eyes

mis, e [mi, miz] pp de **mettre** ♦ adj: **bien ~** well-dressed

mise [miz] nf (argent: au jeu) stake; (tenue) clothing, attire; **être de ~** to be acceptable ou in season; **~ au point** (fig) clarification; **~ de fonds** capital outlay; **~ en examen** charging, indictment; **~ en plis** set; **~ en scène** production

miser [mize] vt (enjeu) to stake, bet; **~ sur** (cheval, numéro) to bet on; (fig) to bank ou count on

misérable [mizeʀabl] adj (lamentable, malheureux) pitiful, wretched; (pauvre) poverty-stricken; (insignifiant, mesquin) miserable ♦ nm/f wretch

misère [mizɛʀ] nf (extreme) poverty, destitution; **~s** nfpl (malheurs) woes, miseries; (ennuis) little troubles; **salaire de ~** starvation wage

missile [misil] nm missile

mission [misjɔ̃] nf mission; **partir en ~** (ADMIN, POL) to go on an assignment; **missionnaire** nm/f missionary

mit [mi] vb voir **mettre**

mité, e [mite], adj moth-eaten

mi-temps [mitɑ̃] nf inv (SPORT: période) half; (: pause) half-time; **à ~-** part-time

miteux, -euse [mitø, øz] adj (lieu) seedy

mitigé, e [mitiʒe] adj: **sentiments ~s** mixed feelings

mitonner [mitɔne] vt to cook with loving care; (fig) to cook up quietly

mitoyen, ne [mitwajɛ̃, jɛn] adj (mur) common, party cpd

mitrailler [mitʀaje] vt to machine-gun; (fig) to pelt, bombard; (: photographier) to take shot after shot of; **mitraillette** nf submachine gun; **mitrailleuse** nf machine gun

mi-voix [mivwa]: **à ~-~** adv in a low ou hushed voice

mixage [miksaʒ] nm (CINÉMA) (sound) mixing

mixer [miksœʀ] nm (food) mixer

mixte [mikst] adj (gén) mixed; (SCOL) mixed, coeducational

mixture [mikstyʀ] nf mixture; (fig) concoction

Mlle (pl **Mlles**) abr = **Mademoiselle**

MM abr = **Messieurs**

Mme (pl **Mmes**) abr = **Madame**

mobile [mɔbil] adj mobile; (pièce de machine) moving ♦ nm (motif) motive; (œuvre d'art) mobile

mobilier, -ière [mɔbilje, jɛʀ] nm furniture

mobiliser [mɔbilize] *vt* to mobilize

mocassin [mɔkasɛ̃] *nm* moccasin

moche [mɔʃ] *(fam) adj (laid)* ugly; *(mauvais)* rotten

modalité [mɔdalite] *nf* form, mode; **~s de paiement** methods of payment

mode [mɔd] *nf* fashion ♦ *nm (manière)* form, mode; **à la ~** fashionable, in fashion; **~ d'emploi** directions *pl* (for use)

modèle [mɔdɛl] *adj, nm* model; *(qui pose: de peintre)* sitter; **~ déposé** registered design; **~ réduit** small-scale model; **modeler** *vt* to model

modem [mɔdɛm] *nm* modem

modéré, e [mɔdeʀe] *adj, nm/f* moderate

modérer [mɔdeʀe] *vt* to moderate; **se ~** *vi* to restrain o.s.

moderne [mɔdɛʀn] *adj* modern ♦ *nm (style)* modern style; *(meubles)* modern furniture; **moderniser** *vt* to modernize

modeste [mɔdɛst] *adj* modest; **modestie** *nf* modesty

modifier [mɔdifje] *vt* to modify, alter; **se ~** *vi* to alter

modique [mɔdik] *adj* modest

modiste [mɔdist] *nf* milliner

module [mɔdyl] *nm* module

moelle [mwal] *nf* marrow; **~ épinière** spinal cord

moelleux, -euse [mwalø, øz] *adj* soft; *(gâteau)* light and moist

mœurs [mœʀ] *nfpl (conduite)* morals; *(manières)* manners; *(pratiques sociales, mode de vie)* habits

mohair [mɔɛʀ] *nm* mohair

moi [mwa] *pron* me; *(emphatique)*: **~, je ...** for my part, I ..., I myself ...; **à ~** mine; **moi-même** *pron* myself; *(emphatique)* I myself

moindre [mwɛ̃dʀ] *adj* lesser; lower; **le(la) ~, les ~s** the least, the slightest; **merci – c'est la ~ des choses!** thank you – it's a pleasure!

moine [mwan] *nm* monk, friar

moineau, x [mwano] *nm* sparrow

MOT-CLÉ

moins [mwɛ̃] *adv* **1** *(comparatif)*: **moins (que)** less (than); **moins grand que** less tall than, not as tall as; **moins je travaille, mieux je me porte** the less I work, the better I feel

2 *(superlatif)*: **le moins** (the) least; **c'est ce que j'aime le moins** it's what I like (the) least; **le(la) moins doué(e)** the least gifted; **au moins, du moins** at least; **pour le moins** at the very least

3: **moins de** *(quantité)* less (than); *(nombre)* fewer (than); **moins de sable/d'eau** less sand/water; **moins de livres/gens** fewer books/people; **moins de 2 ans** less than 2 years; **moins de midi** not yet midday

4: **de moins, en moins**: **100 F/3 jours de moins** 100F/3 days less; **3 livres en moins** 3 books fewer; 3 books too few; **de l'argent en moins** less money; **le soleil en moins** but for the sun, minus the sun; **de moins en moins** less and less

5: **à moins de, à moins que** unless; **à moins de faire** unless we do *(ou* he does *etc)*; **à moins que tu ne fasses** unless you do; **à moins d'un accident** barring any accident

♦ *prép*: **4 moins 2** 4 minus 2; **il est moins 5** it's 5 to; **il fait moins 5** it's 5 (degrees) below (freezing), it's minus 5

---

mois [mwa] *nm* month

moisi [mwazi] *nm* mould, mildew; **odeur de ~** musty smell; **moisir** *vi* to go mouldy; **moisissure** *nf* mould *no pl*

moisson [mwasɔ̃] *nf* harvest; **moissonner** *vt* to harvest, reap; **moissonneuse** *nf (machine)* harvester

moite [mwat] *adj* sweaty, sticky

moitié [mwatje] *nf* half; **la ~** half (of); **la ~ de** half (of); **la ~ du temps** half the time; **à la ~ de** halfway through; **à ~** *(avant le verbe)* half; *(avant l'adjectif)* half-; **à ~ prix** (at) half-price; **~ moitié** half-and-half

moka [mɔka] *nm* coffee gateau

mol [mɔl] *adj voir* **mou**

molaire [mɔlɛʀ] *nf* molar

molester [mɔlɛste] *vt* to manhandle, maul (about)

molle [mɔl] *adj voir* **mou**; **mollement** *adv* (*péj: travailler*) sluggishly; (*protester*) feebly

mollet [mɔlɛ] *nm* calf ♦ *adj m:* **œuf ~** soft-boiled egg

molletonné, e [mɔltɔne] *adj* fleece-lined

mollir [mɔliʀ] *vi* (*fléchir*) to relent; (*substance*) to go soft

mollusque [mɔlysk] *nm* mollusc

môme [mom] *nm/f* (*fam*) (*enfant*) brat

moment [mɔmɑ̃] *nm* moment; **ce n'est pas le ~** this is not the (right) time; **pour un bon ~** for a good while; **pour le ~** for the moment, for the time being; **au ~ de** at the time of; **au ~ où** just as; **à tout ~** (*peut arriver etc*) at any time *ou* moment; (*constamment*) constantly, continually; **en ce ~** at the moment; at present; **sur le ~** at the time; **par ~s** now and then, at times; **du ~ où** *ou* **que** seeing that, since; **momentané, e** *adj* temporary, momentary; **momentanément** *adv* (*court instant*) for a short while

momie [mɔmi] *nf* mummy

mon, ma [mɔ̃, ma] (*pl* **mes**) *adj* my

Monaco [mɔnako] *nm* Monaco

monarchie [mɔnaʀʃi] *nf* monarchy

monastère [mɔnastɛʀ] *nm* monastery

monceau, x [mɔ̃so] *nm* heap

mondain, e [mɔ̃dɛ̃, ɛn] *adj* (*vie*) society *cpd*

monde [mɔ̃d] *nm* world; (*haute société*): **le ~** (high) society; **il y a du ~** (*beaucoup de gens*) there are a lot of people; (*quelques personnes*) there are some people; **beaucoup/peu de ~** many/few people; **mettre au ~** to bring into the world; **pas le moins du ~** not in the least; **faire un ~ de qch** to make a great deal of fuss about sth; **mondial, e, -aux** *adj* (*population*) world *cpd*; (*influence*) world-wide; **mondialement** *adv* throughout the world

monégasque [mɔnegask] *adj* Monegasque, of *ou* from Monaco

monétaire [mɔnetɛʀ] *adj* monetary

moniteur, -trice [mɔnitœʀ, tʀis] *nm/f* (*SPORT*) instructor(-tress); (*de colonie de vacances*) supervisor ♦ *nm* (*écran*) monitor

monnaie [mɔnɛ] *nf* (*ÉCON, gén: moyen d'échange*) currency; (*petites pièces*): **avoir de la ~** to have (some) change; **une pièce de ~** a coin; **faire de la ~** to get (some) change; **avoir/faire la ~ de 20 F** to have change of/get change for 20 F; **rendre à qn la ~ (sur 20 F)** to give sb the change (out of *ou* from 20 F); **monnayer** *vt* to convert into cash; (*talent*) to capitalize on

monologue [mɔnɔlɔg] *nm* monologue, soliloquy; **monologuer** *vi* to soliloquize

monopole [mɔnɔpɔl] *nm* monopoly

monotone [mɔnɔtɔn] *adj* monotonous

Monsieur [məsjø] (*pl* **Messieurs**) *titre* Mr ♦ *nm* (*homme quelconque*): **un/le m~** a/ the gentleman; **~, ...** (*en tête de lettre*) Dear Sir, ...; *voir aussi* **Madame**

monstre [mɔ̃stʀ] *nm* monster ♦ *adj* (*fam: colossal*) monstrous; **un travail ~** a fantastic amount of work; **monstrueux, -euse** *adj* monstrous

mont [mɔ̃] *nm:* **par ~s et par vaux** up hill and down dale; **le M~ Blanc** Mont Blanc

montage [mɔ̃taʒ] *nm* (*assemblage: d'appareil*) assembly; (*PHOTO*) photomontage; (*CINÉMA*) editing

montagnard, e [mɔ̃taɲaʀ, aʀd] *adj* mountain *cpd* ♦ *nm/f* mountain-dweller

montagne [mɔ̃taɲ] *nf* (*cime*) mountain; (*région*): **la ~** the mountains *pl*; **~s russes** big dipper *sg*, switchback *sg*; **montagneux, -euse** *adj* mountainous; (*basse montagne*) hilly

montant, e [mɔ̃tɑ̃, ɑ̃t] *adj* rising; **pull à col ~** high-necked jumper ♦ *nm* (*somme, total*) (sum) total, (total) amount; (*de fenêtre*) upright; (*de lit*) post

monte-charge [mɔ̃tʃaʀʒ] *nm inv* goods

lift, hoist

montée [mɔ̃te] nf (des prix, hostilités) rise; (escalade) climb; (côte) hill; **au milieu de la ~** halfway up

monter [mɔ̃te] vt (escalier, côte) to go (ou come) up; (valise, paquet) to take (ou bring) up; (étagère) to raise; (tente, échafaudage) to put up; (machine) to assemble; (CINÉMA) to edit; (THÉÂTRE) to put on, stage; (société etc) to set up ♦ vi to go (ou come) up; (prix, niveau, température) to go up, rise; (passager) to get on; **se ~ à** (frais etc) to add up to, come to; **~ à pied** to walk up, go up on foot; **~ dans le train/ l'avion** to get into the train/plane, board the train/plane; **~ sur** to climb up onto; **~ à cheval** (faire du cheval) to ride, go riding

montre [mɔ̃tʀ] nf watch; **contre la ~** (SPORT) against the clock; **montre-bracelet** nf wristwatch

montrer [mɔ̃tʀe] vt to show; **~ qch à qn** to show sb sth

monture [mɔ̃tyʀ] nf (cheval) mount; (de lunettes) frame; (d'une bague) setting

monument [mɔnymɑ̃] nm monument; **~ aux morts** war memorial

moquer [mɔke]: **se ~ de** vt to make fun of, laugh at; (fam: se désintéresser de) not to care about; (tromper): **se ~ de qn** to take sb for a ride; **moquerie** nf mockery

moquette [mɔkɛt] nf fitted carpet

moqueur, -euse [mɔkœʀ, øz] adj mocking

moral, e, -aux [mɔʀal, o] adj moral ♦ nm morale; **avoir le ~** (fam) to be in good spirits; **avoir le ~ à zéro** (fam) to be really down; **morale** nf (mœurs) morals pl; (valeurs) moral standards pl, morality; (d'une fable etc) moral; **faire la morale à** to lecture, preach at; **moralité** nf morality; (de fable) moral

morceau, x [mɔʀso] nm piece, bit; (d'une œuvre) passage, extract; (MUS) piece; (CULIN: de viande) cut; (de sucre) lump; **mettre en ~x** to pull to pieces ou bits; **manger**

un ~ to have a bite (to eat)

morceler [mɔʀsəle] vt to break up, divide up

mordant, e [mɔʀdɑ̃, ɑ̃t] adj (ton, remarque) scathing, cutting; (ironie, froid) biting ♦ nm (style) bite, punch

mordiller [mɔʀdije] vt to nibble at, chew at

mordre [mɔʀdʀ] vt to bite ♦ vi (poisson) to bite; **~ sur** (fig) to go over into, overlap into; **~ à l'hameçon** to bite, rise to the bait

mordu, e [mɔʀdy] (fam) nm/f enthusiast; **un ~ de jazz** a jazz fanatic

morfondre [mɔʀfɔ̃dʀ]: **se ~** vi to mope

morgue [mɔʀg] nf (arrogance) haughtiness; (lieu: de la police) morgue; (: à l'hôpital) mortuary

morne [mɔʀn] adj dismal, dreary

morose [mɔʀoz] adj sullen, morose

mors [mɔʀ] nm bit

morse [mɔʀs] nm (ZOOL) walrus; (TÉL) Morse (code)

morsure [mɔʀsyʀ] nf bite

mort[1] [mɔʀ] nf death

mort[2]**, e** [mɔʀ, mɔʀt] pp de **mourir** ♦ adj dead ♦ nm/f (défunt) dead man/woman; (victime): **il y a eu plusieurs ~s** several people were killed, there were several killed; **~ de peur/fatigue** frightened to death/dead tired

mortalité [mɔʀtalite] nf mortality, death rate

mortel, le [mɔʀtɛl] adj (poison etc) deadly, lethal; (accident, blessure) fatal; (silence, ennemi) deadly; (péché) mortal; (fam: ennuyeux) deadly boring

mortier [mɔʀtje] nm (gén) mortar

mort-né, e [mɔʀne] adj (enfant) stillborn

mortuaire [mɔʀtɥɛʀ] adj: **avis ~** death announcement

morue [mɔʀy] nf (ZOOL) cod inv

mosaïque [mɔzaik] nf mosaic

Moscou [mɔsku] n Moscow

mosquée [mɔske] nf mosque

mot [mo] nm word; (message) line, note; **~**

à ~ word for word; ~ **d'ordre** watchword; ~ **de passe** password; **~s croisés** crossword (puzzle) *sg*

motard [mɔtaʀ, aʀd] *nm* biker; (*policier*) motorcycle cop

motel [mɔtɛl] *nm* motel

moteur, -trice [mɔtœʀ, tʀis] *adj* (ANAT, PHYSIOL) motor; (TECH) driving; (AUTO): **à 4 roues motrices** 4-wheel drive ♦ *nm* engine, motor; **à** ~ power-driven, motor *cpd*; ~ **de recherche** search engine

motif [mɔtif] *nm* (*cause*) motive; (*décoratif*) design, pattern, motif; **sans** ~ groundless

motivation [mɔtivasjɔ̃] *nf* motivation

motiver [mɔtive] *vt* to motivate; (*justifier*) to justify, account for

moto [mɔto] *nf* (motor)bike; **motocycliste** *nm/f* motorcyclist

motorisé, e [mɔtɔʀize] *adj* (*personne*) having transport *ou* a car

motrice [mɔtʀis] *adj voir* **moteur**

motte [mɔt] *nf*: ~ **de terre** lump of earth, clod (of earth); ~ **de beurre** lump of butter

mou (mol), molle [mu, mɔl] *adj* soft; (*personne*) lethargic; (*protestations*) weak ♦ *nm*: **avoir du mou** to be slack

moucharder [muʃaʀde] (*fam*) *vt* (SCOL) to sneak on; (POLICE) to grass on

mouche [muʃ] *nf* fly

moucher [muʃe]: **se** ~ *vi* to blow one's nose

moucheron [muʃʀɔ̃] *nm* midge

mouchoir [muʃwaʀ] *nm* handkerchief, hanky; ~ **en papier** tissue, paper hanky

moudre [mudʀ] *vt* to grind

moue [mu] *nf* pout; **faire la** ~ to pout; (*fig*) to pull a face

mouette [mwɛt] *nf* (sea)gull

moufle [mufl] *nf* (*gant*) mitt(en)

mouillé, e [muje] *adj* wet

mouiller [muje] *vt* (*humecter*) to wet, moisten; (*tremper*): ~ **qn/qch** to make sb/sth wet ♦ *vi* (NAVIG) to lie *ou* be at anchor; **se** ~ to get wet; (*fam: prendre des risques*) to commit o.s.

moulant, e [mulɑ̃, ɑ̃t] *adj* figure-hugging

moule [mul] *nf* mussel ♦ *nm* (CULIN) mould; ~ **à gâteaux** ♦ *nm* cake tin (BRIT) *ou* pan (US)

moulent [mul] *vb voir* **moudre; mouler**

mouler [mule] *vt* (*suj: vêtement*) to hug, fit closely round

moulin [mulɛ̃] *nm* mill; ~ **à café/à poivre** coffee/pepper mill; ~ **à légumes** (vegetable) shredder; ~ **à paroles** (*fig*) chatterbox; ~ **à vent** windmill

moulinet [mulinɛ] *nm* (*de canne à pêche*) reel; (*mouvement*): **faire des ~s avec qch** to whirl sth around

moulinette ® [mulinɛt] *nf* (vegetable) shredder

moulu, e [muly] *pp de* **moudre**

mourant, e [muʀɑ̃, ɑ̃t] *adj* dying

mourir [muʀiʀ] *vi* to die; (*civilisation*) to die out; ~ **de froid/faim** to die of exposure/hunger; ~ **de faim/d'ennui** (*fig*) to be starving/to be bored to death; ~ **d'envie de faire** to be dying to do

mousse [mus] *nf* (BOT) moss; (*de savon*) lather; (*écume: sur eau, bière*) froth, foam; (CULIN) mousse ♦ *nm* (NAVIG) ship's boy; ~ **à raser** shaving foam

mousseline [muslin] *nf* muslin; **pommes** ~ mashed potatoes

mousser [muse] *vi* (*bière, détergent*) to foam; (*savon*) to lather; **mousseux, -euse** *adj* frothy ♦ *nm*: **(vin) mousseux** sparkling wine

mousson [musɔ̃] *nf* monsoon

moustache [mustaʃ] *nf* moustache; **~s** *nfpl* (*du chat*) whiskers *pl*; **moustachu, e** *adj* with a moustache

moustiquaire [mustikɛʀ] *nf* mosquito net

moustique [mustik] *nm* mosquito

moutarde [mutaʀd] *nf* mustard

mouton [mutɔ̃] *nm* sheep *inv*; (*peau*) sheepskin; (CULIN) mutton

mouvement [muvmɑ̃] *nm* movement; (*fig: impulsion*) gesture; **avoir un bon** ~ to make a nice gesture; **en** ~ in motion; on the move; **mouvementé, e** *adj* (*vie,* *poursuite*) eventful; (*réunion*) turbulent

mouvoir [muvwaʀ]: **se ~** *vi* to move

moyen, ne [mwajɛ̃, jɛn] *adj* average; (*tailles, prix*) medium; (*de grandeur moyenne*) medium-sized ♦ *nm* (*façon*) means *sg*, way; **~s** *nmpl* (*capacités*) means; **très ~** (*résultats*) pretty poor; **je n'en ai pas les ~s** I can't afford it; **au ~ de** by means of; **par tous les ~s** by every possible means, every possible way; **par ses propres ~s** all by oneself; **~ âge** Middle Ages; **~ de transport** means of transport

moyennant [mwajenɑ̃] *prép* (*somme*) for; (*service, conditions*) in return for; (*travail, effort*) with

moyenne [mwajɛn] *nf* average; (*MATH*) mean; (*SCOL: à l'examen*) pass mark; **en ~** on (an) average; **~ d'âge** average age

Moyen-Orient [mwajɛnɔʀjɑ̃] *nm*: **le ~-~** the Middle East

moyeu, x [mwajø] *nm* hub

MST *sigle f* (= *maladie sexuellement transmissible*) STD

MTC *sigle m* (= *mécanisme du taux de change*) ERM

mû, mue [my] *pp de* **mouvoir**

muer [mɥe] *vi* (*oiseau, mammifère*) to moult; (*serpent*) to slough; (*jeune garçon*): **il mue** his voice is breaking; **se ~ en** to transform into

muet, te [mɥe, mɥɛt] *adj* dumb; (*fig*): **~ d'admiration** *etc* speechless with admiration *etc*; (*CINÉMA*) silent ♦ *nm/f* mute

mufle [myfl] *nm* muzzle; (*fam: goujat*) boor

mugir [myʒiʀ] *vi* (*taureau*) to bellow; (*vache*) to low; (*fig*) to howl

muguet [mygɛ] *nm* lily of the valley

mule [myl] *nf* (*ZOOL*) (she-)mule

mulet [mylɛ] *nm* (*ZOOL*) (he-)mule

multinationale [myltinasjɔnal] *nf* multinational

multiple [myltipl] *adj* multiple, numerous; (*varié*) many, manifold; **multiplier** *vt* to multiply; **se multiplier** *vi* to multiply

municipal, e, -aux [mynisipal, o] *adj* (*élections, stade*) municipal; (*conseil*) town *cpd*; **piscine/bibliothèque ~e** public swimming pool/library; **municipalité** *nf* (*ville*) municipality; (*conseil*) town council

munir [myniʀ] *vt*: **~ qch de** to equip sth with; **se ~ de** to arm o.s. with

munitions [mynisjɔ̃] *nfpl* ammunition *sg*

mur [myʀ] *nm* wall; **~ du son** sound barrier

mûr, e [myʀ] *adj* ripe; (*personne*) mature

muraille [myʀaj] *nf* (high) wall

mural, e, -aux [myʀal, o] *adj* wall *cpd*; (*art*) mural

mûre [myʀ] *nf* blackberry

muret [myʀɛ] *nm* low wall

mûrir [myʀiʀ] *vi* (*fruit, blé*) to ripen; (*abcès*) to come to a head; (*fig: idée, personne*) to mature ♦ *vt* (*projet*) to nurture; (*personne*) to (make) mature

murmure [myʀmyʀ] *nm* murmur; **murmurer** *vi* to murmur

muscade [myskad] *nf* (*aussi:* **noix (de) ~**) nutmeg

muscat [myska] *nm* (*raisins*) muscat grape; (*vin*) muscatel (wine)

muscle [myskl] *nm* muscle; **musclé, e** *adj* muscular; (*fig*) strong-arm

museau, x [myzo] *nm* muzzle; (*CULIN*) brawn

musée [myze] *nm* museum; (*de peinture*) art gallery

museler [myz(ə)le] *vt* to muzzle

musette [myzɛt] *nf* (*sac*) lunchbag

musical, e, -aux [myzikal, o] *adj* musical

music-hall [myzikol] *nm* (*salle*) variety theatre; (*genre*) variety

musicien, ne [myzisjɛ̃, jɛn] *adj* musical ♦ *nm/f* musician

musique [myzik] *nf* music; **~ d'ambiance** background music

musulman, e [myzylmɑ̃, an] *adj, nm/f* Moslem, Muslim

mutation [mytasjɔ̃] *nf* (*ADMIN*) transfer

muter [myte] *vt* to transfer, move

mutilé, e [mytile] *nm/f* disabled person (*through loss of limbs*)

mutiler [mytile] *vt* to mutilate, maim

mutin, e [mytɛ̃, in] *adj* (*air, ton*) mischievous, impish ♦ *nm/f* (*MIL, NAVIG*) mutineer; **mutinerie** *nf* mutiny

mutisme [mytism] *nm* silence

mutuel, le [mytɥɛl] *adj* mutual; **mutuelle** *nf* voluntary insurance premiums for back-up health cover

myope [mjɔp] *adj* short-sighted

myosotis [mjozɔtis] *nm* forget-me-not

myrtille [miʀtij] *nf* bilberry

mystère [mistɛʀ] *nm* mystery; **mystérieux, -euse** *adj* mysterious

mystifier [mistifje] *vt* to fool

mythe [mit] *nm* myth

mythologie [mitɔlɔʒi] *nf* mythology

N, n

n' [n] *adv voir* **ne**

nacre [nakʀ] *nf* mother of pearl

nage [naʒ] *nf* swimming; (*manière*) style of swimming, stroke; **traverser à la ~** to swim across; **en ~** bathed in sweat; **nageoire** *nf* fin; **nager** *vi* to swim; **nageur, -euse** *nm/f* swimmer

naguère [nagɛʀ] *adv* formerly

naïf, -ïve [naif, naiv] *adj* naïve

nain, e [nɛ̃, nɛn] *nm/f* dwarf

naissance [nɛsɑ̃s] *nf* birth; **donner ~ à** to give birth to; (*fig*) to give rise to

naître [nɛtʀ] *vi* to be born; (*fig*): **~ de** to arise from, be born out of; **il est né en 1960** he was born in 1960; **faire ~** (*fig*) to give rise to, arouse

naïve [naiv] *adj voir* **naïf**

naïveté [naivte] *nf* naïvety

nana [nana] (*fam*) *nf* (*fille*) chick, bird (*BRIT*)

nantir [nɑ̃tiʀ] *vt*: **~ qn de** to provide sb with; **les nantis** (*péj*) the well-to-do

nappe [nap] *nf* tablecloth; (*de pétrole, gaz*) layer; **~ phréatique** ground water; **napperon** *nm* table-mat

naquit *etc* [naki] *vb voir* **naître**

narcodollars [naʀkodɔlaʀ] *nmpl* drug money *sg*

narguer [naʀge] *vt* to taunt

narine [naʀin] *nf* nostril

narquois, e [naʀkwa, waz] *adj* mocking

natal, e [natal] *adj* native; **natalité** *nf* birth rate

natation [natasjɔ̃] *nf* swimming

natif, -ive [natif, iv] *adj* native

nation [nasjɔ̃] *nf* nation; **national, e, -aux** *adj* national; **nationale** *nf*: (**route**) **nationale** ≃ A road (*BRIT*), ≃ state highway (*US*); **nationaliser** *vt* to nationalize; **nationalisme** *nm* nationalism; **nationalité** *nf* nationality

natte [nat] *nf* (*cheveux*) plait; (*tapis*) mat

naturaliser [natyʀalize] *vt* to naturalize

nature [natyʀ] *nf* nature ♦ *adj, adv* (*CULIN*) plain, without seasoning or sweetening; (*café, thé*) black, without sugar; (*yaourt*) natural; **payer en ~** to pay in kind; **~ morte** still-life; **naturel, le** *adj* (*gén, aussi enfant*) natural ♦ *nm* (*absence d'affectation*) naturalness; (*caractère*) disposition, nature; **naturellement** *adv* naturally; (*bien sûr*) of course

naufrage [nofʀaʒ] *nm* (ship)wreck; **faire ~** to be shipwrecked

nauséabond, e [nozeabɔ̃, ɔ̃d] *adj* foul

nausée [noze] *nf* nausea

nautique [notik] *adj* nautical, water *cpd*; **sports ~s** water sports

naval, e [naval] *adj* naval; (*industrie*) shipbuilding

navet [navɛ] *nm* turnip; (*péj: film*) rubbishy film

navette [navɛt] *nf* shuttle; **faire la ~ (entre)** to go to and fro *ou* shuttle (between)

navigateur [navigatœʀ, tʀis] *nm* (*NAVIG*) seafarer; (*INFORM*) browser

navigation [navigasjɔ̃] *nf* navigation, sailing

naviguer [navige] *vi* to navigate, sail; **~ sur Internet** to surf the net

navire [naviʀ] *nm* ship

navrer [navʀe] *vt* to upset, distress; **je suis navré** I'm so sorry

ne, n' [n(ə)] *adv voir* **pas**; **plus**; **jamais** *etc*; *(sans valeur négative: non traduit)*: **c'est plus loin que je ~ le croyais** it's further than I thought

né, e [ne] *pp (voir* **naître)**: **~ en 1960** born in 1960; **~e Scott** née Scott

néanmoins [neɑ̃mwɛ̃] *adv* nevertheless

néant [neɑ̃] *nm* nothingness; **réduire à ~** to bring to nought; *(espoir)* to dash

nécessaire [neseseʀ] *adj* necessary ♦ *nm* necessary; *(sac)* kit; **je vais faire le ~** I'll see to it; **~ de couture** sewing kit; **nécessité** *nf* necessity; **nécessiter** *vt* to require

nécrologique [nekʀɔlɔʒik] *adj*: **rubrique ~** obituary column

nectar [nektaʀ] *nm* nectar

néerlandais, e [neɛʀlɑ̃dɛ, ɛz] *adj* Dutch

nef [nɛf] *nf (d'église)* nave

néfaste [nefast] *adj (nuisible)* harmful; *(funeste)* ill-fated

négatif, -ive [negatif, iv] *adj* negative ♦ *nm (PHOTO)* negative

négligé, e [negliʒe] *adj (en désordre)* slovenly ♦ *nm (tenue)* negligee

négligeable [negliʒabl] *adj* negligible

négligent, e [negliʒɑ̃, ɑ̃t] *adj* careless, negligent

négliger [negliʒe] *vt (tenue)* to be careless about; *(avis, précautions)* to disregard; *(épouse, jardin)* to neglect; **~ de faire** to fail to do, not bother to do

négoce [negɔs] *nm* trade

négociant [negɔsjɑ̃, jɑ̃t] *nm* merchant

négociation [negɔsjasjɔ̃] *nf* negotiation

négocier [negɔsje] *vi, vt* to negotiate

nègre [nɛgʀ] *(péj) nm (écrivain)* ghost (writer)

neige [nɛʒ] *nf* snow; **neiger** *vi* to snow

nénuphar [nenyfaʀ] *nm* water-lily

néon [neɔ̃] *nm* neon

néo-zélandais, e [neozelɑ̃dɛ, ɛz] *adj* New Zealand *cpd* ♦ *nm/f*: **N~-Z~, e** New Zealander

nerf [nɛʀ] *nm* nerve; **être sur les ~s** to be all keyed up; **allons, du ~!** come on,

buck up!; **nerveux, -euse** *adj* nervous; *(irritable)* touchy, nervy; *(voiture)* nippy, responsive; **nervosité** *nf* excitability, tenseness; *(irritabilité passagère)* irritability

nervure [nɛʀvyʀ] *nf* vein

n'est-ce pas [nɛspa] *adv* isn't it?, won't you? *etc, selon le verbe qui précède*

Net [nɛt] *nm (Internet)*: **le ~** the Net

net, nette [nɛt] *adj (sans équivoque, distinct)* clear; *(évident: amélioration, différence)* marked, distinct; *(propre)* neat, clean; *(COMM: prix, salaire)* net ♦ *adv (refuser)* flatly ♦ *nm*: **mettre au ~** to copy out; **s'arrêter ~** to stop dead; **nettement** *adv* clearly, distinctly; *(incontestablement)* decidedly, distinctly; **netteté** *nf* clearness

nettoyage [netwajaʒ] *nm* cleaning; **~ à sec** dry cleaning

nettoyer [netwaje] *vt* to clean

neuf¹ [nœf] *num* nine

neuf², neuve [nœf, nœv] *adj* new ♦ *nm*: **remettre à ~** to do up (as good as new), refurbish; **quoi de ~?** what's new?

neutre [nøtʀ] *adj* neutral; *(LING)* neuter

neuve [nœv] *adj voir* **neuf²**

neuvième [nœvjɛm] *num* ninth

neveu, x [n(ə)vø] *nm* nephew

névrosé, e [nevʀoze] *adj, nm/f* neurotic

nez [ne] *nm* nose; **~ à ~ avec** face to face with; **avoir du ~** to have flair

ni [ni] *conj*: **~ ... ~** neither ... nor; **je n'aime ~ les lentilles ~ les épinards** I like neither lentils nor spinach; **il n'a dit ~ oui ~ non** he didn't say either yes or no; **elles ne sont venues ~ l'une ~ l'autre** neither of them came

niais, e [njɛ, njɛz] *adj* silly, thick

niche [niʃ] *nf (du chien)* kennel; *(de mur)* recess, niche; **nicher** *vi* to nest

nid [ni] *nm* nest; **~ de poule** pothole

nièce [njɛs] *nf* niece

nier [nje] *vt* to deny

nigaud, e [nigo, od] *nm/f* booby, fool

Nil [nil] *nm*: **le ~** the Nile

n'importe [nɛ̃pɔʀt] *adv*: **~ qui/quoi/où** anybody/anything/anywhere; **~ quand**

any time; **~ quel/quelle** any; **~ lequel/ laquelle** any (one); **~ comment** (sans soin) carelessly

niveau, x [nivo] nm level; (des élèves, études) standard; **~ de vie** standard of living

niveler [niv(ə)le] vt to level

NN abr (= nouvelle norme) revised standard of hotel classification

noble [nɔbl] adj noble; noble; **noblesse** nf nobility; (d'une action etc) nobleness

noce [nɔs] nf wedding; (gens) wedding party (ou guests pl); **faire la ~** (fam) to go on a binge

nocif, -ive [nɔsif, iv] adj harmful, noxious

nocturne [nɔktyrn] adj nocturnal ♦ nf late-night opening

Noël [nɔɛl] nm Christmas

nœud [nø] nm knot; (ruban) bow; **~ papillon** bow tie

noir, e [nwar] adj black; (obscur, sombre) dark ♦ nm/f black man/woman ♦ nm: **dans le ~** in the dark; **travail au ~** moonlighting; **travailler au ~** to work on the side; **noircir** vt, vi to blacken; **noire** nf (MUS) crotchet (BRIT), quarter note (US)

noisette [nwazet] nf hazelnut

noix [nwa] nf walnut; (CULIN): **une ~ de beurre** a knob of butter; **~ de cajou** cashew nut; **~ de coco** coconut; **à la ~** (fam) worthless

nom [nɔ̃] nm name; (LING) noun; **~ de famille** surname; **~ de jeune fille** maiden name; **~ déposé** trade name; **~ propre** proper noun

nomade [nɔmad] nm/f nomad

nombre [nɔ̃br] nm number; **venir en ~** to come in large numbers; **depuis ~ d'années** for many years; **au ~ de mes amis** among my friends; **nombreux, -euse** adj many, numerous; (avec nom sg: foule etc) large; **peu nombreux** few

nombril [nɔ̃bri(l)] nm navel

nommer [nɔme] vt to name; (élire) to appoint, nominate; **se ~: il se nomme Pascal** his name's Pascal, he's called Pascal

non [nɔ̃] adv (réponse) no; (avec loin, sans, seulement) not; **~ (pas) que** not that; **~ plus** neither do I, I don't either; **c'est bon ~?** (exprimant le doute) it's good, isn't it?

non-alcoolisé, e [nɔ̃alkɔlize] adj non-alcoholic

nonante [nɔnɑ̃t] (BELGIQUE, SUISSE) num ninety

non-fumeur [nɔ̃fymœr, øz] nm non-smoker

non-sens [nɔ̃sɑ̃s] nm absurdity

nonchalant, e [nɔ̃ʃalɑ̃, ɑ̃t] adj nonchalant

nord [nɔr] nm North ♦ adj northern; north; **au ~** (situation) in the north; (direction) to the north; **au ~ de** (to the) north of; **nord-est** nm North-East; **nord-ouest** nm North-West

normal, e, -aux [nɔrmal, o] adj normal; **c'est tout à fait ~** it's perfectly natural; **vous trouvez ça ~?** does it seem right to you?; **normale** nf: **la normale** the norm, the average; **normalement** adv (en général) normally

normand, e [nɔrmɑ̃, ɑ̃d] adj of Normandy

Normandie [nɔrmɑ̃di] nf Normandy

norme [nɔrm] nf norm; (TECH) standard

Norvège [nɔrvɛʒ] nf Norway; **norvégien, ne** adj Norwegian ♦ nm/f: **Norvégien, ne** Norwegian ♦ nm (LING) Norwegian

nos [no] adj voir **notre**

nostalgie [nɔstalʒi] nf nostalgia; **nostalgique** adj nostalgic

notable [nɔtabl] adj (fait) notable, noteworthy; (marqué) noticeable, marked ♦ nm prominent citizen

notaire [nɔtɛr] nm solicitor

notamment [nɔtamɑ̃] adv in particular, among others

note [nɔt] nf (écrite, MUS) note; (SCOL) mark (BRIT), grade; (facture) bill; **~ de service** memorandum

noté, e [nɔte] adj: **être bien/mal ~** (employé etc) to have a good/bad record

noter [nɔte] vt (écrire) to write down; (re-

marquer) to note, notice; (*devoir*) to mark, grade

notice [nɔtis] *nf* summary, short article; (*brochure*) leaflet, instruction book

notifier [nɔtifje] *vt*: ~ **qch à qn** to notify sb of sth, notify sth to sb

notion [nɔsjɔ̃] *nf* notion, idea

notoire [nɔtwaʀ] *adj* widely known; (*en mal*) notorious

notre [nɔtʀ] (*pl* **nos**) *adj* our

nôtre [notʀ] *pron*: **le ~, la ~, les ~s** ours ♦ *adj* ours; **les ~s** ours; (*alliés etc*) our own people; **soyez des ~s** join us

nouer [nwe] *vt* to tie, knot; (*fig: alliance etc*) to strike up

noueux, -euse [nwø, øz] *adj* gnarled

nouilles [nuj] *nfpl* noodles

nourrice [nuʀis] *nf* (*gardienne*) child-minder

nourrir [nuʀiʀ] *vt* to feed; (*fig: espoir*) to harbour, nurse; **se ~** to eat; **se ~ de** to feed (o.s.) on; **nourrissant, e** *adj* nourishing, nutritious; **nourrisson** *nm* (un-weaned) infant; **nourriture** *nf* food

nous [nu] *pron* (*sujet*) we; (*objet*) us; **nous-mêmes** *pron* ourselves

nouveau (nouvel), -elle, X [nuvo, nuvɛl] *adj* new ♦ *nm*: **y a-t-il du ~?** is there anything new on this? ♦ *nm/f* new pupil (*ou* employee); **de ~, à ~** again; ~ **venu, nouvelle venue** newcomer; **~x mariés** newly-weds; **nouveau-né, e** *nm/f* newborn baby; **nouveauté** *nf* no-velty; (*objet*) new thing *ou* article

nouvel [nuvɛl] *adj voir* **nouveau; N~ An** New Year

nouvelle [nuvɛl] *adj voir* **nouveau** ♦ *nf* (piece of) news *sg*; (*LITTÉRATURE*) short story; **les ~s** the news; **je suis sans ~s de lui** I haven't heard from him; **Nouvelle-Calédonie** *nf* New Caledonia; **nouvellement** *adv* recently, newly; **Nouvelle-Zélande** *nf* New Zealand

novembre [nɔvɑ̃bʀ] *nm* November

novice [nɔvis] *adj* inexperienced

noyade [nwajad] *nf* drowning *no pl*

noyau, X [nwajo] *nm* (*de fruit*) stone; (*BIO, PHYSIQUE*) nucleus; (*fig: centre*) core; **noyauter** *vt* (*POL*) to infiltrate

noyer [nwaje] *nm* walnut (tree); (*bois*) wal-nut ♦ *vt* to drown; (*moteur*) to flood; **se ~** *vi* to be drowned, drown; (*suicide*) to drown o.s.

nu, e [ny] *adj* naked; (*membres*) naked, bare; (*pieds, mains, chambre, fil électrique*) bare ♦ *nm* (*ART*) nude; **tout ~** stark naked; **se mettre ~** to strip; **mettre à ~** to bare

nuage [nɥaʒ] *nm* cloud; **nuageux, -euse** *adj* cloudy

nuance [nɥɑ̃s] *nf* (*de couleur, sens*) shade; **il y a une ~ (entre)** there's a slight differ-ence (between); **nuancer** *vt* (*opinion*) to bring some reservations *ou* qualifications to

nucléaire [nykleɛʀ] *adj* nuclear ♦ *nm*: **le ~** nuclear energy

nudiste [nydist] *nm/f* nudist

nuée [nɥe] *nf*: **une ~ de** a cloud *ou* host *ou* swarm of

nues [ny] *nfpl*: **tomber des ~** to be taken aback; **porter qn aux ~** to praise sb to the skies

nuire [nɥiʀ] *vi* to be harmful; ~ **à** to harm, do damage to; **nuisible** *adj* harmful; **ani-mal nuisible** pest

nuit [nɥi] *nf* night; **il fait ~** it's dark; **cette ~** (*hier*) last night; (*aujourd'hui*) tonight; ~ **blanche** sleepless night

nul, nulle [nyl] *adj* (*aucun*) no; (*minime*) nil, non-existent; (*non valable*) null; (*péj*) useless, hopeless ♦ *pron* none, no one; **match** *ou* **résultat ~** draw; **~le part** no-where; **nullement** *adv* by no means; **nullité** *nf* (*personne*) nonentity

numérique [nymeʀik] *adj* numerical; (*affichage*) digital

numéro [nymeʀo] *nm* number; (*spectacle*) act, turn; (*PRESSE*) issue, number; ~ **de té-léphone** (tele)phone number; ~ **vert** ≈ freefone ® number (*BRIT*), ≈ toll-free number (*US*); **numéroter** *vt* to number

nu-pieds [nypje] *adj inv, adv* barefoot
nuque [nyk] *nf* nape of the neck
nu-tête [nytɛt] *adj inv, adv* bareheaded
nutritif, -ive [nytritif, iv] *adj (besoins, valeur)* nutritional; *(nourrissant)* nutritious
nylon [nilɔ̃] *nm* nylon

O, o

oasis [ɔazis] *nf* oasis
obéir [ɔbeiʀ] *vi* to obey; **~ à** to obey; **obéissance** *nf* obedience; **obéissant, e** *adj* obedient
obèse [ɔbɛz] *adj* obese; **obésité** *nf* obesity
objecter [ɔbʒɛkte] *vt (prétexter)* to plead, put forward as an excuse; **~ (à qn) que** to object (to sb) that; **objecteur** *nm*: **objecteur de conscience** conscientious objector
objectif, -ive [ɔbʒɛktif, iv] *adj* objective ♦ *nm* objective; *(PHOTO)* lens *sg,* objective; **objectivité** *nf* objectivity
objection [ɔbʒɛksjɔ̃] *nf* objection
objet [ɔbʒɛ] *nm* object; *(d'une discussion, recherche)* subject; **être** *ou* **faire l'~ de** *(discussion)* to be the subject of; *(soins)* to be given *ou* shown; **sans ~** purposeless; groundless; **~ d'art** objet d'art; **~s trouvés** lost property *sg (BRIT),* lost-and-found *sg (US);* **~s de valeur** valuables
obligation [ɔbligasjɔ̃] *nf* obligation; *(COMM)* bond, debenture; **obligatoire** *adj* compulsory, obligatory; **obligatoirement** *adv* necessarily; *(fam: sans aucun doute)* inevitably
obligé, e [ɔbliʒe] *adj (redevable)*: **être très ~ à qn** to be most obliged to sb
obligeance [ɔbliʒɑ̃s] *nf*: **avoir l'~ de ...** to be kind *ou* good enough to ...; **obligeant, e** *adj (personne)* obliging, kind
obliger [ɔbliʒe] *vt (contraindre)*: **~ qn à faire** to force *ou* oblige sb to do; **je suis bien obligé** I have to
oblique [ɔblik] *adj* oblique; **en ~** diagon-

ally; **obliquer** *vi*: **obliquer vers** to turn off towards
oblitérer [ɔblitere] *vt (timbre-poste)* to cancel
obnubiler [ɔbnybile] *vt* to obsess
obscène [ɔpsɛn] *adj* obscene
obscur, e [ɔpskyʀ] *adj* dark; *(méconnu)* obscure; **obscurcir** *vt* to darken; *(fig)* to obscure; **s'obscurcir** *vi* to grow dark; **obscurité** *nf* darkness; **dans l'obscurité** in the dark, in darkness
obsédé, e [ɔpsede] *nm/f*: **un ~ (sexuel)** a sex maniac
obséder [ɔpsede] *vt* to obsess, haunt
obsèques [ɔpsɛk] *nfpl* funeral *sg*
observateur, -trice [ɔpsɛʀvatœʀ, tʀis] *adj* observant, perceptive ♦ *nm/f* observer
observation [ɔpsɛʀvasjɔ̃] *nf* observation; *(d'un règlement etc)* observance; *(reproche)* reproof; **être en ~** *(MÉD)* to be under observation
observatoire [ɔpsɛʀvatwaʀ] *nm* observatory
observer [ɔpsɛʀve] *vt (regarder)* to observe, watch; *(scientifiquement; aussi règlement etc)* to observe; *(surveiller)* to watch; *(remarquer)* to observe, notice; **faire ~ qch à qn** *(dire)* to point out sth to sb
obsession [ɔpsesjɔ̃] *nf* obsession
obstacle [ɔpstakl] *nm* obstacle; *(ÉQUITATION)* jump, hurdle; **faire ~ à** *(projet)* to hinder, put obstacles in the path of
obstiné, e [ɔpstine] *adj* obstinate
obstiner [ɔpstine]: **s'~** *vi* to insist, dig one's heels in; **s'~ à faire** to persist (obstinately) in doing
obstruer [ɔpstʀye] *vt* to block, obstruct
obtenir [ɔptəniʀ] *vt* to obtain, get; *(résultat)* to achieve, obtain; **~ de pouvoir faire** to obtain permission to do
obturateur [ɔptyʀatœʀ, tʀis] *nm (PHOTO)* shutter
obus [ɔby] *nm* shell
occasion [ɔkazjɔ̃] *nf (aubaine, possibilité)* opportunity; *(circonstance)* occasion;

(COMM: *article non neuf*) secondhand buy; (: *acquisition avantageuse*) bargain; **à plusieurs ~s** on several occasions; **à l'~** sometimes, on occasions; **d'~** secondhand; **occasionnel, le** adj (non régulier) occasional; **occasionnellement** adv occasionally, from time to time

occasionner [ɔkazjɔne] vt to cause

occident [ɔksidɑ̃] nm: **l'O~** the West; **occidental, e** adj western; (POL) Western ♦ nm/f Westerner

occupation [ɔkypasjɔ̃] nf occupation

occupé, e [ɔkype] adj (personne) busy; (place) taken; (toilettes) engaged; (ligne) engaged (BRIT), busy (US); (MIL, POL) occupied

occuper [ɔkype] vt to occupy; (poste) to hold; **s'~ de** (être responsable de) to be in charge of; (se charger de: affaire) to take charge of, deal with; (: clients etc) to attend to; **s'~ (à qch)** to occupy o.s. ou keep o.s. busy (with sth)

occurrence [ɔkyRɑ̃s] nf: **en l'~** in this case

océan [ɔseɑ̃] nm ocean

octante [ɔktɑ̃t] adj (regional) eighty

octet [ɔkte] nm byte

octobre [ɔktɔbR] nm October

octroyer [ɔktRwaje] vt: **s'~** vt (vacances etc) to treat o.s. to

oculiste [ɔkylist] nm/f eye specialist

odeur [ɔdœR] nf smell

odieux, -euse [ɔdjø, jøz] adj hateful

odorant, e [ɔdɔRɑ̃, ɑ̃t] adj fragrant

odorat [ɔdɔRa] nm (sense of) smell

œil [œj] (pl **yeux**) nm eye; **à l'~** (fam) for free; **à l'~ nu** with the naked eye; **tenir qn à l'~** to keep an eye ou a watch on sb; **avoir l'~ à** to keep an eye on; **fermer les yeux (sur)** (fig) to turn a blind eye (to); **voir qch d'un bon/mauvais ~** to look on sth favourably/unfavourably

œillères [œjeR] nfpl blinkers (BRIT), blinders (US)

œillet [œje] nm (BOT) carnation

œuf [œf, pl ø] nm egg; **~ à la coque/sur le plat/dur** boiled/fried/hard-boiled egg;

~ de Pâques Easter egg; **~s brouillés** scrambled eggs

œuvre [œvR] nf (tâche) task, undertaking; (livre, tableau etc) work; (ensemble de la production artistique) works pl ♦ nm (CONSTR): **le gros ~** the shell; **~ (de bienfaisance)** charity; **mettre en ~** (moyens) to make use of; **~ d'art** work of art

offense [ɔfɑ̃s] nf insult; **offenser** vt to offend, hurt

offert, e [ɔfeR, eRt] pp de **offrir**

office [ɔfis] nm (agence) bureau, agency; (REL) service ♦ nm ou nf (pièce) pantry; **faire ~ de** to act as; **d'~** automatically; **~ du tourisme** tourist bureau

officiel, le [ɔfisjɛl] adj, nm/f official

officier [ɔfisje] nm officer

officieux, -euse [ɔfisjø, jøz] adj unofficial

offrande [ɔfRɑ̃d] nf offering

offre [ɔfR] nf offer; (aux enchères) bid; (ADMIN: soumission) tender; (ÉCON): **l'~ et la demande** supply and demand; **"~s d'emploi"** "situations vacant"; **~ d'emploi** job advertised

offrir [ɔfRiR] vt: **~ (à qn)** to offer (to sb); (faire cadeau de) to give (to sb) **s'~** vt (vacances, voiture) to treat o.s. to; **~ (à qn) de faire qch** to offer to do sth (for sb); **~ à boire à qn** (chez soi) to offer sb a drink

offusquer [ɔfyske] vt to offend

OGM sigle m (= organisme génétiquement modifié) GMO

oie [wa] nf (ZOOL) goose

oignon [ɔɲɔ̃] nm onion; (de tulipe etc) bulb

oiseau, x [wazo] nm bird; **~ de proie** bird of prey

oisif, -ive [wazif, iv] adj idle

oléoduc [ɔleɔdyk] nm (oil) pipeline

olive [ɔliv] nf (BOT) olive; **olivier** nm olive (tree)

OLP sigle f (= Organisation de libération de la Palestine) PLO

olympique [ɔlɛ̃pik] adj Olympic

ombragé, e [ɔ̃bRaʒe] adj shaded, shady; **ombrageux, -euse** adj (personne) touchy, easily offended

ombre [5bʀ] nf (espace non ensoleillé) shade; (~ portée, tache) shadow; **à l'~** in the shade; **dans l'~** (fig) in the dark; **~ à paupières** eyeshadow; **ombrelle** nf parasol, sunshade

omelette [ɔmlɛt] nf omelette; **~ norvé-gienne** baked Alaska

omettre [ɔmɛtʀ] vt to omit, leave out

omnibus [ɔmnibys] nm slow ou stopping train

omoplate [ɔmɔplat] nf shoulder blade

MOT-CLÉ

on [5] pron 1 (indéterminé) you, one; **on peut le faire ainsi** you ou one can do it like this, it can be done like this

2 (quelqu'un): **on les a attaqués** they were attacked; **on vous demande au té-léphone** there's a phone call for you, you're wanted on the phone

3 (nous) we; **on va y aller demain** we're going tomorrow

4 (les gens) they; **autrefois, on croyait ...** they used to believe ...

5: **on ne peut plus**

♦ adv: **on ne peut plus stupide** as stupid as can be

---

oncle [5kl] nm uncle

onctueux, -euse [5ktɥø, øz] adj creamy, smooth

onde [5d] nf wave; **sur les ~s** on the radio; **sur ~s courtes** on short wave sg; **moyennes/longues ~s** medium/long wave sg

ondée [5de] nf shower

on-dit [5di] nm inv rumour

onduler [5dyle] vi to undulate; (cheveux) to wave

onéreux, -euse [ɔneʀø, øz] adj costly

ongle [5gl] nm nail

ont [5] vb voir **avoir**

ONU sigle f (= Organisation des Nations Unies) UN

onze ['5z] num eleven; **onzième** num

eleventh

OPA sigle f = **offre publique d'achat**

opaque [ɔpak] adj opaque

opéra [ɔpeʀa] nm opera; (édifice) opera house

opérateur, -trice [ɔpeʀatœʀ, tʀis] nm/f operator; **~ (de prise de vues)** camera-man

opération [ɔpeʀasj5] nf operation; (COMM) dealing

opératoire [ɔpeʀatwaʀ] adj (choc etc) post-operative

opérer [ɔpeʀe] vt (personne) to operate on; (faire, exécuter) to carry out, make ♦ vi (re-mède: faire effet) to act, work; (MÉD) to operate; **s'~** vi (avoir lieu) to occur, take place; **se faire ~** to have an operation

opérette [ɔpeʀɛt] nf operetta, light opera

ophtalmologiste [ɔftalmɔlɔʒist] nm/f ophthalmologist, optician

opiner [ɔpine] vi: **~ de la tête** to nod as-sent

opinion [ɔpinj5] nf opinion; **l'~ (publique)** public opinion

opportun, e [ɔpɔʀtœ̃, yn] adj timely, op-portune; **opportuniste** nm/f opportunist

opposant, e [ɔpozɑ̃, ɑ̃t] nm/f opponent

opposé, e [ɔpoze] adj (direction) opposite; (faction) opposing; (opinions, intérêts) con-flicting; (contre): **~ à** opposed to, against ♦ nm: **l'~** the other ou opposite side (ou direction); (contraire) the opposite; **à l'~** (fig) on the other hand; **à l'~ de** (fig) con-trary to, unlike

opposer [ɔpoze] vt (personnes, équipes) to oppose; (couleurs) to contrast; **s'~** vi (équipes) to confront each other; (opinions) to conflict; (couleurs, styles) to clash; **s'~ à** (interdire) to oppose; **~ qch à** (comme obstacle, défense) to set sth against; (comme objection) to put sth for-ward against

opposition [ɔpozisj5] nf opposition; **par ~ à** as opposed to, in contrast with; **entrer en ~ avec** to come into conflict with; **fai-re ~ à un chèque** to stop a cheque

oppressant, e [ɔpʀesɑ̃, ɑ̃t] *adj* oppressive

oppresser [ɔpʀese] *vt* to oppress; **oppression** *nf* oppression

opprimer [ɔpʀime] *vt* to oppress

opter [ɔpte] *vi*: **~ pour** to opt for

opticien, ne [ɔptisjɛ̃, jɛn] *nm/f* optician

optimisme [ɔptimism] *nm* optimism; **optimiste** *nm/f* optimist ♦ *adj* optimistic

option [ɔpsjɔ̃] *nf* option; **matière à ~** (*SCOL*) optional subject

optique [ɔptik] *adj* (*nerf*) optic; (*verres*) optical ♦ *nf* (*fig: manière de voir*) perspective

opulent, e [ɔpylɑ̃, ɑ̃t] *adj* wealthy, opulent; (*formes, poitrine*) ample, generous

or [ɔʀ] *nm* gold ♦ *conj* now, but; **en ~** (*objet*) gold *cpd*; **une affaire en ~** a real bargain; **il croyait gagner ~ il a perdu** he was sure he would win and yet he lost

orage [ɔʀaʒ] *nm* (thunder)storm; **orageux, -euse** *adj* stormy

oral, e, -aux [ɔʀal, o] *adj, nm* oral; **par voie ~e** (*MÉD*) orally

orange [ɔʀɑ̃ʒ] *nf* orange ♦ *adj inv* orange; **orangeade** *nf* orangeade; **orangé, e** *adj* orangey, orange-coloured; **oranger** *nm* orange tree

orateur [ɔʀatœʀ, tʀis] *nm* speaker

orbite [ɔʀbit] *nf* (*ANAT*) (eye-)socket; (*PHYSIQUE*) orbit

orchestre [ɔʀkɛstʀ] *nm* orchestra; (*de jazz*) band; (*places*) stalls *pl* (*BRIT*), orchestra (*US*); **orchestrer** *vt* to orchestrate

orchidée [ɔʀkide] *nf* orchid

ordinaire [ɔʀdinɛʀ] *adj* ordinary; (*qualité*) standard; (*péj: commun*) common ♦ *nm* ordinary; (*menus*) everyday fare ♦ *nf* (*essence*) ≈ two-star (petrol) (*BRIT*), ≈ regular gas (*US*); **d'~** usually, normally; **comme à l'~** as usual

ordinateur [ɔʀdinatœʀ] *nm* computer

ordonnance [ɔʀdɔnɑ̃s] *nf* (*MÉD*) prescription; (*MIL*) orderly, batman (*BRIT*)

ordonné, e [ɔʀdɔne] *adj* tidy, orderly

ordonner [ɔʀdɔne] *vt* (*agencer*) to organize, arrange; (*donner un ordre*): **~ à qn de faire** to order sb to do; (*REL*) to ordain; (*MÉD*) to prescribe

ordre [ɔʀdʀ] *nm* order; (*propreté et soin*) orderliness, tidiness; (*nature*): **d'~ pratique** of a practical nature; **~s** *nmpl* (*REL*) holy orders; **mettre en ~** to tidy (up), put in order; **être à l'~ de qn** payable to sb; **être aux ~s de qn/sous les ~s de qn** to be at sb's disposal/under sb's command; **jusqu'à nouvel ~** until further notice; **de premier ~** first-rate; **~ du jour** (*d'une réunion*) agenda; **à l'~ du jour** (*fig*) topical

ordure [ɔʀdyʀ] *nf* filth *no pl*; **~s** *nfpl* (*balayures, déchets*) rubbish *sg*, refuse *sg*; **~s ménagères** household refuse

oreille [ɔʀɛj] *nf* ear; **avoir de l'~** to have a good ear (for music)

oreiller [ɔʀeje] *nm* pillow

oreillons [ɔʀɛjɔ̃] *nmpl* mumps *sg*

ores [ɔʀ]: **d'~ et déjà** *adv* already

orfèvrerie [ɔʀfɛvʀəʀi] *nf* goldsmith's (*ou* silversmith's) trade; (*ouvrage*) gold (*ou* silver) plate

organe [ɔʀgan] *nm* organ; (*porte-parole*) representative, mouthpiece

organigramme [ɔʀganigʀam] *nm* (*tableau hiérarchique*) organization chart; (*schéma*) flow chart

organique [ɔʀganik] *adj* organic

organisateur, -trice [ɔʀganizatœʀ, tʀis] *nm/f* organizer

organisation [ɔʀganizasjɔ̃] *nf* organization

organiser [ɔʀganize] *vt* to organize; (*mettre sur pied: service etc*) to set up; **s'~** to get organized

organisme [ɔʀganism] *nm* (*BIO*) organism; (*corps, ADMIN*) body

organiste [ɔʀganist] *nm/f* organist

orgasme [ɔʀgasm] *nm* orgasm, climax

orge [ɔʀʒ] *nf* barley

orgue [ɔʀg] *nm* organ; **~s** *nfpl* (*MUS*) organ *sg*

orgueil [ɔʀgœj] *nm* pride; **orgueilleux, -euse** *adj* proud

Orient [ɔʀjɑ̃] *nm*: **l'~** the East, the Orient; **oriental, e, -aux** *adj* (*langue, produit*) oriental; (*frontière*) eastern

orientation [ɔʀjɑ̃tasjɔ̃] *nf* (*de recherches*) orientation; (*d'une maison etc*) aspect; (*d'un journal*) leanings *pl*; **avoir le sens de l'~** to have a (good) sense of direction; **~ professionnelle** careers advisory service

orienté, e [ɔʀjɑ̃te] *adj* (fig: *article, journal*) slanted; **bien/mal ~** (*appartement*) well/badly positioned; **~ au sud** facing south, with a southern aspect

orienter [ɔʀjɑ̃te] *vt* (*tourner: antenne*) to direct, turn; (*personne, recherches*) to direct; (*fig: élève*) to orientate; **s'~** (*se repérer*) to find one's bearings; **s'~ vers** (*fig*) to turn towards

origan [ɔʀigɑ̃] *nm* oregano

originaire [ɔʀiʒinɛʀ] *adj*: **être ~ de** to be a native of

original, e, -aux [ɔʀiʒinal, o] *adj* original; (*bizarre*) eccentric ♦ *nm/f* eccentric ♦ *nm* (*document etc, ART*) original

origine [ɔʀiʒin] *nf* origin; **dès l'~** at *ou* from the outset; **à l'~** originally; **originel, le** *adj* original

orme [ɔʀm] *nm* elm

ornement [ɔʀnəmɑ̃] *nm* ornament

orner [ɔʀne] *vt* to decorate, adorn

ornière [ɔʀnjɛʀ] *nf* rut

orphelin, e [ɔʀfəlɛ̃, in] *adj* orphan(ed) ♦ *nm/f* orphan; **~ de père/mère** fatherless/motherless; **orphelinat** *nm* orphanage

orteil [ɔʀtɛj] *nm* toe; **gros ~** big toe

orthographe [ɔʀtɔgʀaf] *nf* spelling

ortie [ɔʀti] *nf* (stinging) nettle

os [ɔs] *nm* bone; **tomber sur un ~** (*fam*) to hit a snag

osciller [ɔsile] *vi* (*au vent etc*) to rock; (fig): **~ entre** to waver *ou* fluctuate between

osé, e [oze] *adj* daring, bold

oseille [ozɛj] *nf* sorrel

oser [oze] *vi, vt* to dare; **~ faire** to dare (to) do

osier [ozje] *nm* willow; **d'~, en ~** wicker(work)

ossature [ɔsatyʀ] *nf* (*ANAT*) frame, skeletal

structure; (*fig*) framework

osseux, -euse [ɔsø, øz] *adj* bony; (*tissu, maladie, greffe*) bone *cpd*

ostensible [ɔstɑ̃sibl] *adj* conspicuous

otage [ɔtaʒ] *nm* hostage; **prendre qn comme ~** to take sb hostage

OTAN *sigle f* (= *Organisation du traité de l'Atlantique Nord*) NATO

otarie [ɔtaʀi] *nf* sea-lion

ôter [ote] *vt* to remove; (*soustraire*) to take away; **~ qch à qn** to take sth (away) from sb; **~ qch de** to remove sth from

otite [ɔtit] *nf* ear infection

ou [u] *conj* or; **~ ... ~** either ... or; **~ bien** or (else)

| MOT-CLÉ |
---

où [u] *pron relatif* **1** (*position, situation*) where, that (*souvent omis*); **la chambre où il était** the room (that) he was in, the room where he was; **la ville où je l'ai rencontré** the town where I met him; **la pièce d'où il est sorti** the room he came out of; **le village d'où je viens** the village I come from; **les villes par où il est passé** the towns he went through

2 (*temps, état*) that (*souvent omis*); **le jour où il est parti** the day (that) he left; **au prix où c'est** at the price it is

♦ *adv* **1** (*interrogation*) where; **où est-il/va-t-il?** where is he/is he going?; **par où?** which way?; **d'où vient que ...?** how come ...?

2 (*position*) where; **je sais où il est** I know where he is; **où que l'on aille** wherever you go

---

ouate ['wat] *nf* cotton wool (*BRIT*), cotton (*US*)

oubli [ubli] *nm* (*acte*): **l'~ de** forgetting; (*trou de mémoire*) lapse of memory; (*négligence*) omission, oversight; **tomber dans l'~** to sink into oblivion

oublier [ublije] *vt* to forget; (*laisser quelque part: chapeau etc*) to leave behind; (*ne pas voir: erreurs etc*) to miss oubliettes [ublijɛt] *nfpl* dungeon *sg*

ouest [wɛst] *nm* west ♦ *adj inv* west; (*région*) western; **à l'~** in the west; (*direction*) (to the) west, westwards; **à l'~ de** (to the) west of

ouf ['uf] *excl* phew!

oui ['wi] *adv* yes

ouï-dire ['widiʀ]: **par ~-~** *adv* by hearsay

ouïe [wi] *nf* hearing; **~s** *nfpl* (*de poisson*) gills

ouille ['uj] *excl* ouch!

ouragan [uʀagɑ̃] *nm* hurricane

ourlet [uʀlɛ] *nm* hem

ours [uʀs] *nm* bear; **~ brun/blanc** brown/polar bear; **~ (en peluche)** teddy (bear)

oursin [uʀsɛ̃] *nm* sea urchin

ourson [uʀsɔ̃] *nm* (bear-)cub

ouste [ust] *excl* hop it!

outil [uti] *nm* tool; **outiller** *vt* to equip

outrage [utʀaʒ] *nm* insult; **~ à la pudeur** indecent conduct *no pl*; **outrager** *vt* to offend gravely

outrance [utʀɑ̃s]: **à ~** *adv* excessively, to excess

outre [utʀ] *prép* besides ♦ *adv*: **passer ~ à** to disregard, take no notice of; **en ~** besides, moreover; **~ mesure** to excess; (*manger, boire*) immoderately; **outre-Atlantique** *adv* across the Atlantic; **outre-Manche** *adv* across the Channel; **outre-mer** *adv* overseas; **outrepasser** *vt* to go beyond, exceed

ouvert, e [uvɛʀ, ɛʀt] *pp de* **ouvrir** ♦ *adj* open; (*robinet, gaz etc*) on; **ouvertement** *adv* openly; **ouverture** *nf* opening; (*MUS*) overture; **ouverture d'esprit** open-mindedness

ouvrable [uvʀabl] *adj*: **jour ~** working day, weekday

ouvrage [uvʀaʒ] *nm* (*tâche, de tricot etc*) work *no pl*; (*texte, livre*) work; **ouvragé, e** *adj* finely embroidered (*ou* worked *ou* carved)

ouvre-boîte(s) [uvʀabwat] *nm inv* tin (*BRIT*) *ou* can opener

ouvre-bouteille(s) [uvʀabutɛj] *nm inv* bottle-opener

ouvreuse [uvʀøz] *nf* usherette

ouvrier, -ière [uvʀije, ijɛʀ] *nm/f* worker ♦ *adj* working-class; (*conflit*) industrial; (*mouvement*) labour *cpd*; **classe ouvrière** working class

ouvrir [uvʀiʀ] *vt* (*gén*) to open; (*brèche, passage, MÉD: abcès*) to open up; (*commencer l'exploitation de, créer*) to open (up); (*eau, électricité, chauffage, robinet*) to turn on ♦ *vi* to open; to open up; **s'~** *vi* to open; **s'~ à qn** to open one's heart to sb; **~ l'appétit à qn** to whet sb's appetite

ovaire [ovɛʀ] *nm* ovary

ovale [oval] *adj* oval

ovni [ovni] *sigle m* (= *objet volant non identifié*) UFO

oxyder [ɔkside]: **s'~** *vi* to become oxidized

oxygène [ɔksiʒɛn] *nm* oxygen

oxygéné, e [ɔksiʒene] *adj*: **eau ~e** hydrogen peroxide

oxygéner [ɔksiʒene]: **s'~** (*fam*) *vi* to get some fresh air

ozone [ozon] *nf* ozone; **la couche d'~** the ozone layer

P, p

pacifique [pasifik] *adj* peaceful ♦ *nm*: **le P~, l'océan P~** the Pacific (Ocean)

pacotille [pakɔtij] *nf* cheap junk

pack [pak] *nm* pack

pacte [pakt] *nm* pact, treaty

pagaie [pagɛ] *nf* paddle

pagaille [pagaj] *nf* mess, shambles *sg*

pagayer [pageje] *vi* to paddle

page [paʒ] *nf* page ♦ *nm* page (boy); **à la ~** (*fig*) up-to-date; **~ d'accueil** (*INFORM*) home page

paiement [pemɑ̃] *nm* payment

païen, ne [pajɛ̃, pajɛn] *adj, nm/f* pagan, heathen

paillasson [pajasɔ̃] *nm* doormat

paille [paj] *nf* straw

paillettes [pɑjɛt] *nfpl* (*décoratives*) sequins, spangles

pain [pɛ̃] *nm* (*substance*) bread; (*unité*) loaf (of bread); (*morceau*): ~ **de savon** *etc* bar of soap *etc*; ~ **au chocolat** chocolate-filled pastry; ~ **aux raisins** currant bun; ~ **bis/complet** brown/wholemeal (*BRIT*) *ou* wholewheat (*US*) bread; ~ **d'épice** gingerbread; ~ **de mie** sandwich loaf; ~ **grillé** toast

pair, e [pɛʀ] *adj* (*nombre*) even ♦ *nm* peer; **aller de** ~ to go hand in hand *ou* together; **jeune fille au** ~ au pair; **paire** *nf* pair

paisible [pezibl] *adj* peaceful, quiet

paître [pɛtʀ] *vi* to graze

paix [pɛ] *nf* peace; **faire/avoir la** ~ to make/have peace; **fiche-lui la** ~**!** (*fam*) leave him alone!

Pakistan [pakistɑ̃] *nm*: **le** ~ Pakistan

palace [palas] *nm* luxury hotel

palais [palɛ] *nm* palace; (*ANAT*) palate

pâle [pɑl] *adj* pale; **bleu** ~ pale blue

Palestine [palɛstin] *nf*: **la** ~ Palestine

palet [palɛ] *nm* disc; (*HOCKEY*) puck

paletot [palto] *nm* (thick) cardigan

palette [palɛt] *nf* (*de peintre*) palette; (*produits*) range

pâleur [pɑlœʀ] *nf* paleness

palier [palje] *nm* (*d'escalier*) landing; (*fig*) level, plateau; **par** ~s in stages

pâlir [pɑliʀ] *vi* to turn *ou* go pale; (*couleur*) to fade

palissade [palisad] *nf* fence

pallier [palje]: ~ **à** *vt* to offset, make up for

palmarès [palmaʀɛs] *nm* record (of achievements); (*SPORT*) list of winners

palme [palm] *nf* (*de plongeur*) flipper; **palmé, e** *adj* (*pattes*) webbed

palmier [palmje] *nm* palm tree; (*gâteau*) heart-shaped biscuit made of flaky pastry

pâlot, te [pɑlo, ɔt] *adj* pale, peaky

palourde [paluʀd] *nf* clam

palper [palpe] *vt* to feel, finger

palpitant, e [palpitɑ̃, ɑ̃t] *adj* thrilling

palpiter [palpite] *vi* (*cœur, pouls*) to beat; (: *plus fort*) to pound, throb

paludisme [palydism] *nm* malaria

pamphlet [pɑ̃flɛ] *nm* lampoon, satirical tract

pamplemousse [pɑ̃pləmus] *nm* grapefruit

pan [pɑ̃] *nm* section, piece ♦ *excl* bang!

panache [panaʃ] *nm* plume; (*fig*) spirit, panache

panaché, e [panaʃe] *adj*: **glace** ~**e** mixed-flavour ice cream ♦ *nm* (*bière*) shandy

pancarte [pɑ̃kaʀt] *nf* sign, notice

pancréas [pɑ̃kʀeas] *nm* pancreas

pané, e [pane] *adj* fried in breadcrumbs

panier [panje] *nm* basket; **mettre au** ~ to chuck away; ~ **à provisions** shopping basket; **panier-repas** *nm* packed lunch

panique [panik] *nf, adj* panic; **paniquer** *vi* to panic

panne [pan] *nf* breakdown; **être/tomber en** ~ to have broken down/break down; **être en** ~ **d'essence** *ou* **sèche** to have run out of petrol (*BRIT*) *ou* gas (*US*); ~ **d'électricité** *ou* **de courant** power *ou* electrical failure

panneau, x [pano] *nm* (*écriteau*) sign, notice; ~ **d'affichage** notice board; ~ **de signalisation** roadsign

panoplie [panɔpli] *nf* (*jouet*) outfit; (*fig*) array

panorama [panɔʀama] *nm* panorama

panse [pɑ̃s] *nf* paunch

pansement [pɑ̃smɑ̃] *nm* dressing, bandage; ~ **adhésif** sticking plaster

panser [pɑ̃se] *vt* (*plaie*) to dress, bandage; (*bras*) to put a dressing on, bandage; (*cheval*) to groom

pantalon [pɑ̃talɔ̃] *nm* trousers *pl*, pair of trousers; ~ **de ski** ski pants *pl*

panthère [pɑ̃tɛʀ] *nf* panther

pantin [pɑ̃tɛ̃] *nm* puppet

pantois [pɑ̃twa] *adj m*: **rester** ~ to be flabbergasted

pantoufle [pɑ̃tufl] *nf* slipper

paon [pã] *nm* peacock

papa [papa] *nm* dad(dy)

pape [pap] *nm* pope

paperasse [papʀas] (*péj*) *nf* bumf *no pl*, papers *pl*; **paperasserie** (*péj*) *nf* paperwork *no pl*; (*tracasserie*) red tape *no pl*

papeterie [papetʀi] *nf* (*magasin*) stationer's (shop)

papi *nm* (*fam*) granddad

papier [papje] *nm* paper; (*article*) article; **~s** *nmpl* (*aussi*: **~s d'identité**) (identity) papers; **~ à lettres** writing paper, notepaper; **~ carbone** carbon paper; **~ (d')aluminium** aluminium (*BRIT*) *ou* aluminum (*US*) foil, tinfoil; **~ de verre** sandpaper; **~ hygiénique** *ou* **de toilette** toilet paper; **~ journal** newspaper; **~ peint** wallpaper

papillon [papijɔ̃] *nm* butterfly; (*fam*: *contravention*) (parking) ticket; **~ de nuit** moth

papillote [papijɔt] *nf*: **en ~** cooked in tinfoil

papoter [papɔte] *vi* to chatter

paquebot [pak(ə)bo] *nm* liner

pâquerette [pakʀɛt] *nf* daisy

Pâques [pak] *nm*, *nfpl* Easter

paquet [pakɛ] *nm* packet; (*colis*) parcel; (*fig*: *tas*): **~ de** pile *ou* heap of; **paquet-cadeau** *nm*: **faites-moi un paquet-cadeau** gift-wrap it for me

par [paʀ] *prép* by; **finir** *etc* **~** to end *etc* with; **~ amour** out of love; **passer ~ Lyon/la côte** to go via *ou* through Lyons/along by the coast; **~ la fenêtre** (*jeter*, *regarder*) out of the window; **3 ~ jour/personne** 3 a *ou* per day/head; **2 ~ 2** in twos; **~ ici** this way; (*dans le coin*) round here; **~-ci, ~-là** here and there; **~ temps de pluie** in wet weather

parabolique [paʀabɔlik] *adj*: **antenne ~** parabolic *ou* dish aerial

parachever [paʀaʃ(ə)ve] *vt* to perfect

parachute [paʀaʃyt] *nm* parachute; **parachutiste** *nm/f* parachutist; (*MIL*) paratrooper

parade [paʀad] *nf* (*spectacle*, *défilé*) parade; (*ESCRIME*, *BOXE*) parry

paradis [paʀadi] *nm* heaven, paradise

paradoxe [paʀadɔks] *nm* paradox

paraffine [paʀafin] *nf* paraffin

parages [paʀaʒ] *nmpl*: **dans les ~ (de)** in the area *ou* vicinity (of)

paragraphe [paʀagʀaf] *nm* paragraph

paraître [paʀɛtʀ] *vb* +*attrib* to seem, look, appear ♦ *vi* to appear; (*être visible*) to show; (*PRESSE*, *ÉDITION*) to be published, come out, appear ♦ *vb impers*: **il paraît que** it seems *ou* appears that, they say that; **chercher à ~** to show off

parallèle [paʀalɛl] *adj* parallel; (*non officiel*) unofficial ♦ *nm* (*comparaison*): **faire un ~ entre** to draw a parallel between ♦ *nf* parallel (line)

paralyser [paʀalize] *vt* to paralyse

paramédical, e, -aux [paʀamedikal, o] *adj*: **personnel ~** paramedics *pl*, paramedical workers *pl*

paraphrase [paʀafʀɑz] *nf* paraphrase

parapluie [paʀaplyi] *nm* umbrella

parasite [paʀazit] *nm* parasite; **~s** *nmpl* (*TÉL*) interference *sg*

parasol [paʀasɔl] *nm* parasol, sunshade

paratonnerre [paʀatɔnɛʀ] *nm* lightning conductor

paravent [paʀavã] *nm* folding screen

parc [paʀk] *nm* (*public*) park, gardens *pl*; (*de château etc*) grounds *pl*; (*d'enfant*) playpen; (*ensemble d'unités*) stock; (*de voitures etc*) fleet; **~ d'attractions** theme park; **~ de stationnement** car park

parcelle [paʀsɛl] *nf* fragment, scrap; (*de terrain*) plot, parcel

parce que [paʀsk(ə)] *conj* because

parchemin [paʀʃəmɛ̃] *nm* parchment

parcmètre [paʀkmɛtʀ] *nm* parking meter

parcourir [paʀkuʀiʀ] *vt* (*trajet*, *distance*) to cover; (*article*, *livre*) to skim *ou* glance through; (*lieu*) to go all over, travel up and down; (*suj*: *frisson*) to run through

parcours [paʀkuʀ] *nm* (*trajet*) journey; (*itinéraire*) route

par-derrière [paʀdeʀjeʀ] *adv* round the back; **dire du mal de qn ~-~** to speak ill of sb behind his back

par-dessous [paʀd(ə)su] *prép, adv* under(neath)

pardessus [paʀdəsy] *nm* overcoat

par-dessus [paʀd(ə)sy] *prép* over (the top of) ♦ *adv* over (the top); **~-~ le marché** on top of all that; **~-~ tout** above all; **en avoir ~-~ la tête** to have had enough

par-devant [paʀd(ə)vɑ̃] *adv* (*passer*) round the front

pardon [paʀdɔ̃] *nm* forgiveness *no pl* ♦ *excl* sorry!; (*pour interpeller etc*) excuse me!; **demander ~ à qn (de)** to apologize to sb (for); **je vous demande ~** I'm sorry; (*pour interpeller*) excuse me; **pardonner** *vt* to forgive; **pardonner qch à qn** to forgive sb for sth

pare...: **pare-balles** *adj inv* bulletproof; **pare-brise** *nm inv* windscreen (*BRIT*), windshield (*US*); **pare-chocs** *nm inv* bumper

paré, e [paʀe] *adj* ready, all set

pareil, le [paʀɛj] *adj* (*identique*) the same, alike; (*similaire*) similar; (*tel*): **un courage/livre ~** such courage/a book, courage/a book like this; **de ~s livres** such books; **ne pas avoir son(sa) ~(le)** to be second to none; **~ à** the same as; (*similaire*) similar to; **sans ~** unparalleled, unequalled

parent, e [paʀɑ̃, ɑ̃t] *nm/f*: **un(e) ~(e)** a relative *ou* relation; **~s** *nmpl* (*père et mère*) parents; **parenté** *nf* (*lien*) relationship

parenthèse [paʀɑ̃tɛz] *nf* (*ponctuation*) bracket, parenthesis; (*digression*) parenthesis, digression; **entre ~s** in brackets; (*fig*) incidentally

parer [paʀe] *vt* to adorn; (*éviter*) to ward off; **~ au plus pressé** to attend to the most urgent things first

paresse [paʀɛs] *nf* laziness; **paresseux, -euse** *adj* lazy

parfaire [paʀfɛʀ] *vt* to perfect

parfait, e [paʀfɛ, ɛt] *adj* perfect ♦ *nm* (*LING*) perfect (tense); **parfaitement** *adv* perfectly ♦ *excl* (*most*) certainly

parfois [paʀfwa] *adv* sometimes

parfum [paʀfœ̃] *nm* (*produit*) perfume, scent; (*odeur: de fleur*) scent, fragrance; (*goût*) flavour; **parfumé, e** *adj* (*fleur, fruit*) fragrant; (*femme*) perfumed; **parfumé au café** coffee-flavoured; **parfumer** *vt* (*suj: odeur, bouquet*) to perfume; (*crème, gâteau*) to flavour; **parfumerie** *nf* (*produits*) perfumes *pl*; (*boutique*) perfume shop

pari [paʀi] *nm* bet; **parier** *vt* to bet

Paris [paʀi] *n* Paris; **parisien, ne** *adj* Parisian; (*GÉO, ADMIN*) Paris *cpd* ♦ *nm/f*: **Parisien, ne** Parisian

parjure [paʀʒyʀ] *nm* perjury

parking [paʀkiŋ] *nm* (*lieu*) car park

parlant, e [paʀlɑ̃, ɑ̃t] *adj* (*regard*) eloquent; (*CINÉMA*) talking; **les chiffres sont ~s** the figures speak for themselves

parlement [paʀləmɑ̃] *nm* parliament; **parlementaire** *adj* parliamentary ♦ *nm/f* member of parliament; **parlementer** *vi* to negotiate, parley

parler [paʀle] *vi* to speak, talk; (*avouer*) to talk; **~ (à qn) de** to talk *ou* speak (to sb) about; **~ le/en français** to speak French/in French; **~ affaires** to talk business; **sans ~ de** (*fig*) not to mention, to say nothing of; **tu parles!** (*fam: bien sûr*) you bet!

parloir [paʀlwaʀ] *nm* (*de prison, d'hôpital*) visiting room

parmi [paʀmi] *prép* among(st)

paroi [paʀwa] *nf* wall; (*cloison*) partition; **~ rocheuse** rock face

paroisse [paʀwas] *nf* parish

parole [paʀɔl] *nf* (*faculté*): **la ~** speech; (*mot, promesse*) word; **~s** *nfpl* (*MUS*) words, lyrics; **tenir ~** to keep one's word; **prendre la ~** to speak; **demander la ~** to ask for permission to speak; **je te crois sur ~** I'll take your word for it

parquer [paʀke] *vt* (*voiture, matériel*) to park; (*bestiaux*) to pen (in *ou* up)

parquet [paʀke] *nm* (parquet) floor; (*JUR*):

le ~ the Public Prosecutor's department

parrain [paʀɛ̃] *nm* godfather; **parrainer** *vt* (*suj: entreprise*) to sponsor

pars [paʀ] *vb voir* **partir**

parsemer [paʀsəme] *vt* (*suj: feuilles, papiers*) to be scattered over; ~ **qch de** to scatter sth with

part [paʀ] *nf* (*qui revient à qn*) share; (*fraction, partie*) part; **prendre ~ à** (*débat etc*) to take part in; (*soucis, douleur de qn*) to share in; **faire ~ de qch à qn** to announce sth to sb, inform sb of sth; **pour ma ~** as for me, as far as I'm concerned; **à ~ entière** full; **de la ~ de** (*au nom de*) on behalf of; (*donné par*) from; **de toute(s) ~(s)** from all sides *ou* quarters; **de ~ et d'autre** on both sides, on either side; **d'une ~ ... d'autre ~** on the one hand ... on the other hand; **d'autre ~** (*de plus*) moreover; **à ~** *adv* (*séparément*) separately; (*de côté*) aside ♦ *prép* apart from, except for; **faire la ~ des choses** to make allowances

partage [paʀtaʒ] *nm* (*fractionnement*) dividing up; (*répartition*) sharing (out) *no pl*, share-out

partager [paʀtaʒe] *vt* to share; (*distribuer, répartir*) to share (out); (*morceler, diviser*) to divide (up); **se ~** *vt* (*héritage etc*) to share between themselves (*ou* ourselves)

partance [paʀtɑ̃s] : **en ~** *adv*: **en ~ pour** (bound) for

partenaire [paʀtənɛʀ] *nm/f* partner

parterre [paʀtɛʀ] *nm* (*de fleurs*) (flower) bed; (*THÉÂTRE*) stalls *pl*

parti [paʀti] *nm* (*POL*) party; (*décision*) course of action; (*personne à marier*) match; **tirer ~ de** to take advantage of, turn to good account; **prendre ~ (pour/ contre)** to take sides *ou* a stand (for/ against); ~ **pris** bias

partial, e, -aux [paʀsjal, jo] *adj* biased, partial

participant, e [paʀtisipɑ̃, ɑ̃t] *nm/f* participant; (*à un concours*) entrant

participation [paʀtisipasjɔ̃] *nf* participa-

tion; (*financière*) contribution

participer [paʀtisipe]: ~ **à** *vt* (*course, réunion*) to take part in; (*frais etc*) to contribute to; (*chagrin, succès de qn*) to share (in)

particularité [paʀtikylaʀite] *nf* (*distinctive*) characteristic

particulier, -ière [paʀtikylje, jɛʀ] *adj* (*spécifique*) particular; (*spécial*) special, particular; (*personnel, privé*) private; (*étrange*) peculiar, odd ♦ *nm* (*individu: ADMIN*) private individual; ~ **à** peculiar to; **en ~** (*surtout*) in particular, particularly; (*en privé*) in private; **particulièrement** *adv* particularly

partie [paʀti] *nf* (*gén*) part; (*JUR etc: protagonistes*) party; (*de cartes, tennis etc*) game; **une ~ de pêche** a fishing party *ou* trip; **en ~** partly, in part; **faire ~ de** (*suj: chose*) to be part of; **prendre qn à ~** to take sb to task; **en grande ~** largely, in the main; ~ **civile** (*JUR*) party claiming damages in a criminal case

partiel, le [paʀsjɛl] *adj* partial ♦ *nm* (*SCOL*) class exam

partir [paʀtiʀ] *vi* (*gén*) to go; (*quitter*) to go, leave; (*tache*) to go, come out; ~ **de** (*lieu: quitter*) to leave; (: *commencer à*) to start from; **à ~ de** from

partisan, e [paʀtizɑ̃, an] *nm/f* partisan ♦ *adj*: **être ~ de qch/de faire** to be in favour of sth/doing

partition [paʀtisjɔ̃] *nf* (*MUS*) score

partout [paʀtu] *adv* everywhere; ~ **où il allait** everywhere *ou* wherever he went

paru [paʀy] *pp de* **paraître**

parure [paʀyʀ] *nf* (*bijoux etc*) finery *no pl*; jewellery *no pl*; (*assortiment*) set

parution [paʀysjɔ̃] *nf* publication

parvenir [paʀvəniʀ]: ~ **à** *vt* (*atteindre*) to reach; (*réussir*): ~ **à faire** to manage to do, succeed in doing; ~ **à ses fins** to achieve one's ends

pas[1] [pa] *nm* (*enjambée, DANSE*) step; (*allure, mesure*) pace; (*bruit*) (foot)step; (*trace*) footprint; ~ **à ~** step by step; **au ~** at walking pace; **faire les cent ~** to pace up and down; **faire les premiers ~** to make the first move; **sur le ~ de la porte** on the doorstep

---
MOT-CLÉ
---

pas[2] [pɑ] *adv* 1 (*en corrélation avec ne, non etc*) not; **il ne pleure pas** he does not *ou* doesn't cry; he's not *ou* isn't crying; **il n'a pas pleuré/ne pleurera pas** he did not *ou* didn't/will not *ou* won't cry; **ils n'ont pas de voiture/d'enfants** they haven't got a car/any children, they have no car/children; **il m'a dit de ne pas le faire** he told me not to do it; **non pas que ...** not that ...

2 (*employé sans ne etc*): **pas moi** not me; not I, I don't (*ou* can't *etc*); **une pomme pas mûre** an apple which isn't ripe; **pas plus tard qu'hier** only yesterday; **pas du tout** not at all

3: **pas mal** not bad; not badly; **pas mal de** quite a lot of

---

passage [pɑsaʒ] *nm* (*fait de passer*) voir **passer**; (*lieu, prix de la traversée, extrait*) passage; (*chemin*) way; **de ~** (*touristes*) passing through; **~ à niveau** level crossing; **~ clouté** pedestrian crossing; **"~ interdit"** "no entry"; **~ souterrain** subway (*BRIT*), underpass

passager, -ère [pɑsaʒe, ɛʀ] *adj* passing ♦ *nm/f* passenger; **~ clandestin** stowaway

passant, e [pɑsɑ̃, ɑ̃t] *adj* (*rue, endroit*) busy ♦ *nm/f* passer-by; **en ~** in passing

passe[1] [pɑs] *nf* (*SPORT, NAVIG*) pass; **être en ~ de faire** to be on the way to doing; **être dans une mauvaise ~** to be going through a rough patch

passe[2] [pɑs] *nm* (*~-partout*) master *ou* skeleton key

passé, e [pɑse] *adj* (*révolu*) past; (*dernier: semaine etc*) last; (*couleur*) faded ♦ *prép* after ♦ *nm* past; (*LING*) past (tense); **~ de mode** out of fashion; **~ composé** perfect (tense); **~ simple** past historic

passe-partout [pɑspaʀtu] *nm inv* master *ou* skeleton key ♦ *adj inv* all-purpose

passeport [pɑspɔʀ] *nm* passport

passer [pɑse] *vi* (*aller*) to go; (*voiture, piétons: défiler*) to pass (by), go by; (*facteur, laitier etc*) to come, call; (*pour rendre visite*) to call *ou* drop in; (*film, émission*) to be on; (*temps, jours*) to pass, go by; (*couleur*) to fade; (*mode*) to die out; (*douleur*) to pass, go away; (*SCOL*) to go up (to the next class) ♦ *vt* (*frontière, rivière etc*) to cross; (*douane*) to go through; (*examen*) to sit, take; (*visite médicale etc*) to have; (*journée, temps*) to spend; (*enfiler: vêtement*) to slip on; (*film, pièce*) to show, put on; (*disque*) to play, put on; (*marché, accord*) to agree on; **se ~** *vi* (*avoir lieu: scène, action*) to take place; (*se dérouler: entretien etc*) to go; (*s'écouler: semaine etc*) to pass, go by; (*arriver*): **que s'est-il passé?** what happened?; **~ qch à qn** (*sel etc*) to pass sth to sb; (*prêter*) to lend sb sth; (*lettre, message*) to pass sth on to sb; (*tolérer*) to let sb get away with sth; **~ par** to go through; **~ avant qch/qn** (*fig*) to come before sth/sb; **~ un coup de fil à qn** (*fam*) to give sb a ring; **laisser ~** (*air, lumière, personne*) to let through; (*occasion*) to let slip, miss; (*erreur*) to overlook; **~ la seconde** (*AUTO*) to change into second; **~ le balai/l'aspirateur** to sweep up/ hoover; **je vous passe M. X** (*je vous mets en communication avec lui*) I'm putting you through to Mr X; (*je lui passe l'appareil*) here is Mr X, I'll hand you over to Mr X; **se ~ de** to go *ou* do without

passerelle [pɑsʀɛl] *nf* footbridge; (*de navire, avion*) gangway

passe-temps [pɑstɑ̃] *nm inv* pastime

passible [pɑsibl] *adj*: **~ de** liable to

passif, -ive [pɑsif, iv] *adj* passive

passion [pɑsjɔ̃] *nf* passion; **passionnant, e** *adj* fascinating; **passionné, e** *adj* (*personne*) passionate; (*récit*) impassioned; **être passionné de** to have a passion for; **passionner** *vt* (*personne*) to fascinate, grip; **se passionner pour** (*sport*) to have a passion for

passoire [paswaʀ] *nf* sieve; (*à légumes*) colander; (*à thé*) strainer

pastèque [pastɛk] *nf* watermelon

pasteur [pastœʀ] *nm* (*protestant*) minister, pastor

pasteurisé, e [pastœʀize] *adj* pasteurized

pastille [pastij] *nf* (*à sucer*) lozenge, pastille

patate [patat] *nf* (*fam: pomme de terre*) spud; ~ **douce** sweet potato

patauger [patoʒe] *vi* to splash about

pâte [pat] *nf* (*à tarte*) pastry; (*à pain*) dough; (*à frire*) batter; ~**s** *nfpl* (*macaroni etc*) pasta *sg*; ~ **à modeler** modelling clay, Plasticine ® (*BRIT*); ~ **brisée** shortcrust pastry; ~ **d'amandes** almond paste; ~ **de fruits** crystallized fruit *no pl*; ~ **feuilletée** puff *ou* flaky pastry

pâté [pate] *nm* (*charcuterie*) pâté; (*tache*) ink blot; (*de sable*) sandpie; ~ **de maisons** block (of houses); ~ **en croûte** ≈ pork pie

pâtée [pate] *nf* mash, feed

patente [patɑ̃t] *nf* (*COMM*) trading licence

paternel, le [patɛʀnɛl] *adj* (*amour, soins*) fatherly; (*ligne, autorité*) paternal

pâteux, -euse [patø, øz] *adj* pasty; (*langue*) coated

pathétique [patetik] *adj* moving

patience [pasjɑ̃s] *nf* patience

patient, e [pasjɑ̃, jɑ̃t] *adj, nm/f* patient; **patienter** *vi* to wait

patin [patɛ̃] *nm* skate; (*sport*) skating; ~**s** (*à glace*) (ice) skates; ~**s à roulettes** roller skates

patinage [patinaʒ] *nm* skating

patiner [patine] *vi* to skate; (*roue, voiture*) to spin; **se** ~ *vi* (*meuble, cuir*) to acquire a sheen; **patineur, -euse** *nm/f* skater; **patinoire** *nf* skating rink, (ice) rink

pâtir [patiʀ]: ~ **de** *vt* to suffer because of

pâtisserie [patisʀi] *nf* (*boutique*) cake shop; (*gâteau*) cake, pastry; (*à la maison*) pastry- *ou* cake-making, baking; **pâtissier, -ière** *nm/f* pastrycook

patois [patwa, waz] *nm* dialect, patois

patraque [patʀak] (*fam*) *adj* peaky, off-colour

patrie [patʀi] *nf* homeland

patrimoine [patʀimwan] *nm* (*culture*) heritage

patriotique [patʀijɔtik] *adj* patriotic

patron, ne [patʀɔ̃, ɔn] *nm/f* boss; (*REL*) patron saint ♦ *nm* (*COUTURE*) pattern; **patronat** *nm* employers *pl*; **patronner** *vt* to sponsor, support

patrouille [patʀuj] *nf* patrol

patte [pat] *nf* (*jambe*) leg; (*pied: de chien, chat*) paw; (: *d'oiseau*) foot

pâturage [patyʀaʒ] *nm* pasture

paume [pom] *nf* palm

paumé, e [pome] (*fam*) *nm/f* drop-out

paumer [pome] (*fam*) *vt* to lose

paupière [popjɛʀ] *nf* eyelid

pause [poz] *nf* (*arrêt*) break; (*en parlant, MUS*) pause

pauvre [povʀ] *adj* poor; **pauvreté** *nf* (*état*) poverty

pavaner [pavane]: **se** ~ *vi* to strut about

pavé, e [pave] *adj* (*cour*) paved; (*chaussée*) cobbled ♦ *nm* (*bloc*) paving stone; cobblestone

pavillon [pavijɔ̃] *nm* (*de banlieue*) small (detached) house; pavilion; (*drapeau*) flag

pavoiser [pavwaze] *vi* (*fig*) to rejoice, exult

pavot [pavo] *nm* poppy

payant, e [pɛjɑ̃, ɑ̃t] *adj* (*spectateurs etc*) paying; (*fig: entreprise*) profitable; (*effort*) which pays off; **c'est** ~ you have to pay, there is a charge

paye [pɛj] *nf* pay, wages *pl*

payer [peje] *vt* (*créancier, employé, loyer*) to pay; (*achat, réparations, fig: faute*) to pay for ♦ *vi* to pay; (*métier*) to be well-paid; (*tactique etc*) to pay off; **il me l'a fait ~ 10 euros** he charged me 10 euros for it; ~ **qch à qn** to buy sth for sb, buy sb sth; **se ~ la tête de qn** (*fam*) to take the mickey out of sb

pays [pei] *nm* country; (*région*) region; **du ~** local

paysage [peizaʒ] *nm* landscape

paysan, ne [peizɑ̃, an] *nm/f* farmer; (*péj*) peasant ♦ *adj* (*agricole*) farming; (*rural*) country

Pays-Bas [peiba] *nmpl*: **les ~-~** the Netherlands

PC *nm* (*INFORM*) PC ♦ *sigle m* = **parti communiste**

P.D.G. *sigle m* = **président directeur général**

péage [peaʒ] *nm* toll; (*endroit*) tollgate

peau, x [po] *nf* skin; **gants de ~** fine leather gloves; **être bien/mal dans sa ~** to be quite at ease/ill-at-ease; **~ de chamois** (*chiffon*) chamois leather, shammy; **Peau-Rouge** *nm/f* Red Indian, redskin

pêche [pɛʃ] *nf* (*sport, activité*) fishing; (*poissons pêchés*) catch; (*fruit*) peach; **~ à la ligne** (*en rivière*) angling

péché [peʃe] *nm* sin

pécher [peʃe] *vi* (*REL*) to sin

pêcher [peʃe] *nm* peach tree ♦ *vi* to go fishing ♦ *vt* (*attraper*) to catch; (*être pêcheur de*) to fish for

pécheur, -eresse [peʃœʀ, peʃʀɛs] *nm/f* sinner

pêcheur [peʃœʀ] *nm* fisherman; (*à la ligne*) angler

pécule [pekyl] *nm* savings *pl*, nest egg

pédagogie [pedagɔʒi] *nf* educational methods *pl*, pedagogy; **pédagogique** *adj* educational

pédale [pedal] *nf* pedal

pédalo [pedalo] *nm* pedal-boat

pédant, e [pedɑ̃, ɑ̃t] (*péj*) *adj* pedantic

pédestre [pedɛstʀ] *adj*: **randonnée ~** ramble; **sentier ~** pedestrian footpath

pédiatre [pedjatʀ] *nm/f* paediatrician, child specialist

pédicure [pedikyʀ] *nm/f* chiropodist

pègre [pɛgʀ] *nf* underworld

peignais *etc* [pɛɲɛ] *vb voir* **peindre; peigner**

peigne [pɛɲ] *nm* comb; **peigner** *vt* to comb (the hair of); **se peigner** *vi* to comb one's hair

peignoir *nm* dressing gown; **peignoir de bain** bathrobe

peindre [pɛ̃dʀ] *vt* to paint; (*fig*) to portray, depict

peine [pɛn] *nf* (*affliction*) sorrow, sadness *no pl*; (*mal, effort*) trouble *no pl*, effort; (*difficulté*) difficulty; (*JUR*) sentence; **avoir de la ~** to be sad; **faire de la ~ à qn** to distress *ou* upset sb; **prendre la ~ de faire** to go to the trouble of doing; **se donner de la ~** to make an effort; **ce n'est pas la ~ de faire** there's no point in doing, it's not worth doing; **à ~** scarcely, hardly, barely; **à ~ ... que** hardly ... than; **~ capitale** *ou* **de mort** capital punishment, death sentence; **peiner** *vi* (*personne*) to work hard; (*moteur, voiture*) to labour ♦ *vt* to grieve, sadden

peintre [pɛ̃tʀ] *nm* painter; **~ en bâtiment** house painter

peinture [pɛ̃tyʀ] *nf* painting; (*matière*) paint; (*surfaces peintes: aussi:* **~s**) paintwork; **"~ fraîche"** "wet paint"

péjoratif, -ive [peʒɔʀatif, iv] *adj* pejorative, derogatory

pelage [pəlaʒ] *nm* coat, fur

pêle-mêle [pɛlmɛl] *adv* higgledy-piggledy

peler [pəle] *vt, vi* to peel

pèlerin [pɛlʀɛ̃] *nm* pilgrim

pèlerinage [pɛlʀinaʒ] *nm* pilgrimage

pelle [pɛl] *nf* shovel; (*d'enfant, de terrassier*) spade

pellicule [pelikyl] *nf* film; **~s** *nfpl* (*MÉD*) dandruff *sg*

pelote [p(ə)lɔt] *nf* (*de fil, laine*) ball

peloton [p(ə)lɔtɔ̃] *nm* group, squad; (*CYCLISME*) pack; **~ d'exécution** firing squad

pelotonner [p(ə)lɔtɔne]: **se ~** *vi* to curl (o.s.) up

pelouse [p(ə)luz] *nf* lawn

peluche [p(ə)lyʃ] *nf*: **(animal en) ~** fluffy animal, soft toy; **chien/lapin en ~** fluffy dog/rabbit

pelure [p(ə)lyʀ] *nf* peeling, peel *no pl*

pénal, e, -aux [penal, o] *adj* penal; **pénalité** *nf* penalty

penaud, e [pəno, od] *adj* sheepish, contrite

penchant [pɑ̃ʃɑ̃] *nm* (*tendance*) tendency, propensity; (*faible*) liking, fondness

pencher [pɑ̃ʃe] *vi* to tilt, lean over ♦ *vt* to tilt; **se ~** *vi* to lean over; (*se baisser*) to bend down; **se ~ sur** (*fig: problème*) to look into; **~ pour** to be inclined to favour

pendaison [pɑ̃dɛzɔ̃] *nf* hanging

pendant [pɑ̃dɑ̃] *prép* (*au cours de*) during; (*indique la durée*) for; **~ que** while

pendentif [pɑ̃dɑ̃tif] *nm* pendant

penderie [pɑ̃dʀi] *nf* wardrobe

pendre [pɑ̃dʀ] *vt*, *vi* to hang; **se ~** (*se suicider*) to hang o.s.; **~ la crémaillère** to have a house-warming party

pendule [pɑ̃dyl] *nf* clock ♦ *nm* pendulum

pénétrer [penetre] *vi*, *vt* to penetrate; **~ dans** to enter

pénible [penibl] *adj* (*travail*) hard; (*sujet*) painful; (*personne*) tiresome; **péniblement** *adv* with difficulty

péniche [peniʃ] *nf* barge

pénicilline [penisilin] *nf* penicillin

péninsule [penɛ̃syl] *nf* peninsula

pénis [penis] *nm* penis

pénitence [penitɑ̃s] *nf* (*peine*) penance; (*repentir*) penitence; **pénitencier** *nm* penitentiary

pénombre [penɔ̃bʀ] *nf* (*faible clarté*) half-light; (*obscurité*) darkness

pensée [pɑ̃se] *nf* thought; (*démarche, doctrine*) thinking *no pl*; (*fleur*) pansy; **en ~** in one's mind

penser [pɑ̃se] *vi*, *vt* to think; **~ à** (*ami, vacances*) to think of *ou* about; (*réfléchir à: problème, offre*) to think about *ou* over; (*prévoir*) to think of; **faire ~ à** to remind one of; **~ faire qch** to be thinking of doing sth, intend to do sth; **pensif, -ive** *adj* pensive, thoughtful

pension [pɑ̃sjɔ̃] *nf* (*allocation*) pension; (*prix du logement*) board and lodgings, bed and board; (*école*) boarding school; **~ alimentaire** (*de divorcée*) maintenance allowance, alimony; **~ complète** full board; **~ (de famille)** boarding house, guest-house; **pensionnaire** *nm/f* (SCOL) boarder; **pensionnat** *nm* boarding school

pente [pɑ̃t] *nf* slope; **en ~** sloping

Pentecôte [pɑ̃tkot] *nf*: **la ~** Whitsun (BRIT), Pentecost

pénurie [penyʀi] *nf* shortage

pépé [pepe] (*fam*) *nm* grandad

pépin [pepɛ̃] *nm* (BOT: *graine*) pip; (*ennui*) snag, hitch

pépinière [pepinjɛʀ] *nf* nursery

perçant, e [pɛʀsɑ̃, ɑ̃t] *adj* (*cri*) piercing, shrill; (*regard*) piercing

percée [pɛʀse] *nf* (*trouée*) opening; (MIL, *technologique*) breakthrough

perce-neige [pɛʀsənɛʒ] *nf inv* snowdrop

percepteur [pɛʀsɛptœʀ, tʀis] *nm* tax collector

perception [pɛʀsɛpsjɔ̃] *nf* perception; (*bureau*) tax office

percer [pɛʀse] *vt* to pierce; (*ouverture etc*) to make; (*mystère, énigme*) to penetrate ♦ *vi* to break through; **perceuse** *nf* drill

percevoir [pɛʀsəvwaʀ] *vt* (*distinguer*) to perceive, detect; (*taxe, impôt*) to collect; (*revenu, indemnité*) to receive

perche [pɛʀʃ] *nf* (*bâton*) pole

percher [pɛʀʃe] *vt*, *vi* to perch; **se ~** *vi* to perch; **perchoir** *nm* perch

perçois *etc* [pɛʀswa] *vb voir* **percevoir**

percolateur [pɛʀkɔlatœʀ] *nm* percolator

perçu, e [pɛʀsy] *pp de* **percevoir**

percussion [pɛʀkysjɔ̃] *nf* percussion

percuter [pɛʀkyte] *vt* to strike; (*suj: véhicule*) to crash into

perdant, e [pɛʀdɑ̃, ɑ̃t] *nm/f* loser

perdre [pɛʀdʀ] *vt* to lose; (*gaspiller: temps, argent*) to waste; (*personne: moralement etc*) to ruin ♦ *vi* to lose; (*sur une vente etc*) to lose out; **se ~** *vi* (*s'égarer*) to get lost, lose one's way; (*denrées*) to go to waste

perdrix [pɛʀdʀi] *nf* partridge

perdu, e [pɛʀdy] *pp de* **perdre** ♦ *adj* (*isolé*) out-of-the-way; (COMM: *emballage*) non-returnable; (*malade*): **il est ~** there's no hope left for him; **à vos moments ~s** in your spare time

père [pɛʀ] *nm* father; **~ de famille** father; **le ~ Noël** Father Christmas

perfection [pɛʀfɛksjɔ̃] *nf* perfection; **à la ~** to perfection; **perfectionné, e** *adj* sophisticated; **perfectionner** *vt* to improve, perfect

perforatrice [pɛʀfɔʀatʀis] *nf* (*de bureau*) punch

perforer [pɛʀfɔʀe] *vt* (*poinçonner*) to punch

performant, e [pɛʀfɔʀmɑ̃, ɑ̃t] *adj*: **très ~** high-performance *cpd*

perfusion [pɛʀfyzjɔ̃] *nf*: **faire une ~ à qn** to put sb on a drip

péricliter [peʀiklite] *vi* to collapse

péril [peʀil] *nm* peril

périmé, e [peʀime] *adj* (*ADMIN*) out-of-date, expired

périmètre [peʀimɛtʀ] *nm* perimeter

période [peʀjɔd] *nf* period; **périodique** *adj* periodic ♦ *nm* periodical

péripéties [peʀipesi] *nfpl* events, episodes

périphérique [peʀifeʀik] *adj* (*quartiers*) outlying ♦ *nm* (*AUTO*) ring road

périple [peʀipl] *nm* journey

périr [peʀiʀ] *vi* to die, perish

périssable [peʀisabl] *adj* perishable

perle [pɛʀl] *nf* pearl; (*de plastique, métal, sueur*) bead

permanence [pɛʀmanɑ̃s] *nf* permanence; (*local*) (duty) office; **assurer une ~** (*service public, bureaux*) to operate *ou* maintain a basic service; **être de ~** to be on call *ou* duty; **en ~** continuously

permanent, e [pɛʀmanɑ̃, ɑ̃t] *adj* permanent; (*spectacle*) continuous; **permanente** *nf* perm

perméable [pɛʀmeabl] *adj* (*terrain*) permeable; **~ à** (*fig*) receptive *ou* open to

permettre [pɛʀmɛtʀ] *vt* to allow, permit; **~ à qn de faire/qch** to allow sb to do/ sth; **se ~ de faire** to take the liberty of doing

permis [pɛʀmi, iz] *nm* permit, licence; **~ de chasse** hunting permit; **~ (de conduire)** (driving) licence (*BRIT*), (driver's) license (*US*); **~ de construire** planning permission (*BRIT*), building permit (*US*); **~ de séjour** residence permit; **~ de travail** work permit

permission [pɛʀmisjɔ̃] *nf* permission; (*MIL*) leave; **avoir la ~ de faire** to have permission to do; **en ~** on leave

permuter [pɛʀmyte] *vt* to change around, permutate ♦ *vi* to change, swap

Pérou [peʀu] *nm* Peru

perpétuel, le [pɛʀpetɥɛl] *adj* perpetual; **perpétuité** *nf*: **à perpétuité** for life; **être condamné à perpétuité** to receive a life sentence

perplexe [pɛʀplɛks] *adj* perplexed, puzzled

perquisitionner [pɛʀkizisjɔne] *vi* to carry out a search

perron [pɛʀɔ̃] *nm* steps *pl* (*leading to entrance*)

perroquet [pɛʀɔkɛ] *nm* parrot

perruche [peʀyʃ] *nf* budgerigar (*BRIT*), budgie (*BRIT*), parakeet (*US*)

perruque [peʀyk] *nf* wig

persan, e [pɛʀsɑ̃, an] *adj* Persian

persécuter [pɛʀsekyte] *vt* to persecute

persévérer [pɛʀseveʀe] *vi* to persevere

persiennes [pɛʀsjɛn] *nfpl* shutters

persil [pɛʀsi] *nm* parsley

Persique [pɛʀsik] *adj*: **le golfe ~** the (Persian) Gulf

persistant, e [pɛʀsistɑ̃, ɑ̃t] *adj* persistent

persister [pɛʀsiste] *vi* to persist; **~ à faire qch** to persist in doing sth

personnage [pɛʀsɔnaʒ] *nm* (*individu*) character, individual; (*célébrité*) important person; (*de roman, film*) character; (*PEINTURE*) figure

personnalité [pɛʀsɔnalite] *nf* personality; (*personnage*) prominent figure

personne [pɛʀsɔn] *nf* person ♦ *pron* nobody, no one; (*avec négation en anglais*) anybody, anyone; **~s** *nfpl* (*gens*) people *pl*; **il n'y a ~** there's nobody there, there isn't anybody there; **~ âgée** elderly person; **personnel, le** *adj* personal; (*égoïste*) selfish ♦ *nm* staff, personnel; **personnel-**

lement *adv* personally

perspective [pɛʀspɛktiv] *nf* (ART) perspective; (*vue*) view; (*point de vue*) viewpoint, angle; (*chose envisagée*) prospect; **en ~** in prospect

perspicace [pɛʀspikas] *adj* clear-sighted, gifted with (*ou* showing) insight; **perspicacité** *nf* clear-sightedness

persuader [pɛʀsɥade] *vt*: **~ qn (de faire)** to persuade sb (to do)

persuasif, -ive [pɛʀsɥazif, iv] *adj* persuasive

perte [pɛʀt] *nf* loss; (*de temps*) waste; (*fig: morale*) ruin; **à ~ de vue** as far as the eye can (*ou* could) see; **~s blanches** (vaginal) discharge *sg*

pertinemment [pɛʀtinamɑ̃] *adv* (*savoir*) full well

pertinent, e [pɛʀtinɑ̃, ɑ̃t] *adj* apt, relevant

perturbation [pɛʀtyʀbasjɔ̃] *nf*: **~ (atmosphérique)** atmospheric disturbance

perturber [pɛʀtyʀbe] *vt* to disrupt; (PSYCH) to perturb, disturb

pervers, e [pɛʀvɛʀ, ɛʀs] *adj* perverted

pervertir [pɛʀvɛʀtiʀ] *vt* to pervert

pesant, e [pəzɑ̃, ɑ̃t] *adj* heavy; (*fig: présence*) burdensome

pèse-personne [pɛzpɛʀsɔn] *nm* (bathroom) scales *pl*

peser [pəze] *vt* to weigh ♦ *vi* to weigh; (*fig: avoir de l'importance*) to carry weight; **~ lourd** to be heavy

pessimisme [pesimism] *nm* pessimism

pessimiste [pesimist] *adj* pessimistic ♦ *nm/f* pessimist

peste [pɛst] *nf* plague

pester [pɛste] *vi*: **~ contre** to curse

pétale [petal] *nm* petal

pétanque [petɑ̃k] *nf* type of bowls

---
pétanque
---

i Pétanque, *which originated in the south of France, is a version of the game of* **boules** *played on a variety of hard surfaces. Standing with their feet to-*

gether, *players throw steel bowls towards a wooden jack.*

---

pétarader [petaʀade] *vi* to backfire

pétard [petaʀ] *nm* banger (BRIT), firecracker

péter [pete] *vi* (*fam: casser*) to bust; (*fam!*) to fart (*!*)

pétillant, e [petijɑ̃, ɑ̃t] *adj* sparkling

pétiller [petije] *vi* (*feu*) to crackle; (*champagne*) to bubble; (*yeux*) to sparkle

petit, e [p(ə)ti, it] *adj* small; (*avec nuance affective*) little; (*voyage*) short, little; (*bruit etc*) faint, slight; **~s** *nmpl* (*d'un animal*) young *pl*; **les tout~s** the little ones, the tiny tots; **~ à ~** bit by bit, gradually; **~(e) ami(e)** boyfriend/girlfriend; **~ déjeuner** breakfast; **~ pain** (bread) roll; **les ~es annonces** the small ads; **~s pois** garden peas; **petite-fille** *nf* granddaughter; **petit-fils** *nm* grandson

pétition [petisjɔ̃] *nf* petition

petits-enfants [pətizɑ̃fɑ̃] *nmpl* grandchildren

petit-suisse [pətisɥis] (*pl* **~s-~s**) *nm* small individual pot of cream cheese

pétrin [petʀɛ̃] *nm* (*fig*): **dans le ~** (*fam*) in a jam *ou* fix

pétrir [petʀiʀ] *vt* to knead

pétrole [petʀɔl] *nm* oil; (*pour lampe, réchaud etc*) paraffin (oil); **pétrolier, -ière** *nm* oil tanker

---
MOT-CLÉ
---

peu [pø] *adv* **1** (*modifiant verbe, adjectif, adverbe*): **il boit peu** he doesn't drink (very) much; **il est peu bavard** he's not very talkative; **peu avant/après** shortly before/afterwards

2 (*modifiant nom*): **peu de**: **peu de gens/d'arbres** few *ou* not (very) many people/trees; **il a peu d'espoir** he hasn't (got) much hope, he has little hope; **pour peu de temps** for (only) a short while

3: **peu à peu** little by little; **à peu près** just about, more or less; **à peu près 10**

kg/10 F approximately 10 kg/10F
♦ *nm* **1: le peu de gens qui** the few people who; **le peu de sable qui** what little sand, the little sand which
2: un peu a little; **un petit peu** a little bit; **un peu d'espoir** a little hope
♦ *pron:* **peu le savent** few know (it); **avant** *ou* **sous peu** shortly, before long; **de peu** (only) just

peuple [pœpl] *nm* people; **peupler** *vt* (*pays, région*) to populate; (*étang*) to stock; (*suj: hommes, poissons*) to inhabit
peuplier [pøplije] *nm* poplar (tree)
peur [pœʀ] *nf* fear; **avoir ~ (de/de faire/ que)** to be frightened *ou* afraid (of/of doing/that); **faire ~ à** to frighten; **de ~ de/que** for fear of/that; **peureux, -euse** *adj* fearful, timorous
peut [pø] *vb voir* **pouvoir**
peut-être [pøtetʀ] *adv* perhaps, maybe; **~-~ que** perhaps, maybe; **~-~ bien qu'il fera/est** he may well do/be
peux *etc* [pø] *vb voir* **pouvoir**
phare [faʀ] *nm* lighthouse; (*de véhicule*) headlight; **~s de recul** reversing lights
pharmacie [faʀmasi] *nf* (*magasin*) chemist's (*BRIT*), pharmacy; (*de salle de bain*) medicine cabinet; **pharmacien, ne** *nm/f* pharmacist, chemist (*BRIT*)
phénomène [fenɔmɛn] *nm* phenomenon
philatélie [filateli] *nf* philately, stamp collecting
philosophe [filɔzɔf] *nm/f* philosopher ♦ *adj* philosophical
philosophie [filɔzɔfi] *nf* philosophy
phobie [fɔbi] *nf* phobia
phonétique [fɔnetik] *nf* phonetics *sg*
phoque [fɔk] *nm* seal
phosphorescent, e [fɔsfɔʀesɑ̃, ɑ̃t] *adj* luminous
photo [fɔto] *nf* photo(graph); **prendre en ~** to take a photo of; **faire de la ~** to take photos; **~ d'identité** passport photograph; **photocopie** *nf* photocopy; **photocopier** *vt* to photocopy; **photoco-**

pieuse *nf* photocopier; **photographe** *nm/f* photographer; **photographie** *nf* (*technique*) photography; (*cliché*) photograph; **photographier** *vt* to photograph
phrase [fʀɑz] *nf* sentence
physicien, ne [fizisjɛ̃, jɛn] *nm/f* physicist
physionomie [fizjɔnɔmi] *nf* face
physique [fizik] *adj* physical ♦ *nm* physique ♦ *nf* physics *sg*; **au ~** physically; **physiquement** *adv* physically
piailler [pjɑje] *vi* to squawk
pianiste [pjanist] *nm/f* pianist
piano [pjano] *nm* piano; **pianoter** *vi* to tinkle away (at the piano)
pic [pik] *nm* (*instrument*) pick(axe); (*montagne*) peak; (*ZOOL*) woodpecker; **à ~** vertically; (*fig: tomber, arriver*) just at the right time
pichet [piʃɛ] *nm* jug
picorer [pikɔʀe] *vt* to peck
picoter [pikɔte] *vt* (*suj: oiseau*) to peck ♦ *vi* (*irriter*) to smart, prickle
pie [pi] *nf* magpie
pièce [pjɛs] *nf* (*d'un logement*) room; (*THÉÂTRE*) play; (*de machine*) part; (*de monnaie*) coin; (*document*) document; (*fragment, de collection*) piece; **dix francs la ~** ten francs each; **vendre à la ~** to sell separately; **travailler à la ~** to do piecework; **un maillot une ~** a one-piece swimsuit; **un deux-~s cuisine** a two-room(ed) flat (*BRIT*) *ou* apartment (*US*) with kitchen; **~ à conviction** exhibit; **~ d'identité: avez-vous une ~ d'identité?** have you got any (means of) identification?; **~ montée** tiered cake; **~s détachées** spares, (spare) parts; **~s justificatives** supporting documents
pied [pje] *nm* foot; (*de table*) leg; (*de lampe*) base; **à ~** on foot; **au ~ de la lettre** literally; **avoir ~** to be able to touch the bottom, not to be out of one's depth; **avoir le ~ marin** to be a good sailor; **sur ~** (*debout, rétabli*) up and about; **mettre sur ~** (*entreprise*) to set up; **c'est le ~** (*fam*) it's brilliant; **mettre les ~s dans le**

plat (*fam*) to put one's foot in it; **il se débrouille comme un ~** (*fam*) he's completely useless; **pied-noir** *nm* Algerian-born Frenchman

piège [pjɛʒ] *nm* trap; **prendre au ~** to trap; **piéger** *vt* (*avec une bombe*) to booby-trap; **lettre/voiture piégée** letter-/car-bomb

pierre [pjɛʀ] *nf* stone; **~ précieuse** precious stone, gem; **~ tombale** tombstone; **pierreries** *nfpl* gems, precious stones

piétiner [pjetine] *vi* (*trépigner*) to stamp (one's foot); (*fig*) to be at a standstill ♦ *vt* to trample on

piéton, ne [pjetɔ̃, ɔn] *nm/f* pedestrian; **piétonnier, -ière** *adj*: **rue** *ou* **zone piétonnière** pedestrian precinct

pieu, x [pjø] *nm* post; (*pointu*) stake

pieuvre [pjœvʀ] *nf* octopus

pieux, -euse [pjø, pjøz] *adj* pious

piffer [pife] (*fam*) *vt*: **je ne peux pas le ~** I can't stand him

pigeon [piʒɔ̃] *nm* pigeon

piger [piʒe] (*fam*) *vi, vt* to understand

pigiste [piʒist] *nm/f* freelance(r)

pignon [piɲɔ̃] *nm* (*de mur*) gable

pile [pil] *nf* (*tas*) pile; (*ÉLEC*) battery ♦ *adv* (*fam: s'arrêter etc*) dead; **à deux heures ~** at two on the dot; **jouer à ~ ou face** to toss up (for it); **~ ou face?** heads or tails?

piler [pile] *vt* to crush, pound

pilier [pilje] *nm* pillar

piller [pije] *vt* to pillage, plunder, loot

pilote [pilɔt] *nm* pilot; (*de voiture*) driver ♦ *adj* pilot *cpd*; **~ de course** racing driver; **~ de ligne/d'essai/de chasse** airline/test/fighter pilot; **piloter** *vt* (*avion*) to pilot, fly; (*voiture*) to drive

pilule [pilyl] *nf* pill; **prendre la ~** to be on the pill

piment [pimɑ̃] *nm* (*aussi: ~ rouge*) chilli; (*fig*) spice, piquancy; **~ doux** pepper, capsicum; **pimenté, e** *adj* (*plat*) hot, spicy

pimpant, e [pɛ̃pɑ̃, ɑ̃t] *adj* spruce

pin [pɛ̃] *nm* pine

pinard [pinaʀ] (*fam*) *nm* (cheap) wine,

plonk (*BRIT*)

pince [pɛ̃s] *nf* (*outil*) pliers *pl*; (*de homard, crabe*) pincer, claw; (*COUTURE: pli*) dart; **~ à épiler** tweezers *pl*; **~ à linge** clothes peg (*BRIT*) *ou* pin (*US*)

pincé, e [pɛ̃se] *adj* (*air*) stiff

pinceau, x [pɛ̃so] *nm* (paint)brush

pincée [pɛ̃se] *nf*: **une ~ de** a pinch of

pincer [pɛ̃se] *vt* to pinch; (*fam*) to nab

pinède [pined] *nf* pinewood, pine forest

pingouin [pɛ̃gwɛ̃] *nm* penguin

ping-pong ® [piŋpɔ̃g] *nm* table tennis

pingre [pɛ̃gʀ] *adj* niggardly

pinson [pɛ̃sɔ̃] *nm* chaffinch

pintade [pɛ̃tad] *nf* guinea-fowl

pioche [pjɔʃ] *nf* pickaxe; **piocher** *vt* to dig up (with a pickaxe); **piocher dans** (*le tas, ses économies*) to dig into

pion [pjɔ̃] *nm* (*ÉCHECS*) pawn; (*DAMES*) piece; (*SCOL*) supervisor

pionnier [pjɔnje] *nm* pioneer

pipe [pip] *nf* pipe; **fumer la ~** to smoke a pipe

pipeau, x [pipo] *nm* (reed-)pipe

piquant, e [pikɑ̃, ɑ̃t] *adj* (*barbe, rosier etc*) prickly; (*saveur, sauce*) hot, pungent; (*détail*) titillating; (*froid*) biting ♦ *nm* (*épine*) thorn, prickle; (*fig*) spiciness, spice

pique [pik] *nf* pike; (*fig*) cutting remark ♦ *nm* (*CARTES*) spades *pl*

pique-nique [piknik] *nm* picnic; **pique-niquer** *vi* to have a picnic

piquer [pike] *vt* (*suj: guêpe, fumée, orties*) to sting; (: *moustique*) to bite; (: *barbe*) to prick; (: *froid*) to bite; (*MÉD*) to give a jab to; (: *chien, chat*) to put to sleep; (*intérêt*) to arouse; (*fam: voler*) to pinch ♦ *vi* (*avion*) to go into a dive; **se ~** (*avec une aiguille*) to prick o.s.; (*dans les orties*) to get stung; (*suj: toxicomane*) to shoot up; **~ une colère** to fly into a rage

piquet [pike] *nm* (*pieu*) post, stake; (*de tente*) peg; **~ de grève** (strike-)picket

piqûre [pikyʀ] *nf* (*d'épingle*) prick; (*d'ortie*) sting; (*de moustique*) bite; (*MÉD*) injection, shot (*US*); **faire une ~ à qn** to give sb an injection

pirate [piʀat] *nm, adj* pirate; **~ de l'air** hijacker

pire [piʀ] *adj* worse; *(superlatif):* **le(la) ~ ...** the worst ... ♦ *nm:* **le ~ (de)** the worst (of); **au ~** at (the very) worst

pis [pi] *nm (de vache)* udder; *(pire):* **le ~** the worst ♦ *adj, adv* worse; **de mal en ~** from bad to worse

piscine [pisin] *nf* (swimming) pool; **~ couverte** indoor (swimming) pool

pissenlit [pisɑ̃li] *nm* dandelion

pistache [pistaʃ] *nf* pistachio (nut)

piste [pist] *nf (d'un animal, sentier)* track, trail; *(indice)* lead; *(de stade)* track; *(de cirque)* ring; *(de danse)* floor; *(de patinage)* rink; *(de ski)* run; *(AVIAT)* runway; **~ cyclable** cycle track

pistolet [pistɔlɛ] *nm (arme)* pistol, gun; *(à peinture)* spray gun; **pistolet-mitrailleur** *nm* submachine gun

piston [pistɔ̃] *nm (TECH)* piston; **avoir du ~** *(fam)* to have friends in the right places; **pistonner** *vt (candidat)* to pull strings for

piteux, -euse [pitø, øz] *adj* pitiful, sorry *(avant le nom)*

pitié [pitje] *nf* pity; **il me fait ~** I feel sorry for him; **avoir ~ de** *(compassion)* to pity, feel sorry for; *(merci)* to have pity *ou* mercy on

pitoyable [pitwajabl] *adj* pitiful

pitre [pitʀ] *nm* clown; **pitrerie** *nf* tomfoolery *no pl*

pittoresque [pitɔʀɛsk] *adj* picturesque

pivot [pivo] *nm* pivot; **pivoter** *vi* to revolve; *(fauteuil)* to swivel

P.J. *sigle f* (= *police judiciaire*) ≃ CID *(BRIT)*, ≃ FBI *(US)*

placard [plakaʀ] *nm (armoire)* cupboard; *(affiche)* poster, notice

place [plas] *nf (emplacement, classement)* place; *(de ville, village)* square; *(espace libre)* room, space; *(de parking)* space; *(siège: de train, cinéma, voiture)* seat; *(emploi)* job; **en ~** *(mettre)* in its place; **sur ~** on the spot; **faire ~ à** to give way to; **ça prend de la**

~ it takes up a lot of room *ou* space; **à la ~ de** in place of, instead of; **à ta ~ ...** if I were you ...; **se mettre à la ~ de qn** to put o.s. in sb's place *ou* in sb's shoes

placé, e [plase] *adj:* **être bien/mal ~** *(spectateur)* to have a good/a poor seat; *(concurrent)* to be in a good/bad position; **il est bien ~ pour le savoir** he is in a position to know

placement [plasmɑ̃] *nm (FINANCE)* investment; **bureau de ~** employment agency

placer [plase] *vt (convive, spectateur)* to seat; *(argent)* to place, invest; **il n'a pas pu ~ un mot** he couldn't get a word in; **se ~ au premier rang** to go and stand *ou* sit in the first row

plafond [plafɔ̃] *nm* ceiling

plage [plaʒ] *nf* beach

plagiat [plaʒja] *nm* plagiarism

plaid [plɛd] *nm (tartan)* car rug

plaider [plede] *vi (avocat)* to plead ♦ *vt* to plead; **~ pour** *(fig)* to speak for; **plaidoyer** *nm (JUR)* speech for the defence; *(fig)* plea

plaie [plɛ] *nf* wound

plaignant, e [plɛɲɑ̃, ɑ̃t] *nm/f* plaintiff

plaindre [plɛ̃dʀ] *vt* to pity, feel sorry for; **se ~** *vi (gémir)* to moan; *(protester):* **se ~ (à qn) (de)** to complain (to sb) (about); *(souffrir):* **se ~ de** to complain of

plaine [plɛn] *nf* plain

plain-pied [plɛ̃pje] *adv:* **de ~-~ (avec)** on the same level (as)

plainte [plɛ̃t] *nf (gémissement)* moan, groan; *(doléance)* complaint; **porter ~** to lodge a complaint

plaire [plɛʀ] *vi* to be a success, be successful; **ça plaît beaucoup aux jeunes** it's very popular with young people; **~ à: cela me plaît** I like it; **se ~ quelque part** to like being somewhere *ou* like it somewhere; **j'irai si ça me plaît** I'll go if I feel like it; **s'il vous plaît** please

plaisance [plɛzɑ̃s] *nf (aussi:* **navigation de ~)** (pleasure) sailing, yachting

plaisant, e [plɛzɑ̃, ɑ̃t] *adj* pleasant; *(his-*

toire, anecdote) amusing

plaisanter [plɛzɑ̃te] *vi* to joke; **plaisanterie** *nf* joke

plaise *etc* [plɛz] *vb voir* **plaire**

plaisir [pleziʀ] *nm* pleasure; **faire ~ à qn** *(délibérément)* to be nice to sb, please sb; **ça me fait ~** I like (doing) it; **j'espère que ça te fera ~** I hope you'll like it; **pour le ~** for pleasure

plaît [plɛ] *vb voir* **plaire**

plan, e [plɑ̃, an] *adj* flat ♦ *nm* plan; *(fig)* level, plane; *(CINÉMA)* shot; **au premier/ second ~** in the foreground/middle distance; **à l'arrière ~** in the background; **rester en ~** *(fam)* to be left stranded; **laisser en ~** *(fam: travail)* to drop, abandon; **~ d'eau** lake

planche [plɑ̃ʃ] *nf (pièce de bois)* plank, (wooden) board; *(illustration)* plate; **~ à repasser** ironing board; **~ à roulettes** skateboard; **~ à voile** *(sport)* windsurfing

plancher [plɑ̃ʃe] *nm* floor; floorboards *pl* ♦ *vi (fam)* to work hard

planer [plane] *vi* to glide; *(fam: rêveur)* to have one's head in the clouds; **~ sur** *(fig: danger)* to hang over

planète [planɛt] *nf* planet

planeur [planœʀ] *nm* glider

planification [planifikasjɔ̃] *nf (economic)* planning

planifier [planifje] *vt* to plan

planning [planiŋ] *nm* programme, schedule

planque [plɑ̃k] *nf (fam) (emploi peu fatigant)* cushy *(BRIT)* ou easy number; *(cachette)* hiding place

plant [plɑ̃] *nm* seedling, young plant

plante [plɑ̃t] *nf* plant; **~ d'appartement** house ou pot plant; **~ des pieds** sole (of the foot)

planter [plɑ̃te] *vt (plante)* to plant; *(enfoncer)* to hammer ou drive in; *(tente)* to put up, pitch; *(fam: personne)* to dump; **se ~** *(fam: se tromper)* to get it wrong

plantureux, -euse [plɑ̃tyʀø, øz] *adj* copious, lavish; *(femme)* buxom

plaque [plak] *nf* plate; *(de verglas, d'eczéma)* patch; *(avec inscription)* plaque; **~ chauffante** hotplate; **~ de chocolat** bar of chocolate; **~ (minéralogique ou d'immatriculation)** number *(BRIT)* ou license *(US)* plate; **~ tournante** *(fig)* centre

plaqué, e [plake] *adj*: **~ or/argent** gold-/ silver-plated

plaquer [plake] *vt (aplatir)*: **~ qch sur** ou **contre** to make sth stick ou cling to; *(RUGBY)* to bring down; *(fam: laisser tomber)* to drop

plaquette [plakɛt] *nf (de chocolat)* bar; *(beurre)* pack(et); **~ de frein** brake pad

plastique [plastik] *adj, nm* plastic; **plastiquer** *vt* to blow up *(with a plastic bomb)*

plat, e [pla, -at] *adj* flat; *(cheveux)* straight; *(style)* flat, dull ♦ *nm (récipient, CULIN)* dish; *(d'un repas)* course; **à ~ ventre** face down; **à ~** *(pneu, batterie)* flat; *(fam: personne)* dead beat; **~ cuisiné** pre-cooked meal; **~ de résistance** main course; **~ du jour** dish of the day

platane [platan] *nm* plane tree

plateau, x [plato] *nm (support)* tray; *(GÉO)* plateau; *(CINÉMA)* set; **~ de fromages** cheeseboard

plate-bande [platbɑ̃d] *nf* flower bed

plate-forme [platfɔʀm] *nf* platform; **~-~ de forage/pétrolière** drilling/oil rig

platine [platin] *nm* platinum ♦ *nf (d'un tourne-disque)* turntable

plâtre [platʀ] *nm (matériau)* plaster; *(statue)* plaster statue; *(MÉD)* (plaster) cast; **avoir un bras dans le ~** to have an arm in plaster

plein, e [plɛ̃, plɛn] *adj* full ♦ *nm*: **faire le ~ (d'essence)** to fill up (with petrol); **à ~es mains** *(ramasser)* in handfuls; **à ~ temps** full-time; **en ~ air** in the open air; **en ~ soleil** in direct sunlight; **en ~e nuit/rue** in the middle of the night/street; **en ~ jour** in broad daylight

pleurer [plœʀe] *vi* to cry; *(yeux)* to water ♦ *vt* to mourn (for); **~ sur** to lament (over), to bemoan

pleurnicher [plœʀniʃe] *vi* to snivel, whine

pleurs [plœʀ] *nmpl*: **en ~** in tears

pleut [plø] *vb voir* **pleuvoir**

pleuvoir [pløvwaʀ] *vb impers* to rain ♦ *vi* (*coups*) to rain down; (*critiques, invitations*) to shower down; **il pleut** it's raining

pli [pli] *nm* fold; (*de jupe*) pleat; (*de pantalon*) crease; **prendre le ~ de faire** to get into the habit of doing; **un mauvais ~** a bad habit

pliant, e [plijɑ̃, plijɑ̃t] *adj* folding

plier [plije] *vt* to fold; (*pour ranger*) to fold up; (*genou, bras*) to bend ♦ *vi* to bend; **se ~** *vi* to fold; **se ~ à** to submit to

plinthe [plɛ̃t] *nf* skirting board

plisser [plise] *vt* (*jupe*) to put pleats in; (*yeux*) to screw up; (*front*) to crease

plomb [plɔ̃] *nm* (*métal*) lead; (*d'une cartouche*) (lead) shot; (*PÊCHE*) sinker; (*ÉLEC*) fuse; **sans ~** (*essence etc*) unleaded

plombage [plɔ̃baʒ] *nm* (*de dent*) filling

plomberie [plɔ̃bʀi] *nf* plumbing

plombier [plɔ̃bje] *nm* plumber

plonge [plɔ̃ʒ] *nf* washing-up

plongeant, e [plɔ̃ʒɑ̃, ɑ̃t] *adj* (*vue*) from above; (*décolleté*) plunging

plongée [plɔ̃ʒe] *nf* (*SPORT*) diving *no pl*; (*sans scaphandre*) skin diving; **~ sous-marine** diving

plongeoir [plɔ̃ʒwaʀ] *nm* diving board

plongeon [plɔ̃ʒɔ̃] *nm* dive

plonger [plɔ̃ʒe] *vi* to dive ♦ *vt*: **~ qch dans** to plunge sth into; **se ~ dans** (*études, lecture*) to bury *ou* immerse o.s. in; **plongeur** *nm* diver

ployer [plwaje] *vt, vi* to bend

plu [ply] *pp de* **plaire**; **pleuvoir**

pluie [plɥi] *nf* rain

plume [plym] *nf* feather; (*pour écrire*) (pen) nib; (*fig*) pen

plupart [plypaʀ]: **la ~** *pron* the majority, most (of them); **la ~ des** most, the majority of; **la ~ du temps/d'entre nous** most of the time/of us; **pour la ~** for the most part, mostly

pluriel [plyʀjɛl] *nm* plural

plus¹ [ply] *vb voir* **plaire**

MOT-CLÉ
---

plus² [ply] *adv* **1** (*forme négative*): **ne ... plus** no more, no longer; **je n'ai plus d'argent** I've got no more money *ou* no money left; **il ne travaille plus** he's no longer working, he doesn't work any more

2 (*comparatif*) more, ...+er; (*superlatif*): **le plus** the most, the ...+est; **plus grand/intelligent (que)** bigger/more intelligent (than); **le plus grand/intelligent** the biggest/most intelligent; **tout au plus** at the very most

3 (*davantage*) more; **il travaille plus (que)** he works more (than); **plus il travaille, plus il est heureux** the more he works, the happier he is; **plus de pain** more bread; **plus de 10 personnes** more than 10 people, over 10 people; **3 heures de plus que** 3 hours more than; **de plus** what's more, moreover; **3 kilos en plus** 3 kilos more; **en plus de** in addition to; **de plus en plus** more and more; **plus ou moins** more or less; **ni plus ni moins** no more, no less

♦ *prép*: **4 plus 2** 4 plus 2

---

plusieurs [plyzjœʀ] *dét, pron* several; **ils sont ~** there are several of them

plus-value [plyvaly] *nf* (*bénéfice*) surplus

plut [ply] *vb voir* **plaire**

plutôt [plyto] *adv* rather; **je préfère ~ celui-ci** I'd rather have this one; **~ que (de) faire** rather than *ou* instead of doing

pluvieux, -euse [plyvjø, jøz] *adj* rainy, wet

PME *sigle f* (= *petite(s) et moyenne(s) entreprise(s)*) small business(es)

PMU *sigle m* (= *Pari mutuel urbain*) system of betting on horses; (*café*) betting agency

PNB *sigle m* (= *produit national brut*) GNP

pneu [pnø] *nm* tyre (*BRIT*), tire (*US*)

pneumonie [pnømɔni] *nf* pneumonia

poche [pɔʃ] *nf* pocket; (*sous les yeux*) bag, pouch; **argent de ~** pocket money

pocher [pɔʃe] *vt* (CULIN) to poach

pochette [pɔʃɛt] *nf* (*d'aiguilles etc*) case; (*mouchoir*) breast pocket handkerchief; (*sac à main*) clutch bag; **~ de disque** record sleeve

poêle [pwal] *nm* stove ♦ *nf*: **~ (à frire)** frying pan

poème [pɔɛm] *nm* poem

poésie [pɔezi] *nf* (*poème*) poem; (*art*): **la ~** poetry

poète [pɔɛt] *nm* poet

poids [pwa] *nm* weight; (SPORT) shot; **vendre au ~** to sell by weight; **prendre du ~** to put on weight; **~ lourd** (*camion*) lorry (BRIT), truck (US)

poignant, e [pwaɲɑ̃, ɑ̃t] *adj* poignant

poignard [pwaɲaʁ] *nm* dagger; **poignarder** *vt* to stab, knife

poigne [pwaɲ] *nf* grip; **avoir de la ~** (*fig*) to rule with a firm hand

poignée [pwaɲe] *nf* (*de sel etc, fig*) handful; (*de couvercle, porte*) handle; **~ de main** handshake

poignet [pwaɲɛ] *nm* (ANAT) wrist; (*de chemise*) cuff

poil [pwal] *nm* (ANAT) hair; (*de pinceau, brosse*) bristle; (*de tapis*) strand; (*pelage*) coat; **à ~** (*fam*) starkers; **au ~** (*fam*) hunky-dory; **poilu, e** *adj* hairy

poinçon [pwɛ̃sɔ̃] *nm* (*marque*) hallmark; **poinçonner** *vt* (*bijou*) to hallmark; (*billet*) to punch

poing [pwɛ̃] *nm* fist; **coup de ~** punch

point [pwɛ̃] *nm* point; (*endroit*) spot; (*marque, signe*) dot; (: *de ponctuation*) full stop, period (US); (COUTURE, TRICOT) stitch ♦ *adv* = **pas²**; **faire le ~** (*fig*) to take stock (of the situation); **sur le ~ de faire** (just) about to do; **à tel ~ que** so much so that; **mettre au ~** (*procédé*) to develop; (*affaire*) to settle; **à ~** (CULIN: *viande*) medium; **à ~ (nommé)** just at the right time; **deux ~s** colon; **~ (de côté)** stitch (*pain*); **~ d'exclamation/d'interrogation** exclamation/question mark; **~ de repère** landmark; (*dans le temps*) point of reference; **~ de suture** (MÉD) stitch; **~ de vente** retail outlet; **~ de vue** viewpoint; (*fig: opinion*) point of view; **~ d'honneur: mettre un ~ d'honneur à faire qch** to make it a point of honour to do sth; **~ faible/fort** weak/strong point; **~ noir** blackhead; **~s de suspension** suspension points

pointe [pwɛ̃t] *nf* point; (*clou*) tack; (*fig*): **une ~ de** a hint of; **être à la ~ de** (*fig*) to be in the forefront of; **sur la ~ des pieds** on tiptoe; **en ~** pointed, tapered; **de ~** (*technique etc*) leading; **heures de ~** peak hours

pointer [pwɛ̃te] *vt* (*diriger: canon, doigt*): **~ sur qch** to point at sth ♦ *vi* (*employé*) to clock in

pointillé [pwɛ̃tije] *nm* (*trait*) dotted line

pointilleux, -euse [pwɛ̃tijø, øz] *adj* particular, pernickety

pointu, e [pwɛ̃ty] *adj* pointed; (*voix*) shrill; (*analyse*) precise

pointure [pwɛ̃tyʁ] *nf* size

point-virgule [pwɛ̃viʁgyl] *nm* semi-colon

poire [pwaʁ] *nf* pear; (*fam: péj*) mug

poireau, x [pwaʁo] *nm* leek

poireauter [pwaʁote] *vi* (*fam*) to be left kicking one's heels

poirier [pwaʁje] *nm* pear tree

pois [pwa] *nm* (BOT) pea; (*sur une étoffe*) dot, spot; **~ chiche** chickpea; **à ~** (*cravate etc*) spotted, polka-dot *cpd*

poison [pwazɔ̃] *nm* poison

poisse [pwas] *nf* (*fam*) rotten luck

poisseux, -euse [pwasø, øz] *adj* sticky

poisson [pwasɔ̃] *nm* fish *gén inv*; **les P~s** (*signe*) Pisces; **~ d'avril!** April fool!; **~ rouge** goldfish; **poissonnerie** *nf* fish-shop; **poissonnier, -ière** *nm/f* fishmonger (BRIT), fish merchant (US)

poitrine [pwatʁin] *nf* chest; (*seins*) bust, bosom; (CULIN) breast

poivre [pwavʁ] *nm* pepper

poivron [pwavʁɔ̃] *nm* pepper, capsicum

polaire [pɔlɛʁ] *adj* polar

polar [pɔlaʀ] (fam) nm detective novel

pôle [pol] nm (GÉO, ÉLEC) pole

poli, e [pɔli] adj polite; (lisse) smooth

police [pɔlis] nf police; ~ d'assurance insurance policy; ~ judiciaire ≃ Criminal Investigation Department (BRIT), ≃ Federal Bureau of Investigation (US); ~ secours ≃ emergency services pl (BRIT), ≃ paramedics pl (US); policier, -ière adj police cpd ♦ nm policeman; (aussi: roman policier) detective novel

polio [pɔljo] nf polio

polir [pɔliʀ] vt to polish

polisson, ne [pɔlisɔ̃, ɔn] nm/f (enfant) (little) rascal

politesse [pɔlites] nf politeness

politicien, ne [pɔlitisjɛ̃, jɛn] (péj) nm/f politician

politique [pɔlitik] adj political ♦ nf politics sg; (mesures, méthode) policies pl

pollen [pɔlen] nm pollen

polluant, e [pɔlɥɑ̃, ɑ̃t] adj polluting; produit ~ pollutant

polluer [pɔlɥe] vt to pollute; pollution nf pollution

polo [pɔlo] nm (chemise) polo shirt

Pologne [pɔlɔɲ] nf: la ~ Poland; polonais, e adj Polish ♦ nm/f: Polonais, e Pole ♦ nm (LING) Polish

poltron, ne [pɔltʀɔ̃, ɔn] adj cowardly

polycopier [pɔlikɔpje] vt to duplicate

Polynésie [pɔlinezi] nf: la ~ Polynesia

polyvalent, e [pɔlivalɑ̃, ɑ̃t] adj (rôle) varied; (salle) multi-purpose

pommade [pɔmad] nf ointment, cream

pomme [pɔm] nf apple; tomber dans les ~s (fam) to pass out; ~ d'Adam Adam's apple; ~ de pin pine ou fir cone; ~ de terre potato

pommeau, x [pɔmo] nm (boule) knob; (de selle) pommel

pommette [pɔmɛt] nf cheekbone

pommier [pɔmje] nm apple tree

pompe [pɔ̃p] nf pump; (faste) pomp (and ceremony); ~ à essence petrol pump; ~s funèbres funeral parlour sg, undertaker's

sg; pomper vt to pump; (aspirer) to pump up; (absorber) to soak up

pompeux, -euse [pɔ̃pø, øz] adj pompous

pompier [pɔ̃pje] nm fireman

pompiste [pɔ̃pist] nm/f petrol (BRIT) ou gas (US) pump attendant

poncer [pɔ̃se] vt to sand (down)

ponctuation [pɔ̃ktɥasjɔ̃] nf punctuation

ponctuel, le [pɔ̃ktɥɛl] adj punctual

pondéré, e [pɔ̃deʀe] adj level-headed, composed

pondre [pɔ̃dʀ] vt to lay

poney [pɔnɛ] nm pony

pont [pɔ̃] nm bridge; (NAVIG) deck; faire le ~ to take the extra day off; ~ suspendu suspension bridge; pont-levis nm drawbridge

---

faire le pont

ⓘ The expression **"faire le pont"** refers to the practice of taking a Monday or Friday off to make a long weekend if a public holiday falls on a Tuesday or Thursday. The French often do this at l'Ascension, l'Assomption and le 14 juillet.

---

pop [pɔp] adj inv pop

populace [pɔpylas] (péj) nf rabble

populaire [pɔpylɛʀ] adj popular; (manifestation) mass cpd; (milieux, quartier) working-class; (expression) vernacular

popularité [pɔpylaʀite] nf popularity

population [pɔpylasjɔ̃] nf population; ~ active working population

populeux, -euse [pɔpylø, øz] adj densely populated

porc [pɔʀ] nm pig; (CULIN) pork

porcelaine [pɔʀsəlɛn] nf porcelain, china; piece of china(ware)

porc-épic [pɔʀkepik] nm porcupine

porche [pɔʀʃ] nm porch

porcherie [pɔʀʃəʀi] nf pigsty

pore [pɔʀ] nm pore

porno [pɔʀno] adj porno ♦ nm porn

port [pɔʀ] *nm* harbour, port; (*ville*) port; (*de l'uniforme etc*) wearing; (*pour lettre*) postage; (*pour colis, aussi: posture*) carriage; **~ de pêche/de plaisance** fishing/sailing harbour

portable [pɔʀtabl] *nm* (COMPUT) laptop (computer); (*téléphone*) mobile

portail [pɔʀtaj] *nm* gate

portant, e [pɔʀtɑ̃, ɑ̃t] *adj*: **bien/mal ~** in good/poor health

portatif, -ive [pɔʀtatif, iv] *adj* portable

porte [pɔʀt] *nf* door; (*de ville, jardin*) gate; **mettre à la ~** to throw out; **~ à ~** ♦ *nm* door-to-door selling; **~ d'entrée** front door; porte-avions *nm inv* aircraft carrier; porte-bagages *nm inv* luggage rack; porte-bonheur *nm inv* lucky charm; porte-clefs *nm inv* key ring; porte-documents *nm inv* attaché *ou* document case

porté, e [pɔʀte] *adj*: **être ~ à faire** to be inclined to do; **être ~ sur qch** to be keen on sth; **portée** *nf* (*d'une arme*) range; (*fig: effet*) impact, import; (: *capacité*) scope, capability; (*de chatte etc*) litter; (MUS) stave, staff; **à/hors de portée (de)** within/out of reach (of); **à portée de (la) main** within (arm's) reach; **à la portée de qn** (*fig*) at sb's level, within sb's capabilities

porte...: porte-fenêtre *nf* French window; portefeuille *nm* wallet; portemanteau, x *nm* (*cintre*) coat hanger; (*au mur*) coat rack; porte-monnaie *nm inv* purse; porte-parole *nm inv* spokesman

porter [pɔʀte] *vt* to carry; (*sur soi: vêtement, barbe, bague*) to wear; (*fig: responsabilité etc*) to bear, carry; (*inscription, nom, fruits*) to bear; (*coup*) to deal; (*attention*) to turn; (*apporter*): **~ qch à qn** to take sth to sb ♦ *vi* (*voix*) to carry; (*coup, argument*) to hit home; **se ~** *vi* (*se sentir*): **se ~ bien/mal** to be well/unwell; **~ sur** (*recherches*) to be concerned with; **se faire ~ malade** to report sick

porteur [pɔʀtœʀ, øz] *nm* (*de bagages*) por-

ter; (*de chèque*) bearer

porte-voix [pɔʀtəvwa] *nm inv* megaphone

portier [pɔʀtje] *nm* doorman

portière [pɔʀtjɛʀ] *nf* door

portillon [pɔʀtijɔ̃] *nm* gate

portion [pɔʀsjɔ̃] *nf* (*part*) portion, share; (*partie*) portion, section

porto [pɔʀto] *nm* port (wine)

portrait [pɔʀtʀɛ] *nm* (*peinture*) portrait; (*photo*) photograph; portrait-robot *nm* Identikit ® *ou* photo-fit ® picture

portuaire [pɔʀtɥɛʀ] *adj* port *cpd*, harbour *cpd*

portugais, e [pɔʀtygɛ, ɛz] *adj* Portuguese ♦ *nm/f*: **P~, e** Portuguese ♦ *nm* (LING) Portuguese

Portugal [pɔʀtygal] *nm*: **le ~** Portugal

pose [poz] *nf* (*de moquette*) laying; (*attitude, d'un modèle*) pose; (PHOTO) exposure

posé, e [poze] *adj* serious

poser [poze] *vt* to put; (*installer: moquette, carrelage*) to lay; (*rideaux, papier peint*) to hang; (*question*) to ask; (*principe, conditions*) to lay *ou* set down; (*problème*) to formulate; (*difficulté*) to pose ♦ *vi* (*modèle*) to pose; **se ~** *vi* (*oiseau, avion*) to land; (*question*) to arise; **~ qch (sur)** (*déposer*) to put sth down (on); **~ qch sur/quelque part** (*placer*) to put sth on/somewhere; **~ sa candidature à un poste** to apply for a post

positif, -ive [pozitif, iv] *adj* positive

position [pozisjɔ̃] *nf* position; **prendre ~** (*fig*) to take a stand

posologie [pozɔlɔʒi] *nf* dosage

posséder [posede] *vt* to own, possess; (*qualité, talent*) to have, possess; (*sexuellement*) to possess; possession *nf* ownership *no pl*, possession

possibilité [posibilite] *nf* possibility; **~s** *nfpl* (*potentiel*) potential *sg*

possible [posibl] *adj* possible; (*projet, entreprise*) feasible ♦ *nm*: **faire son ~** to do all one can, do one's utmost; **le plus/moins de livres ~** as many/few books as possible; **le plus vite ~** as quickly as possible; **dès que ~** as soon as possible

postal, e, -aux [pɔstal, o] *adj* postal

poste [pɔst] *nf* (*service*) post, postal service; (*administration, bureau*) post office ♦ *nm* (*fonction, MIL*) post; (*TÉL*) extension; (*de radio etc*) set; **mettre à la ~** to post; **~ (de police)** *nm* police station; **~ de secours** *nm* first-aid post; **~ restante** *nf* poste restante (*BRIT*), general delivery (*US*)

poster¹ [pɔste] *vt* to post

poster² [pɔstɛʀ] *nm* poster

postérieur, e [pɔsteʀjœʀ] *adj* (*date*) later; (*partie*) back ♦ *nm* (*fam*) behind

posthume [pɔstym] *adj* posthumous

postulant, e [pɔstylɑ̃, ɑ̃t] *nm/f* applicant

postuler [pɔstyle] *vi*: **~ à** *ou* **pour un emploi** to apply for a job

posture [pɔstyʀ] *nf* position

pot [po] *nm* (*en verre*) jar; (*en terre*) pot; (*en plastique, carton*) carton; (*en métal*) tin; (*fam: chance*) luck; **avoir du ~** (*fam*) to be lucky; **boire** *ou* **prendre un ~** (*fam*) to have a drink; **petit ~ (pour bébé)** (jar of) baby food; **~ catalytique** catalytic converter; **~ d'échappement** exhaust pipe; **~ de fleurs** plant pot, flowerpot; (*plante*) pot plant

potable [pɔtabl] *adj*: **eau (non) ~** (non-) drinking water

potage [pɔtaʒ] *nm* soup; **potager, -ère** *adj*: **(jardin) potager** kitchen *ou* vegetable garden

pot-au-feu [pɔtofø] *nm inv* (beef) stew

pot-de-vin [podvɛ̃] *nm* bribe

pote [pɔt] (*fam*) *nm* pal

poteau, x [pɔto] *nm* post; **~ indicateur** signpost

potelé, e [pɔt(ə)le] *adj* plump, chubby

potence [pɔtɑ̃s] *nf* gallows *sg*

potentiel, le [pɔtɑ̃sjɛl] *adj, nm* potential

poterie [pɔtʀi] *nf* pottery; (*objet*) piece of pottery

potier [pɔtje, jɛʀ] *nm* potter

potins [pɔtɛ̃] (*fam*) *nmpl* gossip *sg*

potiron [pɔtiʀɔ̃] *nm* pumpkin

pou, x [pu] *nm* louse

poubelle [pubɛl] *nf* (dust)bin

pouce [pus] *nm* thumb

poudre [pudʀ] *nf* powder; (*fard*) (face) powder; (*explosif*) gunpowder; **en ~: café en ~** instant coffee; **lait en ~** dried *ou* powdered milk; **poudreuse** *nf* powder snow; **poudrier** *nm* (powder) compact

pouffer [pufe] *vi*: **~ (de rire)** to burst out laughing

poulailler [pulaje] *nm* henhouse

poulain [pulɛ̃] *nm* foal; (*fig*) protégé

poule [pul] *nf* hen; (*CULIN*) (boiling) fowl

poulet [pulɛ] *nm* chicken; (*fam*) cop

poulie [puli] *nf* pulley

pouls [pu] *nm* pulse; **prendre le ~ de qn** to feel sb's pulse

poumon [pumɔ̃] *nm* lung

poupe [pup] *nf* stern; **en ~** astern

poupée [pupe] *nf* doll

pouponnière [pupɔnjɛʀ] *nf* crèche, day nursery

pour [puʀ] *prép* for ♦ *nm*: **le ~ et le contre** the pros and cons; **~ faire** (so as) to do, in order to do; **~ avoir fait** for having done; **~ que** so that, in order that; **~ 100 francs d'essence** 100 francs' worth of petrol; **~ cent** per cent; **~ ce qui est de** as for

pourboire [puʀbwaʀ] *nm* tip

pourcentage [puʀsɑ̃taʒ] *nm* percentage

pourchasser [puʀʃase] *vt* to pursue

pourparlers [puʀpaʀle] *nmpl* talks, negotiations

pourpre [puʀpʀ] *adj* crimson

pourquoi [puʀkwa] *adv, conj* why ♦ *nm inv*: **le ~ (de)** the reason (for)

pourrai *etc* [puʀe] *vb voir* **pouvoir**

pourri, e [puʀi] *adj* rotten

pourrir [puʀiʀ] *vi* to rot; (*fruit*) to go rotten *ou* bad ♦ *vt* to rot; (*fig*) to spoil thoroughly; **pourriture** *nf* rot

pourrons *etc* [puʀɔ̃] *vb voir* **pouvoir**

poursuite [puʀsɥit] *nf* pursuit, chase; **~s** *nfpl* (*JUR*) legal proceedings

poursuivre [puʀsɥivʀ] *vt* to pursue, chase (after); (*obséder*) to haunt; (*JUR*) to bring proceedings against, prosecute; (: *au civil*) to sue; (*but*) to strive towards; (*continuer: études etc*) to carry on with, continue; **se ~** *vi* to go on, continue

pourtant [puʀtɑ̃] *adv* yet; **c'est ~ facile** (and) yet it's easy

pourtour [puʀtuʀ] *nm* perimeter

pourvoir [puʀvwaʀ] *vt*: **~ qch/qn de** to equip sth/sb with ♦ *vi*: **~ à** to provide for; **pourvoyeur** *nm* supplier; **pourvu, e** *adj*: **pourvu de** equipped with; **pourvu que** (*si*) provided that, so long as; (*espérons que*) let's hope (that)

pousse [pus] *nf* growth; (*bourgeon*) shoot

poussé, e [puse] *adj* (*enquête*) exhaustive; (*études*) advanced; **poussée** *nf* thrust; (*d'acné*) eruption; (*fig: prix*) upsurge

pousser [puse] *vt* to push; (*émettre: cri, soupir*) to give; (*stimuler: élève*) to urge on; (*poursuivre: études, discussion*) to carry on (further) ♦ *vi* to push; (*croître*) to grow; **se ~** *vi* to move over; **~ qn à** (*inciter*) to urge on; press sb to; (*acculer*) to drive sb to; **faire ~** (*plante*) to grow

poussette [puset] *nf* push chair (*BRIT*), stroller (*US*)

poussière [pusjɛʀ] *nf* dust; **poussiéreux; -euse** *adj* dusty

poussin [pusɛ̃] *nm* chick

poutre [putʀ] *nf* beam

MOT-CLÉ

pouvoir [puvwaʀ] *nm* power; (*POL: dirigeants*): **le pouvoir** those in power; **les pouvoirs publics** the authorities; **pouvoir d'achat** purchasing power

♦ *vb semi-aux* 1 (*être en état de*) can, be able to; **je ne peux pas le réparer** I can't *ou* I am not able to repair it; **déçu de ne pas pouvoir le faire** disappointed not to be able to do it

2 (*avoir la permission*) can, may, be allowed to; **vous pouvez aller au cinéma** you can *ou* may go to the pictures

3 (*probabilité, hypothèse*) may, might, could; **il a pu avoir un accident** he may

ou might *ou* could have had an accident; **il aurait pu le dire!** he might *ou* could have said (so)!

♦ *vb impers* may, might, could; **il peut arriver que** it may *ou* might *ou* could happen that

♦ *vt* can, be able to; **j'ai fait tout ce que j'ai pu** I did all I could; **je n'en peux plus** (*épuisé*) I'm exhausted; (*à bout*) I can't take any more; **se pouvoir** *vi*: **il se peut que** it may *ou* might be that; **cela se pourrait** that's quite possible

---

prairie [pʀeʀi] *nf* meadow

praline [pʀalin] *nf* sugared almond

praticable [pʀatikabl] *adj* passable, practicable

pratiquant, e [pʀatikɑ̃, ɑ̃t] *nm/f* (regular) churchgoer

pratique [pʀatik] *nf* practice ♦ *adj* practical; **pratiquement** *adv* (*pour ainsi dire*) practically, virtually; **pratiquer** *vt* to practise; (*l'équitation, la pêche*) to go in for; (*le golf, football*) to play; (*intervention, opération*) to carry out

pré [pʀe] *nm* meadow

préalable [pʀealabl] *adj* preliminary; **au ~** beforehand

préambule [pʀeɑ̃byl] *nm* preamble; (*fig*) prelude; **sans ~** straight away

préau [pʀeo] *nm* (*SCOL*) covered playground

préavis [pʀeavi] *nm* notice

précaution [pʀekosjɔ̃] *nf* precaution; **avec ~** cautiously; **par ~** as a precaution

précédemment [pʀesedamɑ̃] *adv* before, previously

précédent, e [pʀesedɑ̃, ɑ̃t] *adj* previous ♦ *nm* precedent

précéder [pʀesede] *vt* to precede

précepteur, -trice [pʀeseptœʀ, tʀis] *nm/f* (private) tutor

prêcher [pʀeʃe] *vt* to preach

précieux, -euse [pʀesjø, jøz] *adj* precious; (*aide, conseil*) invaluable

précipice [pʀesipis] *nm* drop, chasm

précipitamment [presipitamɑ̃] adv hurriedly, hastily

précipitation [presipitasjɔ̃] nf (hâte) haste; **~s** nfpl (pluie) rain sg

précipité, e [presipite] adj hurried, hasty

précipiter [presipite] vt (hâter: départ) to hasten; (faire tomber): **~ qn/qch du haut de** to throw ou hurl sb/sth off ou from; **se ~** vi to speed up; **se ~ sur/vers** to rush at/towards

précis, e [presi, iz] adj precise; (mesures) accurate, precise; **à 4 heures ~es** at 4 o'clock sharp; **précisément** adv precisely; **préciser** vt (expliquer) to be more specific about, clarify; (spécifier) to state, specify; **se préciser** vi to become clear(er); **précision** nf precision; (détail) point ou detail; **demander des précisions** to ask for further explanation

précoce [prekɔs] adj early; (enfant) precocious

préconçu, e [prekɔ̃sy] adj preconceived

préconiser [prekɔnize] vt to advocate

prédécesseur [predesesœr] nm predecessor

prédilection [predileksjɔ̃] nf: **avoir une ~ pour** to be partial to

prédire [predir] vt to predict

prédominer [predɔmine] vi to predominate

préface [prefas] nf preface

préfecture [prefektyr] nf prefecture; **~ de police** police headquarters pl

préférable [preferabl] adj preferable

préféré, e [prefere] adj, nm/f favourite

préférence [preferɑ̃s] nf preference; **de ~** preferably

préférer [prefere] vt: **~ qn/qch (à)** to prefer sb/sth (to), like sb/sth better (than); **~ faire** to prefer to do; **je ~ais du thé** I would rather have tea, I'd prefer tea

préfet [prefe] nm prefect

préhistorique [preistɔrik] adj prehistoric

préjudice [preʒydis] nm (matériel) loss; (moral) harm no pl; **porter ~ à** to harm, be detrimental to; **au ~ de** at the expense of

préjugé [preʒyʒe] nm prejudice; **avoir un ~ contre** to be prejudiced ou biased against

préjuger [preʒyʒe]: **~ de** vt to prejudge

prélasser [prelase]: **se ~** vi to lounge

prélèvement [prelevmɑ̃] nm (montant) deduction; **faire un ~ de sang** to take a blood sample

prélever [prel(ə)ve] vt (échantillon) to take; **~ (sur)** (montant) to deduct (from); (argent: sur son compte) to withdraw (from)

prématuré, e [prematyre] adj premature
♦ nm premature baby

premier, -ière [prəmje, jɛr] adj first; (rang) front; (fig: objectif) basic; **le ~ venu** the first person to come along; **de ~ ordre** first-rate; **P~ Ministre** Prime Minister; **première** nf (SCOL) lower sixth form; (THÉÂTRE) first night; (AUTO) first (gear); (AVIAT, RAIL etc) first class; (CINÉMA) première; (exploit) first; **premièrement** adv firstly

prémonition [premɔnisjɔ̃] nf premonition

prémunir [premynir]: **se ~** vi: **se ~ contre** to guard against

prenant, e [prənɑ̃, ɑ̃t] adj absorbing, engrossing

prénatal, e [prenatal] adj (MÉD) antenatal

prendre [prɑ̃dr] vt to take; (repas) to have; (se procurer) to get; (malfaiteur, poisson) to catch; (passager) to pick up; (personnel) to take on; (traiter: personne) to handle; (voix, ton) to put on; (ôter): **~ qch à** to take sth from; (coincer): **se ~ les doigts dans** to get one's fingers caught in ♦ vi (liquide, ciment) to set; (greffe, vaccin) to take; (feu: foyer) to go; (se diriger): **~ à gauche** to turn (to the) left; **~ froid** to catch cold; **se ~ pour** to think one is; **s'en ~ à** to attack; **se ~ d'amitié pour** to befriend; **s'y ~** (procéder) to set about it

preneur [prənœr, øz] nm: **être/trouver ~** to be willing to buy/find a buyer

preniez [prənje] vb voir **prendre**

prenne etc [pren] vb voir **prendre**

prénom [pʀenɔ̃] *nm* first *ou* Christian name

préoccupation [pʀeɔkypasjɔ̃] *nf* (*souci*) concern; (*idée fixe*) preoccupation

préoccuper [pʀeɔkype] *vt* (*inquiéter*) to worry; (*absorber*) to preoccupy; **se ~ de** to be concerned with

préparatifs [pʀepaʀatif] *nmpl* preparations

préparation [pʀepaʀasjɔ̃] *nf* preparation

préparer [pʀepaʀe] *vt* to prepare; (*café, thé*) to make; (*examen*) to prepare for; (*voyage, entreprise*) to plan; **se ~** *vi* (*orage, tragédie*) to brew, be in the air; **~ qch à qn** (*surprise etc*) to have sth in store for sb; **se ~ (à qch/faire)** to prepare (o.s.) *ou* get ready (for sth/to do)

prépondérant, e [pʀepɔ̃deʀɑ̃, ɑ̃t] *adj* major, dominating

préposé, e [pʀepoze] *nm/f* employee; (*facteur*) postman

préposition [pʀepozisjɔ̃] *nf* preposition

près [pʀɛ] *adv* near, close; **~ de** near (to), close to; (*environ*) nearly, almost; **de ~** closely; **à 5 kg ~** to within about 5 kg; **à cela ~ que** apart from the fact that; **il n'est pas à 10 minutes ~** he can spare 10 minutes

présage [pʀezaʒ] *nm* omen; **présager** *vt* to foresee

presbyte [pʀɛsbit] *adj* long-sighted

presbytère [pʀɛsbiteʀ] *nm* presbytery

prescription [pʀɛskʀipsjɔ̃] *nf* prescription

prescrire [pʀɛskʀiʀ] *vt* to prescribe

présence [pʀezɑ̃s] *nf* presence; (*au bureau, à l'école*) attendance

présent, e [pʀezɑ̃, ɑ̃t] *adj, nm* present; **à ~ (que)** now (that)

présentation [pʀezɑ̃tasjɔ̃] *nf* presentation; (*de nouveau venu*) introduction; (*allure*) appearance; **faire les ~s** to do the introductions

présenter [pʀezɑ̃te] *vt* to present; (*excuses, condoléances*) to offer; (*invité, conférencier*): **~ qn (à)** to introduce sb (to) ♦ *vi*: **~ bien** to have a pleasing appearance; **se**

~ *vi* (*occasion*) to arise; **se ~ à** (*examen*) to sit; (*élection*) to stand at, run for

préservatif [pʀezɛʀvatif, iv] *nm* sheath, condom

préserver [pʀezɛʀve] *vt*: **~ de** (*protéger*) to protect from

président [pʀezidɑ̃] *nm* (*POL*) president; (*d'une assemblée, COMM*) chairman; **~ directeur général** chairman and managing director; **présidentielles** *nfpl* presidential elections

présider [pʀezide] *vt* to preside over; (*dîner*) to be the guest of honour at

présomptueux, -euse [pʀezɔ̃ptɥø, øz] *adj* presumptuous

presque [pʀɛsk] *adv* almost, nearly; **~ personne** hardly anyone; **~ rien** hardly anything; **~ pas** hardly (at all); **~ pas (de)** hardly any

presqu'île [pʀɛskil] *nf* peninsula

pressant, e [pʀesɑ̃, ɑ̃t] *adj* urgent

presse [pʀɛs] *nf* press; (*affluence*): **heures de ~** busy times

pressé, e [pʀese] *adj* in a hurry; (*travail*) urgent; **orange ~e** freshly-squeezed orange juice

pressentiment [pʀesɑ̃timɑ̃] *nm* foreboding, premonition

pressentir [pʀesɑ̃tiʀ] *vt* to sense

presse-papiers [pʀɛspapje] *nm inv* paperweight

presser [pʀese] *vt* (*fruit, éponge*) to squeeze; (*bouton*) to press; (*allure*) to speed up; (*inciter*): **~ qn de faire** to urge *ou* press sb to do ♦ *vi* to be urgent; **se ~** *vi* (*se hâter*) to hurry (up); **se ~ contre qn** to squeeze up against sb; **rien ne presse** there's no hurry

pressing [pʀesiŋ] *nm* (*magasin*) dry-cleaner's

pression [pʀesjɔ̃] *nf* pressure; (*bouton*) press stud; (*fam: bière*) draught beer; **faire ~ sur** to put pressure on; **~ artérielle** blood pressure

prestance [pʀɛstɑ̃s] *nf* presence, imposing bearing

prestataire [prɛstatɛr] *nm/f* supplier

prestation [prɛstasjɔ̃] *nf* (*allocation*) benefit; (*d'une entreprise*) service provided; (*d'un artiste*) performance

prestidigitateur, -trice [prɛstidiʒitatœr, tris] *nm/f* conjurer

prestige [prɛstiʒ] *nm* prestige; **prestigieux, -euse** *adj* prestigious

présumer [prezyme] *vt*: ~ **que** to presume *ou* assume that

prêt, e [prɛ, prɛt] *adj* ready ♦ *nm* (*somme*) loan; **prêt-à-porter** *nm* ready-to-wear *ou* off-the-peg (*BRIT*) clothes *pl*

prétendre [pretɑ̃dr] *vt* (*affirmer*): ~ **que** to claim that; (*avoir l'intention de*): ~ **faire qch** to mean *ou* intend to do sth; **prétendu, e** *adj* (*supposé*) so-called

prétentieux, -euse [pretɑ̃sjø, jøz] *adj* pretentious

prétention [pretɑ̃sjɔ̃] *nf* claim; (*vanité*) pretentiousness; **~s** *nfpl* (*salaire*) expected salary

prêter [prete] *vt* (*livres, argent*): ~ **qch (à)** to lend sth (to); (*supposer*): ~ **à qn** (*caractère, propos*) to attribute to sb; **se ~ à** to lend o.s. (*ou* itself) to; (*manigances etc*) to go along with; ~ **à** (*critique, commentaires etc*) to be open to, give rise to; ~ **attention à** to pay attention to; ~ **serment** to take the oath

prétexte [pretɛkst] *nm* pretext, excuse; **sous aucun ~** on no account; **prétexter** *vt* to give as a pretext *ou* an excuse

prêtre [prɛtr] *nm* priest

preuve [prœv] *nf* proof; (*indice*) proof, evidence *no pl*; **faire ~ de** to show; **faire ses ~s** to prove o.s. (*ou* itself)

prévaloir [prevalwar] *vi* to prevail

prévenant, e [prev(ə)nɑ̃, ɑ̃t] *adj* thoughtful, kind

prévenir [prev(ə)nir] *vt* (*éviter: catastrophe etc*) to avoid, prevent; (*anticiper: désirs, besoins*) to anticipate; ~ **qn (de)** (*avertir*) to warn sb (about); (*informer*) to tell *ou* inform sb (about)

préventif, -ive [prevɑ̃tif, iv] *adj* preventive

prévention [prevɑ̃sjɔ̃] *nf* prevention; ~ **routière** road safety

prévenu, e [prev(ə)ny] *nm/f* (*JUR*) defendant, accused

prévision [previzjɔ̃] *nf*: **~s** predictions; (*ÉCON*) forecast *sg*; **en ~ de** in anticipation of; **~s météorologiques** weather forecast *sg*

prévoir [prevwar] *vt* (*anticiper*) to foresee; (*s'attendre à*) to expect, reckon on; (*organiser: voyage etc*) to plan; (*envisager*) to allow; **comme prévu** as planned; **prévoyant, e** *adj* gifted with (*ou* showing) foresight; **prévu, e** *pp de* **prévoir**

prier [prije] *vi* to pray ♦ *vt* (*Dieu*) to pray to; (*implorer*) to beg; (*demander*): ~ **qn de faire** to ask sb to do; **se faire ~** to need coaxing *ou* persuading; **je vous en prie** (*allez-y*) please do; (*de rien*) don't mention it; **prière** *nf* prayer; **"prière de ..."** "please ..."

primaire [primɛr] *adj* primary ♦ *nm* (*SCOL*) primary education

prime [prim] *nf* (*bonus*) bonus; (*subvention*) premium; (*COMM: cadeau*) free gift; (*ASSURANCES, BOURSE*) premium ♦ *adj*: **de ~ abord** at first glance; **primer** *vt* (*récompenser*) to award a prize to ♦ *vi* to dominate; to be most important

primeurs [primœr] *nfpl* early fruits and vegetables

primevère [primvɛr] *nf* primrose

primitif, -ive [primitif, iv] *adj* primitive; (*originel*) original

primordial, e, -iaux [primɔrdjal, jo] *adj* essential

prince [prɛ̃s] *nm* prince; **princesse** *nf* princess

principal, e, -aux [prɛ̃sipal, o] *adj* principal, main ♦ *nm* (*SCOL*) principal, head(master); (*essentiel*) main thing

principe [prɛ̃sip] *nm* principle; **par ~** on principle; **en ~** (*habituellement*) as a rule; (*théoriquement*) in principle

printemps [prɛ̃tɑ̃] *nm* spring

priorité [prijɔrite] *nf* priority; (*AUTO*) right of way; **~ à droite** right of way to vehicles coming from the right

pris, e [pri, priz] *pp de* **prendre** ♦ *adj* (*place*) taken; (*mains*) full; (*personne*) busy; **avoir le nez/la gorge ~(e)** to have a stuffy nose/a hoarse throat; **être ~ de panique** to be panic-stricken

prise [priz] *nf* (*d'une ville*) capture; (*PÊCHE, CHASSE*) catch; (*point d'appui ou pour empoigner*) hold; (*ÉLEC: fiche*) plug; (: *femelle*) socket; **être aux ~s avec** to be grappling with; **~ de conscience** awareness, realization; **~ de contact** (*rencontre*) initial meeting, first contact; **~ de courant** power point; **~ de sang** blood test; **~ de vue** (*photo*) shot; **~ multiple** adaptor

priser [prize] *vt* (*estimer*) to prize, value

prison [prizɔ̃] *nf* prison; **aller/être en ~** to go to/be in prison *ou* jail; **prisonnier, -ière** *nm/f* prisoner ♦ *adj* captive

prit [pri] *vb voir* **prendre**

privé, e [prive] *adj* private ♦ *nm* (*COMM*) private sector; **en ~** in private

priver [prive] *vt:* **~ qn de** to deprive sb of; **se ~ de** to go *ou* do without

privilège [privilɛʒ] *nm* privilege

prix [pri] *nm* price; (*récompense, SCOL*) prize; **hors de ~** exorbitantly priced; **à aucun ~** not at any price; **à tout ~** at all costs; **~ d'achat/de vente/de revient** purchasing/selling/cost price

probable [prɔbabl] *adj* likely, probable; **probablement** *adv* probably

probant, e [prɔbɑ̃, ɑ̃t] *adj* convincing

problème [prɔblɛm] *nm* problem

procédé [prɔsede] *nm* (*méthode*) process; (*comportement*) behaviour *no pl*

procéder [prɔsede] *vi* to proceed; (*moralement*) to behave; **~ à** to carry out

procès [prɔsɛ] *nm* trial; (*poursuites*) proceedings *pl*; **être en ~ avec** to be involved in a lawsuit with

processus [prɔsesys] *nm* process

procès-verbal, -aux [prɔsɛverbal, o] *nm* (*de réunion*) minutes *pl*; (*aussi:* **P.V.**) park-

ing ticket

prochain, e [prɔʃɛ̃, ɛn] *adj* next; (*proche: départ, arrivée*) impending ♦ *nm* fellow man; **la ~e fois/semaine ~e** next time/week; **prochainement** *adv* soon, shortly

proche [prɔʃ] *adj* nearby; (*dans le temps*) imminent; (*parent, ami*) close; **~s** *nmpl* (*parents*) close relatives; **être ~ (de)** to be near, be close (to); **le P~ Orient** the Middle East

proclamer [prɔklame] *vt* to proclaim

procuration [prɔkyrasjɔ̃] *nf* proxy

procurer [prɔkyre] *vt:* **~ qch à qn** (*fournir*) to obtain sth for sb; (*causer: plaisir etc*) to bring sb sth; **se ~** *vt* to get; **procureur** *nm* public prosecutor

prodige [prɔdiʒ] *nm* marvel, wonder; (*personne*) prodigy; **prodiguer** *vt* (*soins, attentions*): **prodiguer qch à qn** to give sb sth

producteur, -trice [prɔdyktœr, tris] *nm/f* producer

productif, -ive [prɔdyktif, iv] *adj* productive

production [prɔdyksjɔ̃] *nf* production; (*rendement*) output

productivité [prɔdyktivite] *nf* productivity

produire [prɔdɥir] *vt* to produce; **se ~** *vi* (*événement*) to happen, occur; (*acteur*) to perform, appear

produit [prɔdɥi] *nm* product; **~ chimique** chemical; **~ d'entretien** cleaning product; **~ national brut** gross national product; **~s alimentaires** foodstuffs

prof [prɔf] (*fam*) *nm* teacher

profane [prɔfan] *adj* (*REL*) secular ♦ *nm/f* layman(-woman)

proférer [prɔfere] *vt* to utter

professeur [prɔfesœr] *nm* teacher; (*de faculté*) (university) lecturer; (: *titulaire d'une chaire*) professor

profession [prɔfesjɔ̃] *nf* occupation; **~ libérale** (liberal) profession; **sans ~** unemployed; **professionnel, le** *adj, nm/f* professional

profil [prɔfil] *nm* profile; **de ~** in profile

profit [pʀɔfi] *nm* (*avantage*) benefit, advantage; (*COMM, FINANCE*) profit; **au ~ de** in aid of; **tirer ~ de** to profit from; **profitable** *adj* (*utile*) beneficial; (*lucratif*) profitable; **profiter** *vi*: **profiter de** (*situation, occasion*) to take advantage of; (*vacances, jeunesse etc*) to make the most of

profond, e [pʀɔfɔ̃, ɔ̃d] *adj* deep; (*sentiment, intérêt*) profound; **profondément** *adv* deeply; **il dort profondément** he is sound asleep; **profondeur** *nf* depth

progéniture [pʀɔʒenityʀ] *nf* offspring *inv*

programme [pʀɔgʀam] *nm* programme; (*SCOL*) syllabus, curriculum; (*INFORM*) program; **programmer** *vt* (*émission*) to schedule; (*INFORM*) to program; **programmeur, -euse** *nm/f* programmer

progrès [pʀɔgʀɛ] *nm* progress *no pl*; **faire des ~** to make progress; **progresser** *vi* to progress; **progressif, -ive** *adj* progressive

prohiber [pʀɔibe] *vt* to prohibit, ban

proie [pʀwa] *nf* prey *no pl*

projecteur [pʀɔʒɛktœʀ] *nm* (*pour film*) projector; (*de théâtre, cirque*) spotlight

projectile [pʀɔʒɛktil] *nm* missile

projection [pʀɔʒɛksjɔ̃] *nf* projection; (*séance*) showing

projet [pʀɔʒɛ] *nm* plan; (*ébauche*) draft; **~ de loi** bill; **projeter** *vt* (*envisager*) to plan; (*film, photos*) to project; (*ombre, lueur*) to throw, cast; (*jeter*) to throw up (*ou* off *ou* out)

prolétaire [pʀɔletɛʀ] *adj, nmf* proletarian

prolongement [pʀɔlɔ̃ʒmɑ̃] *nm* extension; **dans le ~ de** running on from

prolonger [pʀɔlɔ̃ʒe] *vt* (*débat, séjour*) to prolong; (*délai, billet, rue*) to extend; **se ~** *vi* to go on

promenade [pʀɔm(ə)nad] *nf* walk (*ou* drive *ou* ride); **faire une ~** to go for a walk; **une ~ en voiture/à vélo** a drive/(bicycle) ride

promener [pʀɔm(ə)ne] *vt* (*chien*) to take out for a walk; (*doigts, regard*): **~ qch sur** to run sth over; **se ~** *vi* to go for (*ou* be

out for) a walk

promesse [pʀɔmɛs] *nf* promise

promettre [pʀɔmɛtʀ] *vt* to promise ♦ *vi* to be *ou* look promising; **~ à qn de faire** to promise sb that one will do

promiscuité [pʀɔmiskɥite] *nf* (*chambre*) lack of privacy

promontoire [pʀɔmɔ̃twaʀ] *nm* headland

promoteur, -trice [pʀɔmɔtœʀ, tʀis] *nm/f*: **~ (immobilier)** property developer (*BRIT*), real estate promoter (*US*)

promotion [pʀɔmɔsjɔ̃] *nf* promotion; **en ~** on special offer

promouvoir [pʀɔmuvwaʀ] *vt* to promote

prompt, e [pʀɔ̃(pt), pʀɔ̃(p)t] *adj* swift, rapid

prôner [pʀone] *vt* (*préconiser*) to advocate

pronom [pʀɔnɔ̃] *nm* pronoun

prononcer [pʀɔnɔ̃se] *vt* to pronounce; (*dire*) to utter; (*discours*) to deliver; **se ~** *vi* to be pronounced; **se ~ (sur)** (*se décider*) to reach a decision (*on ou* about), give a verdict (on); **prononciation** *nf* pronunciation

pronostic [pʀɔnɔstik] *nm* (*MÉD*) prognosis; (*fig: aussi:* **~s**) forecast

propagande [pʀɔpagɑ̃d] *nf* propaganda

propager [pʀɔpaʒe] *vt* to spread; **se ~** *vi* to spread

prophète [pʀɔfɛt] *nm* prophet

prophétie [pʀɔfesi] *nf* prophecy

propice [pʀɔpis] *adj* favourable

proportion [pʀɔpɔʀsjɔ̃] *nf* proportion; **toute(s) ~(s) gardée(s)** making due allowance(s)

propos [pʀɔpo] *nm* (*intention*) intention, aim; (*sujet*): **à quel ~?** what about? ♦ *nmpl* (*paroles*) talk *no pl*, remarks; **à ~ de** about, regarding; **à tout ~** for the slightest thing *ou* reason; **à ~** by the way; (*opportunément*) at the right moment

proposer [pʀɔpoze] *vt* to propose; **~ qch (à qn)** (*suggérer*) to suggest sth (to sb), propose sth (to sb); (*offrir*) to offer (sb) sth; **se ~** to offer one's services; **se ~ de faire** to intend *ou* propose to do; **propo-**

sition *(suggestion)* nf proposal, suggestion; *(LING)* clause

propre [prɔpr] adj clean; *(net)* neat, tidy; *(possessif)* own; *(sens)* literal; *(particulier)*: ~ **à** peculiar to; *(approprié)*: ~ **à** suitable for ♦ nm: **recopier au** ~ to make a fair copy of; **proprement** adv *(avec propreté)* cleanly; **le village proprement dit** the village itself; **à proprement parler** strictly speaking; **propreté** nf cleanliness

propriétaire [prɔprijetɛr] nm/f owner; *(pour le locataire)* landlord(-lady)

propriété [prɔprijete] nf property; *(droit)* ownership

propulser [prɔpylse] vt to propel

proroger [prɔrɔʒe] vt *(prolonger)* to extend

proscrire [prɔskrir] vt *(interdire)* to ban, prohibit

prose [proz] nf *(style)* prose

prospecter [prɔspɛkte] vt to prospect; *(COMM)* to canvass

prospectus [prɔspɛktys] nm leaflet

prospère [prɔspɛr] adj prosperous; **prospérer** vi to prosper

prosterner [prɔstɛrne]: **se** ~ vi to bow low, prostrate o.s.

prostituée [prɔstitɥe] nf prostitute

prostitution [prɔstitysjɔ̃] nf prostitution

protecteur, -trice [prɔtɛktœr, tris] adj *(air, ton: péj)* patronizing ♦ nm/f protector

protection [prɔtɛksjɔ̃] nf protection; *(d'un personnage influent: aide)* patronage

protéger [prɔteʒe] vt to protect; **se** ~ **de** *ou* **contre** to protect o.s. from

protéine [prɔtein] nf protein

protestant, e [prɔtɛstɑ̃, ɑ̃t] adj, nm/f Protestant

protestation [prɔtɛstasjɔ̃] nf *(plainte)* protest

protester [prɔtɛste] vi: ~ **(contre)** to protest (against *ou* about); ~ **de** *(son innocence)* to protest

prothèse [prɔtɛz] nf: ~ **dentaire** denture

protocole [prɔtɔkɔl] nm *(fig)* etiquette

proue [pru] nf bow(s pl), prow

prouesse [prues] nf feat

prouver [pruve] vt to prove

provenance [prɔv(ə)nɑ̃s] nf origin; **avion en** ~ **de** plane (arriving) from

provenir [prɔv(ə)nir]: ~ **de** vt to come from

proverbe [prɔvɛrb] nm proverb

province [prɔvɛ̃s] nf province

proviseur [prɔvizœr] nm ≈ head(teacher) *(BRIT)*, ≈ principal *(US)*

provision [prɔvizjɔ̃] nf *(réserve)* stock, supply; **~s** nfpl *(vivres)* provisions, food *no pl*

provisoire [prɔvizwar] adj temporary; **provisoirement** adv temporarily

provocant, e [prɔvɔkɑ̃, ɑ̃t] adj provocative

provoquer [prɔvɔke] vt *(défier)* to provoke; *(causer)* to cause, bring about; *(inciter)*: ~ **qn à** to incite sb to

proxénète [prɔksenɛt] nm procurer

proximité [prɔksimite] nf nearness, closeness; *(dans le temps)* imminence, closeness; **à** ~ near *ou* close by; **à** ~ **de** near (to), close to

prudemment [prydamɑ̃] adv carefully; wisely, sensibly

prudence [prydɑ̃s] nf carefulness; **avec** ~ carefully; **par** ~ as a precaution

prudent, e [prydɑ̃, ɑ̃t] adj *(pas téméraire)* careful; (: *en général)* safety-conscious; *(sage, conseillé)* wise, sensible; **c'est plus** ~ it's wiser

prune [pryn] nf plum

pruneau, x [pryno] nm prune

prunelle [prynɛl] nf *(BOT)* sloe; **il y tient comme à la** ~ **de ses yeux** he treasures *ou* cherishes it

prunier [prynje] nm plum tree

PS *sigle m* = **parti socialiste**

psaume [psom] nm psalm

pseudonyme [psødɔnim] nm *(gén)* fictitious name; *(d'écrivain)* pseudonym, pen name

psychanalyse [psikanaliz] nf psychoanalysis

psychiatre [psikjatʀ] *nm/f* psychiatrist;
psychiatrique *adj* psychiatric

psychique [psiʃik] *adj* psychological

psychologie [psikɔlɔʒi] *nf* psychology;
psychologique *adj* psychological; **psychologue** *nm/f* psychologist

P.T.T. *sigle fpl* = **Postes, Télécommunications et Télédiffusion**

pu [py] *pp de* **pouvoir**

puanteur [pyɑ̃tœʀ] *nf* stink, stench

pub [pyb] *nf (fam: annonce)* ad, advert;
(pratique) advertising

public, -ique [pyblik] *adj* public; *(école,
instruction)* state *cpd* ♦ *nm* public; *(assistance)* audience; **en ~** in public

publicitaire [pyblisitɛʀ] *adj* advertising
cpd; (film) publicity *cpd*

publicité [pyblisite] *nf (méthode, profession)*
advertising; *(annonce)* advertisement; *(ré-
vélations)* publicity

publier [pyblije] *vt* to publish

publique [pyblik] *adj voir* **public**

puce [pys] *nf* flea; *(INFORM)* chip; **carte à ~**
smart card; **~s** *nfpl (marché)* flea market
sg

pudeur [pydœʀ] *nf* modesty

pudique [pydik] *adj (chaste)* modest; *(discret)* discreet

puer [pɥe] *(péj) vi* to stink

puéricultrice [pɥeʀikyltʀis] *nf* p(a)ediatric
nurse

puéril, e [pɥeʀil] *adj* childish

puis [pɥi] *vb voir* **pouvoir** ♦ *adv* then

puiser [pɥize] *vt:* **~ (dans)** to draw (from)

puisque [pɥisk] *conj* since

puissance [pɥisɑ̃s] *nf* power; **en ~** ♦ *adj*
potential

puissant, e [pɥisɑ̃, ɑ̃t] *adj* powerful

puisse *etc* [pɥis] *vb voir* **pouvoir**

puits [pɥi] *nm* well

pull(-over) [pyl(ɔvɛʀ)] *nm* sweater

pulluler [pylyle] *vi* to swarm

pulpe [pylp] *nf* pulp

pulvérisateur [pylveʀizatœʀ] *nm* spray

pulvériser [pylveʀize] *vt* to pulverize; *(liquide)* to spray

punaise [pynɛz] *nf (ZOOL)* bug; *(clou)*
drawing pin *(BRIT)*, thumbtack *(US)*

punch¹ [pɔ̃ʃ] *nm (boisson)* punch

punch² [pœnʃ] *nm (BOXE, fig)* punch

punir [pyniʀ] *vt* to punish; **punition** *nf*
punishment

pupille [pypij] *nf (ANAT)* pupil ♦ *nm/f (enfant)* ward

pupitre [pypitʀ] *nm (SCOL)* desk

pur, e [pyʀ] *adj* pure; *(vin)* undiluted;
(whisky) neat; **en ~e perte** to no avail;
c'est de la folie ~e it's sheer madness;
purement *adv* purely

purée [pyʀe] *nf:* **~ (de pommes de terre)**
mashed potatoes *pl;* **~ de marrons** chestnut purée

purgatoire [pyʀgatwaʀ] *nm* purgatory

purger [pyʀʒe] *vt (MÉD, POL)* to purge; *(JUR:
peine)* to serve

purin [pyʀɛ̃] *nm* liquid manure

pur-sang [pyʀsɑ̃] *nm inv* thoroughbred

pus [py] *nm* pus

putain [pytɛ̃] *(fam!) nf* whore (!)

puzzle [pœzl] *nm* jigsaw (puzzle)

P.-V. *sigle m* = **procès-verbal**

pyjama [piʒama] *nm* pyjamas *pl (BRIT)*, pajamas *pl (US)*

pyramide [piʀamid] *nf* pyramid

Pyrénées [piʀene] *nfpl:* **les ~** the Pyrenees

Q, q

QI *sigle m* (= *quotient intellectuel*) IQ

quadragénaire [k(w)adʀaʒeneʀ] *nm/f*
man/woman in his/her forties

quadriller [kadʀije] *vt (POLICE)* to keep under tight control

quadruple [k(w)adʀypl] *nm:* **le ~ de** four
times as much as; **quadruplés, -ées**
nm/fpl quadruplets, quads

quai [ke] *nm (de port)* quay; *(de gare)*
platform; **être à ~** *(navire)* to be alongside

qualification [kalifikasjɔ̃] *nf (aptitude)*

qualification

qualifié, e [kalifje] *adj* qualified; (*main d'œuvre*) skilled

qualifier [kalifje] *vt* to qualify; **se ~** *vi* to qualify; **~ qch/qn de** to describe sth/sb as

qualité [kalite] *nf* quality

quand [kɑ̃] *conj, adv* when; **~ je serai riche** when I'm rich; **~ même** all the same; **~ même, il exagère!** really, he overdoes it!; **~ bien même** even though

quant [kɑ̃]: **~ à** *prép* (*pour ce qui est de*) as for, as to; (*au sujet de*) regarding; **quant-à-soi** *nm*: **rester sur son quant-à-soi** to remain aloof

quantité [kɑ̃tite] *nf* quantity, amount; (*grand nombre*): **une** *ou* **des ~(s) de** a great deal of

quarantaine [karɑ̃tɛn] *nf* (*MÉD*) quarantine; **avoir la ~** (*âge*) to be around forty; **une ~ (de)** forty or so, about forty

quarante [karɑ̃t] *num* forty

quart [kar] *nm* (*fraction*) quarter; (*surveillance*) watch; **un ~ de vin** a quarter litre of wine; **le ~ de** a quarter of; **~ d'heure** quarter of an hour; **~s de finale** quarter finals

quartier [kartje] *nm* (*de ville*) district, area; (*de bœuf*) quarter; (*de fruit*) piece; **cinéma de ~** local cinema; **avoir ~ libre** (*fig*) to be free; **~ général** headquarters *pl*

quartz [kwarts] *nm* quartz

quasi [kazi] *adv* almost, nearly; **quasiment** *adv* almost, nearly; **quasiment jamais** hardly ever

quatorze [katɔrz] *num* fourteen

quatre [katr] *num* four; **à ~ pattes** on all fours; **se mettre en ~ pour qn** to go out of one's way for sb; **~ à ~** (*monter, descendre*) four at a time; **quatre-quarts** *nm inv* pound cake; **quatre-vingt-dix** *num* ninety; **quatre-vingts** *num* eighty; **quatre-vingt-un** *num* eighty-one; **quatrième** *num* fourth ♦ *nf* (*SCOL*) third form *ou* year

quatuor [kwatɥɔr] *nm* quartet(te)

MOT-CLÉ

que [kə] *conj* 1 (*introduisant complétive*) that; **il sait que tu es là** he knows (that) you're here; **je veux que tu acceptes** I want you to accept; **il a dit que oui** he said he would (*ou* it was *etc*)

2 (*reprise d'autres conjonctions*): **quand il rentrera et qu'il aura mangé** when he gets back and (when) he has eaten; **si vous y allez ou que vous ...** if you go there or if you ...

3 (*en tête de phrase: hypothèse, souhait etc*): **qu'il le veuille ou non** whether he likes it or not; **qu'il fasse ce qu'il voudra!** let him do as he pleases!

4 (*après comparatif*) than, as; *voir aussi* **plus**; **aussi**; **autant** *etc*

5 (*seulement*): **ne ... que** only; **il ne boit que de l'eau** he only drinks water

♦ *adv* (*exclamation*): **qu'il** *ou* **qu'est-ce qu'il est bête/court vite!** he's so silly!/he runs so fast!; **que de livres!** what a lot of books!

♦ *pron* 1 (*relatif: personne*) whom; (*: chose*) that, which; **l'homme que je vois** the man (whom) I see; **le livre que tu vois** the book (that *ou* which) you see; **un jour que j'étais ...** a day when I was ...

2 (*interrogatif*) what; **que fais-tu?**, **qu'est-ce que tu fais?** what are you doing?; **qu'est-ce que c'est?** what is it?, what's that?; **que faire?** what can one do?

Québec [kebɛk] *n*: **le ~** Quebec; **québécois, e** *adj* Quebec ♦ *nm/f*: **Québécois, e** Quebecker ♦ *nm* (*LING*) Quebec French

---

MOT-CLÉ

quel, quelle [kɛl] *adj* 1 (*interrogatif: personne*) who; (*: chose*) what; which; **quel est cet homme?** who is this man?; **quel est ce livre?** what is this book?; **quel livre/homme?** what book/man?; (*parmi un certain choix*) which book/man?; **quels**

acteurs préférez-vous? which actors do you prefer?; **dans quels pays êtes-vous allé?** which *ou* what countries did you go to?

2 (*exclamatif*): **quelle surprise!** what a surprise!

3: **quel que soit le coupable** whoever is guilty; **quel que soit votre avis** whatever your opinion

quelconque [kɛlkɔ̃k] *adj* (*indéfini*): **un ami/prétexte ~** some friend/pretext or other; (*médiocre: repas*) indifferent, poor; (*laid: personne*) plain-looking

---

MOT-CLÉ

---

quelque [kɛlk] *adj* 1 some; a few; (*tournure interrogative*) any; **quelque espoir** some hope; **il a quelques amis** he has a few *ou* some friends; **a-t-il quelques amis?** has he any *ou* some friends?; **les quelques livres qui** the few books which; **20 kg et quelque(s)** a bit over 20 kg

2: **quelque ... que: quelque livre qu'il choisisse** whatever (*ou* whichever) book he chooses

3: **quelque chose** something; (*tournure interrogative*) anything; **quelque chose d'autre** something else; anything else; **quelque part** somewhere; anywhere; **en quelque sorte** as it were

♦ *adv* 1 (*environ*): **quelque 100 mètres** some 100 metres

2: **quelque peu** rather, somewhat

---

quelquefois [kɛlkəfwa] *adv* sometimes
quelques-uns, -unes [kɛlkəzœ̃, yn] *pron* a few, some
quelqu'un [kɛlkœ̃] *pron* someone, somebody; (+*tournure interrogative*) anyone, anybody; **~ d'autre** someone *ou* somebody else; (+ *tournure interrogative*) anybody else
quémander [kemɑ̃de] *vt* to beg for
qu'en dira-t-on [kɑ̃diRatɔ̃] *nm inv*: **le ~~~~** gossip, what people say

querelle [kəRɛl] *nf* quarrel; **quereller: se quereller** *vi* to quarrel
qu'est-ce que [kɛskə] *voir* **que**
qu'est-ce qui [kɛski] *voir* **qui**
question [kɛstjɔ̃] *nf* question; (*fig*) matter, issue; **il a été ~ de** we (: *ou* they) spoke about; **de quoi est-il ~?** what is it about?; **il n'en est pas ~** there's no question of it; **hors de ~** out of the question; **remettre en ~** to question; **questionnaire** *nm* questionnaire; **questionner** *vt* to question
quête [kɛt] *nf* collection; (*recherche*) quest, search; **faire la ~** (*à l'église*) to take the collection; (*artiste*) to pass the hat round
quetsche [kwɛtʃ] *nf kind of dark-red plum*
queue [kø] *nf* tail; (*fig: du classement*) bottom; (: *de poêle*) handle; (: *de fruit, feuille*) stalk; (: *de train, colonne, file*) rear; **faire la ~** to queue (up) (*BRIT*), line up (*US*); **~ de cheval** ponytail; **~ de poisson** (*AUT*): **faire une ~ de poisson à qn** to cut in front of sb
qui [ki] *pron* (*personne*) who; (+*prép*) whom; (*chose, animal*) which, that; **qu'est-ce ~ est sur la table?** what is on the table?; **~ est-ce ~?** who?; **~ est-ce que?** who?; **à ~ est ce sac?** whose bag is this?; **à ~ parlais-tu?** who were you talking to?, to whom were you talking?; **amenez ~ vous voulez** bring who you like; **~ que ce soit** whoever it may be
quiconque [kikɔ̃k] *pron* (*celui qui*) whoever, anyone who; (*n'importe qui*) anyone, anybody
quiétude [kjetyd] *nf*: **en toute ~** in complete peace
quille [kij] *nf*: **(jeu de) ~s** skittles *sg* (*BRIT*), bowling (*US*)
quincaillerie [kɛ̃kajRi] *nf* (*ustensiles*) hardware; (*magasin*) hardware shop; **quincaillier, -ière** *nm/f* hardware dealer
quinquagénaire [kɛ̃kaʒenɛR] *nm/f* man/woman in his/her fifties
quintal, -aux [kɛ̃tal, o] *nm* quintal (*100 kg*)

quinte [kɛ̃t] *nf:* ~ **(de toux)** coughing fit

quintuple [kɛ̃typl] *nm:* **le** ~ **de** five times as much as; **quintuplés, -ées** *nm/fpl* quintuplets, quins

quinzaine [kɛ̃zɛn] *nf:* **une** ~ **(de)** about fifteen, fifteen or so; **une** ~ **(de jours)** a fortnight (*BRIT*), two weeks

quinze [kɛ̃z] *num* fifteen; **dans** ~ **jours** in a fortnight('s time), in two weeks(' time)

quiproquo [kiprɔko] *nm* misunderstanding

quittance [kitɑ̃s] *nf* (*reçu*) receipt

quitte [kit] *adj:* **être** ~ **envers qn** to be no longer in sb's debt; (*fig*) to be quits with sb; ~ **à faire** even if it means doing

quitter [kite] *vt* to leave; (*vêtement*) to take off; **se** ~ *vi* (*couples, interlocuteurs*) to part; **ne quittez pas** (*au téléphone*) hold the line

qui-vive [kiviv] *nm:* **être sur le ~-~** to be on the alert

quoi [kwa] *pron* (*interrogatif*) what; ~ **de neuf?** what's the news?; **as-tu de** ~ **écrire?** have you anything to write with?; ~ **qu'il arrive** whatever happens; ~ **qu'il en soit** be that as it may; ~ **que ce soit** anything at all; **"il n'y a pas de ~"** "(please) don't mention it"; **il n'y a pas de** ~ **rire** there's nothing to laugh about; **à** ~ **bon?** what's the use?; **en** ~ **puis-je vous aider?** how can I help you?

quoique [kwak] *conj* (al)though

quote-part [kɔtpar] *nf* share

quotidien, ne [kɔtidjɛ̃, jɛn] *adj* daily; (*banal*) everyday ♦ *nm* (*journal*) daily (paper); **quotidiennement** *adv* daily

R, r

r. *abr* = **route; rue**

rab [rab] (*fam*) *nm* (*nourriture*) extra; **est-ce qu'il y a du ~?** is there any extra (left)?

rabâcher [rabaʃe] *vt* to keep on repeating

rabais [rabɛ] *nm* reduction, discount; **rabaisser** *vt* (*dénigrer*) to belittle; (*rabattre:*

prix) to reduce

rabat-joie [rabaʒwa] *nm inv* killjoy

rabattre [rabatr] *vt* (*couvercle, siège*) to pull down; (*déduire*) to reduce; **se** ~ *vi* (*se refermer: couvercle*) to fall shut; (*véhicule, coureur*) to cut in; **se** ~ **sur** to fall back on

rabbin [rabɛ̃] *nm* rabbi

râblé, e [rable] *adj* stocky

rabot [rabo] *nm* plane

rabougri, e [rabugri] *adj* stunted

rabrouer [rabrue] *vt* to snub

racaille [rakaj] (*péj*) *nf* rabble, riffraff

raccommoder [rakɔmɔde] *vt* to mend, repair; **se** ~ *vi* (*fam*) to make it up

raccompagner [rakɔ̃paɲe] *vt* to take *ou* see back

raccord [rakɔr] *nm* link; (*retouche*) touch up; **raccorder** *vt* to join (up), link up; (*suj: pont etc*) to connect, link

raccourci [rakursi] *nm* short cut

raccourcir [rakursir] *vt* to shorten ♦ *vi* (*jours*) to grow shorter, draw in

raccrocher [rakrɔʃe] *vt* (*tableau*) to hang back up; (*récepteur*) to put down ♦ *vi* (*TÉL*) to hang up, ring off; **se** ~ **à** *vt* to cling to, hang on to

race [ras] *nf* race; (*d'animaux, fig*) breed; **de** ~ purebred, pedigree

rachat [raʃa] *nm* buying; (*du même objet*) buying back

racheter [raʃ(ə)te] *vt* (*article perdu*) to buy another; (*après avoir vendu*) to buy back; (*d'occasion*) to buy; (*COMM: part, firme*) to buy up; (*davantage*): ~ **du lait/3 œufs** to buy more milk/another 3 eggs *ou* 3 more eggs; **se** ~ *vi* (*fig*) to make amends

racial, e, -aux [rasjal, jo] *adj* racial

racine [rasin] *nf* root; ~ **carrée/cubique** square/cube root

raciste [rasist] *adj, nm/f* raci(al)ist

racket [raket] *nm* racketeering *no pl*

raclée [rakle] (*fam*) *nf* hiding, thrashing

racler [rakle] *vt* (*surface*) to scrape; **se** ~ **la gorge** to clear one's throat

racoler [rakɔle] *vt* (*suj: prostituée*) to solicit;

(: *parti, marchand*) to tout for

racontars [Rakɔ̃taR] *nmpl* story, lie

raconter [Rakɔ̃te] *vt*: **~ (à qn)** (*décrire*) to relate (to sb), tell (sb) about; (*dire de mauvaise foi*) to tell (sb); **~ une histoire** to tell a story

racorni, e [RakɔRni] *adj* hard(ened)

radar [RadaR] *nm* radar

rade [Rad] *nf* (natural) harbour; **rester en ~** (*fig*) to be left stranded

radeau, x [Rado] *nm* raft

radiateur [RadjatœR] *nm* radiator, heater; (*AUTO*) radiator; **~ électrique/à gaz** electric/gas heater *ou* fire

radiation [Radjasjɔ̃] *nf* (*PHYSIQUE*) radiation

radical, e, -aux [Radikal, o] *adj* radical

radier [Radje] *vt* to strike off

radieux, -euse [Radjø, øz] *adj* radiant

radin, e [Radɛ̃, in] (*fam*) *adj* stingy

radio [Radjo] *nf* radio; (*MÉD*) X-ray ♦ *nm* radio operator; **à la ~** on the radio; **radioactif, -ive** *adj* radioactive; **radiocassette** *nm* cassette radio, radio cassette player; **radiodiffuser** *vt* to broadcast; **radiographie** *nf* radiography; (*photo*) X-ray photograph; **radiophonique** *adj* radio *cpd*; **radio-réveil** (*pl* **radios-réveils**) *nm* radio alarm clock

radis [Radi] *nm* radish

radoter [Radɔte] *vi* to ramble on

radoucir [RadusiR]: **se ~** *vi* (*temps*) to become milder; (*se calmer*) to calm down

rafale [Rafal] *nf* (*vent*) gust (of wind); (*tir*) burst of gunfire

raffermir [RafɛRmiR] *vt* to firm up; **se ~** *vi* (*fig: autorité, prix*) to strengthen

raffiner [Rafine] *vt* to refine; **raffinerie** *nf* refinery

raffoler [Rafɔle]: **~ de** *vt* to be very keen on

rafistoler [Rafistɔle] (*fam*) *vt* to patch up

rafle [Rafl] *nf* (*de police*) raid; **rafler** (*fam*) *vt* to swipe, nick

rafraîchir [RafReʃiR] *vt* (*atmosphère, température*) to cool (down); (*aussi*: **mettre à ~**) to chill; (*fig: rénover*) to brighten up; **se**

~ *vi* (*temps*) to grow cooler; (*en se lavant*) to freshen up; (*en buvant*) to refresh o.s.; **rafraîchissant, e** *adj* refreshing; **rafraîchissement** *nm* (*boisson*) cool drink; **rafraîchissements** *nmpl* (*boissons, fruits etc*) refreshments

rage [Raʒ] *nf* (*MÉD*): **la ~** rabies; (*fureur*) rage, fury; **faire ~** to rage; **~ de dents** (raging) toothache

ragot [Rago] (*fam*) *nm* malicious gossip *no pl*

ragoût [Ragu] *nm* stew

raide [Red] *adj* stiff; (*câble*) taut, tight; (*escarpé*) steep; (*droit: cheveux*) straight; (*fam: sans argent*) flat broke; (*osé*) daring, bold ♦ *adv* (*en pente*) steeply; **~ mort** stone dead; **raidir** *vt* (*muscles*) to stiffen; **se raidir** *vi* (*tissu*) to stiffen; (*personne*) to tense up; (: *se préparer moralement*) to brace o.s.; (*fig: position*) to harden; **raideur** *nf* (*rigidité*) stiffness; **avec raideur** (*répondre*) stiffly, abruptly

raie [Re] *nf* (*ZOOL*) skate, ray; (*rayure*) stripe; (*des cheveux*) parting

raifort [RefɔR] *nm* horseradish

rail [Raj] *nm* rail; (*chemins de fer*) railways *pl*; **par ~** by rail

railler [Raje] *vt* to scoff at, jeer at

rainure [RenyR] *nf* groove

raisin [Rezɛ̃] *nm* (*aussi*: **~s**) grapes *pl*; **~s secs** raisins

raison [Rezɔ̃] *nf* reason; **avoir ~** to be right; **donner ~ à qn** to agree with sb; (*événement*) to prove sb right; **perdre la ~** to become insane; **~ de plus** all the more reason; **à plus forte ~** all the more so; **en ~ de** because of; **à ~ de** at the rate of; **sans ~** for no reason; **raisonnable** *adj* reasonable, sensible

raisonnement [Rezɔnmɑ̃] *nm* (*façon de réfléchir*) reasoning; (*argumentation*) argument

raisonner [Rezɔne] *vi* (*penser*) to reason; (*argumenter, discuter*) to argue ♦ *vt* (*personne*) to reason with

rajeunir [RaʒœniR] *vt* (*suj: coiffure, robe*): **~**

qn to make sb look younger; (*fig: personnel*) to inject new blood into ♦ *vi* to become (*ou* look) younger

rajouter [ʀaʒute] *vt* to add

rajuster [ʀaʒyste] *vt* (*vêtement*) to straighten, tidy; (*salaires*) to adjust

ralenti [ʀalɑ̃ti] *nm*: **au ~** (*fig*) at a slower pace; **tourner au ~** (*AUTO*) to tick over (*AUTO*), idle

ralentir [ʀalɑ̃tiʀ] *vt* to slow down

râler [ʀɑle] *vi* to groan; (*fam*) to grouse, moan (and groan)

rallier [ʀalje] *vt* (*rejoindre*) to rejoin; (*gagner à sa cause*) to win over; **se ~ à** (*avis*) to come over *ou* round to

rallonge [ʀalɔ̃ʒ] *nf* (*de table*) (extra) leaf

rallonger [ʀalɔ̃ʒe] *vt* to lengthen

rallye [ʀali] *nm* rally; (*POL*) march

ramadan [ʀamadɑ̃] *nm* Ramadan

ramassage [ʀamasaʒ] *nm*: **~ scolaire** school bus service

ramassé, e [ʀamɑse] *adj* (*trapu*) squat

ramasser [ʀamɑse] *vt* (*objet tombé ou par terre, fam*) to pick up; (*recueillir: copies, ordures*) to collect; (*récolter*) to gather; **se ~** *vi* (*sur soi-même*) to huddle up; **ramassis** (*péj*) *nm* (*de voyous*) bunch; (*d'objets*) jumble

rambarde [ʀɑ̃baʀd] *nf* guardrail

rame [ʀam] *nf* (*aviron*) oar; (*de métro*) train; (*de papier*) ream

rameau, x [ʀamo] *nm* (small) branch; **les R~x** (*REL*) Palm Sunday *sg*

ramener [ʀam(ə)ne] *vt* to bring back; (*reconduire*) to take back; **~ qch à** (*réduire à*) to reduce sth to

ramer [ʀame] *vi* to row

ramollir [ʀamɔliʀ] *vt* to soften; **se ~** *vi* to go soft

ramoner [ʀamɔne] *vt* to sweep

rampe [ʀɑ̃p] *nf* (*d'escalier*) banister(s *pl*); (*dans un garage*) ramp; (*THÉÂTRE*): **la ~** the footlights *pl*

ramper [ʀɑ̃pe] *vi* to crawl

rancard [ʀɑ̃kaʀ] (*fam*) *nm* (*rendez-vous*) date

rancart [ʀɑ̃kaʀ] *nm*: **mettre au ~** (*fam*) to scrap

rance [ʀɑ̃s] *adj* rancid

rancœur [ʀɑ̃kœʀ] *nf* rancour

rançon [ʀɑ̃sɔ̃] *nf* ransom

rancune [ʀɑ̃kyn] *nf* grudge, rancour; **garder ~ à qn (de qch)** to bear sb a grudge (for sth); **sans ~!** no hard feelings!; **rancunier, -ière** *adj* vindictive, spiteful

randonnée [ʀɑ̃dɔne] *nf* ride; (*pédestre*) walk, ramble; (: *en montagne*) hike, hiking *no pl*

rang [ʀɑ̃] *nm* (*rangée*) row; (*grade, classement*) rank; **~s** *nmpl* (*MIL*) ranks; **se mettre en ~s** to get into *ou* form rows; **au premier ~** in the first row; (*fig*) ranking first

rangé, e [ʀɑ̃ʒe] *adj* (*vie*) well-ordered; (*personne*) steady

rangée [ʀɑ̃ʒe] *nf* row

ranger [ʀɑ̃ʒe] *vt* (*mettre de l'ordre dans*) to tidy up; (*classer, grouper*) to order, arrange; (*mettre à sa place*) to put away; (*fig: classer*): **~ qn/qch parmi** to rank sb/ sth among; **se ~** *vi* (*véhicule, conducteur*) to pull over *ou* in; (*piéton*) to step aside; (*s'assagir*) to settle down; **se ~ à** (*avis*) to come round to

ranimer [ʀanime] *vt* (*personne*) to bring round; (*douleur, souvenir*) to revive; (*feu*) to rekindle

rap [ʀap] *nm* rap (music)

rapace [ʀapas] *nm* bird of prey

râpe [ʀɑp] *nf* (*CULIN*) grater; **râper** *vt* (*CULIN*) to grate

rapetisser [ʀap(ə)tise] *vt* to shorten

rapide [ʀapid] *adj* fast; (*prompt: coup d'œil, mouvement*) quick ♦ *nm* express (train); (*de cours d'eau*) rapid; **rapidement** *adv* fast; quickly

rapiécer [ʀapjese] *vt* to patch

rappel [ʀapel] *nm* (*THÉÂTRE*) curtain call; (*MÉD: vaccination*) booster; (*deuxième avis*) reminder; **rappeler** *vt* to call back; (*ambassadeur, MIL*) to recall; (*faire se souvenir*): **rappeler qch à qn** to remind sb of sth;

se rappeler vt (se souvenir de) to remember, recall

rapport [Rapɔʀ] nm (lien, analogie) connection; (compte rendu) report; (profit) yield, return; **~s** nmpl (entre personnes, pays) relations; **avoir ~ à** to have something to do with; **être/se mettre en ~ avec qn** to be/get in touch with sb; **par ~ à** in relation to; **~s (sexuels)** (sexual) intercourse sg

rapporter [Rapɔʀte] vt (rendre, ramener) to bring back; (bénéfice) to yield, bring in; (mentionner, répéter) to report ♦ vi (investissement) to give a good return ou yield; (: activité) to be very profitable; **se ~ à** vt (correspondre à) to relate to; **rapporteur, -euse** nm/f (péj) telltale ♦ nm (GÉOM) protractor

rapprochement [RapRɔʃmɑ̃] nm (de nations) reconciliation; (rapport) parallel

rapprocher [RapRɔʃe] vt (deux objets) to bring closer together; (fig: ennemis, partis etc) to bring together; (comparer) to establish a parallel between; (chaise d'une table): **~ qch (de)** to bring sth closer (to); **se ~** vi to draw closer ou nearer; **se ~ de** to come closer to; (présenter une analogie avec) to be close to

rapt [Rapt] nm abduction

raquette [Rakεt] nf (de tennis) racket; (de ping-pong) bat

rare [RɑR] adj rare; **se faire ~** to become scarce; **rarement** adv rarely, seldom

ras, e [Rɑ, Rɑz] adj (poil, herbe) short; (tête) close-cropped ♦ adv short; **en ~e campagne** in open country; **à ~ bords** to the brim; **en avoir ~ le bol** (fam) to be fed up; **~ du cou** ♦ adj (pull, robe) crew-neck

rasade [Rɑzad] nf glassful

raser [Rɑze] vt (barbe, cheveux) to shave off; (menton, personne) to shave; (fam: ennuyer) to bore; (démolir) to raze (to the ground); (frôler) to graze, skim; **se ~** vi to shave; (fam) to be bored (to tears); **rasoir** nm razor

rassasier [Rɑsazje] vt: **être rassasié** to have eaten one's fill

rassemblement [Rɑsɑ̃bləmɑ̃] nm (groupe) gathering; (POL) union

rassembler [Rɑsɑ̃ble] vt (réunir) to assemble, gather; (documents, notes) to gather together, collect; **se ~** vi to gather

rassis, e [Rɑsi, iz] adj (pain) stale

rassurer [RɑsyRe] vt to reassure; **se ~** vi to reassure o.s.; **rassure-toi** don't worry

rat [Ra] nm rat

rate [Rat] nf spleen

raté, e [Rate] adj (tentative) unsuccessful, failed ♦ nm/f (fam: personne) failure

râteau, x [Rɑto] nm rake

rater [Rate] vi (affaire, projet etc) to go wrong, fail ♦ vt (fam: cible, train, occasion) to miss; (plat) to spoil; (fam: examen) to fail

ration [Rasjɔ̃] nf ration

ratisser [Ratise] vt (allée) to rake; (feuilles) to rake up; (suj: armée, police) to comb

RATP sigle f (= Régie autonome des transports parisiens) Paris transport authority

rattacher [Rataʃe] vt (animal, cheveux) to tie up again; (fig: relier): **~ qch à** to link sth with

rattrapage [RatRapaʒ] nm: **cours de ~** remedial class

rattraper [RatRape] vt (fugitif) to recapture; (empêcher de tomber) to catch (hold of); (atteindre, rejoindre) to catch up with; (réparer: erreur) to make up for; **se ~** vi to make up for it; **se ~ (à)** (se raccrocher) to stop o.s. falling (by catching hold of)

rature [RatyR] nf deletion, erasure

rauque [Rok] adj (voix) hoarse

ravages [Ravaʒ] nmpl: **faire des ~** to wreak havoc

ravaler [Ravale] vt (mur, façade) to restore; (déprécier) to lower

ravi, e [Ravi] adj: **être ~ de/que** to be delighted with/that

ravigoter [Ravigɔte] (fam) vt to buck up

ravin [Ravɛ̃] nm gully, ravine

ravir [RaviR] vt (enchanter) to delight; **à ~** adv beautifully

raviser [ʀavize]: **se ~** *vi* to change one's mind

ravissant, e [ʀavisɑ̃, ɑ̃t] *adj* delightful

ravisseur, -euse [ʀavisœʀ, øz] *nm/f* abductor, kidnapper

ravitaillement [ʀavitajmɑ̃] *nm* (*réserves*) supplies *pl*

ravitailler [ʀavitaje] *vt* (*en vivres, ammunitions*) to provide with fresh supplies; (*avion*) to refuel; **se ~** *vi* to get fresh supplies; (*avion*) to refuel

raviver [ʀavive] *vt* (*feu, douleur*) to revive; (*couleurs*) to brighten up

rayé, e [ʀeje] *adj* (*à rayures*) striped

rayer [ʀeje] *vt* (*érafler*) to scratch; (*barrer*) to cross out; (*d'une liste*) to cross off

rayon [ʀejɔ̃] *nm* (*de soleil etc*) ray; (*GÉOM*) radius; (*de roue*) spoke; (*étagère*) shelf; (*de grand magasin*) department; **dans un ~ de** within a radius of; **~ de soleil** sunbeam; **~s X** X-rays

rayonnement [ʀejɔnmɑ̃] *nm* (*fig: d'une culture*) influence

rayonner [ʀejɔne] *vi* (*fig*) to shine forth; (*personne: de joie, de beauté*) to be radiant; (*touriste*) to go touring (*from one base*)

rayure [ʀejyʀ] *nf* (*motif*) stripe; (*éraflure*) scratch; **à ~s** striped

raz-de-marée [ʀɑdmaʀe] *nm inv* tidal wave

ré [ʀe] *nm* (*MUS*) D; (*en chantant la gamme*) re

réacteur [ʀeaktœʀ] *nm* (*d'avion*) jet engine; (*nucléaire*) reactor

réaction [ʀeaksjɔ̃] *nf* reaction

réadapter [ʀeadapte]: **se ~ (à)** *vi* to readjust (to)

réagir [ʀeaʒiʀ] *vi* to react

réalisateur, -trice [ʀealizatœʀ, tʀis] *nm/f* (*TV, CINÉMA*) director

réalisation [ʀealizasjɔ̃] *nf* realization; (*cinéma*) production; **en cours de ~** under way

réaliser [ʀealize] *vt* (*projet, opération*) to carry out, realize; (*rêve, souhait*) to realize, fulfil; (*exploit*) to achieve; (*film*) to produce; (*se rendre compte de*) to realize; **se ~** *vi* to be realized

réaliste [ʀealist] *adj* realistic

réalité [ʀealite] *nf* reality; **en ~** in (actual) fact; **dans la ~** in reality

réanimation [ʀeanimasjɔ̃] *nf* resuscitation; **service de ~** intensive care unit

rébarbatif, -ive [ʀebaʀbatif, iv] *adj* forbidding

rebattu, e [ʀ(ə)baty] *adj* hackneyed

rebelle [ʀəbɛl] *nm/f* rebel ♦ *adj* (*troupes*) rebel; (*enfant*) rebellious; (*mèche etc*) unruly

rebeller [ʀ(ə)bele]: **se ~** *vi* to rebel

rebondi, e [ʀ(ə)bɔ̃di] *adj* (*joues*) chubby

rebondir [ʀ(ə)bɔ̃diʀ] *vi* (*ballon: au sol*) to bounce; (*: contre un mur*) to rebound; (*fig*) to get moving again; **rebondissement** *nm* new development

rebord [ʀ(ə)bɔʀ] *nm* edge; **le ~ de la fenêtre** the windowsill

rebours [ʀ(ə)buʀ]: **à ~** *adv* the wrong way

rebrousser [ʀ(ə)bʀuse] *vt*: **~ chemin** to turn back

rebut [ʀəby] *nm*: **mettre au ~** to scrap; **rebutant, e** *adj* off-putting; **rebuter** *vt* to put off

récalcitrant, e [ʀekalsitʀɑ̃, ɑ̃t] *adj* refractory

recaler [ʀ(ə)kale] *vt* (*SCOL*) to fail; **se faire ~** to fail

récapituler [ʀekapityle] *vt* to recapitulate, sum up

receler [ʀ(ə)səle] *vt* (*produit d'un vol*) to receive; (*fig*) to conceal; **receleur, -euse** *nm/f* receiver

récemment [ʀesamɑ̃] *adv* recently

recensement [ʀ(ə)sɑ̃smɑ̃] *nm* (*population*) census

recenser [ʀ(ə)sɑ̃se] *vt* (*population*) to take a census of; (*inventorier*) to list

récent, e [ʀesɑ̃, ɑ̃t] *adj* recent

récépissé [ʀesepise] *nm* receipt

récepteur [ʀeseptœʀ, tʀis] *nm* receiver

réception [ʀesepsjɔ̃] *nf* receiving *no pl*;

(*accueil*) reception, welcome; (*bureau*) reception desk; (*réunion mondaine*) reception, party; **réceptionniste** *nm/f* receptionist

recette [R(ə)sɛt] *nf* recipe; (*COMM*) takings *pl*; **~s** *nfpl* (*COMM*: *rentrées*) receipts

receveur, -euse [R(ə)savœR, øz] *nm/f* (*des contributions*) tax collector; (*des postes*) postmaster(-mistress)

recevoir [R(ə)savwaR] *vt* to receive; (*client, patient*) to see; **être reçu** (*à un examen*) to pass

rechange [R(ə)ʃɑ̃ʒ]: **de ~** *adj* (*pièces, roue*) spare; (*fig*: *solution*) alternative; **des vêtements de ~** a change of clothes

réchapper [Reʃape]: **~ de** *ou* **à** *vt* (*accident, maladie*) to come through

recharge [R(ə)ʃaRʒ] *nf* refill; **rechargeable** *adj* (*stylo etc*) refillable; **recharger** *vt* (*stylo*) to refill; (*batterie*) to recharge

réchaud [Reʃo] *nm* (*portable*) stove

réchauffer [Reʃofe] *vt* (*plat*) to reheat; (*mains, personne*) to warm; **se ~** *vi* (*température*) to get warmer; (*personne*) to warm o.s. (up)

rêche [Rɛʃ] *adj* rough

recherche [R(ə)ʃɛRʃ] *nf* (*action*) search; (*raffinement*) studied elegance; (*scientifique etc*): **la ~** research; **~s** *nfpl* (*de la police*) investigations; (*scientifiques*) research.*sg*; **la ~ de** the search for; **être à la ~ de qch** to be looking for sth

recherché, e [R(ə)ʃɛRʃe] *adj* (*rare, demandé*) much sought-after; (*raffiné*: *style*) mannered; (: *tenue*) elegant

rechercher [R(ə)ʃɛRʃe] *vt* (*objet égaré, personne*) to look for; (*causes, nouveau procédé*) to try to find; (*bonheur, compliments*) to seek

rechigner [R(ə)ʃiɲe] *vi*: **~ à faire qch** to balk *ou* jib at doing sth

rechute [R(ə)ʃyt] *nf* (*MÉD*) relapse

récidiver [Residive] *vi* to commit a subsequent offence; (*fig*) to do it again

récif [Resif] *nm* reef

récipient [Resipjɑ̃] *nm* container

réciproque [ResipRɔk] *adj* reciprocal

récit [Resi] *nm* story; **récital** *nm* recital; **réciter** *vt* to recite

réclamation [Reklamasjɔ̃] *nf* complaint; **~s** *nfpl* (*bureau*) complaints department *sg*

réclame [Reklam] *nf* ad, advert(isement); **en ~** on special offer; **réclamer** *vt* to ask for; (*revendiquer*) to claim, demand ♦ *vi* to complain

réclusion [Reklyzjɔ̃] *nf* imprisonment

recoin [Rəkwɛ̃] *nm* nook, corner

reçois *etc* [Rəswa] *vb voir* **recevoir**

récolte [Rekɔlt] *nf* harvesting, gathering; (*produits*) harvest, crop; **récolter** *vt* to harvest, gather (in); (*fig*) to collect

recommandé [R(ə)kɔmɑ̃de] *nm* (*POSTES*): **en ~** by registered mail

recommander [R(ə)kɔmɑ̃de] *vt* to recommend; (*POSTES*) to register

recommencer [R(ə)kɔmɑ̃se] *vt* (*reprendre*: *lutte, séance*) to resume, start again; (*refaire*: *travail, explications*) to start afresh, start (over) again ♦ *vi* to start again; (*récidiver*) to do it again

récompense [Rekɔ̃pɑ̃s] *nf* reward; (*prix*) award; **récompenser** *vt*: **récompenser qn (de** *ou* **pour)** to reward sb (for)

réconcilier [Rekɔ̃silje] *vt* to reconcile; **se ~ (avec)** to be reconciled (with)

reconduire [R(ə)kɔ̃dɥiR] *vt* (*raccompagner*) to take *ou* see back; (*renouveler*) to renew

réconfort [Rekɔ̃fɔR] *nm* comfort; **réconforter** *vt* (*consoler*) to comfort

reconnaissance [R(ə)kɔnɛsɑ̃s] *nf* (*gratitude*) gratitude, gratefulness; (*action de reconnaître*) recognition; (*MIL*) reconnaissance, recce; **reconnaissant, e** *adj* grateful

reconnaître [R(ə)kɔnɛtR] *vt* to recognize; (*MIL*: *lieu*) to reconnoitre; (*JUR*: *enfant, torts*) to acknowledge; **~ que** to admit *ou* acknowledge that; **reconnu, e** *adj* (*indiscuté, connu*) recognized

reconstituant, e [R(ə)kɔ̃stitɥɑ̃, ɑ̃t] *adj* (*aliment, régime*) strength-building

reconstituer [R(ə)kɔ̃stitɥe] *vt* (*événement, accident*) to reconstruct; (*fresque, vase brisé*) to piece together, reconstitute

reconstruction [R(ə)kɔ̃stryksjɔ̃] *nf* rebuilding

reconstruire [R(ə)kɔ̃stryir] *vt* to rebuild

reconvertir [R(ə)kɔ̃vertir]: **se ~ dans** *vr* (*un métier, une branche*) to go into

record [R(ə)kɔr] *nm, adj* record

recoupement [R(ə)kupmɑ̃] *nm*: **par ~** by cross-checking

recouper: [R(ə)kupe]: **se ~** *vi* (*témoignages*) to tie *ou* match up

recourber [R(ə)kurbe]: **se ~** *vi* to curve (up), bend (up)

recourir [R(ə)kurir]: **~ à** *vt* (*ami, agence*) to turn *ou* appeal to; (*force, ruse, emprunt*) to resort to

recours [R(ə)kur] *nm*: **avoir ~ à = recourir à; en dernier ~** as a last resort

recouvrer [R(ə)kuvre] *vt* (*vue, santé etc*) to recover, regain

recouvrir [R(ə)kuvrir] *vt* (*couvrir à nouveau*) to re-cover; (*couvrir entièrement, aussi fig*) to cover

récréation [Rekreasjɔ̃] *nf* (*SCOL*) break

récrier [Rekrije]: **se ~** *vi* to exclaim

récriminations [Rekriminasjɔ̃] *nfpl* remonstrations, complaints

recroqueviller [R(ə)krɔk(ə)vije]: **se ~** *vi* (*personne*) to huddle up

recrudescence [R(ə)krydesɑ̃s] *nf* fresh outbreak

recrue [Rəkry] *nf* recruit

recruter [R(ə)kryte] *vt* to recruit

rectangle [Rektɑ̃gl] *nm* rectangle; **rectangulaire** *adj* rectangular

rectificatif, iv [Rektifikatif, iv] *nm* correction

rectifier [Rektifje] *vt* (*calcul, adresse, paroles*) to correct; (*erreur*) to rectify

rectiligne [Rektiliɲ] *adj* straight

recto [Rekto] *nm* front (of a page); **~ verso** on both sides of the page

reçu, e [R(ə)sy] *pp de* **recevoir** ♦ *adj* (*candidat*) successful; (*admis, consacré*) accepted ♦ *nm* (*COMM*) receipt

recueil [Rəkœj] *nm* collection; **recueillir** *vt* to collect; (*voix, suffrages*) to win; (*accueillir: réfugiés, chat*) to take in; **se recueillir** *vi* to gather one's thoughts, meditate

recul [R(ə)kyl] *nm* (*éloignement*) distance; (*déclin*) decline; **être en ~** to be on the decline; **avec du ~** with hindsight; **avoir un mouvement de ~** to recoil; **prendre du ~** to stand back; **reculé, e** *adj* remote; **reculer** *vi* to move back, back away; (*AUTO*) to reverse, back (up); (*fig*) to (be on the) decline ♦ *vt* to move back; (*véhicule*) to reverse, back (up); (*date, décision*) to postpone; **reculons: à reculons** *adv* backwards

récupérer [Rekypere] *vt* to recover, get back; (*heures de travail*) to make up; (*déchets*) to salvage ♦ *vi* to recover

récurer [Rekyre] *vt* to scour

récuser [Rekyze] *vt* to challenge; **se ~** *vi* to decline to give an opinion

reçut [Rəsy] *vb voir* **recevoir**

recycler [R(ə)sikle] *vt* (*TECH*) to recycle; **se ~** *vi* to retrain

rédacteur, -trice [Redaktœr, tris] *nm/f* (*journaliste*) writer; subeditor; (*d'ouvrage de référence*) editor, compiler; **~ en chef** chief editor

rédaction [Redaksjɔ̃] *nf* writing; (*rédacteurs*) editorial staff; (*SCOL: devoir*) essay, composition

redemander [Rədmɑ̃de] *vt* (*une nouvelle fois*) to ask again for; (*davantage*) to ask for more of

redescendre [R(ə)desɑ̃dr] *vi* to go back down ♦ *vt* (*pente etc*) to go down

redevance [Rədvɑ̃s] *nf* (*TÉL*) rental charge; (*TV*) licence fee

rédiger [Rediʒe] *vt* to write; (*contrat*) to draw up

redire [R(ə)dir] *vt* to repeat; **trouver à ~ à** to find fault with

redonner [R(ə)dɔne] *vt* (*rendre*) to give back; (*resservir: nourriture*) to give more

redoubler [R(ə)duble] *vi* (*tempête, violence*)

to intensify; (SCOL) to repeat a year; **~ de patience/prudence** to be doubly patient/careful

redoutable [R(ə)dutabl] *adj* formidable, fearsome

redouter [R(ə)dute] *vt* to dread

redressement [R(ə)dRɛsmã] *nm* (*économique*) recovery

redresser [R(ə)dRese] *vt* (*relever*) to set upright; (*pièce tordue*) to straighten out; (*situation, économie*) to put right; **se ~** *vi* (*personne*) to sit (*ou* stand) up (straight); (*économie*) to recover

réduction [Redyksjɔ̃] *nf* reduction

réduire [RedɥiR] *vt* to reduce; (*prix, dépenses*) to cut, reduce; **se ~ à** (*revenir à*) to boil down to; **réduit** *nm* (*pièce*) tiny room

rééducation [Reedykasjɔ̃] *nf* (*d'un membre*) re-education; (*de délinquants, d'un blessé*) rehabilitation

réel, le [Reɛl] *adj* real; **réellement** *adv* really

réexpédier [Reɛkspedje] *vt* (*à l'envoyeur*) to return, send back; (*au destinataire*) to send on

refaire [R(ə)fɛR] *vt* to do again; (*faire de nouveau: sport*) to take up again; (*réparer, restaurer*) to do up

réfection [Refɛksjɔ̃] *nf* repair

réfectoire [RefɛktwaR] *nm* refectory

référence [RefeRãs] *nf* reference; **~s** *nfpl* (*recommandations*) reference *sg*

référer [RefeRe]: **se ~ à** *vt* to refer to

refermer [R(ə)fɛRme] *vt* to close *ou* shut again; **se ~** *vi* (*porte*) to close *ou* shut (again)

refiler [R(ə)file] *vi* (*fam*) to palm off

réfléchi, e [Refleʃi] *adj* (*caractère*) thoughtful; (*action*) well-thought-out; (*LING*) reflexive; **c'est tout ~** my mind's made up

réfléchir [RefleʃiR] *vt* to reflect ♦ *vi* to think; **~ à** to think about

reflet [R(ə)flɛ] *nm* reflection; (*sur l'eau etc*) sheen *no pl*, glint; **refléter** *vt* to reflect;

se refléter *vi* to be reflected

réflexe [Reflɛks] *nm, adj* reflex

réflexion [Reflɛksjɔ̃] *nf* (*de la lumière etc*) reflection; (*fait de penser*) thought; (*remarque*) remark; **~ faite, à la ~** on reflection

refluer [R(ə)flye] *vi* to flow back; (*foule*) to surge back

reflux [Rəfly] *nm* (*de la mer*) ebb

réforme [RefɔRm] *nf* reform; (*REL*): **la R~** the Reformation; **réformer** *vt* to reform; (*MIL*) to declare unfit for service

refouler [R(ə)fule] *vt* (*envahisseurs*) to drive back; (*larmes*) to force back; (*désir, colère*) to repress

refrain [R(ə)fRɛ̃] *nm* refrain, chorus

refréner [RafRene] *vt*, **réfréner** [RefRene] *vt* to curb, check

réfrigérateur [RefRiʒeRatœR] *nm* refrigerator, fridge

refroidir [R(ə)fRwadiR] *vt* to cool; (*fig: personne*) to put off ♦ *vi* to cool (down); **se ~** *vi* (*temps*) to get cooler *ou* colder; (*fig: ardeur*) to cool (off); **refroidissement** *nm* (*grippe etc*) chill

refuge [R(ə)fyʒ] *nm* refuge; **réfugié, e** *adj, nm/f* refugee; **réfugier: se réfugier** *vi* to take refuge

refus [R(ə)fy] *nm* refusal; **ce n'est pas de ~** I won't say no, it's welcome; **refuser** *vt* to refuse; (*SCOL: candidat*) to fail; **refuser qch à qn** to refuse sb sth; **se refuser à faire** to refuse to do

réfuter [Refyte] *vt* to refute

regagner [R(ə)gaɲe] *vt* (*faveur*) to win back; (*lieu*) to get back to

regain [Rəgɛ̃] *nm* (*renouveau*): **un ~ de** renewed +*nom*

régal [Regal] *nm* treat; **régaler: se régaler** *vi* to have a delicious meal; (*fig*) to enjoy o.s.

regard [R(ə)gaR] *nm* (*coup d'œil*) look, glance; (*expression*) look (in one's eye); **au ~ de** (*loi, morale*) from the point of view of; **en ~ de** in comparison with

regardant, e [R(ə)gaRdã, ãt] *adj* (*économe*) tight-fisted; **peu ~ (sur)** very free (about)

regarder [ʀ(ə)ɡaʀde] *vt* to look at; *(film, télévision, match)* to watch; *(concerner)* to concern ♦ *vi* to look; **ne pas ~ à la dépense** to spare no expense; **~ qn/qch comme** to regard sb/sth as

régie [ʀeʒi] *nf* *(COMM, INDUSTRIE)* state-owned company; *(THÉÂTRE, CINÉMA)* production; *(RADIO, TV)* control room

regimber [ʀ(ə)ʒɛ̃be] *vi* to balk, jib

régime [ʀeʒim] *nm* *(POL)* régime; *(MÉD)* diet; *(ADMIN: carcéral, fiscal etc)* system; *(de bananes, dattes)* bunch; **se mettre au/suivre un ~** to go on/be on a diet

régiment [ʀeʒimɑ̃] *nm* regiment

région [ʀeʒjɔ̃] *nf* region; **régional, e, -aux** *adj* regional

régir [ʀeʒiʀ] *vt* to govern

régisseur [ʀeʒisœʀ] *nm* *(d'un domaine)* steward; *(CINÉMA, TV)* assistant director; *(THÉÂTRE)* stage manager

registre [ʀəʒistʀ] *nm* register

réglage [ʀeɡlaʒ] *nm* adjustment

règle [ʀeɡl] *nf* *(instrument)* ruler; *(loi)* rule; **~s** *nfpl* *(menstruation)* period *sg*; **en ~** *(papiers d'identité)* in order; **en ~ générale** as a (general) rule

réglé, e [ʀeɡle] *adj* *(vie)* well-ordered; *(arrangé)* settled

règlement [ʀeɡləmɑ̃] *nm* *(paiement)* settlement; *(arrêté)* regulation; *(règles, statuts)* regulations *pl*, rules *pl*; **~ de compte(s)** settling of old scores; **réglementaire** *adj* conforming to the regulations; *(tenue)* regulation *cpd*; **réglementation** *nf* *(règles)* regulations; **réglementer** *vt* to regulate

régler [ʀeɡle] *vt* *(conflit, facture)* to settle; *(personne)* to settle up with; *(mécanisme, machine)* to regulate, adjust; *(thermostat etc)* to set, adjust

réglisse [ʀeɡlis] *nf* liquorice

règne [ʀɛɲ] *nm* *(d'un roi etc, fig)* reign; **régner** *vi* *(roi)* to rule, reign; *(fig)* to reign

regorger [ʀ(ə)ɡɔʀʒe] *vi*: **~ de** to overflow with, be bursting with

regret [ʀ(ə)ɡʀɛ] *nm* regret; **à ~** with re-

gret; **sans ~** with no regrets; **regrettable** *adj* regrettable; **regretter** *vt* to regret; *(personne)* to miss; **je regrette mais ...** I'm sorry but ...

regrouper [ʀ(ə)ɡʀupe] *vt* *(grouper)* to group together; *(contenir)* to include, comprise; **se ~** *vi* to gather (together)

régulier, -ière [ʀeɡylje, jɛʀ] *adj* *(gén)* regular; *(vitesse, qualité)* steady; *(égal: couche, ligne)* even, *(TRANSPORTS: ligne, service)*, scheduled, regular; *(légal)* lawful, in order; *(honnête)* straight, on the level; **régulièrement** *adv* regularly; *(uniformément)* evenly

rehausser [ʀɑose] *vt* *(relever)* to heighten, raise; *(fig: souligner)* to set off, enhance

rein [ʀɛ̃] *nm* kidney; **~s** *nmpl* *(dos)* back *sg*

reine [ʀɛn] *nf* queen

reine-claude [ʀɛnklod] *nf* greengage

réinsertion [ʀeɛ̃sɛʀsjɔ̃] *nf* *(de délinquant)* reintegration, rehabilitation

réintégrer [ʀeɛ̃teɡʀe] *vt* *(lieu)* to return to; *(fonctionnaire)* to reinstate

rejaillir [ʀ(ə)ʒajiʀ] *vi* to splash up; **~ sur** *(fig: scandale)* to rebound on; *(: gloire)* to be reflected on

rejet [ʀəʒɛ] *nm* rejection; **rejeter** *vt* *(relancer)* to throw back; *(écarter)* to reject; *(déverser)* to throw out, discharge; *(vomir)* to bring *ou* throw up; **rejeter la responsabilité de qch sur qn** to lay the responsibility for sth at sb's door

rejoindre [ʀ(ə)ʒwɛ̃dʀ] *vt* *(famille, régiment)* to rejoin, return to; *(lieu)* to get (back) to; *(suj: route etc)* to meet, join; *(rattraper)* to catch up (with); **se ~** *vi* to meet; **je te rejoins à la gare** I'll see *ou* meet you at the station

réjouir [ʀeʒwiʀ] *vt* to delight; **se ~ (de)** *vi* to be delighted (about); **réjouissances** *nfpl* *(fête)* festivities

relâche [ʀəlɑʃ] *nm ou nf*: **sans ~** without respite *ou* a break; **relâché, e** *adj* loose, lax; **relâcher** *vt* *(libérer)* to release; *(desserrer)* to loosen; **se relâcher** *vi* *(discipline)* to become slack *ou* lax; *(élève etc)* to slacken off

relais [R(ə)lε] *nm* (*SPORT*): **(course de) ~** relay (race); **prendre le ~ (de)** to take over (from); **~ routier** ≃ transport café (*BRIT*), ≃ truck stop (*US*)

relancer [R(ə)lɑ̃se] *vt* (*balle*) to throw back; (*moteur*) to restart; (*fig*) to boost, revive; (*harceler*): **~ qn** to pester sb

relatif, -ive [R(ə)latif, iv] *adj* relative

relation [R(ə)lasjɔ̃] *nf* (*rapport*) relation(ship); (*connaissance*) acquaintance; **~s** *nfpl* (*rapports*) relations; (*connaissances*) connections; **être/entrer en ~(s) avec** to be/get in contact with

relaxe [Rəlaks] (*fam*) *adj* (*tenue*) informal; (*personne*) relaxed; **relaxer: se relaxer** *vi* to relax

relayer [R(ə)leje] *vt* (*collaborateur, coureur etc*) to relieve; **se ~** *vi* (*dans une activité*) to take it in turns

reléguer [R(ə)lege] *vt* to relegate

relent(s) [Rəlɑ̃] *nm(pl)* (foul) smell

relevé, e [Rəl(ə)ve] *adj* (*manches*) rolled-up; (*sauce*) highly-seasoned ♦ *nm* (*de compteur*) reading; (*bancaire*) statement

relève [Rəlεv] *nf* (*personne*) relief; **prendre la ~** to take over

relever [Rəl(ə)ve] *vt* (*meuble*) to stand up again; (*personne tombée*) to help up; (*vitre, niveau de vie*) to raise; (*col*) to turn up; (*style*) to elevate; (*plat, sauce*) to season; (*sentinelle, équipe*) to relieve; (*fautes*) to pick out; (*défi*) to accept, take up; (*noter: adresse etc*) to take down, note; (*: plan*) to sketch; (*compteur*) to read; (*ramasser: cahiers*) to collect, take in; **se ~** *vi* (*se remettre debout*) to get up; **~ de** (*maladie*) to be recovering from; (*être du ressort de*) to be a matter for; (*fig*) to pertain to; **~ qn de** (*fonctions*) to relieve sb of

relief [Rəljεf] *nm* relief; **mettre en ~** (*fig*) to bring out, highlight

relier [Rəlje] *vt* to link up; (*livre*) to bind; **~ qch à** to link sth to

religieuse [R(ə)liʒjøz] *nf* nun; (*gâteau*) cream bun

religieux, -euse [R(ə)liʒjø, jøz] *adj* religious ♦ *nm* monk

religion [R(ə)liʒjɔ̃] *nf* religion

relire [R(ə)liR] *vt* (*à nouveau*) to reread, read again; (*vérifier*) to read over

reliure [RəljyR] *nf* binding

reluire [R(ə)lɥiR] *vi* to gleam

remanier [R(ə)manje] *vt* to reshape, recast; (*POL*) to reshuffle

remarquable [R(ə)maRkabl] *adj* remarkable

remarque [R(ə)maRk] *nf* remark; (*écrite*) note

remarquer [R(ə)maRke] *vt* (*voir*) to notice; **se ~** *vi* to be noticeable; **faire ~ (à qn) que** to point out (to sb) that; **faire ~ qch (à qn)** to point sth out (to sb); **remarquez, ...** mind you ...; **se faire ~** to draw attention to o.s.

rembourrer [Rɑ̃buRe] *vt* to stuff

remboursement [Rɑ̃buRsəmɑ̃] *nm* (*de dette, d'emprunt*) repayment; (*de frais*) refund; **rembourser** *vt* to pay back, repay; (*frais, billet etc*) to refund; **se faire rembourser** to get a refund

remède [R(ə)mεd] *nm* (*médicament*) medicine; (*traitement, fig*) remedy, cure

remémorer [R(ə)memɔRe]: **se ~** *vt* to recall, recollect

remerciements [RəmεRsimɑ̃] *nmpl* thanks

remercier [R(ə)mεRsje] *vt* to thank; (*congédier*) to dismiss; **~ qn de/d'avoir fait** to thank sb for/for having done

remettre [R(ə)mεtR] *vt* (*replacer*) to put back; (*vêtement*) to put back on; (*ajouter*) to add; (*ajourner*): **~ qch (à)** to postpone sth (until); **se ~** *vi*: **se ~ (de)** to recover (from); **~ qch à qn** (*donner: lettre, clé etc*) to hand over sth to sb; (*: prix, décoration*) to present sb with sth; **se ~ à faire qch** to start doing sth again

remise [R(ə)miz] *nf* (*rabais*) discount; (*local*) shed; **~ de peine** reduction of sentence; **~ en jeu** (*FOOTBALL*) throw-in

remontant [R(ə)mɔ̃tɑ̃, ɑ̃t] *nm* tonic, pickme-up

remonte-pente [R(ə)mɔ̃tpɑ̃t] *nm* ski-lift

remonter [R(ə)mɔ̃te] *vi* to go back up; (*prix, température*) to go up again ♦ *vt* (*pente*) to go up; (*fleuve*) to sail (*ou* swim *etc*) up; (*manches, pantalon*) to roll up; (*col*) to turn up; (*niveau, limite*) to raise; (*fig: personne*) to buck up; (*qch de démonté*) to put back together, reassemble; (*montre*) to wind up; **~ le moral à qn** to raise sb's spirits; **~ à** (*dater de*) to date *ou* go back to

remontrance [R(ə)mɔ̃trɑ̃s] *nf* reproof, reprimand

remontrer [R(ə)mɔ̃tre] *vt* (*fig*): **en ~ à** to prove one's superiority over

remords [R(ə)mɔR] *nm* remorse *no pl*; **avoir des ~** to feel remorse

remorque [R(ə)mɔRk] *nf* trailer; **remorquer** *vt* to tow; **remorqueur** *nm* tug(boat)

remous [Rəmu] *nm* (*d'un navire*) (back)wash *no pl*; (*de rivière*) swirl, eddy ♦ *nmpl* (*fig*) stir *sg*

remparts [Rɑ̃paR] *nmpl* walls, ramparts

remplaçant, e [Rɑ̃plasɑ̃, ɑ̃t] *nm/f* replacement, stand-in; (*SCOL*) supply teacher

remplacement [Rɑ̃plasmɑ̃] *nm* replacement; **faire des ~s** (*professeur*) to do supply teaching; (*secrétaire*) to temp

remplacer [Rɑ̃plase] *vt* to replace; **~ qch/qn par** to replace sth/sb with

rempli, e [Rɑ̃pli] *adj* (*emploi du temps*) full, busy; **~ de** full of, filled with

remplir [Rɑ̃pliR] *vt* to fill (up); (*questionnaire*) to fill out *ou* up; (*obligations, fonction, condition*) to fulfil; **se ~** *vi* to fill up

remporter [Rɑ̃pɔRte] *vt* (*marchandise*) to take away; (*fig*) to win, achieve

remuant, e [Rəmɥɑ̃, ɑ̃t] *adj* restless

remue-ménage [R(ə)mymenaʒ] *nm inv* commotion

remuer [Rəmɥe] *vt* to move; (*café, sauce*) to stir ♦ *vi* to move; **se ~** *vi* to move; (*fam: s'activer*) to get a move on

rémunérer [Remynere] *vt* to remunerate

renard [R(ə)naR] *nm* fox

renchérir [Rɑ̃ʃeRiR] *vi* (*fig*): **~ (sur)** (*en paroles*) to add something (to)

rencontre [Rɑ̃kɔ̃tR] *nf* meeting; (*imprévue*) encounter; **aller à la ~ de qn** to go and meet sb; **rencontrer** *vt* to meet; (*mot, expression*) to come across; (*difficultés*) to meet with; **se rencontrer** *vi* to meet

rendement [Rɑ̃dmɑ̃] *nm* (*d'un travailleur, d'une machine*) output; (*d'un champ*) yield

rendez-vous [Rɑ̃devu] *nm* appointment; (*d'amoureux*) date; (*lieu*) meeting place; **donner ~-~ à qn** to arrange to meet sb; **avoir/prendre ~-~ (avec)** to have/make an appointment (with)

rendre [Rɑ̃dR] *vt* (*restituer*) to give back, return; (*invitation*) to return, repay; (*vomir*) to bring up; (*exprimer, traduire*) to render; (*faire devenir*): **~ qn célèbre/qch possible** to make sb famous/sth possible; **se ~** *vi* (*capituler*) to surrender, give o.s. up; (*aller*): **se ~ quelque part** to go somewhere; **~ la monnaie à qn** to give sb his change; **se ~ compte de qch** to realize sth

rênes [Rɛn] *nfpl* reins

renfermé, e [Rɑ̃fɛRme] *adj* (*fig*) withdrawn ♦ *nm*: **sentir le ~** to smell stuffy

renfermer [Rɑ̃fɛRme] *vt* to contain

renflouer [Rɑ̃flue] *vt* to refloat; (*fig*) to set back on its (*ou* his/her *etc*) feet

renfoncement [Rɑ̃fɔ̃smɑ̃] *nm* recess

renforcer [Rɑ̃fɔRse] *vt* to reinforce; **renfort: renforts** *nmpl* reinforcements; **à grand renfort de** with a great deal of

renfrogné, e [Rɑ̃fRɔɲe] *adj* sullen

rengaine [Rɑ̃gɛn] (*péj*) *nf* old tune

renier [Rənje] *vt* (*personne*) to disown, repudiate; (*foi*) to renounce

renifler [R(ə)nifle] *vi, vt* to sniff

renne [Rɛn] *nm* reindeer *inv*

renom [Rənɔ̃] *nm* reputation; (*célébrité*) renown; **renommé, e** *adj* celebrated, renowned; **renommée** *nf* fame

renoncer [R(ə)nɔ̃se] *vt*: **~ à** *vt* to give up; **~ à faire** to give up the idea of doing

renouer [Rənwe] *vt*: **~ avec** (*habitude*) to

take up again
renouvelable [R(ə)nuv(ə)labl] *adj* (*énergie etc*) renewable
renouveler [R(ə)nuv(ə)le] *vt* to renew; (*exploit, méfait*) to repeat; **se ~** *vi* (*incident*) to recur, happen again; **renouvellement** *nm* (*remplacement*) renewal
rénover [Renɔve] *vt* (*immeuble*) to renovate, do up; (*quartier*) to redevelop
renseignement [Rãsɛɲmã] *nm* information *no pl*, piece of information; (**bureau des**) **~s** information office
renseigner [Rãsɛɲe] *vt*: **~ qn (sur)** to give information to sb (about); **se ~** *vi* to ask for information, make inquiries
rentabilité [Rãtabilite] *nf* profitability
rentable [Rãtabl] *adj* profitable
rente [Rãt] *nf* private income; (*pension*) pension
rentrée [Rãtre] *nf*: **~ (d'argent)** cash *no pl* coming in; **la ~ (des classes)** the start of the new school year

---
rentrée (des classes)

🛈 *La rentrée (des classes) in September marks an important point in the French year. Children and teachers return to school, and political and social life begin again after the long summer break.*

---

rentrer [Rãtre] *vi* (*revenir chez soi*) to go (*ou* come) (back) home; (*entrer de nouveau*) to go (*ou* come) back in; (*entrer*) to go (*ou* come) in; (*air, clou: pénétrer*) to go in; (*revenu*) to come in ♦ *vt* to bring in; (*mettre à l'abri: animaux etc*) to bring in; (: *véhicule*) to put away; (*chemise dans pantalon etc*) to tuck in; (*griffes*) to draw in; **~ le ventre** to pull in one's stomach; **~ dans** (*heurter*) to crash into; **~ dans l'ordre** to be back to normal; **~ dans ses frais** to recover one's expenses
renverse [RãvɛRs]: **à la ~** *adv* backwards
renverser [Rãvɛrse] *vt* (*faire tomber: chaise, verre*) to knock over, overturn; (*liquide, contenu*) to spill, upset; (*piéton*) to knock down; (*retourner*) to turn upside down; (: *ordre des mots etc*) to reverse; (*fig: gouvernement etc*) to overthrow; (*fam: stupéfier*) to bowl over; **se ~** *vi* (*verre, vase*) to fall over; (*contenu*) to spill
renvoi [Rãvwa] *nm* (*d'employé*) dismissal; (*d'élève*) expulsion; (*référence*) cross-reference; (*éructation*) belch; **renvoyer** *vt* to send back; (*congédier*) to dismiss; (*élève: définitivement*) to expel; (*lumière*) to reflect; (*ajourner*): **renvoyer qch (à)** to put sth off *ou* postpone sth (until)
repaire [R(ə)pɛR] *nm* den
répandre [Repãdʀ] *vt* (*renverser*) to spill; (*étaler, diffuser*) to spread; (*odeur*) to give off; **se ~** *vi* to spill; (*se propager*) to spread; **répandu, e** *adj* (*opinion, usage*) widespread
réparation [RepaRasjɔ̃] *nf* repair
réparer [Repare] *vt* to repair; (*fig: offense*) to make up for, atone for; (: *oubli, erreur*) to put right
repartie [Reparti] *nf* retort; **avoir de la ~** to be quick at repartee
repartir [R(ə)paʀtiʀ] *vi* to leave again; (*voyageur*) to set off again; (*fig*) to get going again; **~ à zéro** to start from scratch (again)
répartir [Repaʀtiʀ] *vt* (*pour attribuer*) to share out; (*pour disperser, disposer*) to divide up; (*poids*) to distribute; **se ~** *vt* (*travail, rôles*) to share out between themselves; **répartition** *nf* (*des richesses etc*) distribution
repas [R(ə)pɑ] *nm* meal
repassage [R(ə)pɑsaʒ] *nm* ironing
repasser [R(ə)pase] *vi* to come (*ou* go) back ♦ *vt* (*vêtement, tissu*) to iron; (*examen*) to retake, resit; (*film*) to show again; (*leçon: revoir*) to go over (again)
repêcher [R(ə)peʃe] *vt* to fish out; (*candidat*) to pass (*by inflating marks*)
repentir [Rəpãtiʀ] *nm* repentance; **se ~** *vi* to repent; **se ~ d'avoir fait qch** (*regretter*) to regret having done sth
répercussions [RepɛRkysjɔ̃] *nfpl* (*fig*) re-

percussions

répercuter [ʀepɛʀkyte]: **se ~** *vi* (*bruit*) to reverberate; (*fig*): **se ~ sur** to have repercussions on

repère [ʀ(ə)pɛʀ] *nm* mark; (*monument, événement*) landmark

repérer [ʀ(ə)peʀe] *vt* (*fam: erreur, personne*) to spot; (: *endroit*) to locate; **se ~** *vi* to find one's way about

répertoire [ʀepɛʀtwaʀ] *nm* (*liste*) (alphabetical) list; (*carnet*) index notebook; (*INFORM*) folder, directory; (*d'un artiste*) repertoire

répéter [ʀepete] *vt* to repeat; (*préparer: leçon*) to learn, go over; (*THÉÂTRE*) to rehearse; **se ~** *vi* (*redire*) to repeat o.s.; (*se reproduire*) to be repeated, recur

répétition [ʀepetisjɔ̃] *nf* repetition; (*THÉÂTRE*) rehearsal

répit [ʀepi] *nm* respite

replier [ʀ(ə)plije] *vt* (*rabattre*) to fold down *ou* over; **se ~** *vi* (*troupes, armée*) to withdraw, fall back; (*sur soi-même*) to withdraw into o.s.

réplique [ʀeplik] *nf* (*repartie, fig*) reply; (*THÉÂTRE*) line; (*copie*) replica; **répliquer** *vi* to reply; (*riposter*) to retaliate

répondeur [ʀepɔ̃dœʀ, øz] *nm*: **~ automatique** (*TÉL*) answering machine

répondre [ʀepɔ̃dʀ] *vi* to answer, reply; (*freins*) to respond; **~ à** to reply to, answer; (*affection, salut*) to return; (*provocation*) to respond to; (*correspondre à: besoin*) to answer; (: *conditions*) to meet; (: *description*) to match; (*avec impertinence*): **~ à qn** to answer sb back; **~ de** to answer for

réponse [ʀepɔ̃s] *nf* answer, reply; **en ~ à** in reply to

reportage [ʀ(ə)pɔʀtaʒ] *nm* report; **~ en direct** (live) commentary

reporter¹ [ʀəpɔʀtɛʀ] *nm* reporter

reporter² [ʀəpɔʀte] *vt* (*ajourner*): **~ qch (à)** to postpone sth (until); (*transférer*): **~ qch sur** to transfer sth to; **se ~ à** (*époque*) to think back to; (*document*) to refer to

repos [ʀ(ə)po] *nm* rest; (*tranquillité*) peace (and quiet); (*MIL*): **~!** stand at ease!; **ce**

n'est pas de tout ~! it's no picnic!

reposant, e [ʀ(ə)pozɑ̃, ɑ̃t] *adj* restful

reposer [ʀ(ə)poze] *vt* (*verre, livre*) to put down; (*délasser*) to rest ♦ *vi*: **laisser ~** (*pâte*) to leave to stand; **se ~** *vi* to rest; **se ~ sur qn** to rely on sb; **~ sur** (*fig*) to rest on

repoussant, e [ʀ(ə)pusɑ̃, ɑ̃t] *adj* repulsive

repousser [ʀ(ə)puse] *vi* to grow again ♦ *vt* to repel, repulse; (*offre*) to turn down, reject; (*personne*) to push back; (*différer*) to put back

reprendre [ʀ(ə)pʀɑ̃dʀ] *vt* (*objet prêté, donné*) to take back; (*prisonnier, ville*) to recapture; (*firme, entreprise*) to take over; (*le travail*) to resume; (*emprunter: argument, idée*) to take up, use; (*refaire: article etc*) to go over again; (*vêtement*) to alter; (*réprimander*) to tell off; (*corriger*) to correct; (*chercher*): **je viendrai te ~ à 4 h** I'll come and fetch you at 4; (*se resservir de*): **~ du pain/un œuf** to take (*ou* eat) more bread/another egg ♦ *vi* (*classes, pluie*) to start (up) again; (*activités, travaux, combats*) to resume, start (up) again; (*affaires*) to pick up; (*dire*): **reprit-il** he went on; **se ~** *vi* (*se ressaisir*) to recover; **~ des forces** to recover one's strength; **~ courage** to take new heart; **~ la route** to set off again; **~ haleine** *ou* **son souffle** to get one's breath back

représailles [ʀ(ə)pʀezaj] *nfpl* reprisals

représentant, e [ʀ(ə)pʀezɑ̃tɑ̃, ɑ̃t] *nm/f* representative

représentation [ʀ(ə)pʀezɑ̃tasjɔ̃] *nf* (*symbole, image*) representation; (*spectacle*) performance

représenter [ʀ(ə)pʀezɑ̃te] *vt* to represent; (*donner: pièce, opéra*) to perform; **se ~** *vt* (*se figurer*) to imagine

répression [ʀepʀesjɔ̃] *nf* repression

réprimer [ʀepʀime] *vt* (*émotions*) to suppress; (*peuple etc*) to repress

repris [ʀ(ə)pʀi, iz] *nm*: **~ de justice** exprisoner, ex-convict

reprise [ʀ(ə)pʀiz] *nf* (*recommencement*) resumption; (*économique*) recovery; (*TV*) repeat; (*COMM*) trade-in, part exchange; (*raccommodage*) mend; **à plusieurs ~s** on several occasions

repriser [R(ə)pRize] *vt* (*chaussette, lainage*) to darn; (*tissu*) to mend

reproche [R(ə)pRɔʃ] *nm* (*remontrance*) reproach; **faire des ~s à qn** to reproach sb; **sans ~(s)** beyond reproach; **reprocher** *vt*: **reprocher qch à qn** to reproach *ou* blame sb for sth; **reprocher qch à** (*critiquer*) to have sth against

reproduction [R(ə)pRɔdyksjɔ̃] *nf* reproduction

reproduire [R(ə)pRɔdɥiR] *vt* to reproduce; **se ~** *vi* (*BIO*) to reproduce; (*recommencer*) to recur, re-occur

réprouver [RepRuve] *vt* to reprove

reptile [Reptil] *nm* reptile

repu, e [Rəpy] *adj* satisfied, sated

république [Repyblik] *nf* republic

répugnant, e [Repyɲɑ̃, ɑ̃t] *adj* disgusting

répugner [Repyɲe]: **~ à** *vt*: **~ à qn** to repel *ou* disgust sb; **~ à faire** to be loath *ou* reluctant to do

réputation [Repytasjɔ̃] *nf* reputation; **réputé, e** *adj* renowned

requérir [RəkeRiR] *vt* (*nécessiter*) to require, call for

requête [Rəkɛt] *nf* request

requin [Rəkɛ̃] *nm* shark

requis, e [Rəki, iz] *adj* required

RER *sigle m* (= *réseau express régional*) Greater Paris high-speed train service

rescapé, e [Reskape] *nm/f* survivor

rescousse [Reskus] *nf*: **aller à la ~ de qn** to go to sb's aid *ou* rescue

réseau, x [Rezo] *nm* network

réservation [RezeRvasjɔ̃] *nf* booking, reservation

réserve [RezeRv] *nf* (*retenue*) reserve; (*entrepôt*) storeroom; (*restriction, d'Indiens*) reservation; (*de pêche, chasse*) preserve; **de ~** (*provisions etc*) in reserve

réservé, e [RezeRve] *adj* reserved; **chasse/pêche ~e** private hunting/fishing

réserver [RezeRve] *vt* to reserve; (*chambre, billet etc*) to book, reserve; (*fig: destiner*) to have in store; (*garder*) to keep *ou* save sth for; **~ qch pour/à** to keep *ou* save sth for

réservoir [RezeRvwaR] *nm* tank

résidence [Rezidɑ̃s] *nf* residence; **~ secondaire** second home; **résidentiel, le** *adj* residential; **résider** *vi*: **résider à/dans/en** to reside in; **résider dans** (*fig*) to lie in

résidu [Rezidy] *nm* residue *no pl*

résigner [Reziɲe]: **se ~** *vi*: **se ~ (à qch/à faire)** to resign o.s. (to sth/to doing)

résilier [Rezilje] *vt* to terminate

résistance [Rezistɑ̃s] *nf* resistance; (*de réchaud, bouilloire: fil*) element

résistant, e [Rezistɑ̃, ɑ̃t] *adj* (*personne*) robust, tough; (*matériau*) strong, hardwearing

résister [Reziste] *vi* to resist; **~ à** (*assaut, tentation*) to resist; (*supporter: gel etc*) to withstand; (*désobéir à*) to stand up to, oppose

résolu, e [Rezɔly] *pp de* **résoudre** ♦ *adj*: **être ~ à qch/faire** to be set upon sth/doing

résolution [Rezɔlysjɔ̃] *nf* (*fermeté, décision*) resolution; (*d'un problème*) solution

résolve *etc* [Rezɔlv] *vb voir* **résoudre**

résonner [Rezɔne] *vi* (*cloche, pas*) to reverberate, resound; (*salle*) to be resonant

résorber [RezɔRbe]: **se ~** *vi* (*fig: chômage*) to be reduced; (: *déficit*) to be absorbed

résoudre [RezudR] *vt* to solve; **se ~ à faire** to bring o.s. to do

respect [Rɛspɛ] *nm* respect; **tenir en ~** to keep at bay; **respecter** *vt* to respect; **respectueux, -euse** *adj* respectful

respiration [RɛspiRasjɔ̃] *nf* breathing *no pl*

respirer [RɛspiRe] *vi* to breathe; (*fig: se détendre*) to get one's breath; (: *se rassurer*) to breathe again ♦ *vt* to breathe (in), inhale; (*manifester: santé, calme etc*) to exude

resplendir [Rɛsplɑ̃diR] *vi* to shine; (*fig*): **~ (de)** to be radiant (with)

responsabilité [Rɛspɔ̃sabilite] *nf* responsibility; (*légale*) liability

responsable [ʀɛspɔ̃sabl] *adj* responsible ♦ *nm/f* (*coupable*) person responsible; (*personne compétente*) person in charge; (*de parti, syndicat*) official; ~ **de** responsible for

resquiller [ʀɛskije] (*fam*) *vi* to get in without paying; (*ne pas faire la queue*) to jump the queue

ressaisir [ʀ(ə)sezir]: **se** ~ *vi* to regain one's self-control

ressasser [ʀ(ə)sase] *vt* to keep going over

ressemblance [ʀ(ə)sɑ̃blɑ̃s] *nf* resemblance, similarity, likeness

ressemblant, e [ʀ(ə)sɑ̃blɑ̃, ɑ̃t] *adj* (*portrait*) lifelike, true to life

ressembler [ʀ(ə)sɑ̃ble]: ~ **à** *vt* to be like, resemble; (*visuellement*) to look like; **se** ~ *vi* to be (*ou* look) alike

ressemeler [ʀ(ə)səm(ə)le] *vt* to (re)sole

ressentiment [ʀ(ə)sɑ̃timɑ̃] *nm* resentment

ressentir [ʀ(ə)sɑ̃tir] *vt* to feel

resserrer [ʀ(ə)sere] *vt* (*nœud, boulon*) to tighten (up); (*fig: liens*) to strengthen

resservir [ʀ(ə)servir] *vi* to do *ou* serve again; **se** ~ *vi* to help o.s. again

ressort [ʀɔsɔʀ] *nm* (*pièce*) spring; (*énergie*) spirit; (*recours*): **en dernier** ~ as a last resort; (*compétence*): **être du** ~ **de** to fall within the competence of

ressortir [ʀəsɔʀtir] *vi* to go (*ou* come) out (again); (*contraster*) to stand out; ~ **de** to emerge from; **faire** ~ (*fig: souligner*) to bring out

ressortissant, e [ʀ(ə)sɔʀtisɑ̃, ɑ̃t] *nm/f* national

ressources [ʀ(ə)suʀs] *nfpl* (*moyens*) resources

ressusciter [ʀesysite] *vt* (*fig*) to revive, bring back ♦ *vi* to rise (from the dead)

restant, e [ʀɛstɑ̃, ɑ̃t] *adj* remaining ♦ *nm*: **le** ~ **(de)** the remainder (of); **un** ~ **de** (*de trop*) some left-over

restaurant [ʀɛstɔʀɑ̃] *nm* restaurant

restauration [ʀɛstɔʀasjɔ̃] *nf* restoration; (*hôtellerie*) catering; ~ **rapide** fast food

restaurer [ʀɛstɔʀe] *vt* to restore; **se** ~ *vi* to have something to eat

reste [ʀɛst] *nm* (*restant*): **le** ~ **(de)** the rest (of); (*de trop*): **un** ~ **(de)** some left-over; ~**s** *nmpl* (*nourriture*) left-overs; (*d'une cité etc, dépouille mortelle*) remains; **du** ~, **au** ~ besides, moreover

rester [ʀɛste] *vi* to stay, remain; (*subsister*) to remain, be left; (*durer*) to last, live on ♦ *vb impers*: **il reste du pain/2 œufs** there's some bread/there are 2 eggs left (over); **restons-en là** let's leave it at that; **il me reste assez de temps** I have enough time left; **il ne me reste plus qu'à ...** I've just got to ...

restituer [ʀɛstitɥe] *vt* (*objet, somme*): ~ **qch (à qn)** to return sth (to sb)

restreindre [ʀɛstʀɛ̃dʀ] *vt* to restrict, limit

restriction [ʀɛstʀiksjɔ̃] *nf* restriction

résultat [ʀezylta] *nm* result; (*d'examen, d'élection*) results *pl*

résulter [ʀezylte]: ~ **de** *vt* to result from, be the result of

résumé [ʀezyme] *nm* summary, résumé

résumer [ʀezyme] *vt* (*texte*) to summarize; (*récapituler*) to sum up

résurrection [ʀezyʀɛksjɔ̃] *nf* resurrection

rétablir [ʀetablir] *vt* to restore, reestablish; **se** ~ *vi* (*guérir*) to recover; (*silence, calme*) to return, be restored; **rétablissement** *nm* restoring; (*guérison*) recovery

retaper [ʀ(ə)tape] (*fam*) *vt* (*maison, voiture etc*) to do up; (*revigorer*) to buck up

retard [ʀ(ə)taʀ] *nm* (*d'une personne attendue*) lateness *no pl*; (*sur l'horaire, un programme*) delay; (*fig: scolaire, mental etc*) backwardness; **en** ~ **(de 2 heures)** (2 hours) late; **avoir du** ~ to be late; (*sur un programme*) to be behind (schedule); **prendre du** ~ (*train, avion*) to be delayed; **sans** ~ without delay

retardataire [ʀ(ə)taʀdatɛʀ] *nmf* latecomer

retardement [ʀ(ə)taʀdəmɑ̃]: **à** ~ *adj* delayed action *cpd*; **bombe à** ~ time bomb

retarder [ʀ(ə)taʀde] *vt* to delay; (*montre*

to put back ♦ vi (montre) to be slow; ~ **qn (d'une heure)** (sur un horaire) to delay sb (an hour); ~ **qch (de 2 jours)** (départ, date) to put sth back (2 days)

retenir [Rət(ə)niR] vt (garder, retarder) to keep, detain; (maintenir: objet qui glisse, fig: colère, larmes) to hold back; (se rappeler) to retain; (réserver) to reserve; (accepter: proposition etc) to accept; (fig: empêcher d'agir): ~ **qn (de faire)** to hold sb back (from doing); (prélever): ~ **qch (sur)** to deduct sth (from); **se** ~ vi (se raccrocher): **se** ~ **à** to hold onto; (se contenir): **se** ~ **de faire** to restrain o.s. from doing; ~ **son souffle** to hold one's breath

retentir [R(ə)tɑ̃tiR] vi to ring out; (salle): ~ **de** to ring ou resound with; retentissant, e adj resounding; **retentissement** nm repercussion

retenu, e [Rət(ə)ny] adj (place) reserved; (personne: empêché) held up; **retenue** nf (prélèvement) deduction; (SCOL) detention; (modération) (self-)restraint

réticence [Retisɑ̃s] nf hesitation, reluctance no pl; **réticent, e** adj hesitant, reluctant

rétine [Retin] nf retina

retiré, e [R(ə)tiRe] adj (vie) secluded; (lieu) remote

retirer [R(ə)tiRe] vt (vêtement, lunettes) to take off, remove; (argent, plainte) to withdraw; (reprendre: bagages, billets) to collect, pick up; (extraire): ~ **qch de** to take sth out of, remove sth from

retombées [Rətɔ̃be] nfpl (radioactives) fallout sg; (fig: répercussions) effects

retomber [R(ə)tɔ̃be] vi (à nouveau) to fall again; (atterrir: après un saut etc) to land; (échoir): ~ **sur qn** to fall on sb

rétorquer [Retɔrke] vt: ~ **(à qn) que** to retort (to sb) that

retouche [R(ə)tuʃ] nf (sur vêtement) alteration; **retoucher** vt (photographie) to touch up; (texte, vêtement) to alter

retour [R(ə)tuR] nm return; **au** ~ (en route) on the way back; **à mon** ~ when I get/

got back; **être de** ~ **(de)** to be back (from); **par** ~ **du courrier** by return of post

retourner [R(ə)turne] vt (dans l'autre sens: matelas, crêpe etc) to turn (over); (: sac, vêtement) to turn inside out; (fam: bouleverser) to shake; (renvoyer, restituer): ~ **qch à qn** to return sth to sb ♦ vi (aller, revenir): ~ **quelque part/à** to go back ou return somewhere/to; **se** ~ vi (tourner la tête) to turn round; ~ **à** (état, activité) to return to, go back to; **se** ~ **contre** (fig) to turn against

retrait [R(ə)tRɛ] nm (d'argent) withdrawal; **en** ~ set back; ~ **du permis (de conduire)** disqualification from driving (BRIT), revocation of driver's license (US)

retraite [R(ə)tRɛt] nf (d'un employé) retirement; (revenu) pension; (d'une armée, REL) retreat; **prendre sa** ~ to retire; ~ **anticipée** early retirement; **retraité, e** adj retired ♦ nm/f pensioner

retrancher [R(ə)tRɑ̃ʃe] vt (nombre, somme): ~ **qch de** to take ou deduct sth from; **se** ~ **derrière/dans** to take refuge behind/in

retransmettre [R(ə)tRɑ̃smɛtR] vt (RADIO) to broadcast; (TV) to show

rétrécir [RetResiR] vt (vêtement) to take in ♦ vi to shrink

rétribution [Retribysjɔ̃] nf payment

rétro [RetRo] adj inv: **la mode** ~ the nostalgia vogue

rétrograde [RetRɔgRad] adj reactionary, backward-looking

rétroprojecteur [RetRopRɔʒɛktœR] nm overhead projector

rétrospective [RetRɔspɛktiv] nf retrospective exhibition/season; **rétrospectivement** adv in retrospect

retrousser [R(ə)tRuse] vt to roll up

retrouvailles [R(ə)tRuvaj] nfpl reunion sg

retrouver [R(ə)tRuve] vt (fugitif, objet perdu) to find; (calme, santé) to regain; (revoir) to see again; (rejoindre) to meet (again), join; **se** ~ vi to meet; (s'orienter) to find one's way; **se** ~ **quelque part** to find o.s.

somewhere; **s'y ~** (*y voir clair*) to make sense of it; (*rentrer dans ses frais*) to break even

rétroviseur [ʀetʀɔvizœʀ] *nm* (rear-view) mirror

réunion [ʀeynjɔ̃] *nf* (*séance*) meeting

réunir [ʀeyniʀ] *vt* (*rassembler*) to gather together; (*inviter: amis, famille*) to have round, have in; (*cumuler: qualités etc*) to combine; (*rapprocher: ennemis*) to bring together (again), reunite; (*rattacher: parties*) to join (together); **se ~** *vi* (*se rencontrer*) to meet

réussi, e [ʀeysi] *adj* successful

réussir [ʀeysiʀ] *vi* to succeed, be successful; (*à un examen*) to pass ♦ *vt* to make a success of; **~ à faire** to succeed in doing; **~ à qn** (*être bénéfique à*) to agree with sb; **réussite** *nf* success; (*CARTES*) patience

revaloir [ʀ(ə)valwaʀ] *vt*: **je vous revaudrai cela** I'll repay you some day; (*en mal*) I'll pay you back for this

revanche [ʀ(ə)vɑ̃ʃ] *nf* revenge; (*sport*) revenge match; **en ~** on the other hand

rêve [ʀɛv] *nm* dream; **de ~** dream *cpd*; **faire un ~** to have a dream

revêche [ʀəvɛʃ] *adj* surly, sour-tempered

réveil [ʀevɛj] *nm* waking up *no pl*; (*fig*) awakening; (*pendule*) alarm (clock); **au ~** on waking (up); **réveille-matin** *nm inv* alarm clock; **réveiller** *vt* (*personne*) to wake up; (*fig*) to awaken, revive; **se réveiller** *vi* to wake up

réveillon [ʀevɛjɔ̃] *nm* Christmas Eve; (*de la Saint-Sylvestre*) New Year's Eve; **réveillonner** *vi* to celebrate Christmas Eve (*ou* New Year's Eve)

révélateur, -trice [ʀevelatœʀ, tʀis] *adj*: **~ (de qch)** revealing (sth)

révéler [ʀevele] *vt* to reveal; **se ~** *vi* to be revealed, reveal itself ♦ *vb +attrib*: **se ~ difficile/aisé** to prove difficult/easy

revenant, e [ʀ(ə)vənɑ̃, ɑ̃t] *nm/f* ghost

revendeur, -euse [ʀ(ə)vɑ̃dœʀ, øz] *nm/f* (*détaillant*) retailer; (*de drogue*) (drug-) dealer

revendication [ʀ(ə)vɑ̃dikasjɔ̃] *nf* claim, demand

revendiquer [ʀ(ə)vɑ̃dike] *vt* to claim, demand; (*responsabilité*) to claim

revendre [ʀ(ə)vɑ̃dʀ] *vt* (*d'occasion*) to resell; (*détailler*) to sell; **à ~** (*en abondance*) to spare

revenir [ʀəv(ə)niʀ] *vi* to come back; (*coûter*): **~ cher/à 10 euros (à qn)** to cost (sb) a lot/10 euros; **~ à** (*reprendre: études, projet*) to return to, go back to; (*équivaloir à*) to amount to; **~ à qn** (*part, honneur*) to go to sb, be sb's; (*souvenir, nom*) to come back to sb; **~ sur** (*question, sujet*) to go back over; (*engagement*) to go back on; **~ à soi** to come round; **n'en pas ~**: **je n'en reviens pas** I can't get over it; **~ sur ses pas** to retrace one's steps; **cela revient à dire que/au même** it amounts to saying that/the same thing; **faire ~** (*CULIN*) to brown

revenu [ʀəv(ə)ny] *nm* income; **~s** *nmpl* income *sg*

rêver [ʀeve] *vi, vt* to dream; **~ de/à** to dream of

réverbère [ʀevɛʀbɛʀ] *nm* street lamp *ou* light; **réverbérer** *vt* to reflect

révérence [ʀeveʀɑ̃s] *nf* (*salut*) bow; (: *de femme*) curtsey

rêverie [ʀɛvʀi] *nf* daydreaming *no pl*, daydream

revers [ʀ(ə)vɛʀ] *nm* (*de feuille, main*) back; (*d'étoffe*) wrong side; (*de pièce, médaille*) back, reverse; (*TENNIS, PING-PONG*) backhand; (*de veste*) lapel; (*fig: échec*) setback

revêtement [ʀ(ə)vɛtmɑ̃] *nm* (*des sols*) flooring; (*de chaussée*) surface

revêtir [ʀ(ə)vetiʀ] *vt* (*habit*) to don, put on; (*prendre: importance, apparence*) to take on; **~ qch de** to cover sth with

rêveur, -euse [ʀɛvœʀ, øz] *adj* dreamy ♦ *nm/f* dreamer

revient [ʀəvjɛ̃] *vb voir* **revenir**

revigorer [ʀ(ə)vigɔʀe] *vt* (*air frais*) to invigorate, brace up; (*repas, boisson*) to revive, buck up

revirement [R(ə)viRmɑ̃] *nm* change of mind; (*d'une situation*) reversal

réviser [Revize] *vt* to revise; (*machine*) to overhaul, service

révision [Revizjɔ̃] *nf* revision; (*de voiture*) servicing *no pl*

revivre [R(ə)vivR] *vi* (*reprendre des forces*) to come alive again ♦ *vt* (*épreuve, moment*) to relive

revoir [RəvwaR] *vt* to see again; (*réviser*) to revise ♦ *nm*: **au ~** goodbye

révoltant, e [Revɔltɑ̃, ɑ̃t] *adj* revolting, appalling

révolte [Revɔlt] *nf* rebellion, revolt

révolter [Revɔlte] *vt* to revolt; **se ~ (contre)** to rebel (against); **ça me révolte (de voir que ...)** I'm revolted *ou* appalled (to see that ...)

révolu, e [Revɔly] *adj* past; (*ADMIN*): **âgé de 18 ans ~s** over 18 years of age

révolution [Revɔlysjɔ̃] *nf* revolution; **révolutionnaire** *adj, nm/f* revolutionary

revolver [RevɔlvɛR] *nm* gun; (*à barillet*) revolver

révoquer [Revɔke] *vt* (*fonctionnaire*) to dismiss; (*arrêt, contrat*) to revoke

revue [R(ə)vy] *nf* review; (*périodique*) review, magazine; (*de music-hall*) variety show; **passer en ~** (*mentalement*) to go through

rez-de-chaussée [Red(ə)ʃose] *nm inv* ground floor

RF *sigle f* = **République française**

Rhin [Rɛ̃] *nm* Rhine

rhinocéros [RinɔseRɔs] *nm* rhinoceros

Rhône [Ron] *nm* Rhone

rhubarbe [RybaRb] *nf* rhubarb

rhum [Rɔm] *nm* rum

rhumatisme [Rymatism] *nm* rheumatism *no pl*

rhume [Rym] *nm* cold; **~ de cerveau** head cold; **le ~ des foins** hay fever

ri [Ri] *pp de* **rire**

riant, e [R(i)jɑ̃, R(i)jɑ̃t] *adj* smiling, cheerful

ricaner [Rikane] *vi* (*avec méchanceté*) to snigger; (*bêtement*) to giggle

riche [Riʃ] *adj* rich; (*personne, pays*) rich, wealthy; **~ en** rich in; **richesse** *nf* wealth; (*fig: de sol, musée etc*) richness; **richesses** *nfpl* (*ressources, argent*) wealth *sg*; (*fig: trésors*) treasures

ricochet [Rikɔʃɛ] *nm*: **faire des ~s** to skip stones; **par ~** (*fig*) as an indirect result

rictus [Riktys] *nm* grin

ride [Rid] *nf* wrinkle

rideau, x [Rido] *nm* curtain; **~ de fer** (*boutique*) metal shutter(s)

rider [Ride] *vt* to wrinkle; **se ~** *vi* to become wrinkled

ridicule [Ridikyl] *adj* ridiculous ♦ *nm*: **le ~** ridicule; **ridiculiser: se ridiculiser** *vi* to make a fool of o.s.

MOT-CLÉ

rien [Rjɛ̃] *pron* 1: **(ne) ... rien** nothing; *tournure negative + anything*; **qu'est-ce que vous avez? – rien** what have you got? – nothing; **il n'a rien dit/fait** he said/did nothing; he hasn't said/done anything; **il n'a rien** (*n'est pas blessé*) he's all right; **de rien!** not at all!

2 (*quelque chose*): **a-t-il jamais rien fait pour nous?** has he ever done anything for us?

3: **rien de: rien d'intéressant** nothing interesting; **rien d'autre** nothing else; **rien du tout** nothing at all

4: **rien que** just, only; nothing but; **rien que pour lui faire plaisir** only *ou* just to please him; **rien que la vérité** nothing but the truth; **rien que cela** that alone

♦ *nm*: **un petit rien** (*cadeau*) a little something; **des riens** trivia *pl*; **un rien de** a hint of; **en un rien de temps** in no time at all

---

rieur, -euse [R(i)jœR, R(i)jøz] *adj* cheerful

rigide [Riʒid] *adj* stiff; (*fig*) rigid; strict

rigole [Rigɔl] *nf* (*conduit*) channel

rigoler [Rigɔle] *vi* (*fam: rire*) to laugh; (*s'amuser*) to have (some) fun; (*plaisanter*) to be joking *ou* kidding; **rigolo, -ote**

(*fam*) *adj* funny ♦ *nm/f* comic; (*péj*) fraud, phoney

rigoureusement [ʀiguʀøzmɑ̃] *adv* (*vrai*) absolutely; (*interdit*) strictly

rigoureux, -euse [ʀiguʀø, øz] *adj* rigorous; (*hiver*) hard, harsh

rigueur [ʀigœʀ] *nf* rigour; **être de ~** to be the rule; **à la ~** at a pinch; **tenir ~ à qn de qch** to hold sth against sb

rillettes [ʀijɛt] *nfpl* potted meat (*made from pork or goose*)

rime [ʀim] *nf* rhyme

rinçage [ʀɛ̃saʒ] *nm* rinsing (out); (*opération*) rinse

rincer [ʀɛ̃se] *vt* to rinse; (*récipient*) to rinse out

ring [ʀiŋ] *nm* (boxing) ring

ringard, e [ʀɛ̃gaʀ, aʀd] (*fam*) *adj* old-fashioned

rions [ʀjɔ̃] *vb voir* **rire**

riposter [ʀipɔste] *vi* to retaliate ♦ *vt*: **~ que** to retort that

rire [ʀiʀ] *vi* to laugh; (*se divertir*) to have fun ♦ *nm* laugh; **le ~** laughter; **~ de** to laugh at; **pour ~** (*pas sérieusement*) for a joke *ou* a laugh

risée [ʀize] *nf*: **être la ~ de** to be the laughing stock of

risible [ʀizibl] *adj* laughable

risque [ʀisk] *nm* risk; **le ~** danger; **à ses ~s et périls** at his own risk; **risqué, e** *adj* risky; (*plaisanterie*) risqué, daring; **risquer** *vt* to risk; (*allusion, question*) to venture, hazard; **ça ne risque rien** it's quite safe; **risquer de: il risque de se tuer** he could get himself killed; **ce qui risque de se produire** what might *ou* could well happen; **il ne risque pas de recommencer** there's no chance of him doing that again; **se risquer à faire** (*tenter*) to venture *ou* dare to do

rissoler [ʀisɔle] *vi, vt*: **(faire)** **~** to brown

ristourne [ʀistuʀn] *nf* discount

rite [ʀit] *nm* rite; (*fig*) ritual

rivage [ʀivaʒ] *nm* shore

rival, e, -aux [ʀival, o] *adj, nm/f* rival; ri-

valiser *vi*: **rivaliser avec** (*personne*) to rival, vie with; **rivalité** *nf* rivalry

rive [ʀiv] *nf* shore; (*de fleuve*) bank; **riverain, e** *nm/f* riverside (*ou* lakeside) resident; (*d'une route*) local resident

rivet [ʀivɛ] *nm* rivet

rivière [ʀivjɛʀ] *nf* river

rixe [ʀiks] *nf* brawl, scuffle

riz [ʀi] *nm* rice; **rizière** *nf* paddy-field, rice-field

RMI *sigle m* (= *revenu minimum d'insertion*) ≃ income support (*BRIT*), welfare (*US*)

RN *sigle f* = **route nationale**

robe [ʀɔb] *nf* dress; (*de juge*) robe; (*pelage*) coat; **~ de chambre** dressing gown; **~ de soirée/de mariée** evening/wedding dress

robinet [ʀɔbinɛ] *nm* tap

robot [ʀɔbo] *nm* robot

robuste [ʀɔbyst] *adj* robust, sturdy; **robustesse** *nf* robustness, sturdiness

roc [ʀɔk] *nm* rock

rocade [ʀɔkad] *nf* bypass

rocaille [ʀɔkaj] *nf* loose stones *pl*; (*jardin*) rockery, rock garden

roche [ʀɔʃ] *nf* rock

rocher [ʀɔʃe] *nm* rock

rocheux, -euse [ʀɔʃø, øz] *adj* rocky

rodage [ʀɔdaʒ] *nm*: **en ~** running in

roder [ʀɔde] *vt* (*AUTO*) to run in

rôder [ʀode] *vi* to roam about; (*de façon suspecte*) to lurk (about *ou* around); **rôdeur, -euse** *nm/f* prowler

rogne [ʀɔɲ] (*fam*) *nf*: **être en ~** to be in a temper

rogner [ʀɔɲe] *vt* to clip; **~ sur** (*fig*) to cut down *ou* back on

rognons [ʀɔɲɔ̃] *nmpl* (*CULIN*) kidneys

roi [ʀwa] *nm* king; **la fête des R~s, les R~s** Twelfth Night

fête des Rois

ⓘ **La fête des Rois** *is celebrated on January 6. Figurines representing the magi are traditionally added to the Christmas crib and people eat* **la galette des**

Rois, *a plain, flat cake in which a porcelain charm* (**la fève**) *is hidden. Whoever finds the charm is king or queen for the day and chooses a partner.*

---

rôle [ʀol] *nm* role, part

rollers [ʀɔlɛʀ] *mpl* Rollerblades ®

romain, e [ʀɔmɛ̃, ɛn] *adj* Roman ♦ *nm/f:* **R~, e** Roman

roman, e [ʀɔmɑ̃, an] *adj* (ARCHIT) Romanesque ♦ *nm* novel; **~ d'espionnage** spy novel *ou* story; **~ policier** detective story

romance [ʀɔmɑ̃s] *nf* ballad

romancer [ʀɔmɑ̃se] *vt* (*agrémenter*) to romanticize; **romancier, -ière** *nm/f* novelist; **romanesque** *adj* (*amours, aventures*) storybook *cpd*; (*sentimental*) romantic

roman-feuilleton [ʀɔmɑ̃fœjtɔ̃] *nm* serialized novel

romanichel, le [ʀɔmaniʃɛl] (*péj*) *nm/f* gipsy

romantique [ʀɔmɑ̃tik] *adj* romantic

romarin [ʀɔmaʀɛ̃] *nm* rosemary

rompre [ʀɔ̃pʀ] *vt* to break; (*entretien, fiançailles*) to break off ♦ *vi* (*fiancés*) to break it off; **se ~** *vi* to break; **rompu, e** *adj* (*fourbu*) exhausted

ronces [ʀɔ̃s] *nfpl* brambles

ronchonner [ʀɔ̃ʃɔne] (*fam*) *vi* to grouse, grouch

rond, e [ʀɔ̃, ʀɔ̃d] *adj* round; (*joues, mollets*) well-rounded; (*fam: ivre*) tight ♦ *nm* (*cercle*) ring; (*fam: sou*): **je n'ai plus un ~** I haven't a penny left; **en ~** (*s'asseoir, danser*) in a ring; **ronde** (*gén: de surveillance*) rounds *pl*, patrol; (*danse*) round (dance); (*MUS*) semibreve (BRIT), whole note (US); **à la ronde** (*alentour*): **à 10 km à la ronde** for 10 km round; **rondelet, te** *adj* plump

rondelle [ʀɔ̃dɛl] *nf* (*tranche*) slice, round; (*TECH*) washer

rondement [ʀɔ̃dmɑ̃] *adv* (*efficacement*) briskly

rondin [ʀɔ̃dɛ̃] *nm* log

rond-point [ʀɔ̃pwɛ̃] *nm* roundabout

ronflant, e [ʀɔ̃flɑ̃, ɑ̃t] (*péj*) *adj* high-flown, grand

ronflement [ʀɔ̃fləmɑ̃] *nm* snore, snoring

ronfler [ʀɔ̃fle] *vi* to snore; (*moteur, poêle*) to hum

ronger [ʀɔ̃ʒe] *vt* to gnaw (at); (*suj: vers, rouille*) to eat into; **se ~ les ongles** to bite one's nails; **se ~ les sangs** to worry o.s. sick; **rongeur** *nm* rodent

ronronner [ʀɔ̃ʀɔne] *vi* to purr

rosace [ʀozas] *nf* (*vitrail*) rose window

rosbif [ʀɔsbif] *nm:* **du ~** roasting beef; (*cuit*) roast beef

rose [ʀoz] *nf* rose ♦ *adj* pink

rosé, e [ʀoze] *adj* pinkish; **(vin) ~** rosé

roseau, x [ʀozo] *nm* reed

rosée [ʀoze] *nf* dew

rosette [ʀozɛt] *nf* (*nœud*) bow

rosier [ʀozje] *nm* rosebush, rose tree

rosse [ʀɔs] (*fam*) *adj* nasty, vicious

rossignol [ʀɔsiɲɔl] *nm* (ZOOL) nightingale

rot [ʀo] *nm* belch; (*de bébé*) burp

rotatif, -ive [ʀɔtatif, iv] *adj* rotary

rotation [ʀɔtasjɔ̃] *nf* rotation

roter [ʀɔte] (*fam*) *vi* to burp, belch

rôti [ʀoti] *nm:* **du ~** roasting meat; (*cuit*) roast meat; **~ de bœuf/porc** joint of beef/pork

rotin [ʀɔtɛ̃] *nm* rattan (cane); **fauteuil en ~** cane (arm)chair

rôtir [ʀotiʀ] *vi, vt* (*aussi:* **faire ~**) to roast; **rôtisserie** *nf* (*restaurant*) steakhouse; (*traiteur*) roast meat shop; **rôtissoire** *nf* (*roasting*) spit

rotule [ʀɔtyl] *nf* kneecap

roturier, -ière [ʀɔtyʀje, jɛʀ] *nm/f* commoner

rouage [ʀwaʒ] *nm* cog(wheel), gearwheel; **les ~s de l'État** the wheels of State

roucouler [ʀukule] *vi* to coo

roue [ʀu] *nf* wheel; **~ de secours** spare wheel

roué, e [ʀwe] *adj* wily

rouer [ʀwe] *vt:* **~ qn de coups** to give sb a thrashing

rouge [ʀuʒ] *adj, nm/f* red ♦ *nm* red; **(vin)**

~ red wine; **sur la liste** ~ ex-directory (*BRIT*), unlisted (*US*); **passer au** ~ (*signal*) to go red; (*automobiliste*) to go through a red light; ~ **(à lèvres)** lipstick; **rouge-gorge** *nm* robin (redbreast)

rougeole [ʀuʒɔl] *nf* measles *sg*

rougeoyer [ʀuʒwaje] *vi* to glow red

rouget [ʀuʒɛ] *nm* mullet

rougeur [ʀuʒœʀ] *nf* redness; (*MÉD: tache*) red blotch

rougir [ʀuʒiʀ] *vi* to turn red; (*de honte, timidité*) to blush, flush; (*de plaisir, colère*) to flush

rouille [ʀuj] *nf* rust; **rouillé, e** *adj* rusty; **rouiller** *vt* to rust ♦ *vi* to rust, go rusty; **se rouiller** *vi* to rust

roulant, e [ʀulɑ̃, ɑ̃t] *adj* (*meuble*) on wheels; (*tapis etc*) moving; **escalier** ~ escalator

rouleau, x [ʀulo] *nm* roll; (*à mise en plis, à peinture, vague*) roller; ~ **à pâtisserie** rolling pin

roulement [ʀulmɑ̃] *nm* (*rotation*) rotation, (*bruit*) rumbling *no pl*, rumble; **travailler par** ~ to work on a rota (*BRIT*) *ou* rotation (*US*) basis; ~ **à billes** ball bearings *pl*; ~ **de tambour** drum roll

rouler [ʀule] *vt* to roll; (*papier, tapis*) to roll up; (*CULIN: pâte*) to roll out; (*fam: duper*) to do, con ♦ *vi* (*bille, boule*) to roll; (*voiture, train*) to go, run; (*automobiliste*) to drive; (*bateau*) to roll; **se** ~ **dans** (*boue*) to roll in; (*couverture*) to roll o.s. (up) in

roulette [ʀulɛt] *nf* (*de table, fauteuil*) castor; (*de dentiste*) drill; (*jeu*) roulette; **à** ~**s** on castors; **ça a marché comme sur des** ~**s** (*fam*) it went off very smoothly

roulis [ʀuli] *nm* roll(ing)

roulotte [ʀulɔt] *nf* caravan

roumain, e [ʀumɛ̃, ɛn] *adj* Rumanian ♦ *nm/f*: **R~, e** Rumanian

Roumanie [ʀumani] *nf* Rumania

rouquin, e [ʀukɛ̃, in] (*péj*) *nm/f* redhead

rouspéter [ʀuspete] (*fam*) *vi* to moan

rousse [ʀus] *adj voir* **roux**

roussir [ʀusiʀ] *vt* to scorch ♦ *vi* (*CULIN*):

faire ~ to brown

route [ʀut] *nf* road; (*fig: chemin*) way; (*itinéraire, parcours*) route; (*fig: voie*) road, path; **il y a 3h de** ~ it's a 3-hour ride *ou* journey; **en** ~ on the way; **mettre en** ~ to start up; **se mettre en** ~ to set off; ~ **nationale** ≃ A road (*BRIT*), ≃ state highway (*US*); **routier, -ière** *adj* road *cpd* ♦ *nm* (*camionneur*) (long-distance) lorry (*BRIT*) *ou* truck (*US*) driver; (*restaurant*) ≃ transport café (*BRIT*), ≃ truck stop (*US*)

routine [ʀutin] *nf* routine; **routinier, -ière** (*péj*) *adj* (*activité*) humdrum; (*personne*) addicted to routine

rouvrir [ʀuvʀiʀ] *vt, vi* to reopen, open again; **se** ~ *vi* to reopen, open again

roux, rousse [ʀu, ʀus] *adj* red; (*personne*) red-haired ♦ *nm/f* redhead

royal, e, -aux [ʀwajal, o] *adj* royal; (*cadeau etc*) fit for a king

royaume [ʀwajom] *nm* kingdom; (*fig*) realm; **le R~-Uni** the United Kingdom

royauté [ʀwajote] *nf* (*régime*) monarchy

RPR *sigle m*: **Rassemblement pour la République** French right-wing political party

ruban [ʀybɑ̃] *nm* ribbon; ~ **adhésif** adhesive tape

rubéole [ʀybeɔl] *nf* German measles *sg*, rubella

rubis [ʀybi] *nm* ruby

rubrique [ʀybʀik] *nf* (*titre, catégorie*) heading; (*PRESSE: article*) column

ruche [ʀyʃ] *nf* hive

rude [ʀyd] *adj* (*au toucher*) rough; (*métier, tâche*) hard, tough; (*climat*) severe, harsh; (*bourru*) harsh, rough; (*fruste: manières*) rugged, tough; (*fam: fameux*) jolly good; **rudement** (*fam*) *adv* (*très*) terribly

rudimentaire [ʀydimɑ̃tɛʀ] *adj* rudimentary, basic

rudiments [ʀydimɑ̃] *nmpl*: **avoir des** ~ **d'anglais** to have a smattering of English

rudoyer [ʀydwaje] *vt* to treat harshly

rue [ʀy] *nf* street

ruée [ʀɥe] *nf* rush

ruelle [ʀɥɛl] *nf* alley(-way)

ruer [ʀɥe] *vi* (*cheval*) to kick out; **se ~** *vi*: **se ~ sur** to pounce on; **se ~ vers/dans/hors de** to rush *ou* dash towards/into/out of

rugby [ʀygbi] *nm* rugby (football)

rugir [ʀyʒiʀ] *vi* to roar

rugueux, -euse [ʀygø, øz] *adj* rough

ruine [ʀɥin] *nf* ruin; **ruiner** *vt* to ruin; **ruineux, -euse** *adj* ruinous

ruisseau, x [ʀɥiso] *nm* stream, brook

ruisseler [ʀɥis(ə)le] *vi* to stream

rumeur [ʀymœʀ] *nf* (*nouvelle*) rumour; (*bruit confus*) rumbling

ruminer [ʀymine] *vt* (*herbe*) to ruminate; (*fig*) to ruminate on *ou* over, chew over

rupture [ʀyptyʀ] *nf* (*séparation, désunion*) break-up, split; (*de négociations etc*) breakdown; (*de contrat*) breach; (*dans continuité*) break

rural, e, -aux [ʀyʀal, o] *adj* rural, country *cpd*

ruse [ʀyz] *nf*: **la ~** cunning, craftiness; (*pour tromper*) trickery; **une ~** a trick, a ruse; **rusé, e** *adj* cunning, crafty

russe [ʀys] *adj* Russian ♦ *nm/f*: **R~** Russian ♦ *nm* (*LING*) Russian

Russie [ʀysi] *nf*: **la ~** Russia

rustine ® [ʀystin] *nf* rubber repair patch (*for bicycle tyre*)

rustique [ʀystik] *adj* rustic

rustre [ʀystʀ] *nm* boor

rutilant, e [ʀytilɑ̃, ɑ̃t] *adj* gleaming

rythme [ʀitm] *nm* rhythm; (*vitesse*) rate; (: *de la vie*) pace, tempo; **rythmé, e** *adj* rhythmic(al)

S, s

s' [s] *pron voir* **se**

sa [sa] *adj voir* **son**[1]

SA *sigle* (= société anonyme) ≈ Ltd (*BRIT*), ≈ Inc. (*US*)

sable [sabl] *nm* sand; **~s mouvants** quicksand(s)

sablé [sable] *nm* shortbread biscuit

sabler [sable] *vt* (*contre le verglas*) to grit; **~ le champagne** to drink champagne

sablier [sablije] *nm* hourglass; (*de cuisine*) egg timer

sablonneux, -euse [sablɔnø, øz] *adj* sandy

saborder [sabɔʀde] *vt* (*navire*) to scuttle; (*fig: projet*) to put paid to, scupper

sabot [sabo] *nm* clog; (*de cheval*) hoof; **~ de frein** brake shoe

saboter [sabɔte] *vt* to sabotage; (*bâcler*) to make a mess of, botch

sac [sak] *nm* bag; (*à charbon etc*) sack; **~ à dos** rucksack; **~ à main** handbag; **~ de couchage** sleeping bag; **~ de voyage** travelling bag; **~ poubelle** bin liner

saccadé, e [sakade] *adj* jerky; (*respiration*) spasmodic

saccager [sakaʒe] *vt* (*piller*) to sack; (*dévaster*) to create havoc in

saccharine [sakaʀin] *nf* saccharin

sacerdoce [sasɛʀdɔs] *nm* priesthood; (*fig*) calling, vocation

sache *etc* [saʃ] *vb voir* **savoir**

sachet [saʃɛ] *nm* (small) bag; (*de sucre, café*) sachet; **du potage en ~** packet soup; **~ de thé** tea bag

sacoche [sakɔʃ] *nf* (*gén*) bag; (*de bicyclette*) saddlebag

sacquer [sake] (*fam*) *vt* (*employé*) to fire; (*détester*): **je ne peux pas le ~** I can't stand him

sacre [sakʀ] *nm* (*roi*) coronation

sacré, e [sakʀe] *adj* sacred; (*fam: satané*) blasted; (: *fameux*): **un ~ toupet** a heck of a cheek

sacrement [sakʀəmɑ̃] *nm* sacrament

sacrifice [sakʀifis] *nm* sacrifice; **sacrifier** *vt* to sacrifice

sacristie [sakʀisti] *nf* (*catholique*) sacristy; (*protestante*) vestry

sadique [sadik] *adj* sadistic

safran [safʀɑ̃] *nm* saffron

sage [saʒ] *adj* wise; (*enfant*) good

sage-femme [saʒfam] *nf* midwife

sagesse [saʒes] *nf* wisdom

Sagittaire [saʒiteʀ] *nm*: **le ~** Sagittarius

Sahara [saaʀa] *nm*: **le ~** the Sahara (desert)

saignant, e [sɛɲɑ̃, ɑ̃t] *adj* (*viande*) rare

saignée [seɲe] *nf* (*fig*) heavy losses *pl*

saigner [seɲe] *vi* to bleed ♦ *vt* to bleed; (*animal*) to kill (by bleeding); **~ du nez** to have a nosebleed

saillie [saji] *nf* (*sur un mur etc*) projection

saillir [sajiʀ] *vi* to project, stick out; (*veine, muscle*) to bulge

sain, e [sɛ̃, sɛn] *adj* healthy; **~ d'esprit** sound in mind, sane; **~ et sauf** safe and sound, unharmed

saindoux [sɛ̃du] *nm* lard

saint, e [sɛ̃, sɛ̃t] *adj* holy ♦ *nm/f* saint; **le S~ Esprit** the Holy Spirit *ou* Ghost; **la S~e Vierge** the Blessed Virgin; **la S~-Sylvestre** New Year's Eve; **sainteté** *nf* holiness

sais *etc* [sɛ] *vb voir* **savoir**

saisi, e [sezi] *adj*: **~ de panique** panic-stricken; **être ~ (par le froid)** to be struck by the sudden cold

saisie *nf* seizure; **~e (de données)** (data) capture

saisir [seziʀ] *vt* to take hold of, grab; (*fig: occasion*) to seize; (*comprendre*) to grasp; (*entendre*) to get, catch; (*données*) to capture; (*CULIN*) to fry quickly; (*JUR: biens, publication*) to seize; **se ~ de** *vt* to seize; **saisissant, e** *adj* startling, striking

saison [sɛzɔ̃] *nf* season; **morte ~** slack season; **saisonnier, -ière** *adj* seasonal

sait [sɛ] *vb voir* **savoir**

salade [salad] *nf* (*BOT*) lettuce *etc*; (*CULIN*) (green) salad; (*fam: confusion*) tangle, muddle; **~ composée** mixed salad; **~ de fruits** fruit salad; **saladier** *nm* (salad) bowl

salaire [saleʀ] *nm* (*annuel, mensuel*) salary; (*hebdomadaire, journalier*) pay, wages *pl*; **~ minimum interprofessionnel de croissance** index-linked guaranteed minimum wage

salarié, e [salaʀje] *nm/f* salaried em-

ployee; wage-earner

salaud [salo] (*fam!*) *nm* sod (*!*), bastard (*!*)

sale [sal] *adj* dirty, filthy; (*fam: mauvais*) nasty

salé, e [sale] *adj* (*mer, goût*) salty; (*CULIN: amandes, beurre etc*) salted; (*: gâteaux*) savoury; (*fam: grivois*) spicy; (*: facture*) steep

saler [sale] *vt* to salt

saleté [salte] *nf* (*état*) dirtiness; (*crasse*) dirt, filth; (*tache etc*) dirt *no pl*; (*fam: méchanceté*) dirty trick; (*: camelote*) rubbish *no pl*; (*: obscénité*) filthy thing (to say)

salière [saljɛʀ] *nf* saltcellar

salin, e [salɛ̃, in] *adj* saline

salir [saliʀ] *vt* to (make) dirty; (*fig: quelqu'un*) to soil the reputation of; **se ~** *vi* to get dirty; **salissant, e** *adj* (*tissu*) which shows the dirt; (*travail*) dirty, messy

salle [sal] *nf* room; (*d'hôpital*) ward; (*de restaurant*) dining room; (*d'un cinéma*) auditorium; (*: public*) audience; **~ à manger** dining room; **~ d'attente** waiting room; **~ de bain(s)** bathroom; **~ de classe** classroom; **~ de concert** concert hall; **~ d'eau** shower-room; **~ d'embarquement** (*à l'aéroport*) departure lounge; **~ de jeux** (*pour enfants*) playroom; **~ d'opération** (*d'hôpital*) operating theatre; **~ de séjour** living room; **~ des ventes** saleroom

salon [salɔ̃] *nm* lounge, sitting room; (*mobilier*) lounge suite; (*exposition*) exhibition, show; **~ de coiffure** hairdressing salon; **~ de thé** tearoom

salope [salɔp] (*fam!*) *nf* bitch (*!*); **saloperie** (*fam!*) *nf* (*action*) dirty trick; (*chose sans valeur*) rubbish *no pl*

salopette [salɔpet] *nf* dungarees *pl*; (*d'ouvrier*) overall(s)

salsifis [salsifi] *nm* salsify

salubre [salybʀ] *adj* healthy, salubrious

saluer [salɥe] *vt* (*pour dire bonjour, fig*) to greet; (*pour dire au revoir*) to take one's leave; (*MIL*) to salute

salut [saly] *nm* (*geste*) wave; (*parole*) greeting; (*MIL*) salute; (*sauvegarde*) safety; (*REL*) salvation ♦ *excl* (*fam: bonjour*) hi (there);

(: *au revoir*) see you, bye

salutations [salytasjɔ̃] *nfpl* greetings; **Veuillez agréer, Monsieur, mes ~ distinguées** yours faithfully

samedi [samdi] *nm* Saturday

SAMU [samy] *sigle m* (= *service d'assistance médicale d'urgence*) ≃ ambulance (service) (*BRIT*), ≃ paramedics *pl* (*US*)

sanction [sɑ̃ksjɔ̃] *nf* sanction; **sanctionner** *vt* (*loi, usage*) to sanction; (*punir*) to punish

sandale [sɑ̃dal] *nf* sandal

sandwich [sɑ̃dwi(t)ʃ] *nm* sandwich

sang [sɑ̃] *nm* blood; **en ~** covered in blood; **se faire du mauvais ~** to fret, get in a state; **sang-froid** *nm* calm, sangfroid; **de sang-froid** in cold blood; **sanglant, e** *adj* bloody

sangle [sɑ̃gl] *nf* strap

sanglier [sɑ̃glije] *nm* (wild) boar

sanglot [sɑ̃glo] *nm* sob; **sangloter** *vi* to sob

sangsue [sɑ̃sy] *nf* leech

sanguin, e [sɑ̃gɛ̃, in] *adj* blood *cpd*; **sanguinaire** *adj* bloodthirsty

sanitaire [saniteʀ] *adj* health *cpd*; **~s** *nmpl* (*lieu*) bathroom *sg*

sans [sɑ̃] *prép* without; **un pull ~ manches** a sleeveless jumper; **~ faute** without fail; **~ arrêt** without a break; **~ ça** (*fam*) otherwise; **~ qu'il s'en aperçoive** without him *ou* his noticing; **sans-abri** *nmpl* homeless; **sans-emploi** *nm/f inv* unemployed person; **les sans-emploi** the unemployed; **sans-gêne** *adj inv* inconsiderate

santé [sɑ̃te] *nf* health; **en bonne ~** in good health; **boire à la ~ de qn** to drink (to) sb's health; **à ta/votre ~!** cheers!

saoudien, ne [saudjɛ̃, jɛn] *adj* Saudi Arabian ♦ *nm/f*: **S~, ne** Saudi Arabian

saoul, e [su, sul] *adj* = **soûl**

saper [sape] *vt* to undermine, sap

sapeur-pompier [sapœʀpɔ̃pje] *nm* fireman

saphir [safiʀ] *nm* sapphire

sapin [sapɛ̃] *nm* fir (tree); (*bois*) fir; **~ de Noël** Christmas tree

sarcastique [saʀkastik] *adj* sarcastic

sarcler [saʀkle] *vt* to weed

Sardaigne [saʀdɛɲ] *nf*: **la ~** Sardinia

sardine [saʀdin] *nf* sardine

sarrasin [saʀazɛ̃] *nm* buckwheat

SARL *sigle f* (= *société à responsabilité limitée*) ≃ plc (*BRIT*), ≃ Inc. (*US*)

sas [sas] *nm* (*de sous-marin, d'engin spatial*) airlock; (*d'écluse*) lock

satané, e [satane] (*fam*) *adj* confounded

satellite [satelit] *nm* satellite

satin [satɛ̃] *nm* satin

satire [satiʀ] *nf* satire; **satirique** *adj* satirical

satisfaction [satisfaksjɔ̃] *nf* satisfaction

satisfaire [satisfɛʀ] *vt* to satisfy; **~ à** (*conditions*) to meet; **satisfaisant, e** *adj* (*acceptable*) satisfactory; **satisfait, e** *adj* satisfied; **satisfait de** happy *ou* satisfied with

saturer [satyʀe] *vt* to saturate

sauce [sos] *nf* sauce; (*avec un rôti*) gravy; **saucière** *nf* sauceboat

saucisse [sosis] *nf* sausage

saucisson [sosisɔ̃] *nm* (slicing) sausage

sauf, sauve [sof, sov] *adj* unharmed, unhurt; (*fig: honneur*) intact, saved ♦ *prép* except; **laisser la vie sauve à qn** to spare sb's life; **~ si** (*à moins que*) unless; **~ erreur** if I'm not mistaken; **~ avis contraire** unless you hear to the contrary

sauge [soʒ] *nf* sage

saugrenu, e [sogʀəny] *adj* preposterous

saule [sol] *nm* willow (tree)

saumon [somɔ̃] *nm* salmon *inv*

saumure [somyʀ] *nf* brine

saupoudrer [sopudʀe] *vt*: **~ qch de** to sprinkle sth with

saur [sɔʀ] *adj m*: **hareng ~** smoked *ou* red herring, kipper

saurai *etc* [sɔʀe] *vb voir* **savoir**

saut [so] *nm* jump; (*discipline sportive*) jumping; **faire un ~ chez qn** to pop over to sb's (place); **~ à l'élastique** bungee jumping; **~ à la perche** pole vaulting; **~ en hauteur/longueur** high/long jump; **~ périlleux** somersault

saute [sot] *nf*: **~ d'humeur** sudden change of mood

sauter [sote] *vi* to jump, leap; *(exploser)* to blow up, explode; *(: fusibles)* to blow; *(se détacher)* to pop out *(ou* off*)* ♦ *vt* to jump (over), leap (over); *(fig: omettre)* to skip, miss (out); **faire ~** to blow up; *(CULIN)* to sauté; **~ au cou de qn** to fly into sb's arms; **~ sur une occasion** to jump at an opportunity; **~ aux yeux** to be (quite) obvious

sauterelle [sotʀɛl] *nf* grasshopper

sautiller [sotije] *vi (oiseau)* to hop; *(enfant)* to skip

sauvage [sovaʒ] *adj (gén)* wild; *(peuplade)* savage; *(farouche: personne)* unsociable; *(barbare)* wild, savage; *(non officiel)* unauthorized, unofficial; **faire du camping ~** to camp in the wild ♦ *nm/f* savage; *(timide)* unsociable type

sauve [sov] *adj f voir* **sauf**

sauvegarde [sovgaʀd] *nf* safeguard; *(IN-FORM)* backup; **sauvegarder** *vt* to safeguard; *(INFORM: enregistrer)* to save; *(: copier)* to back up

sauve-qui-peut [sovkipø] *excl* run for your life!

sauver [sove] *vt* to save; *(porter secours à)* to rescue; *(récupérer)* to salvage, rescue; **se ~** *vi (s'enfuir)* to run away; *(fam: partir)* to be off; **sauvetage** *nm* rescue; **sauveteur** *nm* rescuer; **sauvette: à la sauvette** *adv (se marier etc)* hastily, hurriedly; **sauveur** *nm* saviour *(BRIT)*, savior *(US)*

savais *etc* [save] *vb voir* **savoir**

savamment [savamɑ̃] *adv (avec érudition)* learnedly; *(habilement)* skilfully, cleverly

savant, e [savɑ̃, ɑ̃t] *adj* scholarly, learned ♦ *nm* scientist

saveur [savœʀ] *nf* flavour; *(fig)* savour

savoir [savwaʀ] *vt* to know; *(être capable de)*: **il sait nager** he can swim ♦ *nm* knowledge; **se ~** *vi (être connu)* to be

known; **à ~** that is, namely; **faire ~ qch à qn** to let sb know sth; **pas que je sache** not as far as I know

savon [savɔ̃] *nm (produit)* soap; *(morceau)* bar of soap; *(fam)*: **passer un ~ à qn** to give sb a good dressing-down; **savonner** *vt* to soap; **savonnette** *nf* bar of soap

savons [savɔ̃] *vb voir* **savoir**

savourer [savuʀe] *vt* to savour; **savoureux, -euse** *adj* tasty; *(fig: anecdote)* spicy, juicy

saxo(phone) [saksɔ(fɔn)] *nm* sax(ophone)

scabreux, -euse [skabʀø, øz] *adj* risky; *(indécent)* improper, shocking

scandale [skɑ̃dal] *nm* scandal; *(tapage)*: **faire un ~** to make a scene, create a disturbance; **faire ~** to scandalize people; **scandaleux, -euse** *adj* scandalous, outrageous

scandinave [skɑ̃dinav] *adj* Scandinavian ♦ *nm/f*: **S~** Scandinavian

Scandinavie [skɑ̃dinavi] *nf* Scandinavia

scaphandre [skafɑ̃dʀ] *nm (de plongeur)* diving suit

scarabée [skaʀabe] *nm* beetle

scarlatine [skaʀlatin] *nf* scarlet fever

scarole [skaʀɔl] *nf* endive

sceau, x [so] *nm* seal

scélérat, e [seleʀa, at] *nm/f* villain

sceller [sele] *vt* to seal

scénario [senaʀjo] *nm* scenario

scène [sɛn] *nf (gén)* scene; *(estrade, fig: théâtre)* stage; **entrer en ~** to come on stage; **mettre en ~** *(THÉÂTRE)* to stage; *(CINÉMA)* to direct; **~ de ménage** domestic scene

sceptique [sɛptik] *adj* sceptical

schéma [ʃema] *nm (diagramme)* diagram, sketch; **schématique** *adj* diagrammatic(al), schematic; *(fig)* oversimplified

sciatique [sjatik] *nf* sciatica

scie [si] *nf* saw; **~ à métaux** hacksaw

sciemment [sjamɑ̃] *adv* knowingly

science [sjɑ̃s] *nf* science; *(savoir)* knowledge; **~s naturelles** *(SCOL)* natural science *sg*, biology *sg*; **~s po** political science *ou* studies *pl*; **science-fiction** *nf* science fiction; **scientifique** *adj* scientific ♦ *nm/f* scientist; (*étudiant*) science student

scier [sje] *vt* to saw; (*retrancher*) to saw off; **scierie** *nf* sawmill

scinder [sɛ̃de] *vt* to split up; **se ~** *vi* to split up

scintiller [sɛ̃tije] *vi* to sparkle; (*étoile*) to twinkle

scission [sisjɔ̃] *nf* split

sciure [sjyʀ] *nf*: **~ (de bois)** sawdust

sclérose [skleʀoz] *nf*: **~ en plaques** multiple sclerosis

scolaire [skɔlɛʀ] *adj* school *cpd*; **scolariser** *vt* to provide with schooling/schools; **scolarité** *nf* schooling

scooter [skutœʀ] *nm* (motor) scooter

score [skɔʀ] *nm* score

scorpion [skɔʀpjɔ̃] *nm* (*signe*): **le S~** Scorpio

Scotch ® [skɔtʃ] *nm* adhesive tape

scout, e [skut] *adj, nm* scout

script [skʀipt] *nm* (*écriture*) printing; (*CINÉMA*) (shooting) script

scrupule [skʀypyl] *nm* scruple

scruter [skʀyte] *vt* to scrutinize; (*l'obscurité*) to peer into

scrutin [skʀytɛ̃] *nm* (*vote*) ballot; (*ensemble des opérations*) poll

sculpter [skylte] *vt* to sculpt; (*bois*) to carve; **sculpteur** *nm* sculptor; **sculpture** *nf* sculpture; **sculpture sur bois** wood carving

SDF *sigle m* (= *sans domicile fixe*) homeless person; **les SDF** the homeless

---

MOT-CLÉ

se [sə], **s'** *pron* **1** (*emploi réfléchi*) oneself; (: *masc*) himself; (: *fém*) herself; (: *sujet non humain*) itself; (: *pl*) themselves; **se voir comme l'on est** to see o.s. as one is

2 (*réciproque*) one another, each other; **ils s'aiment** they love one another *ou* each other

3 (*passif*): **cela se répare facilement** it is easily repaired

4 (*possessif*): **se casser la jambe/laver les mains** to break one's leg/wash one's hands

---

séance [seɑ̃s] *nf* (*d'assemblée*) meeting, session; (*de tribunal*) sitting, session; (*musicale, CINÉMA, THÉÂTRE*) performance; **~ tenante** forthwith

seau, x [so] *nm* bucket, pail

sec, sèche [sɛk, sɛʃ] *adj* dry; (*raisins, figues*) dried; (*cœur: insensible*) hard, cold ♦ *nm*: **tenir au ~** to keep in a dry place ♦ *adv* hard; **je le bois ~** I drink it straight *ou* neat; **à ~** (*puits*) dried up

sécateur [sekatœʀ] *nm* secateurs *pl* (*BRIT*), shears *pl*

sèche [sɛʃ] *adj f voir* **sec**; **sèche-cheveux** *nm inv* hair-drier; **sèche-linge** *nm inv* tumble dryer; **sèchement** *adv* (*répondre*) drily

sécher [seʃe] *vt* to dry; (*dessécher: peau, blé*) to dry (out); (: *étang*) to dry up; (*fam: cours*) to skip ♦ *vi* to dry; to dry out; to dry up; (*fam: candidat*) to be stumped; **se ~** (*après le bain*) to dry o.s.; **sécheresse** *nf* dryness; (*absence de pluie*) drought; **séchoir** *nm* drier

second, e [s(ə)gɔ̃, ɔ̃d] *adj* second ♦ *nm* (*assistant*) second in command; (*NAVIG*) first mate; **voyager en ~e** to travel second-class; **secondaire** *adj* secondary; **seconde** *nf* second; **seconder** *vt* to assist

secouer [s(ə)kwe] *vt* to shake; (*passagers*) to rock; (*traumatiser*) to shake (up); **se ~** *vi* (*fam: faire un effort*) to shake o.s. up; (: *se dépêcher*) to get a move on

secourir [s(ə)kuʀiʀ] *vt* (*venir en aide à*) to assist, aid; **secourisme** *nm* first aid; **secouriste** *nmf* first-aid worker

secours [s(ə)kuʀ] *nm* help, aid, assistance ♦ *nmpl* aid *sg*; **au ~!** help!; **appeler au ~** to shout *ou* call for help; **porter ~ à qn** to give sb assistance, help sb; **les premiers ~** first aid *sg*

secousse [s(ə)kus] *nf* jolt, bump; (*électri-*

que) shock; (*fig: psychologique*) jolt, shock;
~ **sismique** earth tremor

secret, -ète [sakʀɛ, ɛt] *adj* secret; (*fig:
renfermé*) reticent, reserved ♦ *nm* secret;
(*discrétion absolue*): **le ~** secrecy

secrétaire [s(ə)kʀetɛʀ] *nm/f* secretary
♦ *nm* (*meuble*) writing desk; ~ **de direction** private *ou* personal secretary; ~ **d'État**
junior minister; ~ **général** (COMM) company secretary; **secrétariat** *nm* (*profession*) secretarial work; (*bureau*) office;
(: *d'organisation internationale*) secretariat

secteur [sɛktœʀ] *nm* sector; (*zone*) area;
(ÉLEC): **branché sur ~** plugged into the
mains (supply)

section [sɛksjɔ̃] *nf* section; (*de parcours
d'autobus*) fare stage; (MIL: *unité*) platoon;
sectionner *vt* to sever

Sécu [seky] *abr f* = **sécurité sociale**

séculaire [sekylɛʀ] *adj* (*très vieux*) age-old

sécuriser [sekyʀize] *vt* to give (a feeling
of) security to

sécurité [sekyʀite] *nf* (*absence de danger*)
safety; (*absence de troubles*) security; **système de ~** security system; **être en ~** to
be safe; **la ~ routière** road safety; **la ~
sociale** ≈ (the) Social Security (BRIT), ≈
Welfare (US)

sédentaire [sedɑ̃tɛʀ] *adj* sedentary

séduction [sedyksjɔ̃] *nf* seduction;
(*charme, attrait*) appeal, charm

séduire [seduiʀ] *vt* to charm; (*femme: abuser de*) to seduce; **séduisant, e** *adj*
(*femme*) seductive; (*homme, offre*) very attractive

ségrégation [segʀegasjɔ̃] *nf* segregation

seigle [sɛɡl] *nm* rye

seigneur [sɛɲœʀ] *nm* lord

sein [sɛ̃] *nm* breast; (*entrailles*) womb; **au ~
de** (*équipe, institution*) within

séisme [seism] *nm* earthquake

seize [sɛz] *num* sixteen; **seizième** *num*
sixteenth

séjour [seʒuʀ] *nm* stay; (*pièce*) living room;
séjourner *vi* to stay

sel [sɛl] *nm* salt; (*fig: piquant*) spice

sélection [selɛksjɔ̃] *nf* selection; **sélectionner** *vt* to select

self-service [sɛlfsɛʀvis] *adj, nm* self-
service

selle [sɛl] *nf* saddle; ~**s** *nfpl* (MÉD) stools;
seller *vt* to saddle

sellette [sɛlɛt] *nf*: **être sur la ~** to be in
the hot seat

selon [s(ə)lɔ̃] *prép* according to; (*en se con-
formant à*) in accordance with; ~ **que** according to whether; ~ **moi** as I see it

semaine [s(ə)mɛn] *nf* week; **en ~** during
the week, on weekdays

semblable [sɑ̃blabl] *adj* similar; (*de ce
genre*): **de ~s mésaventures** such mis-
haps ♦ *nm* fellow creature *ou* man; ~ **à**
similar to, like

semblant [sɑ̃blɑ̃] *nm*: **un ~ de ...** a semblance of ...; **faire ~ (de faire)** to pretend
(to do)

sembler [sɑ̃ble] *vb +attrib* to seem ♦ *vb
impers*: **il semble (bien) que/inutile de** it
(really) seems *ou* appears that/useless to;
il me semble que it seems to me that;
comme bon lui semble as he sees fit

semelle [s(ə)mɛl] *nf* sole; (*intérieure*) insole, inner sole

semence [s(ə)mɑ̃s] *nf* (*graine*) seed

semer [s(ə)me] *vt* to sow; (*fig: éparpiller*) to
scatter; (: *confusion*) to spread; (*fam: poursuivants*) to lose, shake off; **semé de** (*difficultés*) riddled with

semestre [s(ə)mɛstʀ] *nm* half-year; (SCOL)
semester

séminaire [seminɛʀ] *nm* seminar

semi-remorque [səmiʀəmɔʀk] *nm* articu-
lated lorry (BRIT), semi(trailer) (US)

semoule [s(ə)mul] *nf* semolina

sempiternel, le [sɑ̃pitɛʀnɛl] *adj* eternal,
never-ending

sénat [sena] *nm* senate; **sénateur** *nm*
senator

sens [sɑ̃s] *nm* (PHYSIOL, *instinct*) sense; (*signification*) meaning, sense; (*direction*) direction; **à mon ~** to my mind; **dans le ~
des aiguilles d'une montre** clockwise; ~

dessus dessous upside down; **~ interdit** one-way street; **~ unique** one-way street

sensation [sɑ̃sasjɔ̃] *nf* sensation; **à ~** (*péj*) sensational; **faire ~** to cause *ou* create a sensation; **sensationnel, le** *adj* (*fam*) fantastic, terrific

sensé, e [sɑ̃se] *adj* sensible

sensibiliser [sɑ̃sibilize] *vt*: **~ qn à** to make sb sensitive to

sensibilité [sɑ̃sibilite] *nf* sensitivity

sensible [sɑ̃sibl] *adj* sensitive; (*aux sens*) perceptible; (*appréciable: différence, progrès*) appreciable, noticeable; **sensiblement** *adv* (*à peu près*): **ils sont sensiblement du même âge** they are approximately the same age; **sensiblerie** *nf* sentimentality

sensuel, le [sɑ̃sɥɛl] *adj* (*personne*) sensual; (*musique*) sensuous

sentence [sɑ̃tɑ̃s] *nf* (*jugement*) sentence

sentier [sɑ̃tje] *nm* path

sentiment [sɑ̃timɑ̃] *nm* feeling; **sentimental, e, -aux** *adj* sentimental; (*vie, aventure*) love *cpd*

sentinelle [sɑ̃tinɛl] *nf* sentry

sentir [sɑ̃tiʀ] *vt* (*par l'odorat*) to smell; (*par le goût*) to taste; (*au toucher, fig*) to feel; (*répandre une odeur de*) to smell of; (: *ressemblance*) to smell like ♦ *vi* to smell; **~ mauvais** to smell bad; **~ bien** to feel good; **se ~ mal** (*être indisposé*) to feel unwell *ou* ill; **se ~ le courage/la force de faire** to feel brave/strong enough to do; **il ne peut pas le ~** (*fam*) he can't stand him

séparation [separasjɔ̃] *nf* separation; (*cloison*) division, partition

séparé, e [sepaʀe] *adj* (*distinct*) separate; (*époux*) separated; **séparément** *adv* separately

séparer [sepaʀe] *vt* to separate; (*désunir*) to drive apart; (*détacher*): **~ qch de** to pull sth (off) from; **se ~** *vi* (*époux, amis*) to separate, part; (*se diviser: route etc*) to divide; **se ~ de** (*époux*) to separate *ou* part from; (*employé, objet personnel*) to part with

sept [sɛt] *num* seven; **septante** (*BELGIQUE, SUISSE*) *adj inv* seventy

septembre [sɛptɑ̃bʀ] *nm* September

septennat [sɛptena] *nm* seven year term of office (of French President)

septentrional, e, -aux [sɛptɑ̃tʀijɔnal, o] *adj* northern

septicémie [sɛptisemi] *nf* blood poisoning, septicaemia

septième [sɛtjɛm] *num* seventh

septique [sɛptik] *adj*: **fosse ~** septic tank

sépulture [sepyltyʀ] *nf* (*tombeau*) burial place, grave

séquelles [sekɛl] *nfpl* after-effects; (*fig*) aftermath *sg*

séquestrer [sekɛstʀe] *vt* (*personne*) to confine illegally; (*biens*) to impound

serai *etc* [sɔʀe] *vb voir* **être**

serein, e [sɔʀɛ̃, ɛn] *adj* serene

serez [sɔʀe] *vb voir* **être**

sergent [sɛʀʒɑ̃] *nm* sergeant

série [seʀi] *nf* series *inv*; (*de clés, casseroles, outils*) set; (*catégorie: SPORT*) rank; **en ~** in quick succession; (*COMM*) mass *cpd*; **hors ~** (*COMM*) custom-built

sérieusement [seʀjøzmɑ̃] *adv* seriously

sérieux, -euse [seʀjø, jøz] *adj* serious; (*élève, employé*) reliable, responsible; (*client, maison*) reliable, dependable ♦ *nm* seriousness; (*d'une entreprise etc*) reliability; **garder son ~** to keep a straight face; **prendre qch/qn au ~** to take sth/sb seriously

serin [s(ə)ʀɛ̃] *nm* canary

seringue [s(ə)ʀɛ̃g] *nf* syringe

serions [səʀjɔ̃] *vb voir* **être**

serment [sɛʀmɑ̃] *nm* (*juré*) oath; (*promesse*) pledge, vow

sermon [sɛʀmɔ̃] *nm* sermon

séronégatif, -ive [seʀonegatif, iv] *adj* (*MÉD*) HIV negative

séropositif, -ive [seʀopozitif, iv] *adj* (*MÉD*) HIV positive

serpent [sɛʀpɑ̃] *nm* snake; **serpenter** *vi* to wind

serpillière [sɛʀpijɛʀ] *nf* floorcloth

serre [sɛʀ] *nf* (*AGR*) greenhouse; **~s** *nfpl* (*griffes*) claws, talons

serré, e [seʀe] *adj* (*habits*) tight; (*fig: lutte, match*) tight, close-fought; (*passagers etc*) (tightly) packed; (*réseau*) dense; **avoir le cœur ~** to have a heavy heart

serrer [seʀe] *vt* (*tenir*) to grip *ou* hold tight; (*comprimer, coincer*) to squeeze; (*poings, mâchoires*) to clench; (*suj: vêtement*) to be too tight for; (*ceinture, nœud, vis*) to tighten ♦ *vi*: **~ à droite** to keep *ou* get over to the right; **se ~** *vi* (*se rapprocher*) to squeeze up; **se ~ contre qn** to huddle up to sb; **~ la main à qn** to shake sb's hand; **~ qn dans ses bras** to hug sb, clasp sb in one's arms

serrure [seʀyʀ] *nf* lock; **serrurier** *nm* locksmith

sert *etc* [sɛʀ] *vb voir* **servir**

servante [sɛʀvɑ̃t] *nf* (maid)servant

serveur, -euse [sɛʀvœʀ, øz] *nm/f* waiter (waitress)

serviable [sɛʀvjabl] *adj* obliging, willing to help

service [sɛʀvis] *nm* service; (*assortiment de vaisselle*) set, service; (*bureau: de la vente etc*) department, section; (*travail*) duty; **premier ~** (*série de repas*) first sitting; **être de ~** to be on duty; **faire le ~** to serve; **rendre un ~ à qn** to do sb a favour; (*objet: s'avérer utile*) to come in useful *ou* handy for sb; **mettre en ~** to put into service *ou* operation; **~ compris/non compris** service included/not included; **hors ~** out of order; **~ après-vente** after-sales service; **~ d'ordre** police (*ou* stewards) in charge of maintaining order; **~ militaire** military service; **~s secrets** secret service *sg*

---

service militaire

ⓘ *French men over eighteen are required to do ten months'* **service militaire** *if pronounced fit. The call-up can be delayed if the conscript is in full-time higher education. Conscientious objectors are required*

to do two years' public service. Since 1970, women have been able to do military service, though few do.

---

serviette [sɛʀvjɛt] *nf* (*de table*) (table) napkin, serviette; (*de toilette*) towel; (*porte-documents*) briefcase; **~ hygiénique** sanitary towel

servir [sɛʀviʀ] *vt* to serve; (*au restaurant*) to wait on; (*au magasin*) to serve, attend to ♦ *vi* (*TENNIS*) to serve; (*CARTES*) to deal; **se ~** *vi* (*prendre d'un plat*) to help o.s.; **vous êtes servi?** are you being served?; **~ à qn** (*diplôme, livre*) to be of use to sb; **~ à qch/faire** (*outil etc*) to be used for sth/ doing; **ça ne sert à rien** it's no use; **~ (à qn) de** to serve as (for sb); **se ~ de** (*plat*) to help o.s. to; (*voiture, outil, relations*) to use

serviteur [sɛʀvitœʀ] *nm* servant

ses [se] *adj voir* **son**[1]

set [sɛt] *nm*: **~ (de table)** tablemat, place mat

seuil [sœj] *nm* doorstep; (*fig*) threshold

seul, e [sœl] *adj* (*sans compagnie*) alone; (*unique*): **un ~ livre** only one book, a single book ♦ *adv* (*vivre*) alone, on one's own ♦ *nm, nf*: **il en reste un(e) ~(e)** there's only one left; **le ~ livre** the only book; **parler tout ~** to talk to oneself; **faire qch (tout) ~** to do sth (all) on one's own *ou* (all) by oneself; **à lui (tout) ~** single-handed, on his own; **se sentir ~** to feel lonely; **seulement** *adv* only; **non seulement ... mais aussi** *ou* **encore** not only ... but also

sève [sɛv] *nf* sap

sévère [seveʀ] *adj* severe

sévices [sevis] *nmpl* (physical) cruelty *sg*, ill treatment *sg*

sévir [seviʀ] *vi* (*punir*) to use harsh measures, crack down; (*suj: fléau*) to rage, be rampant

sevrer [səvʀe] *vt* (*enfant etc*) to wean

sexe [sɛks] *nm* sex; (*organes génitaux*) genitals, sex organs; **sexuel, le** *adj* sexual

seyant, e [sejɑ̃, ɑ̃t] *adj* becoming
shampooing [ʃɑ̃pwɛ̃] *nm* shampoo
short [ʃɔʀt] *nm* (pair of) shorts *pl*

MOT-CLÉ

si [si] *nm* (*MUS*) B; (*en chantant la gamme*) ti
♦ *adv* **1** (*oui*) yes
2 (*tellement*) so; **si gentil/rapidement** so kind/fast; **(tant et) si bien que** so much so that; **si rapide qu'il soit** however fast he may be
♦ *conj* if; **si tu veux** if you want; **je me demande si** I wonder if *ou* whether; **si seulement** if only

---

Sicile [sisil] *nf*: **la ~** Sicily
SIDA [sida] *sigle m* (= *syndrome immuno-déficitaire acquis*) AIDS *sg*
sidéré, e [sideʀe] *adj* staggered
sidérurgie [sideʀyʀʒi] *nf* steel industry
siècle [sjɛkl] *nm* century
siège [sjɛʒ] *nm* seat; (*d'entreprise*) head office; (*d'organisation*) headquarters *pl*; (*MIL*) siege; **~ social** registered office; **siéger** *vi* to sit
sien, ne [sjɛ̃, sjɛn] *pron*: **le(la) ~(ne), les ~(ne)s** (*homme*) his; (*femme*) hers; (*chose, animal*) its; **les ~s** (*sa famille*) one's family; **faire des ~nes** (*fam*) to be up to one's (usual) tricks
sieste [sjɛst] *nf* (afternoon) snooze *ou* nap; **faire la ~** to have a snooze *ou* nap
sifflement [siflɑ̃mɑ̃] *nm*: **un ~** a whistle
siffler [sifle] *vi* (*gén*) to whistle; (*en respirant*) to wheeze; (*serpent, vapeur*) to hiss ♦ *vt* (*chanson*) to whistle; (*chien etc*) to whistle for; (*fille*) to whistle at; (*pièce, orateur*) to hiss, boo; (*fin du match, départ*) to blow one's whistle for; (*fam: verre*) to guzzle
sifflet [sifle] *nm* whistle; **coup de ~** whistle
siffloter [siflɔte] *vi*, *vt* to whistle
sigle [sigl] *nm* acronym
signal, -aux [siɲal, o] *nm* signal; (*indice, écriteau*) sign; **donner le ~ de** to give the signal for; **~ d'alarme** alarm signal; **si-**

gnaux (lumineux) (*AUTO*) traffic signals;
signalement *nm* description, particulars *pl*
signaler [siɲale] *vt* to indicate; (*personne: faire un signe*) to signal; (*vol, perte*) to report; (*faire remarquer*): **~ qch à qn/(à qn) que** to point out sth to sb/(to sb) that; **se ~ (par)** to distinguish o.s. (by)
signature [siɲatyʀ] *nf* signature; (*action*) signing
signe [siɲ] *nm* sign; (*TYPO*) mark; **faire un ~ de la main** to give a sign with one's hand; **faire ~ à qn** (*fig: contacter*) to get in touch with sb; **faire ~ à qn d'entrer** to motion (to) sb to come in; **signer** *vt* to sign; **se signer** *vi* to cross o.s.
significatif, -ive [siɲifikatif, iv] *adj* significant
signification [siɲifikasjɔ̃] *nf* meaning
signifier [siɲifje] *vt* (*vouloir dire*) to mean; (*faire connaître*): **~ qch (à qn)** to make sth known (to sb)
silence [silɑ̃s] *nm* silence; (*MUS*) rest; **garder le ~** to keep silent, say nothing; **silencieux, -euse** *adj* quiet, silent ♦ *nm* silencer
silex [silɛks] *nm* flint
silhouette [silwɛt] *nf* outline, silhouette; (*lignes, contour*) outline; (*allure*) figure
silicium [silisjɔm] *nm* silicon
sillage [sijaʒ] *nm* wake
sillon [sijɔ̃] *nm* furrow; (*de disque*) groove; **sillonner** *vt* to criss-cross
simagrées [simagʀe] *nfpl* fuss *sg*
similaire [similɛʀ] *adj* similar; **similicuir** *nm* imitation leather; **similitude** *nf* similarity
simple [sɛ̃pl] *adj* simple; (*non multiple*) single; **~ messieurs** *nm* (*TENNIS*) men's singles *sg*; **~ soldat** private
simplicité [sɛ̃plisite] *nf* simplicity
simplifier [sɛ̃plifje] *vt* to simplify
simulacre [simylakʀ] *nm* (*péj*): **un ~ de** a pretence of
simuler [simyle] *vt* to sham, simulate
simultané, e [simyltane] *adj* simulta-

neous

sincère [sɛ̃sɛʀ] *adj* sincere; **sincèrement** *adv* sincerely; (*pour parler franchement*) honestly, really; **sincérité** *nf* sincerity

sine qua non [sinekwanɔn] *adj*: **condition ~** indispensable condition

singe [sɛ̃ʒ] *nm* monkey; (*de grande taille*) ape; **singer** *vt* to ape, mimic; **singeries** *nfpl* antics

singulariser [sɛ̃gylaʀize]: **se ~** *vi* to call attention to o.s.

singularité [sɛ̃gylaʀite] *nf* peculiarity

singulier, -ière [sɛ̃gylje, jɛʀ] *adj* remarkable, singular ♦ *nm* singular

sinistre [sinistʀ] *adj* sinister ♦ *nm* (*incendie*) blaze; (*catastrophe*) disaster; (*ASSURANCES*) damage (*giving rise to a claim*); **sinistré, e** *adj* disaster-stricken ♦ *nm/f* disaster victim

sinon [sinɔ̃] *conj* (*autrement, sans quoi*) otherwise, or else; (*sauf*) except, other than; (*si ce n'est*) if not

sinueux, -euse [sinɥø, øz] *adj* winding

sinus [sinys] *nm* (*ANAT*) sinus; (*GÉOM*) sine; **sinusite** *nf* sinusitis

siphon [sifɔ̃] *nm* (*tube, d'eau gazeuse*) siphon; (*d'évier etc*) U-bend

sirène [siʀɛn] *nf* siren; **~ d'alarme** fire alarm; (*en temps de guerre*) air-raid siren

sirop [siʀo] *nm* (*à diluer: de fruit etc*) syrup; (*pharmaceutique*) syrup, mixture; **~ pour la toux** cough mixture

siroter [siʀɔte] *vt* to sip

sismique [sismik] *adj* seismic

site [sit] *nm* (*paysage, environnement*) setting; (*d'une ville etc: emplacement*) site; **~ (pittoresque)** beauty spot; **~s touristiques** places of interest; **~ Web** (*INFORM*) website

sitôt [sito] *adv*: **~ parti** as soon as he *etc* had left; **~ que** as soon as; **pas de ~** not for a long time

situation [sitɥasjɔ̃] *nf* situation; (*d'un édifice, d'une ville*) position, location; **~ de famille** marital status

situé, e [sitɥe] *adj* situated

situer [sitɥe] *vt* to site, situate; (*en pensée*) to set, place; **se ~** *vi* to be situated

six [sis] *num* six; **sixième** *num* sixth ♦ *nf* (*SCOL*) first form

Skaï® [skaj] *nm* Leatherette ®

ski [ski] *nm* (*objet*) ski; (*sport*) skiing; **faire du ~** to ski; **~ de fond** cross-country skiing; **~ nautique** water-skiing; **~ de piste** downhill skiing; **~ de randonnée** cross-country skiing; **skier** *vi* to ski; **skieur, -euse** *nm/f* skier

slip [slip] *nm* (*sous-vêtement*) pants *pl*, briefs *pl*; (*de bain: d'homme*) trunks *pl*; (*: du bikini*) (bikini) briefs *pl*

SMIC [smik] *sigle m* = **salaire minimum interprofessionnel de croissance**

SMIC

ⓘ *In France, the* **SMIC** *is the minimum legal hourly rate for workers over eighteen. It is index-linked and is raised each time the cost of living rises by 2%.*

---

smicard, e [smikaʀ, aʀd] (*fam*) *nm/f* minimum wage earner

smoking [smɔkiŋ] *nm* dinner suit

SMS *abr m* (= *Short Message Service*) SMS

SNCF *sigle f* (= *Société nationale des chemins de fer français*) French railways

snob [snɔb] *adj* snobbish ♦ *nm/f* snob; **snobisme** *nm* snobbery, snobbishness

sobre [sɔbʀ] *adj* (*personne*) temperate, abstemious; (*élégance, style*) sober

sobriquet [sɔbʀikɛ] *nm* nickname

social, e, -aux [sɔsjal, jo] *adj* social

socialisme [sɔsjalism] *nm* socialism; **socialiste** *nm/f* socialist

société [sɔsjete] *nf* society; (*sportive*) club; (*COMM*) company; **la ~ de consommation** the consumer society; **~ anonyme** ≈ limited (*BRIT*) *ou* incorporated (*US*) company

sociologie [sɔsjɔlɔʒi] *nf* sociology

socle [sɔkl] *nm* (*de colonne, statue*) plinth, pedestal; (*de lampe*) base

socquette [sɔkɛt] *nf* ankle sock

sœur [sœʀ] *nf* sister; (*religieuse*) nun, sister

soi [swa] *pron* oneself; **en ~** (*intrinsèquement*) in itself; **cela va de ~** that *ou* it goes without saying; **soi-disant** *adj inv* so-called ♦ *adv* supposedly

soie [swa] *nf* silk; **soierie** *nf* (*tissu*) silk

soif [swaf] *nf* thirst; **avoir ~** to be thirsty; **donner ~ à qn** to make sb thirsty

soigné, e [swaɲe] *adj* (*tenue*) well-groomed, neat; (*travail*) careful, meticulous

soigner [swaɲe] *vt* (*malade, maladie: suj: docteur*) to treat; (*suj: infirmière, mère*) to nurse, look after; (*travail, détails*) to take care over; (*jardin, invités*) to look after; **soigneux, -euse** *adj* (*propre*) tidy, neat; (*appliqué*) painstaking, careful

soi-même [swamɛm] *pron* oneself

soin [swɛ̃] *nm* (*application*) care; (*propreté, ordre*) tidiness, neatness; **~s** *nmpl* (*à un malade, blessé*) treatment *sg*, medical attention *sg*; (*hygiène*) care *sg*; **prendre ~ de** to take care of, look after; **prendre ~ de faire** to take care to do; **les premiers ~s** first aid *sg*

soir [swaʀ] *nm* evening; **ce ~** this evening, tonight; **demain ~** tomorrow evening, tomorrow night; **soirée** *nf* evening; (*réception*) party

soit [swa] *vb voir* **être** ♦ *conj* (*à savoir*) namely; (*ou*): **~ ... ~** either ... or ♦ *adv* so be it, very well; **~ que ... ~ que** *ou* **ou que** whether ... or whether

soixantaine [swasɑ̃tɛn] *nf*: **une ~ (de)** sixty or so, about sixty; **avoir la ~** (*âge*) to be around sixty

soixante [swasɑ̃t] *num* sixty; **soixante-dix** *num* seventy

soja [sɔʒa] *nm* soya; (*graines*) soya beans *pl*; **germes de ~** beansprouts

sol [sɔl] *nm* ground; (*de logement*) floor; (*AGR*) soil; (*MUS*) G; (: *en chantant la gamme*) so(h)

solaire [sɔlɛʀ] *adj* (*énergie etc*) solar; (*crème etc*) sun *cpd*

soldat [sɔlda] *nm* soldier

solde [sɔld] *nf* pay ♦ *nm* (*COMM*) balance; **~s** *nm ou f pl* (*articles*) sale goods; (*vente*) sales; **en ~** at sale price; **solder** *vt* (*marchandise*) to sell at sale price, sell off; **se solder par** (*fig*) to end in; **article soldé (à) 10 F** item reduced to 10 F

sole [sɔl] *nf* sole *inv* (*fish*)

soleil [sɔlej] *nm* sun; (*lumière*) sun(light); (*temps ensoleillé*) sun(shine); **il fait du ~** it's sunny; **au ~** in the sun

solennel, le [sɔlanɛl] *adj* solemn

solfège [sɔlfɛʒ] *nm* musical theory

solidaire [sɔlidɛʀ] *adj*: **être ~s** to show solidarity, stand *ou* stick together; **être ~ de** (*collègues*) to stand by; **solidarité** *nf* solidarity; **par solidarité (avec)** in sympathy (with)

solide [sɔlid] *adj* solid; (*mur, maison, meuble*) solid, sturdy; (*connaissances, argument*) sound; (*personne, estomac*) robust, sturdy ♦ *nm* solid

soliste [sɔlist] *nm/f* soloist

solitaire [sɔlitɛʀ] *adj* (*sans compagnie*) solitary, lonely; (*lieu*) lonely ♦ *nm/f* (*ermite*) recluse; (*fig: ours*) loner

solitude [sɔlityd] *nf* loneliness; (*tranquillité*) solitude

solive [sɔliv] *nf* joist

solliciter [sɔlisite] *vt* (*personne*) to appeal to; (*emploi, faveur*) to seek

sollicitude [sɔlisityd] *nf* concern

soluble [sɔlybl] *adj* soluble

solution [sɔlysjɔ̃] *nf* solution; **~ de facilité** easy way out

solvable [sɔlvabl] *adj* solvent

sombre [sɔ̃bʀ] *adj* dark; (*fig*) gloomy; **sombrer** *vi* (*bateau*) to sink; **sombrer dans** (*misère, désespoir*) to sink into

sommaire [sɔmɛʀ] *adj* (*simple*) basic; (*expéditif*) summary ♦ *nm* summary

sommation [sɔmasjɔ̃] *nf* (*JUR*) summons *sg*; (*avant de faire feu*) warning

somme [sɔm] *nf* (*MATH*) sum; (*quantité*) amount; (*argent*) sum, amount ♦ *nm*: **faire un ~** to have a (short) nap; **en ~** all in all; **~ toute** all in all

sommeil [sɔmɛj] *nm* sleep; **avoir ~** to be sleepy; **sommeiller** *vi* to doze

sommer [sɔme] *vt*: **~ qn de faire** to command *ou* order sb to do

sommes [sɔm] *vb voir* **être**

sommet [sɔmɛ] *nm* top; (*d'une montagne*) summit, top; (*fig: de la perfection, gloire*) height

sommier [sɔmje] *nm* (bed) base

somnambule [sɔmnɑ̃byl] *nm/f* sleepwalker

somnifère [sɔmnifɛʀ] *nm* sleeping drug *no pl* (*ou* pill)

somnoler [sɔmnɔle] *vi* to doze

somptueux, -euse [sɔ̃ptɥø, øz] *adj* sumptuous

son¹, sa [sɔ̃, sa] (*pl* **ses**) *adj* (*antécédent humain: mâle*) his; (*: femelle*) her; (*: valeur indéfinie*) one's, his/her; (*antécédent non humain*) its

son² [sɔ̃] *nm* sound; (*de blé*) bran

sondage [sɔ̃daʒ] *nm*: **~ (d'opinion)** (opinion) poll

sonde [sɔ̃d] *nf* (NAVIG) lead *ou* sounding line; (MÉD) probe; (TECH: *de forage*) borer, driller

sonder [sɔ̃de] *vt* (NAVIG) to sound; (TECH) to bore, drill; (*fig: personne*) to sound out; **~ le terrain** (*fig*) to test the ground

songe [sɔ̃ʒ] *nm* dream; **songer** *vi*: **songer à** (*penser à*) to think over; (*envisager*) to consider, think of; **songer que** to think that; **songeur, -euse** *adj* pensive

sonnant, e [sɔnɑ̃, ɑ̃t] *adj*: **à 8 heures ~es** on the stroke of 8

sonné, e [sɔne] *adj* (*fam*) cracked; **il est midi ~** it's gone twelve

sonner [sɔne] *vi* to ring ♦ *vt* (*cloche*) to ring; (*glas, tocsin*) to sound; (*portier, infirmière*) to ring for; **~ faux** (*instrument*) to sound out of tune; (*rire*) to ring false

sonnerie [sɔnʀi] *nf* (*son*) ringing; (*sonnette*) bell; **~ d'alarme** alarm bell

sonnette [sɔnɛt] *nf* bell; **~ d'alarme** alarm bell

sono [sɔno] *abr f* = **sonorisation**

sonore [sɔnɔʀ] *adj* (*voix*) sonorous, ringing; (*salle*) resonant; (*film, signal*) sound *cpd*; **sonorisation** *nf* (*équipement: de salle de conférences*) public address system, P.A. system; (: *de discothèque*) sound system; **sonorité** *nf* (*de piano, violon*) tone; (*d'une salle*) acoustics *pl*

sont [sɔ̃] *vb voir* **être**

sophistiqué, e [sɔfistike] *adj* sophisticated

sorbet [sɔʀbɛ] *nm* water ice, sorbet

sorcellerie [sɔʀsɛlʀi] *nf* witchcraft *no pl*

sorcier [sɔʀsje] *nm* sorcerer; **sorcière** *nf* witch *ou* sorceress

sordide [sɔʀdid] *adj* (*lieu*) squalid; (*action*) sordid

sornettes [sɔʀnɛt] *nfpl* twaddle *sg*

sort [sɔʀ] *nm* (*destinée*) fate; (*condition*) lot; (*magique*) curse, spell; **tirer au ~** to draw lots

sorte [sɔʀt] *nf* sort, kind; **de la ~** in that way; **de (telle) ~ que** so that; **en quelque ~** in a way; **faire en ~ que** to see to it that

sortie [sɔʀti] *nf* (*issue*) way out, exit; (*remarque drôle*) sally; (*promenade*) outing; (*le soir: au restaurant etc*) night out; (COMM: *d'un disque*) release; (: *d'un livre*) publication; (: *d'un modèle*) launching; **~s** *nfpl* (COMM: *somme*) items of expenditure, outgoings; **~ de bain** (*vêtement*) bathrobe; **~ de secours** emergency exit

sortilège [sɔʀtilɛʒ] *nm* (magic) spell

sortir [sɔʀtiʀ] *vi* (*gén*) to come out; (*partir, se promener, aller au spectacle*) to go out; (*numéro gagnant*) to come up ♦ *vt* (*gén*) to take out; (*produit, modèle*) to bring out; (*fam: dire*) to come out with; **~ avec qn** to be going out with sb; **s'en ~** (*malade*) to pull through; (*d'une difficulté etc*) to get through; **~ de** (*endroit*) to go (*ou* come) out of, leave; (*provenir de*) to come from; (*compétence*) to be outside

sosie [sɔzi] *nm* double

sot, sotte [so, sɔt] *adj* silly, foolish ♦ *nm/f* fool; **sottise** *nf* (*caractère*) silliness, foolishness; (action) silly ou foolish thing

sou [su] nm: **près de ses ~s** tight-fisted; **sans le ~** penniless

soubresaut [subʀəso] nm start; (cahot) jolt

souche [suʃ] nf (d'arbre) stump; (de carnet) counterfoil (BRIT), stub

souci [susi] nm (inquiétude) worry; (préoccupation) concern; (BOT) marigold; **se faire du ~** to worry; **soucier**: **se soucier de** vt to care about; **soucieux, -euse** adj concerned, worried

soucoupe [sukup] nf saucer; **~ volante** flying saucer

soudain, e [sudɛ̃, ɛn] adj (douleur, mort) sudden ♦ adv suddenly, all of a sudden

soude [sud] nf soda

souder [sude] vt (avec fil à ~) to solder; (par soudure autogène) to weld; (fig) to bind together

soudoyer [sudwaje] (péj) vt to bribe

soudure [sudyʀ] nf soldering; welding; (joint) soldered joint; weld

souffert, e [sufɛʀ, ɛʀt] pp de **souffrir**

souffle [sufl] nm (en expirant) breath; (en soufflant) puff, blow; (respiration) breathing; (d'explosion, de ventilateur) blast; (du vent) blowing; **être à bout de ~** to be out of breath; **un ~ d'air** a breath of air

soufflé, e [sufle] adj (fam: stupéfié) staggered ♦ nm (CULIN) soufflé

souffler [sufle] vi (gén) to blow; (haleter) to puff (and blow) ♦ vt (feu, bougie) to blow out; (chasser: poussière etc) to blow away; (TECH: verre) to blow; (dire): **~ qch à qn** to whisper sth to sb; **soufflet** nm (instrument) bellows pl; (gifle) slap (in the face); **souffleur** nm (THÉÂTRE) prompter

souffrance [sufʀɑ̃s] nf suffering; **en ~** (affaire) pending

souffrant, e [sufʀɑ̃, ɑ̃t] adj unwell

souffre-douleur [sufʀədulœʀ] nm inv butt, underdog

souffrir [sufʀiʀ] vi to suffer, be in pain ♦ vt to suffer, endure; (supporter) to bear, stand; **~ de** (maladie, froid) to suffer from;

elle ne peut pas le ~ she can't stand ou bear him

soufre [sufʀ] nm sulphur

souhait [swɛ] nm wish; **tous nos ~s de** good wishes ou our best wishes for; **à vos ~s!** bless you!; **souhaitable** adj desirable

souhaiter [swete] vt to wish for; **~ la bonne année à qn** to wish sb a happy New Year; **~ que** to hope that

souiller [suje] vt to dirty, soil; (fig: réputation etc) to sully, tarnish

soûl, e [su, sul] adj drunk ♦ nm: **tout son ~** to one's heart's content

soulagement [sulaʒmɑ̃] nm relief

soulager [sulaʒe] vt to relieve

soûler [sule] vt: **~ qn** to get sb drunk; (suj: boisson) to make sb drunk; (fig) to make sb's head spin ou reel; **se ~** vi to get drunk

soulever [sul(ə)ve] vt to lift; (poussière) to send up; (enthousiasme) to arouse; (question, débat) to raise; **se ~** vi (peuple) to rise up; (personne couchée) to lift o.s. up

soulier [sulje] nm shoe

souligner [suliɲe] vt to underline; (fig) to emphasize, stress

soumettre [sumɛtʀ] vt (pays) to subject, subjugate; (rebelle) to put down, subdue; **se ~ (à)** to submit (to); **~ qch à qn** (projet etc) to submit sth to sb

soumis, e [sumi, iz] adj submissive; **soumission** nf submission

soupape [supap] nf valve

soupçon [supsɔ̃] nm suspicion; (petite quantité): **un ~ de** a hint ou touch of; **soupçonner** vt to suspect; **soupçonneux, -euse** adj suspicious

soupe [sup] nf soup

souper [supe] vi to have supper ♦ nm supper

soupeser [supəze] vt to weigh in one's hand(s); (fig) to weigh up

soupière [supjɛʀ] nf (soup) tureen

soupir [supiʀ] nm sigh; **pousser un ~ de soulagement** to heave a sigh of relief

soupirail, -aux [supiʀaj, o] *nm* (small) basement window

soupirer [supiʀe] *vi* to sigh

souple [supl] *adj* supple; (*fig: règlement, caractère*) flexible; (: *démarche, taille*) lithe, supple; **souplesse** *nf* suppleness; (*de caractère*) flexibility

source [suʀs] *nf* (*point d'eau*) spring; (*d'un cours d'eau, fig*) source; **de bonne ~** on good authority

sourcil [suʀsi] *nm* (eye)brow; **sourciller** *vi*: **sans sourciller** without turning a hair *ou* batting an eyelid

sourd, e [suʀ, suʀd] *adj* deaf; (*bruit*) muffled; (*douleur*) dull ♦ *nm/f* deaf person; **faire la ~e oreille** to turn a deaf ear; **sourdine** *nf* (*MUS*) mute; **en sourdine** softly, quietly; **sourd-muet, sourde-muette** *adj* deaf-and-dumb ♦ *nm/f* deaf-mute

souriant, e [suʀjɑ̃, jɑ̃t] *adj* cheerful

souricière [suʀisjɛʀ] *nf* mousetrap; (*fig*) trap

sourire [suʀiʀ] *nm* smile ♦ *vi* to smile; **~ à qn** to smile at sb; (*fig: plaire à*) to appeal to sb; (*suj: chance*) to smile on sb; **garder le ~** to keep smiling

souris [suʀi] *nf* mouse

sournois, e [suʀnwa, waz] *adj* deceitful, underhand

sous [su] *prép* under; **~ la pluie** in the rain; **~ terre** underground; **~ peu** shortly, before long; **sous-bois** *nm inv* undergrowth

souscrire [suskʀiʀ]: **~ à** *vt* to subscribe to

sous...: **sous-directeur, -trice** *nm/f* assistant manager(-manageress); **sous-entendre** *vt* to imply, infer; **sous-entendu, e** *adj* implied ♦ *nm* innuendo, insinuation; **sous-estimer** *vt* to underestimate; **sous-jacent, e** *adj* underlying; **sous-louer** *vt* to sublet; **sous-marin, e** *adj* (*flore, faune*) submarine; (*pêche*) underwater ♦ *nm* submarine; **sous-officier** *nm* ≃ non-commissioned officer (N.C.O.);

sous-produit *nm* by-product; **sous-pull** *nm* thin poloneck jersey; **soussigné, e** *adj*: **je soussigné** I the undersigned; **sous-sol** *nm* basement; **sous-titre** *nm* subtitle

soustraction [sustʀaksjɔ̃] *nf* subtraction

soustraire [sustʀɛʀ] *vt* to subtract, take away; (*dérober*) **~ qch à qn** to remove sth from sb; **se ~ à** (*autorité etc*) to elude, escape from

sous...: **sous-traitant** *nm* subcontractor; **sous-traiter** *vt* to subcontract; **sous-vêtements** *nmpl* underwear *sg*

soutane [sutan] *nf* cassock, soutane

soute [sut] *nf* hold

soutenir [sut(ə)niʀ] *vt* to support; (*assaut, choc*) to stand up to, withstand; (*intérêt, effort*) to keep up; (*assurer*): **~ que** to maintain that; **soutenu, e** *adj* (*efforts*) sustained, unflagging; (*style*) elevated

souterrain, e [suteʀɛ̃, ɛn] *adj* underground ♦ *nm* underground passage

soutien [sutjɛ̃] *nm* support; **soutien-gorge** *nm* bra

soutirer [sutiʀe] *vt*: **~ qch à qn** to squeeze *ou* get sth out of sb

souvenir [suv(ə)niʀ] *nm* (*réminiscence*) memory; (*objet*) souvenir ♦ *vb*: **se ~ de** ♦ *vt* to remember; **se ~ que** to remember that; **en ~ de** in memory *ou* remembrance of

souvent [suvɑ̃] *adv* often; **peu ~** seldom, infrequently

souverain, e [suv(ə)ʀɛ̃, ɛn] *nm/f* sovereign, monarch

soyeux, -euse [swajø, øz] *adj* silky

soyons *etc* [swajɔ̃] *vb voir* **être**

spacieux, -euse [spasjø, jøz] *adj* spacious, roomy

spaghettis [spageti] *nmpl* spaghetti *sg*

sparadrap [spaʀadʀa] *nm* sticking plaster (*BRIT*), Bandaid ® (*US*)

spatial, e, -aux [spasjal, jo] *adj* (*AVIAT*) space *cpd*

speaker, ine [spikœʀ, kʀin] *nm/f* announcer

spécial, e, -aux [spesjal, jo] adj special; (bizarre) peculiar; **spécialement** adv especially, particularly; (tout exprès) specially; **spécialiser: se spécialiser** vi to specialize; **spécialiste** nm/f specialist; **spécialité** nf speciality; (branche) special field

spécifier [spesifje] vt to specify, state

spécimen [spesimɛn] nm specimen

spectacle [spɛktakl] nm (scène) sight; (représentation) show; (industrie) show business; **spectaculaire** adj spectacular

spectateur, -trice [spɛktatœr, tris] nm/f (CINÉMA etc) member of the audience; (SPORT) spectator; (d'un événement) onlooker, witness

spéculer [spekyle] vi to speculate

spéléologie [speleɔlɔʒi] nf potholing

sperme [spɛrm] nm semen, sperm

sphère [sfɛr] nf sphere

spirale [spiral] nf spiral

spirituel, le [spirituɛl] adj spiritual; (fin, piquant) witty

splendide [splɑ̃did] adj splendid

sponsoriser [spɔ̃sɔrize] vt to sponsor

spontané, e [spɔ̃tane] adj spontaneous; **spontanéité** nf spontaneity

sport [spɔr] nm sport ♦ adj inv (vêtement) casual; **faire du ~** to do sport; **~s d'hiver** winter sports; **sportif, -ive** adj (journal, association, épreuve) sports cpd; (allure, démarche) athletic; (attitude, esprit) sporting

spot [spɔt] nm (lampe) spot(light); (annonce): **~ (publicitaire)** commercial (break)

square [skwar] nm public garden(s)

squelette [skəlɛt] nm skeleton; **squelettique** adj scrawny

stabiliser [stabilize] vt to stabilize

stable [stabl] adj stable, steady

stade [stad] nm (SPORT) stadium; (phase, niveau) stage

stage [staʒ] nm (cours) training course; **~ de formation (professionnelle)** voca-

tional (training) course; **~ de perfectionnement** advanced training course; **stagiaire** nm/f, adj trainee

stagner [stagne] vi to stagnate

stalle [stal] nf stall, box

stand [stɑ̃d] nm (d'exposition) stand; (de foire) stall; **~ de tir** (à la foire, SPORT) shooting range

standard [stɑ̃dar] adj inv standard ♦ nm switchboard; **standardiste** nm/f switchboard operator

standing [stɑ̃diŋ] nm standing; **de grand ~** luxury

starter [starter] nm (AUTO) choke

station [stasjɔ̃] nf station; (de bus) stop; (de villégiature) resort; **~ balnéaire** seaside resort; **~ de ski** ski resort; **~ de taxis** taxi rank (BRIT) ou stand (US); **stationnement** nm parking; **stationner** vi to park; **station-service** nf service station

statistique [statistik] nf (science) statistics sg; (rapport, étude) statistic ♦ adj statistical

statue [staty] nf statue

statu quo [statykwo] nm status quo

statut [staty] nm status; **~s** nmpl (JUR, ADMIN) statutes; **statutaire** adj statutory

Sté abr = **société**

steak [stɛk] nm steak; **~ haché** hamburger

sténo(dactylo) [steno(daktilo)] nf shorthand typist (BRIT), stenographer (US); **sténo(graphie)** [steno(grafi)] nf shorthand

stéréo [stereo] adj stereo

stérile [steril] adj sterile

stérilet [sterilɛ] nm coil, loop

stériliser [sterilize] vt to sterilize

stigmates [stigmat] nmpl scars, marks

stimulant [stimylɑ̃] nm (fig) stimulus, incentive; (physique) stimulant

stimuler [stimyle] vt to stimulate

stipuler [stipyle] vt to stipulate

stock [stɔk] nm stock; **stocker** vt to stock

stop [stɔp] nm (AUTO: écriteau) stop sign; (: feu arrière) brake-light; **faire du ~** (fam) to hitch(hike); **stopper** vt, vi to stop, halt

store [stɔr] nm blind; (de magasin) shade,

awning

strabisme [stʀabism] *nm* squinting

strapontin [stʀapɔ̃tɛ̃] *nm* jump *ou* fold-away seat

stratégie [stʀateʒi] *nf* strategy; **stratégique** *adj* strategic

stress [stʀɛs] *nm* stress; **stressant, e** *adj* stressful; **stresser** *vt*: **stresser qn** to make sb (feel) tense

strict, e [stʀikt] *adj* strict; (*tenue, décor*) severe, plain; **le ~ nécessaire/minimum** the bare essentials/minimum

strident, e [stʀidɑ̃, ɑ̃t] *adj* shrill, strident

strophe [stʀɔf] *nf* verse, stanza

structure [stʀyktyʀ] *nf* structure

studieux, -euse [stydjø, jøz] *adj* studious

studio [stydjo] *nm* (*logement*) (one-roomed) flatlet (*BRIT*) *ou* apartment (*US*); (*d'artiste, TV etc*) studio

stupéfait, e [stypefɛ, ɛt] *adj* astonished

stupéfiant [stypefjɑ̃, jɑ̃t] *adj* (*étonnant*) stunning, astounding ♦ *nm* (*MÉD*) drug, narcotic

stupéfier [stypefje] *vt* (*étonner*) to stun, astonish

stupeur [stypœʀ] *nf* astonishment

stupide [stypid] *adj* stupid; **stupidité** *nf* stupidity; (*parole, acte*) stupid thing (to do *ou* say)

style [stil] *nm* style

stylé, e [stile] *adj* well-trained

styliste [stilist] *nm/f* designer

stylo [stilo] *nm*: **~ (à encre)** (fountain) pen; **~ (à) bille** ball-point pen; **~-feutre** felt-tip pen

su, e [sy] *pp de* **savoir** ♦ *nm*: **au ~ de** with the knowledge of

suave [sɥav] *adj* sweet

subalterne [sybaltɛʀn] *adj* (*employé, officier*) junior; (*rôle*) subordinate, subsidiary ♦ *nm/f* subordinate

subconscient [sypkɔ̃sjɑ̃] *nm* subconscious

subir [sybiʀ] *vt* (*affront, dégâts*) to suffer; (*opération, châtiment*) to undergo

subit, e [sybi, it] *adj* sudden; **subitement** *adv* suddenly, all of a sudden

subjectif, -ive [sybʒɛktif, iv] *adj* subjective

subjonctif [sybʒɔ̃ktif] *nm* subjunctive

subjuguer [sybʒyge] *vt* to captivate

submerger [sybmɛʀʒe] *vt* to submerge; (*fig*) to overwhelm

subordonné, e [sybɔʀdɔne] *adj, nm/f* subordinate

subrepticement [sybʀɛptismɑ̃] *adv* surreptitiously

subside [sybzid] *nm* grant

subsidiaire [sybzidjɛʀ] *adj*: **question ~** deciding question

subsister [sybziste] *vi* (*rester*) to remain, subsist; (*survivre*) to live on

substance [sypstɑ̃s] *nf* substance

substituer [sypstitɥe] *vt*: **~ qn/qch à** to substitute sb/sth for; **se ~ à qn** (*évincer*) to substitute o.s. for sb

substitut [sypstity] *nm* (*succédané*) substitute

subterfuge [s/ptɛʀfyʒ] *nm* subterfuge

subtil, e [syptil] *adj* subtle

subtiliser [syptilize] *vt*: **~ qch (à qn)** to spirit sth away (from sb)

subvenir [sybvəniʀ]: **~ à** *vt* to meet

subvention [sybvɑ̃sjɔ̃] *nf* subsidy, grant; **subventionner** *vt* to subsidize

suc [syk] *nm* (*BOT*) sap; (*de viande, fruit*) juice

succédané [syksedane] *nm* substitute

succéder [syksede]: **~ à** *vt* to succeed; **se ~** *vi* (*accidents, années*) to follow one another

succès [syksɛ] *nm* success; **avoir du ~** to be a success, be successful; **à ~** successful; **~ de librairie** bestseller; **~ (féminins)** conquests

successif, -ive [syksesif, iv] *adj* successive

successeur [syksesœʀ] *nm* successor

succession [syksesjɔ̃] *nf* (*série, POL*) succession; (*JUR: patrimoine*) estate, inheritance

succomber [sykɔ̃be] *vi* to die, succumb;

(fig): ~ **à** to succumb to

succulent, e [sykylɑ̃, ɑ̃t] *adj (repas, mets)* delicious

succursale [sykyʀsal] *nf* branch

sucer [syse] *vt* to suck; **sucette** *nf (bonbon)* lollipop; *(de bébé)* dummy *(BRIT)*, pacifier *(US)*

sucre [sykʀ] *nm (substance)* sugar; *(morceau)* lump of sugar, sugar lump *ou* cube; ~ **d'orge** barley sugar; ~ **en morceaux/ en poudre** lump/caster sugar; ~ **glace/ roux** icing/brown sugar; **sucré, e** *adj (produit alimentaire)* sweetened; *(au goût)* sweet; **sucrer** *vt (thé, café)* to sweeten, put sugar in; **sucreries** *nfpl (bonbons)* sweets, sweet things; **sucrier** *nm (récipient)* sugar bowl

sud [syd] *nm:* **le** ~ the south ♦ *adj inv* south; *(côté)* south, southern; **au** ~ *(situation)* in the south; *(direction)* to the south; **au** ~ **de** (to the) south of; **sud-africain, e** *adj* South African ♦ *nm/f:* **Sud-Africain, e** South African; **sud-américain, e** *adj* South American ♦ *nm/f:* **Sud-Américain, e** South American; **sud-est** *nm, adj inv* south-east; **sud-ouest** *nm, adj inv* south-west

Suède [sɥɛd] *nf:* **la** ~ Sweden; **suédois, e** *adj* Swedish ♦ *nm/f:* **Suédois, e** Swede ♦ *nm (LING)* Swedish

suer [sɥe] *vi* to sweat; *(suinter)* to ooze; **sueur** *nf* sweat; **en sueur** sweating, in a sweat; **donner des sueurs froids à qn** to put sb in(to) a cold sweat

suffire [syfiʀ] *vi (être assez):* ~ **(à qn/pour qch/pour faire)** to be enough *ou* sufficient (for sb/for sth/to do); **il suffit d'une négligence ...** only takes one act of carelessness ...; **il suffit qu'on oublie pour que ...** one only needs to forget for ...; **ça suffit!** that's enough!

suffisamment [syfizamɑ̃] *adv* sufficiently, enough; ~ **de** sufficient, enough

suffisant, e [syfizɑ̃, ɑ̃t] *adj* sufficient; *(résultats)* satisfactory; *(vaniteux)* self-important, bumptious

suffixe [syfiks] *nm* suffix

suffoquer [syfɔke] *vt* to choke, suffocate; *(stupéfier)* to stagger, astound ♦ *vi* to choke, suffocate

suffrage [syfʀaʒ] *nm (POL: voix)* vote

suggérer [sygʒeʀe] *vt* to suggest; **suggestion** *nf* suggestion

suicide [sɥisid] *nm* suicide; **suicider: se suicider** *vi* to commit suicide

suie [sɥi] *nf* soot

suinter [sɥɛ̃te] *vi* to ooze

suis [sɥi] *vb voir* **être; suivre**

suisse [sɥis] *adj* Swiss ♦ *nm:* **S~** Swiss *pl inv* ♦ *nf:* **la S~** Switzerland; **la S~ romande/allemande** French-speaking/ German-speaking Switzerland; **Suisses- se** *nf* Swiss (woman *ou* girl)

suite [sɥit] *nf (continuation: d'énumération etc)* rest, remainder; *(: de feuilleton)* continuation; *(: film etc sur le même thème)* sequel; *(série)* series, succession; *(conséquence)* result; *(ordre, liaison logique)* coherence; *(appartement, MUS)* suite; *(escorte)* retinue, suite; ~**s** *nfpl (d'une maladie etc)* effects; **prendre la** ~ **de** *(directeur etc)* to succeed, take over from; **donner** ~ **à** *(requête, projet)* to follow up; **faire** ~ **à** to follow; **(faisant)** ~ **à votre lettre du ...** further to your letter of the ...; **de** ~ *(d'affilée)* in succession; *(immédiatement)* at once; **par la** ~ afterwards, subsequently; **à la** ~ one after the other; **à la** ~ **de** *(derrière)* behind; *(en conséquence de)* following

suivant, e [sɥivɑ̃, ɑ̃t] *adj* next, following ♦ *prép (selon)* according to; **au** ~! next!

suivi, e [sɥivi] *adj (effort, qualité)* consistent; *(cohérent)* coherent; **très/peu** ~ *(cours)* well-/poorly-attended

suivre [sɥivʀ] *vt (gén)* to follow; *(SCOL: cours)* to attend; *(comprendre)* to keep up with; *(COMM: article)* to continue to stock ♦ *vi* to follow; *(élève: assimiler)* to keep up; **se** ~ *vi (accidents etc)* to follow one after the other; **faire** ~ *(lettre)* to forward; **"à ~"** "to be continued"

sujet, te [syʒɛ, ɛt] *adj:* **être ~ à** *(vertige etc)* to be liable *ou* subject to ♦ *nm/f (d'un souverain)* subject ♦ *nm* subject; **au ~ de** about; **~ de conversation** topic *ou* subject of conversation; **~ d'examen** *(SCOL)* examination question

summum [sɔ(m)mɔm] *nm:* **le ~ de** the height of

super [sypɛR] *(fam) adj inv* terrific, great, fantastic, super

superbe [sypɛRb] *adj* magnificent, superb

super(carburant) [sypɛR(kaRbyRɑ̃)] *nm* ≃ 4-star petrol *(BRIT)*, ≃ high-octane gasoline *(US)*

supercherie [sypɛRʃəRi] *nf* trick

supérette [sypeRɛt] *nf (COMM)* minimarket, superette *(US)*

superficie [sypɛRfisi] *nf* (surface) area

superficiel, le [sypɛRfisjɛl] *adj* superficial

superflu, e [sypɛRfly] *adj* superfluous

supérieur, e [sypeRjœR] *adj (lèvre, étages, classes)* upper; *(plus élevé: température, niveau, enseignement)*: **~ (à)** higher (than); *(meilleur: qualité, produit)*: **~ (à)** superior (to); *(excellent, hautain)* superior ♦ *nm, nf* superior; **supériorité** *nf* superiority

superlatif [sypɛRlatif] *nm* superlative

supermarché [sypɛRmaRʃe] *nm* supermarket

superposer [sypɛRpoze] *vt (faire chevaucher)* to superimpose; **lits superposés** bunk beds

superproduction [sypɛRpRɔdyksjɔ̃] *nf (film)* spectacular

superpuissance [sypɛRpɥisɑ̃s] *nf* superpower

superstitieux, -euse [sypɛRstisjø, jøz] *adj* superstitious

superviser [sypɛRvize] *vt* to supervise

supplanter [syplɑ̃te] *vt* to supplant

suppléance [sypleɑ̃s] *nf:* **faire des ~s** *(professeur)* to do supply teaching; **suppléant, e** *adj (professeur)* supply *cpd;* *(juge, fonctionnaire)* deputy *cpd* ♦ *nm/f (professeur)* supply teacher

suppléer [syplee] *vt (ajouter: mot man-*

quant etc) to supply, provide; *(compenser: lacune)* to fill in; **~ à** to make up for

supplément [syplemɑ̃] *nm* supplement; *(de frites etc)* extra portion; **un ~ de travail** extra *ou* additional work; **payer un ~** to pay an additional charge; **le vin est en ~** wine is extra; **supplémentaire** *adj* additional, further; *(train, bus)* relief *cpd,* extra

supplications [syplikasjɔ̃] *nfpl* pleas, entreaties

supplice [syplis] *nm* torture *no pl*

supplier [syplije] *vt* to implore, beseech

support [sypɔR] *nm* support; *(publicitaire)* medium; *(audio-visuel)* aid

supportable [sypɔRtabl] *adj (douleur)* bearable

supporter¹ [sypɔRtɛR] *nm* supporter, fan

supporter² [sypɔRte] *vt (conséquences, épreuve)* to bear, endure; *(défauts, personne)* to put up with; *(suj: chose: chaleur etc)* to withstand; *(: personne: chaleur, vin)* to be able to take

supposer [sypoze] *vt* to suppose; *(impliquer)* to presuppose; **à ~ que** supposing (that)

suppositoire [sypozitwaR] *nm* suppository

suppression [sypResjɔ̃] *nf (voir supprimer)* cancellation; removal; deletion

supprimer [sypRime] *vt (congés, service d'autobus etc)* to cancel; *(emplois, privilèges, témoin gênant)* to do away with; *(cloison, cause, anxiété)* to remove; *(clause, mot)* to delete

suprême [sypRɛm] *adj* supreme

| MOT-CLÉ |

---

sur [syR] *prép* **1** *(position)* on; *(par-dessus)* over; *(au-dessus)* above; **pose-le sur la table** put it on the table; **je n'ai pas d'argent sur moi** I haven't any money on me **2** *(direction)* towards; **en allant sur Paris** going towards Paris; **sur votre droite** on *ou* to your right

3 *(à propos de)* on, about; **un livre/une conférence sur Balzac** a book/lecture on *ou* about Balzac

4 (*proportion, mesures*) out of, by; **un sur 10** one in 10; (*SCOL*) one out of 10; **4 m sur 2** 4 m by 2

sur ce *adv* hereupon

---

sûr, e [syʀ] *adj* sure, certain; (*digne de confiance*) reliable; (*sans danger*) safe; (*diagnostic, goût*) reliable; **le plus ~ est de** the safest thing is to; **~ de soi** self-confident; **~ et certain** absolutely certain

surcharge [syʀʃaʀʒ] *nf* (*de passagers etc*) excess load; **surcharger** *vt* to overload

surchoix [syʀʃwa] *adj inv* top-quality

surclasser [syʀklase] *vt* to outclass

surcroît [syʀkʀwa] *nm*: **un ~ de** additional +*nom*; **par** *ou* **de ~** moreover; **en ~** in addition

surdité [syʀdite] *nf* deafness

surélever [syʀel(ə)ve] *vt* to raise, heighten

sûrement [syʀmɑ̃] *adv* (*certainement*) certainly; (*sans risques*) safely

surenchère [syʀɑ̃ʃɛʀ] *nf* (*aux enchères*) higher bid; **surenchérir** *vi* to bid higher; (*fig*) to try and outbid each other

surent [syʀ] *vb voir* **savoir**

surestimer [syʀɛstime] *vt* to overestimate

sûreté [syʀte] *nf* (*sécurité*) safety; (*exactitude: de renseignements etc*) reliability; (*d'un geste*) steadiness; **mettre en ~** to put in a safe place; **pour plus de ~** as an extra precaution, to be on the safe side

surf [sœʀf] *nm* surfing

surface [syʀfas] *nf* surface; (*superficie*) surface area; **une grande ~** a supermarket; **faire ~** to surface; **en ~** near the surface; (*fig*) superficially

surfait, e [syʀfɛ, ɛt] *adj* overrated

surfer [syʀfe] *vi* to surf; **~ sur Internet** to surf the net

surgelé, e [syʀʒəle] *adj* (deep-)frozen ♦ *nm*: **les ~s** (deep-)frozen food

surgir [syʀʒiʀ] *vi* to appear suddenly; (*fig: problème, conflit*) to arise

sur...: **surhumain, e** *adj* superhuman; **sur-le-champ** *adv* immediately; **surlen-**

demain *nm*: **le surlendemain (soir)** two days later (in the evening); **le surlendemain de** two days after; **surmenage** *nm* overwork(ing); **surmener**: **se surmener** *vi* to overwork

surmonter [syʀmɔ̃te] *vt* (*vaincre*) to overcome; (*être au-dessus de*) to top

surnaturel, le [syʀnatyʀɛl] *adj, nm* supernatural

surnom [syʀnɔ̃] *nm* nickname

surnombre [syʀnɔ̃bʀ] *nm*: **être en ~** to be too many (*ou* one too many)

surpeuplé, e [syʀpœple] *adj* overpopulated

sur-place [syʀplas] *nm*: **faire du ~-~** to mark time

surplomber [syʀplɔ̃be] *vt, vi* to overhang

surplus [syʀply] *nm* (*COMM*) surplus; (*reste*): **~ de bois** wood left over

surprenant, e [syʀpʀənɑ̃, ɑ̃t] *adj* amazing

surprendre [syʀpʀɑ̃dʀ] *vt* (*étonner*) to surprise; (*tomber sur: intrus etc*) to catch; (*entendre*) to overhear

surpris, e [syʀpʀi, iz] *adj*: **~ (de/que)** surprised (at/that); **surprise** *nf* surprise; **faire une surprise à qn** to give sb a surprise; **surprise-partie** *nf* party

surréservation [syʀʀezɛʀvasjɔ̃] *nf* double booking, overbooking

sursaut [syʀso] *nm* start, jump; **~ de** (*énergie, indignation*) sudden fit *ou* burst of; **en ~** with a start; **sursauter** *vi* to (give a) start, jump

sursis [syʀsi] *nm* (*JUR: gén*) suspended sentence; (*fig*) reprieve

surtaxe [syʀtaks] *nf* surcharge

surtout [syʀtu] *adv* (*avant tout*) above all; (*spécialement*) especially; **~, ne dites rien!** whatever you do don't say anything!; **~ pas!** certainly *ou* definitely not!; **~ que ...** especially as ...

surveillance [syʀvejɑ̃s] *nf* watch; (*POLICE, MIL*) surveillance; **sous ~ médicale** under medical supervision

surveillant, e [syʀvejɑ̃, ɑ̃t] *nm/f* (*de pri-*

son) warder; (*SCOL*) monitor

surveiller [syʀveje] *vt* (*enfant, élèves, bagages*) to watch, keep an eye on; (*prisonnier, suspect*) to keep (a) watch on; (*territoire, bâtiment*) to (keep) watch over; (*travaux, cuisson*) to supervise; (*SCOL: examen*) to invigilate; **~ son langage/sa ligne** to watch one's language/figure

survenir [syʀvəniʀ] *vi* (*incident, retards*) to occur, arise; (*événement*) to take place

survêt(ement) [syʀvɛt(mã)] *nm* tracksuit

survie [syʀvi] *nf* survival; **survivant, e** *nm/f* survivor; **survivre** *vi* to survive; **survivre à** (*accident etc*) to survive

survoler [syʀvɔle] *vt* to fly over; (*fig: livre*) to skim through

survolté, e [syʀvɔlte] *adj* (*fig*) worked up

sus [sy(s)]: **en ~ de** *prép* in addition to, over and above; **en ~** in addition

susceptible [syseptibl] *adj* touchy, sensitive; **~ de faire** (*hypothèse*) liable to do

susciter [sysite] *vt* (*admiration*) to arouse; (*ennuis*) **(à qn)** to create (for sb)

suspect, e [syspe(kt), ɛkt] *adj* suspicious; (*témoignage, opinions*) suspect ♦ *nm/f* suspect; **suspecter** *vt* to suspect; (*honnêteté de qn*) to question, have one's suspicions about

suspendre [syspãdʀ] *vt* (*accrocher: vêtement*): **~ qch (à)** to hang sth up (on); (*interrompre, démettre*) to suspend; **se ~ à** to hang from

suspendu, e [syspãdy] *adj* (*accroché*): **~ à** hanging from (*ou* from); (*perché*): **~ au-dessus de** suspended over

suspens [syspã]: **en ~** *adv* (*affaire*) in abeyance; **tenir en ~** to keep in suspense

suspense [syspens, syspãs] *nm* suspense

suspension [syspãsjɔ̃] *nf* suspension; (*lustre*) light fitting *ou* fitment

sut [sy] *vb voir* **savoir**

suture [sytyʀ] *nf* (*MÉD*): **point de ~** stitch

svelte [svɛlt] *adj* slender, svelte

SVP *abr* (= *s'il vous plaît*) please

sweat-shirt [switʃœʀt] (*pl* **~-~s**) *nm* sweatshirt

syllabe [si(l)lab] *nf* syllable

symbole [sɛ̃bɔl] *nm* symbol; **symbolique** *adj* symbolic(al); (*geste, offrande*) token *cpd*; **symboliser** *vt* to symbolize

symétrique [simetʀik] *adj* symmetrical

sympa [sɛ̃pa] (*fam*) *adj inv* nice; **sois ~, prête-le moi** be a pal and lend it to me

sympathie [sɛ̃pati] *nf* (*inclination*) liking; (*affinité*) friendship; (*condoléances*) sympathy; **j'ai beaucoup de ~ pour lui** I like him a lot; **sympathique** *adj* nice, friendly

sympathisant, e [sɛ̃patizã, ãt] *nm/f* sympathizer

sympathiser [sɛ̃patize] *vi* (*voisins etc: s'entendre*) to get on (*BRIT*) *ou* along (*US*) (well)

symphonie [sɛ̃fɔni] *nf* symphony

symptôme [sɛ̃ptom] *nm* symptom

synagogue [sinagɔg] *nf* synagogue

syncope [sɛ̃kɔp] *nf* (*MÉD*) blackout; **tomber en ~** to faint, pass out

syndic [sɛ̃dik] *nm* (*d'immeuble*) managing agent

syndical, e, -aux [sɛ̃dikal, o] *adj* (trade) union *cpd*; **syndicaliste** *nm/f* trade unionist

syndicat [sɛ̃dika] *nm* (*d'ouvriers, employés*) (trade) union; **~ d'initiative** tourist office; **syndiqué, e** *adj* belonging to a (trade) union; **se syndiquer** *vi* to form a trade union; (*adhérer*) to join a trade union

synonyme [sinɔnim] *adj* synonymous ♦ *nm* synonym; **~ de** synonymous with

syntaxe [sɛ̃taks] *nf* syntax

synthèse [sɛ̃tez] *nf* synthesis

synthétique [sɛ̃tetik] *adj* synthetic

Syrie [siʀi] *nf*: **la ~** Syria

systématique [sistematik] *adj* systematic

système [sistɛm] *nm* system; **~ D** (*fam*) resourcefulness

T, t

t' [t] *pron voir* **te**

ta [ta] *adj voir* **ton**[1]

tabac [taba] *nm* tobacco; (*magasin*) tobacconist's (shop); **~ blond/brun** light/dark tobacco

tabagisme [tabaʒism] *nm*: **~ passif** passive smoking

tabasser [tabase] (*fam*) *vt* to beat up

table [tabl] *nf* table; **à ~!** dinner *etc* is ready!; **se mettre à ~** to sit down to eat; **mettre la ~** to lay the table; **faire ~ rase de** to make a clean sweep of; **~ à repasser** ironing board; **~ de cuisson** (*à l'électricité*) hotplate; (*au gaz*) gas ring; **~ de nuit** *ou* **de chevet** bedside table; **~ des matières** (table of) contents *pl*; **~ d'orientation** viewpoint indicator; **~ roulante** trolley

tableau, x [tablo] *nm* (*peinture*) painting; (*reproduction, fig*) picture; (*panneau*) board; (*schéma*) table, chart; **~ d'affichage** notice board; **~ de bord** dashboard; (*AVIAT*) instrument panel; **~ noir** blackboard

tabler [table] *vi*: **~ sur** to bank on

tablette [tablɛt] *nf* (*planche*) shelf; **~ de chocolat** bar of chocolate

tableur [tablœʀ] *nm* spreadsheet

tablier [tablije] *nm* apron

tabou [tabu] *nm* taboo

tabouret [tabuʀɛ] *nm* stool

tac [tak] *nm*: **il m'a répondu du ~ au ~** he answered me right back

tache [taʃ] *nf* (*saleté*) stain, mark; (*ART, de couleur, lumière*) spot; **~ de rousseur** freckle

tâche [taʃ] *nf* task

tacher [taʃe] *vt* to stain, mark

tâcher [taʃe] *vi*: **~ de faire** to try *ou* endeavour to do

tacheté, e [taʃte] *adj* spotted

tacot [tako] (*péj*) *nm* banger (*BRIT*), (old) heap

tact [takt] *nm* tact; **avoir du ~** to be tactful

tactique [taktik] *adj* tactical ♦ *nf* (*technique*) tactics *sg*; (*plan*) tactic

taie [tɛ] *nf*: **~ (d'oreiller)** pillowslip, pillowcase

taille [taj] *nf* cutting; (*d'arbre etc*) pruning; (*milieu du corps*) waist; (*hauteur*) height; (*grandeur*) size; **de ~ à faire** capable of doing; **de ~** sizeable; **taille-crayon(s)** *nm* pencil sharpener

tailler [taje] *vt* (*pierre, diamant*) to cut; (*arbre, plante*) to prune; (*vêtement*) to cut out; (*crayon*) to sharpen

tailleur [tajœʀ] *nm* (*couturier*) tailor; (*vêtement*) suit; **en ~** (*assis*) cross-legged

taillis [taji] *nm* copse

taire [tɛʀ] *vi*: **faire ~ qn** to make sb be quiet; **se ~** *vi* to be silent *ou* quiet

talc [talk] *nm* talc, talcum powder

talent [talɑ̃] *nm* talent

talkie-walkie [tokiwoki] *nm* walkie-talkie

taloche [talɔʃ] (*fam*) *nf* clout, cuff

talon [talɔ̃] *nm* heel; (*de chèque, billet*) stub, counterfoil (*BRIT*); **~s plats/aiguilles** flat/stiletto heels

talonner [talɔne] *vt* (*suivre*) to follow hot on the heels of; (*harceler*) to hound

talus [taly] *nm* embankment

tambour [tɑ̃buʀ] *nm* (*MUS, aussi*) drum; (*musicien*) drummer; (*porte*) revolving door(s *pl*); **tambourin** *nm* tambourine; **tambouriner** *vi* to drum; **tambouriner à/sur** to drum on

tamis [tami] *nm* sieve

Tamise [tamiz] *nf*: **la ~** the Thames

tamisé, e [tamize] *adj* (*fig*) subdued, soft

tampon [tɑ̃pɔ̃] *nm* (*de coton, d'ouate*) wad, pad; (*amortisseur*) buffer; (*bouchon*) plug, stopper; (*cachet, timbre*) stamp; **(mémoire) ~** (*INFORM*) buffer; **~ (hygiénique)** tampon; **tamponner** *vt* (*timbres*) to stamp; (*heurter*) to crash *ou* ram into; **tamponneuse** *adj f*: **autos tamponneuses** dodgems

tandem [tɑ̃dɛm] *nm* tandem

tandis [tɑ̃di]: ~ **que** *conj* while

tanguer [tɑ̃ge] *vi* to pitch (and toss)

tanière [tanjɛʀ] *nf* lair, den

tanné, e [tane] *adj* weather-beaten

tanner [tane] *vt* to tan; (*fam: harceler*) to badger

tant [tɑ̃] *adv* so much; ~ **de** (*sable, eau*) so much; (*gens, livres*) so many; ~ **que** as long as; (*autant que*) as much as; ~ **mieux** that's great; (*avec une certaine réserve*) so much the better; ~ **pis** too bad; (*conciliant*) never mind

tante [tɑ̃t] *nf* aunt

tantôt [tɑ̃to] *adv* (*parfois*): ~ ... ~ now ... now; (*cet après-midi*) this afternoon

taon [tɑ̃] *nm* horsefly

tapage [tapaʒ] *nm* uproar, din

tapageur, -euse [tapaʒœʀ, øz] *adj* noisy; (*voyant*) loud, flashy

tape [tap] *nf* slap

tape-à-l'œil [tapalœj] *adj inv* flashy, showy

taper [tape] *vt* (*porte*) to bang, slam; (*enfant*) to slap; (*dactylographier*) to type (out); (*fam: emprunter*): ~ **qn de 10 F** to touch sb for 10 F ♦ *vi* (*soleil*) to beat down; **se** ~ *vt* (*repas*) to put away; (*fam: corvée*) to get landed with; ~ **sur qn** to thump sb; (*fig*) to run sb down; ~ **sur un clou** to hit a nail; ~ **à** (*porte etc*) to knock on; ~ **dans** (*se servir*) to dig into; ~ **des mains/pieds** to clap one's hands/stamp one's feet; ~ **(à la machine)** to type; **se** ~ **un travail** (*fam*) to land o.s. a job

tapi, e [tapi] *adj* (*blotti*) crouching; (*caché*) hidden away

tapis [tapi] *nm* carpet; (*petit*) rug; **mettre sur le** ~ (*fig*) to bring up for discussion; ~ **de bain** bath mat; ~ **de sol** (*de tente*) groundsheet; ~ **de souris** mouse mat; ~ **roulant** (*pour piétons*) moving walkway; (*pour bagages*) carousel

tapisser [tapise] *vt* (*avec du papier peint*) to paper; (*recouvrir*): ~ **qch (de)** to cover sth (with); **tapisserie** *nf* (*tenture, broderie*) tapestry; (*papier peint*) wallpaper; **tapissier,**

-ière *nm/f*: **tapissier-décorateur** interior decorator

tapoter [tapote] *vt* (*joue, main*) to pat; (*objet*) to tap

taquin, e [takɛ̃, in] *adj* teasing; **taquiner** *vt* to tease

tarabiscoté, e [taʀabiskɔte] *adj* over-ornate, fussy

tard [taʀ] *adv* late; **plus** ~ later (on); **au plus** ~ at the latest; **sur le** ~ late in life

tarder [taʀde] *vi* (*chose*) to be a long time coming; (*personne*): ~ **à faire** to delay doing; **il me tarde d'être** I am longing to be; **sans (plus)** ~ without (further) delay

tardif, -ive [taʀdif, iv] *adj* late

taré, e [taʀe] *nm/f* cretin

tarif [taʀif] *nm*: ~ **des consommations** price list; ~**s postaux/douaniers** postal/customs rates; ~ **des taxis** taxi fares; ~ **plein/réduit** (*train*) full/reduced fare; (*téléphone*) peak/off-peak rate

tarir [taʀiʀ] *vi* to dry up, run dry

tarte [taʀt] *nf* tart; ~ **aux fraises** strawberry tart; ~ **Tatin** ≈ apple upside-down tart

tartine [taʀtin] *nf* slice of bread; ~ **de miel** slice of bread and honey; **tartiner** *vt* to spread; **fromage à tartiner** cheese spread

tartre [taʀtʀ] *nm* (*des dents*) tartar; (*de bouilloire*) fur, scale

tas [tɑ] *nm* heap, pile; (*fig*): **un** ~ **de** heaps of, lots of; **en** ~ in a heap *ou* pile; **formé sur le** ~ trained on the job

tasse [tɑs] *nf* cup; ~ **à café** coffee cup

tassé, e [tɑse] *adj*: **bien** ~ (*café etc*) strong

tasser [tɑse] *vt* (*terre, neige*) to pack down; (*entasser*): ~ **qch dans** to cram sth into; **se** ~ *vi* (*se serrer*) to squeeze up; (*s'affaisser*) to settle; (*fig*) to settle down

tata [tata] *nf* auntie

tâter [tɑte] *vt* to feel; (*fig*) to try out; **se** ~ (*hésiter*) to be in two minds; ~ **de** (*prison etc*) to have a taste of

tatillon, ne [tatijɔ̃, ɔn] *adj* pernickety

tâtonnement [tɑtɔnmɑ̃] *nm*: **par ~s** (*fig*)

by trial and error

tâtonner [tɑtɔne] *vi* to grope one's way along

tâtons [tatɔ̃]: **à ~** *adv*: **chercher à ~** to grope around for

tatouage [tatwaʒ] *nm* tattoo

tatouer [tatwe] *vt* to tattoo

taudis [todi] *nm* hovel, slum

taule [tol] (*fam*) *nf* nick (*fam*), prison

taupe [top] *nf* mole

taureau, x [tɔro] *nm* bull; (*signe*): **le T~** Taurus

tauromachie [tɔrɔmaʃi] *nf* bullfighting

taux [to] *nm* rate; (*d'alcool*) level; **~ de change** exchange rate; **~ d'intérêt** interest rate

taxe [taks] *nf* tax; (*douanière*) duty; **toutes ~s comprises** inclusive of tax; **la boutique hors ~s** the duty free shop; **~ à la valeur ajoutée** value added tax

taxer [takse] *vt* (*personne*) to tax; (*produit*) to put a tax on, tax

taxi [taksi] *nm* taxi; (*fam*) taxi driver

Tchécoslovaquie [tʃekɔslɔvaki] *nf* Czechoslovakia; **tchèque** *adj* Czech ♦ *nm/f*: **Tchèque** Czech ♦ *nm* (*LING*) Czech; **la République tchèque** the Czech Republic

te, t' [tə] *pron* you; (*réfléchi*) yourself

technicien, ne [teknisjɛ̃, jɛn] *nm/f* technician

technico-commercial, e, -aux [teknikokɔmɛrsjal, jo] *adj*: **agent ~-~** sales technician

technique [teknik] *adj* technical ♦ *nf* technique; **techniquement** *adv* technically

technologie [teknɔlɔʒi] *nf* technology; **technologique** *adj* technological

teck [tek] *nm* teak

tee-shirt [tiʃœrt] *nm* T-shirt, tee-shirt

teignais *etc* [tɛɲɛ] *vb voir* **teindre**

teindre [tɛdr] *vt* to dye; **se ~ les cheveux** to dye one's hair; **teint, e** *adj* dyed ♦ *nm* (*du visage*) complexion; (*momentané*) colour ♦ *nf* shade; **grand teint** colourfast

teinté, e [tɛ̃te] *adj*: **~ de** (*fig*) tinged with

teinter [tɛ̃te] *vt* (*verre, papier*) to tint; (*bois*) to stain

teinture [tɛ̃tyr] *nf* dye; **~ d'iode** tincture of iodine; **teinturerie** *nf* dry cleaner's; **teinturier** *nm* dry cleaner

tel, telle [tɛl] *adj* (*pareil*) such; (*comme*): **~ un/des ...** like a/like ...; (*indéfini*) such-and-such a; (*intensif*): **un ~/de tels ...** such (a)/such ...; **rien de ~** nothing like it; **~ que** like, such as; **~ quel** as it is (*ou* was *etc*); **venez ~ jour** come on such-and-such a day

télé [tele] (*fam*) *nf* TV

télé...: **télécabine** *nf* (*benne*) cable car; **télécarte** *nf* phonecard; **télécharger** *vt* to download; **télécommande** *nf* remote control; **télécopie** *nf* fax; **envoyer qch par télécopie** to fax sth; **télécopieur** *nm* fax machine; **télédistribution** *nf* cable TV; **téléférique** *nm* = **téléphérique**; **télégramme** *nm* telegram; **télégraphier** *vt* to telegraph, cable; **téléguider** *vt* to radio-control; **télématique** *nf* telematics *sg*; **téléobjectif** *nm* telephoto lens *sg*; **télépathie** *nf* telepathy; **téléphérique** *nm* cable car

téléphone [telefɔn] *nm* telephone; **avoir le ~** to be on the (tele)phone; **au ~** on the phone; **~ mobile** mobile phone; **~ rouge** hot line; **~ sans fil** cordless (tele)phone; **~ de voiture** car phone; **téléphoner** *vi* to make a phone call; **téléphoner à** to phone, call up; **téléphonique** *adj* (tele)phone *cpd*

téléréalité [telerealite] *nf* reality TV

télescope [teleskɔp] *nm* telescope

télescoper [teleskɔpe] *vt* to smash up; **se ~** (*véhicules*) to concertina

télé...: **téléscripteur** *nm* teleprinter; **télésiège** *nm* chairlift; **téléski** *nm* ski-tow; **téléspectateur, -trice** *nm/f* (television) viewer; **télévente** *nf* telesales; **téléviseur** *nm* television set; **télévision** *nf* television; **à la télévision** on television; **télévision numérique** digital TV

telle [tɛl] *adj voir* **tel**; **tellement** *adv* (*tant*) so much; (*si*) so; **tellement de** (*sable, eau*) so much; (*gens, livres*) so many; **il s'est endormi tellement il était fatigué** he was so tired (that) he fell asleep; **pas tellement** not (all) that much; not (all) that *+adjectif*

téméraire [temerɛr] *adj* reckless, rash; **témérité** *nf* recklessness, rashness

témoignage [temwaɲaʒ] *nm* (*JUR: déclaration*) testimony *no pl*, evidence *no pl*; (*rapport, récit*) account; (*fig: d'affection etc: cadeau*) token, mark; (*: geste*) expression

témoigner [temwaɲe] *vt* (*intérêt, gratitude*) to show ♦ *vi* (*JUR*) to testify, give evidence; **~ de** to bear witness to, testify to

témoin [temwɛ̃] *nm* witness ♦ *adj*: **appartement ~** show flat (*BRIT*); **être ~ de** to witness; **~ oculaire** eyewitness

tempe [tɑ̃p] *nf* temple

tempérament [tɑ̃peramɑ̃] *nm* temperament, disposition; **à ~** (*vente*) on deferred (payment) terms; (*achat*) by instalments, hire purchase *cpd*

température [tɑ̃peratyr] *nf* temperature; **avoir** *ou* **faire de la ~** to be running *ou* have a temperature

tempéré, e [tɑ̃pere] *adj* temperate

tempête [tɑ̃pɛt] *nf* storm; **~ de sable/neige** sand/snowstorm

temple [tɑ̃pl] *nm* temple; (*protestant*) church

temporaire [tɑ̃pɔrɛr] *adj* temporary

temps [tɑ̃] *nm* (*atmosphérique*) weather; (*durée*) time; (*époque*) time, times *pl*; (*LING*) tense; (*MUS*) beat; (*TECH*) stroke; **un ~ de chien** (*fam*) rotten weather; **quel ~ fait-il?** what's the weather like?; **il fait beau/mauvais** ~ the weather is fine/bad; **avoir le ~/tout son ~** to have time/plenty of time; **en ~ de paix/guerre** in peacetime/wartime; **en ~ utile** *ou* **voulu** in due time *ou* course; **ces derniers ~** lately; **dans quelque ~** in a (little) while; **de ~ en ~, de ~ à autre** from time to time; **à ~** (*partir, arriver*) in time; **à ~**

complet, à plein ~ full-time; **à ~ partiel** part-time; **dans le ~** at one time; **~ d'arrêt** pause, halt; **~ mort** (*COMM*) slack period

tenable [t(ə)nabl] *adj* bearable

tenace [tənas] *adj* persistent

tenailler [tənaje] *vt* (*fig*) to torment

tenailles [tənaj] *nfpl* pincers

tenais *etc* [t(ə)nɛ] *vb voir* **tenir**

tenancier, -ière [tənɑ̃sje] *nm/f* manager/manageress

tenant, e [tənɑ̃, ɑ̃t] *nm/f* (*SPORT*): **~ du titre** title-holder

tendance [tɑ̃dɑ̃s] *nf* tendency; (*opinions*) leanings *pl*, sympathies *pl*; (*évolution*) trend; **avoir ~ à** to have a tendency to, tend to

tendeur [tɑ̃dœr] *nm* (*attache*) elastic strap

tendre [tɑ̃dr] *adj* tender; (*bois, roche, couleur*) soft ♦ *vt* (*élastique, peau*) to stretch; (*corde*) to tighten; (*muscle*) to tense; (*fig: piège*) to set, lay; (*donner*): **~ qch à qn** to hold sth out to sb; (*offrir*) to offer sb sth; **se ~** *vi* (*corde*) to tighten; (*relations*) to become strained; **~ à qch/à faire** to tend towards sth/to do; **~ l'oreille** to prick up one's ears; **~ la main/le bras** to hold out one's hand/stretch out one's arm; **tendrement** *adv* tenderly; **tendresse** *nf* tenderness

tendu, e [tɑ̃dy] *pp de* **tendre** ♦ *adj* (*corde*) tight; (*muscles*) tensed; (*relations*) strained

ténèbres [tenɛbr] *nfpl* darkness *sg*

teneur [tənœr] *nf* content; (*d'une lettre*) terms *pl*, content

tenir [t(ə)nir] *vt* to hold; (*magasin, hôtel*) to run; (*promesse*) to keep ♦ *vi* to hold; (*neige, gel*) to last; **se ~** *vi* (*avoir lieu*) to be held, take place; (*être: personne*) to stand; **~ à** (*personne, objet*) to be attached to; (*réputation*) to care about; **~ à faire** to be determined to do; **~ de** (*ressembler à*) to take after; **ça ne tient qu'à lui** it is entirely up to him; **~ qn pour** to regard sb as; **~ qch de qn** (*histoire*) to have heard *ou* learnt sth from sb; (*qualité,* *défaut*) to have inherited *ou* got sth from sb; **~ dans** to fit into; **~ compte de qch** to take sth into account; **~ les comptes** to keep the books; **~ bon** to stand fast; **~ le coup** to hold out; **~ au chaud** to keep hot; **tiens/tenez, voilà le stylo** there's the pen!; **tiens, voilà Alain!** look, here's Alain!; **tiens?** (*surprise*) really?; **se ~ droit** to stand (*ou* sit) up straight; **bien se ~** to behave well; **se ~ à qch** to hold on to sth; **s'en ~ à qch** to confine o.s. to sth

tennis [tenis] *nm* tennis; (*court*) tennis court ♦ *nm ou f pl* (*aussi:* **chaussures de ~**) tennis *ou* gym shoes; **~ de table** table tennis; **tennisman** *nm* tennis player

tension [tɑ̃sjɔ̃] *nf* tension; (*MÉD*) blood pressure; **avoir de la ~** to have high blood pressure

tentation [tɑ̃tasjɔ̃] *nf* temptation

tentative [tɑ̃tativ] *nf* attempt

tente [tɑ̃t] *nf* tent

tenter [tɑ̃te] *vt* (*éprouver, attirer*) to tempt; (*essayer*): **~ qch/de faire** to attempt *ou* try sth/to do; **~ sa chance** to try one's luck

tenture [tɑ̃tyʀ] *nf* hanging

tenu, e [t(ə)ny] *pp de* **tenir** ♦ *adj* (*maison, comptes*): **bien ~** well-kept; (*obligé*): **~ de faire** obliged to do ♦ *nf* (*vêtements*) clothes *pl*; (*comportement*) (*good*) manners *pl*, good behaviour; (*d'une maison*) upkeep; **en petite ~e** scantily dressed *ou* clad; **~e de route** (*AUTO*) road-holding; **~e de soirée** evening dress

ter [tɛʀ] *adj*: **16 ~** 16b *ou* B

térébenthine [teʀebɑ̃tin] *nf*: (**essence de**) **~** (oil of) turpentine

Tergal ® [tɛʀgal] *nm* Terylene ®

terme [tɛʀm] *nm* term; (*fin*) end; **à court/long ~** ♦ *adj* short-/long-term ♦ *adv* in the short/long term; **avant ~** (*MÉD*) prematurely; **mettre un ~ à** to put an end *ou* a stop to; **en bons ~s** on good terms

terminaison [tɛʀminezɔ̃] *nf* (*LING*) ending

terminal [tɛʀminal, o] *nm* terminal; **termi-**

nale *nf* (*SCOL*) ≈ sixth form *ou* year (*BRIT*), ≈ twelfth grade (*US*)

terminer [tɛʀmine] *vt* to finish; **se ~** *vi* to end

terne [tɛʀn] *adj* dull

ternir [tɛʀniʀ] *vt* to dull; (*fig*) to sully, tarnish; **se ~** *vi* to become dull

terrain [teʀɛ̃] *nm* (*sol, fig*) ground; (*COMM: étendue de terre*) land *no pl*; (*parcelle*) plot (of land); (*à bâtir*) site; **sur le ~** (*fig*) on the field; **~ d'aviation** airfield; **~ de camping** campsite; **~ de football/rugby** football/rugby pitch (*BRIT*) *ou* field (*US*); **~ de golf** golf course; **~ de jeu** games field; (*pour les petits*) playground; **~ de sport** sports ground; **~ vague** waste ground *no pl*

terrasse [teʀas] *nf* terrace; **à la ~** (*café*) outside; **terrasser** *vt* (*adversaire*) to floor; (*suj: maladie etc*) to strike down

terre [tɛʀ] *nf* (*gén, aussi ÉLEC*) earth; (*substance*) soil, earth; (*opposé à mer*) land *no pl*; (*contrée*) land; **~s** *nfpl* (*terrains*) lands, land *sg*; **en ~** (*pipe, poterie*) clay *cpd*; **à ~** *ou* **par ~** (*mettre, être, s'asseoir*) on the ground (*ou* floor); (*jeter, tomber*) to the ground, down; **~ à ~** *adj inv* down-to-earth; **~ cuite** terracotta; **la ~ ferme** dry land; **~ glaise** clay

terreau [teʀo] *nm* compost

terre-plein [tɛʀplɛ̃] *nm* platform; (*sur chaussée*) central reservation

terrer [teʀe]: **se ~** *vi* to hide away

terrestre [teʀɛstʀ] *adj* (*surface*) earth's, of the earth; (*BOT, ZOOL, MIL*) land *cpd*; (*REL*) earthly

terreur [teʀœʀ] *nf* terror *no pl*

terrible [teʀibl] *adj* terrible, dreadful; (*fam*) terrific; **pas ~** nothing special

terrien, ne [teʀjɛ̃, jɛn] *adj*: **propriétaire ~** landowner ♦ *nm/f* (*non martien etc*) earthling

terrier [teʀje] *nm* burrow, hole; (*chien*) terrier

terrifier [teʀifje] *vt* to terrify

terrine [teʀin] *nf* (*récipient*) terrine; (*CULIN*)

pâté

territoire [teritwar] *nm* territory

terroir [terwar] *nm:* **accent du ~** country accent

terroriser [terɔrize] *vt* to terrorize

terrorisme [terɔrism] *nm* terrorism; **terroriste** *nm/f* terrorist

tertiaire [tersjer] *adj* tertiary ♦ *nm* (ÉCON) service industries *pl*

tertre [tertr] *nm* hillock, mound

tes [te] *adj voir* **ton**[1]

tesson [tesɔ̃] *nm:* **~ de bouteille** piece of broken bottle

test [test] *nm* test

testament [testamɑ̃] *nm* (JUR) will; (REL) Testament; (fig) legacy

tester [teste] *vt* to test

testicule [testikyl] *nm* testicle

tétanos [tetanos] *nm* tetanus

têtard [tetar] *nm* tadpole

tête [tet] *nf* head; (cheveux) hair *no pl*; (visage) face; **de ~** adj (wagon etc) front *cpd* ♦ *adv* (calculer) in one's head, mentally; **tenir ~ à qn** to stand up to sb; **la ~ en bas** with one's head down; **la ~ la première** (tomber) headfirst; **faire une ~** (FOOTBALL) to head the ball; **faire la ~** (fig) to sulk; **en ~** at the front; (SPORT) in the lead; **à la ~ de** at the head of; **à ~ reposée** in a more leisurely moment; **n'en faire qu'à sa ~** to do as one pleases; **en avoir par-dessus la ~** to be fed up; **en ~ à ~** in private, alone together; **de la ~ aux pieds** from head to toe; **~ de lecture** (playback) head; **~ de liste** (POL) chief candidate; **~ de série** (TENNIS) seeded player, seed; **tête-à-queue** *nm inv*: **faire un tête-à-queue** to spin round

téter [tete] *vt:* **~ (sa mère)** to suck at one's mother's breast, feed

tétine [tetin] *nf* teat; (sucette) dummy (BRIT), pacifier (US)

têtu, e [tety] *adj* stubborn, pigheaded

texte [tekst] *nm* text; (morceau choisi) passage

textile [tekstil] *adj* textile *cpd* ♦ *nm* textile;

le ~ the textile industry

texto [teksto] (fam) *adj* word for word

texture [tekstyr] *nf* texture

thaïlandais, e [tajlɑ̃dɛ, ɛz] *adj* Thai ♦ *nm/f:* **T~, e** Thai

Thaïlande [tajlɑ̃d] *nf* Thailand

TGV *sigle m* (= *train à grande vitesse*) high-speed train

thé [te] *nm* tea; **~ au citron** lemon tea; **~ au lait** tea with milk; **prendre le ~** to have tea; **faire le ~** to make the tea

théâtral, e, -aux [teatral, o] *adj* theatrical

théâtre [teatr] *nm* theatre; (péj: simulation) playacting; (fig: lieu): **le ~ de** the scene of; **faire du ~** to act

théière [tejer] *nf* teapot

thème [tem] *nm* theme; (SCOL: traduction) prose (composition)

théologie [teɔlɔʒi] *nf* theology

théorie [teɔri] *nf* theory; **théorique** *adj* theoretical

thérapie [terapi] *nf* therapy

thermal, e, -aux [termal, o] *adj:* **station ~e** spa; **cure ~e** water cure

thermes [term] *nmpl* thermal baths

thermomètre [termɔmetr] *nm* thermometer

thermos ® [termos] *nm ou nf:* **(bouteille) ~ vacuum ou Thermos** ® flask

thermostat [termɔsta] *nm* thermostat

thèse [tez] *nf* thesis

thon [tɔ̃] *nm* tuna (fish)

thym [tɛ̃] *nm* thyme

tibia [tibja] *nm* shinbone, tibia; (partie antérieure de la jambe) shin

tic [tik] *nm* tic, (nervous) twitch; (de langage etc) mannerism

ticket [tike] *nm* ticket; **~ de caisse** receipt; **~ de quai** platform ticket

tic-tac [tiktak] *nm* ticking; **faire ~-~** to tick

tiède [tjed] *adj* lukewarm; (vent, air) mild, warm; **tiédir** *vi* to cool; (se réchauffer) to grow warmer

tien, ne [tjɛ̃, tjen] *pron:* **le(la) ~(ne), les**

~(ne)s yours; **à la ~ne!** cheers!

tiens [tjɛ̃] *vb, excl voir* **tenir**

tierce [tjɛʀs] *adj voir* **tiers**

tiercé [tjɛʀse] *nm system of forecast betting giving first 3 horses*

tiers, tierce [tjɛʀ, tjɛʀs] *adj* third ♦ *nm* (*JUR*) third party; (*fraction*) third; **le ~ monde** the Third World

tifs [tif] (*fam*) *nmpl* hair

tige [tiʒ] *nf* stem; (*baguette*) rod

tignasse [tiɲas] (*péj*) *nf* mop of hair

tigre [tigʀ] *nm* tiger; **tigresse** *nf* tigress; **tigré, e** *adj* (*rayé*) striped; (*tacheté*) spotted; (*chat*) tabby

tilleul [tijœl] *nm* lime (tree), linden (tree); (*boisson*) lime(-blossom) tea

timbale [tɛ̃bal] *nf* (metal) tumbler; **~s** *nfpl* (*MUS*) timpani, kettledrums

timbre [tɛ̃bʀ] *nm* (*tampon*) stamp; (*aussi*: **~-poste**) (postage) stamp; (*MUS: de voix, instrument*) timbre, tone

timbré, e [tɛ̃bʀe] (*fam*) *adj* cracked

timide [timid] *adj* shy; (*timoré*) timid; **timidement** *adv* shyly; timidly; **timidité** *nf* shyness; timidity

tins *etc* [tɛ̃] *vb voir* **tenir**

tintamarre [tɛ̃tamaʀ] *nm* din, uproar

tinter [tɛ̃te] *vi* to ring, chime; (*argent, clefs*) to jingle

tique [tik] *nf* (*parasite*) tick

tir [tiʀ] *nm* (*sport*) shooting; (*fait ou manière de ~er*) firing *no pl*; (*rafale*) fire; (*stand*) shooting gallery; **~ à l'arc** archery; **~ au pigeon** clay pigeon shooting

tirage [tiʀaʒ] *nm* (*action*) printing; (*PHOTO*) print; (*de journal*) circulation; (*de livre: nombre d'exemplaires*) (print) run; (*: édition*) edition; (*de loterie*) draw; **par ~ au sort** by drawing lots

tirailler [tiʀaje] *vt*: **être tiraillé entre** to be torn between

tire [tiʀ] *nf*: **vol à la ~** pickpocketing

tiré, e [tiʀe] *adj* (*traits*) drawn; **~ par les cheveux** far-fetched

tire-au-flanc [tiʀɔflɑ̃] (*péj*) *nm inv* skiver

tire-bouchon [tiʀbuʃɔ̃] *nm* corkscrew

tirelire [tiʀliʀ] *nf* moneybox

tirer [tiʀe] *vt* (*gén*) to pull; (*extraire*): **~ qch de** to take *ou* pull sth out of; (*trait, rideau, carte, conclusion, chèque*) to draw; (*langue*) to stick out; (*en faisant feu: balle, coup*) to fire; (*: animal*) to shoot; (*journal, livre, photo*) to print; (*FOOTBALL: corner etc*) to take ♦ *vi* (*faire feu*) to fire; (*faire du tir, FOOTBALL*) to shoot; **se ~** *vi* (*fam*) to push off; **s'en ~** (*éviter le pire*) to get off; (*survivre*) to pull through; (*se débrouiller*) to manage; **~ sur** (*corde*) to pull on *ou* at; (*faire feu sur*) to shoot *ou* fire at; (*pipe*) to draw on; (*approcher de: couleur*) to verge *ou* border on; **~ qn de** (*embarras etc*) to help *ou* get sb out of; **~ à l'arc/la carabine** to shoot with a bow and arrow/with a rifle; **~ à sa fin** to be drawing to a close; **~ qch au clair** to clear sth up; **~ au sort** to draw lots; **~ parti de** to take advantage of; **~ profit de** to profit from

tiret [tiʀe] *nm* dash

tireur [tiʀœʀ] *nm* gunman; **~ d'élite** marksman

tiroir [tiʀwaʀ] *nm* drawer; **tiroir-caisse** *nm* till

tisane [tizan] *nf* herb tea

tisonnier [tizɔnje] *nm* poker

tisser [tise] *vt* to weave; **tisserand** *nm* weaver

tissu [tisy] *nm* fabric, material, cloth *no pl*; (*ANAT, BIO*) tissue; **tissu-éponge** *nm* (terry) towelling *no pl*

titre [titʀ] *nm* (*gén*) title; (*de journal*) headline; (*diplôme*) qualification; (*COMM*) security; **en ~** (*champion*) official; **à juste ~** rightly; **à quel ~?** on what grounds?; **à aucun ~** on no account; **au même ~ (que)** in the same way (as); **à ~ d'information** for (your) information; **à ~ gracieux** free of charge; **à ~ d'essai** on a trial basis; **à ~ privé** in a private capacity; **~ de propriété** title deed; **~ de transport** ticket

tituber [titybe] *vi* to stagger (along)

titulaire [tityleʀ] *adj* (ADMIN) with tenure ♦ *nm/f* (*de permis*) holder

toast [tost] *nm* slice *ou* piece of toast; (*de bienvenue*) (welcoming) toast; **porter un ~ à qn** to propose *ou* drink a toast to sb

toboggan [tɔbɔgã] *nm* slide; (AUTO) fly-over

toc [tɔk] *excl:* ~, ~ knock knock ♦ *nm:* **en ~ toc** fake

tocsin [tɔksɛ̃] *nm* alarm (bell)

toge [tɔʒ] *nf* toga; (*de juge*) gown

tohu-bohu [tɔybɔy] *nm* hubbub

toi [twa] *pron* you

Toile [twal] *nf* Web

toile *nf* (*tableau*) canvas; **de** *ou* **en ~** (*pantalon*) cotton; (*sac*) canvas; **~ cirée** oilcloth; **~ d'araignée** cobweb; **~ de fond** (*fig*) backdrop

toilette [twalɛt] *nf* (*habits*) outfit; **~s** *nfpl* (*w.-c.*) toilet *sg*; **faire sa ~** to get washed; **articles de ~** toiletries

toi-même [twamɛm] *pron* yourself

toiser [twaze] *vt* to eye up and down

toison [twazɔ̃] *nf* (*de mouton*) fleece

toit [twa] *nm* roof; **~ ouvrant** sunroof

toiture [twatyʀ] *nf* roof

tôle [tol] *nf* (*plaque*) steel *ou* iron sheet; **~ ondulée** corrugated iron

tolérable [tɔleʀabl] *adj* tolerable

tolérant, e [tɔleʀɑ̃, ɑ̃t] *adj* tolerant

tolérer [tɔleʀe] *vt* to tolerate; (ADMIN: *hors taxe etc*) to allow

tollé [tɔ(l)le] *nm* outcry

tomate [tɔmat] *nf* tomato; **~s farcies** stuffed tomatoes

tombe [tɔ̃b] *nf* (*sépulture*) grave; (*avec monument*) tomb

tombeau, x [tɔ̃bo] *nm* tomb

tombée [tɔ̃be] *nf:* **à la ~ de la nuit** at nightfall

tomber [tɔ̃be] *vi* to fall; (*fièvre, vent*) to drop; **laisser ~** (*objet*) to drop; (*personne*) to let down; (*activité*) to give up; **laisse ~!** forget it!; **faire ~** to knock over; **~ sur** (*rencontrer*) to bump into; **~ de fatigue/**

sommeil to drop from exhaustion/be falling asleep on one's feet; **ça tombe bien** that's come at the right time; **il est bien tombé** he's been lucky; **~ à l'eau** (*projet*) to fall through; **~ en panne** to break down

tombola [tɔ̃bɔla] *nf* raffle

tome [tɔm] *nm* volume

ton¹, ta [tɔ̃, ta] (*pl* **tes**) *adj* your

ton² [tɔ̃] *nm* (*gén*) tone; (*couleur*) shade, tone; **de bon ~** in good taste

tonalité [tɔnalite] *nf* (*au téléphone*) dialling tone

tondeuse [tɔ̃døz] *nf* (*à gazon*) (lawn)mower; (*du coiffeur*) clippers *pl*; (*pour les moutons*) shears *pl*

tondre [tɔ̃dʀ] *vt* (*pelouse, herbe*) to mow; (*haie*) to cut, clip; (*mouton, toison*) to shear; (*cheveux*) to crop

tongs [tɔ̃g] *nfpl* flip-flops

tonifier [tɔnifje] *vt* (*peau, organisme*) to tone up

tonique [tɔnik] *adj* fortifying ♦ *nm* tonic

tonne [tɔn] *nf* metric ton, tonne

tonneau, x [tɔno] *nm* (*à vin, cidre*) barrel; **faire des ~x** (*voiture, avion*) to roll over

tonnelle [tɔnɛl] *nf* bower, arbour

tonner [tɔne] *vi* to thunder; **il tonne** it is thundering, there's some thunder

tonnerre [tɔnɛʀ] *nm* thunder

tonton [tɔ̃tɔ̃] *nm* uncle

tonus [tɔnys] *nm* energy

top [tɔp] *nm:* **au 3ème ~** at the 3rd stroke

topinambour [tɔpinãbuʀ] *nm* Jerusalem artichoke

topo [tɔpo] (*fam*) *nm* rundown; **c'est le même ~** it's the same old story

toque [tɔk] *nf* (*de fourrure*) fur hat; **~ de cuisinier** chef's hat; **~ de jockey/juge** jockey's/judge's cap

toqué, e [tɔke] (*fam*) *adj* cracked

torche [tɔʀʃ] *nf* torch

torchon [tɔʀʃɔ̃] *nm* cloth; (*à vaisselle*) tea towel *ou* cloth

tordre [tɔʀdʀ] *vt* (*chiffon*) to wring; (*barre, fig: visage*) to twist; **se ~** *vi:* **se ~ le**

poignet/la cheville to twist one's wrist/ ankle; **se ~ de douleur/rire** to be doubled up with pain/laughter; **tordu, e** *adj* bent; *(fig)* crazy

tornade [tɔʀnad] *nf* tornado

torpille [tɔʀpij] *nf* torpedo

torréfier [tɔʀefje] *vt* to roast

torrent [tɔʀɑ̃] *nm* mountain stream

torsade [tɔʀsad] *nf*: **un pull à ~s** a cable sweater

torse [tɔʀs] *nm* chest; *(ANAT, SCULPTURE)* torso; **~ nu** stripped to the waist

tort [tɔʀ] *nm (défaut)* fault; **~s** *nmpl (JUR)* fault *sg*; **avoir ~** to be wrong; **être dans son ~** to be in the wrong; **donner ~ à qn** to lay the blame on sb; **causer du ~ à** to harm; **à ~** wrongly; **à ~ et à travers** wildly

torticolis [tɔʀtikɔli] *nm* stiff neck

tortiller [tɔʀtije] *vt* to twist; *(moustache)* to twirl; **se ~** *vi* to wriggle; *(en dansant)* to wiggle

tortionnaire [tɔʀsjɔnɛʀ] *nm* torturer

tortue [tɔʀty] *nf* tortoise; *(d'eau douce)* terrapin; *(d'eau de mer)* turtle

tortueux, -euse [tɔʀtɥø, øz] *adj (rue)* twisting; *(fig)* tortuous

torture [tɔʀtyʀ] *nf* torture; **torturer** *vt* to torture; *(fig)* to torment

tôt [to] *adv* early; **~ ou tard** sooner or later; **si ~** so early; *(déjà)* so soon; **plus ~** earlier; **au plus ~** at the earliest; **il eut ~ fait de faire** he soon did

total, e, -aux [tɔtal, o] *adj, nm* total; **au ~** in total; *(fig)* on the whole; **faire le ~** to work out the total; **totalement** *adv* totally; **totaliser** *vt* to total; **totalitaire** *adj* totalitarian; **totalité** *nf*: **la totalité de** all (of); the whole +*sg*; **en totalité** entirely

toubib [tubib] *(fam) nm* doctor

touchant, e [tuʃɑ̃, ɑ̃t] *adj* touching

touche [tuʃ] *nf (de piano, de machine à écrire)* key; *(de téléphone)* button; *(PEINTURE etc)* stroke, touch; *(fig: de nostalgie)* touch; *(FOOTBALL: aussi:* **remise en ~)** throw-in; *(aussi:* **ligne de ~)** touch-line

toucher [tuʃe] *nm* touch ♦ *vt* to touch; *(palper)* to feel; *(atteindre: d'un coup de feu etc)* to hit; *(concerner)* to concern, affect; *(contacter)* to reach, contact; *(recevoir: récompense)* to receive, get; *(: salaire)* to draw, get; *(: chèque)* to cash; **se ~** *(être en contact)* to touch; **au ~** to the touch; **~ à** to touch; *(concerner)* to have to do with, concern; **je vais lui en ~ un mot** I'll have a word with him about it; **~ à sa fin** to be drawing to a close

touffe [tuf] *nf* tuft

touffu, e [tufy] *adj* thick, dense

toujours [tuʒuʀ] *adv* always; *(encore)* still; *(constamment)* forever; **~ plus** more and more; **pour ~** forever; **~ est-il que** the fact remains that; **essaie ~** (you can) try anyway

toupet [tupɛ] *(fam) nm* cheek

toupie [tupi] *nf* (spinning) top

tour [tuʀ] *nf* tower; *(immeuble)* high-rise block *(BRIT)* ou building *(US)*; *(ÉCHECS)* castle, rook ♦ *nm (excursion)* trip; *(à pied)* stroll, walk; *(en voiture)* run, ride; *(SPORT: aussi:* **~ de piste)** lap; *(d'être servi ou de jouer etc)* turn; *(de roue etc)* revolution; *(POL: aussi:* **~ de scrutin)** ballot; *(ruse, de prestidigitation)* trick; *(de potier)* wheel; *(à bois, métaux)* lathe; *(circonférence)*: **de 3 m de ~** 3 m round, with a circumference *ou* girth of 3 m; **faire le ~ de** to go round; *(à pied)* to walk round; **c'est au ~ de Renée** it's Renée's turn; **à ~ de rôle, ~ à ~** in turn; **~ de chant** *nm* song recital; **~ de contrôle** *nf* control tower; **~ de garde** *nm* spell of duty; **~ d'horizon** *nm* *(fig)* general survey; **~ de taille/tête** *nm* waist/head measurement; **un 33 ~s** an LP; **un 45 ~s** a single

tourbe [tuʀb] *nf* peat

tourbillon [tuʀbijɔ̃] *nm* whirlwind; *(d'eau)* whirlpool; *(fig)* whirl, swirl; **tourbillonner** *vi* to whirl (round)

tourelle [tuʀɛl] *nf* turret

tourisme [tuʀism] *nm* tourism; **agence de ~** tourist agency; **faire du ~** to go touring; (*en ville*) to go sightseeing; **touriste** *nm/f* tourist; **touristique** *adj* tourist *cpd*; (*région*) touristic

tourment [tuʀmɑ̃] *nm* torment; **tourmenter** *vt* to torment; **se tourmenter** *vi* to fret, worry o.s.

tournage [tuʀnaʒ] *nm* (*CINÉMA*) shooting

tournant [tuʀnɑ̃] *nm* (*de route*) bend; (*fig*) turning point

tournebroche [tuʀnəbʀɔʃ] *nm* roasting spit

tourne-disque [tuʀnədisk] *nm* record player

tournée [tuʀne] *nf* (*du facteur etc*) round; (*d'artiste, politicien*) tour; (*au café*) round (of drinks)

tournemain [tuʀnəmɛ̃]: **en un ~** *adv* (as) quick as a flash

tourner [tuʀne] *vt* to turn; (*sauce, mélange*) to stir; (*CINÉMA: faire les prises de vues*) to shoot; (: *produire*) to make ♦ *vi* to turn; (*moteur*) to run; (*taximètre*) to tick away; (*lait etc*) to turn (sour); **se ~** *vi* to turn round; **mal ~** to go wrong; **~ autour de** to go round; (*péj*) to hang round; **~ à/en** to turn into; **~ à gauche/droite** to turn left/right; **~ le dos à** to turn one's back on; to have one's back to; **~ de l'œil** to pass out; **se ~ vers** to turn towards; (*fig*) to turn to

tournesol [tuʀnəsɔl] *nm* sunflower

tournevis [tuʀnəvis] *nm* screwdriver

tourniquet [tuʀnikɛ] *nm* (*pour arroser*) sprinkler; (*portillon*) turnstile; (*présentoir*) revolving stand

tournoi [tuʀnwa] *nm* tournament

tournoyer [tuʀnwaje] *vi* to swirl (round)

tournure [tuʀnyʀ] *nf* (*LING*) turn of phrase; (*évolution*): **la ~ de qch** the way sth is developing; **~ d'esprit** turn *ou* cast of mind; **la ~ des événements** the turn of events

tourte [tuʀt] *nf* pie

tourterelle [tuʀtəʀɛl] *nf* turtledove

tous [tu] *adj, pron voir* **tout**

Toussaint [tusɛ̃] *nf*: **la ~** All Saints' Day

| **Toussaint** |

i **La Toussaint**, *November 1, is a public holiday in France. People traditionally visit the graves of friends and relatives to lay wreaths of heather and chrysanthemums.*

---

tousser [tuse] *vi* to cough

| *MOT-CLÉ* |

tout, e [tu, tut] (*mpl* **tous**, *fpl* **toutes**) *adj*
1 (*avec article singulier*) all; **tout le lait** all the milk; **toute la nuit** all night, the whole night; **tout le livre** the whole book; **tout un pain** a whole loaf; **tout le temps** all the time; the whole time; **c'est tout le contraire** it's quite the opposite
2 (*avec article pluriel*) every, all; **tous les livres** all the books; **toutes les nuits** every night; **toutes les fois** every time; **toutes les trois/deux semaines** every third/other *ou* second week, every three/two weeks; **tous les deux** both *ou* each of us (*ou* them *ou* you); **toutes les trois** all three of us (*ou* them *ou* you)
3 (*sans article*): **à tout âge** at any age; **pour toute nourriture, il avait ...** his only food was ...
♦ *pron* everything, all; **il a tout fait** he's done everything; **je les vois tous** I can see them all *ou* all of them; **nous y sommes tous allés** all of us went, we all went; **en tout** in all; **tout ce qu'il sait** all he knows
♦ *nm* whole; **le tout** all of it (*ou* them); **le tout est de ...** the main thing is to ...; **pas du tout** not at all
♦ *adv* 1 (*très, complètement*) very; **tout près** very near; **le tout premier** the very first; **tout seul** all alone; **le livre tout entier** the whole book; **tout en haut** right at the top; **tout droit** straight ahead
2: **tout en** while; **tout en travaillant** while working, as he *etc* works
3: **tout d'abord** first of all; **tout à coup**

suddenly; **tout à fait** absolutely; **tout à l'heure** a short while ago; *(futur)* in a short while, shortly; **à tout à l'heure!** see you later!; **tout de même** all the same; **tout le monde** everybody; **tout de suite** immediately, straight away; **tout terrain** *ou* **tous terrains** all-terrain

toutefois [tutfwa] *adv* however

toutes [tut] *adj, pron voir* **tout**

toux [tu] *nf* cough

toxicomane [tɔksikɔman] *nm/f* drug addict

toxique [tɔksik] *adj* toxic

trac [trak] *nm (au théâtre, en public)* stage fright; *(aux examens)* nerves *pl*; **avoir le ~** *(au théâtre, en public)* to have stage fright; *(aux examens)* to be feeling nervous

tracasser [trakase] *vt* to worry, bother; **se ~** to worry

trace [tras] *nf (empreintes)* tracks *pl*; *(marques, aussi fig)* mark; *(quantité infime, indice, vestige)* trace; **~s de pas** footprints

tracé [trase] *nm (parcours)* line; *(plan)* layout

tracer [trase] *vt* to draw; *(piste)* to open up

tract [trakt] *nm* tract, pamphlet

tractations [traktasjɔ̃] *nfpl* dealings, bargaining *sg*

tracteur [traktœr] *nm* tractor

traction [traksjɔ̃] *nf*: **~ avant/arrière** front-wheel/rear-wheel drive

tradition [tradisjɔ̃] *nf* tradition; **traditionnel, le** *adj* traditional

traducteur, -trice [tradyktœr, tris] *nm/f* translator

traduction [tradyksjɔ̃] *nf* translation

traduire [traduir] *vt* to translate; *(exprimer)* to convey; **~ qn en justice** to bring sb before the courts

trafic [trafik] *nm* traffic; **~ d'armes** arms dealing; **trafiquant, e** *nm/f* trafficker; *(d'armes)* dealer; **trafiquer** *(péj) vt (vin)* to doctor; *(moteur, document)* to tamper with

tragédie [traʒedi] *nf* tragedy; **tragique** *adj* tragic

trahir [trair] *vt* to betray; **trahison** *nf* betrayal; *(JUR)* treason

train [trɛ̃] *nm (RAIL)* train; *(allure)* pace; **être en ~ de faire qch** to be doing sth; **mettre qn en ~** to put sb in good spirits; **se sentir en ~** to feel in good form; **~ d'atterrissage** undercarriage; **~ de vie** style of living; **~ électrique** *(jouet)* (electric) train set; **~-autos-couchettes** car-sleeper train

traîne [trɛn] *nf (de robe)* train; **être à la ~** to lag behind

traîneau, x [trɛno] *nm* sleigh, sledge

traînée [trɛne] *nf* trail; *(sur un mur, dans le ciel)* streak; *(péj)* slut

traîner [trɛne] *vt (remorque)* to pull; *(enfant, chien)* to drag *ou* trail along ♦ *vi (robe, manteau)* to trail; *(être en désordre)* to lie around; *(aller lentement)* to dawdle (along); *(vagabonder, agir lentement)* to hang about; *(durer)* to drag on; **se ~** *vi* to drag o.s. along; **~ les pieds** to drag one's feet

train-train [trɛ̃trɛ̃] *nm* humdrum routine

traire [trɛr] *vt* to milk

trait [trɛ] *nm (ligne)* line; *(de dessin)* stroke; *(caractéristique)* feature, trait; **~s** *nmpl (du visage)* features; **d'un ~** *(boire)* in one gulp; **de ~** *(animal)* draught; **avoir ~ à** to concern; **~ d'union** hyphen

traitant, e [trɛtɑ̃, ɑ̃t] *adj (shampooing)* medicated; **votre médecin ~** your usual *ou* family doctor

traite [trɛt] *nf (COMM)* draft; *(AGR)* milking; **d'une ~** without stopping; **la ~ des noirs** the slave trade

traité [trɛte] *nm* treaty

traitement [trɛtmɑ̃] *nm* treatment; *(salaire)* salary; **~ de données** data processing; **~ de texte** word processing; *(logiciel)* word processing package

traiter [trɛte] *vt* to treat; *(qualifier)*: **~ qn d'idiot** to call sb a fool ♦ *vi* to deal; **~ de** to deal with

traiteur [trɛtœr] *nm* caterer

traître, -esse [tʀɛtʀ, tʀɛtʀɛs] *adj* (*dangereux*) treacherous ♦ *nm* traitor

trajectoire [tʀaʒɛktwaʀ] *nf* path

trajet [tʀaʒɛ] *nm* (*parcours, voyage*) journey; (*itinéraire*) route; (*distance à parcourir*) distance

trame [tʀam] *nf* (*de tissu*) weft; (*fig*) framework; **usé jusqu'à la ~** threadbare

tramer [tʀame] *vt*: **il se trame quelque chose** there's something brewing

trampoline [tʀɑ̃pɔlin] *nm* trampoline

tramway [tʀamwɛ] *nm* tram(way); (*voiture*) tram(car) (*BRIT*), streetcar (*US*)

tranchant, e [tʀɑ̃ʃɑ̃, ɑ̃t] *adj* sharp; (*fig*) peremptory ♦ *nm* (*d'un couteau*) cutting edge; (*de la main*) edge; **à double ~** double-edged

tranche [tʀɑ̃ʃ] *nf* (*morceau*) slice; (*arête*) edge; **~ d'âge/de salaires** age/wage bracket

tranché, e [tʀɑ̃ʃe] *adj* (*couleurs*) distinct; (*opinions*) clear-cut; **tranchée** *nf* trench

trancher [tʀɑ̃ʃe] *vt* to cut, sever ♦ *vi* to take a decision; **~ avec** to contrast sharply with

tranquille [tʀɑ̃kil] *adj* quiet; (*rassuré*) easy in one's mind, with one's mind at rest; **se tenir ~** (*enfant*) to be quiet; **laisse-moi/laisse-ça ~** leave me/it alone; **avoir la conscience ~** to have a clear conscience; **tranquillisant** *nm* tranquillizer; **tranquillité** *nf* peace (and quiet); (*d'esprit*) peace of mind

transat [tʀɑ̃zat] *nm* deckchair

transborder [tʀɑ̃sbɔʀde] *vt* to tran(s)ship

transcription [tʀɑ̃skʀipsjɔ̃] *nf* transcription; (*copie*) transcript

transférer [tʀɑ̃sfeʀe] *vt* to transfer; **transfert** *nm* transfer

transformation [tʀɑ̃sfɔʀmasjɔ̃] *nf* change; transformation; alteration; (*RUGBY*) conversion

transformer [tʀɑ̃sfɔʀme] *vt* to change; (*radicalement*) to transform; (*vêtement*) to alter; (*matière première, appartement, RUGBY*) to convert; **(se) ~ en** to turn into

transfusion [tʀɑ̃sfyzjɔ̃] *nf*: **~ sanguine** blood transfusion

transgresser [tʀɑ̃sgʀese] *vt* to contravene

transi, e [tʀɑ̃zi] *adj* numb (with cold), chilled to the bone

transiger [tʀɑ̃ziʒe] *vi* to compromise

transit [tʀɑ̃zit] *nm* transit; **transiter** *vi* to pass in transit

transitif, -ive [tʀɑ̃zitif, iv] *adj* transitive

transition [tʀɑ̃zisjɔ̃] *nf* transition; **transitoire** *adj* transitional

translucide [tʀɑ̃slysid] *adj* translucent

transmettre [tʀɑ̃smɛtʀ] *vt* (*passer*): **~ qch à qn** to pass sth on to sb; (*TECH, TÉL, MÉD*) to transmit; (*TV, RADIO: retransmettre*) to broadcast; **transmission** *nf* transmission

transparent, e [tʀɑ̃spaʀɑ̃, ɑ̃t] *adj* transparent

transpercer [tʀɑ̃spɛʀse] *vt* (*froid, pluie*) to go through, pierce; (*balle*) to go through

transpiration [tʀɑ̃spiʀasjɔ̃] *nf* perspiration

transpirer [tʀɑ̃spiʀe] *vi* to perspire

transplanter [tʀɑ̃splɑ̃te] *vt* (*MÉD, BOT*) to transplant; **transplantation** *nf* (*MÉD*) transplant

transport [tʀɑ̃spɔʀ] *nm* transport; **~s en commun** public transport *sg*; **transporter** *vt* to carry, move; (*COMM*) to transport, convey; **transporteur** *nm* haulage contractor (*BRIT*), trucker (*US*)

transvaser [tʀɑ̃svaze] *vt* to decant

transversal, e, -aux [tʀɑ̃svɛʀsal, o] *adj* (*rue*) which runs across; **coupe ~e** cross section

trapèze [tʀapɛz] *nm* (*au cirque*) trapeze

trappe [tʀap] *nf* trap door

trapu, e [tʀapy] *adj* squat, stocky

traquenard [tʀaknaʀ] *nm* trap

traquer [tʀake] *vt* to track down; (*harceler*) to hound

traumatiser [tʀomatize] *vt* to traumatize

travail, -aux [tʀavaj] *nm* (*gén*) work; (*tâche, métier*) work *no pl*, job; (*ÉCON, MÉD*) labour; **être sans ~** (*employé*) to be out of work *ou* unemployed; *voir aussi* **tra-**

vaux; ~ **(au) noir** moonlighting

travailler [tʀavaje] *vi* to work; *(bois)* to warp ♦ *vt* (*bois, métal*) to work; *(objet d'art, discipline)* to work on; **cela le travaille** it is on his mind; **travailleur, -euse** *adj* ≃ Labour *cpd*

travaux [tʀavo] *nmpl* (*de réparation, agricoles etc*) work *sg*; *(sur route)* roadworks *pl*; *(de construction)* building work; **travaux des champs** farmwork *sg*; **travaux dirigés** (*SCOL*) tutorial; **travaux forcés** hard labour *sg*; **travaux manuels** (*SCOL*) handicrafts; **travaux ménagers** housework *sg*; **travaux pratiques** (*SCOL*) practical work; *(en laboratoire)* lab work

travers [tʀavɛʀ] *nm* fault, failing; **en ~ (de)** across; **au ~ (de)/à ~** through; **de ~** (*nez, bouche*) crooked; *(chapeau)* askew; **comprendre de ~** to misunderstand; **regarder de ~** (*fig*) to look askance at

traverse [tʀavɛʀs] *nf* (*de voie ferrée*) sleeper; **chemin de ~** shortcut

traversée [tʀavɛʀse] *nf* crossing

traverser [tʀavɛʀse] *vt* (*gén*) to cross; *(ville, tunnel, aussi: percer, fig)* to go through; *(suj: ligne, trait)* to run across

traversin [tʀavɛʀsɛ̃] *nm* bolster

travesti [tʀavɛsti] *nm* transvestite

trébucher [tʀebyʃe] *vi*: ~ **(sur)** to stumble (over), trip (against)

trèfle [tʀɛfl] *nm* (*BOT*) clover; *(CARTES: couleur)* clubs *pl*; *(: carte)* club

treille [tʀɛj] *nf* vine arbour

treillis [tʀeji] *nm* (*métallique*) wire-mesh; *(MIL: tenue*) combat uniform; *(pantalon)* combat trousers *pl*

treize [tʀɛz] *num* thirteen; **treizième** *num* thirteenth

---
treizième mois

ⓘ Le treizième mois *is an end-of-year bonus roughly equal to one month's salary. For many employees it is a standard part of their salary package.*

---

tréma [tʀema] *nm* diaeresis

tremblement [tʀɑ̃bləmɑ̃] *nm*: ~ **de terre** earthquake

trembler [tʀɑ̃ble] *vi* to tremble, shake; ~ **de** (*froid, fièvre*) to shiver *ou* tremble with; *(peur)* to shake *ou* tremble with; ~ **pour qn** to fear for sb

trémousser [tʀemuse]: **se** ~ *vi* to jig about, wriggle about

trempe [tʀɑ̃p] *nf* (*fig*): **de cette/sa** ~ of this/his calibre

trempé, e [tʀɑ̃pe] *adj* soaking (wet), drenched; *(TECH)* tempered

tremper [tʀɑ̃pe] *vt* to soak, drench; (*aussi*: **faire** ~, **mettre à** ~) to soak; *(plonger)*: ~ **qch dans** to dip sth in(to) ♦ *vi* to soak; *(fig)*: ~ **dans** to be involved *ou* have a hand in; **se** ~ *vi* to have a quick dip; **trempette** *nf*: **faire trempette** to go paddling

tremplin [tʀɑ̃plɛ̃] *nm* springboard; *(SKI)* ski-jump

trentaine [tʀɑ̃tɛn] *nf*: **une** ~ **(de)** thirty or so, about thirty; **avoir la** ~ (*âge*) to be around thirty

trente [tʀɑ̃t] *num* thirty; **être sur son** ~ **et un** to be wearing one's Sunday best; **trentième** *num* thirtieth

trépidant, e [tʀepidɑ̃, ɑ̃t] *adj* (*fig: rythme*) pulsating; *(: vie)* hectic

trépied [tʀepje] *nm* tripod

trépigner [tʀepiɲe] *vi* to stamp (one's feet)

très [tʀɛ] *adv* very; much +*pp*, highly +*pp*

trésor [tʀezɔʀ] *nm* treasure; **T~ (public)** public revenue; **trésorerie** *nf* (*gestion*) accounts *pl*; *(bureaux)* accounts department; **difficultés de trésorerie** cash problems, shortage of cash *ou* funds; **trésorier, -ière** *nm/f* treasurer

tressaillir [tʀesajiʀ] *vi* to shiver, shudder

tressauter [tʀesote] *vi* to start, jump

tresse [tʀɛs] *nf* braid, plait; **tresser** *vt* (*cheveux*) to braid, plait; *(corbeille)* to weave

tréteau, x [tʀeto] *nm* trestle

treuil [tʀœj] *nm* winch

trêve [tʀɛv] nf (MIL, POL) truce; (fig) respite; **~ de ...** enough of this ...

tri [tʀi] nm: **faire le ~ (de)** to sort out; **(bureau de) ~** (POSTES) the sorting office

triangle [tʀijɑ̃gl] nm triangle; **triangulaire** adj triangular

tribord [tʀibɔʀ] nm: **à ~** to starboard, on the starboard side

tribu [tʀiby] nf tribe

tribunal, -aux [tʀibynal, o] nm (JUR) court; (MIL) tribunal

tribune [tʀibyn] nf (estrade) platform, rostrum; (débat) forum; (d'église, de tribunal) gallery; (de stade) stand

tribut [tʀiby] nm tribute

tributaire [tʀibytɛʀ] adj: **être ~ de** to be dependent on

tricher [tʀiʃe] vi to cheat; **tricheur, -euse** nm/f cheat(er)

tricolore [tʀikɔlɔʀ] adj three-coloured; (français) red, white and blue

tricot [tʀiko] nm (technique, ouvrage) knitting no pl; (vêtement) jersey, sweater; **~ de peau** vest; **tricoter** vt to knit

trictrac [tʀiktʀak] nm backgammon

tricycle [tʀisikl] nm tricycle

triennal, e, -aux [tʀijenal, o] adj three-year

trier [tʀije] vt to sort out; (POSTES, fruits) to sort

trimestre [tʀimɛstʀ] nm (SCOL) term; (COMM) quarter; **trimestriel, le** adj quarterly; (SCOL) end-of-term

tringle [tʀɛ̃gl] nf rod

trinquer [tʀɛ̃ke] vi to clink glasses

triomphe [tʀijɔ̃f] nm triumph; **triompher** vi to triumph, win; **triompher de** to triumph over, overcome

tripes [tʀip] nfpl (CULIN) tripe sg

triple [tʀipl] adj triple ♦ nm: **le ~ (de)** (comparaison) three times as much (as); **en ~ exemplaire** in triplicate; **tripler** vi, vt to triple, treble

triplés, -ées [tʀiple] nm/fpl triplets

tripoter [tʀipɔte] vt to fiddle with

triste [tʀist] adj sad; (couleur, temps, journée) dreary; (péj): **~ personnage/affaire** sorry individual/affair; **tristesse** nf sadness

trivial, e, -aux [tʀivjal, jo] adj coarse, crude; (commun) mundane

troc [tʀɔk] nm barter

troène [tʀɔɛn] nm privet

trognon [tʀɔɲɔ̃] nm (de fruit) core; (de légume) stalk

trois [tʀwa] num three; **troisième** num third; **trois quarts** nmpl: **les trois quarts de** three-quarters of

trombe [tʀɔ̃b] nf: **des ~s d'eau** a downpour; **en ~** like a whirlwind

trombone [tʀɔ̃bɔn] nm (MUS) trombone; (de bureau) paper clip

trompe [tʀɔ̃p] nf (d'éléphant) trunk; (MUS) trumpet, horn

tromper [tʀɔ̃pe] vt to deceive; (vigilance, poursuivants) to elude; **se ~** vi to make a mistake, be mistaken; **se ~ de voiture/jour** to take the wrong car/get the day wrong; **se ~ de 3 cm/20 euros** to be out by 3 cm/20 euros; **tromperie** nf deception, trickery no pl

trompette [tʀɔ̃pɛt] nf trumpet; **en ~** (nez) turned-up

trompeur, -euse [tʀɔ̃pœʀ, øz] adj deceptive

tronc [tʀɔ̃] nm (BOT, ANAT) trunk; (d'église) collection box

tronçon [tʀɔ̃sɔ̃] nm section; **tronçonner** vt to saw up

trône [tʀon] nm throne

trop [tʀo] adv (+vb) too much; (+adjectif, adverbe) too; **~ (nombreux)** too many; **~ peu (nombreux)** too few; **~ (souvent)** too often; **~ (longtemps)** (for) too long; **~ de** (nombre) too many; (quantité) too much; **de ~, en ~: des livres en ~** a few books too many; **du lait en ~** too much milk; **3 livres/3 F de ~** 3 books too many/3 F too much

tropical, e, -aux [tʀɔpikal, o] adj tropical

tropique [tʀɔpik] nm tropic

trop-plein [tʀoplɛ̃] nm (tuyau) overflow ou

outlet (pipe); (*liquide*) overflow

troquer [tʀɔke] *vt*: ~ **qch contre** to barter *ou* trade sth for; (*fig*) to swap sth for

trot [tʀo] *nm* trot; **trotter** *vi* to trot

trotteuse [tʀɔtøz] *nf* (sweep) second hand

trottinette [tʀɔtinɛt] *nf* (child's) scooter

trottoir [tʀɔtwaʀ] *nm* pavement; **faire le ~** (*péj*) to walk the streets; **~ roulant** moving walkway, travellator

trou [tʀu] *nm* hole; (*fig*) gap; (*COMM*) deficit; **~ d'air** air pocket; **~ d'ozone** ozone hole; **le ~ de la serrure** the keyhole; **~ de mémoire** blank, lapse of memory

troublant, e [tʀublɑ̃, ɑ̃t] *adj* disturbing

trouble [tʀubl] *adj* (*liquide*) cloudy; (*image, photo*) blurred; (*affaire*) shady, murky ♦ *nm* agitation; **~s** *nmpl* (*POL*) disturbances, troubles, unrest *sg*; (*MÉD*) trouble *sg*, disorders; **trouble-fête** *nm* spoilsport

troubler [tʀuble] *vt* to disturb; (*liquide*) to make cloudy; (*intriguer*) to bother; **se ~** *vi* (*personne*) to become flustered *ou* confused

trouer [tʀue] *vt* to make a hole (*ou* holes) in

trouille [tʀuj] (*fam*) *nf*: **avoir la ~** to be scared to death

troupe [tʀup] *nf* troop; **~ (de théâtre)** (theatrical) company

troupeau, x [tʀupo] *nm* (*de moutons*) flock; (*de vaches*) herd

trousse [tʀus] *nf* case, kit; (*d'écolier*) pencil case; **aux ~s de** (*fig*) on the heels *ou* tail of; **~ à outils** toolkit; **~ de toilette** toilet bag

trousseau, x [tʀuso] *nm* (*de mariée*) trousseau; **~ de clefs** bunch of keys

trouvaille [tʀuvaj] *nf* find

trouver [tʀuve] *vt* to find; (*rendre visite*): **aller/venir ~ qn** to go/come and see sb; **se ~** *vi* (*être*) to be; **je trouve que** I find *ou* think that; **~ à boire/critiquer** to find something to drink/criticize; **se ~ bien** to feel well; **se ~ mal** to pass out

truand [tʀyɑ̃] *nm* gangster; **truander** *vt*: **se faire truander** to be swindled

truc [tʀyk] *nm* (*astuce*) way, trick; (*de cinéma, prestidigitateur*) trick, effect; (*chose*) thing, thingumajig; **avoir le ~** to have the knack

truelle [tʀyɛl] *nf* trowel

truffe [tʀyf] *nf* truffle; (*nez*) nose

truffé, e [tʀyfe] *adj*: **~ de** (*fig*) peppered with; (*fautes*) riddled with; (*pièges*) bristling with

truie [tʀɥi] *nf* sow

truite [tʀɥit] *nf* trout *inv*

truquage [tʀykaʒ] *nm* special effects

truquer [tʀyke] *vt* (*élections, serrure, dés*) to fix

TSVP *sigle* (= *tournez svp*) PTO

TTC *sigle* (= *toutes taxes comprises*) inclusive of tax

tu¹ [ty] *pron* you

tu², e [ty] *pp de* **taire**

tuba [tyba] *nm* (*MUS*) tuba; (*SPORT*) snorkel

tube [tyb] *nm* tube; (*chanson*) hit

tuberculose [tybɛʀkyloz] *nf* tuberculosis

tuer [tɥe] *vt* to kill; **se ~** *vi* to be killed; (*suicide*) to kill o.s.; **tuerie** *nf* slaughter *no pl*

tue-tête [tytɛt]: **à ~-~** *adv* at the top of one's voice

tueur [tɥœʀ] *nm* killer; **~ à gages** hired killer

tuile [tɥil] *nf* tile; (*fam*) spot of bad luck, blow

tulipe [tylip] *nf* tulip

tuméfié, e [tymefje] *adj* puffed-up, swollen

tumeur [tymœʀ] *nf* growth, tumour

tumulte [tymylt] *nm* commotion; **tumultueux, -euse** *adj* stormy, turbulent

tunique [tynik] *nf* tunic

Tunisie [tynizi] *nf*: **la ~** Tunisia; **tunisien, ne** *adj* Tunisian ♦ *nm/f*: **Tunisien, ne** Tunisian

tunnel [tynɛl] *nm* tunnel; **le ~ sous la Manche** the Channel Tunnel

turbulences [tyʀbylɑ̃s] *nfpl* (*AVIAT*) turbulence *sg*

turbulent, e [tyʀbylɑ̃, ɑ̃t] *adj* boisterous,

unruly

turc, turque [tyʀk] *adj* Turkish ♦ *nm/f*:
T~, -que Turk/Turkish woman ♦ *nm*
(*LING*) Turkish

turf [tyʀf] *nm* racing; **turfiste** *nm/f* race-goer

Turquie [tyʀki] *nf*: **la ~** Turkey

turquoise [tyʀkwaz] *nf* turquoise ♦ *adj inv*
turquoise

tus *etc* [ty] *vb voir* **taire**

tutelle [tytɛl] *nf* (*JUR*) guardianship; (*POL*)
trusteeship; **sous la ~ de** (*fig*) under the
supervision of

tuteur [tytœʀ] *nm* (*JUR*) guardian; (*de
plante*) stake, support

tutoyer [tytwaje] *vt*: **~ qn** to address sb as
"tu"

tuyau, x [tɥijo] *nm* pipe; (*flexible*) tube;
(*fam*) tip; **~ d'arrosage** hosepipe; **~
d'échappement** exhaust pipe; **tuyauterie** *nf* piping *no pl*

TVA *sigle f* (= *taxe à la valeur ajoutée*)
VAT

tympan [tɛ̃pɑ̃] *nm* (*ANAT*) eardrum

type [tip] *nm* type; (*fam*) chap, guy ♦ *adj*
typical, classic

typé, e [tipe] *adj* ethnic

typique [tipik] *adj* typical

tyran [tiʀɑ̃] *nm* tyrant; **tyrannique** *adj*
tyrannical

tzigane [dzigan] *adj* gipsy, tzigane

U, u

UEM *sigle f* (= *union économique et monétaire*) EMU

ulcère [ylsɛʀ] *nm* ulcer; **ulcérer** *vt* (*fig*) to
sicken, appal

ultérieur, e [ylteʀjœʀ] *adj* later, subsequent;
remis à une date ~e postponed
to a later date; **ultérieurement** *adv* later, subsequently

ultime [yltim] *adj* final

ultra... [yltʀa] *préfixe*: **~moderne/-rapide**
ultra-modern/-fast

un, une [œ̃, yn] *art indéf* a; (*devant voyelle*)
an; **un garçon/vieillard** a boy/an old
man; **une fille** a girl
♦ *pron* one; **l'un des meilleurs** one of
the best; **l'un ..., l'autre** (the) one ..., the
other; **les uns ..., les autres** some ...,
others; **l'un et l'autre** both (of them);
l'un ou l'autre either (of them); **l'un
l'autre, les uns les autres** each other,
one another; **pas un seul** not a single
one; **un par un** one by one
♦ *num* one; **une pomme seulement** one
apple only

└───────────────────────────────────────┘

unanime [ynanim] *adj* unanimous; **unanimité** *nf*: **à l'unanimité** unanimously

uni, e [yni] *adj* (*ton, tissu*) plain; (*surface*)
smooth, even; (*famille*) close(-knit); (*pays*)
united

unifier [ynifje] *vt* to unite, unify

uniforme [ynifɔʀm] *adj* uniform; (*surface,
ton*) even ♦ *nm* uniform; **uniformiser** *vt*
(*systèmes*) to standardize

union [ynjɔ̃] *nf* union; **~ de consomma-
teurs** consumers' association; **U~ européenne** European Union; **U~ soviétique**
Soviet Union

unique [ynik] *adj* (*seul*) only; (*exceptionnel*)
unique; (*le même*): **un prix/système ~** a
single price/system; **fils/fille ~** only son/
daughter, only child; **sens ~** one-way
street; **uniquement** *adv* only, solely;
(*juste*) only, merely

unir [yniʀ] *vt* (*nations*) to unite; (*en mariage*) to unite, join together; **s'~** *vi* to
unite; (*en mariage*) to be joined together

unitaire [ynitɛʀ] *adj*: **prix ~** unit price

unité [ynite] *nf* unit; (*harmonie, cohésion*)
unity

univers [yniveʀ] *nm* universe; **universel,
le** *adj* universal

universitaire [yniveʀsitɛʀ] *adj* university
cpd; (*diplôme, études*) academic, university
cpd ♦ *nm/f* academic

université [ynivɛʀsite] *nf* university

urbain, e [yʀbɛ̃, ɛn] *adj* urban, city *cpd*, town *cpd*; **urbanisme** *nm* town planning

urgence [yʀʒɑ̃s] *nf* urgency; (*MÉD etc*) emergency; **d'~** *adj* emergency *cpd* ♦ *adv* as a matter of urgency; **(service des) ~s** casualty

urgent, e [yʀʒɑ̃, ɑ̃t] *adj* urgent

urine [yʀin] *nf* urine; **urinoir** *nm* (public) urinal

urne [yʀn] *nf* (*électorale*) ballot box; (*vase*) urn

urticaire [yʀtikɛʀ] *nf* nettle rash

us [ys] *nmpl*: **~ et coutumes** (habits and) customs

USA *sigle mpl*: **les USA** the USA

usage [yzaʒ] *nm* (*emploi, utilisation*) use; (*coutume*) custom; **à l'~** with use; **à l'~ de** (*pour*) for (use of); **hors d'~** out of service; **à ~ interne** (*MÉD*) to be taken; **à ~ externe** (*MÉD*) for external use only; **usagé, e** *adj* (*usé*) worn; **usager, -ère** *nm/f* user

usé, e [yze] *adj* worn; (*banal: argument etc*) hackneyed

user [yze] *vt* (*outil*) to wear down; (*vêtement*) to wear out; (*matière*) to wear away; (*consommer: charbon etc*) to use; **s'~** *vi* (*tissu, vêtement*) to wear out; **~ de** (*moyen, procédé*) to use, employ; (*droit*) to exercise

usine [yzin] *nf* factory

usité, e [yzite] *adj* common

ustensile [ystɑ̃sil] *nm* implement; **~ de cuisine** kitchen utensil

usuel, le [yzɥɛl] *adj* everyday, common

usure [yzyʀ] *nf* wear

utérus [yteʀys] *nm* uterus, womb

utile [ytil] *adj* useful

utilisation [ytilizasjɔ̃] *nf* use

utiliser [ytilize] *vt* to use

utilitaire [ytilitɛʀ] *adj* utilitarian

utilité [ytilite] *nf* usefulness *no pl*; **de peu d'~** of little use *ou* help

utopie [ytɔpi] *nf* utopia

V, v

va [va] *vb voir* **aller**

vacance [vakɑ̃s] *nf* (*ADMIN*) vacancy; **~s** *nfpl* holiday(s *pl*), vacation *sg*; **les grandes ~s** the summer holidays; **prendre des/ses ~s** to take a holiday/one's holiday(s); **aller en ~s** to go on holiday; **vacancier, -ière** *nm/f* holiday-maker

vacant, e [vakɑ̃, ɑ̃t] *adj* vacant

vacarme [vakaʀm] *nm* (*bruit*) racket

vaccin [vaksɛ̃] *nm* vaccine; (*opération*) vaccination; **vaccination** *nf* vaccination; **vacciner** *vt* to vaccinate; **être vacciné contre qch** (*fam*) to be cured of sth

vache [vaʃ] *nf* (*ZOOL*) cow; (*cuir*) cowhide ♦ *adj* (*fam*) rotten, mean; **vachement** (*fam*) *adv* (*très*) really; (*pleuvoir, travailler*) a hell of a lot; **vacherie** *nf* (*action*) dirty trick; (*remarque*) nasty remark

vaciller [vasije] *vi* to sway, wobble; (*bougie, lumière*) to flicker; (*fig*) to be failing, falter

va-et-vient [vaevjɛ̃] *nm inv* (*de personnes, véhicules*) comings and goings *pl*, to-ings and fro-ings *pl*

vagabond [vagabɔ̃] *nm* (*rôdeur*) tramp, vagrant; (*voyageur*) wanderer; **vagabonder** *vi* to roam, wander

vagin [vaʒɛ̃] *nm* vagina

vague [vag] *nf* wave ♦ *adj* vague; (*regard*) faraway; (*manteau, robe*) loose(-fitting); (*quelconque*): **un ~ bureau/cousin** some office/cousin or other; **~ de fond** ground swell; **~ de froid** cold spell

vaillant, e [vajɑ̃, ɑ̃t] *adj* (*courageux*) gallant; (*robuste*) hale and hearty

vaille [vaj] *vb voir* **valoir**

vain, e [vɛ̃, vɛn] *adj* vain; **en ~** in vain

vaincre [vɛ̃kʀ] *vt* to defeat; (*fig*) to conquer, overcome; **vaincu, e** *nm/f* defeated party; **vainqueur** *nm* victor; (*SPORT*) winner

vais [vɛ] *vb voir* **aller**

vaisseau, x [veso] *nm* (*ANAT*) vessel; (*NA-VIG*) ship, vessel; **~ spatial** spaceship

vaisselier [vesəlje] *nm* dresser

vaisselle [vesɛl] *nf* (*service*) crockery; (*plats etc à laver*) (dirty) dishes *pl*; **faire la ~** to do the washing-up (*BRIT*) *ou* the dishes

val [val, vo] (*pl* **vaux** *ou* **~s**) *nm* valley

valable [valabl] *adj* valid; (*acceptable*) decent, worthwhile

valent *etc* [val] *vb voir* **valoir**

valet [valɛ] *nm* manservant; (*CARTES*) jack

valeur [valœʀ] *nf* (*gén*) value; (*mérite*) worth, merit; (*COMM: titre*) security; **mettre en ~** (*détail*) to highlight; (*objet décoratif*) to show off to advantage; **avoir de la ~** to be valuable; **sans ~** worthless; **prendre de la ~** to go up *ou* gain in value

valide [valid] *adj* (*en bonne santé*) fit; (*valable*) valid; **valider** *vt* to validate

valions [valjɔ̃] *vb voir* **valoir**

valise [valiz] *nf* (suit)case; **faire ses ~s** to pack one's bags

vallée [vale] *nf* valley

vallon [valɔ̃] *nm* small valley; **vallonné, e** *adj* hilly

valoir [valwaʀ] *vi* (*être valable*) to hold, apply ♦ *vt* (*prix, valeur, effort*) to be worth; (*causer*): **~ qch à qn** to earn sb sth; **se ~** *vi* to be of equal merit; (*péj*) to be two of a kind; **faire ~** (*droits, prérogatives*) to assert; **faire ~ que** to point out that; **à ~ sur** to be deducted from; **vaille que vaille** somehow or other; **cela ne me dit rien qui vaille** I don't like the look of it at all; **ce climat ne me vaut rien** this climate doesn't suit me; **~ le coup** *ou* **la peine** to be worth the trouble *ou* worth it; **~ mieux**: **il vaut mieux se taire** it's better to say nothing; **ça ne vaut rien** it's worthless; **que vaut ce candidat?** how good is this applicant?

valse [vals] *nf* waltz

valu, e [valy] *pp de* **valoir**

vandalisme [vɑ̃dalism] *nm* vandalism

vanille [vanij] *nf* vanilla

vanité [vanite] *nf* vanity; **vaniteux, -euse** *adj* vain, conceited

vanne [van] *nf* gate; (*fig*) joke

vannerie [vanʀi] *nf* basketwork

vantard, e [vɑ̃taʀ, aʀd] *adj* boastful

vanter [vɑ̃te] *vt* to speak highly of, praise; **se ~** *vi* to boast, brag; **se ~ de** to pride o.s. on; (*péj*) to boast of

vapeur [vapœʀ] *nf* steam; (*émanation*) vapour, fumes *pl*; **~s** *nfpl* (*bouffées*) vapours; **à ~** steam-powered, steam *cpd*; **cuit à la ~** steamed; **vaporeux, -euse** *adj* (*flou*) hazy, misty; (*léger*) filmy; **vaporisateur** *nm* spray; **vaporiser** *vt* (*parfum etc*) to spray

varappe [vaʀap] *nf* rock climbing

vareuse [vaʀøz] *nf* (*blouson*) pea jacket; (*d'uniforme*) tunic

variable [vaʀjabl] *adj* variable; (*temps, humeur*) changeable; (*divers: résultats*) varied, various

varice [vaʀis] *nf* varicose vein

varicelle [vaʀisɛl] *nf* chickenpox

varié, e [vaʀje] *adj* varied; (*divers*) various

varier [vaʀje] *vi* to vary; (*temps, humeur*) to change ♦ *vt* to vary; **variété** *nf* variety; **variétés** *nfpl*: **spectacle/émission de variétés** variety show

variole [vaʀjɔl] *nf* smallpox

vas [va] *vb voir* **aller**

vase [vaz] *nm* vase ♦ *nf* silt, mud; **vaseux, -euse** *adj* silty, muddy; (*fig: confus*) woolly, hazy; (: *fatigué*) woozy

vasistas [vazistas] *nm* fanlight

vaste [vast] *adj* vast, immense

vaudrai *etc* [vodʀe] *vb voir* **valoir**

vaurien, ne [voʀjɛ̃, jɛn] *nm/f* good-for-nothing

vaut [vo] *vb voir* **valoir**

vautour [votuʀ] *nm* vulture

vautrer [votʀe] *vb*: **se ~ dans/sur** to wallow in/sprawl on

vaux [vo] *nmpl de* **val** ♦ *vb voir* **valoir**

va-vite [vavit]: **à la ~-~** *adv* in a rush *ou* hurry

VDQS

i **VDQS** *(vin délimité de qualité supérieure)* is the second highest French
wine classification after AOC, indicating
high-quality wine from an approved regional vineyard. It is followed by **vin de
pays**. **Vin de table** *or* **vin ordinaire** *is
table wine of unspecified origin, often
blended.*

---

veau, x [vo] *nm (ZOOL)* calf; *(CULIN)* veal;
(peau) calfskin

vécu, e [veky] *pp de* **vivre**

vedette [vədɛt] *nf (artiste etc)* star; *(canot)*
motor boat; *(police)* launch

végétal, e, -aux [veʒetal, o] *adj* vegetable ♦ *nm* vegetable, plant; **végétalien,
ne** *adj, nm/f* vegan

végétarien, ne [veʒetaʀjɛ̃, jɛn] *adj, nm/f*
vegetarian

végétation [veʒetasjɔ̃] *nf* vegetation; **~s**
nfpl (MÉD) adenoids

véhicule [veikyl] *nm* vehicle; **~ utilitaire**
commercial vehicle

veille [vɛj] *nf (état)* wakefulness; *(jour)*: **la
~ (de)** the day before; **la ~ au soir** the
previous evening; **à la ~ de** on the eve
of; **la ~ de Noël** Christmas Eve; **la ~ du
jour de l'An** New Year's Eve

veillée [veje] *nf (soirée)* evening; *(réunion)*
evening gathering; **~ (funèbre)** wake

veiller [veje] *vi* to stay up ♦ *vt (malade,
mort)* to watch over, sit up with; **~ à** to
attend to, see to; **~ à ce que** to make
sure that; **~ sur** to watch over; **veilleur**
nm: **veilleur de nuit** night watchman;
veilleuse *nf (lampe)* night light; *(AUTO)*
sidelight; *(flamme)* pilot light

veinard, e [vɛnaʀ, aʀd] *nm/f* lucky devil

veine [vɛn] *nf (ANAT, du bois etc)* vein;
(filon) vein, seam; *(fam: chance)*: **avoir de
la ~** to be lucky

véliplanchiste [veliplɑ̃ʃist] *nm/f* windsurf-
er

vélo [velo] *nm* bike, cycle; **faire du ~** to
go cycling; **~ tout-terrain** mountain bike;
vélomoteur *nm* moped

velours [v(ə)luʀ] *nm* velvet; **~ côtelé** corduroy; **velouté, e** *adj* velvety ♦ *nm:* **velouté de tomates** cream of tomato soup

velu, e [vəly] *adj* hairy

venais *etc* [vənɛ] *vb voir* **venir**

venaison [vənɛzɔ̃] *nf* venison

vendange [vɑ̃dɑ̃ʒ] *nf (aussi:* **~s**) grape
harvest; **vendanger** *vi* to harvest the
grapes

vendeur, -euse [vɑ̃dœʀ, øz] *nm/f* shop
assistant ♦ *nm (JUR)* vendor, seller; **~ de
journaux** newspaper seller

vendre [vɑ̃dʀ] *vt* to sell; **~ qch à qn** to sell
sb sth; **"à ~"** "for sale"

vendredi [vɑ̃dʀədi] *nm* Friday; **V~ saint**
Good Friday

vénéneux, -euse [venenø, øz] *adj* poi-
sonous

vénérien, ne [veneʀjɛ̃, jɛn] *adj* venereal

vengeance [vɑ̃ʒɑ̃s] *nf* vengeance *no pl*,
revenge *no pl*

venger [vɑ̃ʒe] *vt* to avenge; **se ~** *vi* to
avenge o.s.; **se ~ de qch** to avenge o.s.
for sth, take one's revenge for sth; **se ~
de qn** to take revenge on sb; **se ~ sur** to
take revenge on

venimeux, -euse [vənimø, øz] *adj* poi-
sonous, venomous; *(fig: haineux)* venomous, vicious

venin [vənɛ̃] *nm* venom, poison

venir [v(ə)niʀ] *vi* to come; **~ de** to come
from; **~ de faire: je viens d'y aller/de le
voir** I've just been there/seen him; **s'il
vient à pleuvoir** if it should rain; **j'en
viens à croire que** I have come to believe that; **faire ~** *(docteur)* to call (out)

vent [vɑ̃] *nm* wind; **il y a du ~** it's windy;
c'est du ~ it's all hot air; **au ~** to wind-
ward; **sous le ~** to leeward; **avoir le ~
debout/arrière** to head into the wind/
have the wind astern; **dans le ~** *(fam)*
trendy

vente [vɑ̃t] *nf* sale; **la ~** *(activité)* selling;
(secteur) sales *pl*; **mettre en ~** *(produit)* to

put on sale; (*maison, objet personnel*) to put up for sale; ~ **aux enchères** auction sale; ~ **de charité** jumble sale

venteux, -euse [vãtø, øz] *adj* windy

ventilateur [vãtilatœR] *nm* fan

ventiler [vãtile] *vt* to ventilate

ventouse [vãtuz] *nf* (*de caoutchouc*) suction pad

ventre [vãtR] *nm* (ANAT) stomach; (*légèrement péj*) belly; (*utérus*) womb; **avoir mal au** ~ to have stomach ache (BRIT) *ou* a stomach ache (US)

ventriloque [vãtRilɔk] *nm/f* ventriloquist

venu, e [v(ə)ny] *pp de* **venir ♦** *adj*: **bien** ~ timely; **mal** ~ out of place; **être mal** ~ **à** *ou* **de faire** to have no grounds for doing, be in no position to do

ver [vɛR] *nm* worm; (*des fruits etc*) maggot; (*du bois*) woodworm *no pl*; *voir aussi* **vers;** ~ **à soie** silkworm; ~ **de terre** earthworm; ~ **luisant** glow-worm; ~ **solitaire** tapeworm

verbaliser [vɛRbalize] *vi* (POLICE) to book *ou* report an offender

verbe [vɛRb] *nm* verb

verdâtre [vɛRdatR] *adj* greenish

verdict [vɛRdik(t)] *nm* verdict

verdir [vɛRdiR] *vi, vt* to turn green; **verdure** *nf* greenery

véreux, -euse [veRø, øz] *adj* worm-eaten; (*malhonnête*) shady, corrupt

verge [vɛRʒ] *nf* (ANAT) penis

verger [vɛRʒe] *nm* orchard

verglacé, e [vɛRglase] *adj* icy, iced-over

verglas [vɛRgla] *nm* (black) ice

vergogne [vɛRgɔɲ]: **sans** ~ *adv* shamelessly

véridique [veRidik] *adj* truthful

vérification [veRifikasjɔ̃] *nf* (*action*) checking *no pl*; (*contrôle*) check

vérifier [veRifje] *vt* to check; (*corroborer*) to confirm, bear out

véritable [veRitabl] *adj* real; (*ami, amour*) true

vérité [veRite] *nf* truth; **en** ~ really, actually

vermeil, le [vɛRmɛj] *adj* ruby red

vermine [vɛRmin] *nf* vermin *pl*

vermoulu, e [vɛRmuly] *adj* worm-eaten

verni, e [vɛRni] *adj* (*fam*) lucky; **cuir** ~ patent leather

vernir [vɛRniR] *vt* (*bois, tableau, ongles*) to varnish; (*poterie*) to glaze

vernis *nm* (*enduit*) varnish; glaze; (*fig*) veneer; ~ **à ongles** nail polish *ou* varnish; **vernissage** *nm* (*d'une exposition*) preview

vérole [veRɔl] *nf* (*variole*) smallpox

verrai *etc* [veRe] *vb voir* **voir**

verre [vɛR] *nm* glass; (*de lunettes*) lens *sg*; **boire** *ou* **prendre un** ~ to have a drink; ~ **dépoli** frosted glass; ~**s de contact** contact lenses; **verrerie** *nf* (*fabrique*) glassworks *sg*; (*activité*) glass-making; (*objets*) glassware; **verrière** *nf* (*paroi vitrée*) glass wall; (*toit vitré*) glass roof

verrons *etc* [veRɔ̃] *vb voir* **voir**

verrou [veRu] *nm* (*targette*) bolt; **mettre qn sous les** ~**s** to put sb behind bars; **verrouillage** *nm* locking; **verrouillage centralisé** central locking; **verrouiller** *vt* (*porte*) to bolt; (*ordinateur*) to lock

verrue [veRy] *nf* wart

vers [vɛR] *nm* line **♦** *nmpl* (*poésie*) verse *sg* **♦** *prép* (*en direction de*) toward(s); (*près de*) around (about); (*temporel*) about, around

versant [vɛRsã] *nm* slopes *pl*, side

versatile [vɛRsatil] *adj* fickle, changeable

verse [vɛRs]: **à** ~ *adv*: **il pleut à** ~ it's pouring (with rain)

Verseau [vɛRso] *nm*: **le** ~ Aquarius

versement [vɛRsəmã] *nm* payment; **en 3** ~**s** in 3 instalments

verser [vɛRse] *vt* (*liquide, grains*) to pour; (*larmes, sang*) to shed; (*argent*) to pay **♦** *vi* (*véhicule*) to overturn; (*temporel*): ~ **dans** to lapse into

verset [vɛRse] *nm* verse

version [vɛRsjɔ̃] *nf* version; (SCOL) translation (*into the mother tongue*); **film en** ~ **originale** film in the original language

verso [vɛRso] *nm* back; **voir au** ~ see over(leaf)

vert, e [vɛʀ, vɛʀt] *adj* green; (*vin*) young; (*vigoureux*) sprightly ♦ *nm* green

vertèbre [vɛʀtɛbʀ] *nf* vertebra

vertement [vɛʀtəmɑ̃] *adv* (*réprimander*) sharply

vertical, e, -aux [vɛʀtikal, o] *adj* vertical; **verticale** *nf* vertical; **à la verticale** vertically; **verticalement** *adv* vertically

vertige [vɛʀtiʒ] *nm* (*peur du vide*) vertigo; (*étourdissement*) dizzy spell; (*fig*) fever; **vertigineux, -euse** *adj* breathtaking

vertu [vɛʀty] *nf* virtue; **en ~ de** in accordance with; **vertueux, -euse** *adj* virtuous

verve [vɛʀv] *nf* witty eloquence; **être en ~** to be in brilliant form

verveine [vɛʀvɛn] *nf* (*BOT*) verbena, vervain; (*infusion*) verbena tea

vésicule [vezikyl] *nf* vesicle; **~ biliaire** gall-bladder

vessie [vesi] *nf* bladder

veste [vɛst] *nf* jacket; **~ droite/croisée** single-/double-breasted jacket

vestiaire [vɛstjɛʀ] *nm* (*au théâtre etc*) cloakroom; (*de stade etc*) changing-room (*BRIT*), locker-room (*US*)

vestibule [vɛstibyl] *nm* hall

vestige [vɛstiʒ] *nm* relic; (*fig*) vestige; **~s** *nmpl* (*de ville*) remains

vestimentaire [vɛstimɑ̃tɛʀ] *adj* (*détail*) of dress; (*élégance*) sartorial; **dépenses ~s** clothing expenditure

veston [vɛstɔ̃] *nm* jacket

vêtement [vɛtmɑ̃] *nm* garment, item of clothing; **~s** *nmpl* clothes

vétérinaire [veteʀinɛʀ] *nm/f* vet, veterinary surgeon

vêtir [vetiʀ] *vt* to clothe, dress

veto [veto] *nm* veto; **opposer un ~ à** to veto

vêtu, e [vety] *pp de* **vêtir**

vétuste [vetyst] *adj* ancient; timeworn

veuf, veuve [vœf, vœv] *adj* widowed ♦ *nm* widower

veuille [vœj] *vb voir* **vouloir**

veuillez [vœje] *vb voir* **vouloir**

veule [vøl] *adj* spineless

veuve [vœv] *nf* widow

veux [vø] *vb voir* **vouloir**

vexant, e [vɛksɑ̃, ɑ̃t] *adj* (*contrariant*) annoying; (*blessant*) hurtful

vexation [vɛksasjɔ̃] *nf* humiliation

vexer [vɛkse] *vt*: **~ qn** to hurt sb's feelings; **se ~** *vi* to be offended

viable [vjabl] *adj* viable; (*économie, industrie etc*) sustainable

viaduc [vjadyk] *nm* viaduct

viager, -ère [vjaʒe, ɛʀ] *adj*: **rente viagère** life annuity

viande [vjɑ̃d] *nf* meat

vibrer [vibʀe] *vi* to vibrate; (*son, voix*) to be vibrant; (*fig*) to be stirred; **faire ~** to (cause to) vibrate; (*fig*) to stir, thrill

vice [vis] *nm* vice; (*défaut*) fault ♦ *préfixe*: **~...** vice-; **~ de forme** legal flaw *ou* irregularity

vichy [viʃi] *nm* (*toile*) gingham

vicié, e [visje] *adj* (*air*) polluted, tainted; (*JUR*) invalidated

vicieux, -euse [visjø, jøz] *adj* (*pervers*) lecherous; (*rétif*) unruly ♦ *nm/f* lecher

vicinal, e, -aux [visinal, o] *adj*: **chemin ~** by-road, byway

victime [viktim] *nf* victim; (*d'accident*) casualty

victoire [viktwaʀ] *nf* victory

victuailles [viktɥaj] *nfpl* provisions

vidange [vidɑ̃ʒ] *nf* (*d'un fossé, réservoir*) emptying; (*AUTO*) oil change; (*de lavabo: bonde*) waste outlet; **~s** *nfpl* (*matières*) sewage *sg*; **vidanger** *vt* to empty

vide [vid] *adj* empty ♦ *nm* (*PHYSIQUE*) vacuum; (*espace*) (empty) space, gap; (*futilité, néant*) void; **avoir peur du ~** to be afraid of heights; **emballé sous ~** vacuum packed; **à ~** (*sans occupants*) empty; (*sans charge*) unladen

vidéo [video] *nf* video ♦ *adj*: **cassette ~** video cassette; **jeu ~** video game; **vidéoclip** *nm* music video; **vidéoclub** *nm* video shop

vide-ordures [vidɔʀdyʀ] *nm inv* (rubbish)

chute

vidéothèque [videɔtɛk] *nf* video library
vide-poches [vidpɔʃ] *nm inv* tidy; (*AUTO*) glove compartment
vider [vide] *vt* to empty; (*CULIN: volaille, poisson*) to gut, clean out; **se ~** *vi* to empty; **~ les lieux** to quit *ou* vacate the premises; **videur** *nm* (*de boîte de nuit*) bouncer
vie [vi] *nf* life; **être en ~** to be alive; **sans ~** lifeless; **à ~** for life
vieil [vjɛj] *adj m voir* **vieux**; **vieillard** *nm* old man; **les vieillards** old people, the elderly; **vieille** *adj, nf voir* **vieux**; **vieilleries** *nfpl* old things; **vieillesse** *nf* old age; **vieillir** *vi* (*prendre de l'âge*) to grow old; (*population, vin*) to age; (*doctrine, auteur*) to become dated ♦ *vt* to age; **vieillissement** *nm* growing old; ageing
Vienne [vjɛn] *nf* Vienna
viens [vjɛ̃] *vb voir* **venir**
vierge [vjɛrʒ] *adj* virgin; (*page*) clean, blank ♦ *nf* virgin; (*signe*): **la V~** Virgo
Vietnam, Viet-Nam [vjɛtnam] *nm* Vietnam; **vietnamien, ne** *adj* Vietnamese ♦ *nm/f*: **Vietnamien, ne** Vietnamese
vieux (vieil), vieille [vjø, vjɛj] *adj* old ♦ *nm/f* old man (woman) ♦ *nmpl* old people; **mon ~/ma vieille** (*fam*) old man/girl; **prendre un coup de ~** to put years on; **vieille fille** spinster; **~ garçon** bachelor; **~ jeu** *adj inv* old-fashioned
vif, vive [vif, viv] *adj* (*animé*) lively; (*alerte, brusque, aigu*) sharp; (*lumière, couleur*) bright; (*air*) crisp; (*vent, émotion*) keen; (*fort: regret, déception*) great, deep; (*vivant*): **brûlé ~** burnt alive; **de vive voix** personally; **avoir l'esprit ~** to be quick-witted; **piquer qn au ~** to cut sb to the quick; **à ~** (*plaie*) open; **avoir les nerfs à ~** to be on edge
vigne [viɲ] *nf* (*plante*) vine; (*plantation*) vineyard; **vigneron** *nm* wine grower
vignette [viɲɛt] *nf* (*ADMIN*) ≈ (road) tax disc (*BRIT*), ≈ license plate sticker (*US*); (*de médicament*) price label (*used for reimburse-*

ment)

vignoble [viɲɔbl] *nm* (*plantation*) vineyard; (*vignes d'une région*) vineyards *pl*
vigoureux, -euse [viguRø, øz] *adj* vigorous, robust
vigueur [vigœR] *nf* vigour; **entrer en ~** to come into force; **en ~** current
vil, e [vil] *adj* vile, base
vilain, e [vilɛ̃, ɛn] *adj* (*laid*) ugly; (*affaire, blessure*) nasty; (*pas sage: enfant*) naughty
villa [villa] *nf* (*detached*) house; **~ en multipropriété** time-share villa
village [vilaʒ] *nm* village; **villageois, e** *adj* village *cpd* ♦ *nm/f* villager
ville [vil] *nf* town; (*importante*) city; (*administration*): **la ~** ≈ the Corporation; ≈ the (town) council; **~ d'eaux** spa
villégiature [vi(l)leʒjatyR] *nf* holiday; (**lieu de**) **~** (holiday) resort
vin [vɛ̃] *nm* wine; **avoir le ~ gai** to get happy after a few drinks; **~ d'honneur** reception (*with wine and snacks*); **~ de pays** local wine; **~ ordinaire** table wine
vinaigre [vinɛgR] *nm* vinegar; **vinaigrette** *nf* vinaigrette, French dressing
vindicatif, -ive [vɛ̃dikatif, iv] *adj* vindictive
vineux, -euse [vinø, øz] *adj* win(e)y
vingt [vɛ̃] *num* twenty; **vingtaine** *nf*: **une vingtaine (de)** about twenty, twenty or so; **vingtième** *num* twentieth
vinicole [vinikɔl] *adj* wine *cpd*, winegrowing
vins *etc* [vɛ̃] *vb voir* **venir**
vinyle [vinil] *nm* vinyl
viol [vjɔl] *nm* (*d'une femme*) rape; (*d'un lieu sacré*) violation
violacé, e [vjɔlase] *adj* purplish, mauvish
violemment [vjɔlamɑ̃] *adv* violently
violence [vjɔlɑ̃s] *nf* violence
violent, e [vjɔlɑ̃, ɑ̃t] *adj* violent; (*remède*) drastic
violer [vjɔle] *vt* (*femme*) to rape; (*sépulture, loi, traité*) to violate
violet, te [vjɔlɛ, ɛt] *adj, nm* purple, mauve; **violette** *nf* (*fleur*) violet

violon [vjɔlɔ̃] *nm* violin; (*fam: prison*) lock-up; **~ d'Ingres** hobby; **violoncelle** *nm* cello; **violoniste** *nm/f* violinist

vipère [vipɛʀ] *nf* viper, adder

virage [viʀaʒ] *nm* (*d'un véhicule*) turn; (*d'une route, piste*) bend

virée [viʀe] *nf* trip; (*à pied*) walk; (*longue*) walking tour; (*dans les cafés*) tour

virement [viʀmɑ̃] *nm* (COMM) transfer

virent [viʀ] *vb voir* **voir**

virer [viʀe] *vt* (COMM): **~ qch (sur)** to transfer sth (into); (*fam: expulser*): **~ qn** to kick sb out ♦ *vi* to turn; (CHIMIE) to change colour; **~ de bord** to tack

virevolter [viʀvɔlte] *vi* to twirl around

virgule [viʀgyl] *nf* comma; (MATH) point

viril, e [viʀil] *adj* (*propre à l'homme*) masculine; (*énergique, courageux*) manly, virile

virtuel, le [viʀtɥɛl] *adj* potential; (*théorique*) virtual

virtuose [viʀtɥoz] *nm/f* (MUS) virtuoso; (*gén*) master

virus [viʀys] *nm* virus

vis¹ [vi] *vb voir* **voir**; **vivre**

vis² [vi] *nf* screw

visa [viza] *nm* (*sceau*) stamp; (*validation de passeport*) visa

visage [vizaʒ] *nm* face

vis-à-vis [vizavi] *prép*: **~-~-~ de qn** to(wards) sb; **en ~-~-~** facing each other

viscéral, e, -aux [viseʀal, o] *adj* (*fig*) deep-seated, deep-rooted

visées [vize] *nfpl* (*intentions*) designs

viser [vize] *vi* to aim ♦ *vt* to aim at; (*concerner*) to be aimed *ou* directed at; (*apposer un visa sur*) to stamp, visa; **~ à qch/faire** to aim at sth/at doing *ou* to do; **viseur** *nm* (*d'arme*) sights *pl*; (PHOTO) viewfinder

visibilité [vizibilite] *nf* visibility

visible [vizibl] *adj* visible; (*disponible*): **est-il ~?** can he see me?, will he see visitors?

visière [vizjɛʀ] *nf* (*de casquette*) peak; (*qui s'attache*) eyeshade

vision [vizjɔ̃] *nf* vision; (*sens*) (eye)sight, vision; (*fait de voir*): **la ~ de** the sight of; **visionneuse** *nf* viewer

visite [vizit] *nf* visit; **~ médicale** medical examination; **~ accompagnée** *ou* **guidée** guided tour; **faire une ~ à qn** to call on sb, pay sb a visit; **rendre ~ à qn** to visit sb, pay sb a visit; **être en ~ (chez qn)** to be visiting (sb); **avoir de la ~** to have visitors; **heures de ~** (*hôpital, prison*) visiting hours

visiter [vizite] *vt* to visit; **visiteur, -euse** *nm/f* visitor

vison [vizɔ̃] *nm* mink

visser [vise] *vt*: **~ qch** (*fixer, serrer*) to screw sth on

visuel, le [vizɥɛl] *adj* visual

vit [vi] *vb voir* **voir**; **vivre**

vital, e, -aux [vital, o] *adj* vital

vitamine [vitamin] *nf* vitamin

vite [vit] *adv* (*rapidement*) quickly, fast; (*sans délai*) quickly; (*sous peu*) soon; **~!** quick!; **faire ~** to be quick; **le temps passe ~** time flies

vitesse [vites] *nf* speed; (AUTO: *dispositif*) gear; **prendre de la ~** to pick up *ou* gather speed; **à toute ~** at full *ou* top speed; **en ~** (*rapidement*) quickly; (*en hâte*) in a hurry

viticole [vitikɔl] *adj* wine *cpd*, wine-growing; **viticulteur** *nm* wine grower

vitrage [vitʀaʒ] *nm*: **double ~** double glazing

vitrail, -aux [vitʀaj, o] *nm* stained-glass window

vitre [vitʀ] *nf* (*window*) pane; (*de portière, voiture*) window; **vitré, e** *adj* glass *cpd*; **vitrer** *vt* to glaze; **vitreux, -euse** *adj* (*terne*) glassy

vitrine [vitʀin] *nf* (*shop*) window; (*petite armoire*) display cabinet; **en ~** in the window; **~ publicitaire** display case, showcase

vivable [vivabl] *adj* (*personne*) livable-with; (*maison*) fit to live in

vivace [vivas] *adj* (*arbre, plante*) hardy; (*fig*) indestructible, inveterate

vivacité [vivasite] *nf* liveliness, vivacity

vivant, e [vivã, ãt] *adj (qui vit)* living, alive; *(animé)* lively; *(preuve, exemple)* living ♦ *nm*: **du ~ de qn** in sb's lifetime; **les ~s** the living

vive [viv] *adj voir* **vif** ♦ *vb voir* **vivre** ♦ *excl*: **~ le roi!** long live the king!; **vivement** *adv* deeply ♦ *excl*: **vivement les vacances!** roll on the holidays!

vivier [vivje] *nm (étang)* fish tank; *(réservoir)* fishpond

vivifiant, e [vivifjã, jãt] *adj* invigorating

vivions [vivjɔ̃] *vb voir* **vivre**

vivoter [vivɔte] *vi (personne)* to scrape a living, get by; *(fig: affaire etc)* to struggle along

vivre [vivʀ] *vi, vt* to live; *(période)* to live through; **~ de** to live on; **il vit encore** he is still alive; **se laisser ~** to take life as it comes; **ne plus ~** *(être anxieux)* to live on one's nerves; **il a vécu** *(eu une vie aventureuse)* he has seen life; **être facile à ~** to be easy to get on with; **faire ~ qn** *(pourvoir à sa subsistance)* to provide (a living) for sb; **vivres** *nmpl* provisions, food supplies

vlan [vlã] *excl* wham!, bang!

VO [veo] *nf*: **film en ~** film in the original version; **en ~ sous-titrée** in the original version with subtitles

vocable [vɔkabl] *nm* term

vocabulaire [vɔkabylɛʀ] *nm* vocabulary

vocation [vɔkasjɔ̃] *nf* vocation, calling

vociférer [vɔsifeʀe] *vi, vt* to scream

vœu, x [vø] *nm* wish; *(promesse)* vow; **faire ~ de** to take a vow of; **tous nos ~x de bonne année, meilleurs ~x** best wishes for the New Year

vogue [vɔg] *nf* fashion, vogue

voguer [vɔge] *vi* to sail

voici [vwasi] *prép (pour introduire, désigner)* here is +*sg*, here are +*pl*; **et ~ que ...** and now it *(ou* he) ...; *voir aussi* **voilà**

voie [vwa] *nf* way; *(RAIL)* track, line; *(AUTO)* lane; **être en bonne ~** to be going well; **mettre qn sur la ~** to put sb on the right track; **pays en ~ de développe-**

ment developing country; **être en ~ d'achèvement/de rénovation** to be nearing completion/in the process of renovation; **par ~ buccale** *ou* **orale** orally; **à ~ étroite** narrow-gauge; **~ d'eau** *(NAVIG)* leak; **~ de garage** *(RAIL)* siding; **~ ferrée** track; railway line; **la ~ publique** the public highway

voilà [vwala] *prép (en désignant)* there is +*sg*, there are +*pl*; **les ~** *ou* **voici** here *ou* there they are; **en ~** *ou* **voici un** here's one, there's one; **voici mon frère et ~ ma sœur** this is my brother and that's my sister; **~** *ou* **voici deux ans** two years ago; **~** *ou* **voici deux ans que** it's two years since; **et ~!** there we are!; **~ tout** that's all; **~** *ou* **voici** *(en offrant etc)* there *ou* here you are; **tiens! ~ Paul** look! there's Paul

voile [vwal] *nm* veil; *(tissu léger)* net ♦ *nf* sail; *(sport)* sailing; **voiler** *vt* to veil; *(fausser: roue)* to buckle; (: *bois)* to warp; **se voiler** *vi (lune, regard)* to mist over; *(voix)* to become husky; *(roue, disque)* to buckle; *(planche)* to warp; **voilier** *nm* sailing ship; *(de plaisance)* sailing boat; **voilure** *nf (de voilier)* sails *pl*

voir [vwaʀ] *vi, vt* to see; **se ~** *vt (être visible)* to show; *(se fréquenter)* to see each other; *(se produire)* to happen; **se ~ critiquer/transformer** to be criticized/transformed; **cela se voit** *(c'est visible)* that's obvious, it shows; **faire ~ qch à qn** to show sb sth; **en faire ~ à qn** *(fig)* to give sb a hard time; **ne pas pouvoir ~ qn** not to be able to stand sb; **voyons!** let's see now; *(indignation etc)* come on!; **avoir quelque chose à ~ avec** to have something to do with

voire [vwaʀ] *adv* even

voisin, e [vwazɛ̃, in] *adj (proche)* neighbouring; *(contigu)* next; *(ressemblant)* connected ♦ *nm/f* neighbour; **voisinage** *nm (proximité)* proximity; *(environs)* vicinity; *(quartier, voisins)* neighbourhood

voiture [vwatyʀ] *nf* car; *(wagon)* coach,

carriage; ~ **de course** racing car; ~ **de sport** sports car

voix [vwa] *nf* voice; (*POL*) vote; **à haute ~** aloud; **à ~ basse** in a low voice; **à 2/4 ~** (*MUS*) in 2/4 parts; **avoir ~ au chapitre** to have a say in the matter

vol [vɔl] *nm* (*d'oiseau, d'avion*) flight; (*larcin*) theft; ~ **régulier** scheduled flight; **à d'oiseau** as the crow flies; **au ~: attraper qch au ~** to catch sth as it flies past; **en ~** in flight; ~ **à main armée** armed robbery; ~ **à voile** gliding; ~ **libre** hang-gliding

volage [vɔlaʒ] *adj* fickle

volaille [vɔlaj] *nf* (*oiseaux*) poultry *pl*; (*viande*) poultry *no pl*; (*oiseau*) fowl

volant, e [vɔlɑ̃, ɑ̃t] *adj voir* **feuille** *etc*
♦ *nm* (*d'automobile*) (steering) wheel; (*de commande*) wheel; (*objet lancé*) shuttlecock; (*bande de tissu*) flounce

volcan [vɔlkɑ̃] *nm* volcano

volée [vɔle] *nf* (*TENNIS*) volley; **à la ~: rattraper à la ~** to catch in mid-air; **à toute ~** (*sonner les cloches*) vigorously; (*lancer un projectile*) with full force; ~ **de coups/de flèches** volley of blows/arrows

voler [vɔle] *vi* (*avion, oiseau, fig*) to fly; (*voleur*) to steal ♦ *vt* (*objet*) to steal; (*personne*) to rob; ~ **qch à qn** to steal sth from sb; **il ne l'a pas volé!** he asked for it!

volet [vɔlɛ] *nm* (*de fenêtre*) shutter; (*de feuillet, document*) section

voleur, -euse [vɔlœʀ, øz] *nm/f* thief ♦ *adj* thieving; **"au ~!"** "stop thief!"

volière [vɔljɛʀ] *nf* aviary

volley [vɔlɛ] *nm* volleyball

volontaire [vɔlɔ̃tɛʀ] *adj* (*acte, enrôlement, prisonnier*) voluntary; (*oubli*) intentional; (*caractère, personne: décidé*) self-willed ♦ *nm/f* volunteer

volonté [vɔlɔ̃te] *nf* (*faculté de vouloir*) will; (*énergie, fermeté*) will(power); (*souhait, désir*) wish; **à ~** as much as one likes; **bonne ~** goodwill, willingness; **mauvaise ~** lack of goodwill, unwillingness

volontiers [vɔlɔ̃tje] *adv* (*avec plaisir*) willingly, gladly; (*habituellement, souvent*) readily, willingly; **voulez-vous boire quelque chose? - ~!** would you like something to drink? - yes, please!

volt [vɔlt] *nm* volt

volte-face [vɔltəfas] *nf inv*: **faire ~-~** to turn round

voltige [vɔltiʒ] *nf* (*ÉQUITATION*) trick riding; (*au cirque*) acrobatics *sg*; **voltiger** *vi* to flutter (about)

volubile [vɔlybil] *adj* voluble

volume [vɔlym] *nm* volume; (*GÉOM: solide*) solid; **volumineux, -euse** *adj* voluminous, bulky

volupté [vɔlypte] *nf* sensual delight *ou* pleasure

vomi [vɔmi] *nm* vomit; **vomir** *vi* to vomit, be sick ♦ *vt* to vomit, bring up; (*fig*) to belch out, spew out; (*exécrer*) to loathe, abhor; **vomissements** *nmpl*: **être pris de vomissements** to (suddenly) start vomiting

vont [vɔ̃] *vb voir* **aller**

vorace [vɔʀas] *adj* voracious

vos [vo] *adj voir* **votre**

vote [vɔt] *nm* vote; ~ **par correspondance/procuration** postal/proxy vote; **voter** *vi* to vote ♦ *vt* (*projet de loi*) to vote for; (*loi, réforme*) to pass

votre [vɔtʀ] (*pl* **vos**) *adj* your

vôtre [votʀ] *pron*: **le ~, la ~, les ~s** yours; **les ~s** (*fig*) your family *ou* folks; **à la ~** (*toast*) your (good) health!

voudrai *etc* [vudʀe] *vb voir* **vouloir**

voué, e [vwe] *adj*: ~ **à** doomed to

vouer [vwe] *vt*: ~ **qch à** (*Dieu, un saint*) to dedicate sth to; ~ **sa vie à** (*étude, cause etc*) to devote one's life to; ~ **une amitié éternelle à qn** to vow undying friendship to sb

---

MOT-CLÉ

---

vouloir [vulwaʀ] *nm*: **le bon vouloir de qn** sb's goodwill; sb's pleasure
♦ *vt* **1** (*exiger, désirer*) to want; **vouloir**

faire/**que qn fasse** to want to do/sb to do; **voulez-vous du thé?** would you like *ou* do you want some tea?; **que me veut-il?** what does he want with 'me?; **sans le vouloir** (*involontairement*) without meaning to, unintentionally; **je voudrais ceci/faire** I would *ou* I'd like this/to do
2 (*consentir*): **je veux bien** (*bonne volonté*) I'll be happy to; (*concession*) fair enough, that's fine; **oui, si on veut** (*en quelque sorte*) yes, if you like; **veuillez attendre** please wait; **veuillez agréer ...** (*formule épistolaire*) yours faithfully
3: **en vouloir à qn** to bear a grudge; **s'en vouloir (de)** to be annoyed with o.s. (for); **il en veut à mon argent** he's after my money
4: **vouloir de: l'entreprise ne veut plus de lui** the firm doesn't want him any more; **elle ne veut pas de son aide** she doesn't want his help
5: **vouloir dire** to mean

voulu, e [vuly] *adj* (*requis*) required, requisite; (*délibéré*) deliberate, intentional; *voir aussi* **vouloir**
vous [vu] *pron* you; (*objet indirect*) (to) you; (*réfléchi: sg*) yourself; (: *pl*) yourselves; (*réciproque*) each other; **~-même** yourself; **~-mêmes** yourselves
voûte [vut] *nf* vault; **voûter**: **se voûter** *vi* (*dos, personne*) to become stooped
vouvoyer [vuvwaje] *vt*: **~ qn** to address sb as "vous"
voyage [vwajaʒ] *nm* journey, trip; (*fait de* ~*r*): **le ~** travel(ling); **partir/être en ~** to go off/be away on a journey *ou* trip; **faire bon ~** to have a good journey; **~ d'agrément/d'affaires** pleasure/business trip; **~ de noces** honeymoon; **~ organisé** package tour
voyager [vwajaʒe] *vi* to travel; **voyageur, -euse** *nm/f* traveller; (*passager*) passenger
voyant, e [vwajɑ̃, ɑ̃t] *adj* (*couleur*) loud, gaudy ♦ *nm* (*signal*) (warning) light; **voyante** *nf* clairvoyant

voyelle [vwajɛl] *nf* vowel
voyons *etc* [vwajɔ̃] *vb voir* **voir**
voyou [vwaju] *nm* hooligan
vrac [vʀak]: **en ~** *adv* (*au détail*) loose; (*en gros*) in bulk; (*en désordre*) in a jumble
vrai, e [vʀɛ] *adj* (*véridique: récit, faits*) true; (*non factice, authentique*) real; **à ~ dire** to tell the truth; **vraiment** *adv* really; **vraisemblable** *adj* likely; (*excuse*) convincing; **vraisemblablement** *adj* probably; **vraisemblance** *nf* likelihood; (*romanesque*) verisimilitude
vrille [vʀij] *nf* (*de plante*) tendril; (*outil*) gimlet; (*spirale*) spiral; (*AVIAT*) spin
vrombir [vʀɔ̃biʀ] *vi* to hum
VRP *sigle m* (= *voyageur, représentant, placier*) sales rep (*fam*)
VTT *sigle m* (= *vélo tout-terrain*) mountain bike
vu, e [vy] *pp de* **voir** ♦ *adj*: **bien/mal ~** (*fig: personne*) popular/unpopular; (: *chose*) approved/disapproved of ♦ *prép* (*en raison de*) in view of; **~ que** in view of the fact that
vue [vy] *nf* (*fait de voir*): **la ~ de** the sight of; (*sens, faculté*) (eye)sight; (*panorama, image, photo*) view; **~s** *nfpl* (*idées*) views; (*dessein*) designs; **hors de ~** out of sight; **avoir en ~** to have in mind; **tirer à ~** to shoot on sight; **à ~ d'œil** visibly; **de ~** by sight; **perdre de ~** to lose sight of; **en ~** (*visible*) in sight; (*célèbre*) in the public eye; **en ~ de faire** with a view to doing
vulgaire [vylgɛʀ] *adj* (*grossier*) vulgar, coarse; (*ordinaire*) commonplace, mundane; (*péj: quelconque*) **de ~s touristes** common tourists; (*BOT, ZOOL: non latin*) common; **vulgariser** *vt* to popularize
vulnérable [vylneʀabl] *adj* vulnerable

W, w

wagon [vagɔ̃] *nm* (*de voyageurs*) carriage; (*de marchandises*) truck, wagon; **wagon-lit** *nm* sleeper, sleeping car; **wagon-restaurant** *nm* restaurant *ou* dining car

wallon, ne [walɔ̃, ɔn] *adj* Walloon

waters [watɛʀ] *nmpl* toilet *sg*

watt [wat] *nm* watt

WC *sigle mpl* (= *water-closet(s)*) toilet

Web [wɛb] *nm inv*: **le ~** the (World Wide) Web

week-end [wikɛnd] *nm* weekend

western [wɛstɛʀn] *nm* western

whisky [wiski] (*pl* **whiskies**) *nm* whisky

X, x

xénophobe [gzenɔfɔb] *adj* xenophobic ♦ *nm/f* xenophobe

xérès [gzeʀɛs] *nm* sherry

xylophone [gzilɔfɔn] *nm* xylophone

Y, y

y [i] *adv* (*à cet endroit*) there; (*dessus*) on it (*ou* them); (*dedans*) in it (*ou* them) ♦ *pron* (*about ou* on *ou* of) it (*d'après le verbe employé*); **j'~ pense** I'm thinking about it; **ça ~ est!** that's it!; *voir aussi* **aller**; **avoir**

yacht [jɔt] *nm* yacht

yaourt [jauʀt] *nm* yoghourt; **~ nature/aux fruits** plain/fruit yogurt

yeux [jø] *nmpl de* **œil**

yoga [jɔga] *nm* yoga

yoghourt [jɔguʀt] *nm* = **yaourt**

yougoslave [jugɔslav] (*HISTOIRE*) *adj* Yugoslav(ian) ♦ *nm/f*: **Y~** Yugoslav

Yougoslavie [jugɔslavi] (*HISTOIRE*) *nf* Yugoslavia

Z, z

zapper [zape] *vi* to zap

zapping [zapiŋ] *nm*: **faire du ~** to flick through the channels

zèbre [zɛbʀ(ə)] *nm* (*ZOOL*) zebra; **zébré, e** *adj* striped, streaked

zèle [zɛl] *nm* zeal; **faire du ~** (*péj*) to be over-zealous; **zélé, e** *adj* zealous

zéro [zeʀo] *nm* zero, nought (*BRIT*); **au-dessous de ~** below zero (Centigrade) *ou* freezing; **partir de ~** to start from scratch; **trois (buts) à ~** 3 (goals to) nil

zeste [zɛst] *nm* peel, zest

zézayer [zezeje] *vi* to have a lisp

zigzag [zigzag] *nm* zigzag; **zigzaguer** *vi* to zigzag

zinc [zɛ̃g] *nm* (*CHIMIE*) zinc

zizanie [zizani] *nf*: **semer la ~** to stir up ill-feeling

zizi [zizi] *nm* (*langage enfantin*) willy

zodiaque [zɔdjak] *nm* zodiac

zona [zona] *nm* shingles *sg*

zone [zon] *nf* zone, area; **~ bleue** ≃ restricted parking area; **~ industrielle** industrial estate

zoo [zo(o)] *nm* zoo

zoologie [zɔɔlɔʒi] *nf* zoology; **zoologique** *adj* zoological

zut [zyt] *excl* dash (it)! (*BRIT*), nuts! (*US*)

VERB TABLES

Introduction

The **Verb Tables** in the following section contain 32 tables of French verbs (some regular and some irregular) in alphabetical order. Each table shows you the following forms: **Present, Perfect, Future, Subjunctive, Imperfect, Conditional, Imperative** and the **Present** and **Past Participles**.

In order to help you use the verbs shown in Verb Tables correctly, there are also a number of example phrases at the bottom of each page to show the verb as it is used in context.

In French there are both **regular** verbs (their forms follow the normal rules) and **irregular** verbs (their forms do not follow the normal rules). The regular verbs in these tables are:

donner (regular -er verb, Verb Table 11)
finir (regular -ir verb, Verb Table 16)
attendre (regular -re verb, Verb Table 3)

The irregular verbs are shown in full.

For a further list of French irregular verb forms see pages 585–588.

▶ aller (to go)

PRESENT

je	vais
tu	vas
il/elle/on	va
nous	allons
vous	allez
ils/elles	vont

PRESENT SUBJUNCTIVE

j'	aille
tu	ailles
il/elle/on	aille
nous	allions
vous	alliez
ils/elles	aillent

PERFECT

je	suis allé(e)
tu	es allé(e)
il/elle/on	est allé(e)
nous	sommes allé(e)s
vous	êtes allé(e)(s)
ils/elles	sont allé(e)s

IMPERFECT

j'	allais
tu	allais
il/elle/on	allait
nous	allions
vous	alliez
ils/elles	allaient

FUTURE

j'	irai
tu	iras
il/elle/on	ira
nous	irons
vous	irez
ils/elles	iront

CONDITIONAL

j'	irais
tu	irais
il/elle/on	irait
nous	irions
vous	iriez
ils/elles	iraient

IMPERATIVE

va / allons / allez

PAST PARTICIPLE

allé

PRESENT PARTICIPLE

allant

EXAMPLE PHRASES

*Vous **allez** au cinéma?* Are you going to the cinema?
*Je **suis allé** à Londres.* I went to London.
*Est-ce que tu **es** déjà **allé** en Allemagne?* Have you ever been to Germany?

---

je/j' = I **tu** = you **il** = he/it **elle** = she/it **on** = we/one **nous** = we **vous** = you **ils/elles** = they

▶ **attendre** (to wait)

PRESENT

j'	attends
tu	attends
il/elle/on	attend
nous	attendons
vous	attendez
ils/elles	attendent

PRESENT SUBJUNCTIVE

j'	attende
tu	attendes
il/elle/on	attende
nous	attendions
vous	attendiez
ils/elles	attendent

PERFECT

j'	ai attendu
tu	as attendu
il/elle/on	a attendu
nous	avons attendu
vous	avez attendu
ils/elles	ont attendu

IMPERFECT

j'	attendais
tu	attendais
il/elle/on	attendait
nous	attendions
vous	attendiez
ils/elles	attendaient

FUTURE

j'	attendrai
tu	attendras
il/elle/on	attendra
nous	attendrons
vous	attendrez
ils/elles	attendront

CONDITIONAL

j'	attendrais
tu	attendrais
il/elle/on	attendrait
nous	attendrions
vous	attendriez
ils/elles	attendraient

IMPERATIVE

attends / attendons / attendez

PAST PARTICIPLE

attendu

PRESENT PARTICIPLE

attendant

EXAMPLE PHRASES

***Attends**-moi!* Wait for me!
*Tu **attends** depuis longtemps?* Have you been waiting long?
*Je l'**ai attendu** à la poste.* I waited for him at the post office.
*Je m'**attends** à ce qu'il soit en retard.* I expect he'll be late.

je/j' = I **tu** = you **il** = he/it **elle** = she/it **on** = we/one **nous** = we **vous** = you **ils/elles** = they

▶ **avoir** (to have)

PRESENT

j'	ai
tu	as
il/elle/on	a
nous	avons
vous	avez
ils/elles	ont

PRESENT SUBJUNCTIVE

j'	aie
tu	aies
il/elle/on	ait
nous	ayons
vous	ayez
ils/elles	aient

PERFECT

j'	ai eu
tu	as eu
il/elle/on	a eu
nous	avons eu
vous	avez eu
ils/elles	ont eu

IMPERFECT

j'	avais
tu	avais
il/elle/on	avait
nous	avions
vous	aviez
ils/elles	avaient

FUTURE

j'	aurai
tu	auras
il/elle/on	aura
nous	aurons
vous	aurez
ils/elles	auront

CONDITIONAL

j'	aurais
tu	aurais
il/elle/on	aurait
nous	aurions
vous	auriez
ils/elles	auraient

IMPERATIVE

aie / ayons / ayez

PAST PARTICIPLE

eu

PRESENT PARTICIPLE

ayant

EXAMPLE PHRASES

*Il **a** les yeux bleus.* He's got blue eyes.
*Quel âge **as**-tu?* How old are you?
*Il **a eu** un accident.* He's had an accident.
*J'**avais** faim.* I was hungry.
*Il y **a** beaucoup de monde.* There are lots of people.

---

je/j' = I   **tu** = you   **il** = he/it   **elle** = she/it   **on** = we/one   **nous** = we   **vous** = you   **ils/elles** = they

▶ **boire** (to drink)

PRESENT

je	bois
tu	bois
il/elle/on	boit
nous	buvons
vous	buvez
ils/elles	boivent

PRESENT SUBJUNCTIVE

je	boive
tu	boives
il/elle/on	boive
nous	buvions
vous	buviez
ils/elles	boivent

PERFECT

j'	ai bu
tu	as bu
il/elle/on	a bu
nous	avons bu
vous	avez bu
ils/elles	ont bu

IMPERFECT

je	buvais
tu	buvais
il/elle/on	buvait
nous	buvions
vous	buviez
ils/elles	buvaient

FUTURE

je	boirai
tu	boiras
il/elle/on	boira
nous	boirons
vous	boirez
ils/elles	boiront

CONDITIONAL

je	boirais
tu	boirais
il/elle/on	boirait
nous	boirions
vous	boiriez
ils/elles	boiraient

IMPERATIVE

bois / buvons / buvez

PAST PARTICIPLE

bu

PRESENT PARTICIPLE

buvant

EXAMPLE PHRASES

Qu'est-ce que tu veux boire? What would you like to drink?
Il ne boit jamais d'alcool. He never drinks alcohol.
J'ai bu un litre d'eau. I drank a litre of water.

je/j' = I **tu** = you **il** = he/it **elle** = she/it **on** = we/one **nous** = we **vous** = you **ils/elles** = they

▶ connaître (to know)

PRESENT

je	connais
tu	connais
il/elle/on	connaît
nous	connaissons
vous	connaissez
ils/elles	connaissent

PRESENT SUBJUNCTIVE

je	connaisse
tu	connaisses
il/elle/on	connaisse
nous	connaissions
vous	connaissiez
ils/elles	connaissent

PERFECT

j'	ai connu
tu	as connu
il/elle/on	a connu
nous	avons connu
vous	avez connu
ils/elles	ont connu

IMPERFECT

je	connaissais
tu	connaissais
il/elle/on	connaissait
nous	connaissions
vous	connaissiez
ils/elles	connaissaient

FUTURE

je	connaîtrai
tu	connaîtras
il/elle/on	connaîtra
nous	connaîtrons
vous	connaîtrez
ils/elles	connaîtront

CONDITIONAL

je	connaîtrais
tu	connaîtrais
il/elle/on	connaîtrait
nous	connaîtrions
vous	connaîtriez
ils/elles	connaîtraient

IMPERATIVE

connais / connaissons / connaissez

PAST PARTICIPLE

connu

PRESENT PARTICIPLE

connaissant

EXAMPLE PHRASES

*Je ne **connais** pas du tout cette région.* I don't know the area at all.
*Vous **connaissez** M Amiot?* Do you know Mr Amiot?
*Il n'a pas **connu** son grand-père.* He never knew his granddad.
*Ils **se sont connus** à Rouen.* They first met in Rouen.

▶ **courir** (to run)

PRESENT

je	cours
tu	cours
il/elle/on	court
nous	courons
vous	courez
ils/elles	courent

PRESENT SUBJUNCTIVE

je	coure
tu	coures
il/elle/on	coure
nous	courions
vous	couriez
ils/elles	courent

PERFECT

j'	ai couru
tu	as couru
il/elle/on	a couru
nous	avons couru
vous	avez couru
ils/elles	ont couru

IMPERFECT

je	courais
tu	courais
il/elle/on	courait
nous	courions
vous	couriez
ils/elles	couraient

FUTURE

je	courrai
tu	courras
il/elle/on	courra
nous	courrons
vous	courrez
ils/elles	courront

CONDITIONAL

je	courrais
tu	courrais
il/elle/on	courrait
nous	courrions
vous	courriez
ils/elles	courraient

IMPERATIVE

cours / courons / courez

PRESENT PARTICIPLE

courant

PAST PARTICIPLE

couru

EXAMPLE PHRASES

*Je ne **cours** pas très vite.* I can't run very fast.
*Elle est sortie en **courant**.* She ran out.
*Ne **courez** pas dans le couloir.* Don't run in the corridor.
*J'**ai couru** jusqu'à l'école.* I ran all the way to school.

---

je/j' = I **tu** = you **il** = he/it **elle** = she/it **on** = we/one **nous** = we **vous** = you **ils/elles** = they

▶ croire (to believe)

PRESENT

je	crois
tu	crois
il/elle/on	croit
nous	croyons
vous	croyez
ils/elles	croient

PRESENT SUBJUNCTIVE

je	croie
tu	croies
il/elle/on	croie
nous	croyions
vous	croyiez
ils/elles	croient

PERFECT

j'	ai cru
tu	as cru
il/elle/on	a cru
nous	avons cru
vous	avez cru
ils/elles	ont cru

IMPERFECT

je	croyais
tu	croyais
il/elle/on	croyait
nous	croyions
vous	croyiez
ils/elles	croyaient

FUTURE

je	croirai
tu	croiras
il/elle/on	croira
nous	croirons
vous	croirez
ils/elles	croiront

CONDITIONAL

je	croirais
tu	croirais
il/elle/on	croirait
nous	croirions
vous	croiriez
ils/elles	croiraient

IMPERATIVE

crois / croyons / croyez

PAST PARTICIPLE

cru

PRESENT PARTICIPLE

croyant

EXAMPLE PHRASES

*Je ne te **crois** pas.* I don't believe you.
*J'**ai cru** que tu n'allais pas venir.* I thought you weren't going to come.
*Elle **croyait** encore au père Noël.* She still believed in Santa.

---

je/j' = I **tu** = you **il** = he/it **elle** = she/it **on** = we/one **nous** = we **vous** = you **ils/elles** = they

▶ **devoir** (to have to; to owe)

PRESENT

je	dois
tu	dois
il/elle/on	doit
nous	devons
vous	devez
ils/elles	doivent

PRESENT SUBJUNCTIVE

je	doive
tu	doives
il/elle/on	doive
nous	devions
vous	deviez
ils/elles	doivent

PERFECT

j'	ai dû
tu	as dû
il/elle/on	a dû
nous	avons dû
vous	avez dû
ils/elles	ont dû

IMPERFECT

je	devais
tu	devais
il/elle/on	devait
nous	devions
vous	deviez
ils/elles	devaient

FUTURE

je	devrai
tu	devras
il/elle/on	devra
nous	devrons
vous	devrez
ils/elles	devront

CONDITIONAL

je	devrais
tu	devrais
il/elle/on	devrait
nous	devrions
vous	devriez
ils/elles	devraient

IMPERATIVE

dois / devons / devez

PAST PARTICIPLE

dû (*NB*: due, dus, dues)

PRESENT PARTICIPLE

devant

EXAMPLE PHRASES

*Je **dois** aller faire les courses ce matin.* I have to do the shopping this morning.
*À quelle heure est-ce que tu **dois** partir?* What time do you have to leave?
*Il **a dû** faire ses devoirs hier soir.* He had to do his homework last night.
*Il **devait** prendre le train pour aller travailler.* He had to go to work by train.

je/j' = I **tu** = you **il** = he/it **elle** = she/it **on** = we/one **nous** = we **vous** = you **ils/elles** = they

▶ **dire** (to say)

PRESENT

je	dis
tu	dis
il/elle/on	dit
nous	disons
vous	dites
ils/elles	disent

PRESENT SUBJUNCTIVE

je	dise
tu	dises
il/elle/on	dise
nous	disions
vous	disiez
ils/elles	disent

PERFECT

j'	ai dit
tu	as dit
il/elle/on	a dit
nous	avons dit
vous	avez dit
ils/elles	ont dit

IMPERFECT

je	disais
tu	disais
il/elle/on	disait
nous	disions
vous	disiez
ils/elles	disaient

FUTURE

je	dirai
tu	diras
il/elle/on	dira
nous	dirons
vous	direz
ils/elles	diront

CONDITIONAL

je	dirais
tu	dirais
il/elle/on	dirait
nous	dirions
vous	diriez
ils/elles	diraient

IMPERATIVE

dis / disons / dites

PAST PARTICIPLE

dit

PRESENT PARTICIPLE

disant

EXAMPLE PHRASES

*Qu'est-ce qu'elle **dit**?* What is she saying?
*"Bonjour!", **a-t-il dit**.* "Hello!" he said.
*Ils m'**ont dit** que le film était nul.* They told me that the film was rubbish.
*Comment ça **se dit** en anglais?* How do you say that in English?

---

je/j' = I **tu** = you **il** = he/it **elle** = she/it **on** = we/one **nous** = we **vous** = you **ils/elles** = they

▶ **donner** (to give)

PRESENT

je	donne
tu	donnes
il/elle/on	donne
nous	donnons
vous	donnez
ils/elles	donnent

PRESENT SUBJUNCTIVE

je	donne
tu	donnes
il/elle/on	donne
nous	donnions
vous	donniez
ils/elles	donnent

PERFECT

j'	ai donné
tu	as donné
il/elle/on	a donné
nous	avons donné
vous	avez donné
ils/elles	ont donné

IMPERFECT

je	donnais
tu	donnais
il/elle/on	donnait
nous	donnions
vous	donniez
ils/elles	donnaient

FUTURE

je	donnerai
tu	donneras
il/elle/on	donnera
nous	donnerons
vous	donnerez
ils/elles	donneront

CONDITIONAL

je	donnerais
tu	donnerais
il/elle/on	donnerait
nous	donnerions
vous	donneriez
ils/elles	donneraient

IMPERATIVE

donne / donnons / donnez

PAST PARTICIPLE

donné

PRESENT PARTICIPLE

donnant

EXAMPLE PHRASES

Donne-*moi la main.* Give me your hand.
*Est-ce que je t'**ai donné** mon adresse?* Did I give you my address?
*L'appartement **donne** sur la place.* The flat overlooks the square.

---

je/j' = I **tu** = you **il** = he/it **elle** = she/it **on** = we/one **nous** = we **vous** = you **ils/elles** = they

▶ **écrire** (to write)

PRESENT

j'	écris
tu	écris
il/elle/on	écrit
nous	écrivons
vous	écrivez
ils/elles	écrivent

PRESENT SUBJUNCTIVE

j'	écrive
tu	écrives
il/elle/on	écrive
nous	écrivions
vous	écriviez
ils/elles	écrivent

PERFECT

j'	ai écrit
tu	as écrit
il/elle/on	a écrit
nous	avons écrit
vous	avez écrit
ils/elles	ont écrit

IMPERFECT

j'	écrivais
tu	écrivais
il/elle/on	écrivait
nous	écrivions
vous	écriviez
ils/elles	écrivaient

FUTURE

j'	écrirai
tu	écriras
il/elle/on	écrira
nous	écrirons
vous	écrirez
ils/elles	écriront

CONDITIONAL

j'	écrirais
tu	écrirais
il/elle/on	écrirait
nous	écririons
vous	écririez
ils/elles	écriraient

IMPERATIVE

écris / écrivons / écrivez

PAST PARTICIPLE

écrit

PRESENT PARTICIPLE

écrivant

EXAMPLE PHRASES

*Tu **as écrit** à ta correspondante récemment?* Have you written to your penfriend lately?
*Elle **écrit** des romans.* She writes novels.
*Comment ça s'**écrit**, "brouillard"?* How do you spell "brouillard"?

▶ être (to be)

PRESENT

je	suis
tu	es
il/elle/on	est
nous	sommes
vous	êtes
ils/elles	sont

PRESENT SUBJUNCTIVE

je	sois
tu	sois
il/elle/on	soit
nous	soyons
vous	soyez
ils/elles	soient

PERFECT

j'	ai été
tu	as été
il/elle/on	a été
nous	avons été
vous	avez été
ils/elles	ont été

IMPERFECT

j'	étais
tu	étais
il/elle/on	était
nous	étions
vous	étiez
ils/elles	étaient

FUTURE

je	serai
tu	seras
il/elle/on	sera
nous	serons
vous	serez
ils/elles	seront

CONDITIONAL

je	serais
tu	serais
il/elle/on	serait
nous	serions
vous	seriez
ils/elles	seraient

IMPERATIVE

sois / soyons / soyez

PAST PARTICIPLE

été

PRESENT PARTICIPLE

étant

EXAMPLE PHRASES

Mon père est professeur. My father's a teacher.
Quelle heure est-il? – Il est dix heures. What time is it? – It's 10 o'clock.
Ils ne sont pas encore arrivés. They haven't arrived yet.

---

je/j' = I **tu** = you **il** = he/it **elle** = she/it **on** = we/one **nous** = we **vous** = you **ils/elles** = they

▶ **faire** (to do; to make)

PRESENT

je	fais
tu	fais
il/elle/on	fait
nous	faisons
vous	faites
ils/elles	font

PRESENT SUBJUNCTIVE

je	fasse
tu	fasses
il/elle/on	fasse
nous	fassions
vous	fassiez
ils/elles	fassent

PERFECT

j'	ai fait
tu	as fait
il/elle/on	a fait
nous	avons fait
vous	avez fait
ils/elles	ont fait

IMPERFECT

je	faisais
tu	faisais
il/elle/on	faisait
nous	faisions
vous	faisiez
ils/elles	faisaient

FUTURE

je	ferai
tu	feras
il/elle/on	fera
nous	ferons
vous	ferez
ils/elles	feront

CONDITIONAL

je	ferais
tu	ferais
il/elle/on	ferait
nous	ferions
vous	feriez
ils/elles	feraient

IMPERATIVE

fais / faisons / faites

PAST PARTICIPLE

fait

PRESENT PARTICIPLE

faisant

EXAMPLE PHRASES

*Qu'est-ce que tu **fais**?* What are you doing?
*Qu'est-ce qu'il **a fait**?* What has he done? *or* What did he do?
*J'ai **fait** un gâteau.* I've made a cake *or* I made a cake.
*Il s'est **fait** couper les cheveux.* He's had his hair cut.

---

je/j' = I **tu** = you **il** = he/it **elle** = she/it **on** = we/one **nous** = we **vous** = you **ils/elles** = they

▶ **falloir** (to be necessary)

PRESENT

il faut

PRESENT SUBJUNCTIVE

il faille

PERFECT

il a fallu

IMPERFECT

il fallait

FUTURE

il faudra

CONDITIONAL

il faudrait

IMPERATIVE

not used

PAST PARTICIPLE

fallu

PRESENT PARTICIPLE

not used

EXAMPLE PHRASES

*Il **faut** se dépêcher!* We have to hurry up!
*Il me **fallait** de l'argent.* I needed money.
*Il **faudra** que tu sois là à 8 heures.* You'll have to be there at 8.

---

je/j' = I **tu** = you **il** = he/it **elle** = she/it **on** = we/one **nous** = we **vous** = you **ils/elles** = they

▶ **finir** (to finish)

PRESENT

je	finis
tu	finis
il/elle/on	finit
nous	finissons
vous	finissez
ils/elles	finissent

PRESENT SUBJUNCTIVE

je	finisse
tu	finisses
il/elle/on	finisse
nous	finissions
vous	finissiez
ils/elles	finissent

PERFECT

j'	ai fini
tu	as fini
il/elle/on	a fini
nous	avons fini
vous	avez fini
ils/elles	ont fini

IMPERFECT

je	finissais
tu	finissais
il/elle/on	finissait
nous	finissions
vous	finissiez
ils/elles	finissaient

FUTURE

je	finirai
tu	finiras
il/elle/on	finira
nous	finirons
vous	finirez
ils/elles	finiront

CONDITIONAL

je	finirais
tu	finirais
il/elle/on	finirait
nous	finirions
vous	finiriez
ils/elles	finiraient

IMPERATIVE

finis / finissons / finissez

PAST PARTICIPLE

fini

PRESENT PARTICIPLE

finissant

EXAMPLE PHRASES

Finis ta soupe! Finish your soup!
J'ai fini! I've finished!
Je finirai mes devoirs demain. I'll finish my homework tomorrow.

▶ se laver (to wash oneself)

PRESENT

je	me lave
tu	te laves
il/elle/on	se lave
nous	nous lavons
vous	vous lavez
ils/elles	se lavent

PRESENT SUBJUNCTIVE

je	me lave
tu	te laves
il/elle/on	se lave
nous	nous lavions
vous	vous laviez
ils/elles	se lavent

PERFECT

je	me suis lavé(e)
tu	t'es lavé(e)
il/elle/on	s'est lavé(e)
nous	nous sommes lavé(e)s
vous	vous êtes lavé(e)(s)
ils/elles	se sont lavé(e)s

IMPERFECT

je	me lavais
tu	te lavais
il/elle/on	se lavait
nous	nous lavions
vous	vous laviez
ils/elles	se lavient

FUTURE

je	me laverai
tu	te laveras
il/elle/on	se lavera
nous	nous laverons
vous	vous laverez
ils/elles	se laveront

CONDITIONAL

je	me laverais
tu	te laverais
il/elle/on	se laverait
nous	nous laverions
vous	vous laveriez
ils/elles	se laveraient

IMPERATIVE

lave-toi / lavons-nous / lavez-vous

PAST PARTICIPLE

lavé(e)

PRESENT PARTICIPLE

se lavant

EXAMPLE PHRASES

Lave-toi vite, tu vas être en retard. Have a quick wash, you're going to be late.
Lavez-vous les mains avant de vous mettre à table. Wash your hands before you sit at the table.
Nous nous sommes lavé les dents puis nous sommes allés nous coucher. We cleaned our teeth and went to bed.

---

je/j' = I **tu** = you **il** = he/it **elle** = she/it **on** = we/one **nous** = we **vous** = you **ils/elles** = they

▶ lire (to read)

PRESENT

je	lis
tu	lis
il/elle/on	lit
nous	lisons
vous	lisez
ils/elles	lisent

PRESENT SUBJUNCTIVE

je	lise
tu	lises
il/elle/on	lise
nous	lisions
vous	lisiez
ils/elles	lisent

PERFECT

j'	ai lu
tu	as lu
il/elle/on	a lu
nous	avons lu
vous	avez lu
ils/elles	ont lu

IMPERFECT

je	lisais
tu	lisais
il/elle/on	lisait
nous	lisions
vous	lisiez
ils/elles	lisaient

FUTURE

je	lirai
tu	liras
il/elle/on	lira
nous	lirons
vous	lirez
ils/elles	liront

CONDITIONAL

je	lirais
tu	lirais
il/elle/on	lirait
nous	lirions
vous	liriez
ils/elles	liraient

IMPERATIVE

lis / lisons / lisez

PAST PARTICIPLE

lu

PRESENT PARTICIPLE

lisant

EXAMPLE PHRASES

*Vous **avez lu** "Madame Bovary"?* Have you read "Madame Bovary"?
*Je le **lirai** dans l'avion.* I'll read it on the plane.
*Elle lui **lisait** une histoire.* She was reading him a story.

---

je/j' = I **tu** = you **il** = he/it **elle** = she/it **on** = we/one **nous** = we **vous** = you **ils/elles** = they

▶ **mettre** (to put)

PRESENT

je	mets
tu	mets
il/elle/on	met
nous	mettons
vous	mettez
ils/elles	mettent

PRESENT SUBJUNCTIVE

je	mette
tu	mettes
il/elle/on	mette
nous	mettions
vous	mettiez
ils/elles	mettent

PERFECT

j'	ai mis
tu	as mis
il/elle/on	a mis
nous	avons mis
vous	avez mis
ils/elles	ont mis

IMPERFECT

je	mettais
tu	mettais
il/elle/on	mettait
nous	mettions
vous	mettiez
ils/elles	mettaient

FUTURE

je	mettrai
tu	mettras
il/elle/on	mettra
nous	mettrons
vous	mettrez
ils/elles	mettront

CONDITIONAL

je	mettrais
tu	mettrais
il/elle/on	mettrait
nous	mettrions
vous	mettriez
ils/elles	mettraient

IMPERATIVE

mets / mettons / mettez

PAST PARTICIPLE

mis

PRESENT PARTICIPLE

mettant

EXAMPLE PHRASES

Mets ton manteau! Put your coat on!
Où est-ce que tu as mis les clés? Where have you put the keys?
J'ai mis le livre sur la table. I put the book on the table.
Elle s'est mise à pleurer. She started crying.

---

je/j' = I   **tu** = you   **il** = he/it   **elle** = she/it   **on** = we/one   **nous** = we   **vous** = you   **ils/elles** = they

▶ mourir (to die)

PRESENT

je	meurs
tu	meurs
il/elle/on	meurt
nous	mourons
vous	mourez
ils/elles	meurent

PRESENT SUBJUNCTIVE

je	meure
tu	meures
il/elle/on	meure
nous	mourions
vous	mouriez
ils/elles	meurent

PERFECT

je	suis mort(e)
tu	es mort(e)
il/elle/on	est mort(e)
nous	sommes mort(e)s
vous	êtes mort(e)(s)
ils/elles	sont mort(e)s

IMPERFECT

je	mourais
tu	mourais
il/elle/on	mourait
nous	mourions
vous	mouriez
ils/elles	mouraient

FUTURE

je	mourrai
tu	mourras
il/elle/on	mourra
nous	mourrons
vous	mourrez
ils/elles	mourront

CONDITIONAL

je	mourrais
tu	mourrais
il/elle/on	mourrait
nous	mourrions
vous	mourriez
ils/elles	mourraient

IMPERATIVE

meurs / mourons / mourez

PAST PARTICIPLE

mort

PRESENT PARTICIPLE

mourant

EXAMPLE PHRASES

*Elle **est morte** en 1998.* She died in 1998.
*Ils **sont morts**.* They're dead.
*On **meurt** de froid ici!* We're freezing to death in here!

je/j' = I **tu** = you **il** = he/it **elle** = she/it **on** = we/one **nous** = we **vous** = you **ils/elles** = they

▶ naître (to be born)

PRESENT

je	nais
tu	nais
il/elle/on	naît
nous	naissons
vous	naissez
ils/elles	naissent

PRESENT SUBJUNCTIVE

je	naisse
tu	naisses
il/elle/on	naisse
nous	naissions
vous	naissiez
ils/elles	naissent

PERFECT

je	suis né(e)
tu	es né(e)
il/elle/on	est né(e)
nous	sommes né(e)s
vous	êtes né(e)(s)
ils/elles	sont né(e)s

IMPERFECT

je	naissais
tu	naissais
il/elle/on	naissait
nous	naissions
vous	naissiez
ils/elles	naissaient

FUTURE

je	naîtrai
tu	naîtras
il/elle/on	naîtra
nous	naîtrons
vous	naîtrez
ils/elles	naîtront

CONDITIONAL

je	naîtrais
tu	naîtrais
il/elle/on	naîtrait
nous	naîtrions
vous	naîtriez
ils/elles	naîtraient

IMPERATIVE

nais / naissons / naissez

PAST PARTICIPLE

né

PRESENT PARTICIPLE

naissant

EXAMPLE PHRASES

Je suis née le 12 février. I was born on 12 February.
Le bébé de Delphine naîtra en mars. Delphine is going to have a baby in March.
Quand est-ce que tu es né? When were you born?

---

je/j' = I **tu** = you **il** = he/it **elle** = she/it **on** = we/one **nous** = we **vous** = you **ils/elles** = they

▶ ouvrir (to open)

PRESENT

j'	ouvre
tu	ouvres
il/elle/on	ouvre
nous	ouvrons
vous	ouvrez
ils/elles	ouvrent

PRESENT SUBJUNCTIVE

j'	ouvre
tu	ouvres
il/elle/on	ouvre
nous	ouvrions
vous	ouvriez
ils/elles	ouvrent

PERFECT

j'	ai ouvert
tu	as ouvert
il/elle/on	a ouvert
nous	avons ouvert
vous	avez ouvert
ils/elles	ont ouvert

IMPERFECT

j'	ouvrais
tu	ouvrais
il/elle/on	ouvrait
nous	ouvrions
vous	ouvriez
ils/elles	ouvraient

FUTURE

j'	ouvrirai
tu	ouvriras
il/elle/on	ouvrira
nous	ouvrirons
vous	ouvrirez
ils/elles	ouvriront

CONDITIONAL

j'	ouvrirais
tu	ouvrirais
il/elle/on	ouvrirait
nous	ouvririons
vous	ouvririez
ils/elles	ouvriraient

IMPERATIVE

ouvre / ouvrons / ouvrez

PAST PARTICIPLE

ouvert

PRESENT PARTICIPLE

ouvrant

EXAMPLE PHRASES

*Elle **a ouvert** la porte.* She opened the door.
*Est-ce que tu pourrais **ouvrir** la fenêtre?* Could you open the window?
*Je me suis coupé en **ouvrant** une boîte de conserve.* I cut myself opening a tin.
*La porte s'est **ouverte**.* The door opened.

---

je/j' = I **tu** = you **il** = he/it **elle** = she/it **on** = we/one **nous** = we **vous** = you **ils/elles** = they

▶ pouvoir (to be able)

PRESENT

je	peux
tu	peux
il/elle/on	peut
nous	pouvons
vous	pouvez
ils/elles	peuvent

PRESENT SUBJUNCTIVE

je	puisse
tu	puisses
il/elle/on	puisse
nous	puissions
vous	puissiez
ils/elles	puissent

PERFECT

j'	ai pu
tu	as pu
il/elle/on	a pu
nous	avons pu
vous	avez pu
ils/elles	ont pu

IMPERFECT

je	pouvais
tu	pouvais
il/elle/on	pouvait
nous	pouvions
vous	pouviez
ils/elles	pouvaient

FUTURE

je	pourrai
tu	pourras
il/elle/on	pourra
nous	pourrons
vous	pourrez
ils/elles	pourront

CONDITIONAL

je	pourrais
tu	pourrais
il/elle/on	pourrait
nous	pourrions
vous	pourriez
ils/elles	pourraient

IMPERATIVE

not used

PAST PARTICIPLE

pu

PRESENT PARTICIPLE

pouvant

EXAMPLE PHRASES

Je **peux** t'aider, si tu veux. I can help you if you like.
J'ai fait tout ce que j'**ai pu**. I did all I could.
Je ne **pourrai** pas venir samedi. I won't be able to come on Saturday.

---

je/j' = I **tu** = you **il** = he/it **elle** = she/it **on** = we/one **nous** = we **vous** = you **ils/elles** = they

▶ **prendre** (to take)

PRESENT

je	prends
tu	prends
il/elle/on	prend
nous	prenons
vous	prenez
ils/elles	prennent

PRESENT SUBJUNCTIVE

je	prenne
tu	prennes
il/elle/on	prenne
nous	prenions
vous	preniez
ils/elles	prennent

PERFECT

j'	ai pris
tu	as pris
il/elle/on	a pris
nous	avons pris
vous	avez pris
ils/elles	ont pris

IMPERFECT

je	prenais
tu	prenais
il/elle/on	prenait
nous	prenions
vous	preniez
ils/elles	prenaient

FUTURE

je	prendrai
tu	prendras
il/elle/on	prendra
nous	prendrons
vous	prendrez
ils/elles	prendront

CONDITIONAL

je	prendrais
tu	prendrais
il/elle/on	prendrait
nous	prendrions
vous	prendriez
ils/elles	prendraient

IMPERATIVE

prends / prenons / prenez

PAST PARTICIPLE

pris

PRESENT PARTICIPLE

prenant

EXAMPLE PHRASES

J'**ai pris** plein de photos. I took lots of pictures.
N'oublie pas de **prendre** ton passeport. Don't forget to take your passport.
Il **prendra** le train de 8h20. He'll take the 8.20 train.
Pour qui est-ce qu'il **se prend**? Who does he think he is?

---

je/j' = I **tu** = you **il** = he/it **elle** = she/it **on** = we/one **nous** = we **vous** = you **ils/elles** = they

▶ **rire** (to laugh)

PRESENT

je	ris
tu	ris
il/elle/on	rit
nous	rions
vous	riez
ils/elles	rient

PRESENT SUBJUNCTIVE

je	rie
tu	ries
il/elle/on	rie
nous	riions
vous	riiez
ils/elles	rient

PERFECT

j'	ai ri
tu	as ri
il/elle/on	a ri
nous	avons ri
vous	avez ri
ils/elles	ont ri

IMPERFECT

je	riais
tu	riais
il/elle/on	riait
nous	riions
vous	riiez
ils/elles	riaient

FUTURE

je	rirai
tu	riras
il/elle/on	rira
nous	rirons
vous	rirez
ils/elles	riront

CONDITIONAL

je	rirais
tu	rirais
il/elle/on	rirait
nous	ririons
vous	ririez
ils/elles	riraient

IMPERATIVE

ris / rions / riez

PAST PARTICIPLE

ri

PRESENT PARTICIPLE

riant

EXAMPLE PHRASES

*On **a** bien **ri**.* We had a good laugh.
*Ne **ris** pas, ce n'est pas drôle!* Don't laugh, it's not funny!
*C'était juste pour **rire**.* It was only for a laugh.

---

je/j' = I **tu** = you **il** = he/it **elle** = she/it **on** = we/one **nous** = we **vous** = you **ils/elles** = they

▶ savoir (to know)

PRESENT

je	sais
tu	sais
il/elle/on	sait
nous	savons
vous	savez
ils/elles	savent

PRESENT SUBJUNCTIVE

je	sache
tu	saches
il/elle/on	sache
nous	sachions
vous	sachiez
ils/elles	sachent

PERFECT

j'	ai su
tu	as su
il/elle/on	a su
nous	avons su
vous	avez su
ils/elles	ont su

IMPERFECT

je	savais
tu	savais
il/elle/on	savait
nous	savions
vous	saviez
ils/elles	savaient

FUTURE

je	saurai
tu	sauras
il/elle/on	saura
nous	saurons
vous	saurez
ils/elles	sauront

CONDITIONAL

je	saurais
tu	saurais
il/elle/on	saurait
nous	saurions
vous	sauriez
ils/elles	sauraient

IMPERATIVE

sache / sachons / sachez

PAST PARTICIPLE

su

PRESENT PARTICIPLE

sachant

EXAMPLE PHRASES

*Tu **sais** ce que tu vas faire l'année prochaine?* Do you know what you're doing next year?
*Je ne **sais** pas.* I don't know.
*Elle ne **sait** pas nager.* She can't swim.
*Tu **savais** que son père était pakistanais?* Did you know her father was Pakistani?

---

je/j' = I **tu** = you **il** = he/it **elle** = she/it **on** = we/one **nous** = we **vous** = you **ils/elles** = they

▶ **sortir** (to go out)

PRESENT

je	sors
tu	sors
il/elle/on	sort
nous	sortons
vous	sortez
ils/elles	sortent

PRESENT SUBJUNCTIVE

je	sorte
tu	sortes
il/elle/on	sorte
nous	sortions
vous	sortiez
ils/elles	sortent

PERFECT

je	suis sorti(e)
tu	es sorti(e)
il/elle/on	est sorti(e)
nous	sommes sorti(e)s
vous	êtes sorti(e)(s)
ils/elles	sont sorti(e)s

IMPERFECT

je	sortais
tu	sortais
il/elle/on	sortait
nous	sortions
vous	sortiez
ils/elles	sortaient

FUTURE

je	sortirai
tu	sortiras
il/elle/on	sortira
nous	sortirons
vous	sortirez
ils/elles	sortiront

CONDITIONAL

je	sortirais
tu	sortirais
il/elle/on	sortirait
nous	sortirions
vous	sortiriez
ils/elles	sortiraient

IMPERATIVE

sors / sortons / sortez

PRESENT PARTICIPLE

sortant

PAST PARTICIPLE

sorti

EXAMPLE PHRASES

*Je ne **suis** pas **sortie** ce week-end.* I didn't go out this weekend.
*Aurélie **sort** avec Bruno.* Aurélie is going out with Bruno.
*Elle **est sortie** de l'hôpital hier.* She came out of hospital yesterday.
*Je n'**ai** pas **sorti** le chien parce qu'il pleuvait.* I didn't take the dog out for a walk because it was raining.

i Note that **sortir** takes **avoir** in the perfect tense when it is used with a direct object.

je/j' = I **tu** = you **il** = he/it **elle** = she/it **on** = we/one **nous** = we **vous** = you **ils/elles** = they

▶ **tenir** (to hold)

PRESENT

je	tiens
tu	tiens
il/elle/on	tient
nous	tenons
vous	tenez
ils/elles	tiennent

PRESENT SUBJUNCTIVE

je	tienne
tu	tiennes
il/elle/on	tienne
nous	tenions
vous	teniez
ils/elles	tiennent

PERFECT

j'	ai tenu
tu	as tenu
il/elle/on	a tenu
nous	avons tenu
vous	avez tenu
ils/elles	ont tenu

IMPERFECT

je	tenais
tu	tenais
il/elle/on	tenait
nous	tenions
vous	teniez
ils/elles	tenaient

FUTURE

je	tiendrai
tu	tiendras
il/elle/on	tiendra
nous	tiendrons
vous	tiendrez
ils/elles	tiendront

CONDITIONAL

je	tiendrais
tu	tiendrais
il/elle/on	tiendrait
nous	tiendrions
vous	tiendriez
ils/elles	tiendraient

IMPERATIVE

tiens / tenons / tenez

PAST PARTICIPLE

tenu

PRESENT PARTICIPLE

tenant

EXAMPLE PHRASES

Tiens-moi la main. Hold my hand.
*Elle **tenait** beaucoup à son chat.* She was really attached to her cat.
Tiens, prends mon stylo. Here, have my pen.
Tiens-toi droit! Sit up straight!

---

je/j' = I **tu** = you **il** = he/it **elle** = she/it **on** = we/one **nous** = we **vous** = you **ils/elles** = they

▶ **venir** (to come)

PRESENT

je	viens
tu	viens
il/elle/on	vient
nous	venons
vous	venez
ils/elles	viennent

PRESENT SUBJUNCTIVE

je	vienne
tu	viennes
il/elle/on	vienne
nous	venions
vous	veniez
ils/elles	viennent

PERFECT

je	suis venu(e)
tu	es venu(e)
il/elle/on	est venu(e)
nous	sommes venu(e)s
vous	êtes venu(e)(s)
ils/elles	sont venu(e)s

IMPERFECT

je	venais
tu	venais
il/elle/on	venait
nous	venions
vous	veniez
ils/elles	venaient

FUTURE

je	viendrai
tu	viendras
il/elle/on	viendra
nous	viendrons
vous	viendrez
ils/elles	viendront

CONDITIONAL

je	viendrais
tu	viendrais
il/elle/on	viendrait
nous	viendrions
vous	viendriez
ils/elles	viendraient

IMPERATIVE

viens / venons / venez

PAST PARTICIPLE

venu

PRESENT PARTICIPLE

venant

EXAMPLE PHRASES

*Elle ne **viendra** pas cette année.* She won't be coming this year.
*Fatou et Malik **viennent** du Sénégal.* Fatou and Malik come from Senegal.
*Je **viens** de manger.* I've just eaten.

---

je/j' = I **tu** = you **il** = he/it **elle** = she/it **on** = we/one **nous** = we **vous** = you **ils/elles** = they

▶ vivre (to live)

PRESENT		PRESENT SUBJUNCTIVE	
je	vis	je	vive
tu	vis	tu	vives
il/elle/on	vit	il/elle/on	vive
nous	vivons	nous	vivions
vous	vivez	vous	viviez
ils/elles	vivent	ils/elles	vivent

PERFECT		IMPERFECT	
j'	ai vécu	je	vivais
tu	as vécu	tu	vivais
il/elle/on	a vécu	il/elle/on	vivait
nous	avons vécu	nous	vivions
vous	avez vécu	vous	viviez
ils/elles	ont vécu	ils/elles	vivaient

FUTURE		CONDITIONAL	
je	vivrai	je	vivrais
tu	vivras	tu	vivrais
il/elle/on	vivra	il/elle/on	vivrait
nous	vivrons	nous	vivrions
vous	vivrez	vous	vivriez
ils/elles	vivront	ils/elles	vivraient

IMPERATIVE

vis / vivons / vivez

PAST PARTICIPLE

vécu

PRESENT PARTICIPLE

vivant

EXAMPLE PHRASES

*Ma sœur **vit** en Espagne.* My sister lives in Spain.
*Il **a vécu** dix ans à Lyon.* He lived in Lyons for 10 years.
*Les gorilles **vivent** surtout dans la forêt.* Gorillas mostly live in the forest.

---

je/j' = I **tu** = you **il** = he/it **elle** = she/it **on** = we/one **nous** = we **vous** = you **ils/elles** = they

▶ **voir** (to see)

PRESENT

je	vois
tu	vois
il/elle/on	voit
nous	voyons
vous	voyez
ils/elles	voient

PRESENT SUBJUNCTIVE

je	voie
tu	voies
il/elle/on	voie
nous	voyions
vous	voyiez
ils/elles	voient

PERFECT

j'	ai vu
tu	as vu
il/elle/on	a vu
nous	avons vu
vous	avez vu
ils/elles	ont vu

IMPERFECT

je	voyais
tu	voyais
il/elle/on	voyait
nous	voyions
vous	voyiez
ils/elles	voyaient

FUTURE

je	verrai
tu	verras
il/elle/on	verra
nous	verrons
vous	verrez
ils/elles	verront

CONDITIONAL

je	verrais
tu	verrais
il/elle/on	verrait
nous	verrions
vous	verriez
ils/elles	verraient

IMPERATIVE

vois / voyons / voyez

PAST PARTICIPLE

vu

PRESENT PARTICIPLE

voyant

EXAMPLE PHRASES

*Venez me **voir** quand vous serez à Paris.* Come and see me when you're in Paris.
*Je ne **vois** rien sans mes lunettes.* I can't see anything without my glasses.
*Est-ce que tu l'**as vu**?* Did you see him? or Have you seen him?
*Est-ce que cette tache **se voit**?* Does that stain show?

---

je/j' = I **tu** = you **il** = he/it **elle** = she/it **on** = we/one **nous** = we **vous** = you **ils/elles** = they

▶ **vouloir** (to want)

PRESENT

je	veux
tu	veux
il/elle/on	veut
nous	voulons
vous	voulez
ils/elles	veulent

PRESENT SUBJUNCTIVE

je	veuille
tu	veuilles
il/elle/on	veuille
nous	voulions
vous	vouliez
ils/elles	veuillent

PERFECT

j'	ai voulu
tu	as voulu
il/elle/on	a voulu
nous	avons voulu
vous	avez voulu
ils/elles	ont voulu

IMPERFECT

je	voulais
tu	voulais
il/elle/on	voulait
nous	voulions
vous	vouliez
ils/elles	voulaient

FUTURE

je	voudrai
tu	voudras
il/elle/on	voudra
nous	voudrons
vous	voudrez
ils/elles	voudront

CONDITIONAL

je	voudrais
tu	voudrais
il/elle/on	voudrait
nous	voudrions
vous	voudriez
ils/elles	voudraient

IMPERATIVE

veuille / veuillons / veuillez

PAST PARTICIPLE

voulu

PRESENT PARTICIPLE

voulant

EXAMPLE PHRASES

*Elle **veut** un vélo pour Noël.* She wants a bike for Christmas.
*Ils **voulaient** aller au cinéma.* They wanted to go to the cinema.
*Tu **voudrais** une tasse de thé?* Would you like a cup of tea?

---

je/j' = I **tu** = you **il** = he/it **elle** = she/it **on** = we/one **nous** = we **vous** = you **ils/elles** = they

A, a

A [eɪ] n (MUS) la m

a [eɪ, ə] (before vowel or silent h: an) indef art
1 un(e); **a book** un livre; **an apple** une pomme; **she's a doctor** elle est médecin
2 (instead of the number "one") un(e); **a year ago** il y a un an; **a hundred/ thousand** etc **pounds** cent/mille livres
3 (in expressing ratios, prices etc): **3 a day/ week** 3 par jour/semaine; **10 km an hour** 10 km à l'heure; **30p a kilo** 30p le kilo

---

A.A. n abbr = **Alcoholics Anonymous**; (BRIT: Automobile Association) ≃ TCF m

A.A.A. (US) n abbr (= American Automobile Association) ≃ TCF m

aback [əˈbæk] adv: **to be taken ~** être stupéfait(e), être décontenancé(e)

abandon [əˈbændən] vt abandonner

abate [əˈbeɪt] vi s'apaiser, se calmer

abbey [ˈæbɪ] n abbaye f

abbot [ˈæbət] n père supérieur

abbreviation [əbriːvɪˈeɪʃən] n abréviation f

abdicate [ˈæbdɪkeɪt] vt, vi abdiquer

abdomen [ˈæbdəmen] n abdomen m

abduct [æbˈdʌkt] vt enlever

aberration [æbəˈreɪʃən] n anomalie f

abide [əˈbaɪd] vt: **I can't ~ it/him** je ne peux pas le souffrir or supporter; **~ by** vt fus observer, respecter

ability [əˈbɪlɪtɪ] n compétence f; capacité f; (skill) talent m

abject [ˈæbdʒekt] adj (poverty) sordide; (apology) plat(e)

ablaze [əˈbleɪz] adj en feu, en flammes

able [ˈeɪbl] adj capable, compétent(e); **to be ~ to do sth** être capable de faire qch, pouvoir faire qch; **~-bodied** adj robuste; **ably** adv avec compétence or talent, ha-bilement

abnormal [æbˈnɔːməl] adj anormal(e)

aboard [əˈbɔːd] adv à bord ♦ prep à bord de

abode [əˈbəud] n (LAW): **of no fixed ~** sans domicile fixe

abolish [əˈbɒlɪʃ] vt abolir

aborigine [æbəˈrɪdʒɪnɪ] n aborigène m/f

abort [əˈbɔːt] vt faire avorter; **~ion** n avortement m; **to have an ~ion** se faire avorter; **~ive** [əˈbɔːtɪv] adj manqué(e)

about [əˈbaut] adv 1 (approximately) environ, à peu près; **about a hundred/ thousand** etc environ cent/mille etc, une centaine/un millier etc; **it takes about 10 hours** ça prend environ or à peu près 10 heures; **at about 2 o'clock** vers 2 heures; **I've just about finished** j'ai presque fini
2 (referring to place) çà et là, de côté et d'autre; **to run about** courir çà et là; **to walk about** se promener, aller et venir
3: **to be about to do sth** être sur le point de faire qch
♦ prep 1 (relating to) au sujet de, à propos de; **a book about London** un livre sur Londres; **what is it about?** de quoi s'agit-il?; **we talked about it** nous en avons parlé; **what** or **how about doing this?** et si nous faisions ceci?
2 (referring to place) dans; **to walk about the town** se promener dans la ville

---

about-face [əˈbautˈfeɪs] n demi-tour m

about-turn [əˈbautˈtɜːn] n (MIL) demi-tour m; (fig) volte-face f

above [əˈbʌv] adv au-dessus ♦ prep au-dessus de; (more) plus de; **mentioned ~** mentionné ci-dessus; **~ all** par-dessus tout, surtout; ~**board** *adj* franc (franche); honnête

abrasive [əˈbreɪzɪv] *adj* abrasif(-ive); *(fig)* caustique, agressif(-ive)

abreast [əˈbrest] *adv* de front; **to keep ~ of** se tenir au courant de

abroad [əˈbrɔːd] *adv* à l'étranger

abrupt [əˈbrʌpt] *adj (steep, blunt)* abrupt(e); *(sudden, gruff)* brusque; ~**ly** *adv (speak, end)* brusquement

abscess [ˈæbsɪs] *n* abcès *m*

absence [ˈæbsəns] *n* absence *f*

absent [ˈæbsənt] *adj* absent(e); ~**ee** [æbsənˈtiː] *n* absent(e); *(habitual)* absentéiste *m/f*; ~**-minded** *adj* distrait(e)

absolute [ˈæbsəluːt] *adj* absolu(e); ~**ly** [æbsəˈluːtlɪ] *adv* absolument

absolve [abˈzɔlv] *vt*: **to ~ sb (from)** *(blame, responsibility, sin)* absoudre qn (de)

absorb [abˈzɔːb] *vt* absorber; **to be ~ed in a book** être plongé(e) dans un livre; ~**ent cotton** *(US)* *n* coton *m* hydrophile

abstain [abˈsteɪn] *vi*: **to ~ (from)** s'abstenir (de)

abstract [ˈæbstrækt] *adj* abstrait(e)

absurd [abˈsəːd] *adj* absurde

abundant [əˈbʌndənt] *adj* abondant(e)

abuse [*n* əˈbjuːs, *vb* əˈbjuːz] *n* abus *m*; *(insults)* insultes *fpl*, injures *fpl* ♦ *vt* abuser de; *(insult)* insulter; **abusive** [əˈbjuːsɪv] *adj* grossier(-ère), injurieux(-euse)

abysmal [əˈbɪzməl] *adj* exécrable; *(ignorance etc)* sans bornes

abyss [əˈbɪs] *n* abîme *m*, gouffre *m*

AC *abbr* (= *alternating current*) courant alternatif

academic [ækəˈdemɪk] *adj* universitaire; *(person: scholarly)* intellectuel(le); *(pej: issue)* oiseux(-euse), purement théorique ♦ *n* universitaire *m/f*; ~ **year** *n* année *f* universitaire

academy [əˈkædəmɪ] *n (learned body)* académie *f*; *(school)* collège *m*; ~ **of music** conservatoire *m*

accelerate [ækˈseləreɪt] *vt*, *vi* accélérer; **accelerator** *n* accélérateur *m*

accent [ˈæksənt] *n* accent *m*

accept [əkˈsept] *vt* accepter; ~**able** *adj* acceptable; ~**ance** *n* acceptation *f*

access [ˈækses] *n* accès *m*; *(LAW: in divorce)* droit *m* de visite; ~**ible** [ækˈsesəbl] *adj* accessible

accessory [ækˈsesərɪ] *n* accessoire *m*

accident [ˈæksɪdənt] *n* accident *m*; *(chance)* hasard *m*; **by ~** accidentellement; par hasard; ~**al** [æksɪˈdentl] *adj* accidentel(le); ~**ally** [æksɪˈdentəlɪ] *adv* accidentellement; ~ **insurance** *n* assurance *f* accident; ~**-prone** *adj* sujet(te) aux accidents

acclaim [əˈkleɪm] *n* acclamations *fpl* ♦ *vt* acclamer

accommodate [əˈkɔmədeɪt] *vt* loger, recevoir; *(oblige, help)* obliger; *(car etc)* contenir; **accommodating** *adj* obligeant(e), arrangeant(e); **accommodation** [əkɔməˈdeɪʃən] *(US* **accommodations)** *n* logement *m*

accompany [əˈkʌmpənɪ] *vt* accompagner

accomplice [əˈkʌmplɪs] *n* complice *m/f*

accomplish [əˈkʌmplɪʃ] *vt* accomplir; ~**ment** *n* accomplissement *m*; réussite *f*; *(skill: gen pl)* talent *m*

accord [əˈkɔːd] *n* accord *m* ♦ *vt* accorder; **of his own ~** de son plein gré; ~**ance** [əˈkɔːdəns] *n*: **in ~ance with** conformément à; ~**ing**: ~**ing to** *prep* selon; ~**ingly** *adv* en conséquence

accordion [əˈkɔːdɪən] *n* accordéon *m*

account [əˈkaunt] *n (COMM)* compte *m*; *(report)* compte rendu; récit *m*; ~**s** *npl (COMM)* comptabilité *f*, comptes; **of no ~** sans importance; **on ~** en acompte; **on no ~** en aucun cas; **on ~ of** à cause de; **to take into ~, take ~ of** tenir compte de; ~ **for** *vt fus* expliquer, rendre compte de; ~**able** *adj*: ~**able (to)** responsable (devant); ~**ancy** *n* comptabilité *f*; ~**ant** *n* comptable *m/f*; ~ **number** *n (at bank etc)* numéro *m* de compte

accrued interest [əˈkruːd-] *n* intérêt *m* cumulé

accumulate [əˈkjuːmjuleɪt] *vt* accumuler, amasser ♦ *vi* s'accumuler, s'amasser

accuracy [ˈækjurəsɪ] *n* exactitude *f*, précision f

accurate [ˈækjʊrɪt] *adj* exact(e), précis(e); **~ly** *adv* avec précision

accusation [ækjuːˈzeɪʃən] *n* accusation f

accuse [əˈkjuːz] *vt*: **to ~ sb (of sth)** accuser qn (de qch); **the ~d** l'accusé(e)

accustom [əˈkʌstəm] *vt* accoutumer, habituer; **~ed** *adj* (*usual*) habituel(le); (*in the habit*): **~ed to** habitué(e) *or* accoutumé(e) à

ace [eɪs] *n* as m

ache [eɪk] *n* mal m, douleur f ♦ *vi* (*yearn*): **to ~ to do sth** mourir d'envie de faire qch; **my head ~s** j'ai mal à la tête

achieve [əˈtʃiːv] *vt* (*aim*) atteindre; (*victory, success*) remporter, obtenir; **~ment** *n* exploit m, réussite f

acid [ˈæsɪd] *adj* acide ♦ *n* acide m; **~ rain** *n* pluies fpl acides

acknowledge [əkˈnɔlɪdʒ] *vt* (*letter: also:* **~ receipt of**) accuser réception de; (*fact*) reconnaître; **~ment** *n* (*of letter*) accusé m de réception

acne [ˈæknɪ] *n* acné m

acorn [ˈeɪkɔːn] *n* gland m

acoustic [əˈkuːstɪk] *adj* acoustique; **~s** *n, npl* acoustique f

acquaint [əˈkweɪnt] *vt*: **to ~ sb with sth** mettre qn au courant de qch; **to be ~ed with** connaître; **~ance** *n* connaissance f

acquire [əˈkwaɪəʳ] *vt* acquérir

acquit [əˈkwɪt] *vt* acquitter; **to ~ o.s. well** bien se comporter, s'en tirer très honorablement

acre [ˈeɪkəʳ] *n* acre f (= 4047 m²)

acrid [ˈækrɪd] *adj* âcre

acrobat [ˈækrəbæt] *n* acrobate m/f

across [əˈkrɔs] *prep* (*on the other side*) de l'autre côté de; (*crosswise*) en travers de ♦ *adv* de l'autre côté; en travers; **to run/ swim ~** traverser en courant/à la nage; **~ from** en face de

acrylic [əˈkrɪlɪk] *adj* acrylique

act [ækt] *n* acte m, action f; (*of play*) acte; (*in music-hall etc*) numéro m; (*LAW*) loi f ♦ *vi* agir; (*THEATRE*) jouer; (*pretend*) jouer la comédie ♦ *vt* (*part*) jouer, tenir; **in the ~**

of en train de; **to ~ as** servir de; **~ing** *adj* suppléant(e), par intérim ♦ *n* (*activity*): **to do some ~ing** faire du théâtre (*or* du cinéma)

action [ˈækʃən] *n* action f; (*MIL*) combat(s) m(pl); **out of ~** hors de combat; (*machine*) hors d'usage; **to take ~** agir, prendre des mesures; **~ replay** *n* (*TV*) ralenti m

activate [ˈæktɪveɪt] *vt* (*mechanism*) actionner, faire fonctionner

active [ˈæktɪv] *adj* actif(-ive); (*volcano*) en activité; **~ly** *adv* activement; **activity** [ækˈtɪvɪtɪ] *n* activité f; **activity holiday** *n* vacances actives

actor [ˈæktəʳ] *n* acteur m

actress [ˈæktrɪs] *n* actrice f

actual [ˈæktjuəl] *adj* réel(le), véritable; **~ly** *adv* (*really*) réellement, véritablement; (*in fact*) en fait

acute [əˈkjuːt] *adj* aigu(ë); (*mind, observer*) pénétrant(e), perspicace

ad [æd] *n abbr* = **advertisement**

A.D. *adv abbr* (= *anno Domini*) ap. J.-C.

adamant [ˈædəmənt] *adj* inflexible

adapt [əˈdæpt] *vt* adapter ♦ *vi*: **to ~ (to)** s'adapter (à); **~able** *adj* (*device*) adaptable; (*person*) qui s'adapte facilement; **~er, ~or** *n* (*ELEC*) adaptateur m

add [æd] *vt* ajouter; (*figures: also:* **to ~ up**) additionner ♦ *vi*: **to ~ to** (*increase*) ajouter à, accroître

adder [ˈædəʳ] *n* vipère f

addict [ˈædɪkt] *n* intoxiqué(e); (*fig*) fanatique m/f; **~ed** [əˈdɪktɪd] *adj*: **to be ~ed to** (*drugs, drink etc*) être adonné(e) à; (*fig: football etc*) être un(e) fanatique de; **~ion** *n* (*MED*) dépendance f; **~ive** *adj* qui crée une dépendance

addition [əˈdɪʃən] *n* addition f; (*thing added*) ajout m; **in ~** de plus; de surcroît; **in ~ to** en plus de; **~al** *adj* supplémentaire

additive [ˈædɪtɪv] *n* additif m

address [əˈdrɛs] *n* adresse f; (*talk*) discours m, allocution f ♦ *vt* adresser; (*speak to*) s'adresser à; **to ~ (o.s. to) a problem** s'attaquer à un problème

adept [ˈædɛpt] *adj*: **~ at** expert(e) à *or* en

adequate ['ædɪkwɪt] *adj* adéquat(e); suffisant(e)

adhere [əd'hɪər] *vi*: **to ~ to** adhérer à; *(fig: rule, decision)* se tenir à

adhesive [əd'hiːzɪv] *n* adhésif *m*; **~ tape** *n (BRIT)* ruban adhésif; *(US: MED)* sparadrap *m*

ad hoc [æd'hɔk] *adj* improvisé(e), ad hoc

adjacent [ə'dʒeɪsənt] *adj*: **~ (to)** adjacent (à)

adjective ['ædʒɛktɪv] *n* adjectif *m*

adjoining [ə'dʒɔɪnɪŋ] *adj* voisin(e), adjacent(e), attenant(e)

adjourn [ə'dʒəːn] *vt* ajourner ♦ *vi* suspendre la séance; clore la session

adjust [ə'dʒʌst] *vt (machine)* ajuster, régler; *(prices, wages)* rajuster ♦ *vi*: **to ~ (to)** s'adapter (à); **~able** *adj* réglable; **~ment** *n (PSYCH)* adaptation *f*; *(to machine)* ajustage *m*, réglage *m*; *(of prices, wages)* rajustement *m*

ad-lib [æd'lɪb] *vt, vi* improviser; **ad lib** *adv* à volonté, à loisir

administer [əd'mɪnɪstər] *vt* administrer; *(justice)* rendre; **administration** [ədmɪnɪs'treɪʃən] *n* administration *f*; **administrative** [əd'mɪnɪstrətɪv] *adj* administratif(-ive)

admiral ['ædmərəl] *n* amiral *m*; **A~ty** ['ædmərəltɪ] *(BRIT)* n: **the A~ty** ministère *m* de la Marine

admire [əd'maɪər] *vt* admirer

admission [əd'mɪʃən] *n* admission *f*; *(to exhibition, night club etc)* entrée *f*; *(confession)* aveu *m*; **~ charge** *n* droits *mpl* d'admission

admit [əd'mɪt] *vt* laisser entrer; admettre; *(agree)* reconnaître, admettre; **~ to** *vt fus* reconnaître, avouer; **~tance** *n* admission *f*, (droit *m* d')entrée *f*; **~tedly** *adv* il faut en convenir

ado [ə'duː] *n*: **without (any) more ~** sans plus de cérémonies

adolescence [ædəu'lɛsns] *n* adolescence *f*; **adolescent** *adj, n* adolescent(e)

adopt [ə'dɔpt] *vt* adopter; **~ed** *adj* adoptif(-ive), adopté(e); **~ion** *n* adoption *f*

adore [ə'dɔːr] *vt* adorer

adorn [ə'dɔːn] *vt* orner

Adriatic (Sea) [eɪdrɪ'ætɪk-] *n* Adriatique *f*

adrift [ə'drɪft] *adv* à la dérive

adult ['ædʌlt] *n* adulte *m/f* ♦ *adj* adulte; *(literature, education)* pour adultes

adultery [ə'dʌltərɪ] *n* adultère *m*

advance [əd'vɑːns] *n* avance *f* ♦ *adj*: **~ booking** réservation *f* ♦ *vt* avancer ♦ *vi* avancer, s'avancer; **~ notice** avertissement *m*; **to make ~s (to sb)** faire des propositions (à qn); *(amorously)* faire des avances (à qn); **in ~** à l'avance, d'avance; **~d** *adj* avancé(e); *(SCOL: studies)* supérieur(e)

advantage [əd'vɑːntɪdʒ] *n (also TENNIS)* avantage *m*; **to take ~ of** *(person)* exploiter

advent ['ædvənt] *n* avènement *m*, venue *f*; **A~** Avent *m*

adventure [əd'vɛntʃər] *n* aventure *f*

adverb ['ædvəːb] *n* adverbe *m*

adverse ['ædvəːs] *adj* défavorable, contraire

advert ['ædvəːt] *(BRIT)* *n abbr* = **advertisement**

advertise ['ædvətaɪz] *vi, vt* faire de la publicité (pour); *(in classified ads etc)* mettre une annonce (pour vendre); **to ~ for** *(staff, accommodation)* faire paraître une annonce pour trouver; **~ment** [əd'vəːtɪsmənt] *n (COMM)* réclame *f*, publicité *f*; *(in classified ads)* annonce *f*; **advertising** *n* publicité *f*

advice [əd'vaɪs] *n* conseils *mpl*; *(notification)* avis *m*; **piece of ~** conseil; **to take legal ~** consulter un avocat

advisable [əd'vaɪzəbl] *adj* conseillé(e), indiqué(e)

advise [əd'vaɪz] *vt* conseiller; **to ~ sb of sth** aviser *or* informer qn de qch; **to ~ against sth/doing sth** déconseiller qch/conseiller de ne pas faire qch; **~r**, **advisor** *n* conseiller(-ère); **advisory** *adj* consultatif(-ive)

advocate [*n* 'ædvəkɪt, *vb* 'ædvəkeɪt] *n (upholder)* défenseur *m*, avocat(e); *(LAW)* avocat(e) ♦ vt recommander, prôner

Aegean (Sea) [iːˈdʒiːən-] n (mer f) Égée f

aerial [ˈɛərɪəl] n antenne f ♦ adj aérien(ne)

aerobics [ɛəˈrəubɪks] n aérobic f

aeroplane [ˈɛərəpleɪn] (BRIT) n avion m

aerosol [ˈɛərəsɔl] n aérosol m

aesthetic [iːsˈθɛtɪk] adj esthétique

afar [əˈfɑː] adv: **from ~** de loin

affair [əˈfɛə] n affaire f; (also: **love ~**) liaison f; aventure f

affect [əˈfɛkt] vt affecter; (disease) atteindre; **~ed** adj affecté(e); **~ion** n affection f; **~ionate** adj affectueux(-euse)

affinity [əˈfɪnɪtɪ] n (bond, rapport): **to have an ~ with/for** avoir une affinité avec/pour

afflict [əˈflɪkt] vt affliger

affluence [ˈæfluəns] n abondance f, opulence f

affluent [ˈæfluənt] adj (person, family, surroundings) aisé(e), riche; **the ~ society** la société d'abondance

afford [əˈfɔːd] vt se permettre; (provide) fournir, procurer

afloat [əˈfləut] adj, adv à flot; **to stay ~** surnager

afoot [əˈfut] adv: **there is something ~** il se prépare quelque chose

afraid [əˈfreɪd] adj effrayé(e); **to be ~ of** or **to** avoir peur de; **I am ~ that ...** je suis désolé(e), mais ...; **I am ~ so/not** hélas oui/non

Africa [ˈæfrɪkə] n Afrique f; **~n** adj africain(e) ♦ n Africain(e)

after [ˈɑːftə] prep, adv après ♦ conj après que, après avoir or être +pp; **what/who are you ~?** que/qui cherchez-vous?; **~ he left/having done** après qu'il fut parti/après avoir fait; **ask ~ him** demandez de ses nouvelles; **to name sb ~ sb** donner à qn le nom de qn; **twenty ~ eight** (US) huit heures vingt; **~ all** après tout; **~ you!** après vous, Monsieur (or Madame etc); **~effects** npl (of disaster, radiation, drink etc) répercussions fpl; (of illness) séquelles fpl, suites fpl; **~math** n conséquences fpl, suites fpl; **~noon** n après-midi m or f; **~s**
(inf) n (dessert) dessert m; **~-sales service** (BRIT) n (for car, washing machine etc) service m après-vente; **~-shave (lotion)** n after-shave m; **~sun** n après-soleil m inv; **~thought** n: **I had an ~thought** il m'est venu une idée après coup; **~wards** (US **afterward**) adv après

again [əˈɡɛn] adv de nouveau; encore (une fois); **to do sth ~** refaire qch; **not ... ~** ne ... plus; **~ and ~** à plusieurs reprises

against [əˈɡɛnst] prep contre; (compared to) par rapport à

age [eɪdʒ] n âge m ♦ vt, vi vieillir; **it's been ~s since** ça fait une éternité que ... ne; **he is 20 years of ~** il a 20 ans; **to come of ~** atteindre sa majorité; **~d** [adj eɪdʒd, npl ˈeɪdʒɪd] adj: **~d 10** âgé(e) de 10 ans ♦ npl: **the ~d** les personnes âgées; **~ group** n tranche f d'âge; **~ limit** n limite f d'âge

agency [ˈeɪdʒənsɪ] n agence f; (government body) organisme m, office m

agenda [əˈdʒɛndə] n ordre m du jour

agent [ˈeɪdʒənt] n agent m, représentant m; (firm) concessionnaire m

aggravate [ˈæɡrəveɪt] vt aggraver; (annoy) exaspérer

aggressive [əˈɡrɛsɪv] adj agressif(-ive)

agitate [ˈædʒɪteɪt] vt (person) agiter, émouvoir, troubler ♦ vi: **to ~ for/against** faire campagne pour/contre

AGM n abbr (= annual general meeting) AG f

ago [əˈɡəu] adv: **2 days ~** il y a deux jours; **not long ~** il n'y a pas longtemps; **how long ~?** il y a combien de temps (de cela)?

agony [ˈæɡənɪ] n (pain) douleur f atroce; **to be in ~** souffrir le martyre

agree [əˈɡriː] vt (price) convenir de ♦ vi: **to ~ with** (person) être d'accord avec; (statements etc) concorder avec; (LING) s'accorder avec; **to ~ to do** accepter de or consentir à faire; **to ~ to sth** consentir à qch; **to ~ that** (admit) convenir or reconnaître que; **garlic doesn't ~ with me** je ne supporte pas l'ail; **~able** adj agréable; (*willing*) consentant(e), d'accord; **~d** *adj* (*time, place*) convenu(e); **~ment** *n* accord *m*; **in ~ment** d'accord

agricultural [ægrɪˈkʌltʃərəl] *adj* agricole

agriculture [ˈægrɪkʌltʃər] *n* agriculture *f*

aground [əˈɡraʊnd] *adv*: **to run ~** échouer, s'échouer

ahead [əˈhɛd] *adv* (*in front: of position, place*) devant; (: *at the head*) en avant; (*look, plan, think*) en avant; **~ of** devant; (*fig: schedule etc*) en avance sur; **~ of time** en avance; **go right** *or* **straight ~** allez tout droit; **go ~!** (*fig: permission*) allez-y!

aid [eɪd] *n* aide *f*; (*device*) appareil *m* ♦ *vt* aider; **in ~ of** en faveur de; *see also* **hearing**

aide [eɪd] *n* (*person*) aide *mf*, assistant(e)

AIDS [eɪdz] *n abbr* (= *acquired immune deficiency syndrome*) SIDA *m*; **AIDS-related** *adj* associé(e) au sida

aim [eɪm] *vt*: **to ~ sth (at)** (*gun, camera*) braquer *or* pointer qch (sur); (*missile*) lancer qch (à *or* contre *or* en direction de); (*blow*) allonger qch (à); (*remark*) destiner *or* adresser qch (à) ♦ *vi* (*also*: **to take ~**) viser ♦ *n* but *m*; (*skill*): **his ~ is bad** il vise mal; **to ~ at** viser; (*fig*) viser (à); **to ~ to do** avoir l'intention de faire; **~less** *adj* sans but

ain't [eɪnt] (*inf*) = **am not; aren't; isn't**

air [ɛər] *n* air *m* ♦ *vt* (*room, bed, clothes*) aérer; (*grievances, views, ideas*) exposer, faire connaître ♦ *cpd* (*currents, attack etc*) aérien(ne); **to throw sth into the ~** jeter qch en l'air; **by ~** (*travel*) par avion; **to be on the ~** (*RADIO, TV: programme*) être diffusé(e); (: *station*) diffuser; **~bed** *n* matelas *m* pneumatique; **~-conditioned** *adj* climatisé(e); **~ conditioning** *n* climatisation *f*; **~craft** *n inv* avion *m*; **~craft carrier** *n* porte-avions *m inv*; **~field** *n* terrain *m* d'aviation; **A~ Force** *n* armée *f* de l'air; **~ freshener** *n* désodorisant *m*; **~gun** *n* fusil *m* à air comprimé; **~ hostess** *n* (*BRIT*) hôtesse *f* de l'air; **~ letter** *n* (*BRIT*) aérogramme *m*; **~lift** *n* pont aérien; **~line** *n* ligne aérienne, compagnie *f*

d'aviation; **~liner** *n* avion *m* de ligne; **~mail** *n*: **by ~mail** par avion; **~ mile** *n* air mile *m*; **~plane** *n* (*US*) avion *m*; **~port** *n* aéroport *m*; **~ raid** *n* attaque *or* raid aérien(ne); **~sick** *adj*: **to be ~sick** avoir le mal de l'air; **~tight** *adj* hermétique; **~-traffic controller** *n* aiguilleur *m* du ciel; **~y** *adj* bien aéré(e); (*manners*) dégagé(e)

aisle [aɪl] *n* (*of church*) allée centrale; nef latérale; (*of theatre etc*) couloir *m*, passage *m*, allée; **~ seat** *n* place *m* côté couloir

ajar [əˈdʒɑːr] *adj* entrouvert(e)

akin [əˈkɪn] *adj*: **~ to** (*similar*) qui tient de *or* ressemble à

alarm [əˈlɑːm] *n* alarme *f* ♦ *vt* alarmer; **~ call** *n* coup de fil *m* pour réveiller; **~ clock** *n* réveille-matin *m inv*, réveil *m*

alas [əˈlæs] *excl* hélas!

album [ˈælbəm] *n* album *m*

alcohol [ˈælkəhɒl] *n* alcool *m*; **~-free** *adj* sans alcool; **~ic** [ælkəˈhɒlɪk] *adj* alcoolique ♦ *n* alcoolique *m/f*; **A~ics Anonymous** Alcooliques anonymes

ale [eɪl] *n* bière *f*

alert [əˈlɜːt] *adj* alerte, vif (vive); vigilant(e) ♦ *n* alerte *f* ♦ *vt* alerter; **on the ~** sur le qui-vive; (*MIL*) en état d'alerte

algebra [ˈældʒɪbrə] *n* algèbre *m*

Algeria [ælˈdʒɪərɪə] *n* Algérie *f*

alias [ˈeɪlɪəs] *adv* alias ♦ *n* faux nom, nom d'emprunt; (*writer*) pseudonyme *m*

alibi [ˈælɪbaɪ] *n* alibi *m*

alien [ˈeɪlɪən] *n* étranger(-ère); (*from outer space*) extraterrestre *mf* ♦ *adj*: **~ (to)** étranger(-ère) (à)

alight [əˈlaɪt] *adj, adv* en feu ♦ *vi* mettre pied à terre; (*passenger*) descendre

alike [əˈlaɪk] *adj* semblable, pareil(le) ♦ *adv* de même; **to look ~** se ressembler

alimony [ˈælɪmənɪ] *n* (*payment*) pension *f* alimentaire

alive [əˈlaɪv] *adj* vivant(e); (*lively*) plein(e) de vie

KEYWORD

all [ɔːl] *adj* (*singular*) tout(e); (*plural*) tous (toutes); **all day** toute la journée; **all**

night toute la nuit; **all men** tous les hommes; **all five** tous les cinq; **all the food** toute la nourriture; **all the books** tous les livres; **all the time** tout le temps; **all his life** toute sa vie
♦ *pron* 1 tout; **I ate it all, I ate all of it** j'ai tout mangé; **all of us went** nous y sommes tous allés; **all of the boys went** tous les garçons y sont allés
2 (*in phrases*): **above all** surtout, pardessus tout; **after all** après tout; **not at all** (*in answer to question*) pas du tout; (*in answer to thanks*) je vous en prie!; **I'm not at all tired** je ne suis pas du tout fatigué(e); **anything at all will do** n'importe quoi fera l'affaire; **all in all** tout bien considéré, en fin de compte
♦ *adv*: **all alone** tout(e) seul(e); **it's not as hard as all that** ce n'est pas si difficile que ça; **all the more/the better** d'autant plus/mieux; **all but** presque, pratiquement; **the score is 2 all** le score est de 2 partout

allege [əˈlɛdʒ] *vt* alléguer, prétendre; ~**dly** [əˈlɛdʒɪdlɪ] *adv* à ce que l'on prétend, paraît-il
allegiance [əˈliːdʒəns] *n* allégeance *f*, fidélité *f*, obéissance *f*
allergic [əˈlɜːdʒɪk] *adj*: ~ **to** allergique à
allergy [ˈælədʒɪ] *n* allergie *f*
alleviate [əˈliːvɪeɪt] *vt* soulager, adoucir
alley [ˈælɪ] *n* ruelle *f*
alliance [əˈlaɪəns] *n* alliance *f*
allied [ˈælaɪd] *adj* allié(e)
all-in [ˈɔːlɪn] (BRIT) *adj* (*also adv*: *charge*) tout compris
all-night [ˈɔːlˈnaɪt] *adj* ouvert(e) *or* qui dure toute la nuit
allocate [ˈæləkeɪt] *vt* (*share out*) répartir, distribuer; ~ **sth to** (*duties*) assigner *or* attribuer qch à; (*sum, time*) allouer qch à
allot [əˈlɒt] *vt*: **to** ~ **(to)** (*money*) répartir (entre), distribuer (à); (*time*) allouer (à); ~**ment** *n* (*share*) part *f*; (*garden*) lopin *m* de terre (*loué à la municipalité*)
all-out [ˈɔːˈlaut] *adj* (*effort etc*) total(e)

♦ *adv*: **all out** à fond
allow [əˈlau] *vt* (*practice, behaviour*) permettre, autoriser; (*sum to spend etc*) accorder, allouer; (*sum, time estimated*) compter, prévoir; (*claim, goal*) admettre; (*concede*): **to** ~ **that** convenir que; **to** ~ **sb to do** permettre à qn de faire, autoriser qn à faire; **he is** ~**ed to ...** on lui permet de ...; ~ **for** *vt fus* tenir compte de; ~**ance** [əˈlauəns] *n* (*money received*) allocation *f*; subside *m*; indemnité *f*; (TAX) somme *f* déductible du revenu imposable, abattement *m*; **to make** ~**ances for** tenir compte de
alloy [ˈælɔɪ] *n* alliage *m*
all: ~ **right** *adv* (*feel, work*) bien; (*as answer*) d'accord; ~**-rounder** *n*: **to be a good** ~**-rounder** être doué(e) en tout; ~-**time** *adj* (*record*) sans précédent, absolu(e)
ally [*n* ˈælaɪ, *vb* əˈlaɪ] *n* allié *m* ♦ *vt*: **to** ~ **o.s. with** s'allier avec
almighty [ɔːlˈmaɪtɪ] *adj* tout-puissant; (*tremendous*) énorme
almond [ˈɑːmənd] *n* amande *f*
almost [ˈɔːlməust] *adv* presque
alone [əˈləun] *adj, adv* seul(e); **to leave sb** ~ laisser qn tranquille; **to leave sth** ~ ne pas toucher à qch; **let** ~ **...** sans parler de ...; encore moins ...
along [əˈlɒŋ] *prep* le long de ♦ *adv*: **is he coming** ~ **with us?** vient-il avec nous?; **he was hopping/limping** ~ il avançait en sautillant/boitant; ~ **with** (*together with: person*) en compagnie de; (: *thing*) avec, en plus de; **all** ~ (*all the time*) depuis le début; ~**side** *prep* le long de; à côté de ♦ *adv* bord à bord
aloof [əˈluːf] *adj* distant(e) ♦ *adv*: **to stand** ~ se tenir à distance *or* à l'écart
aloud [əˈlaud] *adv* à haute voix
alphabet [ˈælfəbet] *n* alphabet *m*; ~**ical** [ælfəˈbetɪkl] *adj* alphabétique
alpine [ˈælpaɪn] *adj* alpin(e), alpestre
Alps [ælps] *npl*: **the** ~ les Alpes *fpl*
already [ɔːlˈredɪ] *adv* déjà
alright [ˈɔːlˈraɪt] (BRIT) *adv* = **all right**

Alsatian [æl'seɪʃən] (*BRIT*) *n* (*dog*) berger allemand

also ['ɔːlsəu] *adv* aussi

altar ['ɔltər] *n* autel *m*

alter ['ɔltər] *vt, vi* changer

alternate [*adj* ɔl'təːnɪt, *vb* 'ɔltəːneɪt] *adj* alterné(e), alternant(e), alternatif(-ive) ♦ *vi* alterner; **on ~ days** un jour sur deux, tous les deux jours; **alternating current** *n* courant alternatif

alternative [ɔl'təːnətɪv] *adj* (*solutions*) possible, au choix; (*plan*) autre, de rechange; (*lifestyle etc*) parallèle ♦ *n* (*choice*) alternative *f*; (*other possibility*) autre possibilité *f*; **an ~ comedian** un nouveau comique; **~ medicine** médicines *fpl* parallèles *or* douces; **~ly** *adv*: **~ly one could** une autre *or* l'autre solution serait de, on pourrait aussi

alternator ['ɔltəːneɪtər] *n* (*AUT*) alternateur *m*

although [ɔːl'ðəu] *conj* bien que +*sub*

altitude ['æltɪtjuːd] *n* altitude *f*

alto ['æltəu] *n* (*female*) contralto *m*; (*male*) haute-contre *f*

altogether [ɔːltə'geðər] *adv* entièrement, tout à fait; (*on the whole*) tout compte fait; (*in all*) en tout

aluminium [ælju'mɪnɪəm] (*BRIT*), **aluminum** [ə'luːmɪnəm] (*US*) *n* aluminium *m*

always ['ɔːlweɪz] *adv* toujours

Alzheimer's (disease) ['æltshaɪməz-] *n* maladie *f* d'Alzheimer

AM *n abbr* (= *Assembly Member*) député *m* au Parlement gallois

am [æm] *vb see* **be**

a.m. *adv abbr* (= *ante meridiem*) du matin

amalgamate [ə'mælgəmeɪt] *vt, vi* fusionner

amateur ['æmətər] *n* amateur *m*; **~ish** (*pej*) *adj* d'amateur

amaze [ə'meɪz] *vt* stupéfier; **to be ~d (at)** être stupéfait(e) (de); **~ment** *n* stupéfaction *f*, stupeur *f*; **amazing** *adj* étonnant(e); exceptionnel(le)

ambassador [æm'bæsədər] *n* ambassadeur *m*

amber ['æmbər] *n* ambre *m*; **at ~** (*BRIT*:

AUT) à l'orange

ambiguous [æm'bɪgjuəs] *adj* ambigu(ë)

ambition [æm'bɪʃən] *n* ambition *f*; **ambitious** *adj* ambitieux(-euse)

ambulance ['æmbjuləns] *n* ambulance *f*

ambush ['æmbuʃ] *n* embuscade *f* ♦ *vt* tendre une embuscade à

amenable [ə'miːnəbl] *adj*: **~ to** (*advice etc*) disposé(e) à écouter

amend [ə'mɛnd] *vt* (*law*) amender; (*text*) corriger; **to make ~s** réparer ses torts, faire amende honorable

amenities [ə'miːnɪtɪz] *npl* aménagements *mpl*, équipements *mpl*

America [ə'mɛrɪkə] *n* Amérique *f*; **~n** *adj* américain(e) ♦ *n* Américain(e)

amiable ['eɪmɪəbl] *adj* aimable, affable

amicable ['æmɪkəbl] *adj* amical(e); (*LAW*) à l'amiable

amid(st) [ə'mɪd(st)] *prep* parmi, au milieu de

amiss [ə'mɪs] *adj, adv*: **there's something ~** il y a quelque chose qui ne va pas *or* qui cloche; **to take sth ~** prendre qch mal *or* de travers

ammonia [ə'məunɪə] *n* (*gas*) ammoniac *m*; (*liquid*) ammoniaque *f*

ammunition [æmju'nɪʃən] *n* munitions *fpl*

amok [ə'mɔk] *adv*: **to run ~** être pris(e) d'un accès de folie furieuse

among(st) [ə'mʌŋ(st)] *prep* parmi, entre

amorous ['æmərəs] *adj* amoureux(-euse)

amount [ə'maunt] *n* (*sum*) somme *f*, montant *m*; (*quantity*) quantité *f*, nombre *m* ♦ *vi*: **to ~ to** (*total*) s'élever à; (*be same as*) équivaloir à, revenir à

amp(ere) ['æmp(ɛər)] *n* ampère *m*

ample ['æmpl] *adj* ample; spacieux(-euse); (*enough*): **this is ~** c'est largement suffisant; **to have ~ time/room** avoir bien assez de temps/place

amplifier ['æmplɪfaɪər] *n* amplificateur *m*

amuse [ə'mjuːz] *vt* amuser, divertir; **~ment** *n* amusement *m*; **~ment arcade** *n* salle *f* de jeu; **~ment park** *n* parc *m* d'attractions

an [æn, ən] *indef art see* **a**

anaemic [ə'ni:mɪk] (*US* **anemic**) *adj* anémique

anaesthetic [ænɪs'θetɪk] (*US* **anesthetic**) *n* anesthésique *m*

analog(ue) ['ænəlɒg] *adj* (*watch, computer*) analogique

analyse ['ænəlaɪz] (*US* **analyze**) *vt* analyser; **analysis** [ə'næləsɪs] (*pl* **analyses**) *n* analyse *f*; **analyst** ['ænəlɪst] *n* (*POL etc*) spécialiste *m/f*; (*US*) psychanalyste *m/f*

analyze ['ænəlaɪz] (*US*) *vt* = **analyse**

anarchist ['ænəkɪst] *n* anarchiste *m/f*

anarchy ['ænəkɪ] *n* anarchie *f*

anatomy [ə'nætəmɪ] *n* anatomie *f*

ancestor ['ænsɪstə*] *n* ancêtre *m*, aïeul *m*

anchor ['æŋkə*] *n* ancre *f* ♦ *vi* (*also:* **to drop** ~) jeter l'ancre, mouiller ♦ *vt* mettre à l'ancre; (*fig*): **to** ~ **sth to** fixer qch à

anchovy ['æntʃəvɪ] *n* anchois *m*

ancient ['eɪnʃənt] *adj* ancien(ne), antique; (*person*) d'un âge vénérable; (*car*) antédiluvien(ne)

ancillary [æn'sɪlərɪ] *adj* auxiliaire

and [ænd] *conj* et; ~ **so on** et ainsi de suite; **try** ~ **come** tâchez de venir; **he talked** ~ **talked** il n'a pas arrêté de parler; **better** ~ **better** de mieux en mieux

anew [ə'nju:] *adv* à nouveau

angel ['eɪndʒəl] *n* ange *m*

anger ['æŋgə*] *n* colère *f*

angina [æn'dʒaɪnə] *n* angine *f* de poitrine

angle ['æŋgl] *n* angle *m*; **from their** ~ de leur point de vue

angler ['æŋglə*] *n* pêcheur(-euse) à la ligne

Anglican ['æŋglɪkən] *adj, n* anglican(e)

angling ['æŋglɪŋ] *n* pêche *f* à la ligne

Anglo- ['æŋgləʊ] *prefix* anglo(-)

angrily ['æŋgrɪlɪ] *adv* avec colère

angry ['æŋgrɪ] *adj* en colère, furieux(-euse); (*wound*) enflammé(e); **to be** ~ **with sb/at sth** être furieux contre qn/de qch; **to get** ~ se fâcher, se mettre en colère

anguish ['æŋgwɪʃ] *n* (*mental*) angoisse *f*

animal ['ænɪml] *n* animal *m* ♦ *adj* animal(e)

animate [*vb* 'ænɪmeɪt, *adj* 'ænɪmɪt] *vt* animer ♦ *adj* animé(e), vivant(e); ~**d** *adj* animé(e)

aniseed ['ænɪsi:d] *n* anis *m*

ankle ['æŋkl] *n* cheville *f*; ~ **sock** *n* socquette *f*

annex [*n* 'æneks, *vb* ə'neks] *n* (*BRIT:* ~**e**) annexe *f* ♦ *vt* annexer

anniversary [ænɪ'vɜ:sərɪ] *n* anniversaire *m*

announce [ə'naʊns] *vt* annoncer; (*birth, death*) faire part de; ~**ment** *n* annonce *f*; (*for births etc: in newspaper*) avis *m* de faire-part; (: *letter, card*) faire-part *m*; ~**r** *n* (*RADIO, TV: between programmes*) speaker(ine)

annoy [ə'nɔɪ] *vt* agacer, ennuyer, contrarier; **don't get** ~**ed!** ne vous fâchez pas!; ~**ance** *n* mécontentement *m*, contrariété *f*; ~**ing** *adj* agaçant(e), contrariant(e)

annual ['ænjuəl] *adj* annuel(le) ♦ *n* (*BOT*) plante annuelle; (*children's book*) album *m*

annul [ə'nʌl] *vt* annuler

annum ['ænəm] *n* see **per**

anonymous [ə'nɒnɪməs] *adj* anonyme

anorak ['ænəræk] *n* anorak *m*

anorexia [ænə'reksɪə] *n* (*also:* ~ **nervosa**) anorexie *f*

another [ə'nʌðə*] *adj*: ~ **book** (*one more*) un autre livre, encore un livre, un livre de plus; (*a different one*) un autre livre ♦ *pron* un(e) autre, encore un(e), un(e) de plus; *see also* **one**

answer ['ɑ:nsə*] *n* réponse *f*; (*to problem*) solution *f* ♦ *vi* répondre ♦ *vt* (*reply to*) répondre à; (*problem*) résoudre; (*prayer*) exaucer; **in** ~ **to your letter** en réponse à votre lettre; **to** ~ **the phone** répondre (au téléphone); **to** ~ **the bell** *or* **the door** aller *or* venir ouvrir (la porte); ~ **back** *vi* répondre, répliquer; ~ **for** *vt fus* (*person*) répondre de, se porter garant de; (*crime, one's actions*) être responsable de; ~ **to** *vt fus* (*description*) répondre *or* correspondre à; ~**able** *adj*: ~**able** (**to sb/for sth**) responsable (devant qn/de qch); ~**ing machine** *n* répondeur *m* automatique

ant [ænt] *n* fourmi *f*

antagonism [æn'tægənɪzəm] *n* antagonisme *m*

antagonize [ænˈtæɡənaɪz] *vt* éveiller l'hostilité de, contrarier

Antarctic [æntˈɑːktɪk] *n*: **the ~** l'Antarctique *m*

antenatal [ˈæntɪˈneɪtl] *adj* prénatal(e); **~ clinic** *n* service *m* de consultation prénatale

anthem [ˈænθəm] *n*: **national ~** hymne national

anti: **~-aircraft** *adj* (*missile*) anti-aérien(ne); **~biotic** [ˈæntɪbaɪˈɒtɪk] *n* antibiotique *m*; **~body** *n* anticorps *m*

anticipate [ænˈtɪsɪpeɪt] *vt* s'attendre à; prévoir; (*wishes, request*) aller au devant de, devancer

anticipation [æntɪsɪˈpeɪʃən] *n* attente *f*; **in ~** par anticipation, à l'avance

anticlimax [ˈæntɪˈklaɪmæks] *n* déception *f*, douche froide (*fam*)

anticlockwise [ˈæntɪˈklɒkwaɪz] *adj, adv* dans le sens inverse des aiguilles d'une montre

antics [ˈæntɪks] *npl* singeries *fpl*

antidepressant [ˈæntɪdɪˈpresənt] *n* antidépresseur *m*

antifreeze [ˈæntɪfriːz] *n* antigel *m*

antihistamine [ˈæntɪˈhɪstəmɪn] *n* antihistaminique *m*

antiquated [ˈæntɪkweɪtɪd] *adj* vieilli(e), suranné(e), vieillot(te)

antique [ænˈtiːk] *n* objet *m* d'art ancien, meuble ancien *or* d'époque, antiquité *f* ♦ *adj* ancien(ne); **~ dealer** *n* antiquaire *m*; **~ shop** *n* magasin *m* d'antiquités

anti: **~-Semitism** [ˈæntɪˈsemɪtɪzəm] *n* antisémitisme *m*; **~septic** [æntɪˈseptɪk] *n* antiseptique *m*; **~social** [ˈæntɪˈsəʊʃəl] *adj* peu liant(e), sauvage, insociable; (*against society*) antisocial(e)

antlers [ˈæntləz] *npl* bois *mpl*, ramure *f*

anvil [ˈænvɪl] *n* enclume *f*

anxiety [æŋˈzaɪətɪ] *n* anxiété *f*; (*keenness*): **~ to do** grand désir *or* impatience *f* de faire

anxious [ˈæŋkʃəs] *adj* anxieux(-euse); (*worrying: time, situation*) inquiétant(e); (*keen*): **~ to do/that** qui tient beaucoup à faire/à

ce que; impatient(e) de faire/que

KEYWORD

any [ˈenɪ] *adj* **1** (*in questions etc: singular*) du, de l', de la; (: *plural*) des; **have you any butter/children/ink?** avez-vous du beurre/des enfants/de l'encre?

2 (*with negative*) de, d'; **I haven't any books** je n'ai pas de livres

3 (*no matter which*) n'importe quel(le); **choose any book you like** vous pouvez choisir n'importe quel livre

4 (*in phrases*): **in any case** de toute façon; **any day now** d'un jour à l'autre; **at any moment** à tout moment, d'un instant à l'autre; **at any rate** en tout cas

♦ *pron* **1** (*in questions etc*) en; **have you got any?** est-ce que vous en avez?; **can any of you sing?** est-ce que parmi vous il y en a qui savent chanter?

2 (*with negative*) en; **I haven't any (of them)** je n'en ai pas, je n'en ai aucun

3 (*no matter which one(s)*) n'importe lequel (*or* laquelle); **take any of those books (you like)** vous pouvez prendre n'importe lequel de ces livres

♦ *adv* **1** (*in questions etc*): **do you want any more soup/sandwiches?** voulez-vous encore de la soupe/des sandwichs?; **are you feeling any better?** est-ce que vous vous sentez mieux?

2 (*with negative*): **I can't hear him any more** je ne l'entends plus; **don't wait any longer** n'attendez pas plus longtemps

any: **~body** *pron* n'importe qui; (*in interrogative sentences*) quelqu'un; (*in negative sentences*): **I don't see ~body** je ne vois personne; **~how** *adv* (*at any rate*) de toute façon, quand même; (*haphazard*) n'importe comment; **~one** *pron* = **anybody**; **~thing** *pron* n'importe quoi, quelque chose, ne ... rien; **~way** *adv* de toute façon; **~where** *adv* n'importe où, quelque part; **I don't see him ~where** je ne le vois nulle part

apart [əˈpɑːt] *adv* (*to one side*) à part; de

côté; à l'écart; (*separately*) séparément; **10 miles ~** à 10 miles l'un de l'autre; **to take ~** démonter; **~ from** à part, excepté
apartheid [əˈpɑːteɪt] *n* apartheid *m*
apartment [əˈpɑːtmənt] *n* (*US*) appartement *m*, logement *m*; (*room*) chambre *f*; **~ building** (*US*) *n* immeuble *m*; (*divided house*) maison divisée en appartements
ape [eɪp] *n* (grand) singe ♦ *vt* singer
apéritif [əˈperɪtiːf] *n* apéritif *m*
aperture [ˈæpətʃjuəʳ] *n* orifice *m*, ouverture *f*; (*PHOT*) ouverture (du diaphragme)
APEX [ˈeɪpeks] *n abbr* (*AVIAT*) (= *advance purchase excursion*) APEX *m*
apologetic [əpɔləˈdʒetɪk] *adj* (*tone, letter*) d'excuse; (*person*): **to be ~** s'excuser
apologize [əˈpɔlədʒaɪz] *vi*: **to ~ (for sth to sb)** s'excuser (de qch auprès de qn), présenter des excuses (à qn pour qch)
apology [əˈpɔlədʒi] *n* excuses *fpl*
apostle [əˈpɔsl] *n* apôtre *m*
apostrophe [əˈpɔstrəfi] *n* apostrophe *f*
appalling [əˈpɔːlɪŋ] *adj* épouvantable; (*stupidity*) consternant(e)
apparatus [æpəˈreɪtəs] *n* appareil *m*, dispositif *m*; (*in gymnasium*) agrès *mpl*; (*of government*) dispositif *m*
apparel [əˈpærəl] (*US*) *n* habillement *m*
apparent [əˈpærənt] *adj* apparent(e); ~**ly** *adv* apparemment
appeal [əˈpiːl] *vi* (*LAW*) faire *or* interjeter appel ♦ *n* appel *m*; (*request*) prière *f*; appel *m*; (*charm*) attrait *m*, charme *m*; **to ~ for** lancer un appel pour; **to ~ to** (*beg*) faire appel à; (*be attractive*) plaire à; **it doesn't ~ to me** cela ne m'attire pas; ~**ing** *adj* (*attractive*) attrayant(e)
appear [əˈpɪəʳ] *vi* apparaître, se montrer; (*LAW*) comparaître; (*publication*) paraître, sortir, être publié(e); (*seem*) paraître, sembler; **it would ~ that** il semble que; **to ~ in Hamlet** jouer dans Hamlet; **to ~ on TV** passer à la télé; ~**ance** *n* apparition *f*; parution *f*; (*look, aspect*) apparence *f*, aspect *m*
appease [əˈpiːz] *vt* apaiser, calmer
appendicitis [əpendɪˈsaɪtɪs] *n* appendicite

f
appendix [əˈpendɪks] (*pl* **appendices**) *n* appendice *m*
appetite [ˈæpɪtaɪt] *n* appétit *m*; **appetizer** *n* amuse-gueule *m*; (*drink*) apéritif *m*
applaud [əˈplɔːd] *vt, vi* applaudir
applause [əˈplɔːz] *n* applaudissements *mpl*
apple [ˈæpl] *n* pomme *f*; **~ tree** *n* pommier *m*
appliance [əˈplaɪəns] *n* appareil *m*
applicable [əˈplɪkəbl] *adj* (*relevant*): **to be ~ to** valoir pour
applicant [ˈæplɪkənt] *n*: **~ (for)** candidat(e) (à)
application [æplɪˈkeɪʃən] *n* application *f*; (*for a job, a grant etc*) demande *f*; candidature *f*; **~ form** *n* formulaire *m* de demande
applied [əˈplaɪd] *adj* appliqué(e)
apply [əˈplaɪ] *vt*: **to ~ (to)** (*paint, ointment*) appliquer (sur); (*law etc*) appliquer (à) ♦ *vi*: **to ~ to** (*be suitable for, relevant to*) s'appliquer à; (*ask*) s'adresser à; **to ~ (for)** (*permit, grant*) faire une demande (en vue d'obtenir); (*job*) poser sa candidature (pour), faire une demande d'emploi (concernant); **to ~ o.s. to** s'appliquer à
appoint [əˈpɔɪnt] *vt* nommer, engager; ~**ed** *adj*: **at the ~ed time** à l'heure dite; ~**ment** *n* nomination *f*; (*meeting*) rendez-vous *m*; **to make an ~ment (with)** prendre rendez-vous (avec)
appraisal [əˈpreɪzl] *n* évaluation *f*
appreciate [əˈpriːʃieɪt] *vt* (*like*) apprécier; (*be grateful for*) être reconnaissant(e) de; (*understand*) comprendre; se rendre compte de ♦ *vi* (*FINANCE*) prendre de la valeur
appreciation [əpriːʃiˈeɪʃən] *n* appréciation *f*; (*gratitude*) reconnaissance *f*; (*COMM*) hausse *f*, valorisation *f*
appreciative [əˈpriːʃiətɪv] *adj* (*person*) sensible; (*comment*) élogieux(-euse)
apprehensive [æprɪˈhensɪv] *adj* inquiet(-ète), appréhensif(-ive)
apprentice [əˈprentɪs] *n* apprenti *m*; ~**ship** *n* apprentissage *m*

approach [ə'prəʊtʃ] *vi* approcher ♦ *vt*
(*come near*) approcher de; (*ask, apply to*)
s'adresser à; (*situation, problem*) aborder
♦ *n* approche *f*; (*access*) accès *m*; ~**able**
adj accessible

appropriate [*adj* ə'prəʊpriit, *vb*
ə'prəʊprieit] *adj* (*moment, remark*) oppor-
tun(e); (*tool etc*) approprié(e) ♦ *vt* (*take*)
s'approprier

approval [ə'pruːvəl] *n* approbation *f*; **on ~**
(COMM) à l'examen

approve [ə'pruːv] *vt* approuver; ~ **of** *vt
fus* approuver

approximate [*adj* ə'prɔksimit, *vb*
ə'prɔksimeit] *adj* approximatif(-ive) ♦ *vt* se
rapprocher de, être proche de; ~**ly** *adv*
approximativement

apricot ['eiprikɔt] *n* abricot *m*

April ['eiprəl] *n* avril *m*; ~ **Fool's Day** le
premier avril

April Fool's Day

i April Fool's Day *est le 1er avril, à
l'occasion duquel on fait des farces de
toutes sortes. Les victimes de ces farces
sont les "April fools". Les médias britanniques se prennent aussi au jeu, diffusant de
fausses nouvelles, comme la découverte
d'îles de la taille de l'Irlande, ou faisant
des reportages bidon, montrant par exemple la culture d'arbres à spaghettis en Italie.*

---

apron ['eiprən] *n* tablier *m*

apt [æpt] *adj* (*suitable*) approprié(e); (*likely*):
~ **to do** susceptible de faire; qui a tendance à faire

Aquarius [ə'kwɛəriəs] *n* le Verseau

Arab ['ærəb] *adj* arabe ♦ *n* Arabe *m/f*; ~**ian**
[ə'reibiən] *adj* arabe; ~**ic** *adj* arabe ♦ *n*
arabe *m*

arbitrary ['ɑːbitrəri] *adj* arbitraire

arbitration [ɑːbi'treiʃən] *n* arbitrage *m*

arcade [ɑː'keid] *n* arcade *f*; (*passage with
shops*) passage *m*, galerie marchande;
(*with video games*) salle *f* de jeu

arch [ɑːtʃ] *n* arc *m*; (*of foot*) cambrure *f*,

voûte *f* plantaire ♦ *vt* arquer, cambrer

archaeologist [ɑːki'ɔlədʒist] *n* archéologue *m/f*

archaeology [ɑːki'ɔlədʒi] *n* archéologie *f*

archbishop [ɑːtʃ'biʃəp] *n* archevêque *m*

archeology *etc* (US) [ɑːki'ɔlədʒi] = **archaeology** *etc*

archery ['ɑːtʃəri] *n* tir *m* à l'arc

architect ['ɑːkitekt] *n* architecte *m*; ~**ure**
n architecture *f*

archives ['ɑːkaivz] *npl* archives *fpl*

Arctic ['ɑːktik] *adj* arctique ♦ *n* Arctique *m*

ardent ['ɑːdənt] *adj* fervent(e)

are [ɑːʳ] *vb see* **be**

area ['ɛəriə] *n* (GEOM) superficie *f*; (*zone*)
région *f*; (: *smaller*) secteur *m*, partie *f*; (*in
room*) coin *m*; (*knowledge, research*) domaine *m*; ~ **code** (US) *n* (TEL) indicatif *m* téléphonique

aren't [ɑːnt] = **are not**

Argentina [ɑːdʒən'tiːnə] *n* Argentine *f*;
Argentinian [ɑːdʒən'tiniən] *adj* argen-
tin(e) ♦ *n* Argentin(e)

arguably ['ɑːgjuəbli] *adv*: **it is ~ ...** on
peut soutenir que c'est ...

argue ['ɑːgjuː] *vi* (*quarrel*) se disputer; (*reason*) argumenter; **to ~ that** objecter *or* alléguer que

argument ['ɑːgjumənt] *n* (*reasons*) argument *m*; (*quarrel*) dispute *f*; ~**ative**
[ɑːgju'mentətiv] *adj* ergoteur(-euse),
raisonneur(-euse)

Aries ['ɛəriz] *n* le Bélier

arise [ə'raiz] (*pt* **arose**, *pp* **arisen**) *vi* survenir, se présenter

aristocrat ['æristəkræt] *n* aristocrate *m/f*

arithmetic [ə'riθmətik] *n* arithmétique *f*

ark [ɑːk] *n*: **Noah's A~** l'Arche *f* de Noé

arm [ɑːm] *n* bras *m* ♦ *vt* armer; ~**s** *npl*
(*weapons, HERALDRY*) armes *fpl*; ~ **in ~** bras
dessus bras dessous

armaments ['ɑːməmənts] *npl* armement
m

armchair ['ɑːmtʃɛəʳ] *n* fauteuil *m*

armed [ɑːmd] *adj* armé(e); ~ **robbery** *n*
vol *m* à main armée

armour ['ɑːməʳ] (US **armor**) *n* armure *f*;

(MIL: *tanks*) blindés *mpl*; **~ed car** *n* véhicule blindé

armpit ['ɑːmpɪt] *n* aisselle *f*

armrest ['ɑːmrest] *n* accoudoir *m*

army ['ɑːmɪ] *n* armée *f*

A road (BRIT) *n* (AUT) route nationale

aroma [ə'rəumə] *n* arôme *m*; **~therapy** *n* aromathérapie *f*

arose [ə'rəuz] *pt of* **arise**

around [ə'raund] *adv* autour; (*nearby*) dans les parages ♦ *prep* autour de; (*near*) près de; (*fig: about*) environ; (: *date, time*) vers

arouse [ə'rauz] *vt* (*sleeper*) éveiller; (*curiosity, passions*) éveiller, susciter; (*anger*) exciter

arrange [ə'reɪndʒ] *vt* arranger; **to ~ to do sth** prévoir de faire qch; **~ment** *n* arrangement *m*; **~ments** *npl* (*plans etc*) arrangements *mpl*, dispositions *fpl*

array [ə'reɪ] *n*: **~ of** déploiement *m* or étalage *m* de

arrears [ə'rɪəz] *npl* arriéré *m*; **to be in ~ with one's rent** devoir un arriéré de loyer

arrest [ə'rest] *vt* arrêter; (*sb's attention*) retenir, attirer ♦ *n* arrestation *f*; **under ~** en état d'arrestation

arrival [ə'raɪvl] *n* arrivée *f*; **new ~** nouveau venu, nouvelle venue; (*baby*) nouveau-né(e)

arrive [ə'raɪv] *vi* arriver

arrogant ['ærəgənt] *adj* arrogant(e)

arrow ['ærəu] *n* flèche *f*

arse [ɑːs] (BRIT: *inf!*) *n* cul *m* (!)

arson ['ɑːsn] *n* incendie criminel

art [ɑːt] *n* art *m*; **A~s** *npl* (SCOL) les lettres *fpl*

artery ['ɑːtərɪ] *n* artère *f*

art gallery *n* musée *m* d'art; (*small and private*) galerie *f* de peinture

arthritis [ɑː'θraɪtɪs] *n* arthrite *f*

artichoke ['ɑːtɪtʃəuk] *n* (*also:* **globe ~**) artichaut *m*; (*also:* **Jerusalem ~**) topinambour *m*

article ['ɑːtɪkl] *n* article *m*; **~s** *npl* (BRIT: LAW: *training*) ≈ stage *m*; **~ of clothing** vêtement *m*

articulate [*adj* ɑː'tɪkjulɪt, *vb* ɑː'tɪkjuleɪt] *adj*

(*person*) qui s'exprime bien; (*speech*) bien articulé(e), prononcé(e) clairement ♦ *vt* exprimer; **~d lorry** *n* (BRIT) (camion *m*) semi-remorque *m*

artificial [ɑːtɪ'fɪʃəl] *adj* artificiel(le); **~ respiration** *n* respiration artificielle

artist ['ɑːtɪst] *n* artiste *m/f*; **~ic** [ɑː'tɪstɪk] *adj* artistique; **~ry** *n* art *m*, talent *m*

art school *n* ≈ école *f* des beaux-arts

as [æz, əz] *conj* 1 (*referring to time*) comme, alors que; à mesure que; **he came in as I was leaving** il est arrivé comme je partais; **as the years went by** à mesure que les années passaient; **as from tomorrow** à partir de demain

2 (*in comparisons*): **as big as** aussi grand que; **twice as big as** deux fois plus grand que; **as much** or **many as** autant que; **as much money/many books** autant d'argent/de livres que; **as soon as** dès que

3 (*since, because*) comme, puisque; **as he had to be home by 10 ...** comme il or puisqu'il devait être de retour avant 10 h ...

4 (*referring to manner, way*): **do as you wish** faites comme vous voudrez

5 (*concerning*): **as for** or **to that** quant à cela, pour ce qui est de cela

6: **as if** or **though** comme si; **he looked as if he was ill** il avait l'air d'être malade; *see also* **long**; **such**; **well**

♦ *prep*: **he works as a driver** il travaille comme chauffeur; **as chairman of the company, he ...** en tant que président de la société, il ...; **dressed up as a cowboy** déguisé en cowboy; **he gave me it as a present** il me l'a offert, il m'en a fait cadeau

a.s.a.p. *abbr* (= *as soon as possible*) dès que possible

asbestos [æz'bestəs] *n* amiante *f*

ascend [ə'send] *vt* gravir; (*throne*) monter sur

ascertain [æsə'teɪn] vt vérifier

ash [æʃ] n (dust) cendre f; (also: ~ **tree**) frêne m

ashamed [ə'ʃeɪmd] adj honteux(-euse), confus(e); **to be ~ of** avoir honte de

ashore [ə'ʃɔːr] adv à terre

ashtray ['æʃtreɪ] n cendrier m

Ash Wednesday n mercredi m des cendres

Asia ['eɪʃə] n Asie f; ~**n** n Asiatique m/f ♦ adj asiatique

aside [ə'saɪd] adv de côté; à l'écart ♦ n aparté m

ask [ɑːsk] vt demander; (invite) inviter; **to ~ sb sth/to do sth** demander qch à qn/à qn de faire qch; **to ~ sb about sth** questionner qn sur qch; se renseigner auprès de qn sur qch; **to ~ (sb) a question** poser une question (à qn); **to ~ sb out to dinner** inviter qn au restaurant; ~ **after** vt fus demander des nouvelles de; ~ **for** vt fus demander; (trouble) chercher

asking price ['ɑːskɪŋ-] n: **the ~** le prix de départ

asleep [ə'sliːp] adj endormi(e); **to fall ~** s'endormir

asparagus [əs'pærəgəs] n asperges fpl

aspect ['æspɛkt] n aspect m; (direction in which a building etc faces) orientation f, exposition f

aspire [əs'paɪər] vi: **to ~ to** aspirer à

aspirin ['æsprɪn] n aspirine f

ass [æs] n âne m; (inf) imbécile m/f; (US: inf!) cul m (!)

assailant [ə'seɪlənt] n agresseur m; assaillant m

assassinate [ə'sæsɪneɪt] vt assassiner; **assassination** [əsæsɪ'neɪʃən] n assassinat m

assault [ə'sɔːlt] n (MIL) assaut m; (gen: attack) agression f ♦ vt attaquer; (sexually) violenter

assemble [ə'sɛmbl] vt assembler ♦ vi s'assembler, se rassembler; **assembly** n assemblée f, réunion f; (institution) assemblée; (construction) assemblage m; **assembly line** n chaîne f de montage

assent [ə'sɛnt] n assentiment m, consentement m

assert [ə'sɜːt] vt affirmer, déclarer; (one's authority) faire valoir; (one's innocence) protester de

assess [ə'sɛs] vt évaluer; (tax, payment) établir or fixer le montant de; (property etc: for tax) calculer la valeur imposable de; (person) juger la valeur de; ~**ment** n évaluation f, fixation f, calcul m de la valeur imposable de, jugement m; ~**or** n expert m (impôt et assurance)

asset ['æsɛt] n avantage m, atout m; ~**s** npl (FINANCE) capital m; avoir(s) m(pl); actif m

assign [ə'saɪn] vt (date) fixer; (task) assigner à; (resources) affecter à; ~**ment** n tâche f, mission f

assist [ə'sɪst] vt aider, assister; ~**ance** n aide f, assistance f; ~**ant** n assistant(e), adjoint(e); (BRIT: also: **shop** ~**ant**) vendeur(-euse)

associate [n, adj ə'səuʃɪɪt, vb ə'səuʃɪeɪt] adj, n associé(e) ♦ vt associer ♦ vi: **to ~ with sb** fréquenter qn; **association** [əsəusɪ'eɪʃən] n association f

assorted [ə'sɔːtɪd] adj assorti(e)

assortment [ə'sɔːtmənt] n assortiment m

assume [ə'sjuːm] vt supposer; (responsibilities etc) assumer; (attitude, name) prendre, adopter; **assumption** [ə'sʌmpʃən] n supposition f, hypothèse f; (of power) assomption f, prise f

assurance [ə'ʃuərəns] n assurance f

assure [ə'ʃuər] vt assurer

asthma ['æsmə] n asthme m

astonish [ə'stɔnɪʃ] vt étonner, stupéfier; ~**ment** n étonnement m

astound [ə'staund] vt stupéfier, sidérer

astray [ə'streɪ] adv: **to go ~** s'égarer; (fig) quitter le droit chemin; **to lead ~** détourner du droit chemin

astride [ə'straɪd] prep à cheval sur

astrology [əs'trɔlədʒɪ] n astrologie f

astronaut ['æstrənɔːt] n astronaute m/f

astronomy [əs'trɔnəmɪ] n astronomie f

asylum [ə'saɪləm] n asile m

KEYWORD

at [æt] *prep* **1** (*referring to position, direction*) à; **at the top** au sommet; **at home/school** à la maison *or* chez soi/à l'école; **at the baker's** à la boulangerie, chez le boulanger; **to look at sth** regarder qch
2 (*referring to time*): **at 4 o'clock** à 4 heures; **at Christmas** à Noël; **at night** la nuit; **at times** par moments, parfois
3 (*referring to rates, speed etc*) à; **at £1 a kilo** une livre le kilo; **two at a time** deux à la fois; **at 50 km/h** à 50 km/h
4 (*referring to manner*): **at a stroke** d'un seul coup; **at peace** en paix
5 (*referring to activity*): **to be at work** être au travail, travailler; **to play at cowboys** jouer aux cowboys; **to be good at sth** être bon en qch
6 (*referring to cause*): **shocked/surprised/annoyed at sth** choqué par/étonné de/agacé par qch; **I went at his suggestion** j'y suis allé sur son conseil

---

ate [eɪt] *pt of* **eat**
atheist [ˈeɪθɪɪst] *n* athée *m/f*
Athens [ˈæθɪnz] *n* Athènes
athlete [ˈæθliːt] *n* athlète *m/f*; **athletic** [æθˈletɪk] *adj* athlétique; **athletics** *n* athlétisme *m*
Atlantic [ətˈlæntɪk] *adj* atlantique ♦ *n*: **the ~ (Ocean)** l'(océan *m*) Atlantique *m*
atlas [ˈætləs] *n* atlas *m*
ATM *n abbr* (= *automated telling machine*) guichet *m* automatique
atmosphere [ˈætməsfɪər] *n* atmosphère *f*
atom [ˈætəm] *n* atome *m*; **~ic** [əˈtɔmɪk] *adj* atomique; **~(ic) bomb** *n* bombe *f* atomique; **~izer** *n* atomiseur *m*
atone [əˈtəʊn] *vi*: **to ~ for** expier, racheter
atrocious [əˈtrəʊʃəs] *adj* (*very bad*) atroce, exécrable
attach [əˈtætʃ] *vt* attacher; (*document, letter*) joindre; **to be ~ed to sb/sth** être attaché à qn/qch
attaché case [əˈtæʃeɪ] *n* mallette *f*, attaché-case *m*

attachment [əˈtætʃmənt] *n* (*tool*) accessoire *m*; (*love*): **~ (to)** affection *f* (pour), attachement *m* (à)
attack [əˈtæk] *vt* attaquer; (*task etc*) s'attaquer à ♦ *n* attaque *f*; (*also:* **heart ~**) crise *f* cardiaque
attain [əˈteɪn] *vt* (*also:* **to ~ to**) parvenir à, atteindre; (: *knowledge*) acquérir
attempt [əˈtempt] *n* tentative *f* ♦ *vt* essayer, tenter; **to make an ~ on sb's life** attenter à la vie de qn; **~ed** *adj*: **~ed murder/suicide** tentative *f* de meurtre/suicide
attend [əˈtend] *vt* (*course*) suivre; (*meeting, talk*) assister à; (*school, church*) aller à, fréquenter; (*patient*) soigner, s'occuper de; **~ to** *vt fus* (*needs, affairs etc*) s'occuper de; (*customer, patient*) s'occuper de; **~ance** (*being present*) présence *f*; (*people present*) assistance *f*; **~ant** *n* employé(e) *f* ♦ *adj* (*dangers*) inhérent(e), concomitant(e)
attention [əˈtenʃən] *n* attention *f*; **~!** (MIL) garde-à-vous!; **for the ~ of** (ADMIN) à l'attention de
attentive [əˈtentɪv] *adj* attentif(-ive); (*kind*) prévenant(e)
attest [əˈtest] *vi*: **to ~ to** (*demonstrate*) démontrer; (*confirm*) témoigner
attic [ˈætɪk] *n* grenier *m*
attitude [ˈætɪtjuːd] *n* attitude *f*; pose *f*, maintien *m*
attorney [əˈtɜːnɪ] *n* (US: *lawyer*) avoué *m*; **A~ General** *n* (BRIT) ≈ procureur général; (US) ≈ garde *m* des Sceaux, ministre *m* de la Justice
attract [əˈtrækt] *vt* attirer; **~ion** *n* (*gen pl*: *pleasant things*) attraction *f*, attrait *m*; (PHYSICS) attraction *f*; (*fig*: *towards sb or sth*) attirance *f*; **~ive** *adj* attrayant(e); (*person*) séduisant(e)
attribute [*n* ˈætrɪbjuːt, *vb* əˈtrɪbjuːt] *n* attribut *m* ♦ *vt*: **to ~ sth to** attribuer qch à
attrition [əˈtrɪʃən] *n*: **war of ~** guerre *f* d'usure
aubergine [ˈəʊbəʒiːn] *n* aubergine *f*
auction [ˈɔːkʃən] *n* (*also:* **sale by ~**) vente *f* aux enchères ♦ *vt* (*also:* **sell by ~**) ven-

dre aux enchères; *(also:* **put up for ~)** mettre aux enchères; **~eer** [ɔːkʃəˈnɪər] *n* commissaire-priseur *m*

audience [ˈɔːdɪəns] *n (people)* assistance *f*; public *m*; spectateurs *mpl*; *(interview)* audience *f*

audiovisual [ˈɔːdɪəʊˈvɪzjuəl] *adj* audiovisuel(le); **~ aids** *npl* supports *or* moyens audiovisuels

audit [ˈɔːdɪt] *vt* vérifier

audition [ɔːˈdɪʃən] *n* audition *f*

auditor [ˈɔːdɪtər] *n* vérificateur *m* des comptes

augur [ˈɔːgər] *vi:* **it ~s well** c'est bon signe *or* de bon augure

August [ˈɔːgəst] *n* août *m*

aunt [ɑːnt] *n* tante *f*; **~ie, ~y** [ˈɑːntɪ] *n dimin of* **aunt**

au pair [ˈəʊˈpɛər] *n (also:* **~ girl)** jeune fille *f* au pair

auspicious [ɔːsˈpɪʃəs] *adj* de bon augure, propice

Australia [ɒsˈtreɪlɪə] *n* Australie *f*; **~n** *adj* australien(ne) ♦ *n* Australien(ne)

Austria [ˈɒstrɪə] *n* Autriche *f*; **~n** *adj* autrichien(ne) ♦ *n* Autrichien(ne)

authentic [ɔːˈθɛntɪk] *adj* authentique

author [ˈɔːθər] *n* auteur *m*

authoritarian [ɔːθɒrɪˈtɛərɪən] *adj* autoritaire

authoritative [ɔːˈθɒrɪtətɪv] *adj (account)* digne de foi; *(study, treatise)* qui fait autorité; *(person, manner)* autoritaire

authority [ɔːˈθɒrɪtɪ] *n* autorité *f*; *(permission)* autorisation (formelle); **the authorities** *npl (ruling body)* les autorités *fpl*, l'administration *f*

authorize [ˈɔːθəraɪz] *vt* autoriser

auto [ˈɔːtəʊ] *(US) n* auto *f*, voiture *f*

auto: **~biography** [ɔːtəbaɪˈɒgrəfɪ] *n* autobiographie *f*; **~graph** [ˈɔːtəgrɑːf] *n* autographe *m* ♦ *vt* signer, dédicacer; **~mated** [ˈɔːtəmeɪtɪd] *adj* automatisé(e), automatique; **~matic** [ɔːtəˈmætɪk] *adj* automatique ♦ *n (gun)* automatique *m*; *(washing machine)* machine *f* à laver automatique; *(BRIT: AUT)* voiture *f* à transmission auto-

matique; **~matically** *adv* automatiquement; **~mation** [ɔːtəˈmeɪʃən] *n* automatisation *f* (électronique); **~mobile** [ˈɔːtəməbiːl] *(US) n* automobile *f*; **~nomy** [ɔːˈtɒnəmɪ] *n* autonomie *f*

autumn [ˈɔːtəm] *n* automne *m*; **in ~** en automne

auxiliary [ɔːgˈzɪlɪərɪ] *adj* auxiliaire ♦ *n* auxiliaire *m/f*

avail [əˈveɪl] *vt:* **to ~ o.s. of** profiter de ♦ *n:* **to no ~** sans résultat, en vain, en pure perte

availability [əveɪləˈbɪlɪtɪ] *n* disponibilité *f*

available [əˈveɪləbl] *adj* disponible

avalanche [ˈævəlɑːnʃ] *n* avalanche *f*

Ave *abbr* = **avenue**

avenge [əˈvɛndʒ] *vt* venger

avenue [ˈævənjuː] *n* avenue *f*; *(fig)* moyen *m*

average [ˈævərɪdʒ] *n* moyenne *f*; *(fig)* moyen *m* ♦ *adj* moyen(ne) ♦ *vt (a certain figure)* atteindre *or* faire *etc* en moyenne; **on ~** en moyenne; **~ out** *vi:* **to ~ out at** représenter en moyenne, donner une moyenne de

averse [əˈvɜːs] *adj:* **to be ~ to sth/doing sth** éprouver une forte répugnance envers qch/à faire qch

avert [əˈvɜːt] *vt (danger)* prévenir, écarter; *(one's eyes)* détourner

aviary [ˈeɪvɪərɪ] *n* volière *f*

avocado [ævəˈkɑːdəʊ] *n (BRIT: ~ pear)* avocat *m*

avoid [əˈvɔɪd] *vt* éviter

await [əˈweɪt] *vt* attendre

awake [əˈweɪk] *(pt* **awoke,** *pp* **awoken)** *adj* éveillé(e) ♦ *vt* éveiller ♦ *vi* s'éveiller; **~ to** *(dangers, possibilities)* conscient(e) de; **to be ~** être réveillé(e); **he was still ~** il ne dormait pas encore; **~ning** *n* réveil *m*

award [əˈwɔːd] *n* récompense *f*, prix *m*; *(LAW: damages)* dommages-intérêts *mpl* ♦ *vt (prize)* décerner; *(LAW: damages)* accorder

aware [əˈwɛər] *adj:* **~ (of)** *(conscious)* conscient(e) (de); *(informed)* au courant (de); **to become ~ of/that** prendre conscience de/que; se rendre compte de/que; **~ness** n conscience f, connaissance f

away [ə'weɪ] adj, adv (au) loin; absent(e); **two kilometres ~** à (une distance de) deux kilomètres, à deux kilomètres de distance; **two hours ~ by car** à deux heures de voiture or de route; **the holiday was two weeks ~** il restait deux semaines jusqu'aux vacances; **~ from** loin de; **he's ~ for a week** il est parti (pour) une semaine; **to pedal/work/laugh ~** être en train de pédaler/travailler/rire; **to fade ~** (sound) s'affaiblir; (colour) s'estomper; **to wither ~** (plant) se dessécher; **to take ~** emporter; (subtract) enlever; **~ game** n (SPORT) match m à l'extérieur

awe [ɔː] n respect mêlé de crainte; **~-inspiring** ['ɔːɪnspaɪərɪŋ] adj impressionnant(e)

awful ['ɔːfəl] adj affreux(-euse); **an ~ lot (of)** un nombre incroyable (de); **~ly** adv (very) terriblement, vraiment

awkward ['ɔːkwəd] adj (clumsy) gauche, maladroit(e); (inconvenient) peu pratique; (embarrassing) gênant(e), délicat(e)

awning ['ɔːnɪŋ] n (of tent) auvent m; (of shop) store m; (of hotel etc) marquise f

awoke [ə'wəuk] pt of **awake**; **~n** [ə'wəukən] pp of **awake**

axe [æks] (US **ax**) n hache f ♦ vt (project etc) abandonner; (jobs) supprimer

axes[1] ['æksɪz] npl of **axe**

axes[2] ['æksiːz] npl of **axis**

axis ['æksɪs] (pl **axes**) n axe m

axle ['æksl] n (also: **~-tree**: AUT) essieu m

ay(e) [aɪ] excl (yes) oui

B, b

B [biː] n (MUS) si m; **~ road** (BRIT) route départmentale

B.A. abbr = **Bachelor of Arts**

babble ['bæbl] vi bredouiller; (baby, stream) gazouiller

baby ['beɪbɪ] n bébé m; (US: inf: darling):

come on, ~! viens ma belle/mon gars!; **~ carriage** (US) n voiture f d'enfant; **~ food** n aliments mpl pour bébé(s); **~-sit** vi garder les enfants; **~-sitter** n babysitter m/f; **~ wipe** n lingette f (pour bébé)

bachelor ['bætʃələʳ] n célibataire m; **B~ of Arts/Science** ≈ licencié(e) ès or en lettres/sciences

back [bæk] n (of person, horse, book) dos m; (of hand) dos, revers m; (of house) derrière m; (of car, train) arrière m; (of chair) dossier m; (of page) verso m; (of room, audience) fond m; (SPORT) arrière m ♦ vt (candidate: also: **~ up**) soutenir, appuyer; (horse: at races) parier or miser sur; (car) (faire) reculer ♦ vi (also: **~ up**) reculer; (also: **~ up**: car etc) faire marche arrière ♦ adj (in compounds) de derrière, à l'arrière ♦ adv (not forward) en arrière; (returned): **he's ~** il est rentré, il est de retour; (restitution): **throw the ball ~** renvoie la balle; (again): **he called ~** il a rappelé; **~ seat/wheels** (AUT) sièges mpl/roues fpl arrières; **~ payments/rent** arriéré m de paiements/loyer; **he ran ~** il est revenu en courant; **~ down** vi rabattre de ses prétentions; **~ out** vi (of promise) se dédire; **~ up** vt (candidate etc) soutenir, appuyer; (COMPUT) sauvegarder; **~ache** n mal m de dos; **~bencher** (BRIT) n membre du parlement sans portefeuille; **~bone** n colonne vertébrale, épine dorsale; **~date** vt (letter) antidater; **~dated pay rise** augmentation f avec effet rétroactif; **~fire** vi (AUT) pétarader; (plans) mal tourner; **~ground** n arrière-plan m; (of events) situation f, conjoncture f; (basic knowledge) éléments mpl de base; (experience) formation f; **family ~ground** milieu familial; **~hand** n (TENNIS: also: **~hand stroke**) revers m; **~hander** (BRIT) n (bribe) pot-de-vin m; **~ing** n (fig) soutien m, appui m; **~lash** n contre-coup m, répercussion f; **~log** n: **~log of work** travail m en retard; **~ number** n (of magazine etc) vieux numéro; **~pack** n sac m à dos; **~packer** n randonneur(-euse); **~ pain** n mal m de dos; ~ **pay** *n* rappel *m* de salaire; ~**side** (*inf*) *n* derrière *m*, postérieur *m*; ~**stage** *adv* ♦ *n* derrière la scène, dans la coulisse; ~**stroke** *n* dos crawlé; ~**up** *adj* (*train, plane*) supplémentaire, de réserve; (*COMPUT*) de sauvegarde ♦ *n* (*support*) appui *m*, soutien *m*; (*also*: ~**up disk/file**) sauvegarde *f*; ~**ward** *adj* (*movement*) en arrière; (*person, country*) arriéré(e); attardé(e); ~**wards** *adv* (*move, go*) en arrière; (*read a list*) à l'envers, à rebours; (*fall*) à la renverse; (*walk*) à reculons; ~**water** *n* (*fig*) coin reculé; bled perdu (*péj*); ~**yard** *n* arrière-cour *f*

bacon ['beɪkən] *n* bacon *m*, lard *m*

bacteria [bæk'tɪərɪə] *npl* bactéries *fpl*

bad [bæd] *adj* mauvais(e); (*child*) vilain(e); (*mistake, accident etc*) grave; (*meat, food*) gâté(e), avarié(e); **his ~ leg** sa jambe malade; **to go ~** (*meat, food*) se gâter

badge [bædʒ] *n* insigne *m*; (*of policeman*) plaque *f*

badger ['bædʒəʳ] *n* blaireau *m*

badly ['bædlɪ] *adv* (*work, dress etc*) mal; ~ **wounded** grièvement blessé; **he needs it ~** il en a absolument besoin; ~ **off** *adj, adv* dans la gêne

badminton ['bædmɪntən] *n* badminton *m*

bad-tempered ['bæd'tempəd] *adj* (*person: by nature*) ayant mauvais caractère; (: *on one occasion*) de mauvaise humeur

baffle ['bæfl] *vt* (*puzzle*) déconcerter

bag [bæg] *n* sac *m* ♦ *vt* (*inf: take*) empocher; s'approprier; ~**s of** (*inf: lots of*) des masses de; ~**gage** *n* bagages *mpl*; ~**gage allowance** *n* franchise *f* de bagages; ~**gage reclaim** *n* livraison *f* de bagages; ~**gy** *adj* avachi(e), qui fait des poches; ~**pipes** *npl* cornemuse *f*

bail [beɪl] *n* (*payment*) caution *f*; (*release*) mise *f* en liberté sous caution ♦ *vt* (*prisoner: also*: **grant ~ to**) mettre en liberté sous caution; (*boat: also*: **~ out**) écoper; **on ~** (*prisoner*) sous caution; *see also* **bale**; ~ **out** *vt* (*prisoner*) payer la caution de

bailiff ['beɪlɪf] *n* (*BRIT*) ≈ huissier *m*; (*US*) ≈

huissier-audiencier *m*

bait [beɪt] *n* appât *m* ♦ *vt* appâter; (*fig: tease*) tourmenter

bake [beɪk] *vt* (faire) cuire au four ♦ *vi* (*bread etc*) cuire (au four); (*make cakes etc*) faire de la pâtisserie; ~**d beans** *npl* haricots blancs à la sauce tomate; ~**d potato** *n* pomme *f* de terre en robe des champs; ~**r** *n* boulanger *m*; ~**ry** *n* boulangerie *f*; boulangerie industrielle; **baking** *n* cuisson *f*; **baking powder** *n* levure *f* (chimique)

balance ['bæləns] *n* équilibre *m*; (*COMM: sum*) solde *m*; (*remainder*) reste *m*; (*scales*) balance *f* ♦ *vt* mettre *or* faire tenir en équilibre; (*pros and cons*) peser; (*budget*) équilibrer; (*account*) balancer; ~ **of trade/ payments** balance commerciale/des comptes *or* paiements; ~**d** *adj* (*personality, diet*) équilibré(e); (*report*) objectif(-ive); ~ **sheet** *n* bilan *m*

balcony ['bælkənɪ] *n* balcon *m*; (*in theatre*) deuxième balcon

bald [bɔːld] *adj* chauve; (*tyre*) lisse

bale [beɪl] *n* balle *f*, ballot *m*; ~ **out** *vi* (*of a plane*) sauter en parachute

ball [bɔːl] *n* boule *f*; (*football*) ballon *m*; (*for tennis, golf*) balle *f*; (*of wool*) pelote *f*; (*of string*) bobine *f*; (*dance*) bal *m*; **to play ~ (with sb)** (*fig*) coopérer (avec qn)

ballast ['bæləst] *n* lest *m*

ball bearings *npl* roulement *m* à billes

ballerina [bælə'riːnə] *n* ballerine *f*

ballet ['bæleɪ] *n* ballet *m*; (*art*) danse *f* (classique); ~ **dancer** *n* danseur(-euse) *m/f* de ballet; ~ **shoe** *n* chausson *m* de danse

balloon [bə'luːn] *n* ballon *m*; (*in comic strip*) bulle *f*

ballot ['bælət] *n* scrutin *m*; ~ **paper** *n* bulletin *m* de vote

ballpoint (pen) ['bɔːlpɔɪnt(-)] *n* stylo *m* à bille

ballroom ['bɔːlrum] *n* salle *f* de bal

ban [bæn] *n* interdiction *f* ♦ *vt* interdire

banana [bə'nɑːnə] *n* banane *f*

band [bænd] *n* bande *f*; (*at a dance*) orchestre *m*; (*MIL*) musique *f*, fanfare *f*; ~

together vi se liguer

bandage ['bændɪdʒ] n bandage m, pansement m ♦ vt bander

Bandaid ® ['bændeɪd] (US) n pansement adhésif

bandit n bandit m

bandy-legged ['bændɪ'legɪd] adj aux jambes arquées

bang [bæŋ] n détonation f; (of door) claquement m; (blow) coup (violent) ♦ vt frapper (violemment); (door) claquer ♦ vi détoner; claquer ♦ excl pan!; ~s (US) npl (fringe) frange f

banish ['bænɪʃ] vt bannir

banister(s) ['bænɪstə(z)] n(pl) rampe f (d'escalier)

bank [bæŋk] n banque f; (of river, lake) bord m, rive f; (of earth) talus m, remblai m ♦ vi (AVIAT) virer sur l'aile; ~ **on** vt fus miser or tabler sur; ~ **account** n compte m en banque; ~ **card** n carte f d'identité bancaire; ~**er** n banquier m; ~**er's card** (BRIT) n = **bank card**; ~ **holiday** (BRIT) n jour férié (les banques sont fermées); ~**ing** n opérations fpl bancaires; profession f de banquier; ~**note** n billet m de banque; ~ **rate** n taux m de l'escompte

---

bank holiday

---

i Un **bank holiday** en Grande-Bretagne est un lundi férié et donc l'occasion d'un week-end prolongé. La circulation sur les routes et le trafic dans les gares et les aéroports augmentent considérablement à ces périodes. Les principaux bank holidays, à part Pâques et Noël, ont lieu au mois de mai et fin août.

---

bankrupt ['bæŋkrʌpt] adj en faillite; **to go ~** faire faillite; ~**cy** n faillite f

bank statement n relevé m de compte

banner ['bænər] n bannière f

bannister(s) ['bænɪstə(z)] n(pl) = **banister(s)**

baptism ['bæptɪzəm] n baptême m

bar [bɑːr] n (pub) bar m; (counter: in pub) comptoir m, bar; (rod: of metal etc) barre f; (on window etc) barreau m; (of chocolate) tablette f, plaque f; (fig) obstacle m; (prohibition) mesure f d'exclusion; (MUS) mesure f ♦ vt (road) barrer; (window) munir de barreaux; (person) exclure; (activity) interdire; ~ **of soap** savonnette f; **the B~** (LAW) le barreau; **behind ~s** (prisoner) sous les verrous; ~ **none** sans exception

barbaric [bɑː'bærɪk] adj barbare

barbecue ['bɑːbɪkjuː] n barbecue m

barbed wire ['bɑːbd-] n fil m de fer barbelé

barber ['bɑːbər] n coiffeur m (pour hommes)

bar code n (on goods) code m à barres

bare [bɛər] adj nu(e) ♦ vt mettre à nu, dénuder; (teeth) montrer; **the ~ necessities** le strict nécessaire; ~**back** adv à cru, sans selle; ~**faced** adj impudent(e), effronté(e); ~**foot** adj, adv nu-pieds, (les) pieds nus; ~**ly** adv à peine

bargain ['bɑːgɪn] n (transaction) marché m; (good buy) affaire f, occasion f ♦ vi (haggle) marchander; (negotiate): **to ~ (with sb)** négocier (avec qn), traiter (avec qn); **into the ~** par-dessus le marché; ~ **for** vt fus: **he got more than he ~ed for** il ne s'attendait pas à un coup pareil

barge [bɑːdʒ] n péniche f; ~ **in** vi (walk in) faire irruption; (interrupt talk) intervenir mal à propos

bark [bɑːk] n (of tree) écorce f; (of dog) aboiement m ♦ vi aboyer

barley ['bɑːlɪ] n orge f; ~ **sugar** n sucre m d'orge

bar: ~**maid** n serveuse f de bar, barmaid f; ~**man** (irreg) n barman m; ~ **meal** n repas m de bistrot; **to go for a ~ meal** aller manger au bistrot

barn [bɑːn] n grange f

barometer [bə'rɒmɪtər] n baromètre m

baron ['bærən] n baron m; ~**ess** ['bærənɪs] n baronne f

barracks ['bærəks] npl caserne f

barrage ['bærɑːʒ] n (MIL) tir m de barrage; (dam) barrage m; (fig) pluie f

barrel ['bærəl] n tonneau m; (of oil) baril

m; (of gun) canon m

barren ['bærən] adj stérile

barricade [bærɪ'keɪd] n barricade f

barrier ['bærɪər] n barrière f; (fig: to progress etc) obstacle m

barring ['bɑːrɪŋ] prep sauf

barrister ['bærɪstər] (BRIT) n avocat (plaidant)

barrow ['bærəu] n (wheelbarrow) charrette f à bras

bartender ['bɑːtɛndər] (US) n barman m

barter ['bɑːtər] vt: to ~ sth for échanger qch contre

base [beɪs] n base f; (of tree, post) pied m
♦ vt: to ~ sth on baser or fonder qch sur
♦ adj vil(e), bas(se)

baseball ['beɪsbɔːl] n base-ball m

basement ['beɪsmənt] n sous-sol m

bases¹ ['beɪsɪz] npl of **base**

bases² ['beɪsiːz] npl of **basis**

bash [bæʃ] (inf) vt frapper, cogner

bashful ['bæʃful] adj timide; modeste

basic ['beɪsɪk] adj fondamental(e), de base; (minimal) rudimentaire; ~**ally** adv fondamentalement, à la base; (in fact) en fait, au fond; ~**s** npl: **the ~s** l'essentiel m

basil ['bæzl] n basilic m

basin ['beɪsn] n (vessel, also GEO) cuvette f, bassin m; (also: **washbasin**) lavabo m

basis ['beɪsɪs] (pl **bases**) n base f; **on a trial ~** à titre d'essai; **on a part-time ~** à temps partiel

bask [bɑːsk] vi: to ~ in the sun se chauffer au soleil

basket ['bɑːskɪt] n corbeille f; (with handle) panier m; ~**ball** n basket-ball m

bass [beɪs] n (MUS) basse f; ~ **drum** n grosse caisse f

bassoon [bə'suːn] n (MUS) basson m

bastard ['bɑːstəd] n enfant naturel(le), bâtard(e); (inf!) salaud m (!)

bat [bæt] n chauve-souris f; (for baseball etc) batte f; (BRIT: for table tennis) raquette f
♦ vt: **he didn't ~ an eyelid** il n'a pas sourcillé or bronché

batch [bætʃ] n (of bread) fournée f; (of papers) liasse f

bated ['beɪtɪd] adj: **with ~ breath** en retenant son souffle

bath [bɑːθ] n bain m; (~tub) baignoire f
♦ vt baigner, donner un bain à; **to have a ~** prendre un bain; see also **baths**

bathe [beɪð] vi se baigner ♦ vt (wound) laver; **bathing** n baignade f; **bathing costume, bathing suit** (US) n maillot m (de bain)

bath: ~**robe** n peignoir m de bain; ~**room** n salle f de bains; ~**s** npl (also: **swimming ~s**) piscine f; ~ **towel** n serviette f de bain

baton ['bætən] n bâton m; (MUS) baguette f; (club) matraque f

batter ['bætər] vt battre ♦ n pâte f à frire; ~**ed** ['bætəd] adj (hat, pan) cabossé(e)

battery ['bætərɪ] n batterie f; (of torch) pile f; ~ **farming** n élevage m en batterie

battle ['bætl] n bataille f, combat m ♦ vi se battre, lutter; ~**field** n champ m de bataille; ~**ship** n cuirassé m

Bavaria [bə'vɛərɪə] n Bavière f

bawl [bɔːl] vi hurler; (child) brailler

bay [beɪ] n (of sea) baie f; **to hold sb at ~** tenir qn à distance or en échec; ~ **leaf** n laurier m; ~ **window** n baie vitrée

bazaar [bə'zɑːr] n bazar m; vente f de charité

B & B n abbr = **bed and breakfast**

BBC n abbr (= British Broadcasting Corporation) office de la radiodiffusion et télévision britannique

B.C. adv abbr (= before Christ) av. J.-C.

KEYWORD

be [biː] (pt **was, were**, pp **been**) aux vb 1 (with present participle: forming continuous tenses): **what are you doing?** que faites-vous?; **they're coming tomorrow** ils viennent demain; **I've been waiting for you for 2 hours** je t'attends depuis 2 heures

2 (with pp: forming passives) être; **to be killed** être tué(e); **he was nowhere to be seen** on ne le voyait nulle part

3 (in tag questions): **it was fun, wasn't it?** c'était drôle, n'est-ce pas?; **she's back, is**

she? elle est rentrée, n'est-ce pas or alors?
4 (+*to* +*infinitive*): **the house is to be sold** la maison doit être vendue; **he's not to open it** il ne doit pas l'ouvrir
♦ *vb* + *complement* 1 (*gen*) être; **I'm English** je suis anglais(e); **I'm tired** je suis fatigué(e); **I'm hot/cold** j'ai chaud/froid; **he's a doctor** il est médecin; **2 and 2 are 4** 2 et 2 font 4
2 (*of health*) aller; **how are you?** comment allez-vous?; **he's fine now** il va bien maintenant; **he's very ill** il est très malade
3 (*of age*) avoir; **how old are you?** quel âge avez-vous?; **I'm sixteen (years old)** j'ai seize ans
4 (*cost*) coûter; **how much was the meal?** combien a coûté le repas?; **that'll be £5, please** ça fera 5 livres, s'il vous plaît
♦ *vi* 1 (*exist, occur etc*) être, exister; **the prettiest girl that ever was** la fille la plus jolie qui ait jamais existé; **be that as it may** quoi qu'il en soit; **so be it** soit
2 (*referring to place*) être, se trouver; **I won't be here tomorrow** je ne serai pas là demain; **Edinburgh is in Scotland** Édimbourg est or se trouve en Écosse
3 (*referring to movement*) aller; **where have you been?** où êtes-vous allé(s)?
♦ *impers vb* 1 (*referring to time, distance*) être; **it's 5 o'clock** il est 5 heures; **it's the 28th of April** c'est le 28 avril; **it's 10 km to the village** le village est à 10 km
2 (*referring to the weather*) faire; **it's too hot/cold** il fait trop chaud/froid; **it's windy** il y a du vent
3 (*emphatic*): **it's me/the postman** c'est moi/le facteur

beach [bi:tʃ] *n* plage *f* ♦ *vt* échouer
beacon ['bi:kən] *n* (*lighthouse*) fanal *m*; (*marker*) balise *f*
bead [bi:d] *n* perle *f*
beak [bi:k] *n* bec *m*
beaker ['bi:kər] *n* gobelet *m*

beam [bi:m] *n* poutre *f*; (*of light*) rayon *m*
♦ *vi* rayonner
bean [bi:n] *n* haricot *m*; (*of coffee*) grain *m*; **runner ~** haricot *m* (à rames); **broad ~** fève *f*; **~sprouts** *npl* germes *mpl* de soja
bear [beər] (*pt* **bore**, *pp* **borne**) *n* ours *m*
♦ *vt* porter; (*endure*) supporter ♦ *vi*: **to ~ right/left** obliquer à droite/gauche, se diriger vers la droite/gauche; **~ out** *vt* corroborer, confirmer; **~ up** *vi* (*person*) tenir le coup
beard [biəd] *n* barbe *f*; **~ed** *adj* barbu(e)
bearer ['beərər] *n* porteur *m*; (*of passport*) titulaire *m/f*
bearing ['beərɪŋ] *n* maintien *m*, allure *f*; (*connection*) rapport *m*; **~s** *npl* (*also:* **ball ~s**) roulement *m* (à billes); **to take a ~** faire le point
beast [bi:st] *n* bête *f*; (*inf: person*) brute *f*; **~ly** *adj* infect(e)
beat [bi:t] (*pt* **beat**, *pp* **beaten**) *n* battement *m*; (*MUS*) temps *m*, mesure *f*; (*of policeman*) ronde *f* ♦ *vt*, *vi* battre; **off the ~en track** hors des chemins or sentiers battus; **~ it!** (*inf*) fiche(-moi) le camp!; **~ off** *vt* repousser; **~ up** *vt* (*inf: person*) tabasser; (*eggs*) battre; **~ing** *n* raclée *f*
beautiful ['bju:tɪful] *adj* beau (belle); **~ly** *adv* admirablement
beauty ['bju:tɪ] *n* beauté *f*; **~ salon** *n* institut *m* de beauté; **~ spot** (*BRIT*) (*TOURISM*) site naturel (d'une grande beauté)
beaver ['bi:vər] *n* castor *m*
because [bɪ'kɒz] *conj* parce que; **~ of** *prep* à cause de
beck [bek] *n*: **to be at sb's ~ and call** être à l'entière disposition de qn
beckon ['bekən] *vt* (*also:* **~ to**) faire signe (de venir) à
become [bɪ'kʌm] (*irreg: like* **come**) *vi* devenir; **to ~ fat/thin** grossir/maigrir; **becoming** *adj* (*behaviour*) convenable, bienséant(e); (*clothes*) seyant(e)
bed [bed] *n* lit *m*; (*of flowers*) parterre *m*; (*of coal, clay*) couche *f*; (*of sea*) fond *m*; **to go to ~** aller se coucher; **~ and breakfast** *n* (*terms*) chambre et petit déjeuner;

(*place*) ≃ chambre *f* d'hôte; ~**clothes** *npl* couvertures *fpl* et draps *mpl*; ~**ding** *n* literie *f*; ~ **linen** *n* draps *mpl* de lit (et taies *fpl* d'oreillers), literie *f*

> **bed and breakfast**

ⓘ *Un* **bed and breakfast** *est une petite pension dans une maison particulière ou une ferme où l'on peut louer une chambre avec petit déjeuner compris pour un prix modique par rapport à ce que l'on paierait dans un hôtel. Ces établissements sont communément appelés B & B, et sont signalés par une pancarte dans le jardin ou au-dessus de la porte.*

bedraggled [bɪˈdrægld] *adj* (*person, clothes*) débraillé(e); (*hair: wet*) trempé(e)

bed: ~**ridden** *adj* cloué(e) au lit; ~**room** *n* chambre *f* (à coucher); ~**side** *n*: **at sb's ~side** au chevet de qn; ~**sit(ter)** *n* (*BRIT*) chambre meublée, studio *m*; ~**spread** *n* couvre-lit *m*, dessus-de-lit *m inv*; ~**time** *n* heure *f* du coucher

bee [biː] *n* abeille *f*

beech [biːtʃ] *n* hêtre *m*

beef [biːf] *n* bœuf *m*; **roast ~** rosbif *m*; ~**burger** *n* hamburger *m*; ~**eater** *n* hallebardier de la Tour de Londres

bee: ~**hive** *n* ruche *f*; ~**line** *n*: **to make a ~line for** se diriger tout droit vers

been [biːn] *pp* of **be**

beer [bɪəʳ] *n* bière *f*

beet [biːt] *n* (*vegetable*) betterave *f*; (*US: also:* **red ~**) betterave (potagère)

beetle [ˈbiːtl] *n* scarabée *m*

beetroot [ˈbiːtruːt] (*BRIT*) *n* betterave *f*

before [bɪˈfɔːʳ] *prep* (*in time*) avant; (*in space*) devant ♦ *conj* avant que +*sub*; avant de ♦ *adv* avant; devant; ~ **going** avant de partir; ~ **she goes** avant qu'elle ne parte; **the week ~** la semaine précédente *or* d'avant; **I've seen it ~** je l'ai déjà vu; ~**hand** *adv* au préalable, à l'avance

beg [beg] *vi* mendier ♦ *vt* mendier; (*forgiveness, mercy etc*) demander; (*entreat*) supplier; *see also* **pardon**

began [bɪˈgæn] *pt* of **begin**

beggar [ˈbegəʳ] *n* mendiant(e)

begin [bɪˈgɪn] (*pt* **began**, *pp* **begun**) *vt, vi* commencer; **to ~ doing** *or* **to do sth** commencer à *or* de faire qch; ~**ner** *n* débutant(e); ~**ning** *n* commencement *m*, début *m*

behalf [bɪˈhɑːf] *n*: **on ~ of**, (*US*) **in ~ of** (*representing*) de la part de; (*for benefit of*) pour le compte de; **on my/his ~** pour moi/lui

behave [bɪˈheɪv] *vi* se conduire, se comporter; (*well: also:* ~ **o.s.**) se conduire bien *or* comme il faut; **behaviour** (*US* **behavior**) [bɪˈheɪvjəʳ] *n* comportement *m*, conduite *f*

behead [bɪˈhed] *vt* décapiter

behind [bɪˈhaɪnd] *prep* derrière; (*time, progress*) en retard sur; (*work, studies*) en retard dans ♦ *adv* derrière ♦ *n* derrière *m*; **to be ~** (*schedule*) avoir du retard; ~ **the scenes** dans les coulisses

behold [bɪˈhəʊld] (*irreg: like* **hold**) *vt* apercevoir, voir

beige [beɪʒ] *adj* beige

Beijing [ˈbeɪˈdʒɪŋ] *n* Bei-jing, Pékin

being [ˈbiːɪŋ] *n* être *m*

Beirut [beɪˈruːt] *n* Beyrouth

Belarus [belaˈrus] *n* Bélarus *f*

belated [bɪˈleɪtɪd] *adj* tardif(-ive)

belch [beltʃ] *vi* avoir un renvoi, roter ♦ *vt* (*also:* ~ **out**: *smoke etc*) vomir, cracher

Belgian [ˈbeldʒən] *adj* belge, de Belgique ♦ *n* Belge *m/f*

Belgium [ˈbeldʒəm] *n* Belgique *f*

belie [bɪˈlaɪ] *vt* démentir

belief [bɪˈliːf] *n* (*opinion*) conviction *f*; (*trust, faith*) foi *f*

believe [bɪˈliːv] *vt, vi* croire; **to ~ in** (*God*) croire en; (*method, ghosts*) croire à; ~**r** *n* (*in idea, activity*): ~**r in** partisan(e) de; (*REL*) croyant(e)

belittle [bɪˈlɪtl] *vt* déprécier, rabaisser

bell [bel] *n* cloche *f*; (*small*) clochette *f*, grelot *m*; (*on door*) sonnette *f*; (*electric*) sonnerie *f*

belligerent [bɪˈlɪdʒərənt] *adj* (*person, atti-*

tude) agressif(-ive)
bellow ['bɛləʊ] *vi* (*bull*) meugler; (*person*) brailler
belly ['bɛlɪ] *n* ventre *m*
belong [bɪ'lɒŋ] *vi*: **to ~ to** appartenir à; (*club etc*) faire partie de; **this book ~s here** ce livre va ici; **~ings** *npl* affaires *fpl*, possessions *fpl*
beloved [bɪ'lʌvɪd] *adj* (bien-)aimé(e)
below [bɪ'ləʊ] *prep* sous, au-dessous de ♦ *adv* en dessous; **see ~** voir plus bas *or* plus loin *or* ci-dessous
belt [bɛlt] *n* ceinture *f*; (*of land*) région *f*; (*TECH*) courroie *f* ♦ *vt* (*thrash*) donner une raclée à; **~way** (*US*) *n* (*AUT*) route *f* de ceinture; (: *motorway*) périphérique *m*
bemused [bɪ'mjuːzd] *adj* stupéfié(e)
bench [bɛntʃ] *n* (*gen, also BRIT: POL*) banc *m*; (*in workshop*) établi *m*; **the B~** (*LAW: judge*) le juge; (: *judges collectively*) la magistrature, la Cour
bend [bɛnd] (*pt, pp* **bent**) *vt* courber; (*leg, arm*) plier ♦ *vi* se courber ♦ *n* (*BRIT: in road*) virage *m*, tournant *m*; (*in pipe, river*) coude *m*; **~ down** *vi* se baisser; **~ over** *vi* se pencher
beneath [bɪ'niːθ] *prep* sous, au-dessous de; (*unworthy of*) indigne de ♦ *adv* dessous, au-dessous, en bas
benefactor ['bɛnɪfæktəʳ] *n* bienfaiteur *m*
beneficial [bɛnɪ'fɪʃəl] *adj* salutaire; avantageux(-euse); **~ to the health** bon(ne) pour la santé
benefit ['bɛnɪfɪt] *n* avantage *m*, profit *m*; (*allowance of money*) allocation *f* ♦ *vt* faire du bien à, profiter à ♦ *vi*: **he'll ~ from it** cela lui fera du bien, il y gagnera *or* s'en trouvera bien
Benelux ['bɛnɪlʌks] *n* Bénélux *m*
benevolent [bɪ'nevələnt] *adj* bienveillant(e); (*organization*) bénévole
benign [bɪ'naɪn] *adj* (*person, smile*) bienveillant(e), affable; (*MED*) bénin(-igne)
bent [bɛnt] *pt, pp of* **bend** ♦ *n* inclination *f*, penchant *m*; **to be ~ on** être résolu(e) à
bequest [bɪ'kwɛst] *n* legs *m*
bereaved [bɪ'riːvd] *n*: **the ~** la famille du

disparu
beret ['bɛreɪ] *n* béret *m*
Berlin [bəː'lɪn] *n* Berlin
berm [bəːm] (*US*) *n* (*AUT*) accotement *m*
Bermuda [bəː'mjuːdə] *n* Bermudes *fpl*
berry ['bɛrɪ] *n* baie *f*
berserk [bə'səːk] *adj*: **to go ~** (*madman, crowd*) se déchaîner
berth [bəːθ] *n* (*bed*) couchette *f*; (*for ship*) poste *m* d'amarrage, mouillage *m* ♦ *vi* (*in harbour*) venir à quai; (*at anchor*) mouiller
beseech [bɪ'siːtʃ] (*pt, pp* **besought**) *vt* implorer, supplier
beset [bɪ'sɛt] (*pt, pp* **beset**) *vt* assaillir
beside [bɪ'saɪd] *prep* à côté de; **to be ~ o.s. (with anger)** être hors de soi; **that's ~ the point** cela n'a rien à voir; **~s** *adv* en outre, de plus; (*in any case*) d'ailleurs ♦ *prep* (*as well as*) en plus de
besiege [bɪ'siːdʒ] *vt* (*town*) assiéger; (*fig*) assaillir
best [bɛst] *adj* meilleur(e) ♦ *adv* le mieux; **the ~ part of** (*quantity*) le plus clair de, la plus grande partie de; **at ~** au mieux; **to make the ~ of sth** s'accommoder de qch (du mieux que l'on peut); **to do one's ~** faire de son mieux; **to the ~ of my knowledge** pour autant que je sache; **to the ~ of my ability** du mieux que je pourrai; **~ before date** *n* date *f* de limite d'utilisation *or* de consommation; **~ man** *n* garçon *m* d'honneur
bestow [bɪ'stəʊ] *vt*: **to ~ sth on sb** accorder qch à qn; (*title*) conférer qch à qn
bet [bɛt] (*pt, pp* **bet** *or* **betted**) *n* pari *m* ♦ *vt, vi* parier
betray [bɪ'treɪ] *vt* trahir
better ['bɛtəʳ] *adj* meilleur(e) ♦ *adv* mieux ♦ *vt* améliorer ♦ *n*: **to get the ~ of** triompher de, l'emporter sur; **you had ~ do it** vous feriez mieux de le faire; **he thought ~ of it** il s'est ravisé; **to get ~** aller mieux; s'améliorer; **~ off** *adj* plus à l'aise financièrement; (*fig*): **you'd be ~ off this way** vous vous en trouveriez mieux ainsi
betting ['bɛtɪŋ] *n* paris *mpl*; **~ shop** (*BRIT*) *n* bureau *m* de paris

between [bɪ'twiːn] *prep* entre ♦ *adv*: **(in) ~** au milieu; dans l'intervalle; (*in time*) dans l'intervalle

beverage ['bɛvərɪdʒ] *n* boisson *f* (*gén sans alcool*)

beware [bɪ'wɛəʳ] *vi*: **to ~ (of)** prendre garde (à); **"~ of the dog"** "attention! chien méchant"

bewildered [bɪ'wɪldəd] *adj* dérouté(e), ahuri(e)

beyond [bɪ'jɔnd] *prep* (*in space, time*) au-delà de; (*exceeding*) au-dessus de ♦ *adv* au-delà; **~ doubt** hors de doute; **~ repair** irréparable

bias ['baɪəs] *n* (*prejudice*) préjugé *m*, parti pris; **~(s)ed** *adj* partial(e), montrant un parti pris

bib [bɪb] *n* bavoir *m*, bavette *f*

Bible ['baɪbl] *n* Bible *f*

bicarbonate of soda [baɪ'kɑːbənɪt-] *n* bicarbonate *m* de soude

bicker ['bɪkəʳ] *vi* se chamailler

bicycle ['baɪsɪkl] *n* bicyclette *f*

bid [bɪd] (*pt* **bid** *or* **bade**, *pp* **bid(den)**) *n* offre *f*; (*at auction*) enchère *f*; (*attempt*) tentative *f* ♦ *vi* faire une enchère *or* offre ♦ *vt* faire une enchère *or* offre de; **to ~ sb good day** souhaiter le bonjour à qn; **~der** *n*: **the highest ~der** le plus offrant; **~ding** *n* enchères *fpl*

bide [baɪd] *vt*: **to ~ one's time** attendre son heure

bifocals [baɪ'fəʊklz] *npl* verres *mpl* à double foyer, lunettes bifocales

big [bɪg] *adj* grand(e); gros(se); **~headed** *adj* prétentieux(-euse)

bigot ['bɪgət] *n* fanatique *m/f*, sectaire *m/f*; **~ed** *adj* fanatique, sectaire; **~ry** *n* fanatisme *m*, sectarisme *m*

big top *n* grand chapiteau

bike [baɪk] *n* vélo *m*, bécane *f*

bikini [bɪ'kiːnɪ] *n* bikini *m*

bilingual [baɪ'lɪŋgwəl] *adj* bilingue

bill [bɪl] *n* note *f*, facture *f*; (*POL*) projet *m* de loi; (*US: banknote*) billet *m* (de banque); (*of bird*) bec *m*; (*THEATRE*): **on the ~** à l'affiche; **"post no ~s"** "défense d'affi-

cher"; **to fit** *or* **fill the ~** (*fig*) faire l'affaire; **~board** *n* panneau *m* d'affichage

billet ['bɪlɪt] *n* cantonnement *m* (chez l'habitant)

billfold ['bɪlfəʊld] (*US*) *n* portefeuille *m*

billiards ['bɪljədz] *n* (jeu *m* de) billard *m*

billion ['bɪljən] *n* (*BRIT*) billion *m* (*million de millions*); (*US*) milliard *m*

bimbo ['bɪmbəʊ] (*inf*) *n* ravissante idiote *f*, potiche *f*

bin [bɪn] *n* boîte *f*; (*also*: **dustbin**) poubelle *f*; (*for coal*) coffre *m*

bind [baɪnd] (*pt, pp* **bound**) *vt* attacher; (*book*) relier; (*oblige*) obliger, contraindre ♦ *n* (*inf: nuisance*) scie *f*; **~ing** *adj* (*contract*) constituant une obligation

binge [bɪndʒ] (*inf*) *n*: **to go on a/the ~** aller faire la bringue

bingo ['bɪngəʊ] *n* jeu de loto pratiqué dans des établissements publics

binoculars [bɪ'nɔkjuləz] *npl* jumelles *fpl*

bio *prefix*: **~chemistry** *n* biochimie *f*; **~degradable** *adj* biodégradable; **~graphy** *n* biographie *f*; **~logical** *adj* biologique; **~logy** *n* biologie *f*

birch [bəːtʃ] *n* bouleau *m*

bird [bəːd] *n* oiseau *m*; (*BRIT: inf: girl*) nana *f*; **~'s-eye view** *n* vue *f* à vol d'oiseau; (*fig*) vue d'ensemble *or* générale; **~watcher** *n* ornithologue *m/f* amateur

Biro ['baɪərəʊ] ® *n* stylo *m* à bille

birth [bəːθ] *n* naissance *f*; **to give ~ to** (*subj: woman*) donner naissance à; (: *animal*) mettre bas; **~ certificate** *n* acte *m* de naissance; **~ control** *n* (*policy*) limitation *f* des naissances; (*method*) méthode(s) contraceptive(s); **~day** *n* anniversaire *m* ♦ *cpd* d'anniversaire; **~place** *n* lieu *m* de naissance; (*fig*) berceau *m*; **~ rate** *n* (taux *m* de) natalité *f*

biscuit ['bɪskɪt] *n* (*BRIT*) biscuit *m*; (*US*) petit pain au lait

bisect [baɪ'sɛkt] *vt* couper *or* diviser en deux

bishop ['bɪʃəp] *n* évêque *m*; (*CHESS*) fou *m*

bit [bɪt] *pt of* **bite** ♦ *n* morceau *m*; (*of tool*) mèche *f*; (*of horse*) mors *m*; (*COMPUT*) élément *m* binaire; **a ~ of** un peu de; **a ~ mad** un peu fou; **~ by ~** petit à petit

bitch [bɪtʃ] *n* (*dog*) chienne *f*; (*inf!*) salope *f* (*!*), garce *f*

bite [baɪt] (*pt* **bit**, *pp* **bitten**) *vt, vi* mordre; (*insect*) piquer ♦ *n* (*insect ~*) piqûre *f*; (*mouthful*) bouchée *f*; **let's have a ~ (to eat)** (*inf*) mangeons un morceau; **to ~ one's nails** se ronger les ongles

bitter [ˈbɪtəʳ] *adj* amer(-ère); (*weather, wind*) glacial(e); (*criticism*) cinglant(e); (*struggle*) acharné(e) ♦ *n* (*BRIT: beer*) bière *f* (forte); **~ness** *n* amertume *f*; (*taste*) goût amer

black [blæk] *adj* noir(e) ♦ *n* (*colour*) noir *m*; (*person*): **B~** noir(e) ♦ *vt* (*BRIT: INDUSTRY*) boycotter; **to give sb a ~ eye** pocher l'œil à qn, faire un œil au beurre noir à qn; **~ and blue** couvert(e) de bleus; **to be in the ~** (*in credit*) être créditeur(-trice); **~berry** *n* mûre *f*; **~bird** *n* merle *m*; **~board** *n* tableau noir; **~ coffee** *n* café noir; **~currant** *n* cassis *m*; **~en** *vt* noircir; **~ ice** *n* verglas *m*; **~leg** (*BRIT*) *n* briseur *m* de grève, jaune *m*; **~list** *n* liste noire; **~mail** *n* chantage *m* ♦ *vt* faire chanter, soumettre au chantage; **~ market** *n* marché noir; **~out** *n* panne *f* d'électricité; (*TV etc*) interruption *f* d'émission; (*fainting*) syncope *f*; **~ pudding** *n* boudin (noir); **B~ Sea** *n*: **the B~ Sea** la mer Noire; **~ sheep** *n* brebis galeuse; **~smith** *n* forgeron *m*; **~ spot** (*AUT*) *n* point noir

bladder [ˈblædəʳ] *n* vessie *f*

blade [bleɪd] *n* lame *f*; (*of propeller*) pale *f*; **~ of grass** brin *m* d'herbe

blame [bleɪm] *n* faute *f*, blâme *m* ♦ *vt*: **to ~ sb/sth for sth** attribuer à qn/qch la responsabilité de qch; reprocher qch à qn/qch; **who's to ~?** qui est le fautif *or* coupable *or* responsable?

bland [blænd] *adj* (*taste, food*) doux (douce), fade

blank [blæŋk] *adj* blanc (blanche); (*look*) sans expression, dénué(e) d'expression ♦ *n* espace *m* vide, blanc *m*; (*cartridge*) cartouche *f* à blanc; **his mind was a ~** il avait la tête vide; **~ cheque** chèque *m* en blanc

blanket [ˈblæŋkɪt] *n* couverture *f*; (*of snow, cloud*) couche *f*

blare [blɛəʳ] *vi* beugler

blast [blɑːst] *n* souffle *m*; (*of explosive*) explosion *f* ♦ *vt* faire sauter *or* exploser; **~off** *n* (*SPACE*) lancement *m*

blatant [ˈbleɪtənt] *adj* flagrant(e), criant(e)

blaze [bleɪz] *n* (*fire*) incendie *m*; (*fig*) flamboiement *m* ♦ *vi* (*fire*) flamber; (*fig: eyes*) flamboyer; (: *guns*) crépiter ♦ *vt*: **to ~ a trail** (*fig*) montrer la voie

blazer [ˈbleɪzəʳ] *n* blazer *m*

bleach [bliːtʃ] *n* (*also:* **household ~**) eau *f* de Javel ♦ *vt* (*linen etc*) blanchir; **~ed** *adj* (*hair*) oxygéné(e), décoloré(e)

bleak [bliːk] *adj* morne, (*countryside*) désolé(e)

bleat [bliːt] *vi* bêler

bleed [bliːd] (*pt, pp* **bled**) *vt, vi* saigner; **my nose is ~ing** je saigne du nez

bleeper [ˈbliːpəʳ] *n* (*device*) bip *m*

blemish [ˈblemɪʃ] *n* défaut *m*; (*on fruit, reputation*) tache *f*

blend [blend] *n* mélange *m* ♦ *vt* mélanger ♦ *vi* (*colours etc: also:* **~ in**) se mélanger, se fondre; **~er** *n* mixeur *m*

bless [bles] (*pt, pp* **blessed** *or* **blest**) *vt* bénir; **~ you!** (*after sneeze*) à vos souhaits!; **~ing** *n* bénédiction *f*; (*godsend*) bienfait *m*

blew [bluː] *pt of* **blow**

blight [blaɪt] *vt* (*hopes etc*) anéantir; (*life*) briser

blimey [ˈblaɪmɪ] (*BRIT: inf*) *excl* mince alors!

blind [blaɪnd] *adj* aveugle ♦ *n* (*for window*) store *m* ♦ *vt* aveugler; **~ alley** *n* impasse *f*; **~ corner** (*BRIT*) *n* virage *m* sans visibilité; **~fold** *n* bandeau *m* ♦ *adj, adv* les yeux bandés ♦ *vt* bander les yeux à; **~ly** *adv* aveuglément; **~ness** *n* cécité *f*; **~ spot** *n* (*AUT etc*) angle mort; **that is her ~ spot** (*fig*) elle refuse d'y voir clair sur ce point

blink [blɪŋk] *vi* cligner des yeux; (*light*) clignoter; **~ers** *npl* œillères *fpl*

bliss [blɪs] *n* félicité *f*, bonheur *m* sans mélange

blanc

blanc

blister ['blɪstər] n (on skin) ampoule f, cloque f; (on paintwork, rubber) boursouflure f ♦ vi (paint) se boursoufler, se cloquer

blizzard ['blɪzəd] n blizzard m, tempête f de neige

bloated ['bləʊtɪd] adj (face) bouffi(e); (stomach, person) gonflé(e)

blob [blɒb] n (drop) goutte f; (stain, spot) tache f

block [blɒk] n bloc m; (in pipes) obstruction f; (toy) cube m; (of buildings) pâté m (de maisons) ♦ vt bloquer; (fig) faire obstacle à; ~ **of flats** (BRIT) immeuble (locatif); **mental** ~ trou m de mémoire; ~**ade** [blɒ'keɪd] n blocus m; ~**age** n obstruction f; ~**buster** n (film, book) grand succès; ~ **letters** npl majuscules fpl

bloke [bləʊk] (BRIT: inf) n type m

blond(e) [blɒnd] adj, n blond(e)

blood [blʌd] n sang m; ~ **donor** n donneur(-euse) de sang; ~ **group** n groupe sanguin; ~**hound** n limier m; ~ **poisoning** n empoisonnement m du sang; ~ **pressure** n tension f (artérielle); ~**shed** n effusion f de sang, carnage m; ~ **sports** npl sports mpl sanguinaires; ~**shot** adj: ~**shot eyes** yeux injectés de sang; ~**stream** n sang m, système sanguin; ~ **test** n prise f de sang; ~**thirsty** adj sanguinaire; ~ **vessel** n vaisseau sanguin; ~**y** adj sanglant(e); (nose) en sang; (BRIT: inf!): **this ~y ...** ce foutu ... (!), ce putain de ... (!); ~**y strong/good** vachement or sacrément fort/bon; ~**y-minded** (BRIT: inf) adj contrariant(e), obstiné(e)

bloom [blu:m] n fleur f ♦ vi être en fleur

blossom ['blɒsəm] n fleur(s) f(pl) ♦ vi être en fleurs; (fig) s'épanouir; **to ~ into** devenir

blot [blɒt] n tache f ♦ vt tacher; ~ **out** vt (memories) effacer; (view) cacher, masquer

blotchy ['blɒtʃɪ] adj (complexion) couvert(e) de marbrures

blotting paper ['blɒtɪŋ-] n buvard m

blouse [blaʊz] n chemisier m, corsage m

blow [bləʊ] (pt **blew**, pp **blown**) n coup m ♦ vi souffler ♦ vt souffler; (fuse) faire sauter; (instrument) jouer de; **to ~ one's nose** se moucher; **to ~ a whistle** siffler; ~ **away** vt chasser, faire s'envoler; ~ **down** vt faire tomber, renverser; ~ **off** vt emporter; ~ **out** vi (fire, flame) s'éteindre; ~ **over** vi s'apaiser; ~ **up** vi faire sauter; (tyre) gonfler; (PHOT) agrandir ♦ vi exploser, sauter; ~**-dry** n brushing m; ~**lamp** (BRIT) n chalumeau m; ~**-out** n (of tyre) éclatement m; ~**-torch** n = **blowlamp**

blue [blu:] adj bleu(e); (fig) triste; ~**s** n (MUS): **the ~s** les blues; ~ **film/joke** film m/histoire f pornographique; **to come out of the ~** (fig) être complètement inattendu; ~**bell** n jacinthe f des bois; ~**bottle** n mouche f à viande; ~**print** n (fig) projet m, plan directeur

bluff [blʌf] vi bluffer ♦ n bluff m; **to call sb's ~** mettre qn au défi d'exécuter ses menaces

blunder ['blʌndər] n gaffe f, bévue f ♦ vi faire une gaffe or une bévue

blunt [blʌnt] adj (person) brusque, ne mâchant pas ses mots; (knife) émoussé(e), peu tranchant(e); (pencil) mal taillé

blur [blɜːr] n tache or masse floue or confuse ♦ vt brouiller

blush [blʌʃ] vi rougir ♦ n rougeur f

blustery ['blʌstərɪ] adj (weather) à bourrasques

boar [bɔːr] n sanglier m

board [bɔːd] n planche f; (on wall) panneau m; (for chess) échiquier m; (cardboard) carton m; (committee) conseil m, comité m; (in firm) conseil d'administration; (NAUT, AVIAT): **on ~** à bord ♦ vt (ship) monter à bord de; (train) monter dans; **full ~** (BRIT) pension complète; **half ~** demi-pension f; ~ **and lodging** chambre f avec pension; **which goes by the ~** (fig) qu'on laisse tomber, qu'on abandonne; ~ **up** vt (door, window) boucher; ~**er** n (SCOL) interne m/f, pensionnaire; ~ **game** n jeu m de société; ~**ing card** n = **boarding pass**; ~**ing house** n pension f; ~**ing pass** n (AVIAT, NAUT) carte f d'embarquement; ~**ing school** n internat m, pensionnat *m*; ~ **room** *n* salle *f* du conseil d'administration

boast [bəust] *vi*: **to ~ (about** *or* **of)** se vanter (de)

boat [bəut] *n* bateau *m*; (*small*) canot *m*; barque *f*; ~ **train** *n* train *m* (qui assue correspondance avec le ferry)

bob [bɔb] *vi* (*boat, cork on water: also:* ~ **up and down**) danser, se balancer

bobby ['bɔbɪ] (*BRIT: inf*) *n* ≃ agent *m* (de police)

bobsleigh ['bɔbsleɪ] *n* bob *m*

bode [bəud] *vi*: **to ~ well/ill (for)** être de bon/mauvais augure (pour)

bodily ['bɔdɪlɪ] *adj* corporel(le) ♦ *adv* dans ses bras

body ['bɔdɪ] *n* corps *m*; (*of car*) carrosserie *f*; (*of plane*) fuselage *m*; (*fig: society*) organe *m*, organisme *m*; (: *quantity*) ensemble *m*, masse *f*; (*of wine*) corps *m*; ~-**building** *n* culturisme *m*; ~**guard** *n* garde *m* du corps; ~**work** *n* carrosserie *f*

bog [bɔg] *n* tourbière *f* ♦ *vt*: **to get ~ged down** (*fig*) s'enliser

bog-standard (*inf*) *adj* tout à fait ordinaire

bogus ['bəugəs] *adj* bidon *inv*; fantôme

boil [bɔɪl] *vt* (*faire*) bouillir ♦ *vi* bouillir ♦ *n* (*MED*) furoncle *m*; **to come to the** (*BRIT*) ~ *or* **a** (*US*) ~ bouillir; ~ **down to** *vt fus* (*fig*) se réduire *or* ramener à; ~ **over** *vi* déborder; ~**ed egg** *n* œuf *m* à la coque; ~**ed potatoes** *npl* pommes *fpl* à l'anglaise *or* à l'eau; ~**er** *n* chaudière *f*; ~**ing point** *n* point *m* d'ébullition

boisterous ['bɔɪstərəs] *adj* bruyant(e), tapageur(-euse)

bold [bəuld] *adj* hardi(e), audacieux(-euse); (*pej*) effronté(e); (*outline, colour*) franc (franche), tranché(e), marqué(e); (*pattern*) grand(e)

bollard ['bɔləd] (*BRIT*) *n* (*AUT*) borne lumineuse *or* de signalisation

bolt [bəult] *n* (*lock*) verrou *m*; (*with nut*) boulon *m* ♦ *adv*: ~ **upright** droit(e) comme un piquet ♦ *vt* verrouiller; (*TECH: also:* ~ **on,** ~ **together**) boulonner; (*food*) engloutir ♦ *vi* (*horse*) s'emballer

bomb [bɔm] *n* bombe *f* ♦ *vt* bombarder; ~**ing** *n* (*by terrorist*) attentat *m* à la bombe; ~ **disposal unit** *n* section *f* de déminage; ~**er** *n* (*AVIAT*) bombardier *m*; ~**shell** *n* (*fig*) bombe *f*

bond [bɔnd] *n* lien *m*; (*binding promise*) engagement *m*, obligation *f*; (*COMM*) obligation; **in ~** (*of goods*) en douane

bondage ['bɔndɪdʒ] *n* esclavage *m*

bone [bəun] *n* os *m*; (*of fish*) arête *f* ♦ *vt* désosser; ôter les arêtes de; ~ **dry** *adj* complètement sec (sèche); ~ **idle** *adj* fainéant(e); ~ **marrow** *n* moelle *f* osseuse

bonfire ['bɔnfaɪər] *n* feu *m* (de joie); (*for rubbish*) feu

bonnet ['bɔnɪt] *n* bonnet *m*; (*BRIT: of car*) capot *m*

bonus ['bəunəs] *n* prime *f*, gratification *f*

bony ['bəunɪ] *adj* (*arm, face, MED: tissue*) osseux(-euse); (*meat*) plein(e) d'os; (*fish*) plein d'arêtes

boo [bu:] *excl* hou!, peuh! ♦ *vt* huer

booby trap ['bu:bɪ-] *n* engin piégé

book [buk] *n* livre *m*; (*of stamps, tickets*) carnet *m* ♦ *vt* (*ticket*) prendre; (*seat, room*) réserver; (*driver*) dresser un procès-verbal à; (*football player*) prendre le nom de; ~**s** *npl* (*accounts*) comptes *mpl*, comptabilité *f*; ~**case** *n* bibliothèque *f* (*meuble*); ~**ing office** (*BRIT*) *n* bureau *m* de location; ~-**keeping** *n* comptabilité *f*; ~**let** *n* brochure *f*; ~**maker** *n* bookmaker *m*; ~**seller** *n* libraire *m/f*; ~**shelf** *n* (*single*) étagère *f* (à livres); ~**shop** *n* librairie *f*; ~**store** *n* librairie *f*

boom [bu:m] *n* (*noise*) grondement *m*; (*in prices, population*) forte augmentation ♦ *vi* gronder; prospérer

boon [bu:n] *n* bénédiction *f*, grand avantage

boost [bu:st] *n* stimulant *m*, remontant *m* ♦ *vt* stimuler; ~**er** *n* (*MED*) rappel *m*

boot [bu:t] *n* botte *f*; (*for hiking*) chaussure *f* (de marche); (*for football etc*) soulier *m*; (*BRIT: of car*) coffre *m* ♦ *vt* (*COMPUT*) amorcer, initialiser; **to ~** (*in addition*) par-dessus le marché

booth [buːð] n (at fair) baraque (foraine); (telephone etc) cabine f; (also: **voting ~**) isoloir m

booze [buːz] (inf) n boissons fpl alcooliques, alcool m

border ['bɔːdəʳ] n bordure f; bord m; (of a country) frontière f ♦ vt border; (also: **~ on**: country) être limitrophe de; (GEO): **the B~s** la région frontière entre l'Écosse et l'Angleterre; **~ on** vt fus être voisin(e) de, toucher à; **~line** n (fig) ligne f de démarcation; **~line case** n cas m limite

bore [bɔːʳ] pt of **bear** ♦ vt (hole) percer; (oil well, tunnel) creuser; (person) ennuyer, raser ♦ n raseur(-euse); (of gun) calibre m; **to be ~d** s'ennuyer; **~dom** n ennui m; **boring** adj ennuyeux(-euse)

born [bɔːn] adj: **to be ~** naître; **I was ~ in 1960** je suis né en 1960

borne [bɔːn] pp of **bear**

borough ['bʌrə] n municipalité f

borrow ['bɔrəu] vt: **to ~ sth (from sb)** emprunter qch (à qn)

Bosnia (and) Herzegovina ['bɔznɪə-(ənd)hɜːtsəgəuˈviːnə] n Bosnie-Herzégovine f; **Bosnian** adj bosniaque, bosnien(ne) ♦ n Bosniaque m/f

bosom ['buzəm] n poitrine f; (fig) sein m

boss [bɔs] n patron(ne) ♦ vt (also: **~ around/about**) mener à la baguette; **~y** adj autoritaire

bosun ['bəusn] n maître m d'équipage

botany ['bɔtənɪ] n botanique f

botch [bɔtʃ] vt (also: **~ up**) saboter, bâcler

both [bəuθ] adj les deux, l'un(e) et l'autre ♦ pron: **~ (of them)** les deux, tous (toutes) (les) deux, l'un(e) et l'autre; **they sell ~ the fabric and the finished curtains** ils vendent (et) le tissu et les rideaux (finis), ils vendent à la fois le tissu et les rideaux (finis); **~ of us went, we ~ went** nous y sommes allés (tous) les deux

bother ['bɔðəʳ] vt (worry) tracasser; (disturb) déranger ♦ vi (also: **~ o.s.**) se tracasser, se faire du souci ♦ n: **it is a ~ to have to do** c'est vraiment ennuyeux d'avoir à faire;

it's no ~ aucun problème; **to ~ doing** prendre la peine de faire

bottle ['bɔtl] n bouteille f; (baby's) biberon m ♦ vt mettre en bouteille(s); **~d beer** bière f en canette; **~d water** eau minérale; **~ up** vt refouler, contenir; **~ bank** n conteneur m à verre; **~neck** n étranglement m; **~-opener** n ouvre-bouteille m

bottom ['bɔtəm] n (of container, sea etc) fond m; (buttocks) derrière m; (of page, list) bas m ♦ adj du fond; du bas; **the ~ of the class** le dernier de la classe

bough [bau] n branche f, rameau m

bought [bɔːt] pt, pp of **buy**

boulder ['bəuldəʳ] n gros rocher

bounce [bauns] vi (ball) rebondir; (cheque) être refusé(e) (étant sans provision) ♦ vt faire rebondir ♦ n (rebound) rebond m; **~r** (inf) n (at dance, club) videur m

bound [baund] pt, pp of **bind** ♦ n (gen pl) limite f; (leap) bond m ♦ vi (leap) bondir ♦ vt (limit) borner ♦ adj: **to be ~ to do sth** (obliged) être obligé(e) or avoir obligation de faire qch; **he's ~ to fail** (likely) il est sûr d'échouer, son échec est inévitable or assuré; **~ by** (law, regulation) engagé(e) par; **~ for** à destination de; **out of ~s** dont l'accès est interdit

boundary ['baundrɪ] n frontière f

bout [baut] n période f; (of malaria etc) accès m, crise f, attaque f; (BOXING etc) combat m, match m

bow[1] [bəu] n nœud m; (weapon) arc m; (MUS) archet m

bow[2] [bau] n (with body) révérence f, inclination f (du buste or corps); (NAUT: also: **~s**) proue f ♦ vi faire une révérence, s'incliner; (yield): **to ~ to** or **before** s'incliner devant, se soumettre à

bowels ['bauəlz] npl intestins mpl; (fig) entrailles fpl

bowl [bəul] n (for eating) bol m; (ball) boule f ♦ vi (CRICKET, BASEBALL) lancer (la balle)

bow-legged ['bəu'lɛgɪd] adj aux jambes arquées

bowler ['bəuləʳ] n (CRICKET, BASEBALL) lanceur m (de la balle); (BRIT: also: **~ hat**) (chapeau *m*) melon *m*

bowling [ˈbəʊlɪŋ] *n* (*game*) jeu *m* de boules; jeu *m* de quilles; ~ **alley** *n* bowling *m*; ~ **green** *n* terrain *m* de boules (*gazonné et carré*)

bowls [bəʊlz] *n* (*game*) (jeu *m* de) boules *fpl*

bow tie [bəʊ-] *n* nœud *m* papillon

box [bɒks] *n* boîte *f*; (*also:* **cardboard ~**) carton *m*; (THEATRE) loge *f* ♦ *vt* mettre en boîte; (SPORT) boxer avec ♦ *vi* boxer, faire de la boxe; ~**er** *n* (*person*) boxeur *m*; ~**er shorts** *npl* caleçon *msg*; ~**ing** *n* (SPORT) boxe *f*; B~**ing Day** (BRIT) le lendemain de Noël; ~**ing gloves** *npl* gants *mpl* de boxe; ~**ing ring** *n* ring *m*; ~ **office** *n* bureau *m* de location; ~**room** *n* débarras *m*; chambrette *f*

Boxing Day

ⓘ **Boxing Day** est le lendemain de Noël, férié en Grande-Bretagne. Si Noël tombe un samedi, le jour férié est reculé jusqu'au lundi suivant. Ce nom vient d'une coutume du XIXe siècle qui consistait à donner des cadeaux de Noël (dans des boîtes) à ses employés etc le 26 décembre.

---

boy [bɔɪ] *n* garçon *m*

boycott [ˈbɔɪkɔt] *n* boycottage *m* ♦ *vt* boycotter

boyfriend [ˈbɔɪfrɛnd] *n* (petit) ami

boyish [ˈbɔɪɪʃ] *adj* (*behaviour*) de garçon; (*girl*) garçonnier(-ière)

BR *n abbr* = **British Rail**

bra [brɑː] *n* soutien-gorge *m*

brace [breɪs] *n* (*on teeth*) appareil *m* (dentaire); (*tool*) vilbrequin *m* ♦ *vt* (*knees, shoulders*) appuyer; ~**s** *npl* (BRIT: *for trousers*) bretelles *fpl*; **to ~ o.s.** (*lit*) s'arc-bouter; (*fig*) se préparer mentalement

bracelet [ˈbreɪslɪt] *n* bracelet *m*

bracing [ˈbreɪsɪŋ] *adj* tonifiant(e), tonique

bracket [ˈbrækɪt] *n* (TECH) tasseau *m*, support *m*; (*group*) classe *f*, tranche *f*; (*also:* **brace ~**) accolade *f*; (*also:* **round ~**) parenthèse *f*; (*also:* **square ~**) crochet *m* ♦ *vt* mettre entre parenthèse(s); (*fig: also:* ~ **together**) regrouper

brag [bræg] *vi* se vanter

braid [breɪd] *n* (*trimming*) galon *m*; (*of hair*) tresse *f*

brain [breɪn] *n* cerveau *m*; ~**s** *npl* (*intellect*, CULIN) cervelle *f*; **he's got ~s** il est intelligent; ~**wash** *vt* faire subir un lavage de cerveau à; ~**wave** *n* idée géniale; ~**y** *adj* intelligent(e), doué(e)

braise [breɪz] *vt* braiser

brake [breɪk] *n* (*on vehicle, also fig*) frein *m* ♦ *vi* freiner; ~ **light** *n* feu *m* de stop

bran [bræn] *n* son *m*

branch [brɑːntʃ] *n* branche *f*; (COMM) succursale *f* ♦ *vi* bifurquer; ~ **out** *vi* (*fig*): **to ~ out into** étendre ses activités à

brand [brænd] *n* marque (commerciale) ♦ *vt* (*cattle*) marquer (au fer rouge); ~-**new** *adj* tout(e) neuf (neuve), flambant neuf (neuve)

brandy [ˈbrændɪ] *n* cognac *m*, fine *f*

brash [bræʃ] *adj* effronté(e)

brass [brɑːs] *n* cuivre (jaune), laiton *m*; **the ~** (MUS) les cuivres; ~ **band** *n* fanfare *f*

brat [bræt] (*pej*) *n* mioche *m/f*, môme *m/f*

brave [breɪv] *adj* courageux(-euse), brave ♦ *n* guerrier indien ♦ *vt* braver, affronter; ~**ry** *n* bravoure *f*, courage *m*

brawl [brɔːl] *n* rixe *f*, bagarre *f*

brazen [ˈbreɪzn] *adj* impudent(e), effronté(e) ♦ *vt*: **to ~ it out** payer d'effronterie, crâner

brazier [ˈbreɪzɪər] *n* brasero *m*

Brazil [brəˈzɪl] *n* Brésil *m*

breach [briːtʃ] *vt* ouvrir une brèche dans ♦ *n* (*gap*) brèche *f*; (*breaking*): ~ **of contract** rupture *f* de contrat; ~ **of the peace** attentat *m* à l'ordre public

bread [brɛd] *n* pain *m*; ~ **and butter** *n* tartines (beurrées); (*fig*) subsistance *f*; ~**bin** (BRIT) *n* boîte *f* à pain; (*bigger*) huche *f* à pain; ~**crumbs** *npl* miettes *fpl* de pain; (CULIN) chapelure *f*, panure *f*; ~**line** *n*: **to be on the ~line** être sans le sou or dans l'indigence

breadth [brɛtθ] *n* largeur *f*; (*fig*) ampleur *f*

breadwinner ['brɛdwɪnəʳ] *n* soutien *m* de famille

break [breɪk] (*pt* **broke**, *pp* **broken**) *vt* casser, briser; (*promise*) rompre; (*law*) violer ♦ *vi* (se) casser, se briser; (*weather*) tourner; (*story, news*) se répandre; (*day*) se lever ♦ *vi* (*gap*) brèche *f*; (*fracture*) cassure *f*; (*pause, interval*) interruption *f*, arrêt *m*; (*: short*) pause *f*; (*: at school*) récréation *f*; (*chance*) chance *f*, occasion *f* favorable; **to ~ one's leg** *etc* se casser la jambe *etc*; **to ~ a record** battre un record; **to ~ the news to sb** annoncer la nouvelle à qn; **~ even** rentrer dans ses frais; **~ free** *or* **loose** se dégager, s'échapper; **~ open** (*door etc*) forcer, fracturer; **~ down** *vt* (*figures, data*) décomposer, analyser ♦ *vi* s'effondrer; (*MED*) faire une dépression (nerveuse); (*AUT*) tomber en panne; **~ in** *vt* (*horse etc*) dresser ♦ *vi* (*burglar*) entrer par effraction; (*interrupt*) interrompre; **~ into** *vt fus* (*house*) s'introduire *or* pénétrer par effraction dans; **~ off** *vi* (*speaker*) s'interrompre; (*branch*) se rompre; **~ out** *vi* éclater, se déclarer; (*prisoner*) s'évader; **to ~ out in spots** *or* **a rash** avoir une éruption de boutons; **~ up** *vi* (*ship*) se disloquer; (*crowd, meeting*) se disperser, se séparer; (*marriage*) se briser; (*SCOL*) entrer en vacances ♦ *vt* casser; (*fight etc*) interrompre, faire cesser; **~age** *n* casse *f*; **~down** *n* (*AUT*) panne *f*; (*in communications, marriage*) rupture *f*; (*MED: also:* **nervous ~down**) dépression (nerveuse) *f*; (*of statistics*) ventilation *f*; **~down van** (*BRIT*) *n* dépanneuse *f*; **~er** *n* brisant *m*

breakfast ['brɛkfəst] *n* petit déjeuner

break: **~-in** *n* cambriolage *m*; **~ing and entering** *n* (*LAW*) effraction *f*; **~through** *n* percée *f*; **~water** *n* brise-lames *m inv*, digue *f*

breast [brɛst] *n* (*of woman*) sein *m*; (*chest, of meat*) poitrine *f*; **~-feed** (*irreg: like* **feed**) *vt, vi* allaiter; **~stroke** *n* brasse *f*

breath [brɛθ] *n* haleine *f*; **out of ~** à bout

de souffle, essoufflé(e); **B~alyser** ® ['brɛθəlaɪzəʳ] *n* Alcootest ® *m*

breathe [briːð] *vt, vi* respirer; **~ in** *vt, vi* aspirer, inspirer; **~ out** *vt, vi* expirer; **~r** *n* moment *m* de repos *or* de répit; **breathing** *n* respiration *f*

breathless ['brɛθlɪs] *adj* essoufflé(e), haletant(e)

breathtaking ['brɛθteɪkɪŋ] *adj* stupéfiant(e)

breed [briːd] (*pt,pp* **bred**) *vt* élever, faire l'élevage de ♦ *vi* se reproduire ♦ *n* race *f*, variété *f*; **~ing** *n* (*upbringing*) éducation *f*

breeze [briːz] *n* brise *f*; **breezy** *adj* frais (fraîche); aéré(e); (*manner etc*) désinvolte, jovial(e)

brevity ['brɛvɪtɪ] *n* brièveté *f*

brew [bruː] *vt* (*tea*) faire infuser; (*beer*) brasser ♦ *vi* (*fig*) se préparer, couver; **~ery** *n* brasserie *f* (*fabrique*)

bribe [braɪb] *n* pot-de-vin *m* ♦ *vt* acheter, soudoyer; **~ry** *n* corruption *f*

brick [brɪk] *n* brique *f*; **~layer** *n* maçon *m*

bridal ['braɪdl] *adj* nuptial(e)

bride [braɪd] *n* mariée *f*, épouse *f*; **~groom** *n* marié *m*, époux *m*; **~smaid** *n* demoiselle *f* d'honneur

bridge [brɪdʒ] *n* pont *m*; (*NAUT*) passerelle *f* (de commandement); (*of nose*) arête *f*; (*CARDS, DENTISTRY*) bridge *m* ♦ *vt* (*fig: gap, gulf*) combler

bridle ['braɪdl] *n* bride *f*; **~ path** *n* piste *or* allée cavalière

brief [briːf] *adj* bref (brève) ♦ *n* (*LAW*) dossier *m*, cause *f*; (*gen*) tâche *f* ♦ *vt* mettre au courant; **~s** *npl* (*undergarment*) slip *m*; **~case** *n* serviette *f*, porte-documents *m inv*; **~ly** *adv* brièvement

bright [braɪt] *adj* brillant(e); (*room, weather*) clair(e); (*clever: person, idea*) intelligent(e); (*cheerful: colour, person*) vif (vive)

brighten ['braɪtn] (*also:* **~ up**) *vt* (*room*) éclaircir, égayer; (*event*) égayer ♦ *vi* s'éclaircir; (*person*) retrouver un peu de sa gaieté; (*face*) s'éclairer; (*prospects*) s'améliorer

brilliance ['brɪljəns] *n* éclat *m*

brilliant ['brɪljənt] adj brillant(e); (sunshine, light) éclatant(e); (inf: holiday etc) super

brim [brɪm] n bord m

brine [braɪn] n (CULIN) saumure f

bring [brɪŋ] (pt, pp **brought**) vt apporter; (person) amener; ~ **about** vt provoquer, entraîner; ~ **back** vt rapporter; ramener; (restore: hanging) réinstaurer; ~ **down** vt (price) faire baisser; (enemy plane) descendre; (government) faire tomber; ~ **forward** vt avancer; ~ **off** vt (task, plan) réussir, mener à bien; ~ **out** vt (meaning) faire ressortir; (book) publier; (object) sortir; ~ **round** vt (unconscious person) ranimer; ~ **up** vt (child) élever; (carry up) monter; (question) soulever; (food: vomit) vomir, rendre

brink [brɪŋk] n bord m

brisk [brɪsk] adj vif (vive)

bristle ['brɪsl] n poil m ♦ vi se hérisser

Britain ['brɪtən] n (also: **Great ~**) Grande-Bretagne f

British ['brɪtɪʃ] adj britannique ♦ npl: **the ~** les Britanniques mpl; ~ **Isles** npl: **the ~ Isles** les Iles fpl Britanniques; ~ **Rail** n compagnie ferroviaire britannique

Briton ['brɪtən] n Britannique m/f

Brittany ['brɪtənɪ] n Bretagne f

brittle ['brɪtl] adj cassant(e), fragile

broach [brəutʃ] vt (subject) aborder

broad [brɔːd] adj large; (general: outlines) grand(e); (: distinction) général(e); (accent) prononcé(e); **in ~ daylight** en plein jour; ~**band** n haut débit m; ~**cast** (pt, pp **broadcast**) n émission f ♦ vt radiodiffuser; téléviser ♦ vi émettre; ~**en** vt élargir ♦ vi s'élargir; **to ~en one's mind** élargir ses horizons; ~**ly** adv en gros, généralement; ~**-minded** adj large d'esprit

broccoli ['brɔkəlɪ] n brocoli m

brochure ['brəuʃjuər] n prospectus m, dépliant m

broil [brɔɪl] vt griller

broke [brəuk] pt of **break** ♦ adj (inf) fauché(e)

broken ['brəukn] pp of **break** ♦ adj cassé(e); (machine: also: ~ **down**) fichu(e); **in**

~ English/French dans un anglais/français approximatif or hésitant; ~ **leg** etc jambe etc cassée; ~**-hearted** adj (ayant) le cœur brisé

broker ['brəukər] n courtier m

brolly ['brɔlɪ] (BRIT: inf) n pépin m, parapluie m

bronchitis [brɔŋ'kaɪtɪs] n bronchite f

brooch [brəutʃ] n broche f

brood [bruːd] n couvée f ♦ vi (person) méditer (sombrement), ruminer

broom [brum] n balai m; (BOT) genêt m; ~**stick** n manche m à balai

Bros. abbr = **Brothers**

broth [brɔθ] n bouillon m de viande et de légumes

brothel ['brɔθl] n maison close, bordel m

brother ['brʌðər] n frère m; ~**-in-law** n beau-frère m

brought [brɔːt] pt, pp of **bring**

brow [brau] n front m; (eyebrow) sourcil m; (of hill) sommet m

brown [braun] adj brun(e), marron inv; (hair) châtain inv, brun; (eyes) marron inv; (tanned) bronzé(e) ♦ n (colour) brun m ♦ vt (CULIN) faire dorer; ~ **bread** n pain m bis; B~**ie** n (also: B~**ie Guide**) jeannette f, éclaireuse (cadette); ~**ie** (US) n (cake) gâteau m au chocolat et aux noix; ~ **paper** n papier m d'emballage; ~ **sugar** n cassonade f

browse [brauz] vi (among books) bouquiner, feuilleter les livres; **to ~ through a book** feuilleter un livre; ~**r** n navigateur m

bruise [bruːz] n bleu m, contusion f ♦ vt contusionner, meurtrir

brunette [bruː'net] n (femme) brune

brunt [brʌnt] n: **the ~ of** (attack, criticism etc) le plus gros de

brush [brʌʃ] n brosse f; (painting) pinceau m; (shaving) blaireau m; (quarrel) accrochage m, prise f de bec ♦ vt brosser; (also: ~ **against**) effleurer, frôler; ~ **aside** vt écarter, balayer; ~ **up** vt (knowledge) rafraîchir, réviser; ~**wood** n broussailles fpl, taillis m

Brussels ['brʌslz] *n* Bruxelles; ~ **sprout** *n* chou *m* de Bruxelles

brutal ['bru:tl] *adj* brutal(e)

brute [bru:t] *n* brute *f* ♦ *adj*: **by ~ force** par la force

BSc *abbr* = **Bachelor of Science**

BSE *n abbr* (= *bovine spongiform encephalopathy*) ESB *f*, BSE *f*

bubble ['bʌbl] *n* bulle *f* ♦ *vi* bouillonner, faire des bulles; (*sparkle*) pétiller; ~ **bath** *n* bain moussant; ~ **gum** *n* bubblegum *m*

buck [bʌk] *n* mâle *m* (*d'un lapin, daim etc*); (*US: inf*) dollar *m* ♦ *vi* ruer, lancer une ruade; **to pass the ~ (to sb)** se décharger de la responsabilité (sur qn); ~ **up** *vi* (*cheer up*) reprendre du poil de la bête, se remonter

bucket ['bʌkɪt] *n* seau *m*

i *Buckingham Palace est la résidence officielle londonienne du souverain britannique depuis 1762. Construit en 1703, il fut à l'origine le palais du duc de Buckingham. Il a été partiellement reconstruit au début du siècle.*

buckle ['bʌkl] *n* boucle *f* ♦ *vt* (*belt etc*) boucler, attacher ♦ *vi* (*warp*) tordre, gauchir; (*: wheel*) se voiler; se déformer

bud [bʌd] *n* bourgeon *m*; (*of flower*) bouton *m* ♦ *vi* bourgeonner; (*flower*) éclore

Buddhism ['budɪzəm] *n* bouddhisme *m*

Buddhist *adj* bouddhiste ♦ *n* Bouddhiste *m/f*

budding ['bʌdɪŋ] *adj* (*poet etc*) en herbe; (*passion etc*) naissant(e)

buddy ['bʌdɪ] (*US*) *n* copain *m*

budge [bʌdʒ] *vt* faire bouger; (*fig: person*) faire changer d'avis ♦ *vi* bouger; changer d'avis

budgerigar ['bʌdʒərɪgɑːʳ] (*BRIT*) *n* perruche *f*

budget ['bʌdʒɪt] *n* budget *m* ♦ *vi*: **to ~ for sth** inscrire qch au budget

budgie ['bʌdʒɪ] (*BRIT*) *n* = **budgerigar**

buff [bʌf] *adj* (couleur *f*) chamois *m* ♦ *n* (*inf: enthusiast*) mordu(e); **he's a ... ~** c'est un mordu de ...

buffalo ['bʌfələu] (*pl* ~ *or* ~**es**) *n* buffle *m*; (*US*) bison *m*

buffer ['bʌfəʳ] *n* tampon *m*; (*COMPUT*) mémoire *f* tampon

buffet[1] ['bʌfɪt] *vt* secouer, ébranler

buffet[2] ['bufeɪ] *n* (*food, BRIT: bar*) buffet *m*; ~ **car** (*BRIT*) (*RAIL*) voiture-buffet *f*

bug [bʌg] *n* (*insect*) punaise *f*; (*: gen*) insecte *m*, bestiole *f*; (*fig: germ*) virus *m*, microbe *m*; (*COMPUT*) erreur *f*; (*fig: spy device*) dispositif *m* d'écoute (électronique) ♦ *vt* garnir de dispositifs d'écoute; (*inf: annoy*) embêter; ~**ged** *adj* sur écoute

bugle ['bju:gl] *n* clairon *m*

build [bɪld] (*pt, pp* **built**) *n* (*of person*) carrure *f*, charpente *f* ♦ *vt* construire, bâtir; ~ **up** *vt* accumuler, amasser; accroître; ~**er** *n* entrepreneur *m*; ~**ing** *n* (*trade*) construction *f*; (*house, structure*) bâtiment *m*, construction; (*offices, flats*) immeuble *m*; ~**ing society** (*BRIT*) *n* société *f* de crédit immobilier

i *Une building society est une mutuelle dont les épargnants et emprunteurs sont les propriétaires. Ces mutuelles offrent deux services principaux: on peut y avoir un compte d'épargne duquel on peut retirer son argent sur demande ou moyennant un court préavis; et on peut également y faire des emprunts à long terme, par exemple pour acheter une maison.*

built [bɪlt] *pt, pp of* **build**; ~-**in** ['bɪlt'ɪn] *adj* (*cupboard, oven*) encastré(e); (*device*) incorporé(e); intégré(e); ~-**up area** ['bɪltʌp-] *n* zone urbanisée

bulb [bʌlb] *n* (*BOT*) bulbe *m*, oignon *m*; (*ELEC*) ampoule *f*

Bulgaria [bʌl'gɛərɪə] *n* Bulgarie *f*

bulge [bʌldʒ] *n* renflement *m*, gonflement *m* ♦ *vi* (*pocket, file etc*) être plein(e) à craquer; (*cheeks*) être gonflé(e)

bulk [bʌlk] *n* masse *f*, volume *m*; (*of per-*

son) corpulence f; **in ~** (COMM) en vrac; **the ~ of** la plus grande or grosse partie de; **~y** adj volumineux(-euse), encombrant(e)

bull [bul] n taureau m; (male elephant/whale) mâle m; **~dog** n bouledogue m

bulldozer ['buldəuzə^r] n bulldozer m

bullet ['bulɪt] n balle f (de fusil etc)

bulletin ['bulɪtɪn] n bulletin m, communiqué m; (news ~) (bulletin d')informations fpl; **~ board** n (Internet) messagerie f électronique

bulletproof ['bulɪtpru:f] adj (car) blindé(e); (vest etc) pare-balles inv

bullfight ['bulfaɪt] n corrida f, course f de taureaux; **~er** n torero m; **~ing** n tauromachie f

bullion ['buljən] n or m or argent m en lingots

bullock ['bulək] n bœuf m

bullring ['bulrɪŋ] n arènes fpl

bull's-eye ['bulzaɪ] n centre m (de la cible)

bully ['bulɪ] n brute f, tyran m ♦ vt tyranniser, rudoyer

bum [bʌm] n (inf: backside) derrière m; (esp US: tramp) vagabond(e), traîne-savates m/f inv

bumblebee ['bʌmblbi:] n bourdon m

bump [bʌmp] n (in car: minor accident) accrochage m; (jolt) cahot m; (on road etc, on head) bosse f ♦ vt heurter, cogner; **~ into** vt fus rentrer dans, tamponner; (meet) tomber sur; **~er** n pare-chocs m inv ♦ adj: **~er crop/harvest** récolte/moisson exceptionnelle; **~er cars** (US) npl autos tamponneuses; **~y** adj cahoteux(-euse)

bun [bʌn] n petit pain au lait; (of hair) chignon m

bunch [bʌntʃ] n (of flowers) bouquet m; (of keys) trousseau m; (of bananas) régime m; (of people) groupe m; **~es** npl (in hair) couettes fpl; **~ of grapes** grappe f de raisin

bundle ['bʌndl] n paquet m ♦ vt (also: **~ up**) faire un paquet de; (put): **to ~ sth/sb into** fourrer or enfourner qch/qn dans

bungalow ['bʌŋgələu] n bungalow m

bungle ['bʌŋgl] vt bâcler, gâcher

bunion ['bʌnjən] n oignon m (au pied)

bunk [bʌŋk] n couchette f; **~ beds** npl lits superposés

bunker ['bʌŋkə^r] n (coal store) soute f à charbon; (MIL, GOLF) bunker m

bunting ['bʌntɪŋ] n pavoisement m, drapeaux mpl

buoy [bɔɪ] n bouée f; **~ up** vt faire flotter; (fig) soutenir, épauler; **~ant** adj capable de flotter; (carefree) gai(e), plein(e) d'entrain; (economy) ferme, actif

burden ['bə:dn] n fardeau m ♦ vt (trouble) accabler, surcharger

bureau ['bjuərəu] (pl **~x**) n (BRIT: writing desk) bureau m, secrétaire m; (US: chest of drawers) commode f; (office) bureau, office m; **~cracy** [bjuə'rɔkrəsɪ] n bureaucratie f

burglar ['bə:glə^r] n cambrioleur m; **~ alarm** n sonnerie f d'alarme

Burgundy ['bə:gəndɪ] n Bourgogne f

burial ['berɪəl] n enterrement m

burly ['bə:lɪ] adj de forte carrure, costaud(e)

Burma ['bə:mə] n Birmanie f

burn [bə:n] (pt, pp **burned** or **burnt**) vt, vi brûler ♦ n brûlure f; **~ down** vt incendier, détruire par le feu; **~er** n brûleur m; **~ing** adj brûlant(e); (house) en flammes; (ambition) dévorant(e)

burrow ['bʌrəu] n terrier m ♦ vt creuser

bursary ['bə:sərɪ] n (BRIT) bourse f (d'études)

burst [bə:st] (pt, pp **burst**) vt crever; faire éclater; (subj: river: banks etc) rompre ♦ vi éclater; (tyre) crever ♦ n (of gunfire) rafale f (de tir); (also: **~ pipe**) rupture f, fuite f; **a ~ of enthusiasm/energy** un accès d'enthousiasme/d'énergie; **to ~ into flames** s'enflammer soudainement; **to ~ out laughing** éclater de rire; **to ~ into tears** fondre en larmes; **to be ~ing with** être plein (à craquer) de; (fig) être débordant(e) de; **~ into** vt fus (room etc) faire irruption dans

bury ['berɪ] vt enterrer

bus [bʌs] (*pl* **~es**) *n* autobus *m*

bush [buʃ] *n* buisson *m*; (*scrubland*) brousse *f*; **to beat about the ~** tourner autour du pot; **~y** *adj* broussailleux(-euse), touffu(e)

busily ['bɪzɪlɪ] *adv* activement

business ['bɪznɪs] *n* (*matter, firm*) affaire *f*; (*trading*) affaires *fpl*; (*job, duty*) travail *m*; **to be away on ~** être en déplacement d'affaires; **it's none of my ~** cela ne me regarde pas, ce ne sont pas mes affaires; **he means ~** il ne plaisante pas, il est sérieux; **~like** *adj* (*firm*) sérieux(-euse); (*method*) efficace; **~man** (*irreg*) *n* homme *m* d'affaires; **~ trip** *n* voyage *m* d'affaires; **~woman** (*irreg*) *n* femme *f* d'affaires

busker ['bʌskər] (*BRIT*) *n* musicien ambulant

bus: **~ shelter** *n* abribus *m*; **~ station** *n* gare routière; **~ stop** *n* arrêt *m* d'autobus

bust [bʌst] *n* buste *m*; (*measurement*) tour *m* de poitrine ♦ *adj* (*inf: broken*) fichu(e), fini(e); **to go ~** faire faillite

bustle ['bʌsl] *n* remue-ménage *m*, affairement *m* ♦ *vi* s'affairer, se démener; **bustling** *adj* (*town*) bruyant(e), affairé(e)

busy ['bɪzɪ] *adj* occupé(e); (*shop, street*) très fréquenté(e) ♦ *vt*: **to ~ o.s.** s'occuper; **~body** *n* mouche *f* du coche, âme *f* charitable; **~ signal** (*US*) *n* (*TEL*) tonalité *f* occupé *inv*

KEYWORD

but [bʌt] *conj* mais; **I'd love to come, but I'm busy** j'aimerais venir mais je suis occupé

♦ *prep* (*apart from, except*) sauf, excepté; **we've had nothing but trouble** nous n'avons eu que des ennuis; **no-one but him can do it** lui seul peut le faire; **but for you/your help** sans toi/ton aide; **anything but that** tout sauf *or* excepté ça, tout mais pas ça

♦ *adv* (*just, only*) ne ... que; **she's but a child** elle n'est qu'une enfant; **had I but known** si seulement j'avais su; **all but finished** pratiquement terminé

butcher ['butʃər] *n* boucher *m* ♦ *vt* massacrer; (*cattle etc for meat*) tuer; **~'s (shop)** *n* boucherie *f*

butler ['bʌtlər] *n* maître *m* d'hôtel

butt [bʌt] *n* (*large barrel*) gros tonneau; (*of gun*) crosse *f*; (*of cigarette*) mégot *m*; (*BRIT: fig: target*) cible *f* ♦ *vt* donner un coup de tête à; **~ in** *vi* (*interrupt*) s'immiscer dans la conversation

butter ['bʌtər] *n* beurre *m* ♦ *vt* beurrer; **~cup** *n* bouton *m* d'or

butterfly ['bʌtəflaɪ] *n* papillon *m*; (*SWIMMING: also:* **~ stroke**) brasse *f* papillon

buttocks ['bʌtəks] *npl* fesses *fpl*

button ['bʌtn] *n* bouton *m*; (*US: badge*) pin *m* ♦ *vt* (*also:* **~ up**) boutonner ♦ *vi* se boutonner

buttress ['bʌtrɪs] *n* contrefort *m*

buy [baɪ] (*pt, pp* **bought**) *vt* acheter ♦ *n* achat *m*; **to ~ sb sth/sth from sb** acheter qch à qn; **to ~ sb a drink** offrir un verre *or* à boire à qn; **~er** *n* acheteur(-euse)

buzz [bʌz] *n* bourdonnement *m*; (*inf: phone call*): **to give sb a ~** passer un coup *m* de fil à qn ♦ *vi* bourdonner; **~er** *n* timbre *m* électrique; **~ word** *n* (*inf*) mot *m* à la mode

---

KEYWORD

by [baɪ] *prep* **1** (*referring to cause, agent*) par, de; **killed by lightning** tué par la foudre; **surrounded by a fence** entouré d'une barrière; **a painting by Picasso** un tableau de Picasso

2 (*referring to method, manner, means*): **by bus/car** en autobus/voiture; **by train** par le *or* en train; **to pay by cheque** payer par chèque; **by saving hard, he ...** à force d'économiser, il ...

3 (*via, through*) par; **we came by Dover** nous sommes venus par Douvres

4 (*close to, past*) à côté de; **the house by the school** la maison à côté de l'école; **a holiday by the sea** des vacances au bord de la mer; **she sat by his bed** elle était assise à son chevet; **she went by me** elle

est passée à côté de moi; **I go by the post office every day** je passe devant la poste tous les jours
5 (*with time: not later than*) avant; (: *during*): **by daylight** à la lumière du jour; **by night** la nuit, de nuit; **by 4 o'clock** avant 4 heures; **by this time tomorrow** d'ici demain à la même heure; **by the time I got here it was too late** lorsque je suis arrivé il était déjà trop tard
6 (*amount*) à; **by the kilo/metre** au kilo/au mètre; **paid by the hour** payé à l'heure
7 (*MATH, measure*): **to divide/multiply by 3** diviser/multiplier par 3; **a room 3 metres by 4** une pièce de 3 mètres sur 4; **it's broader by a metre** c'est plus large d'un mètre; **one by one** un à un; **little by little** petit à petit, peu à peu
8 (*according to*) d'après, selon; **it's 3 o'clock by my watch** il est 3 heures à ma montre; **it's all right by me** je n'ai rien contre
9: (all) by oneself *etc* tout(e) seul(e)
10: by the way au fait, à propos
♦ *adv* **1** *see* **go**; **pass** *etc*
2: by and by un peu plus tard, bientôt; **by and large** dans l'ensemble

bye(-bye) ['baɪ('baɪ)] *excl* au revoir!, salut!
by(e)-law ['baɪlɔ:] *n* arrêté municipal
by-: ~**-election** (*BRIT*) *n* élection (législative) partielle; ~**gone** *adj* passé(e) ♦ *n*: **let ~gones be ~gones** passons l'éponge, oublions le passé; ~**pass** *n* (route *f* de) contournement *m*; (*MED*) pontage *m* ♦ *vt* éviter; ~**product** *n* sous-produit *m*, dérivé *m*; (*fig*) conséquence *f* secondaire, retombée *f*; ~**stander** *n* spectateur(-trice), badaud(e)
byte [baɪt] *n* (*COMPUT*) octet *m*
byword ['baɪwə:d] *n*: **to be a ~ for** être synonyme de (*fig*)

C, c

C [si:] *n* (*MUS*) do *m*
CA *abbr* = **chartered accountant**
cab [kæb] *n* taxi *m*; (*of train, truck*) cabine *f*
cabaret ['kæbəreɪ] *n* (*show*) spectacle *m* de cabaret
cabbage ['kæbɪdʒ] *n* chou *m*
cabin ['kæbɪn] *n* (*house*) cabane *f*, hutte *f*; (*on ship*) cabine *f*; (*on plane*) compartiment *m*; ~ **crew** *n* (*AVIAT*) équipage *m*; ~ **cruiser** *n* cruiser *m*
cabinet ['kæbɪnɪt] *n* (*POL*) cabinet *m*; (*furniture*) petit meuble à tiroirs et rayons; (*also*: **display ~**) vitrine *f*, petite armoire vitrée
cable ['keɪbl] *n* câble *m* ♦ *vt* câbler, télégraphier; ~**-car** *n* téléphérique *m*; ~ **television** *n* télévision *f* par câble
cache [kæʃ] *n* stock *m*
cackle ['kækl] *vi* caqueter
cactus ['kæktəs] (*pl* **cacti**) *n* cactus *m*
cadet [kə'dɛt] *n* (*MIL*) élève *m* officier
cadge [kædʒ] (*inf*) *vt*: **to ~ (from or off)** se faire donner (par)
Caesarian [sɪ'zɛərɪən] *n* (*also*: ~ **section**) césarienne *f*
café ['kæfeɪ] *n* ≃ café(-restaurant) *m* (*sans alcool*)
cage [keɪdʒ] *n* cage *f*
cagey ['keɪdʒɪ] (*inf*) *adj* réticent(e); méfiant(e)
cagoule [kə'gu:l] *n* K-way ® *m*
Cairo ['kaɪərəu] *n* le Caire
cajole [kə'dʒəul] *vt* couvrir de flatteries *or* de gentillesses
cake [keɪk] *n* gâteau *m*; ~**d** *adj*: ~**d with** raidi(e) par, couvert(e) d'une croûte de
calculate ['kælkjuleɪt] *vt* calculer; (*estimate: chances, effect*) évaluer; **calculation** *n* calcul *m*; **calculator** *n* machine *f* à calculer, calculatrice *f*; (*pocket*) calculette *f*
calendar ['kæləndəʳ] *n* calendrier *m*; ~ **year** *n* année civile
calf [kɑ:f] (*pl* **calves**) *n* (*of cow*) veau *m*; (*of*

other animals) petit *m*; (*also:* **~skin**) veau *m*, vachette *f*; (*ANAT*) mollet *m*

calibre ['kælɪbə'] (*US* **caliber**) *n* calibre *m*

call [kɔ:l] *vt* appeler; (*meeting*) convoquer ♦ *vi* appeler; (*visit: also:* **~ in, ~ round**) passer ♦ *n* (*shout*) appel *m*, cri *m*; (*also:* **telephone ~**) coup *m* de téléphone; (*visit*) visite *f*; **she's ~ed Suzanne** elle s'appelle Suzanne; **to be on ~** être de permanence; **~ back** *vi* (*return*) repasser; (*TEL*) rappeler; **~ for** *vt fus* (*demand*) demander; (*fetch*) passer prendre; **~ off** *vt* annuler; **~ on** *vt fus* (*visit*) rendre visite à; (*request*): **to ~ on sb to do** inviter qn à faire; **~ out** *vi* pousser un cri *or* des cris; **~ up** *vt* (*MIL*) appeler, mobiliser; (*TEL*) appeler; **~box** *n* (*TEL*) cabine *f* téléphonique; **~ centre** *n* centre *m* d'appels; **~er** *n* (*TEL*) personne *f* qui appelle; (*visitor*) visiteur *m*; **~ girl** *n* call-girl *f*; **~-in** (*US*) *n* (*RADIO, TV: phone-in*) programme *m* à ligne ouverte; **~ing** *n* vocation *f*; (*trade, occupation*) état *m*; **~ing card** (*US*) *n* carte *f* de visite

callous ['kæləs] *adj* dur(e), insensible

calm [kɑ:m] *adj* calme ♦ *n* calme *m* ♦ *vt* calmer, apaiser; **~ down** *vi* se calmer ♦ *vt* calmer, apaiser

Calor gas ® ['kælə'-] *n* butane *m*, butagaz *m* ®

calorie ['kælərɪ] *n* calorie *f*

calves [kɑ:vz] *npl of* **calf**

camber ['kæmbə'] *n* (*of road*) bombement *m*

Cambodia [kæm'bəudɪə] *n* Cambodge *m*

camcorder ['kæmkɔ:də'] *n* caméscope *m*

came [keɪm] *pt of* **come**

camel ['kæməl] *n* chameau *m*

camera ['kæmərə] *n* (*PHOT*) appareil-photo *m*; (*also:* **cine-~, movie ~**) caméra *f*; **in ~** à huis clos; **~man** (*irreg*) *n* caméraman *m*; **~phone** *n* téléphone *m* avec appareil-photo numérique intégré

camouflage ['kæməflɑ:ʒ] *n* camouflage *m* ♦ *vt* camoufler

camp [kæmp] *n* camp *m* ♦ *vi* camper ♦ *adj* (*man*) efféminé(e)

campaign [kæm'peɪn] *n* (*MIL, POL etc*) cam-

pagne *f* ♦ *vi* faire campagne

camp: **~bed** (*BRIT*) *n* lit *m* de camp; **~er** *n* campeur(-euse); (*vehicle*) camping-car *m*; **~ing** *n* camping *m*; **to go ~ing** faire du camping; **~ing gas** ® *n* butane *m*; **~site** *n* (terrain *m* de) camping *m*

can[1] [kæn] *n* (*of milk, oil, water*) bidon *m*; (*tin*) boîte *f* de conserve ♦ *vt* mettre en conserve

---

KEYWORD

can[2] [kæn] (*negative* **cannot, can't**, *conditional and pt* **could**) *aux vb* 1 (*be able to*) pouvoir; **you can do it if you try** vous pouvez le faire si vous essayez; **I can't hear you** je ne t'entends pas

2 (*know how to*) savoir; **I can swim/play tennis/drive** je sais nager/jouer au tennis/conduire; **can you speak French?** parlez-vous français?

3 (*may*) pouvoir; **can I use your phone?** puis-je me servir de votre téléphone?

4 (*expressing disbelief, puzzlement etc*): **it can't be true!** ce n'est pas possible!; **what CAN he want?** qu'est-ce qu'il peut bien vouloir?

5 (*expressing possibility, suggestion etc*): **he could be in the library** il est peut-être dans la bibliothèque; **she could have been delayed** il se peut qu'elle ait été retardée

---

Canada ['kænədə] *n* Canada *m*; **Canadian** [kə'neɪdɪən] *adj* canadien(ne) ♦ *n* Canadien(ne)

canal [kə'næl] *n* canal *m*

canapé ['kænəpeɪ] *n* canapé *m*

canary [kə'nɛərɪ] *n* canari *m*, serin *m*

cancel ['kænsəl] *vt* annuler; (*train*) supprimer; (*party, appointment*) décommander; (*cross out*) barrer, rayer; **~lation** [kænsə'leɪʃən] *n* annulation *f*; suppression *f*

cancer ['kænsə'] *n* (*MED*) cancer *m*; **C~** (*ASTROLOGY*) le Cancer

candid ['kændɪd] *adj* (très) franc (franche), sincère

candidate ['kændɪdeɪt] *n* candidat(e)

candle ['kændl] *n* bougie *f*; (*of tallow*) chandelle *f*; (*in church*) cierge *m*; **~light** *n*: **by ~light** à la lumière d'une bougie; (*dinner*) aux chandelles; **~stick** *n* (*also:* **~ holder**) bougeoir *m*; (*bigger, ornate*) chandelier *m*

candour ['kændə^r] (*US* **candor**) *n* (grande) franchise *or* sincérité

candy ['kændı] *n* sucre candi; (*US*) bonbon *m*; **~floss** (*BRIT*) *n* barbe *f* à papa

cane [keın] *n* canne *f*; (*for furniture, baskets etc*) rotin *m* ♦ *vt* (*BRIT: SCOL*) administrer des coups de bâton à

canister ['kænıstə^r] *n* boîte *f*; (*of gas, pressurized substance*) bombe *f*

cannabis ['kænəbıs] *n* (*drug*) cannabis *m*

canned [kænd] *adj* (*food*) en boîte, en conserve

cannon ['kænən] (*pl* **~** *or* **~s**) *n* (*gun*) canon *m*

cannot ['kænɔt] = **can not**

canoe [kə'nu:] *n* pirogue *f*; (*SPORT*) canoë *m*; **~ing** *n*: **to go ~ing** faire du canoë

canon ['kænən] *n* (*clergyman*) chanoine *m*; (*standard*) canon *m*

can-opener ['kænəupnə^r] *n* ouvre-boîte *m*

canopy ['kænəpı] *n* baldaquin *m*; dais *m*

can't [kænt] = **cannot**

canteen [kæn'ti:n] *n* cantine *f*; (*BRIT: of cutlery*) ménagère *f*

canter ['kæntə^r] *vi* (*horse*) aller au petit galop

canvas ['kænvəs] *n* toile *f*

canvass ['kænvəs] *vi* (*POL*): **to ~ for** faire campagne pour ♦ *vt* (*investigate: opinions etc*) sonder

canyon ['kænjən] *n* cañon *m*, gorge (profonde)

cap [kæp] *n* casquette *f*; (*of pen*) capuchon *m*; (*of bottle*) capsule *f*; (*contraceptive: also:* **Dutch ~**) diaphragme *m*; (*for toy gun*) amorce *f* ♦ *vt* (*outdo*) surpasser; (*put limit on*) plafonner

capability [keıpə'bılıtı] *n* aptitude *f*, capacité *f*

capable ['keıpəbl] *adj* capable

capacity [kə'pæsıtı] *n* capacité *f*; (*capabili-* ty) aptitude *f*; (*of factory*) rendement *m*

cape [keıp] *n* (*garment*) cape *f*; (*GEO*) cap *m*

caper ['keıpə^r] *n* (*CULIN: gen pl*) câpre *f*; (*prank*) farce *f*

capital ['kæpıtl] *n* (*also:* **~ city**) capitale *f*; (*money*) capital *m*; (*also:* **~ letter**) majuscule *f*; **~ gains tax** *n* (*COMM*) impôt *m* sur les plus-values; **~ism** *n* capitalisme *m*; **~ist** *adj* capitaliste ♦ *n* capitaliste *m/f*; **~ize** ['kæpıtlaız] *vi*: **to ~ize on** tirer parti de; **~ punishment** *n* peine capitale

---

Capitol

i Le **Capitol** est le siège du **Congress**, à Washington. Il est situé sur Capitol Hill.

Capricorn ['kæprıkɔ:n] *n* le Capricorne

capsize [kæp'saız] *vt* faire chavirer ♦ *vi* chavirer

capsule ['kæpsju:l] *n* capsule *f*

captain ['kæptın] *n* capitaine *m*

caption ['kæpʃən] *n* légende *f*

captive ['kæptıv] *adj*, *n* captif(-ive)

capture ['kæptʃə^r] *vt* capturer, prendre; (*attention*) capter; (*COMPUT*) saisir ♦ *n* capture *f*; (*data ~*) saisie *f* de données

car [kɑ:^r] *n* voiture *f*, auto *f*; (*RAIL*) wagon *m*, voiture

caramel ['kærəməl] *n* caramel *m*

caravan ['kærəvæn] *n* caravane *f*; **~ning** *n*: **to go ~ning** faire du caravaning; **~ site** (*BRIT*) *n* camping *m* pour caravanes

carbohydrate [kɑ:bəu'haıdreıt] *n* hydrate *m* de carbone; (*food*) féculent *m*

carbon ['kɑ:bən] *n* carbone *m*; **~ dioxide** *n* gaz *m* carbonique; **~ monoxide** *n* oxyde *m* de carbone; **~ paper** *n* papier *m* carbone

car boot sale *n* marché aux puces où les particuliers vendent des objets entreposés dans le coffre de leur voiture

carburettor [kɑ:bju'retə^r] (*US* **carburetor**) *n* carburateur *m*

card [kɑ:d] *n* carte *f*; (*material*) carton *m*; **~board** *n* carton *m*; **~ game** *n* jeu *m* de

cartes
cardiac ['kɑːdɪæk] *adj* cardiaque
cardigan ['kɑːdɪgən] *n* cardigan *m*
cardinal ['kɑːdɪnl] *adj* cardinal(e) ♦ *n* cardinal *m*
card index *n* fichier *m*
cardphone *n* téléphone *m* à carte
care [kɛəʳ] *n* soin *m*, attention *f*; (*worry*) souci *m*; (*charge*) charge *f*, garde *f* ♦ *vi*: **to ~ about** se soucier de, s'intéresser à; (*person*) être attaché(e) à; **~ of** chez, aux bons soins de; **in sb's ~** à la garde de qn, confié(e) à qn; **to take ~ (to do)** faire attention (à faire); **to take ~ of** s'occuper de; **I don't ~** ça m'est bien égal; **I couldn't ~ less** je m'en fiche complètement (*inf*); **~ for** *vt fus* s'occuper de; (*like*) aimer
career [kə'rɪəʳ] *n* carrière *f* ♦ *vi* (*also:* **~ along**) aller à toute allure; **~ woman** (*irreg*) *n* femme ambitieuse
care: **~free** *adj* sans souci, insouciant(e); **~ful** *adj* (*thorough*) soigneux(-euse); (*cautious*) prudent(e); **(be) ~ful!** (fais) attention!; **~fully** *adv* avec soin, soigneusement; prudemment; **~less** *adj* négligent(e); (*heedless*) insouciant(e); **~r** *n* (*MED*) aide *f*
caress [kə'rɛs] *n* caresse *f* ♦ *vt* caresser
caretaker ['kɛəteɪkəʳ] *n* gardien(ne), concierge *m/f*
car-ferry ['kɑːfɛrɪ] *n* (*on sea*) ferry(-boat) *m*
cargo ['kɑːgəu] (*pl* **~es**) *n* cargaison *f*, chargement *m*
car hire *n* location *f* de voitures
Caribbean [kærɪ'biːən] *adj*: **the ~ (Sea)** la mer des Antilles *or* Caraïbes
caring ['kɛərɪŋ] *adj* (*person*) bienveillant(e); (*society, organization*) humanitaire
carnation [kɑː'neɪʃən] *n* œillet *m*
carnival ['kɑːnɪvl] *n* (*public celebration*) carnaval *m*; (*US: funfair*) fête foraine
carol ['kærəl] *n*: **(Christmas) ~** chant *m* de Noël
carp [kɑːp] *n* (*fish*) carpe *f*
car park (*BRIT*) *n* parking *m*, parc *m* de stationnement

carpenter ['kɑːpɪntəʳ] *n* charpentier *m*;
carpentry *n* menuiserie *f*
carpet ['kɑːpɪt] *n* tapis *m* ♦ *vt* recouvrir d'un tapis; **~ sweeper** *n* balai *m* mécanique
car phone *n* (*TEL*) téléphone *m* de voiture
car rental *n* location *f* de voitures
carriage ['kærɪdʒ] *n* voiture *f*; (*of goods*) transport *m*; (*: cost*) port *m*; **~way** (*BRIT*) *n* (*part of road*) chaussée *f*
carrier ['kærɪəʳ] *n* transporteur *m*, camionneur *m*; (*company*) entreprise *f* de transport; (*MED*) porteur(-euse); **~ bag** (*BRIT*) *n* sac *m* (en papier *or* en plastique)
carrot ['kærət] *n* carotte *f*
carry ['kærɪ] *vt* (*subj: person*) porter; (*: vehicle*) transporter; (*involve: responsibilities etc*) comporter, impliquer ♦ *vi* (*sound*) porter; **to get carried away** (*fig*) s'emballer, s'enthousiasmer; **~ on** *vi*: **to ~ on with sth/doing** continuer qch/de faire ♦ *vt* poursuivre; **~ out** *vt* (*orders*) exécuter; (*investigation*) mener; **~cot** (*BRIT*) *n* porte-bébé *m*; **~-on** (*inf*) *n* (*fuss*) histoires *fpl*
cart [kɑːt] *n* charrette *f* ♦ *vt* (*inf*) transporter, trimballer (*inf*)
carton ['kɑːtən] *n* (*box*) carton *m*; (*of yogurt*) pot *m*; (*of cigarettes*) cartouche *f*
cartoon [kɑː'tuːn] *n* (*PRESS*) dessin *m* (humoristique), caricature *f*; (*BRIT: comic strip*) bande dessinée; (*CINEMA*) dessin animé
cartridge ['kɑːtrɪdʒ] *n* cartouche *f*
carve [kɑːv] *vt* (*meat*) découper; (*wood, stone*) tailler, sculpter; **~ up** *vt* découper; (*fig: country*) morceler; **carving** *n* sculpture *f*; **carving knife** *n* couteau *m* à découper
car wash *n* station *f* de lavage (de voitures)
case [keɪs] *n* cas *m*; (*LAW*) affaire *f*, procès *m*; (*box*) caisse *f*, boîte *f*, étui *m*; (*BRIT: also: suitcase*) valise *f*; **in ~ of** en cas de; **in ~ he ...** au cas où il ...; **just in ~** à tout hasard; **in any ~** en tout cas, de toute façon
cash [kæʃ] *n* argent *m*; (*COMM*) argent li-

quide, espèces *fpl* ♦ *vt* encaisser; **to pay (in)** ~ payer comptant; ~ **on delivery** payable *or* paiement à la livraison; ~-**book** *n* livre *m* de caisse; ~ **card** (*BRIT*) *n* carte *f* de retrait; ~ **desk** (*BRIT*) *n* caisse *f*; ~ **dispenser** (*BRIT*) *n* distributeur *m* automatique de billets, billeterie *f*

cashew [kæ'ʃuː] *n* (*also*: ~ **nut**) noix *f* de cajou

cashier [kæ'ʃɪəʳ] *n* caissier(-ère)

cashmere ['kæʃmɪəʳ] *n* cachemire *m*

cash register *n* caisse (enregistreuse)

casing ['keɪsɪŋ] *n* revêtement (protecteur), enveloppe (protectrice)

casino [kə'siːnəu] *n* casino *m*

casket ['kɑːskɪt] *n* coffret *m*; (*US*: *coffin*) cercueil *m*

casserole ['kæsərəul] *n* (*container*) cocotte *f*; (*food*) ragoût *m* (en cocotte)

cassette [kæ'set] *n* cassette *f*, musicassette *f*; ~ **player** *n* lecteur *m* de cassettes; ~ **recorder** *n* magnétophone *m* à cassettes

cast [kɑːst] (*pt*, *pp* **cast**) *vt* (*throw*) jeter; (*shed*) perdre; se dépouiller de; (*statue*) mouler; (*THEATRE*): **to** ~ **sb as Hamlet** attribuer à qn le rôle de Hamlet ♦ *n* (*THEATRE*) distribution *f*; (*also*: **plaster** ~) plâtre *m*; **to** ~ **one's vote** voter; ~ **off** *vi* (*NAUT*) larguer les amarres; (*KNITTING*) arrêter les mailles; ~ **on** *vi* (*KNITTING*) monter les mailles

castaway ['kɑːstəweɪ] *n* naufragé(e)

caster sugar ['kɑːstə-] (*BRIT*) *n* sucre *m* semoule

casting vote (*BRIT*) *n* voix prépondérante (*pour départager*)

cast iron *n* fonte *f*

castle ['kɑːsl] *n* château (fort); (*CHESS*) tour *f*

castor ['kɑːstəʳ] *n* (*wheel*) roulette *f*; ~ **oil** *n* huile *f* de ricin

castrate [kæs'treɪt] *vt* châtrer

casual ['kæʒjul] *adj* (*by chance*) de hasard, fait(e) au hasard, fortuit(e); (*irregular*: *work etc*) temporaire; (*unconcerned*) désinvolte; ~**ly** *adv* avec désinvolture, négligemment; (*dress*) de façon décontractée

casualty ['kæʒjultɪ] *n* accidenté(e), blessé(e); (*dead*) victime *f*, mort(e); (*MED*: *department*) urgences *fpl*

casual wear *n* vêtements *mpl* décontractés

cat [kæt] *n* chat *m*

catalogue ['kætəlɔg] (*US* **catalog**) *n* catalogue *m* ♦ *vt* cataloguer

catalyst ['kætəlɪst] *n* catalyseur *m*

catalytic converter [kætə'lɪtɪk kən'vɜːtəʳ] *n* pot *m* catalytique

catapult ['kætəpʌlt] (*BRIT*) *n* (*sling*) lance-pierres *m inv*, fronde *m*

catarrh [kə'tɑːʳ] *n* rhume *m* chronique, catarrhe *m*

catastrophe [kə'tæstrəfɪ] *n* catastrophe *f*

catch [kætʃ] (*pt*, *pp* **caught**) *vt* attraper; (*person*: *by surprise*) prendre, surprendre; (*understand*, *hear*) saisir ♦ *vi* (*fire*) prendre; (*become trapped*) se prendre, s'accrocher ♦ *n* prise *f*; (*trick*) attrape *f*; (*of lock*) loquet *m*; **to** ~ **sb's attention** *or* **eye** attirer l'attention de qn; **to** ~ **one's breath** retenir son souffle; **to** ~ **fire** prendre feu; **to** ~ **sight of** apercevoir; ~ **on** *vi* saisir; (*grow popular*) prendre; ~ **up** *vi* se rattraper, combler son retard ♦ *vt* (*also*: ~ **up with**) rattraper; ~**ing** *adj* (*MED*) contagieux(-euse); ~**ment area** ['kætʃmənt-] (*BRIT*) *n* (*SCOL*) secteur *m* de recrutement; (*of hospital*) circonscription hospitalière; ~ **phrase** *n* slogan *m*; expression *f* (à la mode); ~**y** *adj* (*tune*) facile à retenir

category ['kætɪgərɪ] *n* catégorie *f*

cater ['keɪtəʳ] *vi* (*provide food*): **to** ~ **(for)** préparer des repas (pour), se charger de la restauration (pour); ~ **for** (*BRIT*) *vt fus* (*needs*) satisfaire, pourvoir à; (*readers*, *consumers*) s'adresser à, pourvoir aux besoins de; ~ **er** *n* traiteur *m*; fournisseur *m*; ~**ing** *n* restauration *f*; approvisionnement *m*, ravitaillement *m*

caterpillar ['kætəpɪləʳ] *n* chenille *f*

cathedral [kə'θiːdrəl] *n* cathédrale *f*

catholic ['kæθəlɪk] *adj* (*tastes*) éclectique, varié(e); **C~** *adj* catholique ♦ *n* catholique *m/f*

Catseye ® ['kæts'aɪ] (*BRIT*) *n* (*AUT*) cata-dioptre *m*

cattle ['kætl] *npl* bétail *m*

catty ['kætɪ] *adj* méchant(e)

caucus ['kɔːkəs] *n* (*POL: group*) comité local d'un parti politique; (*US: POL*) comité électoral (pour désigner des candidats)

caught [kɔːt] *pt, pp of* **catch**

cauliflower ['kɒlɪflauər] *n* chou-fleur *m*

cause [kɔːz] *n* cause *f* ♦ *vt* causer

caution ['kɔːʃən] *n* prudence *f*; (*warning*) avertissement *m* ♦ *vt* avertir, donner un avertissement à; **cautious** *adj* prudent(e)

cavalry ['kævəlrɪ] *n* cavalerie *f*

cave [keɪv] *n* caverne *f*, grotte *f*; ~ **in** *vi* (*roof etc*) s'effondrer; **~man** ['keɪvmæn] (*irreg*) *n* homme *m* des cavernes

caviar(e) ['kævɪɑːʳ] *n* caviar *m*

CB *n abbr* (= *Citizens' Band (Radio*)) CB *f*

CBI *n abbr* (= *Confederation of British Industries*) groupement du patronat

cc *abbr* = **carbon copy**; **cubic centimetres**

CCTV *n abbr* (= *closed-circuit television*) télévision *f* en circuit fermé

CD *n abbr* (= *compact disc (player*)) CD *m*; **CDI** *n abbr* (= *Compact Disk Interactive*) CD-I *m*; **CD player** *n* platine *f* laser; **CD-ROM** [siːdiːˈrɔm] *n abbr* (= *compact disc read-only memory*) CD-Rom *m*

cease [siːs] *vt, vi* cesser; **~fire** *n* cessez-le-feu *m*; **~less** *adj* incessant(e), continuel(le)

cedar ['siːdər] *n* cèdre *m*

ceiling ['siːlɪŋ] *n* plafond *m*

celebrate ['sɛlɪbreɪt] *vt, vi* célébrer; **~d** *adj* célèbre; **celebration** [sɛlɪˈbreɪʃən] *n* célébration *f*; **celebrity** [sɪˈlɛbrɪtɪ] *n* célébrité *f*

celery ['sɛlərɪ] *n* céleri *m* (à côtes)

cell [sɛl] *n* cellule *f*; (*ELEC*) élément *m* (de pile)

cellar ['sɛlər] *n* cave *f*

cello ['tʃɛləu] *n* violoncelle *m*

cellphone ['sɛlfəun] *n* téléphone *m* cellulaire

Celt [kɛlt, sɛlt] *n* Celte *m/f*; **~ic** *adj* celte

cement [sə'mɛnt] *n* ciment *m*

cemetery ['sɛmɪtrɪ] *n* cimetière *m*

censor ['sɛnsər] *n* censeur *m* ♦ *vt* censurer; **~ship** *n* censure *f*

censure ['sɛnʃər] *vt* blâmer, critiquer

census ['sɛnsəs] *n* recensement *m*

cent [sɛnt] *n* (*US etc: coin*) cent *m* (= *un centième du dollar, de l'euro*); *see also* **per**

centenary [sɛn'tiːnərɪ] *n* centenaire *m*

center ['sɛntər] (*US*) *n* = **centre**

centigrade ['sɛntɪgreɪd] *adj* centigrade

centimetre ['sɛntɪmiːtər] (*US* **centimeter**) *n* centimètre *m*

centipede ['sɛntɪpiːd] *n* mille-pattes *m inv*

central ['sɛntrəl] *adj* central(e); **C~ America** *n* Amérique centrale; **~ heating** *n* chauffage central; **~ reservation** (*BRIT*) *n* (*AUT*) terre-plein central

centre ['sɛntər] (*US* **center**) *n* centre *m* ♦ *vt* centrer; **~-forward** *n* (*SPORT*) avant-centre *m*; **~-half** *n* (*SPORT*) demi-centre *m*

century ['sɛntjurɪ] *n* siècle *m*; **20th ~** XXe siècle

ceramic [sɪ'ræmɪk] *adj* céramique

cereal ['siːrɪəl] *n* céréale *f*

ceremony ['sɛrɪmənɪ] *n* cérémonie *f*; **to stand on ~** faire des façons

certain ['sɜːtən] *adj* certain(e); **for ~** certainement, sûrement; **~ly** *adv* certainement; **~ty** *n* certitude *f*

certificate [sə'tɪfɪkɪt] *n* certificat *m*

certified ['sɜːtɪfaɪd] *adj*: **by ~ mail** (*US*) en recommandé, avec avis de réception; **~ public accountant** (*US*) expert-comptable *m*

certify ['sɜːtɪfaɪ] *vt* certifier; (*award diploma to*) conférer un diplôme *etc* à; (*declare insane*) déclarer malade mental(e)

cervical ['sɜːvɪkl] *adj*: **~ cancer** cancer *m* du col de l'utérus; **~ smear** frottis vaginal

cervix ['sɜːvɪks] *n* col *m* de l'utérus

cf. *abbr* (= *compare*) cf., voir

CFC *n abbr* (= *chlorofluorocarbon*) CFC *m*

ch. *abbr* (= *chapter*) chap.

chafe [tʃeɪf] *vt* irriter, frotter contre

chain [tʃeɪn] *n* chaîne *f* ♦ *vt* (*also:* ~ **up**) enchaîner, attacher (avec une chaîne); ~ **reaction** *n* réaction *f* en chaîne; ~-

smoke vi fumer cigarette sur cigarette; ~ **store** n magasin m à succursales multiples

chair [tʃɛəʳ] n chaise f; (armchair) fauteuil m; (of university) chaire f; (of meeting, committee) présidence f ♦ vt (meeting) présider; **~lift** n télésiège m; **~man** (irreg) n président m

chalet ['ʃæleɪ] n chalet m

chalk [tʃɔːk] n craie f

challenge ['tʃælɪndʒ] n défi m ♦ vt défier; (statement, right) mettre en question, contester; **to ~ sb to do** mettre au défi de faire; **challenging** adj (tone, look) de défi, provocateur(-trice); (task, career) qui représente un défi or une gageure

chamber ['tʃeɪmbəʳ] n chambre f; **~ of commerce** chambre de commerce; **~maid** n femme f de chambre; **~ music** n musique f de chambre

champagne [ʃæm'peɪn] n champagne m

champion ['tʃæmpɪən] n champion(ne); **~ship** n championnat m

chance [tʃɑːns] n (opportunity) occasion f, possibilité f; (hope, likelihood) chance f; (risk) risque m ♦ vt: **to ~ it** risquer (le coup), essayer ♦ adj fortuit(e), de hasard; **to take a ~** prendre un risque; **by ~** par hasard

chancellor ['tʃɑːnsələʳ] n chancelier m; **C~ of the Exchequer** (BRIT) n chancelier m de l'Échiquier; ≈ ministre m des Finances

chandelier [ʃændə'lɪəʳ] n lustre m

change [tʃeɪndʒ] vt (alter, replace, COMM: money) changer; (hands, trains, clothes, one's name) changer de; (transform): **to ~ sb into** changer or transformer qn en ♦ vi (gen) changer; (one's clothes) se changer; (be transformed): **to ~ into** se changer or transformer en ♦ n changement m; (money) monnaie f; **to ~ gear** (AUT) changer de vitesse; **to ~ one's mind** changer d'avis; **a ~ of clothes** des vêtements de rechange; **for a ~** pour changer; **~able** adj (weather) variable; **~ machine** n distributeur m de monnaie; **~over** n (to new

system) changement m, passage m; **changing** adj changeant(e); **changing room** (BRIT) n (in shop) salon m d'essayage; (SPORT) vestiaire m

channel ['tʃænl] n (TV) chaîne f; (navigable passage) chenal m; (irrigation) canal m ♦ vt canaliser; **the (English) C~** la Manche; **the C~ Islands** les îles de la Manche, les îles Anglo-Normandes; **the C~ Tunnel** le tunnel sous la Manche; **~-hopping** n (TV) zapping m

chant [tʃɑːnt] n chant m; (REL) psalmodie f ♦ vt chanter, scander

chaos ['keɪɔs] n chaos m

chap [tʃæp] (BRIT: inf) n (man) type m

chapel ['tʃæpl] n chapelle f; (BRIT: nonconformist ~) église f

chaplain ['tʃæplɪn] n aumônier m

chapped [tʃæpt] adj (skin, lips) gercé(e)

chapter ['tʃæptəʳ] n chapitre m

char [tʃɑːʳ] vt (burn) carboniser

character ['kærɪktəʳ] n caractère m; (in novel, film) personnage m; (eccentric) numéro m, phénomène m; **~istic** [kærɪktə'rɪstɪk] adj caractéristique ♦ n caractéristique f

charcoal ['tʃɑːkəʊl] n charbon m de bois; (for drawing) charbon m

charge [tʃɑːdʒ] n (cost) prix (demandé); (accusation) accusation f; (LAW) inculpation f ♦ vt: **to ~ sb (with)** inculper qn (de); (battery, enemy) charger; (customer, sum) faire payer ♦ vi foncer; **~s** npl (costs) frais mpl; **to reverse the ~s** (TEL) téléphoner en P.C.V.; **to take ~ of** se charger de; **to be in ~ of** être responsable de, s'occuper de; **how much do you ~?** combien prenez-vous?; **to ~ an expense (up) to sb** mettre une dépense sur le compte de qn; **~ card** n carte f de client

charity ['tʃærɪtɪ] n charité f; (organization) institution f charitable or de bienfaisance, œuvre f (de charité)

charm [tʃɑːm] n charme m; (on bracelet) breloque f ♦ vt charmer, enchanter; **~ing** adj charmant(e)

chart [tʃɑːt] n tableau m, diagramme m; graphique m; (map) carte marine ♦ vt dresser _or_ établir la carte de; **~s** npl (_hit parade_) hit-parade m

charter ['tʃɑːtəʳ] vt (_plane_) affréter ♦ n (_document_) charte f; **~ed accountant** (_BRIT_) n expert-comptable m; ~ **flight** n charter m

chase [tʃeɪs] vt poursuivre, pourchasser; (_also:_ ~ **away**) chasser ♦ n poursuite f, chasse f

chasm ['kæzəm] n gouffre m, abîme m

chat [tʃæt] vi (_also:_ **have a ~**) bavarder, causer ♦ n conversation f; ~ **show** (_BRIT_) n causerie télévisée

chatter ['tʃætəʳ] vi (_person_) bavarder; (_animal_) jacasser ♦ n bavardage m; jacassement m; **my teeth are ~ing** je claque des dents; **~box** (_inf_) n moulin à paroles

chatty ['tʃætɪ] adj (_style_) familier(-ère); (_person_) bavard(e)

chauffeur ['ʃəufəʳ] n chauffeur m (de maître)

chauvinist ['ʃəuvɪnɪst] n (_male ~_) phallocrate m; (_nationalist_) chauvin(e)

cheap [tʃiːp] adj bon marché inv, pas cher (chère); (_joke_) facile, d'un goût douteux; (_poor quality_) à bon marché, de qualité médiocre ♦ adv à bon marché, pour pas cher; ~ **day return** billet m d'aller et retour réduit (_valable pour la journée_); **~er** adj moins cher (chère); **~ly** adv à bon marché, à bon compte

cheat [tʃiːt] vi tricher ♦ vt tromper, duper; (_rob_): **to ~ sb out of sth** escroquer qch à qn ♦ n tricheur(-euse); escroc m

check [tʃɛk] vt vérifier; (_passport, ticket_) contrôler; (_halt_) arrêter; (_restrain_) maîtriser ♦ n vérification f; contrôle m; (_curb_) frein m; (_US: bill_) addition f; (_pattern: gen pl_) carreaux mpl; (_US_) = **cheque** ♦ adj (_pattern, cloth_) à carreaux; ~ **in** vi (_in hotel_) remplir sa fiche (d'hôtel); (_at airport_) se présenter à l'enregistrement ♦ vt (_luggage_) (faire) enregistrer; ~ **out** vi (_in hotel_) régler sa note; ~ **up** vi: **to ~ up (on sth)** vérifier (qch); **to ~ up on sb** se renseigner sur le compte de qn; **~ered** (_US_) adj = **chequered**; **~ers** (_US_) npl jeu m de dames;

~**in** (**desk**) n enregistrement m; ~**ing account** (_US_) n (_current account_) compte courant; ~**mate** n échec et mat m; ~**out** n (_in shop_) caisse f; ~**point** n contrôle m; ~**room** n (_US_) (_left-luggage office_) consigne f; ~**up** n (_MED_) examen médical, check-up m

cheek [tʃiːk] n joue f; (_impudence_) toupet m, culot m; ~**bone** n pommette f; ~**y** adj effronté(e), culotté(e)

cheep [tʃiːp] vi piauler

cheer [tʃɪəʳ] vt acclamer, applaudir; (_gladden_) réjouir, réconforter ♦ vi applaudir ♦ n (_gen pl_) acclamations fpl, applaudissements mpl; bravos mpl, hourras mpl; **~s!** à la vôtre!; ~ **up** vi se dérider, reprendre courage ♦ vt remonter le moral à _or_ de, dérider; ~**ful** adj gai(e), joyeux(-euse)

cheerio [tʃɪərɪ'əu] (_BRIT_) excl salut!, au revoir!

cheese [tʃiːz] n fromage m; ~**board** n plateau m de fromages

cheetah ['tʃiːtə] n guépard m

chef [ʃɛf] n chef (cuisinier)

chemical ['kɛmɪkl] adj chimique ♦ n produit m chimique

chemist ['kɛmɪst] n (_BRIT: pharmacist_) pharmacien(ne); (_scientist_) chimiste m/f; ~**ry** n chimie f; ~**'s (shop)** (_BRIT_) n pharmacie f

cheque [tʃɛk] (_BRIT_) n chèque m; ~**book** n chéquier m, carnet m de chèques; ~ **card** n carte f (d'identité) bancaire

chequered ['tʃɛkəd] (_US_ **checkered**) adj (_fig_) varié(e)

cherish ['tʃɛrɪʃ] vt chérir

cherry ['tʃɛrɪ] n cerise f; (_also:_ ~ **tree**) cerisier m

chess [tʃɛs] n échecs mpl; ~**board** n échiquier m

chest [tʃɛst] n poitrine f; (_box_) coffre m, caisse f; ~ **of drawers** n commode f

chestnut ['tʃɛsnʌt] n châtaigne f; (_also:_ ~ **tree**) châtaignier m

chew [tʃuː] vt mâcher; ~**ing gum** n chewing-gum m

chic [ʃiːk] *adj* chic *inv*, élégant(e)

chick [tʃik] *n* poussin *m*; (*inf*) nana *f*

chicken ['tʃikin] *n* poulet *m*; (*inf: coward*) poule mouillée; ~ **out** (*inf*) *vi* se dégonfler; ~**pox** *n* varicelle *f*

chicory ['tʃikəri] *n* (*for coffee*) chicorée *f*; (*salad*) endive *f*

chief [tʃiːf] *n* chef ♦ *adj* principal(e); ~ **executive** (*US* **chief executive officer**) *n* directeur(-trice) général(e); ~**ly** *adv* principalement, surtout

chiffon ['ʃifɔn] *n* mousseline *f* de soie

chilblain ['tʃilblein] *n* engelure *f*

child [tʃaild] (*pl* ~**ren**) *n* enfant *m/f*; ~**birth** *n* accouchement *m*; ~**hood** *n* enfance *f*; ~**ish** *adj* puéril(e), enfantin(e); ~**like** *adj* d'enfant, innocent(e); ~ **minder** (*BRIT*) *n* garde *f* d'enfants; ~**ren** ['tʃildrən] *npl of* **child**

Chile ['tʃili] *n* Chili *m*

chill [tʃil] *n* (*of water*) froid *m*; (*of air*) fraîcheur *f*; (*MED*) refroidissement *m*, coup *m* de froid ♦ *vt* (*person*) faire frissonner; (*CULIN*) mettre au frais, rafraîchir

chil(l)i ['tʃili] *n* piment *m* (rouge)

chilly ['tʃili] *adj* froid(e), glacé(e); (*sensitive to cold*) frileux(-euse); **to feel ~** avoir froid

chime [tʃaim] *n* carillon *m* ♦ *vi* carillonner, sonner

chimney ['tʃimni] *n* cheminée *f*; ~ **sweep** *n* ramoneur *m*

chimpanzee [tʃimpæn'ziː] *n* chimpanzé *m*

chin [tʃin] *n* menton *m*

China ['tʃainə] *n* Chine *f*

china ['tʃainə] *n* porcelaine *f*; (*crockery*) (vaisselle *f* en) porcelaine

Chinese [tʃai'niːz] *adj* chinois(e) ♦ *n inv* (*person*) Chinois(e); (*LING*) chinois *m*

chink [tʃiŋk] *n* (*opening*) fente *f*, fissure *f*; (*noise*) tintement *m*

chip [tʃip] *n* (*gen pl: CULIN: BRIT*) frite *f*; (: *US: potato* ~) chip *m*; (*of wood*) copeau *m*; (*of glass, stone*) éclat *m*; (*also:* **microchip**) puce *f* ♦ *vt* (*cup, plate*) ébrécher

---

chip shop

ⓘ Un *chip shop*, que l'on appelle également un *"fish-and-chip shop"*, est un magasin où l'on vend des plats à emporter. Les chip shops sont d'ailleurs à l'origine des **takeaways**. On y achète en particulier du poisson frit et des frites, mais on y trouve également des plats traditionnels britanniques (steak pies, saucisses, etc). Tous les plats étaient à l'origine emballés dans du papier journal. Dans certains de ces magasins, on peut s'asseoir pour consommer sur place.

---

chiropodist [ki'rɔpədist] (*BRIT*) *n* pédicure *m/f*

chirp [tʃəːp] *vi* pépier, gazouiller

chisel ['tʃizl] *n* ciseau *m*

chit [tʃit] *n* mot *m*, note *f*

chitchat ['tʃittʃæt] *n* bavardage *m*

chivalry ['ʃivəlri] *n* esprit *m* chevaleresque, galanterie *f*

chives [tʃaivz] *npl* ciboulette *f*, civette *f*

chock-a-block ['tʃɔkə'blɔk], **chock-full** [tʃɔk'ful] *adj* plein(e) à craquer

chocolate ['tʃɔklit] *n* chocolat *m*

choice [tʃɔis] *n* choix *m* ♦ *adj* de choix

choir ['kwaiər] *n* chœur *m*, chorale *f*; ~**boy** *n* jeune choriste *m*

choke [tʃəuk] *vi* étouffer ♦ *vt* étrangler; étouffer ♦ *n* (*AUT*) starter *m*; **street ~d with traffic** rue engorgée *or* embouteillée

cholesterol [kə'lestərɔl] *n* cholestérol *m*

choose [tʃuːz] (*pt* **chose**, *pp* **chosen**) *vt* choisir; **to ~ to do** décider de faire, juger bon de faire; **choosy** *adj*: (**to be**) **choosy** (faire le/la) difficile

chop [tʃɔp] *vt* (*wood*) couper (à la hache); (*CULIN: also:* ~ **up**) couper (fin), émincer, hacher (en morceaux) ♦ *n* (*CULIN*) côtelette *f*; ~**s** *npl* (*jaws*) mâchoires *fpl*

chopper ['tʃɔpər] *n* (*helicopter*) hélicoptère *m*, hélico *m*

choppy ['tʃɔpi] *adj* (*sea*) un peu agité(e)

chopsticks ['tʃɔpstiks] *npl* baguettes *fpl*

chord [kɔːd] *n* (*MUS*) accord *m*

chore [tʃɔːr] n travail m de routine; **household ~s** travaux mpl du ménage

chortle [ˈtʃɔːtl] vi glousser

chorus [ˈkɔːrəs] n chœur m; (repeated part of song: also fig) refrain m

chose [tʃəuz] pt of **choose**; **~n** pp of **choose**

chowder [ˈtʃaudər] n soupe f de poisson

Christ [kraist] n Christ m

christen [ˈkrɪsn] vt baptiser

christening n baptême m

Christian [ˈkrɪstɪən] adj, n chrétien(ne); **~ity** [krɪstɪˈænɪtɪ] n christianisme m; **~ name** n prénom m

Christmas [ˈkrɪsməs] n Noël m or f; **Happy** or **Merry ~!** joyeux Noël!; **~ card** n carte f de Noël; **~ Day** n le jour de Noël; **~ Eve** n la veille de Noël; la nuit de Noël; **~ tree** n arbre m de Noël

chrome [krəum] n chrome·m

chromium [ˈkrəumɪəm] n chrome m

chronic [ˈkrɒnɪk] adj chronique

chronicle [ˈkrɒnɪkl] n chronique f

chronological [krɒnəˈlɒdʒɪkl] adj chronologique

chrysanthemum [krɪˈsænθəməm] n chrysanthème m

chubby [ˈtʃʌbɪ] adj potelé(e), rondelet(te)

chuck [tʃʌk] (inf) vt (throw) lancer, jeter; (BRIT: person) plaquer; (: also: **~ up**: job) lâcher; **~ out** vt flanquer dehors or à la porte; (rubbish) jeter

chuckle [ˈtʃʌkl] vi glousser

chug [tʃʌg] vi faire teuf-teuf; (also: **~ along**) avancer en faisant teuf-teuf

chum [tʃʌm] n copain (copine)

chunk [tʃʌŋk] n gros morceau

church [tʃəːtʃ] n église f; **~yard** n cimetière m

churn [tʃəːn] n (for butter) baratte f; (also: **milk ~**) (grand) bidon m à lait; **~ out** vt débiter

chute [ʃuːt] n glissoire f; (also: **rubbish ~**) vide-ordures m inv

chutney [ˈtʃʌtnɪ] n condiment m à base de fruits au vinaigre

CIA n abbr (= Central Intelligence Agency)

CIA f

CID (BRIT) n abbr (= Criminal Investigation Department) P.J. f

cider [ˈsaɪdər] n cidre m

cigar [sɪˈgɑːr] n cigare m

cigarette [sɪgəˈret] n cigarette f; **~ case** n étui m à cigarettes; **~ end** n mégot m

Cinderella [sɪndəˈrelə] n Cendrillon

cinders [ˈsɪndəz] npl cendres fpl

cine-camera [ˈsɪnɪˈkæmərə] (BRIT) n caméra f

cinema [ˈsɪnəmə] n cinéma m

cinnamon [ˈsɪnəmən] n cannelle f

circle [ˈsəːkl] n cercle m; (in cinema, theatre) balcon m ♦ vi faire or décrire des cercles ♦ vt (move round) faire le tour de, tourner autour de; (surround) entourer, encercler

circuit [ˈsəːkɪt] n circuit m; **~ous** [səːˈkjuːtəs] adj indirect(e), qui fait un détour

circular [ˈsəːkjulər] adj circulaire ♦ n circulaire f

circulate [ˈsəːkjuleɪt] vi circuler ♦ vt faire circuler; **circulation** [səːkjuˈleɪʃən] n circulation f; (of newspaper) tirage m

circumflex [ˈsəːkəmfleks] n (also: **~ accent**) accent m circonflexe

circumstances [ˈsəːkəmstənsɪz] npl circonstances fpl; (financial condition) moyens mpl, situation financière

circus [ˈsəːkəs] n cirque m

CIS n abbr (= Commonwealth of Independent States) CEI f

cistern [ˈsɪstən] n réservoir m (d'eau); (in toilet) réservoir de la chasse d'eau

citizen [ˈsɪtɪzn] n citoyen(ne); (resident): **the ~s of this town** les habitants de cette ville; **~ship** n citoyenneté f

citrus fruit [ˈsɪtrəs-] n agrume m

city [ˈsɪtɪ] n ville f, cité f; **the C~** la Cité de Londres (centre des affaires); **~ technology college** n établissement m d'enseignement technologique

civic [ˈsɪvɪk] adj civique; (authorities) municipal(e); **~ centre** (BRIT) n centre administratif (municipal)

civil ['sɪvɪl] *adj* civil(e); *(polite)* poli(e), courtois(e); *(disobedience, defence)* passif(-ive); **~ engineer** *n* ingénieur *m* des travaux publics; **~ian** [sɪ'vɪlɪən] *adj, n* civil(e)

civilization [sɪvɪlaɪ'zeɪʃən] *n* civilisation *f*

civilized ['sɪvɪlaɪzd] *adj* civilisé(e); *(fig)* où règnent les bonnes manières

civil: ~ law *n* code civil; *(study)* droit civil; **~ servant** *n* fonctionnaire *m/f*; **C~ Service** *n* fonction publique, administration *f*; **~ war** *n* guerre civile

clad [klæd] *adj:* **~ (in)** habillé(e) (de)

claim [kleɪm] *vt* revendiquer; *(rights, inheritance)* demander, prétendre à; *(assert)* déclarer, prétendre ♦ *vi (for insurance)* faire une déclaration de sinistre ♦ *n* revendication *f*; demande *f*; prétention *f*, déclaration *f*; *(right)* droit *m*, titre *m*; **~ant** *n (ADMIN, LAW)* requérant(e)

clairvoyant [kleə'vɔɪənt] *n* voyant(e), extra-lucide *m/f*

clam [klæm] *n* palourde *f*

clamber ['klæmbəʳ] *vi* grimper, se hisser

clammy ['klæmɪ] *adj* humide (et froid(e)), moite

clamour ['klæməʳ] *(US* **clamor)** *vi:* **to ~ for** réclamer à grands cris

clamp [klæmp] *n* agrafe *f*, crampon *m* ♦ *vt* serrer; *(sth to sth)* fixer; *(wheel)* mettre un sabot à; **~ down on** *vt fus* sévir *or* prendre des mesures draconiennes contre

clan [klæn] *n* clan *m*

clang [klæŋ] *vi* émettre un bruit *or* fracas métallique

clap [klæp] *vi* applaudir; **~ping** *n* applaudissements *mpl*

claret ['klærət] *n* (vin *m* de) bordeaux *m* (rouge)

clarinet [klærɪ'net] *n* clarinette *f*

clarity ['klærɪtɪ] *n* clarté *f*

clash [klæʃ] *n* choc *m*; *(fig)* conflit *m* ♦ *vi* se heurter; être *or* entrer en conflit; *(colours)* jurer; *(two events)* tomber en même temps

clasp [klɑ:sp] *n (of necklace, bag)* fermoir *m*; *(hold, embrace)* étreinte *f* ♦ *vt* serrer, étreindre

class [klɑ:s] *n* classe *f* ♦ *vt* classer, classifier

classic ['klæsɪk] *adj* classique ♦ *n (author, work)* classique *m*; **~al** *adj* classique

classified ['klæsɪfaɪd] *adj (information)* secret(-ète); **~ advertisement** *n* petite annonce

classmate ['klɑ:smeɪt] *n* camarade *m/f* de classe

classroom ['klɑ:srum] *n (salle f de) classe f*

clatter ['klætəʳ] *n* cliquetis *m* ♦ *vi* cliqueter

clause [klɔ:z] *n* clause *f*; *(LING)* proposition *f*

claw [klɔ:] *n* griffe *f*; *(of bird of prey)* serre *f*; *(of lobster)* pince *f*

clay [kleɪ] *n* argile *f*

clean [kli:n] *adj* propre; *(clear, smooth)* net(te); *(record, reputation)* sans tache; *(joke, story)* correct(e) ♦ *vt* nettoyer; **~ out** *vt* nettoyer (à fond); **~ up** *vt* nettoyer; *(fig)* remettre de l'ordre dans; **~-cut** *adj (person)* net(te), soigné(e); **~er** *n (person)* nettoyeur(-euse), femme *f* de ménage; *(product)* détachant *m*; **~er's** *n (also:* **dry ~er's)** teinturier *m*; **~ing** *n* nettoyage *m*; **~liness** ['klenlɪnɪs] *n* propreté *f*

cleanse [klenz] *vt* nettoyer; *(purify)* purifier; **~r** *n (for face)* démaquillant *m*

clean-shaven ['kli:n'ʃeɪvn] *adj* rasé(e) de près

cleansing department ['klenzɪŋ-] *(BRIT)* *n* service *m* de voirie

clear [klɪəʳ] *adj* clair(e); *(glass, plastic)* transparent(e); *(road, way)* libre, dégagé(e); *(conscience)* net(te) ♦ *vt (room)* débarrasser; *(of people)* faire évacuer; *(cheque)* compenser; *(LAW: suspect)* innocenter; *(obstacle)* franchir *or* sauter sans heurter ♦ *vi (weather)* s'éclaircir; *(fog)* se dissiper ♦ *adv:* **~ of** à distance de, à l'écart de; **to ~ the table** débarrasser la table, desservir; **~ up** *vt* ranger, mettre en ordre; *(mystery)* éclaircir, résoudre; **~ance** *n (removal)* déblaiement *m*; *(permission)* autorisation *f*; **~-cut** *adj* clair(e), nettement défini(e); **~ing** *n (in forest)* clairière *f*; **~ing bank** *(BRIT)* *n* banque qui appartient à une *chambre de compensation;* ~**ly** *adv* clairement; (*evidently*) de toute évidence; ~**way** (*BRIT*) *n* route *f* à stationnement interdit

clef [klɛf] *n* (*MUS*) clé *f*

cleft [klɛft] *n* (*in rock*) crevasse *f*, fissure *f*

clementine [ˈklɛməntaɪn] *n* clémentine *f*

clench [klɛntʃ] *vt* serrer

clergy [ˈkləːdʒɪ] *n* clergé *m*; ~**man** (*irreg*) *n* ecclésiastique *m*

clerical [ˈklɛrɪkl] *adj* de bureau, d'employé de bureau; (*REL*) clérical(e), du clergé

clerk [klɑːk, (*US*) kləːrk] *n* employé(e) de bureau; (*US: salesperson*) vendeur(-euse)

clever [ˈklɛvəʳ] *adj* (*mentally*) intelligent(e); (*crafty*) habile, adroit(e); (*device, arrangement*) ingénieux(-euse), astucieux(-euse)

click [klɪk] *vi* faire un bruit sec ou un déclic; ~ **on** *vt* (*COMPUT*) cliquer sur

client [ˈklaɪənt] *n* client(e)

cliff [klɪf] *n* falaise *f*

climate [ˈklaɪmɪt] *n* climat *m*

climax [ˈklaɪmæks] *n* apogée *m*, point culminant; (*sexual*) orgasme *m*

climb [klaɪm] *vi* grimper, monter ♦ *vt* gravir, escalader, monter sur ♦ *n* montée *f*, escalade *f*; ~-**down** *n* reculade *f*; ~**er** *n* (*mountaineer*) grimpeur(-euse), varappeur(-euse); (*plant*) plante grimpante; ~**ing** *n* (*mountaineering*) escalade *f*, varappe *f*

clinch [klɪntʃ] *vt* (*deal*) conclure, sceller

cling [klɪŋ] (*pt, pp* **clung**) *vi*: **to ~ (to)** se cramponner (à), s'accrocher (à); (*of clothes*) coller (à)

clinic [ˈklɪnɪk] *n* centre médical; ~**al** *adj* clinique; (*attitude*) froid(e), détaché(e)

clink [klɪŋk] *vi* tinter, cliqueter

clip [klɪp] *n* (*for hair*) barrette *f*; (*also:* **paper ~**) trombone *m* ♦ *vt* (*fasten*) attacher; (*hair, nails*) couper; (*hedge*) tailler; ~**pers** *npl* (*for hedge*) sécateur *m*; (*also:* **nail ~pers**) coupe-ongles *m inv*; ~**ping** *n* (*from newspaper*) coupure *f* de journal

cloak [kləuk] *n* grande cape *f* (*fig*) masquer, cacher; ~**room** *n* (*for coats etc*) vestiaire *m*; (*BRIT: WC*) toilettes *fpl*

clock [klɔk] *n* (*large*) horloge *f*; (*small*) pendule *f*; ~ **in** (*BRIT*) *vi* pointer (en arrivant);

~ **off** (*BRIT*) *vi* pointer (en partant); ~ **on** (*BRIT*) *vi* = **clock in**; ~ **out** (*BRIT*) *vi* = **clock off**; ~**wise** *adv* dans le sens des aiguilles d'une montre; ~**work** *n* rouages *mpl*, mécanisme *m*; (*of clock*) mouvement *m* (d'horlogerie) ♦ *adj* mécanique

clog [klɔg] *n* sabot *m* ♦ *vt* boucher ♦ *vi* (*also:* ~ **up**) se boucher

cloister [ˈklɔɪstəʳ] *n* cloître *m*

clone [kləun] *n* clone *m* ♦ *vt* cloner

close¹ [kləus] *adj* (*near*) près, proche; (*contact, link*) étroit(e); (*contest*) très serré(e); (*watch*) étroit(e), strict(e); (*examination*) attentif(-ive), minutieux(-euse); (*weather*) lourd(e), étouffant(e) ♦ *adv* près, à proximité; ~ **to** près de, proche de; ~ **by** *adj* proche ♦ *adv* tout(e) près; ~ **at hand** = **close by**; **a ~ friend** un ami intime; **to have a ~ shave** (*fig*) l'échapper belle

close² [kləuz] *vt* fermer ♦ *vi* (*shop etc*) fermer; (*lid, door etc*) se fermer; (*end*) se terminer, se conclure ♦ *n* (*end*) conclusion *f*, fin *f*; ~ **down** *vt, vi* fermer (définitivement); ~**d** *adj* fermé(e); ~**d shop** *n* organisation *f* qui n'admet que des travailleurs syndiqués

close-knit [ˈkləusˈnɪt] *adj* (*family, community*) très uni(e)

closely [ˈkləuslɪ] *adv* (*examine, watch*) de près

closet [ˈklɔzɪt] *n* (*cupboard*) placard *m*, réduit *m*

close-up [ˈkləusʌp] *n* gros plan

closure [ˈkləuʒəʳ] *n* fermeture *f*

clot [klɔt] *n* (*gen: blood*) ~ caillot *m*; (*inf: person*) ballot *m* ♦ *vi* (*blood*) se coaguler; ~**ted cream** *crème fraîche très épaisse*

cloth [klɔθ] *n* (*material*) tissu *m*, étoffe *f*; (*also:* **teacloth**) torchon *m*; lavette *f*

clothe [kləuð] *vt* habiller, vêtir; ~**s** *npl* vêtements *mpl*, habits *mpl*; ~**s brush** *n* brosse *f* à habits; ~**s line** *n* corde *f* (à linge); ~**s peg** (*US* **clothes pin**) *n* pince *f* à linge; **clothing** *n* = **clothes**

cloud [klaud] *n* nuage *m*; ~**burst** *n* grosse averse; ~**y** *adj* nuageux(-euse), couvert(e); (*liquid*) trouble

clout [klaut] vt flanquer une taloche à

clove [kləuv] n (CULIN: spice) clou m de girofle; **~ of garlic** gousse f d'ail

clover ['kləuvə^r] n trèfle m

clown [klaun] n clown m ♦ vi (also: ~ **about, ~ around**) faire le clown

cloying ['klɔɪɪŋ] adj (taste, smell) écœurant(e)

club [klʌb] n (society, place: also: **golf ~**) club m; (weapon) massue f, matraque f ♦ vt matraquer ♦ vi: **to ~ together** s'associer; **~s** npl (CARDS) trèfle m; **~ class** n (AVIAT) classe f club; **~house** n club m

cluck [klʌk] vi glousser

clue [klu:] n indice m; (in crosswords) définition f; **I haven't a ~** je n'en ai pas la moindre idée

clump [klʌmp] n: **~ of trees** bouquet m d'arbres

clumsy ['klʌmzɪ] adj gauche, maladroit(e)

clung [klʌŋ] pt, pp of **cling**

cluster ['klʌstə^r] n (of people) (petit) groupe; (of flowers) grappe f; (of stars) amas m ♦ vi se rassembler

clutch [klʌtʃ] n (grip, grasp) étreinte f, prise f; (AUT) embrayage m ♦ vt (grasp) agripper; (hold tightly) serrer fort; (hold on to) se cramponner à

clutter ['klʌtə^r] vt (also: ~ **up**) encombrer

CND n abbr (= Campaign for Nuclear Disarmament) mouvement pour le désarmement nucléaire

Co. abbr = **county; company**

c/o abbr (= care of) c/o, aux bons soins de

coach [kəutʃ] n (bus) autocar m; (horsedrawn) diligence f; (of train) voiture f, wagon m; (SPORT: trainer) entraîneur(-euse); (SCOL: tutor) répétiteur(-trice) ♦ vt entraîner; (student) faire travailler; **~ trip** n excursion f en car

coal [kəul] n charbon m; **~ face** n front m de taille; **~field** n bassin houiller

coalition [kəuə'lɪʃən] n coalition f

coalman (irreg) n charbonnier m, marchand m de charbon

coalmine n mine f de charbon

coarse [kɔ:s] adj grossier(-ère), rude

coast [kəust] n côte f ♦ vi (car, cycle etc) descendre en roue libre; **~al** adj côtier(-ère); **~guard** n garde-côte m; (service) gendarmerie f maritime; **~line** n côte f, littoral m

coat [kəut] n manteau m; (of animal) pelage m, poil m; (of paint) couche f ♦ vt couvrir; **~ hanger** n cintre m; **~ing** n couche f, revêtement m; **~ of arms** n blason m, armoiries fpl

coax [kəuks] vt persuader par des cajoleries

cobbler ['kɔblə^r] n cordonnier m

cobbles ['kɔblz] (also: **~tones**) npl pavés (ronds)

cobweb ['kɔbwɛb] n toile f d'araignée

cocaine [kə'keɪn] n cocaïne f

cock [kɔk] n (rooster) coq m; (male bird) mâle m ♦ vt (gun) armer; **~erel** n jeune coq m

cockle ['kɔkl] n coque f

cockney ['kɔknɪ] n cockney m, habitant des quartiers populaires de l'East End de Londres, ≈ faubourien(ne)

cockpit ['kɔkpɪt] n (in aircraft) poste m de pilotage, cockpit m

cockroach ['kɔkrəutʃ] n cafard m

cocktail ['kɔkteɪl] n cocktail m; (fruit ~ etc) salade f; **~ cabinet** n (meuble-)bar m; **~ party** n cocktail m

cocoa ['kəukəu] n cacao m

coconut ['kəukənʌt] n noix f de coco

COD abbr = **cash on delivery**

cod [kɔd] n morue fraîche, cabillaud m

code [kəud] n code m

cod-liver oil n huile f de foie de morue

coercion [kəu'ə:ʃən] n contrainte f

coffee ['kɔfɪ] n café m; **~ bar** (BRIT) n café m; **~ bean** n grain m de café; **~ break** n pause-café f; **~pot** n cafetière f; **~ table** n (petite) table basse

coffin ['kɔfɪn] n cercueil m

cog [kɔg] n dent f (d'engrenage); (wheel) roue dentée

cogent ['kəudʒənt] adj puissant(e), convaincant(e)

coil [kɔɪl] n rouleau m, bobine f; (contraceptive) stérilet m ♦ vt enrouler

coin [kɔɪn] *n* pièce *f* de monnaie ♦ *vt* (*word*) inventer; ~**age** *n* monnaie *f*, système *m* monétaire; ~ **box** (*BRIT*) *n* cabine *f* téléphonique

coincide [kəʊɪnˈsaɪd] *vi* coïncider; ~**nce** [kəʊˈɪnsɪdəns] *n* coïncidence *f*

Coke [kəʊk] ® *n* coca *m*

coke [kəʊk] *n* coke *m*

colander [ˈkɔləndər] *n* passoire *f*

cold [kəʊld] *adj* froid(e) ♦ *n* froid *m*; (*MED*) rhume *m*; **it's ~** il fait froid; **to be** *or* **feel ~** (*person*) avoir froid; **to catch ~** prendre *or* attraper froid; **to catch a ~** attraper un rhume; **in ~ blood** de sang-froid; ~-**shoulder** *vt* se montrer froid(e) envers, snober; ~ **sore** *n* bouton *m* de fièvre

coleslaw [ˈkəʊlslɔː] *n* sorte de salade de chou cru

colic [ˈkɔlɪk] *n* colique(s) *f(pl)*

collapse [kəˈlæps] *vi* s'effondrer, s'écrouler ♦ *n* effondrement *m*, écroulement *m*; **collapsible** *adj* pliant(e); télescopique

collar [ˈkɔlər] *n* (*of coat, shirt*) col *m*; (*for animal*) collier *m*; ~**bone** *n* clavicule *f*

collateral [kəˈlætərl] *n* nantissement *m*

colleague [ˈkɔliːg] *n* collègue *m/f*

collect [kəˈlekt] *vt* rassembler; ramasser; (*as a hobby*) collectionner; (*BRIT: call and pick up*) (passer) prendre; (*mail*) faire la levée de, ramasser; (*money owed*) encaisser; (*donations, subscriptions*) recueillir ♦ *vi* (*people*) se rassembler; (*things*) s'amasser; **to call ~** (*US: TEL*) téléphoner en P.C.V.; ~**ion** *n* collection *f*; (*of mail*) levée *f*; (*for money*) collecte *f*, quête *f*; ~**or** *n* collectionneur *m*

college [ˈkɔlɪdʒ] *n* collège *m*

collide [kəˈlaɪd] *vi* entrer en collision

colliery [ˈkɔlɪərɪ] (*BRIT*) *n* mine *f* de charbon, houillère *f*

collision [kəˈlɪʒən] *n* collision *f*

colloquial [kəˈləʊkwɪəl] *adj* familier(-ère)

colon [ˈkəʊlən] *n* (*sign*) deux-points *m inv*; (*MED*) côlon *m*

colonel [ˈkɜːnl] *n* colonel *m*

colony [ˈkɔlənɪ] *n* colonie *f*

colour [ˈkʌlər] (*US* **color**) *n* couleur *f* ♦ *vt* (*paint*) peindre; (*dye*) teindre; (*news*) fausser, exagérer ♦ *vi* (*blush*) rougir; ~**s** *npl* (*of party, club*) couleurs *fpl*; ~ **in** *vt* colorier; ~ **bar** *n* discrimination raciale (*dans un établissement*); ~-**blind** *adj* daltonien(ne); ~**ed** *adj* (*person*) de couleur; (*illustration*) en couleur; ~ **film** *n* (*for camera*) pellicule *f* (en) couleur; ~**ful** *adj* coloré(e), vif (vive); (*personality*) pittoresque, haut(e) en couleurs; ~**ing** [ˈkʌlərɪŋ] *n* colorant *m*; (*complexion*) teint *m*; ~ **scheme** *n* combinaison *f* de(s) couleur(s); ~ **television** *n* télévision *f* (en) couleur

colt [kəʊlt] *n* poulain *m*

column [ˈkɔləm] *n* colonne *f*; ~**ist** [ˈkɔləmnɪst] *n* chroniqueur(-euse)

coma [ˈkəʊmə] *n* coma *m*

comb [kəʊm] *n* peigne *m* ♦ *vt* (*hair*) peigner; (*area*) ratisser, passer au peigne fin

combat [ˈkɔmbæt] *n* combat *m* ♦ *vt* combattre, lutter contre

combination [kɔmbɪˈneɪʃən] *n* combinaison *f*

combine [*vb* kəmˈbaɪn, *n* ˈkɔmbaɪn] *vt*: **to ~ sth with sth** combiner qch avec qch; (*one quality with another*) joindre *or* allier qch à qch ♦ *vi* s'associer; (*CHEM*) se combiner ♦ *n* (*ECON*) trust *m*; ~ (**harvester**) *n* moissonneuse-batteuse(-lieuse) *f*

come [kʌm] (*pt* **came**, *pp* **come**) *vi* venir; arriver; **to ~** (*to*) (*decision etc*) parvenir *or* arriver à; **to ~ undone/loose** se défaire; desserrer; ~ **about** *vi* se produire, arriver; ~ **across** *vt fus* rencontrer par hasard, tomber sur; ~ **along** *vi* = **come on**; ~ **away** *vi* partir, s'en aller, se détacher; ~ **back** *vi* revenir; ~ **by** *vt fus* (*acquire*) obtenir, se procurer; ~ **down** *vi* descendre; (*prices*) baisser; (*buildings*) s'écrouler, être démoli(e); ~ **forward** *vi* s'avancer, se présenter, s'annoncer; ~ **from** *vt fus* être originaire de, venir de; ~ **in** *vi* entrer; ~ **in for** *vi* (*criticism etc*) être l'objet de; ~ **into** *vt fus* (*money*) hériter de; ~ **off** *vi* (*button*) se détacher; (*stain*) s'enlever; (*attempt*) réussir; ~ **on** *vi* (*pupil, work, project*) faire des progrès, s'avancer; (*lights, electri-*

city) s'allumer; (*central heating*) se mettre en marche; ~ **on!** viens!, allons!, allez!; ~ **out** *vi* sortir; (*book*) paraître; (*strike*) cesser le travail, se mettre en grève; ~ **round** *vi* (*after faint, operation*) revenir à soi, reprendre connaissance; ~ **to** *vi* revenir à soi; ~ **up** *vi* monter; ~ **up against** *vt fus* (*resistance, difficulties*) rencontrer; ~ **up with** *vt fus*: **he came up with an idea** il a eu une idée, il a proposé quelque chose; ~ **upon** *vt fus* tomber sur; ~**back** *n* (*THEATRE etc*) rentrée *f*

comedian [kə'mi:dɪən] *n* (*in music hall etc*) comique *m*; (*THEATRE*) comédien *m*

comedy ['kɒmɪdɪ] *n* comédie *f*

comeuppance [kʌm'ʌpəns] *n*: **to get one's ~** recevoir ce qu'on mérite

comfort ['kʌmfət] *n* confort *m*, bien-être *m*; (*relief*) soulagement *m*, réconfort *m* ♦ *vt* consoler, réconforter; **the ~s of home** les commodités *fpl* de la maison; ~**able** *adj* confortable; (*person*) à l'aise; (*patient*) dont l'état est stationnaire; (*walk etc*) facile; ~**ably** *adv* (*sit*) confortablement; (*live*) à l'aise; ~ **station** (*US*) *n* toilettes *fpl*

comic ['kɒmɪk] *adj* (*also*: ~**al**) comique ♦ *n* comique *m*; (*BRIT: magazine*) illustré *m*; ~ **strip** *n* bande dessinée

coming ['kʌmɪŋ] *n* arrivée *f* ♦ *adj* prochain(e), à venir; ~**(s) and going(s)** *n(pl)* va-et-vient *m inv*

comma ['kɒmə] *n* virgule *f*

command [kə'mɑ:nd] *n* ordre *m*, commandement *m*; (*MIL: authority*) commandement; (*mastery*) maîtrise *f* ♦ *vt* (*troops*) commander; **to ~ sb to do** ordonner à qn de faire; ~**eer** [kɒmən'dɪər] *vt* réquisitionner; ~**er** *n* (*MIL*) commandant *m*

commando [kə'mɑ:ndəu] *n* commando *m*; membre *m* d'un commando

commemorate [kə'meməreɪt] *vt* commémorer

commence [kə'mɛns] *vt, vi* commencer

commend [kə'mɛnd] *vt* louer; (*recommend*) recommander

commensurate [kə'mɛnʃərɪt] *adj*: ~ **with**

or **to** en proportion de, proportionné(e) à

comment ['kɒmɛnt] *n* commentaire *m* ♦ *vi*: **to ~ (on)** faire des remarques (sur); **"no ~"** "je n'ai rien à dire"; ~**ary** ['kɒməntərɪ] *n* commentaire *m*; (*SPORT*) reportage *m* (en direct); ~**ator** ['kɒmənteɪtər] *n* commentateur *m*; reporter *m*

commerce ['kɒmə:s] *n* commerce *m*

commercial [kə'mə:ʃəl] *adj* commercial(e) ♦ *n* (*TV, RADIO*) annonce *f* publicitaire, spot *m* (publicitaire)

commiserate [kə'mɪzəreɪt] *vi*: **to ~ with sb** témoigner de la sympathie pour qn

commission [kə'mɪʃən] *n* (*order for work*) commande *f*; (*committee, fee*) commission *f* ♦ *vt* (*work of art*) commander, charger un artiste de l'exécution de; **out of ~** (*not working*) hors service; ~**aire** [kəmɪʃə'neər] (*BRIT*) *n* (*at shop, cinema etc*) portier *m* (en uniforme); ~**er** *n* (*POLICE*) préfet *m* (de police)

commit [kə'mɪt] *vt* (*act*) commettre; (*resources*) consacrer; (*to sb's care*) confier (à); **to ~ o.s. (to do)** s'engager (à faire); **to ~ suicide** se suicider; ~**ment** *n* engagement *m*; (*obligation*) responsabilité(s) *f(pl)*

committee [kə'mɪtɪ] *n* comité *m*

commodity [kə'mɒdɪtɪ] *n* produit *m*, marchandise *f*, article *m*

common ['kɒmən] *adj* commun(e); (*usual*) courant(e) ♦ *n* terrain communal; **the C~s** (*BRIT*) *npl* la chambre des Communes; **in ~** en commun; ~**er** *n* roturier(-ière); ~ **law** *n* droit coutumier; ~**ly** *adv* communément, généralement; couramment; **C~ Market** *n* Marché commun; ~**place** *adj* banal(e), ordinaire; ~ **room** *n* salle commune; ~ **sense** *n* bon sens; **C~wealth** (*BRIT*) *n* Commonwealth *m*

commotion [kə'məuʃən] *n* désordre *m*, tumulte *m*

communal ['kɒmju:nl] *adj* (*life*) communautaire; (*for common use*) commun(e)

commune [*n* 'kɒmju:n, *vb* kə'mju:n] *n* (*group*) communauté *f* ♦ *vi*: **to ~ with** communier avec

communicate [kəˈmjuːnɪkeɪt] *vt, vi* communiquer; **communication** [kəmjuːnɪˈkeɪʃən] *n* communication *f*; **communication cord** (*BRIT*) *n* sonnette *f* d'alarme

communion [kəˈmjuːnɪən] *n* (*also:* **Holy C~**) communion *f*

communism [ˈkɔmjunɪzəm] *n* communisme *m*; **communist** *adj* communiste ♦ *n* communiste *m/f*

community [kəˈmjuːnɪtɪ] *n* communauté *f*; **~ centre** *n* centre *m* de loisirs; **~ chest** (*US*) *n* fonds commun

commutation ticket [kɔmjuˈteɪʃən-] (*US*) *n* carte *f* d'abonnement

commute [kəˈmjuːt] *vi* faire un trajet journalier pour se rendre à son travail ♦ *vt* (*LAW*) commuer; **~r** *n* banlieusard(e) (*qui fait un trajet journalier pour se rendre à son travail*)

compact [*adj* kəmˈpækt, *n* ˈkɔmpækt] *adj* compact(e) ♦ *n* (*also:* **powder ~**) poudrier *m*; **~ disc** *n* disque compact; **~ disc player** *n* lecteur *m* de disque compact

companion [kəmˈpænjən] *n* compagnon (compagne); **~ship** *n* camaraderie *f*

company [ˈkʌmpənɪ] *n* compagnie *f*; **to keep sb ~** tenir compagnie à qn; **~ secretary** (*BRIT*) *n* (*COMM*) secrétaire général (*d'une société*)

comparative [kəmˈpærətɪv] *adj* (*study*) comparatif(-ive); (*relative*) relatif(-ive); **~ly** *adv* (*relatively*) relativement

compare [kəmˈpeəʳ] *vt*: **to ~ sth/sb with/to** comparer qch/qn avec *or* et/à ♦ *vi*: **to ~ (with)** se comparer (à); être comparable (à); **comparison** [kəmˈpærɪsn] *n* comparaison *f*

compartment [kəmˈpɑːtmənt] *n* compartiment *m*

compass [ˈkʌmpəs] *n* boussole *f*; **~es** *npl* (*GEOM: also:* **pair of ~es**) compas *m*

compassion [kəmˈpæʃən] *n* compassion *f*; **~ate** *adj* compatissant(e)

compatible [kəmˈpætɪbl] *adj* compatible

compel [kəmˈpɛl] *vt* contraindre, obliger

compensate [ˈkɔmpənseɪt] *vt* indemniser, dédommager ♦ *vi*: **to ~ for** compenser; **compensation** [kɔmpənˈseɪʃən] *n* compensation *f*; (*money*) dédommagement *m*, indemnité *f*

compère [ˈkɔmpeəʳ] *n* (*TV*) animateur(-trice)

compete [kəmˈpiːt] *vi*: **to ~ (with)** rivaliser (avec), faire concurrence (à)

competent [ˈkɔmpɪtənt] *adj* compétent(e), capable

competition [kɔmpɪˈtɪʃən] *n* (*contest*) compétition *f*, concours *m*; (*ECON*) concurrence *f*

competitive [kəmˈpetɪtɪv] *adj* (*ECON*) concurrentiel(le); (*sport*) de compétition; (*person*) qui a l'esprit de compétition; **competitor** *n* concurrent(e)

complacency [kəmˈpleɪsnsɪ] *n* suffisance *f*, vaine complaisance

complain [kəmˈpleɪn] *vi*: **to ~ (about)** se plaindre (de); (*in shop etc*) réclamer (au sujet de); **to ~ of** (*pain*) se plaindre de; **~t** *n* plainte *f*; réclamation *f*; (*MED*) affection *f*

complement [*n* ˈkɔmplɪmənt, *vb* ˈkɔmplɪment] *n* complément *m*; (*especially of ship's crew etc*) effectif complet ♦ *vt* (*enhance*) compléter; **~ary** [kɔmplɪˈmentərɪ] *adj* complémentaire

complete [kəmˈpliːt] *adj* complet(-ète) ♦ *vt* achever, parachever; (*set, group*) compléter; (*a form*) remplir; **~ly** *adv* complètement; **completion** *n* achèvement *m*; (*of contract*) exécution *f*

complex [ˈkɔmpleks] *adj* complexe ♦ *n* complexe *m*

complexion [kəmˈplekʃən] *n* (*of face*) teint *m*

compliance [kəmˈplaɪəns] *n* (*submission*) docilité *f*; (*agreement*): **~ with** le fait de se conformer à; **in ~ with** en accord avec

complicate [ˈkɔmplɪkeɪt] *vt* compliquer; **~d** *adj* compliqué(e); **complication** [kɔmplɪˈkeɪʃən] *n* complication *f*

compliment [*n* ˈkɔmplɪmənt, *vb* ˈkɔmplɪment] *n* compliment *m* ♦ *vt* complimenter; **~s** *npl* (*respects*) compliments *mpl*, hommages *mpl*; **to pay sb a ~** faire *or* adresser un compliment à qn; **~ary** [kɔmplɪ'mentərɪ] *adj* flatteur(-euse); *(free)* (offert(e)) à titre gracieux; **~ary ticket** *n* billet *m* de faveur

comply [kəm'plaɪ] *vi*: **to ~ with** se soumettre à, se conformer à

component [kəm'pəunənt] *n* composant *m*, élément *m*

compose [kəm'pəuz] *vt* composer; *(form)*: **to be ~d of** se composer de; **to ~ o.s.** se calmer, se maîtriser; prendre une contenance; **~d** *adj* calme, posé(e); **~r** *n (MUS)* compositeur *m*; **composition** [kɔmpə'zɪʃən] *n* composition *f*; **composure** [kəm'pəuʒə*r*] *n* calme *m*, maîtrise *f* de soi

compound ['kɔmpaund] *n* composé *m*; *(enclosure)* enclos *m*, enceinte *f*; **~ fracture** *n* fracture compliquée; **~ interest** *n* intérêt composé

comprehend [kɔmprɪ'hend] *vt* comprendre; **comprehension** *n* compréhension *f*

comprehensive [kɔmprɪ'hensɪv] *adj* (très) complet(-ète); **~ policy** *n (INSURANCE)* assurance *f* tous risques; **~ (school)** *(BRIT)* école secondaire polyvalente; ≈ C.E.S. *m*

compress [*vb* kəm'pres, *n* 'kɔmpres] *vt* comprimer; *(text, information)* condenser ♦ *n (MED)* compresse *f*

comprise [kəm'praɪz] *vt (also:* **be ~d of)** comprendre; *(constitute)* constituer, représenter

compromise ['kɔmprəmaɪz] *n* compromis *m* ♦ *vt* compromettre ♦ *vi* transiger, accepter un compromis

compulsion [kəm'pʌlʃən] *n* contrainte *f*, force *f*

compulsive [kəm'pʌlsɪv] *adj (PSYCH)* compulsif(-ive); *(book, film etc)* captivant(e)

compulsory [kəm'pʌlsərɪ] *adj* obligatoire

computer [kəm'pju:tə*r*] *n* ordinateur *m*; **~ game** *n* jeu *m* vidéo; **~-generated** *adj* de synthèse; **~ize** *vt* informatiser; **~ programmer** *n* programmeur(-euse); **~ programming** *n* programmation *f*; **~ sci-**

ence *n* informatique *f*; **computing** *n* = **computer science**

comrade ['kɔmrɪd] *n* camarade *m/f*

con [kɔn] *vt* duper; *(cheat)* escroquer ♦ *n* escroquerie *f*

conceal [kən'si:l] *vt* cacher, dissimuler

conceit [kən'si:t] *n* vanité *f*, suffisance *f*, prétention *f*; **~ed** *adj* vaniteux(-euse), suffisant(e)

conceive [kən'si:v] *vt, vi* concevoir

concentrate ['kɔnsəntreɪt] *vi* se concentrer ♦ *vt* concentrer; **concentration** *n* concentration *f*; **concentration camp** *n* camp *m* de concentration

concept ['kɔnsept] *n* concept *m*

concern [kən'sə:n] *n* affaire *f*; *(COMM)* entreprise *f*, firme *f*; *(anxiety)* inquiétude *f*, souci *m* ♦ *vt* concerner; **to be ~ed (about)** s'inquiéter (de), être inquiet(-ète) (au sujet de); **~ing** *prep* en ce qui concerne, à propos de

concert ['kɔnsət] *n* concert *m*; **~ed** [kən'sə:tɪd] *adj* concerté(e); **~ hall** *n* salle *f* de concert

concerto [kən'tʃə:təu] *n* concerto *m*

concession [kən'seʃən] *n* concession *f*; **tax ~** dégrèvement fiscal

conclude [kən'klu:d] *vt* conclure; **conclusion** [kən'klu:ʒən] *n* conclusion *f*; **conclusive** [kən'klu:sɪv] *adj* concluant(e), définitif(-ive)

concoct [kən'kɔkt] *vt* confectionner, composer; *(fig)* inventer; **~ion** *n* mélange *m*

concourse ['kɔŋkɔ:s] *n (hall)* hall *m*, salle *f* des pas perdus

concrete ['kɔŋkri:t] *n* béton *m* ♦ *adj* concret(-ète); *(floor etc)* en béton

concur [kən'kə:*r*] *vi (agree)* être d'accord

concurrently [kən'kʌrntlɪ] *adv* simultanément

concussion [kən'kʌʃən] *n (MED)* commotion (cérébrale)

condemn [kən'dem] *vt* condamner

condensation [kɔndεn'seɪʃən] *n* condensation *f*

condense [kən'dens] *vi* se condenser ♦ *vt*

condenser; ~**d milk** *n* lait concentré (sucré)

condition [kən'dɪʃən] *n* condition *f*; (MED) état *m* ♦ *vt* déterminer, conditionner; **on ~ that** à condition que +*sub*, à condition de; ~**al** *adj* conditionnel(le); ~**er** *n* (*for hair*) baume après-shampooing *m*; (*for fabrics*) assouplissant *m*

condolences [kən'dəʊlənsɪz] *npl* condoléances *fpl*

condom ['kɔndəm] *n* préservatif *m*

condominium [kɔndə'mɪnɪəm] (US) *n* (*building*) immeuble *m* (en copropriété)

condone [kən'dəʊn] *vt* fermer les yeux sur, approuver (tacitement)

conducive [kən'dju:sɪv] *adj*: ~ **to** favorable à, qui contribue à

conduct [*n* 'kɔndʌkt, *vb* kən'dʌkt] *n* conduite *f* ♦ *vt* conduire; (MUS) diriger; **to ~ o.s.** se conduire, se comporter; ~**ed tour** *n* voyage organisé; (*of building*) visite guidée; ~**or** *n* (*of orchestra*) chef *m* d'orchestre; (*on bus*) receveur *m*; (US: *on train*) chef *m* de train; (ELEC) conducteur *m*; ~**ress** *n* (*on bus*) receveuse *f*

cone [kəʊn] *n* cône *m*; (*for ice-cream*) cornet *m*; (BOT) pomme *f* de pin, cône

confectioner [kən'fekʃənər] *n* confiseur(-euse); ~**'s (shop)** *n* confiserie *f*; ~**y** *n* confiserie *f*

confer [kən'fə:r] *vt*: **to ~ sth on** conférer qch à ♦ *vi* conférer, s'entretenir

conference ['kɔnfərəns] *n* conférence *f*

confess [kən'fes] *vt* confesser, avouer ♦ *vi* se confesser; ~**ion** *n* confession *f*

confetti [kən'fetɪ] *n* confettis *mpl*

confide [kən'faɪd] *vi*: **to ~ in** se confier à

confidence ['kɔnfɪdns] *n* confiance *f*; (*also*: **self-~**) assurance *f*, confiance en soi; (*secret*) confidence *f*; **in ~** (*speak, write*) en confidence, confidentiellement; ~ **trick** *n* escroquerie *f*; **confident** *adj* sûr(e), assuré(e); **confidential** [kɔnfɪ'denʃəl] *adj* confidentiel(le)

confine [kən'faɪn] *vt* limiter, borner; (*shut up*) confiner, enfermer; ~**d** *adj* (*space*) restreint(e), réduit(e); ~**ment** *n* emprisonne-

ment *m*, détention *f*; ~**s** ['kɔnfaɪnz] *npl* confins *mpl*, bornes *fpl*

confirm [kən'fə:m] *vt* confirmer; (*appointment*) ratifier; ~**ation** [kɔnfə'meɪʃən] *n* confirmation *f*; ~**ed** *adj* invétéré(e), incorrigible

confiscate ['kɔnfɪskeɪt] *vt* confisquer

conflict [*n* 'kɔnflɪkt, *vb* kən'flɪkt] *n* conflit *m*, lutte *f* ♦ *vi* être or entrer en conflit; (*opinions*) s'opposer, se heurter; ~**ing** [kən'flɪktɪŋ] *adj* contradictoire

conform [kən'fɔ:m] *vi*: **to ~ (to)** se conformer (à)

confound [kən'faʊnd] *vt* confondre

confront [kən'frʌnt] *vt* confronter, mettre en présence; (*enemy, danger*) affronter, faire face à; ~**ation** [kɔnfrən'teɪʃən] *n* confrontation *f*

confuse [kən'fju:z] *vt* (*person*) troubler; (*situation*) embrouiller; (*one thing with another*) confondre; ~**d** *adj* (*person*) dérouté(e), désorienté(e); **confusing** *adj* peu clair(e), déroutant(e); **confusion** [kən'fju:ʒən] *n* confusion *f*

congeal [kən'dʒi:l] *vi* (*blood*) se coaguler; (*oil etc*) se figer

congenial [kən'dʒi:nɪəl] *adj* sympathique, agréable

congested [kən'dʒestɪd] *adj* (MED) congestionné(e); (*area*) surpeuplé(e); (*road*) bloqué(e); **congestion** *n* congestion *f*; (*fig*) encombrement *m*

congratulate [kən'grætjuleɪt] *vt*: **to ~ sb (on)** féliciter qn (de); **congratulations** [kəngrætju'leɪʃənz] *npl* félicitations *fpl*

congregate ['kɔngrɪgeɪt] *vi* se rassembler, se réunir; **congregation** [kɔngrɪ'geɪʃən] *n* assemblée *f* (des fidèles)

congress ['kɔngres] *n* congrès *m*; ~**man** (*irreg*) (US) *n* membre *m* du Congrès

conjunction [kən'dʒʌŋkʃən] *n* (LING) conjonction *f*

conjunctivitis [kəndʒʌŋktɪ'vaɪtɪs] *n* conjonctivite *f*

conjure ['kʌndʒər] *vi* faire des tours de passe-passe; ~ **up** *vt* (*ghost, spirit*) faire apparaître; (*memories*) évoquer; ~**r** *n* pres-

tidigitateur *m*, illusionniste *m/f*

con man (*irreg*) *n* escroc *m*

connect [kə'nɛkt] *vt* joindre, relier; (*ELEC*) connecter; (*TEL: caller*) mettre en connection (*with* avec); (: *new subscriber*) brancher; (*fig*) établir un rapport entre, faire un rapprochement entre ♦ *vi* (*train*): **to ~ with** assurer la correspondance avec; **to be ~ed with** (*fig*) avoir un rapport avec, avoir des rapports avec, être en relation avec; **~ion** *n* relation *f*, lien *m*; (*ELEC*) connexion *f*; (*train, plane etc*) correspondance *f*; (*TEL*) branchement *m*, communication *f*

connive [kə'naɪv] *vi*: **to ~ at** se faire le complice de

conquer ['kɔŋkəʳ] *vt* conquérir; (*feelings*) vaincre, surmonter; **conquest** ['kɔŋkwɛst] *n* conquête *f*

cons [kɔnz] *npl see* **convenience; pro**

conscience ['kɔnʃəns] *n* conscience *f*; **conscientious** [kɔnʃɪ'ɛnʃəs] *adj* consciencieux(-euse)

conscious ['kɔnʃəs] *adj* conscient(e); **~ness** *n* conscience *f*; (*MED*) connaissance *f*

conscript ['kɔnskrɪpt] *n* conscrit *m*

consent [kən'sɛnt] *n* consentement *m* ♦ *vi*: **to ~ (to)** consentir (à)

consequence ['kɔnsɪkwəns] *n* conséquence *f*, suites *fpl*; (*significance*) importance *f*; **consequently** *adv* par conséquent, donc

conservation [kɔnsə'veɪʃən] *n* préservation *f*, protection *f*

conservative [kən'sə:vətɪv] *adj* conservateur(-trice); **at a ~ estimate** au bas mot; **C~** (*BRIT*) *adj*, *n* (*POL*) conservateur(-trice)

conservatory [kən'sə:vətrɪ] *n* (*greenhouse*) serre *f*

conserve [kən'sə:v] *vt* conserver, préserver; (*supplies, energy*) économiser ♦ *n* confiture *f*

consider [kən'sɪdəʳ] *vt* (*study*) considérer, réfléchir à; (*take into account*) penser à, prendre en considération; (*regard, judge*) considérer, estimer; **to ~ doing sth** envisager de faire qch; **~able** *adj* considérable; **~ably** *adv* nettement, sensiblement; **~ate** *adj* prévenant(e), plein(e) d'égards; **~ation** [kənsɪdə'reɪʃən] *n* considération *f*; **~ing** *prep* étant donné

consign [kən'saɪn] *vt* expédier; (*to sb's care*) confier; (*fig*) livrer; **~ment** *n* arrivage *m*, envoi *m*

consist [kən'sɪst] *vi*: **to ~ of** consister en, se composer de

consistency [kən'sɪstənsɪ] *n* consistance *f*; (*fig*) cohérence *f*

consistent [kən'sɪstənt] *adj* logique, cohérent(e)

consolation [kɔnsə'leɪʃən] *n* consolation *f*

console[1] [kən'səul] *vt* consoler

console[2] ['kɔnsəul] *n* (*COMPUT*) console *f*

consonant ['kɔnsənənt] *n* consonne *f*

conspicuous [kən'spɪkjuəs] *adj* voyant(e), qui attire l'attention

conspiracy [kən'spɪrəsɪ] *n* conspiration *f*, complot *m*

constable ['kʌnstəbl] (*BRIT*) *n* ≈ agent *m* de police, gendarme *m*; **chief ~** ≈ préfet *m* de police; **constabulary** [kən'stæbjulərɪ] (*BRIT*) *n* ≈ police *f*, gendarmerie *f* .

constant ['kɔnstənt] *adj* constant(e); incessant(e); **~ly** *adv* constamment, sans cesse

constipated ['kɔnstɪpeɪtɪd] *adj* constipé(e); **constipation** [kɔnstɪ'peɪʃən] *n* constipation *f*

constituency [kən'stɪtjuənsɪ] *n* circonscription électorale

constituent [kən'stɪtjuənt] *n* (*POL*) électeur(-trice); (*part*) élément constitutif, composant *m*

constitution [kɔnstɪ'tju:ʃən] *n* constitution *f*; **~al** *adj* constitutionnel(le)

constraint [kən'streɪnt] *n* contrainte *f*

construct [kən'strʌkt] *vt* construire; **~ion** *n* construction *f*; **~ive** *adj* constructif(-ive); **~ive dismissal** démission forcée

consul ['kɔnsl] *n* consul *m*; **~ate** ['kɔnsjulɪt] *n* consulat *m*

consult [kən'sʌlt] *vt* consulter; **~ant** *n*

(*MED*) médecin consultant; (*other specialist*) consultant *m*, (expert-)conseil *m*; ~ing room (*BRIT*) *n* cabinet *m* de consultation

consume [kən'sju:m] *vt* consommer; ~r *n* consommateur(-trice); ~r goods *npl* biens *mpl* de consommation; ~r society *n* société *f* de consommation

consummate ['kɔnsʌmeɪt] *vt* consommer

consumption [kən'sʌmpʃən] *n* consommation *f*

cont. *abbr* (= *continued*) suite

contact ['kɔntækt] *n* contact *m*; (*person*) connaissance *f*, relation *f* ♦ *vt* contacter, se mettre en contact *or* en rapport avec; ~ lenses *npl* verres *mpl* de contact, lentilles *fpl*

contagious [kən'teɪdʒəs] *adj* contagieux(-euse)

contain [kən'teɪn] *vt* contenir; to ~ o.s. se contenir, se maîtriser; ~er *n* récipient *m*; (*for shipping etc*) container *m*

contaminate [kən'tæmɪneɪt] *vt* contaminer

cont'd *abbr* (= *continued*) suite

contemplate ['kɔntəmpleɪt] *vt* contempler; (*consider*) envisager

contemporary [kən'tempərərɪ] *adj* contemporain(e); (*design, wallpaper*) moderne ♦ *n* contemporain(e)

contempt [kən'tempt] *n* mépris *m*, dédain *m*; ~ of court (*LAW*) outrage *m* à l'autorité de la justice; ~uous [kən'temptjuəs] *adj* dédaigneux(-euse), méprisant(e)

contend [kən'tend] *vt*: to ~ that soutenir *or* prétendre que ♦ *vi*: to ~ with (*compete*) rivaliser avec; (*struggle*) lutter avec; ~er *n* concurrent(e); (*POL*) candidat(e)

content [*adj, vb* kən'tent, *n* 'kɔntent] *adj* content(e), satisfait(e) ♦ *vt* contenter, satisfaire ♦ *n* contenu *m*; (*of fat, moisture*) teneur *f*; ~s *npl* (*of container etc*) contenu *m*; (table of) ~s table *f* des matières; ~ed *adj* content(e), satisfait(e)

contention [kən'tenʃən] *n* dispute *f*, contestation *f*; (*argument*) assertion *f*, affirmation *f*

contest [*n* 'kɔntest, *vb* kən'test] *n* combat *m*, lutte *f*; (*competition*) concours *m* ♦ *vt* (*decision, statement*) contester, discuter; (*compete for*) disputer; ~ant [kən'testənt] *n* concurrent(e); (*in fight*) adversaire *m/f*

context ['kɔntekst] *n* contexte *m*

continent ['kɔntɪnənt] *n* continent *m*; the C~ (*BRIT*) l'Europe continentale; ~al [kɔntɪ'nentl] *adj* continental(e); ~al breakfast *n* petit déjeuner *m* à la française; ~al quilt (*BRIT*) *n* couette *f*

contingency [kən'tɪndʒənsɪ] *n* éventualité *f*, événement imprévu

continual [kən'tɪnjuəl] *adj* continuel(le)

continuation [kəntɪnju'eɪʃən] *n* continuation *f*; (*after interruption*) reprise *f*; (*of story*) suite *f*

continue [kən'tɪnju:] *vi*, *vt* continuer; (*after interruption*) reprendre, poursuivre; **continuity** [kɔntɪ'nju:ɪtɪ] *n* continuité *f*; (*TV etc*) enchaînement *m*; **continuous** [kən'tɪnjuəs] *adj* continu(e); (*LING*) progressif(-ive)

contort [kən'tɔ:t] *vt* tordre, crisper

contour ['kɔntuər] *n* contour *m*, profil *m*; (*on map: also:* ~ line) courbe *f* de niveau

contraband ['kɔntrəbænd] *n* contrebande *f*

contraceptive [kɔntrə'septɪv] *adj* contraceptif(-ive), anticonceptionnel(le) ♦ *n* contraceptif *m*

contract [*n* 'kɔntrækt, *vb* kən'trækt] *n* contrat *m* ♦ *vi* (*become smaller*) se contracter, se resserrer; (*COMM*): to ~ to do sth s'engager (par contrat) à faire qch; ~ion [kən'trækʃən] *n* contraction *f*; ~or [kən'træktər] *n* entrepreneur *m*

contradict [kɔntrə'dɪkt] *vt* contredire

contraflow ['kɔntrəfləu] *n* (*AUT*): ~ lane voie *f* à contresens; **there's a ~ system in operation on ...** une voie a été mise en sens inverse sur ...

contraption [kən'træpʃən] (*pej*) *n* machin *m*, truc *m*

contrary¹ ['kɔntrərɪ] *adj* contraire, opposé(e) ♦ *n* contraire *m*; **on the ~** au contraire; **unless you hear to the ~** sauf avis contraire contrary² [kən'treəri] adj (perverse) contrariant(e), entêté(e)

contrast [n 'kɔntrɑːst, vb kən'trɑːst] n contraste m ♦ vt mettre en contraste, contraster; in ~ to or with contrairement à

contravene [kɔntrə'viːn] vt enfreindre, violer, contrevenir à

contribute [kən'trɪbjuːt] vi contribuer ♦ vt: to ~ £10/an article to donner 10 livres/un article à; to ~ to contribuer à; (newspaper) collaborer à; contribution [kɔntrɪ'bjuːʃən] n contribution f; contributor [kən'trɪbjutər] n (to newspaper) collaborateur(-trice)

contrive [kən'traɪv] vi: to ~ to do s'arranger pour faire, trouver le moyen de faire

control [kən'trəul] vt maîtriser, commander; (check) contrôler ♦ n contrôle m, autorité f; maîtrise f; ~s npl (of machine etc) commandes fpl; (on radio, TV) boutons mpl de réglage; ~led substance narcotique m; everything is under ~ tout va bien, j'ai (or il a etc) la situation en main; to be in ~ of être maître de, maîtriser; the car went out of ~ j'ai (or il a etc) perdu le contrôle du véhicule; ~ panel n tableau m de commande; ~ room n salle f des commandes; ~ tower n (AVIAT) tour f de contrôle

controversial [kɔntrə'vəːʃl] adj (topic) discutable, controversé(e); (person) qui fait beaucoup parler de lui; controversy ['kɔntrəvəːsɪ] n controverse f, polémique f

convalesce [kɔnvə'les] vi relever de maladie, se remettre (d'une maladie)

convector [kən'vektər] n (heater) radiateur m (à convexion)

convene [kən'viːn] vt convoquer, assembler ♦ vi se réunir, s'assembler

convenience [kən'viːniəns] n commodité f; at your ~ quand or comme cela vous convient; all modern ~s, (BRIT) all mod cons avec tout le confort moderne, tout confort

convenient [kən'viːniənt] adj commode

convent ['kɔnvənt] n couvent m; ~

school n couvent m

convention [kən'venʃən] n convention f; ~al adj conventionnel(le)

conversant [kən'vəːsnt] adj: to be ~ with s'y connaître en; être au courant de

conversation [kɔnvə'seɪʃən] n conversation f

converse [n 'kɔnvəːs, vb kən'vəːs] n contraire m, inverse m ♦ vi s'entretenir; ~ly [kɔn'vəːslɪ] adv inversement, réciproquement

convert [vb kən'vəːt, n 'kɔnvəːt] vt (REL, COMM) convertir; (alter) transformer; (house) aménager ♦ n converti(e); ~ible [kən'vəːtəbl] n (voiture f) décapotable f

convey [kən'veɪ] vt transporter; (thanks) transmettre; (idea) communiquer; ~or belt n convoyeur m, tapis roulant

convict [vb kən'vɪkt, n 'kɔnvɪkt] vt déclarer (or reconnaître) coupable ♦ n forçat m, détenu m; ~ion [kən'vɪkʃən] n (LAW) condamnation f; (belief) conviction f

convince [kən'vɪns] vt convaincre, persuader; convincing adj persuasif(-ive), convaincant(e)

convoluted ['kɔnvəluːtɪd] adj (argument) compliqué(e)

convulse [kən'vʌls] vt: to be ~d with laughter/pain se tordre de rire/douleur

cook [kuk] vt (faire) cuire ♦ vi cuire; (person) faire la cuisine ♦ n cuisinier(-ière); ~book n livre m de cuisine; ~er n cuisinière f; ~ery n cuisine f; ~ery book (BRIT) n = cookbook; ~ie (US) n biscuit m, petit gâteau sec; ~ing n cuisine f

cool [kuːl] adj frais (fraîche); (calm, unemotional) calme; (unfriendly) froid(e) ♦ vt, vi rafraîchir, refroidir

coop [kuːp] n poulailler m; (for rabbits) clapier m ♦ vt: to ~ up (fig) cloîtrer, enfermer

cooperate [kəu'ɔpəreɪt] vi coopérer, collaborer; cooperation [kəuɔpə'reɪʃən] n coopération f, collaboration f; cooperative [kəu'ɔpərətɪv] adj coopératif(-ive) ♦ n coopérative f

coordinate [vb kəu'ɔːdɪneɪt, n kəu'ɔːdɪnət]

vt· coordonner ♦ *n* (*MATH*) coordonnée *f*; **~s** *npl* (*clothes*) ensemble *m*, coordonnés *mpl*

co-ownership [kəu'əunəʃɪp] *n* co-propriété *f*

cop [kɒp] (*inf*) *n* flic *m*

cope [kəup] *vi*: **to ~ with** faire face à; (*solve*) venir à bout de

copper ['kɒpər] *n* cuivre *m*; (*BRIT: inf: policeman*) flic *m*; **~s** *npl* (*coins*) petite monnaie

copy ['kɒpɪ] *n* copie *f*; (*of book etc*) exemplaire *m* ♦ *vt* copier; **~right** *n* droit *m* d'auteur, copyright *m*

coral ['kɒrəl] *n* corail *m*

cord [kɔːd] *n* corde *f*; (*fabric*) velours côtelé, (*ELEC*) cordon *m*, fil *m*

cordial ['kɔːdɪəl] *adj* cordial(e), chaleureux(-euse) ♦ *n* cordial *m*

cordon ['kɔːdn] *n* cordon *m*; **~ off** *vt* boucler (*par cordon de police*)

corduroy ['kɔːdərɔɪ] *n* velours côtelé

core [kɔːr] *n* noyau *m*, (*of fruit*) trognon *m*, cœur *m*; (*of building, problem*) cœur ♦ *vt* enlever le trognon *or* le cœur de

cork [kɔːk] *n* liège *m*; (*of bottle*) bouchon *m*; **~screw** *n* tire-bouchon *m*

corn [kɔːn] *n* (*BRIT: wheat*) blé *m*; (*US: maize*) maïs *m*; (*on foot*) cor *m*; **~ on the cob** (*CULIN*) épi *m* de maïs; **~ed beef** *n* corned-beef *m*

corner ['kɔːnər] *n* coin *m*; (*AUT*) tournant *m*, virage *m*; (*FOOTBALL: also: ~ kick*) corner *m* ♦ *vt* acculer, mettre au pied du mur; coincer; (*COMM: market*) accaparer ♦ *vi* prendre un virage; **~stone** *n* pierre *f* angulaire

cornet ['kɔːnɪt] *n* (*MUS*) cornet *m* à pistons; (*BRIT: of ice-cream*) cornet (de glace)

cornflakes ['kɔːnfleɪks] *npl* corn-flakes *mpl*

cornflour ['kɔːnflauər] (*BRIT*), **cornstarch** ['kɔːnstɑːtʃ] (*US*) *n* farine *f* de maïs, maïzena *f* ®

Cornwall ['kɔːnwəl] *n* Cornouailles *f*

corny ['kɔːnɪ] (*inf*) *adj* rebattu(e)

coronary ['kɒrənərɪ] *n* (*also: ~ thrombosis*) infarctus *m* (du myocarde), thrombo-

se *f* coronarienne

coronation [kɒrə'neɪʃən] *n* couronnement *m*

coroner ['kɒrənər] *n* officiel chargé de déterminer les causes d'un décès

corporal ['kɔːpərl] *n* caporal *m*, brigadier *m* ♦ *adj*: **~ punishment** châtiment corporel

corporate ['kɔːpərɪt] *adj* en commun, collectif(-ive); (*COMM*) de l'entreprise

corporation [kɔːpə'reɪʃən] *n* (*of town*) municipalité *f*, conseil municipal; (*COMM*) société *f*

corps [kɔːr] (*pl* **~**) *n* corps *m*

corpse [kɔːps] *n* cadavre *m*

correct [kə'rekt] *adj* (*accurate*) correct(e), exact(e); (*proper*) correct, convenable ♦ *vt* corriger; **~ion** *n* correction *f*

correspond [kɒrɪs'pɒnd] *vi* correspondre; **~ence** *n* correspondance *f*; **~ence course** *n* cours *m* par correspondance; **~ent** *n* correspondant(e)

corridor ['kɒrɪdɔːr] *n* couloir *m*, corridor *m*

corrode [kə'rəud] *vt* corroder, ronger ♦ *vi* se corroder

corrugated ['kɒrəgeɪtɪd] *adj* plissé(e); ondulé(e); **~ iron** *n* tôle ondulée

corrupt [kə'rʌpt] *adj* corrompu(e) ♦ *vt* corrompre; **~ion** *n* corruption *f*

Corsica ['kɔːsɪkə] *n* Corse *f*

cosmetic [kɒz'metɪk] *n* produit *m* de beauté, cosmétique *m*

cost [kɒst] (*pt, pp* **cost**) *n* coût *m* ♦ *vi* coûter ♦ *vt* établir *or* calculer le prix de revient de; **~s** *npl* (*COMM*) frais *mpl*; (*LAW*) dépens *mpl*; **it ~s £5/too much** cela coûte cinq livres/c'est trop cher; **at all ~s** coûte que coûte, à tout prix

co-star ['kəustɑːr] *n* partenaire *m/f*

cost: **~-effective** *adj* rentable; **~ly** *adj* coûteux(-euse); **~-of-living** *adj*: **~-of-living allowance** indemnité *f* de vie chère; **~-of-living index** index *m* du coût de la vie; **~ price** (*BRIT*) *n* prix coûtant *or* de revient

costume ['kɒstjuːm] *n* costume *m*; (*lady's suit*) tailleur *m*; (*BRIT: also:* **swimming ~**)

maillot *m* (de bain); ~ **jewellery** *n* bijoux *mpl* fantaisie

cosy ['kəuzi] (*US* **cozy**) *adj* douillet(te); (*person*) à l'aise, au chaud

cot [kɔt] *n* (*BRIT: child's*) lit *m* d'enfant, petit lit; (*US: campbed*) lit de camp

cottage ['kɔtidʒ] *n* petite maison (à la campagne), cottage *m*; ~ **cheese** *n* fromage blanc (*maigre*)

cotton ['kɔtn] *n* coton *m*; ~ **on** (*inf*) *vi*: to ~ **on to** piger; ~ **candy** (*US*) *n* barbe *f* à papa; ~ **wool** (*BRIT*) *n* ouate *f*, coton *m* hydrophile

couch [kautʃ] *n* canapé *m*; divan *m*

couchette [ku:'ʃet] *n* couchette *f*

cough [kɔf] *vi* tousser ♦ *n* toux *f*; ~ **sweet** *n* pastille *f* pour *or* contre la toux

could [kud] *pt* of **can²**; ~**n't** = **could not**

council ['kaunsl] *n* conseil *m*; **city** *or* **town** ~ conseil municipal; ~ **estate** (*BRIT*) *n* (zone *f* de) logements loués à/par la municipalité; ~ **house** (*BRIT*) *n* maison *f* (à loyer modéré) louée par la municipalité; ~**lor** *n* conseiller(-ère)

counsel ['kaunsl] *n* (*lawyer*) avocat(e); (*advice*) conseil *m*, consultation *f*; ~**lor** *n* conseiller(-ère); (*US: lawyer*) avocat(e)

count [kaunt] *vt, vi* compter ♦ *n* compte *m*; (*nobleman*) comte *m*; ~ **on** *vt fus* compter sur; ~**down** *n* compte *m* à rebours

countenance ['kauntinəns] *n* expression *f* ♦ *vt* approuver

counter ['kauntər] *n* comptoir *m*; (*in post office, bank*) guichet *m*; (*in game*) jeton *m* ♦ *vt* aller à l'encontre de, opposer ♦ *adv*: ~ **to** contrairement à; ~**act** *vt* neutraliser, contrebalancer; ~**feit** *n* faux *m*, contrefaçon *f* ♦ *vt* contrefaire ♦ *adj* faux (fausse); ~**foil** *n* talon *m*, souche *f*; ~**part** *n* (of person etc) homologue *m/f*

countess ['kauntis] *n* comtesse *f*

countless ['kauntlis] *adj* innombrable

country ['kʌntri] *n* pays *m*; (*native land*) patrie *f*; (*as opposed to town*) campagne *f*; (*region*) région *f*, pays; ~ **dancing** (*BRIT*) *n* danse *f* folklorique; ~ **house** *n* manoir *m*, (petit) château; ~**man** (*irreg*) *n* (*compatriot*) compatriote *m*; (*country dweller*) habitant *m* de la campagne, campagnard *m*; ~**side** *n* campagne *f*

county ['kaunti] *n* comté *m*

coup [ku:] (*pl* ~**s**) *n* beau coup; (*also:* ~ **d'état**) coup d'État

couple ['kʌpl] *n* couple *m*; **a** ~ **of** deux; (*a few*) quelques

coupon ['ku:pɔn] *n* coupon *m*, bon-prime *m*, bon-réclame *m*; (*COMM*) coupon

courage ['kʌridʒ] *n* courage *m*

courier ['kuriər] *n* messager *m*, courrier *m*; (*for tourists*) accompagnateur(-trice), guide *m/f*

course [kɔ:s] *n* cours *m*; (*of ship*) route *f*; (*for golf*) terrain *m*; (*part of meal*) plat *m*; **first** ~ entrée *f*; **of** ~ bien sûr; ~ **of action** parti *m*, ligne *f* de conduite; ~ **of treatment** (*MED*) traitement *m*

court [kɔ:t] *n* cour *f*; (*LAW*) cour, tribunal *m*; (*TENNIS*) court *m* ♦ *vt* (*woman*) courtiser, faire la cour à; **to take to** ~ actionner *or* poursuivre en justice

courteous ['kə:tiəs] *adj* courtois(e), poli(e); **courtesy** ['kə:təsi] *n* courtoisie *f*, politesse *f*; **(by) courtesy of** avec l'aimable autorisation de; **courtesy bus** *or* **coach** *n* navette gratuite

court: ~-**house** (*US*) *n* palais *m* de justice; ~**ier** *n* courtisan *m*, dame *f* de la cour; ~-**martial** (*pl* **courts martial**) *n* cour martiale, conseil *m* de guerre; ~**room** *n* salle *f* de tribunal; ~**yard** *n* cour *f*

cousin ['kʌzn] *n* cousin(e); **first** ~ cousin(e) germain(e)

cove [kəuv] *n* petite baie, anse *f*

covenant ['kʌvənənt] *n* engagement *m*

cover ['kʌvər] *vt* couvrir ♦ *n* couverture *f*; (*of pan*) couvercle *m*; (*over furniture*) housse *f*; (*shelter*) abri *m*; **to take** ~ se mettre à l'abri; **under** ~ à l'abri; **under** ~ **of darkness** à la faveur de la nuit; **under separate** ~ (*COMM*) sous pli séparé; **to** ~ **up for sb** couvrir qn; ~**age** *n* (*TV, PRESS*) reportage *m*; ~ **charge** *n* couvert *m* (*supplément à payer*); ~**ing** *n* couche *f*; ~**ing**

letter (_US_ **cover letter**) _n_ lettre explicative; **~ note** _n_ (_INSURANCE_) police _f_ provisoire

covert ['kʌvət] _adj_ (_threat_) voilé(e), caché(e); (_glance_) furtif(-ive)

cover-up ['kʌvərʌp] _n_ tentative _f_ pour étouffer une affaire

covet ['kʌvɪt] _vt_ convoiter

cow [kau] _n_ vache _f_ ♦ _vt_ effrayer, intimider

coward ['kauəd] _n_ lâche _m/f_; **~ice** _n_ lâcheté _f_; **~ly** _adj_ lâche

cowboy ['kaubɔɪ] _n_ cow-boy _m_

cower ['kauə*] _vi_ se recroqueviller

coy [kɔɪ] _adj_ faussement effarouché(e) _or_ timide

cozy ['kəuzɪ] (_US_) _adj_ = **cosy**

CPA (_US_) _n abbr_ = **certified public accountant**

crab [kræb] _n_ crabe _m_; **~ apple** _n_ pomme _f_ sauvage

crack [kræk] _n_ (_split_) fente _f_, fissure _f_; (_in cup, bone etc_) fêlure _f_; (_in wall_) lézarde _f_; (_noise_) craquement _m_, coup (sec); (_drug_) crack _m_ ♦ _vt_ fendre, fissurer; fêler; lézarder; (_whip_) faire claquer; (_nut_) casser; (_code_) déchiffrer; (_problem_) résoudre ♦ _adj_ (_athlete_) de première classe, d'élite; **~ down on** _vt fus_ mettre un frein à; **~ up** _vi_ être au bout du rouleau, s'effondrer; **~ed** _adj_ (_cup, bone_) fêlé(e); (_broken_) cassé(e); (_wall_) lézardé(e); (_surface_) craquelé(e); (_inf: mad_) cinglé(e); **~er** _n_ (_Christmas cracker_) pétard _m_; (_biscuit_) biscuit (salé)

crackle ['krækl] _vi_ crépiter, grésiller

cradle ['kreidl] _n_ berceau _m_

craft [krɑ:ft] _n_ métier (artisanal); (_pl inv: boat_) embarcation _f_, barque _f_; (_: plane_) appareil _m_; **~sman** (_irreg_) _n_ artisan _m_, ouvrier (qualifié); **~smanship** _n_ travail _m_; **~y** _adj_ rusé(e), malin(-igne)

crag [kræg] _n_ rocher escarpé

cram [kræm] _vt_ (_fill_): **to ~ sth with** bourrer qch de; (_put_): **to ~ sth into** fourrer qch dans ♦ _vi_ (_for exams_) bachoter

cramp [kræmp] _n_ crampe _f_ ♦ _vt_ gêner, entraver; **~ed** _adj_ à l'étroit, très serré(e)

cranberry ['krænbəri] _n_ canneberge _f_

crane [krein] _n_ grue _f_

crank [kræŋk] _n_ manivelle _f_; (_person_) excentrique _m/f_

cranny ['krænɪ] _n see_ **nook**

crash [kræʃ] _n_ fracas _m_; (_of car_) collision _f_; (_of plane_) accident _m_ ♦ _vt_ avoir un accident avec ♦ _vi_ (_plane_) s'écraser; (_two cars_) se percuter, s'emboutir; (_COMM_) s'effondrer; **to ~ into** se jeter _or_ se fracasser contre; **~ course** _n_ cours intensif; **~ helmet** _n_ casque (protecteur); **~ landing** _n_ atterrissage forcé _or_ en catastrophe

crate [kreit] _n_ cageot _m_; (_for bottles_) caisse _f_

cravat(e) [krə'væt] _n_ foulard (noué autour du cou)

crave [kreiv] _vt_, _vi_: **to ~ (for)** avoir une envie irrésistible de

crawl [krɔ:l] _vi_ ramper; (_vehicle_) avancer au pas ♦ _n_ (_SWIMMING_) crawl _m_

crayfish ['kreifiʃ] _n inv_ (_freshwater_) écrevisse _f_; (_saltwater_) langoustine _f_

crayon ['kreiən] _n_ crayon _m_ (de couleur)

craze [kreiz] _n_ engouement _m_

crazy ['kreizɪ] _adj_ fou (folle)

creak [kri:k] _vi_ grincer; craquer

cream [kri:m] _n_ crème _f_ ♦ _adj_ (_colour_) crème _inv_; **~ cake** _n_ (petit) gâteau à la crème; **~ cheese** _n_ fromage _m_ à la crème, fromage blanc; **~y** _adj_ crémeux(-euse)

crease [kri:s] _n_ pli _m_ ♦ _vt_ froisser, chiffonner ♦ _vi_ se froisser, se chiffonner

create [kri:'eit] _vt_ créer; **creation** _n_ création _f_; **creative** _adj_ (_artistic_) créatif(-ive); (_ingenious_) ingénieux(-euse)

creature ['kri:tʃə*] _n_ créature _f_

crèche [krɛʃ] _n_ garderie _f_, crèche _f_

credence ['kri:dns] _n_: **to lend** _or_ **give ~ to** ajouter foi à

credentials [krɪ'dɛnʃlz] _npl_ (_references_) références _fpl_; (_papers of identity_) pièce _f_ d'identité

credit ['krɛdɪt] _n_ crédit _m_; (_recognition_) honneur _m_ ♦ _vt_ (_COMM_) créditer; (_believe: also_: **give ~ to**) ajouter foi à, croire; **~s** _npl_ (_CINEMA, TV_) générique _m_; **to be in ~**

(person, bank account) être créditeur(-trice); **to ~ sb with** (fig) prêter or attribuer à qn; **~ card** n carte f de crédit; **~or** n créancier(-ière)

creed [kri:d] n croyance f; credo m

creek [kri:k] n crique f, anse f; (US: stream) ruisseau m, petit cours d'eau

creep [kri:p] (pt, pp **crept**) vi ramper; **~er** n plante grimpante; **~y** adj (frightening) qui fait frissonner, qui donne la chair de poule

cremate [krɪ'meɪt] vt incinérer; **crematorium** [kremə'tɔ:rɪəm] (pl **crematoria**) n four m crématoire

crêpe [kreɪp] n crêpe m; **~ bandage** (BRIT) n bande f Velpeau ®

crept [krept] pt, pp of **creep**

crescent ['kresnt] n croissant m; (street) rue f (en arc de cercle)

cress [kres] n cresson m

crest [krest] n crête f; **~fallen** adj déconfit(e), découragé(e)

Crete [kri:t] n Crète f

crevice ['krevɪs] n fissure f, lézarde f, fente f

crew [kru:] n équipage m; (CINEMA) équipe f; **~-cut** n: **to have a ~-cut** avoir les cheveux en brosse; **~-neck** n col ras du cou

crib [krɪb] n lit m d'enfant; (for baby) berceau m ♦ vt (inf) copier

crick [krɪk] n: **~ in the neck** torticolis m; **~ in the back** tour m de reins

cricket ['krɪkɪt] n (insect) grillon m, cri-cri m inv; (game) cricket m

crime [kraɪm] n crime m; **criminal** ['krɪmɪnl] adj, n criminel(le)

crimson ['krɪmzn] adj cramoisi(e)

cringe [krɪndʒ] vi avoir un mouvement de recul

crinkle ['krɪŋkl] vt froisser, chiffonner

cripple ['krɪpl] n boiteux(-euse), infirme m/f ♦ vt estropier

crisis ['kraɪsɪs] (pl **crises**) n crise f

crisp [krɪsp] adj croquant(e); (weather) vif (vive); (manner etc) brusque; **~s** (BRIT) npl (pommes) chips fpl

crisscross ['krɪskrɔs] adj entrecroisé(e)

criterion [kraɪ'tɪərɪən] (pl **criteria**) n critère m

critic ['krɪtɪk] n critique m; **~al** adj critique; **~ally** adv (examine) d'un œil critique; (speak etc) sévèrement; **~ally ill** gravement malade; **~ism** ['krɪtɪsɪzəm] n critique f; **~ize** ['krɪtɪsaɪz] vt critiquer

croak [krəuk] vi (frog) coasser; (raven) croasser; (person) parler d'une voix rauque

Croatia [krəu'eɪʃə] n Croatie f

crochet ['krəuʃeɪ] n travail m au crochet

crockery ['krɔkərɪ] n vaisselle f

crocodile ['krɔkədaɪl] n crocodile m

crocus ['krəukəs] n crocus m

croft [krɔft] (BRIT) n petite ferme

crony ['krəunɪ] (inf: pej) n copain (copine)

crook [kruk] n escroc m; (of shepherd) houlette f; **~ed** ['krukɪd] adj courbé(e), tordu(e); (action) malhonnête

crop [krɔp] n (produce) culture f; (amount produced) récolte f; (riding ~) cravache f ♦ vt (hair) tondre; **~ up** vi surgir, se présenter, survenir

cross [krɔs] n croix f; (BIO etc) croisement m ♦ vt (street etc) traverser; (arms, legs, BIO) croiser; (cheque) barrer ♦ adj en colère, fâché(e); **~ out** vt barrer, biffer; **~over** vi traverser; **~bar** n barre (transversale); **~-country (race)** n cross(-country) m; **~-examine** vt (LAW) faire subir un examen contradictoire à; **~-eyed** adj qui louche; **~fire** n feux croisés; **~ing** n (sea passage) traversée f; (also: **pedestrian ~ing**) passage clouté; **~ing guard** (US) n contractuel qui fait traverser la rue aux enfants; **~ purposes** npl: **to be at ~ purposes with sb** comprendre qn de travers; **~-reference** n renvoi m, référence f; **~roads** n carrefour m; **~ section** n (of object) coupe transversale; (in population) échantillon m; **~walk** (US) n passage clouté; **~wind** n vent m de travers; **~word** n mots mpl croisés

crotch [krɔtʃ] n (ANAT, of garment) entrejambes m inv

crouch [krautʃ] vi s'accroupir; se tapir

crow [krəu] n (bird) corneille f; (of cock)

chant *m* du coq, cocorico *m* ♦ *vi* (*cock*) chanter

crowbar [ˈkrəʊbɑːʳ] *n* levier *m*

crowd [kraʊd] *n* foule *f* ♦ *vt* remplir ♦ *vi* affluer, s'attrouper, s'entasser; **to ~ in** entrer en foule; **~ed** *adj* bondé(e), plein(e)

crown [kraʊn] *n* couronne *f*; (*of head*) sommet *m* de la tête; (*of hill*) sommet *m* ♦ *vt* couronner; **~ jewels** *npl* joyaux *mpl* de la Couronne

crow's-feet [ˈkrəʊzfiːt] *npl* pattes *fpl* d'oie

crucial [ˈkruːʃl] *adj* crucial(e), décisif(-ive)

crucifix [ˈkruːsɪfɪks] *n* (*REL*) crucifix *m*; **~ion** [kruːsɪˈfɪkʃən] *n* (*REL*) crucifixion *f*

crude [kruːd] *adj* (*materials*) brut(e); non raffiné(e); (*fig: basic*) rudimentaire, sommaire; (: *vulgar*) cru(e), grossier(-ère); **~ (oil)** *n* (pétrole) brut *m*

cruel [ˈkruəl] *adj* cruel(le); **~ty** *n* cruauté *f*

cruise [kruːz] *n* croisière *f* ♦ *vi* (*ship*) croiser; (*car*) rouler; **~r** *n* croiseur *m*; (*motorboat*) yacht *m* de croisière

crumb [krʌm] *n* miette *f*

crumble [ˈkrʌmbl] *vt* émietter ♦ *vi* (*plaster etc*) s'effriter; (*land, earth*) s'ébouler; (*building*) s'écrouler, crouler; (*fig*) s'effondrer; **crumbly** *adj* friable

crumpet [ˈkrʌmpɪt] *n* petite crêpe (épaisse)

crumple [ˈkrʌmpl] *vt* froisser, friper

crunch [krʌntʃ] *vt* croquer; (*underfoot*) faire craquer or crisser, écraser ♦ *n* (*fig*) instant *m* or moment *m* critique, moment de vérité; **~y** *adj* croquant(e), croustillant(e)

crusade [kruːˈseɪd] *n* croisade *f*

crush [krʌʃ] *n* foule *f*, cohue *f*; (*love*): **to have a ~ on sb** avoir le béguin pour qn (*inf*); (*drink*): **lemon ~** citron pressé ♦ *vt* écraser; (*crumple*) froisser; (*fig: hopes*) anéantir

crust [krʌst] *n* croûte *f*

crutch [krʌtʃ] *n* béquille *f*

crux [krʌks] *n* point crucial

cry [kraɪ] *vi* pleurer; (*shout: also:* **~ out**) crier ♦ *n* cri *m*; **~ off** (*inf*) *vi* se dédire; se décommander

cryptic [ˈkrɪptɪk] *adj* énigmatique

crystal [ˈkrɪstl] *n* cristal *m*; **~-clear** *adj* clair(e) comme de l'eau de roche

CSA *n abbr* (= *Child Support Agency*) organisme pour la protection des enfants de parents séparés, qui contrôle le versement des pensions alimentaires

CTC *n abbr* = **city technology college**

cub [kʌb] *n* petit *m* (*d'un animal*); (*also:* **C~ scout**) louveteau *m*

Cuba [ˈkjuːbə] *n* Cuba *m*

cube [kjuːb] *n* cube *m* ♦ *vt* (*MATH*) élever au cube; **cubic** *adj* cubique; **cubic metre** *etc* mètre *m etc* cube; **cubic capacity** *n* cylindrée *f*

cubicle [ˈkjuːbɪkl] *n* (*in hospital*) box *m*; (*at pool*) cabine *f*

cuckoo [ˈkuːkuː] *n* coucou *m*; **~ clock** *n* (pendule *f* à) coucou *m*

cucumber [ˈkjuːkʌmbəʳ] *n* concombre *m*

cuddle [ˈkʌdl] *vt* câliner, caresser ♦ *vi* se blottir l'un contre l'autre

cue [kjuː] *n* (*snooker ~*) queue *f* de billard; (*THEATRE etc*) signal *m*

cuff [kʌf] *n* (*BRIT: of shirt, coat etc*) poignet *m*, manchette *f*; (*US: of trousers*) revers *m*; (*blow*) tape *f*; **off the ~** à l'improviste; **~ links** *npl* boutons *mpl* de manchette

cul-de-sac [ˈkʌldəsæk] *n* cul-de-sac *m*, impasse *f*

cull [kʌl] *vt* sélectionner ♦ *n* (*of animals*) massacre *m*

culminate [ˈkʌlmɪneɪt] *vi*: **to ~ in** finir or se terminer par; (*end in*) mener à; **culmination** [kʌlmɪˈneɪʃən] *n* point culminant

culottes [kjuːˈlɒts] *npl* jupe-culotte *f*

culprit [ˈkʌlprɪt] *n* coupable *m/f*

cult [kʌlt] *n* culte *m*

cultivate [ˈkʌltɪveɪt] *vt* cultiver; **cultivation** [kʌltɪˈveɪʃən] *n* culture *f*

cultural [ˈkʌltʃərəl] *adj* culturel(le)

culture [ˈkʌltʃəʳ] *n* culture *f*; **~d** *adj* (*person*) cultivé(e)

cumbersome [ˈkʌmbəsəm] *adj* encombrant(e), embarrassant(e)

cunning [ˈkʌnɪŋ] *n* ruse *f*, astuce *f* ♦ *adj* rusé(e), malin(-igne); (*device, idea*) astucieux(-euse)

cup [kʌp] n tasse f; (as prize) coupe f; (of bra) bonnet m

cupboard ['kʌbəd] n armoire f; (built-in) placard m

cup tie (BRIT) n match m de coupe

curate ['kjuərɪt] n vicaire m

curator [kjuə'reɪtə] n conservateur m (d'un musée etc)

curb [kə:b] vt refréner, mettre un frein à ♦ n (fig) frein m, restriction f; (US: kerb) bord m du trottoir

curdle ['kə:dl] vi se cailler

cure [kjuə] vt guérir; (CULIN: salt) saler; (: smoke) fumer; (: dry) sécher ♦ n remède m

curfew ['kə:fju:] n couvre-feu m

curiosity [kjuərɪ'ɔsɪtɪ] n curiosité f

curious ['kjuərɪəs] adj curieux(-euse)

curl [kə:l] n boucle f (de cheveux) ♦ vt, vi boucler; (tightly) friser; ~ **up** vi s'enrouler; se pelotonner; ~**er** n bigoudi m, rouleau m; ~**y** adj bouclé(e); frisé(e)

currant ['kʌrnt] n (dried) raisin m de Corinthe, raisin sec; (bush) groseiller m; (fruit) groseille f

currency ['kʌrnsɪ] n monnaie f; **to gain ~** (fig) s'accréditer

current ['kʌrnt] n courant m ♦ adj courant(e); ~ **account** (BRIT) n compte courant; ~ **affairs** npl (questions fpl d')actualité f; ~**ly** adv actuellement

curriculum [kə'rɪkjuləm] (pl ~s or **curricula**) n programme m d'études; ~ **vitae** n curriculum vitae m

curry ['kʌrɪ] n curry m ♦ vt: **to ~ favour with** chercher à s'attirer les bonnes grâces de

curse [kə:s] vi jurer, blasphémer ♦ vt maudire ♦ n (spell) malédiction f; (problem, scourge) fléau m; (swearword) juron m

cursor ['kə:sə] n (COMPUT) curseur m

cursory ['kə:sərɪ] adj superficiel(le), hâtif(-ive)

curt [kə:t] adj brusque, sec (sèche)

curtail [kə:'teɪl] vt (visit etc) écourter; (expenses, freedom etc) réduire

curtain ['kə:tn] n rideau m

curts(e)y ['kə:tsɪ] vi faire une révérence

curve [kə:v] n courbe f; (in the road) tournant m, virage m ♦ vi se courber; (road) faire une courbe

cushion ['kuʃən] n coussin m ♦ vt (fall, shock) amortir

custard ['kʌstəd] n (for pouring) crème anglaise

custody ['kʌstədɪ] n (of child) garde f; **to take sb into ~** (suspect) placer qn en détention préventive

custom ['kʌstəm] n coutume f, usage m; (COMM) clientèle f; ~**ary** adj habituel(le)

customer ['kʌstəmə] n client m

customized ['kʌstəmaɪzd] adj (car etc) construit(e) sur commande

custom-made ['kʌstəm'meɪd] adj (clothes) fait(e) sur mesure; (other goods) hors série, fait(e) sur commande

customs ['kʌstəmz] npl douane f; ~ **officer** n douanier(-ière)

cut [kʌt] (pt, pp **cut**) vt couper; (meat) découper; (reduce) réduire ♦ vi couper ♦ n coupure f; (of clothes) coupe f; (in salary etc) réduction f; (of meat) morceau m; **to ~ one's hand** se couper la main; **to ~ a tooth** percer une dent; ~ **down** vt fus (tree etc) abattre; (consumption) réduire; ~ **off** vt couper; (fig) isoler; ~ **out** vi découper; (stop) arrêter; (remove) ôter; ~ **up** vt (meat) découper; ~**back** n réduction f

cute [kju:t] adj mignon(ne), adorable

cutlery ['kʌtlərɪ] n couverts mpl

cutlet ['kʌtlɪt] n côtelette f

cut: ~**out** n (switch) coupe-circuit m inv; (cardboard cutout) découpage m; ~**-price** (US **cut-rate**) adj au rabais, à prix réduit; ~**-throat** n assassin m ♦ adj acharné(e); ~**ting** adj tranchant(e), coupant(e); (fig) cinglant(e), mordant(e) ♦ n (BRIT: from newspaper) coupure f (de journal); (from plant) bouture f

CV n abbr = **curriculum vitae**

cwt abbr = **hundredweight(s)**

cyanide ['saɪənaɪd] n cyanure m

cybercafé ['saɪbəkæfeɪ] n cybercafé m

cyberspace ['saɪbəspeɪs] n cyberspace m

cycle ['saɪkl] n cycle m; (bicycle) bicyclette f, vélo m ♦ vi faire de la bicyclette; ~ hire n location f de vélos; ~ lane or path n piste f cyclable; cycling n cyclisme m; cyclist ['saɪklɪst] n cycliste m/f

cygnet ['sɪgnɪt] n jeune cygne m

cylinder ['sɪlɪndəʳ] n cylindre m; ~-head gasket n joint m de culasse

cymbals ['sɪmblz] npl cymbales fpl

cynic ['sɪnɪk] n cynique m/f; ~al adj cynique; ~ism ['sɪnɪsɪzəm] n cynisme m

Cypriot ['sɪprɪət] adj cypriote, chypriote ♦ n Cypriote m/f, Chypriote m/f

Cyprus ['saɪprəs] n Chypre f

cyst [sɪst] n kyste m

cystitis [sɪs'taɪtɪs] n cystite f

czar [zɑːʳ] n tsar m

Czech [tʃɛk] adj tchèque ♦ n Tchèque m/f; (LING) tchèque m

Czechoslovak [tʃɛkə'sləuvæk] adj tchécoslovaque ♦ n Tchécoslovaque m/f

Czechoslovakia [tʃɛkəslə'vækɪə] n Tchécoslovaquie f

D, d

D [diː] n (MUS) ré m

dab [dæb] vt (eyes, wound) tamponner; (paint, cream) appliquer (par petites touches or rapidement)

dabble ['dæbl] vi: to ~ in faire or se mêler or s'occuper un peu de

dad [dæd] n, daddy ['dædɪ] n papa m

daffodil ['dæfədɪl] n jonquille f

daft [dɑːft] adj idiot(e), stupide

dagger ['dægəʳ] n poignard m

daily ['deɪlɪ] adj quotidien(ne), journalier(-ère) ♦ n quotidien m ♦ adv tous les jours

dainty ['deɪntɪ] adj délicat(e), mignon(ne)

dairy ['dɛərɪ] n (BRIT: shop) crémerie f, laiterie f; (on farm) laiterie f; ~ products npl produits laitiers; ~ store n (US) crémerie f, laiterie f

daisy ['deɪzɪ] n pâquerette f

dale [deɪl] n vallon m

dam [dæm] n barrage m ♦ vt endiguer

damage ['dæmɪdʒ] n dégâts mpl, dommages mpl; (fig) tort m ♦ vt endommager, abîmer; (fig) faire du tort à; ~s npl (LAW) dommages-intérêts mpl

damn [dæm] vt condamner; (curse) maudire ♦ n (inf): I don't give a ~ je m'en fous ♦ adj (inf: also: ~ed): this ~ ... ce sacré or foutu ...; ~ (it)! zut!; ~ing adj accablant(e)

damp [dæmp] adj humide ♦ n humidité f ♦ vt (also: ~en: cloth, rag) humecter; (: enthusiasm) refroidir

damson ['dæmzən] n prune f de Damas

dance [dɑːns] n danse f; (social event) bal m ♦ vi danser; ~ hall n salle f de bal, dancing m; ~r n danseur(-euse); dancing n danse f

dandelion ['dændɪlaɪən] n pissenlit m

dandruff ['dændrəf] n pellicules fpl

Dane [deɪn] n Danois(e)

danger ['deɪndʒəʳ] n danger m; there is a ~ of fire il y a (un) risque d'incendie; in ~ en danger; he was in ~ of falling il risquait de tomber; ~ous adj dangereux(-euse)

dangle ['dæŋgl] vt balancer ♦ vi pendre

Danish ['deɪnɪʃ] adj danois(e) ♦ n (LING) danois m

dare [dɛəʳ] vt: to ~ sb to do défier qn de faire ♦ vi: to ~ (to) do sth oser faire qch; I ~ say (I suppose) il est probable (que); daring adj hardi(e), audacieux(-euse); (dress) osé(e) ♦ n audace f, hardiesse f

dark [dɑːk] adj (night, room) obscur(e), sombre; (colour, complexion) foncé(e), sombre ♦ n: in the ~ dans le noir; in the ~ about (fig) ignorant tout de; after ~ après la tombée de la nuit; ~en vt obscurcir, assombrir ♦ vi s'obscurcir, s'assombrir; ~ glasses npl lunettes noires; ~ness n obscurité f; ~room n chambre noire

darling ['dɑːlɪŋ] adj chéri(e) ♦ n chéri(e); (favourite): to be the ~ of être la coqueluche de

darn [dɑːn] vt repriser, raccommoder

dart [dɑːt] n fléchette f; (sewing) pince f

♦ *vi:* **to ~ towards** (*also:* **make a ~ towards**) se précipiter *or* s'élancer vers; **to ~ away/along** partir/passer comme une flèche; **~board** *n* cible *f* (de jeu de fléchettes); **~s** *n* (jeu *m* de) fléchettes *fpl*

dash [dæʃ] *n* (*sign*) tiret *m*; (*small quantity*) goutte *f*, larme *f* ♦ *vt* (*missile*) jeter *or* lancer violemment; (*hopes*) anéantir ♦ *vi:* **to ~ towards** (*also:* **make a ~ towards**) se précipiter *or* se ruer vers; **~ away** *vi* partir à toute allure, filer; **~ off** *vi* = **dash away**

dashboard ['dæʃbɔːd] *n* (AUT) tableau *m* de bord

dashing ['dæʃɪŋ] *adj* fringant(e)

data ['deɪtə] *npl* données *fpl*; **~base** *n* (COMPUT) base *f* de données; **~ processing** *n* traitement *m* de données

date [deɪt] *n* date *f*; (*with sb*) rendez-vous *m*; (*fruit*) datte *f* ♦ *vt* dater; (*person*) sortir avec; **~ of birth** date de naissance; **to ~** (*until now*) à ce jour; **out of ~** (*passport*) périmé(e); (*theory etc*) dépassé(e); (*clothes etc*) démodé(e); **up to ~** moderne; (*news*) très récent; **~d** ['deɪtɪd] *adj* démodé(e); **~ rape** *n* viol *m* (*à l'issue d'un rendez-vous galant*)

daub [dɔːb] *vt* barbouiller

daughter ['dɔːtər] *n* fille *f*; **~-in-law** *n* belle-fille *f*, bru *f*

daunting ['dɔːntɪŋ] *adj* décourageant(e)

dawdle ['dɔːdl] *vi* traîner, lambiner

dawn [dɔːn] *n* aube *f*, aurore *f* ♦ *vi* (*day*) se lever, poindre; (*fig*): **it ~ed on him that ...** il lui vint à l'esprit que ...

day [deɪ] *n* jour *m*; (*as duration*) journée *f*; (*period of time, age*) époque *f*, temps *m*; **the ~ before** la veille, le jour précédent; **the ~ after, the following ~** le lendemain, le jour suivant; **the ~ after tomorrow** après-demain; **the ~ before yesterday** avant-hier; **by ~** de jour; **~break** *n* point *m* du jour; **~dream** *vi* rêver (tout éveillé); **~light** *n* (lumière *f* du) jour *m*; **~ return** (BRIT) *n* billet *m* d'aller-retour (valable pour la journée); **~time** *n* jour *m*, journée *f*; **~-to-~** *adj* quotidien(ne);

(*event*) journalier(-ère)

daze [deɪz] *vt* (*stun*) étourdir ♦ *n:* **in a ~** étourdi(e), hébété(e)

dazzle ['dæzl] *vt* éblouir, aveugler

DC *abbr* (= *direct current*) courant continu

D-day ['diːdeɪ] *n* le jour J

dead [ded] *adj* mort(e); (*numb*) engourdi(e), insensible; (*battery*) à plat; (*telephone*): **the line is ~** la ligne est coupée ♦ *adv* absolument, complètement ♦ *npl:* **the ~** les morts; **he was shot ~** il a été tué d'un coup de revolver; **~ on time** à l'heure pile; **~ tired** éreinté(e), complètement fourbu(e); **to stop ~** s'arrêter pile *or* net; **~en** *vt* (*blow, sound*) amortir; (*pain*) calmer; **~ end** *n* impasse *f*; **~ heat** *n* (SPORT): **to finish in a ~ heat** terminer ex-æquo; **~line** *n* date *f or* heure *f* limite; **~lock** (*fig*) *n* impasse *f*; **~ loss** *n:* **to be a ~ loss** (*inf: person*) n'être bon(ne) à rien; **~ly** *adj* mortel(le); (*weapon*) meurtrier(-ère); (*accuracy*) extrême; **~pan** *adj* impassible; **D~ Sea** *n:* **the D~ Sea** la mer Morte

deaf [def] *adj* sourd(e); **~en** *vt* rendre sourd; **~ening** *adj* assourdissant(e); **~-mute** *n* sourd(e)-muet(te); **~ness** *n* surdité *f*

deal [diːl] (*pt, pp* **dealt**) *n* affaire *f*, marché *m* ♦ *vt* (*blow*) porter; (*cards*) donner, distribuer; **a great ~ (of)** beaucoup (de); **~ in** *vt fus* faire le commerce de; **~ with** *vt fus* (*person, problem*) s'occuper *or* se charger de; (*be about: book etc*) traiter de; **~er** *n* marchand *m*; **~ings** *npl* (COMM) transactions *fpl*; (*relations*) relations *fpl*, rapports *mpl*

dean [diːn] *n* (REL, BRIT: SCOL) doyen *m*; (US: SCOL) conseiller(-ère) (principal(e)) d'éducation

dear [dɪər] *adj* cher (chère); (*expensive*) cher, coûteux(-euse) ♦ *n:* **my ~** mon cher/ma chère; **~ me!** mon Dieu!; **D~ Sir/Madam** (*in letter*) Monsieur/Madame; **D~ Mr/Mrs X** Cher Monsieur/Chère Madame; **~ly** *adv* (*love*) tendrement; (*pay*) cher

death [dɛθ] n mort f; (*fatality*) mort m; (*ADMIN*) décès m; ~ **certificate** n acte m de décès; ~**ly** adj de mort; ~ **penalty** n peine f de mort; ~ **rate** n (taux m de) mortalité f; ~ **toll** n nombre m de morts

debase [dɪ'beɪs] vt (*value*) déprécier, dévaloriser

debatable [dɪ'beɪtəbl] adj discutable

debate [dɪ'beɪt] n discussion f, débat m ♦ vt discuter, débattre

debit ['dɛbɪt] n débit m ♦ vt: **to ~ a sum to sb** or **to sb's account** porter une somme au débit de qn, débiter qn d'une somme; *see also* **direct**

debt [dɛt] n dette f; **to be in ~** avoir des dettes, être endetté(e); ~**or** n débiteur(-trice)

decade ['dɛkeɪd] n décennie f, décade f

decadence ['dɛkədəns] n décadence f

decaff ['di:kæf] (*inf*) n déca m

decaffeinated [dɪ'kæfɪneɪtɪd] adj décaféiné(e)

decanter [dɪ'kæntəʳ] n carafe f

decay [dɪ'keɪ] n (*of building*) délabrement m; (*also:* **tooth ~**) carie f (dentaire) ♦ vi (*rot*) se décomposer, pourrir; (: *teeth*) se carier

deceased [dɪ'si:st] n défunt(e)

deceit [dɪ'si:t] n tromperie f, supercherie f; ~**ful** adj trompeur(-euse); **deceive** vt tromper

December [dɪ'sɛmbəʳ] n décembre m

decent ['di:sənt] adj décent(e), convenable

deception [dɪ'sɛpʃən] n tromperie f

deceptive [dɪ'sɛptɪv] adj trompeur(-euse)

decide [dɪ'saɪd] vt (*person*) décider; (*question, argument*) trancher, régler ♦ vi se décider, décider; **to ~ to do/that** décider de faire/que; **to ~ on** décider, se décider pour; ~**d** adj (*resolute*) résolu(e), décidé(e); (*clear, definite*) net(te), marqué(e); ~**dly** adv résolument; (*distinctly*) incontestablement, nettement

deciduous [dɪ'sɪdjuəs] adj à feuilles caduques

decimal ['dɛsɪməl] adj décimal(e) ♦ n décimale f; ~ **point** n ≃ virgule f

decipher [dɪ'saɪfəʳ] vt déchiffrer

decision [dɪ'sɪʒən] n décision f

decisive [dɪ'saɪsɪv] adj décisif(-ive); (*person*) décidé(e)

deck [dɛk] n (*NAUT*) pont m; (*of bus*): **top ~** impériale f; (*of cards*) jeu m; (*record ~*) platine f; ~**chair** n chaise longue

declare [dɪ'klɛəʳ] vt déclarer

decline [dɪ'klaɪn] n (*decay*) déclin m; (*lessening*) baisse f ♦ vt refuser, décliner ♦ vi décliner; (*business*) baisser

decoder [di:'kəudəʳ] n (*TV*) décodeur m

decorate ['dɛkəreɪt] vt (*adorn, give a medal to*) décorer; (*paint and paper*) peindre et tapisser; **decoration** [dɛkə'reɪʃən] n (*medal etc, adornment*) décoration f; **decorator** n peintre-décorateur m

decoy ['di:kɔɪ] n piège m; (*person*) compère m

decrease [n 'di:kri:s, vb di:'kri:s] n: ~ **(in)** diminution f (de) ♦ vt, vi diminuer

decree [dɪ'kri:] n (*POL, REL*) décret m; (*LAW*) arrêt m, jugement m; ~ **nisi** [-'naɪsaɪ] n jugement m provisoire de divorce

dedicate ['dɛdɪkeɪt] vt consacrer; (*book etc*) dédier; ~**d** adj (*person*) dévoué(e); (*COMPUT*) spécialisé(e), dédié(e); **dedication** [dɛdɪ'keɪʃən] n (*devotion*) dévouement m; (*in book*) dédicace f

deduce [dɪ'dju:s] vt déduire, conclure

deduct [dɪ'dʌkt] vt: **to ~ sth (from)** déduire qch (de), retrancher qch (de); ~**ion** n (*deducting, deducing*) déduction f; (*from wage etc*) prélèvement m, retenue f

deed [di:d] n action f, acte m; (*LAW*) acte notarié, contrat m

deep [di:p] adj profond(e); (*voice*) grave ♦ adv: **spectators stood 20 ~** il y avait 20 rangs de spectateurs; **4 metres ~** de 4 mètres de profondeur; ~ **end** (*of swimming pool*) grand bain; ~**en** vt approfondir ♦ vi (*fig*) s'épaissir; ~**freeze** n congélateur m; ~**fry** vt faire frire (en friteuse); ~**ly** adv profondément; (*interested*) vivement; ~**-sea diver** n sous-marin(e); ~**-sea diving** n plongée sous-marine; ~**-sea fishing** n grande pêche; ~**-seated** adj

deer → deliver

profond(e), profondément enraciné(e)

deer [dɪəʳ] n inv: **(red) ~** cerf m, biche f; **(fallow) ~** daim m; **(roe) ~** chevreuil m; **~skin** n daim

deface [dɪˈfeɪs] vt dégrader; (notice, poster) barbouiller

default [dɪˈfɔːlt] n (COMPUT: also: **~ value**) valeur f par défaut; **by ~** (LAW) par défaut, par contumace; (SPORT) par forfait

defeat [dɪˈfiːt] n défaite f ♦ vt (team, opponents) battre

defect [n ˈdiːfɛkt, vb dɪˈfɛkt] n défaut m ♦ vi: **to ~ to the enemy** passer à l'ennemi; **~ive** [dɪˈfɛktɪv] adj défectueux(-euse)

defence [dɪˈfɛns] (US **defense**) n défense f; **~less** adj sans défense

defend [dɪˈfɛnd] vt défendre; **~ant** n défendeur(-deresse); (in criminal case) accusé(e), prévenu(e); **~er** n défenseur m

defer [dɪˈfəːʳ] vt (postpone) différer, ajourner

defiance [dɪˈfaɪəns] n défi m; **in ~ of** au mépris de; **defiant** adj provocant(e), de défi; (person) rebelle, intraitable

deficiency [dɪˈfɪʃənsɪ] n insuffisance f, déficience f; **deficient** adj (inadequate) insuffisant(e); **to be deficient in** manquer de

deficit [ˈdɛfɪsɪt] n déficit m

define [dɪˈfaɪn] vt définir

definite [ˈdɛfɪnɪt] adj (fixed) défini(e), (bien) déterminé(e); (clear, obvious) net(te), manifeste; (certain) sûr(e); **he was ~ about it** il a été catégorique; **~ly** adv sans aucun doute

definition [dɛfɪˈnɪʃən] n définition f; (clearness) netteté f

deflate [diːˈfleɪt] vt dégonfler

deflect [dɪˈflɛkt] vt détourner, faire dévier

deformed [dɪˈfɔːmd] adj difforme

defraud [dɪˈfrɔːd] vt frauder; **to ~ sb of sth** escroquer qch à qn

defrost [diːˈfrɒst] vt dégivrer; (food) décongeler; **~er** n (US) (demister) dispositif m anti-buée inv

deft [dɛft] adj adroit(e), preste

defunct [dɪˈfʌŋkt] adj défunt(e)

defuse [diːˈfjuːz] vt désamorcer

defy [dɪˈfaɪ] vt défier; (efforts etc) résister à

degenerate [vb dɪˈdʒɛnəreɪt, adj dɪˈdʒɛnərɪt] vi dégénérer ♦ adj dégénéré(e)

degree [dɪˈɡriː] n degré m; (SCOL) diplôme m (universitaire); **a (first) ~ in maths** une licence en maths; **by ~s** (gradually) par degrés; **to some ~, to a certain ~** jusqu'à un certain point, dans une certaine mesure

dehydrated [diːhaɪˈdreɪtɪd] adj déshydraté(e); (milk, eggs) en poudre

de-ice [diːˈaɪs] vt (windscreen) dégivrer

deign [deɪn] vi: **to ~ to do** daigner faire

dejected [dɪˈdʒɛktɪd] adj abattu(e), déprimé(e)

delay [dɪˈleɪ] vt retarder ♦ vi s'attarder ♦ n délai m, retard m; **to be ~ed** être en retard

delectable [dɪˈlɛktəbl] adj délicieux(-euse)

delegate [n ˈdɛlɪɡɪt, vb ˈdɛlɪɡeɪt] n délégué(e) ♦ vt déléguer

delete [dɪˈliːt] vt rayer, supprimer

deliberate [adj dɪˈlɪbərɪt, vb dɪˈlɪbəreɪt] adj (intentional) délibéré(e); (slow) mesuré(e) ♦ vi délibérer, réfléchir; **~ly** [dɪˈlɪbərɪtlɪ] adv (on purpose) exprès, délibérément

delicacy [ˈdɛlɪkəsɪ] n délicatesse f; (food) mets fin or délicat, friandise f

delicate [ˈdɛlɪkɪt] adj délicat(e)

delicatessen [dɛlɪkəˈtɛsn] n épicerie fine

delicious [dɪˈlɪʃəs] adj délicieux(-euse)

delight [dɪˈlaɪt] n (grande) joie, grand plaisir ♦ vt enchanter; **to take (a) ~ in** prendre grand plaisir à; **~ed** adj: **~ed (at or with/to do)** ravi(e) (de/de faire); **~ful** adj (person) adorable; (meal, evening) merveilleux(-euse)

delinquent [dɪˈlɪŋkwənt] adj, n délinquant(e)

delirious [dɪˈlɪrɪəs] adj: **to be ~** délirer

deliver [dɪˈlɪvəʳ] vt (mail) distribuer; (goods) livrer; (message) remettre; (speech) prononcer; (MED: baby) mettre au monde; **~y** n distribution f; livraison f; (of speaker) élocution f; (MED) accouchement m; **to take ~y of** prendre livraison de

delude [dɪ'luːd] vt tromper, leurrer; delusion n illusion f

demand [dɪ'mɑːnd] vt réclamer, exiger ♦ n exigence f; (claim) revendication f; (ECON) demande f; in ~ demandé(e), recherché(e); on ~ sur demande; ~ing adj (person) exigeant(e); (work) astreignant(e)

demean [dɪ'miːn] vt: to ~ o.s. s'abaisser

demeanour [dɪ'miːnəʳ] (US demeanor) n comportement m; maintien m

demented [dɪ'mɛntɪd] adj dément(e), fou (folle)

demise [dɪ'maɪz] n mort f

demister [diː'mɪstəʳ] (BRIT) n (AUT) dispositif m anti-buée inv

demo ['dɛməu] (inf) n abbr (= demonstration) manif f

democracy [dɪ'mɔkrəsɪ] n démocratie f; democrat ['dɛməkræt] n démocrate m/f; democratic [dɛmə'krætɪk] adj démocratique

demolish [dɪ'mɔlɪʃ] vt démolir

demonstrate ['dɛmənstreɪt] vt démontrer, prouver; (show) faire une démonstration de ♦ vi: to ~ (for/against) manifester (en faveur de/contre); demonstration [dɛmən'streɪʃən] n démonstration f, manifestation f; demonstrator n (POL) manifestant(e)

demote [dɪ'məut] vt rétrograder

demure [dɪ'mjuəʳ] adj sage, réservé(e)

den [dɛn] n tanière f, antre m

denial [dɪ'naɪəl] n démenti m; (refusal) dénégation f

denim ['dɛnɪm] n jean m; ~s npl (jeans) (blue-)jean(s) m(pl)

Denmark ['dɛnmɑːk] n Danemark m

denomination [dɪnɔmɪ'neɪʃən] n (of money) valeur f; (REL) confession f

denounce [dɪ'nauns] vt dénoncer

dense [dɛns] adj dense; (stupid) obtus(e), bouché(e); ~ly adv: ~ly populated à forte densité de population; density ['dɛnsɪtɪ] n densité f; double/high-density diskette disquette f double densité/haute densité

dent [dɛnt] n bosse f ♦ vt (also: make a ~ in) cabosser

dental ['dɛntl] adj dentaire; ~ surgeon n (chirurgien(ne)) dentiste

dentist ['dɛntɪst] n dentiste m/f

dentures ['dɛntʃəz] npl dentier m sg

deny [dɪ'naɪ] vt nier; (refuse) refuser

deodorant [diː'əudərənt] n déodorant m, désodorisant m

depart [dɪ'pɑːt] vi partir; to ~ from (fig: differ from) s'écarter de

department [dɪ'pɑːtmənt] n (COMM) rayon m; (SCOL) section f; (POL) ministère m, département m; ~ store n grand magasin

departure [dɪ'pɑːtʃəʳ] n départ m; a new ~ une nouvelle voie; ~ lounge n (at airport) salle f d'embarquement

depend [dɪ'pɛnd] vi: to ~ on dépendre de; (rely on) compter sur; it ~s cela dépend; ~ing on the result selon le résultat; ~able adj (person) sérieux(-euse), sûr(e); (car, watch) solide, fiable; ~ant n personne f à charge; ~ent adj: to be ~ent (on) dépendre (de) ♦ n = dependant

depict [dɪ'pɪkt] vt (in picture) représenter; (in words) (dé)peindre, décrire

depleted [dɪ'pliːtɪd] adj (considérablement) réduit(e) or diminué(e)

deport [dɪ'pɔːt] vt expulser

deposit [dɪ'pɔzɪt] n (CHEM, COMM, GEO) dépôt m; (of ore, oil) gisement m; (part payment) arrhes fpl, acompte m; (on bottle etc) consigne f; (for hired goods etc) cautionnement m, garantie f ♦ vt déposer; ~ account n compte m sur livret

depot ['dɛpəu] n dépôt m; (US: RAIL) gare f

depress [dɪ'prɛs] vt déprimer; (press down) appuyer sur, abaisser; (prices, wages) faire baisser; ~ed adj (person) déprimé(e); (area) en déclin, touché(e) par le sous-emploi; ~ing adj déprimant(e); ~ion n dépression f; (hollow) creux m

deprivation [dɛprɪ'veɪʃən] n privation f; (loss) perte f

deprive [dɪ'praɪv] vt: to ~ sb of priver qn de; ~d adj déshérité(e)

depth [dɛpθ] n profondeur f; in the ~s of despair au plus profond du désespoir; to be out of one's ~ avoir perdu pied, nager

deputize [ˈdɛpjutaɪz] *vi*: **to ~ for** assurer l'intérim de

deputy [ˈdɛpjutɪ] *adj* adjoint(e) ♦ *n* (*second in command*) adjoint(e); (*US: also:* **~ sheriff**) shérif adjoint; **~ head** directeur adjoint, sous-directeur *m*

derail [dɪˈreɪl] *vt*: **to be ~ed** dérailler

deranged [dɪˈreɪndʒd] *adj*: **to be (mentally) ~** avoir le cerveau dérangé

derby [ˈdɑːrbɪ] (*US*) *n* (*bowler hat*) (chapeau *m*) melon *m*

derelict [ˈdɛrɪlɪkt] *adj* abandonné(e), à l'abandon

derisory [dɪˈraɪsərɪ] *adj* (*sum*) dérisoire; (*smile, person*) moqueur(-euse)

derive [dɪˈraɪv] *vt*: **to ~ sth from** tirer qch de; trouver qch dans ♦ *vi*: **to ~ from** provenir de, dériver de

derogatory [dɪˈrɒɡətərɪ] *adj* désobligeant(e); péjoratif(-ive)

descend [dɪˈsɛnd] *vt, vi* descendre; **to ~ from** descendre de, être issu(e) de; **to ~ to (doing) sth** s'abaisser à (faire) (qch); **descent** *n* descente *f*; (*origin*) origine *f*

describe [dɪsˈkraɪb] *vt* décrire; **description** [dɪsˈkrɪpʃən] *n* description *f*; (*sort*) sorte *f*, espèce *f*

desecrate [ˈdɛsɪkreɪt] *vt* profaner

desert [*n* ˈdɛzət, *vb* dɪˈzɜːt] *n* désert *m* ♦ *vt* déserter, abandonner ♦ *vi* (*MIL*) déserter; **~s** *npl*: **to get one's just ~s** n'avoir que ce qu'on mérite; **~er** [dɪˈzɜːtəʳ] *n* déserteur *m*; **~ion** [dɪˈzɜːʃən] *n* (*MIL*) désertion *f*; (*LAW: of spouse*) abandon *m* du domicile conjugal; **~ island** *n* île déserte

deserve [dɪˈzɜːv] *vt* mériter; **deserving** *adj* (*person*) méritant(e); (*action, cause*) méritoire

design [dɪˈzaɪn] *n* (*sketch*) plan *m*, dessin *m*; (*layout, shape*) conception *f*, ligne *f*; (*pattern*) dessin *m*, motif(s) *m(pl)*; (*COMM, art*) design *m*, stylisme *m*; (*intention*) dessein *m* ♦ *vt* dessiner; élaborer; **~er** *n* (*TECH*) concepteur-projeteur *m*; (*ART*) dessinateur(-trice), designer *m*; (*fashion*) styliste *m/f*

desire [dɪˈzaɪəʳ] *n* désir *m* ♦ *vt* désirer

desk [dɛsk] *n* (*in office*) bureau *m*; (*for pupil*) pupitre *m*; (*BRIT: in shop, restaurant*) caisse *f*; (*in hotel, at airport*) réception *f*; **~-top publishing** *n* publication assistée par ordinateur, PAO *f*

desolate [ˈdɛsəlɪt] *adj* désolé(e); (*person*) affligé(e)

despair [dɪsˈpɛəʳ] *n* désespoir *m* ♦ *vi*: **to ~ of** désespérer de

despatch [dɪsˈpætʃ] *n, vt* = **dispatch**

desperate [ˈdɛspərɪt] *adj* désespéré(e); (*criminal*) prêt(e) à tout; **to be ~ for sth/ to do sth** avoir désespérément besoin de qch/de faire qch; **~ly** *adv* désespérément; (*very*) terriblement, extrêmement; **desperation** [dɛspəˈreɪʃən] *n* désespoir *m*; **in (sheer) desperation** en désespoir de cause

despicable [dɪsˈpɪkəbl] *adj* méprisable

despise [dɪsˈpaɪz] *vt* mépriser

despite [dɪsˈpaɪt] *prep* malgré, en dépit de

despondent [dɪsˈpɒndənt] *adj* découragé(e), abattu(e)

dessert [dɪˈzɜːt] *n* dessert *m*; **~spoon** *n* cuiller *f* à dessert

destination [dɛstɪˈneɪʃən] *n* destination *f*

destined [ˈdɛstɪnd] *adj*: **to be ~ to do/for sth** être destiné(e) à faire/à qch

destiny [ˈdɛstɪnɪ] *n* destinée *f*, destin *m*

destitute [ˈdɛstɪtjuːt] *adj* indigent(e)

destroy [dɪsˈtrɔɪ] *vt* détruire; (*injured horse*) abattre; (*dog*) faire piquer; **~er** *n* (*NAUT*) contre-torpilleur *m*

destruction [dɪsˈtrʌkʃən] *n* destruction *f*

detach [dɪˈtætʃ] *vt* détacher; **~ed** *adj* (*attitude, person*) détaché(e); **~ed house** *n* pavillon *m*, maison(nette) (individuelle); **~ment** *n* (*MIL*) détachement *m*; (*fig*) détachement, indifférence *f*

detail [ˈdiːteɪl] *n* détail *m* ♦ *vt* raconter en détail, énumérer; **in ~** en détail; **~ed** *adj* détaillé(e)

detain [dɪˈteɪn] *vt* retenir; (*in captivity*) détenir; (*in hospital*) hospitaliser

detect [dɪˈtɛkt] *vt* déceler, percevoir; (*MED, POLICE*) dépister; (*MIL, RADAR, TECH*) détecter; ~**ion** *n* découverte *f*; ~**ive** *n* agent *m* de la sûreté, policier *m*; **private ~ive** détective privé; ~**ive story** *n* roman policier

detention [dɪ'tenʃən] *n* détention *f*; (SCOL) retenue *f*, consigne *f*

deter [dɪ'təːʳ] *vt* dissuader

detergent [dɪ'təːdʒənt] *n* détergent *m*, détersif *m*

deteriorate [dɪ'tɪərɪəreɪt] *vi* se détériorer, se dégrader

determine [dɪ'təːmɪn] *vt* déterminer; **to ~ to do** résoudre de faire, se déterminer à faire; ~**d** *adj* (*person*) déterminé(e), décidé(e)

deterrent [dɪ'terənt] *n* effet *m* de dissuasion; force *f* de dissuasion

detest [dɪ'test] *vt* détester, avoir horreur de

detonate ['detəneɪt] *vt* faire détoner *or* exploser

detour ['diːtuəʳ] *n* détour *m*; (US: AUT: diversion) déviation *f*

detract [dɪ'trækt] *vt*: **to ~ from** (*quality, pleasure*) diminuer; (*reputation*) porter atteinte à

detriment ['detrɪmənt] *n*: **to the ~ of** au détriment de, au préjudice de; ~**al** [detrɪ'mentl] *adj*: ~**al to** préjudiciable *or* nuisible à

devaluation [dɪvæljuˈeɪʃən] *n* dévaluation *f*

devastate ['devəsteɪt] *vt* dévaster; ~**d** *adj* (*fig*) anéanti(e); **devastating** *adj* dévastateur(-trice); (*news*) accablant(e)

develop [dɪ'veləp] *vt* (*gen*) développer; (*disease*) commencer à souffrir de; (*resources*) mettre en valeur, exploiter ♦ *vi* se développer; (*situation, disease: evolve*) évoluer; (*facts, symptoms: appear*) se manifester, se produire; ~**ing country** pays *m* en voie de développement; **the machine has ~ed a fault** un problème s'est manifesté dans cette machine; ~**er** [dɪ'veləpəʳ] *n* (*also:* **property ~er**) promoteur *m*; ~**ment** [dɪ'veləpmənt] *n* développement *m*; (*of affair, case*) rebondissement *m*, fait(s) nouveau(x)

device [dɪ'vaɪs] *n* (*apparatus*) engin *m*, dispositif *m*

devil ['devl] *n* diable *m*; démon *m*

devious ['diːvɪəs] *adj* (*person*) sournois(e), dissimulé(e)

devise [dɪ'vaɪz] *vt* imaginer, concevoir

devoid [dɪ'vɔɪd] *adj*: ~ **of** dépourvu(e) de, dénué(e) de

devolution [diːvə'luːʃən] *n* (POL) décentralisation *f*

devote [dɪ'vəut] *vt*: **to ~ sth to** consacrer qch à; ~**d** [dɪ'vəutɪd] *adj* dévoué(e); **to be ~d to** (*book etc*) être consacré(e) à; (*person*) être très attaché(e) à; ~**e** [devəu'tiː] *n* (REL) adepte *m/f*; (MUS, SPORT) fervent(e); **devotion** *n* dévouement *m*, attachement *m*; (REL) dévotion *f*, piété *f*

devour [dɪ'vauəʳ] *vt* dévorer

devout [dɪ'vaut] *adj* pieux(-euse), dévot(e)

dew [djuː] *n* rosée *f*

diabetes [daɪə'biːtiːz] *n* diabète *m*; **diabetic** [daɪə'betɪk] *adj* diabétique ♦ *n* diabétique *m/f*

diabolical [daɪə'bɔlɪkl] (*inf*) *adj* (*weather*) atroce; (*behaviour*) infernal(e)

diagnosis [daɪəg'nəusɪs] (*pl* **diagnoses**) *n* diagnostic *m*

diagonal [daɪ'ægənl] *adj* diagonal(e) ♦ *n* diagonale *f*

diagram ['daɪəgræm] *n* diagramme *m*, schéma *m*

dial ['daɪəl] *n* cadran *m* ♦ *vt* (*number*) faire, composer

dialect ['daɪəlekt] *n* dialecte *m*

dialling code (BRIT) *n* indicatif *m* (téléphonique)

dialling tone (BRIT) *n* tonalité *f*

dialogue ['daɪəlɔg] *n* dialogue *m*

dial tone (US) *n* = **dialling tone**

diameter [daɪ'æmɪtəʳ] *n* diamètre *m*

diamond ['daɪəmənd] *n* diamant *m*; (*shape*) losange *m*; ~**s** *npl* (CARDS) carreau *m*

diaper ['daɪəpəʳ] (US) *n* couche *f*

diaphragm ['daɪəfræm] *n* diaphragme *m*

diarrhoea [daɪə'riːə] (US **diarrhea**) *n* diarrhée *f*

diary ['daɪərɪ] *n* (*daily account*) journal *m*;

(book) agenda m
dice [daɪs] n inv dé m ♦ vt (CULIN) couper en dés or en cubes
dictate [dɪk'teɪt] vt dicter; **dictation** n dictée f
dictator [dɪk'teɪtər] n dictateur m; **~ship** n dictature f
dictionary ['dɪkʃənrɪ] n dictionnaire m
did [dɪd] pt of **do**; **~n't = did not**
die [daɪ] vi mourir; **to be dying for sth** avoir une envie folle de qch; **to be dying to do sth** mourir d'envie de faire qch; **~ away** vi s'éteindre; **~ down** vi se calmer, s'apaiser; **~ out** vi disparaître
diesel ['diːzl] n (vehicle) diesel m; (also: **~ oil**) carburant m diesel, gas-oil m; **~ engine** n moteur m diesel
diet ['daɪət] n alimentation f; (restricted food) régime m ♦ vi (also: **be on a ~**) suivre un régime
differ ['dɪfər] vi (be different): **to ~ (from)** être différent (de); différer (de); (disagree): **to ~ (from sb over sth)** ne pas être d'accord (avec qn au sujet de qch); **~ence** n différence f; (quarrel) différend m, désaccord m; **~ent** adj différent(e); **~entiate** [dɪfə'renʃɪeɪt] vi: **to ~entiate (between)** faire une différence (entre)
difficult ['dɪfɪkəlt] adj difficile; **~y** n difficulté f
diffident ['dɪfɪdənt] adj qui manque de confiance or d'assurance
dig [dɪg] (pt, pp **dug**) vt (hole) creuser; (garden) bêcher ♦ n (prod) coup m de coude; (fig) coup de griffe or de patte; (archeological) fouilles fpl; **~ in** vi (MIL: also: **o.s. in**) se retrancher; **~ into** vt fus (savings) puiser dans; **to ~ one's nails into sth** enfoncer ses ongles dans qch; **~ up** vt déterrer
digest [vb daɪ'dʒɛst, n 'daɪdʒɛst] vt digérer ♦ n sommaire m, résumé m; **~ion** [dɪ'dʒɛstʃən] n digestion f
digit ['dɪdʒɪt] n (number) chiffre m; (finger) doigt m; **~al** adj digital(e), à affichage numérique or digital; **~al camera** appareil m photo numérique; **~al computer** cal-

culateur m numérique; **~al TV** télévision f numérique; **~al watch** montre f à affichage numérique
dignified ['dɪgnɪfaɪd] adj digne
dignity ['dɪgnɪtɪ] n dignité f
digress [daɪ'grɛs] vi: **to ~ from** s'écarter de, s'éloigner de
digs [dɪgz] (BRIT: inf) npl piaule f, chambre meublée
dilapidated [dɪ'læpɪdeɪtɪd] adj délabré(e)
dilemma [daɪ'lɛmə] n dilemme m
diligent ['dɪlɪdʒənt] adj appliqué(e)
dilute [daɪ'luːt] vt diluer
dim [dɪm] adj (light) faible; (memory, outline) vague, indécis(e); (room) sombre; (stupid) borné(e), obtus(e) ♦ vt (light) réduire, baisser; (US: AUT) mettre en code
dime [daɪm] (US) n = **10 cents**
dimension [daɪ'mɛnʃən] n dimension f
diminish [dɪ'mɪnɪʃ] vt, vi diminuer
diminutive [dɪ'mɪnjutɪv] adj minuscule, tout(e) petit(e)
dimmers ['dɪməz] (US) npl (AUT) phares mpl code inv; feux mpl de position
dimple ['dɪmpl] n fossette f
din [dɪn] n vacarme m
dine [daɪn] vi dîner; **~r** n (person) dîneur(-euse); (US: restaurant) petit restaurant
dinghy ['dɪŋgɪ] n youyou m; (also: **rubber ~**) canot m pneumatique; (also: **sailing ~**) voilier m, dériveur m
dingy ['dɪndʒɪ] adj miteux(-euse), minable
dining car (BRIT) n wagon-restaurant m
dining room n salle f à manger
dinner ['dɪnər] n dîner m; (lunch) déjeuner m; (public) banquet m; **~ jacket** n smoking m; **~ party** n dîner m; **~ time** n heure f du dîner; (midday) heure du déjeuner
dinosaur ['daɪnəsɔːr] n dinosaure m
dip [dɪp] n déclivité f; (in sea) baignade f, bain m; (CULIN) ≈ sauce f ♦ vt tremper, plonger; (BRIT: AUT: lights) mettre en code, baisser ♦ vi plonger
diploma [dɪ'pləumə] n diplôme m
diplomacy [dɪ'pləuməsɪ] n diplomatie f
diplomat ['dɪpləmæt] n diplomate m; **~ic**

[dɪplə'mætɪk] *adj* diplomatique

dipstick ['dɪpstɪk] *n* (AUT) jauge *f* de niveau d'huile

dipswitch ['dɪpswɪtʃ] (BRIT) *n* (AUT) interrupteur *m* de lumière réduite

dire [daɪəʳ] *adj* terrible, extrême, affreux(-euse)

direct [daɪ'rɛkt] *adj* direct(e) ♦ *vt* diriger, orienter; (*letter, remark*) adresser; (*film, programme*) réaliser; (*play*) mettre en scène; (*order*): **to ~ sb to do sth** ordonner à qn de faire qch ♦ *adv* directement; **can you ~ me to ...?** pouvez-vous m'indiquer le chemin de ...?; **~ debit** (BRIT) *n* prélèvement *m* automatique

direction [dɪ'rɛkʃən] *n* direction *f*; **~s** *npl* (*advice*) indications *fpl*; **sense of ~** sens *m* de l'orientation; **~s for use** mode *m* d'emploi

directly [dɪ'rɛktlɪ] *adv* (*in a straight line*) directement, tout droit; (*at once*) tout de suite, immédiatement

director [dɪ'rɛktəʳ] *n* directeur *m*; (THEATRE) metteur *m* en scène; (CINEMA, TV) réalisateur(-trice)

directory [dɪ'rɛktərɪ] *n* annuaire *m*; (COMPUT) répertoire *m*; **~ enquiries** (US **directory assistance**) *n* renseignements *mpl*

dirt [dəːt] *n* saleté *f*; crasse *f*; (*earth*) terre *f*, boue *f*; **~-cheap** *adj* très bon marché *inv*; **~y** *adj* sale ♦ *vt* salir; **~y trick** coup tordu

disability [dɪsə'bɪlɪtɪ] *n* invalidité *f*, infirmité *f*

disabled [dɪs'eɪbld] *adj* infirme, invalide ♦ *npl*: **the ~** les handicapés

disadvantage [dɪsəd'vɑːntɪdʒ] *n* désavantage *m*, inconvénient *m*

disagree [dɪsə'griː] *vi* (*be different*) ne pas concorder; (*be against, think otherwise*): **to ~ (with)** ne pas être d'accord (avec); **~able** *adj* désagréable; **~ment** *n* désaccord *m*, différend *m*

disallow ['dɪsə'lau] *vt* rejeter

disappear [dɪsə'pɪəʳ] *vi* disparaître; **~ance** *n* disparition *f*

disappoint [dɪsə'pɔɪnt] *vt* décevoir; **~ed** *adj* déçu(e); **~ing** *adj* décevant(e); **~ment** *n* déception *f*

disapproval [dɪsə'pruːvəl] *n* désapprobation *f*

disapprove [dɪsə'pruːv] *vi*: **to ~ (of)** désapprouver

disarmament [dɪs'ɑːməmənt] *n* désarmement *m*

disarray [dɪsə'reɪ] *n*: **in ~** (*army*) en déroute; (*organization*) en désarroi; (*hair, clothes*) en désordre

disaster [dɪ'zɑːstəʳ] *n* catastrophe *f*, désastre *m*; **disastrous** *adj* désastreux(-euse)

disband [dɪs'bænd] *vt* démobiliser; disperser ♦ *vi* se séparer; se disperser

disbelief ['dɪsbə'liːf] *n* incrédulité *f*

disc [dɪsk] *n* disque *m*; (COMPUT) = **disk**

discard [dɪs'kɑːd] *vt* (*old things*) se débarrasser de; (*fig*) écarter, renoncer à

discern [dɪ'səːn] *vt* discerner, distinguer; **~ing** *adj* perspicace

discharge [*vb* dɪs'tʃɑːdʒ, *n* 'dɪstʃɑːdʒ] *vt* décharger; (*duties*) s'acquitter de; (*patient*) renvoyer (chez lui); (*employee*) congédier, licencier; (*soldier*) rendre à la vie civile, réformer; (*defendant*) relaxer, élargir ♦ *n* décharge *f*; (*dismissal*) renvoi *m*; licenciement *m*; élargissement *m*; (MED) écoulement *m*

discipline ['dɪsɪplɪn] *n* discipline *f*

disc jockey *n* disc-jockey *m*

disclaim [dɪs'kleɪm] *vt* nier

disclose [dɪs'kləuz] *vt* révéler, divulguer; **disclosure** *n* révélation *f*

disco ['dɪskəu] *n abbr* = **discotheque**

discomfort [dɪs'kʌmfət] *n* malaise *m*, gêne *f*; (*lack of comfort*) manque *m* de confort

disconcert [dɪskən'səːt] *vt* déconcerter

disconnect [dɪskə'nɛkt] *vt* (ELEC, RADIO, *pipe*) débrancher; (TEL, *water*) couper

discontent [dɪskən'tɛnt] *n* mécontentement *m*; **~ed** *adj* mécontent(e)

discontinue [dɪskən'tɪnjuː] *vt* cesser, interrompre; **"~d"** (COMM) "fin de série"

discord ['dɪskɔːd] *n* discorde *f*, dissension

f; (MUS) dissonance f

discotheque ['dɪskəutek] n discothèque f

discount [n 'dɪskaunt, vb dɪs'kaunt] n remise f, rabais m ♦ vt (sum) faire une remise de; (fig) ne pas tenir compte de

discourage [dɪs'kʌrɪdʒ] vt décourager

discover [dɪs'kʌvəʳ] vt découvrir; ~**y** n découverte f

discredit [dɪs'krɛdɪt] vt (idea) mettre en doute; (person) discréditer

discreet [dɪs'kriːt] adj discret(-ète)

discrepancy [dɪs'krɛpənsɪ] n divergence f, contradiction f

discretion [dɪs'krɛʃən] n discrétion f; **use your own ~** à vous de juger

discriminate [dɪs'krɪmɪnɛɪt] vi: **to ~ between** établir une distinction entre, faire la différence entre; **to ~ against** pratiquer une discrimination contre; **discriminating** adj qui a du discernement; **discrimination** [dɪskrɪmɪ'neɪʃən] n discrimination f; (judgment) discernement m

discuss [dɪs'kʌs] vt discuter de; (debate) discuter; ~**ion** n discussion f

disdain [dɪs'deɪn] n dédain m

disease [dɪ'ziːz] n maladie f

disembark [dɪsɪm'bɑːk] vi débarquer

disentangle [dɪsɪn'tæŋgl] vt (wool, wire) démêler, débrouiller; (from wreckage) dégager

disfigure [dɪs'fɪgəʳ] vt défigurer

disgrace [dɪs'greɪs] n honte f; (disfavour) disgrâce f ♦ vt déshonorer, couvrir de honte; ~**ful** adj scandaleux(-euse), honteux(-euse)

disgruntled [dɪs'grʌntld] adj mécontent(e)

disguise [dɪs'gaɪz] n déguisement m ♦ vt déguiser; **in ~** déguisé(e)

disgust [dɪs'gʌst] n dégoût m, aversion f ♦ vt dégoûter, écœurer; ~**ing** adj dégoûtant(e); révoltant(e)

dish [dɪʃ] n plat m; **to do** or **wash the ~es** faire la vaisselle; **~ out** vt servir, distribuer; **~ up** vt servir; **~cloth** n (for washing) lavette f

dishearten [dɪs'hɑːtn] vt décourager

dishevelled [dɪ'ʃevəld] (US **disheveled**) adj ébouriffé(e); décoiffé(e); débraillé(e)

dishonest [dɪs'ɔnɪst] adj malhonnête

dishonour [dɪs'ɔnəʳ] (US **dishonor**) n déshonneur m; ~**able** adj (behaviour) déshonorant(e); (person) peu honorable

dishtowel ['dɪʃtauəl] (US) n torchon m

dishwasher ['dɪʃwɔʃəʳ] n lave-vaisselle m

disillusion [dɪsɪ'luːʒən] vt désabuser, désillusionner

disinfect [dɪsɪn'fekt] vt désinfecter; ~**ant** n désinfectant m

disintegrate [dɪs'ɪntɪgreɪt] vi se désintégrer

disinterested [dɪs'ɪntrəstɪd] adj désintéressé(e)

disjointed [dɪs'dʒɔɪntɪd] adj décousu(e), incohérent(e)

disk [dɪsk] n (COMPUT) disque m; (: floppy ~) disquette f; **single-/double-sided ~** disquette simple/double face; ~ **drive** n lecteur m de disquettes; ~**ette** [dɪs'kɛt] n disquette f, disque m souple

dislike [dɪs'laɪk] n aversion f, antipathie f ♦ vt ne pas aimer

dislocate ['dɪsləkeɪt] vt disloquer; déboiter

dislodge [dɪs'lɔdʒ] vt déplacer, faire bouger

disloyal [dɪs'lɔɪəl] adj déloyal(e)

dismal ['dɪzml] adj lugubre, maussade

dismantle [dɪs'mæntl] vt démonter

dismay [dɪs'meɪ] n consternation f

dismiss [dɪs'mɪs] vt congédier, renvoyer; (soldiers) faire rompre les rangs à; (idea) écarter; (LAW): **to ~ a case** rendre une fin de non-recevoir; ~**al** n renvoi m

dismount [dɪs'maunt] vi mettre pied à terre, descendre

disobedient [dɪsə'biːdɪənt] adj désobéissant(e)

disobey [dɪsə'beɪ] vt désobéir à

disorder [dɪs'ɔːdəʳ] n désordre m; (rioting) désordres mpl; (MED) troubles mpl; ~**ly** adj en désordre; désordonné(e)

disorientated [dɪs'ɔːrɪenteɪtɪd] adj désorienté(e)

disown [dɪs'əun] vt renier

disparaging [dɪs'pærɪdʒɪŋ] _adj_ désobligeant(e)

dispassionate [dɪs'pæʃənət] _adj_ calme, froid(e); impartial(e), objectif(-ive)

dispatch [dɪs'pætʃ] _vt_ expédier, envoyer ♦ _n_ envoi _m_, expédition _f_; (_MIL, PRESS_) dépêche _f_

dispel [dɪs'pɛl] _vt_ dissiper, chasser

dispense [dɪs'pɛns] _vt_ distribuer, administrer; ~ **with** _vt fus_ se passer de; ~**r** _n_ (_machine_) distributeur _m_; **dispensing chemist** (_BRIT_) _n_ pharmacie _f_

disperse [dɪs'pɜːs] _vt_ disperser ♦ _vi_ se disperser

dispirited [dɪs'pɪrɪtɪd] _adj_ découragé(e), déprimé(e)

displace [dɪs'pleɪs] _vt_ déplacer

display [dɪs'pleɪ] _n_ étalage _m_; déploiement _m_; affichage _m_; (_screen_) écran _m_, visuel _m_; (_of feeling_) manifestation _f_ ♦ _vt_ montrer; (_goods_) mettre à l'étalage, exposer; (_results, departure times_) afficher; (_pej_) faire étalage de

displease [dɪs'pliːz] _vt_ mécontenter, contrarier; ~**d** _adj_: ~**d with** mécontent(e) de; **displeasure** [dɪs'plɛʒəʳ] _n_ mécontentement _m_

disposable [dɪs'pəuzəbl] _adj_ (_pack etc_) jetable, à jeter; (_income_) disponible; ~ **nappy** (_BRIT_) _n_ couche _f_ à jeter, couche-culotte _f_

disposal [dɪs'pəuzl] _n_ (_of goods for sale_) vente _f_; (_of property_) disposition _f_, cession _f_; (_of rubbish_) enlèvement _m_; destruction _f_; **at one's** ~ à sa disposition

dispose [dɪs'pəuz] _vt_ disposer; ~ **of** _vt fus_ (_unwanted goods etc_) se débarrasser de, se défaire de; (_problem_) expédier; ~**d** _adj_: **to be** ~**d to do sth** être disposé(e) à faire qch; **disposition** [dɪspə'zɪʃən] _n_ disposition _f_; (_temperament_) naturel _m_

disprove [dɪs'pruːv] _vt_ réfuter

dispute [dɪs'pjuːt] _n_ discussion _f_; (_also:_ **industrial** ~) conflit _m_ ♦ _vt_ contester; (_matter_) discuter; (_victory_) disputer

disqualify [dɪs'kwɔlɪfaɪ] _vt_ (_SPORT_) disqualifier; **to** ~ **sb for sth/from doing** rendre qn inapte à qch/à faire

disquiet [dɪs'kwaɪət] _n_ inquiétude _f_, trouble _m_

disregard [dɪsrɪ'ɡɑːd] _vt_ ne pas tenir compte de

disrepair ['dɪsrɪ'pɛəʳ] _n_: **to fall into** ~ (_building_) tomber en ruine

disreputable [dɪs'rɛpjutəbl] _adj_ (_person_) de mauvaise réputation; (_behaviour_) déshonorant(e)

disrespectful [dɪsrɪ'spɛktful] _adj_ irrespectueux(-euse)

disrupt [dɪs'rʌpt] _vt_ (_plans_) déranger; (_conversation_) interrompre

dissatisfied [dɪs'sætɪsfaɪd] _adj_: ~ **(with)** insatisfait(e) (de)

dissect [dɪ'sɛkt] _vt_ disséquer

dissent [dɪ'sɛnt] _n_ dissentiment _m_, différence _f_ d'opinion

dissertation [dɪsə'teɪʃən] _n_ mémoire _m_

disservice [dɪs'səːvɪs] _n_: **to do sb a** ~ rendre un mauvais service à qn

dissimilar [dɪ'sɪmɪləʳ] _adj_: ~ **(to)** dissemblable (à), différent(e) (de)

dissipate ['dɪsɪpeɪt] _vt_ dissiper; (_money, efforts_) disperser

dissolute ['dɪsəluːt] _adj_ débauché(e), dissolu(e)

dissolve [dɪ'zɔlv] _vt_ dissoudre ♦ _vi_ se dissoudre, fondre; **to** ~ **in(to) tears** fondre en larmes

distance ['dɪstns] _n_ distance _f_; **in the** ~ au loin

distant ['dɪstnt] _adj_ lointain(e), éloigné(e); (_manner_) distant(e), froid(e)

distaste [dɪs'teɪst] _n_ dégoût _m_; ~**ful** _adj_ déplaisant(e), désagréable

distended [dɪs'tɛndɪd] _adj_ (_stomach_) dilaté(e)

distil [dɪs'tɪl] (_US_ **distill**) _vt_ distiller; ~**lery** _n_ distillerie _f_

distinct [dɪs'tɪŋkt] _adj_ distinct(e); (_clear_) marqué(e); **as** ~ **from** par opposition à; ~**ion** _n_ distinction _f_; (_in exam_) mention _f_ très bien; ~**ive** _adj_ distinctif(-ive)

distinguish [dɪs'tɪŋgwɪʃ] _vt_ distinguer; ~**ed** _adj_ (_eminent_) distingué(e); ~**ing** _adj_ (feature) distinctif(-ive), caractéristique

distort [dɪs'tɔ:t] vt déformer

distract [dɪs'trækt] vt distraire, déranger; ~ed adj distrait(e); (anxious) éperdu(e), égaré(e); ~ion n distraction f; égarement m

distraught [dɪs'trɔ:t] adj éperdu(e)

distress [dɪs'trɛs] n détresse f ♦ vt affliger; ~ing adj douloureux(-euse), pénible

distribute [dɪs'trɪbju:t] vt distribuer; distribution [dɪstrɪ'bju:ʃən] n distribution f; distributor n distributeur m

district ['dɪstrɪkt] n (of country) région f; (of town) quartier m; (ADMIN) district m; ~ attorney (US) n ≈ procureur m de la République; ~ nurse (BRIT) n infirmière visiteuse

distrust [dɪs'trʌst] n méfiance f ♦ vt se méfier de

disturb [dɪs'tə:b] vt troubler; (inconvenience) déranger; ~ance n dérangement m; (violent event, political etc) troubles mpl; ~ed adj (worried, upset) agité(e), troublé(e); to be emotionally ~ed avoir des problèmes affectifs; ~ing adj troublant(e), inquiétant(e)

disuse [dɪs'ju:s] n: to fall into ~ tomber en désuétude; ~d [dɪs'ju:zd] adj désaffecté(e)

ditch [dɪtʃ] n fossé m; (irrigation) rigole f ♦ vt (inf) abandonner; (person) plaquer

dither ['dɪðəʳ] vi hésiter

ditto ['dɪtəu] adv idem

dive [daɪv] n plongeon m; (of submarine) plongée f ♦ vi plonger; to ~ into (bag, drawer etc) plonger la main dans; (shop, car etc) se précipiter dans; ~r n plongeur m

diversion [daɪ'və:ʃən] n (BRIT: AUT) déviation f; (distraction, MIL) diversion f

divert [daɪ'və:t] vt (funds, BRIT: traffic) dévier; (river, attention) détourner

divide [dɪ'vaɪd] vt diviser; (separate) séparer ♦ vi se diviser; ~d highway (US) n route f à quatre voies

dividend ['dɪvɪdɛnd] n dividende m

divine [dɪ'vaɪn] adj divin(e)

diving ['daɪvɪŋ] n plongée (sous-marine); ~ board n plongeoir m

divinity [dɪ'vɪnɪtɪ] n divinité f; (SCOL) théologie f

division [dɪ'vɪʒən] n division f

divorce [dɪ'vɔ:s] n divorce m ♦ vt divorcer d'avec; (dissociate) séparer; ~d adj divorcé(e); ~e n divorcé(e)

D.I.Y. (BRIT) n abbr = **do-it-yourself**

dizzy ['dɪzɪ] adj: to make sb ~ donner le vertige à qn; to feel ~ avoir la tête qui tourne

DJ n abbr = **disc jockey**

DNA fingerprinting n technique f des empreintes génétiques

KEYWORD

do [du:] (pt did, pp done) n (inf: party etc) soirée f, fête f

♦ vb 1 (in negative constructions) non traduit; I don't understand je ne comprends pas

2 (to form questions) non traduit; didn't you know? vous ne le saviez pas?; why didn't you come? pourquoi n'êtes-vous pas venu?

3 (for emphasis, in polite expressions): she does seem rather late je trouve qu'elle est bien en retard; do sit down/help yourself asseyez-vous/servez-vous je vous en prie

4 (used to avoid repeating vb): she swims better than I do elle nage mieux que moi; do you agree? - yes, I do/no, I don't vous êtes d'accord? - oui/non; she lives in Glasgow - so do I elle habite Glasgow - moi aussi; who broke it? - I did qui l'a cassé? - c'est moi

5 (in question tags): he laughed, didn't he? il a ri, n'est-ce pas?; I don't know him, do I? je ne crois pas le connaître

♦ vt (gen: carry out, perform etc) faire; what are you doing tonight? qu'est-ce que vous faites ce soir?; to do the cooking/washing-up faire la cuisine/la vaisselle; to do one's teeth/hair/nails se brosser les dents/se coiffer/se faire les ongles; the

car was doing 100 ≃ la voiture faisait du 160 (à l'heure)
♦ *vi* 1 (*act, behave*) faire; **do as I do** faites comme moi

2 (*get on, fare*) marcher; **the firm is doing well** l'entreprise marche bien; **how do you do?** comment allez-vous?; (*on being introduced*) enchanté(e)!

3 (*suit*) aller; **will it do?** est-ce que ça ira?

4 (*be sufficient*) suffire, aller; **will £10 do?** est-ce que 10 livres suffiront?; **that'll do** ça suffit, ça ira; **that'll do!** (*in annoyance*) ça va *or* suffit comme ça!; **to make do (with)** se contenter (de)

do away with *vt fus* supprimer

do up *vt* (*laces, dress*) attacher; (*buttons*) boutonner; (*zip*) fermer; (*renovate: room*) refaire; (*: house*) remettre à neuf

do with *vt fus* (*need*): **I could do with a drink/some help** quelque chose à boire/un peu d'aide ne serait pas de refus; (*be connected*): **that has nothing to do with you** cela ne vous concerne pas; **I won't have anything to do with it** je ne veux pas m'en mêler

do without *vi* s'en passer ♦ *vt fus* se passer de

dock [dɔk] *n* dock *m*; (*LAW*) banc *m* des accusés ♦ *vi* se mettre à quai; (*SPACE*) s'arrimer; ~**er** *n* docker *m*; ~**yard** *n* chantier *m* de construction navale

doctor ['dɔktər] *n* médecin *m*, docteur *m*; (*PhD etc*) docteur ♦ *vt* (*drink*) frelater; **D~ of Philosophy** (*degree*) doctorat *m*; (*person*) Docteur *m* en Droit *or* Lettres *etc*, titulaire *m/f* d'un doctorat

document ['dɔkjumənt] *n* document *m*; ~**ary** [dɔkju'mɛntəri] *adj* documentaire ♦ *n* documentaire

dodge [dɔdʒ] *n* truc *m*; combine *f* ♦ *vt* esquiver, éviter

dodgems ['dɔdʒəmz] (*BRIT*) *npl* autos tamponneuses

doe [dəu] *n* (*deer*) biche *f*; (*rabbit*) lapine *f*

does [dʌz] *vb see* **do**; ~**n't** = **does not**

dog [dɔg] *n* chien(ne) ♦ *vt* suivre de près;

poursuivre, harceler; ~ **collar** *n* collier *m* de chien; (*fig*) faux-col *m* d'ecclésiastique; ~-**eared** *adj* corné(e); ~**ged** ['dɔgɪd] *adj* obstiné(e), opiniâtre; ~**sbody** *n* bonne *f* à tout faire, tâcheron *m*

doings ['duɪŋz] *npl* activités *fpl*

do-it-yourself ['du:ɪtjɔ:'sɛlf] *n* bricolage *m*

doldrums ['dɔldrəmz] *npl*: **to be in the ~** avoir le cafard; (*business*) être dans le marasme

dole [dəul] *n* (*BRIT: payment*) allocation *f* de chômage; **on the ~** au chômage; ~ **out** *vt* donner au compte-goutte

doll [dɔl] *n* poupée *f*

dollar ['dɔlər] *n* dollar *m*

dolled up (*inf*) *adj*: **(all) ~** sur son trente et un

dolphin ['dɔlfɪn] *n* dauphin *m*

dome [dəum] *n* dôme *m*

domestic [də'mɛstɪk] *adj* (*task, appliances*) ménager(-ère); (*of country: trade, situation etc*) intérieur(e); (*animal*) domestique; ~**ated** *adj* (*animal*) domestiqué(e); (*husband*) pantouflard(e)

dominate ['dɔmɪneɪt] *vt* dominer

domineering [dɔmɪ'nɪərɪŋ] *adj* dominateur(-trice), autoritaire

dominion [də'mɪnɪən] *n* (*territory*) territoire *m*; **to have ~ over** contrôler

domino ['dɔmɪnəu] (*pl* ~**es**) *n* domino *m*; ~**es** *n* (*game*) dominos *mpl*

don [dɔn] (*BRIT*) *n* professeur *m* d'université

donate [də'neɪt] *vt* faire don de, donner

done [dʌn] *pp of* **do**

donkey ['dɔŋkɪ] *n* âne *m*

donor ['dəunər] *n* (*of blood etc*) donneur(-euse); (*to charity*) donateur(-trice); ~ **card** *n* carte *f* de don d'organes

don't [dəunt] *vb* = **do not**

donut ['dəunʌt] (*US*) *n* = **doughnut**

doodle ['du:dl] *vi* griffonner, gribouiller

doom [du:m] *n* destin *m* ♦ *vt*: **to be ~ed (to failure)** être voué(e) à l'échec

door [dɔ:r] *n* porte *f*; (*RAIL, car*) portière *f*; ~**bell** *n* sonnette *f*; ~**handle** *n* poignée *f* de la porte; (*car*) poignée de portière; ~**man** (*irreg*) *n* (*in hotel*) portier *m*; ~**mat**

n paillasson *m*; ~**step** *n* pas *m* de (la) porte, seuil *m*; ~**way** *n* (embrasure *f* de la) porte *f*

dope [dəup] *n* (*inf*: *drug*) drogue *f*; (: *person*) andouille *f* ♦ *vt* (*horse etc*) doper

dormant ['dɔːmənt] *adj* assoupi(e), en veilleuse

dormitory ['dɔːmɪtrɪ] *n* dortoir *m*; (*US: building*) résidence *f* universitaire

dormouse ['dɔːmaus] (*pl* **dormice**) *n* loir *m*

DOS [dɔs] *n abbr* (= *disk operating system*) DOS

dose [dəus] *n* dose *f*

dosh [dɔʃ] (*inf*) *n* fric *m*

doss house ['dɔs-] (*BRIT*) *n* asile *m* de nuit

dot [dɔt] *n* point *m*; (*on material*) pois *m* ♦ *vt*: ~**ted with** parsemé(e) de; **on the ~** à l'heure tapante *or* pile; ~**ted line** *n* pointillé(s) *m(pl)*

double ['dʌbl] *adj* double ♦ *adv* (*twice*): **to cost ~** (**sth**) coûter le double (de qch) *or* deux fois plus (que qch) ♦ *n* double *m* ♦ *vt* doubler; (*fold*) plier en deux ♦ *vi* doubler; ~**s** *n* (*TENNIS*) double *m*; **on** (*BRIT*) **at the ~** au pas de course; ~ **bass** (*BRIT*) *n* contrebasse *f*; ~ **bed** *n* grand lit; ~ **bend** (*BRIT*) *n* virage *m* en S; ~**breasted** *adj* croisé(e); ~**click** *vi* (*COMPUT*) double-cliquer; ~**cross** *vt* doubler, trahir; ~**decker** *n* autobus *m* à impériale; ~ **glazing** (*BRIT*) *n* double vitrage *m*; ~ **room** *n* chambre *f* pour deux personnes; **doubly** *adv* doublement, deux fois plus

doubt [daut] *n* doute *m* ♦ *vt* douter de; **to ~ that** douter que; ~**ful** *adj* douteux(-euse); (*person*) incertain(e); ~**less** *adv* sans doute, sûrement

dough [dəu] *n* pâte *f*; ~**nut** (*US* **donut**) *n* beignet *m*

dove [dʌv] *n* colombe *f*

Dover ['dəuvə'] *n* Douvres

dovetail ['dʌvteɪl] *vi* (*fig*) concorder

dowdy ['daudɪ] *adj* démodé(e); mal fagoté(e) (*inf*)

down [daun] *n* (*soft feathers*) duvet *m*

♦ *adv* en bas, vers le bas; (*on the ground*) par terre ♦ *prep* en bas de ♦ *vt* (*inf*: *drink, food*) s'envoyer; ~ **with X!** à bas X!; ~**and-out** *n* clochard(e); ~**at-heel** *adj* (*fig*) miteux(-euse); ~**cast** *adj* démoralisé(e); ~**fall** *n* chute *f*; ruine *f*; ~**hearted** *adj* découragé(e); ~**hill** *adv*: **to go ~hill** descendre; (*fig*) péricliter; ~**load** *vt* (*COMPUT*) télécharger; ~ **payment** *n* acompte *m*; ~**pour** *n* pluie torrentielle, déluge *m*; ~**right** *adj* (*lie etc*) effronté(e); (*refusal*) catégorique; ~**size** *vt* (*ECON*) réduire ses effectifs

---

Downing Street

i **Downing Street** est une rue de Westminster (à Londres) où se trouve la résidence officielle du Premier ministre (numéro 10) et celle du ministre des Finances (numéro 11). Le nom **"Downing Street"** est souvent utilisé pour désigner le gouvernement britannique.

Down's syndrome [daunz-] *n* (*MED*) trisomie *f*

down: ~**stairs** *adv* au rez-de-chaussée; à l'étage inférieur; ~**stream** *adv* en aval; ~**to-earth** *adj* terre à terre *inv*; ~**town** *adv* en ville; ~ **under** *adv* en Australie/Nouvelle-Zélande; ~**ward** *adj*, *adv* vers le bas; ~**wards** *adv* vers le bas

dowry ['dauri] *n* dot *f*

doz. *abbr* = **dozen**

doze [dəuz] *vi* sommeiller; ~ **off** *vi* s'assoupir

dozen ['dʌzn] *n* douzaine *f*; **a ~ books** une douzaine de livres; ~**s of** des centaines de

Dr. *abbr* = **doctor; drive**

drab [dræb] *adj* terne, morne

draft [drɑːft] *n* ébauche *f*; (*of letter, essay etc*) brouillon *m*; (*COMM*) traite *f*; (*US: call-up*) conscription *f* ♦ *vt* faire le brouillon *or* un projet de; (*MIL: send*) détacher; *see also* **draught**

draftsman ['drɑːftsmən] (*irreg*) (*US*) *n* = **draughtsman**

drag [dræg] *vt* traîner; (*river*) draguer ♦ *vi*

traîner ♦ n (inf) casse-pieds m/f; (women's clothing): **in ~** (en) travesti; **~ on** vi s'éterniser

dragon ['drægn] n dragon m

dragonfly ['drægənflaɪ] n libellule f

drain [dreɪn] n égout m, canalisation f; (on resources) saignée f ♦ vt (land, marshes etc) drainer, assécher; (vegetables) égoutter; (glass) vider ♦ vi (water) s'écouler; **~age** n drainage m; système m d'égouts or de canalisations; **~ing board** (US **drain board**) n égouttoir m; **~pipe** n tuyau m d'écoulement

drama ['drɑːmə] n (art) théâtre m, art m dramatique; (play) pièce f (de théâtre); (event) drame m; **~tic** [drə'mætɪk] adj dramatique; spectaculaire; **~tist** ['dræmətɪst] n auteur m dramatique; **~tize** ['dræmətaɪz] vt (events) dramatiser; (adapt: for TV/cinema) adapter pour la télévision/pour l'écran

drank [dræŋk] pt of **drink**

drape [dreɪp] vt draper; **~s** (US) npl rideaux mpl

drastic ['dræstɪk] adj sévère; énergique; (change) radical(e)

draught [drɑːft] (US **draft**) n courant m d'air; (NAUT) tirant m d'eau; **on ~** (beer) à la pression; **~board** (BRIT) n damier m; **~s** (BRIT) n (jeu m de) dames fpl

draughtsman ['drɑːftsmən] (irreg) n dessinateur(-trice) (industriel(le))

draw [drɔː] (pt **drew**, pp **drawn**) vt tirer; (tooth) arracher, extraire; (attract) attirer; (picture) dessiner; (line, circle) tracer; (money) retirer; (wages) toucher ♦ vi (SPORT) faire match nul ♦ n match nul; (lottery) tirage m au sort; loterie f; **to ~ near** s'approcher; approcher; **~ out** vi (lengthen) s'allonger ♦ vt (money) retirer; **~ up** vi (stop) s'arrêter ♦ vt (chair) approcher; (document) établir, dresser; **~back** n inconvénient m, désavantage m; **~bridge** n pont-levis m

drawer [drɔːr] n tiroir m

drawing ['drɔːɪŋ] n dessin m; **~ board** n planche f à dessin; **~ pin** (BRIT) n punaise

f; **~ room** n salon m

drawl [drɔːl] n accent traînant

drawn [drɔːn] pp of **draw**

dread [dred] n terreur f, effroi m ♦ vt redouter, appréhender; **~ful** adj affreux(-euse)

dream [driːm] (pt, pp **dreamed** or **dreamt**) n rêve m ♦ vt, vi rêver; **~y** adj rêveur(-euse); (music) langoureux(-euse)

dreary ['drɪərɪ] adj morne; monotone

dredge [dredʒ] vt draguer

dregs [dregz] npl lie f

drench [drentʃ] vt tremper

dress [dres] n robe f; (no pl: clothing) habillement m, tenue f ♦ vi s'habiller ♦ vt habiller; (wound) panser; **to get ~ed** s'habiller; **~ up** vi s'habiller; (in fancy ~) se déguiser; **~ circle** (BRIT) n (THEATRE) premier balcon; **~er** n (furniture) vaisselier m; (: US) coiffeuse f, commode f; **~ing** n (MED) pansement m; (CULIN) sauce f, assaisonnement m; **~ing gown** (BRIT) n robe f de chambre; **~ing room** n (THEATRE) loge f; (SPORT) vestiaire m; **~ing table** n coiffeuse f; **~maker** n couturière f; **~ rehearsal** n (répétition) générale f

drew [druː] pt of **draw**

dribble ['drɪbl] vi (baby) baver ♦ vt (ball) dribbler

dried [draɪd] adj (fruit, beans) sec (sèche); (eggs, milk) en poudre

drier ['draɪər] n = **dryer**

drift [drɪft] n (of current etc) force f; direction f, mouvement m; (of snow) rafale f; (: on ground) congère f; (general meaning) sens (général) ♦ vi (boat) aller à la dérive, dériver; (sand, snow) s'amonceler, s'entasser; **~wood** n bois flotté

drill [drɪl] n perceuse f; (~ bit) foret m, mèche f; (of dentist) roulette f, fraise f; (MIL) exercice m ♦ vt percer; (troops) entraîner ♦ vi (for oil) faire un or des forage(s)

drink [drɪŋk] (pt **drank**, pp **drunk**) n boisson f; (alcoholic) verre m ♦ vt, vi boire; **to have a ~** boire quelque chose, boire un verre; prendre l'apéritif; **a ~ of water** un verre d'eau; ~er n buveur(-euse); ~ing water n eau f potable

drip [drɪp] n goutte f; (MED) goutte-à-goutte m inv, perfusion f ♦ vi tomber goutte à goutte; (tap) goutter; ~-dry adj (shirt) sans repassage; ~ping n graisse f (de rôti)

drive [draɪv] (pt **drove**, pp **driven**) n promenade f or trajet m en voiture; (also: ~way) allée f; (energy) dynamisme m, énergie f; (push) effort (concerté), campagne f; (also: **disk** ~) lecteur m de disquettes ♦ vt conduire; (push) chasser, pousser; (TECH: motor, wheel) faire fonctionner, entraîner; (nail, stake etc): **to ~ sth into sth** enfoncer qch dans qch ♦ vi (AUT: at controls) conduire; (: travel) aller en voiture; **left-/right-hand** ~ conduite f à gauche/droite; **to ~ sb mad** rendre qn fou (folle); **to ~ sb home/to the airport** reconduire chez lui/conduire qn à l'aéroport; ~-**by** shooting n (tentative d')assassinat par coups de feu tirés d'un voiture

drivel ['drɪvl] (inf) n idioties fpl

driver ['draɪvər] n conducteur(-trice); (of taxi, bus) chauffeur m; ~'**s license** n (US) permis m de conduire

driveway ['draɪvweɪ] n allée f

driving ['draɪvɪŋ] n conduite f; ~ **instructor** n moniteur m d'auto-école; ~ **lesson** n leçon f de conduite; ~ **licence** n (BRIT) permis m de conduire; ~ **school** n auto-école f; ~ **test** n examen m du permis de conduire

drizzle ['drɪzl] n bruine f, crachin m

drool [druːl] vi baver

droop [druːp] vi (shoulders) tomber; (head) pencher; (flower) pencher la tête

drop [drɒp] n goutte f; (fall) baisse f; (also: **parachute** ~) saut m ♦ vt laisser tomber; (voice, eyes, price) baisser; (set down from car) déposer ♦ vi tomber; ~**s** npl (MED) gouttes; ~ **off** vi (sleep) s'assoupir ♦ vt (passenger) déposer; ~ **out** vi (withdraw) se retirer; (student etc) abandonner, décrocher; ~**out** n marginal(e); ~**per** n

compte-gouttes m inv; ~**pings** npl crottes fpl

drought [draut] n sécheresse f

drove [drəuv] pt of **drive**

drown [draun] vt noyer ♦ vi se noyer

drowsy ['drauzɪ] adj somnolent(e)

drug [drʌg] n médicament m; (narcotic) drogue f ♦ vt droguer; **to be on ~s** se droguer; ~ **addict** n toxicomane m/f; ~**gist** (US) n pharmacien(ne)-droguiste; ~**store** (US) n pharmacie-droguerie f, drugstore m

drum [drʌm] n tambour m; (for oil, petrol) bidon m; ~**s** npl (kit) batterie f; ~**mer** n (joueur m de) tambour m

drunk [drʌŋk] pp of **drink** ♦ adj ivre, soûl(e) ♦ n (also: ~**ard**) ivrogne m/f; ~**en** adj (person) ivre, soûl(e); (rage, stupor) ivrogne, d'ivrogne

dry [draɪ] adj sec (sèche); (day) sans pluie; (humour) pince-sans-rire inv; (lake, riverbed, well) à sec ♦ vt sécher; (clothes) faire sécher ♦ vi sécher; ~ **up** vi tarir; ~-**cleaner's** n teinturerie f; ~**er** n séchoir m; (spin-dryer) essoreuse f; ~**ness** n sécheresse f; ~ **rot** n pourriture sèche (du bois)

DSS n abbr (= Department of Social Security) ≈ Sécurité sociale

DTP n abbr (= desk-top publishing) PAO f

dual ['djuəl] adj double; ~ **carriageway** (BRIT) n route f à quatre voies or à chaussées séparées; ~-**purpose** adj à double usage

dubbed [dʌbd] adj (CINEMA) doublé(e)

dubious ['djuːbɪəs] adj hésitant(e), incertain(e); (reputation, company) douteux(-euse)

duchess ['dʌtʃɪs] n duchesse f

duck [dʌk] n canard m ♦ vi se baisser vivement, baisser subitement la tête; ~**ling** ['dʌklɪŋ] n caneton m

duct [dʌkt] n conduite f, canalisation f; (ANAT) conduit m

dud [dʌd] n (object, tool): **it's a ~** c'est de la camelote, ça ne marche pas ♦ adj: ~ **cheque** (BRIT) chèque sans provision

due [djuː] *adj* dû (due); (*expected*) attendu(e); (*fitting*) qui convient ♦ *n*: **to give sb his** (*or* **her**) **~** être juste envers qn ♦ *adv*: **~ north** droit vers le nord; **~s** *npl* (*for club, union*) cotisation *f*; **in ~ course** en temps utile *or* voulu; finalement; **~ to** (*due*) à; causé(e) par; **he's ~ to finish tomorrow** normalement il doit finir demain

duet [djuːˈɛt] *n* duo *m*

duffel bag [ˈdʌfl-] *n* sac *m* marin

duffel coat *n* duffel-coat *m*

dug [dʌg] *pt, pp of* **dig**

duke [djuːk] *n* duc *m*

dull [dʌl] *adj* terne, morne; (*boring*) ennuyeux(-euse); (*sound, pain*) sourd(e); (*weather, day*) gris(e), maussade ♦ *vt* (*pain, grief*) atténuer; (*mind, senses*) engourdir

duly [ˈdjuːli] *adv* (*on time*) en temps voulu; (*as expected*) comme il se doit

dumb [dʌm] *adj* muet(te); (*stupid*) bête; **~founded** *adj* sidéré(e)

dummy [ˈdʌmi] *n* (*tailor's model*) mannequin *m*; (*mock-up*) factice *m*, maquette *f*; (*BRIT: for baby*) tétine *f* ♦ *adj* faux (fausse), factice

dump [dʌmp] *n* (*also:* **rubbish ~**) décharge (publique); (*pej*) trou *m* ♦ *vt* (*put down*) déposer; déverser; (*get rid of*) se débarrasser de; (*COMPUT: data*) vider

dumpling [ˈdʌmplɪŋ] *n* boulette *f* (de pâte)

dumpy [ˈdʌmpɪ] *adj* boulot(te)

dunce [dʌns] *n* âne *m*, cancre *m*

dune [djuːn] *n* dune *f*

dung [dʌŋ] *n* fumier *m*

dungarees [dʌŋɡəˈriːz] *npl* salopette *f*; bleu(s) *m(pl)*

dungeon [ˈdʌndʒən] *n* cachot *m*

duplex [ˈdjuːplɛks] (*US*) *n* maison jumelée; (*apartment*) duplex *m*

duplicate [*n* ˈdjuːplɪkət, *vb* ˈdjuːplɪkeɪt] *n* double *m* ♦ *vt* faire un double de; (*on machine*) polycopier; photocopier; **in ~** en deux exemplaires

durable [ˈdjuərəbl] *adj* durable; (*clothes, metal*) résistant(e), solide

duration [djuəˈreɪʃən] *n* durée *f*

during [ˈdjuərɪŋ] *prep* pendant, au cours de

dusk [dʌsk] *n* crépuscule *m*

dust [dʌst] *n* poussière *f* ♦ *vt* (*furniture*) épousseter, essuyer; (*cake etc*): **to ~ with** saupoudrer de; **~bin** (*BRIT*) *n* poubelle *f*; **~er** *n* chiffon *m*; **~man** (*BRIT*) (*irreg*) *n* boueux *m*, éboueur *m*; **~y** *adj* poussiéreux(-euse)

Dutch [dʌtʃ] *adj* hollandais(e), néerlandais(e) ♦ *n* (*LING*) hollandais *m* ♦ *adv* (*inf*): **to go ~** partager les frais; **the ~** *npl* (*people*) les Hollandais; **~man** (*irreg*) *n* Hollandais; **~woman** (*irreg*) *n* Hollandaise *f*

duty [ˈdjuːti] *n* devoir *m*; (*tax*) droit *m*, taxe *f*; **on ~** de service; (*at night etc*) de garde; **off ~** libre, pas de service *or* de garde; **~-free** *adj* exempté(e) de douane, hors taxe *inv*

duvet [ˈduːveɪ] (*BRIT*) *n* couette *f*

DVD *n abbr* (= *digital versatile disc*) DVD *m*

dwarf [dwɔːf] (*pl* **dwarves**) *n* nain(e) ♦ *vt* écraser

dwell [dwɛl] (*pt, pp* **dwelt**) *vi* demeurer; **~ on** *vt fus* s'appesantir sur

dwindle [ˈdwɪndl] *vi* diminuer, décroître

dye [daɪ] *n* teinture *f* ♦ *vt* teindre

dying [ˈdaɪɪŋ] *adj* mourant(e), agonisant(e)

dyke [daɪk] (*BRIT*) *n* digue *f*

dynamic [daɪˈnæmɪk] *adj* dynamique

dynamite [ˈdaɪnəmaɪt] *n* dynamite *f*

dynamo [ˈdaɪnəməu] *n* dynamo *f*

dyslexia [dɪsˈlɛksɪə] *n* dyslexie *f*

E, e

E [iː] *n* (*MUS*) mi *m*

each [iːtʃ] *adj* chaque ♦ *pron* chacun(e); **~ other** l'un(e) l'autre; **they hate ~ other** ils se détestent (mutuellement); **you are jealous of ~ other** vous êtes jaloux l'un de l'autre; **they have 2 books ~** ils ont 2 livres chacun

eager [ˈiːɡər] *adj* (*keen*) avide; **to be ~ to do sth** avoir très envie de faire qch; **to be**

~ for désirer vivement, être avide de

eagle ['i:gl] n aigle m

ear [iəʳ] n oreille f; (of corn) épi m; **~ache** n mal m aux oreilles; **~drum** n tympan m

earl [ə:l] (BRIT) n comte m

earlier ['ə:liəʳ] adj (date etc) plus rapproché(e); (edition, fashion etc) plus ancien(ne), antérieur(e) ♦ adv plus tôt

early ['ə:li] adv tôt, de bonne heure; (ahead of time) en avance; (near the beginning) au début ♦ adj qui se manifeste (or se fait) tôt or de bonne heure; (work) de jeunesse; (settler, Christian) premier(-ère); (reply) rapide; (death) prématuré(e); **to have an ~ night** se coucher tôt or de bonne heure; **in the ~ or ~ in the spring/19th century** au début du printemps/19ème siècle; **~ retirement** n: **to take ~ retirement** prendre sa retraite anticipée

earmark ['iəmɑ:k] vt: **to ~ sth for** réserver or destiner qch à

earn [ə:n] vt gagner; (COMM: yield) rapporter

earnest ['ə:nist] adj sérieux(-euse); **in ~** ♦ adv sérieusement

earnings ['ə:niŋz] npl salaire m; (of company) bénéfices mpl

ear: **~phones** npl écouteurs mpl; **~ring** n boucle f d'oreille; **~shot** n: **within ~shot** à portée de voix

earth [ə:θ] n (gen, also BRIT: ELEC) terre f ♦ vt relier à la terre; **~enware** n poterie f; faïence f; **~quake** n tremblement m de terre, séisme m; **~y** adj (vulgar: humour) truculent(e)

ease [i:z] n facilité f, aisance f; (comfort) bien-être m ♦ vt (soothe) calmer; (loosen) relâcher, détendre; **to ~ sth in/out** faire pénétrer/sortir qch délicatement or avec douceur; faciliter la pénétration/la sortie de qch; **at ~!** (MIL) repos!; **~ off or up** vi diminuer; (slow down) ralentir

easel ['i:zl] n chevalet m

easily ['i:zili] adv facilement

east [i:st] n est m ♦ adj (wind) d'est; (side) est inv ♦ adv à l'est, vers l'est; **the E~** l'Orient m; (POL) les pays mpl de l'Est

Easter ['i:stəʳ] n Pâques fpl; **~ egg** n œuf m de Pâques

east: **~erly** ['i:stəli] adj (wind) d'est; (direction) est inv; (point) à l'est; **~ern** ['i:stən] adj de l'est, oriental(e); **~ward(s)** ['i:stwəd(z)] adv vers l'est, à l'est

easy ['i:zi] adj facile; (manner) aisé(e) ♦ adv: **to take it** or **things ~** ne pas se fatiguer; (not worry) ne pas (trop) s'en faire; **~ chair** n fauteuil m; **~-going** adj accommodant(e), facile à vivre

eat [i:t] (pt **ate**, pp **eaten**) vt, vi manger; **~ away vt**, **~ into vt fus** ronger, attaquer; (savings) entamer

eaves [i:vz] npl avant-toit m

eavesdrop ['i:vzdrɔp] vi: **to ~ (on a conversation)** écouter (une conversation) de façon indiscrète

ebb [ɛb] n reflux m ♦ vi refluer; (fig: also: **~ away**) décliner

ebony ['ɛbəni] n ébène f

EC n abbr (= European Community) C.E. f

ECB n abbr (= European Central Bank) BCE f

eccentric [ik'sentrik] adj excentrique

echo ['ɛkəu] (pl **~es**) n écho m ♦ vt répéter ♦ vi résonner, faire écho

eclipse [i'klips] n éclipse f

ecology [i'kɔlədʒi] n écologie f

e-commerce ['i:kɔmə:s] n commerce m électronique

economic [i:kə'nɔmik] adj économique; (business etc) rentable; **economical** adj économique; (person) économe

economics [i:kə'nɔmiks] n économie f politique ♦ npl (of project, situation) aspect m financier

economize [i'kɔnəmaiz] vi économiser, faire des économies

economy [i'kɔnəmi] n économie f; **~ class** n classe f touriste; **~ size** n format m économique

ecstasy ['ɛkstəsi] n extase f (drogue aussi); **ecstatic** [ɛks'tætik] adj extatique

ECU ['eikju:] n abbr (= European Currency Unit) ECU m

eczema ['ɛksɪmə] *n* eczéma *m*

edge [edʒ] *n* bord *m*; (*of knife etc*) tranchant *m*, fil *m* ♦ *vt* border; **on ~** (*fig*) crispé(e), tendu(e); **to ~ away from** s'éloigner furtivement de; **~ways** *adv*: **he couldn't get a word in ~ways** il ne pouvait pas placer un mot

edgy ['ɛdʒɪ] *adj* crispé(e), tendu(e)

edible ['ɛdɪbl] *adj* comestible

Edinburgh ['ɛdɪnbərə] *n* Édimbourg

edit ['ɛdɪt] *vt* (*text, book*) éditer; (*report*) préparer; (*film*) monter; (*broadcast*) réaliser; **~ion** [ɪ'dɪʃən] *n* édition *f*; **~or** *n* (*of column*) rédacteur(-trice); (*of newspaper*) rédacteur(-trice) en chef; (*of sb's work*) éditeur(-trice); **~orial** [ɛdɪ'tɔːrɪəl] *adj* de la rédaction, éditorial(e) ♦ *n* éditorial *m*

educate ['ɛdjukeɪt] *vt* (*teach*) instruire; (*instruct*) éduquer; **~d** *adj* (*person*) cultivé(e); **education** [ɛdju'keɪʃən] *n* éducation *f*; (*studies*) études *fpl*; (*teaching*) enseignement *m*, instruction *f*; **educational** *adj* (*experience, toy*) pédagogique; (*institution*) scolaire; (*policy*) d'éducation

eel [iːl] *n* anguille *f*

eerie ['ɪərɪ] *adj* inquiétant(e)

effect [ɪ'fɛkt] *n* effet *m* ♦ *vt* effectuer; **to take ~** (*law*) entrer en vigueur, prendre effet; (*drug*) agir, faire son effet; **in ~** en fait; **~ive** [ɪ'fɛktɪv] *adj* efficace; (*actual*) véritable; **~ively** *adv* efficacement; (*in reality*) effectivement; **~iveness** *n* efficacité *f*

effeminate [ɪ'fɛmɪnɪt] *adj* efféminé(e)

effervescent [ɛfə'vɛsnt] *adj* (*drink*) gazeux(-euse)

efficiency [ɪ'fɪʃənsɪ] *n* efficacité *f*; (*of machine*) rendement *m*

efficient [ɪ'fɪʃənt] *adj* efficace; (*machine*) qui a un bon rendement

effort ['ɛfət] *n* effort *m*; **~less** *adj* (*style*) aisé(e); (*achievement*) facile

effusive [ɪ'fjuːsɪv] *adj* chaleureux(-euse)

e.g. *adv abbr* (= *exempli gratia*) par exemple, p. ex.

egg [ɛg] *n* œuf *m*; **hard-boiled/soft-boiled ~** œuf dur/à la coque; **~ on** *vt* pousser; **~cup** *n* coquetier *m*; **~plant** *n*

(*esp US*) aubergine *f*; **~shell** *n* coquille *f* d'œuf

ego ['iːgəu] *n* (*self-esteem*) amour-propre *m*

egotism ['ɛgəutɪzəm] *n* égotisme *m*

egotist ['ɛgəutɪst] *n* égotiste *m/f*

Egypt ['iːdʒɪpt] *n* Égypte *f*; **~ian** [ɪ'dʒɪpʃən] *adj* égyptien(ne) ♦ *n* Égyptien(ne)

eiderdown ['aɪdədaun] *n* édredon *m*

Eiffel Tower ['aɪfəl-] *n* tour *f* Eiffel

eight [eɪt] *num* huit; **~een** [eɪ'tiːn] *num* dix-huit; **~h** [eɪtθ] *num* huitième; **~y** ['eɪtɪ] *num* quatre-vingt(s)

Eire ['ɛərə] *n* République *f* d'Irlande

either ['aɪðər] *adj* l'un ou l'autre; (*both, each*) chaque ♦ *pron*: **~ (of them)** l'un ou l'autre ♦ *adv* non plus ♦ *conj*: **~ good or bad** ou bon ou mauvais, soit bon soit mauvais; **on ~ side** de chaque côté; **I don't like ~** je n'aime ni l'un ni l'autre; **no, I don't ~** moi non plus

eject [ɪ'dʒɛkt] *vt* (*tenant etc*) expulser; (*object*) éjecter

elaborate [*adj* ɪ'læbərɪt, *vb* ɪ'læbəreɪt] *adj* compliqué(e), recherché(e) ♦ *vt* élaborer ♦ *vi*: **to ~ (on)** entrer dans les détails (de)

elastic [ɪ'læstɪk] *adj* élastique ♦ *n* élastique *m*; **~ band** *n* élastique *m*

elated [ɪ'leɪtɪd] *adj* transporté(e) de joie

elation [ɪ'leɪʃən] *n* allégresse *f*

elbow ['ɛlbəu] *n* coude *m*

elder ['ɛldər] *adj* aîné(e) ♦ *n* (*tree*) sureau *m*; **one's ~s** ses aînés; **~ly** *adj* âgé(e) ♦ *npl*: **the ~ly** les personnes âgées

eldest ['ɛldɪst] *adj, n*: **the ~ (child)** l'aîné(e) (des enfants)

elect [ɪ'lɛkt] *vt* élire ♦ *adj*: **the president ~** le président désigné; **to ~ to do** choisir de faire; **~ion** *n* élection *f*; **~ioneering** [ɪlɛkʃə'nɪərɪŋ] *n* propagande électorale, manœuvres électorales; **~or** *n* électeur(-trice); **~orate** *n* électorat *m*

electric [ɪ'lɛktrɪk] *adj* électrique; **~al** *adj* électrique; **~ blanket** *n* couverture chauffante; **~ fire** (*BRIT*) *n* radiateur *m* électrique; **~ian** [ɪlɛk'trɪʃən] *n* électricien *m*; **~ity** [ɪlɛk'trɪsɪtɪ] *n* électricité *f*; **electrify** [ɪ'lɛktrɪfaɪ] *vt* (*RAIL, fence*) électrifier; (*audi-*

ence) électriser
electronic [ɪlɛk'trɒnɪk] *adj* électronique; **~ mail** *n* courrier *m* électronique; **~s** *n* électronique *f*
elegant ['ɛlɪɡənt] *adj* élégant(e)
element ['ɛlɪmənt] *n* (*gen*) élément *m*; (*of heater, kettle etc*) résistance *f*; **~ary** [ɛlɪ'mɛntərɪ] *adj* élémentaire; (*school, education*) primaire
elephant ['ɛlɪfənt] *n* éléphant *m*
elevation [ɛlɪ'veɪʃən] *n* (*raising, promotion*) avancement *m*, promotion *f*; (*height*) hauteur *f*
elevator ['ɛlɪveɪtə'] *n* (*in warehouse etc*) élévateur *m*, monte-charge *m inv*; (*US: lift*) ascenseur *m*
eleven [ɪ'lɛvn] *num* onze; **~ses** [ɪ'lɛvnzɪz] *npl* ≃ pause-café *f*; **~th** *num* onzième
elicit [ɪ'lɪsɪt] *vt*: **to ~ (from)** obtenir (de), arracher (à)
eligible ['ɛlɪdʒəbl] *adj*: **to be ~ for** remplir les conditions requises pour; **an ~ young man/woman** un beau parti
elm [ɛlm] *n* orme *m*
elongated ['iːlɒŋɡeɪtɪd] *adj* allongé(e)
elope [ɪ'ləup] *vi* (*lovers*) s'enfuir (ensemble)
eloquent ['ɛləkwənt] *adj* éloquent(e)
else [ɛls] *adv* d'autre; **something ~** quelque chose d'autre, autre chose; **somewhere ~** ailleurs, autre part; **everywhere ~** partout ailleurs; **nobody ~** personne d'autre; **where ~?** à quel autre endroit?; **little ~** pas grand-chose d'autre; **~where** *adv* ailleurs, autre part
elude [ɪ'luːd] *vt* échapper à
elusive [ɪ'luːsɪv] *adj* insaisissable
emaciated [ɪ'meɪsɪeɪtɪd] *adj* émacié(e), décharné(e)
e-mail ['iːmeɪl] *n* courrier *m* électronique ♦ *vt* (*person*) envoyer un message électronique à
emancipate [ɪ'mænsɪpeɪt] *vt* émanciper
embankment [ɪm'bæŋkmənt] *n* (*of road, railway*) remblai *m*, talus *m*; (*of river*) berge *f*, quai *m*
embark [ɪm'bɑːk] *vi* embarquer; **to ~ on** (*journey*) entreprendre; (*fig*) se lancer or

s'embarquer dans; **~ation** [ɛmbɑː'keɪʃən] *n* embarquement *m*
embarrass [ɪm'bærəs] *vt* embarrasser, gêner; **~ed** *adj* gêné(e); **~ing** *adj* gênant(e), embarrassant(e); **~ment** *n* embarras *m*, gêne *f*
embassy ['ɛmbəsɪ] *n* ambassade *f*
embedded [ɪm'bɛdɪd] *adj* enfoncé(e)
embellish [ɪm'bɛlɪʃ] *vt* orner, décorer; (*fig: account*) enjoliver
embers ['ɛmbəz] *npl* braise *f*
embezzle [ɪm'bɛzl] *vt* détourner; **~ment** *n* détournement *m* de fonds
embitter [ɪm'bɪtə'] *vt* aigrir; (*relations*) envenimer
embody [ɪm'bɒdɪ] *vt* (*features*) réunir, comprendre; (*ideas*) formuler, exprimer
embossed [ɪm'bɒst] *adj* (*metal*) estampé(e); (*leather*) frappé(e); **~ wallpaper** papier gaufré
embrace [ɪm'breɪs] *vt* embrasser, étreindre; (*include*) embrasser ♦ *vi* s'étreindre, s'embrasser ♦ *n* étreinte *f*
embroider [ɪm'brɔɪdə'] *vt* broder; **~y** *n* broderie *f*
emerald ['ɛmərəld] *n* émeraude *f*
emerge [ɪ'mɜːdʒ] *vi* apparaître; (*from room, car*) surgir; (*from sleep, imprisonment*) sortir
emergency [ɪ'mɜːdʒənsɪ] *n* urgence *f*; **in an ~** en cas d'urgence; **~ cord** *n* sonnette *f* d'alarme; **~ exit** *n* sortie *f* de secours; **~ landing** *n* atterrissage forcé; **~ services** *npl*: **the ~ services** (*fire, police, ambulance*) les services *mpl* d'urgence
emery board ['ɛmərɪ-] *n* lime *f* à ongles (*en carton émerisé*)
emigrate ['ɛmɪɡreɪt] *vi* émigrer
eminent ['ɛmɪnənt] *adj* éminent(e)
emissions [ɪ'mɪʃənz] *npl* émissions *fpl*
emit [ɪ'mɪt] *vt* émettre
emotion [ɪ'məuʃən] *n* émotion *f*; **~al** *adj* (*person*) émotif(-ive), très sensible; (*needs, exhaustion*) affectif(-ive); (*scene*) émouvant(e); (*tone, speech*) qui fait appel aux sentiments; **emotive** *adj* chargé(e) d'émotion; (*subject*) sensible
emperor ['ɛmpərə'] *n* empereur *m*

emphasis ['emfəsɪs] (*pl* **-ases**) *n* (*stress*) accent *m*; (*importance*) insistance *f*

emphasize ['emfəsaɪz] *vt* (*syllable, word, point*) appuyer *or* insister sur; (*feature*) souligner, accentuer

emphatic [ɪm'fætɪk] *adj* (*strong*) énergique, vigoureux(-euse); (*unambiguous, clear*) catégorique

empire ['empaɪər] *n* empire *m*

employ [ɪm'plɔɪ] *vt* employer; **~ee** *n* employé(e); **~er** *n* employeur(-euse); **~ment** *n* emploi *m*; **~ment agency** *n* agence *f* *or* bureau *m* de placement

empower [ɪm'pauər] *vt*: **to ~ sb to do** autoriser *or* habiliter qn à faire

empress ['emprɪs] *n* impératrice *f*

emptiness ['emptɪnɪs] *n* (*of area, region*) aspect *m* désertique; (*of life*) vide *m*, vacuité *f*

empty ['emptɪ] *adj* vide; (*threat, promise*) en l'air, vain(e) ♦ *vt* vider ♦ *vi* se vider; (*liquid*) s'écouler; **~-handed** *adj* les mains vides

EMU *n abbr* (= *economic and monetary union*) UME *f*

emulate ['emjuleɪt] *vt* rivaliser avec, imiter

emulsion [ɪ'mʌlʃən] *n* émulsion *f*; (*also: ~ paint*) peinture mate

enable [ɪ'neɪbl] *vt*: **to ~ sb to do** permettre à qn de faire

enamel [ɪ'næməl] *n* émail *m*; (*also: ~ paint*) peinture laquée

enchant [ɪn'tʃɑːnt] *vt* enchanter; **~ing** *adj* ravissant(e), enchanteur(-teresse)

encl. *abbr* = **enclosed**

enclose [ɪn'kləuz] *vt* (*land*) clôturer; (*space, object*) entourer; (*letter etc*): **to ~ (with)** joindre (à); **please find ~d** veuillez trouver ci-joint; **enclosure** *n* enceinte *f*

encompass [ɪn'kʌmpəs] *vt* (*include*) contenir, inclure

encore [ɔŋ'kɔːr] *excl* bis ♦ *n* bis *m*

encounter [ɪn'kauntər] *n* rencontre *f* ♦ *vt* rencontrer

encourage [ɪn'kʌrɪdʒ] *vt* encourager; **~ment** *n* encouragement *m*

encroach [ɪn'krəutʃ] *vi*: **to ~ (up)on** em-

piéter sur

encyclop(a)edia [ensaɪkləu'piːdɪə] *n* encyclopédie *f*

end [end] *n* (*gen, also: aim*) fin *f*; (*of table, street, rope etc*) bout *m*, extrémité *f* ♦ *vt* terminer; (*also:* **bring to an ~, put an ~ to**) mettre fin à ♦ *vi* se terminer, finir; **in the ~** finalement; **on ~** (*object*) debout, dressé(e); **to stand on ~** (*hair*) se dresser sur la tête; **for hours on ~** pendant des heures et des heures; **~ up** *vi*: **to ~ up in** (*condition*) finir *or* se terminer par; (*place*) finir *or* aboutir à

endanger [ɪn'deɪndʒər] *vt* mettre en danger; **an ~ed species** une espèce en voie de disparition

endearing [ɪn'dɪərɪŋ] *adj* attachant(e)

endeavour [ɪn'devər] (*US* **endeavor**) *n* tentative *f*, effort *m* ♦ *vi*: **to ~ to do** tenter *or* s'efforcer de faire

ending ['endɪŋ] *n* dénouement *m*, fin *f*; (*LING*) terminaison *f*

endive ['endaɪv] *n* chicorée *f*; (*smooth*) endive *f*

endless ['endlɪs] *adj* sans fin, interminable

endorse [ɪn'dɔːs] *vt* (*cheque*) endosser; (*approve*) appuyer, approuver, sanctionner; **~ment** *n* (*approval*) appui *m*, aval *m*; (*BRIT: on driving licence*) contravention portée au permis de conduire

endure [ɪn'djuər] *vt* supporter, endurer ♦ *vi* durer

enemy ['enəmɪ] *adj, n* ennemi(e)

energetic [enə'dʒetɪk] *adj* énergique; (*activity*) qui fait se dépenser (physiquement)

energy ['enədʒɪ] *n* énergie *f*

enforce [ɪn'fɔːs] *vt* (*law*) appliquer, faire respecter

engage [ɪn'geɪdʒ] *vt* engager; (*attention etc*) retenir ♦ *vi* (*TECH*) s'enclencher, s'engrener; **to ~ in** se lancer dans; **~d** *adj* (*BRIT: busy, in use*) occupé(e); (*betrothed*) fiancé(e); **to get ~d** se fiancer; **~d tone** *n* (*TEL*) tonalité *f* occupé *inv or* pas libre; **~ment** *n* obligation *f*, engagement *m*; rendez-vous *m inv*; (*to marry*) fiançailles *fpl*; **~ment ring** *n* bague *f* de fiançailles;

engaging *adj* engageant(e), attirant(e)
engine ['ɛndʒɪn] *n* (AUT) moteur *m*; (RAIL) locomotive *f*; ~ **driver** *n* mécanicien *m*
engineer [ɛndʒɪ'nɪər] *n* ingénieur *m*; (BRIT: *repairer*) dépanneur *m*; (NAVY, US RAIL) mécanicien *m*; ~**ing** *n* engineering *m*, ingénierie *f*; (*of bridges, ships*) génie *m*; (*of machine*) mécanique *f*
England ['ɪŋglənd] *n* Angleterre *f*; **English** *adj* anglais(e) ♦ *n* (LING) anglais *m*; **the English** *npl* (*people*) les Anglais; **the English Channel** la Manche; **Englishman** (*irreg*) *n* Anglais; **Englishwoman** (*irreg*) *n* Anglaise *f*
engraving [ɪn'ɡreɪvɪŋ] *n* gravure *f*
engrossed [ɪn'ɡrəust] *adj*: ~ **in** absorbé(e) par, plongé(e) dans
engulf [ɪn'ɡʌlf] *vt* engloutir
enhance [ɪn'hɑ:ns] *vt* rehausser, mettre en valeur
enjoy [ɪn'dʒɔɪ] *vt* aimer, prendre plaisir à; (*have: health, fortune*) jouir de; (: *success*) connaître; **to ~ o.s.** s'amuser; ~**able** *adj* agréable; ~**ment** *n* plaisir *m*
enlarge [ɪn'lɑ:dʒ] *vt* accroître; (PHOT) agrandir ♦ *vi*: **to ~ on** (*subject*) s'étendre sur; ~**ment** [ɪn'lɑ:dʒmənt] *n* (PHOT) agrandissement *m*
enlighten [ɪn'laɪtn] *vt* éclairer; ~**ed** *adj* éclairé(e); ~**ment** *n*: **the E~ment** (HISTORY) ≃ le Siècle des lumières
enlist [ɪn'lɪst] *vt* recruter; (*support*) s'assurer ♦ *vi* s'engager
enmity ['ɛnmɪtɪ] *n* inimitié *f*
enormous [ɪ'nɔ:məs] *adj* énorme
enough [ɪ'nʌf] *adj*, *pron*: ~ **time/books** assez *or* suffisamment de temps/livres ♦ *adv*: **big ~** assez *or* suffisamment grand; **have you got ~?** en avez-vous assez?; **he has not worked ~** il n'a pas assez *or* suffisamment travaillé; ~ **to eat** assez à manger; ~**!** assez!, ça suffit!; **that's ~, thanks** cela suffit *or* c'est assez, merci; **I've had ~ of him** j'en ai assez de lui; **... which, funnily** *or* **oddly ~** ... qui, chose curieuse
enquire [ɪn'kwaɪər] *vt*, *vi* = **inquire**
enrage [ɪn'reɪdʒ] *vt* mettre en fureur *or* en rage, rendre furieux(-euse)
enrol [ɪn'rəul] (US **enroll**) *vt* inscrire ♦ *vi* s'inscrire; ~**ment** (US **enrollment**) *n* inscription *f*
en suite ['ɒnswi:t] *adj*: **with ~ bathroom** avec salle de bains en attenante
ensure [ɪn'ʃuər] *vt* assurer; garantir; **to ~ that** s'assurer que
entail [ɪn'teɪl] *vt* entraîner, occasionner
entangled [ɪn'tæŋld] *adj*: **to become ~ (in)** s'empêtrer (dans)
enter ['ɛntər] *vt* (*room*) entrer dans, pénétrer dans; (*club, army*) entrer à; (*competition*) s'inscrire à *or* pour; (*sb for a competition*) (faire) inscrire; (*write down*) inscrire, noter; (COMPUT) entrer, introduire ♦ *vi* entrer; ~ **for** *vt fus* s'inscrire à, se présenter pour *or* à; ~ **into** *vt fus* (*explanation*) se lancer dans; (*discussion, negotiations*) entamer; (*agreement*) conclure
enterprise ['ɛntəpraɪz] *n* entreprise *f*; (*initiative*) (esprit *m* d')initiative *f*; **free ~** libre entreprise; **private ~** entreprise privée; **enterprising** *adj* entreprenant(e), dynamique; (*scheme*) audacieux(-euse)
entertain [ɛntə'teɪn] *vt* amuser, distraire; (*invite*) recevoir (à dîner); (*idea, plan*) envisager; ~**er** *n* artiste *m/f* de variétés; ~**ing** *adj* amusant(e), distrayant(e); ~**ment** *n* (*amusement*) divertissement *m*, amusement *m*; (*show*) spectacle *m*
enthralled [ɪn'θrɔ:ld] *adj* captivé(e)
enthusiasm [ɪn'θu:zɪæzəm] *n* enthousiasme *m*
enthusiast [ɪn'θu:zɪæst] *n* enthousiaste *m/f*; ~**ic** [ɪnθu:zɪ'æstɪk] *adj* enthousiaste; **to be ~ic about** être enthousiasmé(e) par
entire [ɪn'taɪər] *adj* (tout) entier(-ère); ~**ly** *adv* entièrement, complètement; ~**ty** [ɪn'taɪərətɪ] *n*: **in its ~ty** dans sa totalité
entitle [ɪn'taɪtl] *vt*: **to ~ sb to sth** donner droit à qch à qn; ~**d** [ɪn'taɪtld] *adj* (*book*) intitulé(e); **to be ~d to do** avoir le droit de *or* être habilité à faire
entrance [*n* 'ɛntrns, *vb* ɪn'trɑ:ns] *n* entrée *f* ♦ *vt* enchanter, ravir; **to gain ~ to** (*university etc*) être admis à; ~ **examination**

n examen *m* d'entrée; ~ **fee** *n* (*to museum etc*) prix *m* d'entrée; (*to join club etc*) droit *m* d'inscription; ~ **ramp** (*US*) *n* (*AUT*) bretelle *f* d'accès; **entrant** *n* participant(e); concurrent(e); (*BRIT: in exam*) candidat(e)

entrenched [ɛn'trɛntʃt] *adj* retranché(e); (*ideas*) arrêté(e)

entrepreneur ['ɔntrəprə'nəːʳ] *n* entrepreneur *m*

entrust [ɪn'trʌst] *vt*: **to ~ sth to** confier qch à

entry ['ɛntrɪ] *n* entrée *f*; (*in register*) inscription *f*; **no ~** défense d'entrer, entrée interdite; (*AUT*) sens interdit; ~ **form** *n* feuille *f* d'inscription; ~ **phone** (*BRIT*) *n* interphone *m*

envelop [ɪn'vɛləp] *vt* envelopper

envelope ['ɛnvələup] *n* enveloppe *f*

envious ['ɛnvɪəs] *adj* envieux(-euse)

environment [ɪn'vaɪərnmənt] *n* environnement *m*; (*social, moral*) milieu *m*; ~**al** [ɪnvaɪərn'mɛntl] *adj* écologique; du milieu; ~**-friendly** *adj* écologique

envisage [ɪn'vɪzɪdʒ] *vt* (*foresee*) prévoir

envoy ['ɛnvɔɪ] *n* (*diplomat*) ministre *m* plénipotentiaire

envy ['ɛnvɪ] *n* envie *f* ♦ *vt* envier; **to ~ sb sth** envier qch à qn

epic ['ɛpɪk] *n* épopée *f* ♦ *adj* épique

epidemic [ɛpɪ'dɛmɪk] *n* épidémie *f*

epilepsy ['ɛpɪlɛpsɪ] *n* épilepsie *f*; **epileptic** *n* épileptique *m/f*

episode ['ɛpɪsəud] *n* épisode *m*

epitome [ɪ'pɪtəmɪ] *n* modèle *m*; **epitomize** *vt* incarner

equal ['iːkwl] *adj* égal(e) ♦ *n* égal(e) ♦ *vt* égaler; ~ **to** (*task*) à la hauteur de; ~**ity** [iː'kwɔlɪtɪ] *n* égalité *f*; ~**ize** *vi* (*SPORT*) égaliser; ~**ly** *adv* également; (*just as*) tout aussi

equanimity [ɛkwə'nɪmɪtɪ] *n* égalité *f* d'humeur

equate [ɪ'kweɪt] *vt*: **to ~ sth with** comparer qch à; assimiler qch à; **equation** *n* (*MATH*) équation *f*

equator [ɪ'kweɪtəʳ] *n* équateur *m*

equilibrium [iːkwɪ'lɪbrɪəm] *n* équilibre *m*

equip [ɪ'kwɪp] *vt*: **to ~ (with)** équiper (de); **to be well ~ped** être bien équipé(e); ~**ment** *n* équipement *m*; (*electrical etc*) appareillage *m*, installation *f*

equities ['ɛkwɪtɪz] (*BRIT*) *npl* (*COMM*) actions cotées en Bourse

equivalent [ɪ'kwɪvələnt] *adj*: ~ **(to)** équivalent(e) (à) ♦ *n* équivalent *m*

era ['ɪərə] *n* ère *f*, époque *f*

eradicate [ɪ'rædɪkeɪt] *vt* éliminer

erase [ɪ'reɪz] *vt* effacer; ~**r** *n* gomme *f*

erect [ɪ'rɛkt] *adj* droit(e) ♦ *vt* construire; (*monument*) ériger, élever; (*tent etc*) dresser; ~**ion** *n* érection *f*

ERM *n abbr* (= *Exchange Rate Mechanism*) MTC *m*

erode [ɪ'rəud] *vt* éroder; (*metal*) ronger

erotic [ɪ'rɔtɪk] *adj* érotique

errand ['ɛrənd] *n* course *f*, commission *f*

erratic [ɪ'rætɪk] *adj* irrégulier(-ère); inconstant(e)

error ['ɛrəʳ] *n* erreur *f*

erupt [ɪ'rʌpt] *vi* entrer en éruption; (*fig*) éclater; ~**ion** *n* éruption *f*

escalate ['ɛskəleɪt] *vi* s'intensifier

escalator ['ɛskəleɪtəʳ] *n* escalier roulant

escapade [ɛskə'peɪd] *n* (*misdeed*) fredaine *f*; (*adventure*) équipée *f*

escape [ɪs'keɪp] *n* fuite *f*; (*from prison*) évasion *f* ♦ *vi* s'échapper, fuir; (*from jail*) s'évader; (*fig*) s'en tirer; (*leak*) s'échapper ♦ *vt* échapper à; **to ~ from** (*person*) échapper à; (*place*) s'échapper de; (*fig*) fuir; **escapism** *n* (*fig*) évasion *f*

escort [*n* 'ɛskɔːt, *vb* ɪs'kɔːt] *n* escorte *f* ♦ *vt* escorter

Eskimo ['ɛskɪməu] *n* Esquimau(de)

especially [ɪs'pɛʃlɪ] *adv* (*particularly*) particulièrement; (*above all*) surtout

espionage ['ɛspɪənɑːʒ] *n* espionnage *m*

Esquire [ɪs'kwaɪəʳ] *n*: **J. Brown, ~** Monsieur J. Brown

essay ['ɛseɪ] *n* (*SCOL*) dissertation *f*; (*LITERATURE*) essai *m*

essence ['ɛsns] *n* essence *f*

essential [ɪ'sɛnʃl] *adj* essentiel(le); (*basic*) fondamental(e) ♦ *n*: ~**s** éléments essen-

tiels; ~ly *adv* essentiellement
establish [ɪsˈtæblɪʃ] *vt* établir; (*business*) fonder, créer; (*one's power etc*) asseoir, affermir; ~ed *adj* bien établi(e); ~ment *n* établissement *m*; (*founding*) création *f*
estate [ɪsˈteɪt] *n* (*land*) domaine *m*, propriété *f*; (*LAW*) biens *mpl*, succession *f*; (*BRIT: also:* **housing** ~) lotissement *m*, cité *f*; ~ **agent** *n* agent immobilier; ~ **car** (*BRIT*) *n* break *m*
esteem [ɪsˈtiːm] *n* estime *f*
esthetic [ɪsˈθetɪk] (*US*) *adj* = **aesthetic**
estimate [*n* ˈestɪmət, *vb* ˈestɪmeɪt] *n* estimation *f*; (*COMM*) devis *m* ♦ *vt* estimer; **estimation** [estɪˈmeɪʃən] *n* opinion *f*; (*calculation*) estimation *f*
estranged [ɪsˈtreɪndʒd] *adj* séparé(e); dont on s'est séparé(e)
eternal [ɪˈtɜːnl] *adj* éternel(le)
eternity [ɪˈtɜːnɪtɪ] *n* éternité *f*
ethical [ˈeθɪkl] *adj* moral(e); **ethics** *n* éthique *f* ♦ *npl* moralité *f*
Ethiopia [iːθɪˈəʊpɪə] *n* Éthiopie *f*
ethnic [ˈeθnɪk] *adj* ethnique; (*music etc*) folklorique; ~ **minority** minorité *f* ethnique
ethos [ˈiːθɒs] *n* génie *m*
e-ticket *n* billet *m* électronique
etiquette [ˈetɪket] *n* convenances *fpl*, étiquette *f*
EU *n abbr* (= *European Union*) UE *f*
euro [ˈjʊərəʊ] *n* (*currency*) euro *m*
Eurocheque [ˈjʊərəʊtʃek] *n* eurochèque *m*
Euroland [ˈjʊərəʊlænd] *n* Euroland *m*
Europe [ˈjʊərəp] *n* Europe *f*; ~**an** [jʊərəˈpiːən] *adj* européen(ne) ♦ *n* Européen(ne); ~**an Community** Communauté européenne
evacuate [ɪˈvækjueɪt] *vt* évacuer
evade [ɪˈveɪd] *vt* échapper à; (*question etc*) éluder; (*duties*) se dérober à; **to** ~ **tax** frauder le fisc
evaporate [ɪˈvæpəreɪt] *vi* s'évaporer; ~**d milk** *n* lait condensé non sucré
evasion [ɪˈveɪʒən] *n* dérobade *f*; **tax** ~ fraude fiscale
eve [iːv] *n*: **on the** ~ **of** à la veille de

even [ˈiːvn] *adj* (*level, smooth*) régulier(-ère); (*equal*) égal(e); (*number*) pair(e) ♦ *adv* même; ~ **if** même si +*indic*; ~ **though** alors même que +*cond*; ~ **more** encore plus; ~ **so** quand même; **not** ~ pas même; **to get** ~ **with sb** prendre sa revanche sur qn
evening [ˈiːvnɪŋ] *n* soir *m*; (*as duration, event*) soirée *f*; **in the** ~ le soir; ~ **class** *n* cours *m* du soir; ~ **dress** *n* tenue *f* de soirée
event [ɪˈvent] *n* événement *m*; (*SPORT*) épreuve *f*; **in the** ~ **of** en cas de; ~**ful** *adj* mouvementé(e)
eventual [ɪˈventʃuəl] *adj* final(e); ~**ity** [ɪventʃuˈælɪtɪ] *n* possibilité *f*, éventualité *f*; ~**ly** *adv* finalement
ever [ˈevər] *adv* jamais; (*at all times*) toujours; **the best** ~ le meilleur qu'on ait jamais vu; **have you** ~ **seen it?** l'as-tu déjà vu?, as-tu eu l'occasion *or* t'est-il arrivé de le voir?; **why** ~ **not?** mais enfin, pourquoi pas?; ~ **since** *adv* depuis ♦ *conj* depuis que; ~**green** *n* arbre *m* à feuilles persistantes; ~**lasting** *adj* éternel(le)
every [ˈevrɪ] *adj* chaque; ~ **day** tous les jours, chaque jour; ~ **other/third day** tous les deux/trois jours; ~ **other car** une voiture sur deux; ~ **now and then** de temps en temps; ~**body** *pron* tout le monde, tous *pl*; ~**day** *adj* quotidien(ne), de tous les jours; ~**one** *pron* = **everybody**; ~**thing** *pron* tout; ~**where** *adv* partout
evict [ɪˈvɪkt] *vt* expulser; ~**ion** *n* expulsion *f*
evidence [ˈevɪdns] *n* (*proof*) preuve(s) *f(pl)*; (*of witness*) témoignage *m*; (*sign*): **to show** ~ **of** présenter des signes de; **to give** ~ témoigner, déposer
evident [ˈevɪdnt] *adj* évident(e); ~**ly** *adv* de toute évidence; (*apparently*) apparemment
evil [ˈiːvl] *adj* mauvais(e) ♦ *n* mal *m*
evoke [ɪˈvəʊk] *vt* évoquer
evolution [iːvəˈluːʃən] *n* évolution *f*
evolve [ɪˈvɒlv] *vt* élaborer ♦ *vi* évoluer

ewe [juː] n brebis f

ex- [eks] prefix ex-

exact [ɪgˈzækt] adj exact(e) ♦ vt: **to ~ sth (from)** extorquer qch (à); exiger qch (de); ~ing adj exigeant(e); (work) astreignant(e); ~ly adv exactement

exaggerate [ɪgˈzædʒəreɪt] vt, vi exagérer; exaggeration [ɪgzædʒəˈreɪʃən] n exagération f

exalted [ɪgˈzɔːltɪd] adj (prominent) élevé(e) (: person) haut placé(e)

exam [ɪgˈzæm] n abbr (SCOL) = **examination**

examination [ɪgzæmɪˈneɪʃən] n (SCOL, MED) examen m

examine [ɪgˈzæmɪn] vt (gen) examiner; (SCOL: person) interroger; ~r n examinateur(-trice)

example [ɪgˈzɑːmpl] n exemple m; **for ~** par exemple

exasperate [ɪgˈzɑːspəreɪt] vt exaspérer; exasperation [ɪgzɑːspəˈreɪʃən] n exaspération f, irritation f

excavate [ˈekskəveɪt] vt excaver; excavation [ekskəˈveɪʃən] n fouilles fpl

exceed [ɪkˈsiːd] vt dépasser; (one's powers) outrepasser; ~ingly adv extrêmement

excellent [ˈeksələnt] adj excellent(e)

except [ɪkˈsept] prep (also: ~ for, ~ing) sauf, excepté ♦ vt excepter; ~ **if/when** sauf si/quand; ~ **that** sauf que, si ce n'est que; ~ion n exception f; **to take ~ion to** s'offusquer de; ~ional adj exceptionnel(le)

excerpt [ˈeksəːpt] n extrait m

excess [ɪkˈses] n excès m; ~ **baggage** n excédent m de bagages; ~ **fare** (BRIT) n supplément m; ~ive adj excessif(-ive)

exchange [ɪksˈtʃeɪndʒ] n échange m; (also: **telephone ~**) central m ♦ vt: **to ~ (for)** échanger (contre); ~ **rate** n taux m de change

Exchequer [ɪksˈtʃekər] (BRIT) n: **the ~** l'Échiquier m, ≈ le ministère des Finances

excise [n ˈeksaɪz, vb ekˈsaɪz] n taxe f ♦ vt exciser

excite [ɪkˈsaɪt] vt exciter; **to get ~d** s'exci-

ter; ~ment n excitation f; exciting adj passionnant(e)

exclaim [ɪksˈkleɪm] vi s'exclamer; exclamation [ekskləˈmeɪʃən] n exclamation f; exclamation mark n point m d'exclamation

exclude [ɪksˈkluːd] vt exclure; exclusion zone n zone interdite; exclusive adj exclusif(-ive); (club, district) sélect(e); (item of news) en exclusivité; **exclusive of VAT** TVA non comprise; **mutually exclusive** qui s'excluent l'un(e) l'autre

excruciating [ɪksˈkruːʃieɪtɪŋ] adj atroce

excursion [ɪksˈkəːʃən] n excursion f

excuse [n ɪksˈkjuːs, vb ɪksˈkjuːz] n excuse f ♦ vt excuser; **to ~ sb from** (activity) dispenser qn de; (club, district) **~ me!** excusez-moi!, pardon!; **now if you will ~ me, ...** maintenant, si vous (le) permettez ...

ex-directory [ˈeksdɪˈrektəri] (BRIT) adj sur la liste rouge

execute [ˈeksɪkjuːt] vt exécuter; execution n exécution f

executive [ɪgˈzekjutɪv] n (COMM) cadre m; (of organization, political party) bureau m ♦ adj exécutif(-ive)

exemplify [ɪgˈzemplɪfaɪ] vt illustrer; (typify) incarner

exempt [ɪgˈzempt] adj: ~ **from** exempté(e) or dispensé(e) de ♦ vt: **to ~ sb from** exempter or dispenser qn de

exercise [ˈeksəsaɪz] n exercice m ♦ vt exercer; (patience etc) faire preuve de; (dog) promener ♦ vi prendre de l'exercice; ~ **book** n cahier m

exert [ɪgˈzəːt] vt exercer, employer; **to ~ o.s.** se dépenser; ~ion n effort m

exhale [eksˈheɪl] vt exhaler ♦ vi expirer

exhaust [ɪgˈzɔːst] n (also: ~ **fumes**) gaz mpl d'échappement; (also: ~ **pipe**) tuyau m d'échappement ♦ vt épuiser; ~ed adj épuisé(e); ~ion n épuisement m; **nervous ~ion** fatigue nerveuse; surmenage mental; ~ive adj très complet(-ète)

exhibit [ɪgˈzɪbɪt] n (ART) pièce exposée, objet exposé; (LAW) pièce à conviction ♦ vt exposer; (courage, skill) faire preuve de;

~ion [ɛksɪ'bɪʃən] *n* exposition *f*; (*of ill-temper, talent etc*) démonstration *f*
exhilarating [ɪg'zɪləreɪtɪŋ] *adj* grisant(e); stimulant(e)
ex-husband *n* ex-mari *m*
exile ['ɛksaɪl] *n* exil *m*; (*person*) exilé(e) ♦ *vt* exiler
exist [ɪg'zɪst] *vi* exister; **~ence** *n* existence *f*; **~ing** *adj* actuel(le)
exit ['ɛksɪt] *n* sortie *f* ♦ *vi* (*COMPUT, THEATRE*) sortir; **~ poll** *n* sondage *m* (fait à la sortie de l'isoloir); **~ ramp** *n* (*AUT*) bretelle *f* d'accès
exodus ['ɛksədəs] *n* exode *m*
exonerate [ɪg'zɔnəreɪt] *vt*: **to ~ from** disculper de
exotic [ɪg'zɔtɪk] *adj* exotique
expand [ɪks'pænd] *vt* agrandir; accroître ♦ *vi* (*trade etc*) se développer, s'accroître; (*gas, metal*) se dilater
expanse [ɪks'pæns] *n* étendue *f*
expansion [ɪks'pænʃən] *n* développement *m*, accroissement *m*
expect [ɪks'pɛkt] *vt* (*anticipate*) s'attendre à, s'attendre à ce que +*sub*; (*count on*) compter sur, escompter; (*require*) demander, exiger; (*suppose*) supposer; (*await, also baby*) attendre ♦ *vi*: **to be ~ing** être enceinte; **~ancy** *n* (*anticipation*) attente *f*; **life ~ancy** espérance *f* de vie; **~ant mother** *n* future maman *f*; **~ation** [ɛkspɛk'teɪʃən] *n* attente *f*, espérance(s) *f(pl)*
expedient [ɪks'pi:dɪənt] *adj* indiqué(e), opportun(e) ♦ *n* expédient *m*
expedition [ɛkspə'dɪʃən] *n* expédition *f*
expel [ɪks'pɛl] *vt* chasser, expulser; (*SCOL*) renvoyer
expend [ɪks'pɛnd] *vt* consacrer; (*money*) dépenser; **~iture** [ɪks'pɛndɪtʃər] *n* dépense *f*; dépenses *fpl*
expense [ɪks'pɛns] *n* dépense *f*, frais *mpl*; (*high cost*) coût *m*; **~s** *npl* (*COMM*) frais *mpl*; **at the ~ of** aux dépens de; **~ account** *n* (note *f* de) frais *mpl*; **expensive** *adj* cher (chère), coûteux(-euse); **to be expensive** coûter cher

experience [ɪks'pɪərɪəns] *n* expérience *f* ♦ *vt* connaître, faire l'expérience de; (*feeling*) éprouver; **~d** *adj* expérimenté(e)
experiment [ɪks'pɛrɪmənt] *n* expérience *f* ♦ *vi* faire une expérience; **to ~ with** expérimenter
expert ['ɛkspə:t] *adj* expert(e) ♦ *n* expert *m*; **~ise** [ɛkspə:'ti:z] *n* (grande) compétence
expire [ɪks'paɪər] *vi* expirer; **expiry** *n* expiration *f*
explain [ɪks'pleɪn] *vt* expliquer; **explanation** [ɛksplə'neɪʃən] *n* explication *f*; **explanatory** [ɪks'plænətrɪ] *adj* explicatif(-ive)
explicit [ɪks'plɪsɪt] *adj* explicite; (*definite*) formel(le)
explode [ɪks'pləud] *vi* exploser
exploit [*n* 'ɛksplɔɪt, *vb* ɪks'plɔɪt] *n* exploit *m* ♦ *vt* exploiter; **~ation** [ɛksplɔɪ'teɪʃən] *n* exploitation *f*
exploratory [ɪks'plɔrətrɪ] *adj* (*expedition*) d'exploration; (*fig: talks*) préliminaire
explore [ɪks'plɔ:ʳ] *vt* explorer; (*possibilities*) étudier, examiner; **~r** *n* explorateur(-trice)
explosion [ɪks'pləuʒən] *n* explosion *f*; **explosive** *adj* explosif(-ive) ♦ *n* explosif *m*
exponent [ɪks'pəunənt] *n* (*of school of thought etc*) interprète *m*, représentant *m*
export [*vb* ɛks'pɔ:t, *n* 'ɛkspɔ:t] *vt* exporter ♦ *n* exportation *f* ♦ *cpd* d'exportation; **~er** *n* exportateur *m*
expose [ɪks'pəuz] *vt* exposer; (*unmask*) démasquer, dévoiler; **~d** *adj* (*position, house*) exposé(e); **exposure** *n* exposition *f*; (*publicity*) couverture *f*; (*PHOT*) (temps *m* de) pose *f*; (*: shot*) pose; **to die from exposure** (*MED*) mourir de froid; **exposure meter** *n* posemètre *m*
express [ɪks'prɛs] *adj* (*definite*) formel(le), exprès(-esse); (*BRIT: letter etc*) exprès *inv* ♦ *n* (*train*) rapide *m*; (*bus*) car *m* express ♦ *vt* exprimer; **~ion** *n* expression *f*; **~ly** *adv* expressément, formellement; **~way** *n* (*US*) (*urban motorway*) voie *f* express (à plusieurs files)
exquisite [ɛks'kwɪzɪt] *adj* exquis(e)
extend [ɪks'tɛnd] *vt* (*visit, street*) prolonger;

(*building*) agrandir; (*offer*) présenter, offrir; (*hand, arm*) tendre ♦ *vi* s'étendre; **extension** *n* prolongation *f*; agrandissement *m*; (*building*) annexe *f*; (*to wire, table*) rallonge *f*; (*telephone: in offices*) poste *m*; (: *in private house*) téléphone *m* supplémentaire; **extensive** *adj* étendu(e), vaste; (*damage, alterations*) considérable; (*inquiries*) approfondi(e); **extensively** *adv*: **he's travelled extensively** il a beaucoup voyagé

extent [ɪks'tɛnt] *n* étendue *f*; **to some ~** dans une certaine mesure; **to what ~?** dans quelle mesure?, jusqu'à quel point? ; **to the ~ of ...** au point de ...; **to such an ~ that ...** à tel point que ...

extenuating [ɪks'tɛnjueɪtɪŋ] *adj*: **~ circumstances** circonstances atténuées

exterior [ɛks'tɪərɪər] *adj* extérieur(e) ♦ *n* extérieur *m*; dehors *m*

external [ɛks'tɔːnl] *adj* externe

extinct [ɪks'tɪŋkt] *adj* éteint(e)

extinguish [ɪks'tɪŋgwɪʃ] *vt* éteindre

extort [ɪks'tɔːt] *vt*: **to ~ sth (from)** extorquer qch (à); **~ionate** *adj* exorbitant(e)

extra ['ɛkstrə] *adj* supplémentaire, de plus ♦ *adv* (*in addition*) en plus ♦ *n* supplément *m*; (*perk*) à-côté *m*; (THEATRE) figurant(e) ♦ *prefix* extra...

extract [*vb* ɪks'trækt, *n* 'ɛkstrækt] *vt* extraire; (*tooth*) arracher; (*money, promise*) soutirer ♦ *n* extrait *m*

extracurricular ['ɛkstrəkə'rɪkjulər] *adj* parascolaire

extradite ['ɛkstrədaɪt] *vt* extrader

extra...: **~marital** ['ɛkstrə'mærɪtl] *adj* extra-conjugal(e); **~mural** ['ɛkstrə'mjuərl] *adj* hors faculté *inv*; (*lecture*) public(-que); **~ordinary** [ɪks'trɔːdnrɪ] *adj* extraordinaire

extravagance [ɪks'trævəgəns] *n* prodigalités *fpl*; (*thing bought*) folie *f*, dépense excessive; **extravagant** *adj* extravagant(e); (*in spending: person*) prodigue, dépensier(-ère); (: *tastes*) dispendieux(-euse)

extreme [ɪks'triːm] *adj* extrême ♦ *n* extrême *m*; **~ly** *adv* extrêmement; **extremist** *adj*, *n* extrémiste *m/f*

extricate ['ɛkstrɪkeɪt] *vt*: **to ~ sth (from)**

dégager qch (de)

extrovert ['ɛkstrəvɔːt] *n* extraverti(e)

ex-wife *n* ex-femme *f*

eye [aɪ] *n* œil *m* (*pl yeux*); (*of needle*) trou *m*, chas *m* ♦ *vt* examiner; **to keep an ~ on** surveiller; **~brow** *n* sourcil *m*; **~drops** *npl* gouttes *fpl* pour les yeux; **~lash** *n* cil *m*; **~lid** *n* paupière *f*; **~liner** *n* eye-liner *m*; **~-opener** *n* révélation *f*; **~shadow** *n* ombre *f* à paupières; **~sight** *n* vue *f*; **~sore** *n* horreur *f*; **~ witness** *n* témoin *m* oculaire

F, f

F [ɛf] *n* (MUS) fa *m*

fable ['feɪbl] *n* fable *f*

fabric ['fæbrɪk] *n* tissu *m*

fabulous ['fæbjuləs] *adj* fabuleux(-euse); (*inf: super*) formidable

face [feɪs] *n* visage *m*, figure *f*; (*expression*) expression *f*; (*of clock*) cadran *m*; (*of cliff*) paroi *f*; (*of mountain*) face *f*; (*of building*) façade *f* ♦ *vt* faire face à; **~ down** (*person*) à plat ventre; (*card*) face en dessous; **to lose/save ~** perdre/sauver la face; **to make** *or* **pull a ~** faire une grimace; **in the ~ of** (*difficulties etc*) face à, devant; **on the ~ of it** à première vue; **~ to ~** face à face; **~ up to** *vt fus* faire face à, affronter; **~ cloth** (BRIT) *n* gant *m* de toilette; **~ cream** *n* crème *f* pour le visage; **~ lift** *n* lifting *m*; (*of building etc*) ravalement *m*, retapage *m*; **~ powder** *n* poudre *f* de riz; **~ value** *n* (*of coin*) valeur nominale; **to take sth at ~ value** (*fig*) prendre qch pour argent comptant

facilities [fə'sɪlɪtɪz] *npl* installations *fpl*, équipement *m*; **credit ~** facilités *fpl* de paiement

facing ['feɪsɪŋ] *prep* face à, en face de

facsimile [fæk'sɪmɪlɪ] *n* (*exact replica*) facsimilé *m*; (*fax*) télécopie *f*

fact [fækt] *n* fait *m*; **in ~** en fait

factor ['fæktər] *n* facteur *m*

factory ['fæktərɪ] *n* usine *f*, fabrique *f*

factual ['fæktjuəl] *adj* basé(e) sur les faits

faculty ['fækəltɪ] *n* faculté *f*; (*US: teaching staff*) corps enseignant

fad [fæd] *n* (*craze*) engouement *m*

fade [feɪd] *vi* se décolorer, passer; (*light, sound*) s'affaiblir; (*flower*) se faner

fag [fæg] (*BRIT: inf*) *n* (*cigarette*) sèche *f*

fail [feɪl] *vt* (*exam*) échouer à; (*candidate*) recaler; (*subj: courage, memory*) faire défaut à ♦ *vi* échouer; (*brakes*) lâcher; (*eyesight, health, light*) baisser, s'affaiblir; **to ~ to do sth** (*neglect*) négliger de faire qch; (*be unable*) ne pas arriver or parvenir à faire qch; **without ~** à coup sûr; sans faute; **~ing** *n* défaut *m* ♦ *prep* faute de; **~ure** *n* échec *m*; (*person*) raté(e); (*mechanical etc*) défaillance *f*

faint [feɪnt] *adj* faible; (*recollection*) vague; (*mark*) à peine visible ♦ *n* évanouissement *m* ♦ *vi* s'évanouir; **to feel ~** défaillir

fair [fɛəʳ] *adj* équitable, juste, impartial(e); (*hair*) blond(e); (*skin, complexion*) pâle, blanc (blanche); (*weather*) beau (belle); (*good enough*) assez bon(ne); (*sizeable*) considérable ♦ *adv*: **to play ~** jouer franc-jeu ♦ *n* foire *f*; (*BRIT: funfair*) fête (foraine); **~ly** *adv* équitablement; (*quite*) assez; **~ness** *n* justice *f*, équité *f*, impartialité *f*

fairy ['fɛərɪ] *n* fée *f*; **~ tale** *n* conte *m* de fées

faith [feɪθ] *n* foi *f*; (*trust*) confiance *f*; (*specific religion*) religion *f*; **~ful** *adj* fidèle; **~fully** *adv* see **yours**

fake [feɪk] *n* (*painting etc*) faux *m*; (*person*) imposteur *m* ♦ *adj* faux (fausse) ♦ *vt* simuler; (*painting*) faire un faux de

falcon ['fɔːlkən] *n* faucon *m*

fall [fɔːl] (*pt fell, pp fallen*) *n* chute *f*; (*US: autumn*) automne *m* ♦ *vi* tomber; (*price, temperature, dollar*) baisser; **~s** *npl* (*waterfall*) chute *f* d'eau, cascade *f*; **to ~ flat** (*on one's face*) tomber de tout son long, s'étaler; (*joke*) tomber à plat; (*plan*) échouer; **~ back** *vi* reculer, se retirer; **~ back on** *vt fus* se rabattre sur; **~ behind** *vi* prendre du retard; **~ down** *vi* (*person*) tomber;

(*building*) s'effondrer, s'écrouler; **~ for** *vt fus* (*trick, story etc*) se laisser prendre à; (*person*) tomber amoureux de; **~ in** *vi* s'effondrer; (*MIL*) se mettre en rangs; **~ off** *vi* (*diminish*) baisser, diminuer; **~ out** *vi* (*hair, teeth*) tomber; (*MIL*) rompre les rangs; (*friends etc*) se brouiller; **~ through** *vi* (*plan, project*) tomber à l'eau

fallacy ['fæləsɪ] *n* erreur *f*, illusion *f*

fallout ['fɔːlaut] *n* retombées (radioactives)

fallow ['fæləu] *adj* en jachère; en friche

false [fɔːls] *adj* faux (fausse); **~ alarm** *n* fausse alerte; **~ pretences** *npl*: **under ~ pretences** sous un faux prétexte; **~ teeth** (*BRIT*) *npl* fausses dents

falter ['fɔːltəʳ] *vi* chanceler, vaciller

fame [feɪm] *n* renommée *f*, renom *m*

familiar [fə'mɪlɪəʳ] *adj* familier(-ère); **to be ~ with** (*subject*) connaître

family ['fæmɪlɪ] *n* famille *f* ♦ *cpd* (*business, doctor etc*) de famille; **has he any ~?** (*children*) a-t-il des enfants?

famine ['fæmɪn] *n* famine *f*

famished ['fæmɪʃt] (*inf*) *adj* affamé(e)

famous ['feɪməs] *adj* célèbre; **~ly** *adv* (*get on*) fameusement, à merveille

fan [fæn] *n* (*folding*) éventail *m*; (*ELEC*) ventilateur *m*; (*of person*) fan *m*, admirateur(-trice); (*of team, sport etc*) supporter *m/f* ♦ *vt* éventer; (*fire, quarrel*) attiser

fanatic [fə'nætɪk] *n* fanatique *m/f*

fan belt *n* courroie *f* de ventilateur

fancy ['fænsɪ] *n* fantaisie *f*, envie *f*; imagination *f* ♦ *adj* (*de*) fantaisie *inv* ♦ *vt* (*feel like, want*) avoir envie de; (*imagine, think*) imaginer; **to take a ~ to** se prendre d'affection pour; s'enticher de; **he fancies her** (*inf*) elle lui plaît; **~ dress** *n* déguisement *m*, travesti *m*; **~-dress ball** *n* bal masqué or costumé

fang [fæŋ] *n* croc *m*; (*of snake*) crochet *m*

fantastic [fæn'tæstɪk] *adj* fantastique

fantasy ['fæntəsɪ] *n* imagination *f*, fantaisie *f*; (*dream*) chimère *f*

far [fɑːʳ] *adj* lointain(e), éloigné(e) ♦ *adv* loin; **~ away** or **off** au loin, dans le lointain; **at the ~ side/end** à l'autre côté/

bout; **~ better** beaucoup mieux; **~ from** loin de; **by ~** de loin, de beaucoup; **go as ~ as the farm** allez jusqu'à la ferme; **as ~ as I know** pour autant que je sache; **how ~ is it to ...?** combien y a-t-il jusqu'à ...?; **how ~ have you got?** où en êtes-vous?; ~**away** ['fɑːrəweɪ] *adj* lointain(e); (*look*) distrait(e)

farce [fɑːs] *n* farce *f*

fare [feəʳ] *n* (*on trains, buses*) prix *m* du billet; (*in taxi*) prix de la course; (*food*) table *f*, chère *f*; **half ~** demi-tarif; **full ~** plein tarif

Far East *n* Extrême-Orient *m*

farewell [feə'wel] *excl* adieu ♦ *n* adieu *m*

farm [fɑːm] *n* ferme *f* ♦ *vt* cultiver; ~**er** *n* fermier(-ère); cultivateur(-trice); ~**hand** *n* ouvrier(-ère) agricole; ~**house** *n* (maison *f* de) ferme *f*; ~**ing** *n* agriculture *f*; (*of animals*) élevage *m*; ~**land** *n* terres cultivées; ~ **worker** *n* = **farmhand**; ~**yard** *n* cour *f* de ferme

far-reaching ['fɑː'riːtʃɪŋ] *adj* d'une grande portée

fart [fɑːt] (*inf!*) *vi* péter

farther ['fɑːðəʳ] *adv* plus loin ♦ *adj* plus éloigné(e), plus lointain(e)

farthest ['fɑːðɪst] *superl of* **far**

fascinate ['fæsɪneɪt] *vt* fasciner; **fascinating** *adj* fascinant(e)

fascism ['fæʃɪzəm] *n* fascisme *m*

fashion ['fæʃən] *n* mode *f*; (*manner*) façon *f*, manière *f* ♦ *vt* façonner; **in ~** à la mode; **out of ~** démodé(e); ~**able** *adj* à la mode; ~ **show** *n* défilé *m* de mannequins *or* de mode

fast [fɑːst] *adj* rapide; (*clock*): **to be ~** avancer; (*dye, colour*) grand *or* bon teint *inv* ♦ *adv* vite, rapidement; (*stuck, held*) solidement ♦ *n* jeûne *m* ♦ *vi* jeûner; ~ **asleep** profondément endormi

fasten ['fɑːsn] *vt* attacher, fixer; (*coat*) attacher, fermer ♦ *vi* se fermer, s'attacher; ~**er**, ~**ing** *n* attache *f*

fast food *n* fast food *m*, restauration *f* rapide

fastidious [fæs'tɪdɪəs] *adj* exigeant(e), difficile

fat [fæt] *adj* gros(se) ♦ *n* graisse *f*; (*on meat*) gras *m*; (*for cooking*) matière grasse

fatal ['feɪtl] *adj* (*injury etc*) mortel(le); (*mistake*) fatal(e); ~**ity** [fə'tælɪtɪ] *n* (*road death etc*) victime *f*, décès *m*

fate [feɪt] *n* destin *m*; (*of person*) sort *m*; ~**ful** *adj* fatidique

father ['fɑːðəʳ] *n* père *m*; ~-**in-law** *n* beau-père *m*; ~**ly** *adj* paternel(le)

fathom ['fæðəm] *n* brasse *f* (= *1828 mm*) ♦ *vt* (*mystery*) sonder, pénétrer

fatigue [fə'tiːg] *n* fatigue *f*

fatten ['fætn] *vt*, *vi* engraisser

fatty ['fætɪ] *adj* (*food*) gras(se) ♦ *n* (*inf*) gros(se)

fatuous ['fætjuəs] *adj* stupide

faucet ['fɔːsɪt] (*US*) *n* robinet *m*

fault [fɔːlt] *n* faute *f*; (*defect*) défaut *m*; (*GEO*) faille *f* ♦ *vt* trouver des défauts à; **it's my ~** c'est de ma faute; **to find ~ with** trouver à redire *or* à critiquer à; **at ~** fautif(-ive), coupable; ~**y** *adj* défectueux(-euse)

fauna ['fɔːnə] *n* faune *f*

favour ['feɪvəʳ] (*US* **favor**) *n* faveur *f*; (*help*) service *m* ♦ *vt* (*proposition*) être en faveur de; (*pupil etc*) favoriser; (*team, horse*) donner gagnant; **to do sb a ~** rendre un service à qn; **to find ~ with** trouver grâce aux yeux de; **in ~ of** en faveur de; ~**able** *adj* favorable; ~**ite** ['feɪvrɪt] *adj*, *n* favori(te)

fawn [fɔːn] *n* faon *m* ♦ *adj* (*colour*) fauve ♦ *vi*: **to ~ (up)on** flatter servilement

fax [fæks] *n* (*document*) télécopie *f*; (*machine*) télécopieur *m* ♦ *vt* envoyer par télécopie

FBI *n abbr* (*US: Federal Bureau of Investigation*) F.B.I. *m*

fear [fɪəʳ] *n* crainte *f*, peur *f* ♦ *vt* craindre; **for ~ of** de peur que +*sub*, de peur de +*infin*; ~**ful** *adj* craintif(-ive); (*sight, noise*) affreux(-euse), épouvantable; ~**less** *adj* intrépide

feasible ['fiːzəbl] *adj* faisable, réalisable

feast [fiːst] *n* festin *m*, banquet *m*; (*REL:*

also: **~ day**) fête f ♦ vi festoyer

feat [fiːt] n exploit m, prouesse f

feather ['feðəʳ] n plume f

feature ['fiːtʃəʳ] n caractéristique f; (article) chronique f, rubrique f ♦ vt (subj: film) avoir pour vedette(s) ♦ vi: **to ~ in** figurer (en bonne place) dans; (in film) jouer dans; **~s** npl (of face) traits mpl; **~ film** n long métrage

February ['fɛbruərɪ] n février m

fed [fɛd] pt, pp of **feed**

federal ['fɛdərəl] adj fédéral(e)

fed up adj: **to be ~** en avoir marre, en avoir plein le dos

fee [fiː] n rémunération f; (of doctor, lawyer) honoraires mpl; (for examination) droits mpl; **school ~s** frais mpl de scolarité

feeble ['fiːbl] adj faible; (pathetic: attempt, excuse) pauvre; (: joke) piteux(-euse)

feed [fiːd] (pt, pp **fed**) n (of animal) fourrage m; pâture f; (on printer) mécanisme m d'alimentation ♦ vt (person) nourrir; (BRIT: baby) allaiter; (: with bottle) donner le biberon à; (horse etc) donner à manger à; (machine) alimenter; (data, information): **to ~ sth into** fournir qch à; **~ on** vt fus se nourrir de; **~back** n feed-back m inv

feel [fiːl] (pt, pp **felt**) n sensation f; (impression) impression f ♦ vt toucher; (explore) tâter, palper; (cold, pain) sentir; (grief, anger) ressentir, éprouver; (think, believe) trouver; **to ~ hungry/cold** avoir faim/froid; **to ~ lonely/better** se sentir seul/mieux; **I don't ~ well** je ne me sens pas bien; **it ~s soft** c'est doux (douce) au toucher; **to ~ like** (want) avoir envie de; **~ about** vi fouiller, tâtonner; **~er** n (of insect) antenne f; **~ing** n (physical) sensation f; (emotional) sentiment m

feet [fiːt] npl of **foot**

feign [feɪn] vt feindre, simuler

fell [fɛl] pt of **fall** ♦ vt (tree, person) abattre

fellow ['fɛləu] n type m; (comrade) compagnon m; (of learned society) membre m ♦ cpd: **their ~ prisoners/students** leurs camarades prisonniers/d'étude; **~ citizen** n concitoyen(ne) m/f; **~ countryman** (irreg) n compatriote m; **~ men** npl semblables mpl; **~ship** n (society) association f; (comradeship) amitié f, camaraderie f; (grant) sorte de bourse universitaire

felony ['fɛlənɪ] n crime m, forfait m

felt [fɛlt] pt, pp of **feel** ♦ n feutre m; **~-tip pen** n stylo-feutre m

female ['fiːmeɪl] n (ZOOL) femelle f; (pej: woman) bonne femme ♦ adj (BIO) femelle; (sex, character) féminin(e); (vote etc) des femmes

feminine ['fɛmɪnɪn] adj féminin(e)

feminist ['fɛmɪnɪst] n féministe m/f

fence [fɛns] n barrière f ♦ vt (also: **~ in**) clôturer ♦ vi faire de l'escrime; **fencing** n escrime m

fend [fɛnd] vi: **to ~ for o.s.** se débrouiller (tout seul); **~ off** vt (attack etc) parer

fender ['fɛndəʳ] n garde-feu m inv; (on boat) défense f; (US: of car) aile f

ferment [vb fə'mɛnt, n 'fɜːmɛnt] vi fermenter ♦ n agitation f, effervescence f

fern [fɜːn] n fougère f

ferocious [fə'rəuʃəs] adj féroce

ferret ['fɛrɪt] n furet m

ferry ['fɛrɪ] n (small) bac m; (large: also: **~boat**) ferry(-boat) m ♦ vt transporter

fertile ['fɜːtaɪl] adj fertile; (BIO) fécond(e);

fertilizer ['fɜːtɪlaɪzəʳ] n engrais m

fester ['fɛstəʳ] vi suppurer

festival ['fɛstɪvəl] n (REL) fête f; (ART, MUS) festival m

festive ['fɛstɪv] adj de fête; **the ~ season** (BRIT: Christmas) la période des fêtes; **festivities** npl réjouissances fpl

festoon [fɛs'tuːn] vt: **to ~ with** orner de

fetch [fɛtʃ] vt aller chercher; (sell for) se vendre

fête [feɪt] n fête f, kermesse f

feud [fjuːd] n dispute f, dissension f

fever ['fiːvəʳ] n fièvre f; **~ish** adj fiévreux(-euse), fébrile

few [fjuː] adj (not many) peu de; **a ~** ♦ adj quelques ♦ pron quelques-uns(-unes); **~er** ['fjuːəʳ] adj moins de; moins (nombreux); **~est** ['fjuːɪst] adj le moins (de)

fiancé, e [fɪ'ɑ̃ːnseɪ] n fiancé(e) m/f

fib [fɪb] *n* bobard *m*

fibre, (*US* **fiber**) ['faɪbə'] *n* fibre *f*; **~glass**, (*US* **Fiberglass** ®) ['faɪbəglɑːs] *n* fibre de verre

fickle ['fɪkl] *adj* inconstant(e), volage, capricieux(-euse)

fiction ['fɪkʃən] *n* romans *mpl*, littérature *f* romanesque; (*invention*) fiction *f*; **~al** *adj* fictif(-ive)

fictitious *adj* fictif(-ive), imaginaire

fiddle ['fɪdl] *n* (*MUS*) violon *m*; (*cheating*) combine *f*; escroquerie *f* ♦ *vt* (*BRIT: accounts*) falsifier, maquiller; **~ with** *vt fus* tripoter

fidget ['fɪdʒɪt] *vi* se trémousser, remuer

field [fiːld] *n* champ *m*; (*fig*) domaine *m*, champ; (*SPORT: ground*) terrain *m*; **~work** *n* travaux *mpl* pratiques (sur le terrain)

fiend [fiːnd] *n* démon *m*

fierce [fɪəs] *adj* (*look, animal*) féroce, sauvage; (*wind, attack, person*) (très) violent(e); (*fighting, enemy*) acharné(e)

fiery ['faɪərɪ] *adj* ardent(e), brûlant(e); (*temperament*) fougueux(-euse)

fifteen [fɪf'tiːn] *num* quinze

fifth [fɪfθ] *num* cinquième

fifty ['fɪftɪ] *num* cinquante; **~-fifty** *adj*: **a ~-fifty chance** etc une chance etc sur deux ♦ *adv* moitié-moitié

fig [fɪg] *n* figue *f*

fight [faɪt] (*pt, pp* **fought**) *n* (*MIL*) combat *m*; (*between persons*) bagarre *f*; (*against cancer etc*) lutte *f* ♦ *vt* se battre contre; (*cancer, alcoholism, emotion*) combattre, lutter contre; (*election*) se présenter à ♦ *vi* se battre; **~er** *n* (*fig*) lutteur *m*; (*plane*) chasseur *m*; **~ing** *n* combats *mpl*; (*brawl*) bagarres *fpl*

figment ['fɪgmənt] *n*: **a ~ of the imagination** une invention

figurative ['fɪgjurətɪv] *adj* figuré(e)

figure ['fɪgə'] *n* figure *f*; (*number, cipher*) chiffre *m*; (*body, outline*) silhouette *f*; (*shape*) ligne *f*, formes *fpl* ♦ *vt* (*think: esp US*) supposer ♦ *vi* (*appear*) figurer; **~ out** *vt* (*work out*) calculer; **~head** *n* (*NAUT*) figure *f* de proue; (*pej*) prête-nom *m*; **~**

of speech *n* figure *f* de rhétorique

file [faɪl] *n* (*dossier*) dossier *m*; (*folder*) dossier, chemise *f*; (*: with hinges*) classeur *m*; (*COMPUT*) fichier *m*; (*row*) file *f*; (*tool*) lime *f* ♦ *vt* (*nails, wood*) limer; (*papers*) classer; (*LAW: claim*) faire enregistrer; déposer ♦ *vi*: **to ~ in/out** entrer/sortir l'un derrière l'autre; **to ~ for divorce** faire une demande en divorce; **filing cabinet** *n* classeur *m* (*meuble*)

fill [fɪl] *vt* remplir; (*need*) répondre à ♦ *n*: **to eat one's ~** manger à sa faim; **to ~ with** remplir de; **~ in** *vt* (*hole*) boucher; (*form*) remplir; **~ up** *vt* remplir; **~ it up, please** (*AUT*) le plein, s'il vous plaît

fillet ['fɪlɪt] *n* filet *m*; **~ steak** *n* filet *m* de bœuf, tournedos *m*

filling ['fɪlɪŋ] *n* (*CULIN*) garniture *f*, farce *f*; (*for tooth*) plombage *m*; **~ station** *n* station-service *f*

film [fɪlm] *n* film *m*; (*PHOT*) pellicule *f*, film *m*; (*of powder, liquid*) couche *f*, pellicule ♦ *vt* (*scene*) filmer ♦ *vi* tourner; **~ star** *n* vedette *f* de cinéma

filter ['fɪltə'] *n* filtre *m* ♦ *vt* filtrer; **~ lane** *n* (*AUT*) voie *f* de sortie; **~-tipped** *adj* à bout filtre

filth [fɪlθ] *n* saleté *f*; **~y** *adj* sale, dégoûtant(e); (*language*) ordurier(-ère)

fin [fɪn] *n* (*of fish*) nageoire *f*

final ['faɪnl] *adj* final(e); (*definitive*) définitif(-ive) ♦ *n* (*SPORT*) finale *f*; **~s** *npl* (*SCOL*) examens *mpl* de dernière année; **~e** [fɪ'nɑːlɪ] *n* finale *m*; **~ist** *n* finaliste *m/f*; **~ize** *vt* mettre au point; **~ly** *adv* (*eventually*) enfin, finalement; (*lastly*) en dernier lieu

finance [faɪ'næns] *n* finance *f* ♦ *vt* financer; **~s** *npl* (*financial position*) finances *fpl*; **financial** [faɪ'nænʃəl] *adj* financier(-ère)

find [faɪnd] (*pt, pp* **found**) *vt* trouver; (*lost object*) retrouver ♦ *n* trouvaille *f*, découverte *f*; **to ~ sb guilty** (*LAW*) déclarer qn coupable; **~ out** *vt* (*truth, secret*) découvrir; (*person*) démasquer ♦ *vi*: **to ~ out about** (*make enquiries*) se renseigner; (*by chance*) apprendre; **~ings** *npl* (*LAW*) conclusions *fpl*, verdict *m*; (*of report*) conclusions

fine [faɪn] *adj* (*excellent*) excellent(e); (*thin, not coarse, subtle*) fin(e); (*weather*) beau (belle) ♦ *adv* (*well*) très bien ♦ *n* (LAW) amende *f*; contravention *f* ♦ *vt* (LAW) condamner à une amende; donner une contravention à; **to be ~** (*person*) aller bien; (*weather*) être beau; **~ arts** *npl* beaux-arts *mpl*; **~ry** *n* parure *f*

finger ['fɪŋgəʳ] *n* doigt *m* ♦ *vt* palper, toucher; **little ~** auriculaire *m*, petit doigt; **index ~** index *m*; **~nail** *n* ongle *m* (de la main); **~print** *n* empreinte digitale; **~tip** *n* bout *m* du doigt

finish ['fɪnɪʃ] *n* fin *f*; (SPORT) arrivée *f*; (*polish etc*) finition *f* ♦ *vt* finir, terminer ♦ *vi* finir, se terminer; **to ~ doing sth** finir de faire qch; **to ~ third** arriver *or* terminer troisième; **~ off** *vt* finir, terminer; (*kill*) achever; **~ up** *vi*, *vt* finir; **~ing line** *n* ligne *f* d'arrivée

finite ['faɪnaɪt] *adj* fini(e); (*verb*) conjugué(e)

Finland ['fɪnlənd] *n* Finlande *f*; **Finn** [fɪn] *n* Finlandais(e); **Finnish** *adj* finlandais(e) ♦ *n* (LING) finnois *m*

fir [fəːʳ] *n* sapin *m*

fire ['faɪəʳ] *n* feu *m*; (*accidental*) incendie *m*; (*heater*) radiateur *m* ♦ *vt* (*fig*) enflammer, animer; (*inf: dismiss*) mettre à la porte, renvoyer; (*discharge*): **to ~ a gun** tirer un coup de feu ♦ *vi* (*shoot*) tirer, faire feu; **on ~** en feu; **~ alarm** *n* avertisseur *m* d'incendie; **~arm** *n* arme *f* à feu; **~ brigade** *n* (sapeurs-)pompiers *mpl*; **~ department** (US) *n* = **fire brigade**; **~ engine** *n* (*vehicle*) voiture *f* des pompiers; **~ escape** *n* escalier *m* de secours; **~ extinguisher** *n* extincteur *m*; **~man** *n* pompier *m*; **~place** *n* cheminée *f*; **~side** *n* foyer *m*, coin *m* du feu; **~ station** *n* caserne *f* de pompiers; **~wood** *n* bois *m* de chauffage; **~works** *npl* feux *mpl* d'artifice; (*display*) feu(x) d'artifice

firing squad ['faɪərɪŋ-] *n* peloton *m* d'exécution

firm [fəːm] *adj* ferme ♦ *n* compagnie *f*, firme *f*

first [fəːst] *adj* premier(-ère) ♦ *adv* (*before all others*) le premier, la première; (*before all other things*) en premier, d'abord; (*when listing reasons etc*) en premier lieu, premièrement ♦ *n* (*person: in race*) premier(-ère); (BRIT: SCOL) mention *f* très bien; (AUT) première *f*; **at ~** au commencement, au début; **~ of all** tout d'abord, pour commencer; **~ aid** *n* premiers secours *or* soins; **~-aid kit** *n* trousse *f* à pharmacie; **~-class** *adj* de première classe; (*excellent*) excellent(e), exceptionnel(le); **~-hand** *adj* de première main; **~ lady** (US) *n* femme *f* du président; **~ly** *adv* premièrement, en premier lieu; **~ name** *n* prénom *m*; **~-rate** *adj* excellent(e)

fish [fɪʃ] *n inv* poisson *m* ♦ *vt*, *vi* pêcher; **to go ~ing** aller à la pêche; **~erman** *n* pêcheur *m*; **~ farm** *n* établissement *m* piscicole; **~ fingers** (BRIT) *npl* bâtonnets de poisson (congelés); **~ing boat** *n* barque *f or* bateau *m* de pêche; **~ing line** *n* ligne *f* (de pêche); **~ing rod** *n* canne *f* à pêche; **~ing tackle** *n* attirail *m* de pêche; **~monger's (shop)** *n* poissonnerie *f*; **~ slice** *n* pelle *f* à poisson; **~ sticks** (US) *npl* = **fish fingers**; **~y** (*inf*) *adj* suspect(e), louche

fist [fɪst] *n* poing *m*

fit [fɪt] *adj* (*healthy*) en (bonne) forme; (*proper*) convenable; approprié(e) ♦ *vt* (*subj: clothes*) aller à; (*put in, attach*) installer, poser; adapter; (*equip*) équiper, garnir, munir; (*suit*) convenir à ♦ *vi* (*clothes*) aller; (*parts*) s'adapter; (*in space, gap*) entrer, s'adapter ♦ *n* (MED) accès *m*, crise *f* (*of anger*) accès; (*of hysterics, jealousy*) crise; **~ to** en état de; **~ for** digne de; apte à; **~ of coughing** quinte *f* de toux; **a ~ of giggles** le fou rire; **this dress is a good ~** cette robe (me) va très bien; **by ~s and starts** par à-coups; **~ in** *vi* s'accorder; s'adapter; **~ful** *adj* (*sleep*) agité(e); **~ment** *n* meuble encastré, élément *m*; **~ness** *n*

(MED) forme *f* physique; **~ted carpet** *n* moquette *f*; **~ted kitchen** *(BRIT)* *n* cuisine équipée; **~ter** *n* monteur *m*; **~ting** *adj* approprié(e) ♦ *n* *(of dress)* essayage *m*; *(of piece of equipment)* pose *f*, installation *f*; **~tings** *npl* *(in building)* installations *fpl*; **~ting room** *n* cabine *f* d'essayage

five [faɪv] *num* cinq; **~r** *(inf)* *n* *(BRIT)* billet *m* de cinq livres; *(US)* billet de cinq dollars

fix [fɪks] *vt* *(date, amount etc)* fixer; *(organize)* arranger; *(mend)* réparer; *(meal, drink)* préparer ♦ *n*: **to be in a ~** être dans le pétrin; **~ up** *vt* *(meeting)* arranger; **to ~ sb up with sth** faire avoir qch à qn; **~ation** [fɪk'seɪʃən] *n* *(PSYCH)* fixation *f*; *(fig)* obsession *f*; **~ed** *adj* *(prices etc)* fixe; *(smile)* figé(e); **~ture** *n* installation *f* (fixe); *(SPORT)* rencontre *f* (au programme)

fizzy ['fɪzɪ] *adj* pétillant(e); gazeux(-euse)

flabbergasted ['flæbəgɑːstɪd] *adj* sidéré(e), ahuri(e)

flabby ['flæbɪ] *adj* mou (molle)

flag [flæg] *n* drapeau *m*; *(also:* **~stone**) dalle *f* ♦ *vi* faiblir; fléchir; **~ down** *vt* héler, faire signe (de s'arrêter) à; **~pole** *n* mât *m*; **~ship** *n* vaisseau *m* amiral; *(fig)* produit *m* vedette

flair [flɛər] *n* flair *m*

flak [flæk] *n* *(MIL)* tir antiaérien; *(inf: criticism)* critiques *fpl*

flake [fleɪk] *n* *(of rust, paint)* écaille *f*; *(of snow, soap powder)* flocon *m* ♦ *vi* *(also: ~ off)* s'écailler

flamboyant [flæm'bɔɪənt] *adj* flamboyant(e), éclatant(e); *(person)* haut(e) en couleur

flame [fleɪm] *n* flamme *f*

flamingo [flə'mɪŋgəu] *n* flamant *m* (rose)

flammable ['flæməbl] *adj* inflammable

flan [flæn] *(BRIT)* *n* tarte *f*

flank [flæŋk] *n* flanc *m* ♦ *vt* flanquer

flannel ['flænl] *n* *(fabric)* flanelle *f*; *(BRIT: also:* **face ~**) gant *m* de toilette

flap [flæp] *n* *(of pocket, envelope)* rabat *m* ♦ *vt* *(wings)* battre (de) ♦ *vi* *(sail, flag)* claquer; *(inf: also:* **be in a ~**) paniquer

flare [flɛər] *n* *(signal)* signal lumineux; *(in skirt etc)* évasement *m*; **~ up** *vi* s'embraser; *(fig: person)* se mettre en colère, s'emporter; *(: revolt etc)* éclater

flash [flæʃ] *n* éclair *m*; *(also:* **news ~**) flash *m* (d'information); *(PHOT)* flash ♦ *vt* *(light)* projeter; *(send: message)* câbler; *(look)* jeter; *(smile)* lancer ♦ *vi* *(light)* clignoter; **a ~ of lightning** un éclair; **in a ~** en un clin d'œil; **to ~ one's headlights** faire un appel de phares; **to ~ by or past** *(person)* passer (devant) comme un éclair; **~bulb** *n* ampoule *f* de flash; **~cube** *n* cube-flash *m*; **~light** *n* lampe *f* de poche; **~y** *(pej)* *adj* tape-à-l'œil *inv*, tapageur(-euse)

flask [flɑːsk] *n* flacon *m*, bouteille *f*; *(also:* **vacuum ~**) thermos ® *m* or *f*

flat [flæt] *adj* plat(e); *(tyre)* dégonflé(e), à plat; *(beer)* éventé(e); *(denial)* catégorique; *(MUS)* bémol *inv*; *(: voice)* faux (fausse); *(fee, rate)* fixe ♦ *n* *(BRIT: apartment)* appartement *m*; *(AUT)* crevaison *f*; *(MUS)* bémol *m*; **to work ~ out** travailler d'arrache-pied; **~ly** *adv* catégoriquement; **~ten** *vt* *(also:* **~ten out**) aplatir; *(crop)* coucher; *(building(s))* raser

flatter ['flætər] *vt* flatter; **~ing** *adj* flatteur(-euse); **~y** *n* flatterie *f*

flaunt [flɔːnt] *vt* faire étalage de

flavour ['fleɪvər] *(US* **flavor**) *n* goût *m*, saveur *f*; *(of ice cream etc)* parfum *m* ♦ *vt* parfumer; **vanilla-~ed** à l'arôme de vanille, à la vanille; **~ing** *n* arôme *m*

flaw [flɔː] *n* défaut *m*; **~less** *adj* sans défaut

flax [flæks] *n* lin *m*

flea [fliː] *n* puce *f*

fleck [flɛk] *n* tacheture *f*; moucheture *f*

flee [fliː] *(pt, pp* **fled**) *vt* fuir ♦ *vi* fuir, s'enfuir

fleece [fliːs] *n* toison *f* ♦ *vt* *(inf)* voler, filouter

fleet [fliːt] *n* flotte *f*; *(of lorries etc)* parc *m*, convoi *m*

fleeting ['fliːtɪŋ] *adj* fugace, fugitif(-ive); *(visit)* très bref (brève)

Flemish ['flɛmɪʃ] *adj* flamand(e)

flesh [flɛʃ] *n* chair *f*; **~ wound** *n* blessure

superficielle

flew [fluː] *pt of* **fly**

flex [flɛks] *n* fil *m or* câble *m* électrique ♦ *vt* (*knee*) fléchir; (*muscles*) tendre; ~**ible** *adj* flexible

flick [flɪk] *n* petite tape; chiquenaude *f*; (*of duster*) petit coup ♦ *vt* donner un petit coup à; (*switch*) appuyer sur; ~ **through** *vt fus* feuilleter

flicker [ˈflɪkəʳ] *vi* (*light*) vaciller; **his eyelids ~ed** il a cillé

flier [ˈflaɪəʳ] *n* aviateur *m*

flight [flaɪt] *n* vol *m*; (*escape*) fuite *f*; (*also:* ~ **of steps**) escalier *m*; ~ **attendant** (*US*) *n* steward *m*, hôtesse *f* de l'air; ~ **deck** *n* (*AVIAT*) poste *m* de pilotage; (*NAUT*) pont *m* d'envol

flimsy [ˈflɪmzɪ] *adj* peu solide; (*clothes*) trop léger(-ère); (*excuse*) pauvre, mince

flinch [flɪntʃ] *vi* tressaillir; **to ~ from** se dérober à, reculer devant

fling [flɪŋ] (*pt, pp* **flung**) *vt* jeter, lancer

flint [flɪnt] *n* silex *m*; (*in lighter*) pierre *f* (à briquet)

flip [flɪp] *vt* (*throw*) lancer (d'une chiquenaude); **to ~ sth over** retourner qch

flippant [ˈflɪpənt] *adj* désinvolte, irrévérencieux(-euse)

flipper [ˈflɪpəʳ] *n* (*of seal etc*) nageoire *f*; (*for swimming*) palme *f*

flirt [flɜːt] *vi* flirter ♦ *n* flirteur(-euse) *m/f*

float [fləʊt] *n* flotteur *m*; (*in procession*) char *m*; (*money*) réserve *f* ♦ *vi* flotter

flock [flɒk] *n* troupeau *m*; (*of birds*) vol *m*; (*REL*) ouailles *fpl* ♦ *vi:* **to ~ to** se rendre en masse à

flog [flɒg] *vt* fouetter

flood [flʌd] *n* inondation *f*; (*of letters, refugees etc*) flot *m* ♦ *vt* inonder ♦ *vi* (*people*): **to ~ into** envahir; ~**ing** *n* inondation *f*; ~**light** *n* projecteur *m*

floor [flɔːʳ] *n* sol *m*; (*storey*) étage *m*; (*of sea, valley*) fond *m* ♦ *vt* (*subj: question*) décontenancer; (: *blow*) terrasser; **on the ~** par terre; **ground ~,** (*US*) **first ~** rez-de-chaussée *m inv*; **first ~,** (*US*) **second ~** premier étage; ~**board** *n* planche *f* (du

plancher); ~ **show** *n* spectacle *m* de variétés

flop [flɒp] *n* fiasco *m* ♦ *vi* être un fiasco; (*fall: into chair*) s'affaler, s'effondrer; ~**py** *adj* lâche, flottant(e) ♦ *n* (*COMPUT: also:* ~**py disk**) disquette *f*

flora [ˈflɔːrə] *n* flore *f*

floral [ˈflɔːrl] *adj* (*dress*) à fleurs

florid [ˈflɒrɪd] *adj* (*complexion*) coloré(e); (*style*) plein(e) de fioritures

florist [ˈflɒrɪst] *n* fleuriste *m/f*; ~**'s** (**shop**) *n* magasin *m or* boutique *f* de fleuriste

flounder [ˈflaʊndəʳ] *vi* patauger ♦ *n* (*ZOOL*) flet *m*

flour [ˈflaʊəʳ] *n* farine *f*

flourish [ˈflʌrɪʃ] *vi* prospérer ♦ *n* (*gesture*) moulinet *m*

flout [flaʊt] *vt* se moquer de, faire fi de

flow [fləʊ] *n* (*ELEC, of river*) courant *m*; (*of blood in veins*) circulation *f*; (*of tide*) flux *m*; (*of orders, data*) flot *m* ♦ *vi* couler; (*traffic*) s'écouler; (*robes, hair*) flotter; **the ~ of traffic** l'écoulement *m* de la circulation; ~ **chart** *n* organigramme *m*

flower [ˈflaʊəʳ] *n* fleur *f* ♦ *vi* fleurir; ~ **bed** *n* plate-bande *f*; ~**pot** *n* pot *m* (de fleurs); ~**y** *adj* fleuri(e)

flown [fləʊn] *pp of* **fly**

flu [fluː] *n* grippe *f*

fluctuate [ˈflʌktjʊeɪt] *vi* varier, fluctuer

fluent [ˈfluːənt] *adj* (*speech*) coulant(e), aisé(e); **he speaks ~ French, he's ~ in French** il parle couramment le français

fluff [flʌf] *n* duvet *m*; (*on jacket, carpet*) peluche *f*; ~**y** *adj* duveteux(-euse); (*toy*) en peluche

fluid [ˈfluːɪd] *adj* fluide ♦ *n* fluide *m*

fluke [fluːk] (*inf*) *n* (*luck*) coup *m* de veine

flung [flʌŋ] *pt, pp of* **fling**

fluoride [ˈflʊəraɪd] *n* fluorure *f*; ~ **toothpaste** dentifrice *m* au fluor

flurry [ˈflʌrɪ] *n* (*of snow*) rafale *f*, bourrasque *f*; ~ **of activity/excitement** affairement *m*/excitation *f* soudain(e)

flush [flʌʃ] *n* (*on face*) rougeur *f*; (*fig: of youth, beauty etc*) éclat *m* ♦ *vt* nettoyer à grande eau ♦ *vi* rougir ♦ *adj:* ~ **with** au ras de, de niveau avec; **to ~ the toilet** tirer la chasse (d'eau); **~ed** adj (tout(e)) rouge

flustered ['flʌstəd] adj énervé(e)

flute [fluːt] n flûte f

flutter ['flʌtə'] n (of panic, excitement) agitation f; (of wings) battement m ♦ vi (bird) battre des ailes, voleter

flux [flʌks] n: **in a state of ~** fluctuant sans cesse

fly [flaɪ] (pt **flew**, pp **flown**) n (insect) mouche f; (on trousers: also: **flies**) braguette f ♦ vt piloter; (passengers, cargo) transporter (par avion); (distances) parcourir ♦ vi voler; (passengers) aller en avion; (escape) s'enfuir, fuir; (flag) se déployer; **~ away** vi (bird, insect) s'envoler; **~ off** vi = **fly away**; **~-drive** n formule f avion plus voiture; **~ing** n (activity) aviation f; (action) vol m ♦ adj: **a ~ing visit** une visite éclair; **with ~ing colours** haut la main; **~ing saucer** n soucoupe volante; **~ing start** n: **to get off to a ~ing start** prendre un excellent départ; **~over** (BRIT) n (bridge) saut-de-mouton m; **~sheet** n (for tent) double toit m

foal [fəul] n poulain m

foam [fəum] n écume f; (on beer) mousse f; (also: **~ rubber**) caoutchouc mousse m ♦ vi (liquid) écumer; (soapy water) mousser

fob [fɔb] vt: **to ~ sb off** se débarrasser de qn

focal point ['fəukl-] n (fig) point central

focus ['fəukəs] (pl **~es**) n foyer m; (of interest) centre m ♦ vt (camera etc) mettre au point ♦ vi: **to ~ (on)** (with camera) régler la mise au point (sur); (person) fixer son regard (sur); **out of/in ~** (picture) flou(e)/net(te); (camera) mal au point/au point

fodder ['fɔdə'] n fourrage m

foe [fəu] n ennemi m

fog [fɔg] n brouillard m; **~gy** adj: **it's ~gy** il y a du brouillard; **~ lamp** (US **fog light**) n (AUT) phare m antibrouillard

foil [fɔɪl] vt déjouer, contrecarrer ♦ n feuille f de métal; (kitchen ~) papier m alu(minium); (complement) repoussoir m

fold [fəuld] n (bend, crease) pli m; (AGR) parc m à moutons; (fig) bercail m ♦ vt plier; (arms) croiser; **~ up** vi (map, table etc) se plier; (business) fermer boutique ♦ vt (map, clothes) plier; **~er** n (for papers) chemise f; (: with hinges) classeur m; (COMPUT) répertoire m; **~ing** adj (chair, bed) pliant(e)

foliage ['fəulɪdʒ] n feuillage m

folk [fəuk] npl gens mpl ♦ cpd folklorique; **~s** (inf) npl (parents) parents mpl; **~lore** ['fəuklɔː'] n folklore m; **~ song** n chanson f folklorique

follow ['fɔləu] vt suivre ♦ vi suivre; (result) s'ensuivre; **to ~ suit** (fig) faire de même; **~ up** vt (letter, offer) donner suite à; (case) suivre; **~er** n disciple m/f, partisan(e); **~ing** adj suivant(e) ♦ n partisans mpl, disciples mpl

folly ['fɔlɪ] n inconscience f; folie f

fond [fɔnd] adj (memory, look) tendre; (hopes, dreams) un peu fou (folle); **to be ~ of** aimer beaucoup

fondle ['fɔndl] vt caresser

font [fɔnt] n (in church: for baptism) fonts baptismaux; (TYP) fonte f

food [fuːd] n nourriture f; **~ mixer** n mixer m; **~ poisoning** n intoxication f alimentaire; **~ processor** n robot m de cuisine; **~stuffs** npl denrées fpl alimentaires

fool [fuːl] n idiot(e); (CULIN) mousse f de fruits ♦ vt berner, duper ♦ vi faire l'idiot or l'imbécile; **~hardy** adj téméraire, imprudent(e); **~ish** adj idiot(e), stupide; (rash) imprudent(e); insensé(e); **~proof** adj (plan etc) infaillible

foot [fut] (pl **feet**) n pied m; (of animal) patte f; (measure) pied (= 30,48 cm; 12 inches) ♦ vt (bill) payer; **on ~** à pied; **~age** n (CINEMA: length) ≃ métrage m; (: material) séquences fpl; **~ball** n ballon m (de football); (sport: BRIT) football m, foot m; (: US) football américain; **~ball player** (BRIT) n (also: **~baller**) joueur m de football; **~brake** n frein m à pédale; **~bridge** n passerelle f; **~hills** npl contreforts mpl; **~hold** n prise f (de pied); **~ing**

n (*fig*) position *f*; **to lose one's ~ing** perdre pied; **~lights** *npl* rampe *f*; **~note** *n* note *f* (en bas de page); **~path** *n* sentier *m*; (*in street*) trottoir *m*; **~print** *n* trace *f* (de pas); **~step** *n* pas *m*; **~wear** *n* chaussure(s) *f(pl)*

---

football pools

ⓘ *Les* **football pools** - *ou plus familièrement les "*pools*" - consistent à parier sur les résultats des matches de football qui se jouent tous les samedis. L'expression consacrée en anglais est "to do the pools". Les parieurs envoient à l'avance les fiches qu'ils ont complétées à l'organisme qui gère les paris et ils attendent 17 h le samedi que les résultats soient annoncés. Les sommes gagnées se comptent parfois en milliers (ou même en millions) de livres sterling.*

KEYWORD

for [fɔːʳ] *prep* **1** (*indicating destination, intention, purpose*) pour; **the train for London** le train pour (ou (à destination) de Londres; **he went for the paper** il est allé chercher le journal; **it's time for lunch** c'est l'heure du déjeuner; **what's it for?** ça sert à quoi?; **what for?** (*why*) pourquoi?
2 (*on behalf of, representing*) pour; **the MP for Hove** le député de Hove; **to work for sb/sth** travailler pour qn/qch; **G for George** G comme Georges
3 (*because of*) pour; **for this reason** pour cette raison; **for fear of being criticized** de peur d'être critiqué
4 (*with regard to*) pour; **it's cold for July** il fait froid pour juillet; **a gift for languages** un don pour les langues
5 (*in exchange for*): **I sold it for £5** je l'ai vendu 5 livres; **to pay 50 pence for a ticket** payer un billet 50 pence
6 (*in favour of*) pour; **are you for or against us?** êtes-vous pour ou contre nous?

7 (*referring to distance*) pendant, sur; **there are roadworks for 5 km** il y a des travaux sur 5 km; **we walked for miles** nous avons marché pendant des kilomètres
8 (*referring to time*) pendant; depuis; pour; **he was away for 2 years** il a été absent pendant 2 ans; **she will be away for a month** elle sera absente (pendant) un mois; **I have known her for years** je la connais depuis des années; **can you do it for tomorrow?** est-ce que tu peux le faire pour demain?
9 (*with infinitive clauses*): **it is not for me to decide** ce n'est pas à moi de décider; **it would be best for you to leave** le mieux serait que vous partiez; **there is still time for you to do it** vous avez encore le temps de le faire; **for this to be possible ...** pour que cela soit possible ...
10 (*in spite of*): **for all his work/efforts** malgré tout son travail/tous ses efforts; **for all his complaints, he's very fond of her** il a beau se plaindre, il l'aime beaucoup
♦ *conj* (*since, as: rather formal*) car

forage ['fɒrɪdʒ] *vi* fourrager
foray ['fɒreɪ] *n* incursion *f*
forbid [fə'bɪd] (*pt* **forbad(e)**, *pp* **forbidden**) *vt* défendre, interdire; **to ~ sb to do** défendre *or* interdire à qn de faire; **~ding** *adj* sévère, sombre
force [fɔːs] *n* force *f* ♦ *vt* forcer; (*push*) pousser (de force); **the F~s** *npl* (MIL) l'armée *f*; **in ~** en vigueur; **~-feed** *vt* nourrir de force; **~ful** *adj* énergique, volontaire; **forcibly** *adv* par la force, de force; (*express*) énergiquement
ford [fɔːd] *n* gué *m*
fore [fɔːʳ] *n*: **to come to the ~** se faire remarquer; **~arm** *n* avant-bras *m inv*; **~boding** *n* pressentiment *m* (néfaste); **~cast** (*irreg: like* **cast**) *n* prévision *f* ♦ *vt* prévoir; **~court** *n* (*of garage*) devant *m*; **~finger** *n* index *m*; **~front** *n*: **in the ~front of** au premier rang *or* plan de

foregone ['fɔːgɒn] *adj*: **it's a ~ conclusion** c'est couru d'avance

foreground ['fɔːgraund] *n* premier plan

forehead ['fɒrɪd] *n* front *m*

foreign ['fɒrɪn] *adj* étranger(-ère); (*trade*) extérieur(-e); **~er** *n* étranger(-ère); **~ exchange** *n* change *m*; **F~ Office** (*BRIT*) *n* ministère *m* des affaires étrangères; **F~ Secretary** (*BRIT*) *n* ministre *m* des affaires étrangères

fore: **~leg** *n* (*of cat, dog*) patte *f* de devant; (*of horse*) jambe antérieure; **~man** (*irreg*) *n* (*of factory, building site*) contremaître *m*, chef *m* d'équipe; **~most** *adj* le (la) plus en vue; premier(-ère) ♦ *adv*: **first and ~most** avant tout, tout d'abord

forensic [fə'rensɪk] *adj*: **~ medicine** médecine légale; **~ scientist** médecin *m* légiste

fore: **~runner** *n* précurseur *m*; **~see** (*irreg*: *like* **see**) *vt* prévoir; **~seeable** *adj* prévisible; **~shadow** *vt* présager, annoncer, laisser prévoir; **~sight** *n* prévoyance *f*

forest ['fɒrɪst] *n* forêt *f*; **~ry** *n* sylviculture *f*

foretaste ['fɔːteɪst] *n* avant-goût *m*

foretell [fɔː'tel] (*irreg*: *like* **tell**) *vt* prédire

forever [fə'revə'] *adv* pour toujours; (*fig*) continuellement

foreword ['fɔːwɜːd] *n* avant-propos *m inv*

forfeit ['fɔːfɪt] *vt* (*lose*) perdre

forgave [fə'geɪv] *pt of* **forgive**

forge [fɔːdʒ] *n* forge *f* ♦ *vt* (*signature*) contrefaire; (*wrought iron*) forger; **to ~ money** (*BRIT*) fabriquer de la fausse monnaie; **~ ahead** *vi* pousser de l'avant, prendre de l'avance; **~d** *adj* faux (fausse); **~r** *n* faussaire *m*; **~ry** *n* faux *m*, contrefaçon *f*

forget [fə'get] (*pt* **forgot**, *pp* **forgotten**) *vt, vi* oublier; **~ful** *adj* distrait(e), étourdi(e); **~-me-not** *n* myosotis *m*

forgive [fə'gɪv] (*pt* **forgave**, *pp* **forgiven**) *vt* pardonner; **to ~ sb for sth/for doing sth** pardonner qch à qn/à qn de faire qch; **~ness** *n* pardon *m*

forgo [fɔː'gəu] (*pt* **forwent**, *pp* **forgone**) *vt* renoncer à

fork [fɔːk] *n* (*for eating*) fourchette *f*; (*for gardening*) fourche *f*; (*of roads*) bifurcation *f*; (*of railways*) embranchement *m* ♦ *vi* (*road*) bifurquer; **~ out** *vt* (*inf*) allonger; **~-lift truck** *n* chariot élévateur

forlorn [fə'lɔːn] *adj* (*deserted*) abandonné(e); (*attempt, hope*) désespéré(e)

form [fɔːm] *n* forme *f*; (*SCOL*) classe *f*; (*questionnaire*) formulaire *m* ♦ *vt* former; (*habit*) contracter; **in top ~** en pleine forme

formal ['fɔːməl] *adj* (*offer, receipt*) en bonne et due forme; (*person*) cérémonieux(-euse); (*dinner*) officiel(le); (*clothes*) de soirée; (*garden*) à la française; (*education*) à proprement parler; **~ly** *adv* officiellement; cérémonieusement

format ['fɔːmæt] *n* format *m* ♦ *vt* (*COMPUT*) formater

formation [fɔː'meɪʃən] *n* formation *f*

formative ['fɔːmətɪv] *adj*: **~ years** années *fpl* d'apprentissage *or* de formation

former ['fɔːmə'] *adj* ancien(ne) (*before n*), précédent(e); **the ~ ... the latter** le premier ... le second, celui-là ... celui-ci; **~ly** *adv* autrefois

formidable ['fɔːmɪdəbl] *adj* redoutable

formula ['fɔːmjulə] (*pl* **~s** *or* **~e**) *n* formule *f*

forsake [fə'seɪk] (*pt* **forsook**, *pp* **forsaken**) *vt* abandonner

fort [fɔːt] *n* fort *m*

forte ['fɔːtɪ] *n* (*point*) fort *m*

forth [fɔːθ] *adv* en avant; **to go back and ~** aller et venir; **and so ~** et ainsi de suite; **~coming** *adj* (*event*) qui va avoir lieu prochainement; (*character*) ouvert(e), communicatif(-ive); (*available*) disponible; **~right** *adj* franc (franche), direct(e); **~with** *adv* sur-le-champ

fortify ['fɔːtɪfaɪ] *vt* fortifier

fortitude ['fɔːtɪtjuːd] *n* courage *m*

fortnight ['fɔːtnaɪt] (*BRIT*) *n* quinzaine *f*, quinze jours *mpl*; **~ly** (*BRIT*) *adj* bimensuel(le) ♦ *adv* tous les quinze jours

fortunate ['fɔːtʃənɪt] *adj* heureux(-euse); (*person*) chanceux(-euse); **it is ~ that** c'est une chance que; **~ly** *adv* heureusement

fortune ['fɔːtʃən] *n* chance *f*; (*wealth*) fortune *f*; **~-teller** *n* diseuse *f* de bonne aventure

forty ['fɔːti] *num* quarante

forward ['fɔːwəd] *adj* (*ahead of schedule*) en avance; (*movement, position*) en avant, vers l'avant; (*not shy*) direct(e); effronté(e) ♦ *n* (*SPORT*) avant *m* ♦ *vt* (*letter*) faire suivre; (*parcel, goods*) expédier; (*fig*) promouvoir, favoriser; **~(s)** *adv* en avant; **to move ~** avancer

fossil ['fɔsl] *n* fossile *m*

foster ['fɔstə^r] *vt* encourager, favoriser; (*child*) élever (*sans obligation d'adopter*); **~ child** *n* enfant adoptif(-ive)

fought [fɔːt] *pt, pp of* **fight**

foul [faul] *adj* (*weather, smell, food*) infect(e); (*language*) ordurier(-ère) ♦ *n* (*SPORT*) faute *f* ♦ *vt* (*dirty*) salir, encrasser; **he's got a ~ temper** il a un caractère de chien; **~ play** *n* (*LAW*) acte criminel

found [faund] *pt, pp of* **find** ♦ *vt* (*establish*) fonder; **~ation** [faun'deɪʃən] *n* (*act*) fondation *f*; (*base*) fondement *m*; (*also:* **~ation cream**) fond *m* de teint; **~ations** *npl* (*of building*) fondations *fpl*

founder ['faundə^r] *n* fondateur *m* ♦ *vi* couler, sombrer

foundry ['faundrɪ] *n* fonderie *f*

fountain ['fauntɪn] *n* fontaine *f*; **~ pen** *n* stylo *m* (à encre)

four [fɔː^r] *num* quatre; **on all ~s** à quatre pattes; **~-poster** *n* (*also:* **~-poster bed**) lit *m* à baldaquin; **~teen** *num* quatorze; **~th** *num* quatrième

fowl [faul] *n* volaille *f*

fox [fɔks] *n* renard *m* ♦ *vt* mystifier

foyer ['fɔɪeɪ] *n* (*hotel*) hall *m*; (*THEATRE*) foyer *m*

fraction ['frækʃən] *n* fraction *f*

fracture ['fræktʃə^r] *n* fracture *f*

fragile ['frædʒaɪl] *adj* fragile

fragment ['frægmənt] *n* fragment *m*

fragrant ['freɪgrənt] *adj* parfumé(e), odorant(e)

frail [freɪl] *adj* fragile, délicat(e)

frame [freɪm] *n* charpente *f*; (*of picture, bicycle*) cadre *m*; (*of door, window*) encadrement *m*, chambranle *m*; (*of spectacles: also:* **~s**) monture *f* ♦ *vt* encadrer; **~ of mind** disposition *f* d'esprit; **~work** *n* structure *f*

France [frɑːns] *n* France *f*

franchise ['fræntʃaɪz] *n* (*POL*) droit *m* de vote; (*COMM*) franchise *f*

frank [fræŋk] *adj* franc (franche) ♦ *vt* (*letter*) affranchir; **~ly** *adv* franchement

frantic ['fræntɪk] *adj* (*hectic*) frénétique; (*distraught*) hors de soi

fraternity [frə'tɜːnɪtɪ] *n* (*spirit*) fraternité *f*; (*club*) communauté *f*, confrérie *f*

fraud [frɔːd] *n* supercherie *f*, fraude *f*, tromperie *f*; (*person*) imposteur *m*

fraught [frɔːt] *adj*: **~ with** chargé(e) de, plein(e) de

fray [freɪ] *vi* s'effilocher

freak [friːk] *n* (*also cpd*) phénomène *m*, créature ou événement exceptionnel par sa rareté

freckle ['frekl] *n* tache *f* de rousseur

free [friː] *adj* libre; (*gratis*) gratuit(e) ♦ *vt* (*prisoner etc*) libérer; (*jammed object or person*) dégager; **~ (of charge), for ~** gratuitement; **~dom** *n* liberté *f*; **F~fone** ® *n* numéro vert; **~-for-all** *n* mêlée générale; **~ gift** *n* prime *f*; **~hold** *n* propriété foncière libre; **~ kick** *n* coup franc; **~lance** *adj* indépendant(e); **~ly** *adv* librement; (*liberally*) libéralement; **F~mason** *n* franc-maçon *m*; **F~post** ® *n* port payé; **~-range** *adj* (*hen, eggs*) de ferme; **~ trade** *n* libre-échange *m*; **~way** (*US*) *n* autoroute *f*; **~ will** *n* libre arbitre *m*; **of one's own ~ will** de son plein gré

freeze [friːz] (*pt* **froze**, *pp* **frozen**) *vi* geler ♦ *vt* geler; (*food*) congeler; (*prices, salaries*) bloquer, geler ♦ *n* gel *m*; (*fig*) blocage *m*; **~-dried** *adj* lyophilisé(e); **~r** *n* congélateur *m*; **freezing** *adj*: **freezing (cold)** (*weather, water*) glacial(e) ♦ *n*: **3 degrees below freezing** 3 degrés au-dessous de zéro; **freezing point** *n* point *m* de congélation

freight [freɪt] *n* (*goods*) fret *m*, cargaison *f*;

(money charged) fret, prix m du transport; ~ **train** n train m de marchandises
French [frɛntʃ] adj français(e) ♦ n (LING) français m; **the** ~ npl (people) les Français; ~ **bean** n haricot vert; ~ **fried potatoes** (US ~ **fries**) npl (pommes de terre fpl) frites fpl; ~ **horn** n (MUS) cor m (d'harmonie); ~ **kiss** n baiser profond; ~ **loaf** n baguette f; ~**man** (irreg) n Français m; ~ **window** n porte-fenêtre f; ~**woman** (irreg) n Française f
frenzy ['frɛnzɪ] n frénésie f
frequency ['fri:kwənsɪ] n fréquence f
frequent [adj 'fri:kwənt, vb frɪ'kwɛnt] adj fréquent(e) ♦ vt fréquenter; ~**ly** adv fréquemment
fresh [frɛʃ] adj frais (fraîche); (new) nouveau (nouvelle); (cheeky) familier(-ère), culotté(e); ~**en** vi (wind, air) fraîchir; ~**en up** vi faire un brin de toilette; ~**er** (BRIT: inf) n (SCOL) bizuth m, étudiant(e) de 1ère année; ~**ly** adv nouvellement, récemment; ~**man** (US) (irreg) n = **fresher**; ~**ness** n fraîcheur f; ~**water** adj (fish) d'eau douce
fret [frɛt] vi s'agiter, se tracasser
friar ['fraɪə*] n moine m, frère m
friction ['frɪkʃən] n friction f
Friday ['fraɪdɪ] n vendredi m
fridge [frɪdʒ] (BRIT) n frigo m, frigidaire ® m
fried [fraɪd] adj frit(e); ~ **egg** œuf m sur le plat
friend [frɛnd] n ami(e); ~**ly** adj amical(e); gentil(le); (place) accueillant(e); **they were killed by** ~**ly fire** ils sont morts sous les tirs de leur propre camp; ~**ship** n amitié f
frieze [fri:z] n frise f
fright [fraɪt] n peur f, effroi m; **to take** ~ prendre peur, s'effrayer; ~**en** vt effrayer, faire peur à; ~**ened** adj: **to be** ~**ened (of)** avoir peur (de); ~**ening** adj effrayant(e); ~**ful** adj affreux(-euse)
frigid ['frɪdʒɪd] adj frigide
frill [frɪl] n (on dress) volant m; (on shirt) jabot m

fringe [frɪndʒ] n (BRIT: of hair) frange f; (edge: of forest etc) bordure f; ~ **benefits** npl avantages sociaux or en nature
Frisbee ® ['frɪzbɪ] n Frisbee ® m
frisk [frɪsk] vt fouiller
fritter ['frɪtə*] n beignet m; ~ **away** vt gaspiller
frivolous ['frɪvələs] adj frivole
frizzy ['frɪzɪ] adj crépu(e)
fro [frəu] adv: **to go to and** ~ aller et venir
frock [frɔk] n robe f
frog [frɔg] n grenouille f; ~**man** n homme-grenouille m
frolic ['frɔlɪk] vi folâtrer, batifoler

KEYWORD

from [frɔm] prep **1** (indicating starting place, origin etc) de; **where do you come from?, where are you from?** d'où venez-vous?; **from London to Paris** de Londres à Paris; **a letter from my sister** une lettre de ma sœur; **to drink from the bottle** boire à (même) la bouteille
2 (indicating time) (à partir) de; **from one o'clock to** or **until** or **till two** d'une heure à deux heures; **from January (on)** à partir de janvier
3 (indicating distance) de; **the hotel is one kilometre from the beach** l'hôtel est à un kilomètre de la plage
4 (indicating price, number etc) de; **the interest rate was increased from 9% to 10%** le taux d'intérêt est passé de 9 à 10%
5 (indicating difference) de; **he can't tell red from green** il ne peut pas distinguer le rouge du vert
6 (because of, on the basis of): **from what he says** d'après ce qu'il dit; **weak from hunger** affaibli par la faim

front [frʌnt] n (of house, dress) devant m; (of coach, train) avant m; (promenade: also: **sea** ~) bord m de mer; (MIL, METEOROLOGY) front m; (fig: appearances) contenance f, façade f ♦ adj de devant; (seat) avant inv; **in** ~ **(of)** devant; ~**age** n (of building) façade f; ~ **door** n porte f d'entrée; (of car) portière f avant; ~**ier** ['frʌntɪəʳ] n frontière f; ~ **page** n première page; ~ **room** (BRIT) n pièce f de devant, salon m; ~-**wheel drive** n traction f avant

frost [frɔst] n gel m, gelée f; (also: **hoar-frost**) givre m; ~**bite** n gelures fpl; ~**ed** adj (glass) dépoli(e); ~**y** adj (weather, welcome) glacial(e)

froth [frɔθ] n mousse f; écume f

frown [fraun] vi froncer les sourcils

froze [frauz] pt of **freeze**

frozen ['frauzn] pp of **freeze**

fruit [fruːt] n inv fruit m; ~**erer** n fruitier m, marchand(e) de fruits; ~**ful** adj (fig) fructueux(-euse); ~**ion** [fruːˈɪʃən] n: **to come to ~ion** se réaliser; ~ **juice** n jus m de fruit; ~ **machine** (BRIT) n machine f à sous; ~ **salad** n salade f de fruits

frustrate [frʌsˈtreɪt] vt frustrer

fry [fraɪ] (pt, pp **fried**) vt (faire) frire; see also **small**; ~**ing pan** n poêle f (à frire)

ft. abbr = **foot**; **feet**

fudge [fʌdʒ] n (CULIN) caramel m

fuel ['fjuəl] n (for heating) combustible m; (for propelling) carburant m; ~ **oil** n mazout m; ~ **tank** n (in vehicle) réservoir m

fugitive ['fjuːdʒɪtɪv] n fugitif(-ive)

fulfil [fulˈfil] (US **fulfill**) vt (function, condition) remplir; (order) exécuter; (wish, desire) satisfaire, réaliser; ~**ment** (US **fulfillment**) n (of wishes etc) réalisation f; (feeling) contentement m

full [ful] adj plein(e); (details, information) complet(-ète); (skirt) ample, large ♦ adv: **to know ~ well that** savoir fort bien que; **I'm ~ (up)** j'ai bien mangé; **a ~ two hours** deux bonnes heures; **at ~ speed** à toute vitesse; **in ~** (reproduce, quote) intégralement; (write) en toutes lettres; ~ **employment** n plein emploi; **to pay in ~** tout payer; ~-**length** adj (film) long métrage; (portrait, mirror) en pied; (coat) long(ue); ~ **moon** n pleine lune; ~-**scale** adj (attack, war) complet(-ète), total(e); (model) grandeur nature inv; ~ **stop** n point m; ~-**time** adj, adv (work) à plein temps; ~**y**

adv entièrement, complètement; (at least) au moins; ~**y licensed** adj (hotel, restaurant) autorisé(e) à vendre des boissons alcoolisées; ~**y-fledged** adj (barrister etc) diplômé(e); (citizen, member) à part entière

fumble ['fʌmbl] vi: ~ **with** tripoter

fume [fjuːm] vi rager; ~**s** npl vapeurs fpl, émanations fpl, gaz mpl

fun [fʌn] n amusement m, divertissement m; **to have ~** s'amuser; **for ~** pour rire; **to make ~ of** se moquer de

function ['fʌŋkʃən] n fonction f; (social occasion) cérémonie f, soirée officielle ♦ vi fonctionner; ~**al** adj fonctionnel(le)

fund [fʌnd] n caisse f, fonds m; (source, store) source f, mine f; ~**s** npl (money) fonds mpl

fundamental [fʌndəˈmɛntl] adj fondamental(e)

funeral ['fjuːnərəl] n enterrement m, obsèques fpl; ~ **parlour** n entreprise f de pompes funèbres; ~ **service** n service m funèbre

funfair ['fʌnfɛəʳ] (BRIT) n fête (foraine)

fungi ['fʌŋgaɪ] npl of **fungus**

fungus ['fʌŋgəs] (pl **fungi**) n champignon m; (mould) moisissure f

funnel ['fʌnl] n entonnoir m; (of ship) cheminée f

funny ['fʌnɪ] adj amusant(e), drôle; (strange) curieux(-euse), bizarre

fur [fəːʳ] n fourrure f; (BRIT: in kettle etc) (dépôt m de) tartre m

furious ['fjuərɪəs] adj furieux(-euse); (effort) acharné(e)

furlong ['fəːlɔŋ] n = 201,17 m

furnace ['fəːnɪs] n fourneau m

furnish ['fəːnɪʃ] vt meubler; (supply): **to ~ sb with sth** fournir qch à qn; ~**ings** npl mobilier m, ameublement m

furniture ['fəːnɪtʃəʳ] n meubles mpl, mobilier m; **piece of ~** meuble m

furrow ['fʌrəu] n sillon m

furry ['fəːrɪ] adj (animal) à fourrure; (toy) en peluche

further ['fəːðəʳ] adj (additional) supplémentaire, autre; nouveau (nouvelle) ♦ adv plus loin; (*more*) davantage; (*moreover*) de plus ♦ *vt* faire avancer *or* progresser, promouvoir; **~ education** *n* enseignement *m* postscolaire; **~more** *adv* de plus, en outre

furthest ['fɜːðɪst] *superl of* **far**

fury ['fjʊərɪ] *n* fureur *f*

fuse [fjuːz] (*US* **fuze**) *n* fusible *m*; (*for bomb etc*) amorce *f*, détonateur *m* ♦ *vt, vi* (*metal*) fondre; **to ~ the lights** (*BRIT*) faire sauter les plombs; **~ box** *n* boîte *f* à fusibles

fuss [fʌs] *n* (*excitement*) agitation *f*; (*complaining*) histoire(s) *f(pl)*; **to make a ~** faire des histoires; **to make a ~ of sb** être aux petits soins pour qn; **~y** *adj* (*person*) tatillon(ne), difficile; (*dress, style*) tarabiscoté(e)

future ['fjuːtʃəʳ] *adj* futur(e) ♦ *n* avenir *m*; (*LING*) futur *m*; **in ~** à l'avenir

fuze [fjuːz] (*US*) *n, vt, vi* = **fuse**

fuzzy ['fʌzɪ] *adj* (*PHOT*) flou(e); (*hair*) crépu(e)

G, g

G [dʒiː] *n* (*MUS*) sol *m*

G7 *n abbr* (= *Group of 7*) le groupe des 7

gabble ['gæbl] *vi* bredouiller

gable ['geɪbl] *n* pignon *m*

gadget ['gædʒɪt] *n* gadget *m*

Gaelic ['geɪlɪk] *adj* gaélique ♦ *n* (*LING*) gaélique *m*

gag [gæg] *n* (*on mouth*) bâillon *m*; (*joke*) gag *m* ♦ *vt* bâillonner

gaiety ['geɪɪtɪ] *n* gaieté *f*

gain [geɪn] *n* (*improvement*) gain *m*; (*profit*) gain, profit *m*; (*increase*): **~ (in)** augmentation *f* (de) ♦ *vt* gagner ♦ *vi* (*watch*) avancer; **to ~ 3 lbs (in weight)** prendre 3 livres; **to ~ on sb** (*catch up*) rattraper qn; **to ~ from/by** gagner de/à

gal. *abbr* = **gallon**

gale [geɪl] *n* coup *m* de vent

gallant ['gælənt] *adj* vaillant(e), brave; (*towards ladies*) galant

gall bladder ['gɔːl-] *n* vésicule *f* biliaire

gallery ['gælərɪ] *n* galerie *f*; (*also:* **art ~**) musée *m*; (: *private*) galerie

gallon ['gæln] *n* gallon *m* (*BRIT* = 4,5 *l*; *US* = 3,8 *l*)

gallop ['gæləp] *n* galop *m* ♦ *vi* galoper

gallows ['gæləʊz] *n* potence *f*

gallstone ['gɔːlstəʊn] *n* calcul *m* biliaire

galore [gə'lɔːʳ] *adv* en abondance, à gogo

Gambia ['gæmbɪə] *n:* **(The) ~** la Gambie

gambit ['gæmbɪt] *n* (*fig*): **(opening) ~** manœuvre *f* stratégique

gamble ['gæmbl] *n* pari *m*, risque calculé ♦ *vt, vi* jouer; **to ~ on** (*fig*) miser sur; **~r** *n* joueur *m*; **gambling** *n* jeu *m*

game [geɪm] *n* jeu *m*; (*match*) match *m*; (*strategy, scheme*) plan *m*; projet *m*; (*HUNTING*) gibier *m* ♦ *adj* (*willing*): **to be ~ (for)** être prêt(e) (à *or* pour); **big ~** gros gibier; **~keeper** *n* garde-chasse *m*

gammon ['gæmən] *n* (*bacon*) quartier *m* de lard fumé; (*ham*) jambon fumé

gamut ['gæmət] *n* gamme *f*

gang [gæŋ] *n* bande *f*; (*of workmen*) équipe *f*; **~ up** *vi:* **to ~ up on sb** se liguer contre qn; **~ster** *n* gangster *m*; **~way** ['gæŋweɪ] *n* passerelle *f*; (*BRIT: of bus, plane*) couloir central; (: *in cinema*) allée centrale

gaol [dʒeɪl] (*BRIT*) *n* = **jail**

gap [gæp] *n* trou *m*; (*in time*) intervalle *m*; (*difference*): **~ between** écart *m* entre

gape [geɪp] *vi* (*person*) être *or* rester bouche bée; (*hole, shirt*) être ouvert(e); **gaping** *adj* (*hole*) béant(e)

garage ['gærɑːʒ] *n* garage *m*

garbage ['gɑːbɪdʒ] *n* (*US: rubbish*) ordures *fpl*, détritus *mpl*; (*inf: nonsense*) foutaises *fpl*; **~ can** (*US*) *n* poubelle *f*, boîte *f* à ordures

garbled ['gɑːbld] *adj* (*account, message*) embrouillé(e)

garden ['gɑːdn] *n* jardin *m*; **~s** *npl* jardin public; **~er** *n* jardinier *m*; **~ing** *n* jardinage *m*

gargle ['gɑːgl] *vi* se gargariser

garish ['gɛərɪʃ] *adj* criard(e), voyant(e); (*light*) cru(e)

garland ['gɑːlənd] *n* guirlande *f*; couronne

f

garlic ['gɑːlɪk] *n* ail *m*

garment ['gɑːmənt] *n* vêtement *m*

garrison ['gærɪsn] *n* garnison *f*

garter ['gɑːtəʳ] *n* jarretière *f*; (US) jarretelle *f*

gas [gæs] *n* gaz *m*; (US: *gasoline*) essence *f* ♦ *vt* asphyxier; ~ **cooker** (*BRIT*) *n* cuisinière *f* à gaz; ~ **cylinder** *n* bouteille *f* de gaz; ~ **fire** (*BRIT*) *n* radiateur *m* à gaz

gash [gæʃ] *n* entaille *f*; (*on face*) balafre *f*

gasket ['gæskɪt] *n* (*AUT*) joint *m* de culasse

gas mask *n* masque *m* à gaz

gas meter *n* compteur *m* à gaz

gasoline ['gæsəliːn] (US) *n* essence *f*

gasp [gɑːsp] *vi* haleter

gas: ~ **ring** *n* brûleur *m*; ~ **station** (US) *n* station-service *f*; ~ **tap** *n* bouton *m* (de cuisinière à gaz); (*on pipe*) robinet *m* à gaz

gastric ['gæstrɪk] *adj* gastrique; ~ **flu** grippe *f* intestinale

gate [geɪt] *n* (*of garden*) portail *m*; (*of field*) barrière *f*; (*of building, at airport*) porte *f*

gateau ['gætəu] *n* (*pl* ~**x**) (gros) gâteau à la crème

gatecrash *vt* s'introduire sans invitation dans

gateway *n* porte *f*

gather ['gæðəʳ] *vt* (*flowers, fruit*) cueillir; (*pick up*) ramasser; (*assemble*) rassembler, réunir; recueillir; (*understand*) comprendre; (*SEWING*) froncer ♦ *vi* (*assemble*) se rassembler; **to ~ speed** prendre de la vitesse; ~**ing** *n* rassemblement *m*

gaudy ['gɔːdɪ] *adj* voyant(e)

gauge [geɪdʒ] *n* (*instrument*) jauge *f* ♦ *vt* jauger

gaunt [gɔːnt] *adj* (*thin*) décharné(e); (*grim, desolate*) désolé(e)

gauntlet ['gɔːntlɪt] *n* (*glove*) gant *m*

gauze [gɔːz] *n* gaze *f*

gave [geɪv] *pt of* **give**

gay [geɪ] *adj* (*homosexual*) homosexuel(le); (*cheerful*) gai(e), réjoui(e); (*colour etc*) gai, vif (vive)

gaze [geɪz] *n* regard *m* fixe ♦ *vi*: **to ~ at** fixer du regard

gazump [gə'zʌmp] (*BRIT*) *vi* revenir sur une promesse de vente (*pour accepter une offre plus intéressante*)

GB *abbr* = **Great Britain**

GCE *n abbr* (*BRIT*) = **General Certificate of Education**

GCSE *n abbr* (*BRIT*) = **General Certificate of Secondary Education**

gear [gɪəʳ] *n* matériel *m*, équipement *m*; attirail *m*; (*TECH*) engrenage *m*; (*AUT*) vitesse *f* ♦ *vt* (*fig: adapt*): **to ~ sth to** adapter qch à; **top** *or* (US) **high** ~ quatrième (*or* cinquième) vitesse; **low** ~ première vitesse; **in** ~ en prise; ~ **box** *n* boîte *f* de vitesses; ~ **lever** (US **gear shift**) *n* levier *m* de vitesse

geese [giːs] *npl of* **goose**

gel [dʒɛl] *n* gel *m*

gem [dʒɛm] *n* pierre précieuse

Gemini ['dʒɛmɪnaɪ] *n* les Gémeaux *mpl*

gender ['dʒɛndəʳ] *n* genre *m*

gene [dʒiːn] *n* gène *m*

general ['dʒɛnərl] *n* général *m* ♦ *adj* général(e); **in** ~ en général; ~ **delivery** *n* poste restante; ~ **election** *n* élection(s) législative(s); ~ **knowledge** *n* connaissances générales; ~**ly** *adv* généralement; ~ **practitioner** *n* généraliste *m/f*

generate ['dʒɛnəreɪt] *vt* engendrer; (*electricity etc*) produire; **generation** *n* génération *f*; (*of electricity etc*) production *f*; **generator** *n* générateur *m*

generosity [dʒɛnə'rɔsɪtɪ] *n* générosité *f*

generous ['dʒɛnərəs] *adj* généreux(-euse); (*copious*) copieux(-euse)

genetic [dʒɪ'nɛtɪk] *adj*: ~ **engineering** ingéniérie *f* génétique; ~ **fingerprinting** système *m* d'empreinte génétique

genetics [dʒɪ'nɛtɪks] *n* génétique *f*

Geneva [dʒɪ'niːvə] *n* Genève *f*

genial ['dʒiːnɪəl] *adj* cordial(e), chaleureux(-euse)

genitals ['dʒɛnɪtlz] *npl* organes génitaux

genius ['dʒiːnɪəs] *n* génie *m*

genteel [dʒɛn'tiːl] *adj* de bon ton, distingué(e)

gentle ['dʒɛntl] *adj* doux (douce)
gentleman ['dʒɛntlmən] *n* monsieur *m*; (*well-bred man*) gentleman *m*
gently ['dʒɛntlɪ] *adv* doucement
gentry ['dʒɛntrɪ] *n inv*: **the ~** la petite noblesse
gents [dʒɛnts] *n* W.-C. *mpl* (pour hommes)
genuine ['dʒɛnjuɪn] *adj* véritable, authentique; (*person*) sincère
geographical [dʒɪə'græfɪkl] *adj* géographique
geography [dʒɪ'ɔgrəfɪ] *n* géographie *f*
geology [dʒɪ'ɔlədʒɪ] *n* géologie *f*
geometric(al) [dʒɪə'mɛtrɪk(l)] *adj* géométrique
geometry [dʒɪ'ɔmətrɪ] *n* géométrie *f*
geranium [dʒɪ'reɪnɪəm] *n* géranium *m*
geriatric [dʒɛrɪ'ætrɪk] *adj* gériatrique
germ [dʒə:m] *n* (*MED*) microbe *m*
German ['dʒə:mən] *adj* allemand(e) ♦ *n* Allemand(e); (*LING*) allemand *m*; ~ **measles** (*BRIT*) *n* rubéole *f*
Germany ['dʒə:mənɪ] *n* Allemagne *f*
gesture ['dʒɛstjə*r*] *n* geste *m*

KEYWORD
---

get [gɛt] (*pt, pp* **got**, *pp* **gotten** (*US*)) *vi* 1 (*become, be*) devenir; **to get old/tired** devenir vieux/fatigué, vieillir/se fatiguer; **to get drunk** s'enivrer; **to get killed** se faire tuer; **when do I get paid?** quand est-ce que je serai payé?; **it's getting late** il se fait tard
2 (*go*): **to get to/from** aller à/de; **to get home** rentrer chez soi; **how did you get here?** comment es-tu arrivé ici?
3 (*begin*) commencer *or* se mettre à; **I'm getting to like him** je commence à l'apprécier; **let's get going** *or* **started** allons-y
4 (*modal aux vb*): **you've got to do it** il faut que vous le fassiez; **I've got to tell the police** je dois le dire à la police
♦ *vt* 1: **to get sth done** (*do*) faire qch; (*have done*) faire faire qch; **to get one's hair cut** se faire couper les cheveux; **to**

get sb to do sth faire faire qch à qn; **to get sb drunk** enivrer qn
2 (*obtain: money, permission, results*) obtenir, avoir; (*find: job, flat*) trouver; (*fetch: person, doctor, object*) aller chercher; **to get sth for sb** procurer qch à qn; **get me Mr Jones, please** (*on phone*) passez-moi Mr Jones, s'il vous plaît; **can I get you a drink?** est-ce que je peux vous servir à boire?
3 (*receive: present, letter*) recevoir, avoir; (*acquire: reputation*) avoir; (*: prize*) obtenir; **what did you get for your birthday?** qu'est-ce que tu as eu pour ton anniversaire?
4 (*catch*) prendre, saisir, attraper; (*hit: target etc*) atteindre; **to get sb by the arm/ throat** prendre *or* saisir *or* attraper qn par le bras/à la gorge; **get him!** arrête-le!
5 (*take, move*) faire parvenir; **do you think we'll get it through the door?** on arrivera à le faire passer par la porte?; **I'll get you there somehow** je me débrouillerai pour t'y emmener
6 (*catch, take: plane, bus etc*) prendre
7 (*understand*) comprendre, saisir; (*hear*) entendre; **I've got it!** j'ai compris!, je saisis!; **I didn't get your name** je n'ai pas entendu votre nom
8 (*have, possess*): **to have got** avoir; **how many have you got?** vous en avez combien?
get about *vi* se déplacer; (*news*) se répandre
get along *vi* (*agree*) s'entendre; (*depart*) s'en aller; (*manage*) = **get by**
get at *vt fus* (*attack*) s'en prendre à; (*reach*) attraper, atteindre
get away *vi* partir, s'en aller; (*escape*) s'échapper
get away with *vt fus* en être quitte pour; se faire passer *or* pardonner
get back *vi* (*return*) rentrer ♦ *vt* récupérer, recouvrer
get by *vi* (*pass*) passer; (*manage*) se débrouiller
get down *vi, vt fus* descendre ♦ *vt* des-

cendre; (*depress*) déprimer

get down to vt fus (*work*) se mettre à (faire)

get in vi rentrer; (*train*) arriver

get into vt fus entrer dans; (*car, train etc*) monter dans; (*clothes*) mettre, enfiler, endosser; **to get into bed/a rage** se mettre au lit/en colère

get off vi (*from train etc*) descendre; (*depart: person, car*) s'en aller; (*escape*) s'en tirer ♦ vt (*remove: clothes, stain*) enlever ♦ vt fus (*train, bus*) descendre de

get on vi (*at exam etc*) se débrouiller; (*agree*): **to get on (with)** s'entendre (avec) ♦ vt fus monter dans; (*horse*) monter sur

get out vi sortir; (*of vehicle*) descendre ♦ vt sortir

get out of vt fus sortir de; (*duty etc*) échapper à, se soustraire à

get over vt fus (*illness*) se remettre de

get round vt fus contourner; (*fig: person*) entortiller

get through vi (*TEL*) avoir la communication; **to get through to sb** atteindre qn

get together vi se réunir ♦ vt assembler

get up vi (*rise*) se lever ♦ vt fus monter

get up to vt fus (*reach*) arriver à; (*prank etc*) faire

getaway ['gɛtəweɪ] n: **to make one's ~** filer

geyser ['giːzəʳ] n (*GEO*) geyser m; (*BRIT: water heater*) chauffe-eau m inv

Ghana ['gɑːnə] n Ghana m

ghastly ['gɑːstlɪ] adj atroce, horrible; (*pale*) livide, blême

gherkin ['gəːkɪn] n cornichon m

ghetto blaster ['gɛtəu'blɑːstəʳ] n stéréo f portable

ghost [gəust] n fantôme m, revenant m

giant ['dʒaɪənt] n géant(e) ♦ adj géant(e), énorme

gibberish ['dʒɪbərɪʃ] n charabia m

giblets ['dʒɪblɪts] npl abats mpl

Gibraltar [dʒɪ'brɔːltəʳ] n Gibraltar m

giddy ['gɪdɪ] adj (*dizzy*): **to be** or **feel ~** avoir le vertige

gift [gɪft] n cadeau m; (*donation, ability*) don m; **~ed** adj doué(e); **~ shop** n boutique f de cadeaux; **~ token** n chèque-cadeau m

gigantic [dʒaɪ'gæntɪk] adj gigantesque

giggle ['gɪgl] vi pouffer (de rire), rire sottement

gill [dʒɪl] n (*measure*) = 0.25 pints (*BRIT* = 0.15 l, *US* = 0.12 l)

gills [gɪlz] npl (*of fish*) ouïes fpl, branchies fpl

gilt [gɪlt] adj doré(e) ♦ n dorure f; **~-edged** adj de premier ordre

gimmick ['gɪmɪk] n truc m

gin [dʒɪn] n (*liquor*) gin m

ginger ['dʒɪndʒəʳ] n gingembre m; **~ ale**, **~ beer** n boisson gazeuse au gingembre; **~bread** n pain m d'épices

gingerly ['dʒɪndʒəlɪ] adv avec précaution

gipsy ['dʒɪpsɪ] n = **gypsy**

giraffe [dʒɪ'rɑːf] n girafe f

girder ['gəːdəʳ] n poutrelle f

girl [gəːl] n fille f, fillette f; (*young unmarried woman*) jeune fille; (*daughter*) fille; **an English ~** une jeune Anglaise; **~friend** n (*of girl*) amie f; (*of boy*) petite amie; **~ish** adj de petite or de jeune fille; (*for a boy*) efféminé(e)

giro ['dʒaɪrəu] n (*bank ~*) virement m bancaire; (*post office ~*) mandat m; (*BRIT: welfare cheque*) mandat m d'allocation chômage

gist [dʒɪst] n essentiel m

give [gɪv] (*pt* **gave**, *pp* **given**) vt donner ♦ vi (*break*) céder; (*stretch: fabric*) prêter; **to ~ sb sth**, **~ sth to sb** donner qch à qn; **to ~ a cry/sigh** pousser un cri/un soupir; **~ away** vt donner; (*~ free*) faire cadeau de; (*betray*) donner, trahir; (*disclose*) révéler; (*bride*) conduire à l'autel; **~ back** vt rendre; **~ in** vi céder ♦ vt donner; **~ off** vt dégager; **~ out** vt distribuer; annoncer; **~ up** vi renoncer ♦ vt renoncer à; **to ~ up smoking** arrêter de fumer; **to ~ o.s. up** se rendre; **~ way** (*BRIT*) vi céder; (*AUT*) céder la priorité

glacier ['glæsɪəʳ] n glacier m

glad [glæd] _adj_ content(e); **~ly** _adv_ volontiers

glamorous ['glæmərəs] _adj_ (_person_) séduisant(e); (_job_) prestigieux(-euse)

glamour ['glæmə^r] _n_ éclat _m_, prestige _m_

glance [glɑːns] _n_ coup _m_ d'œil ♦ _vi_: **to ~ at** jeter un coup d'œil à; **glancing** _adj_ (_blow_) oblique

gland _n_ glande _f_

glare [glɛə^r] _n_ (_of anger_) regard furieux; (_of light_) lumière éblouissante; (_of publicity_) feux _mpl_ ♦ _vi_ briller d'un éclat aveuglant; **to ~ at** lancer un regard furieux à; **glaring** _adj_ (_mistake_) criant(e), qui saute aux yeux

glass [glɑːs] _n_ verre _m_; **~es** _npl_ (_spectacles_) lunettes _fpl_; **~house** (BRIT) _n_ (_for plants_) serre _f_; **~ware** _n_ verrerie _f_

glaze [gleɪz] _vt_ (_door, window_) vitrer; (_pottery_) vernir ♦ _n_ (_on pottery_) vernis _m_; **~d** _adj_ (_pottery_) verni(e); (_eyes_) vitreux(-euse)

glazier ['gleɪzɪə^r] _n_ vitrier _m_

gleam [gliːm] _vi_ luire, briller

glean [gliːn] _vt_ (_information_) glaner

glee [gliː] _n_ joie _f_

glib [glɪb] _adj_ (_person_) qui a du bagou; (_response_) désinvolte, facile

glide [glaɪd] _vi_ glisser; (AVIAT, _birds_) planer; **~r** _n_ (AVIAT) planeur _m_; **gliding** _n_ (SPORT) vol _m_ à voile

glimmer ['glɪmə^r] _n_ lueur _f_

glimpse [glɪmps] _n_ vision passagère, aperçu _m_ ♦ _vt_ entrevoir, apercevoir

glint [glɪnt] _vi_ étinceler

glisten ['glɪsn] _vi_ briller, luire

glitter ['glɪtə^r] _vi_ scintiller, briller

gloat [gləut] _vi_: **to ~ (over)** jubiler (à propos de)

global ['gləubl] _adj_ mondial(e); **~ warming** réchauffement _m_ de la planète

globe [gləub] _n_ globe _m_

gloom [gluːm] _n_ obscurité _f_; (_sadness_) tristesse _f_, mélancolie _f_; **~y** _adj_ sombre, triste, lugubre

glorious ['glɔːrɪəs] _adj_ glorieux(-euse); splendide

glory ['glɔːrɪ] _n_ gloire _f_; splendeur _f_

gloss [glɔs] _n_ (_shine_) brillant _m_, vernis _m_; **~ over** _vt fus_ glisser sur

glossary ['glɔsərɪ] _n_ glossaire _m_

glossy ['glɔsɪ] _adj_ brillant(e); **~ magazine** magazine _m_ de luxe

glove [glʌv] _n_ gant _m_; **~ compartment** _n_ (AUT) boîte _f_ à gants, vide-poches _m inv_

glow [gləu] _vi_ rougeoyer; (_face_) rayonner; (_eyes_) briller

glower ['glauə^r] _vi_: **to ~ (at)** lancer des regards mauvais (à)

glucose ['gluːkəus] _n_ glucose _m_

glue [gluː] _n_ colle _f_ ♦ _vt_ coller

glum [glʌm] _adj_ sombre, morne

glut [glʌt] _n_ surabondance _f_

glutton ['glʌtn] _n_ glouton(ne); **a ~ for work** un bourreau de travail; **a ~ for punishment** un masochiste (_fig_)

GM _abbr_ (= _genetically modified_) génétiquement modifié(e)

gnat [næt] _n_ moucheron _m_

gnaw [nɔː] _vt_ ronger

go [gəu] (_pt_ **went**, _pp_ **gone**, _pl_ **~es**) _vi_ aller; (_depart_) partir, s'en aller; (_work_) marcher; (_break etc_) céder; (_be sold_): **to ~ for £10** se vendre 10 livres; (_fit, suit_): **to ~ with** aller avec; (_become_): **to ~ pale/mouldy** pâlir/moisir ♦ _n_: **to have a ~ (at)** essayer (de faire); **to be on the ~** être en mouvement; **whose ~ is it?** à qui est-ce de jouer?; **he's ~ing to do** il va faire, il est sur le point de faire; **to ~ for a walk** aller se promener; **to ~ dancing** aller danser; **how did it ~?** comment est-ce que ça s'est passé?; **to ~ round the back/by the shop** passer par derrière/devant le magasin; **~ about** _vi_ (_rumour_) se répandre ♦ _vt fus_: **how do I ~ about this?** comment dois-je m'y prendre (pour faire ceci)?; **~ after** _vt fus_ (_pursue_) poursuivre, courir après; (_job, record etc_) essayer d'obtenir; **~ ahead** _vi_ (_make progress_) avancer; (_get ~ing_) (_work_): **to ~ along** vi aller, avancer ♦ _vt fus_ longer, parcourir; **~ away** _vi_ partir, s'en aller; **~ back** _vi_ rentrer; revenir; (~ _again_) retourner; **~ back on** _vt fus_ (_promise_) revenir sur; **~ by** _vi_ (_years, time_) passer, s'écouler ♦ vt fus s'en tenir à; en croire; ~ **down** vi descendre; (ship) couler; (sun) se coucher ♦ vt fus descendre; ~ **for** vt fus (fetch) aller chercher; (like) aimer; (attack) s'en prendre à, attaquer; ~ **in** vi entrer; ~ **in for** vt fus (competition) se présenter à; (like) aimer; ~ **into** vt fus entrer dans; (investigate) étudier, examiner; (embark on) se lancer dans; ~ **off** vi partir, s'en aller; (food) se gâter, (explode) sauter; (event) se dérouler ♦ vt fus ne plus aimer; **the gun went off** le coup est parti; ~ **on** vi continuer; (happen) se passer; **to ~ on doing** continuer à faire; ~ **out** vi sortir, (fire, light) s'éteindre; ~ **over** vt fus (check) revoir, vérifier; ~ **past** vt fus: **to ~ past sth** passer devant qch; ~ **round** vi (circulate: news, rumour) circuler; (revolve) tourner; (suffice) suffire (pour tout le monde); **to ~ round to sb's** (visit) passer chez qn; **to ~ round (by)** (make a detour) faire un détour (par); ~ **through** vt fus (town etc) traverser; ~ **up** vi monter; (price) augmenter ♦ vt fus gravir; ~ **with** vt fus (suit) aller avec; ~ **without** vt fus se passer de

goad [gəud] vt aiguillonner

go-ahead adj dynamique, entreprenant(e) ♦ n feu vert

goal [gəul] n but m; ~**keeper** n gardien m de but; ~**post** n poteau m de but

goat [gəut] n chèvre f

gobble ['gɔbl] vt (also: ~ **down**, ~ **up**) engloutir

go-between ['gəubɪtwiːn] n intermédiaire m/f

god [gɔd] n dieu m; G~ n Dieu m; ~**child** n filleul(e); ~**daughter** n filleule f; ~**dess** n déesse f; ~**father** n parrain m; ~**forsaken** adj maudit(e); ~**mother** n marraine f; ~**send** n aubaine f; ~**son** n filleul m

goggles ['gɔglz] npl (for skiing etc) lunettes protectrices

going ['gəuɪŋ] n (conditions) état m du terrain ♦ adj: **the ~ rate** le tarif (en vigueur)

gold [gəuld] n or m ♦ adj en or; (reserves) d'or; ~**en** adj (made of gold) en or; (gold in colour) doré(e); ~**fish** n poisson m rouge; ~**-plated** adj plaqué(e) or inv; ~**smith** n orfèvre m

golf [gɔlf] n golf m; ~ **ball** n balle f de golf; (on typewriter) boule f; ~ **club** n club m de golf; (stick) club m, crosse f de golf; ~ **course** n (terrain m de) golf m; ~**er** n joueur(-euse) de golf

gone [gɔn] pp of **go**

gong [gɔŋ] n gong m

good [gud] adj bon(ne); (kind) gentil(le); (child) sage ♦ n bien m; ~**s** npl (COMM) marchandises fpl, articles mpl; ~! très bien!; **to be ~ at** être bon en; **to be ~ for** être bon pour; **would you be ~ enough to ...?** auriez-vous la bonté or l'amabilité de ...?; **a ~ deal (of)** beaucoup (de); **a ~ many** beaucoup (de); **to make ~** vi (succeed) faire son chemin, réussir ♦ vt (deficit) combler; (losses) compenser; **it's no ~ complaining** cela ne sert à rien de se plaindre; **for ~** pour de bon, une fois pour toutes; ~ **morning/afternoon!** bonjour!; ~ **evening!** bonsoir!; ~ **night!** bonsoir!; (on going to bed) bonne nuit!; ~**bye** excl au revoir!; G~ **Friday** n Vendredi saint; ~**-looking** adj beau (belle), bien inv; ~**-natured** adj (person) qui a un bon naturel; ~**ness** n (of person) bonté f; **for ~ness sake!** je vous en prie!; ~**ness gracious!** mon Dieu!; ~**s train** (BRIT) n train m de marchandises; ~**will** n bonne volonté

goose [guːs] (pl **geese**) n oie f

gooseberry ['guzbəri] n groseille f à maquereau; **to play ~** (BRIT) tenir la chandelle

gooseflesh ['guːsfleʃ] n, **goose pimples** npl chair f de poule

gore [gɔːr] vt encorner ♦ n sang m

gorge [gɔːdʒ] n gorge f ♦ vt: **to ~ o.s. (on)** se gorger (de)

gorgeous ['gɔːdʒəs] adj splendide, superbe

gorilla [gə'rɪlə] n gorille m

gorse [gɔːs] n ajoncs mpl

gory ['gɔːrɪ] adj sanglant(e); (details) horrible

go-slow ['gəu'sləu] (BRIT) n grève perlée

gospel ['gɔspl] n évangile m

gossip ['gɔsɪp] n (chat) bavardages mpl; commérage m, cancans mpl; (person) commère f ♦ vi bavarder; (maliciously) cancaner, faire des commérages

got [gɔt] pt, pp of **get**; **~ten** (US) pp of **get**

gout [gaut] n goutte f

govern ['gʌvən] vt gouverner; **~ess** n gouvernante f; **~ment** n gouvernement m; (BRIT: ministers) ministère m; **~or** n (of state, bank) gouverneur m; (of school, hospital) ≃ membre m/f du conseil d'établissement; (BRIT: of prison) directeur(-trice)

gown [gaun] n robe f; (of teacher, BRIT: of judge) toge f

GP n abbr = **general practitioner**

grab [græb] vt saisir, empoigner ♦ vi: **to ~ at** essayer de saisir

grace [greɪs] n grâce f ♦ vt honorer; (adorn) orner; **5 days' ~** cinq jours de répit; **~ful** adj gracieux(-euse), élégant(e); **gracious** ['greɪʃəs] adj bienveillant(e)

grade [greɪd] n (COMM) qualité f; (in hierarchy) catégorie f, grade m, échelon m; (SCOL) note f; (US: school class) classe f ♦ vt classer; **~ crossing** (US) n passage m à niveau; **~ school** (US) n école f primaire

gradient ['greɪdɪənt] n inclinaison f, pente f

gradual ['grædjuəl] adj graduel(le), progressif(-ive); **~ly** adv peu à peu, graduellement

graduate [n 'grædjuit, vb 'grædjueit] n diplômé(e), licencié(e); (US: of high school) bachelier(-ère) ♦ vi obtenir son diplôme; (US) obtenir son baccalauréat; **graduation** [grædju'eɪʃən] n (cérémonie f de) remise f des diplômes

graffiti [grə'fi:tɪ] npl graffiti mpl

graft [grɑ:ft] n (AGR, MED) greffe f; (bribery) corruption f ♦ vt greffer; **hard ~** (BRIT: inf) boulot acharné

grain [greɪn] n grain m

gram [græm] n gramme m

grammar ['græmər] n grammaire f; **~**

school (BRIT) n ≃ lycée m; **grammatical** [grə'mætɪkl] adj grammatical(e)

gramme [græm] n = **gram**

grand [grænd] adj magnifique, splendide; (gesture etc) noble; **~children** npl petits-enfants mpl; **~dad** (inf) n grand-papa m; **~daughter** n petite-fille f; **~father** n grand-père m; **~ma** (inf) n grand-maman f; **~mother** n grand-mère f; **~pa** (inf) n = **granddad**; **~parents** npl grands-parents mpl; **~ piano** n piano m à queue; **~son** n petit-fils m; **~stand** n (SPORT) tribune f

granite ['grænit] n granit m

granny ['grænɪ] (inf) n grand-maman f

grant [grɑ:nt] vt accorder; (a request) accéder à; (admit) concéder ♦ n (SCOL) bourse f; (ADMIN) subside m, subvention f; **to take it for ~ed that** trouver tout naturel que +sub; **to take sb for ~ed** considérer qn comme faisant partie du décor

granulated sugar ['grænjuleɪtɪd-] n sucre m en poudre

grape [greɪp] n raisin m

grapefruit ['greɪpfruːt] n pamplemousse m

graph [grɑ:f] n graphique m; **~ic** ['græfɪk] adj graphique; (account, description) vivant(e); **~ics** n arts mpl graphiques; graphisme m ♦ npl représentations fpl graphiques

grapple ['græpl] vi: **to ~ with** être aux prises avec

grasp [grɑ:sp] vt saisir ♦ n (grip) prise f; (understanding) compréhension f, connaissance f; **~ing** adj cupide

grass [grɑ:s] n herbe f; (lawn) gazon m; **~hopper** n sauterelle f; **~-roots** adj de la base, du peuple

grate [greɪt] n grille f de cheminée ♦ vi grincer ♦ vt (CULIN) râper

grateful ['greɪtful] adj reconnaissant(e)

grater ['greɪtər] n râpe f

gratifying ['grætɪfaɪɪŋ] adj agréable

grating ['greɪtɪŋ] n (iron bars) grille f ♦ adj (noise) grinçant(e)

gratitude ['grætɪtjuːd] n gratitude f

gratuity [grə'tjuːɪtɪ] n pourboire m

grave [greɪv] n tombe f ♦ adj grave,

sérieux(-euse)

gravel ['grævl] n gravier m

gravestone ['greɪvstəun] n pierre tombale

graveyard ['greɪvjɑːd] n cimetière m

gravity ['grævɪtɪ] n (PHYSICS) gravité f; pesanteur f; (seriousness) gravité

gravy ['greɪvɪ] n jus m (de viande); sauce f

gray [greɪ] (US) adj = **grey**

graze [greɪz] vi paître, brouter ♦ vt (touch lightly) frôler, effleurer; (scrape) écorcher ♦ n écorchure f

grease [griːs] n (fat) graisse f; (lubricant) lubrifiant m ♦ vt graisser; lubrifier; ~proof paper (BRIT) n papier sulfurisé; **greasy** adj gras(se), graisseux(-euse)

great [greɪt] adj grand(e); (inf) formidable; **G~ Britain** n Grande-Bretagne f; ~-grandfather n arrière-grand-père m; ~-grandmother n arrière-grand-mère f; ~ly adv très, grandement; (with verbs) beaucoup; ~ness n grandeur f

Greece [griːs] n Grèce f

greed [griːd] n (also: **~iness**) avidité f; (for food) gourmandise f, gloutonnerie f; ~y adj avide; gourmand(e), glouton(ne)

Greek [griːk] adj grec (grecque) ♦ n Grec (Grecque); (LING) grec m

green [griːn] adj vert(e); (inexperienced) (bien) jeune, naïf (naïve); (POL) vert(e), écologiste; (ecological) écologique ♦ n vert m; (stretch of grass) pelouse f; ~s npl (vegetables) légumes verts; (POL): **the G~s** les Verts mpl; **the G~ Party** (BRIT: POL) le parti écologiste; ~ belt n (round town) ceinture verte; ~ card n (AUT) carte verte; (US) permis m de travail; ~ery n verdure f; ~grocer's (BRIT) n marchand m de fruits et légumes; ~house n serre f; ~house effect n effet m de serre; ~house gas n gas m à effet de serre; ~ish adj verdâtre

Greenland ['griːnlənd] n Groenland m

greet [griːt] vt accueillir; ~ing n salutation f; ~ing(s) card n carte f de vœux

gregarious [grə'gɛərɪəs] adj (person) sociable

grenade [grə'neɪd] n grenade f

grew [gruː] pt of **grow**

grey [greɪ] (US **gray**) adj gris(e); (dismal) sombre; ~-haired adj grisonnant(e); ~hound n lévrier m

grid [grɪd] n grille f; (ELEC) réseau m; ~lock n (traffic jam) embouteillage m; ~locked adj: **to be ~locked** (roads) être bloqué par un embouteillage; (talks etc) être suspendu

grief [griːf] n chagrin m, douleur f

grievance ['griːvəns] n doléance f, grief m

grieve [griːv] vi avoir du chagrin; se désoler ♦ vt faire de la peine à, affliger; **to ~ for sb** (dead person) pleurer qn; **grievous** adj (LAW): **grievous bodily harm** coups mpl et blessures fpl

grill [grɪl] n (on cooker) gril m; (food: also mixed ~) grillade(s) f(pl) ♦ vt (BRIT) griller; (inf: question) cuisiner

grille [grɪl] n grille f, grillage m; (AUT) calandre f

grim [grɪm] adj sinistre, lugubre; (serious, stern) sévère

grimace [grɪ'meɪs] n grimace f ♦ vi grimacer, faire une grimace

grime [graɪm] n crasse f, saleté f

grin [grɪn] n large sourire m ♦ vi sourire

grind [graɪnd] (pt, pp **ground**) vt écraser; (coffee, pepper etc) moudre; (US: meat) hacher; (make sharp) aiguiser ♦ n (work) corvée f

grip [grɪp] n (hold) prise f, étreinte f; (control) emprise f; (grasp) connaissance f; (handle) poignée f; (holdall) sac m de voyage ♦ vt saisir, empoigner; **to come to ~s with** en venir aux prises avec; ~ping adj prenant(e), palpitant(e)

grisly ['grɪzlɪ] adj sinistre, macabre

gristle ['grɪsl] n cartilage m

grit [grɪt] n gravillon m; (courage) cran m ♦ vt (road) sabler; **to ~ one's teeth** serrer les dents

groan [grəun] n (of pain) gémissement m ♦ vi gémir

grocer ['grəusər] n épicier m; ~ies npl provisions fpl; ~'s (shop) n épicerie f

groin [grɔɪn] n aine f

groom [gruːm] n palefrenier m; (also:

bridegroom) marié *m* ♦ *vt* (*horse*) panser; (*fig*): **to ~** former qn pour; **well-~ed** très soigné(e)

groove [gru:v] *n* rainure *f*

grope [grəup] *vi*: **to ~ for** chercher à tâtons

gross [grəus] *adj* grossier(-ère); (*COMM*) brut(e); **~ly** *adv* (*greatly*) très, grandement

grotto ['grɔtəu] *n* grotte *f*

grotty ['grɔtɪ] (*inf*) *adj* minable, affreux(-euse)

ground [graund] *pt, pp of* **grind** ♦ *n* sol *m*, terre *f*; (*land*) terrain *m*, terres *fpl*; (*SPORT*) terrain *m*; (*US: also*: ~ **wire**) terre; (*reason: gen pl*) raison *f* ♦ *vt* (*plane*) empêcher de décoller, retenir au sol; (*US: ELEC*) équiper d'une prise de terre; **~s** *npl* (*of coffee etc*) marc *m*; (*gardens etc*) parc *m*, domaine *m*; **on the ~, to the ~** par terre; **to gain/lose ~** gagner/perdre du terrain; **~ cloth** (*US*) *n* = **groundsheet**; **~ing** *n* (*in education*) connaissances *fpl* de base; **~less** *adj* sans fondement; **~sheet** (*BRIT*) *n* tapis *m* de sol; **~ staff** *n* personnel *m* au sol; **~work** *n* préparation *f*

group [gru:p] *n* groupe *m* ♦ *vt* (*also*: ~ **together**) grouper ♦ *vi* se grouper

grouse [graus] *n inv* (*bird*) grouse *f* ♦ *vi* (*complain*) rouspéter, râler

grove [grəuv] *n* bosquet *m*

grovel ['grɔvl] *vi* (*fig*) ramper

grow [grəu] (*pt* **grew**, *pp* **grown**) *vi* pousser, croître; (*person*) grandir; (*increase*) augmenter, se développer; (*become*): **to ~ rich/weak** s'enrichir/s'affaiblir; (*develop*): **he's ~n out of his jacket** sa veste est (devenue) trop petite pour lui ♦ *vt* cultiver, faire pousser; (*beard*) laisser pousser; **he'll ~ out of it!** ça lui passera!; **~ up** *vi* grandir; **~er** *n* producteur *m*; **~ing** *adj* (*fear, amount*) croissant(e), grandissant(e)

growl [graul] *vi* grogner

grown [grəun] *pp of* **grow**; **~-up** *n* adulte *m/f*, grande personne

growth [grəuθ] *n* croissance *f*, développement *m*; (*what has grown*) pousse *f*; pous-

sée *f*; (*MED*) grosseur *f*, tumeur *f*

grub [grʌb] *n* larve *f*; (*inf: food*) bouffe *f*

grubby ['grʌbɪ] *adj* crasseux(-euse)

grudge [grʌdʒ] *n* rancune *f* ♦ *vt*: **to ~ sb sth** (*in giving*) donner qch à qn à contre-cœur; (*resent*) reprocher qch à qn; **to bear sb a ~ (for)** garder rancune *or* en vouloir à qn (de)

gruelling ['gruəlɪŋ] (*US* **grueling**) *adj* exté-nuant(e)

gruesome ['gru:səm] *adj* horrible

gruff [grʌf] *adj* bourru(e)

grumble ['grʌmbl] *vi* rouspéter, ronchon-ner

grumpy ['grʌmpɪ] *adj* grincheux(-euse)

grunt [grʌnt] *vi* grogner

G-string ['dʒi:strɪŋ] *n* (*garment*) cache-sexe *m inv*

guarantee [gærən'ti:] *n* garantie *f* ♦ *vt* ga-rantir

guard [gɑ:d] *n* garde *f*; (*one man*) garde *m*; (*BRIT: RAIL*) chef *m* de train; (*on machine*) dispositif *m* de sûreté; (*also*: **fire-guard**) garde-feu *m* ♦ *vt* garder, surveil-ler; (*protect*): **to ~ (against** *or* **from)** proté-ger (contre); **~ against** *vt* (*prevent*) em-pêcher, se protéger de; **~ed** *adj* (*fig*) pru-dent(e); **~ian** *n* gardien(ne); (*of minor*) tuteur(-trice); **~'s van** (*BRIT*) *n* (*RAIL*) four-gon *m*

guerrilla [gə'rɪlə] *n* guérillero *m*

guess [ges] *vt* deviner; (*estimate*) évaluer; (*US*) croire, penser ♦ *vi* deviner ♦ *n* sup-position *f*, hypothèse *f*; **to take** *or* **have a ~** essayer de deviner; **~work** *n* hypo-thèse *f*

guest [gest] *n* invité(e); (*in hotel*) client(e); **~-house** *n* pension *f*; **~ room** *n* cham-bre *f* d'amis

guffaw [gʌ'fɔ:] *vi* pouffer de rire

guidance ['gaɪdəns] *n* conseils *mpl*

guide [gaɪd] *n* (*person, book etc*) guide *m*; (*BRIT: also*: **girl ~**) guide *f* ♦ *vt* guider; **~book** *n* guide *m*; **~ dog** *n* chien *m* d'aveugle; **~lines** *npl* (*fig*) instructions (générales), conseils *mpl*

guild [gɪld] *n* corporation *f*; cercle *m*, asso-

ciation f
guillotine ['gɪləti:n] n guillotine f
guilt [gɪlt] n culpabilité f; ~**y** adj coupable
guinea pig ['gɪnɪ-] n cobaye m
guise [gaɪz] n aspect m, apparence f
guitar [gɪ'tɑ:ʳ] n guitare f
gulf [gʌlf] n golfe m; (abyss) gouffre m
gull [gʌl] n mouette f; (larger) goéland m
gullible ['gʌlɪbl] adj crédule
gully ['gʌlɪ] n ravin m; ravine f; couloir m
gulp [gʌlp] vi avaler sa salive ♦ vt (also: ~ **down**) avaler
gum [gʌm] n (ANAT) gencive f; (glue) colle f; (sweet: also ~drop) boule f de gomme; (also: chewing ~) chewing-gum m ♦ vt coller; ~**boots** (BRIT) npl bottes fpl en caoutchouc
gun [gʌn] n (small) revolver m, pistolet m; (rifle) fusil m, carabine f; (cannon) canon m; ~**boat** n canonnière f; ~**fire** n fusillade f; ~**man** n bandit armé; ~**point** n: **at ~point** sous la menace du pistolet (or fusil); ~**powder** n poudre f à canon; ~**shot** n coup m de feu
gurgle ['gɜ:gl] vi gargouiller; (baby) gazouiller
gush [gʌʃ] vi jaillir; (fig) se répandre en effusions
gust [gʌst] n (of wind) rafale f; (of smoke) bouffée f
gusto ['gʌstəu] n enthousiasme m
gut [gʌt] n intestin m, boyau m; ~**s** npl (inf: courage) cran m
gutter ['gʌtəʳ] n (in street) caniveau m; (of roof) gouttière f
guy [gaɪ] n (inf: man) type m; (also: ~**rope**) corde f; (BRIT: figure) effigie de Guy Fawkes (brûlée en plein air le 5 novembre)

Guy Fawkes' Night

ⓘ Guy Fawkes' Night, que l'on appelle également "bonfire night", commémore l'échec du complot (le "Gunpowder Plot") contre James Ist et son parlement le 5 no-

vembre 1605. L'un des conspirateurs, Guy Fawkes, avait été surpris dans les caves du parlement alors qu'il s'apprêtait à y mettre le feu. Chaque année pour le 5 novembre, les enfants préparent à l'avance une effigie de Guy Fawkes et ils demandent aux passants "un penny pour le guy" avec lequel ils pourront s'acheter des fusées de feu d'artifice. Beaucoup de gens font encore un feu dans leur jardin sur lequel ils brûlent le "guy".

---

guzzle ['gʌzl] vt avaler gloutonnement
gym [dʒɪm] n (also: ~**nasium**) gymnase m; (also: ~**nastics**) gym f; ~**nast** n gymnaste m/f; ~**nastics** [dʒɪm'næstɪks] n, npl gymnastique f; ~ **shoes** npl chaussures fpl de gym; ~**slip** (BRIT) n tunique f (d'écolière)
gynaecologist [gaɪnɪ'kɔlədʒɪst] (US **gynecologist**) n gynécologue m/f
gypsy ['dʒɪpsɪ] n gitan(e), bohémien(ne)

H, h

haberdashery [hæbə'dæʃərɪ] (BRIT) n mercerie f
habit ['hæbɪt] n habitude f; (REL: costume) habit m; ~**ual** adj habituel(le); (drinker, liar) invétéré(e)
hack [hæk] vt hacher, tailler ♦ n (pej: writer) nègre m; ~**er** n (COMPUT) pirate m (informatique); (: enthusiast) passionné(e) m/f des ordinateurs
hackneyed ['hæknɪd] adj usé(e), rebattu(e)
had [hæd] pt, pp of **have**
haddock ['hædək] (pl ~ or ~**s**) n églefin m; **smoked** ~ haddock m
hadn't ['hædnt] = **had not**
haemorrhage ['hemərɪdʒ] (US **hemorrhage**) n hémorragie f
haemorrhoids ['hemərɔɪdz] (US **hemorrhoids**) npl hémorroïdes fpl
haggle ['hægl] vi marchander
Hague [heɪg] n: **The** ~ La Haye

hail [heɪl] n grêle f ♦ vt (call) héler; (acclaim) acclamer ♦ vi grêler; **~stone** n grêlon m

hair [hɛər] n cheveux mpl; (of animal) pelage m; (single ~: on head) cheveu m; (: on body; of animal) poil m; **to do one's ~** se coiffer; **~brush** n brosse f à cheveux; **~cut** n coupe f (de cheveux); **~do** n coiffure f; **~dresser** n coiffeur(-euse); **~dresser's** n salon m de coiffure, coiffeur m; **~ dryer** n sèche-cheveux m; **~ gel** n gel m pour cheveux; **~grip** n pince f à cheveux; **~net** n filet m à cheveux; **~piece** n perruque f; **~pin** n épingle f à cheveux; **~pin bend** (US **hairpin curve**) n virage m en épingle à cheveux; **~-raising** adj à (vous) faire dresser les cheveux sur la tête; **~ removing cream** n crème f dépilatoire; **~ spray** n laque f (pour les cheveux); **~style** n coiffure f; **~y** adj poilu(e); (inf: fig) effrayant(e)

hake [heɪk] (pl ~ or ~s) n colin m, merlu m

half [hɑːf] (pl **halves**) n moitié f; (of beer: also: ~ **pint**) ≃ demi m; (RAIL, bus: also: ~ **fare**) demi-tarif m ♦ adj demi(e) ♦ adv (à) moitié, à demi; ~ **a dozen** une demi-douzaine; ~ **a pound** une demi-livre, ≃ 250 g; **two and a** ~ deux et demi; **to cut sth in** ~ couper qch en deux; **~caste** ['hɑːfkɑːst] n métis(se); **~-hearted** adj tiède, sans enthousiasme; **~-hour** n demi-heure f; **~-mast: at ~-mast** adv (flag) en berne; **~penny** (BRIT) n demi-penny m; **~-price** adj, adv: **(at) ~-price** à moitié prix; **~ term** (BRIT) n (SCOL) congé m de demi-trimestre; **~-time** n mi-temps f; **~way** adv à mi-chemin

hall [hɔːl] n salle f; (entrance way) hall m, entrée f

hallmark ['hɔːlmɑːk] n poinçon m; (fig) marque f

hallo [hə'ləu] excl = **hello**

hall of residence (BRIT) (pl **halls of residence**) n résidence f universitaire

Hallowe'en ['hæləu'iːn] n veille f de la Toussaint

hallucination [həluːsɪ'neɪʃən] n hallucination f

hallway ['hɔːlweɪ] n vestibule m

halo ['heɪləu] n (of saint etc) auréole f

halt [hɔːlt] n halte f, arrêt m ♦ vt (progress etc) interrompre ♦ vi faire halte, s'arrêter

halve [hɑːv] vt (apple etc) partager or diviser en deux; (expense) réduire de moitié; **~s** npl of **half**

ham [hæm] n jambon m

hamburger ['hæmbɜːgər] n hamburger m

hamlet ['hæmlɪt] n hameau m

hammer ['hæmər] n marteau m ♦ vt (nail) enfoncer; (fig) démolir ♦ vi (on door) frapper à coups redoublés; **to ~ an idea into sb** faire entrer de force une idée dans la tête de qn

hammock ['hæmək] n hamac m

hamper ['hæmpər] vt gêner ♦ n panier m (d'osier)

hamster ['hæmstər] n hamster m

hand [hænd] n main f; (of clock) aiguille f; (~writing) écriture f; (worker) ouvrier(-ère); (at cards) jeu m ♦ vt passer, donner; **to give or lend sb a ~** donner un coup de main à qn; **at ~** à portée de la main; **in ~** (time) à disposition; (job, situation) en main; **to be on ~** (person) être disponible; (emergency services) se tenir prêt(e) (à intervenir); **to ~** (information etc) sous la main, à portée de la main; **on the one ~ ..., on the other ~** d'une part ..., d'autre part; **~ in** vt remettre; **~ out** vt distribuer; **~ over** vt transmettre; céder; **~bag** n sac m à main; **~book** n manuel m; **~brake** n frein m à main; **~cuffs** npl menottes fpl;

~ful n poignée f

handicap ['hændɪkæp] n handicap m ♦ vt handicaper; **mentally/physically ~ped** handicapé(e) mentalement/physiquement

handicraft ['hændɪkrɑ:ft] n (travail m d')artisanat m, technique artisanale; (object) objet artisanal

handiwork ['hændɪwɜ:k] n ouvrage m

handkerchief ['hæŋkətʃɪf] n mouchoir m

handle ['hændl] n (of door etc) poignée f; (of cup etc) anse f; (of knife etc) manche m; (of saucepan) queue f; (for winding) manivelle f ♦ vt toucher, manier; (deal with) s'occuper de; (treat: people) prendre; **"~ with care"** "fragile"; **to fly off the ~** s'énerver; ~**bar(s)** n(pl) guidon m

hand: ~**luggage** n bagages mpl à main; ~**made** adj fait(e) à la main; ~**out** n (from government, parents) aide f, don m; (leaflet) documentation f, prospectus m; (summary of lecture) polycopié m; ~**rail** n rampe f, main courante; ~**set** n (TEL) combiné m; **please replace the ~set** raccrochez s'il vous plaît; ~**shake** n poignée f de main

handsome ['hænsəm] adj beau (belle), (profit, return) considérable

handwriting ['hændraɪtɪŋ] n écriture f

handy ['hændɪ] adj (person) adroit(e); (close at hand) sous la main; (convenient) pratique

hang [hæŋ] (pt, pp **hung**) vt accrocher; (criminal: pt, pp: ~ed) pendre ♦ vi pendre; (hair, drapery) tomber; **to get the ~ of (doing) sth** (inf) attraper le coup pour faire qch; ~ **about** vi traîner; ~ **around** vi = **hang about**; ~ **on** vi (wait) attendre; ~ **up** vi (TEL): **to ~ up (on sb)** raccrocher (au nez de qn) ♦ vt (coat, painting etc) accrocher, suspendre

hangar ['hæŋəʳ] n hangar m

hanger ['hæŋəʳ] n cintre m, portemanteau m; ~**-on** n parasite m

hang: ~**-gliding** n deltaplane m, vol m libre; ~**over** n (after drinking) gueule f de bois; ~**-up** n complexe m

hanker ['hæŋkəʳ] vi: **to ~ after** avoir envie de

hankie, hanky ['hæŋkɪ] n abbr = **handkerchief**

haphazard [hæp'hæzəd] adj fait(e) au hasard, fait(e) au petit bonheur

happen ['hæpən] vi arriver; se passer, se produire; **it so ~s that** il se trouve que; **as it ~s** justement; ~**ing** n événement m

happily ['hæpɪlɪ] adv heureusement; (cheerfully) joyeusement

happiness ['hæpɪnɪs] n bonheur m

happy ['hæpɪ] adj heureux(-euse); ~ **with** (arrangements etc) satisfait(e) de; **to be ~ to do** faire volontiers; ~ **birthday!** bon anniversaire!; ~**-go-lucky** adj insouciant(e); ~ **hour** n heure pendant laquelle les consommations sont à prix réduit

harass ['hærəs] vt accabler, tourmenter; ~**ment** n tracasseries fpl

harbour ['hɑ:bəʳ] (US **harbor**) n port m ♦ vt héberger, abriter; (hope, fear etc) entretenir

hard [hɑ:d] adj dur(e); (question, problem) difficile, dur(e); (facts, evidence) concret(-ète) ♦ adv (work) dur; (think, try) sérieusement; **to look ~ at** regarder fixement; (thing) regarder de près; **no ~ feelings!** sans rancune!; **to be ~ of hearing** être dur(e) d'oreille; **to be ~ done by** être traité(e) injustement; ~**back** n livre relié; ~ **cash** n espèces fpl; ~ **disk** n (COMPUT) disque dur; ~**en** vt durcir; (fig) endurcir ♦ vi durcir; ~**-headed** adj réaliste, décidé(e); ~ **labour** n travaux forcés

hardly ['hɑ:dlɪ] adv (scarcely, no sooner) à peine; ~ **anywhere/ever** presque nulle part/jamais

hard: ~**ship** n épreuves fpl; ~ **shoulder** (BRIT) n (AUT) accotement stabilisé; ~ **up** (inf) adj fauché(e); ~**ware** n quincaillerie f; (COMPUT, MIL) matériel m; ~**ware shop** n quincaillerie f; ~**-wearing** adj solide; ~**-working** adj travailleur(-euse)

hardy ['hɑ:dɪ] adj robuste; (plant) résistant(e) au gel

hare [hɛəʳ] n lièvre m; ~**-brained** adj farfelu(e)

harm [hɑːm] *n* mal *m*; (*wrong*) tort *m* ♦ *vt* (*person*) faire du mal *or* du tort à; (*thing*) endommager; **out of ~'s way** à l'abri du danger, en lieu sûr; **~ful** *adj* nuisible; **~less** *adj* inoffensif(-ive); sans méchanceté

harmony ['hɑːmənɪ] *n* harmonie *f*

harness ['hɑːnɪs] *n* harnais *m*; (*safety ~*) harnais de sécurité ♦ *vt* (*horse*) harnacher; (*resources*) exploiter

harp [hɑːp] *n* harpe *f* ♦ *vi*: **to ~ on about** rabâcher

harrowing ['hærəuɪŋ] *adj* déchirant(e), très pénible

harsh [hɑːʃ] *adj* (*hard*) dur(e); (*severe*) sévère; (*unpleasant*: *sound*) discordant(e); (: *light*) cru(e)

harvest ['hɑːvɪst] *n* (*of corn*) moisson *f*; (*of fruit*) récolte *f*; (*of grapes*) vendange *f* ♦ *vt* moissonner; récolter; vendanger

has [hæz] *vb see* **have**

hash [hæʃ] *n* (CULIN) hachis *m*; (*fig*: *mess*) gâchis *m*

hasn't ['hæznt] = **has not**

hassle ['hæsl] *n* (*inf*: *bother*) histoires *fpl*, tracas *mpl*

haste [heɪst] *n* hâte *f*; précipitation *f*; **~n** ['heɪsn] *vt* hâter, accélérer ♦ *vi* se hâter, s'empresser; **hastily** *adv* à la hâte; précipitamment; **hasty** *adj* hâtif(-ive); précipité(e)

hat [hæt] *n* chapeau *m*

hatch [hætʃ] *n* (NAUT: *also*: **~way**) écoutille *f*; (*also*: **service ~**) passe-plats *m inv* ♦ *vi* éclore; **~back** *n* (AUT) modèle *m* avec hayon arrière

hatchet ['hætʃɪt] *n* hachette *f*

hate [heɪt] *vt* haïr, détester ♦ *n* haine *f*; **~ful** *adj* odieux(-euse), détestable; **hatred** ['heɪtrɪd] *n* haine *f*

haughty ['hɔːtɪ] *adj* hautain(e), arrogant(e)

haul [hɔːl] *vt* traîner, tirer ♦ *n* (*of fish*) prise *f*; (*of stolen goods etc*) butin *m*; **~age** *n* transport routier; (*costs*) frais *mpl* de transport

haulier ['hɔːlɪər] (US **hauler**) *n* (*company*) transporteur (routier); (*driver*) camionneur

m

haunch [hɔːntʃ] *n* hanche *f*; (*of meat*) cuissot *m*

haunt [hɔːnt] *vt* (*subj*: *ghost, fear*) hanter; (: *person*) fréquenter ♦ *n* repaire *m*

KEYWORD

have [hæv] (*pt, pp* **had**) *aux vb* **1** (*gen*) avoir; être; **to have arrived/gone** être arrivé(e)/allé(e); **to have eaten/slept** avoir mangé/dormi; **he has been promoted** il a eu une promotion

2 (*in tag questions*): **you've done it, haven't you?** vous l'avez fait, n'est-ce pas?

3 (*in short answers and questions*): **no I haven't!/yes we have!** mais non!/mais si!; **so I have!** ah oui!, oui c'est vrai!; **I've been there before, have you?** j'y suis déjà allé, et vous?

♦ *modal aux vb* (*be obliged*): **to have (got) to do sth** devoir faire qch; être obligé(e) de faire qch; **she has (got) to do it** elle doit le faire, il faut qu'elle le fasse; **you haven't to tell her** vous ne devez pas le lui dire

♦ *vt* **1** (*possess, obtain*) avoir; **he has (got) blue eyes/dark hair** il a les yeux bleus/les cheveux bruns; **may I have your address?** puis-je avoir votre adresse?

2 (+*noun*: *take, hold etc*): **to have breakfast/a bath/a shower** prendre le petit déjeuner/un bain/une douche; **to have dinner/lunch** dîner/déjeuner; **to have a swim** nager; **to have a meeting** se réunir; **to have a party** organiser une fête

3: **to have sth done** faire faire qch; **to have one's hair cut** se faire couper les cheveux; **to have sb do sth** faire faire qch à qn

4 (*experience, suffer*) avoir; **to have a cold/flu** avoir un rhume/la grippe; **to have an operation** se faire opérer

5 (*inf*: *dupe*) avoir; **he's been had** il s'est fait avoir *or* rouler

have out *vt*: **to have it out with sb** (*set-*

tle a problem etc) s'expliquer (franchement) avec qn

haven ['heɪvn] n port m; (*fig*) havre m
haven't ['hævnt] = **have not**
havoc ['hævək] n ravages mpl
hawk [hɔːk] n faucon m
hay [heɪ] n foin m; ~ **fever** n rhume m
des foins; ~**stack** n meule f de foin
haywire (*inf*) adj: **to go** ~ (*machine*) se
détraquer; (*plans*) mal tourner
hazard ['hæzəd] n danger m, risque m ♦ vt
risquer, hasarder; ~ (**warning**) **lights** npl
(*AUT*) feux mpl de détresse
haze [heɪz] n brume f
hazelnut ['heɪzlnʌt] n noisette f
hazy ['heɪzɪ] adj brumeux(-euse); (*idea*) vague
he [hiː] pron il; **it is** ~ **who ...** c'est lui qui ...
head [hɛd] n tête f; (*leader*) chef m; (*of
school*) directeur(-trice) ♦ vt (*list*) être en
tête de; (*group*) être à la tête de; ~**s (or
tails)** pile (ou face); ~ **first** la tête la première; ~ **over heels in love** follement *or*
éperdument amoureux(-euse); **to** ~ **a ball**
faire une tête; ~ **for** vt fus se diriger vers;
~**ache** n mal m de tête; ~**dress** (*BRIT*) n
(*of Red Indian etc*) coiffure f; ~**ing** n titre
m; ~**lamp** (*BRIT*) n = **headlight**; ~**land** n
promontoire m, cap m; ~**light** n phare
m; ~**line** n titre m; ~**long** adv (*fall*) la
tête la première; (*rush*) tête baissée;
~**master** n directeur m; ~**mistress** n directrice f; ~ **office** n bureau central,
siège m; ~**-on** adj (*collision*) de plein
fouet; (*confrontation*) en face à face;
~**phones** npl casque m (à écouteurs);
~**quarters** npl bureau *or* siège central;
(*MIL*) quartier général; ~**rest** n appui-tête
m; ~**room** n (*in car*) hauteur f de plafond; (*under bridge*) hauteur limite; ~**scarf**
n foulard m; ~**strong** adj têtu(e), en-
têté(e); ~ **teacher** n directeur(-trice), (*of
secondary school*) proviseur m; ~ **waiter** n
maître m d'hôtel; ~**way** n: **to make**
~**way** avancer, faire des progrès; ~**wind** n
vent m contraire; (*NAUT*) vent debout; ~**y**

adj capiteux(-euse); enivrant(e); (*experience*) grisant(e)
heal [hiːl] vt, vi guérir
health [hɛlθ] n santé f; ~ **food** n ali-
ment(s) naturel(s); ~ **food shop** n magasin m diététique; **H~ Service** (*BRIT*) n:
the H~ Service ≃ la Sécurité sociale; ~**y**
adj (*person*) en bonne santé; (*climate, food,
attitude etc*) sain(e), bon(ne) pour la santé
heap [hiːp] n tas m ♦ vt: **to** ~ **(up)** entasser, amonceler; **she ~ed her plate with
cakes** elle a chargé son assiette de
gâteaux
hear [hɪər] (*pt, pp* **heard**) vt entendre;
(*news*) apprendre ♦ vi entendre; **to** ~
about entendre parler de; avoir des nouvelles de; **to** ~ **from sb** recevoir *or* avoir
des nouvelles de qn; ~**ing** n (*sense*) ouïe
f; (*of witnesses*) audition f; (*of a case*)
audience f; ~**ing aid** n appareil m acoustique; ~**say:** **by ~say** adv par ouï-dire m
hearse [hɜːs] n corbillard m
heart [hɑːt] n cœur m; ~**s** npl (*CARDS*)
cœur; **to lose/take** ~ perdre/prendre
courage; **at** ~ au fond; **by** ~ (*learn,
know*) par cœur; ~ **attack** n crise f cardiaque; ~**beat** n battement m du cœur;
~**breaking** adj déchirant(e), qui fend le
cœur; ~**broken** adj: **to be ~broken** avoir
beaucoup de chagrin *or* le cœur brisé;
~**burn** n brûlures fpl d'estomac; ~ **failure** n arrêt m du cœur; ~**felt** adj sincère
hearth [hɑːθ] n foyer m, cheminée f
heartily ['hɑːtɪlɪ] adv chaleureusement;
(*laugh*) de bon cœur; (*eat*) de bon appétit; **to agree** ~ être entièrement d'accord
hearty ['hɑːtɪ] adj chaleureux(-euse); (*appetite*) robuste; (*dislike*) cordial(e)
heat [hiːt] n chaleur f; (*fig*) feu m, agitation f; (*SPORT: also:* **qualifying** ~) éliminatoire f ♦ vt chauffer; ~ **up** vi (*water*)
chauffer; (*room*) se réchauffer ♦ vt réchauffer; ~**ed** adj chauffé(e); (*fig*) passion-
né(e), échauffé(e); ~**er** n appareil m de
chauffage; radiateur m; (*in car*) chauffage
m; (*water heater*) chauffe-eau m
heath [hiːθ] (*BRIT*) n lande f

heather ['hɛðəʳ] *n* bruyère *f*

heating ['hi:tɪŋ] *n* chauffage *m*

heatstroke ['hi:tstrəuk] *n* (*MED*) coup *m* de chaleur

heat wave *n* vague *f* de chaleur

heave [hi:v] *vt* soulever (avec effort); (*drag*) traîner ♦ *vi* se soulever; (*retch*) avoir un haut-le-cœur; **to ~ a sigh** pousser un soupir

heaven ['hɛvn] *n* ciel *m*, paradis *m*; (*fig*) paradis *m*; ~**ly** *adj* céleste, divin(e)

heavily ['hɛvɪlɪ] *adv* lourdement; (*drink, smoke*) beaucoup; (*sleep, sigh*) profondément

heavy ['hɛvɪ] *adj* lourd(e); (*work, sea, rain, eater*) gros(se); (*snow*) beaucoup de; (*drinker, smoker*) grand(e); (*breathing*) bruyant(e); (*schedule, week*) chargé(e); ~ **goods vehicle** *n* poids lourd; ~**weight** *n* (*SPORT*) poids lourd

Hebrew ['hi:bru:] *adj* hébraïque ♦ *n* (*LING*) hébreu *m*

Hebrides ['hɛbrɪdi:z] *npl*: **the ~** les Hébrides *fpl*

heckle ['hɛkl] *vt* interpeller (*un orateur*)

hectic ['hɛktɪk] *adj* agité(e), trépidant(e)

he'd [hi:d] = **he would**; **he had**

hedge [hɛdʒ] *n* haie *f* ♦ *vi* se dérober; **to ~ one's bets** (*fig*) se couvrir

hedgehog ['hɛdʒhɔg] *n* hérisson *m*

heed [hi:d] *vt* (*also*: **take ~ of**) tenir compte de; ~**less** *adj* insouciant(e)

heel [hi:l] *n* talon *m* ♦ *vt* retalonner

hefty ['hɛftɪ] *adj* (*person*) costaud(e); (*parcel*) lourd(e); (*profit*) gros(se)

heifer ['hɛfəʳ] *n* génisse *f*

height [haɪt] *n* (*of person*) taille *f*, grandeur *f*; (*of object*) hauteur *f*; (*of plane, mountain*) altitude *f*; (*high ground*) hauteur, éminence *f*; (*fig: of glory*) sommet *m*; (: *of luxury, stupidity*) comble *m*; ~**en** *vt* (*fig*) augmenter

heir [ɛəʳ] *n* héritier *m*; ~**ess** *n* héritière *f*; ~**loom** *n* héritage *m*, meuble *m* (*or* bijou *m or* tableau *m*) de famille

held [hɛld] *pt, pp of* **hold**

helicopter ['hɛlɪkɔptəʳ] *n* hélicoptère *m*

hell [hɛl] *n* enfer *m*; ~**!** (*inf!*) merde!

he'll [hi:l] = **he will**; **he shall**

hellish ['hɛlɪʃ] (*inf*) *adj* infernal(e)

hello [hə'ləu] *excl* bonjour!; (*to attract attention*) hé!; (*surprise*) tiens!

helm [hɛlm] *n* (*NAUT*) barre *f*

helmet ['hɛlmɪt] *n* casque *m*

help [hɛlp] *n* aide *f*; (*charwoman*) femme *f* de ménage ♦ *vt* aider; ~**!** au secours!; ~ **yourself** servez-vous; **he can't ~ it** il ne peut pas s'en empêcher; ~**er** *n* aide *m/f*, assistant(e); ~**ful** *adj* serviable, obligeant(e); (*useful*) utile; ~**ing** *n* portion *f*; ~**less** *adj* impuissant(e); (*defenceless*) faible

hem [hɛm] *n* ourlet *m* ♦ *vt* ourler; ~ **in** *vt* cerner

hemorrhage ['hɛmərɪdʒ] (*US*) *n* = **haemorrhage**

hemorrhoids ['hɛmərɔɪdz] (*US*) *npl* = **haemorrhoids**

hen [hɛn] *n* poule *f*

hence [hɛns] *adv* (*therefore*) d'où, de là; **2 years ~** d'ici 2 ans, dans 2 ans; ~**forth** *adv* dorénavant

her. [hə:ʳ] *pron* (*direct*) la, l'; (*indirect*) lui; (*stressed, after prep*) elle ♦ *adj* son (sa), ses *pl; see also* **me**; **my**

herald ['hɛrəld] *n* héraut *m* ♦ *vt* annoncer; ~**ry** *n* (*study*) héraldique *f*; (*coat of arms*) blason *m*

herb [hə:b] *n* herbe *f*

herd [hə:d] *n* troupeau *m*

here [hɪəʳ] *adv* ici; (*time*) alors ♦ *excl* tiens!, tenez!; ~**!** présent!; ~ **is**, ~ **are** voici; ~ **he/she is!** le/la voici!; ~**after** *adv* après, plus tard; ~**by** *adv* (*formal: in letter*) par la présente

hereditary [hɪ'rɛdɪtrɪ] *adj* héréditaire

heresy ['hɛrəsɪ] *n* hérésie *f*

heritage ['hɛrɪtɪdʒ] *n* (*of country*) patrimoine *m*

hermit ['hə:mɪt] *n* ermite *m*

hernia ['hə:nɪə] *n* hernie *f*

hero ['hɪərəu] (*pl* ~**es**) *n* héros *m*

heroin ['hɛrəuɪn] *n* héroïne *f*

heroine ['hɛrəuɪn] *n* héroïne *f*

heron ['herən] n héron m

herring ['herɪŋ] n hareng m

hers [hɜ:z] pron le (la) sien(ne), les siens (siennes); see also **mine¹**

herself [hɜ:'self] pron (reflexive) se; (emphatic) elle-même; (after prep) elle; see also **oneself**

he's [hi:z] = **he is**; **he has**

hesitant ['hezɪtənt] adj hésitant(e), indécis(e)

hesitate ['hezɪteɪt] vi hésiter; **hesitation** [hezɪ'teɪʃən] n hésitation f

heterosexual ['hetərəʊ'seksjʊəl] adj, n hétérosexuel(le)

heyday ['heɪdeɪ] n: **the ~ of** l'âge m d'or de, les beaux jours de

HGV n abbr = **heavy goods vehicle**

hi [haɪ] excl salut!; (to attract attention) hé!

hiatus [haɪ'eɪtəs] n (gap) lacune f; (interruption) pause f

hibernate ['haɪbəneɪt] vi hiberner

hiccough, hiccup ['hɪkʌp] vi hoqueter; **~s** npl hoquet m

hide [haɪd] (pt hid, pp hidden) n (skin) peau f ♦ vt cacher ♦ vi: **to ~ (from sb)** se cacher (de qn); **~-and-seek** n cache-cache m

hideous ['hɪdɪəs] adj hideux(-euse)

hiding ['haɪdɪŋ] n (beating) correction f, volée f de coups; **to be in ~** (concealed) se tenir caché(e)

hierarchy ['haɪərɑːkɪ] n hiérarchie f

hi-fi ['haɪfaɪ] n hi-fi f inv ♦ adj hi-fi inv

high [haɪ] adj haut(e); (speed, respect, number) grand(e); (price) élevé(e); (wind) fort(e), violent(e); (voice) aigu (aiguë) ♦ adv haut; **20 m ~** haut(e) de 20 m; **~brow** adj, n intellectuel(le); **~chair** n (child's) chaise haute; **~er education** n études supérieures; **~-handed** adj très autoritaire; très cavalier(-ère); **~-heeled** adj à hauts talons; **~ jump** n (SPORT) saut m en hauteur; **~lands** npl Highlands mpl; **~light** n (fig: of event) point culminant ♦ vt faire ressortir, souligner; **~lights** npl (in hair) reflets mpl; **~ly** adv très, fort, hautement; **to speak/think ~ly of sb**

dire/penser beaucoup de bien de qn; **~ly paid** adj très bien payé(e); **~ly strung** adj nerveux(-euse), toujours tendu(e); **~ness** n: **Her (or His) H~ness** Son Altesse f; **~-pitched** adj aigu (aiguë); **~-rise** adj: **~-rise block, ~-rise flats** tour f (d'habitation); **~ school** n lycée m; (US) établissement m d'enseignement supérieur; **~ season** (BRIT) n haute saison; **~ street** (BRIT) n grand-rue f; **~way** n route nationale; **H~way Code** (BRIT) n code m de la route

hijack ['haɪdʒæk] vt (plane) détourner; **~er** n pirate m de l'air

hike [haɪk] vi aller or faire des excursions à pied ♦ n excursion f à pied, randonnée f; **~r** n promeneur(-euse), excursionniste m/f; **hiking** n excursions fpl à pied

hilarious [hɪ'lɛərɪəs] adj (account, event) désopilant(e)

hill [hɪl] n colline f; (fairly high) montagne f; (on road) côte f; **~side** n (flanc m de) coteau m; **~-walking** n randonnée f de basse montagne; **~y** adj vallonné(e); montagneux(-euse)

hilt [hɪlt] n (of sword) garde f; **to the ~** (fig: support) à fond

him [hɪm] pron (direct) le, l'; (stressed, indirect, after prep) lui; see also **me**; **~self** pron (reflexive) se; (emphatic) lui-même; (after prep) lui; see also **oneself**

hinder ['hɪndər] vt gêner; (delay) retarder; **hindrance** n gêne f, obstacle m

hindsight ['haɪndsaɪt] n: **with ~** avec du recul, rétrospectivement

Hindu ['hɪnduː] adj hindou(e)

hinge [hɪndʒ] n charnière f ♦ vi (fig): **to ~ on** dépendre de

hint [hɪnt] n allusion f; (advice) conseil m ♦ vt: **to ~ that** insinuer que ♦ vi: **to ~ at** faire une allusion à

hip [hɪp] n hanche f

hippie ['hɪpɪ] n hippie m/f

hippo ['hɪpəʊ] (pl **~s**), **hippopotamus** [hɪpə'pɒtəməs] (pl **~potamuses** or **~potami**) n hippopotame m

hire ['haɪər] vt (BRIT: car, equipment) louer;

(*worker*) embaucher, engager ♦ *n* location *f*; **for ~** à louer; (*taxi*) libre; **~(d) car** *n* voiture *f* de location; **~ purchase** (*BRIT*) *n* achat *m* (*or* vente *f*) à tempérament *or* crédit

his [hɪz] *pron* le (la) sien(ne), les siens (siennes) ♦ *adj* son (sa), ses *pl*; *see also* **my**; **mine**[1]

hiss [hɪs] *vi* siffler

historic [hɪˈstɔrɪk] *adj* historique; **~al** *adj* historique

history [ˈhɪstərɪ] *n* histoire *f*

hit [hɪt] (*pt, pp* **hit**) *vt* frapper; (*reach: target*) atteindre, toucher; (*collide with: car*) entrer en collision avec, heurter; (*fig: affect*) toucher ♦ *n* coup *m*; (*success*) succès *m*; (: *song*) tube *m*; **to ~ it off with sb** bien s'entendre avec qn; **~-and-run driver** *n* chauffard *m* (coupable du délit de fuite)

hitch [hɪtʃ] *vt* (*fasten*) accrocher, attacher; (*also:* **~ up**) remonter d'une saccade ♦ *n* (*difficulty*) anicroche *f*, contretemps *m*; **to ~ a lift** faire du stop; **~hike** *vi* faire de l'auto-stop; **~hiker** *n* auto-stoppeur(-euse)

hi-tech [ˈhaɪˈtɛk] *adj* de pointe

hitherto [hɪðəˈtuː] *adv* jusqu'ici

hit man *n* tueur *m* à gages

HIV *n*: **~-negative/-positive** *adj* séro-négatif(-ive)/-positif(-ive)

hive [haɪv] *n* ruche *f*

HMS *abbr* = **Her/His Majesty's Ship**

hoard [hɔːd] *n* (*of food*) provisions *fpl*, réserves *fpl*; (*of money*) trésor *m* ♦ *vt* amasser; **~ing** (*BRIT*) *n* (*for posters*) panneau *m* d'affichage *or* publicitaire

hoarse [hɔːs] *adj* enroué(e)

hoax [həuks] *n* canular *m*

hob [hɔb] *n* plaque (chauffante)

hobble [ˈhɔbl] *vi* boitiller

hobby [ˈhɔbɪ] *n* passe-temps favori

hobo [ˈhəubəu] (*US*) *n* vagabond *m*

hockey [ˈhɔkɪ] *n* hockey *m*

hog [hɔg] *n* porc (châtré) ♦ *vt* (*fig*) accaparer; **to go the whole ~** aller jusqu'au bout

hoist [hɔɪst] *n* (*apparatus*) palan *m* ♦ *vt* hisser

hold [həuld] (*pt, pp* **held**) *vt* tenir; (*contain*) contenir; (*believe*) considérer; (*possess*) avoir; (*detain*) détenir ♦ *vi* (*withstand pressure*) tenir (bon); (*be valid*) valoir ♦ *n* (*also fig*) prise *f*; (*NAUT*) cale *f*; **~ the line!** (*TEL*) ne quittez pas!; **to ~ one's own** (*fig*) (bien) se défendre; **to catch** *or* **get (a) ~ of** saisir; **to get ~ of** (*fig*) trouver; **~ back** *vt* retenir; (*secret*) taire; **~ down** *vt* (*person*) maintenir à terre; (*job*) occuper; **~ off** *vt* tenir à distance; **~ on** *vi* tenir bon; (*wait*) attendre; **~ on!** (*TEL*) ne quittez pas!; **~ on to** *vt fus* se cramponner à; (*keep*) conserver, garder; **~ out** *vt* offrir ♦ *vi* (*resist*) tenir bon; **~ up** *vt* (*raise*) lever; (*support*) soutenir; (*delay*) retarder; (*rob*) braquer; **~all** (*BRIT*) *n* fourre-tout *m* *inv*; **~er** *n* (*of ticket, record*) détenteur(-trice); (*of office, title etc*) titulaire *m/f*; (*container*) support *m*; **~ing** *n* (*share*) intérêts *mpl*; (*farm*) ferme *f*; **~-up** *n* (*robbery*) hold-up *m*; (*delay*) retard *m*; (*BRIT: in traffic*) bouchon *m*

hole [həul] *n* trou *m*; **~-in-the-wall** *n* (*cash dispenser*) distributeur *m* de billets

holiday [ˈhɔlɪdeɪ] *n* vacances *fpl*; (*day off*) jour *m* de congé; (*public*) jour férié; **on ~** en congé; **~ camp** *n* (*also:* **~ centre**) camp *m* de vacances; **~-maker** (*BRIT*) *n* vacancier(-ère); **~ resort** *n* centre *m* de villégiature *or* vacances

Holland [ˈhɔlənd] *n* Hollande *f*

hollow [ˈhɔləu] *adj* creux(-euse) ♦ *n* creux *m* ♦ *vt*: **to ~ out** creuser, évider

holly [ˈhɔlɪ] *n* houx *m*

holocaust [ˈhɔləkɔːst] *n* holocauste *m*

holster [ˈhəulstər] *n* étui *m* de revolver

holy [ˈhəulɪ] *adj* saint(e); (*bread, water*) bénit(e); (*ground*) sacré(e); **H~ Ghost** *n* Saint-Esprit *m*

homage [ˈhɔmɪdʒ] *n* hommage *m*; **to pay ~ to** rendre hommage à

home [həum] *n* foyer *m*, maison *f*; (*country*) pays natal, patrie *f*; (*institution*) maison ♦ *adj* de famille; (*ECON, POL*) national(e), intérieur(e); (SPORT: game) sur leur (or notre) terrain; (team) qui reçoit ♦ adv chez soi, à la maison; au pays natal; (right in: nail etc) à fond; **at ~** chez soi, à la maison; **make yourself at ~** faites comme chez vous; ~**address** n domicile permanent; ~**land** n patrie f; ~**less** adj sans foyer; sans abri; ~**ly** adj (plain) simple, sans prétention; ~**made** adj fait(e) à la maison; ~ **match** n match m à domicile; **H~ Office** (BRIT) n ministère m de l'Intérieur; ~ **page** n (COMPUT) page f d'accueil; ~ **rule** n autonomie f; **H~ Secretary** (BRIT) n ministre m de l'Intérieur; ~**sick** adj: **to be ~sick** avoir le mal du pays; s'ennuyer de sa famille; ~ **town** n ville natale; ~**ward** adj (journey) du retour; ~**work** n devoirs mpl

homoeopathic [həumiəu'pæθik] (US **homeopathic**) adj (medicine, methods) homéopathique; (doctor) homéopathe

homogeneous [homəu'dʒi:niəs] adj homogène

homosexual [homəu'seksjuəl] adj, n homosexuel(le)

honest ['onist] adj honnête; (sincere) franc (franche); ~**ly** adv honnêtement; franchement; ~**y** n honnêteté f

honey ['hʌni] n miel m; ~**comb** n rayon m de miel; ~**moon** n lune f de miel, voyage m de noces; ~**suckle** n (BOT) n chèvrefeuille m

honk [hoŋk] vi (AUT) klaxonner

honorary ['onərəri] adj honoraire; (duty, title) honorifique

honour ['onər] (US **honor**) vt honorer ♦ n honneur m; **hono(u)rable** adj honorable; **hono(u)rs degree** n (SCOL) licence avec mention

hood [hud] n capuchon m; (of cooker) hotte f; (AUT: BRIT) capote f; (: US) capot m

hoof [hu:f] (pl **hooves**) n sabot m

hook [huk] n crochet m; (on dress) agrafe f; (for fishing) hameçon m ♦ vt accrocher; (fish) prendre

hooligan ['hu:ligən] n voyou m

hoop [hu:p] n cerceau m

hooray [hu:'rei] excl hourra

hoot [hu:t] vi (AUT) klaxonner; (siren) mugir; (owl) hululer; ~**er** n (BRIT: AUT) klaxon m; (NAUT, factory) sirène f

Hoover ® ['hu:vər] (BRIT) n aspirateur m ♦ vt: **h~** passer l'aspirateur dans or sur

hooves [hu:vz] npl of **hoof**

hop [hop] vi (on one foot) sauter à cloche-pied; (bird) sautiller

hope [həup] vt, vi espérer ♦ n espoir m; **I ~ so** je l'espère; **I ~ not** j'espère que non; ~**ful** adj (person) plein(e) d'espoir; (situation) prometteur(-euse), encourageant(e); ~**fully** adv (expectantly) avec espoir, avec optimisme; ~**less** adj désespéré(e); (useless) nul(le)

hops [hops] npl houblon m

horizon [hə'raizn] n horizon m; ~**tal** [hori'zontl] adj horizontal(e)

horn [ho:n] n corne f; (MUS: also: **French ~**) cor m; (AUT) klaxon m

hornet ['ho:nit] n frelon m

horoscope ['horəskəup] n horoscope m

horrendous [hə'rendəs] adj horrible, affreux(-euse)

horrible ['horibl] adj horrible, affreux(-euse)

horrid ['horid] adj épouvantable

horrify ['horifai] vt horrifier

horror ['horər] n horreur f; ~ **film** n film m d'épouvante

hors d'oeuvre [ɔ:'də:vrə] n (CULIN) hors-d'œuvre m inv

horse [ho:s] n cheval m; ~**back** n: **on ~back** à cheval; ~ **chestnut** n marron m (d'Inde); ~**man** (irreg) n cavalier m; ~**power** n puissance f (en chevaux); ~**racing** n courses fpl de chevaux; ~**radish** n raifort m; ~**shoe** n fer m à cheval

hose [həuz] n (also: ~**pipe**) tuyau m; (also: **garden ~**) tuyau d'arrosage

hospitable ['hospitəbl] adj hospitalier(-ère)

hospital ['hospitl] n hôpital m; **in ~** à l'hôpital

hospitality [hospi'tæliti] n hospitalité f

host [həust] n hôte m; (TV, RADIO)

animateur(-trice); (*REL*) hostie *f*; (*large number*): **a ~ of** une foule de

hostage ['hɔstɪdʒ] *n* otage *m*

hostel ['hɔstl] *n* foyer *m*; (*also:* **youth ~**) auberge *f* de jeunesse

hostess ['həustɪs] *n* hôtesse *f*; (*TV, RADIO*) animatrice *f*

hostile ['hɔstaɪl] *adj* hostile; **hostility** [hɔ'stɪlɪtɪ] *n* hostilité *f*

hot [hɔt] *adj* chaud(e); (*as opposed to only warm*) très chaud(e); (*spicy*) fort(e); (*fig*) acharné(e); (*temper*) passionné(e); **to be ~** (*person*) avoir chaud; (*object*) être (très) chaud; (*weather*) faire chaud; **~bed** *n* (*fig*) foyer *m*, pépinière *f*; **~ dog** *n* hot-dog *m*

hotel [həu'tel] *n* hôtel *m*

hot: **~house** *n* serre (chaude); **~line** *n* (*POL*) téléphone *m* rouge, ligne directe; **~ly** *adv* passionnément, violemment; **~plate** *n* (*on cooker*) plaque chauffante; **~pot** (*BRIT*) *n* ragoût *m*; **~-water bottle** *n* bouillotte *f*

hound [haund] *vt* poursuivre avec acharnement ♦ *n* chien courant

hour ['auər] *n* heure *f*; **~ly** *adj, adv* toutes les heures; (*rate*) horaire

house [*n* haus, *vb* hauz] *n* maison *f*; (*POL*) chambre *f*; (*THEATRE*) salle *f*; auditoire *m* ♦ *vt* (*person*) loger, héberger; (*objects*) abriter; **on the ~** (*fig*) aux frais de la maison; **~ arrest** *n* assignation *f* à résidence; **~boat** *n* bateau *m* (aménagé en habitation); **~bound** *adj* confiné(e) chez soi; **~breaking** *n* cambriolage *m* (avec effraction); **~hold** *n* (*persons*) famille *f*, maisonnée *f*; (*ADMIN etc*) ménage *m*; **~keeper** *n* gouvernante *f*; **~keeping** *n* (*work*) ménage *m*; **~keeping (money)** argent *m* du ménage; (*pl*) pendaison *f* de crémaillère; **~wife** (*irreg*) *n* ménagère *f*; femme *f* au foyer; **~work** *n* (travaux *mpl* du) ménage *m*

housing ['hauzɪŋ] *n* logement *m*; **~ development**, **~ estate** *n* lotissement *m*

hovel ['hɔvl] *n* taudis *m*

hover ['hɔvər] *vi* planer; **~craft** *n* aéroglisseur *m*

how [hau] *adv* comment; **~ are you?** comment allez-vous?; **~ do you do?** bonjour; enchanté(e); **~ far is it to?** combien y a-t-il jusqu'à ...?; **~ long have you been here?** depuis combien de temps êtes-vous là?; **~ lovely!** que *or* comme c'est joli!; **~ many/much?** combien?; **~ many people/much milk?** combien de gens/ lait?; **~ old are you?** quel âge avez-vous?

however [hau'evər] *adv* de quelque façon *or* manière que +*subj*; (+*adj*) quelque *or* si ... que +*subj*; (*in questions*) comment ♦ *conj* pourtant, cependant

howl [haul] *vi* hurler

H.P. *abbr* = **hire purchase**

h.p. *abbr* = **horsepower**

HQ *abbr* = **headquarters**

HTML *n abbr* (= Hypertext Mark-up Language) HTML

hub [hʌb] *n* (*of wheel*) moyeu *m*; (*fig*) centre *m*, foyer *m*; **~cap** *n* enjoliveur *m*

huddle ['hʌdl] *vi*: **to ~ together** se blottir les uns contre les autres

hue [hju:] *n* teinte *f*, nuance *f*

huff [hʌf] *n*: **in a ~** fâché(e)

hug [hʌg] *vt* serrer dans ses bras; (*shore, kerb*) serrer

huge [hju:dʒ] *adj* énorme, immense

hulk [hʌlk] *n* (*ship*) épave *f*; (*car, building*) carcasse *f*; (*person*) mastodonte *m*

hull [hʌl] *n* coque *f*

hullo [hə'ləu] *excl* = **hello**

hum [hʌm] *vt* (*tune*) fredonner ♦ *vi* fredonner; (*insect*) bourdonner; (*plane, tool*) vrombir

human ['hju:mən] *adj* humain(e) ♦ *n*: **~ being** être humain; **~e** [hju:'meɪn] *adj* humain(e), humanitaire; **~itarian** [hju:mænɪ'teərɪən] *adj* humanitaire; **~ity** [hju:'mænɪtɪ] *n* humanité *f*

humble ['hʌmbl] *adj* humble, modeste ♦ *vt* humilier

humdrum ['hʌmdrʌm] *adj* monotone

humid ['hju:mɪd] *adj* humide

humiliate [hju:'mɪlɪeɪt] *vt* humilier; **humiliation** [hju:mɪlɪ'eɪʃən] *n* humiliation *f*

humorous ['hju:mərəs] *adj* humoristique;

(*person*) plein(e) d'humour

humour ['hju:mə^r] (*US* **humor**) *n* humour *m*; (*mood*) humeur *f* ♦ *vt* (*person*) faire plaisir à; se prêter aux caprices de

hump [hʌmp] *n* bosse *f*

hunch [hʌntʃ] *n* (*premonition*) intuition *f*; ~**back** *n* bossu(e); ~**ed** *adj* voûté(e)

hundred ['hʌndrəd] *num* cent; ~**s of** des centaines de; ~**weight** *n* (*BRIT*) 50.8 kg, 112 lb; (*US*) 45.3 kg, 100 lb

hung [hʌŋ] *pt, pp of* **hang**

Hungary ['hʌŋgəri] *n* Hongrie *f*

hunger ['hʌŋgə^r] *n* faim *f* ♦ *vi*: **to ~ for** avoir faim de, désirer ardemment

hungry ['hʌŋgri] *adj* affamé(e); (*keen*): ~ **for** avide de; **to be ~** avoir faim

hunk [hʌŋk] *n* (*of bread etc*) gros morceau

hunt [hʌnt] *vt* chasser; (*criminal*) pourchasser ♦ *vi* chasser; (*search*): **to ~ for** chercher (partout) ♦ *n* chasse *f*; ~**er** *n* chasseur *m*; ~**ing** *n* chasse *f*

hurdle ['hə:dl] *n* (*SPORT*) haie *f*; (*fig*) obstacle *m*

hurl [hə:l] *vt* lancer (avec violence); (*abuse, insults*) lancer

hurrah [hu'rɑ:] *excl* = **hooray**

hurray [hu'rei] *excl* = **hooray**

hurricane ['hʌrikən] *n* ouragan *m*

hurried ['hʌrid] *adj* pressé(e), précipité(e); (*work*) fait(e) à la hâte; ~**ly** *adv* précipitamment, à la hâte

hurry ['hʌri] (*vb: also*: ~ **up**) *n* hâte *f*, précipitation *f* ♦ *vi* se presser, se dépêcher ♦ *vt* (*person*) faire presser, faire se dépêcher; (*work*) presser; **to be in a ~** être pressé(e); **to do sth in a ~** faire qch en vitesse; **to ~ in/out** entrer/sortir précipitamment

hurt [hə:t] (*pt, pp* **hurt**) *vt* (*cause pain to*) faire mal à; (*injure, fig*) blesser ♦ *vi* faire mal ♦ *adj* blessé(e); ~**ful** *adj* (*remark*) blessant(e)

hurtle ['hə:tl] *vi*: **to ~ past** passer en trombe; **to ~ down** dégringoler

husband ['hʌzbənd] *n* mari *m*

hush [hʌʃ] *n* calme *m*, silence *m* ♦ *vt* faire taire; ~**!** chut!; ~ **up** *vt* (*scandal*) étouffer

husk [hʌsk] *n* (*of wheat*) balle *f*; (*of rice,*

maize) enveloppe *f*

husky ['hʌski] *adj* rauque ♦ *n* chien *m* esquimau *or* de traîneau

hustle ['hʌsl] *vt* pousser, bousculer ♦ *n*: ~ **and bustle** tourbillon *m* (d'activité)

hut [hʌt] *n* hutte *f*; (*shed*) cabane *f*

hutch [hʌtʃ] *n* clapier *m*

hyacinth ['haiəsinθ] *n* jacinthe *f*

hydrant ['haidrənt] *n* (*also*: **fire ~**) bouche *f* d'incendie

hydraulic [hai'drɔ:lik] *adj* hydraulique

hydroelectric ['haidrəu'lektrik] *adj* hydro-électrique

hydrofoil ['haidrəfɔil] *n* hydrofoil *m*

hydrogen ['haidrədʒən] *n* hydrogène *m*

hyena [hai'i:nə] *n* hyène *f*

hygiene ['haidʒi:n] *n* hygiène *f*; **hygienic** *adj* hygiénique

hymn [him] *n* hymne *m*; cantique *m*

hype [haip] *n* (*inf*) battage *m* publicitaire

hypermarket ['haipəmɑ:kit] (*BRIT*) *n* hypermarché *m*

hypertext ['haipətekst] *n* (*COMPUT*) hypertexte *m*

hyphen ['haifn] *n* trait *m* d'union

hypnotize ['hipnətaiz] *vt* hypnotiser

hypocrisy [hi'pɔkrisi] *n* hypocrisie *f*; **hypocrite** ['hipəkrit] *n* hypocrite *m/f*; **hypocritical** *adj* hypocrite

hypothesis [hai'pɔθisis] (*pl* **hypotheses**) *n* hypothèse *f*

hysterical [hi'sterikl] *adj* hystérique; (*funny*) hilarant(e); ~ **laughter** fou rire *m*

hysterics [hi'steriks] *npl*: **to be in/have ~** (*anger, panic*) avoir une crise de nerfs; (*laughter*) attraper un fou rire

I, i

I [ai] *pron* je; (*before vowel*) j'; (*stressed*) moi

ice [ais] *n* glace *f*; (*on road*) verglas *m* ♦ *vt* (*cake*) glacer ♦ *vi* (*also*: ~ **over**, ~ **up**) geler; (*window*) se givrer; ~**berg** *n* iceberg *m*; ~**box** *n* (*US*) réfrigérateur *m*; (*BRIT*) compartiment *m* à glace; (*insulated box*) glacière *f*; ~ **cream** *n* glace *f*; ~ **cube** *n* glaçon m; ~d adj glacé(e); ~ hockey n hockey m sur glace; Iceland n Islande f; ~ lolly n (BRIT) esquimau m (glace); ~ rink n patinoire f; ~-skating n patinage m (sur glace)

icicle ['aɪsɪkl] n glaçon m (naturel)

icing ['aɪsɪŋ] n (CULIN) glace f; ~ sugar (BRIT) n sucre m glace

icon ['aɪkɔn] n (COMPUT) icône f

icy ['aɪsɪ] adj (cold) glacé(e); (road) verglacé(e); (weather, temperature) glacial(e)

I'd [aɪd] = I would; I had

idea [aɪ'dɪə] n idée f

ideal [aɪ'dɪəl] n idéal m ♦ adj idéal(e)

identical [aɪ'dɛntɪkl] adj identique

identification [aɪdɛntɪfɪ'keɪʃən] n identification f; means of ~ pièce f d'identité

identify [aɪ'dɛntɪfaɪ] vt identifier

Identikit picture ® [aɪ'dɛntɪkɪt-] n portrait-robot m

identity [aɪ'dɛntɪtɪ] n identité f; ~ card n carte f d'identité

ideology [aɪdɪ'ɔlədʒɪ] n idéologie f

idiom ['ɪdɪəm] n expression f idiomatique; (style) style m

idiosyncrasy [ɪdɪəʊ'sɪŋkrəsɪ] n (of person) particularité f, petite manie

idiot ['ɪdɪət] n idiot(e), imbécile m/f; ~ic [ɪdɪ'ɔtɪk] adj idiot(e), bête, stupide

idle ['aɪdl] adj sans occupation, désœuvré(e); (lazy) oisif(-ive), paresseux(-euse); (unemployed) au chômage; (question, pleasures) vain(e), futile ♦ vi (engine) tourner au ralenti; to lie ~ être arrêté(e), ne pas fonctionner

idol ['aɪdl] n idole f; ~ize vt idolâtrer, adorer

i.e. adv abbr (= id est) c'est-à-dire

if [ɪf] conj si; ~ so si c'est le cas; ~ not si-non; ~ only si seulement

ignite [ɪg'naɪt] vt mettre le feu à, enflammer ♦ vi s'enflammer; ignition n (AUT) allumage m; to switch on/off the ignition mettre/couper le contact; ignition key n clé f de contact

ignorant ['ɪgnərənt] adj ignorant(e); to be ~ of (subject) ne rien connaître à; (events) ne pas être au courant de

ignore [ɪg'nɔːr] vt ne tenir aucun compte de; (person) faire semblant de ne pas reconnaître, ignorer; (fact) méconnaître

ill [ɪl] adj (sick) malade; (bad) mauvais(e) ♦ n mal m ♦ adv: to speak/think ~ of dire/penser du mal de; ~s npl (misfortunes) maux mpl, malheurs mpl; to be taken ~ tomber malade; ~-advised adj (decision) peu judicieux(-euse); (person) malavisé(e); ~-at-ease adj mal à l'aise

I'll [aɪl] = I will; I shall

illegal [ɪ'liːgl] adj illégal(e)

illegible [ɪ'lɛdʒəbl] adj illisible

illegitimate [ɪlɪ'dʒɪtɪmət] adj illégitime

ill-fated [ɪl'feɪtɪd] adj malheureux(-euse); (day) néfaste

ill feeling n ressentiment m, rancune f

illiterate [ɪ'lɪtərət] adj illettré(e)

ill: ~-mannered adj (child) mal élevé(e); ~ness n maladie f; ~-treat vt maltraiter

illuminate [ɪ'luːmɪneɪt] vt (room, street) éclairer; (for special effect) illuminer; illumination [ɪluːmɪ'neɪʃən] n éclairage m; illumination f

illusion [ɪ'luːʒən] n illusion f

illustrate ['ɪləstreɪt] vt illustrer; illustration [ɪlə'streɪʃən] n illustration f

ill will n malveillance f

I'm [aɪm] = I am

image ['ɪmɪdʒ] n image f; (public face) image de marque; ~ry n images fpl

imaginary [ɪ'mædʒɪnərɪ] adj imaginaire

imagination [ɪmædʒɪ'neɪʃən] n imagination f

imaginative [ɪ'mædʒɪnətɪv] adj imaginatif(-ive); (person) plein(e) d'imagination

imagine [ɪ'mædʒɪn] vt imaginer, s'imaginer; (suppose) imaginer, supposer

imbalance [ɪm'bæləns] n déséquilibre m

imitate ['ɪmɪteɪt] vt imiter; imitation [ɪmɪ'teɪʃən] n imitation f

immaculate [ɪ'mækjulət] adj impeccable; (REL) immaculé(e)

immaterial [ɪmə'tɪərɪəl] adj sans importance, insignifiant(e)

immature [ɪmə'tjuər] adj (fruit) (qui n'est

pas mûr(e); (person) qui manque de maturité

immediate [ɪˈmiːdɪət] adj immédiat(e); **~ly** adv (at once) immédiatement; **~ly next to** juste à côté de

immense [ɪˈmɛns] adj immense; énorme

immerse [ɪˈmɜːs] vt immerger, plonger; **immersion heater** (BRIT) n chauffe-eau m électrique

immigrant [ˈɪmɪɡrənt] n immigrant(e); immigré(e); **immigration** [ɪmɪˈɡreɪʃən] n immigration f

imminent [ˈɪmɪnənt] adj imminent(e)

immoral [ɪˈmɔrl] adj immoral(e)

immortal [ɪˈmɔːtl] adj, n immortel(le)

immune [ɪˈmjuːn] adj: **~ (to)** immunisé(e) (contre); (fig) à l'abri de; **immunity** n immunité f

impact [ˈɪmpækt] n choc m, impact m; (fig) impact

impair [ɪmˈpɛər] vt détériorer, diminuer

impart [ɪmˈpɑːt] vt communiquer, transmettre; (flavour) donner

impartial [ɪmˈpɑːʃl] adj impartial(e)

impassable [ɪmˈpɑːsəbl] adj infranchissable; (road) impraticable

impassive [ɪmˈpæsɪv] adj impassible

impatience [ɪmˈpeɪʃəns] n impatience f

impatient [ɪmˈpeɪʃənt] adj impatient(e); **to get or grow ~** s'impatienter; **~ly** adv avec impatience

impeccable [ɪmˈpɛkəbl] adj impeccable, parfait(e)

impede [ɪmˈpiːd] vt gêner; **impediment** n obstacle m; (also: **speech impediment**) défaut m d'élocution

impending [ɪmˈpɛndɪŋ] adj imminent(e)

imperative [ɪmˈpɛrətɪv] adj (need) urgent(e), pressant(e); (tone) impérieux(-euse) ♦ n (LING) impératif m

imperfect [ɪmˈpɜːfɪkt] adj imparfait(e); (goods etc) défectueux(-euse)

imperial [ɪmˈpɪərɪəl] adj impérial(e); (BRIT: measure) légal(e)

impersonal [ɪmˈpɜːsənl] adj impersonnel(le)

impersonate [ɪmˈpɜːsəneɪt] vt se faire

passer pour; (THEATRE) imiter

impertinent [ɪmˈpɜːtɪnənt] adj impertinent(e), insolent(e)

impervious [ɪmˈpɜːvɪəs] adj (fig): **~ to** insensible à

impetuous [ɪmˈpɛtjuəs] adj impétueux(-euse), fougueux(-euse)

impetus [ˈɪmpətəs] n impulsion f; (of runner) élan m

impinge [ɪmˈpɪndʒ]: **to ~ on** vt fus (person) affecter, toucher; (rights) empiéter sur

implement [n ˈɪmplɪmənt, vb ˈɪmplɪment] n outil m, instrument m; (for cooking) ustensile m ♦ vt exécuter

implicit [ɪmˈplɪsɪt] adj implicite; (complete) absolu(e), sans réserve

imply [ɪmˈplaɪ] vt suggérer, laisser entendre; indiquer, supposer

impolite [ɪmpəˈlaɪt] adj impoli(e)

import [vb ɪmˈpɔːt, n ˈɪmpɔːt] vt importer ♦ n (COMM) importation f

importance [ɪmˈpɔːtns] n importance f

important [ɪmˈpɔːtənt] adj important(e)

importer [ɪmˈpɔːtər] n importateur(-trice)

impose [ɪmˈpəuz] vt imposer ♦ vi: **to ~ on sb** abuser de la gentillesse de qn; **imposing** adj imposant(e), impressionnant(e); **imposition** [ɪmpəˈzɪʃən] n (of tax etc) imposition f; **to be an imposition on** (person) abuser de la gentillesse or la bonté de

impossible [ɪmˈpɔsɪbl] adj impossible

impotent [ˈɪmpətnt] adj impuissant(e)

impound [ɪmˈpaund] vt confisquer, saisir

impoverished [ɪmˈpɔvərɪʃt] adj appauvri(e), pauvre

impractical [ɪmˈpræktɪkl] adj pas pratique; (person) qui manque d'esprit pratique

impregnable [ɪmˈprɛgnəbl] adj (fortress) imprenable

impress [ɪmˈprɛs] vt impressionner, faire impression sur; (mark) imprimer, marquer; **to ~ sth on sb** faire bien comprendre qch à qn; **~ed** adj impressionné(e)

impression [ɪmˈprɛʃən] n impression f; (of stamp, seal) empreinte f; (imitation) imitation f; **to be under the ~ that** avoir l'impression que; **~ist** *n* (*ART*) impressioniste *m/f*; (*entertainer*) imitateur(-trice) *m/f*

impressive [ɪmˈpresɪv] *adj* impressionnant(e)

imprint [ˈɪmprɪnt] *n* (*outline*) marque *f*, empreinte *f*

imprison [ɪmˈprɪzn] *vt* emprisonner, mettre en prison

improbable [ɪmˈprɔbəbl] *adj* improbable; (*excuse*) peu plausible

improper [ɪmˈprɔpəʳ] *adj* (*unsuitable*) déplacé(e), de mauvais goût; indécent(e); (*dishonest*) malhonnête

improve [ɪmˈpruːv] *vt* améliorer ♦ *vi* s'améliorer; (*pupil etc*) faire des progrès; **~ment** *n* amélioration *f* (*in* de); progrès *m*

improvise [ˈɪmprəvaɪz] *vt*, *vi* improviser

impudent [ˈɪmpjudnt] *adj* impudent(e)

impulse [ˈɪmpʌls] *n* impulsion *f*; **on ~** impulsivement, sur un coup de tête; **impulsive** *adj* impulsif(-ive)

⸻ KEYWORD ⸻

in [ɪn] *prep* **1** (*indicating place, position*): dans; **in the house/the fridge** dans la maison/le frigo; **in the garden** dans le *or* au jardin; **in town** en ville; **in the country** à la campagne; **in school** à l'école; **in here/there** ici/là

2 (*with place names: of town, region, country*): **in London** à Londres; **in England** en Angleterre; **in Japan** au Japon; **in the United States** aux États-Unis

3 (*indicating time: during*): **in spring** au printemps; **in summer** en été; **in May/1992** en mai/1992; **in the afternoon** (dans) l'après-midi; **at 4 o'clock in the afternoon** à 4 heures de l'après-midi

4 (*indicating time: in the space of*): en; (*: future*) dans; **I did it in 3 hours/days** je l'ai fait en 3 heures/jours; **I'll see you in 2 weeks** *or* **in 2 weeks' time** je te verrai dans 2 semaines

5 (*indicating manner etc*): à; **in a loud/soft voice** à voix haute/basse; **in pencil** au crayon; **in French** en français; **the boy in**

the blue shirt le garçon à *or* avec la chemise bleue

6 (*indicating circumstances*): **in the sun** au soleil; **in the shade** à l'ombre; **in the rain** sous la pluie

7 (*indicating mood, state*): **in tears** en larmes; **in anger** sous le coup de la colère; **in despair** au désespoir; **in good condition** en bon état; **to live in luxury** vivre dans le luxe

8 (*with ratios, numbers*): **1 in 10 (households)**, **1 (household) in 10** 1 (ménage) sur 10; **20 pence in the pound** 20 pence par livre sterling; **they lined up in twos** ils se mirent en rangs (deux) par deux; **in hundreds** par centaines

9 (*referring to people, works*) chez; **the disease is common in children** c'est une maladie courante chez les enfants; **in (the works of) Dickens** chez Dickens, dans (l'œuvre de) Dickens

10 (*indicating profession etc*) dans; **to be in teaching** être dans l'enseignement

11 (*after superlative*) de; **the best pupil in the class** le meilleur élève de la classe

12 (*with present participle*): **in saying this** en disant ceci

♦ *adv*: **to be in** (*person: at home, work*) être là; (*train, ship, plane*) être arrivé(e); (*in fashion*) être à la mode; **to ask sb in** inviter qn à entrer; **to run/limp** *etc* **in** entrer en courant/boitant *etc*

♦ *n*: **the ins and outs (of)** (*of proposal, situation etc*) les tenants et aboutissants (de)

in. *abbr* = **inch**

inability [ɪnəˈbɪlɪtɪ] *n* incapacité *f*

inaccurate [ɪnˈækjurət] *adj* inexact(e); (*person*) qui manque de précision

inadequate [ɪnˈædɪkwət] *adj* insuffisant(e), inadéquat(e)

inadvertently [ɪnədˈvəːtntlɪ] *adv* par mégarde

inadvisable [ɪnədˈvaɪzəbl] *adj* (*action*) à déconseiller

inane [ɪˈneɪn] *adj* inepte, stupide

inanimate [ɪnˈænɪmət] *adj* inanimé(e)

inappropriate [ɪnə'prəʊprɪət] *adj* inopportun(e), mal à propos; (*word, expression*) impropre

inarticulate [ɪnɑː'tɪkjʊlət] *adj* (*person*) qui s'exprime mal; (*speech*) indistinct(e)

inasmuch [ɪnəz'mʌtʃ-] *adv* (*insofar as*) dans la mesure où; (*seeing that*) attendu que

inauguration [ɪnɔːgju'reɪʃən] *n* inauguration *f*; (*of president*) investiture *f*

inborn [ɪn'bɔːn] *adj* (*quality*) inné(e)

inbred [ɪn'brɛd] *adj* inné(e), naturel(le); (*family*) consanguin(e)

Inc. *abbr* = **incorporated**

incapable [ɪn'keɪpəbl] *adj* incapable

incapacitate [ɪnkə'pæsɪteɪt] *vt*: **to ~ sb from doing** rendre qn incapable de faire

incense [*n* 'ɪnsɛns, *vb* ɪn'sɛns] *n* encens *m*
♦ *vt* (*anger*) mettre en colère

incentive [ɪn'sɛntɪv] *n* encouragement *m*, raison *f* de se donner de la peine

incessant [ɪn'sɛsnt] *adj* incessant(e); **~ly** *adv* sans cesse, constamment

inch [ɪntʃ] *n* pouce *m* (= 25 mm; 12 in a foot); **within an ~ of** à deux doigts de; **he didn't give an ~** (*fig*) il n'a pas voulu céder d'un pouce

incident ['ɪnsɪdnt] *n* incident *m*; **~al** [ɪnsɪ'dɛntl] *adj* (*additional*) accessoire; **~al to** qui accompagne; **~ally** *adv* (*by the way*) à propos

inclination [ɪnklɪ'neɪʃən] *n* (*fig*) inclination *f*

incline [*n* 'ɪnklaɪn, *vb* ɪn'klaɪn] *n* pente *f*
♦ *vt* incliner ♦ *vi* (*surface*) s'incliner; **to be ~d to do** avoir tendance à faire

include [ɪn'kluːd] *vt* inclure, comprendre; **including** *prep* y compris; **inclusive** *adj* inclus(e), compris(e); **inclusive of tax** *etc* taxes *etc* comprises

income ['ɪnkʌm] *n* revenu *m*; **~ tax** *n* impôt *m* sur le revenu

incoming ['ɪnkʌmɪŋ] *adj* qui arrive; (*president*) entrant(e); **~ mail** courrier *m* du jour; **~ tide** marée montante

incompetent [ɪn'kɔmpɪtnt] *adj* incompétent(e), incapable

incomplete [ɪnkəm'pliːt] *adj* incomplet(-ète)

incongruous [ɪn'kɔŋgrʊəs] *adj* incongru(e)

inconsiderate [ɪnkən'sɪdərət] *adj* (*person*) qui manque d'égards; (*action*) inconsidéré(e)

inconsistency [ɪnkən'sɪstənsɪ] *n* (*of actions etc*) inconséquence *f*; (*of work*) irrégularité *f*; (*of statement etc*) incohérence *f*

inconsistent [ɪnkən'sɪstnt] *adj* inconséquent(e); irrégulier(-ère); peu cohérent(e); **~ with** incompatible avec

inconspicuous [ɪnkən'spɪkjʊəs] *adj* qui passe inaperçu(e); (*colour, dress*) discret(-ète)

inconvenience [ɪnkən'viːnjəns] *n* inconvénient *m*; (*trouble*) dérangement *m*
♦ *vt* déranger

inconvenient [ɪnkən'viːnjənt] *adj* (*house*) malcommode; (*time, place*) mal choisi(e), qui ne convient pas; (*visitor*) importun(e)

incorporate [ɪn'kɔːpəreɪt] *vt* incorporer; (*contain*) contenir; **~d company** (*US*) *n* ≈ société *f* anonyme

incorrect [ɪnkə'rɛkt] *adj* incorrect(e)

increase [*n* 'ɪnkriːs, *vb* ɪn'kriːs] *n* augmentation *f* ♦ *vi*, *vt* augmenter; **increasing** *adj* (*number*) croissant(e); **increasingly** *adv* de plus en plus

incredible [ɪn'krɛdɪbl] *adj* incroyable

incubator ['ɪnkjubeɪtər] *n* (*for babies*) couveuse *f*

incumbent [ɪn'kʌmbənt] *n* (*president*) président *m* en exercice; (*REL*) titulaire *m/f*
♦ *adj*: **it is ~ on him to ...** il lui incombe *or* appartient de ...

incur [ɪn'kɜːr] *vt* (*expenses*) encourir; (*anger, risk*) s'exposer à; (*debt*) contracter; (*loss*) subir

indebted [ɪn'dɛtɪd] *adj*: **to be ~ to sb (for)** être redevable à qn (de)

indecent [ɪn'diːsnt] *adj* indécent(e), inconvenant(e); **~ assault** (*BRIT*) *n* attentat *m* à la pudeur; **~ exposure** *n* outrage *m* (public) à la pudeur

indecisive [ɪndɪ'saɪsɪv] *adj* (*person*) indécis(e)

indeed [ɪnˈdiːd] *adv* vraiment; en effet; (*furthermore*) d'ailleurs; **yes ~!** certainement!

indefinitely [ɪnˈdɛfɪnɪtlɪ] *adv* (*wait*) indéfiniment

indemnity [ɪnˈdɛmnɪtɪ] *n* (*safeguard*) assurance *f*, garantie *f*; (*compensation*) indemnité *f*

independence [ɪndɪˈpɛndns] *n* indépendance *f*

Independence Day
---

i L'**Independence Day** *est la fête nationale aux États-Unis, le 4 juillet. Il commémore l'adoption de la déclaration d'Indépendance, en 1776, écrite par Thomas Jefferson et proclamant la séparation des 13 colonies américaines de la Grande-Bretagne.*

independent [ɪndɪˈpɛndnt] *adj* indépendant(e); (*school*) privé(e); (*radio*) libre

index [ˈɪndɛks] *n* (*pl*: ~es: *in book*) index *m*; (: *in library etc*) catalogue *m*; (*pl*: **indices**: *ratio, sign*) indice *m*; **~ card** *n* fiche *f*; **~ finger** *n* index *m*; **~-linked** *adj* indexé(e) (sur le coût de la vie *etc*)

India [ˈɪndɪə] *n* Inde *f*; **~n** *adj* indien(ne) ♦ *n* Indien(ne); **(American) ~n** Indien(ne) (d'Amérique); **~n Ocean** *n* océan Indien

indicate [ˈɪndɪkeɪt] *vt* indiquer; **indication** [ɪndɪˈkeɪʃən] *n* indication *f*, signe *m*; **indicative** [ɪnˈdɪkətɪv] *adj*: **indicative of** symptomatique de ♦ *n* (*LING*) indicatif *m*; **indicator** *n* (*sign*) indicateur *m*; (*AUT*) clignotant *m*

indices [ˈɪndɪsiːz] *npl of* **index**

indictment [ɪnˈdaɪtmənt] *n* accusation *f*

indifferent [ɪnˈdɪfrənt] *adj* indifférent(e); (*poor*) médiocre, quelconque

indigenous [ɪnˈdɪdʒɪnəs] *adj* indigène

indigestion [ɪndɪˈdʒɛstʃən] *n* indigestion *f*, mauvaise digestion

indignant [ɪnˈdɪgnənt] *adj*: **~ (at sth/with sb)** indigné(e) (de qch/contre qn)

indignity [ɪnˈdɪgnɪtɪ] *n* indignité *f*, affront

m

indirect [ɪndɪˈrɛkt] *adj* indirect(e)

indiscreet [ɪndɪsˈkriːt] *adj* indiscret(-ète); (*rash*) imprudent(e)

indiscriminate [ɪndɪsˈkrɪmɪnət] *adj* (*person*) qui manque de discernement; (*killings*) commis(e) au hasard

indisputable [ɪndɪsˈpjuːtəbl] *adj* incontestable, indiscutable

individual [ɪndɪˈvɪdjuəl] *n* individu *m* ♦ *adj* individuel(le); (*characteristic*) particulier(-ère), original(e)

indoctrination [ɪndɒktrɪˈneɪʃən] *n* endoctrinement *m*

Indonesia [ɪndəˈniːzɪə] *n* Indonésie *f*

indoor [ˈɪndɔːʳ] *adj* (*plant*) d'appartement; (*swimming pool*) couvert(e); (*sport, games*) pratiqué(e) en salle; **~s** *adv* à l'intérieur

induce [ɪnˈdjuːs] *vt* (*persuade*) persuader; (*bring about*) provoquer; **~ment** *n* (*incentive*) récompense *f*; (*pej*: *bribe*) pot-de-vin *m*

indulge [ɪnˈdʌldʒ] *vt* (*whim*) céder à, satisfaire; (*child*) gâter ♦ *vi*: **to ~ in sth** (*luxury*) se permettre qch; (*fantasies etc*) se livrer à qch; **~nce** *n* fantaisie *f* (que l'on s'offre); (*leniency*) indulgence *f*; **~nt** *adj* indulgent(e)

industrial [ɪnˈdʌstrɪəl] *adj* industriel(le); (*injury*) du travail; **~ action** *n* action revendicative; **~ estate** (*BRIT*) *n* zone industrielle; **~ist** *n* industriel *m*; **~ park** (*US*) *n* = **industrial estate**

industrious [ɪnˈdʌstrɪəs] *adj* travailleur(-euse)

industry [ˈɪndəstrɪ] *n* industrie *f*; (*diligence*) zèle *m*, application *f*

inebriated [ɪˈniːbrɪeɪtɪd] *adj* ivre

inedible [ɪnˈɛdɪbl] *adj* immangeable; (*plant etc*) non comestible

ineffective [ɪnɪˈfɛktɪv], **ineffectual** [ɪnɪˈfɛktʃuəl] *adj* inefficace

inefficient [ɪnɪˈfɪʃənt] *adj* inefficace

inequality [ɪnɪˈkwɒlɪtɪ] *n* inégalité *f*

inescapable [ɪnɪˈskeɪpəbl] *adj* inéluctable, inévitable

inevitable [ɪnˈɛvɪtəbl] *adj* inévitable; **inevitably** *adv* inévitablement

inexpensive [ɪnɪk'spensɪv] *adj* bon marché *inv*

inexperienced [ɪnɪk'spɪərɪənst] *adj* inexpérimenté(e)

infallible [ɪn'fælɪbl] *adj* infaillible

infamous ['ɪnfəməs] *adj* infâme, abominable

infancy ['ɪnfənsɪ] *n* petite enfance, bas âge

infant ['ɪnfənt] *n* (baby) nourrisson *m*; (young child) petit(e) enfant; ~ **school** (BRIT) *n* classes *fpl* préparatoires (entre 5 et 7 ans)

infatuated [ɪn'fætjueɪtɪd] *adj*: ~ **with** entiché(e) de; **infatuation** [ɪnfætju'eɪʃən] *n* engouement *m*

infect [ɪn'fekt] *vt* infecter, contaminer; ~**ion** *n* infection *f*; (contagion) contagion *f*; ~**ious** *adj* infectieux(-euse); (also fig) contagieux(-euse)

infer [ɪn'fəːr] *vt* conclure, déduire

inferior [ɪn'fɪərɪər] *adj* inférieur(e); (goods) de qualité inférieure ♦ *n* inférieur(e); (in rank) subalterne *m/f*; ~**ity** [ɪnfɪərɪ'ɔrɪtɪ] *n* infériorité *f*

infertile [ɪn'fəːtaɪl] *adj* stérile

infighting ['ɪnfaɪtɪŋ] *n* querelles *fpl* internes

infinite ['ɪnfɪnɪt] *adj* infini(e)

infinitive [ɪn'fɪnɪtɪv] *n* infinitif *m*

infinity [ɪn'fɪnɪtɪ] *n* infinité *f*; (also MATH) infini *m*

infirmary [ɪn'fəːmərɪ] *n* (hospital) hôpital *m*

inflamed [ɪn'fleɪmd] *adj* enflammé(e)

inflammable [ɪn'flæməbl] (BRIT) *adj* inflammable

inflammation [ɪnflə'meɪʃən] *n* inflammation *f*

inflatable [ɪn'fleɪtəbl] *adj* gonflable

inflate [ɪn'fleɪt] *vt* (tyre, balloon) gonfler; (price) faire monter; **inflation** *n* (ECON) inflation *f*; **inflationary** *adj* inflationniste

inflict [ɪn'flɪkt] *vt*: **to ~ on** infliger à

influence ['ɪnfluəns] *n* influence *f* ♦ *vt* influencer; **under the ~ of alcohol** en état d'ébriété; **influential** [ɪnflu'enʃl] *adj* influent(e)

influenza [ɪnflu'enzə] *n* grippe *f*

influx ['ɪnflʌks] *n* afflux *m*

infomercial [ɪnfəuməːʃl] (US) *n* (for product) publi-information *f*; (POL) émission où un candidat présente son programme électoral

inform [ɪn'fɔːm] *vt*: **to ~ sb (of)** informer *or* avertir qn (de) ♦ *vi*: **to ~ on sb** dénoncer qn

informal [ɪn'fɔːml] *adj* (person, manner, party) simple; (visit, discussion) dénué(e) de formalités; (announcement, invitation) non officiel(le); (colloquial) familier(-ère); ~**ity** [ɪnfɔː'mælɪtɪ] *n* simplicité *f*, absence *f* de cérémonie; caractère non officiel

informant [ɪn'fɔːmənt] *n* informateur(-trice)

information [ɪnfə'meɪʃən] *n* information *f*; renseignements *mpl*; (knowledge) connaissances *fpl*; **a piece of ~** un renseignement; ~ **desk** *n* accueil *m*; ~ **office** *n* bureau *m* de renseignements

informative [ɪn'fɔːmətɪv] *adj* instructif(-ive)

informer [ɪn'fɔːmər] *n* (also: **police ~**) indicateur(-trice)

infringe [ɪn'frɪndʒ] *vt* enfreindre ♦ *vi*: **to ~ on** empiéter sur; ~**ment** *n*: ~**ment (of)** infraction *f* (à)

infuriating [ɪn'fjuərɪeɪtɪŋ] *adj* exaspérant(e)

ingenious [ɪn'dʒiːnjəs] *adj* ingénieux(-euse); **ingenuity** [ɪndʒɪ'njuːɪtɪ] *n* ingéniosité *f*

ingenuous [ɪn'dʒɛnjuəs] *adj* naïf (naïve), ingénu(e)

ingot ['ɪŋgət] *n* lingot *m*

ingrained [ɪn'greɪnd] *adj* enraciné(e)

ingratiate [ɪn'greɪʃɪeɪt] *vt*: **to ~ o.s. with** s'insinuer dans les bonnes grâces de, se faire bien voir de

ingredient [ɪn'griːdɪənt] *n* ingrédient *m*; (fig) élément *m*

inhabit [ɪn'hæbɪt] *vt* habiter; ~**ant** *n* habitant(e)

inhale [ɪn'heɪl] *vt* respirer; (smoke) avaler ♦ *vi* aspirer; (in smoking) avaler la fumée

inherent [ɪn'hɪərənt] *adj*: ~ **(in** or **to)** inhérent(e) (à)

inherit [ɪnˈhɛrɪt] *vt* hériter (de); **~ance** *n* héritage *m*

inhibit [ɪnˈhɪbɪt] *vt* (PSYCH) inhiber; (growth) freiner; **~ion** [ɪnhɪˈbɪʃən] *n* inhibition *f*

inhuman [ɪnˈhjuːmən] *adj* inhumain(e)

initial [ɪˈnɪʃl] *adj* initial(e) ♦ *n* initiale *f* ♦ *vt* parafer; **~s** *npl* (letters) initiales *fpl*; (as signature) parafe *m*; **~ly** *adv* initialement, au début

initiate [ɪˈnɪʃɪeɪt] *vt* (start) entreprendre, amorcer; (entreprise) lancer; (person) initier; **to ~ proceedings against sb** intenter une action à qn; **initiative** *n* initiative *f*

inject [ɪnˈdʒɛkt] *vt* injecter; (person): **to ~ sb with sth** faire une piqûre de qch à qn; **~ion** *n* injection *f*, piqûre *f*

injure [ˈɪndʒər] *vt* blesser; (reputation etc) compromettre; **~d** *adj* blessé(e); **injury** *n* blessure *f*; **~ time** *n* (SPORT) arrêts *mpl* de jeu

injustice [ɪnˈdʒʌstɪs] *n* injustice *f*

ink [ɪŋk] *n* encre *f*

inkling [ˈɪŋklɪŋ] *n*: **to have an/no ~ of** avoir une (vague) idée de/n'avoir aucune idée de

inlaid [ˈɪnleɪd] *adj* incrusté(e); (table etc) marqueté(e)

inland [adj ˈɪnlænd, adv ɪnˈlænd] *adj* intérieur(e) ♦ *adv* à l'intérieur, dans les terres; **Inland Revenue** (BRIT) *n* fisc *m*

in-laws [ˈɪnlɔːz] *npl* beaux-parents *mpl*; belle famille

inlet [ˈɪnlɛt] *n* (GEO) crique *f*

inmate [ˈɪnmeɪt] *n* (in prison) détenu(e); (in asylum) interné(e)

inn [ɪn] *n* auberge *f*

innate [ɪˈneɪt] *adj* inné(e)

inner [ˈɪnər] *adj* intérieur(e); **~ city** *n* centre *m* de zone urbaine; **~ tube** *n* (of tyre) chambre *f* à air

innings [ˈɪnɪŋz] *n* (CRICKET) tour *m* de batte

innocent [ˈɪnəsnt] *adj* innocent(e)

innocuous [ɪˈnɔkjuəs] *adj* inoffensif(-ive)

innuendo [ɪnjuˈɛndəu] (*pl* **~es**) *n* insinuation *f*, allusion (malveillante)

innumerable [ɪˈnjuːmrəbl] *adj* innombra-

ble

inpatient [ˈɪnpeɪʃənt] *n* malade hospitalisé(e)

input [ˈɪnput] *n* (resources) ressources *fpl*; (COMPUT) entrée *f* (de données); (: data) données *fpl*

inquest [ˈɪnkwɛst] *n* enquête *f*; **(coroner's) ~** enquête judiciaire

inquire [ɪnˈkwaɪər] *vi* demander ♦ *vt* demander; **to ~ about** se renseigner sur; **~ into** *vt fus* faire une enquête sur; **inquiry** *n* demande *f* de renseignements; (investigation) enquête *f*, investigation *f*; **inquiries** *npl*: **the inquiries** (RAIL etc) les renseignements; **inquiry** or **inquiries office** (BRIT) *n* bureau *m* des renseignements

inquisitive [ɪnˈkwɪzɪtɪv] *adj* curieux(-euse)

ins *abbr* = **inches**

insane [ɪnˈseɪn] *adj* fou (folle); (MED) aliéné(e); **insanity** [ɪnˈsænɪtɪ] *n* folie *f*; (MED) aliénation (mentale)

inscription [ɪnˈskrɪpʃən] *n* inscription *f*; (in book) dédicace *f*

inscrutable [ɪnˈskruːtəbl] *adj* impénétrable; (comment) obscur(e)

insect [ˈɪnsɛkt] *n* insecte *m*; **~icide** [ɪnˈsɛktɪsaɪd] *n* insecticide *m*; **~ repellent** *n* crème *f* anti-insecte

insecure [ɪnsɪˈkjuər] *adj* peu solide; peu sûr(e); (person) anxieux(-euse)

insensitive [ɪnˈsɛnsɪtɪv] *adj* insensible

insert [ɪnˈsəːt] *vt* insérer; **~ion** *n* insertion *f*

in-service [ˈɪnˈsəːvɪs] *adj* (training) continu(e), en cours d'emploi; (course) de perfectionnement; de recyclage

inshore [ˈɪnˈʃɔːr] *adj* côtier(-ère) ♦ *adv* près de la côte; (move) vers la côte

inside [ˈɪnˈsaɪd] *n* intérieur *m* ♦ *adj* intérieur(e) ♦ *adv* à l'intérieur, dedans ♦ *prep* à l'intérieur de; (of time): **~ 10 minutes** en moins de 10 minutes; **~s** *npl* (inf) intestins *mpl*; **~ information** *n* renseignements obtenus à la source; **~ lane** *n* (AUT: in Britain) voie *f* de gauche; (: in US, Europe etc) voie de droite; **~ out** *adv* à l'envers; (know) à fond; **~r dealing**, **~r trading** *n* (St Ex) délit *m* d'initié

insight ['ɪnsaɪt] n perspicacité f; (glimpse, idea) aperçu m

insignificant [ɪnsɪg'nɪfɪknt] adj insignifiant(e)

insincere [ɪnsɪn'sɪər] adj hypocrite

insinuate [ɪn'sɪnjueɪt] vt insinuer

insist [ɪn'sɪst] vi insister; **to ~ on doing** insister pour faire; **to ~ on sth** exiger qch; **to ~ that** insister pour que; (claim) maintenir or soutenir que; **~ent** adj insistant(e), pressant(e); (noise, action) ininterrompu(e)

insole ['ɪnsəʊl] n (removable) semelle intérieure

insolent ['ɪnsələnt] adj insolent(e)

insolvent [ɪn'sɒlvənt] adj insolvable

insomnia [ɪn'sɒmnɪə] n insomnie f

inspect [ɪn'spekt] vt inspecter; (ticket) contrôler; **~ion** n inspection f; contrôle m; **~or** n inspecteur(-trice); (BRIT: on buses, trains) contrôleur(-euse)

inspire [ɪn'spaɪər] vt inspirer

install [ɪn'stɔ:l] vt installer; **~ation** [ɪnstə'leɪʃən] n installation f

instalment [ɪn'stɔ:lmənt] (US **installment**) n acompte m, versement partiel; (of TV serial etc) épisode m; **in ~s** (pay) à tempérament; (receive) en plusieurs fois

instance ['ɪnstəns] n exemple m; **for ~** par exemple; **in the first ~** tout d'abord, en premier lieu

instant ['ɪnstənt] n instant m ♦ adj immédiat(e); (coffee, food) instantané(e), en poudre; **~ly** adv immédiatement, tout de suite

instead [ɪn'sted] adv au lieu de cela; **~ of** au lieu de; **~ of sb** à la place de qn

instep ['ɪnstep] n cou-de-pied m; (of shoe) cambrure f

instigate ['ɪnstɪgeɪt] vt (rebellion) fomenter, provoquer; (talks etc) promouvoir

instil [ɪn'stɪl] vt: **to ~ (into)** inculquer (à); (courage) insuffler (à)

instinct ['ɪnstɪŋkt] n instinct m

institute ['ɪnstɪtju:t] n institut m ♦ vt instituer, établir; (inquiry) ouvrir; (proceedings) entamer

institution [ɪnstɪ'tju:ʃən] n institution f; (educational) établissement m (scolaire); (mental home) établissement (psychiatrique)

instruct [ɪn'strʌkt] vt: **to ~ sb in sth** enseigner qch à qn; **to ~ sb to do** charger qn or ordonner à qn de faire; **~ion** n instruction f; **~ions** npl (orders) directives fpl; **~ions (for use)** mode m d'emploi; **~or** n professeur m; (for skiing, driving) moniteur m

instrument ['ɪnstrumənt] n instrument m; **~al** [ɪnstru'mentl] adj: **to be ~al in** contribuer à; **~ panel** n tableau m de bord

insufficient [ɪnsə'fɪʃənt] adj insuffisant(e)

insular ['ɪnsjulər] adj (outlook) borné(e); (person) aux vues étroites

insulate ['ɪnsjuleɪt] vt isoler; (against sound) insonoriser; **insulation** [ɪnsju'leɪʃən] n isolation f; insonorisation f

insulin ['ɪnsjulɪn] n insuline f

insult [n 'ɪnsʌlt, vb ɪn'sʌlt] n insulte f, affront m ♦ vt insulter, faire affront à

insurance [ɪn'ʃʊərəns] n assurance f; **fire/life ~** assurance-incendie/-vie; **~ policy** n police f d'assurance

insure [ɪn'ʃʊər] vt assurer; **to ~ (o.s.) against** (fig) parer à

intact [ɪn'tækt] adj intact(e)

intake ['ɪnteɪk] n (of food, oxygen) consommation f; (BRIT: SCOL): **an ~ of 200 a year** 200 admissions fpl par an

integral ['ɪntɪgrəl] adj (part) intégrant(e)

integrate ['ɪntɪgreɪt] vt intégrer ♦ vi s'intégrer

intellect ['ɪntəlekt] n intelligence f; **~ual** [ɪntə'lektjuəl] adj, n intellectuel(le)

intelligence [ɪn'telɪdʒəns] n intelligence f; (MIL etc) informations fpl, renseignements mpl; **~ service** n services secrets; **intelligent** adj intelligent(e)

intend [ɪn'tend] vt (gift etc): **to ~ sth for** destiner qch à; **to ~ to do** avoir l'intention de faire

intense [ɪn'tens] adj intense; (person) véhément(e); **~ly** adv intensément; profondément

intensive [ɪn'tensɪv] adj intensif(-ive); ~ **care unit** n service m de réanimation

intent [ɪn'tent] n intention f ♦ adj attentif(-ive); **to all ~s and purposes** en fait, pratiquement; **to be ~ on doing sth** être (bien) décidé à faire qch; ~**ion** n intention f; ~**ional** adj intentionnel(le), délibéré(e); ~**ly** adv attentivement

interact [ɪntər'ækt] vi avoir une action réciproque; (people) communiquer; ~**ive** adj (COMPUT) interactif(-ive)

interchange [n 'ɪntətʃeɪndʒ, vb ɪntə'tʃeɪndʒ] n (exchange) échange m; (on motorway) échangeur m; ~**able** adj interchangeable

intercom ['ɪntəkɒm] n interphone m

intercourse ['ɪntəkɔːs] n (sexual) rapports mpl

interest ['ɪntrɪst] n intérêt m; (pastime): **my main ~** ce qui m'intéresse le plus; (COMM) intérêts mpl ♦ vt intéresser; **to be ~ed in sth** s'intéresser à qch; **I am ~ed in going** ça m'intéresse d'y aller; ~**ing** adj intéressant(e); ~ **rate** n taux m d'intérêt

interface ['ɪntəfeɪs] n (COMPUT) interface f

interfere [ɪntə'fɪər] vi: **to ~ in** (quarrel) s'immiscer dans; (other people's business) se mêler de; **to ~ with** (object) toucher à; (plans) contrecarrer; (duty) être en conflit avec; ~**nce** n (in affairs) ingérance f; (RADIO, TV) parasites mpl

interim ['ɪntərɪm] adj provisoire ♦ n: **in the ~** dans l'intérim, entre-temps

interior [ɪn'tɪərɪər] n intérieur m ♦ adj intérieur(e); (minister, department) de l'Intérieur; ~ **designer** n styliste m/f, designer m/f

interjection [ɪntə'dʒekʃən] n (interruption) interruption f; (LING) interjection f

interlock [ɪntə'lɒk] vi s'enclencher

interlude ['ɪntəluːd] n intervalle m; (THEATRE) intermède m

intermediate [ɪntə'miːdɪət] adj intermédiaire; (SCOL: course, level) moyen(ne)

intermission [ɪntə'mɪʃən] n pause f; (THEATRE, CINEMA) entracte m

intern [vb ɪn'tɜːn, n 'ɪntɜːn] vt interner ♦ n (US) interne m/f

internal [ɪn'tɜːnl] adj interne; (politics) intérieur(e); ~**ly** adv: **"not to be taken ~ly"** "pour usage externe"; **I~ Revenue Service** (US) n fisc m

international [ɪntə'næʃənl] adj international(e)

Internet ['ɪntənet] n Internet m; ~ **café** n cybercafé m; ~ **service provider** n fournisseur m d'accès à Internet

interplay ['ɪntəpleɪ] n effet m réciproque, interaction f

interpret [ɪn'tɜːprɪt] vt interpréter ♦ vi servir d'interprète; ~**er** n interprète m/f

interrelated [ɪntərɪ'leɪtɪd] adj en corrélation, en rapport étroit

interrogate [ɪn'terəʊgeɪt] vt interroger; (suspect etc) soumettre à un interrogatoire; **interrogation** [ɪnterəʊ'geɪʃən] n interrogation f; interrogatoire m

interrupt [ɪntə'rʌpt] vt, vi interrompre

intersect [ɪntə'sekt] vi (roads) se croiser, se couper; ~**ion** n (of roads) croisement m

intersperse [ɪntə'spɜːs] vt: **to ~ with** parsemer de

intertwine [ɪntə'twaɪn] vi s'entrelacer

interval ['ɪntəvl] n intervalle m; (BRIT: THEATRE) entracte m; (: SPORT) mi-temps f; **at ~s** par intervalles

intervene [ɪntə'viːn] vi (person) intervenir; (event) survenir; (time) s'écouler (entretemps); **intervention** n intervention f

interview ['ɪntəvjuː] n (RADIO, TV etc) interview f; (for job) entrevue f ♦ vt interviewer; avoir une entrevue avec; ~**er** n (RADIO, TV) interviewer m

intestine [ɪn'testɪn] n intestin m

intimacy ['ɪntɪməsɪ] n intimité f

intimate [adj 'ɪntɪmət, vb 'ɪntɪmeɪt] adj intime; (friendship) profond(e); (knowledge) approfondi(e) ♦ vt (hint) suggérer, laisser entendre

into ['ɪntu] prep dans; ~ **pieces/French** en morceaux/français

intolerant [ɪn'tɒlərnt] adj: ~ **(of)** intolérant(e) (de)

intoxicated [ɪn'tɒksɪkeɪtɪd] adj (drunk) ivre

intractable [ɪnˈtræktəbl] *adj* (*child*) indocile, insoumis(e); (*problem*) insoluble

intranet [ˈɪntrənet] *n* intranet *m*

intransitive [ɪnˈtrænsɪtɪv] *adj* intransitif(-ive)

intravenous [ɪntrəˈviːnəs] *adj* intraveineux(-euse)

in-tray [ˈɪntreɪ] *n* courrier *m* "arrivée"

intricate [ˈɪntrɪkət] *adj* complexe, compliqué(e)

intrigue [ɪnˈtriːg] *n* intrigue *f* ♦ *vt* intriguer; **intriguing** *adj* fascinant(e)

intrinsic [ɪnˈtrɪnsɪk] *adj* intrinsèque

introduce [ɪntrəˈdjuːs] *vt* introduire; (*TV show, people to each other*) présenter; **to ~ sb to** (*pastime, technique*) initier qn à; **introduction** *n* introduction *f*; (*of person*) présentation *f*; (*to new experience*) initiation *f*; **introductory** *adj* préliminaire, d'introduction; **introductory offer** *n* (*COMM*) offre *f* de lancement

intrude [ɪnˈtruːd] *vi* (*person*) être importun(e); **to ~ on** (*conversation etc*) s'immiscer dans; **~r** *n* intrus(e)

intuition [ɪntjuːˈɪʃən] *n* intuition *f*

inundate [ˈɪnʌndeɪt] *vt*: **to ~ with** inonder de

invade [ɪnˈveɪd] *vt* envahir

invalid [*n* ˈɪnvəlɪd, *adj* ɪnˈvælɪd] *n* malade *m/f*; (*with disability*) invalide *m/f* ♦ *adj* (*not valid*) non valide *or* valable

invaluable [ɪnˈvæljuəbl] *adj* inestimable, inappréciable

invariably [ɪnˈveərɪəblɪ] *adv* invariablement; toujours

invent [ɪnˈvent] *vt* inventer; **~ion** *n* invention *f*; **~ive** *adj* inventif(-ive); **~or** *n* inventeur(-trice)

inventory [ˈɪnvəntrɪ] *n* inventaire *m*

invert [ɪnˈvɜːt] *vt* intervertir; (*cup, object*) retourner; **~ed commas** (*BRIT*) *npl* guillemets *mpl*

invest [ɪnˈvest] *vt* investir ♦ *vi*: **to ~ in sth** placer son argent dans qch; (*fig*) s'offrir qch

investigate [ɪnˈvestɪgeɪt] *vt* (*crime etc*) faire une enquête sur; **investigation** [ɪnvestɪˈgeɪʃən] *n* (*of crime*) enquête *f*

investment [ɪnˈvestmənt] *n* investissement *m*, placement *m*

investor [ɪnˈvestər] *n* investisseur *m*; actionnaire *m/f*

invigilator [ɪnˈvɪdʒɪleɪtər] *n* surveillant(e)

invigorating [ɪnˈvɪgəreɪtɪŋ] *adj* vivifiant(e); (*fig*) stimulant(e)

invisible [ɪnˈvɪzɪbl] *adj* invisible

invitation [ɪnvɪˈteɪʃən] *n* invitation *f*

invite [ɪnˈvaɪt] *vt* inviter; (*opinions etc*) demander; **inviting** *adj* engageant(e), attrayant(e)

invoice [ˈɪnvɔɪs] *n* facture *f*

involuntary [ɪnˈvɒləntrɪ] *adj* involontaire

involve [ɪnˈvɒlv] *vt* (*entail*) entraîner, nécessiter; (*concern*) concerner; (*associate*): **to ~ sb (in)** impliquer qn (dans), mêler qn (à); faire participer qn (à); **~d** *adj* (*complicated*) complexe; **to be ~d in** participer à; **~ment** *n*: **~ment (in)** participation *f* (à); rôle *m* (dans); (*enthusiasm*) enthousiasme *m* (pour)

inward [ˈɪnwəd] *adj* (*thought, feeling*) profond(e), intime; (*movement*) vers l'intérieur; **~(s)** *adv* vers l'intérieur

I/O *abbr* (*COMPUT*: = *input/output*) E/S

iodine [ˈaɪəʊdiːn] *n* iode *m*

iota [aɪˈəʊtə] *n* (*fig*) brin *m*, grain *m*

IOU *n abbr* (= *I owe you*) reconnaissance *f* de dette

IQ *n abbr* (= *intelligence quotient*) Q.I. *m*

IRA *n abbr* (= *Irish Republican Army*) IRA *m*

Iran [ɪˈrɑːn] *n* Iran *m*

Iraq [ɪˈrɑːk] *n* Irak *m*

irate [aɪˈreɪt] *adj* courroucé(e)

Ireland [ˈaɪələnd] *n* Irlande *f*

iris [ˈaɪrɪs] (*pl* **~es**) *n* iris *m*

Irish [ˈaɪrɪʃ] *adj* irlandais(e) ♦ *npl*: **the ~** les Irlandais *mpl*; **~man** (*irreg*) *n* Irlandais *m*; **~ Sea** *n* mer *f* d'Irlande; **~woman** (*irreg*) *n* Irlandaise *f*

iron [ˈaɪən] *n* fer *m*; (*for clothes*) fer *m* à repasser ♦ *cpd* de *or* en fer; (*fig*) de fer ♦ *vt* (*clothes*) repasser; **~ out** *vt* (*fig*) aplanir; faire disparaître

ironic(al) [aɪˈrɒnɪk(l)] *adj* ironique

ironing [ˈaɪənɪŋ] *n* repassage *m*; ~ **board** *n* planche *f* à repasser

ironmonger's (shop) [ˈaɪənmʌŋgəz-] *n* quincaillerie *f*

irony [ˈaɪrənɪ] *n* ironie *f*

irrational [ɪˈræʃənl] *adj* irrationnel(le)

irregular [ɪˈregjulər] *adj* irrégulier(-ère); (*surface*) inégal(e)

irrelevant [ɪˈreləvənt] *adj* sans rapport, hors de propos

irresistible [ɪrɪˈzɪstɪbl] *adj* irrésistible

irrespective [ɪrɪˈspektɪv]: ~ **of** *prep* sans tenir compte de

irresponsible [ɪrɪˈspɒnsɪbl] *adj* (*act*) irréfléchi(e); (*person*) irresponsable, inconscient(e)

irrigate [ˈɪrɪgeɪt] *vt* irriguer; **irrigation** [ɪrɪˈgeɪʃən] *n* irrigation *f*

irritate [ˈɪrɪteɪt] *vt* irriter

irritating *adj* irritant(e); **irritation** [ɪrɪˈteɪʃən] *n* irritation *f*

IRS (*US*) *n abbr* = **Internal Revenue Service**

is [ɪz] *vb see* **be**

Islam [ˈɪzlɑːm] *n* Islam *m*; ~**ic** *adj* islamique; ~**ic fundamentalists** intégristes *mpl* musulmans

island [ˈaɪlənd] *n* île *f*; ~**er** *n* habitant(e) d'une île, insulaire *m/f*

isle [aɪl] *n* île *f*

isn't [ˈɪznt] = **is not**

isolate [ˈaɪsəleɪt] *vt* isoler; ~**d** *adj* isolé(e); **isolation** *n* isolation *f*

ISP *n abbr* = **Internet Service Provider**

Israel [ˈɪzreɪl] *n* Israël *m*; ~**i** [ɪzˈreɪlɪ] *adj* israélien(ne) ♦ *n* Israélien(ne)

issue [ˈɪʃuː] *n* question *f*, problème *m*; (*of book*) publication *f*, parution *f*; (*of banknotes etc*) émission *f*; (*of newspaper etc*) numéro *m* ♦ *vt* (*rations, equipment*) distribuer; (*statement*) publier, faire; (*banknotes etc*) émettre, mettre en circulation; **at** ~ en jeu, en cause; **to take** ~ **with sb (over)** exprimer son désaccord avec qn (sur); **to make an** ~ **of sth** faire une montagne de qch

---

it [ɪt] *pron* 1 (*specific: subject*) il (elle); (: *direct object*) le (la, l'); (: *indirect object*) lui; **it's on the table** c'est *or* il (*or* elle) est sur la table; **about/from/of it** en; **I spoke to him about it** je lui en ai parlé; **what did you learn from it?** qu'est-ce que vous en avez retiré?; **I'm proud of it** j'en suis fier; **in/to it** y; **put the book in it** mettez-y le livre; **he agreed to it** il y a consenti; **did you go to it?** (*party, concert etc*) est-ce que vous y êtes allé(s)?

2 (*impersonal*) il; ce; **it's raining** il pleut; **it's Friday tomorrow** demain c'est vendredi *or* nous sommes vendredi; **it's 6 o'clock** il est 6 heures; **who is it? - it's me** qui est-ce? - c'est moi

---

Italian [ɪˈtæljən] *adj* italien(ne) ♦ *n* Italien(ne); (*LING*) italien *m*

italics [ɪˈtælɪks] *npl* italiques *fpl*

Italy [ˈɪtəlɪ] *n* Italie *f*

itch [ɪtʃ] *n* démangeaison *f* ♦ *vi* (*person*) éprouver des démangeaisons; (*part of body*) démanger; **I'm ~ing to do** l'envie me démange de faire; ~**y** *adj* qui démange; **to be ~y** avoir des démangeaisons

it'd [ˈɪtd] = **it would**; **it had**

item [ˈaɪtəm] *n* article *m*; (*on agenda*) question *f*, point *m*; (*also: news* ~) nouvelle *f*; ~**ize** *vt* détailler, faire une liste de

itinerary [aɪˈtɪnərərɪ] *n* itinéraire *m*

it'll [ˈɪtl] = **it will**; **it shall**

its [ɪts] *adj* son (sa), ses *pl*

it's [ɪts] = **it is**; **it has**

itself [ɪtˈself] *pron* (*reflexive*) se; (*emphatic*) lui-même (elle-même)

ITV *n abbr* (*BRIT: Independent Television*) chaîne privée

IUD *n abbr* (= *intra-uterine device*) DIU *m*, stérilet *m*

I've [aɪv] = **I have**

ivory [ˈaɪvərɪ] *n* ivoire *m*

ivy [ˈaɪvɪ] *n* lierre *m*

J, j

jab [dʒæb] *vt*: **to ~ sth into** enfoncer *or* planter qch dans ♦ *n* (*inf: injection*) piqûre *f*

jack [dʒæk] *n* (*AUT*) cric *m*; (*CARDS*) valet *m*; **~ up** *vt* soulever (au cric)

jackal [ˈdʒækl] *n* chacal *m*

jacket [ˈdʒækɪt] *n* veste *f*, veston *m*; (*of book*) jaquette *f*, couverture *f*; **~ potato** *n* pomme *f* de terre en robe des champs

jack: **~knife** *vi*: **the lorry ~knifed** la remorque (du camion) s'est mise en travers; **~ plug** *n* (*ELEC*) prise jack mâle *f*; **~pot** *n* gros lot

jaded [ˈdʒeɪdɪd] *adj* éreinté(e), fatigué(e)

jagged [ˈdʒægɪd] *adj* dentelé(e)

jail [dʒeɪl] *n* prison *f* ♦ *vt* emprisonner, mettre en prison

jam [dʒæm] *n* confiture *f*; (*also*: **traffic ~**) embouteillage *m* ♦ *vt* (*passage etc*) encombrer, obstruer; (*mechanism, drawer etc*) bloquer, coincer; (*RADIO*) brouiller ♦ *vi* se coincer, se bloquer; (*gun*) s'enrayer; **to be in a ~** (*inf*) être dans le pétrin; **to ~ sth into** entasser qch dans; enfoncer qch dans

Jamaica [dʒəˈmeɪkə] *n* Jamaïque *f*

jam: **~ jar** *n* pot *m* à confiture; **~med** *adj* (*window etc*) coincé(e); **~-packed** *adj*: **~-packed (with)** bourré(e) (de)

jangle [ˈdʒæŋgl] *vi* cliqueter

janitor [ˈdʒænɪtəʳ] *n* concierge *m*

January [ˈdʒænjuərɪ] *n* janvier *m*

Japan [dʒəˈpæn] *n* Japon *m*; **~ese** [dʒæpəˈniːz] *adj* japonais(e) ♦ *n inv* Japonais(e); (*LING*) japonais *m*

jar [dʒɑːʳ] *n* (*stone, earthenware*) pot *m*; (*glass*) bocal *m* ♦ *vi* (*sound discordant*) produire un son grinçant *or* discordant; (*colours etc*) jurer

jargon [ˈdʒɑːgən] *n* jargon *m*

jaundice [ˈdʒɔːndɪs] *n* jaunisse *f*

javelin [ˈdʒævlɪn] *n* javelot *m*

jaw [dʒɔː] *n* mâchoire *f*

jay [dʒeɪ] *n* geai *m*; **~walker** *n* piéton indiscipliné

jazz [dʒæz] *n* jazz *m*; **~ up** *vt* animer, égayer

jealous [ˈdʒeləs] *adj* jaloux(-ouse); **~y** *n* jalousie *f*

jeans [dʒiːnz] *npl* jean *m*

jeer [dʒɪəʳ] *vi*: **to ~ (at)** se moquer cruellement (de), railler

Jehovah's Witness [dʒɪˈhəʊvəz-] *n* témoin *m* de Jéhovah

jelly [ˈdʒelɪ] *n* gelée *f*; **~fish** [ˈdʒelɪfɪʃ] *n* méduse *f*

jeopardy [ˈdʒepədɪ] *n*: **to be in ~** être en danger *or* péril

jerk [dʒɜːk] *n* secousse *f*; saccade *f*; sursaut *m*, spasme *m*; (*inf: idiot*) pauvre type *m* ♦ *vt* (*pull*) tirer brusquement ♦ *vi* (*vehicles*) cahoter

jersey [ˈdʒɜːzɪ] *n* (*pullover*) tricot *m*; (*fabric*) jersey *m*

Jesus [ˈdʒiːzəs] *n* Jésus

jet [dʒet] *n* (*gas, liquid*) jet *m*; (*AVIAT*) avion *m* à réaction, jet *m*; **~-black** *adj* (d'un noir) de jais; **~ engine** *n* moteur *m* à réaction; **~ lag** *n* (fatigue due au) décalage *m* horaire

jettison [ˈdʒetɪsn] *vt* jeter par-dessus bord

jetty [ˈdʒetɪ] *n* jetée *f*, digue *f*

Jew [dʒuː] *n* Juif *m*

jewel [ˈdʒuːəl] *n* bijou *m*, joyau *m*; (*in watch*) rubis *m*; **~ler** (*US* **jeweler**) *n* bijoutier(-ère), joaillier *m*; **~ler's (shop)** *n* bijouterie *f*, joaillerie *f*; **~lery** (*US* **jewelry**) *n* bijoux *mpl*

Jewess [ˈdʒuːɪs] *n* Juive *f*

Jewish [ˈdʒuːɪʃ] *adj* juif (juive)

jibe [dʒaɪb] *n* sarcasme *m*

jiffy [ˈdʒɪfɪ] (*inf*) *n*: **in a ~** en un clin d'œil

jigsaw [ˈdʒɪgsɔː] *n* (*also*: **~ puzzle**) puzzle *m*

jilt [dʒɪlt] *vt* laisser tomber, plaquer

jingle [ˈdʒɪŋgl] *n* (*for advert*) couplet *m* publicitaire ♦ *vi* cliqueter, tinter

jinx [dʒɪŋks] (*inf*) *n* (mauvais) sort

jitters [ˈdʒɪtəz] (*inf*) *npl*: **to get the ~** (*inf*) avoir la trouille *or* la frousse

job [dʒɔb] *n* (*chore, task*) travail *m*, tâche *f*; (*employment*) emploi *m*, poste *m*, place *f*; **it's a good ~ that ...** c'est heureux *or* c'est une chance que ...; **just the ~!** (*c'est*) juste *or* exactement ce qu'il faut!; **~ centre** (*BRIT*) *n* agence *f* pour l'emploi; **~less** *adj* sans travail, au chômage

jockey ['dʒɔki] *n* jockey *m* ♦ *vi*: **to ~ for position** manœuvrer pour être bien placé

jog [dʒɔg] *vt* secouer ♦ *vi* (*SPORT*) faire du jogging; **to ~ sb's memory** rafraîchir la mémoire de qn; **~ along** *vi* cheminer; trotter; **~ging** *n* jogging *m*

join [dʒɔin] *vt* (*put together*) unir, assembler; (*become member of*) s'inscrire à; (*meet*) rejoindre, retrouver; (*queue*) se joindre à ♦ *vi* (*roads, rivers*) se rejoindre, se rencontrer ♦ *n* raccord *m*; **~ in** *vi* se mettre de la partie, participer ♦ *vt fus* participer à, se mêler à; **~ up** *vi* (*meet*) se rejoindre; (*MIL*) s'engager

joiner ['dʒɔinə*ʳ*] (*BRIT*) *n* menuisier *m*

joint [dʒɔint] *n* (*TECH*) jointure *f*, joint *m*; (*ANAT*) articulation *f*, jointure; (*BRIT*: *CULIN*) rôti *m*; (*inf*: *place*) boîte *f*; (: *of cannabis*) joint *m* ♦ *adj* commun(e); **~ account** *n* (*with bank etc*) compte joint

joke [dʒəuk] *n* plaisanterie *f*; (*also*: **practical ~**) farce *f* ♦ *vi* plaisanter; **to play a ~ on** jouer un tour à, faire une farce à; **~r** *n* (*CARDS*) joker *m*

jolly ['dʒɔli] *adj* gai(e), enjoué(e); (*enjoyable*) amusant(e), plaisant(e) ♦ *adv* (*BRIT*: *inf*) drôlement

jolt [dʒəult] *n* cahot *m*, secousse *f*; (*shock*) choc *m* ♦ *vt* cahoter, secouer

Jordan ['dʒɔːdən] *n* (*country*) Jordanie *f*

jostle ['dʒɔsl] *vt* bousculer, pousser

jot [dʒɔt] *n*: **not one ~** pas un brin; **~ down** *vt* noter; **~ter** (*BRIT*) *n* cahier *m* (de brouillon); (*pad*) bloc-notes *m*

journal ['dʒəːnl] *n* journal *m*; **~ism** *n* journalisme *m*; **~ist** *n* journaliste *m/f*

journey ['dʒəːni] *n* voyage *m*; (*distance covered*) trajet *m*

joy [dʒɔi] *n* joie *f*; **~ful** *adj* joyeux(-euse); **~rider** *n* personne qui fait une virée dans une voiture volée; **~stick** *n* (*AVIAT, COMPUT*) manche *m* à balai

JP *n abbr* = **Justice of the Peace**

Jr *abbr* = **junior**

jubilant ['dʒuːbilnt] *adj* triomphant(e); réjoui(e)

judge [dʒʌdʒ] *n* juge *m* ♦ *vt* juger; **judg(e)ment** *n* jugement *m*

judicial [dʒuːˈdiʃl] *adj* judiciaire; **judiciary** *n* (*pouvoir m*) judiciaire *m*

judo ['dʒuːdəu] *n* judo *m*

jug [dʒʌg] *n* pot *m*, cruche *f*

juggernaut ['dʒʌgənɔːt] (*BRIT*) *n* (*huge truck*) énorme poids lourd

juggle ['dʒʌgl] *vi* jongler; **~r** *n* jongleur *m*

juice [dʒuːs] *n* jus *m*; **juicy** *adj* juteux(-euse)

jukebox ['dʒuːkbɔks] *n* juke-box *m*

July [dʒuːˈlai] *n* juillet *m*

jumble ['dʒʌmbl] *n* fouillis *m* ♦ *vt* (*also*: **~ up**) mélanger, brouiller; **~ sale** (*BRIT*) *n* vente *f* de charité

---
jumble sale
---

i Les **jumble sales** ont lieu dans les églises, salles de fêtes ou halls d'écoles, et l'on y vend des articles de toutes sortes, en général bon marché et surtout d'occasion, pour collecter des fonds pour une œuvre de charité, une école ou encore une église.
---

jumbo (jet) ['dʒʌmbəu-] *n* jumbo-jet *m*, gros porteur

jump [dʒʌmp] *vi* sauter, bondir; (*start*) sursauter; (*increase*) monter en flèche ♦ *vt* sauter, franchir ♦ *n* saut *m*, bond *m*; sursaut *m*; **to ~ the queue** (*BRIT*) passer avant son tour

jumper ['dʒʌmpə*ʳ*] *n* (*BRIT*: *pullover*) pullover *m*; (*US*: *dress*) robe-chasuble *f*

jumper cables (*US*), **jump leads** (*BRIT*) *npl* câbles *mpl* de démarrage

jumpy ['dʒʌmpi] *adj* nerveux(-euse), agité(e)

Jun. *abbr* = **junior**

junction ['dʒʌŋkʃən] (*BRIT*) *n* (*of roads*) carrefour m; (of rails) embranchement m

juncture ['dʒʌŋktʃəʳ] n: **at this ~** à ce moment-là, sur ces entrefaites

June [dʒuːn] n juin m

jungle ['dʒʌŋgl] n jungle f

junior ['dʒuːnɪəʳ] adj, n: **he's ~ to me (by 2 years), he's my ~ (by 2 years)** il est mon cadet (de 2 ans), il est plus jeune que moi (de 2 ans); **he's ~ to me** (seniority) il est en dessous de moi (dans la hiérarchie), j'ai plus d'ancienneté que lui; **~ school** (BRIT) n ≈ école f primaire

junk [dʒʌŋk] n (rubbish) camelote f; (cheap goods) bric-à-brac m inv; **~ food** n aliments mpl sans grande valeur nutritive; **~ mail** n prospectus mpl (non sollicités); **~ shop** n (boutique f de) brocanteur m

Junr abbr = **junior**

juror ['dʒuərəʳ] n juré m

jury ['dʒuərɪ] n jury m

just [dʒʌst] adj juste ♦ adv: **he's ~ done it/left** il vient de le faire/partir; **~ right/ two o'clock** exactement or juste ce qu'il faut/deux heures; **she's ~ as clever as you** elle est tout aussi intelligente que vous; **it's ~ as well (that) ...** heureusement que ...; **~ as he was leaving** au moment or à l'instant précis où il partait; **~ before/enough/here** juste avant/ assez/ici; **it's ~ me/a mistake** ce n'est que moi/(rien) qu'une erreur; **~ missed/ caught** manqué/attrapé de justesse; **~ listen to this!** écoutez un peu ça!

justice ['dʒʌstɪs] n justice f; (US: judge) juge m de la Cour suprême; **J~ of the Peace** n juge m de paix

justify ['dʒʌstɪfaɪ] vt justifier

jut [dʒʌt] vi (also: **~ out**) dépasser, faire saillie

juvenile ['dʒuːvənaɪl] adj juvénile; (court, books) pour enfants ♦ n adolescent(e)

K, k

K abbr (= one thousand) K; (= kilobyte) Ko

kangaroo [kæŋgəˈruː] n kangourou m

karate [kəˈrɑːtɪ] n karaté m

kebab [kəˈbæb] n kébab m

keel [kiːl] n quille f; **on an even ~** (fig) à flot

keen [kiːn] adj (eager) plein(e) d'enthousiasme; . (interest, desire, competition) vif (vive); (eye, intelligence) pénétrant(e); (edge) effilé(e); **to be ~ to do** or **on doing sth** désirer vivement faire qch, tenir beaucoup à faire qch; **to be ~ on sth/sb** aimer beaucoup qch/qn

keep [kiːp] (pt, pp **kept**) vt (retain, preserve) garder; (detain) retenir; (shop, accounts, diary, promise) tenir; (house) avoir; (support) entretenir; (chickens, bees etc) élever ♦ vi (remain) rester; (food) se conserver ♦ n (of castle) donjon m; (food etc): **enough for his ~** assez pour (assurer) sa subsistance; (inf): **for ~s** pour de bon, pour toujours; **to ~ doing sth** ne pas arrêter de faire qch; **to ~ sb from doing** empêcher qn de faire or que qn ne fasse; **to ~ sb happy/a place tidy** faire que qn soit content/ qu'un endroit reste propre; **to ~ sth to o.s.** garder qch pour soi, tenir qch secret; **to ~ sth (back) from sb** cacher qch à qn; **to ~ time** (clock) être à l'heure, ne pas retarder; **well kept** bien entretenu(e); **~ on** vi: **to ~ on doing** continuer à faire; **don't ~ on about it!** arrête (d'en parler)!; **~ out** vt empêcher d'entrer; **"~ out"** "défense d'entrer"; **~ up** vt continuer, maintenir ♦ vi: **to ~ up with** (in race etc) aller aussi vite que qn; (in work etc) se maintenir au niveau de qn; **~er** n gardien(ne); **~-fit** n gymnastique f d'entretien; **~ing** n (care) garde f; **in ~ing with** en accord avec; **~sake** n souvenir m

kennel ['kɛnl] n niche f; **~s** npl (boarding ~s) chenil m

kerb [kəːb] (BRIT) n bordure f du trottoir

kernel ['kə:nl] *n* (*of nut*) amande *f*; (*fig*) noyau *m*

kettle ['kɛtl] *n* bouilloire *f*; ~**drum** *n* timbale *f*

key [ki:] *n* (*gen , MUS*) clé *f*; (*of piano, typewriter*) touche *f* ♦ *cpd* clé ♦ *vt* (*also:* ~ **in**) introduire (au clavier), saisir; ~**board** *n* clavier *m*; ~**ed up** *adj* (*person*) surexcité(e); ~**hole** *n* trou *m* de la serrure; ~**hole surgery** *n* chirurgie très minutieuse où l'incision est minimale; ~**note** *n* (*of speech*) note dominante; (*MUS*) tonique *f*; ~ **ring** *n* porte-clés *m*

khaki ['kɑ:kɪ] *n* kaki *m*

kick [kɪk] *vt* donner un coup de pied à ♦ *vi* (*horse*) ruer ♦ *n* coup *m* de pied; (*thrill*): **he does it for ~s** il le fait parce que ça l'excite, il le fait pour le plaisir; **to ~ the habit** (*inf*) arrêter; ~ **off** *vi* (*SPORT*) donner le coup d'envoi

kid [kɪd] *n* (*inf: child*) gamin(e), gosse *m/f*; (*animal, leather*) chevreau *m* ♦ *vi* (*inf*) plaisanter, blaguer

kidnap ['kɪdnæp] *vt* enlever, kidnapper; ~**per** *n* ravisseur(-euse); ~**ping** *n* enlèvement *m*

kidney ['kɪdnɪ] *n* (*ANAT*) rein *m*; (*CULIN*) rognon *m*

kill [kɪl] *vt* tuer ♦ *n* mise *f* à mort; ~**er** *n* tueur(-euse); meurtrier(-ère); ~**ing** *n* meurtre *m*; (*of group of people*) tuerie *f*, massacre *m*; **to make a ~ing** (*inf*) réussir un beau coup (de filet); ~**joy** *n* rabat-joie *m/f*

kiln [kɪln] *n* four *m*

kilo ['ki:ləu] *n* kilo *m*; ~**byte** *n* (*COMPUT*) kilo-octet *m*; ~**gram(me)** *n* kilogramme *m*; ~**metre** (*US* **kilometer**) *n* kilomètre *m*; ~**watt** *n* kilowatt *m*

kilt [kɪlt] *n* kilt *m*

kin [kɪn] *n* see **next**

kind [kaɪnd] *adj* gentil(le), aimable ♦ *n* sorte *f*, espèce *f*, genre *m*; **to be two of a ~** se ressembler; **in ~** (*COMM*) en nature

kindergarten ['kɪndəgɑ:tn] *n* jardin *m* d'enfants

kind-hearted [kaɪnd'hɑ:tɪd] *adj* bon (bon-

ne)

kindle ['kɪndl] *vt* allumer, enflammer

kindly ['kaɪndlɪ] *adj* bienveillant(e), plein(e) de gentillesse ♦ *adv* avec bonté; **will you ~ ...!** auriez-vous la bonté *or* l'obligeance de ...?

kindness ['kaɪndnɪs] *n* bonté *f*, gentillesse *f*

king [kɪŋ] *n* roi *m*; ~**dom** *n* royaume *m*; ~**fisher** *n* martin-pêcheur *m*; ~**-size bed** *n* grand lit (*de 1,95 m de large*); ~**-size(d)** *adj* format géant *inv*; (*cigarettes*) long (longue)

kiosk ['ki:ɔsk] *n* kiosque *m*; (*BRIT: TEL*) cabine *f* (téléphonique)

kipper ['kɪpər] *n* hareng fumé et salé

kiss [kɪs] *n* baiser *m* ♦ *vt* embrasser; **to ~ (each other)** s'embrasser; ~ **of life** (*BRIT*) *n* bouche à bouche *m*

kit [kɪt] *n* équipement *m*, matériel *m*; (*set of tools etc*) trousse *f*; (*for assembly*) kit *m*

kitchen ['kɪtʃɪn] *n* cuisine *f*; ~ **sink** *n* évier *m*

kite [kaɪt] *n* (*toy*) cerf-volant *m*

kitten ['kɪtn] *n* chaton *m*, petit chat *m*

kitty ['kɪtɪ] *n* (*money*) cagnotte *f*

km *abbr* = **kilometre**

knack [næk] *n*: **to have the ~ of doing** avoir le coup pour faire

knapsack ['næpsæk] *n* musette *f*

knead [ni:d] *vt* pétrir

knee [ni:] *n* genou *m*; ~**cap** *n* rotule *f*

kneel [ni:l] (*pt, pp* **knelt**) *vi* (*also:* ~ **down**) s'agenouiller

knew [nju:] *pt of* **know**

knickers ['nɪkəz] (*BRIT*) *npl* culotte *f* (de femme)

knife [naɪf] (*pl* **knives**) *n* couteau *m* ♦ *vt* poignarder, frapper d'un coup de couteau

knight [naɪt] *n* chevalier *m*; (*CHESS*) cavalier *m*; ~**hood** (*BRIT*) *n* (*title*): **to get a ~hood** être fait chevalier

knit [nɪt] *vt* tricoter ♦ *vi* tricoter; (*broken bones*) se ressouder; **to ~ one's brows** froncer les sourcils; ~**ting** *n* tricot *m*; ~**ting needle** *n* aiguille *f* à tricoter; ~**wear** *n* tricots *mpl*, lainages *mpl*

knives [naɪvz] *npl of* **knife**

knob [nɔb] *n* bouton *m*

knock [nɔk] *vt* frapper; (*bump into*) heurter; (*inf*) dénigrer ♦ *vi* (*at door etc*): **to ~ at** *or* **on** frapper à ♦ *n* coup *m*; ~ **down** *vt* renverser; ~ **off** *vi* (*inf: finish*) s'arrêter (de travailler) ♦ *vt* (*from price*) faire un rabais de; (*inf: steal*) piquer; ~ **out** *vt* assommer; (*BOXING*) mettre k.-o.; (*defeat*) éliminer; ~ **over** *vt* renverser, faire tomber; **~er** *n* (*on door*) heurtoir *m*; **~out** *n* (*BOXING*) knockout *m*, K.-O. *m*; **~out competition** compétition *f* avec épreuves éliminatoires

knot [nɔt] *n* (*gen*) nœud *m* ♦ *vt* nouer

know [nəu] (*pt* **knew**, *pp* **known**) *vt* savoir; (*person, place*) connaître; **to ~ how to do** savoir (comment) faire; **to ~ how to swim** savoir nager; **to ~ about** *or* **of sth** être au courant de qch; **to ~ about** *or* **of sb** avoir entendu parler de qn; **~-all** (*pej*) *n* je-sais-tout *m/f*; **~-how** *n* savoir-faire *m*; **~ing** *adj* (*look etc*) entendu(e); **~ingly** *adv* sciemment; (*smile, look*) d'un air entendu

knowledge [ˈnɔlɪdʒ] *n* connaissance *f*; (*learning*) connaissances, savoir *m*; **~able** *adj* bien informé(e)

knuckle [ˈnʌkl] *n* articulation *f* (des doigts), jointure *f*

Koran [kɔˈrɑːn] *n* Coran *m*

Korea [kəˈrɪə] *n* Corée *f*

kosher [ˈkəuʃər] *adj* kascher *inv*

Kosovo [ˈkɔsəvəu] *n* Kosovo *m*

L, l

L *abbr* (= *lake, large*) L; (= *left*) g; (*BRIT: AUT: learner*) signale un conducteur débutant

lab [læb] *n abbr* (= *laboratory*) labo *m*

label [ˈleɪbl] *n* étiquette *f* ♦ *vt* étiqueter

labor *etc* [ˈleɪbər] (*US*) = **labour** *etc*

laboratory [ləˈbɔrətərɪ] *n* laboratoire *m*

labour [ˈleɪbər] (*US* **labor**) *n* (*work*) travail *m*; (*workforce*) main-d'œuvre *f* ♦ *vi*: **to ~ (at)** travailler dur (à), peiner (sur) ♦ *vt*: **to ~ a point** insister sur un point; **in ~** (*MED*) en travail, en train d'accoucher; **L~, the**

L~ party (*BRIT*) le parti travailliste, les travaillistes *mpl*; **~ed** *adj* (*breathing*) pénible, difficile; **~er** *n* manœuvre *m*; **farm ~er** ouvrier *m* agricole

lace [leɪs] *n* dentelle *f*; (*of shoe etc*) lacet *m* ♦ *vt* (*shoe: also:* ~ **up**) lacer

lack [læk] *n* manque *m* ♦ *vt* manquer de; **through** *or* **for ~ of** faute de, par manque de; **to be ~ing** manquer, faire défaut; **to be ~ing in** manquer de

lacquer [ˈlækər] *n* laque *f*

lad [læd] *n* garçon *m*, gars *m*

ladder [ˈlædər] *n* échelle *f*; (*BRIT: in tights*) maille filée

laden [ˈleɪdn] *adj*: ~ **(with)** chargé(e) (de)

ladle [ˈleɪdl] *n* louche *f*

lady [ˈleɪdɪ] *n* dame *f*; (*in address*): **ladies and gentlemen** Mesdames (et) Messieurs; **young ~** jeune fille *f*; (*married*) jeune femme *f*; **the ladies' (room)** les toilettes *fpl* (pour dames); **~bird** (*US* **ladybug**) *n* coccinelle *f*; **~like** *adj* distingué(e); **~ship** *n*: **your ~ship** Madame la comtesse/la baronne *etc*

lag [læg] *n* retard *m* ♦ *vi* (*also:* ~ **behind**) rester en arrière, traîner; (*fig*) rester en traîne ♦ *vt* (*pipes*) calorifuger

lager [ˈlɑːgər] *n* bière blonde

lagoon [ləˈguːn] *n* lagune *f*

laid [leɪd] *pt, pp of* **lay**; **~-back** (*inf*) *adj* relaxe, décontracté(e); ~ **up** *adj* alité(e)

lain [leɪn] *pp of* **lie**

lake [leɪk] *n* lac *m*

lamb [læm] *n* agneau *m*; ~ **chop** *n* côtelette *f* d'agneau

lame [leɪm] *adj* boiteux(-euse)

lament [ləˈmɛnt] *n* lamentation *f* ♦ *vt* pleurer, se lamenter sur

laminated [ˈlæmɪnentɪd] *adj* laminé(e); (*windscreen*) (en verre) feuilleté

lamp [læmp] *n* lampe *f*; **~post** (*BRIT*) *n* réverbère *m*; **~shade** *n* abat-jour *m inv*

land [lænd] *n* (*as opposed to sea*) terre *f* (*ferme*); (*soil*) terre; terrain *m*; (*estate*) terre(s), domaine(s) *m(pl)*; (*country*) pays *m* ♦ *vi* (*AVIAT*) atterrir; (*fig*) (re)tomber ♦ *vt* (*passengers, goods*) débarquer; **to ~ sb**

with sth (*inf*) coller qch à qn; ~ **up** *vi* atterrir, (finir par) se retrouver; **~fill site** *n* décharge *f*; **~ing** *n* (AVIAT) atterrissage *m*; (*of staircase*) palier *m*; (*of troops*) débarquement *m*; **~ing strip** *n* piste *f* d'atterrissage; **~lady** *n* propriétaire *f*, logeuse *f*; (*of pub*) patronne *f*; **~locked** *adj* sans littoral; **~lord** *n* propriétaire *m*, logeur *m*; (*of pub etc*) patron *m*; **~mark** *n* (point *m* de) repère *m*; **to be a ~mark** (*fig*) faire date *or* époque; **~owner** *n* propriétaire foncier *or* terrien; **~scape** *n* paysage *m*; **~scape gardener** *n* jardinier(-ère) paysagiste; **~slide** *n* (GEO) glissement *m* (de terrain); (*fig: POL*) raz-de-marée (électoral)

lane [leɪn] *n* (*in country*) chemin *m*; (AUT) voie *f*; file *f*; (*in race*) couloir *m*; **"get in ~"** (AUT) "mettez-vous dans *or* sur la bonne file"

language ['læŋgwɪdʒ] *n* langue *f*; (*way one speaks*) langage *m*; **bad ~** grossièretés *fpl*, langage grossier; **~ laboratory** *n* laboratoire *m* de langues

lank [læŋk] *adj* (*hair*) raide et terne

lanky ['læŋkɪ] *adj* grand(e) et maigre, efflanqué(e)

lantern ['læntən] *n* lanterne *f*

lap [læp] *n* (*of track*) tour *m* (de piste); (*of body*): **in** *or* **on one's ~** sur les genoux ♦ *vt* (*also: ~ up*) laper ♦ *vi* (*waves*) clapoter; **~ up** *vt* (*fig*) accepter béatement, gober

lapel [lə'pel] *n* revers *m*

Lapland ['læplænd] *n* Laponie *f*

lapse [læps] *n* défaillance *f*; (*in behaviour*) écart *m* de conduite ♦ *vi* (LAW) cesser d'être en vigueur; (*contract*) expirer; **to ~ into bad habits** prendre de mauvaises habitudes; **~ of time** laps *m* de temps, intervalle *m*

laptop (computer) ['læptɒp(-)] *n* portable *m*

larceny ['lɑːsənɪ] *n* vol *m*

larch [lɑːtʃ] *n* mélèze *m*

lard [lɑːd] *n* saindoux *m*

larder ['lɑːdəʳ] *n* garde-manger *m inv*

large [lɑːdʒ] *adj* grand(e); (*person, animal*) gros(se); **at ~** (*free*) en liberté; (*generally*)

en général; *see also* **by**; **~ly** *adv* en grande partie; (*principally*) surtout; **~-scale** *adj* (*action*) d'envergure; (*map*) à grande échelle

lark [lɑːk] *n* (*bird*) alouette *f*; (*joke*) blague *f*, farce *f*

laryngitis [lærɪn'dʒaɪtɪs] *n* laryngite *f*

laser ['leɪzəʳ] *n* laser *m*; ~ **printer** *n* imprimante *f* laser

lash [læʃ] *n* coup *m* de fouet; (*also:* **eyelash**) cil *m* ♦ *vt* fouetter; (*tie*) attacher; ~ **out** *vi*: **to ~ out at** *or* **against** attaquer violemment

lass [læs] (BRIT) *n* (jeune) fille *f*

lasso [læ'suː] *n* lasso *m*

last [lɑːst] *adj* dernier(-ère) ♦ *adv* en dernier; (*finally*) finalement ♦ *vi* durer; ~ **week** la semaine dernière; ~ **night** (*evening*) hier soir; (*night*) la nuit dernière; **at ~** enfin; ~ **but one** avant-dernier(-ère); **~-ditch** *adj* (*attempt*) ultime, désespéré(e); **~ing** *adj* durable; **~ly** *adv* en dernier lieu, pour finir; **~-minute** *adj* de dernière minute

latch [lætʃ] *n* loquet *m*

late [leɪt] *adj* (*not on time*) en retard; (*far on in day etc*) tardif(-ive); (*edition, delivery*) dernier(-ère); (*former*) ancien(ne) ♦ *adv* tard; (*behind time, schedule*) en retard; **of ~** dernièrement; **in ~ May** vers la fin (du mois) de mai, fin mai; **the ~ Mr X** feu M. X; **~comer** *n* retardataire *m/f*; **~ly** *adv* récemment; **~r** *adj* (*date etc*) ultérieur(e); (*version etc*) plus récent(e) ♦ *adv* plus tard; **~r on** plus tard; **~st** *adj* tout(e) dernier(-ère); **at the ~st** au plus tard

lathe [leɪð] *n* tour *m*

lather ['lɑːðəʳ] *n* mousse *f* (de savon) ♦ *vt* savonner

Latin ['lætɪn] *n* latin *m* ♦ *adj* latin(e); ~ **America** *n* Amérique latine; ~ **American** *adj* latino-américain(e)

latitude ['lætɪtjuːd] *n* latitude *f*

latter ['lætəʳ] *adj* deuxième, dernier(-ère) ♦ *n*: **the ~** ce dernier, celui-ci; **~ly** *adv* dernièrement, récemment

laudable ['lɔːdəbl] *adj* louable

laugh [lɑːf] n rire m ♦ vi rire; ~ **at** vt fus se moquer de; rire de; ~ **off** vt écarter par une plaisanterie or par une boutade; ~**able** adj risible, ridicule; ~**ing stock** n: **the ~ing stock of** la risée de; ~**ter** n rire m; rires mpl

launch [lɔːntʃ] n lancement m; (motorboat) vedette f ♦ vt lancer; ~ **into** vt fus se lancer dans

Launderette ® [lɔːnˈdrɛt] (BRIT), **Laundromat** ® [ˈlɔːndrəmæt] (US) n laverie f (automatique)

laundry [ˈlɔːndrɪ] n (clothes) linge m; (business) blanchisserie f; (room) buanderie f

laurel [ˈlɔrl] n laurier m

lava [ˈlɑːvə] n lave f

lavatory [ˈlævətərɪ] n toilettes fpl

lavender [ˈlævəndər] n lavande f

lavish [ˈlævɪʃ] adj (amount) copieux(-euse); (person): ~ **with** prodigue de ♦ vt: **to ~ sth on sb** prodiguer qch à qn; (money) dépenser qch sans compter pour qn/qch

law [lɔː] n loi f; (science) droit m; ~-**abiding** adj respectueux(-euse) des lois; ~ **and order** l'ordre public; ~ **court** n tribunal m, cour f de justice; ~**ful** adj légal(e); ~**less** adj (action) illégal(e)

lawn [lɔːn] n pelouse f; ~**mower** n tondeuse f à gazon; ~ **tennis** n tennis m

law school (US) n faculté f de droit

lawsuit [ˈlɔːsuːt] n procès m

lawyer [ˈlɔːjər] n (consultant, with company) juriste m; (for sales, wills etc) notaire m; (partner, in court) avocat m

lax [læks] adj relâché(e)

laxative [ˈlæksətɪv] n laxatif m

lay [leɪ] (pt, pp **laid**) pt of **lie** ♦ adj laïque; (not expert) profane ♦ vt poser, mettre; (eggs) pondre; ~ **the table** mettre la table; ~ **aside** vt mettre de côté; ~ **by** vt = **lay aside**; ~ **down** vt poser; **to ~ down the law** faire la loi; **to ~ down one's life** sacrifier sa vie; ~ **off** vt (workers) licencier; ~ **on** vt (provide) fournir; ~ **out** vt (display) disposer, étaler; ~**about** (inf) n fainéant(e); ~**-by** (BRIT) n aire f de stationnement (sur le bas-côté)

layer [ˈleɪər] n couche f

layman [ˈleɪmən] (irreg) n profane m

layout [ˈleɪaut] n disposition f, plan m, agencement m; (PRESS) mise f en page

laze [leɪz] vi (also: ~ **about**) paresser

lazy [ˈleɪzɪ] adj paresseux(-euse)

lb abbr = **pound** (weight)

lead[1] [liːd] (pt, pp **led**) n (distance, time ahead) avance f; (clue) piste f; (THEATRE) rôle principal; (ELEC) fil m; (for dog) laisse f ♦ vt mener, conduire; (be ~er of) être à la tête de ♦ vi (street etc) mener, conduire; (SPORT) mener, être en tête; **in the ~** en tête; **to ~ the way** montrer le chemin; ~ **away** vt emmener; ~ **back** vt: **to ~ back to** ramener à; ~ **on** vt (tease) faire marcher; ~ **to** vt fus mener à; conduire à; ~ **up to** vt fus conduire à

lead[2] [lɛd] n (metal) plomb m; (in pencil) mine f; ~**ed petrol** n essence f au plomb; ~**en** adj (sky, sea) de plomb

leader [ˈliːdər] n chef m; dirigeant(e), leader m; (SPORT: in league) leader; (: in race) coureur m de tête; ~**ship** n direction f; (quality) qualités fpl de chef

lead-free [ˈlɛdfriː] adj (petrol) sans plomb

leading [ˈliːdɪŋ] adj principal(e); de premier plan; (in race) de tête; ~ **lady** n (THEATRE) vedette (féminine); ~ **light** n (person) vedette f, sommité f; ~ **man** (irreg) n vedette (masculine)

lead singer [liːd-] n (in pop group) (chanteur m) vedette f

leaf [liːf] (pl **leaves**) n feuille f ♦ vi: **to ~ through** feuilleter; **to turn over a new ~** changer de conduite or d'existence

leaflet [ˈliːflɪt] n prospectus m, brochure f; (POL, REL) tract m

league [liːg] n ligue f; (FOOTBALL) championnat m; **to be in ~ with** avoir partie liée avec, être de mèche avec

leak [liːk] n fuite f ♦ vi (pipe, liquid etc) fuir; (shoes) prendre l'eau; (ship) faire eau ♦ vt (information) divulguer

lean [liːn] (pt, pp **leaned** or **leant**) adj maigre ♦ vt: **to ~ sth on sth** appuyer qch sur qch ♦ vi (slope) pencher; (rest): **to ~**

against s'appuyer contre; être appuyé(e) contre; **to ~ on** s'appuyer sur; **to ~ back/forward** se pencher en arrière/avant; **~ out** *vi* se pencher au dehors; **~ over** *vi* se pencher; **~ing** *n*: **~ing (to-wards)** tendance *f* (à), penchant *m* (pour); **~t** [lɛnt] *pt, pp of* **lean**

leap [liːp] (*pt, pp* **leaped** *or* **leapt**) *n* bond *m*, saut *m* ♦ *vi* bondir, sauter; **~frog** *n* saute-mouton *m*; **~t** [lɛpt] *pt, pp of* **leap**; **~ year** *n* année *f* bissextile

learn [lɜːn] (*pt, pp* **learned** *or* **learnt**) *vt, vi* apprendre; **to ~ to do sth** apprendre à faire qch; **to ~ about** *or* **of sth** (*hear, read*) apprendre qch; **~ed** ['lɜːnɪd] *adj* érudit(e), savant(e); **~er** (*BRIT*) *n* (*also:* **~er driver**) (conducteur(-trice)) débutant(e); **~ing** *n* (*knowledge*) savoir *m*; **~t** *pt, pp of* **learn**

lease [liːs] *n* bail *m* ♦ *vt* louer à bail

leash [liːʃ] *n* laisse *f*

least [liːst] *adj*: **the ~** (*+noun*) le (la) plus petit(e), le (la) moindre; (: *smallest amount of*) le moins de ♦ *adv* (*+verb*) le moins; (*+adj*): **the ~** le (la) moins; **at ~** au moins; (*or rather*) du moins; **not in the ~** pas le moins du monde

leather ['lɛðər] *n* cuir *m*

leave [liːv] (*pt, pp* **left**) *vt* laisser; (*go away from*) quitter; (*forget*) oublier ♦ *vi* partir, s'en aller ♦ *n* (*time off*) congé *m*; (*MIL also: consent*) permission *f*; **to be left** rester; **there's some milk left over** il reste du lait; **on ~** en permission; **~ behind** *vt* (*person, object*) laisser; (*forget*) oublier; **~ out** *vt* oublier, omettre; **~ of absence** *n* congé exceptionnel; (*MIL*) permission spéciale

leaves [liːvz] *npl of* **leaf**

Lebanon ['lɛbənən] *n* Liban *m*

lecherous ['lɛtʃərəs] (*pej*) *adj* lubrique

lecture ['lɛktʃər] *n* conférence *f*; (*SCOL*) cours *m* ♦ *vi* donner des cours; enseigner ♦ *vt* (*scold*) sermonner, réprimander; **to give a ~ on** faire une conférence sur; donner un cours sur; **~r** (*BRIT*) *n* (*at university*) professeur *m* (d'université)

led [lɛd] *pt, pp of* **lead**[1]

ledge [lɛdʒ] *n* (*of window, on wall*) rebord *m*; (*of mountain*) saillie *f*, corniche *f*

ledger ['lɛdʒər] *n* (*COMM*) registre *m*, grand livre

leech [liːtʃ] *n* (*also fig*) sangsue *f*

leek [liːk] *n* poireau *m*

leer [lɪər] *vi*: **to ~ at sb** regarder qn d'un air mauvais *or* concupiscent

leeway ['liːweɪ] *n* (*fig*): **to have some ~** avoir une certaine liberté d'action

left [lɛft] *pt, pp of* **leave** ♦ *adj* (*not right*) gauche ♦ *n* gauche *f* ♦ *adv* à gauche; **on the ~, to the ~** à gauche; **the L~** (*POL*) la gauche; **~-handed** *adj* gaucher(-ère); **~-hand side** *n* gauche *f*; **~-luggage locker** *n* (*casier m* à) consigne *f* automatique; **~-luggage (office)** (*BRIT*) *n* consigne *f*; **~overs** *npl* restes *mpl*; **~-wing** *adj* (*POL*) de gauche

leg [lɛg] *n* jambe *f*; (*of animal*) patte *f*; (*of furniture*) pied *m*; (*CULIN: of chicken, pork*) cuisse *f*; (: *of lamb*) gigot *m*; (*of journey*) étape *f*; **1st/2nd ~** (*SPORT*) match *m* aller/retour

legacy ['lɛgəsɪ] *n* héritage *m*, legs *m*

legal ['liːgl] *adj* légal(e); **~ holiday** (*US*) *n* jour férié; **~ tender** *n* monnaie légale

legend ['lɛdʒənd] *n* légende *f*

leggings ['lɛgɪnz] *npl* caleçon *m*

legible ['lɛdʒəbl] *adj* lisible

legislation [lɛdʒɪs'leɪʃən] *n* législation *f*; **legislature** ['lɛdʒɪslətʃər] *n* (*corps m*) législatif *m*

legitimate [lɪ'dʒɪtɪmət] *adj* légitime

leg-room ['lɛgruːm] *n* place *f* pour les jambes

leisure ['lɛʒər] *n* loisir *m*, temps *m* libre; loisirs *mpl*; **at ~** (tout) à loisir; à tête reposée; **~ centre** *n* centre *m* de loisirs; **~ly** *adj* tranquille; fait(e) sans se presser

lemon ['lɛmən] *n* citron *m*; **~ade** [lɛmə'neɪd] *n* limonade *f*; **~ tea** *n* thé *m* au citron

lend [lɛnd] (*pt, pp* **lent**) *vt*: **to ~ sth (to sb)** prêter qch (à qn)

length [lɛŋθ] *n* longueur *f*; (*section: of road, pipe etc*) morceau *m*, bout *m*; (*of time*) du-

rée f; **at ~** (at last) enfin, à la fin; (~ily)
longuement, en long; ~ **ways** adv dans le sens
de la longueur, en long; ~ **y** adj (très)
long (longue)

lenient ['li:niənt] adj indulgent(e), clé-
ment(e)

lens [lɛnz] n lentille f; (of spectacles) verre
m; (of camera) objectif m

Lent [lɛnt] n carême m

lent [lɛnt] pt, pp of **lend**

lentil ['lɛntil] n lentille f

Leo ['li:əu] n le Lion

leotard ['li:əta:d] n maillot m (de danseur
etc), collant m

leprosy ['lɛprəsi] n lèpre f

lesbian ['lɛzbiən] n lesbienne f

less [lɛs] adj moins de ♦ pron, adv moins
♦ prep moins; ~ **than that/you** moins que
cela/vous; ~ **than half** moins de la moitié;
~ **than ever** moins que jamais; ~ **and** ~
de moins en moins; **the ~ he works ...**
moins il travaille ...; ~ **en** vi diminuer, s'atténuer ♦ vt diminuer, réduire, atténuer;
~ **er** adj moindre; **to a ~ er extent** à un
degré moindre

lesson ['lɛsn] n leçon f; **to teach sb a ~**
(fig) donner une bonne leçon à qn

let [lɛt] (pt, pp **let**) vt laisser; (BRIT: lease)
louer; **to ~ sb do sth** laisser qn faire qch;
to ~ sb know sth faire savoir qch à qn,
prévenir qn de qch; ~**'s go** allons-y; ~
him come qu'il vienne; **"to ~"** "à louer";
~ **down** vt (tyre) dégonfler; (person) décevoir, faire faux bond à; ~ **go** vi lâcher prise ♦ vt lâcher; ~ **in** vt laisser entrer; (visitor etc) faire entrer; ~ **off** vt (culprit) ne
pas punir; (firework etc) faire partir; ~ **on**
(inf) vi dire; ~ **out** vt laisser sortir;
(scream) laisser échapper; ~ **up** vi diminuer; (cease) s'arrêter

lethal ['li:θl] adj mortel(le), fatal(e)

letter ['lɛtər] n lettre f; ~ **bomb** n lettre
piégée; ~**box** (BRIT) n boîte f aux or à lettres; ~**ing** n lettres fpl; caractères mpl

lettuce ['lɛtis] n laitue f, salade f

let-up ['lɛtʌp] n répit m, arrêt m

leukaemia [lu:'ki:miə] (US **leukemia**) n
leucémie f

level ['lɛvl] adj plat(e), plan(e), uni(e); ho-
rizontal(e) ♦ n niveau m ♦ vt niveler, aplanir; **to be ~ with** être au même niveau
que; **to draw ~ with** (person, vehicle) arriver à la hauteur de; **"A" ~s** (BRIT) ≃ baccalauréat m; **"O" ~s** (BRIT) ≃ B.E.P.C.; **on
the ~** (fig: honest) régulier(-ère); ~ **off** vi
(prices etc) se stabiliser; ~ **out** vi = **level
off**; ~ **crossing** (BRIT) n passage m à niveau; ~**-headed** adj équilibré(e)

lever ['li:vər] n levier m; ~**age** n: ~**age (on**
or with) prise f (sur)

levy ['lɛvi] n taxe f, impôt m ♦ vt prélever,
imposer; percevoir

lewd [lu:d] adj obscène, lubrique

liability [laiə'biliti] n responsabilité f;
(handicap) handicap m; **liabilities** npl (on
balance sheet) passif m

liable ['laiəbl] adj (subject): ~ **to** sujet(te) à;
passible de; (responsible): ~ **(for)** responsable (de); (likely): ~ **to do** susceptible de
faire

liaise [li:'eiz] vi: **to ~ (with)** assurer la liaison avec; **liaison** n liaison f

liar ['laiər] n menteur(-euse)

libel ['laibl] n diffamation f; (document)
écrit m diffamatoire ♦ vt diffamer

liberal ['libərl] adj libéral(e); (generous): ~
with prodigue de, généreux(-euse) avec;
the L~ Democrats (BRIT) le parti libéral-
démocrate

liberation [libə'reiʃən] n libération f

liberty ['libəti] n liberté f; **to be at ~ to do**
être libre de faire

Libra ['li:brə] n la Balance

librarian [lai'brɛəriən] n bibliothécaire m/f

library ['laibrəri] n bibliothèque f

libretto [li'brɛtəu] n livret m

Libya ['libiə] n Libye f

lice [lais] npl of **louse**

licence ['laisns] (US **license**) n autorisation
f, permis m; (RADIO, TV) redevance f; **driving ~,** (US) **driver's license** permis m (de
conduire); ~ **number** n numéro m d'immatriculation; ~ **plate** n plaque f minéra-

logique

license ['laɪsns] *n* (*US*) = **licence** ♦ *vt* donner une licence à; **~d** *adj* (*car*) muni(e) de la vignette; (*to sell alcohol*) patenté(e) pour la vente des spiritueux, qui a une licence de débit de boissons

lick [lɪk] *vt* lécher; (*inf: defeat*) écraser; **to ~ one's lips** (*fig*) se frotter les mains

licorice ['lɪkərɪs] (*US*) *n* = **liquorice**

lid [lɪd] *n* couvercle *m*; (*eyelid*) paupière *f*

lie [laɪ] (*pt* **lay**, *pp* **lain**) *vi* (*rest*) être étendu(e) *or* allongé(e) *or* couché(e); (*in grave*) être enterré(e), reposer; (*be situated*) se trouver, être; (*be untruthful: pt, pp* ~**d**) mentir ♦ *n* mensonge *m*; **to ~ low** (*fig*) se cacher; **~ about** *vi* traîner; **~ around** *vi* = **lie about**; **~-down** (*BRIT*) *n*: **to have a ~-down** s'allonger, se reposer; **~-in** (*BRIT*) *n*: **to have a ~-in** faire la grasse matinée

lieutenant [lef'tenənt, (*US*) luː'tenənt] *n* lieutenant *m*

life [laɪf] (*pl* **lives**) *n* vie *f*; **to come to ~** (*fig*) s'animer; **~ assurance** (*BRIT*) *n* = **life insurance**; **~belt** (*BRIT*) *n* bouée *f* de sauvetage; **~boat** *n* canot *m* *or* chaloupe *f* de sauvetage; **~buoy** *n* bouée *f* de sauvetage; **~guard** *n* surveillant *m* de baignade; **~ insurance** *n* assurance-vie *f*; **~ jacket** *n* gilet *m* *or* ceinture *f* de sauvetage; **~less** *adj* sans vie, inanimé(e); (*dull*) qui manque de vie *or* de vigueur; **~like** *adj* qui semble vrai(e) *or* vivant(e); (*painting*) réaliste; **~long** *adj* de toute une vie, de toujours; **~ preserver** (*US*) *n* = **lifebelt**; **life jacket**; **~-saving** *n* sauvetage *m*; **~ sentence** *n* condamnation *f* à perpétuité; **~-size(d)** *adj* grandeur nature *inv*; **~ span** *n* (durée *f* de) vie *f*; **~style** *n* style *m* *or* mode *m* de vie; **~-support system** *n* (*MED*) respirateur artificiel; **~time** *n* vie *f*; **in his ~time** de son vivant

lift [lɪft] *vt* soulever, lever; (*end*) supprimer, lever ♦ *vi* (*fog*) se lever ♦ *n* (*BRIT: elevator*) ascenseur *m*; **to give sb a ~** (*BRIT: AUT*) emmener *or* prendre qn en voiture; **~-off** *n* décollage *m*

light [laɪt] (*pt, pp* **lit**) *n* lumière *f*; (*lamp*)

lampe *f*; (*AUT: rear* ~) feu *m*; (: *headlight*) phare *m*; (*for cigarette etc*): **have you got a ~?** avez-vous du feu? ♦ *vt* (*candle, cigarette, fire*) allumer; (*room*) éclairer ♦ *adj* (*room, colour*) clair(e); (*not heavy*) léger(-ère); (*not strenuous*) peu fatigant(e); **~s** *npl* (*AUT: traffic ~s*) feux *mpl*; **to come to ~** être dévoilé(e) *or* découvert(e); **~ up** *vi* (*face*) s'éclairer ♦ *vt* (*illuminate*) éclairer, illuminer; **~ bulb** *n* ampoule *f*; **~en** *vt* (*make less heavy*) alléger; **~er** *n* (*also:* **cigarette ~er**) briquet *m*; **~-headed** *adj* étourdi(e); (*excited*) grisé(e); **~-hearted** *adj* gai(e), joyeux(-euse), enjoué(e); **~house** *n* phare *m*; **~ing** *n* (*on road*) éclairage *m*; (*in theatre*) éclairages; **~ly** *adv* légèrement; **to get off ~ly** s'en tirer à bon compte; **~ness** *n* (*in weight*) légèreté *f*

lightning ['laɪtnɪŋ] *n* éclair *m*, foudre *f*; **~ conductor** (*US* **lightning rod**) *n* paratonnerre *m*

light pen *n* crayon *m* optique

lightweight ['laɪtweɪt] *adj* (*suit*) léger(-ère) ♦ *n* (*BOXING*) poids léger

like [laɪk] *vt* aimer (bien) ♦ *prep* comme ♦ *adj* semblable, pareil(le) ♦ *n*: **and the ~** et d'autres du même genre; **his ~s and dislikes** ses goûts *mpl* *or* préférences *fpl*; **I would ~, I'd ~** je voudrais, j'aimerais; **would you ~ a coffee?** voulez-vous du café?; **to be/look ~ sb/sth** ressembler à qn/qch; **what does it look ~?** de quoi est-ce que ça a l'air?; **what does it taste ~?** quel goût est-ce que ça a?; **that's just ~ him** c'est bien de lui, ça lui ressemble; **do it ~ this** fais-le comme ceci; **it's nothing ~ ...** ce n'est pas du tout comme ...; **~able** *adj* sympathique, agréable

likelihood ['laɪklɪhud] *n* probabilité *f*

likely ['laɪklɪ] *adj* probable; plausible; **he's ~ to leave** il va sûrement partir, il risque fort de partir; **not ~!** (*inf*) pas de danger!

likeness ['laɪknɪs] *n* ressemblance *f*; **that's a good ~** c'est très ressemblant

likewise ['laɪkwaɪz] *adv* de même, pareillement

liking ['laıkıŋ] n (for person) affection f; (for thing) penchant m, goût m

lilac ['laılək] n lilas m

lily ['lılı] n lis m; ~ **of the valley** n muguet m

limb [lım] n membre m

limber up ['lımbər-] vi se dégourdir, faire des exercices d'assouplissement

limbo ['lımbəu] n: **to be in** ~ (fig) être tombé(e) dans l'oubli

lime [laım] n (tree) tilleul m; (fruit) lime f, citron vert; (GEO) chaux f

limelight ['laımlaıt] n: **in the** ~ (fig) en vedette, au premier plan

limerick ['lımərık] n poème m humoristique (de 5 vers)

limestone ['laımstəun] n pierre f à chaux; (GEO) calcaire m

limit ['lımıt] n limite f ♦ vt limiter; ~**ed** adj limité(e), restreint(e); **to be ~ed to** se limiter à, ne concerner que; ~**ed (liability) company** (BRIT) n ≃ société f anonyme

limousine ['lıməzi:n] n limousine f

limp [lımp] n: **to have a** ~ boiter ♦ vi boiter ♦ adj mou (molle)

limpet ['lımpıt] n patelle f

line [laın] n ligne f; (stroke) trait m; (wrinkle) ride f; (rope) corde f; (wire) fil m; (of poem) vers m; (row, series) rangée f; (of people) file f, queue f; (railway track) voie f; (COMM: series of goods) article(s) m(pl); (work) métier m, type m d'activité; (attitude, policy) position f ♦ vt (subj: trees, crowd) border; **in a** ~ aligné(e); **in his** ~ **of business** dans sa partie, dans son rayon; **in** ~ **with** en accord avec; **to** ~ **(with)** (clothes) doubler (de); (box) garnir or tapisser (de); ~ **up** vi s'aligner, se mettre en rang(s) ♦ vt aligner; (event) prévoir, préparer; ~**d** adj (face) ridé(e), marqué(e); (paper) réglé(e)

linen ['lının] n linge m (de maison); (cloth) lin m

liner ['laınər] n paquebot m (de ligne); (for bin) sac m à poubelle

linesman ['laınzmən] (irreg) n juge m de touche; (TENNIS) juge m de ligne

line-up ['laınʌp] n (US: queue) file f; (SPORT) (composition f de l')équipe f

linger ['lıŋgər] vi s'attarder; traîner; (smell, tradition) persister

linguist ['lıŋgwıst] n: **to be a good** ~ être doué(e) pour les langues; ~**ics** [lıŋ'gwıstıks] n linguistique f

lining ['laınıŋ] n doublure f

link [lıŋk] n lien m, rapport m; (of a chain) maillon m ♦ vt relier, lier, unir; ~**s** npl (GOLF) (terrain m de) golf m; ~ **up** vt relier ♦ vi se rejoindre; s'associer

lino ['laınəu] n = **linoleum**

linoleum [lı'nəulıəm] n linoléum m

lion ['laıən] n lion m; ~**ess** n lionne f

lip [lıp] n lèvre f

liposuction ['lıpəusʌkʃən] n liposuccion f

lip: ~-**read** vi lire sur les lèvres; ~ **salve** n pommade f rosat or pour les lèvres; ~ **service** n: **to pay** ~ **service to sth** ne reconnaître le mérite de qch que pour la forme; ~**stick** n rouge m à lèvres

liqueur [lı'kjuər] n liqueur f

liquid ['lıkwıd] adj liquide ♦ n liquide m; ~**ize** vt (CULIN) passer au mixer; ~**izer** n mixer m

liquor ['lıkər] (US) n spiritueux m, alcool m

liquorice ['lıkərıs] (BRIT) n réglisse f

liquor store (US) n magasin m de vins et spiritueux

lisp [lısp] vi zézayer

list [lıst] n liste f ♦ vt (write down) faire une or la liste de; (mention) énumérer; ~**ed building** (BRIT) n monument classé

listen ['lısn] vi écouter; **to** ~ **to** écouter; ~**er** n auditeur(-trice)

listless ['lıstlıs] adj indolent(e), apathique

lit [lıt] pt, pp of **light**

liter ['li:tər] (US) n = **litre**

literacy ['lıtərəsı] n degré m d'alphabétisation, fait m de savoir lire et écrire

literal ['lıtərəl] adj littéral(e); ~**ly** adv littéralement; (really) réellement

literary ['lıtərərı] adj littéraire

literate ['lıtərət] adj qui sait lire et écrire, instruit(e)

literature ['lɪtrɪtʃəʳ] *n* littérature *f*; (*brochures etc*) documentation *f*

lithe [laɪð] *adj* agile, souple

litigation [lɪtɪ'geɪʃən] *n* litige *m*; contentieux *m*

litre ['liːtəʳ] (*US* **liter**) *n* litre *m*

litter ['lɪtəʳ] *n* (*rubbish*) détritus *mpl*, ordures *fpl*; (*young animals*) portée *f*; **~ bin** (*BRIT*) *n* boîte *f* à ordures, poubelle *f*; **~ed** *adj*: **~ed with** jonché(e) de, couvert(e) de

little ['lɪtl] *adj* (*small*) petit(e) ♦ *adv* peu; **~ milk/time** peu de lait/temps; **a ~** un peu (de); **a ~ bit** un peu; **~ by ~** petit à petit, peu à peu

live¹ [laɪv] *adj* (*animal*) vivant(e), en vie; (*wire*) sous tension; (*bullet, bomb*) non explosé(e); (*broadcast*) en direct; (*performance*) en public

live² [lɪv] *vi* vivre; (*reside*) vivre, habiter; **~ down** *vt* faire oublier (avec le temps); **~ on** *vt fus* (*food, salary*) vivre de; **~ together** *vi* vivre ensemble, cohabiter; **~ up to** *vt fus* se montrer à la hauteur de

livelihood ['laɪvlɪhud] *n* moyens *mpl* d'existence

lively ['laɪvlɪ] *adj* vif (vive), plein(e) d'entrain; (*place, book*) vivant(e)

liven up ['laɪvn-] *vt* animer ♦ *vi* s'animer

liver ['lɪvəʳ] *n* foie *m*

lives [laɪvz] *npl of* **life**

livestock ['laɪvstɔk] *n* bétail *m*, cheptel *m*

livid ['lɪvɪd] *adj* livide, blafard(e); (*inf: furious*) furieux(-euse), furibond(e)

living ['lɪvɪŋ] *adj* vivant(e), en vie ♦ *n*: **to earn** *or* **make a ~** gagner sa vie; **~ conditions** *npl* conditions *fpl* de vie; **~ room** *n* salle *f* de séjour; **~ standards** *npl* niveau *m* de vie; **~ wage** *n* salaire *m* permettant de vivre (décemment)

lizard ['lɪzəd] *n* lézard *m*

load [ləud] *n* (*weight*) poids *m*; (*thing carried*) chargement *m*, charge *f* ♦ *vt* (*also: ~ up*): **to ~ (with)** charger (de); (*gun, camera*) charger (avec); (*COMPUT*) charger; **a ~ of, ~s of** (*fig*) un *or* des tas de, des masses de; **to talk a ~ of rubbish** dire des bêtises; **~ed** *adj* (*question*) insidieux(-

euse); (*inf: rich*) bourré(e) de fric

loaf [ləuf] (*pl* **loaves**) *n* pain *m*, miche *f*

loan [ləun] *n* prêt *m* ♦ *vt* prêter; **on ~** prêté(e), en prêt

loath [ləuθ] *adj*: **to be ~ to do** répugner à faire

loathe [ləuð] *vt* détester, avoir en horreur

loaves [ləuvz] *npl of* **loaf**

lobby ['lɔbɪ] *n* hall *m*, entrée *f*; (*POL*) groupe *m* de pression, lobby *m* ♦ *vt* faire pression sur

lobster ['lɔbstəʳ] *n* homard *m*

local ['ləukl] *adj* local(e) ♦ *n* (*BRIT: pub*) pub *m* *or* café *m* du coin; **the ~s** *npl* (*inhabitants*) les gens *mpl* du pays *or* du coin; **~ anaesthetic** *n* anesthésie locale; **~ authority** *n* collectivité locale, municipalité *f*; **~ call** *n* communication urbaine; **~ government** *n* administration locale *or* municipale; **~ity** [ləu'kælɪtɪ] *n* région *f*, environs *mpl*; (*position*) lieu *m*

locate [ləu'keɪt] *vt* (*find*) trouver, repérer; (*situate*): **to be ~d in** être situé(e) à *or* en; **location** *n* emplacement *m*; **on location** (*CINEMA*) en extérieur

loch [lɔx] *n* lac *m*, loch *m*

lock [lɔk] *n* (*of door, box*) serrure *f*; (*of canal*) écluse *f*; (*of hair*) mèche *f*, boucle *f* ♦ *vt* (*with key*) fermer à clé ♦ *vi* (*door etc*) fermer à clé; (*wheels*) se bloquer; **~ in** *vt* enfermer; **~ out** *vt* enfermer dehors; (*deliberately*) mettre à la porte; **~ up** *vt* (*person*) enfermer; (*house*) fermer à clé ♦ *vi* tout fermer (à clé)

locker ['lɔkəʳ] *n* casier *m*; (*in station*) consigne *f* automatique

locket ['lɔkɪt] *n* médaillon *m*

locksmith ['lɔksmɪθ] *n* serrurier *m*

lockup ['lɔkʌp] *n* (*prison*) prison *f*

locum ['ləukəm] *n* (*MED*) suppléant(e) (de médecin)

lodge [lɔdʒ] *n* pavillon *m* (de gardien); (*hunting ~*) pavillon de chasse ♦ *vi* (*person*): **to ~ (with)** être logé(e) (chez), être en pension (chez); (*bullet*) se loger ♦ *vt*: **to ~ a complaint** porter plainte; **~r** *n* locataire *m/f*; (*with meals*) pensionnaire *m/f*;

lodgings *npl* chambre *f*; meublé *m*

loft [lɔft] *n* grenier *m*

lofty ['lɔftɪ] *adj* (*noble*) noble, élevé(e); (*haughty*) hautain(e)

log [lɔg] *n* (*of wood*) bûche *f*; (*book*) = **logbook** ♦ *vt* (*record*) noter; **~book** *n* (*NAUT*) livre *m* or journal *m* de bord; (*AVIAT*) carnet *m* de vol; (*of car*) ≈ carte grise

loggerheads ['lɔgəhɛdz] *npl*: **at ~ (with)** à couteaux tirés (avec)

logic ['lɔdʒɪk] *n* logique *f*; **~al** *adj* logique

log on *vi* (*COMPUT*) se connecter

log off *or* **out** *vi* (*COMPUT*) se déconnecter

loin [lɔɪn] *n* (*CULIN*) filet *m*, longe *f*

loiter ['lɔɪtə*r*] *vi* traîner

loll [lɔl] *vi* (*also*: **~ about**) se prélasser, fainéanter

lollipop ['lɔlɪpɔp] *n* sucette *f*; **~ man/lady** *n* (*BRIT*) *voir encadré*

---

lollipop men/ladies

ⓘ Les **lollipop men/ladies** sont employés pour aider les enfants à traverser la rue à proximité des écoles à l'heure où ils entrent en classe et à la sortie. On les repère facilement à cause de leur long ciré blanc et ils portent une pancarte ronde pour faire signe aux automobilistes de s'arrêter. On les appelle ainsi car la forme circulaire de cette pancarte rappelle une sucette.

---

lolly ['lɔlɪ] (*inf*) *n* (*lollipop*) sucette *f*; (*money*) fric *m*

London ['lʌndən] *n* Londres *m*; **~er** *n* Londonien(ne)

lone [ləun] *adj* solitaire

loneliness ['ləunlɪnɪs] *n* solitude *f*, isolement *m*

lonely ['ləunlɪ] *adj* seul(e); solitaire, isolé(e)

long [lɔŋ] *adj* long (longue) ♦ *adv* longtemps ♦ *vi*: **to ~ for sth** avoir très envie de qch; attendre qch avec impatience; **so** *or* **as ~ as** pourvu que; **don't be ~!** dépêchez-vous!; **how ~ is this river/course?** quelle est la longueur de ce fleuve/la durée de ce cours?; **6 metres ~** (long) de 6 mètres; **6 months ~** qui dure 6 mois, de 6 mois; **all night ~** toute la nuit; **he no ~er comes** il ne vient plus; **I can't stand it any ~er** je ne peux plus le supporter; **~ before/after** longtemps avant/après; **before ~** (+*future*) avant peu, dans peu de temps; (+*past*) peu (de temps) après; **at ~ last** enfin; **~-distance** *adj* (*call*) interurbain(e); **~er** ['lɔŋgə*r*] *adv see* **long**; **~hand** *n* écriture normale *or* courante; **~ing** *n* désir *m*, envie *f*, nostalgie *f*

longitude ['lɔŋgɪtjuːd] *n* longitude *f*

long: **~ jump** *n* saut *m* en longueur; **~-life** *adj* (*batteries etc*) longue durée *inv*; (*milk*) longue conservation; **~-lost** *adj* (*person*) perdu(e) de vue depuis longtemps; **~-range** *adj* à longue portée; **~-sighted** *adj* (*MED*) presbyte; **~-standing** *adj* de longue date; **~-suffering** *adj* empreint(e) d'une patience résignée; extrêmement patient(e); **~-term** *adj* à long terme; **~ wave** *n* grandes ondes; **~-winded** *adj* intarissable, interminable

loo [luː] (*BRIT*: *inf*) *n* W.-C. *mpl*, petit coin

look [luk] *vi* regarder; (*seem*) sembler, paraître, avoir l'air; (*building etc*): **to ~ south/(out) onto the sea** donner au sud/sur la mer ♦ *n* regard *m*; (*appearance*) air *m*, allure *f*, aspect *m*; **~s** *npl* (*good ~s*) physique *m*, beauté *f*; **to have a ~** regarder; **~!** regardez!; **~ (here)!** (*annoyance*) écoutez!; **~ after** *vt fus* (*care for, deal with*) s'occuper de; **~ at** *vt fus* regarder; (*problem etc*) examiner; **~ back** *vi*: **to ~ back on** (*event etc*) évoquer, repenser à; **~ down on** *vt fus* (*fig*) regarder de haut, dédaigner; **~ for** *vt fus* chercher; **~ forward to** *vt fus* attendre avec impatience; **we ~ forward to hearing from you** (*in letter*) dans l'attente de vous lire; **~ into** *vt fus* examiner, étudier; **~ on** *vi* regarder (en spectateur); **~ out** *vi* (*beware*): **to ~ out (for)** prendre garde (à), faire attention (à); **~ out for** *vt fus* être à la recherche de; guetter; **~ round** *vi* regarder derrière soi, se retourner; **~ to** *vt fus* (*rely on*) compter sur; ~ **up** *vi* lever les yeux; (*improve*) s'améliorer ♦ *vt* (*word, name*) chercher; ~ **up to** *vt fus* avoir du respect pour ♦ *n* poste *m* de guet; (*person*) guetteur *m*; **to be on the ~ out (for)** guetter

loom [luːm] *vi* (*also:* ~ **up**) surgir; (*approach: event etc*) être imminent(e); (*threaten*) menacer ♦ *n* (*for weaving*) métier *m* à tisser

loony ['luːnɪ] (*inf*) *adj, n* timbré(e), cinglé(e)

loop [luːp] *n* boucle *f*; ~**hole** *n* (*fig*) porte *f* de sortie; échappatoire *f*

loose [luːs] *adj* (*knot, screw*) desserré(e); (*clothes*) ample, lâche; (*hair*) dénoué(e), épars(e); (*not firmly fixed*) pas solide; (*morals, discipline*) relâché(e) ♦ *n*: **on the ~** en liberté; ~ **change** *n* petite monnaie; ~ **chippings** *npl* (*on road*) gravillons *mpl*; ~ **end** *n*: **to be at a ~ end** *or* (*US*) **at ~ ends** ne pas trop savoir quoi faire; ~**ly** *adv* sans serrer; (*imprecisely*) approximativement; ~**n** *vt* desserrer

loot [luːt] *n* (*inf: money*) pognon *m*, fric *m* ♦ *vt* piller

lopsided ['lɔpˈsaɪdɪd] *adj* de travers, asymétrique

lord [lɔːd] *n* seigneur *m*; **L~ Smith** lord Smith; **the L~** le Seigneur; **good L~!** mon Dieu!; **the (House of) L~s** (*BRIT*) la Chambre des lords; **my L~** = **your Lordship**; **L~ship** *n*: **your L~ship** Monsieur le comte/le baron/le juge; (*to bishop*) Monseigneur

lore [lɔː^r] *n* tradition(s) *f(pl)*

lorry ['lɔrɪ] (*BRIT*) *n* camion *m*; ~ **driver** (*BRIT*) *n* camionneur *m*, routier *m*

lose [luːz] (*pt, pp* **lost**) *vt, vi* perdre; **to ~ (time)** (*clock*) retarder; **to get lost** ♦ *vi* se perdre; ~**r** *n* perdant(e)

loss [lɔs] *n* perte *f*; **to be at a ~** être perplexe *or* embarrassé(e)

lost [lɔst] *pt, pp of* **lose** ♦ *adj* perdu(e); ~ **and found** (*US*), ~ **property** *n* objets trouvés

lot [lɔt] *n* (*set*) lot *m*; **the ~** le tout; **a ~ (of)** beaucoup (de); ~**s of** des tas de; **to**

draw ~s (for sth) tirer (qch) au sort

lotion ['ləʊʃən] *n* lotion *f*

lottery ['lɔtərɪ] *n* loterie *f*

loud [laʊd] *adj* bruyant(e), sonore; (*voice*) fort(e); (*support, condemnation*) vigoureux(-euse); (*gaudy*) voyant(e), tapageur(-euse) ♦ *adv* (*speak etc*) fort; **out ~** tout haut; ~**-hailer** (*BRIT*) *n* porte-voix *m inv*; ~**ly** *adv* fort, bruyamment; ~**speaker** *n* haut-parleur *m*

lounge [laʊndʒ] *n* salon *m*; (*at airport*) salle *f*; (*BRIT: also:* ~ **bar**) (salle de) café *m* or bar *m* ♦ *vi* (*also:* ~ **about or around**) se prélasser, paresser; ~ **suit** (*BRIT*) *n* complet *m*; (*on invitation*) "tenue de ville"

louse [laʊs] (*pl* **lice**) *n* pou *m*

lousy ['laʊzɪ] (*inf*) *adj* infect(e), moche; **I feel ~** je suis mal fichu(e)

lout [laʊt] *n* rustre *m*, butor *m*

lovable ['lʌvəbl] *adj* adorable; très sympathique

love [lʌv] *n* amour *m* ♦ *vt* aimer; (*caringly, kindly*) aimer beaucoup; **"~ (from) Anne"** "affectueusement, Anne"; **I ~ chocolate** j'adore le chocolat; **to be/fall in ~ with** être/tomber amoureux(-euse) de; **to make ~** faire l'amour; **"15 ~"** (*TENNIS*) "15 à rien or zéro"; ~ **affair** *n* liaison (amoureuse); ~ **life** *n* vie sentimentale

lovely ['lʌvlɪ] *adj* (très) joli(e), ravissant(e); (*delightful: person*) charmant(e); (*holiday etc*) (très) agréable

lover ['lʌvə^r] *n* amant *m*; (*person in love*) amoureux(-euse); (*amateur*): **a ~ of** un amateur de; un(e) amoureux(-euse) de

loving ['lʌvɪŋ] *adj* affectueux(-euse), tendre

low [ləʊ] *adj* bas (basse); (*quality*) mauvais(e), inférieur(e); (*person: depressed*) déprimé(e); (: *ill*) bas (basse), affaibli(e) ♦ *adv* bas ♦ *n* (*METEOROLOGY*) dépression *f*; **to be ~ on** être à court de; **to feel ~** se sentir déprimé(e); **to reach an all-time ~** être au plus bas; ~**-alcohol** *adj* peu alcoolisé(e); ~**-calorie** *adj* hypocalorique; ~**-cut** *adj* (*dress*) décolleté(e); ~**er** *adj* inférieur(e) ♦ *vt* abaisser, baisser; ~**er sixth** (*BRIT*) *n* (*SCOL*) première *f*; ~**-fat** *adj* maigre; **~lands** npl (GEO) plaines fpl; **~ly** adj humble, modeste

loyal ['lɔɪəl] adj loyal(e), fidèle; **~ty** n loyauté f, fidélité f; **~ty card** n carte f de fidélité

lozenge ['lɔzɪndʒ] n (MED) pastille f

LP n abbr = **long-playing record**

L-plates ['elpleɪts] (BRIT) npl plaques fpl d'apprenti conducteur

L-plates

i *Les **L-plates** sont des carrés blancs portant un "L" rouge que l'on met à l'avant et à l'arrière de sa voiture pour montrer qu'on n'a pas encore son permis de conduire. Jusqu'à l'obtention du permis, l'apprenti conducteur a un permis provisoire et n'a le droit de conduire que si un conducteur qualifié est assis à côté de lui. Il est interdit aux apprentis conducteurs de circuler sur les autoroutes, même s'ils sont accompagnés.*

Ltd abbr (= limited) ≈ S.A.

lubricant ['lu:brɪkənt] n lubrifiant m

lubricate ['lu:brɪkeɪt] vt lubrifier, graisser

luck [lʌk] n chance f; **bad ~** malchance f, malheur m; **bad** or **hard** or **tough ~!** pas de chance!; **good ~!** bonne chance!; **~ily** adv heureusement, par bonheur; **~y** adj (person) qui a de la chance; (coincidence, event) heureux(-euse); (object) porte-bonheur inv

ludicrous ['lu:dɪkrəs] adj ridicule, absurde

lug [lʌg] (inf) vt traîner, tirer

luggage ['lʌgɪdʒ] n bagages mpl; **~ rack** n (on car) galerie f

lukewarm ['lu:kwɔ:m] adj tiède

lull [lʌl] n accalmie f; (in conversation) pause f ♦ vt: **to ~ sb to sleep** bercer qn pour qu'il s'endorme; **to be ~ed into a false sense of security** s'endormir dans une fausse sécurité

lullaby ['lʌləbaɪ] n berceuse f

lumbago [lʌm'beɪgəu] n lumbago m

lumber ['lʌmbəʳ] n (wood) bois m de charpente; (junk) bric-à-brac m inv; **~jack** n

bûcheron m

luminous ['lu:mɪnəs] adj lumineux(-euse)

lump [lʌmp] n morceau m; (swelling) grosseur f ♦ vt: **to ~ together** réunir, mettre en tas; **~ sum** n somme globale or forfaitaire; **~y** adj (sauce) avec des grumeaux; (bed) défoncé(e), peu confortable

lunar ['lu:nəʳ] adj lunaire

lunatic ['lu:nətɪk] adj fou (folle), cinglé(e) (inf)

lunch [lʌntʃ] n déjeuner m

luncheon ['lʌntʃən] n déjeuner m (chic); **~ meat** n sorte de mortadelle; **~ voucher** (BRIT) n chèque-repas m

lung [lʌŋ] n poumon m

lunge [lʌndʒ] vi (also: **~ forward**) faire un mouvement brusque en avant; **to ~ at** envoyer or assener un coup à

lurch [lə:tʃ] vi vaciller, tituber ♦ n écart m brusque; **to leave sb in the ~** laisser qn se débrouiller or se dépêtrer tout(e) seul(e)

lure [luəʳ] n (attraction) attrait m, charme m ♦ vt attirer or persuader par la ruse

lurid ['luərɪd] adj affreux(-euse), atroce; (pej: colour, dress) criard(e)

lurk [lə:k] vi se tapir, se cacher

luscious ['lʌʃəs] adj succulent(e); appétissant(e)

lush [lʌʃ] adj luxuriant(e)

lust [lʌst] n (sexual) désir m; (fig): **~ for** soif f de; **~y** adj vigoureux(-euse), robuste

Luxembourg ['lʌksəmbə:g] n Luxembourg m

luxurious [lʌg'zjuərɪəs] adj luxueux(-euse)

luxury ['lʌkʃərɪ] n luxe m ♦ cpd de luxe

lying ['laɪɪŋ] n mensonge(s) m(pl) ♦ vb see **lie**

lyrical ['lɪrɪkl] adj lyrique

lyrics ['lɪrɪks] npl (of song) paroles fpl

M, m

m. *abbr* = **metre; mile; million.**

M.A. *abbr* = **Master of Arts**

mac [mæk] *n* (BRIT) imper(méable) *m*

macaroni [mækəˈrəʊnɪ] *n* macaroni *mpl*

machine [məˈʃiːn] *n* machine *f* ♦ *vt* (TECH) façonner à la machine; (*dress etc*) coudre à la machine; ~ **gun** *n* mitrailleuse *f*; ~ **language** *n* (COMPUT) langage-machine *m*; ~**ry** *n* machinerie *f*, machines *fpl*; (*fig*) mécanisme(s) *m(pl)*

mackerel [ˈmækrl] *n inv* maquereau *m*

mackintosh [ˈmækɪntɒʃ] *n* (BRIT) imperméable *m*

mad [mæd] *adj* fou (folle); (*foolish*) insensé(e); (*angry*) furieux(-euse); (*keen*): **to be ~ about** être fou (folle) de

madam [ˈmædəm] *n* madame *f*

madden [ˈmædn] *vt* exaspérer

made [meɪd] *pt, pp of* **make**

Madeira [məˈdɪərə] *n* (GEO) Madère *f*; (*wine*) madère *m*

made-to-measure [ˈmeɪdtəˈmeʒəʳ] (BRIT) *adj* fait(e) sur mesure

madly [ˈmædlɪ] *adv* follement; ~ **in love** éperdument amoureux(-euse)

madman [ˈmædmən] (*irreg*) *n* fou *m*

madness [ˈmædnɪs] *n* folie *f*

magazine [mægəˈziːn] *n* (PRESS) magazine *m*, revue *f*; (RADIO, TV: *also:* ~ **programme**) magazine

maggot [ˈmægət] *n* ver *m*, asticot *m*

magic [ˈmædʒɪk] *n* magie *f* ♦ *adj* magique; ~**al** *adj* magique; (*experience, evening*) merveilleux(-euse); ~**ian** [məˈdʒɪʃən] *n* magicien(ne); (*conjurer*) prestidigitateur *m*

magistrate [ˈmædʒɪstreɪt] *n* magistrat *m*; juge *m*

magnet [ˈmægnɪt] *n* aimant *m*; ~**ic** [mægˈnetɪk] *adj* magnétique

magnificent [mægˈnɪfɪsnt] *adj* superbe, magnifique; (*splendid*: *robe, building*) somptueux(-euse), magnifique

magnify [ˈmægnɪfaɪ] *vt* grossir; (*sound*) amplifier; ~**ing glass** *n* loupe *f*

magnitude [ˈmægnɪtjuːd] *n* ampleur *f*

magpie [ˈmægpaɪ] *n* pie *f*

mahogany [məˈhɒɡənɪ] *n* acajou *m*

maid [meɪd] *n* bonne *f*; **old ~** (*pej*) vieille fille

maiden [ˈmeɪdn] *n* jeune fille *f* ♦ *adj* (*aunt etc*) non mariée; (*speech, voyage*) inaugural(e); ~ **name** *n* nom *m* de jeune fille

mail [meɪl] *n* poste *f*; (*letters*) courrier *m* ♦ *vt* envoyer (par la poste); ~**box** *n* (US) boîte *f* aux lettres; ~**ing list** *n* liste *f* d'adresses; ~-**order** *n* vente *f* or achat *m* par correspondance

maim [meɪm] *vt* mutiler

main [meɪn] *adj* principal(e) ♦ *n*: **the ~(s)** ♦ *n(pl)* (*gas, water*) conduite principale, canalisation *f*; **the ~s** *npl* (ELEC) le secteur; **the ~ thing** l'essentiel; **in the ~** dans l'ensemble; ~**frame** *n* (COMPUT) (gros) ordinateur, unité centrale; ~**land** *n* continent *m*; ~**ly** *adv* principalement, surtout; ~ **road** *n* grand-route *f*; ~**stay** *n* (*fig*) pilier *m*; ~**stream** *n* courant principal

maintain [meɪnˈteɪn] *vt* entretenir; (*continue*) maintenir; (*affirm*) soutenir; **maintenance** [ˈmeɪntənəns] *n* entretien *m*; (*alimony*) pension *f* alimentaire

maize [meɪz] *n* maïs *m*

majestic [məˈdʒestɪk] *adj* majestueux(-euse)

majesty [ˈmædʒɪstɪ] *n* majesté *f*

major [ˈmeɪdʒəʳ] *n* (MIL) commandant *m* ♦ *adj* (*important*) important(e); (*most important*) principal(e); (MUS) majeur(e)

Majorca [məˈjɔːkə] *n* Majorque *f*

majority [məˈdʒɒrɪtɪ] *n* majorité *f*

make [meɪk] (*pt, pp* **made**) *vt* faire; (*manufacture*) faire, fabriquer; (*earn*) gagner; (*cause to be*): **to ~ sb sad** *etc* rendre qn triste *etc*; (*force*): **to ~ sb do sth** obliger qn à faire qch, faire faire qch à qn; (*equal*): **2 and 2 ~ 4** 2 et 2 font 4 ♦ *n* fabrication *f*; (*brand*) marque *f*; **to ~ a fool of sb** (*ridicule*) ridiculiser qn; (*trick*) avoir *or* duper qn; **to ~ a profit** faire *or* des bénéfice(s); **to ~ a loss** essuyer une perte;

to ~ it (*arrive*) arriver; (*achieve sth*) parvenir à qch, réussir; **what time do you ~ it?** quelle heure avez-vous?; **to ~ do with** se contenter de; se débrouiller avec; **~ for** *vt fus* (*place*) se diriger vers; **~ out** *vt* (*write out: cheque*) faire; (*decipher*) déchiffrer; (*understand*) comprendre; (*see*) distinguer; **~ up** *vt* (*constitute*) constituer; (*invent*) inventer, imaginer; (*parcel, bed*) faire ♦ *vi* se réconcilier; (*with cosmetics*) se maquiller; **~ up for** *vt fus* compenser; **~-believe** *n*: **it's just ~-believe** (*game*) c'est pour faire semblant; (*invention*) c'est de l'invention pure; **~r** *n* fabricant *m*; **~shift** *adj* provisoire, improvisé(e); **~-up** *n* maquillage *m*

making ['meɪkɪŋ] *n* (*fig*): **in the ~** en formation *or* gestation; **to have the ~s of** (*actor, athlete etc*) avoir l'étoffe de

malaria [mə'leərɪə] *n* malaria *f*

Malaysia [mə'leɪzɪə] *n* Malaisie *f*

male [meɪl] *n* (*BIO*) mâle *m* ♦ *adj* mâle; (*sex, attitude*) masculin(e); (*child etc*) du sexe masculin

malevolent [mə'lɛvələnt] *adj* malveillant(e)

malfunction [mæl'fʌŋkʃən] *n* fonctionnement défectueux

malice ['mælɪs] *n* méchanceté *f*, malveillance *f*; **malicious** [mə'lɪʃəs] *adj* méchant(e), malveillant(e)

malignant [mə'lɪgnənt] *adj* (*MED*) malin(-igne)

mall [mɔːl] *n* (*also*: **shopping ~**) centre commercial

mallet ['mælɪt] *n* maillet *m*

malpractice [mæl'præktɪs] *n* faute professionnelle; négligence *f*

malt [mɔːlt] *n* malt *m* ♦ *cpd* (*also*: **~ whisky**) pur malt

Malta ['mɔːltə] *n* Malte *f*

mammal ['mæml] *n* mammifère *m*

mammoth ['mæməθ] *n* mammouth *m* ♦ *adj* géant(e), monstre

man [mæn] (*pl* **men**) *n* homme *m* ♦ *vt* (*NAUT: ship*) garnir d'hommes; (*MIL: gun*) servir; (*: post*) être de service à; (*machine*) assurer le fonctionnement de; **an old ~**

un vieillard; **~ and wife** mari et femme

manage ['mænɪdʒ] *vi* se débrouiller ♦ *vt* (*be in charge of*) s'occuper de; (*: business etc*) gérer; (*control: ship*) manier, manœuvrer; (*: person*) savoir s'y prendre avec; **to ~ to do** réussir à faire; **~able** *adj* (*task*) faisable; (*number*) raisonnable; **~ment** *n* gestion *f*, administration *f*, direction *f*; **~r** *n* directeur *m*; administrateur *m*; (*SPORT*) manager *m*; (*of artist*) impresario *m*; **~ress** [mænɪdʒə'rɛs] *n* directrice *f*; gérante *f*; **~rial** [mænɪ'dʒɪərɪəl] *adj* directorial(e); (*skills*) de cadre, de gestion; **managing director** *n* directeur général

mandarin ['mændərɪn] *n* (*also*: **~ orange**) mandarine *f*; (*person*) mandarin *m*

mandatory ['mændətərɪ] *adj* obligatoire

mane [meɪn] *n* crinière *f*

maneuver [mə'nuːvər] (*US*) *vt, vi, n* = **manoeuvre**

manfully ['mænfəlɪ] *adv* vaillamment

mangle ['mæŋgl] *vt* déchiqueter; mutiler

mango ['mæŋgəu] (*pl* **~es**) *n* mangue *f*

mangy ['meɪndʒɪ] *adj* galeux(-euse)

man: **~handle** *vt* malmener; **~hole** *n* trou *m* d'homme; **~hood** *n* âge *m* d'homme; virilité *f*; **~-hour** *n* heure *f* de main-d'œuvre; **~hunt** *n* (*POLICE*) chasse *f* à l'homme

mania ['meɪnɪə] *n* manie *f*; **~c** ['meɪnɪæk] *n* maniaque *m/f*; (*fig*) fou (folle) *m/f*; **manic** ['mænɪk] *adj* maniaque

manicure ['mænɪkjuər] *n* manucure *f*

manifest ['mænɪfɛst] *vt* manifester ♦ *adj* manifeste, évident(e); **~o** [mænɪ'fɛstəu] *n* manifeste *m*

manipulate [mə'nɪpjuleɪt] *vt* manipuler; (*system, situation*) exploiter

man: **~kind** [mæn'kaɪnd] *n* humanité *f*, genre humain; **~ly** *adj* viril(e); **~-made** *adj* artificiel(le); (*fibre*) synthétique

manner ['mænər] *n* manière *f*, façon *f*; (*behaviour*) attitude *f*, comportement *m*; (*sort*): **all ~ of** toutes sortes de; **~s** *npl* (*behaviour*) manières *fpl*; **~ism** *n* particularité *f* de langage (*or* de comportement), tic *m*

manoeuvre [mə'nuːvər] (*US* **maneuver**) *vt*

(*move*) manœuvrer; (*manipulate: person*) manipuler; (: *situation*) exploiter ♦ *vi* manœuvrer ♦ *n* manœuvre *f*

manor ['mænə^r] *n* (*also:* ~ **house**) manoir *m*

manpower ['mænpauə^r] *n* main-d'œuvre *f*

mansion ['mænʃən] *n* château *m*, manoir *m*

manslaughter ['mænslɔːtə^r] *n* homicide *m* involontaire

mantelpiece ['mæntlpiːs] *n* cheminée *f*

manual ['mænjuəl] *adj* manuel(le) ♦ *n* manuel *m*

manufacture [mænju'fæktʃə^r] *vt* fabriquer ♦ *n* fabrication *f*; ~**r** *n* fabricant *m*

manure [mə'njuə^r] *n* fumier *m*

manuscript ['mænjuskrɪpt] *n* manuscrit *m*

many ['mɛnɪ] *adj* beaucoup de, de nombreux(-euses) ♦ *pron* beaucoup, un grand nombre; **a great** ~ un grand nombre (de); ~ **a ...** bien des ..., plus d'un(e) ...

map [mæp] *n* carte *f*; (*of town*) plan *m*; ~ **out** *vt* tracer; (*task*) planifier

maple ['meɪpl] *n* érable *m*

mar [mɑː^r] *vt* gâcher, gâter

marathon ['mærəθən] *n* marathon *m*

marble ['mɑːbl] *n* marbre *m*; (*toy*) bille *f*

March [mɑːtʃ] *n* mars *m*

march [mɑːtʃ] *vi* marcher au pas; (*fig: protesters*) défiler ♦ *n* marche *f*; (*demonstration*) manifestation *f*

mare [mɛə^r] *n* jument *f*

margarine [mɑːdʒə'riːn] *n* margarine *f*

margin ['mɑːdʒɪn] *n* marge *f*; ~**al** (**seat**) *n* (*POL*) siège disputé

marigold ['mærɪgəuld] *n* souci *m*

marijuana [mærɪ'wɑːnə] *n* marijuana *f*

marina [mə'riːnə] *n* (*harbour*) marina *f*

marine [mə'riːn] *adj* marin(e) ♦ *n* fusilier marin; (*US*) marine *m*

marital ['mærɪtl] *adj* matrimonial(e); ~ **status** situation *f* de famille

marjoram ['mɑːdʒərəm] *n* marjolaine *f*

mark [mɑːk] *n* marque *f*; (*of skid etc*) trace *f*; (*BRIT: SCOL*) note *f*; (*currency*) mark *m* ♦ *vt* marquer; (*stain*) tacher; (*BRIT: SCOL*) no-

ter; corriger; **to** ~ **time** marquer le pas; ~**er** *n* (*sign*) jalon *m*; (*bookmark*) signet *m*

market ['mɑːkɪt] *n* marché *m* ♦ *vt* (*COMM*) commercialiser; ~ **garden** (*BRIT*) *n* jardin maraîcher; ~**ing** *n* marketing *m*; ~**place** *n* place *f* du marché; (*COMM*) marché *m*; ~ **research** *n* étude *f* de marché

marksman ['mɑːksmən] (*irreg*) *n* tireur *m* d'élite

marmalade ['mɑːməleɪd] *n* confiture *f* d'oranges

maroon [mə'ruːn] *vt*: **to be ~ed** être abandonné(e); (*fig*) être bloqué(e) ♦ *adj* bordeaux *inv*

marquee [mɑː'kiː] *n* chapiteau *m*

marriage ['mærɪdʒ] *n* mariage *m*; ~ **certificate** *n* extrait *m* d'acte de mariage

married ['mærɪd] *adj* marié(e); (*life, love*) conjugal(e)

marrow ['mærəu] *n* moelle *f*; (*vegetable*) courge *f*

marry ['mærɪ] *vt* épouser, se marier avec; (*subj: father, priest etc*) marier ♦ *vi* (*also:* **get married**) se marier

Mars [mɑːz] *n* (*planet*) Mars *m*

marsh [mɑːʃ] *n* marais *m*, marécage *m*

marshal ['mɑːʃl] *n* maréchal *m*; (*US: fire, police*) ≃ capitaine *m*; (*SPORT*) membre *m* du service d'ordre ♦ *vt* rassembler

marshy ['mɑːʃɪ] *adj* marécageux(-euse)

martyr ['mɑːtə^r] *n* martyr(e); ~**dom** *n* martyre *m*

marvel ['mɑːvl] *n* merveille *f* ♦ *vi*: **to** ~ (**at**) s'émerveiller (de); ~**lous** (*US* **marvelous**) *adj* merveilleux(-euse)

Marxist ['mɑːksɪst] *adj* marxiste ♦ *n* marxiste *m/f*

marzipan ['mɑːzɪpæn] *n* pâte *f* d'amandes

mascara [mæs'kɑːrə] *n* mascara *m*

masculine ['mæskjulɪn] *adj* masculin(e)

mash [mæʃ] *vt* écraser, réduire en purée; ~**ed potatoes** *npl* purée *f* de pommes de terre

mask [mɑːsk] *n* masque *m* ♦ *vt* masquer

mason ['meɪsn] *n* (*also:* **stonemason**) maçon *m*; (*also:* **freemason**) franc-maçon *m*; ~**ry** *n* maçonnerie *f*

masquerade [mæskə'reɪd] *vi*: **to ~ as** se faire passer pour

mass [mæs] *n* multitude *f*, masse *f*; (*PHYSICS*) masse; (*REL*) messe *f* ♦ *cpd* (*communication*) de masse; (*unemployment*) massif(-ive) ♦ *vi* se masser; **the ~es** les masses; **~es of** des tas de

massacre ['mæsəkər] *n* massacre *m*

massage ['mæsɑːʒ] *n* massage *m* ♦ *vt* masser

massive ['mæsɪv] *adj* énorme, massif(-ive)

mass media *n inv* mass-media *mpl*

mass production *n* fabrication *f* en série

mast [mɑːst] *n* mât *m*; (*RADIO*) pylône *m*

master ['mɑːstər] *n* maître *m*; (*in secondary school*) professeur *m*; (*title for boys*): **M~ X** Monsieur X ♦ *vt* maîtriser; (*learn*) apprendre à fond; **~ly** *adj* magistral(e); **~mind** *n* esprit supérieur ♦ *vt* diriger, être le cerveau de; **M~ of Arts/Science** *n* ≈ maîtrise *f* (en lettres/sciences); **~piece** *n* chef-d'œuvre *m*; **~plan** *n* stratégie *f* d'ensemble; **~y** *n* maîtrise *f*; connaissance parfaite

mat [mæt] *n* petit tapis; (*also:* **doormat**) paillasson *m*; (*also:* **tablemat**) napperon *m* ♦ *adj* = **matt**

match [mætʃ] *n* allumette *f*; (*game*) match *m*, partie *f*; (*fig*) égal(e) ♦ *vt* (*also:* **~ up**) assortir; (*go well with*) aller bien avec, s'assortir à; (*equal*) égaler, valoir ♦ *vi* être assorti(e); **to be a good ~** être bien assorti(e); **~box** *n* boîte *f* d'allumettes; **~ing** *adj* assorti(e)

mate [meɪt] *n* (*inf*) copain (copine); (*animal*) partenaire *m/f*, mâle/femelle; (*in merchant navy*) second *m* ♦ *vi* s'accoupler

material [mə'tɪərɪəl] *n* (*substance*) matière *f*, matériau *m*; (*cloth*) tissu *m*, étoffe *f*; (*information, data*) données *fpl* ♦ *adj* matériel(le); (*relevant: evidence*) pertinent(e); **~s** *npl* (*equipment*) matériaux *mpl*

maternal [mə'tə:nl] *adj* maternel(le)

maternity [mə'tə:nɪtɪ] *n* maternité *f*; **~ dress** *n* robe *f* de grossesse; **~ hospital** *n* maternité *f*

mathematical [mæθə'mætɪkl] *adj* mathématique

mathematics [mæθə'mætɪks] *n* mathématiques *fpl*

maths [mæθs] (*US* **math**) *n* math(s) *fpl*

matinée ['mætɪneɪ] *n* matinée *f*

mating call *n* appel *m* du mâle

matrices ['meɪtrɪsi:z] *npl of* **matrix**

matriculation [mətrɪkju'leɪʃən] *n* inscription *f*

matrimonial [mætrɪ'məunɪəl] *adj* matrimonial(e), conjugal(e)

matrimony ['mætrɪmənɪ] *n* mariage *m*

matrix ['meɪtrɪks] (*pl* **matrices**) *n* matrice *f*

matron ['meɪtrən] *n* (*in hospital*) infirmière-chef *f*; (*in school*) infirmière

mat(t) [mæt] *adj* mat(e)

matted ['mætɪd] *adj* emmêlé(e)

matter ['mætər] *n* question *f*; (*PHYSICS*) matière *f*; (*content*) contenu *m*, fond *m*; (*MED: pus*) pus *m* ♦ *vi* importer; **~s** *npl* (*affairs, situation*) la situation; **it doesn't ~** cela n'a pas d'importance; (*I don't mind*) cela ne fait rien; **what's the ~?** qu'est-ce qu'il y a?, qu'est-ce qui ne va pas?; **no ~ what** quoiqu'il arrive; **as a ~ of course** tout naturellement; **as a ~ of fact** en fait; **~-of-fact** *adj* terre à terre; (*voice*) neutre

mattress ['mætrɪs] *n* matelas *m*

mature [mə'tjuər] *adj* mûr(e); (*cheese*) fait(e); (*wine*) arrivé(e) à maturité ♦ *vi* (*person*) mûrir; (*wine, cheese*) se faire

maul [mɔːl] *vt* lacérer

mauve [məuv] *adj* mauve

maximum ['mæksɪməm] (*pl* **maxima**) *adj* maximum ♦ *n* maximum *m*

May [meɪ] *n* mai *m*; **~ Day** *n* le Premier Mai; *see also* **mayday**

may [meɪ] (*conditional* **might**) *vi* (*indicating possibility*): **he ~ come** il se peut qu'il vienne; (*be allowed to*): **~ I smoke?** puis-je fumer?; (*wishes*): **~ God bless you!** (que) Dieu vous bénisse!; **you ~ as well go** à votre place, je partirais

maybe ['meɪbiː] *adv* peut-être; **~ he'll ...** peut-être qu'il ...

mayday ['meɪdeɪ] *n* SOS *m*

mayhem ['meɪhɛm] *n* grabuge *m*

mayonnaise [meɪə'neɪz] *n* mayonnaise *f*

mayor [mɛəʳ] *n* maire *m*; **~ess** *n* épouse *f* du maire

maze [meɪz] *n* labyrinthe *m*, dédale *m*

M.D. *n abbr* (= Doctor of Medicine) titre *universitaire*; = **managing director**

me [miː] *pron* me, m' +*vowel*; (*stressed, after prep*) moi; **he heard ~** il m'a entendu(e); **give ~ a book** donnez-moi un livre; **after ~** après moi

meadow ['mɛdəu] *n* prairie *f*, pré *m*

meagre ['miːgəʳ] (*US* **meager**) *adj* maigre

meal [miːl] *n* repas *m*; (*flour*) farine *f*; **~time** *n* l'heure *f* du repas

mean [miːn] (*pt, pp* **meant**) *adj* (*with money*) avare, radin(e); **he heard ~** méchant(e); (*shabby*) misérable; (*average*) moyen(ne) ♦ *vt* signifier, vouloir dire; (*refer to*) faire allusion à, parler de; (*intend*): **to ~ to do** avoir l'intention de faire ♦ *n* moyenne *f*; **~s** *npl* (*way, money*) moyens *mpl*; **by ~s of** par l'intermédiaire de; au moyen de; **by all ~s!** je vous en prie!; **to be ~t for sb/sth** être destiné(e) à qn/qch; **do you ~ it?** vous êtes sérieux?; **what do you ~?** que voulez-vous dire?

meander [mɪ'ændəʳ] *vi* faire des méandres

meaning ['miːnɪŋ] *n* signification *f*, sens *m*; **~ful** *adj* significatif(-ive); (*relationship, occasion*) important(e); **~less** *adj* dénué(e) de sens

meanness ['miːnnɪs] *n* (*with money*) avarice *f*; (*unkindness*) méchanceté *f*; (*shabbiness*) médiocrité *f*

meant [mɛnt] *pt, pp of* **mean**

meantime ['miːntaɪm] *adv* (*also:* **in the ~**) pendant ce temps

meanwhile ['miːnwaɪl] *adv* = **meantime**

measles ['miːzlz] *n* rougeole *f*

measure ['mɛʒəʳ] *vt, vi* mesurer ♦ *n* mesure *f*; (*ruler*) règle (graduée); **~ments** *npl* mesures *fpl*; **chest/hip ~ment(s)** tour *m* de poitrine/hanches

meat [miːt] *n* viande *f*; **~ball** *n* boulette *f* de viande

Mecca ['mɛkə] *n* La Mecque

mechanic [mɪ'kænɪk] *n* mécanicien *m*; **~al** *adj* mécanique; **~s** *n* (*PHYSICS*) mécanique *f* ♦ *npl* (*of reading, government etc*) mécanisme *m*

mechanism ['mɛkənɪzəm] *n* mécanisme *m*

medal ['mɛdl] *n* médaille *f*; **~lion** [mɪ'dælɪən] *n* médaillon *m*; **~list** (*US* **medalist**) *n* (*SPORT*) médaillé(e)

meddle ['mɛdl] *vi*: **to ~ in** se mêler de, s'occuper de; **to ~ with** toucher à

media ['miːdɪə] *npl* media *mpl*

mediaeval [mɛdɪ'iːvl] *adj* = **medieval**

median ['miːdɪən] (*US*) *n* (*also:* **~ strip**) bande médiane

mediate ['miːdɪeɪt] *vi* servir d'intermédiaire

Medicaid ® ['mɛdɪkeɪd] (*US*) *n* assistance *médicale aux indigents*

medical ['mɛdɪkl] *adj* médical(e) ♦ *n* visite médicale

Medicare ® ['mɛdɪkɛəʳ] (*US*) *n* assistance *médicale aux personnes âgées*

medication [mɛdɪ'keɪʃən] *n* (*drugs*) médicaments *mpl*

medicine ['mɛdsɪn] *n* médecine *f*; (*drug*) médicament *m*

medieval [mɛdɪ'iːvl] *adj* médiéval(e)

mediocre [miːdɪ'əukəʳ] *adj* médiocre

meditate ['mɛdɪteɪt] *vi* méditer

Mediterranean [mɛdɪtə'reɪnɪən] *adj* méditerranéen(ne); **the ~ (Sea)** la (mer) Méditerranée

medium ['miːdɪəm] (*pl* **media**) *adj* moyen(ne) ♦ *n* (*means*) moyen *m*; (*pl* ~s: *person*) médium *m*; **the happy ~** le juste milieu; **~-sized** *adj* de taille moyenne; **~ wave** *n* ondes moyennes

medley ['mɛdlɪ] *n* mélange *m*; (*MUS*) pot-pourri *m*

meek [miːk] *adj* doux (douce), humble

meet [miːt] (*pt, pp* **met**) *vt* rencontrer; (*by arrangement*) retrouver, rejoindre; (*for the first time*) faire la connaissance de; (*go and fetch*): **I'll ~ you at the station** j'irai te chercher à la gare; (*opponent, danger*) faire face à; (*obligations*) satisfaire à ♦ *vi* (*friends*) se rencontrer, se retrouver; (*in* session) se réunir; (join: lines, roads) se rejoindre; ~ with vt fus rencontrer; ~ing n rencontre f; (session: of club etc) réunion f; (POL) meeting m; **she's at a ~ing** (COMM) elle est en conférence

mega ['mɛgə] (inf) adv: **he's ~ rich** il est hyper-riche; **~byte** n (COMPUT) mégaoctet m; **~phone** n porte-voix m inv

melancholy ['mɛlənkəlɪ] n mélancolie f ♦ adj mélancolique

mellow ['mɛləʊ] adj velouté(e); doux (douce); (sound) mélodieux(-euse) ♦ vi (person) s'adoucir

melody ['mɛlədɪ] n mélodie f

melon ['mɛlən] n melon m

melt [mɛlt] vi fondre ♦ vt faire fondre; (metal) fondre; ~ **away** vi fondre complètement; ~ **down** vt fondre; **~down** n fusion f (du cœur d'un réacteur nucléaire); **~ing pot** n (fig) creuset m

member ['mɛmbər] n membre m; **M~ of Parliament** (BRIT) député m; **M~ of the European Parliament** Eurodéputé m; **~ship** n adhésion f; statut m de membre; (members) membres mpl, adhérents mpl; **~ship card** n carte f de membre

memento [mə'mɛntəʊ] n souvenir m

memo ['mɛməʊ] n note f (de service)

memoirs ['mɛmwɑːz] npl mémoires mpl

memorandum [mɛmə'rændəm] (pl **memoranda**) n note f (de service)

memorial [mɪ'mɔːrɪəl] n mémorial m ♦ adj commémoratif(-ive)

memorize ['mɛmərɑɪz] vt apprendre par cœur; retenir

memory ['mɛmərɪ] n mémoire f; (recollection) souvenir m

men [mɛn] npl of **man**

menace ['mɛnɪs] n menace f; (nuisance) plaie f ♦ vt menacer; **menacing** adj menaçant(e)

mend [mɛnd] vt réparer; (darn) raccommoder, repriser ♦ n: **on the ~** en voie de guérison; **to ~ one's ways** s'amender; **~ing** n réparation f; (clothes) raccommodage m

menial ['miːnɪəl] adj subalterne

meningitis [mɛnɪn'dʒɑɪtɪs] n méningite f

menopause ['mɛnəʊpɔːz] n ménopause f

menstruation [mɛnstru'eɪʃən] n menstruation f

mental ['mɛntl] adj mental(e); **~ity** [mɛn'tælɪtɪ] n mentalité f

mention ['mɛnʃən] n mention f ♦ vt mentionner, faire mention de; **don't ~ it!** je vous en prie, il n'y a pas de quoi!

menu ['mɛnjuː] n (set ~, COMPUT) menu m; (list of dishes) carte f

MEP n abbr = **Member of the European Parliament**

mercenary ['mɜːsɪnərɪ] adj intéressé(e), mercenaire ♦ n mercenaire m

merchandise ['mɜːtʃəndɑɪz] n marchandises fpl

merchant ['mɜːtʃənt] n négociant m, marchand m; ~ **bank** (BRIT) n banque f d'affaires; ~ **navy** (US **merchant marine**) n marine marchande

merciful ['mɜːsɪful] adj miséricordieux(-euse), clément(e); **a ~ release** une délivrance

merciless ['mɜːsɪlɪs] adj impitoyable, sans pitié

mercury ['mɜːkjurɪ] n mercure m

mercy ['mɜːsɪ] n pitié f, indulgence f; (REL) miséricorde f; **at the ~ of** à la merci de

mere [mɪər] adj simple; (chance) pur(e); **a ~ two hours** seulement deux heures; **~ly** adv simplement, purement

merge [mɜːdʒ] vt unir ♦ vi (colours, shapes, sounds) se mêler; (roads) se joindre; (COMM) fusionner; **~r** n (COMM) fusion f

meringue [mə'ræŋ] n meringue f

merit ['mɛrɪt] n mérite m, valeur f

mermaid ['mɜːmeɪd] n sirène f

merry ['mɛrɪ] adj gai(e); **M~ Christmas!** Joyeux Noël!; **~-go-round** n manège m

mesh [mɛʃ] n maille f

mesmerize ['mɛzmərɑɪz] vt hypnotiser; fasciner

mess [mɛs] n désordre m, fouillis m, pagaille f; (muddle: of situation) gâchis m; (dirt) saleté f; (MIL) mess m, cantine f; ~ **about** (inf) vi perdre son temps; ~ **about**

with (*inf*) *vt fus* tripoter; ~ **around** (*inf*) *vi* = **mess about**; ~ **around with** *vt fus* = **mess about with**; ~ **up** *vt* (*dirty*) salir; (*spoil*) gâcher

message ['mɛsɪdʒ] *n* message *m*; **messenger** ['mɛsɪndʒəʳ] *n* messager *m*

Messrs ['mɛsəz] *abbr* (*on letters*) MM

messy ['mɛsɪ] *adj* sale; en désordre

met [mɛt] *pt, pp of* **meet**

metal ['mɛtl] *n* métal *m*; **~lic** [mɪ'tælɪk] *adj* métallique

meteorology [miːtɪə'rɔlədʒɪ] *n* météorologie *f*

meter ['miːtəʳ] *n* (*instrument*) compteur *m*; (*also:* **parking ~**) parcomètre *m*; (*US: unit*) = **metre**

method ['mɛθəd] *n* méthode *f*; **~ical** [mɪ'θɔdɪkl] *adj* méthodique; **M~ist** *n* méthodiste *m/f*

meths [mɛθs] (*BRIT*), **methylated spirit** ['mɛθɪleɪtɪd-] (*BRIT*) *n* alcool *m* à brûler

metre ['miːtəʳ] (*US* **meter**) *n* mètre *m*; **metric** ['mɛtrɪk] *adj* métrique

metropolitan [mɛtrə'pɔlɪtn] *adj* métropolitain(e); **the M~ Police** (*BRIT*) la police londonienne

mettle ['mɛtl] *n*: **to be on one's ~** être d'attaque

mew [mjuː] *vi* (*cat*) miauler

mews [mjuːz] (*BRIT*) *n*: **~ cottage** cottage aménagé dans une ancienne écurie

Mexico ['mɛksɪkəu] *n* Mexique *m*

miaow [miː'au] *vi* miauler

mice [maɪs] *npl of* **mouse**

micro ['maɪkrəu] *n* (*also:* **~computer**) micro-ordinateur *m*; **~chip** *n* puce *f*; **~phone** *n* microphone *m*; **~scope** *n* microscope *m*; **~wave** *n* (*also:* **~wave oven**) four *m* à micro-ondes

mid [mɪd] *adj*: **in ~ May** à la mi-mai; ~ **afternoon** le milieu de l'après-midi; **in ~ air** en plein ciel; **~day** *n* midi *m*

middle ['mɪdl] *n* milieu *m*; (*waist*) taille *f* ♦ *adj* du milieu; (*average*) moyen(ne); **in the ~ of the night** au milieu de la nuit; **~-aged** *adj* d'un certain âge; **M~ Ages** *npl*: **the M~ Ages** le moyen âge; **~-class**

adj ≈ bourgeois(e); ~ **class(es)** *n(pl)*: **the ~ class(es)** ≈ les classes moyennes; **M~ East** *n* Proche-Orient *m*, Moyen-Orient *m*; **~man** (*irreg*) *n* intermédiaire *m*; ~ **name** *n* deuxième nom *m*; **~-of-the-road** *adj* (*politician*) modéré(e); (*music*) neutre; **~weight** *n* (*BOXING*) poids moyen; **middling** *adj* moyen(ne)

midge [mɪdʒ] *n* moucheron *m*

midget ['mɪdʒɪt] *n* nain(e)

Midlands ['mɪdləndz] *npl* comtés du centre de l'Angleterre

midnight ['mɪdnaɪt] *n* minuit *m*

midriff ['mɪdrɪf] *n* estomac *m*, taille *f*

midst [mɪdst] *n*: **in the ~ of** au milieu de

midsummer [mɪd'sʌməʳ] *n* milieu *m* de l'été

midway [mɪd'weɪ] *adj, adv*: ~ **(between)** à mi-chemin (entre); ~ **through ...** au milieu de ..., en plein(e) ...

midweek [mɪd'wiːk] *adj* au milieu de la semaine

midwife ['mɪdwaɪf] (*pl* **midwives**) *n* sage-femme *f*

might [maɪt] *vb see* **may** ♦ *n* puissance *f*, force *f*; **~y** *adj* puissant(e)

migraine ['miːgreɪn] *n* migraine *f*

migrant ['maɪgrənt] *adj* (*bird*) migrateur(-trice); (*worker*) saisonnier(-ère)

migrate [maɪ'greɪt] *vi* émigrer

mike [maɪk] *n abbr* (= **microphone**) micro *m*

mild [maɪld] *adj* doux (douce); (*reproach, infection*) léger(-ère); (*illness*) bénin(-igne); (*interest*) modéré(e); (*taste*) peu relevé(e) ♦ *n* (*beer*) bière légère; **~ly** *adv* doucement; légèrement; **to put it ~ly** c'est le moins qu'on puisse dire

mile [maɪl] *n* mi(l)le *m* (= 1609 m); **~age** *n* distance *f* en miles; ≈ kilométrage *m*; **~ometer** [maɪ'lɔmɪtəʳ] *n* compteur *m* (kilométrique); **~stone** *n* borne *f*; (*fig*) jalon *m*

militant ['mɪlɪtnt] *adj* militant(e)

military ['mɪlɪtərɪ] *adj* militaire

militia [mɪ'lɪʃə] *n* milice(s) *f(pl)*

milk [mɪlk] *n* lait *m* ♦ *vt* (*cow*) traire; (*fig: person*) dépouiller, plumer; (: *situation*) exploiter à fond; ~ **chocolate** n chocolat m au lait; ~**man** (*irreg*) n laitier m; ~ **shake** n milk-shake m; ~**y** adj (*drink*) au lait; (*colour*) laiteux(-euse); **M~y Way** n voie lactée

mill [mɪl] n moulin m; (*steel* ~) aciérie f; (*spinning* ~) filature f; (*flour* ~) minoterie f ♦ vt moudre, broyer ♦ vi (*also:* ~ **about**) grouiller; ~**er** n meunier m

millennium bug [mɪˈlɛnɪəm-] n bogue m or bug m de l'an 2000

milligram(me) [ˈmɪlɪɡræm] n milligramme m

millimetre [ˈmɪlɪmiːtəʳ] (*US* **millimeter**) n millimètre m

million [ˈmɪljən] n million m

milometer [maɪˈlɔmɪtəʳ] n ≈ compteur m kilométrique

mime [maɪm] n mime m ♦ vt, vi mimer; **mimic** [ˈmɪmɪk] n imitateur(-trice) ♦ vt imiter, contrefaire

min. *abbr* = **minute(s)**; **minimum**

mince [mɪns] vt hacher ♦ n (*BRIT: CULIN*) viande hachée, hachis m; ~**meat** n (*fruit*) hachis de fruits secs utilisé en pâtisserie; (*US: meat*) viande hachée, hachis; ~ **pie** n (*sweet*) sorte de tarte aux fruits secs; ~**r** n hachoir m

mind [maɪnd] n esprit m ♦ vt (*attend to, look after*) s'occuper de; (*be careful*) faire attention à; (*object to*): **I don't ~ the noise** le bruit ne me dérange pas; **I don't ~** cela ne me dérange pas; **it is on my ~** cela me préoccupe; **to my ~** à mon avis *or* sens; **to be out of one's ~** ne plus avoir toute sa raison; **to keep** *or* **bear sth in ~** tenir compte de qch; **to make up one's ~** se décider; ~ **you, ...** remarquez ...; **never ~** ça ne fait rien; (*don't worry*) ne vous en faites pas; **"~ the step"** "attention à la marche"; ~**er** n (*child-minder*) gardienne f; (*inf: bodyguard*) ange gardien (*fig*); ~**ful** adj: ~**ful of** attentif(-ive) à, soucieux(-euse) de; ~**less** adj irréfléchi(e); (*boring: job*) idiot(e)

mine[1] [maɪn] *pron* le (la) mien(ne), les miens (miennes) ♦ adj: **this book is ~** ce livre est à moi

mine[2] [maɪn] n mine f ♦ vt (*coal*) extraire; (*ship*) miner; ~**field** n champ m de mines; (*fig*) situation (très délicate); ~**r** n mineur m

mineral [ˈmɪnərəl] adj minéral(e) ♦ n minéral m; ~**s** npl (*BRIT: soft drinks*) boissons gazeuses; ~ **water** n eau minérale

mingle [ˈmɪŋɡl] vi: **to ~ with** se mêler à

miniature [ˈmɪnətʃəʳ] adj (en) miniature ♦ n miniature f

minibus [ˈmɪnɪbʌs] n minibus m

Minidisc ® [ˈmɪnɪdɪsk] n minidisque m, Minidisc ® f

minimal [ˈmɪnɪml] adj minime

minimize [ˈmɪnɪmaɪz] vt (*reduce*) réduire au minimum; (*play down*) minimiser

minimum [ˈmɪnɪməm] (*pl* **minima**) adj, n minimum m

mining [ˈmaɪnɪŋ] n exploitation minière

minister [ˈmɪnɪstəʳ] n (*BRIT: POL*) ministre m; (*REL*) pasteur m ♦ vi: **to ~ to sb('s needs)** pourvoir aux besoins de qn; ~**ial** [mɪnɪsˈtɪərɪəl] (*BRIT*) adj (*POL*) ministériel(le); **ministry** n (*BRIT: POL*) ministère m; (*REL*): **to go into the ministry** devenir pasteur

mink [mɪŋk] n vison m

minor [ˈmaɪnəʳ] adj petit(e), de peu d'importance; (*MUS, poet, problem*) mineur(e) ♦ n (*LAW*) mineur(e)

minority [maɪˈnɔrɪtɪ] n minorité f

mint [mɪnt] n (*plant*) menthe f; (*sweet*) bonbon m à la menthe ♦ vt (*coins*) battre; **the (Royal) M~**, (*US*) **the (US) M~** ≈ l'Hôtel m de la Monnaie; **in ~ condition** à l'état de neuf

minus [ˈmaɪnəs] n (*also:* ~ **sign**) signe m moins ♦ *prep* moins

minute[1] [maɪˈnjuːt] adj minuscule; (*detail, search*) minutieux(-euse)

minute[2] [ˈmɪnɪt] n minute f; ~**s** npl (*official record*) procès-verbal, compte rendu

miracle [ˈmɪrəkl] n miracle m

mirror [ˈmɪrəʳ] n miroir m, glace f; (*in car*) rétroviseur m

mirth [mɜːθ] n gaieté f

misadventure [mɪsədˈvɛntʃəʳ] n mésaventure f

misapprehension ['mɪsæprɪ'henʃən] n malentendu m, méprise f

misappropriate [mɪsə'prəuprɪeɪt] vt détourner

misbehave [mɪsbɪ'heɪv] vi mal se conduire

miscalculate [mɪs'kælkjuleɪt] vt mal calculer

miscarriage ['mɪskærɪdʒ] n (MED) fausse couche; **~ of justice** erreur f judiciaire

miscellaneous [mɪsɪ'leɪnɪəs] adj (items) divers(es); (selection) varié(e)

mischief ['mɪstʃɪf] n (naughtiness) sottises fpl; (fun) farce f; (playfulness) espièglerie f; (maliciousness) méchanceté f; **mischievous** ['mɪstʃɪvəs] adj (playful, naughty) coquin(e), espiègle

misconception [mɪskən'sepʃən] n idée fausse

misconduct [mɪs'kɔndʌkt] n inconduite f; **professional ~** faute professionnelle

misdemeanour [mɪsdɪ'miːnər] (US **misdemeanor**) n écart m de conduite; infraction f

miser ['maɪzər] n avare m/f

miserable ['mɪzərəbl] adj (person, expression) malheureux(-euse); (conditions) misérable; (weather) maussade; (offer, donation) minable; (failure) pitoyable

miserly ['maɪzəlɪ] adj avare

misery ['mɪzərɪ] n (unhappiness) tristesse f; (pain) souffrances fpl; (wretchedness) misère f

misfire [mɪs'faɪər] vi rater

misfit ['mɪsfɪt] n (person) inadapté(e)

misfortune [mɪs'fɔːtʃən] n malchance f, malheur m

misgiving [mɪs'gɪvɪŋ] n (apprehension) craintes fpl; **to have ~s about** avoir des doutes quant à

misguided [mɪs'gaɪdɪd] adj malavisé(e)

mishandle [mɪs'hændl] vt (mismanage) mal s'y prendre pour faire or résoudre etc

mishap ['mɪshæp] n mésaventure f

misinform [mɪsɪn'fɔːm] vt mal renseigner

misinterpret [mɪsɪn'tɜːprɪt] vt mal interpréter

misjudge [mɪs'dʒʌdʒ] vt méjuger

mislay [mɪs'leɪ] (irreg: like **lay**) vt égarer

mislead [mɪs'liːd] (irreg: like **lead**) vt induire en erreur; **~ing** adj trompeur(-euse)

mismanage [mɪs'mænɪdʒ] vt mal gérer

misplace [mɪs'pleɪs] vt égarer

misprint ['mɪsprɪnt] n faute f d'impression

Miss [mɪs] n Mademoiselle

miss [mɪs] vt (fail to get, attend or see) manquer, rater; (regret the absence of): **I ~ him/it** il/cela me manque ♦ vi manquer ♦ n (shot) coup manqué; **~ out** (BRIT) vt oublier

misshapen [mɪs'ʃeɪpən] adj difforme

missile ['mɪsaɪl] n (MIL) missile m; (object thrown) projectile m

missing ['mɪsɪŋ] adj manquant(e); (after escape, disaster: person) disparu(e); **to go ~** disparaître; **to be ~** avoir disparu

mission ['mɪʃən] n mission f; **~ary** ['mɪʃənrɪ] n missionnaire m/f; **~ statement** n déclaration f d'intention

mist [mɪst] n brume f ♦ vi (also: **~ over**: eyes) s'embuer; (: windows etc) s'embuer; **~ over** vi (windows etc) s'embuer; **~ up** vi = **mist over**

mistake [mɪs'teɪk] (irreg: like **take**) n erreur f, faute f ♦ vt (meaning, remark) mal comprendre; se méprendre sur; **to make a ~** se tromper, faire une erreur; **by ~** par erreur, par inadvertance; **to ~ for** prendre pour; **~n** pp of **mistake** ♦ adj (idea etc) erroné(e); **to be ~n** faire erreur, se tromper

mister ['mɪstər] (inf) n Monsieur m; see also **Mr**

mistletoe ['mɪsltəu] n gui m

mistook [mɪs'tuk] pt of **mistake**

mistress ['mɪstrɪs] n maîtresse f; (BRIT: in primary school) institutrice f; (: in secondary school) professeur m

mistrust [mɪs'trʌst] vt se méfier de

misty ['mɪstɪ] adj brumeux(-euse); (glasses, window) embué(e)

misunderstand [mɪsʌndə'stænd] (irreg) vt, vi mal comprendre; **~ing** n méprise f, malentendu m

misuse [n mɪs'juːs, vb mɪs'juːz] n mauvais

emploi; (*of power*) abus *m* ♦ *vt* mal employer; abuser de; **~ of funds** détournement *m* de fonds

mitigate ['mɪtɪgeɪt] *vt* atténuer

mitt(en) ['mɪt(n)] *n* mitaine *f*; moufle *f*

mix [mɪks] *vt* mélanger; (*sauce, drink etc*) préparer ♦ *vi* se mélanger; (*socialize*): **he doesn't ~ well** il est peu sociable ♦ *n* mélange *m*; **to ~ with** (*people*) fréquenter; **~ up** *vt* mélanger; (*confuse*) confondre; **~ed** *adj* (*feelings, reactions*) contradictoire; (*salad*) mélangé(e); (*school, marriage*) mixte; **~ed grill** *n* assortiment *m* de grillades; **~ed-up** *adj* (*confused*) désorienté(e), embrouillé(e); **~er** *n* (*for food*) batteur *m*, mixer *m*; (*person*): **he is a good ~er** il est très liant; **~ture** *n* assortiment *m*, mélange *m*; (*MED*) préparation *f*; **~-up** *n* confusion *f*

mm *abbr* (= *millimetre*) mm

moan [məʊn] *n* gémissement *m* ♦ *vi* gémir; (*inf: complain*): **to ~ (about)** se plaindre (de)

moat [məʊt] *n* fossé *m*, douves *fpl*

mob [mɒb] *n* foule *f*; (*disorderly*) cohue *f* ♦ *vt* assaillir

mobile ['məʊbaɪl] *adj* mobile ♦ *n* mobile *m*; **~ home** *n* (grande) caravane *f*; **~ phone** *n* téléphone portatif

mock [mɒk] *vt* ridiculiser; (*laugh at*) se moquer de ♦ *adj* faux (fausse); **~ exam** examen blanc; **~ery** *n* moquerie *f*, raillerie *f*; **to make a ~ery of** tourner en dérision; **~-up** *n* maquette *f*

mod [mɒd] *adj see* **convenience**

mode [məʊd] *n* mode *m*

model ['mɒdl] *n* modèle *m*; (*person: for fashion*) mannequin *m*; (: *for artist*) modèle *m* ♦ *vt* (*with clay etc*) modeler ♦ *vi* travailler comme mannequin ♦ *adj* (*railway: toy*) modèle réduit *inv*; (*child, factory*) modèle; **to ~ clothes** présenter des vêtements; **to ~ o.s. on** imiter

modem ['məʊdɛm] *n* (*COMPUT*) modem *m*

moderate [*adj* 'mɒdərət, *vb* 'mɒdəreɪt] *adj* modéré(e); (*amount, change*) peu important(e) ♦ *vi* se calmer ♦ *vt* modérer

modern ['mɒdən] *adj* moderne; **~ize** *vt* moderniser

modest ['mɒdɪst] *adj* modeste; **~y** *n* modestie *f*

modify ['mɒdɪfaɪ] *vt* modifier

mogul ['məʊgl] *n* (*fig*) nabab *m*

mohair ['məʊhɛə*r*] *n* mohair *m*

moist [mɔɪst] *adj* humide, moite; **~en** *vt* humecter, mouiller légèrement; **~ure** *n* humidité *f*; **~urizer** *n* produit hydratant

molar ['məʊlə*r*] *n* molaire *f*

molasses [mə'læsɪz] *n* mélasse *f*

mold [məʊld] (*US*) *n*, *vt* = **mould**

mole [məʊl] *n* (*animal, fig: spy*) taupe *f*; (*spot*) grain *m* de beauté

molest [mə'lɛst] *vt* (*harass*) molester; (*LAW: sexually*) attenter à la pudeur de

mollycoddle ['mɒlɪkɒdl] *vt* chouchouter, couver

molt [məʊlt] (*US*) *vi* = **moult**

molten ['məʊltən] *adj* fondu(e); (*rock*) en fusion

mom [mɒm] (*US*) *n* = **mum**

moment ['məʊmənt] *n* moment *m*, instant *m*; **at the ~** en ce moment; **at that ~** à ce moment-là; **~ary** *adj* momentané(e), passager(-ère); **~ous** [məʊ'mɛntəs] *adj* important(e), capital(e)

momentum [məʊ'mɛntəm] *n* élan *m*, vitesse acquise; (*fig*) dynamique *f*; **to gather ~** prendre de la vitesse

mommy ['mɒmɪ] (*US*) *n* maman *f*

Monaco ['mɒnəkəʊ] *n* Monaco *m*

monarch ['mɒnək] *n* monarque *m*; **~y** *n* monarchie *f*

monastery ['mɒnəstərɪ] *n* monastère *m*

Monday ['mʌndɪ] *n* lundi *m*

monetary ['mʌnɪtərɪ] *adj* monétaire

money ['mʌnɪ] *n* argent *m*; **to make ~** gagner de l'argent; **~ belt** *n* ceinture-portefeuille *f*; **~ order** *n* mandat *m*; **~-spinner** (*inf*) *n* mine *f* d'or (*fig*)

mongrel ['mʌŋgrəl] *n* (*dog*) bâtard *m*

monitor ['mɒnɪtə*r*] *n* (*TV, COMPUT*) moniteur *m* ♦ *vt* contrôler; (*broadcast*) être à l'écoute de; (*progress*) suivre (de près)

monk [mʌŋk] *n* moine *m*

monkey ['mʌŋkı] *n* singe *m*; ~ **nut** (BRIT) *n* cacahuète *f*

monopoly [mə'nɒpəlı] *n* monopole *m*

monotone ['mɒnətəun] *n* ton *m* (*or* voix *f*) monocorde; **monotonous** [mə'nɒtənəs] *adj* monotone

monsoon [mɒn'su:n] *n* mousson *f*

monster ['mɒnstəʳ] *n* monstre *m*; **monstrous** ['mɒnstrəs] *adj* monstrueux(-euse); (*huge*) gigantesque

month [mʌnθ] *n* mois *m*; ~**ly** *adj* mensuel(le) ♦ *adv* mensuellement

monument ['mɒnjumənt] *n* monument *m*

moo [mu:] *vi* meugler, beugler

mood [mu:d] *n* humeur *f*, disposition *f*; **to be in a good/bad ~** être de bonne/mauvaise humeur; ~**y** *adj* (*variable*) d'humeur changeante, lunatique; (*sullen*) morose, maussade

moon [mu:n] *n* lune *f*; ~**light** *n* clair *m* de lune; ~**lighting** *n* travail *m* au noir; ~**lit** *adj*: **a ~lit night** une nuit de lune

moor [muəʳ] *n* lande *f* ♦ *vt* (*ship*) amarrer ♦ *vi* mouiller; ~**land** *n* lande *f*

moose [mu:s] *n inv* élan *m*

mop [mɒp] *n* balai *m* à laver; (*for dishes*) lavette *f* (à vaisselle) ♦ *vt* essuyer; ~ **of hair** tignasse *f*; ~ **up** *vt* éponger

mope [məup] *vi* avoir le cafard, se morfondre

moped ['məupɛd] *n* cyclomoteur *m*

moral ['mɒrl] *adj* moral(e) ♦ *n* morale *f*; ~**s** *npl* (*attitude, behaviour*) moralité *f*

morale [mɒ'rɑ:l] *n* moral *m*

morality [mə'rælıtı] *n* moralité *f*

morass [mə'ræs] *n* marais *m*, marécage *m*

KEYWORD

more [mɔ:ʳ] *adj* **1** (*greater in number etc*) plus (de), davantage; **more people/work (than)** plus de gens/de travail (que)

2 (*additional*) encore (de); **do you want (some) more tea?** voulez-vous encore de thé?; **I have no** *or* **I don't have any more money** je n'ai plus d'argent; **it'll take a few more weeks** ça prendra encore quelques semaines

♦ *pron* plus, davantage; **more than 10** plus de 10; **it cost more than we expected** cela a coûté plus que prévu; **I want more** j'en veux plus *or* davantage; **is there any more?** est-ce qu'il en reste?; **there's no more** il n'y en a plus; **a little more** un peu plus; **many/much more** beaucoup plus, bien davantage

♦ *adv*: **more dangerous/easily (than)** plus dangereux/facilement (que); **more and more expensive** de plus en plus cher; **more or less** plus ou moins; **more than ever** plus que jamais

moreover [mɔ:'rəuvəʳ] *adv* de plus

morning ['mɔ:nıŋ] *n* matin *m*; matinée *f* ♦ *cpd* matinal(e); (*paper*) du matin; **in the ~** le matin; **7 o'clock in the ~** 7 heures du matin; ~ **sickness** *n* nausées matinales

Morocco [mə'rɒkəu] *n* Maroc *m*

moron ['mɔ:rɒn] (*inf*) *n* idiot(e)

Morse [mɔ:s] *n*: ~ **code** morse *m*

morsel ['mɔ:sl] *n* bouchée *f*

mortar ['mɔ:təʳ] *n* mortier *m*

mortgage ['mɔ:gɪdʒ] *n* hypothèque *f*; (*loan*) prêt *m* (*or* crédit *m*) hypothécaire ♦ *vt* hypothéquer; ~ **company** (US) *n* société *f* de crédit immobilier

mortuary ['mɔ:tjuərı] *n* morgue *f*

mosaic [məu'zeıık] *n* mosaïque *f*

Moscow ['mɒskəu] *n* Moscou

Moslem ['mɒzləm] *adj*, *n* = **Muslim**

mosque [mɒsk] *n* mosquée *f*

mosquito [mɒs'ki:təu] (*pl* ~**es**) *n* moustique *m*

moss [mɒs] *n* mousse *f*

most [məust] *adj* la plupart de; le plus de ♦ *pron* la plupart ♦ *adv* le plus; (*very*) très, extrêmement; **the ~** (*also:* + *adjective*) le plus; ~ **of** la plus grande partie de; ~ **of them** la plupart d'entre eux; **I saw (the)** ~ j'en ai vu la plupart; c'est moi qui en ai vu le plus; **at the (very) ~** au plus; **to make the ~ of** profiter au maximum de; ~**ly** *adv* (*chiefly*) surtout; (*usually*) généralement

MOT *n abbr* (BRIT: *Ministry of Transport*):

the MOT (test) la visite technique (annuelle) obligatoire des véhicules à moteur

motel [məʊˈtɛl] n motel m

moth [mɒθ] n papillon m de nuit; (in clothes) mite f

mother [ˈmʌðəʳ] n mère f ♦ vt (act as ~ to) servir de mère à; (pamper, protect) materner; **~ country** mère patrie; **~hood** n maternité f; **~-in-law** n belle-mère f; **~ly** adj maternel(le); **~-of-pearl** n nacre f; **M~'s Day** n fête f des Mères; **~-to-be** n future maman; **~ tongue** n langue maternelle

motion [ˈməʊʃən] n mouvement m; (gesture) geste m; (at meeting) motion f ♦ vt, vi: **to ~ (to) sb to do** faire signe à qn de faire; **~less** adj immobile, sans mouvement; **~ picture** n film m

motivated [ˈməʊtɪveɪtɪd] adj motivé(e); **motivation** [məʊtɪˈveɪʃən] n motivation f

motive [ˈməʊtɪv] n motif m, mobile m

motley [ˈmɒtlɪ] adj hétéroclite

motor [ˈməʊtəʳ] n moteur m; (BRIT: inf: vehicle) auto f ♦ cpd (industry, vehicle) automobile; **~bike** n moto f; **~boat** n bateau m à moteur; **~car** (BRIT) n automobile f; **~cycle** n vélomoteur m; **~cycle racing** n course f de motos; **~cyclist** n motocycliste m/f; **~ing** (BRIT) n tourisme m automobile; **~ist** n automobiliste m/f; **~ mechanic** n mécanicien m garagiste; **~ racing** (BRIT) n course f automobile; **~way** (BRIT) n autoroute f

mottled [ˈmɒtld] adj tacheté(e), marbré(e)

motto [ˈmɒtəʊ] (pl **~es**) n devise f

mould [məʊld] (US **mold**) n moule m; (mildew) moisissure f ♦ vt mouler, modeler; (fig) façonner; **mo(u)ldy** adj moisi(e); (smell) de moisi

moult [məʊlt] (US **molt**) vi muer

mound [maʊnd] n monticule m, tertre m; (heap) monceau m, tas m

mount [maʊnt] n mont m, montagne f ♦ vt monter ♦ vi (inflation, tension) augmenter; (also: **~ up**: problems etc) s'accumuler; **~ up** vi (bills, costs, savings) s'accumuler

mountain [ˈmaʊntɪn] n montagne f ♦ cpd de montagne; **~ bike** n VTT m, vélo tout-terrain; **~eer** [maʊntɪˈnɪəʳ] n alpiniste m/f; **~eering** n alpinisme m; **~ous** adj montagneux(-euse); **~ rescue team** n équipe f de secours en montagne; **~side** n flanc m or versant m de la montagne

mourn [mɔːn] vt pleurer ♦ vi: **to ~ (for)** (person) pleurer (la mort de); **~er** n parent(e) or ami(e) du défunt; personne f en deuil; **~ing** n deuil m; **in ~ing** en deuil

mouse [maʊs] (pl **mice**) n (also COMPUT) souris f; **~ mat**, **~ pad** n (COMPUT) tapis m de souris; **~trap** n souricière f

mousse [muːs] n mousse f

moustache [məsˈtɑːʃ] (US **mustache**) n moustache(s) f(pl)

mousy [ˈmaʊsɪ] adj (hair) d'un châtain terne

mouth [maʊθ] (pl **~s**) n bouche f; (of dog, cat) gueule f; (of river) embouchure f; (of hole, cave) ouverture f; **~ful** n bouchée f; **~ organ** n harmonica m; **~piece** n (of musical instrument) embouchure f; (spokesman) porte-parole m inv; **~wash** n eau f dentifrice; **~-watering** adj qui met l'eau à la bouche

movable [ˈmuːvəbl] adj mobile

move [muːv] n (~ment) mouvement m; (in game) coup m; (: turn to play) tour m; (change: of house) déménagement m; (: of job) changement m d'emploi ♦ vt déplacer, bouger; (emotionally) émouvoir; (POL: resolution etc) proposer; (in game) jouer ♦ vi (gen) bouger, remuer; (traffic) circuler; (also: **~ house**) déménager; (situation) progresser; **that was a good ~** bien joué!; **to get a ~ on** se dépêcher, se remuer; **to ~ sb to do sth** pousser or inciter qn à faire qch; **~ about** vi (fidget) remuer; (travel) voyager, se déplacer; (change residence, job) ne pas rester au même endroit; **~ along** vi se pousser; **~ around** vi = **move about**; **~ away** vi s'en aller; **~ back** vi revenir, retourner; **~ forward** vi avancer; **~ in** vi (to a house) emménager; (police, soldiers) intervenir; **~ on** vi se remettre en route; **~ out** vi (of house) déménager; **~ over** vi se pousser, se déplacer; **~ up** *vi* (*pupil*) passer dans la classe supérieure; (*employee*) avoir de l'avancement; **~able** *adj* = **movable**

movement ['mu:vmənt] *n* mouvement *m*

movie ['mu:vi] *n* film *m*; **the ~s** le cinéma

moving ['mu:vɪŋ] *adj* en mouvement; (*emotional*) émouvant(e)

mow [məu] (*pt* **mowed**, *pp* **mowed** or **mown**) *vt* faucher; (*lawn*) tondre; **~ down** *vt* faucher; **~er** *n* (*also:* **lawn-mower**) tondeuse *f* à gazon

MP *n abbr* = **Member of Parliament**

MP3 *abbr:* **~player** lecteur *m* MP3

mph *abbr* = **miles per hour**

Mr ['mɪstər] *n:* **~ Smith** Monsieur Smith, M. Smith

Mrs ['mɪsɪz] *n:* **~ Smith** Madame Smith, Mme Smith

Ms [mɪz] *n* (= **Miss** or **Mrs**): **~ Smith** Madame Smith, Mme Smith

MSc *abbr* = **Master of Science**

MSP *n abbr* = (**Member of the Scottish Parliament**) député *m* au Parlement écossais

much [mʌtʃ] *adj* beaucoup de ♦ *adv*, *n*, *pron* beaucoup; **how ~ is it?** combien est-ce que ça coûte?; **too ~** trop (de); **as ~ as** autant de

muck [mʌk] *n* (*dirt*) saleté *f*; **~ about** or **around** (*inf*) *vi* faire l'imbécile; **~ up** (*inf*) *vt* (*exam, interview*) se planter à (*fam*); **~y** *adj* (*très*) sale

mud [mʌd] *n* boue *f*

muddle ['mʌdl] *n* (*mess*) pagaille *f*, désordre *m*; (*mix-up*) confusion *f* ♦ *vt* (*also:* **~ up**) embrouiller; **~ through** *vi* se débrouiller

muddy ['mʌdɪ] *adj* boueux(-euse)

mudguard ['mʌdgɑːd] *n* garde-boue *m inv*

muesli ['mju:zlɪ] *n* muesli *m*

muffle ['mʌfl] *vt* (*sound*) assourdir, étouffer; (*against cold*) emmitoufler; **~d** *adj* (*sound*) étouffé(e); **~r** *n* (*US*) (*AUT*) silencieux *m*

mug [mʌg] *n* (*cup*) grande tasse (*sans soucoupe*); (: *for beer*) chope *f*; (*inf: face*) bouille *f*; (: *fool*) poire *f* ♦ *vt* (*assault*) agresser; **~ger** *n* agresseur *m*; **~ging** *n* agression *f*

muggy ['mʌgɪ] *adj* lourd(e), moite

multi-level ['mʌltɪlevl] (*US*) *adj* = **multi-storey**

multiple ['mʌltɪpl] *adj* multiple ♦ *n* multiple *m*; **~ sclerosis** [-sklɪ'rəusɪs] *n* sclérose *f* en plaques

multiplex cinema ['mʌltɪpleks-] *n* cinéma *m* multisalles

multiplication [mʌltɪplɪ'keɪʃən] *n* multiplication *f*; **multiply** ['mʌltɪplaɪ] *vt* multiplier ♦ *vi* se multiplier

multistorey ['mʌltɪ'stɔːrɪ] (*BRIT*) *adj* (*building*) à étages; (*car park*) à étages or niveaux multiples ♦ *n* (*car park*) parking *m* à plusieurs étages

mum [mʌm] (*BRIT*: *inf*) *n* maman *f* ♦ *adj:* **to keep ~** ne pas souffler mot

mumble ['mʌmbl] *vt*, *vi* marmotter, marmonner

mummy ['mʌmɪ] *n* (*BRIT*: *mother*) maman *f*; (*embalmed*) momie *f*

mumps [mʌmps] *n* oreillons *mpl*

munch [mʌntʃ] *vt*, *vi* mâcher

mundane [mʌn'deɪn] *adj* banal(e), terre à terre *inv*

municipal [mju:'nɪsɪpl] *adj* municipal(e)

murder ['mɜːdər] *n* meurtre *m*, assassinat *m* ♦ *vt* assassiner; **~er** *n* meurtrier *m*, assassin *m*; **~ous** *adj* meurtrier(-ère)

murky ['mɜːkɪ] *adj* sombre, ténébreux(-euse); (*water*) trouble

murmur ['mɜːmər] *n* murmure *m* ♦ *vt*, *vi* murmurer

muscle ['mʌsl] *n* muscle *m*; (*fig*) force *f*; **~ in** *vi* (*on territory*) envahir; (*on success*) exploiter; **muscular** ['mʌskjulər] *adj* musculaire; (*person, arm*) musclé(e)

muse [mju:z] *vi* méditer, songer

museum [mju:'zɪəm] *n* musée *m*

mushroom ['mʌʃrum] *n* champignon *m* ♦ *vi* pousser comme un champignon

music ['mju:zɪk] *n* musique *f*; **~al** *adj* musical(e); (*person*) musicien(ne) ♦ *n* (*show*) comédie musicale; **~al instrument** *n* instrument *m* de musique; **~ centre** *n* chaîne compacte; ~ian [mjuːˈzɪʃən] n musicien(ne)

Muslim [ˈmʌzlɪm] adj, n musulman(e)

muslin [ˈmʌzlɪn] n mousseline f

mussel [ˈmʌsl] n moule f

must [mʌst] aux vb (obligation): **I ~ do it** je dois le faire, il faut que je le fasse; (probability): **he ~ be there by now** il doit y être maintenant, il y est probablement maintenant; (suggestion, invitation): **you ~ come and see me** il faut que vous veniez me voir; (indicating sth unwelcome): **why ~ he behave so badly?** qu'est-ce qui le pousse à se conduire si mal? ♦ n nécessité f, impératif m; **it's a ~** c'est indispensable

mustache [ˈmʌstæʃ] (US) n = **moustache**

mustard [ˈmʌstəd] n moutarde f

muster [ˈmʌstər] vt rassembler

mustn't [ˈmʌsnt] = **must not**

mute [mjuːt] adj muet(te); ~d adj (colour) sourd(e); (reaction) voilé(e)

mutiny [ˈmjuːtɪnɪ] n mutinerie f ♦ vi se mutiner

mutter [ˈmʌtər] vt, vi marmonner, marmotter

mutton [ˈmʌtn] n mouton m

mutual [ˈmjuːtʃuəl] adj mutuel(le), réciproque; (benefit, interest) commun(e); ~ly adv mutuellement

muzzle [ˈmʌzl] n museau m; (protective device) muselière f; (of gun) gueule f ♦ vt museler

my [maɪ] adj mon (ma), mes pl; ~ **house/ car/gloves** ma maison/mon auto/mes gants; **I've washed ~ hair/cut ~ finger** je me suis lavé les cheveux/coupé le doigt; ~**self** [maɪˈself] pron (reflexive) me; (emphatic) moi-même; (after prep) moi; see also **oneself**

mysterious [mɪsˈtɪərɪəs] adj mystérieux(-euse)

mystery [ˈmɪstərɪ] n mystère m

mystify [ˈmɪstɪfaɪ] vt mystifier; (puzzle) ébahir

myth [mɪθ] n mythe m; ~**ology** [mɪˈθɒlədʒɪ] n mythologie f

N, n

n/a abbr = **not applicable**

naff [næf] (BRIT: inf) adj nul(le)

nag [næg] vt (scold) être toujours après, reprendre sans arrêt; ~**ging** adj (doubt, pain) persistant(e)

nail [neɪl] n (human) ongle m; (metal) clou m ♦ vt clouer; **to ~ sb down to a date/ price** contraindre qn à accepter or donner une date/un prix; ~**brush** n brosse f à ongles; ~**file** n lime f à ongles; ~ **polish** n vernis m à ongles; ~ **polish remover** n dissolvant m; ~ **scissors** npl ciseaux mpl à ongles; ~ **varnish** (BRIT) n = **nail polish**

naïve [naɪˈiːv] adj naïf(-ïve)

naked [ˈneɪkɪd] adj nu(e)

name [neɪm] n nom m; (reputation) réputation f ♦ vt nommer; (identify: accomplice etc) citer; (price, date) fixer, donner; **by ~** par son nom; **in the ~ of** au nom de; **what's your ~?** comment vous appelez-vous?; ~**less** adj sans nom; (witness, contributor) anonyme; ~**ly** adv à savoir; ~**sake** n homonyme m

nanny [ˈnænɪ] n bonne f d'enfants

nap [næp] n (sleep) (petit) somme ♦ vi: **to be caught ~ping** être pris à l'improviste or en défaut

nape [neɪp] n: ~ **of the neck** nuque f

napkin [ˈnæpkɪn] n serviette f (de table)

nappy [ˈnæpɪ] (BRIT) n couche f (gen pl); ~ **rash** n: **to have ~ rash** avoir les fesses rouges

narcissus [nɑːˈsɪsəs] (pl **narcissi**) n narcisse m

narcotic [nɑːˈkɒtɪk] n (drug) stupéfiant m; (MED) narcotique m

narrative [ˈnærətɪv] n récit m

narrow [ˈnærəʊ] adj étroit(e); (fig) restreint(e), limité(e) ♦ vi (road) devenir plus étroit, se rétrécir; (gap, difference) se réduire; **to have a ~ escape** l'échapper belle; **to ~ sth down to** réduire qch à; ~**ly** adv:

he ~ly missed injury/the tree il a failli se blesser/rentrer dans l'arbre; ~-minded *adj* à l'esprit étroit, borné(e); (*attitude*) borné

nasty ['nɑːstɪ] *adj* (*person: malicious*) méchant(e); (: *rude*) très désagréable; (*smell*) dégoûtant(e); (*wound, situation, disease*) mauvais(e)

nation ['neɪʃən] *n* nation *f*

national ['næʃənl] *adj* national(e) ♦ *n* (*abroad*) ressortissant(e); (*when home*) national(e); ~ **anthem** *n* hymne national; ~ **dress** *n* costume national; **N~ Health Service** (*BRIT*) *n* service national de santé; ≈ Sécurité Sociale; **N~ Insurance** (*BRIT*) *n* ≈ Sécurité Sociale; ~**ism** *n* nationalisme *m*; ~**ist** *adj* nationaliste ♦ *n* nationaliste *m/f*; ~**ity** [næʃə'nælɪtɪ] *n* nationalité *f*; ~**ize** *vt* nationaliser; ~**ly** *adv* (*as a nation*) du point de vue national; (*nationwide*) dans le pays entier; ~ **park** *n* parc national

---

National Trust

ⓘ Le **National Trust** *est un organisme indépendant, à but non lucratif, dont la mission est de protéger et de mettre en valeur les monuments et les sites britanniques en raison de leur intérêt historique ou de leur beauté naturelle.*

---

nationwide ['neɪʃənwaɪd] *adj* s'étendant à l'ensemble du pays; (*problem*) à l'échelle du pays entier ♦ *adv* à travers *or* dans tout le pays

native ['neɪtɪv] *n* autochtone *m/f*, habitant(e) du pays ♦ *adj* du pays, indigène; (*country*) natal(e); (*ability*) inné(e); **a ~ of Russia** une personne originaire de Russie; **a ~ speaker of French** une personne de langue maternelle française; **N~ American** *n* Indien(ne) d'Amérique; ~ **language** *n* langue maternelle

NATO ['neɪtəʊ] *n abbr* (= *North Atlantic Treaty Organization*) OTAN *f*

natural ['nætʃrəl] *adj* naturel(le); ~ **gas** *n* gaz naturel; ~**ist** *n* naturaliste *m/f*; ~**ly**

adv naturellement

nature ['neɪtʃəʳ] *n* nature *f*; **by ~** par tempérament, de nature

naught [nɔːt] *n* = **nought**

naughty ['nɔːtɪ] *adj* (*child*) vilain(e), pas sage

nausea ['nɔːsɪə] *n* nausée *f*

naval ['neɪvl] *adj* naval(e); ~ **officer** *n* officier *m* de marine

nave [neɪv] *n* nef *f*

navel ['neɪvl] *n* nombril *m*

navigate ['nævɪgeɪt] *vt* (*steer*) diriger; (*plot course*) naviguer ♦ *vi* naviguer; **navigation** [nævɪ'geɪʃən] *n* navigation *f*

navvy ['nævɪ] (*BRIT*) *n* terrassier *m*

navy ['neɪvɪ] *n* marine *f*; ~**(-blue)** *adj* bleu marine *inv*

Nazi ['nɑːtsɪ] *n* Nazi(e)

NB *abbr* (= *nota bene*) NB

near [nɪəʳ] *adj* proche ♦ *adv* près ♦ *prep* (*also:* ~ **to**) près de ♦ *vt* approcher de; ~**by** [nɪə'baɪ] *adj* proche ♦ *adv* tout près, à proximité; ~**ly** *adv* presque; **I ~ly fell** j'ai failli tomber; ~ **miss** *n* (*AVIAT*) quasi-collision *f*; **that was a ~ miss** (*gen*) il s'en est fallu de peu; (*of shot*) c'est passé très près; ~**side** *n* (*AUT: in Britain*) côté *m* gauche; (: *in US, Europe etc*) côté droit; ~-**sighted** *adj* myope

neat [niːt] *adj* (*person, work*) soigné(e); (*room etc*) bien tenu(e) *or* rangé(e); (*skilful*) habile; (*spirits*) pur(e); ~**ly** *adv* avec soin *or* ordre; habilement

necessarily ['nesɪsrɪlɪ] *adv* nécessairement

necessary ['nesɪsrɪ] *adj* nécessaire; **necessity** [nɪ'sesɪtɪ] *n* nécessité *f*; (*thing needed*) chose nécessaire *or* essentielle; **necessities** *npl* nécessaire *m*

neck [nek] *n* cou *m*; (*of animal, garment*) encolure *f*; (*of bottle*) goulot *m* ♦ *vi* (*inf*) se peloter; ~ **and ~** à égalité; ~**lace** *n* collier *m*; ~**line** *n* encolure *f*; ~**tie** *n* cravate *f*

need [niːd] *n* besoin *m* ♦ *vt* avoir besoin de; **to ~ to do** devoir faire; avoir besoin de faire; **you don't ~ to go** vous n'avez pas besoin *or* vous n'êtes pas obligé de partir

needle ['niːdl] n aiguille f ♦ vt asticoter, tourmenter

needless ['niːdlɪs] adj inutile

needlework ['niːdlwəːk] n (activity) travaux mpl d'aiguille; (object(s)) ouvrage m

needn't ['niːdnt] = **need not**

needy ['niːdɪ] adj nécessiteux(-euse)

negative ['nɛgətɪv] n (PHOT, ELEC) négatif m; (LING) terme m de négation ♦ adj négatif(-ive); ~ **equity** situation dans laquelle la valeur d'une maison est inférieure à celle de l'emprunt-logement contracté pour la payer

neglect [nɪ'glɛkt] vt négliger ♦ n (of person, duty, garden) le fait de négliger; (state of ~) abandon m; ~ed adj négligé(e), à l'abandon

negligee ['nɛglɪʒeɪ] n déshabillé m

negotiate [nɪ'gəʊʃɪeɪt] vi, vt négocier; ne-**gotiation** [nɪgəʊʃɪ'eɪʃən] n négociation f, pourparlers mpl

neigh [neɪ] vi hennir

neighbour ['neɪbər] (US **neighbor**) n voisin(e); ~**hood** n (place) quartier m; (people) voisinage m; ~**ing** adj voisin(e), avoisinant(e); ~**ly** adj obligeant(e); (action etc) amical(e)

neither ['naɪðə*] adj, pron aucun(e) (des deux), ni l'un(e) ni l'autre ♦ conj: **I didn't move and ~ did Claude** je n'ai pas bougé, (et) Claude non plus ♦ adv: ~ **good nor bad** ni bon ni mauvais; ..., ~ **did I refuse** ..., (et or mais) je n'ai pas non plus refusé

neon ['niːɔn] n néon m; ~ **light** n lampe f au néon

nephew ['nevjuː] n neveu m

nerve [nəːv] n nerf m; (fig: courage) sang-froid m, courage m; (: impudence) aplomb m, toupet m; **to have a fit of ~s** avoir le trac; ~-**racking** adj angoissant(e)

nervous ['nəːvəs] adj nerveux(-euse); (anxious) inquiet(-ète), plein(e) d'appréhension; (timid) intimidé(e); ~ **breakdown** n dépression nerveuse

nest [nɛst] n nid m ♦ vi (se) nicher, faire son nid; ~ **egg** n (fig) bas m de laine, magot m

nestle ['nɛsl] vi se blottir

net [nɛt] n filet m; **the Net** (INTERNET) le Net ♦ adj net(te) ♦ vt (fish etc) prendre au filet; (profit) rapporter; ~**ball** n netball m

Netherlands ['nɛðələndz] npl: **the ~** les Pays-Bas mpl

nett [nɛt] adj = **net**

netting ['nɛtɪŋ] n (for fence etc) treillis m, grillage m

nettle ['nɛtl] n ortie f

network ['nɛtwəːk] n réseau m

neurotic [njuə'rɔtɪk] adj névrosé(e)

neuter ['njuːtər] adj neutre ♦ vt (cat etc) châtrer, couper

neutral ['njuːtrəl] adj neutre ♦ n (AUT) point mort; ~**ize** vt neutraliser

never ['nɛvər] adv (ne ...) jamais; ~ **again** plus jamais; ~ **in my life** jamais de ma vie; see also **mind**; ~-**ending** adj interminable; ~**theless** adv néanmoins, malgré tout

new [njuː] adj nouveau (nouvelle); (brand ~) neuf (neuve); **N~ Age** n New Age m; ~**born** adj nouveau-né(e); ~**comer** n nouveau venu/nouvelle venue; ~-**fangled** ['njuː'fæŋgld] (pej) adj ultramoderne (et farfelu(e)); ~-**found** adj (enthusiasm) de fraîche date; (friend) nouveau (nouvelle); ~**ly** adv nouvellement, récemment; ~**ly-weds** npl jeunes mariés mpl

news [njuːz] n nouvelle(s) f(pl); (RADIO, TV) informations fpl, actualités fpl; **a piece of ~** une nouvelle; ~ **agency** n agence f de presse; ~**agent** (BRIT) n marchand m de journaux; ~**caster** n présentateur(-trice); ~ **flash** n flash m d'information; ~**letter** n bulletin m; ~**paper** n journal m; ~**print** n papier m (de) journal; ~**reader** n = **newscaster**; ~**reel** n actualités (filmées); ~ **stand** n kiosque m à journaux

newt [njuːt] n triton m

New Year n Nouvel An; ~'**s Day** n le jour de l'An; ~'**s Eve** n la Saint-Sylvestre

New Zealand [-'ziːlənd] n la Nouvelle-Zélande; ~**er** n Néo-zélandais(e)

next [nɛkst] *adj* (*seat, room*) voisin(e), d'à côté; (*meeting, bus stop*) suivant(e); (*in time*) prochain(e) ♦ *adv* (*place*) à côté; (*time*) la fois suivante, la prochaine fois; (*afterwards*) ensuite; **the ~ day** le lendemain, le jour suivant *or* d'après; **~ year** l'année prochaine; **~ time** la prochaine fois; **~ to** à côté de; **~ to nothing** presque rien; **~, please!** (*at doctor's etc*) au suivant!; **~ door** *adv* à côté ♦ *adj* d'à côté; **~-of-kin** *n* parent *m* le plus proche

NHS *n abbr* = **National Health Service**

nib [nɪb] *n* (bec *m* de) plume *f*

nibble ['nɪbl] *vt* grignoter

nice [naɪs] *adj* (*pleasant, likeable*) agréable; (*pretty*) joli(e); (*kind*) gentil(le); **~ly** *adv* agréablement; joliment; gentiment

niceties ['naɪsɪtɪz] *npl* subtilités *fpl*

nick [nɪk] *n* (*indentation*) encoche *f*; (*wound*) entaille *f* ♦ *vt* (BRIT: *inf*) faucher, piquer; **in the ~ of time** juste à temps

nickel ['nɪkl] *n* nickel *m*; (US) pièce *f* de 5 cents

nickname ['nɪkneɪm] *n* surnom *m* ♦ *vt* surnommer

nicotine patch ['nɪkəti:n-] *n* timbre *m* anti-tabac, patch *m*

niece [ni:s] *n* nièce *f*

Nigeria [naɪˈdʒɪərɪə] *n* Nigéria *m or f*

niggling ['nɪglɪŋ] *adj* (*person*) tatillon(ne); (*detail*) insignifiant(e); (*doubts, injury*) persistant(e)

night [naɪt] *n* nuit *f*; (*evening*) soir *m*; **at ~** la nuit; **by ~** de nuit; **the ~ before last** avant-hier soir; **~cap** *n* boisson prise avant de se coucher; **~ club** *n* boîte *f* de nuit; **~dress** *n* chemise *f* de nuit; **~fall** *n* tombée *f* de la nuit; **~gown** *n* chemise *f* de nuit; **~ie** ['naɪtɪ] *n* chemise *f* de nuit; **~ingale** ['naɪtɪŋgeɪl] *n* rossignol *m*; **~life** *n* vie *f* nocturne; **~ly** *adj* de chaque nuit *or* soir; (*by night*) nocturne ♦ *adv* chaque nuit *or* soir; **~mare** *n* cauchemar *m*; **~ porter** *n* gardien *m* de nuit, concierge *m* de service la nuit; **~ school** *n* cours *mpl* du soir; **~ shift** *n* équipe *f* de nuit; **~-time** *n* nuit *f*; **~ watchman** *n* veilleur *m* *or* gardien *m* de nuit

nil [nɪl] *n* rien *m*; (BRIT: SPORT) zéro *m*

Nile [naɪl] *n*: **the ~** le Nil

nimble ['nɪmbl] *adj* agile

nine [naɪn] *num* neuf; **~teen** ['naɪn'ti:n] *num* dix-neuf; **~ty** ['naɪntɪ] *num* quatre-vingt-dix; **ninth** [naɪnθ] *num* neuvième

nip [nɪp] *vt* pincer

nipple ['nɪpl] *n* (ANAT) mamelon *m*, bout *m* du sein

nitrogen ['naɪtrədʒən] *n* azote *m*

KEYWORD

---

no [nəʊ] (*pl* **noes**) *adv* (*opposite of "yes"*) non; **are you coming? - no (I'm not)** est-ce que vous venez? - non; **would you like some more? - no thank you** vous en voulez encore? - non merci
♦ *adj* (*not any*) pas de, aucun(e) (*used with "ne"*); **I have no money/books** je n'ai pas d'argent/de livres; **no student would have done it** aucun étudiant ne l'aurait fait; **"no smoking"** "défense de fumer"; **"no dogs"** "les chiens ne sont pas admis"
♦ *n* non *m*

---

nobility [nəʊˈbɪlɪtɪ] *n* noblesse *f*

noble ['nəʊbl] *adj* noble

nobody ['nəʊbədɪ] *pron* personne

nod [nɒd] *vi* faire un signe de tête (*affirmatif ou amical*); (*sleep*) somnoler ♦ *vt*: **to ~ one's head** faire un signe de (la) tête; (*in agreement*) faire signe que oui ♦ *n* signe *m* de (la) tête; **~ off** *vi* s'assoupir

noise [nɔɪz] *n* bruit *m*; **noisy** *adj* bruyant(e)

nominal ['nɒmɪnl] *adj* symbolique

nominate ['nɒmɪneɪt] *vt* (*propose*) proposer; (*appoint*) nommer; **nominee** [nɒmɪ'ni:] *n* candidat agréé; personne nommée

non... [nɒn] *prefix* non-; **~alcoholic** *adj* non-alcoolisé(e); **~committal** *adj* évasif(ive); **~descript** *adj* quelconque, indéfinissable

none [nʌn] *pron* aucun(e); **~ of you** aucun

d'entre vous, personne parmi vous; **I've ~ left** je n'en ai plus; **he's ~ the worse for it** il ne s'en porte pas plus mal

nonentity [nɔ'nentɪtɪ] *n* personne insignifiante

nonetheless ['nʌnðə'les] *adv* néanmoins

non-existent [nɔnɪg'zɪstənt] *adj* inexistant(e)

non-fiction [nɔn'fɪkʃən] *n* littérature *f* non-romanesque

nonplussed [nɔn'plʌst] *adj* perplexe

nonsense ['nɔnsəns] *n* absurdités *fpl*, idioties *fpl*; **~!** ne dites pas d'idioties!

non: ~-smoker *n* non-fumeur *m*; **~-smoking** *adj* non-fumeur; **~-stick** *adj* qui n'attache pas; **~-stop** *adj* direct(e), sans arrêt (*or* escale) ♦ *adv* sans arrêt

noodles ['nu:dlz] *npl* nouilles *fpl*

nook [nʊk] *n:* **~s and crannies** recoins *mpl*

noon [nu:n] *n* midi *m*

no one ['nəʊwʌn] *pron* = **nobody**

noose [nu:s] *n* nœud coulant; (*hangman's*) corde *f* .

nor [nɔːʳ] *conj* = **neither** ♦ *adv see* **neither**

norm [nɔːm] *n* norme *f*

normal *adj* normal(e); **~ly** ['nɔːməlɪ] *adv* normalement

Normandy ['nɔːməndɪ] *n* Normandie *f*

north [nɔːθ] *n* nord *m* ♦ *adj* du nord, nord *inv* ♦ *adv* au *or* vers le nord; **N~ America** *n* Amérique *f* du Nord; **~-east** *n* nord-est *m*; **~erly** ['nɔːðəlɪ] *adj* du nord; **~ern** ['nɔːðən] *adj* du nord, septentrional(e); **N~ern Ireland** *n* Irlande *f* du Nord; **N~ Pole** *n* pôle *m* Nord; **N~ Sea** *n* mer *f* du Nord; **~ward(s)** *adv* vers le nord; **~-west** *n* nord-ouest *m*

Norway ['nɔːweɪ] *n* Norvège *f*; **Norwegian** [nɔː'wiːdʒən] *adj* norvégien(ne) ♦ *n* Norvégien(ne); (*LING*) norvégien *m*

nose [nəʊz] *n* nez *m*; **~ about, ~ around** *vi* fouiner *or* fureter (partout); **~bleed** *n* saignement *m* du nez; **~-dive** *n* (descente *f* en) piqué *m*; **~y** (*inf*) *adj* = **nosy**

nostalgia [nɔs'tældʒɪə] *n* nostalgie *f*

nostril ['nɔstrɪl] *n* narine *f*; (*of horse*) naseau *m*

nosy ['nəʊzɪ] (*inf*) *adj* curieux(-euse)

not [nɔt] *adv* (ne ...) pas; **he is ~** *or* **isn't here** il n'est pas ici; **you must ~** *or* **you mustn't do that** tu ne dois pas faire ça; **it's too late, isn't it** *or* **is it ~?** c'est trop tard, n'est-ce pas?; **~ yet/now** pas encore/maintenant; **~ at all** pas du tout; *see also* **all; only**

notably ['nəʊtəblɪ] *adv* (*particularly*) en particulier; (*markedly*) spécialement

notary ['nəʊtərɪ] *n* notaire *m*

notch [nɔtʃ] *n* encoche *f*

note [nəʊt] *n* note *f*; (*letter*) mot *m*; (*banknote*) billet *m* ♦ *vt* (*also:* **~ down**) noter; (*observe*) constater; **~book** *n* carnet *m*; **~d** *adj* réputé(e); **~pad** *n* bloc-notes *m*; **~paper** *n* papier *m* à lettres

nothing ['nʌθɪŋ] *n* rien *m*; **he does ~** il ne fait rien; **~ new** rien de nouveau; **for ~** pour rien

notice ['nəʊtɪs] *n* (*announcement, warning*) avis *m*; (*period of time*) délai *m*; (*resignation*) démission *f*; (*dismissal*) congé *m* ♦ *vt* remarquer, s'apercevoir de; **to take ~ of** prêter attention à; **to bring sth to sb's ~** porter qch à la connaissance de qn; **at short ~** dans un délai très court; **until further ~** jusqu'à nouvel ordre; **to hand in one's ~** donner sa démission, démissionner; **~able** *adj* visible; **~ board** (*BRIT*) *n* panneau *m* d'affichage

notify ['nəʊtɪfaɪ] *vt:* **to ~ sth to sb** notifier qch à qn; **to ~ sb (of sth)** avertir qn (de qch)

notion ['nəʊʃən] *n* idée *f*; (*concept*) notion *f*

notorious [nəʊ'tɔːrɪəs] *adj* notoire (*souvent en mal*)

nought [nɔːt] *n* zéro *m*

noun [naʊn] *n* nom *m*

nourish ['nʌrɪʃ] *vt* nourrir; **~ing** *adj* nourrissant(e); **~ment** *n* nourriture *f*

novel ['nɔvl] *n* roman *m* ♦ *adj* nouveau (nouvelle), original(e); **~ist** *n* romancier *m*; **~ty** *n* nouveauté *f*

November [nəʊ'vembəʳ] *n* novembre *m*

now [naʊ] *adv* maintenant ♦ *conj:* **~ (that)**

maintenant que; **right ~** tout de suite; **by ~** à l'heure qu'il est; **just ~: that's the fashion just ~** c'est la mode en ce moment; **~ and then, ~ and again** de temps en temps; **from ~ on** dorénavant; **~adays** *adv* de nos jours

nowhere ['nəʊwεəᵉ] *adv* nulle part

nozzle ['nɒzl] *n* (*of hose etc*) ajutage *m*; (*of vacuum cleaner*) suceur *m*

nuclear ['njuːklɪəᵉ] *adj* nucléaire

nucleus ['njuːklɪəs] (*pl* **nuclei**) *n* noyau *m*

nude [njuːd] *adj* nu(e) ♦ *n* nu *m*; **in the ~** (tout(e)) nu(e)

nudge [nʌdʒ] *vt* donner un (petit) coup de coude à

nudist ['njuːdɪst] *n* nudiste *m/f*

nuisance ['njuːsns] *n*: **it's a ~** c'est (très) embêtant; **he's a ~** il est assommant *or* casse-pieds; **what a ~!** quelle barbe!

null [nʌl] *adj*: **~ and void** nul(le) et non avenu(e)

numb [nʌm] *adj* engourdi(e); (*with fear*) paralysé(e)

number ['nʌmbəᵉ] *n* nombre *m*; (*numeral*) chiffre *m*; (*of house, bank account etc*) numéro *m* ♦ *vt* numéroter; (*amount to*) compter; **a ~ of** un certain nombre de; **they were seven in ~** ils étaient (au nombre de) sept; **to be ~ed among** compter parmi; **~ plate** *n* (*AUT*) plaque *f* minéralogique *or* d'immatriculation

numeral ['njuːmərəl] *n* chiffre *m*

numerate ['njuːmərɪt] (*BRIT*) *adj*: **to be ~** avoir des notions d'arithmétique

numerical [njuː'mεrɪkl] *adj* numérique

numerous ['njuːmərəs] *adj* nombreux(-euse)

nun [nʌn] *n* religieuse *f*, sœur *f*

nurse [nəːs] *n* infirmière *f* ♦ *vt* (*patient, cold*) soigner

nursery ['nəːsərɪ] *n* (*room*) nursery *f*; (*institution*) crèche *f*; (*for plants*) pépinière *f*; **~ rhyme** *n* comptine *f*, chansonnette *f* pour enfants; **~ school** *n* école maternelle; **~ slope** *n* (*SKI*) piste *f* pour débutants

nursing ['nəːsɪŋ] *n* (*profession*) profession *f* d'infirmière; (*care*) soins *mpl*; **~ home** *n*

clinique *f*; maison *f* de convalescence

nut [nʌt] *n* (*of metal*) écrou *m*; (*fruit*) noix *f*; noisette *f*; cacahuète *f*; **~crackers** *npl* casse-noix *m inv*, casse-noisette(s) *m*

nutmeg ['nʌtmεg] *n* (*noix f*) muscade *f*

nutritious [njuː'trɪʃəs] *adj* nutritif(-ive), nourrissant(e)

nuts [nʌts] (*inf*) *adj* dingue

nutshell ['nʌtʃεl] *n*: **in a ~** en un mot

nutter ['nʌtəᵉ] (*BRIT: inf*) *n*: **he's a complete ~** il est complètement cinglé

nylon ['naɪlɒn] *n* nylon *m* ♦ *adj* de *or* en nylon

O, o

oak [əʊk] *n* chêne *m* ♦ *adj* de *or* en (bois de) chêne

OAP (*BRIT*) *n abbr* = **old-age pensioner**

oar [ɔːᵉ] *n* aviron *m*, rame *f*

oasis [əʊ'eɪsɪs] (*pl* **oases**) *n* oasis *f*

oath [əʊθ] *n* serment *m*; (*swear word*) juron *m*; **under ~**, (*BRIT*) **on ~** sous serment

oatmeal ['əʊtmiːl] *n* flocons *mpl* d'avoine

oats [əʊts] *n* avoine *f*

obedience [ə'biːdɪəns] *n* obéissance *f*; **obedient** *adj* obéissant(e)

obey [ə'beɪ] *vt* obéir à; (*instructions*) se conformer à

obituary [ə'bɪtjʊərɪ] *n* nécrologie *f*

object [*n* 'ɒbdʒɪkt, *vb* əb'dʒεkt] *n* objet *m*; (*purpose*) but *m*, objet; (*LING*) complément *m* d'objet ♦ *vi*: **to ~ to** (*attitude*) désapprouver; (*proposal*) protester contre; **expense is no ~** l'argent n'est pas un problème; **he ~ed that ...** il a fait valoir *or* a objecté que ...; **I ~!** je proteste!; **~ion** [əb'dʒεkʃən] *n* objection *f*; **~ionable** *adj* très désagréable; (*language*) choquant(e); **~ive** *n* objectif *m* ♦ *adj* objectif(-ive)

obligation [ɔblɪ'geɪʃən] *n* obligation *f*, devoir *m*; **without ~** sans engagement; **obligatory** [ə'blɪgətərɪ] *adj* obligatoire

oblige [ə'blaɪdʒ] *vt* (*force*): **to ~ sb to do** obliger *or* forcer qn à faire; (*do a favour*) rendre service à, obliger; **to be ~d to sb**

for sth être obligé(e) à qn de qch; **obliging** *adj* obligeant(e), serviable

oblique [ə'bliːk] *adj* oblique; (*allusion*) indirect(e)

obliterate [ə'blitəreit] *vt* effacer

oblivion [ə'blɪvɪən] *n* oubli *m*; **oblivious** *adj*: **oblivious of** oublieux(-euse) de

oblong ['ɔblɔŋ] *adj* oblong (oblongue) ♦ *n* rectangle *m*

obnoxious [əb'nɔkʃəs] *adj* odieux(-euse), (*smell*) nauséabond(e)

oboe ['əubəu] *n* hautbois *m*

obscene [əb'siːn] *adj* obscène

obscure [əb'skjuəʳ] *adj* obscur(e) ♦ *vt* obscurcir; (*hide: sun*) cacher

observant [əb'zɑːvənt] *adj* observateur(-trice)

observation [ɔbzə'veɪʃən] *n* (*remark*) observation *f*; (*watching*) surveillance *f*

observatory [əb'zɔːvətri] *n* observatoire *m*

observe [əb'zɔːv] *vt* observer; (*remark*) faire observer *or* remarquer; **~r** *n* observateur(-trice)

obsess [əb'sɛs] *vt* obséder; **~ive** *adj* obsédant(e)

obsolete ['ɔbsəliːt] *adj* dépassé(e); démodé(e)

obstacle ['ɔbstəkl] *n* obstacle *m*; **~ race** *n* course *f* d'obstacles

obstinate ['ɔbstɪnɪt] *adj* obstiné(e)

obstruct [əb'strʌkt] *vt* (*block*) boucher, obstruer; (*hinder*) entraver

obtain [əb'teɪn] *vt* obtenir

obvious ['ɔbvɪəs] *adj* évident(e), manifeste; **~ly** *adv* manifestement; **~ly not!** bien sûr que non!

occasion [ə'keɪʒən] *n* occasion *f*; (*event*) événement *m*; **~al** *adj* pris(e) *or* fait(e) *etc* de temps en temps; occasionnel(le); **~ally** *adv* de temps en temps, quelquefois

occupation [ɔkju'peɪʃən] *n* occupation *f*; (*job*) métier *m*, profession *f*; **~al hazard** *n* risque *m* du métier

occupier ['ɔkjupaɪəʳ] *n* occupant(e)

occupy ['ɔkjupaɪ] *vt* occuper; **to ~ o.s. in** *or* **with doing** s'occuper à faire

occur [ə'kɔːʳ] *vi* (*event*) se produire; (*phe-

nomenon, error*) se rencontrer; **to ~ to sb** venir à l'esprit de qn; **~rence** *n* (*existence*) présence *f*, existence *f*; (*event*) cas *m*, fait *m*

ocean ['əuʃən] *n* océan *m*

o'clock [ə'klɔk] *adv*: **it is 5 ~** il est 5 heures

OCR *n abbr* = **optical character reader**; **optical character recognition**

October [ɔk'təubəʳ] *n* octobre *m*

octopus ['ɔktəpəs] *n* pieuvre *f*

odd [ɔd] *adj* (*strange*) bizarre, curieux(-euse); (*number*) impair(e); (*not of a set*) dépareillé(e); **60-** 60 et quelques; **at ~ times** de temps en temps; **the ~ one out** l'exception *f*; **~ity** *n* (*person*) excentrique *m/f*; (*thing*) curiosité *f*; **~-job man** *n* homme *m* à tout faire; **~ jobs** *npl* petits travaux divers; **~ly** *adv* bizarrement, curieusement; **~ments** *npl* (*COMM*) fins *fpl* de série; **~s** *npl* (*in betting*) cote *f*; **it makes no ~s** cela n'a pas d'importance; **at ~s** en désaccord; **~s and ends** de petites choses

odour ['əudəʳ] (*US* **odor**) *n* odeur *f*

KEYWORD

of [ɔv, əv] *prep* 1 (*gen*) de; **a friend of ours** un de nos amis; **a boy of 10** un garçon de 10 ans; **that was kind of you** c'était gentil de votre part

2 (*expressing quantity, amount, dates etc*) de; **a kilo of flour** un kilo de farine; **how much of this do you need?** combien vous en faut-il?; **there were 3 of them** (*people*) ils étaient 3; (*objects*) il y en avait 3; **3 of us went** 3 d'entre nous y sont allé(e)s; **the 5th of July** le 5 juillet

3 (*from, out of*) en, de; **a statue of marble** une statue de *or* en marbre; **made of wood** (fait) en bois

---

off [ɔf] *adj, adv* (*engine*) coupé(e); (*tap*) fermé(e); (*BRIT: food: bad*) mauvais(e); (: *milk: bad*) tourné(e); (*absent*) absent(e); (*cancelled*) annulé(e) ♦ *prep* de; sur; **to be ~** (*to leave*) partir, s'en aller; **to be ~ sick**

être absent pour cause de maladie; **a day ~** un jour de congé; **to have an ~ day** n'être pas en forme; **he had his coat ~** il avait enlevé son manteau; **10% ~** (*COMM*) 10% de rabais; **~ the coast** au large de la côte; **I'm ~ meat** je ne mange plus de viande, je n'aime plus la viande; **on the ~ chance** à tout hasard

offal ['ɔfl] *n* (*CULIN*) abats *mpl*

off-colour ['ɔf'kʌlə'] (*BRIT*) *adj* (*ill*) malade, mal fichu(e)

offence [ə'fɛns] (*US* **offense**) *n* (*crime*) délit *m*, infraction *f*; **to take ~ at** se vexer de, s'offenser de

offend [ə'fɛnd] *vt* (*person*) offenser, blesser; **~er** *n* délinquant(e)

offense [ə'fɛns] (*US*) *n* = **offence**

offensive [ə'fɛnsɪv] *adj* offensant(e), choquant(e); (*smell etc*) très déplaisant(e); (*weapon*) offensif(-ive) ♦ *n* (*MIL*) offensive *f*

offer ['ɔfə'] *n* offre *f*, proposition *f* ♦ *vt* offrir, proposer; **"on ~"** (*COMM*) "en promotion"; **~ing** *n* offrande *f*

offhand [ɔf'hænd] *adj* désinvolte ♦ *adv* spontanément

office ['ɔfɪs] *n* (*place, room*) bureau *m*; (*position*) charge *f*, fonction *f*; **doctor's ~** (*US*) cabinet (médical); **to take ~** entrer en fonctions; **~ automation** *n* bureautique *f*; **~ block** (*US* **office building**) *n* immeuble *m* de bureaux; **~ hours** *npl* heures *fpl* de bureau; (*US: MED*) heures de consultation

officer ['ɔfɪsə'] *n* (*MIL etc*) officier *m*; (*also*: **police ~**) agent *m* (de police); (*of organization*) membre *m* du bureau directeur

office worker *n* employé(e) de bureau

official [ə'fɪʃl] *adj* officiel(le) ♦ *n* officiel *m*; (*civil servant*) fonctionnaire *m/f*; employé(e)

officiate [ə'fɪʃɪeɪt] *vi* (*REL*) officier; **to ~ at a marriage** célébrer un mariage

officious [ə'fɪʃəs] *adj* trop empressé(e)

offing ['ɔfɪŋ] *n*: **in the ~** (*fig*) en perspective

off: **~-licence** (*BRIT*) *n* (*shop*) débit *m* de vins et de spiritueux; **~-line** *adj*, *adv*

(*COMPUT*) (en mode) autonome; (: *switched off*) non connecté(e); **~-peak** *adj* aux heures creuses; (*electricity, heating, ticket*) au tarif heures creuses; **~-putting** (*BRIT*) *adj* (*remark*) rébarbatif(-ive); (*person*) rebutant(e), peu engageant(e); **~-road vehicle** *n* véhicule *m* tout-terrain; **~-season** *adj, adv* hors-saison *inv*; **~set** (*irreg*) *vt* (*counteract*) contrebalancer, compenser; **~shoot** *n* (*fig*) ramification *f*, antenne *f*; **~shore** *adj* (*breeze*) de terre; (*fishing*) côtier(-ère); **~side** *adj* (*SPORT*) hors jeu; (*AUT: in Britain*) de droite; (: *in US, Europe*) de gauche; **~spring** *n inv* progéniture *f*; **~stage** *adv* dans les coulisses; **~-the-peg** (*US* **off-the-rack**) *adv* en prêt-à-porter; **~-white** *adj* blanc cassé *inv*

---

off-licence

> *Un **off-licence** est un magasin où l'on vend de l'alcool (à emporter) aux heures où les pubs sont fermés. On peut également y acheter des boissons non alcoolisées, des cigarettes, des chips, des bonbons, des chocolats etc.*

Oftel ['ɔftɛl] *n organisme qui supervise les télécommunications*

often ['ɔfn] *adv* souvent; **how ~ do you go?** vous y allez tous les combien?; **how ~ have you gone there?** vous y êtes allé combien de fois?

Ofwat ['ɔfwɔt] *n organisme qui surveille les activités des compagnies des eaux*

oh [əu] *excl* ô!, oh!, ah!

oil [ɔɪl] *n* huile *f*; (*petroleum*) pétrole *m*; (*for central heating*) mazout *m* ♦ *vt* (*machine*) graisser; **~can** *n* burette *f* de graissage; (*for storing*) bidon *m* à huile; **~field** *n* (*for storing*) bidon *m* à huile; **~field** *n* gisement *m* de pétrole; **~ filter** *n* (*AUT*) filtre *m* à huile; **~ painting** *n* peinture *f* à l'huile; **~ refinery** *n* raffinerie *f*; **~ rig** *n* derrick *m*; (*at sea*) plate-forme pétrolière; **~ slick** *n* nappe *f* de mazout; **~ tanker** *n* (*ship*) pétrolier *m*; (*truck*) camion-citerne *m*; **~ well** *n* puits *m* de pétrole; **~y** *adj* huileux(-euse); (*food*) gras(se)

ointment ['ɔɪntmənt] *n* onguent *m*

O.K., okay ['əu'keɪ] *excl* d'accord! ♦ *adj* (*average*) pas mal ♦ *vt* approuver, donner son accord à; **is it ~?, are you ~?** ça va?

old [əuld] *adj* vieux (vieille); (*person*) vieux, âgé(e); (*former*) ancien(ne), vieux; **how ~ are you?** quel âge avez-vous?; **he's 10 years ~** il a 10 ans, il est âgé de 10 ans; **~er brother/sister** frère/sœur aîné(e); **~ age** vieillesse *f*; **~ age pensioner** (*BRIT*) *n* retraité(e); **~-fashioned** *adj* démodé(e); (*person*) vieux jeu *inv*

olive ['ɔlɪv] *n* (*fruit*) olive *f*; (*tree*) olivier *m* ♦ *adj* (*also:* **~-green**) (vert) olive *inv*; **~ oil** *n* huile *f* d'olive

Olympic [əu'lɪmpɪk] *adj* olympique; **the ~ Games, the ~s** les Jeux *mpl* olympiques

omelet(te) ['ɔmlɪt] *n* omelette *f*

omen ['əumən] *n* présage *m*

ominous ['ɔmɪnəs] *adj* menaçant(e), inquiétant(e); (*event*) de mauvais augure

omit [əu'mɪt] *vt* omettre; **to ~ to do** omettre de faire

KEYWORD

on [ɔn] *prep* **1** (*indicating position*) sur; **on the table** sur la table; **on the wall** sur le *or* au mur; **on the left** à gauche

2 (*indicating means, method, condition etc*): **on foot** à pied; **on the train/plane** (*be*) dans le train/l'avion; (*go*) en train/avion; **on the telephone/radio/television** au téléphone/à la radio/à la télévision; **to be on drugs** se droguer; **on holiday** en vacances

3 (*referring to time*): **on Friday** vendredi; **on Fridays** le vendredi; **on June 20th** le 20 juin; **a week on Friday** vendredi en huit; **on arrival** à l'arrivée; **on seeing this** en voyant cela

4 (*about, concerning*) sur, de; **a book on Balzac/physics** un livre sur Balzac/de physique

♦ *adv* **1** (*referring to dress, covering*): **to have one's coat on** avoir (mis) son manteau; **to put one's coat on** mettre son manteau; **what's she got on?** qu'est-ce qu'elle porte?; **screw the lid on tightly** vissez bien le couvercle

2 (*further, continuously*): **to walk** *etc* **on** continuer à marcher *etc*; **on and off** de temps à autre

♦ *adj* **1** (*in operation: machine*) en marche; (: *radio, TV, light*) allumé(e); (: *tap, gas*) ouvert(e); (: *brakes*) mis(e); **is the meeting still on?** (*not cancelled*) est-ce que la réunion a bien lieu?; (*in progress*) la réunion dure-t-elle encore?; **when is this film on?** quand passe ce film?

2 (*inf*): **that's not on!** (*not acceptable*) cela ne se fait pas!; (*not possible*) pas question!

---

once [wʌns] *adv* une fois; (*formerly*) autrefois ♦ *conj* une fois que; **~ he had left/it was done** une fois qu'il fut parti/que ce fut terminé; **at ~** tout de suite, immédiatement; (*simultaneously*) à la fois; **~ a week** une fois par semaine; **~ more** encore une fois; **~ and for all** une fois pour toutes; **~ upon a time** il y avait une fois, il était une fois

oncoming ['ɔnkʌmɪŋ] *adj* (*traffic*) venant en sens inverse

KEYWORD

one [wʌn] *num* un(e); **one hundred and fifty** cent cinquante; **one day** un jour

♦ *adj* **1** (*sole*) seul(e), unique; **the one book which** l'unique *or* le seul livre qui; **the one man who** le seul (homme) qui

2 (*same*) même; **they came in the one car** ils sont venus dans la même voiture

♦ *pron* **1**: **this one** celui-ci (celle-ci); **that one** celui-là (celle-là); **I've already got one/a red one** j'en ai déjà un(e)/un(e) rouge; **one by one** un(e) à *or* par un(e)

2: **one another** l'un(e) l'autre; **to look at one another** se regarder

3 (*impersonal*) on; **one never knows** on ne sait jamais; **to cut one's finger** se couper le doigt

---

one: **~-day excursion** (*US*) *n* billet *m* d'aller-retour (valable pour la journée);

~-man *adj* (*business*) dirigé(e) *etc* par un seul homme; **~-man band** *n* homme-orchestre *m*; **~-off** (*BRIT: inf*) *n* exemplaire *m* unique

oneself [wʌn'sɛlf] *pron* (*reflexive*) se; (*after prep*) soi(-même); (*emphatic*) soi-même; **to hurt ~** se faire mal; **to keep sth for ~** garder qch pour soi; **to talk to ~** se parler à soi-même

one: **~-sided** *adj* (*argument*) unilatéral; **~-to-~** *adj* (*relationship*) univoque; **~-way** *adj* (*street, traffic*) à sens unique

ongoing ['ɒŋɡəʊɪŋ] *adj* en cours; (*relationship*) suivi(e)

onion ['ʌnjən] *n* oignon *m*

on-line ['ɒnlaɪn] *adj, adv* (*COMPUT*) en ligne; (*: switched on*) connecté(e)

onlooker ['ɒnlʊkə^r] *n* spectateur(-trice)

only ['əʊnlɪ] *adv* seulement ♦ *adj* seul(e), unique ♦ *conj* seulement, mais; **an ~ child** un enfant unique; **not ~ ... but also** non seulement ... mais aussi

onset ['ɒnsɛt] *n* début *m*; (*of winter, old age*) approche *f*

onshore ['ɒnʃɔː^r] *adj* (*wind*) du large

onslaught ['ɒnslɔːt] *n* attaque *f*, assaut *m*

onto ['ɒntʊ] *prep* = **on to**

onward(s) ['ɒnwəd(z)] *adv* (*move*) en avant; **from that time ~** à partir de ce moment

ooze [uːz] *vi* suinter

opaque [əʊ'peɪk] *adj* opaque

OPEC ['əʊpɛk] *n abbr* (= *Organization of Petroleum-Exporting Countries*) O.P.E.P. *f*

open ['əʊpn] *adj* ouvert(e); (*car*) découvert(e); (*road, view*) dégagé(e); (*meeting*) public(-ique); (*admiration*) manifeste ♦ *vt* ouvrir ♦ *vi* (*flower, eyes, door, debate*) s'ouvrir; (*shop, bank, museum*) ouvrir; (*book star, commence*) commencer, débuter; **in the ~ (air)** en plein air; **~ on to** *vt fus* (*subj: room, door*) donner sur; **~ up** *vt* ouvrir; (*blocked road*) dégager ♦ *vi* s'ouvrir; **~ing** *n* ouverture *f*; (*opportunity*) occasion *f* ♦ *adj* (*remarks*) préliminaire; **~ing hours** *npl* heures *fpl* d'ouverture; **~ly** *adv* ouvertement; **~-minded** *adj* à l'esprit ouvert;

~-necked *adj* à col ouvert; **~-plan** *adj* sans cloisons

Open University

---

opera ['ɒpərə] *n* opéra *m*; **~ singer** *n* chanteur(-euse) d'opéra

operate ['ɒpəreɪt] *vt* (*machine*) faire marcher, faire fonctionner ♦ *vi* fonctionner; (*MED*): **to ~ (on sb)** opérer (qn)

operatic [ɒpə'rætɪk] *adj* d'opéra

operating table *n* table *f* d'opération

operating theatre *n* salle *f* d'opération

operation [ɒpə'reɪʃən] *n* opération *f*; (*of machine*) fonctionnement *m*; **to be in ~** (*system, law*) être en vigueur; **to have an ~** (*MED*) se faire opérer

operative ['ɒpərətɪv] *adj* (*measure*) en vigueur

operator ['ɒpəreɪtə^r] *n* (*of machine*) opérateur(-trice); (*TEL*) téléphoniste *m/f*

opinion [ə'pɪnjən] *n* opinion *f*, avis *m*; **in my ~** à mon avis; **~ated** *adj* aux idées bien arrêtées; **~ poll** *n* sondage *m* (d'opinion)

opponent [ə'pəʊnənt] *n* adversaire *m/f*

opportunity [ɒpə'tjuːnɪtɪ] *n* occasion *f*; **to take the ~ of doing** profiter de l'occasion pour faire; **en profiter pour faire**

oppose [ə'pəʊz] *vt* s'opposer à; **~d to** opposé(e) à; **as ~d to** par opposition à; **opposing** *vt* (*side*) opposé(e)

opposite ['ɒpəzɪt] *adj* opposé(e); (*house etc*) d'en face ♦ *adv* en face ♦ *prep* en face de ♦ *n* opposé *m*, contraire *m*; **the ~**

sex l'autre sexe, le sexe opposé; **opposition** [əpə'zɪʃən] n opposition f

oppressive [ə'presɪv] adj (political regime) oppressif(-ive); (weather) lourd(e); (heat) accablant(e)

opt [ɔpt] vi: **to ~ for** opter pour; **to ~ to do** choisir de faire; **~ out** vi: **to ~ out of** choisir de ne pas participer à or de ne pas faire

optical ['ɔptɪkl] adj optique; (instrument) d'optique; **~ character recognition/reader** n lecture f/lecteur m optique

optician [ɔp'tɪʃən] n opticien(ne)

optimist ['ɔptɪmɪst] n optimiste m/f; **~ic** [ɔptɪ'mɪstɪk] adj optimiste

option ['ɔpʃən] n choix m, option f; (SCOL) matière f à option; (COMM) option; **~al** adj facultatif(-ive); (COMM) en option

or [ɔːr] conj ou; (with negative): **he hasn't seen ~ heard anything** il n'a rien vu ni entendu; **~ else** sinon; ou bien

oral ['ɔːrəl] adj oral(e) ♦ n oral m

orange ['ɔrɪndʒ] n (fruit) orange f ♦ adj orange inv

orbit ['ɔːbɪt] n orbite f ♦ vt graviter autour de; **~al** (motorway) n périphérique m

orchard ['ɔːtʃəd] n verger m

orchestra ['ɔːkɪstrə] n orchestre m; (US: seating) (fauteuils mpl d')orchestre

orchid ['ɔːkɪd] n orchidée f

ordain [ɔː'deɪn] vt (REL) ordonner

ordeal [ɔː'diːl] n épreuve f

order ['ɔːdər] n ordre m; (COMM) commande f ♦ ♦ vt ordonner; (COMM) commander; **in ~** en ordre; (document) en règle; **in (working) ~** en état de marche; **out of ~** (not in correct ~) en désordre; (not working) en dérangement; **in ~ to do/that** pour faire/que +sub; **on ~** (COMM) en commande; **to ~ sb to do** ordonner à qn de faire; **~ form** n bon m de commande; **~ly** n (MIL) ordonnance f; (MED) garçon m de salle ♦ adj (room) en ordre; (person) qui a le sens de l'ordre

ordinary ['ɔːdnrɪ] adj ordinaire, normal(e); (pej) ordinaire, quelconque; **out of the ~** exceptionnel(le)

Ordnance Survey map ['ɔːdnəns-] n ≃ carte f d'Etat-Major

ore [ɔːr] n minerai m

organ ['ɔːgən] n organe m; (MUS) orgue m, orgues fpl; **~ic** [ɔː'gænɪk] adj organique; (food) biologique

organization [ɔːgənaɪ'zeɪʃən] n organisation f

organize ['ɔːgənaɪz] vt organiser; **~r** n organisateur(-trice)

orgasm ['ɔːgæzəm] n orgasme m

Orient ['ɔːrɪənt] n: **the ~** l'Orient m; **o~al** [ɔːrɪ'entl] adj oriental(e)

origin ['ɔrɪdʒɪn] n origine f

original [ə'rɪdʒɪnl] adj original(e); (earliest) originel(le) ♦ n original m; **~ly** adv (at first) à l'origine

originate [ə'rɪdʒɪneɪt] vi: **to ~ from** (person) être originaire de; (suggestion) provenir de; **to ~ in** prendre naissance dans; avoir son origine dans

Orkney ['ɔːknɪ] n (also: **the ~ Islands**) les Orcades fpl

ornament ['ɔːnəmənt] n ornement m; (trinket) bibelot m; **~al** [ɔːnə'mentl] adj décoratif(-ive); (garden) d'agrément

ornate [ɔː'neɪt] adj très orné(e)

orphan ['ɔːfn] n orphelin(e)

orthopaedic [ɔːθə'piːdɪk] (US **orthopedic**) adj orthopédique

ostensibly [ɔs'tensɪblɪ] adv en apparence

ostentatious [ɔsten'teɪʃəs] adj prétentieux(-euse)

ostracize ['ɔstrəsaɪz] vt frapper d'ostracisme

ostrich ['ɔstrɪtʃ] n autruche f

other ['ʌðər] adj autre ♦ pron: **the ~ (one)** l'autre; **~s** (~ people) d'autres; **~ than** autrement que; à part; **~wise** adv, conj autrement

otter ['ɔtər] n loutre f

ouch [autʃ] excl aïe!

ought [ɔːt] (pt **ought**) aux vb: **I ~ to do it** je devrais le faire, il faudrait que je le fasse; **this ~ to have been corrected** cela aurait dû être corrigé; **he ~ to win** il devrait gagner

ounce [auns] *n* once *f* (= *28.35g; 16 in a pound*)

our ['auə^r] *adj* notre, nos *pl*; *see also* **my**; **~s** *pron* le (la) nôtre, les nôtres; *see also* **mine**[1]; **~selves** [auə'selvz] *pron pl* (*reflexive, after preposition*) nous; (*emphatic*) nous-mêmes; *see also* **oneself**

oust [aust] *vt* évincer

out [aut] *adv* dehors; (*published, not at home etc*) sorti(e); (*light, fire*) éteint(e); **~ here** ici; **~ there** là-bas; **he's ~** (*absent*) il est sorti; (*unconscious*) il est sans connaissance; **to be ~ in one's calculations** s'être trompé dans ses calculs; **to run/back** *etc* **~** sortir en courant/en reculant *etc*; **~ loud** à haute voix; **~ of** (*~side*) en dehors de; (*because of: anger etc*) par; (*from among*): **~ of 10** sur 10; (*without*): **~ of petrol** sans essence, à court d'essence; **~ of order** (*machine*) en panne; (TEL: *line*) en dérangement; **~-and-~** *adj* (*liar, thief etc*) véritable; **~back** *n* (*in Australia*): **the ~back** l'intérieur *m*; **~board** *n* (*also:* **~board motor**) (moteur *m*) hors-bord *m*; **~break** *n* (*of war, disease*) début *m*; (*of violence*) éruption *f*; **~burst** *n* explosion *f*, accès *m*; **~cast** *n* exilé(e); (*socially*) paria *m*; **~come** *n* issue *f*, résultat *m*; **~crop** *n* (*of rock*) affleurement *m*; **~cry** *n* tollé (général); **~dated** *adj* démodé(e); **~do** (*irreg*) *vt* surpasser; **~door** *adj* de or en plein air; **~doors** *adv* dehors; au grand air

outer ['autə^r] *adj* extérieur(e); **~ space** *n* espace *m* cosmique

outfit ['autfit] *n* (*clothes*) tenue *f*

out: **~going** *adj* (*character*) ouvert(e), extraverti(e); (*departing*) sortant(e); **~goings** (BRIT) *npl* (*expenses*) dépenses *fpl*; **~grow** (*irreg*) *vt* (*clothes*) devenir trop grand(e) pour; **~house** *n* appentis *m*, remise *f*

outing ['autɪŋ] *n* sortie *f*; excursion *f*

out: **~law** *n* hors-la-loi *m inv* ♦ *vt* mettre hors-la-loi; **~lay** *n* dépenses *fpl*; (*investment*) mise *f* de fonds; **~let** *n* (*for liquid etc*) issue *f*, sortie *f*; (US: ELEC) prise *f* de courant; (*also:* **retail ~let**) point *m* de

vente; **~line** *n* (*shape*) contour *m*; (*summary*) esquisse *f*, grandes lignes *fpl* ♦ *vt* (*fig: theory, plan*) exposer à grands traits; **~live** *vt* survivre à; **~look** *n* perspective *f*; **~lying** *adj* écarté(e); **~moded** *adj* démodé(e); dépassé(e); **~number** *vt* surpasser en nombre; **~-of-date** *adj* (*passport*) périmé(e); (*theory etc*) dépassé(e); (*clothes etc*) démodé(e); **~-of-the-way** *adj* (*place*) loin de tout; **~patient** *n* malade *m/f* en consultation externe; **~post** *n* avant-poste *m*; **~put** *n* rendement *m*, production *f*; (COMPUT) sortie *f*

outrage ['autreɪdʒ] *n* (*anger*) indignation *f*; (*violent act*) atrocité *f*; (*scandal*) scandale *m* ♦ *vt* outrager; **~ous** [aut'reɪdʒəs] *adj* atroce; scandaleux(-euse)

outright [*adv* aut'raɪt, *adj* 'autraɪt] *adv* complètement; (*deny, refuse*) catégoriquement; (*ask*) carrément; (*kill*) sur le coup ♦ *adj* complet(-ète); catégorique

outset ['autset] *n* début *m*

outside [aut'saɪd] *n* extérieur *m* ♦ *adj* extérieur(e) ♦ *adv* (au) dehors, à l'extérieur ♦ *prep* hors de, à l'extérieur de; **at the ~** (*fig*) au plus *or* maximum; **~ lane** *n* (AUT: *in Britain*) voie *f* de droite; (: *in US, Europe*) voie de gauche; **~ line** *n* (TEL) ligne extérieure; **~r** *n* (*stranger*) étranger(-ère)

out: **~size** ['autsaɪz] *adj* énorme; (*clothes*) grande taille *inv*; **~skirts** *npl* faubourgs *mpl*; **~spoken** *adj* très franc (franche); **~standing** *adj* remarquable, exceptionnel(le); (*unfinished*) en suspens; (*debt*) impayé(e); (*problem*) non réglé(e); **~stay** *vt*: **to ~stay one's welcome** abuser de l'hospitalité de son hôte; **~stretched** [aut'stretʃt] *adj* (*hand*) tendu(e); **~strip** [aut'strɪp] *vt* (*competitors, demand*) dépasser; **~ tray** *n* courrier *m* "départ"

outward ['autwəd] *adj* (*sign, appearances*) extérieur(e); (*journey*) (d')aller

outweigh [aut'weɪ] *vt* l'emporter sur

outwit [aut'wɪt] *vt* se montrer plus malin que

oval ['əuvl] *adj* ovale ♦ *n* ovale *m*

Oval Office

i *L'Oval Office est le bureau personnel du président des États-Unis à la Maison-Blanche, ainsi appelé du fait de sa forme ovale. Par extension, ce terme désigne la présidence elle-même.*

---

ovary ['əʊvərɪ] *n* ovaire *m*

oven ['ʌvn] *n* four *m*; **~proof** *adj* allant au four

over ['əʊvər] *adv* (par-)dessus ♦ *adj* (*finished*) fini(e), terminé(e); (*too much*) en plus ♦ *prep* sur; par-dessus; (*above*) au-dessus de; (*on the other side of*) de l'autre côté de; (*more than*) plus de; (*during*) pendant; **~ here** ici; **~ there** là-bas; **all ~** (*everywhere*) partout, fini(e); **~ and ~ (again)** à plusieurs reprises; **~ and above** en plus de; **to ask sb ~** inviter qn (à passer)

overall [*adj, n* 'əʊvərɔːl, *adv* əʊvər'ɔːl] *adj* (*length, cost etc*) total(e); (*study*) d'ensemble ♦ *n* (*BRIT*) blouse *f* ♦ *adv* dans l'ensemble, en général; **~s** *npl* bleus *mpl* (de travail)

over: ~awe *vt* impressionner; **~balance** *vi* basculer; **~board** *adv* (*NAUT*) pardessus bord; **~book** *vt* faire du surbooking; **~cast** *adj* couvert(e)

overcharge [əʊvə'tʃɑːdʒ] *vt*: **to ~ sb for sth** faire payer qch trop cher à qn

overcoat ['əʊvəkəʊt] *n* pardessus *m*

overcome [əʊvə'kʌm] (*irreg*) *vt* (*defeat*) triompher de; (*difficulty*) surmonter

over: ~crowded *adj* bondé(e); **~do** (*irreg*) *vt* exagérer; (*overcook*) trop cuire; **to ~do it** (*work etc*) se surmener; **~dose** *n* dose excessive; **~draft** *n* découvert *m*; **~drawn** *adj* (*account*) à découvert; (*person*) dont le compte est à découvert; **~due** *adj* en retard; (*change, reform*) qui tarde; **~estimate** *vt* surestimer

overflow [*vb* əʊvə'fləʊ *n* 'əʊvəfləʊ] *vi* déborder ♦ *n* (*also*: **~ pipe**) tuyau *m* d'écoulement, trop-plein *m*

overgrown [əʊvə'grəʊn] *adj* (*garden*) envahi(e) par la végétation

overhaul [*vb* əʊvə'hɔːl, *n* 'əʊvəhɔːl] *vt* réviser ♦ *n* révision *f*

overhead [*adv* əʊvə'hɛd, *adj, n* 'əʊvəhɛd] *adv* au-dessus ♦ *adj* aérien(ne); (*lighting*) vertical(e) ♦ *n* (*US*) = **overheads**; **~s** *npl* (*expenses*) frais généraux; **~ projector** *n* rétroprojecteur *m*

over: ~hear (*irreg*) *vt* entendre (par hasard); **~heat** *vi* (*engine*) chauffer; **~joyed** *adj*: **~joyed (at)** ravi(e) (de), enchanté(e) (de)

overland ['əʊvəlænd] *adj, adv* par voie de terre

overlap [əʊvə'læp] *vi* se chevaucher

over: ~leaf *adv* au verso; **~load** *vt* surcharger; **~look** *vt* (*have view of*) donner sur; (*miss: by mistake*) oublier; (*forgive*) fermer les yeux sur

overnight [*adv* əʊvə'naɪt, *adj* 'əʊvənaɪt] *adv* (*happen*) durant la nuit; (*fig*) soudain ♦ *adj* d'une (*or* de) nuit; **he stayed there ~** il y a passé la nuit

overpass ['əʊvəpɑːs] *n* pont autoroutier

overpower [əʊvə'paʊər] *vt* vaincre; (*fig*) accabler; **~ing** *adj* (*heat, stench*) suffocant(e)

over: ~rate *vt* surestimer; **~ride** (*irreg: like* **ride**) *vt* (*order, objection*) passer outre à; **~riding** *adj* prépondérant(e); **~rule** *vt* (*decision*) annuler; (*claim*) rejeter; (*person*) rejeter l'avis de; **~run** (*irreg: like* **run**) *vt* (*country*) occuper; (*time limit*) dépasser

overseas [əʊvə'siːz] *adv* outre-mer; (*abroad*) à l'étranger ♦ *adj* (*trade*) extérieur(e); (*visitor*) étranger(-ère)

overshadow [əʊvə'ʃædəʊ] *vt* (*fig*) éclipser

oversight ['əʊvəsaɪt] *n* omission *f*, oubli *m*

oversleep [əʊvə'sliːp] (*irreg*) *vi* se réveiller (trop) tard

overstep [əʊvə'stɛp] *vt*: **to ~ the mark** dépasser la mesure

overt [əʊ'vɜːt] *adj* non dissimulé(e)

overtake [əʊvə'teɪk] (*irreg*) *vt* (*AUT*) dépasser, doubler

over: ~throw (*irreg*) *vt* (*government*) renverser; **~time** *n* heures *fpl* supplémentaires; **~tone** *n* (*also*: **~tones**) note *f*, sous-entendus *mpl*

overture [ˈəuvətjuəʳ] *n* (MUS, fig) ouverture *f*

over: ~**turn** *vt* renverser ♦ *vi* se retourner; ~**weight** *adj* (person) trop gros(se); ~**whelm** *vt* (subj: emotion) accabler; (enemy, opponent) écraser; ~**whelming** *adj* (victory, defeat) écrasant(e); (desire) irrésistible

overwrought [əuvəˈrɔːt] *adj* excédé(e)

owe [əu] *vt:* **to ~ sb sth, to ~ sth to sb** devoir qch à qn; **owing to** *prep* à cause de, en raison de

owl [aul] *n* hibou *m*

own [əun] *vt* posséder ♦ *adj* propre; **a room of my ~** une chambre à moi, ma propre chambre; **to get one's ~ back** prendre sa revanche; **on one's ~** tout(e) seul(e); ~ **up** *vi* avouer; ~**er** *n* propriétaire *m/f*; ~**ership** *n* possession *f*

ox [ɔks] (pl ~**en**) *n* bœuf *m*; ~**tail** *n:* ~**tail soup** soupe *f* à la queue de bœuf

oxygen [ˈɔksɪdʒən] *n* oxygène *m*

oyster [ˈɔɪstəʳ] *n* huître *f*

oz. *abbr* = **ounce(s)**

ozone [ˈəuzəun]: ~**-friendly** *adj* qui n'attaque pas *or* qui préserve la couche d'ozone; ~ **hole** *n* trou *m* d'ozone; ~ **layer** *n* couche *f* d'ozone

P, p

p *abbr* = **penny; pence**

PA *n abbr* = **personal assistant; public address system**

pa [pɑː] (inf) *n* papa *m*

p.a. *abbr* = **per annum**

pace [peɪs] *n* pas *m*; (speed) allure *f*; vitesse *f* ♦ *vi:* **to ~ up and down** faire les cent pas; **to keep ~ with** aller à la même vitesse que; ~**maker** *n* (MED) stimulateur *m* cardiaque; (SPORT: also: ~**setter**) meneur(-euse) de train

Pacific [pəˈsɪfɪk] *n:* **the ~ (Ocean)** le Pacifique, l'océan *m* Pacifique

pack [pæk] *n* (~**et**, US: of cigarettes) paquet

m; (of hounds) meute *f*; (of thieves etc) bande *f*; (back ~) sac *m* à dos; (of cards) jeu *m* ♦ *vt* (goods) empaqueter, emballer; (box) remplir; (cram) entasser; **to ~ one's suitcase** faire sa valise; **to ~ (one's bags)** faire ses bagages; **to ~ sb off** expédier qn à; ~ **it in!** laisse tomber!, écrase!

package [ˈpækɪdʒ] *n* paquet *m*; (also: ~ **deal**) forfait *m*; ~ **tour** (BRIT) *n* voyage organisé

packed *adj* (crowded) bondé(e); ~ **lunch** (BRIT) *n* repas froid

packet [ˈpækɪt] *n* paquet *m*

packing [ˈpækɪŋ] *n* emballage *m*; ~ **case** *n* caisse *f* (d'emballage)

pact [pækt] *n* pacte *m*; traité *m*

pad [pæd] *n* bloc(-notes) *m*; (to prevent friction) tampon *m*; (inf: home) piaule *f* ♦ *vt* rembourrer; ~**ding** *n* rembourrage *m*

paddle [ˈpædl] *n* (oar) pagaie *f*; (US: for table tennis) raquette *f* de ping-pong ♦ *vt:* **to ~ a canoe** *etc* pagayer ♦ *vi* barboter, faire trempette; **paddling pool** (BRIT) *n* petit bassin

paddock [ˈpædək] *n* enclos *m*; (RACING) paddock *m*

padlock [ˈpædlɔk] *n* cadenas *m*

paediatrics [piːdɪˈætrɪks] (US **pediatrics**) *n* pédiatrie *f*

pagan [ˈpeɪgən] *adj, n* païen(ne)

page [peɪdʒ] *n* (of book) page *f*; (also: ~ **boy**) groom *m*, chasseur *m*; (at wedding) garçon *m* d'honneur ♦ *vt* (in hotel etc) (faire) appeler

pageant [ˈpædʒənt] *n* spectacle *m* historique; ~**ry** *n* apparat *m*, pompe *f*

pager [ˈpeɪdʒəʳ], **paging device** *n* (TEL) récepteur *m* d'appels

paid [peɪd] *pt, pp of* **pay** ♦ *adj* (work, official) rémunéré(e); (holiday) payé(e); **to put ~ to** (BRIT) mettre fin à, régler

pail [peɪl] *n* seau *m*

pain [peɪn] *n* douleur *f*; **to be in ~** souffrir, avoir mal; **to take ~s to do** se donner du mal pour faire; ~**ed** *adj* peiné(e), chagrin(e); ~**ful** *adj* douloureux(-euse); (fig) difficile, pénible; ~**fully** *adv* (fig: very) terriblement; **~killer** n analgésique m; **~less** adj indolore; **~staking** ['peɪnzteɪkɪŋ] adj (person) soigneux(-euse); (work) soigné(e)

paint [peɪnt] n peinture f ♦ vt peindre; **to ~ the door blue** peindre la porte en bleu; **~brush** n pinceau m; **~er** n peintre m; **~ing** n peinture f; (picture) tableau m; **~work** n peinture f

pair [peər] n (of shoes, gloves etc) paire f; (of people) couple m; **~ of scissors** (paire de) ciseaux mpl; **~ of trousers** pantalon m

pajamas [pə'dʒɑːməz] (US) npl pyjama(s) m(pl)

Pakistan [pɑːkɪ'stɑːn] n Pakistan m; **~i** adj pakistanais(e) ♦ n Pakistanais(e)

pal [pæl] (inf) n copain (copine)

palace ['pæləs] n palais m

palatable ['pælɪtəbl] adj bon (bonne), agréable au goût

palate ['pælɪt] n palais m (ANAT)

pale [peɪl] adj pâle ♦ n: **beyond the ~** (behaviour) inacceptable; **to grow ~** pâlir

Palestine ['pælɪstaɪn] n Palestine f; **Palestinian** [pælɪs'tɪnɪən] adj palestinien(ne) ♦ n Palestinien(ne)

palette ['pælɪt] n palette f

pall [pɔːl] n (of smoke) voile m ♦ vi devenir lassant(e)

pallet ['pælɪt] n (for goods) palette f

pallid ['pælɪd] adj blême

palm [pɑːm] n (of hand) paume f; (also: **~ tree**) palmier m ♦ vt: **to ~ sth off on sb** (inf) refiler qch à qn; **P~ Sunday** n le dimanche des Rameaux

paltry ['pɔːltrɪ] adj dérisoire

pamper ['pæmpər] vt gâter, dorloter

pamphlet ['pæmflət] n brochure f

pan [pæn] n (also: **saucepan**) casserole f; (also: **frying ~**) poêle f; **~cake** n crêpe f

panda ['pændə] n panda m

pandemonium [pændɪ'məʊnɪəm] n tohu-bohu m

pander ['pændər] vi: **to ~ to** flatter bassement; obéir servilement à

pane [peɪn] n carreau m, vitre f

panel ['pænl] n (of wood, cloth etc) panneau m; (RADIO, TV) experts mpl; (for interview, exams) jury m; **~ling** (US **paneling**) n boiseries fpl

pang [pæŋ] n: **~s of remorse/jealousy** affres mpl du remords/de la jalousie; **~s of hunger/conscience** tiraillements mpl d'estomac/de la conscience

panic ['pænɪk] n panique f, affolement m ♦ vi s'affoler, paniquer; **~ky** adj (person) qui panique or s'affole facilement; **~-stricken** adj affolé(e)

pansy ['pænzɪ] n (BOT) pensée f; (inf: pej) tapette f, pédé m

pant [pænt] vi haleter

panther ['pænθər] n panthère f

panties ['pæntɪz] npl slip m

pantomime ['pæntəmaɪm] (BRIT) n spectacle m de Noël

---

pantomime

i Une **pantomime**, que l'on appelle également de façon familière "panto", est un genre de farce où le personnage principal est souvent un jeune garçon et où il y a toujours une **dame**, c'est-à-dire une vieille femme jouée par un homme, et un méchant. La plupart du temps, l'histoire est basée sur un conte de fées comme Cendrillon ou Le Chat botté, et le public est encouragé à participer en prévenant le héros d'un danger imminent. Ce genre de spectacle, qui s'adresse surtout aux enfants, vise également un public d'adultes au travers des nombreuses plaisanteries faisant allusion à des faits d'actualité.

---

pantry ['pæntrɪ] n garde-manger m inv

pants [pænts] npl (BRIT: woman's) slip m; (: man's) slip m, caleçon m; (US: trousers) pantalon m

pantyhose ['pæntɪhəʊz] (US) npl collant m

paper ['peɪpər] n papier m; (also: **wallpaper**) papier peint; (also: **newspaper**) journal m; (academic essay) article m; (exam) épreuve écrite ♦ adj en or de papier ♦ vt tapisser (de papier peint); **~s** npl (also: **identity ~s**) papiers (d'identité);

~**back** *n* livre *m* de poche; livre broché *or* non relié; ~ **bag** *n* sac *m* en papier; ~ **clip** *n* trombone *m*; ~ **hankie** *n* mouchoir *m* en papier; ~**weight** *n* presse-papiers *m inv*; ~**work** *n* papiers *mpl*; *(pej)* paperasserie *f*

par [pɑːʳ] *n* pair *m*; *(GOLF)* normale *f* du parcours; **on a** ~ **with** à égalité avec, au même niveau que

parachute ['pærəʃuːt] *n* parachute *m*

parade [pə'reɪd] *n* défilé *m* ♦ *vt (fig)* faire étalage de ♦ *vi* défiler

paradise ['pærədaɪs] *n* paradis *m*

paradox ['pærədɔks] *n* paradoxe *m*; ~**ically** [pærə'dɔksɪklɪ] *adv* paradoxalement

paraffin ['pærəfɪn] *(BRIT) n (also: ~ oil)* pétrole *(lampant)*

paragon ['pærəgən] *n* modèle *m*

paragraph ['pærəgrɑːf] *n* paragraphe *m*

parallel ['pærəlel] *adj* parallèle; *(fig)* semblable ♦ *n (line)* parallèle *f*; *(fig, GEO)* parallèle *m*

paralyse ['pærəlaɪz] *(BRIT) vt* paralyser; **paralysis** [pə'rælɪsɪs] *n* paralysie *f*; **paralyze** *(US) vt* = **paralyse**

paramount ['pærəmaunt] *adj*: **of** ~ **importance** de la plus haute *or* grande importance

paranoid ['pærənɔɪd] *adj (PSYCH)* paranoïaque

paraphernalia [pærəfə'neɪlɪə] *n* attirail *m*

parasol ['pærəsɔl] *n* ombrelle *f*; *(over table)* parasol *m*

paratrooper ['pærətruːpəʳ] *n* parachutiste *m (soldat)*

parcel ['pɑːsl] *n* paquet *m*, colis *m* ♦ *vt (also: ~ up)* empaqueter

parchment ['pɑːtʃmənt] *n* parchemin *m*

pardon ['pɑːdn] *n* pardon *m*; grâce *f* ♦ *vt* pardonner à; ~ **me!, I beg your ~!** pardon!, je suis désolé!; **(I beg your) ~?,** *(US)* ~ **me?** pardon?

parent ['pɛərənt] *n* père *m or* mère *f*; ~**s** *npl* parents *mpl*

Paris ['pærɪs] *n* Paris

parish ['pærɪʃ] *n* paroisse *f*; *(BRIT: civil)* ≃ commune *f*

Parisian [pə'rɪzɪən] *adj* parisien(ne) ♦ *n* Parisien(ne)

park [pɑːk] *n* parc *m*, jardin public ♦ *vt* garer ♦ *vi* se garer

parking ['pɑːkɪŋ] *n* stationnement *m*; **"no ~"** "stationnement interdit"; ~ **lot** *(US)* parking *m*, parc *m* de stationnement; ~ **meter** *n* parcomètre *m*; ~ **ticket** *n* P.V. *m*

parliament ['pɑːləmənt] *n* parlement *m*; ~**ary** [pɑːlə'mentərɪ] *adj* parlementaire

parlour ['pɑːləʳ] *(US* **parlor)** *n* salon *m*

parochial [pə'rəukɪəl] *(pej) adj* à l'esprit de clocher

parole [pə'rəul] *n*: **on** ~ en liberté conditionnelle

parrot ['pærət] *n* perroquet *m*

parry ['pærɪ] *vt (blow)* esquiver

parsley ['pɑːslɪ] *n* persil *m*

parsnip ['pɑːsnɪp] *n* panais *m*

parson ['pɑːsn] *n* ecclésiastique *m*; *(Church of England)* pasteur *m*

part [pɑːt] *n* partie *f*; *(of machine)* pièce *f*; *(THEATRE etc)* rôle *m*; *(of serial)* épisode *m*; *(US: in hair)* raie *f* ♦ *adv* = **partly** ♦ *vt* séparer ♦ *vi (people)* se séparer; *(crowd)* s'ouvrir; **to take** ~ **in** participer à, prendre part à; **to take sth in good** ~ prendre qch du bon côté; **to take sb's** ~ prendre le parti de qn, prendre parti pour qn; **for my** ~ en ce qui me concerne; **for the most** ~ dans la plupart des cas; ~ **with** *vt fus* se séparer de; ~ **exchange** *(BRIT) n*: **in** ~ **exchange** en reprise

partial ['pɑːʃl] *adj (not complete)* partiel(le); **to be** ~ **to** avoir un faible pour

participate [pɑː'tɪsɪpeɪt] *vi*: **to** ~ **(in)** participer (à), prendre part (à); **participation** [pɑːtɪsɪ'peɪʃən] *n* participation *f*

participle ['pɑːtɪsɪpl] *n* participe *m*

particle ['pɑːtɪkl] *n* particule *f*

particular [pə'tɪkjuləʳ] *adj* particulier(-ère); *(special)* spécial(e); *(fussy)* difficile; méticuleux(-euse); ~**s** *npl (details)* détails *mpl*; *(personal)* nom, adresse etc; **in** ~ en particulier; ~**ly** *adv* particulièrement

parting ['pɑːtɪŋ] *n* séparation *f*; *(BRIT: in*

hair) raie f ♦ *adj* d'adieu

partisan [pɑ:tɪ'zæn] *n* partisan(e) ♦ *adj* partisan(e); de parti

partition [pɑ:'tɪʃən] *n* (*wall*) cloison f; (*POL*) partition f, division f

partly ['pɑ:tlɪ] *adv* en partie, partiellement

partner ['pɑ:tnər] *n* partenaire m/f; (*in marriage*) conjoint(e); (*boyfriend, girlfriend*) ami(e); (*COMM*) associé(e); (*at dance*) cavalier(-ère); ~**ship** *n* association f

partridge ['pɑ:trɪdʒ] *n* perdrix f

part-time ['pɑ:t'taɪm] *adj, adv* à mi-temps, à temps partiel

party ['pɑ:tɪ] *n* (*POL*) parti m; (*group*) groupe m; (*LAW*) partie f; (*celebration*) réception f; soirée f; fête f ♦ *cpd* (*POL*) de or du parti; ~ **dress** *n* robe habillée

pass [pɑ:s] *vt* passer; (*place*) passer devant; (*friend*) croiser; (*overtake*) dépasser; (*exam*) être reçu(e) à, réussir; (*approve*) approuver, accepter ♦ *vi* passer; (*SCOL*) être reçu(e) or admis(e), réussir ♦ *n* (*permit*) laissez-passer m inv; carte f d'accès or d'abonnement; (*in mountains*) col m; (*SPORT*) passe f; (*SCOL: also*: ~ **mark**): **to get a** ~ être reçu(e) (sans mention); **to make a** ~ **at sb** (*inf*) faire des avances à qn; ~ **away** *vi* mourir; ~ **by** *vi* passer ♦ *vt* négliger; ~ **on** *vt* (*news, object*) transmettre; (*illness*) passer; ~ **out** *vi* s'évanouir; ~ **up** *vt* (*opportunity*) laisser passer; ~**able** *adj* (*road*) praticable; (*work*) acceptable

passage ['pæsɪdʒ] *n* (*also*: ~**way**) couloir m; (*gen, in book*) passage m; (*by boat*) traversée f

passbook ['pɑ:sbʊk] *n* livret m

passenger ['pæsɪndʒər] *n* passager(-ère)

passer-by [pɑ:sə'baɪ] (*pl* ~**s-**~) *n* passant(e)

passing ['pɑ:sɪŋ] *adj* (*fig*) passager(-ère); **in** ~ en passant; ~ **place** *n* (*AUT*) aire f de croisement

passion ['pæʃən] *n* passion f; ~**ate** *adj* passionné(e)

passive ['pæsɪv] *adj* (*also LING*) passif(-ive); ~ **smoking** *n* tabagisme m passif

Passover ['pɑ:səʊvər] *n* Pâque f (*juive*)

passport ['pɑ:spɔ:t] *n* passeport m; ~ **control** *n* contrôle m des passeports; ~ **office** *n* bureau m de délivrance des passeports

password ['pɑ:swɜ:d] *n* mot m de passe

past [pɑ:st] *prep* (*in front of*) devant; (*further than*) au delà de, plus loin que; après; (*later than*) après ♦ *adj* passé(e); (*president etc*) ancien(ne) ♦ *n* passé m; **he's** ~ **forty** il a dépassé la quarantaine, il a plus de or passé quarante ans; **for the** ~ **few/3 days** depuis quelques/3 jours; ces derniers/3 derniers jours; **ten/quarter** ~ **eight** huit heures dix/un et quart

pasta ['pæstə] *n* pâtes fpl

paste [peɪst] *n* pâte f; (*meat* ~) pâté m (à tartiner); (*tomato* ~) purée f, concentré m; (*glue*) colle f (de pâte) ♦ *vt* coller

pasteurized ['pæstʃəraɪzd] *adj* pasteurisé(e)

pastille ['pæstɪl] *n* pastille f

pastime ['pɑ:staɪm] *n* passe-temps m inv

pastry ['peɪstrɪ] *n* pâte f; (*cake*) pâtisserie f

pasture ['pɑ:stʃər] *n* pâturage m

pasty [*n* 'pæstɪ, *adj* 'peɪstɪ] *n* petit pâté (en croûte) ♦ *adj* (*complexion*) terreux(-euse)

pat [pæt] *vt* tapoter; (*dog*) caresser

patch [pætʃ] *n* (*of material*) pièce f; (*eye* ~) cache m; (*spot*) tache f; (*on tyre*) rustine f ♦ *vt* (*clothes*) rapiécer; **(to go through) a bad** ~ (passer par) une période difficile; ~ **up** *vt* réparer (grossièrement); **to** ~ **up a quarrel** se raccommoder; ~**y** *adj* inégal(e); (*incomplete*) fragmentaire

pâté ['pæteɪ] *n* pâté m, terrine f

patent ['peɪtnt] *n* brevet m (d'invention) ♦ *vt* faire breveter ♦ *adj* patent(e), manifeste; ~ **leather** *n* cuir verni

paternal [pə'tɜ:nl] *adj* paternel(le)

path [pɑ:θ] *n* chemin m, sentier m; (*in garden*) allée f; (*trajectory*) trajectoire f

pathetic [pə'θetɪk] *adj* (*pitiful*) pitoyable; (*very bad*) lamentable, minable

pathological [pæθə'lɒdʒɪkl] *adj* pathologique

pathway ['pɑ:θweɪ] *n* sentier m, passage

m

patience ['peɪʃns] *n* patience *f*; (*BRIT: CARDS*) réussite *f*

patient ['peɪʃnt] *n* malade *m/f*; (*of dentist etc*) patient(e) ♦ *adj* patient(e)

patio ['pætɪəu] *n* patio *m*

patriotic [pætrɪ'ɔtɪk] *adj* patriotique; (*person*) patriote

patrol [pə'trəul] *n* patrouille *f* ♦ *vt* patrouiller dans; ~ **car** *n* voiture *f* de police; ~**man** (*irreg*) (*US*) *n* agent *m* de police

patron ['peɪtrən] *n* (*in shop*) client(e); (*of charity*) patron(ne); ~ **of the arts** mécène *m*; ~**ize** ['pætrənaɪz] *vt* (*pej*) traiter avec condescendance; (*shop, club*) être (un) client *or* un habitué de

patter ['pætə'] *n* crépitement *m*, tapotement *m*; (*sales talk*) boniment *m*

pattern ['pætən] *n* (*design*) motif *m*; (*SEWING*) patron *m*

pauper ['pɔːpə'] *n* indigent(e)

pause [pɔːz] *n* pause *f*, arrêt *m* ♦ *vi* faire une pause, s'arrêter

pave [peɪv] *vt* paver, daller; **to ~ the way for** ouvrir la voie à

pavement ['peɪvmənt] (*BRIT*) *n* trottoir *m*

pavilion [pə'vɪlɪən] *n* pavillon *m*; tente *f*

paving ['peɪvɪŋ] *n* (*material*) pavé *m*, dalle *f*; ~ **stone** *n* pavé *m*

paw [pɔː] *n* patte *f*

pawn [pɔːn] *n* (*CHESS, also fig*) pion *m* ♦ *vt* mettre en gage; ~**broker** *n* prêteur *m* sur gages; ~**shop** *n* mont-de-piété *m*

pay [peɪ] (*pt, pp* **paid**) *n* salaire *m*; paie *f* ♦ *vt* payer ♦ *vi* payer; (*be profitable*) être rentable; **to ~ attention (to)** prêter attention (à); **to ~ sb a visit** rendre visite à qn; **to ~ one's respects to sb** présenter ses respects à qn; ~ **back** *vt* rembourser; ~ **for** *vt fus* payer; ~ **in** *vt* verser; ~ **off** *vt* régler, acquitter; (*person*) rembourser ♦ *vi* (*scheme, decision*) se révéler payant(e); ~ **up** *vt* (*money*) payer; ~**able** *adj*: ~**able to sb** (*cheque*) à l'ordre de qn; ~**ee** [peɪ'iː] *n* bénéficiaire *m/f*; ~ **envelope** (*US*) *n* = **pay packet**; ~**ment** *n* paiement *m*; règlement *m*; **monthly ~ment** mensualité

f; ~ **packet** (*BRIT*) *n* paie *f*; ~ **phone** *n* cabine *f* téléphonique, téléphone public; ~**roll** *n* registre *m* du personnel; ~ **slip** (*BRIT*) *n* bulletin *m* de paie; ~ **television** *n* chaînes *fpl* payantes

PC *n abbr* = **personal computer**

p.c. *abbr* = **per cent**

pea [piː] *n* (petit) pois

peace [piːs] *n* paix *f*; (*calm*) calme *m*, tranquillité *f*; ~**ful** *adj* paisible, calme

peach [piːtʃ] *n* pêche *f*

peacock ['piːkɔk] *n* paon *m*

peak [piːk] *n* (*mountain*) pic *m*, cime *f*; (*of cap*) visière *f*; (*fig: highest level*) maximum *m*; (: *of career, fame*) apogée *m*; ~ **hours** *npl* heures *fpl* de pointe

peal [piːl] *n* (*of bells*) carillon *m*; ~ **of laughter** éclat *m* de rire

peanut ['piːnʌt] *n* arachide *f*, cacahuète *f*; ~ **butter** *n* beurre *m* de cacahuète

pear [pɛə'] *n* poire *f*

pearl [pɜːl] *n* perle *f*

peasant ['pɛznt] *n* paysan(ne)

peat [piːt] *n* tourbe *f*

pebble ['pɛbl] *n* caillou *m*, galet *m*

peck [pɛk] *vt* (*also:* ~ **at**) donner un coup de bec à ♦ *n* coup *m* de bec; (*kiss*) bise *f*; ~**ing order** *n* ordre *m* des préséances; ~**ish** (*BRIT: inf*) *adj*: **I feel ~ish** je mangerais bien quelque chose

peculiar [pɪ'kjuːlɪə'] *adj* étrange, bizarre, curieux(-euse); ~ **to** particulier(-ère) à

pedal ['pɛdl] *n* pédale *f* ♦ *vi* pédaler

pedantic [pɪ'dæntɪk] *adj* pédant(e)

peddler ['pɛdlə'] *n* (*of drugs*) revendeur(-euse)

pedestal ['pɛdəstl] *n* piédestal *m*

pedestrian [pɪ'dɛstrɪən] *n* piéton *m*; ~ **crossing** (*BRIT*) *n* passage clouté; ~**ized** *adj*: **a ~ized street** une rue piétonne

pediatrics [piːdɪ'ætrɪks] (*US*) *n* = **paediatrics**

pedigree ['pɛdɪgriː] *n* ascendance *f*; (*of animal*) pedigree *m* ♦ *cpd* (*animal*) de race

pee [piː] *n* (*inf*) *vi* faire pipi, pisser

peek [piːk] *vi* jeter un coup d'œil (furtif)

peel [piːl] *n* pelure *f*, épluchure *f*; (*of or-*

ange, lemon) écorce f ♦ vt peler, éplucher ♦ vi *(paint etc)* s'écailler; *(wallpaper)* se décoller; *(skin)* peler

peep [piːp] n *(BRIT: look)* coup d'œil furtif; *(sound)* pépiement m ♦ vi *(BRIT)* jeter un coup d'œil furtif; **~ out** vi *(BRIT)* se montrer (furtivement); **~hole** n judas m

peer [pɪəʳ] vi: **to ~ at** regarder attentivement, scruter ♦ n *(noble)* pair m; *(equal)* pair, égal(e); **~age** [ˈpɪərɪdʒ] n pairie f

peeved [piːvd] adj irrité(e), fâché(e)

peg [pɛg] n *(for coat etc)* patère f; *(BRIT: also:* **clothes ~)** pince f à linge

Pekin(g)ese [piːkɪˈniːz] n *(dog)* pékinois m

pelican [ˈpɛlɪkən] n pélican m; **~ crossing** *(BRIT)* n *(AUT)* feu m à commande manuelle

pellet [ˈpɛlɪt] n boulette f; *(of lead)* plomb m

pelt [pɛlt] vt: **to ~ sb (with)** bombarder qn (de) ♦ vi *(rain)* tomber à seaux; *(inf: run)* courir à toutes jambes ♦ n peau f

pelvis [ˈpɛlvɪs] n bassin m

pen [pɛn] n *(for writing)* stylo m; *(for sheep)* parc m

penal [ˈpiːnl] adj pénal(e); *(system, colony)* pénitentiaire; **~ize** [ˈpiːnəlaɪz] vt pénaliser

penalty [ˈpɛnltɪ] n pénalité f; sanction f; *(fine)* amende f; *(SPORT)* pénalisation f; *(FOOTBALL)* penalty m; *(RUGBY)* pénalité f

penance [ˈpɛnəns] n pénitence f

pence [pɛns] *(BRIT)* npl of **penny**

pencil [ˈpɛnsl] n crayon m; **~ case** n trousse f (d'écolier); **~ sharpener** n taille-crayon(s) m inv

pendant [ˈpɛndnt] n pendentif m

pending [ˈpɛndɪŋ] prep en attendant ♦ adj en suspens

pendulum [ˈpɛndjuləm] n *(of clock)* balancier m

penetrate [ˈpɛnɪtreɪt] vt pénétrer dans; pénétrer

penfriend [ˈpɛnfrɛnd] *(BRIT)* n correspondant(e)

penguin [ˈpɛŋgwɪn] n pingouin m

penicillin [pɛnɪˈsɪlɪn] n pénicilline f

peninsula [pəˈnɪnsjulə] n péninsule f

penis [ˈpiːnɪs] n pénis m, verge f

penitentiary [pɛnɪˈtɛnʃərɪ] n prison f

penknife [ˈpɛnnaɪf] n canif m

pen name n nom m de plume, pseudonyme m

penniless [ˈpɛnɪlɪs] adj sans le sou

penny [ˈpɛnɪ] *(pl* **pennies** *or (BRIT)* **pence)** n penny m

penpal [ˈpɛnpæl] n correspondant(e)

pension [ˈpɛnʃən] n pension f; *(from company)* retraite f; **~er** *(BRIT)* n retraité(e); **~ fund** n caisse f de pension; **~ plan** n plan m de retraite

---

Pentagon

ⓘ Le **Pentagon** est le nom donné aux bureaux du ministère de la Défense américain, situés à Arlington en Virginie, à cause de la forme pentagonale du bâtiment dans lequel ils se trouvent. Par extension, ce terme est également utilisé en parlant du ministère lui-même.

---

pentathlon [pɛnˈtæθlən] n pentathlon m

Pentecost [ˈpɛntɪkɔst] n Pentecôte f

penthouse [ˈpɛnthaus] n appartement m (de luxe) (en attique)

pent-up [ˈpɛntʌp] adj *(feelings)* refoulé(e)

penultimate [peˈnʌltɪmət] adj avant-dernier(-ère)

people [ˈpiːpl] npl gens mpl; personnes fpl; *(inhabitants)* population f; *(POL)* peuple m ♦ n *(nation, race)* peuple m; **several ~ came** plusieurs personnes sont venues; **~ say that ...** on dit que ...

pep up [ˈpɛp-] *(inf)* vt remonter

pepper [ˈpɛpəʳ] n poivre m; *(vegetable)* poivron m ♦ vt *(fig)*: **to ~ with** bombarder de; **~ mill** n moulin m à poivre; **~mint** n *(sweet)* pastille f de menthe

peptalk [ˈpɛptɔːk] *(inf)* n (petit) discours d'encouragement

per [pəːʳ] prep par; **~ hour** *(miles etc)* à l'heure; *(fee)* (de) l'heure; **~ kilo** etc le kilo etc; **~ annum** par an; **~ capita** par personne, par habitant

perceive [pə'siːv] *vt* percevoir; *(notice)* remarquer, s'apercevoir de

per cent *adv* pour cent; **percentage** *n* pourcentage *m*

perception [pə'sɛpʃən] *n* perception *f*; *(insight)* perspicacité *f*

perceptive [pə'sɛptɪv] *adj* pénétrant(e); *(person)* perspicace

perch [pəːtʃ] *n* (fish) perche *f*; (for bird) perchoir *m* ♦ *vi*: **to ~ on** se percher sur

percolator ['pəːkəleɪtəʳ] *n* cafetière *f* (électrique)

percussion [pə'kʌʃən] *n* percussion *f*

perennial [pə'rɛnɪəl] *adj* perpétuel(le); *(BOT)* vivace

perfect [adj, n 'pəːfɪkt, vb pə'fɛkt] *adj* parfait(e) ♦ *n* (also: ~ **tense**) parfait *m* ♦ *vt* parfaire; mettre au point; **~ly** *adv* parfaitement

perforate ['pəːfəreɪt] *vt* perforer, percer; **perforation** [pəːfə'reɪʃən] *n* perforation *f*

perform [pə'fɔːm] *vt* (carry out) exécuter; (concert etc) jouer, donner ♦ *vi* jouer; **~ance** *n* représentation *f*, spectacle *m*; (of an artist) interprétation *f*; (SPORT) performance *f*; (of car, engine) fonctionnement *m*; (of company, economy) résultats *mpl*; **~er** *n* artiste *m/f*, interprète *m/f*

perfume ['pəːfjuːm] *n* parfum *m*

perhaps [pə'hæps] *adv* peut-être

peril ['pɛrɪl] *n* péril *m*

perimeter [pə'rɪmɪtəʳ] *n* périmètre *m*

period ['pɪərɪəd] *n* période *f*; (of history) époque *f*; (SCOL) cours *m*; (full stop) point *m*; (MED) règles *fpl* ♦ *adj* (costume, furniture) d'époque; **~ic(al)** [pɪərɪ'ɔdɪk(l)] *adj* périodique; **~ical** [pɪərɪ'ɔdɪkl] *n* périodique *m*

peripheral [pə'rɪfərəl] *adj* périphérique ♦ *n* (COMPUT) périphérique *m*

perish ['pɛrɪʃ] *vi* périr; (decay) se détériorer; **~able** *adj* périssable

perjury ['pəːdʒərɪ] *n* parjure *m*, faux serment

perk [pəːk] *n* avantage *m* accessoire, à-côté *m*; **~ up** *vi* (cheer up) se ragaillardir; **~y** *adj* (cheerful) guilleret(te)

perm [pəːm] *n* (for hair) permanente *f*

permanent ['pəːmənənt] *adj* permanent(e)

permeate ['pəːmɪeɪt] *vi* s'infiltrer ♦ *vt* s'infiltrer dans; pénétrer

permissible [pə'mɪsɪbl] *adj* permis(e), acceptable

permission [pə'mɪʃən] *n* permission *f*, autorisation *f*

permissive [pə'mɪsɪv] *adj* tolérant(e), permissif(-ive)

permit [n 'pəːmɪt, vb pə'mɪt] *n* permis *m* ♦ *vt* permettre

perpendicular [pəːpən'dɪkjuləʳ] *adj* perpendiculaire

perplex [pə'plɛks] *vt* rendre perplexe

persecute ['pəːsɪkjuːt] *vt* persécuter

persevere [pəːsɪ'vɪəʳ] *vi* persévérer

Persian ['pəːʃən] *adj* persan(e) ♦ *n* (LING) persan *m*; **the ~ Gulf** le golfe Persique

persist [pə'sɪst] *vi*: **to ~ (in doing)** persister or s'obstiner (à faire); **~ent** [pə'sɪstənt] *adj* persistant(e), tenace; **~ent vegetative state** état *m* végétatif persistant

person ['pəːsn] *n* personne *f*, **in ~** en personne; **~al** *adj* personnel(le); **~al assistant** *n* secrétaire privé(e); **~al column** *n* annonces personnelles; **~al computer** *n* ordinateur personnel; **~ality** [pəːsə'nælɪtɪ] *n* personnalité *f*; **~ally** *adv* personnellement; **to take sth ~ally** se sentir visé(e) (par qch); **~al organizer** *n* filofax ® *m*; **~al stereo** *n* Walkman ® *m*, baladeur *m*

personnel [pəːsə'nɛl] *n* personnel *m*

perspective [pə'spɛktɪv] *n* perspective *f*; **to get things into ~** faire la part des choses

Perspex ® ['pəːspɛks] *n* plexiglas ® *m*

perspiration [pəːspɪ'reɪʃən] *n* transpiration *f*

persuade [pə'sweɪd] *vt*: **to ~ sb to do sth** persuader qn de faire qch; **persuasion** [pə'sweɪʒən] *n* persuasion *f*; (creed) religion *f*

perverse [pə'vəːs] *adj* pervers(e); (contrary) contrariant(e); **pervert** [n 'pəːvəːt, vb pə'vəːt] *n* perverti(e) ♦ *vt* pervertir; (words) déformer

pessimist ['pesɪmɪst] n pessimiste m/f; **~ic** [pesɪ'mɪstɪk] adj pessimiste

pest [pest] n animal m (or insecte m) nuisible; (fig) fléau m

pester ['pestə^r] vt importuner, harceler

pet [pet] n animal familier ♦ cpd (favourite) favori(te) ♦ vt (stroke) caresser, câliner; **teacher's ~** chouchou m du professeur; **~ hate** bête noire

petal ['petl] n pétale m

peter out ['pi:tə-] vi (stream, conversation) tarir; (meeting) tourner court; (road) se perdre

petite [pə'ti:t] adj menu(e)

petition [pə'tɪʃən] n pétition f

petrified ['petrɪfaɪd] adj (fig) mort(e) de peur

petrol ['petrəl] (BRIT) n essence f; **four-star ~** super m; **~ can** n bidon m à essence

petroleum [pə'trəulɪəm] n pétrole m

petrol: **~ pump** (BRIT) n pompe f à essence; **~ station** (BRIT) n station-service f; **~ tank** (BRIT) n réservoir m d'essence

petticoat ['petɪkəut] n combinaison f

petty ['petɪ] adj (mean) mesquin(e); (unimportant) insignifiant(e), sans importance; **~ cash** n caisse f des dépenses courantes; **~ officer** n second-maître m

petulant ['petjulənt] adj boudeur(-euse), irritable

pew [pju:] n banc m (d'église)

pewter ['pju:tə^r] n étain m

phantom ['fæntəm] n fantôme m

pharmacy ['fɑ:məsɪ] n pharmacie f

phase [feɪz] n phase f ♦ vt: **to ~ sth in/ out** introduire/supprimer qch progressivement

PhD abbr = **Doctor of Philosophy** ♦ abbr (title) ≈ docteur m (en droit or lettres etc), ≈ doctorat m; (person) titulaire m/f d'un doctorat

pheasant ['feznt] n faisan m

phenomenon [fə'nɔmɪnən] (pl **phenomena**) n phénomène m

philosophical [fɪlə'sɔfɪkl] adj philosophique

philosophy [fɪ'lɔsəfɪ] n philosophie f

phobia ['fəubjə] n phobie f

phone [fəun] n téléphone m ♦ vt téléphoner; **to be on the ~** avoir le téléphone; (be calling) être au téléphone; **~ back** vt, vi rappeler; **~ up** vt téléphoner à ♦ vi téléphoner; **~ bill** n facture f de téléphone; **~ book** n annuaire m; **~ booth**, **~ box** (BRIT) n cabine f téléphonique; **~ call** n coup m de fil or de téléphone; **~card** n carte f de téléphone; **~-in** (BRIT) n (RADIO, TV) programme m à ligne ouverte; **~ number** n numéro m de téléphone

phonetics [fə'netɪks] n phonétique f

phoney ['fəunɪ] adj faux (fausse), factice; (person) pas franc (franche), poseur(-euse)

photo ['fəutəu] n photo f; **~copier** n photocopieuse f; **~copy** n photocopie f ♦ vt photocopier; **~graph** n photographie f ♦ vt photographier; **~grapher** [fə'tɔgrəfə^r] n photographe m/f; **~graphy** [fə'tɔgrəfɪ] n photographie f

phrase [freɪz] n expression f; ~(LING) locution f ♦ vt exprimer; **~ book** n recueil m d'expressions (pour touristes)

physical ['fɪzɪkl] adj physique; **~ education** n éducation f physique; **~ly** adv physiquement

physician [fɪ'zɪʃən] n médecin m

physicist ['fɪzɪsɪst] n physicien(ne)

physics ['fɪzɪks] n physique f

physiotherapist [fɪzɪəu'θerəpɪst] n kinésithérapeute m/f

physiotherapy [fɪzɪəu'θerəpɪ] n kinésithérapie f

physique [fɪ'zi:k] n physique m; constitution f

pianist ['pi:ənɪst] n pianiste m/f

piano [pɪ'ænəu] n piano m

pick [pɪk] n (tool: also: **~axe**) pic m, pioche f ♦ vt choisir; (fruit etc) cueillir; (remove) prendre; (lock) forcer; **take your ~** faites votre choix; **the ~ of** le (la) meilleur(e) de; **to ~ one's nose** se mettre les doigts dans le nez; **to ~ one's teeth** se curer les dents; **to ~ a quarrel with sb** chercher noise à qn; **~ at** vt fus: **to ~ at one's**

food manger du bout des dents, chipoter; ~ **on** *vt fus* (*person*) harceler; ~ **out** *vt* (*knowledge*) soutirer; ~ **up** *vi* (*improve*) s'améliorer ♦ *vt* ramasser; (*collect*) passer prendre; (*AUT: give lift to*) prendre, emmener; (*learn*) apprendre; (*RADIO*) capter; **to ~ up speed** prendre de la vitesse; **to ~ o.s. up** se relever

picket ['pɪkɪt] *n* (*in strike*) piquet *m* de grève ♦ *vt* mettre un piquet de grève devant

pickle ['pɪkl] *n* (*also:* ~**s**: *as condiment*) pickles *mpl*; *petits légumes macérés dans du vinaigre* ♦ *vt* conserver dans du vinaigre *or* dans de la saumure; **to be in a ~** (*mess*) être dans le pétrin

pickpocket ['pɪkpɔkɪt] *n* pickpocket *m*

pick-up ['pɪkʌp] *n* (*small truck*) pick-up *m inv*

picnic ['pɪknɪk] *n* pique-nique *m*

picture ['pɪktʃər] *n* image *f*; (*painting*) peinture *f*, tableau *m*; (*etching*) gravure *f*; (*photograph*) photo(graphie) *f*; (*drawing*) dessin *m*; (*film*) film *m*; (*fig*) description *f*, tableau *m* ♦ *vt* se représenter; **the ~s** (*BRIT: inf*) le cinéma; ~ **book** *n* livre *m* d'images

picturesque [pɪktʃə'resk] *adj* pittoresque

pie [paɪ] *n* tourte *f*; (*of fruit*) tarte *f*; (*of meat*) pâté *m* en croûte

piece [piːs] *n* morceau *m*; (*item*): **a ~ of furniture/advice** un meuble/conseil ♦ *vt*: **to ~ together** rassembler; **to take to ~s** démonter; ~**meal** *adv* (*irregularly*) au coup par coup; (*bit by bit*) par bouts; ~**work** *n* travail *m* aux pièces

pie chart *n* graphique *m* circulaire, camembert *m*

pier [pɪər] *n* jetée *f*

pierce [pɪəs] *vt* percer, transpercer; ~**d** *adj* (*ears*) percé(e)

pig [pɪg] *n* cochon *m*, porc *m*

pigeon ['pɪdʒən] *n* pigeon *m*; ~**hole** *n* casier *m*

piggy bank ['pɪgɪ-] *n* tirelire *f*

pig: ~**headed** *adj* entêté(e), têtu(e); ~**let** *n* porcelet *m*, petit cochon *m*; ~**skin** *n* peau *m* de porc; ~**sty** *n* porcherie *f*; ~**tail** *n* natte *f*, tresse *f*

pike [paɪk] *n* (*fish*) brochet *m*

pilchard ['pɪltʃəd] *n* pilchard *m* (*sorte de sardine*)

pile [paɪl] *n* (*pillar, of books*) pile *f*; (*heap*) tas *m*; (*of carpet*) poils *mpl* ♦ *vt* (*also:* ~ **up**) empiler, entasser ♦ *vi* (*also:* ~ **up**) s'entasser, s'accumuler; **to ~ into** (*car*) s'entasser dans; ~**s** *npl* hémorroïdes *fpl*; ~-**up** *n* (*AUT*) télescopage *m*, collision *f* en série

pilfering ['pɪlfərɪŋ] *n* chapardage *m*

pilgrim ['pɪlgrɪm] *n* pèlerin *m*

pill [pɪl] *n* pilule *f*

pillage ['pɪlɪdʒ] *vt* piller

pillar ['pɪlər] *n* pilier *m*; ~ **box** (*BRIT*) *n* boîte *f* aux lettres (*publique*)

pillion ['pɪljən] *n*: **to ride ~** (*on motorcycle*) monter derrière

pillow ['pɪləʊ] *n* oreiller *m*; ~**case** *n* taie *f* d'oreiller

pilot ['paɪlət] *n* pilote *m* ♦ *cpd* (*scheme etc*) pilote, expérimental(e) ♦ *vt* piloter; ~ **light** *n* veilleuse *f*

pimp [pɪmp] *n* souteneur *m*, maquereau *m*

pimple ['pɪmpl] *n* bouton *m*

pin [pɪn] *n* épingle *f*; (*TECH*) cheville *f* ♦ *vt* épingler; ~**s and needles** fourmis *fpl*; **to ~ sb down** (*fig*) obliger qn à répondre; **to ~ sth on sb** (*fig*) mettre qch sur le dos de qn

PIN [pɪn] *n abbr* (= *personal identification number*) numéro *m* d'identification personnel

pinafore ['pɪnəfɔːr] *n* tablier *m*

pinball ['pɪnbɔːl] *n* flipper *m*

pincers ['pɪnsəz] *npl* tenailles *fpl*; (*of crab etc*) pinces *fpl*

pinch [pɪntʃ] *n* (*of salt etc*) pincée *f* ♦ *vt* pincer; (*inf: steal*) piquer, chiper; **at a ~** à la rigueur

pincushion ['pɪnkuʃən] *n* pelote *f* à épingles

pine [paɪn] *n* (*also:* ~ **tree**) pin *m* ♦ *vi*: **to ~ for** s'ennuyer de, désirer ardemment; ~ **away** *vi* dépérir

pineapple ['paɪnæpl] n ananas m

ping [pɪŋ] n (noise) tintement m; **~-pong**
® n ping-pong ® m

pink [pɪŋk] adj rose ♦ n (colour) rose m;
(BOT) œillet m, mignardise f

PIN (number) ['pɪn(-)] n code m confidentiel

pinpoint ['pɪnpɔɪnt] vt indiquer or localiser
(avec précision); (problem) mettre le doigt
sur

pint [paɪnt] n pinte f (BRIT = 0.57l; US = 0.47l);
(BRIT: inf) ≈ demi m

pioneer [paɪə'nɪə*] n pionnier m

pious ['paɪəs] adj pieux(-euse)

pip [pɪp] n (seed) pépin m; **the ~s** npl (BRIT:
time signal on radio) le(s) top(s) sonore(s)

pipe [paɪp] n tuyau m, conduite f; (for smoking) pipe f ♦ vt amener par tuyau; **~s** npl
(also: **bagpipes**) cornemuse f; **~ cleaner**
n cure-pipe m; **~ dream** n chimère f,
château m en Espagne; **~line** n pipe-line
m; **~r** n joueur(-euse) de cornemuse

piping ['paɪpɪŋ] adv: **~ hot** très chaud(e)

pique ['piːk] n dépit m

pirate ['paɪərət] n pirate m; **~d** adj pirate

Pisces ['paɪsiːz] n les Poissons mpl

piss [pɪs] (inf!) vi pisser; **~ed** (inf!) adj
(drunk) bourré(e)

pistol ['pɪstl] n pistolet m

piston ['pɪstən] n piston m

pit [pɪt] n trou m, fosse f; (also: **coal ~**)
puits m de mine; (quarry) carrière f ♦ vt:
to ~ one's wits against sb se mesurer à
qn; **~s** npl (AUT) aire f de service

pitch [pɪtʃ] n (MUS) ton m; (BRIT: SPORT) terrain m; (tar) poix f; (fig) degré m; point m
♦ vt (throw) lancer ♦ vi (fall) tomber; **to ~
a tent** dresser une tente; **~-black** adj
noir(e) (comme du cirage); **~ed battle** n
bataille rangée

pitfall ['pɪtfɔːl] n piège m

pith [pɪθ] n (of orange etc) intérieur m de
l'écorce; **~y** adj piquant(e)

pitiful ['pɪtɪful] adj (touching) pitoyable

pitiless ['pɪtɪlɪs] adj impitoyable

pittance ['pɪtns] n salaire m de misère

pity ['pɪtɪ] n pitié f ♦ vt plaindre; **what a ~!**
quel dommage!

pizza ['piːtsə] n pizza f

placard ['plækɑːd] n affiche f; (in march)
pancarte f

placate [plə'keɪt] vt apaiser, calmer

place [pleɪs] n endroit m, lieu m; (proper
position, job, rank, seat) place f; (home):
at/to his ~ chez lui ♦ vt (object) placer,
mettre; (identify) situer; reconnaître; **to
take ~** avoir lieu; **out of ~** (not suitable)
déplacé(e), inopportun(e); **to change ~s
with sb** changer de place avec qn; **in the
first ~** d'abord, en premier

plague [pleɪg] n fléau m; (MED) peste f
♦ vt (fig) tourmenter

plaice [pleɪs] n inv carrelet m

plaid [plæd] n tissu écossais

plain [pleɪn] adj (in one colour) uni(e); (simple) simple; (clear) clair(e), évident(e); (not
handsome) quelconque, ordinaire ♦ adv
franchement, carrément ♦ n plaine f; **~
chocolate** n chocolat m à croquer; **~
clothes** adj (police officer) en civil; **~ly**
adv clairement; (frankly) carrément, sans
détours

plaintiff ['pleɪntɪf] n plaignant(e)

plait [plæt] n tresse f, natte f

plan [plæn] n plan m; (scheme) projet m
♦ vt (think in advance) projeter; (prepare)
organiser; (house) dresser les plans de,
concevoir ♦ vi faire des projets; **to ~ to
do** prévoir de faire

plane [pleɪn] n (AVIAT) avion m; (ART, MATH
etc) plan m; (fig) niveau m, plan; (tool) rabot m; (also: **~ tree**) platane m ♦ vt rabo-
ter

planet ['plænɪt] n planète f

plank [plæŋk] n planche f

planner ['plænə*] n planificateur(-trice);
(town ~) urbaniste m/f

planning ['plænɪŋ] n planification f; **family
~** planning familial; **~ permission** n
permis m de construire

plant [plɑːnt] n plante f; (machinery) matériel m; (factory) usine f ♦ vt planter;
(bomb) poser; (microphone, incriminating
evidence) cacher

plaster ['plɑːstəʳ] *n* plâtre *m*; (*also:* ~ **of Paris**) plâtre à mouler; (*BRIT: also:* **sticking ~**) pansement adhésif ♦ *vt* plâtrer; (*cover*): **to ~ with** couvrir de; **~ed** (*inf*) *adj* soûl(e)

plastic ['plæstɪk] *n* plastique *m* ♦ *adj* (*made of ~*) en plastique; **~ bag** *n* sac *m* en plastique

Plasticine ® ['plæstɪsiːn] *n* pâte *f* à modeler

plastic surgery *n* chirurgie *f* esthétique

plate [pleɪt] *n* (*dish*) assiette *f*; (*in book*) gravure *f*, planche *f*; (*dental ~*) dentier *m*

plateau ['plætəu] (*pl* **~s** *or* **~x**) *n* plateau *m*

plate glass *n* verre *m* (de vitrine)

platform ['plætfɔːm] *n* plate-forme *f*; (*at meeting*) tribune *f*; (*stage*) estrade *f*; (*RAIL*) quai *m*

platinum ['plætɪnəm] *n* platine *m*

platter ['plætəʳ] *n* plat *m*

plausible ['plɔːzɪbl] *adj* plausible; (*person*) convaincant(e)

play [pleɪ] *n* (*THEATRE*) pièce *f* (de théâtre) ♦ *vt* (*game*) jouer à; (*team, opponent*) jouer contre; (*instrument*) jouer de; (*part, piece of music, note*) jouer; (*record etc*) passer ♦ *vi* jouer; **to ~ safe** ne pas prendre aucun risque; **~ down** *vt* minimiser; **~ up** *vi* (*cause trouble*) faire des siennes; **~boy** *n* playboy *m*; **~er** *n* joueur(-euse); (*THEATRE*) acteur(-trice); (*MUS*) musicien(ne); **~ful** *adj* enjoué(e); **~ground** *n* cour *f* de récréation; (*in park*) aire *f* de jeux; **~group** *n* garderie *f*; **~ing card** *n* carte *f* à jouer; **~ing field** *n* terrain *m* de sport; **~mate** *n* camarade *m/f*, copain (copine); **~-off** *n* (*SPORT*) belle *f*; **~pen** *n* parc *m* (pour bébé); **~thing** *n* jouet *m*; **~time** *n* récréation *f*; **~wright** *n* dramaturge *m*

plc *abbr* (= *public limited company*) SARL *f*

plea [pliː] *n* (*request*) appel *m*; (*LAW*) défense *f*

plead [pliːd] *vt* plaider; (*give as excuse*) invoquer ♦ *vi* (*LAW*) plaider; (*beg*): **to ~ with sb** implorer qn

pleasant ['plɛznt] *adj* agréable; **~ries** *npl*

(*polite remarks*) civilités *fpl*

please [pliːz] *excl* s'il te (*or* vous) plaît ♦ *vt* plaire à ♦ *vi* plaire; (*think fit*): **do as you ~** faites comme il vous plaira; **~ yourself!** à ta (*or* votre) guise!; **~d** *adj*: **~d (with)** content(e) (de); **~d to meet you** enchanté (de faire votre connaissance); **pleasing** *adj* plaisant(e), qui fait plaisir

pleasure ['plɛʒəʳ] *n* plaisir *m*; **"it's a ~"** "je vous en prie"

pleat [pliːt] *n* pli *m*

pledge [plɛdʒ] *n* (*promise*) promesse *f* ♦ *vt* engager; promettre

plentiful ['plɛntɪful] *adj* abondant(e), copieux(-euse)

plenty ['plɛntɪ] *n*: **~ of** beaucoup de; (*bien*) assez de

pliable ['plaɪəbl] *adj* flexible; (*person*) malléable

pliers ['plaɪəz] *npl* pinces *fpl*

plight [plaɪt] *n* situation *f* critique

plimsolls ['plɪmsəlz] (*BRIT*) *npl* chaussures *fpl* de tennis, tennis *mpl*

plinth [plɪnθ] *n* (*of statue*) socle *m*

P.L.O. *n abbr* (= *Palestine Liberation Organization*) OLP *f*

plod [plɔd] *vi* avancer péniblement; (*fig*) peiner

plonk [plɔŋk] (*inf*) *n* (*BRIT: wine*) pinard *m*, piquette *f* ♦ *vt*: **to ~ sth down** poser brusquement qch

plot [plɔt] *n* complot *m*, conspiration *f*; (*of story, play*) intrigue *f*; (*of land*) lot *m* de terrain, lopin *m* ♦ *vt* (*sb's downfall*) comploter; (*mark out*) pointer; relever, déterminer ♦ *vi* comploter

plough [plau] (*US* **plow**) *n* charrue *f* ♦ *vt* (*earth*) labourer; **to ~ money into** investir dans; **~ through** *vt fus* (*snow etc*) avancer péniblement dans; **~man's lunch** (*BRIT*) *n* assiette froide avec du pain, du fromage et des pickles

ploy [plɔɪ] *n* stratagème *m*

pluck [plʌk] *vt* (*fruit*) cueillir; (*musical instrument*) pincer; (*bird*) plumer; (*eyebrow*) épiler ♦ *n* courage *m*, cran *m*; **to ~ up courage** prendre son courage à deux mains

plug [plʌg] n (ELEC) prise f de courant; (stopper) bouchon m, bonde f; (AUT: also: **spark(ing) ~**) bougie f ♦ vt (hole) boucher; (inf: advertise) faire du battage pour; **~ in** vt (ELEC) brancher

plum [plʌm] n (fruit) prune f ♦ cpd: **~ job** (inf) travail m en or

plumb [plʌm] vt: **to ~ the depths** (fig) toucher le fond (du désespoir)

plumber ['plʌmə^r] n plombier m

plumbing ['plʌmɪŋ] n (trade) plomberie f; (piping) tuyauterie f

plummet ['plʌmɪt] vi: **to ~ (down)** plonger, dégringoler

plump [plʌmp] adj rondelet(te), dodu(e), bien en chair ♦ vi: **to ~ for** (inf: choose) se décider pour

plunder ['plʌndə^r] n pillage m; (loot) butin m ♦ vt piller

plunge [plʌndʒ] n plongeon m; (fig) chute f ♦ vt plonger ♦ vi (dive) plonger; (fall) tomber, dégringoler; **to take the ~** se jeter à l'eau; **plunging** ['plʌndʒɪŋ] adj: **plunging neckline** décolleté plongeant

pluperfect [plu:'pə:fɪkt] n plus-que-parfait m

plural ['pluərl] adj pluriel(le) ♦ n pluriel m

plus [plʌs] n (also: **~ sign**) signe m plus ♦ prep plus; **ten/twenty ~** plus de dix/vingt

plush [plʌʃ] adj somptueux(-euse)

ply [plaɪ] vt (a trade) exercer ♦ vi (ship) faire la navette ♦ n (of wool, rope) fil m, brin m; **to ~ sb with drink** donner continuellement à boire à qn; **to ~ sb with questions** presser qn de questions; **~wood** n contre-plaqué m

PM abbr = **Prime Minister**

p.m. adv abbr (= post meridiem) de l'après-midi

pneumatic drill [nju:'mætɪk-] n marteau-piqueur m

pneumonia [nju:'məunɪə] n pneumonie f

poach [pəutʃ] vt (cook) pocher; (steal) pêcher (or chasser) sans permis ♦ vi braconner; **~ed egg** n œuf poché; **~er** n braconnier m

P.O. box n abbr = **post office box**

pocket ['pɔkɪt] n poche f ♦ vt empocher; **to be out of ~** (BRIT) en être de sa poche; **~book** (US) n (wallet) portefeuille m; **~ calculator** n calculette f; **~ knife** n canif m; **~ money** n argent m de poche

pod [pɔd] n cosse f

podgy ['pɔdʒɪ] adj rondelet(te)

podiatrist [pɔ'di:ətrɪst] (US) n pédicure m/f, podologue m/f

poem ['pəuɪm] n poème m

poet ['pəuɪt] n poète m; **~ic** [pəu'etɪk] adj poétique; **~ry** ['pəuɪtrɪ] n poésie f

poignant ['pɔɪnjənt] adj poignant(e); (sharp) vif (vive)

point [pɔɪnt] n point m; (tip) pointe f; (in time) moment m; (in space) endroit m; (subject, idea) point, sujet m; (purpose) sens m; (ELEC) prise f; (also: **decimal ~**): **2 ~ 3 (2.3)** 2 virgule 3 (2,3) ♦ vt (show) indiquer; (gun etc): **to ~ sth at** braquer or diriger qch sur ♦ vi: **to ~ at** montrer du doigt; **~s** npl (AUT) vis platinées, (RAIL) aiguillage m; **to be on the ~ of doing sth** être sur le point de faire qch; **to make a ~ of doing** ne pas manquer de faire; **to get the ~** comprendre, saisir; **to miss the ~** ne pas comprendre; **to come to the ~** en venir au fait; **there's no ~ (in doing)** cela ne sert à rien (de faire); **~ out** vt faire remarquer, souligner; **~ to** vt fus (fig) indiquer; **~-blank** adv (fig) catégoriquement; (also: **at ~-blank range**) à bout portant; **~ed** adj (shape) pointu(e); (remark) plein(e) de sous-entendus; **~er** n (needle) aiguille f; (piece of advice) conseil m; (clue) indice m; **~less** adj inutile, vain(e); **~ of view** n point m de vue

poise [pɔɪz] n (composure) calme m

poison ['pɔɪzn] n poison m ♦ vt empoisonner; **~ous** adj (snake) venimeux(-euse); (plant) vénéneux(-euse); (fumes etc) toxique

poke [pəuk] vt (fire) tisonner; (jab with finger, stick etc) piquer; pousser du doigt; (put): **to ~ sth in(to)** fourrer or enfoncer qch dans; **~ about** vi fureter; **~r** n tisonnier *m*; (CARDS) poker *m*

poky ['pəʊkɪ] *adj* exigu(ë)

Poland ['pəʊlənd] *n* Pologne *f*

polar ['pəʊlər] *adj* polaire; **~ bear** *n* ours blanc

Pole [pəʊl] *n* Polonais(e)

pole [pəʊl] *n* poteau *m*; (of wood) mât *m*, perche *f*; (GEO) pôle *m*; **~ bean** (US) *n* haricot *m* (à rames); **~ vault** *n* saut *m* à la perche

police [pə'liːs] *npl* police *f* ♦ *vt* maintenir l'ordre dans; **~ car** *n* voiture *f* de police; **~man** (irreg) *n* agent *m* de police, policier *m*; **~ station** *n* commissariat *m* de police; **~woman** (irreg) *n* femme-agent *f*

policy ['pɒlɪsɪ] *n* politique *f*; (also: **insurance ~**) police *f* (d'assurance)

polio ['pəʊlɪəʊ] *n* polio *f*

Polish ['pəʊlɪʃ] *adj* polonais(e) ♦ *n* (LING) polonais *m*

polish ['pɒlɪʃ] *n* (for shoes) cirage *m*; (for floor) cire *f*, encaustique *f*; (shine) éclat *m*, poli *m*; (fig: refinement) raffinement *m* ♦ *vt* (put ~ on shoes, wood) cirer; (make shiny) astiquer, faire briller; **~ off** (inf) *vt* (food) liquider; **~ed** *adj* (fig) raffiné(e)

polite [pə'laɪt] *adj* poli(e); **in ~ society** dans la bonne société; **~ly** *adv* poliment; **~ness** *n* politesse *f*

political [pə'lɪtɪkl] *adj* politique; **~ly correct** *adj* politiquement correct(e)

politician [pɒlɪ'tɪʃən] *n* homme *m*/femme *f* politique

politics ['pɒlɪtɪks] *npl* politique *f*

poll [pəʊl] *n* scrutin *m*, vote *m*; (also: **opinion ~**) sondage *m* (d'opinion) ♦ *vt* obtenir

pollen ['pɒlən] *n* pollen *m*

polling day ['pəʊlɪŋ-] (BRIT) *n* jour *m* des élections

polling station (BRIT) *n* bureau *m* de vote

pollute [pə'luːt] *vt* polluer; **pollution** *n* pollution *f*

polo ['pəʊləʊ] *n* polo *m*; **~-necked** *adj* à col roulé; **~ shirt** *n* polo *m*

polyester [pɒlɪ'estər] *n* polyester *m*

polystyrene [pɒlɪ'staɪriːn] *n* polystyrène *m*

polythene ['pɒlɪθiːn] *n* polyéthylène *m*; **~ bag** *n* sac *m* en plastique

pomegranate ['pɒmɪgrænɪt] *n* grenade *f*

pomp [pɒmp] *n* pompe *f*, faste *f*, apparat *m*; **~ous** *adj* pompeux(-euse)

pond [pɒnd] *n* étang *m*; mare *f*

ponder ['pɒndər] *vt* considérer, peser; **~ous** *adj* pesant(e), lourd(e)

pong [pɒŋ] (BRIT: inf) *n* puanteur *f*

pony ['pəʊnɪ] *n* poney *m*; **~tail** *n* queue *f* de cheval; **~ trekking** (BRIT) *n* randonnée *f* à cheval

poodle ['puːdl] *n* caniche *m*

pool [puːl] *n* (of rain) flaque *f*; (pond) mare *f*; (also: **swimming ~**) piscine *f*; (billiards) poule *f* ♦ *vt* mettre en commun; **~s** *npl* (football ~s) ≈ loto sportif

poor [puər] *adj* pauvre; (mediocre) médiocre, faible, mauvais(e) ♦ *npl*: **the ~** les pauvres *mpl*; **~ly** *adj* souffrant(e), malade ♦ *adv* mal; médiocrement

pop [pɒp] *n* (MUS) musique *f* pop; (drink) boisson gazeuse; (US: inf: father) papa *m*; (noise) bruit sec ♦ *vt* (put) mettre (rapidement) ♦ *vi* éclater; (cork) sauter; **~ in** *vi* entrer en passant; **~ out** *vi* sortir (brièvement); **~ up** *vi* apparaître, surgir; **~corn** *n* pop-corn *m*

pope [pəʊp] *n* pape *m*

poplar ['pɒplər] *n* peuplier *m*

popper ['pɒpər] (BRIT: inf) *n* bouton-pression *m*

poppy ['pɒpɪ] *n* coquelicot *m*; pavot *m*

Popsicle ® ['pɒpsɪkl] (US) *n* esquimau *m* (glace)

popular ['pɒpjulər] *adj* populaire; (fashionable) à la mode

population [pɒpju'leɪʃən] *n* population *f*

porcelain ['pɔːslɪn] *n* porcelaine *f*

porch [pɔːtʃ] *n* porche *m*; (US) véranda *f*

porcupine ['pɔːkjupaɪn] *n* porc-épic *m*

pore [pɔːr] *n* pore *m* ♦ *vi*: **to ~ over** s'absorber dans, être plongé(e) dans

pork [pɔːk] *n* porc *m*

porn [pɔːn] (inf) *adj*, *n* porno *m*

pornographic [pɔːnə'græfɪk] *adj* pornographique

pornography [pɔːˈnɔgrəfɪ] n pornographie f

porpoise [ˈpɔːpəs] n marsouin m

porridge [ˈpɔrɪdʒ] n porridge m

port [pɔːt] n (harbour) port m; (NAUT: left side) bâbord m; (wine) porto m; **~ of call** escale f

portable [ˈpɔːtəbl] adj portatif(-ive)

porter [ˈpɔːtər] n (for luggage) porteur m; (doorkeeper) gardien(ne); portier m

portfolio [pɔːtˈfəulɪəu] n portefeuille m; (of artist) portfolio m

porthole [ˈpɔːthəul] n hublot m

portion [ˈpɔːʃən] n portion f, part f

portrait [ˈpɔːtreɪt] n portrait m

portray [pɔːˈtreɪ] vt faire le portrait de; (in writing) dépeindre, représenter; (subj: actor) jouer

Portugal [ˈpɔːtjugl] n Portugal m; **Portuguese** [ˈpɔːtjuˈgiːz] adj portugais(e) ♦ n inv Portugais(e); (LING) portugais m

pose [pəuz] n pose f ♦ vi (pretend): **to ~ as** se poser en ♦ vt poser; (problem) créer

posh [pɔʃ] (inf) adj chic inv

position [pəˈzɪʃən] n position f; (job) situation f ♦ vt placer

positive [ˈpɔzɪtɪv] adj positif(-ive); (certain) sûr(e), certain(e); (definite) formel(le), catégorique

possess [pəˈzɛs] vt posséder; **~ion** n possession f

possibility [pɔsɪˈbɪlɪtɪ] n possibilité f; éventualité f

possible [ˈpɔsɪbl] adj possible; **as big as ~** aussi gros que possible; **possibly** adv (perhaps) peut-être; **if you possibly can** si cela vous est possible; **I cannot possibly come** il m'est impossible de venir

post [pəust] n poste f; (BRIT: letters, delivery) courrier m; (job, situation, MIL) poste m; (pole) poteau m ♦ vt (BRIT: send by ~) poster; (: appoint): **to ~ to** affecter à; **~age** n tarifs mpl d'affranchissement; **~al order** n mandat(-poste) m; **~box** (BRIT) n boîte f aux lettres; **~card** n carte postale; **~code** (BRIT) n code postal

poster [ˈpəustər] n affiche f

poste restante [pəustˈrestɑ̃ːnt] (BRIT) n poste restante

postgraduate [ˈpəustˈgrædjuət] n ≈ étudiant(e) de troisième cycle

posthumous [ˈpɔstjuməs] adj posthume

postman [ˈpəustmən] (irreg) n facteur m

postmark [ˈpəustmɑːk] n cachet m (de la poste)

postmortem [pəustˈmɔːtəm] n autopsie f

post office n (building) poste f; (organization): **the P~ O~** les Postes; **~ box** n boîte postale

postpone [pəusˈpəun] vt remettre (à plus tard)

posture [ˈpɔstʃər] n posture f; (fig) attitude f

postwar [pəustˈwɔːr] adj d'après-guerre

postwoman n factrice f

posy [ˈpəuzɪ] n petit bouquet

pot [pɔt] n pot m; (for cooking) marmite f; casserole f; (teapot) théière f; (coffeepot) cafetière f; (inf: marijuana) herbe f ♦ vt (plant) mettre en pot; **to go to ~** (inf: work, performance) aller à vau-l'eau

potato [pəˈteɪtəu] (pl **~es**) n pomme f de terre; **~ peeler** n épluche-légumes m inv

potent [ˈpəutnt] adj puissant(e); (drink) fort(e), très alcoolisé(e); (man) viril

potential [pəˈtɛnʃl] adj potentiel(le) ♦ n potentiel m

pothole [ˈpɔthəul] n (in road) nid m de poule; (BRIT: underground) gouffre m, caverne f; **potholing** (BRIT) n: **to go potholing** faire de la spéléologie

potluck [pɔtˈlʌk] n: **to take ~** tenter sa chance

pot plant n plante f d'appartement

potted [ˈpɔtɪd] adj (food) en conserve; (plant) en pot; (abbreviated) abrégé(e)

potter [ˈpɔtər] n potier m ♦ vi: **to ~ around, ~ about** (BRIT) bricoler; **~y** n poterie f

potty [ˈpɔtɪ] adj (inf: mad) dingue ♦ n (child's) pot m

pouch [pautʃ] n (ZOOL) poche f; (for tobacco) blague f; (for money) bourse f

poultry ['pəultrı] *n* volaille *f*

pounce [pauns] *vi*: **to ~ (on)** bondir (sur), sauter (sur)

pound [paund] *n* (*unit of money*) livre *f*; (*unit of weight*) livre ♦ *vt* (*beat*) bourrer de coups, marteler; (*crush*) piler, pulvériser ♦ *vi* (*heart*) battre violemment, taper

pour [pɔːr] *vt* verser ♦ *vi* couler à flots; **to ~ (with rain)** pleuvoir à verse; **to ~ sb a drink** verser *or* servir à boire à qn; **~ away** *vt* vider; **~ in** *vi* (*people*) affluer, se précipiter; (*news, letters etc*) arriver en masse; **~ off** *vt* = **pour away**; **~ out** *vi* (*people*) sortir en masse ♦ *vt* vider; (*fig*) déverser; (*serve: a drink*) verser; **~ing** ['pɔːrɪŋ] *adj*: **~ing rain** pluie torrentielle

pout [paut] *vi* faire la moue

poverty ['pɔvətɪ] *n* pauvreté *f*, misère *f*; **~-stricken** *adj* pauvre, déshérité(e)

powder ['paudər] *n* poudre *f* ♦ *vt*: **to ~ one's face** se poudrer; **~ compact** *n* poudrier *m*; **~ed milk** *n* lait *m* en poudre; **~ room** *n* toilettes *fpl* (pour dames)

power ['pauər] *n* (*strength*) puissance *f*, force *f*; (*ability, authority*) pouvoir *m*; (*of speech, thought*) faculté *f*; (*ELEC*) courant *m*; **to be in ~** (*POL etc*) être au pouvoir; **~ cut** *n* coupure *f* de courant; **~ed** *adj*: **~ed by** actionné(e) par, fonctionnant à; **~ failure** *n* panne *f* de courant; **~ful** *adj* puissant(e); **~less** *adj* impuissant(e); **~ point** (*BRIT*) *n* prise *f* de courant; **~ station** *n* centrale *f* électrique; **~ struggle** *n* lutte *f* pour le pouvoir

p.p. *abbr* (= *per procurationem*): **p.p. J. Smith** pour M. J. Smith

PR *n abbr* = **public relations**

practical ['præktɪkl] *adj* pratique; **~ity** [præktɪ'kælɪtɪ] (*no pl*) (*of person*) sens *m* pratique; **~ities** *npl* (*of situation*) aspect *m* pratique; **~ joke** *n* farce *f*; **~ly** *adv* (*almost*) pratiquement

practice ['præktɪs] *n* pratique *f*; (*of profession*) exercice *m*; (*at football etc*) entraînement *m*; (*business*) cabinet *m* ♦ *vt*, *vi* (*US*) = **practise**; **in ~** (*in reality*) en pratique; **out of ~** rouillé(e)

practise ['præktɪs] (*US* **practice**) *vt* (*musical instrument*) travailler; (*train for: sport*) s'entraîner à; (*a sport, religion*) pratiquer; (*profession*) exercer ♦ *vi* s'exercer, travailler; (*train*) s'entraîner; (*lawyer, doctor*) exercer; **practising** *adj* (*Christian etc*) pratiquant(e); (*lawyer*) en exercice

practitioner [præk'tɪʃənər] *n* praticien(ne)

prairie ['prɛərɪ] *n* steppe *f*, prairie *f*

praise [preɪz] *n* éloge(s) *m(pl)*, louange(s) *f(pl)* ♦ *vt* louer, faire l'éloge de; **~worthy** *adj* digne d'éloges

pram [præm] (*BRIT*) *n* landau *m*, voiture *f* d'enfant

prance [prɑːns] *vi* (*also*: **~ about**: *person*) se pavaner

prank [præŋk] *n* farce *f*

prawn [prɔːn] *n* crevette *f* (rose); **~ cocktail** *n* cocktail *m* de crevettes

pray [preɪ] *vi* prier; **~er** [prɛər] *n* prière *f*

preach [priːtʃ] *vt*, *vi* prêcher

precaution [prɪ'kɔːʃən] *n* précaution *f*

precede [prɪ'siːd] *vt* précéder

precedent ['prɛsɪdənt] *n* précédent *m*

preceding *adj* qui précède/précédait *etc*

precinct ['priːsɪŋkt] *n* (*US*) circonscription *f*, arrondissement *m*; **~s** *npl* (*neighbourhood*) alentours *mpl*, environs *mpl*; **pedestrian ~** (*BRIT*) zone piétonnière *or* piétonne; **shopping ~** (*BRIT*) centre commercial

precious ['prɛʃəs] *adj* précieux(-euse)

precipitate [prɪ'sɪpɪteɪt] *vt* précipiter

precise [prɪ'saɪs] *adj* précis(e); **~ly** *adv* précisément

precocious [prɪ'kəuʃəs] *adj* précoce

precondition ['priːkən'dɪʃən] *n* condition *f* nécessaire

predecessor ['priːdɪsɛsər] *n* prédécesseur *m*

predicament [prɪ'dɪkəmənt] *n* situation *f* difficile

predict [prɪ'dɪkt] *vt* prédire; **~able** *adj* prévisible

predominantly [prɪ'dɔmɪnəntlɪ] *adv* en majeure partie; surtout

pre-empt [priː'ɛmt] *vt* anticiper, devancer

preen [priːn] vt: **to ~ itself** (bird) se lisser les plumes; **to ~ o.s.** s'admirer

prefab ['priːfæb] n bâtiment préfabriqué

preface ['prefəs] n préface f

prefect ['priːfɛkt] (BRIT) n (in school) élève chargé(e) de certaines fonctions de discipline

prefer [prɪ'fəːʳ] vt préférer; **~ably** ['prefrəblɪ] adv de préférence; **~ence** ['prefrəns] n préférence f; **~ential** [prefə'renʃəl] adj: **~ential treatment** traitement m de faveur or préférentiel

prefix ['priːfɪks] n préfixe m

pregnancy ['pregnənsɪ] n grossesse f

pregnant ['pregnənt] adj enceinte; (animal) pleine

prehistoric ['priːhɪs'tɔrɪk] adj préhistorique

prejudice ['predʒudɪs] n préjugé m; **~d** adj (person) plein(e) de préjugés; (in a matter) partial(e)

premarital ['priː'mærɪtl] adj avant le mariage

premature ['premətʃuəʳ] adj prématuré(e)

premenstrual syndrome [priː'menstruəl-] n syndrome prémenstruel

premier ['premɪəʳ] adj premier(-ère), principal(e) ♦ n (POL) Premier ministre

première ['premɪɛəʳ] n première f

Premier League n première division

premise ['premɪs] n prémisse f; **~s** npl (building) locaux mpl; **on the ~s** sur les lieux; sur place

premium ['priːmɪəm] n prime f; **to be at a ~** faire prime; **~ bond** (BRIT) n bon m à lot, obligation f à prime

premonition [premə'nɪʃən] n prémonition f

preoccupied [priː'ɔkjupaɪd] adj préoccupé(e)

prep [prep] n (SCOL) étude f

prepaid [priː'peɪd] adj payé(e) d'avance

preparation [prepə'reɪʃən] n préparation f; **~s** npl (for trip, war) préparatifs mpl

preparatory [prɪ'pærətərɪ] adj préliminaire; **~ school** (BRIT) n école primaire privée

prepare [prɪ'pɛəʳ] vt préparer ♦ vi: **to ~ for** se préparer à; **~d to** prêt(e) à

preposition [prepə'zɪʃən] n préposition f

preposterous [prɪ'pɔstərəs] adj absurde

prep school n = **preparatory school**

prerequisite [priː'rekwɪzɪt] n condition f préalable

Presbyterian [prezbɪ'tɪərɪən] adj, n presbytérien(ne) m/f

prescribe [prɪ'skraɪb] vt prescrire; **prescription** [prɪ'skrɪpʃən] n (MED) ordonnance f; (: medicine) médicament (obtenu sur ordonnance)

presence ['prezns] n présence f; **~ of mind** présence d'esprit

present [adj, n 'preznt, vb prɪ'zent] adj présent(e) ♦ n (gift) cadeau m; (actuality) présent m ♦ vt présenter; (prize, medal) remettre; (give): **to ~ sb with sth** or **sth to sb** offrir qch à qn; **to give sb a ~** offrir un cadeau à qn; **at ~** en ce moment; **~ation** [prezn'teɪʃən] n présentation f; (ceremony) remise f du cadeau (or de la médaille etc); **~-day** adj contemporain(e), actuel(le); **~er** n (RADIO, TV) présentateur(-trice); **~ly** adv (with verb in past) peu après; (soon) tout à l'heure, bientôt; (at present) en ce moment

preservative [prɪ'zəːvətɪv] n agent m de conservation

preserve [prɪ'zəːv] vt (keep safe) préserver, protéger; (maintain) conserver, garder; (food) mettre en conserve ♦ n (often pl: jam) confiture f

president ['prezɪdənt] n président(e); **~ial** [prezɪ'denʃl] adj présidentiel(le)

press [pres] n presse f; (for wine) pressoir m ♦ vt (squeeze) presser, serrer; (push) appuyer sur; (clothes: iron) repasser; (put pressure on) faire pression sur; (insist): **to ~ sth on sb** presser qn d'accepter qch ♦ vi appuyer, peser; **to ~ for sth** faire pression pour obtenir qch; **we are ~ed for time/money** le temps/l'argent nous manque; **~ on** vi continuer; **~ conference** n conférence f de presse; **~ing** adj urgent(e), pressant(e); **~ stud** (BRIT) n bouton-pression *m*; ~**-up** (*BRIT*) *n* traction *f*

pressure ['prɛʃəʳ] *n* pression *f*; (*stress*) tension *f*; **to put ~ on sb (to do)** faire pression sur qn (pour qu'il/elle fasse); ~ **cooker** *n* cocotte-minute *f*; ~ **gauge** *n* manomètre *m*; ~ **group** *n* groupe *m* de pression

prestige [prɛs'tiːʒ] *n* prestige *m*; **prestigious** [prɛs'tɪdʒəs] *adj* prestigieux(-euse)

presumably [prɪ'zjuːməblɪ] *adv* vraisemblablement

presume [prɪ'zjuːm] *vt* présumer, supposer

pretence [prɪ'tɛns] (*US* **pretense**) *n* (*claim*) prétention *f*; **under false ~s** sous des prétextes fallacieux

pretend [prɪ'tɛnd] *vt* (*feign*) feindre, simuler ♦ *vi* faire semblant

pretext ['priːtɛkst] *n* prétexte *m*

pretty ['prɪtɪ] *adj* joli(e) ♦ *adv* assez

prevail [prɪ'veɪl] *vi* (*be usual*) avoir cours; (*win*) l'emporter, prévaloir; ~**ing** *adj* dominant(e); **prevalent** ['prɛvələnt] *adj* répandu(e), courant(e)

prevent [prɪ'vɛnt] *vt*: **to ~ (from doing)** empêcher (de faire); ~**ative** [prɪ'vɛntətɪv], ~**ive** [prɪ'vɛntɪv] *adj* préventif(-ive)

preview ['priːvjuː] *n* (*of film etc*) avant-première *f*

previous ['priːvɪəs] *adj* précédent(e); antérieur(e); ~**ly** *adv* précédemment, auparavant

prewar [priː'wɔːʳ] *adj* d'avant-guerre

prey [preɪ] *n* proie *f* ♦ *vi*: **to ~ on** s'attaquer à; **it was ~ing on his mind** cela le travaillait

price [praɪs] *n* prix *m* ♦ *vt* (*goods*) fixer le prix de; ~**less** *adj* sans prix, inestimable; ~ **list** *n* liste *f* des prix, tarif *m*

prick [prɪk] *n* piqûre *f* ♦ *vt* piquer; **to ~ up one's ears** dresser *or* tendre l'oreille

prickle ['prɪkl] *n* (*of plant*) épine *f*; (*sensation*) picotement *m*; **prickly** *adj* piquant(e), épineux(-euse); **prickly heat** *n* fièvre *f* miliaire

pride [praɪd] *n* orgueil *m*; fierté *f* ♦ *vt*: **to ~ o.s. on** se flatter de; s'enorgueillir de

priest [priːst] *n* prêtre *m*; ~**hood** *n* prêtrise *f*, sacerdoce *m*

prim [prɪm] *adj* collet monté *inv*, guindé(e)

primarily ['praɪmərɪlɪ] *adv* principalement, essentiellement

primary ['praɪmərɪ] *adj* (*first in importance*) premier(-ère), primordial(e), principal(e) ♦ *n* (*US: election*) (élection *f*) primaire *f*; ~ **school** (*BRIT*) *n* école primaire *f*

prime [praɪm] *adj* primordial(e), fondamental(e); (*excellent*) excellent(e) ♦ *n*: **in the ~ of life** dans la fleur de l'âge ♦ *vt* (*wood*) apprêter; (*fig*) mettre au courant; **P~ Minister** *n* Premier ministre *m*

primeval [praɪ'miːvəl] *adj* primitif(-ive); ~ **forest** forêt *f* vierge

primitive ['prɪmɪtɪv] *adj* primitif(-ive)

primrose ['prɪmrəuz] *n* primevère *f*

primus (stove) ® ['praɪməs-] (*BRIT*) *n* réchaud *m* de camping

prince [prɪns] *n* prince *m*

princess [prɪn'sɛs] *n* princesse *f*

principal ['prɪnsɪpl] *adj* principal(e) ♦ *n* (*headmaster*) directeur(-trice), principal *m*

principle ['prɪnsɪpl] *n* principe *m*; **in/on ~** en/par principe

print [prɪnt] *n* (*mark*) empreinte *f*; (*letters*) caractères *mpl*; (*ART*) gravure *f*, estampe *f*; (: *photograph*) photo *f* ♦ *vt* imprimer; (*publish*) publier; (*write in block letters*) écrire en caractères d'imprimerie; **out of ~** épuisé(e); ~**ed matter** *n* imprimé(s) *m(pl)*; ~**er** *n* imprimeur *m*; (*machine*) imprimante *f*; ~**ing** *n* impression *f*; ~**-out** *n* copie *f* papier

prior ['praɪəʳ] *adj* antérieur(e), précédent(e); (*more important*) prioritaire ♦ *adv*: ~ **to doing** avant de faire; ~**ity** [praɪ'ɔrɪtɪ] *n* priorité *f*

prise [praɪz] *vt*: **to ~ open** forcer

prison ['prɪzn] *n* prison *f* ♦ *cpd* pénitentiaire; ~**er** *n* prisonnier(-ère)

pristine ['prɪstiːn] *adj* parfait(e)

privacy ['prɪvəsɪ] *n* intimité *f*, solitude *f*

private ['praɪvɪt] *adj* privé(e); (*personal*) personnel(le); (*house, lesson*) particulier(-ère); (*quiet: place*) tranquille; (*reserved: per-*

son) secret(-ète) ♦ *n* soldat *m* de deuxième classe; **"~"** (*on envelope*) "personnelle"; **in ~** en privé; **~ detective** *n* détective privé; **~ enterprise** *n* l'entreprise privée; **~ property** *n* propriété privée; **privatize** *vt* privatiser

privet ['prɪvɪt] *n* troène *m*

privilege ['prɪvɪlɪdʒ] *n* privilège *m*

privy ['prɪvɪ] *adj*: **to be ~ to** être au courant de

prize [praɪz] *n* prix *m* ♦ *adj* (*example, idiot*) parfait(e); (*bull, novel*) primé(e) ♦ *vt* priser, faire grand cas de; **~-giving** *n* distribution *f* des prix; **~winner** *n* gagnant(e)

pro [prəu] *n* (*SPORT*) professionnel(le); **the ~s and cons** le pour et le contre

probability [prɒbə'bɪlɪtɪ] *n* probabilité *f*

probable ['prɒbəbl] *adj* probable; **probably** *adv* probablement

probation [prə'beɪʃən] *n*: **on ~** (*LAW*) en liberté surveillée, en sursis; (*employee*) à l'essai

probe [prəub] *n* (*MED, SPACE*) sonde *f*; (*enquiry*) enquête *f*, investigation *f* ♦ *vt* sonder, explorer

problem ['prɒbləm] *n* problème *m*

procedure [prə'si:dʒər] *n* (*ADMIN, LAW*) procédure *f*; (*method*) marche *f* à suivre, façon *f* de procéder

proceed [prə'si:d] *vi* continuer; (*go forward*) avancer; **to ~ (with)** continuer, poursuivre; **to ~ to do** se mettre à faire; **~ings** *npl* (*LAW*) poursuites *fpl*; (*meeting*) réunion *f*, séance *f*; **~s** ['prəusi:dz] *npl* produit *m*, recette *f*

process ['prəuses] *n* processus *m*; (*method*) procédé *m* ♦ *vt* traiter; **~ing** *n* (*PHOT*) développement *m*; **~ion** [prə'seʃən] *n* défilé *m*, cortège *m*; (*REL*) procession *f*; **funeral ~ion** (*on foot*) cortège *m* funèbre; (*in cars*) convoi *m* mortuaire

proclaim [prə'kleɪm] *vt* déclarer, proclamer

procrastinate [prəu'kræstɪneɪt] *vi* faire traîner les choses, vouloir tout remettre au lendemain

procure [prə'kjuər] *vt* obtenir

prod [prɒd] *vt* pousser

prodigal ['prɒdɪgl] *adj* prodigue

prodigy ['prɒdɪdʒɪ] *n* prodige *m*

produce [*n* 'prɒdju:s, *vb* prə'dju:s] *n* (*AGR*) produits *mpl* ♦ *vt* produire; (*to show*) présenter; (*cause*) provoquer, causer; (*THEATRE*) mettre en scène; **~r** *n* producteur *m*; (*THEATRE*) metteur *m* en scène

product ['prɒdʌkt] *n* produit *m*

production [prə'dʌkʃən] *n* production *f*; (*THEATRE*) mise *f* en scène; **~ line** *n* chaîne *f* (de fabrication)

productivity [prɒdʌk'tɪvɪtɪ] *n* productivité *f*

profession [prə'feʃən] *n* profession *f*; **~al** *n* professionnel(le) ♦ *adj* professionnel(le); (*work*) de professionnel; **~ally** *adv* professionnellement; (*SPORT: play*) en professionnel; **she sings ~ally** c'est une chanteuse professionnelle; **I only know him ~ally** je n'ai avec lui que des relations de travail

professor [prə'fesər] *n* professeur *m* (*titulaire d'une chaire*)

proficiency [prə'fɪʃənsɪ] *n* compétence *f*, aptitude *f*

profile ['prəufaɪl] *n* profil *m*

profit ['prɒfɪt] *n* bénéfice *m*; profit *m* ♦ *vi*: **to ~ (by** or **from)** profiter (de); **~able** *adj* lucratif(-ive), rentable

profound [prə'faund] *adj* profond(e)

profusely [prə'fju:slɪ] *adv* abondamment; avec effusion

prognosis [prɒg'nəusɪs] (*pl* **prognoses**) *n* pronostic *m*

programme ['prəugræm] (*US* **program**) *n* programme *m*; (*RADIO, TV*) émission *f* ♦ *vt* programmer; **~r** (*US* **programer**) *n* programmeur(-euse); **programming** (*US* **programing**) *n* programmation *f*

progress [*n* 'prəugres, *vb* prə'gres] *n* progrès *m*(*pl*) ♦ *vi* progresser, avancer; **in ~** en cours; **~ive** [prə'gresɪv] *adj* progressif(-ive); (*person*) progressiste

prohibit [prə'hɪbɪt] *vt* interdire, défendre

project [*n* 'prɒdʒɛkt, *vb* prə'dʒɛkt] *n* (*plan*) projet *m*, plan *m*; (*venture*) opération *f*, entreprise *f*; (*research*) étude *f*, dossier *m*

♦ *vt* projeter ♦ *vi* faire saillie, s'avancer; **~ion** *n* projection *f*; (*overhang*) saillie *f*; **~or** *n* projecteur *m*

prolong [prə'lɒŋ] *vt* prolonger

prom [prɒm] *n abbr* = **promenade**; (*US: ball*) bal *m* d'étudiants

promenade [prɒmə'nɑːd] *n* (*by sea*) esplanade *f*, promenade *f*; **~ concert** (*BRIT*) *n* concert *m* populaire (de musique classique)

---
promenade concert

i En Grande-Bretagne, un **promenade concert** (*ou* **prom**) est un concert de musique classique, ainsi appelé car, à l'origine, le public restait debout et se promenait au lieu de rester assis. De nos jours, une partie du public reste debout, mais il y a également des places assises (plus chères). Les Proms les plus connus sont les Proms londoniens. La dernière séance (*the Last Night of the Proms*) est un grand événement médiatique où se jouent des airs traditionnels et patriotiques. Aux États-Unis et au Canada, le **prom** *ou* **promenade** *est un bal organisé par le lycée.*

---

prominent ['prɒmɪnənt] *adj* (*standing out*) proéminent(e); (*important*) important(e)

promiscuous [prə'mɪskjuəs] *adj* (*sexually*) de mœurs légères

promise ['prɒmɪs] *n* promesse *f* ♦ *vt, vi* promettre; **promising** *adj* prometteur(-euse)

promote [prə'məut] *vt* promouvoir; (*new product*) faire la promotion de; **~r** *n* (*of event*) organisateur(-trice); (*of cause, idea*) promoteur(-trice); **promotion** *n* promotion *f*

prompt [prɒmpt] *adj* rapide ♦ *adv* (*punctually*) à l'heure ♦ *n* (*COMPUT*) message *m* (de guidage) ♦ *vt* provoquer; (*person*) inciter, pousser; (*THEATRE*) souffler (son rôle *or* ses répliques) à; **~ly** *adv* rapidement, sans délai; ponctuellement

prone [prəun] *adj* (*lying*) couché(e) (face contre terre); **~ to** enclin(e) à

prong [prɒŋ] *n* (*of fork*) dent *f*

pronoun ['prəunaun] *n* pronom *m*

pronounce [prə'nauns] *vt* prononcer; **pronunciation** [prənʌnsɪ'eɪʃən] *n* prononciation *f*

proof [pruːf] *n* preuve *f*; (*TYP*) épreuve *f* ♦ *adj*: **~ against** à l'épreuve de

prop [prɒp] *n* support *m*, étai *m*; (*fig*) soutien *m* ♦ *vt* (*also*: **~ up**) étayer, soutenir; (*lean*): **to ~ sth against** appuyer qch contre *or* à

propaganda [prɒpə'gændə] *n* propagande *f*

propel [prə'pel] *vt* propulser, faire avancer; **~ler** *n* hélice *f*

propensity [prə'pensɪtɪ] *n*: **a ~ for** *or* **to/ to do** une propension à/à faire

proper ['prɒpər] *adj* (*suited, right*) approprié(e), bon (bonne); (*seemly*) correct(e), convenable; (*authentic*) vrai(e), véritable; (*referring to place*): **the village ~** le village proprement dit; **~ly** *adv* correctement, convenablement; **~ noun** *n* nom *m* propre

property ['prɒpətɪ] *n* propriété *f*; (*things owned*) biens *mpl*; propriété(s) *f(pl)*; (*land*) terres *fpl*

prophecy ['prɒfɪsɪ] *n* prophétie *f*

prophesy ['prɒfɪsaɪ] *vt* prédire

prophet ['prɒfɪt] *n* prophète *m*

proportion [prə'pɔːʃən] *n* proportion *f*; (*share*) part *f*; partie *f*; **~al, ~ate** *adj* proportionnel(le)

proposal [prə'pəuzl] *n* proposition *f*, offre *f*; (*plan*) projet *m*; (*of marriage*) demande *f* en mariage

propose [prə'pəuz] *vt* proposer, suggérer ♦ *vi* faire sa demande en mariage; **to ~ to do** avoir l'intention de faire; **proposition** [prɒpə'zɪʃən] *n* proposition *f*

proprietor [prə'praɪətər] *n* propriétaire *m/f*

propriety [prə'praɪətɪ] *n* (*seemliness*) bienséance *f*, convenance *f*

prose [prəuz] *n* (*not poetry*) prose *f*

prosecute ['prɒsɪkjuːt] *vt* poursuivre; **prosecution** [prɒsɪ'kjuːʃən] *n* poursuites *fpl* judiciaires; (*accusing side*) partie plaignante; **prosecutor** n (US: plaintiff) plaignant(e); (also: **public prosecutor**) procureur m, ministère public

prospect [n 'prɔspekt, vb prə'spekt] n perspective f ♦ vt, vi prospecter; **~s** npl (for work etc) possibilités fpl d'avenir, débouchés mpl; (for gold, oil etc) prospection f; **~ing** adj (possible) éventuel(le); (future) futur(e)

prospectus [prə'spektəs] n prospectus m

prosperity [prɔ'spɛrɪtɪ] n prospérité f

prostitute ['prɔstɪtjuːt] n prostitué(e)

protect [prə'tɛkt] vt protéger; **~ion** n protection f; **~ive** adj protecteur(-trice); (clothing) de protection

protein ['prəutiːn] n protéine f

protest [n 'prəutɛst, vb prə'tɛst] n protestation f ♦ vi, vt: **to ~ (that)** protester (que)

Protestant ['prɔtɪstənt] adj, n protestant(e)

protester [prə'tɛstər] n manifestant(e)

protracted [prə'træktɪd] adj prolongé(e)

protrude [prə'truːd] vi avancer, dépasser

proud [praud] adj fier(-ère); (pej) orgueilleux(-euse)

prove [pruːv] vt prouver, démontrer ♦ vi: **to ~ (to be) correct** etc s'avérer juste etc; **to ~ o.s.** montrer ce dont on est capable

proverb ['prɔvəːb] n proverbe m

provide [prə'vaɪd] vt fournir; **to ~ sb with sth** fournir qch à qn; **~ for** vt fus (person) subvenir aux besoins de; (future event) prévoir; **~d (that)** conj à condition que +sub; **providing** conj: **providing (that)** à condition que +sub

province ['prɔvɪns] n province f; (fig) domaine m; **provincial** [prə'vɪnʃəl] adj provincial(e)

provision [prə'vɪʒən] n (supplying) fourniture f; approvisionnement m; (stipulation) disposition f; **~s** npl (food) provisions fpl; **~al** adj provisoire

proviso [prə'vaɪzəu] n condition f

provocative [prə'vɔkətɪv] adj provocateur(-trice), provocant(e)

provoke [prə'vəuk] vt provoquer

prowess ['prauɪs] n prouesse f

prowl [praul] vi (also: **~ about, ~ around**) rôder ♦ n: **on the ~** à l'affût; **~er** n rôdeur(-euse)

proxy ['prɔksɪ] n procuration f

prudent ['pruːdnt] adj prudent(e)

prune [pruːn] n pruneau m ♦ vt élaguer

pry [praɪ] vi: **to ~ into** fourrer son nez dans

PS n abbr (= postscript) p.s.

psalm [sɑːm] n psaume m

pseudonym ['sjuːdənɪm] n pseudonyme m

psyche ['saɪkɪ] n psychisme m

psychiatrist [saɪ'kaɪətrɪst] n psychiatre m/f

psychic ['saɪkɪk] adj (also: **~al**) (méta)psychique; (person) doué(e) d'un sixième sens

psychoanalyst [saɪkəu'ænəlɪst] n psychanalyste m/f

psychological [saɪkə'lɔdʒɪkl] adj psychologique

psychologist [saɪ'kɔlədʒɪst] n psychologue m/f

psychology [saɪ'kɔlədʒɪ] n psychologie f

PTO abbr (= please turn over) T.S.V.P.

pub [pʌb] n (public house) pub m

___pub___

❶ Un **pub** comprend en général deux salles: l'une ("the lounge") est plutôt confortable, avec des fauteuils et des bancs capitonnés, tandis que l'autre ("the public bar") est simplement un bar où les consommations sont en général moins chères. Cette dernière est souvent aussi une salle de jeux, les jeux les plus courants étant les fléchettes, les dominos et le billard. Il y a parfois aussi une petite arrière-salle douillette appelée "the snug". Beaucoup de pubs servent maintenant des repas, surtout à l'heure du déjeuner, et c'est alors le seul moment où les enfants sont acceptés, à condition d'être accompagnés. Les pubs sont en général ouverts de 11 h à 23 h, mais cela peut varier selon leur licence; certains pubs ferment l'après-midi.

public ['pʌblɪk] adj public(-ique) ♦ n public

m; **in ~** en public; **to make ~** rendre public; **~ address system** *n* (système *m* de) sonorisation *f*; hauts-parleurs *mpl*

publican ['pʌblɪkən] *n* patron *m* de pub

public: **~ company** *n* société *f* anonyme (*cotée en Bourse*); **~ convenience** (*BRIT*) *n* toilettes *fpl*; **~ holiday** *n* jour férié; **~ house** (*BRIT*) *n* pub *m*

publicity [pʌb'lɪsɪtɪ] *n* publicité *f*

publicize ['pʌblɪsaɪz] *vt* faire connaître, rendre public(-ique)

public: **~ opinion** *n* opinion publique; **~ relations** *n* relations publiques; **~ school** (*BRIT*) *n* école (secondaire) privée; (*US*) école publique; **~-spirited** *adj* qui fait preuve de civisme; **~ transport** *n* transports *mpl* en commun

publish ['pʌblɪʃ] *vt* publier; **~er** *n* éditeur *m*; **~ing** *n* édition *f*

pub lunch *n* repas *m* de bistrot

pucker ['pʌkər] *vt* plisser

pudding ['pudɪŋ] *n* pudding *m*; (*BRIT: sweet*) dessert *m*, entremets *m*; **black ~**, (*US*) **blood ~** boudin (noir)

puddle ['pʌdl] *n* flaque *f* (d'eau)

puff [pʌf] *n* bouffée *f* ♦ *vt*: **to ~ one's pipe** tirer sur sa pipe ♦ *vi* (*pant*) haleter; **~ out** *vt* (*fill with air*) gonfler; **~ pastry** (*US* **puff paste**) *n* pâte feuilletée; **~y** *adj* bouffi(e), boursouflé(e)

pull [pul] *n* (*tug*): **to give sth a ~** tirer sur qch ♦ *vt* tirer; (*trigger*) presser ♦ *vi* tirer; **to ~ to pieces** mettre en morceaux; **to ~ one's punches** ménager son adversaire; **to ~ one's weight** faire sa part (du travail); **to ~ o.s. together** se ressaisir; **to ~ sb's leg** (*fig*) faire marcher qn; **~ apart** *vt* (*break*) mettre en pièces, démantibuler; **~ down** *vt* (*house*) démolir; **~ in** *vi* (*AUT*) entrer; (*RAIL*) entrer en gare; **~ off** *vt* enlever, ôter; (*deal etc*) mener à bien, conclure; **~ out** *vi* démarrer, partir ♦ *vt* sortir; arracher; **~ over** *vi* (*AUT*) se ranger; **~ through** *vi* s'en sortir; **~ up** *vi* (*stop*) s'arrêter ♦ *vt* remonter; (*uproot*) déraciner, arracher

pulley ['pulɪ] *n* poulie *f*

pullover ['puləuvər] *n* pull(-over) *m*, tricot *m*

pulp [pʌlp] *n* (*of fruit*) pulpe *f*

pulpit ['pulpɪt] *n* chaire *f*

pulsate [pʌl'seɪt] *vi* battre, palpiter; (*music*) vibrer

pulse [pʌls] *n* (*of blood*) pouls *m*; (*of heart*) battement *m*; (*of music, engine*) vibrations *fpl*; (*BOT, CULIN*) légume sec

pump [pʌmp] *n* pompe *f*; (*shoe*) escarpin *m* ♦ *vt* pomper; **~ up** *vt* gonfler

pumpkin ['pʌmpkɪn] *n* potiron *m*, citrouille *f*

pun [pʌn] *n* jeu *m* de mots, calembour *m*

punch [pʌntʃ] *n* (*blow*) coup *m* de poing; (*tool*) poinçon *m*; (*drink*) punch *m* ♦ *vt* (*hit*): **to ~ sb/sth** donner un coup de poing à qn/sur qch; **~line** *n* (*of joke*) conclusion *f*; **~-up** (*BRIT: inf*) *n* bagarre *f*

punctual ['pʌŋktjuəl] *adj* ponctuel(le)

punctuation [pʌŋktju'eɪʃən] *n* ponctuation *f*

puncture ['pʌŋktʃər] *n* crevaison *f*

pundit ['pʌndɪt] *n* individu *m* qui pontifie, pontife *m*

pungent ['pʌndʒənt] *adj* piquant(e), âcre

punish ['pʌnɪʃ] *vt* punir; **~ment** *n* punition *f*, châtiment *m*

punk [pʌŋk] *n* (*also:* **~ rocker**) punk *m/f*; (*also:* **~ rock**) le punk rock; (*US: inf: hoodlum*) voyou *m*

punt [pʌnt] *n* (*boat*) bachot *m*

punter ['pʌntər] (*BRIT*) *n* (*gambler*) parieur(-euse); (*inf*): **the ~s** le public

puny ['pju:nɪ] *adj* chétif(-ive); (*effort*) piteux(-euse)

pup [pʌp] *n* chiot *m*

pupil ['pju:pl] *n* (*SCOL*) élève *m/f*; (*of eye*) pupille *f*

puppet ['pʌpɪt] *n* marionnette *f*, pantin *m*

puppy ['pʌpɪ] *n* chiot *m*, jeune chien(ne)

purchase ['pə:tʃɪs] *n* achat *m* ♦ *vt* acheter; **~r** *n* acheteur-(euse)

pure [pjuər] *adj* pur(e); **~ly** *adv* purement

purge [pə:dʒ] *n* purge *f* ♦ *vt* purger

purple ['pə:pl] *adj* violet(te); (*face*) cramoisi(e)

purpose ['pə:pəs] n intention f, but m; **on ~** exprès; **~ful** adj déterminé(e), résolu(e)

purr [pə:ʳ] vi ronronner

purse [pə:s] n (BRIT: for money) porte-monnaie m inv; (US: handbag) sac m à main ♦ vt serrer, pincer

purser n (NAUT) commissaire m du bord

pursue [pə'sju:] vt poursuivre; **pursuit** [pə'sju:t] n poursuite f; (occupation) occupation f, activité f

push [puʃ] n poussée f ♦ vt pousser; (button) appuyer sur; (product) faire de la publicité pour; (thrust): **to ~ sth (into)** enfoncer qch (dans) ♦ vi pousser; (demand): **to ~ for** exiger, demander avec insistance; **~ aside** vt écarter; **~ off** (inf) vi filer, ficher le camp; **~ on** vi (continue) continuer; **~ through** vt se frayer un chemin ♦ vt (measure) faire accepter; **~ up** vt (total, prices) faire monter; **~chair** (BRIT) n poussette f; **~er** n (drug pusher) revendeur(-euse) (de drogue), ravitailleur(-euse) (en drogue); **~over** (inf) n: **it's a ~over** c'est un jeu d'enfant; **~-up** (US) n traction f; **~y** (pej) adj arriviste

puss [pus], **pussy (cat)** ['pusi(kæt)] (inf) n minet m

put [put] (pt, pp put) vt mettre, poser, placer; (say) dire, exprimer; (a question) poser; (case, view) exposer, présenter; (estimate) estimer; **~ about** vt (rumour) faire courir; **~ across** vt (ideas etc) communiquer; **~ away** vt (store) ranger; **~ back** vt (replace) remettre, replacer; (postpone) remettre; (delay) retarder; **~ by** vt (money) mettre de côté, économiser; **~ down** vt (parcel etc) poser, déposer; (in writing) mettre par écrit, inscrire; (suppress: revolt etc) réprimer, faire cesser; (animal) abattre; (dog, cat) faire piquer; (attribute) attribuer; **~ forward** vt (ideas) avancer; **~ in** vt (gas, electricity) installer; (application, complaint) soumettre; (time, effort) consacrer; **~ off** vt (light etc) éteindre; (postpone) remettre à plus tard, ajourner; (discourage) dissuader; **~ on** vt (clothes, lipstick, record) mettre; (light etc) allumer;

(play etc) monter; (food: cook) mettre à cuire or à chauffer; (gain): **to ~ on weight** prendre du poids, grossir; **to ~ the brakes on** freiner; **to ~ the kettle on** mettre l'eau à chauffer; **~ out** vt (take out) mettre dehors; (one's hand) tendre; (light etc) éteindre; (person: inconvenience) déranger, gêner; **~ through** vt (TEL: call) passer; (: person) mettre en communication; (plan) faire accepter; **~ up** vt (raise) lever, relever, remonter; (pin up) afficher; (hang) accrocher; (build) construire, ériger; (tent) monter; (umbrella) ouvrir; (increase) augmenter; (accommodate) loger; **~ up with** vt fus supporter

putt [pʌt] n coup roulé; **~ing green** n green m

putty ['pʌti] n mastic m

put-up ['putʌp] (BRIT) adj: **~-~ job** coup monté

puzzle ['pʌzl] n énigme f, mystère m; (jigsaw) puzzle m ♦ vt intriguer, rendre perplexe ♦ vi se creuser la tête; **~d** adj perplexe; **puzzling** adj déconcertant(e)

pyjamas [pə'dʒɑ:məz] (BRIT) npl pyjama(s) m(pl)

pylon ['paɪlən] n pylône m

pyramid ['pɪrəmɪd] n pyramide f

Pyrenees [pɪrə'ni:z] npl: **the ~** les Pyrénées fpl

Q, q

quack [kwæk] n (of duck) coin-coin m inv; (pej: doctor) charlatan m

quad [kwɔd] n abbr = **quadrangle**; **quadruplet**

quadrangle ['kwɔdræŋgl] n (courtyard) cour f

quadruple [kwɔ'dru:pl] vt, vi quadrupler; **~ts** npl quadruplés

quail [kweɪl] n (ZOOL) caille f ♦ vi: **to ~ at** or **before** reculer devant

quaint [kweɪnt] adj bizarre; (house, village) au charme vieillot, pittoresque

quake [kweɪk] vi trembler

qualification [kwɔlɪfɪ'keɪʃən] n (often pl: degree etc) diplôme m; (training) qualification(s) f(pl), expérience f; (ability) compétence(s) f(pl); (limitation) réserve f, restriction f

qualified ['kwɔlɪfaɪd] adj (trained) qualifié(e), (professionally) diplômé(e); (fit, competent) compétent(e), qualifié(e); (limited) conditionnel(le)

qualify ['kwɔlɪfaɪ] vt qualifier; (modify) atténuer, nuancer ♦ vi: **to ~ (as)** obtenir son diplôme (de); **to ~ (for)** remplir les conditions requises (pour); (SPORT) se qualifier (pour)

quality ['kwɔlɪtɪ] n qualité f; **~ time** n moments privilégiés

> **quality (news)papers**

> ⓘ Les **quality (news)papers** (ou la **quality press**) englobent les journaux sérieux, quotidiens ou hebdomadaires, par opposition aux journaux populaires (**tabloid press**). Ces journaux visent un public qui souhaite des informations détaillées sur un éventail très vaste de sujets et qui est prêt à consacrer beaucoup de temps à leur lecture. Les **quality newspapers** sont en général de grand format.

qualm [kwɑːm] n doute m; scrupule m

quandary ['kwɔndrɪ] n: **in a ~** devant un dilemme, dans l'embarras

quantity ['kwɔntɪtɪ] n quantité f; **~ surveyor** n métreur m vérificateur

quarantine ['kwɔrəntiːn] n quarantaine f

quarrel ['kwɔrl] n querelle f, dispute f ♦ vi se disputer, se quereller

quarry ['kwɔrɪ] n (for stone) carrière f; (animal) proie f, gibier m

quart [kwɔːt] n ≈ litre m

quarter ['kwɔːtər] n quart m; (US: coin: 25 cents) quart de dollar; (of year) trimestre m; (district) quartier m ♦ vt (divide) partager en quartiers ou en quatre; **~s** npl (living ~) logement m; (MIL) quartiers mpl, cantonnement m; **a ~ of an hour** un quart d'heure; **~ final** n quart m de fina-

le; **~ly** adj trimestriel(le) ♦ adv tous les trois mois

quartet(te) [kwɔː'tet] n quatuor m; (jazz players) quartette m

quartz [kwɔːts] n quartz m

quash [kwɔʃ] vt (verdict) annuler

quaver ['kweɪvər] vi trembler

quay [kiː] n (also: **~side**) quai m

queasy ['kwiːzɪ] adj: **to feel ~** avoir mal au cœur

queen [kwiːn] n reine f; (CARDS etc) dame f; **~ mother** n reine mère f

queer [kwɪər] adj étrange, curieux(-euse); (suspicious) louche ♦ n (inf!) homosexuel m

quell [kwel] vt réprimer, étouffer

quench [kwentʃ] vt: **to ~ one's thirst** se désaltérer

query ['kwɪərɪ] n question f ♦ vt remettre en question, mettre en doute

quest [kwest] n recherche f, quête f

question ['kwestʃən] n question f ♦ vt (person) interroger; (plan, idea) remettre en question, mettre en doute; **beyond ~** sans aucun doute; **out of the ~** hors de question; **~able** adj discutable; **~ mark** n point m d'interrogation; **~naire** [kwestʃə'neər] n questionnaire m

queue [kjuː] (BRIT) n queue f, file f ♦ vi (also: **~ up**) faire la queue

quibble ['kwɪbl] vi: **~ (about sth)** or **(over sth)** or **(with sth)** ergoter (sur qch)

quick [kwɪk] adj rapide; (agile) agile, vif (vive) ♦ n: **cut to the ~** (fig) touché(e) au vif; **be ~!** dépêche-toi!; **~en** vt accélérer, presser ♦ vi s'accélérer, devenir plus rapide; **~ly** adv vite, rapidement; **~sand** n sables mouvants; **~-witted** adj à l'esprit vif

quid [kwɪd] (BRIT: inf) n, pl inv livre f

quiet ['kwaɪət] adj tranquille, calme; (voice) bas(se); (ceremony, colour) discret(-ète) ♦ n tranquillité f, calme m; (silence) silence m ♦ vt, vi (US) = **quieten**; **keep ~!** tais-toi!; **~en** vi (also: **~en down**) se calmer, s'apaiser ♦ vt calmer, apaiser; **~ly** adv tranquillement, calmement; (silently) silencieusement; ~**ness** n tranquillité f, calme m; (silence) silence m

quilt [kwɪlt] n édredon m; (continental ~) couette f

quin [kwɪn] n abbr = **quintuplet**

quintuplets [kwɪn'tjuːplɪts] npl quintuplé(e)s

quip [kwɪp] n remarque piquante or spirituelle, pointe f

quirk [kwɜːk] n bizarrerie f

quit [kwɪt] (pt, pp **quit** or **quitted**) vt quitter; (smoking, grumbling) arrêter de ♦ vi (give up) abandonner, renoncer; (resign) démissionner

quite [kwaɪt] adv (rather) assez, plutôt; (entirely) complètement, tout à fait; (following a negative = almost): **that's not ~ big enough** ce n'est pas tout à fait assez grand; **I ~ understand** je comprends très bien; **~ a few of them** un assez grand nombre d'entre eux; **~ (so)!** exactement!

quits [kwɪts] adj: **~ (with)** quitte (envers); **let's call it ~** restons-en là

quiver ['kwɪvəʳ] vi trembler, frémir

quiz [kwɪz] n (game) jeu-concours m ♦ vt interroger; ~**zical** adj narquois(e)

quota ['kwəʊtə] n quota m

quotation [kwəʊ'teɪʃən] n citation f; (estimate) devis m; **~ marks** npl guillemets mpl

quote [kwəʊt] n citation f; (estimate) devis m ♦ vt citer; (price) indiquer; **~s** npl guillemets mpl

R, r

rabbi ['ræbaɪ] n rabbin m

rabbit ['ræbɪt] n lapin m; ~ **hutch** n clapier m

rabble ['ræbl] (pej) n populace f

rabies ['reɪbiːz] n rage f

RAC n abbr (BRIT) = **Royal Automobile Club**

rac(c)oon [rə'kuːn] n raton laveur

race [reɪs] n (species) race f; (competition, rush) course f ♦ vt (horse) faire courir ♦ vi (compete) faire la course, courir; (hurry) al-

ler à toute vitesse, courir; (engine) s'emballer; (pulse) augmenter; ~ **car** (US) n = **racing car**; ~ **car driver** (US) = **racing driver**; ~**course** n champ m de courses; ~**horse** n cheval m de course; ~**r** n (bike) vélo m de course; ~**track** n piste f

racial ['reɪʃl] adj racial(e)

racing ['reɪsɪŋ] n courses fpl; ~ **car** (BRIT) n voiture f de course; ~ **driver** (BRIT) n pilote m de course

racism ['reɪsɪzəm] n racisme m; **racist** adj raciste ♦ n raciste m/f

rack [ræk] n (for guns, tools) râtelier m; (also: luggage ~) porte-bagages m inv, filet m à bagages; (also: roof ~) galerie f; (dish ~) égouttoir m ♦ vt tourmenter; **to ~ one's brains** se creuser la cervelle

racket ['rækɪt] n (for tennis) raquette f; (noise) tapage m; vacarme m; (swindle) escroquerie f

racquet ['rækɪt] n raquette f

racy ['reɪsɪ] adj plein(e) de verve; (slightly indecent) osé(e)

radar ['reɪdɑːʳ] n radar m

radial ['reɪdɪəl] adj (also: ~-ply) à carcasse radiale

radiant ['reɪdɪənt] adj rayonnant(e)

radiate ['reɪdɪeɪt] vt (heat) émettre, dégager; (emotion) rayonner de ♦ vi (lines) rayonner; **radiation** [reɪdɪ'eɪʃən] n rayonnement m; (radioactive) radiation f; **radiator** ['reɪdɪeɪtəʳ] n radiateur m

radical ['rædɪkl] adj radical(e)

radii ['reɪdɪaɪ] npl of **radius**

radio ['reɪdɪəʊ] n radio f ♦ vt appeler par radio; **on the ~** à la radio; ~**active** ['reɪdɪəʊ'æktɪv] adj radioactif(-ive); ~ **cassette** n radiocassette m; ~**-controlled** adj téléguidé(e); ~ **station** n station f de radio

radish ['rædɪʃ] n radis m

radius ['reɪdɪəs] n (pl **radii**) n rayon m

RAF n abbr = **Royal Air Force**

raffle ['ræfl] n tombola f

raft [rɑːft] n (craft; also: life ~) radeau m

rafter ['rɑːftəʳ] n chevron m

rag [ræg] n chiffon m; (pej: newspaper) feuille *f* de chou, torchon *m*; (*student ~*) attractions organisées au profit d'œuvres de charité; **~s** *npl* (*torn clothes etc*) haillons *mpl*; **~ doll** *n* poupée *f* de chiffon

rage [reɪdʒ] *n* (*fury*) rage *f*, fureur *f* ♦ *vi* (*person*) être fou (folle) de rage; (*storm*) faire rage, être déchaîné(e); **it's all the ~** cela fait fureur

ragged [ˈrægɪd] *adj* (*edge*) inégal(e); (*clothes*) en loques; (*appearance*) déguenillé(e)

raid [reɪd] *n* (*attack, also:* MIL) raid *m*; (*criminal*) hold-up *m inv*; (*by police*) descente *f*, rafle *f* ♦ *vt* faire un raid sur *or* un hold-up *or* une descente dans

rail [reɪl] *n* (*on stairs*) rampe *f*; (*on bridge, balcony*) balustrade *f*; (*of ship*) bastingage *m*; **~s** *npl* (*track*) rails *mpl*, voie ferrée; **by ~** par chemin de fer, en train; **~ing(s)** *n(pl)* grille *f*; **~road** (US), **~way** (BRIT) *n* (*track*) voie ferrée; (*company*) chemin *m* de fer; **~way line** (BRIT) *n* ligne *f* de chemin de fer; **~wayman** (BRIT) (*irreg*) *n* cheminot *m*; **~way station** (BRIT) *n* gare *f*

rain [reɪn] *n* pluie *f* ♦ *vi* pleuvoir; **in the ~** sous la pluie; **it's ~ing** il pleut; **~bow** *n* arc-en-ciel *m*; **~coat** *n* imperméable *m*; **~drop** *n* goutte *f* de pluie; **~fall** *n* chute *f* de pluie; (*measurement*) hauteur *f* des précipitations; **~forest** *n* forêt *f* tropicale humide; **~y** *adj* pluvieux(-euse)

raise [reɪz] *n* augmentation *f* ♦ *vt* (*lift*) lever; hausser; (*increase*) augmenter; (*morale*) remonter; (*standards*) améliorer; (*question, doubt*) provoquer, soulever; (*cattle, family*) élever; (*crop*) faire pousser; (*funds*) rassembler; (*loan*) obtenir; (*army*) lever; **to ~ one's voice** élever la voix

raisin [ˈreɪzn] *n* raisin sec

rake [reɪk] *n* (*tool*) râteau *m* ♦ *vt* ratisser

rally [ˈrælɪ] *n* (POL *etc*) meeting *m*, rassemblement *m*; (AUT) rallye *m*; (TENNIS) échange *m* ♦ *vt* (*support*) gagner ♦ *vi* (*sick person*) aller mieux; (Stock Exchange) reprendre; **~ round** *vt fus* venir en aide à

RAM [ræm] *n abbr* (= *random access memory*) mémoire vive

ram [ræm] *n* bélier *m* ♦ *vt* enfoncer; (*crash into*) emboutir; percuter

Ramadan [ˈræmədæn] *n* ramadan *m*

ramble [ˈræmbl] *n* randonnée *f* ♦ *vi* (*walk*) se promener, faire une randonnée; (*talk: also:* **~ on**) discourir, pérorer; **~r** *n* promeneur(-euse), randonneur(-euse); (BOT) rosier grimpant; **rambling** *adj* (*speech*) décousu(e); (*house*) plein(e) de coins et de recoins; (BOT) grimpant(e)

ramp [ræmp] *n* (*incline*) rampe *f*; dénivellation *f*; **on ~, off ~** (US: AUT) bretelle *f* d'accès

rampage [ræmˈpeɪdʒ] *n*: **to be on the ~** se déchaîner

rampant [ˈræmpənt] *adj* (*disease etc*) qui sévit

ram raiding [-reɪdɪŋ] *n* pillage d'un magasin en enfonçant la vitrine avec une voiture

ramshackle [ˈræmʃækl] *adj* (*house*) délabré(e); (*car etc*) déglingué(e)

ran [ræn] *pt of* **run**

ranch [rɑːntʃ] *n* ranch *m*; **~er** *n* propriétaire *m* de ranch

rancid [ˈrænsɪd] *adj* rance

rancour [ˈræŋkər] (US **rancor**) *n* rancune *f*

random [ˈrændəm] *adj* fait(e) *or* établi(e) au hasard; (MATH) aléatoire ♦ *n*: **at ~** au hasard; **~ access** *n* (COMPUT) accès sélectif

randy [ˈrændɪ] (BRIT: *inf*) *adj* excité(e); lubrique

rang [ræŋ] *pt of* **ring**

range [reɪndʒ] *n* (*of mountains*) chaîne *f*; (*of missile, voice*) portée *f*; (*of products*) choix *m*, gamme *f*; (MIL: *also:* **shooting ~**) champ *m* de tir; (*indoor*) stand *m* de tir; (*also:* **kitchen ~**) fourneau *m* (de cuisine) ♦ *vt* (*place in a line*) mettre en rang, ranger **to ~ from ... to** aller de ... à; **a ~ of** (*series: of proposals etc*) divers(e)

ranger [ˈreɪndʒər] *n* garde forestier

rank [ræŋk] *n* rang *m*; (MIL) grade *m*; (BRIT: *also:* **taxi ~**) station *f* de taxis ♦ *vi*: **to ~ among** compter *or* se classer parmi ♦ *adj* (*stinking*) fétide, puant(e); **the ~ and file** (*fig*) la masse, la base

ransack ['rænsæk] *vt* fouiller (à fond); (*plunder*) piller

ransom ['rænsəm] *n* rançon *f*; **to hold to ~** (*fig*) exercer un chantage sur

rant [rænt] *vi* fulminer

rap [ræp] *vt* frapper sur *or* à; taper sur ♦ *n*: **~ music** rap *m*

rape [reɪp] *n* viol *m*; (*BOT*) colza *m* ♦ *vt* violer; **~(seed) oil** *n* huile *f* de colza

rapid ['ræpɪd] *adj* rapide; **~s** *npl* (*GEO*) rapides *mpl*

rapist ['reɪpɪst] *n* violeur *m*

rapport [ræ'pɔːʳ] *n* entente *f*

rapturous ['ræptʃərəs] *adj* enthousiaste, frénétique

rare [reəʳ] *adj* rare; (*CULIN: steak*) saignant(e)

raring ['reərɪŋ] *adj*: **~ to go** (*inf*) très impatient(e) de commencer

rascal ['rɑːskl] *n* vaurien *m*

rash [ræʃ] *adj* imprudent(e), irréfléchi(e) ♦ *n* (*MED*) rougeur *f*, éruption *f*; (*spate: of events*) série (noire)

rasher ['ræʃəʳ] *n* fine tranche (de lard)

raspberry ['rɑːzbərɪ] *n* framboise *f*; **~ bush** *n* framboisier *m*

rasping ['rɑːspɪŋ] *adj*: **~ noise** grincement *m*

rat [ræt] *n* rat *m*

rate [reɪt] *n* taux *m*; (*speed*) vitesse *f*, rythme *m*; (*price*) tarif *m* ♦ *vt* classer; évaluer; **~s** *npl* (*BRIT: tax*) impôts locaux; (*fees*) tarifs *mpl*; **to ~ sb/sth as** considérer qn/qch comme; **~able value** (*BRIT*) *n* valeur locative imposable; **~payer** ['reɪtpeɪəʳ] (*BRIT*) *n* contribuable *m/f* (*payant les impôts locaux*)

rather ['rɑːðəʳ] *adv* plutôt; **it's ~ expensive** c'est assez cher; (*too much*) c'est un peu cher; **there's ~ a lot** il y en a beaucoup; **I would** *or* **I'd ~ go** j'aimerais mieux *or* je préférerais partir

rating ['reɪtɪŋ] *n* (*assessment*) évaluation *f*; (*score*) classement *m*; **~s** *npl* (*RADIO, TV*) indice *m* d'écoute

ratio ['reɪʃɪəu] *n* proportion *f*

ration ['ræʃən] *n* (*gen pl*) ration(s) *f(pl)*

rational ['ræʃənl] *adj* raisonnable, sensé(e); (*solution, reasoning*) logique; **~e** [ræʃə'nɑːl] *n* raisonnement *m*; **~ize** *vt* rationaliser; (*conduct*) essayer d'expliquer *or* de motiver

rat race *n* foire *f* d'empoigne

rattle ['rætl] *n* (*of door, window*) battement *m*; (*of coins, chain*) cliquetis *m*; (*of train, engine*) bruit *m* de ferraille; (*object: for baby*) hochet *m* ♦ *vi* cliqueter; (*car, bus*): **to ~ along** rouler dans un bruit de ferraille ♦ *vt* agiter (bruyamment); (*unnerve*) décontenancer; **~snake** *n* serpent *m* à sonnettes

raucous ['rɔːkəs] *adj* rauque; (*noisy*) bruyant(e), tapageur(-euse)

rave [reɪv] *vi* (*in anger*) s'emporter; (*with enthusiasm*) s'extasier; (*MED*) délirer ♦ *n* (*BRIT: inf: party*) rave *f*, soirée *f* techno

raven ['reɪvən] *n* corbeau *m*

ravenous ['rævənəs] *adj* affamé(e)

ravine [rə'viːn] *n* ravin *m*

raving ['reɪvɪŋ] *adj*: **~ lunatic** ♦ *n* fou (folle) furieux(-euse)

ravishing ['rævɪʃɪŋ] *adj* enchanteur(-eresse)

raw [rɔː] *adj* (*uncooked*) cru(e); (*not processed*) brut(e); (*sore*) à vif, irrité(e); (*inexperienced*) inexpérimenté(e); (*weather, day*) froid(e) et humide; **~ deal** (*inf*) *n* sale coup *m*; **~ material** *n* matière première

ray [reɪ] *n* rayon *m*; **~ of hope** lueur *f* d'espoir

raze [reɪz] *vt* (*also*: **~ to the ground**) raser, détruire

razor ['reɪzəʳ] *n* rasoir *m*; **~ blade** *n* lame *f* de rasoir

Rd *abbr* = **road**

RE *n abbr* = **religious education**

re [riː] *prep* concernant

reach [riːtʃ] *n* portée *f*, atteinte *f*; (*of river etc*) étendue *f* ♦ *vt* atteindre; (*conclusion, decision*) parvenir à ♦ *vi* s'étendre, étendre le bras; **out of ~** hors de/à portée; **within ~ of the shops** pas trop loin des *or* à proximité des magasins; **~ out** *vt* tendre ♦ *vi*: **to ~ out (for)** allonger le bras (pour prendre)

react [ri:ˈækt] vi réagir; **~ion** n réaction f

reactor [ri:ˈæktəʳ] n réacteur m

read [ri:d, pt, pp red] (pt, pp **read**) vi lire ♦ vt lire; (understand) comprendre, interpréter; (study) étudier; (meter) relever; ~ out vt lire à haute voix; **~able** adj facile or agréable à lire; (writing) lisible; **~er** n lecteur(-trice); (BRIT: at university) chargé(e) d'enseignement; **~ership** n (of paper etc) (nombre m de) lecteurs mpl

readily [ˈredɪlɪ] adv volontiers, avec empressement; (easily) facilement

readiness [ˈredɪnɪs] n empressement m; **in ~** (prepared) prêt(e)

reading [ˈri:dɪŋ] n lecture f; (understanding) interprétation f; (on instrument) indications fpl

ready [ˈredɪ] adj prêt(e); (willing) prêt, disposé(e); (available) disponible ♦ n: **at the ~** (MIL) prêt à faire feu; **to get ~** se préparer ♦ vt préparer; **~-made** adj tout(e) fait(e); **~-to-wear** adj prêt(e) à porter

real [rɪəl] adj véritable; réel(le); **in ~ terms** dans la réalité; **~ estate** n biens fonciers or immobiliers; **~istic** [rɪəˈlɪstɪk] adj réaliste; **~ity** [ri:ˈælɪtɪ] n réalité f

realization [rɪəlaɪˈzeɪʃən] n (awareness) prise f de conscience; (fulfilment; also: of asset) réalisation f

realize [ˈrɪəlaɪz] vt (understand) se rendre compte de; (a project, COMM: asset) réaliser

really [ˈrɪəlɪ] adv vraiment; **~?** vraiment?, c'est vrai?

realm [relm] n royaume m; (fig) domaine m

realtor ® [ˈrɪəltɔːʳ] n (US) agent immobilier

reap [ri:p] vt moissonner; (fig) récolter

reappear [ri:əˈpɪəʳ] vi réapparaître, reparaître

rear [rɪəʳ] adj de derrière, arrière inv; (AUT: wheel etc) arrière ♦ n arrière m ♦ vt (cattle, family) élever ♦ vi (also: ~ up: animal) se cabrer; **~guard** n (MIL) arrière-garde f; **~-view mirror** n (AUT) rétroviseur m

reason [ˈri:zn] n raison f ♦ vi: **to ~ with**

sb raisonner qn, faire entendre raison à qn; **to have ~ to think** avoir lieu de penser; **it stands to ~ that** il va sans dire que; **~able** adj raisonnable; (not bad) acceptable; **~ably** adv raisonnablement; **~ing** n raisonnement m

reassurance [ri:əˈʃuərəns] n réconfort m; (factual) assurance f, garantie f

reassure [ri:əˈʃuəʳ] vt rassurer

rebate [ˈri:beɪt] n (on tax etc) dégrèvement m

rebel [n ˈrebl, vb riˈbel] n rebelle m/f ♦ vi se rebeller, se révolter; **~lious** [riˈbeljəs] adj rebelle

rebound [vb riˈbaund, n ˈri:baund] vi (ball) rebondir ♦ n rebond m; **to marry on the ~** se marier immédiatement après une déception amoureuse

rebuff [riˈbʌf] n rebuffade f

rebuke [riˈbju:k] vt réprimander

rebut [riˈbʌt] vt réfuter

recall [vb riˈkɔ:l, n riˈkɔl] vt rappeler; (remember) se rappeler, se souvenir de ♦ n rappel m; (ability to remember) mémoire f

recant [riˈkænt] vi se rétracter; (REL) abjurer

recap [ˈri:kæp], **recapitulate** [ri:kəˈpɪtjuleɪt] vt, vi récapituler

rec'd abbr = **received**

recede [riˈsi:d] vi (tide) descendre; (disappear) disparaître peu à peu; (memory, hope) s'estomper; **receding** adj (chin) fuyant(e); **receding hairline** front dégarni

receipt [riˈsi:t] n (document) reçu m; (for parcel etc) accusé m de réception; (act of receiving) réception f; **~s** npl (COMM) recettes fpl

receive [riˈsi:v] vt recevoir; **~r** n (TEL) récepteur m, combiné m; (RADIO) récepteur m; (of stolen goods) receleur m; (LAW) administrateur m judiciaire

recent [ˈri:snt] adj récent(e); **~ly** adv récemment

receptacle [riˈseptɪkl] n récipient m

reception [riˈsepʃən] n réception f; (welcome) accueil m, réception; **~ desk** n réception f; **~ist** n réceptionniste m/f

recess [rɪ'sɛs] n (in room) renfoncement m, alcôve f; (secret place) recoin m; (POL etc: holiday) vacances fpl

recession [rɪ'sɛʃən] n récession f

recipe ['rɛsɪpɪ] n recette f

recipient [rɪ'sɪpɪənt] n (of payment) bénéficiaire m/f; (of letter) destinataire m/f

recital [rɪ'saɪtl] n récital m

recite [rɪ'saɪt] vt (poem) réciter

reckless ['rɛkləs] adj (driver etc) imprudent(e)

reckon ['rɛkən] vt (count) calculer, compter; (think): **I ~ that ...** je pense que ...; **~ on** vt fus compter sur, s'attendre à; **~ing** n compte m, calcul m; estimation f

reclaim [rɪ'kleɪm] vt (demand back) réclamer (le remboursement or la restitution de); (land: from sea) assécher; (waste materials) récupérer

recline [rɪ'klaɪn] vi être allongé(e) or étendu(e); **reclining** adj (seat) à dossier réglable

recluse [rɪ'kluːs] n reclus(e), ermite m

recognition [rɛkəg'nɪʃən] n reconnaissance f; **to gain ~** être reconnu(e); **transformed beyond ~** méconnaissable

recognizable ['rɛkəgnaɪzəbl] adj: **~ (by)** reconnaissable (à)

recognize ['rɛkəgnaɪz] vt: **to ~ (by/as)** reconnaître (à/comme étant)

recoil [vb rɪ'kɔɪl, n 'riːkɔɪl] vi (person): **to ~ (from sth/doing sth)** reculer (devant qch/l'idée de faire qch) ♦ n (of gun) recul m

recollect [rɛkə'lɛkt] vt se rappeler, se souvenir de; **~ion** n souvenir m

recommend [rɛkə'mɛnd] vt recommander

reconcile ['rɛkənsaɪl] vt (two people) réconcilier; (two facts) concilier, accorder; **to ~ o.s. to** se résigner à

recondition [riːkən'dɪʃən] vt remettre à neuf; réviser entièrement

reconnoitre [rɛkə'nɔɪtər] (US **reconnoiter**) vt (MIL) reconnaître

reconsider [riːkən'sɪdər] vt reconsidérer

reconstruct [riːkən'strʌkt] vt (building) reconstruire; (crime, policy, system) reconstituer

record [n 'rɛkɔːd, vb rɪ'kɔːd] n rapport m, récit m; (of meeting etc) procès-verbal m; (register) registre m; (file) dossier m; (also: **criminal ~**) casier m judiciaire; (MUS: disc) disque m; (SPORT) record m; (COMPUT) article m ♦ vt (set down) noter; (MUS: song etc) enregistrer; **in ~ time** en un temps record inv; **off the ~** ♦ adj officieux(-euse) ♦ adv officieusement; **~ card** n (in file) fiche f; **~ed delivery** n (BRIT: POST): **~ed delivery letter** etc lettre etc recommandée; **~er** n (MUS) flûte f à bec; **~ holder** n (SPORT) détenteur(-trice) du record; **~ing** n (MUS) enregistrement m; **~ player** n tourne-disque m

recount [rɪ'kaunt] vt raconter

re-count ['riːkaunt] n (POL: of votes) deuxième compte m

recoup [rɪ'kuːp] vt: **to ~ one's losses** récupérer ce qu'on a perdu, se refaire

recourse [rɪ'kɔːs] n: **to have ~ to** avoir recours à

recover [rɪ'kʌvər] vt récupérer ♦ vi: **to ~ (from)** (illness) se rétablir (de); (from shock) se remettre (de); **~y** n récupération f; rétablissement m; (ECON) redressement m

recreation [rɛkrɪ'eɪʃən] n récréation f, détente f; **~al** adj pour la détente, récréatif(-ive)

recruit [rɪ'kruːt] n recrue f ♦ vt recruter

rectangle ['rɛktæŋgl] n rectangle m; **rectangular** [rɛk'tæŋgjulər] adj rectangulaire

rectify ['rɛktɪfaɪ] vt (error) rectifier, corriger

rector ['rɛktər] n (REL) pasteur m

recuperate [rɪ'kjuːpəreɪt] vi récupérer; (from illness) se rétablir

recur [rɪ'kəːr] vi se reproduire; (symptoms) réapparaître; **~rence** n répétition f; réapparition f; **~rent** adj périodique, fréquent(e)

recycle [riːˈsaɪkl] vt recycler; **recycling** n recyclage m

red [rɛd] n rouge m; (POL: pej) rouge m/f ♦ adj rouge; (hair) roux (rousse); **in the ~** (account) à découvert; (business) en déficit; **~ carpet treatment** n réception f en grande pompe; **R~ Cross** *n* Croix-Rouge *f*; **~currant** *n* groseille *f* (rouge); **~den** *vt*, *vi* rougir

redecorate [riː'dɛkəreɪt] *vi* (*with wallpaper*) retapisser; (*with paint*) refaire les peintures

redeem [rɪ'diːm] *vt* (*debt*) rembourser; (*sth in pawn*) dégager; (*fig, also REL*) racheter; **~ing** *adj* (*feature*) qui sauve, qui rachète (le reste)

redeploy [riːdɪ'plɔɪ] *vt* (*resources*) réorganiser

red: **~-haired** *adj* roux (rousse); **~-handed** *adj*: **to be caught ~-handed** être pris(e) en flagrant délit *or* la main dans le sac; **~head** *n* roux (rousse); **~herring** *n* (*fig*) diversion *f*, fausse piste; **~-hot** *adj* chauffé(e) au rouge, brûlant(e)

redirect [riːdaɪ'rɛkt] *vt* (*mail*) faire suivre

red light *n*: **to go through a ~** (AUT) brûler un feu rouge; **red-light district** *n* quartier *m* des prostituées

redo [riː'duː] *vt* (*irreg*) refaire

redress [rɪ'drɛs] *n* réparation *f* ♦ *vt* redresser

red: **R~ Sea** *n* mer Rouge *f*; **~skin** *n* Peau-Rouge *m/f*; **~ tape** *n* (*fig*) paperasserie (administrative)

reduce [rɪ'djuːs] *vt* réduire; (*lower*) abaisser; **"~ speed now"** (AUT) "ralentir"; **~duction** [rɪ'dʌkʃən] *n* réduction *f*; (*discount*) rabais *m*

redundancy [rɪ'dʌndənsɪ] (BRIT) *n* licenciement *m*, mise *f* au chômage

redundant [rɪ'dʌndnt] *adj* (BRIT: *worker*) mis(e) au chômage, licencié(e); (*detail, object*) superflu(e); **to be made ~** être licencié(e), être mis(e) au chômage

reed [riːd] *n* (BOT) roseau *m*; (MUS: *of clarinet etc*) hanche *f*

reef [riːf] *n* (*at sea*) récif *m*, écueil *m*

reek [riːk] *vi*: **to ~ (of)** puer, empester

reel [riːl] *n* bobine *f*; (FISHING) moulinet *m*; (CINEMA) bande *f*; (*dance*) quadrille écossais ♦ *vi* (*sway*) chanceler; **~ in** *vt* (*fish, line*) ramener

ref [rɛf] (*inf*) *n abbr* (= *referee*) arbitre *m*

refectory [rɪ'fɛktərɪ] *n* réfectoire *m*

refer [rɪ'fəːʳ] *vt*: **to ~ sb to** (*inquirer: for information, patient: to specialist*) adresser qn à; (*reader: to text*) renvoyer qn à; (*dispute, decision*): **to ~ sth to** soumettre qch à ♦ *vi*: **~ to** (*allude to*) parler de, faire allusion à; (*consult*) se reporter à

referee [rɛfə'riː] *n* arbitre *m*; (BRIT: *for job application*) répondant(e)

reference ['rɛfrəns] *n* référence *f*, renvoi *m*; (*mention*) allusion *f*, mention *f*; (*for job application: letter*) références, lettre *f* de recommandation; **with ~ to** (COMM: *in letter*) me référant à, suite à; **~ book** *n* ouvrage *m* de référence

refill [*vb* riː'fɪl, *n* 'riːfɪl] *vt* remplir à nouveau; (*pen, lighter etc*) recharger ♦ *n* (*for pen etc*) recharge *f*

refine [rɪ'faɪn] *vt* (*sugar, oil*) raffiner; (*taste*) affiner; (*theory, idea*) fignoler (*inf*); **~d** *adj* (*person, taste*) raffiné(e); **~ry** *n* raffinerie *f*

reflect [rɪ'flɛkt] *vt* (*light, image*) réfléchir, refléter; (*fig*) refléter ♦ *vi* (*think*) réfléchir, méditer; **it ~s badly on him** cela le discrédite; **it ~s well on him** c'est tout à son honneur; **~ion** *n* réflexion *f*; (*image*) reflet *m*; (*criticism*): **~ion on** critique *f* de; atteinte *f* à; **on ~ion** réflexion faite

reflex ['riːflɛks] *adj* réflexe ♦ *n* réflexe *m*; **~ive** [rɪ'flɛksɪv] *adj* (LING) réfléchi(e)

reform [rɪ'fɔːm] *n* réforme *f* ♦ *vt* réformer; **~atory** [rɪ'fɔːmətərɪ] (US) *n* ≃ centre *m* d'éducation surveillée

refrain [rɪ'freɪn] *vi*: **to ~ from doing** s'abstenir de faire ♦ *n* refrain *m*

refresh [rɪ'frɛʃ] *vt* rafraîchir; (*subj: sleep*) reposer; **~er course** (BRIT) *n* cours *m* de recyclage; **~ing** *adj* (*drink*) rafraîchissant(e); (*sleep*) réparateur(-trice); **~ments** *npl* rafraîchissements *mpl*

refrigerator [rɪ'frɪdʒəreɪtəʳ] *n* réfrigérateur *m*, frigidaire ® *m*

refuel [riː'fjuəl] *vi* se ravitailler en carburant

refuge ['rɛfjuːdʒ] *n* refuge *m*; **to take ~ in** se réfugier dans; **~e** [rɛfju'dʒiː] *n* réfugié(e)

refund [*n* 'riːfʌnd, *vb* rɪ'fʌnd] *n* remboursement *m* ♦ *vt* rembourser

refurbish [riː'fɜːbɪʃ] *vt* remettre à neuf

refusal [rɪ'fjuːzəl] *n* refus *m*; **to have first ~ on** avoir droit de préemption sur

refuse[1] [rɪ'fjuːz] *vt, vi* refuser

refuse[2] ['refjuːs] *n* ordures *fpl*, détritus *mpl*; **~ collection** *n* ramassage *m* d'ordures

regain [rɪ'geɪn] *vt* regagner; retrouver

regal ['riːgl] *adj* royal(e)

regard [rɪ'gɑːd] *n* respect *m*, estime *f*, considération *f* ♦ *vt* considérer; **to give one's ~s to** faire ses amitiés à; **"with kindest ~s"** "bien amicalement"; **as ~s, with ~ to = regarding**; **~ing** *prep* en ce qui concerne; **~less** *adv* quand même; **~less of** sans se soucier de

régime [reɪ'ʒiːm] *n* régime *m*

regiment ['redʒɪmənt] *n* régiment *m*; **~al** [redʒɪ'mentl] *adj* d'un *or* du régiment

region ['riːdʒən] *n* région *f*; **in the ~ of** (*fig*) aux alentours de; **~al** *adj* régional(e)

register ['redʒɪstər] *n* registre *m*; (*also:* **electoral ~**) liste électorale ♦ *vt* enregistrer; (*birth, death*) déclarer; (*vehicle*) immatriculer; (*POST: letter*) envoyer en recommandé; (*subj: instrument*) marquer ♦ *vi* s'inscrire; (*at hotel*) signer le registre; (*make impression*) être (bien) compris(e); **~ed** *adj* (*letter, parcel*) recommandé(e); **~ed trademark** *n* marque déposée.

registrar ['redʒɪstrɑːr] *n* officier *m* de l'état civil; **registration** [redʒɪs'treɪʃən] *n* enregistrement *m*; (*BRIT: AUT: also:* **registration number**) numéro *m* d'immatriculation

registry ['redʒɪstrɪ] *n* bureau *m* de l'enregistrement; **~ office** (*BRIT*) *n* bureau *m* de l'état civil; **to get married in a ~ office** ≈ se marier à la mairie

regret [rɪ'gret] *n* regret *m* ♦ *vt* regretter; **~fully** *adv* à *or* avec regret

regular ['regjulər] *adj* régulier(-ère); (*usual*) habituel(le); (*soldier*) de métier ♦ *n* (*client etc*) habitué(e); **~ly** *adv* régulièrement

regulate ['regjuleɪt] *vt* régler; **regulation** [regju'leɪʃən] *n* (*rule*) règlement *m*; (*adjust-*

ment) réglage *m*

rehabilitation ['riːəbɪlɪ'teɪʃən] *n* (*of offender*) réinsertion *f*; (*of addict*) réadaptation *f*

rehearsal [rɪ'hɜːsəl] *n* répétition *f*

rehearse [rɪ'hɜːs] *vt* répéter

reign [reɪn] *n* règne *m* ♦ *vi* régner

reimburse [riːɪm'bɜːs] *vt* rembourser

rein [reɪn] *n* (*for horse*) rêne *f*

reindeer ['reɪndɪər] *n, pl inv* renne *m*

reinforce [riːɪn'fɔːs] *vt* renforcer; **~d concrete** *n* béton armé; **~ments** *npl* (*MIL*) renfort(s) *m(pl)*

reinstate [riːɪn'steɪt] *vt* rétablir, réintégrer

reject [*n* 'riːdʒekt, *vb* rɪ'dʒekt] *n* (*COMM*) article *m* de rebut ♦ *vt* refuser; (*idea*) rejeter; **~ion** *n* rejet *m*, refus *m*

rejoice [rɪ'dʒɔɪs] *vi*: **to ~ (at *or* over)** se réjouir (de)

rejuvenate [rɪ'dʒuːvəneɪt] *vt* rajeunir

relapse [rɪ'læps] *n* (*MED*) rechute *f*

relate [rɪ'leɪt] *vt* (*tell*) raconter; (*connect*) établir un rapport entre ♦ *vi*: **this ~s to** cela se rapporte à; **to ~ to sb** entretenir des rapports avec qn; **~d** *adj* apparenté(e); **relating to** *prep* concernant

relation [rɪ'leɪʃən] *n* (*person*) parent(e); (*link*) rapport *m*, lien *m*; **~ship** *n* rapport *m*, lien *m*; (*personal ties*) relations *fpl*, rapports; (*also:* **family ~ship**) lien de parenté

relative ['relətɪv] *n* parent(e) ♦ *adj* relatif(-ive); **all her ~s** toute sa famille; **~ly** *adv* relativement

relax [rɪ'læks] *vi* (*muscle*) se relâcher; (*person: unwind*) se détendre ♦ *vt* relâcher; (*mind, person*) détendre; **~ation** [riːlæk'seɪʃən] *n* relâchement *m*; (*of mind*) détente *f*, relaxation *f*; (*recreation*) détente *f*, délassement *m*; **~ed** *adj* détendu(e); **~ing** *adj* délassant(e)

relay [*n* 'riːleɪ, *vb* rɪ'leɪ] *n* (*SPORT*) course *f* de relais ♦ *vt* (*message*) retransmettre, relayer

release [rɪ'liːs] *n* (*from prison, obligation*) libération *f*; (*of gas etc*) émission *f*; (*of film etc*) sortie *f*; (*new recording*) disque *m* ♦ *vt* (*prisoner*) libérer; (*gas etc*) émettre, dégager; (*free: from wreckage etc*) dégager;

(*TECH: catch, spring etc*) faire jouer; (*book, film*) sortir; (*report, news*) rendre public, publier

relegate ['rɛləgeɪt] *vt* reléguer; (*BRIT: SPORT*): **to be ~d** descendre dans une division inférieure

relent [rɪ'lɛnt] *vi* se laisser fléchir; **~less** *adj* implacable; (*unceasing*) continuel(le)

relevant ['rɛləvənt] *adj* (*question*) pertinent(e); (*fact*) significatif(-ive); (*information*) utile; **~ to** ayant rapport à, approprié à

reliable [rɪ'laɪəbl] *adj* (*person, firm*) sérieux(-euse), fiable; (*method, machine*) fiable; (*news, information*) sûr(e); **reliably** *adv*: **to be reliably informed** savoir de source sûre

reliance [rɪ'laɪəns] *n*: **~ (on)** (*person*) confiance *f* (en); (*drugs, promises*) besoin *m* (de), dépendance *f* (de)

relic ['rɛlɪk] *n* (*REL*) relique *f*; (*of the past*) vestige *m*

relief [rɪ'liːf] *n* (*from pain, anxiety etc*) soulagement *m*; (*help, supplies*) secours *m(pl)*; (*ART, GEO*) relief *m*

relieve [rɪ'liːv] *vt* (*pain, patient*) soulager; (*fear, worry*) dissiper; (*bring help*) secourir; (*take over from: gen*) relayer; (*: guard*) relever; **to ~ sb of sth** débarrasser qn de qch; **to ~ o.s.** se soulager

religion [rɪ'lɪdʒən] *n* religion *f*; **religious** *adj* religieux(-euse); (*book*) de piété

relinquish [rɪ'lɪŋkwɪʃ] *vt* abandonner; (*plan, habit*) renoncer à

relish ['rɛlɪʃ] *n* (*CULIN*) condiment *m*; (*enjoyment*) délectation *f* ♦ *vt* (*food etc*) savourer; **to ~ doing** se délecter à faire

relocate [riːˈləʊˈkeɪt] *vt* installer ailleurs ♦ *vi* déménager, s'installer ailleurs

reluctance [rɪ'lʌktəns] *n* répugnance *f*

reluctant [rɪ'lʌktənt] *adj* peu disposé(e), qui hésite; **~ly** *adv* à contrecœur

rely on [rɪ'laɪ-] *vt fus* (*be dependent*) dépendre de; (*trust*) compter sur

remain [rɪ'meɪn] *vi* rester; **~der** *n* reste *m*; **~ing** *adj* qui reste; **~s** *npl* restes *mpl*

remake ['riːmeɪk] *n* (*CINEMA*) remake *m*

remand [rɪ'mɑːnd] *n*: **on ~** en détention préventive ♦ *vt*: **to be ~ed in custody** être placé(e) en détention préventive

remark [rɪ'mɑːk] *n* remarque *f*, observation *f* ♦ *vt* (faire) remarquer, dire; **~able** *adj* remarquable; **~ably** *adv* remarquablement

remarry [riːˈmærɪ] *vi* se remarier

remedial [rɪ'miːdɪəl] *adj* (*tuition, classes*) de rattrapage; **~ exercises** gymnastique corrective

remedy ['rɛmədɪ] *n*: **~ (for)** remède *m* (contre *or* à) ♦ *vt* remédier à

remember [rɪ'mɛmbər] *vt* se rappeler, se souvenir de; (*send greetings*): **~ me to him** saluez-le de ma part; **remembrance** *n* souvenir *m*; mémoire *f*; **Remembrance Day** *n* le jour de l'Armistice

---

Remembrance Sunday

ⓘ **Remembrance Sunday** *ou* **Remembrance Day** *est le dimanche le plus proche du 11 novembre, jour où la Première Guerre mondiale a officiellement pris fin, et rend hommage aux victimes des deux guerres mondiales. À cette occasion, un silence de deux minutes est observé à 11 h, heure de la signature de l'armistice avec l'Allemagne en 1918; certains membres de la famille royale et du gouvernement déposent des gerbes de coquelicots au cénotaphe de Whitehall, et des couronnes sont placées sur les monuments aux morts dans toute la Grande-Bretagne; par ailleurs, les gens portent des coquelicots artificiels fabriqués et vendus par des membres de la légion britannique blessés au combat, au profit des blessés de guerre et de leur famille.*

---

remind [rɪ'maɪnd] *vt*: **to ~ sb of** rappeler à qn; **to ~ sb to do** faire penser à qn à faire, rappeler à qn qu'il doit faire; **~er** *n* (*souvenir*) souvenir *m*; (*letter*) rappel *m*

reminisce [rɛmɪ'nɪs] *vi*: **to ~ (about)** évoquer ses souvenirs (de); **~nt** *adj*: **to be ~nt of** rappeler, faire penser à

remiss [rɪ'mɪs] *adj* négligent(e); **~ion** *n* (*of illness, sins*) rémission *f*; (*of debt, prison sentence*) remise *f*

remit [rɪ'mɪt] *vt* (*send: money*) envoyer; **~tance** *n* paiement *m*

remnant ['rɛmnənt] *n* reste *m*, restant *m*; (*of cloth*) coupon *m*; **~s** *npl* (COMM) fins *fpl* de série

remorse [rɪ'mɔːs] *n* remords *m*; **~ful** *adj* plein(e) de remords; **~less** *adj* (*fig*) impitoyable

remote [rɪ'məut] *adj* éloigné(e), lointain(e); (*person*) distant(e); (*possibility*) vague; **~ control** *n* télécommande *f*; **~ly** *adv* au loin; (*slightly*) très vaguement

remould ['riːməuld] (BRIT) *n* (*tyre*) pneu rechapé

removable [rɪ'muːvəbl] *adj* (*detachable*) amovible

removal [rɪ'muːvəl] *n* (*taking away*) enlèvement *m*; suppression *f*; (BRIT: *from house*) déménagement *m*; (*from office: dismissal*) renvoi *m*; (*of stain*) nettoyage *m*; (MED) ablation *f*; **~ van** (BRIT) *n* camion *m* de déménagement

remove [rɪ'muːv] *vt* enlever, retirer; (*employee*) renvoyer; (*stain*) faire partir; (*abuse*) supprimer; (*doubt*) chasser

render ['rɛndər] *vt* rendre; **~ing** *n* (MUS *etc*) interprétation *f*

rendezvous ['rɔndɪvuː] *n* rendez-vous *m inv*

renew [rɪ'njuː] *vt* renouveler; (*negotiations*) reprendre; (*acquaintance*) renouer; **~able** *adj* (*energy*) renouvelable; **~al** *n* renouvellement *m*; reprise *f*

renounce [rɪ'nauns] *vt* renoncer à

renovate ['rɛnəveɪt] *vt* rénover; (*art work*) restaurer

renown [rɪ'naun] *n* renommée *f*; **~ed** *adj* renommé(e)

rent [rɛnt] *n* loyer *m* ♦ *vt* louer; **~al** *n* (*for television, car*) prix *m* de) location *f*

reorganize [riː'ɔːgənaɪz] *vt* réorganiser

rep [rɛp] *n abbr* = **representative**; **repertory**

repair [rɪ'pɛər] *n* réparation *f* ♦ *vt* réparer;

in good/bad ~ en bon/mauvais état; **~ kit** *n* trousse *f* de réparation

repatriate [riː'pætrɪeɪt] *vt* rapatrier

repay [riː'peɪ] (*irreg*) *vt* (*money, creditor*) rembourser; (*sb's efforts*) récompenser; **~ment** *n* remboursement *m*

repeal [rɪ'piːl] *n* (*of law*) abrogation *f* ♦ *vt* (*law*) abroger

repeat [rɪ'piːt] *n* (RADIO, TV) reprise *f* ♦ *vt* répéter; (COMM: *order*) renouveler; (SCOL: *a class*) redoubler ♦ *vi* répéter; **~edly** *adv* souvent, à plusieurs reprises

repel [rɪ'pɛl] *vt* repousser; **~lent** *adj* repoussant(e) ♦ *n*: **insect ~lent** insectifuge *m*

repent [rɪ'pɛnt] *vi*: **to ~ (of)** se repentir (de); **~ance** *n* repentir *m*

repertory ['rɛpətərɪ] *n* (*also:* **~ theatre**) théâtre *m* de répertoire

repetition [rɛpɪ'tɪʃən] *n* répétition *f*

repetitive [rɪ'pɛtɪtɪv] *adj* (*movement, work*) répétitif(-ive); (*speech*) plein(e) de redites

replace [rɪ'pleɪs] *vt* (*put back*) remettre, replacer; (*take the place of*) remplacer; **~ment** *n* (*substitution*) remplacement *m*; (*person*) remplaçant(e)

replay ['riːpleɪ] *n* (*of match*) match rejoué; (*of tape, film*) répétition *f*

replenish [rɪ'plɛnɪʃ] *vt* (*glass*) remplir (de nouveau); (*stock etc*) réapprovisionner

replica ['rɛplɪkə] *n* réplique *f*, copie exacte

reply [rɪ'plaɪ] *n* réponse *f* ♦ *vi* répondre

report [rɪ'pɔːt] *n* rapport *m*; (PRESS *etc*) reportage *m*; (BRIT: *also:* **school ~**) bulletin *m* (scolaire); (*of gun*) détonation *f* ♦ *vt* rapporter, faire un compte rendu de; (PRESS *etc*) faire un reportage sur; (*bring to notice: occurrence*) signaler ♦ *vi* (*make a ~*) faire un rapport (*or* un reportage); (*present o.s.*): **to ~ (to sb)** se présenter (chez qn); (*be responsible to*): **to ~ to sb** être sous les ordres de qn; **~ card** (US, SCOT-TISH) *n* bulletin *m* scolaire; **~edly** *adv*: **she is ~edly living in ...** elle habiterait ...; **he ~edly told them to ...** il leur aurait ordonné de ...; **~er** *n* reporter *m*

repose [rɪ'pəuz] *n*: **in ~** en *or* au repos

represent [rɛprɪˈzɛnt] *vt* représenter; (*view, belief*) présenter, expliquer; (*describe*): **to ~ sth as** présenter *or* décrire qch comme; **~ation** [rɛprɪzɛnˈteɪʃən] *n* représentation *f*; **~ations** *npl* (*protest*) démarche *f*; **~ative** [rɛprɪˈzɛntətɪv] *n* représentant(e); (US: POL) député *m* ♦ *adj* représentatif(-ive), caractéristique *f*

repress [rɪˈprɛs] *vt* réprimer; **~ion** *n* répression *f*

reprieve [rɪˈpriːv] *n* (LAW) grâce *f*; (*fig*) sursis *m*, délai *m*

reprisal [rɪˈpraɪzl] *n*: **~s** ♦ *npl* représailles *fpl*

reproach [rɪˈprəʊtʃ] *vt*: **to ~ sb with sth** reprocher qch à qn; **~ful** *adj* de reproche

reproduce [riːprəˈdjuːs] *vt* reproduire ♦ *vi* se reproduire; **reproduction** [riːprəˈdʌkʃən] *n* reproduction *f*

reproof [rɪˈpruːf] *n* reproche *m*

reptile [ˈrɛptaɪl] *n* reptile *m*

republic [rɪˈpʌblɪk] *n* république *f*; **~an** *adj* républicain(e)

repudiate [rɪˈpjuːdɪeɪt] *vt* répudier, rejeter

repulsive [rɪˈpʌlsɪv] *adj* repoussant(e), répulsif(-ive)

reputable [ˈrɛpjʊtəbl] *adj* de bonne réputation; (*occupation*) honorable

reputation [rɛpjuˈteɪʃən] *n* réputation *f*

reputed [rɪˈpjuːtɪd] *adj* (*supposed*) supposé(e); **~ly** *adv* d'après ce qu'on dit

request [rɪˈkwɛst] *n* demande *f*; (*formal*) requête *f* ♦ *vt*: **to ~ (of** *or* **from sb)** demander (à qn); **~ stop** (BRIT) *n* (*for bus*) arrêt facultatif

require [rɪˈkwaɪə*] *vt* (*need: subj: person*) avoir besoin de; (: *thing, situation*) demander; (*want*) exiger; (*order*): **to ~ sb to do sth/sth of sb** exiger que qn fasse qch/qch de qn; **~ment** *n* exigence *f*; besoin *m*; condition requise

requisition [rɛkwɪˈzɪʃən] *n*: **~ (for)** demande *f* (de) ♦ *vt* (MIL) réquisitionner

rescue [ˈrɛskjuː] *n* (*from accident*) sauvetage *m*; (*help*) secours *mpl* ♦ *vt* sauver; **~ party** *n* équipe *f* de sauvetage; **~r** *n* sauveteur *m*

research [rɪˈsəːtʃ] *n* recherche(s) *f(pl)* ♦ *vt* faire des recherches sur

resemblance [rɪˈzɛmbləns] *n* ressemblance *f*

resemble [rɪˈzɛmbl] *vt* ressembler à

resent [rɪˈzɛnt] *vt* être contrarié(e) par; **~ful** *adj* irrité(e), plein(e) de ressentiment; **~ment** *n* ressentiment *m*

reservation [rɛzəˈveɪʃən] *n* (*booking*) réservation *f*; (*doubt*) réserve *f*; (*for tribe*) réserve; **to make a ~ (in a hotel/a restaurant/on a plane)** réserver *or.* retenir une chambre/une table/une place

reserve [rɪˈzəːv] *n* réserve *f*; (SPORT) remplaçant(e) ♦ *vt* (*seats etc*) réserver, retenir; **~s** *npl* (MIL) réservistes *mpl*; **in ~** en réserve; **~d** *adj* réservé(e)

reshuffle [riːˈʃʌfl] *n*: **Cabinet ~** (POL) remaniement ministériel

residence [ˈrɛzɪdəns] *n* résidence *f*; **~ permit** (BRIT) *n* permis *m* de séjour

resident [ˈrɛzɪdənt] *n* résident(e) ♦ *adj* résidant(e); **~ial** [rɛzɪˈdɛnʃəl] *adj* résidentiel(le); (*course*) avec hébergement sur place; **~ial school** *n* internat *m*

residue [ˈrɛzɪdjuː] *n* reste *m*; (CHEM, PHYSICS) résidu *m*

resign [rɪˈzaɪn] *vt* (*one's post*) démissionner de ♦ *vi* démissionner; **to ~ o.s. to** se résigner à; **~ation** [rɛzɪgˈneɪʃən] *n* (*of post*) démission *f*; (*state of mind*) résignation *f*; **~ed** *adj* résigné(e)

resilient [rɪˈzɪlɪənt] *adj* (*material*) élastique; (*person*) qui réagit, qui a du ressort

resist [rɪˈzɪst] *vt* résister à; **~ance** *n* résistance *f*

resit [riːˈsɪt] *vt* (*exam*) repasser ♦ *n* deuxième session *f* (*d'un examen*)

resolution [rɛzəˈluːʃən] *n* résolution *f*

resolve [rɪˈzɔlv] *n* résolution *f* ♦ *vt* (*problem*) résoudre ♦ *vi*: **to ~ to do** résoudre *or* décider de faire

resort [rɪˈzɔːt] *n* (*seaside town*) station *f* balnéaire; (*ski ~*) station de ski; (*recourse*) recours *m* ♦ *vi*: **to ~ to** avoir recours à; **in the last ~** en dernier ressort

resounding [rɪˈzaundɪŋ] *adj* retentissant(e)

resource [rɪ'sɔːs] *n* ressource *f*; **~s** *npl* (*supplies, wealth etc*) ressources; **~ful** *adj* ingénieux(-euse), débrouillard(e)

respect [rɪs'pekt] *n* respect *m* ♦ *vt* respecter; **~s** *npl* (*compliments*) respects, hommages *mpl*; **with ~ to** en ce qui concerne; **in this ~** à cet égard; **~able** *adj* respectable; **~ful** *adj* respectueux(-euse); **~ively** *adv* respectivement

respite ['respaɪt] *n* répit *m*

respond [rɪs'pɔnd] *vi* répondre; (*react*) réagir; **response** *n* réponse *f*; réaction *f*

responsibility [rɪspɔnsɪ'bɪlɪtɪ] *n* responsabilité *f*

responsible [rɪs'pɔnsɪbl] *adj* (*liable*): **~ (for)** responsable (de); (*person*) digne de confiance; (*job*) qui comporte des responsabilités

responsive [rɪs'pɔnsɪv] *adj* qui réagit; (*person*) qui n'est pas réservé(e) *or* indifférent(e)

rest [rest] *n* repos *m*; (*stop*) arrêt *m*, pause *f*; (*MUS*) silence *m*; (*support*) support *m*, appui *m*; (*remainder*) reste *m*, restant *m* ♦ *vi* se reposer; (*be supported*): **to ~ on** appuyer *or* reposer sur; (*remain*) rester ♦ *vt* (*lean*): **to ~ sth on/against** appuyer qch sur/contre; **the ~ of them** les autres; **it ~s with him to ...** c'est à lui de ...

restaurant ['restərɔŋ] *n* restaurant *m*; **~ car** (*BRIT*) *n* wagon-restaurant *m*

restful ['restful] *adj* reposant(e)

restive ['restɪv] *adj* agité(e), impatient(e); (*horse*) rétif(-ive)

restless ['restlɪs] *adj* agité(e)

restoration [restə'reɪʃən] *n* restauration *f*; restitution *f*; rétablissement *m*

restore [rɪ'stɔː] *vt* (*building*) restaurer; (*sth stolen*) restituer; (*peace, health*) rétablir; **to ~ to** (*former state*) ramener à

restrain [rɪs'treɪn] *vt* contenir; (*person*): **to ~ (from doing)** retenir (de faire); **~ed** *adj* (*style*) sobre; (*manner*) mesuré(e); **~t** *n* (*restriction*) contrainte *f*; (*moderation*) retenue *f*

restrict [rɪs'trɪkt] *vt* restreindre, limiter;

~ion *n* restriction *f*, limitation *f*

rest room (*US*) *n* toilettes *fpl*

result [rɪ'zʌlt] *n* résultat *m* ♦ *vi*: **to ~ in** aboutir à, se terminer par; **as a ~ of** à la suite de

resume [rɪ'zjuːm] *vt, vi* (*work, journey*) reprendre

résumé ['reɪzjuːmeɪ] *n* résumé *m*; (*US*) curriculum vitae *m*

resumption [rɪ'zʌmpʃən] *n* reprise *f*

resurgence [rɪ'səːdʒəns] *n* (*of energy, activity*) regain *m*

resurrection [rezə'rekʃən] *n* résurrection *f*

resuscitate [rɪ'sʌsɪteɪt] *vt* (*MED*) réanimer

retail ['riːteɪl] *adj* de *or* au détail ♦ *adv* au détail; **~er** *n* détaillant(e); **~ price** *n* prix *m* de détail

retain [rɪ'teɪn] *vt* (*keep*) garder, conserver; **~er** *n* (*fee*) acompte *m*, provision *f*

retaliate [rɪ'tælɪeɪt] *vi*: **to ~ (against)** se venger (de); **retaliation** [rɪtælɪ'eɪʃən] *n* représailles *fpl*, vengeance *f*

retarded [rɪ'tɑːdɪd] *adj* retardé(e)

retch [retʃ] *vi* avoir des haut-le-cœur

retentive [rɪ'tentɪv] *adj*: **~ memory** excellente mémoire

retina ['retɪnə] *n* rétine *f*

retire [rɪ'taɪə] *vi* (*give up work*) prendre sa retraite; (*withdraw*) se retirer, partir; (*go to bed*) (aller) se coucher; **~d** *adj* (*person*) retraité(e); **~ment** *n* retraite *f*; **retiring** *adj* (*shy*) réservé(e); (*leaving*) sortant(e)

retort [rɪ'tɔːt] *vi* riposter

retrace [riː'treɪs] *vt*: **to ~ one's steps** revenir sur ses pas

retract [rɪ'trækt] *vt* (*statement, claws*) rétracter; (*undercarriage, aerial*) rentrer, escamoter

retrain [riː'treɪn] *vt* (*worker*) recycler

retread ['riːtred] *n* (*tyre*) pneu rechapé

retreat [rɪ'triːt] *n* retraite *f* ♦ *vi* battre en retraite

retribution [retrɪ'bjuːʃən] *n* châtiment *m*

retrieval [rɪ'triːvəl] *n* (*see vb*) récupération *f*; réparation *f*

retrieve [rɪ'triːv] *vt* (*sth lost*) récupérer; (*situation, honour*) sauver; (*error, loss*) réparer; **~r** n chien m d'arrêt

retrospect ['retrəspekt] n: **in ~** rétrospectivement, après coup; **~ive** [retrə'spektɪv] adj rétrospectif(-ive); (law) rétroactif(-ive)

return [rɪ'tə:n] n (going or coming back) retour m; (of sth stolen etc) restitution f; (FINANCE: from land, shares) rendement m, rapport m ♦ cpd (journey) de retour; (BRIT: ticket) aller et retour; (match) retour ♦ vi (come back) revenir; (go back) retourner ♦ vt rendre; (bring back) rapporter; (send back; also: ball) renvoyer; (put back) remettre; (POL: candidate) élire; **~s** npl (COMM) recettes fpl; (FINANCE) bénéfices mpl; **in ~ (for)** en échange (de); **by ~ (of post)** par retour (du courrier); **many happy ~s (of the day)!** bon anniversaire!

reunion [ri:'ju:nɪən] n réunion f

reunite [ri:ju:'naɪt] vt réunir

reuse [ri:'ju:z] vt réutiliser

rev [rev] n abbr (AUT: = revolution) tour m ♦ vt (also: **rev up**) emballer

revamp [ri:'væmp] vt (firm, system etc) réorganiser

reveal [rɪ'vi:l] vt (make known) révéler; (display) laisser voir; **~ing** adj révélateur(-trice); (dress) au décolleté généreux or suggestif

revel ['revl] vi: **to ~ in sth/in doing** se délecter de qch/à faire

revenge [rɪ'vendʒ] n vengeance f; **to take ~ on** (enemy) se venger sur

revenue ['revənju:] n revenu m

reverberate [rɪ'və:bəreɪt] vi (sound) retentir, se répercuter; (fig: shock etc) se propager

reverence ['revərəns] n vénération f, révérence f

Reverend ['revərənd] adj (in titles): **the ~ John Smith** (Anglican) le révérend John Smith; (Catholic) l'abbé (John) Smith; (Protestant) le pasteur (John) Smith

reversal [rɪ'və:sl] n (of opinion) revirement m; (of order) renversement m; (of direction) changement m

reverse [rɪ'və:s] n contraire m, opposé m; (back) dos m, envers m; (of paper) verso m; (of coin; also: setback) revers m; (AUT: also: ~ **gear**) marche f arrière ♦ adj (order, direction) opposé(e), inverse ♦ vt (order, position) changer, inverser; (direction, policy) changer complètement de; (decision) annuler; (roles) renverser; (car) faire marche arrière avec ♦ vi (BRIT: AUT) faire marche arrière; **he ~d (the car) into a wall** il a embouti un mur en marche arrière; **~d charge call** (BRIT) n (TEL) communication f en PCV; **reversing lights** (BRIT) npl (AUT) feux mpl de marche arrière or de recul

revert [rɪ'və:t] vi: **to ~ to** revenir à, retourner à

review [rɪ'vju:] n revue f; (of book, film) critique f, compte rendu; (of situation, policy) examen m, bilan m ♦ vt passer en revue; faire la critique de; examiner; **~er** n critique m

revise [rɪ'vaɪz] vt réviser, modifier; (manuscript) revoir, corriger ♦ vi (study) réviser; **revision** [rɪ'vɪʒən] n révision f

revival [rɪ'vaɪvəl] n reprise f; (recovery) rétablissement m; (of faith) renouveau m

revive [rɪ'vaɪv] vt (person) ranimer; (custom) rétablir; (economy) relancer; (hope, courage) raviver, faire renaître; (play) reprendre ♦ vi (person) reprendre connaissance; (: from ill health) se rétablir; (hope etc) renaître; (activity) reprendre

revoke [rɪ'vəuk] vt révoquer; (law) abroger

revolt [rɪ'vəult] n révolte f ♦ vi se révolter, se rebeller ♦ vt révolter, dégoûter; **~ing** adj dégoûtant(e)

revolution [revə'lu:ʃən] n révolution f; (of wheel etc) tour m, révolution; **~ary** adj révolutionnaire ♦ n révolutionnaire m/f

revolve [rɪ'vɔlv] vi tourner

revolver [rɪ'vɔlvə*] n revolver m

revolving [rɪ'vɔlvɪŋ] adj tournant(e); (chair) pivotant(e); **~ door** n (porte f à) tambour m

revulsion [rɪ'vʌlʃən] n dégoût m, répugnance f

reward [rɪ'wɔ:d] n récompense f ♦ vt: **to ~ (for)** récompenser (de); **~ing** adj (fig) qui (en) vaut la peine, gratifiant(e)

rewind [ri:'waɪnd] *(irreg)* vt *(tape)* rembobiner

rewire [ri:'waɪəʳ] vt *(house)* refaire l'installation électrique de

rheumatism ['ru:mətɪzəm] *n* rhumatisme *m*

Rhine [raɪn] *n* Rhin *m*

rhinoceros [raɪ'nɔsərəs] *n* rhinocéros *m*

Rhone [rəun] *n* Rhône *m*

rhubarb ['ru:bɑ:b] *n* rhubarbe *f*

rhyme [raɪm] *n* rime *f*; *(verse)* vers *mpl*

rhythm ['rɪðm] *n* rythme *m*

rib [rɪb] *n (ANAT)* côte *f*

ribbon ['rɪbən] *n* ruban *m*; **in ~s** *(torn)* en lambeaux

rice [raɪs] *n* riz *m*; **~ pudding** *n* riz au lait

rich [rɪtʃ] *adj* riche; *(gift, clothes)* somptueux(-euse) ♦ *npl*: **the ~** les riches *mpl*; **~es** *npl* richesses *fpl*; **~ly** *adv* richement; *(deserved, earned)* largement

rickets ['rɪkɪts] *n* rachitisme *m*

rid [rɪd] *(pt, pp* rid*)* vt: **to ~ sb of** débarrasser qn de; **to get ~ of** se débarrasser de

riddle ['rɪdl] *n (puzzle)* énigme *f* ♦ vt: **to be ~d with** être criblé(e) de; *(fig: guilt, corruption, doubts)* être en proie à

ride [raɪd] *(pt* rode, *pp* ridden*)* n promenade *f*, tour *m*; *(distance covered)* trajet *m* ♦ *vi (as sport)* monter (à cheval), faire du cheval; *(go somewhere: on horse, bicycle)* aller (à cheval or bicyclette *etc*); *(journey: on bicycle, motorcycle, bus)* rouler ♦ vt *(a certain horse)* monter; *(distance)* parcourir, faire; **to take sb for a ~** *(fig)* faire marcher qn; **to ~ a horse/bicycle** monter à cheval/à bicyclette; **~r** *n* cavalier(-ère); *(in race)* jockey *m*; *(on bicycle)* cycliste *m/f*; *(on motorcycle)* motocycliste *m/f*

ridge [rɪdʒ] *n (of roof, mountain)* arête *f*; *(of hill)* faîte *m*; *(on object)* strie *f*

ridicule ['rɪdɪkju:l] *n* ridicule *m*; dérision *f*

ridiculous [rɪ'dɪkjuləs] *adj* ridicule

riding ['raɪdɪŋ] *n* équitation *f*; **~ school** *n* manège *m*, école *f* d'équitation

rife [raɪf] *adj* répandu(e); **~ with** abondant(e) en, plein(e) de

riffraff ['rɪfræf] *n* racaille *f*

rifle ['raɪfl] *n* fusil *m* (à canon rayé) ♦ vt vider, dévaliser; **~ through** vt *(belongings)* fouiller; *(papers)* feuilleter; **~ range** *n* champ *m* de tir; *(at fair)* stand *m* de tir

rift [rɪft] *n* fente *f*, fissure *f*; *(fig: disagreement)* désaccord *m*

rig [rɪg] *n (also:* oil ~: *at sea)* plate-forme pétrolière ♦ vt *(election etc)* truquer; **~ out** *(BRIT)* vt: **to ~ out as/in** habiller en/de; **~ up** vt arranger, faire avec des moyens de fortune; **~ging** *n (NAUT)* gréement *m*

right [raɪt] *adj (correctly chosen: answer, road etc)* bon (bonne); *(true)* juste, exact(e); *(suitable)* approprié(e), convenable; *(just)* juste, équitable; *(morally good)* bien *inv*; *(not left)* droit(e) ♦ *n (what is morally ~)* bien *m*; *(title, claim)* droit *m*; *(not left)* droite *f* ♦ *adv (answer)* correctement, juste; *(treat)* bien, comme il faut; *(not on the left)* à droite ♦ vt redresser ♦ *excl* bon!; **to be ~** *(person)* avoir raison; *(answer)* être juste or correct(e); *(clock)* à l'heure (juste); **by ~s** toute justice; **on the ~** à droite; **to be in the ~** avoir raison; **~ now** en ce moment même; tout de suite; **~ in the middle** en plein milieu; **~ away** immédiatement; **~ angle** *n (MATH)* angle droit; **~eous** ['raɪtʃəs] *adj* droit(e), vertueux(-euse); *(anger)* justifié(e); **~ful** *adj* légitime; **~-handed** *adj (person)* droitier(-ère); **~-hand man** *n* bras droit *m (fig)*; **~-hand side** *n* la droite; **~ly** *adv (with reason)* à juste titre; **~ of way** *n* droit *m* de passage; *(AUT)* priorité *f*; **~-wing** *adj (POL)* de droite

rigid ['rɪdʒɪd] *adj* rigide; *(principle, control)* strict(e)

rigmarole ['rɪgmərəul] *n* comédie *f*

rigorous ['rɪgərəs] *adj* rigoureux(-euse)

rile [raɪl] *vt* agacer

rim [rɪm] *n* bord *m*; *(of spectacles)* monture *f*; *(of wheel)* jante *f*

rind [raɪnd] *n (of bacon)* couenne *f*; *(of lemon etc)* écorce *f*, zeste *m*; *(of cheese)* croûte *f*

ring [rɪŋ] *(pt* rang, *pp* rung*)* n anneau *m*;

(*on finger*) bague *f*; (*also:* **wedding ~**) alliance *f*; (*of people, objects*) cercle *m*; (*of spies*) réseau *m*; (*of smoke etc*) rond *m*; (*arena*) piste *f*, arène *f*; (*for boxing*) ring *m*; (*sound of bell*) sonnerie *f* ♦ *vi* (*telephone, bell*) sonner; (*person: by telephone*) téléphoner; (*also:* **~ out**: *voice, words*) retentir; (*ears*) bourdonner ♦ *vt* (*BRIT: TEL: also:* **~ up**) téléphoner à, appeler; (*bell*) faire sonner; **to ~ the bell** sonner; **to give sb a ~** (*BRIT: TEL*) appeler qn; **~ back** (*BRIT*) *vt, vi* (*TEL*) rappeler; **~ off** (*BRIT*) *vi* (*TEL*) raccrocher; **~ up** (*BRIT*) *vt* (*TEL*) appeler; **~binder** *n* classeur *m* à anneaux; **~ing** ['rɪŋɪŋ] *n* (*of telephone*) sonnerie *f*; (*of bell*) tintement *m*; (*in ears*) bourdonnement *m*; **~ing tone** (*BRIT*) *n* (*TEL*) sonnerie *f*; **~leader** *n* (*of gang*) chef *m*, meneur *m*; **~lets** *npl* anglaises *fpl*; **~ road** (*BRIT*) *n* route *f* de ceinture; (*motorway*) périphérique *m*; **~tone** *n* sonnerie *f* (*de téléphone portable*)

rink [rɪŋk] *n* (*also:* **ice ~**) patinoire *f*

rinse [rɪns] *vt* rincer

riot ['raɪət] *n* émeute *f*; (*of flowers, colour*) profusion *f* ♦ *vi* faire une émeute, manifester avec violence; **to run ~** se déchaîner; **~ous** *adj* (*mob, assembly*) séditieux(-euse), déchaîné(e); (*living, behaviour*) débauché(e); (*party*) très animé(e); (*welcome*) délirant(e)

rip [rɪp] *n* déchirure *f* ♦ *vt* déchirer ♦ *vi* se déchirer; **~cord** *n* poignée *f* d'ouverture

ripe [raɪp] *adj* (*fruit*) mûr(e); (*cheese*) fait(e); **~n** *vt* mûrir ♦ *vi* mûrir

rip-off (*inf*) *n*: **it's a ~-~!** c'est de l'arnaque!

ripple ['rɪpl] *n* ondulation *f*; (*of applause, laughter*) cascade *f* ♦ *vi* onduler

rise [raɪz] (*pt* **rose**, *pp* **risen**) *n* (*slope*) côte *f*, pente *f*; (*hill*) hauteur *f*; (*increase: in wages: BRIT*) augmentation *f*; (*: in prices, temperature*) hausse *f*, augmentation; (*fig: to power etc*) ascension *f* ♦ *vi* s'élever, monter; (*prices, numbers*) augmenter; (*waters*) monter; (*sun; person: from chair, bed*) se lever; (*also:* **~ up**: *tower, building*) s'élever;

(*: rebel*) se révolter; se rebeller; (*in rank*) s'élever; **to give ~ to** donner lieu à; **to ~ to the occasion** se montrer à la hauteur; **~r** *n*: **to be an early ~r** être matinal(e); **rising** *adj* (*number, prices*) en hausse; (*tide*) montant(e); (*sun, moon*) levant(e)

risk [rɪsk] *n* risque *m* ♦ *vt* risquer; **at ~** en danger; **at one's own ~** à ses risques et périls; **~y** *adj* risqué(e)

rite [raɪt] *n* rite *m*; **last ~s** derniers sacrements

ritual ['rɪtjuəl] *adj* rituel(le) ♦ *n* rituel *m*

rival ['raɪvl] *adj, n* rival(e); (*in business*) concurrent(e) ♦ *vt* (*match*) égaler; **~ry** ['raɪvlrɪ] *n* rivalité *f*, concurrence *f*

river ['rɪvəʳ] *n* rivière *f*; (*major, also fig*) fleuve *m* ♦ *cpd* (*port, traffic*) fluvial(e); **up/down ~** en amont/aval; **~bank** *n* rive *f*, berge *f*; **~bed** *n* lit *m* (*de rivière/fleuve*)

rivet ['rɪvɪt] *n* rivet *m* ♦ *vt* (*fig*) river, fixer

Riviera [rɪvɪ'eərə] *n*: **the (French) ~** la Côte d'Azur; **the Italian ~** la Riviera (italienne)

road [rəud] *n* route *f*; (*in town*) rue *f*; (*fig*) chemin, voie *f*; **major/minor ~** route principale *or* à priorité/voie secondaire; **~ accident** *n* accident *m* de la circulation; **~block** *n* barrage routier; **~hog** *n* chauffard *m*; **~ map** *n* carte routière; **~ rage** *n* comportement très agressif de certains usagers de la route; **~ safety** *n* sécurité routière; **~side** *n* bord *m* de la route, bas-côté *m*; **~ sign** *n* panneau *m* de signalisation; **~way** *n* chaussée *f*; **~ works** *npl* travaux *mpl* (*de réfection des routes*); **~worthy** *adj* en bon état de marche

roam [rəum] *vi* errer, vagabonder

roar [rɔːʳ] *n* rugissement *m*; (*of crowd*) hurlements *mpl*; (*of vehicle, thunder, storm*) grondement *m* ♦ *vi* rugir; hurler; gronder; **to ~ with laughter** éclater de rire; **to do a ~ing trade** faire des affaires d'or

roast [rəust] *n* rôti *m* ♦ *vt* (*faire*) rôtir; (*coffee*) griller, torréfier; **~ beef** *n* rôti *m* de bœuf, rosbif *m*

rob [rɔb] *vt* (*person*) voler; (*bank*) dévaliser; **to ~ sb of sth** voler *or* dérober qch à qn;

(fig: deprive) priver qn de qch; **~ber** *n* bandit *m*, voleur *m*; **~bery** *n* vol *m*

robe [rəʊb] *n* *(for ceremony etc)* robe *f*; *(also:* **bathrobe***)* peignoir *m*; *(US)* couverture *f*

robin ['rɒbɪn] *n* rouge-gorge *m*

robot ['rəʊbɒt] *n* robot *m*

robust [rəʊ'bʌst] *adj* robuste; *(material, appetite)* solide

rock [rɒk] *n* *(substance)* roche *f*, roc *m*; *(boulder)* rocher *m*; *(US: small stone)* caillou *m*; *(BRIT: sweet)* ≃ sucre *m* d'orge ♦ *vt* *(swing gently: cradle)* balancer; *(: child)* bercer; *(shake)* ébranler, secouer ♦ *vi* (se) balancer; être ébranlé(e) *or* secoué(e); **on the ~s** *(drink)* avec des glaçons; *(marriage etc)* en train de craquer; **~ and roll** *n* rock *(and roll)* *m*, rock'n'roll *m*; **~-bottom** *adj* *(fig: prices)* sacrifié(e); **~ery** *n* *(jardin m de)* rocaille *f*

rocket ['rɒkɪt] *n* fusée *f*; *(MIL)* fusée, roquette *f*

rocking chair *n* fauteuil *m* à bascule

rocking horse *n* cheval *m* à bascule

rocky ['rɒkɪ] *adj* *(hill)* rocheux(-euse); *(path)* rocailleux(-euse)

rod [rɒd] *n* *(wooden)* baguette *f*; *(metallic)* tringle *f*; *(TECH)* tige *f*; *(also:* **fishing ~***)* canne *f* à pêche

rode [rəʊd] *pt of* **ride**

rodent ['rəʊdnt] *n* rongeur *m*

rodeo ['rəʊdɪəʊ] *(US)* *n* rodéo *m*

roe [rəʊ] *n* *(species: also:* **~ deer***)* chevreuil *m*; *(of fish: also:* **hard ~***)* œufs *mpl* de poisson; **soft ~** laitance *f*

rogue [rəʊg] *n* coquin(e)

role [rəʊl] *n* rôle *m*; **~ play** *n* jeu *m* de rôle

roll [rəʊl] *n* rouleau *m*; *(of banknotes)* liasse *f*; *(also:* **bread ~***)* petit pain; *(register)* liste *f*; *(sound: of drums etc)* roulement *m* ♦ *vt* rouler; *(also:* **~ up***: string)* enrouler; *(: sleeves)* retrousser; *(also:* **~ out***: pastry)* étendre au rouleau, abaisser ♦ *vi* rouler; **~ about** *vi* rouler ça et là; *(person)* se rouler par terre; **~ around** *vi* = **roll about**; **~ by** *vi* *(time)* s'écouler, passer; **~ over** *vi* se

retourner; **~ up** *vi* *(inf: arrive)* arriver, s'amener ♦ *vt* rouler; **~ call** *n* appel *m*; **~er** *n* rouleau *m*; *(wheel)* roulette *f*; *(for road)* rouleau compresseur; **~er blade** *n* patin *m* en ligne; **~er coaster** *n* montagnes *fpl* russes; **~er skates** *npl* patins *mpl* à roulettes; **~er skating** *n* patin *m* à roulettes; **~ing** *adj* *(landscape)* onduleux(-euse); **~ing pin** *n* rouleau *m* à pâtisserie; **~ing stock** *n* *(RAIL)* matériel roulant

ROM [rɒm] *n abbr* *(= read only memory)* mémoire morte

Roman ['rəʊmən] *adj* romain(e); **~ Catholic** *adj, n* catholique *m/f*

romance [rə'mæns] *n* *(love affair)* idylle *f*; *(charm)* poésie *f*; *(novel)* roman *m* à l'eau de rose

Romania [rəʊ'meɪnɪə] *n* Roumanie *f*; **~n** *adj* roumain(e) ♦ *n* Roumain(e); *(LING)* roumain *m*

Roman numeral *n* chiffre romain

romantic [rə'mæntɪk] *adj* romantique; sentimental(e)

Rome [rəʊm] *n* Rome

romp [rɒmp] *n* jeux bruyants ♦ *vi* *(also:* **~ about***)* s'ébattre, jouer bruyamment; **~ers** *npl* barboteuse *f*

roof [ruːf] *(pl* **~s***)* *n* toit *m* ♦ *vt* couvrir *(d'un toit)*; **the ~ of the mouth** la voûte du palais; **~ing** *n* toiture *f*; **~ rack** *n* *(AUT)* galerie *f*

rook [rʊk] *n* *(bird)* freux *m*; *(CHESS)* tour *f*

room [ruːm] *n* *(in house)* pièce *f*; *(also:* **bedroom***)* chambre *f* *(à coucher)*; *(in school etc)* salle *f*; *(space)* place *f*; **~s** *npl* *(lodging)* meublé *m*; **"~s to let"** *(BRIT)* *or* **"~s for rent"** *(US)* "chambres à louer"; **single/double ~** chambre pour une personne/deux personnes; **there is ~ for improvement** cela laisse à désirer; **~ing house** *(US)* *n* maison *f* *or* immeuble *m* de rapport; **~mate** *n* camarade *m/f* de chambre; **~ service** *n* service *m* des chambres *(dans un hôtel)*; **~y** *adj* spacieux(-euse); *(garment)* ample

roost [ruːst] *vi* se jucher

rooster ['ruːstər] *n* *(esp US)* coq *m*

root [ruːt] *n* (BOT, MATH) racine *f*; (fig: of problem) origine *f*, fond *m* ♦ *vi* (plant) s'enraciner; ~ **about** *vi* (fig) fouiller; ~ **for** *vt fus* encourager, applaudir; ~ **out** *vt* (find) dénicher

rope [rəup] *n* corde *f*; (NAUT) cordage *m* ♦ *vt* (tie up or together) attacher; (climbers: also: ~ **together**) encorder; (area: ~ off) interdire l'accès de; (: divide off) séparer; **to know the ~s** (fig) être au courant, connaître les ficelles; ~ **in** *vt* (fig: person) embringuer

rosary ['rəuzəri] *n* chapelet *m*

rose [rəuz] *pt of* **rise** ♦ *n* rose *f*; (also: ~**bush**) rosier *m*; (on watering can) pomme *f*

rosé ['rəuzeɪ] *n* rosé *m*

rosebud ['rəuzbʌd] *n* bouton *m* de rose

rosemary ['rəuzməri] *n* romarin *m*

roster ['rɔstə*] *n*: **duty ~** tableau *m* de service

rostrum ['rɔstrəm] *n* tribune *f* (pour un orateur etc)

rosy ['rəuzi] *adj* rose; **a ~ future** un bel avenir

rot [rɔt] *n* (decay) pourriture *f*; (fig: pej) idioties *fpl* ♦ *vt, vi* pourrir

rota ['rəutə] *n* liste *f*, tableau *m* de service; **on a ~ basis** par roulement

rotary ['rəutəri] *adj* rotatif(-ive)

rotate [rəu'teɪt] *vt* (revolve) faire tourner; (change round: jobs) faire à tour de rôle ♦ *vi* (revolve) tourner; **rotating** *adj* (movement) tournant(e)

rotten ['rɔtn] *adj* (decayed) pourri(e); (dishonest) corrompu(e); (inf: bad) mauvais(e), moche; **to feel ~** (ill) être mal fichu(e)

rotund [rəu'tʌnd] *adj* (person) rondelet(te)

rough [rʌf] *adj* (cloth, skin) rêche, rugueux(-euse); (terrain) accidenté(e); (path) rocailleux(-euse); (voice) rauque, rude; (person, manner: coarse) rude, fruste; (: violent) brutal(e); (district, weather) mauvais(e); (sea) houleux(-euse); (plan etc) ébauché(e); (guess) approximatif(-ive) ♦ *n* (GOLF) rough *m* ♦ *vt*: **to ~ it** vivre à la dure; **to sleep ~** (BRIT) coucher à la dure;

~**age** *n* fibres *fpl* alimentaires; ~**-and-ready** *adj* rudimentaire; ~ **copy** ~ **draft** *n* brouillon *m*; ~**ly** *adv* (handle) rudement, brutalement; (speak) avec brusquerie; (make) grossièrement; (approximately) à peu près, en gros

roulette [ruː'let] *n* roulette *f*

Roumania [ruː'meɪnɪə] *n* = **Romania**

round [raund] *adj* rond(e) ♦ *n* (BRIT: of toast) tranche *f*; (duty: of policeman, milkman etc) tournée *f*; (: of doctor) visites *fpl*; (game: of cards, in competition) partie *f*; (BOXING) round *m*; (of talks) série *f* ♦ *vt* (corner) tourner ♦ *prep* autour de ♦ *adv*: **all ~** tout autour; **the long way ~** (par) le chemin le plus long; **all the year ~** toute l'année; **it's just ~ the corner** (fig) c'est tout près; **the clock** 24 heures sur 24; **to go ~ to sb's (house)** aller chez qn; **go ~ the back** passez par derrière; **enough to go ~** assez pour tout le monde; ~ **of ammunition** cartouche *f*; ~ **of applause** ban *m*, applaudissements *mpl*; ~ **of drinks** tournée *f*; ~ **of sandwiches** sandwich *m*; ~ **off** *vt* (speech etc) terminer; ~ **up** *vt* rassembler; (criminals) effectuer une rafle de; (price, figure) arrondir (au chiffre supérieur); ~**about** *n* (BRIT: AUT) rond-point *m* (à sens giratoire); (: at fair) manège *m* (de chevaux de bois) ♦ *adj* (route, means) détourné(e); ~**ers** *n* (game) sorte de baseball; ~**ly** *adv* (fig) tout net, carrément; ~ **trip** *n* (voyage *m*) aller et retour *m*; ~**up** *n* rassemblement *m*; (of criminals) rafle *f*

rouse [rauz] *vt* (wake up) réveiller; (stir up) susciter; provoquer; éveiller; **rousing** *adj* (welcome) enthousiaste

route [ruːt] *n* itinéraire *m*; (of bus) parcours *m*; (of trade, shipping) route *f*

routine [ruː'tiːn] *adj* (work) ordinaire, courant(e); (procedure) d'usage ♦ *n* (habits) habitudes *fpl*; (pej) train-train *m*; (THEATRE) numéro *m*

rove [rəuv] *vt* (area, streets) errer dans

row¹ [rəu] *n* (line) rangée *f*; (of people, seats, KNITTING) rang *m*; (behind one another: of cars, people) file f ♦ vi (in boat) ramer; (as sport) faire de l'aviron ♦ vt (boat) faire aller à la rame or à l'aviron; **in a ~** (fig) d'affilée

row² [rau] n (noise) vacarme m; (dispute) dispute f, querelle f; (scolding) réprimande f, savon m ♦ vi se disputer, se quereller

rowboat ['rəubəut] (US) n canot m (à rames)

rowdy ['raudɪ] adj chahuteur(-euse); (occasion) tapageur(-euse)

rowing ['rəuɪŋ] n canotage m; (as sport) aviron m; ~ **boat** (BRIT) n canot m (à rames)

royal ['rɔɪəl] adj royal(e); R~ **Air Force** (BRIT) n armée de l'air britannique; ~**ty** n (royal persons) (membres mpl de la) famille royale; (payment: to author) droits mpl d'auteur; (: to inventor) royalties fpl

rpm abbr (AUT) (= revolutions per minute) tr/mn

RSVP abbr (= répondez s'il vous plaît) R.S.V.P.

Rt Hon. abbr (BRIT: Right Honourable) titre donné aux députés de la Chambre des communes

rub [rʌb] vt frotter; frictionner; (hands) se frotter ♦ n (with cloth) coup m chiffon or de torchon; **to give sth a ~** donner un coup de chiffon or de torchon à; **to ~ sb up** (BRIT) or **to ~ sb** (US) **the wrong way** prendre qn à rebrousse-poil; ~ **off** vi partir; ~ **off on** vt fus déteindre sur; ~ **out** vt effacer

rubber ['rʌbər] n caoutchouc m; (BRIT: eraser) gomme f (à effacer); ~ **band** n élastique m; ~ **plant** n caoutchouc m (plante verte)

rubbish ['rʌbɪʃ] n (from household) ordures fpl; (fig: pej) camelote f; (: nonsense) bêtises fpl, idioties fpl; ~ **bin** (BRIT) n poubelle f; ~ **dump** n décharge publique, dépotoir m

rubble ['rʌbl] n décombres mpl; (smaller) gravats mpl; (CONSTR) blocage m

ruby ['ru:bɪ] n rubis m

rucksack ['rʌksæk] n sac m à dos

rudder ['rʌdər] n gouvernail m

ruddy ['rʌdɪ] adj (face) coloré(e); (inf: damned) sacré(e), fichu(e)

rude [ru:d] adj (impolite) impoli(e); (coarse) grossier(-ère); (shocking) indécent(e), inconvenant(e)

ruffle ['rʌfl] vt (hair) ébouriffer; (clothes) chiffonner; (fig: person): **to get ~d** s'énerver

rug [rʌg] n petit tapis; (BRIT: blanket) couverture f

rugby ['rʌgbɪ] n (also: ~ **football**) rugby m

rugged ['rʌgɪd] adj (landscape) accidenté(e); (features, character) rude

ruin ['ru:ɪn] n ruine f ♦ vt ruiner; (spoil, clothes) abîmer; (event) gâcher; ~**s** npl (of building) ruine(s)

rule [ru:l] n règle f; (regulation) règlement m; (government) autorité f, gouvernement m ♦ vt (country) gouverner; (person) dominer ♦ vi commander; (LAW) statuer; **as a ~** normalement, en règle générale; ~ **out** vt exclure; ~**d** adj (paper) réglé(e); ~**r** n (sovereign) souverain(e); (for measuring) règle f; **ruling** adj (party) au pouvoir; (class) dirigeant(e) ♦ n (LAW) décision f

rum [rʌm] n rhum m

Rumania [ru:ˈmeɪnɪə] n = **Romania**

rumble ['rʌmbl] vi gronder; (stomach, pipe) gargouiller

rummage ['rʌmɪdʒ] vi fouiller

rumour ['ru:mər] (US **rumor**) n rumeur f, bruit m (qui court) ♦ vt: **it is ~ed that** le bruit court que

rump [rʌmp] n (of animal) croupe f; (inf: of person) postérieur m; ~ **steak** n rumsteck m

rumpus ['rʌmpəs] (inf) n tapage m, chahut m

run [rʌn] (pt **ran**, pp **run**) n (fast pace) (pas m de) course f; (outing) tour m or promenade f (en voiture); (distance travelled) parcours m, trajet m; (series) suite f, série f; (THEATRE) série de représentations; (SKI) piste f; (CRICKET, BASEBALL) point m; (in tights, stockings) maille filée, échelle f ♦ vt (operate: business) diriger; (: competition, *course)* organiser; (: *hotel, house)* tenir; *(race)* participer à; *(COMPUT)* exécuter; *(to pass: hand, finger)* passer; *(water, bath)* faire couler; *(PRESS: feature)* publier ♦ *vi* courir; *(flee)* s'enfuir; *(work: machine, factory)* marcher; *(bus, train)* circuler; *(continue: play)* se jouer; (: *contract)* être valide; *(flow: river, bath; nose)* couler; *(colours, washing)* déteindre; *(in election)* être candidat, se présenter; **to go for a ~** faire un peu de course à pied; **there was a ~ on ...** *(meat, tickets)* les gens se sont rués sur ...; **in the long ~** à longue échéance; **in the long**, en fin de compte; **on the ~** en fuite; **I'll ~ you to the station** je vais vous emmener *or* conduire à la gare; **to ~ a risk** courir un risque; **~ about** *vi (children)* courir çà et là; **~ across** *vt fus (find)* trouver par hasard; **~ around** *vi* = **run about**; **~ away** *vi* s'enfuir; **~ down** *vt (production)* réduire progressivement; *(factory)* réduire progressivement la production de; *(AUT)* renverser; *(criticize)* critiquer, dénigrer; **to be ~ down** *(person: tired)* être fatigué(e) *or* à plat; **~ in** *(BRIT)* *vt (car)* roder; **~ into** *vt fus (meet: person)* rencontrer par hasard; *(trouble)* se heurter à; *(collide with)* heurter; **~ off** *vi* s'enfuir ♦ *vt (water)* laisser s'écouler; *(copies)* tirer; **~ out** *vi (person)* sortir en courant; *(liquid)* couler; *(lease)* expirer; *(money)* être épuisé(e); **~ out of** *vt fus* se trouver à court de; **~ over** *vt (AUT)* écraser ♦ *vt fus (revise)* revoir, reprendre; **~ through** *vt fus (recapitulate)* reprendre; *(play)* répéter; **~ up** *vt*: **to ~ up against** *(difficulties)* se heurter à; **to ~ up a debt** s'endetter; **~away** *adj (horse)* emballé(e); *(truck)* fou (folle); *(person)* fugitif(-ive); *(teenager)* fugueur(-euse)

rung [rʌŋ] *pp* of **ring** ♦ *n (of ladder)* barreau *m*

runner ['rʌnəʳ] *n (in race: person)* coureur(-euse); (: *horse)* partant *m*; *(on sledge)* patin *m*; *(for drawer etc)* coulisseau *m*; **~ bean** *(BRIT)* haricot *m* (à rames); **~-up** *n* second(e)

running ['rʌnɪŋ] *n* course *f*; *(of business, organization)* gestion *f*, direction *f* ♦ *adj (water)* courant(e); **to be in/out of the ~ for sth** être/ne pas être sur les rangs pour qch; **6 days ~** 6 jours de suite; **~ commentary** *n* commentaire détaillé; **~ costs** *npl* frais *mpl* d'exploitation

runny ['rʌnɪ] *adj* qui coule

run-of-the-mill ['rʌnəvðə'mɪl] *adj* ordinaire, banal(e)

runt [rʌnt] *n* avorton *m*

run-up ['rʌnʌp] *n*: **~-~ to sth** *(election etc)* période *f* précédant qch

runway ['rʌnweɪ] *n (AVIAT)* piste *f*

rupture ['rʌptʃəʳ] *n (MED)* hernie *f*

rural ['ruərl] *adj* rural(e)

rush [rʌʃ] *n (hurry)* hâte *f*, précipitation *f*; *(of crowd, COMM: sudden demand)* ruée *f*; *(current)* flot *m*; *(of emotion)* vague *f*; *(BOT)* jonc *m* ♦ *vt (hurry)* transporter *or* envoyer d'urgence ♦ *vi* se précipiter; **~ hour** *n* heures *fpl* de pointe

rusk [rʌsk] *n* biscotte *f*

Russia ['rʌʃə] *n* Russie *f*; **~n** *adj* russe ♦ *n* Russe *m/f*; *(LING)* russe *m*

rust [rʌst] *n* rouille *f* ♦ *vi* rouiller

rustic ['rʌstɪk] *adj* rustique

rustle ['rʌsl] *vi* bruire, produire un bruissement ♦ *vt* froisser

rustproof ['rʌstpruːf] *adj* inoxydable

rusty ['rʌstɪ] *adj* rouillé(e)

rut [rʌt] *n* ornière *f*; *(ZOOL)* rut *m*; **to be in a ~** suivre l'ornière, s'encroûter

ruthless ['ruːθlɪs] *adj* sans pitié, impitoyable

rye [raɪ] *n* seigle *m*

S, s

Sabbath ['sæbəθ] *n (Jewish)* sabbat *m*; *(Christian)* dimanche *m*

sabotage ['sæbətɑːʒ] *n* sabotage *m* ♦ *vt* saboter

saccharin(e) ['sækərɪn] *n* saccharine *f*

sachet ['sæʃeɪ] *n* sachet *m*

sack [sæk] *n (bag)* sac *m* ♦ *vt (dismiss)* renvoyer, mettre à la porte; (*plunder*) piller, mettre à sac; **to get the ~** être renvoyé(e), être mis(e) à la porte; **~ing** *n* (*material*) toile *f* à sac; (*dismissal*) renvoi *m*

sacrament ['sækrəmənt] *n* sacrement *m*

sacred ['seɪkrɪd] *adj* sacré(e)

sacrifice ['sækrɪfaɪs] *n* sacrifice *m* ♦ *vt* sacrifier

sad [sæd] *adj* triste; (*deplorable*) triste, fâcheux(-euse)

saddle ['sædl] *n* selle *f* ♦ *vt* (*horse*) seller; **to be ~d with sth** (*inf*) avoir qch sur les bras; **~bag** *n* sacoche *f*

sadistic [sə'dɪstɪk] *adj* sadique

sadly ['sædlɪ] *adv* tristement; (*unfortunately*) malheureusement; (*seriously*) fort

sadness ['sædnɪs] *n* tristesse *f*

s.a.e. *n abbr* = **stamped addressed envelope**

safe [seɪf] *adj* (*out of danger*) hors de danger, en sécurité; (*not dangerous*) sans danger; (*cautious*) prudent(e); (*sure: bet etc*) assuré(e) ♦ *n* coffre-fort *m*; **~ from** à l'abri de; **~ and sound** sain(e) et sauf (sauve); **(just) to be on the ~ side** pour plus de sûreté, par précaution; **~ journey!** bon voyage!; **~-conduct** *n* sauf-conduit *m*; **~-deposit** *n* (*vault*) dépôt *m* de coffres-forts; (*box*) coffre-fort *m*; **~guard** *n* sauvegarde *f*, protection *f* ♦ *vt* sauvegarder, protéger; **~keeping** *n* bonne garde; **~ly** *adv* (*assume, say*) sans risque d'erreur; (*drive, arrive*) sans accident; **~ sex** *n* rapports *mpl* sexuels sans risque

safety ['seɪftɪ] *n* sécurité *f*; **~ belt** *n* ceinture *f* de sécurité; **~ pin** *n* épingle *f* de sûreté *or* de nourrice; **~ valve** *n* soupape *f* de sûreté

sag [sæg] *vi* s'affaisser; (*hem, breasts*) pendre

sage [seɪdʒ] *n* (*herb*) sauge *f*; (*person*) sage *m*

Sagittarius [sædʒɪ'tɛərɪəs] *n* le Sagittaire

Sahara [sə'hɑːrə] *n*: **the ~ (Desert)** le (désert du) Sahara

said [sɛd] *pt, pp of* **say**

sail [seɪl] *n* (*on boat*) voile *f*; (*trip*): **to go**

for a ~ faire un tour en bateau ♦ *vt* (*boat*) manœuvrer, piloter ♦ *vi* (*travel: ship*) avancer, naviguer; (*set off*) partir, prendre la mer; (*SPORT*) faire de la voile; **they ~ed into Le Havre** ils sont entrés dans le port du Havre; **~ through** *vi, vt fus* (*fig*) réussir haut la main; **~boat** (*US*) *n* bateau *m* à voiles, voilier *m*; **~ing** *n* (*SPORT*) voile *f*; **to go ~ing** faire de la voile; **~ing boat** *n* bateau *m* à voiles, voilier *m*; **~ing ship** *n* grand voilier; **~or** *n* marin *m*, matelot *m*

saint [seɪnt] *n* saint(e)

sake [seɪk] *n*: **for the ~ of** pour (l'amour de), dans l'intérêt de; par égard pour

salad ['sæləd] *n* salade *f*; **~ bowl** *n* saladier *m*; **~ cream** (*BRIT*) *n* (sorte *f* de) mayonnaise *f*; **~ dressing** *n* vinaigrette *f*

salami [sə'lɑːmɪ] *n* salami *m*

salary ['sælərɪ] *n* salaire *m*

sale [seɪl] *n* vente *f*; (*at reduced prices*) soldes *mpl*; **"for ~"** "à vendre"; **on ~** en vente; **on ~ or return** vendu(e) avec faculté de retour; **~room** *n* salle *f* des ventes; **~s assistant** (*US* **sales clerk**) *n* vendeur(-euse); **~sman** (*irreg*) *n* vendeur *m*; (*representative*) représentant *m*; **~s rep** *n* (*COMM*) représentant(e) *m/f*; **~swoman** (*irreg*) *n* vendeuse *f*; (*representative*) représentante *f*

salmon ['sæmən] *n inv* saumon *m*

salon ['sælɔn] *n* salon *m*

saloon [sə'luːn] *n* (*US*) bar *m*; (*BRIT: AUT*) berline *f*; (*ship's lounge*) salon *m*

salt [sɔːlt] *n* sel *m* ♦ *vt* saler; **~ cellar** *n* salière *f*; **~water** *adj* de mer; **~y** *adj* salé(e)

salute [sə'luːt] *n* salut *m* ♦ *vt* saluer

salvage ['sælvɪdʒ] *n* (*saving*) sauvetage *m*; (*things saved*) biens sauvés *or* récupérés ♦ *vt* sauver, récupérer

salvation [sæl'veɪʃən] *n* salut *m*; **S~ Army** *n* armée *f* du Salut

same [seɪm] *adj* même ♦ *pron*: **the ~** le (la) même, les mêmes; **the ~ book as** le même livre que; **at the ~ time** en même temps; **all** *or* **just the ~** tout de même, quand même; **to do the ~** faire de même, en faire autant; **to do the ~ as sb** faire comme qn; **the ~ to you!** à vous de même!; (*after insult*) toi-même!

sample ['sɑ:mpl] *n* échantillon *m*; (*blood*) prélèvement *m* ♦ *vt* (*food, wine*) goûter

sanction ['sæŋkʃən] *n* approbation *f*, sanction *f*

sanctity ['sæŋktɪtɪ] *n* sainteté *f*, caractère sacré

sanctuary ['sæŋktjuərɪ] *n* (*holy place*) sanctuaire *m*; (*refuge*) asile *m*; (*for wild life*) réserve *f*

sand [sænd] *n* sable *m* ♦ *vt* (*furniture: also:* **~ down**) poncer

sandal ['sændl] *n* sandale *f*

sand: **~box** (*US*) *n* tas *m* de sable; **~castle** *n* château *m* de sable; **~paper** *n* papier *m* de verre; **~pit** (*BRIT*) *n* (*for children*) tas *m* de sable; **~stone** *n* grès *m*

sandwich ['sændwɪtʃ] *n* sandwich *m*; **cheese/ham ~** sandwich au fromage/jambon; **~ course** (*BRIT*) *n* cours *m* de formation professionnelle

sandy ['sændɪ] *adj* sablonneux(-euse); (*colour*) sable *inv*, blond roux *inv*

sane [seɪn] *adj* (*person*) sain(e) d'esprit; (*outlook*) sensé(e), sain(e)

sang [sæŋ] *pt of* **sing**

sanitary ['sænɪtərɪ] *adj* (*system, arrangements*) sanitaire; (*clean*) hygiénique; **~ towel** (*US* **sanitary napkin**) *n* serviette *f* hygiénique

sanitation [sænɪ'teɪʃən] *n* (*in house*) installations *fpl* sanitaires; (*in town*) système *m* sanitaire; **~ department** (*US*) *n* service *m* de voirie

sanity ['sænɪtɪ] *n* santé mentale; (*common sense*) bon sens

sank [sæŋk] *pt of* **sink**

Santa Claus [sæntə'klɔːz] *n* le père Noël

sap [sæp] *n* (*of plants*) sève *f* ♦ *vt* (*strength*) saper, miner

sapling ['sæplɪŋ] *n* jeune arbre *m*

sapphire ['sæfaɪəʳ] *n* saphir *m*

sarcasm ['sɑ:kæzm] *n* sarcasme *m*, raillerie *f*; **sarcastic** [sɑ:'kæstɪk] *adj* sarcastique

sardine [sɑ:'di:n] *n* sardine *f*

Sardinia [sɑ:'dɪnɪə] *n* Sardaigne *f*

sash [sæʃ] *n* écharpe *f*

sat [sæt] *pt, pp of* **sit**

satchel ['sætʃl] *n* cartable *m*

satellite ['sætəlaɪt] *n* satellite *m*; **~ dish** *n* antenne *f* parabolique; **~ television** *n* télévision *f* par câble

satin ['sætɪn] *n* satin *m* ♦ *adj* en *or* de satin, satiné(e)

satire ['sætaɪəʳ] *n* satire *f*

satisfaction [sætɪs'fækʃən] *n* satisfaction *f*

satisfactory [sætɪs'fæktərɪ] *adj* satisfaisant(e)

satisfied ['sætɪsfaɪd] *adj* satisfait(e)

satisfy ['sætɪsfaɪ] *vt* satisfaire, contenter; (*convince*) convaincre, persuader; **~ing** *adj* satisfaisant(e)

Saturday ['sætədɪ] *n* samedi *m*

sauce [sɔ:s] *n* sauce *f*; **~pan** *n* casserole *f*

saucer ['sɔ:səʳ] *n* soucoupe *f*

Saudi ['saudɪ]: **~ Arabia** *n* Arabie Saoudite; **~ (Arabian)** *adj* saoudien(ne)

sauna ['sɔ:nə] *n* sauna *m*

saunter ['sɔ:ntəʳ] *vi*: **to ~ along/in/out** *etc* marcher/entrer/sortir *etc* d'un pas nonchalant

sausage ['sɔsɪdʒ] *n* saucisse *f*; (*cold meat*) saucisson *m*; **~ roll** *n* ≈ friand *m*

savage ['sævɪdʒ] *adj* (*cruel, fierce*) brutal(e), féroce; (*primitive*) primitif(-ive), sauvage ♦ *n* sauvage *m/f*

save [seɪv] *vt* (*person, belongings*) sauver; (*money*) mettre de côté, économiser; (*time*) (faire) gagner; (*keep*) garder; (*COMPUT*) sauvegarder; (*SPORT: stop*) arrêter; (*avoid: trouble*) éviter ♦ *vi* (*also:* **~ up**) mettre de l'argent de côté ♦ *n* (*SPORT*) arrêt *m* (du ballon) ♦ *prep* sauf, à l'exception de

saving ['seɪvɪŋ] *n* économie *f* ♦ *adj*: **the ~ grace of sth** ce qui rachète qch; **~s** *npl* (*money saved*) économies *fpl*; **~s account** *n* compte *m* d'épargne; **~s bank** *n* caisse *f* d'épargne

saviour ['seɪvjəʳ] (*US* **savior**) *n* sauveur *m*

savour ['seɪvəʳ] (*US* **savor**) *vt* savourer; **~y** (*US* **savory**) *adj* (*dish: not sweet*) salé(e)

saw [sɔː] (pt **sawed**, pp **sawed** or **sawn**) vt scier ♦ n (tool) scie f ♦ pt of **see**; ~**dust** n sciure f; ~**mill** n scierie f; ~**n-off** adj: ~**n-off shotgun** carabine f à canon scié

sax [sæks] (inf) n saxo m

saxophone ['sæksəfəʊn] n saxophone m

say [seɪ] (pt, pp **said**) n: **to have one's** ~ dire ce qu'on a à dire ♦ vt dire; **to have a** or **some** ~ **in sth** avoir voix au chapitre; **could you** ~ **that again?** pourriez-vous répéter ce que vous venez de dire?; **that goes without** ~**ing** cela va sans dire, cela va de soi; ~**ing** n dicton m, proverbe m

scab [skæb] n croûte f; (pej) jaune m

scaffold ['skæfəld] n échafaud m; ~**ing** n échafaudage m

scald [skɔːld] n brûlure f ♦ vt ébouillanter

scale [skeɪl] n (of fish) écaille f; (MUS) gamme f; (of ruler, thermometer etc) graduation f, échelle (graduée); (of salaries, fees etc) barème m; (of map, also size, extent) échelle ♦ vt (mountain) escalader; ~**s** npl (for weighing) balance f; (also: **bathroom** ~) pèse-personne m inv; **on a large** ~ sur une grande échelle, en grand; ~ **of charges** tableau m des tarifs; ~ **down** vt réduire

scallop ['skɒləp] n coquille f Saint-Jacques; (SEWING) feston m

scalp [skælp] n cuir chevelu ♦ vt scalper

scampi ['skæmpi] npl langoustines (frites), scampi mpl

scan [skæn] vt scruter, examiner; (glance at quickly) parcourir; (TV, RADAR) balayer ♦ n (MED) scanographie f

scandal ['skændl] n scandale m; (gossip) ragots mpl

Scandinavia [skændɪ'neɪvɪə] n Scandinavie f; ~**n** adj scandinave

scant [skænt] adj insuffisant(e); ~**y** ['skænti] adj peu abondant(e), insuffisant(e); (underwear) minuscule

scapegoat ['skeɪpgəʊt] n bouc m émissaire

scar [skɑː] n cicatrice f ♦ vt marquer (d'une cicatrice)

scarce [skɛəs] adj rare, peu abondant(e); **to make o.s.** ~ (inf) se sauver; ~**ly** adv à peine; **scarcity** n manque m, pénurie f

scare [skɛəʳ] n peur f, panique f ♦ vt effrayer, faire peur à; **to** ~ **sb stiff** faire une peur bleue à qn; **bomb** ~ alerte f à la bombe; ~ **away** vt faire fuir; ~ **off** vt = **scare away**; ~**crow** n épouvantail m; ~**d** adj: **to be** ~**d** avoir peur

scarf [skɑːf] (pl ~**s** or **scarves**) n (long) écharpe f; (square) foulard m

scarlet ['skɑːlɪt] adj écarlate; ~ **fever** n scarlatine f

scary ['skɛərɪ] (inf) adj effrayant(e)

scathing ['skeɪðɪŋ] adj cinglant(e), acerbe

scatter ['skætəʳ] vt éparpiller, répandre; (crowd) disperser ♦ vi se disperser; ~**brained** adj écervelé(e), étourdi(e)

scavenger ['skævɪndʒəʳ] n (person: in bins etc) pilleur m de poubelles

scene [siːn] n (THEATRE, fig etc) scène f; (of crime, accident) lieu(x) m(pl); (sight, view) spectacle m, vue f; ~**ry** ['siːnərɪ] n (THEATRE) décor(s) m(pl); (landscape) paysage m; **scenic** adj (picturesque) offrant de beaux paysages or panoramas

scent [sɛnt] n parfum m, odeur f; (track) piste f

sceptical ['skɛptɪkl] (US **skeptical**) adj sceptique

schedule ['ʃɛdjuːl, (US) 'skɛdjuːl] n programme m, plan m; (of trains) horaire m; (of prices etc) barème m, tarif m ♦ vt prévoir; **on** ~ à l'heure (prévue); **to be ahead of/behind** ~ avoir de l'avance/du retard; ~**d flight** n vol régulier

scheme [skiːm] n plan m, projet m; (dishonest plan, plot) complot m, combine f; (arrangement) arrangement m, classification f; (pension ~ etc) régime m ♦ vi comploter, manigancer; **scheming** adj rusé(e), intrigant(e) ♦ n manigances fpl, intrigues fpl

scholar ['skɒləʳ] n érudit(e); (pupil) boursier(-ère); ~**ship** n (knowledge) érudition f; (grant) bourse f (d'études)

school [skuːl] n école f; (secondary ~) collège m, lycée m; (US: university) université f; (in university) faculté f ♦ cpd scolaire; **~book** n livre m scolaire or de classe; **~boy** n écolier m; collégien m, lycéen m; **~children** npl écoliers mpl; collégiens mpl, lycéens mpl; **~girl** n écolière f; collégienne f, lycéenne f; **~ing** n instruction f, études fpl; **~master** n professeur m; **~mistress** n professeur m; **~teacher** n instituteur(-trice); professeur m

science ['saɪəns] n science f; **~ fiction** n science-fiction f; **scientific** [saɪən'tɪfɪk] adj scientifique; **scientist** n scientifique m/f; (eminent) savant m

scissors ['sɪzəz] npl ciseaux mpl

scoff [skɔf] vt (BRIT: inf: eat) avaler, bouffer ♦ vi: **to ~ (at)** (mock) se moquer (de)

scold [skəuld] vt gronder

scone [skɔn] n sorte de petit pain rond au lait

scoop [sku:p] n pelle f (à main); (for ice cream) boule f à glace; (PRESS) scoop m; **~ out** vt évider, creuser; **~ up** vt ramasser

scooter ['sku:tə'] n (also: **motor ~**) scooter m; (toy) trottinette f

scope [skəup] n (capacity: of plan, undertaking) portée f, envergure f; (: of person) compétence f, capacités fpl; (opportunity) possibilités fpl; **within the ~ of** dans les limites de

scorch [skɔːtʃ] vt (clothes) brûler (légèrement), roussir; (earth, grass) dessécher, brûler

score [skɔː'] n score m, décompte m des points; (MUS) partition f; (twenty) vingt ♦ vt (goal, point) marquer; (success) remporter ♦ vi marquer des points; (FOOTBALL) marquer un but; (keep ~) compter les points; **~s of** (very many) beaucoup de, un tas de (fam); **on that ~** sur ce chapitre, à cet égard; **to ~ 6 out of 10** obtenir 6 sur 10; **~ out** vt rayer, barrer, biffer; **~board** n tableau m

scorn [skɔːn] n mépris m, dédain m

Scorpio ['skɔːpɪəu] n le Scorpion

Scot [skɔt] n Écossais(e)

Scotch [skɔtʃ] n whisky m, scotch m

scot-free ['skɔt'fri:] adv: **to get off ~-~** s'en tirer sans être puni(e)

Scotland ['skɔtlənd] n Écosse f; **Scots** adj écossais(e); **Scotsman** (irreg) n Écossais; **Scotswoman** (irreg) n Écossaise f; **Scottish** adj écossais(e); **Scottish Parliament** n Parlement m écossais

scoundrel ['skaundrl] n vaurien m

scour ['skauə'] vt (search) battre, parcourir

scout [skaut] n (MIL) éclaireur m; (also: **boy ~**) scout m; **girl ~** (US) guide f; **~ around** vi explorer, chercher

scowl [skaul] vi se renfrogner, avoir l'air maussade; **to ~ at** regarder de travers

scrabble ['skræbl] vi (also: **~ around**: search) chercher à tâtons; (claw): **to ~ (at)** gratter ♦ n: **S~** ® Scrabble ® m

scram [skræm] (inf) vi ficher le camp

scramble ['skræmbl] n (rush) bousculade f, ruée f ♦ vi: **to ~ up/down** grimper/descendre tant bien que mal; **to ~ out** sortir or descendre à toute vitesse; **to ~ through** se frayer un passage (à travers); **to ~ for** se bousculer or se disputer pour (avoir); **~d eggs** npl œufs brouillés

scrap [skræp] n bout m, morceau m; (fight) bagarre f; (also: **~ iron**) ferraille f ♦ vt jeter, mettre au rebut; (fig) abandonner, laisser tomber ♦ vi (fight) se bagarrer; **~s** npl (waste) déchets mpl; **~book** n album m; **~ dealer** n marchand m de ferraille

scrape [skreɪp] vt, vi gratter, racler ♦ n: **to get into a ~** s'attirer des ennuis; **to ~ through** réussir de justesse; **~ together** vt (money) racler ses fonds de tiroir pour réunir

scrap: ~ heap n: **on the ~ heap** (fig) au rancart or rebut; **~ merchant** (BRIT) n marchand m de ferraille; **~ paper** n papier m brouillon

scratch [skrætʃ] n égratignure f, rayure f; éraflure f; (from claw) coup m de griffe ♦ cpd: **~ team** équipe de fortune or improvisée ♦ vt (rub) (se) gratter; (record) rayer; (paint etc) érafler; (with claw, nail) griffer

♦ *vi* (se) gratter; **to start from ~** partir de zéro; **to be up to ~** être à la hauteur

scrawl [skrɔːl] *vi* gribouiller

scrawny ['skrɔːnɪ] *adj* décharné(e)

scream [skriːm] *n* cri perçant, hurlement *m* ♦ *vi* crier, hurler

screech [skriːtʃ] *vi* hurler; (*tyres*) crisser; (*brakes*) grincer

screen [skriːn] *n* écran *m*; (*in room*) paravent *m*; (*fig*) écran, rideau *m* ♦ *vt* (*conceal*) masquer, cacher; (*from the wind etc*) abriter, protéger; (*film*) projeter; (*candidates etc*) filtrer; **~ing** *n* (*MED*) test *m* (*or* tests) de dépistage; **~play** *n* scénario *m*

screw [skruː] *n* vis *f* ♦ *vt* visser; **~ up** *vt* (*paper etc*) froisser; **to ~ up one's eyes** plisser les yeux; **~driver** *n* tournevis *m*

scribble ['skrɪbl] *vt, vi* gribouiller, griffonner

script [skrɪpt] *n* (*CINEMA etc*) scénario *m*, texte *m*; (*system of writing*) (écriture *f*) script *m*

Scripture(s) ['skrɪptʃəʳ(-əz)] *n(pl)* (*Christian*) Écriture sainte; (*other religions*) écritures saintes

scroll [skrəʊl] *n* rouleau *m*

scrounge [skraʊndʒ] (*inf*) *vt*: **to ~ sth off** *or* **from sb** taper qn de qch; **~r** (*inf*) *n* parasite *m*

scrub [skrʌb] *n* (*land*) broussailles *fpl* ♦ *vt* (*floor*) nettoyer à la brosse; (*pan*) récurer; (*washing*) frotter; (*inf: cancel*) annuler

scruff [skrʌf] *n*: **by the ~ of the neck** par la peau du cou

scruffy ['skrʌfɪ] *adj* débraillé(e)

scrum(mage) ['skrʌm(ɪdʒ)] *n* (*RUGBY*) mêlée *f*

scruple ['skruːpl] *n* scrupule *m*

scrutiny ['skruːtɪnɪ] *n* examen minutieux

scuff [skʌf] *vt* érafler

scuffle ['skʌfl] *n* échauffourée *f*, rixe *f*

sculptor ['skʌlptəʳ] *n* sculpteur *m*

sculpture ['skʌlptʃəʳ] *n* sculpture *f*

scum [skʌm] *n* écume *f*, mousse *f*; (*pej: people*) rebut *m*, lie *f*

scurry ['skʌrɪ] *vi* filer à toute allure; **to ~ off** détaler, se sauver

scuttle ['skʌtl] *n* (*also:* **coal ~**) seau *m* (à charbon) ♦ *vt* (*ship*) saborder ♦ *vi* (*scamper*): **to ~ away** *or* **off** détaler

scythe [saɪð] *n* faux *f*

SDP *n abbr* = **Social Democratic Party**

sea [siː] *n* mer *f* ♦ *cpd* marin(e), de (la) mer; **by ~** (*travel*) par mer, en bateau; **on the ~** (*boat*) en mer; (*town*) au bord de la mer; **to be all at ~** (*fig*) nager complètement; **out to ~** au large; (**out**) **at ~** en mer; **~board** *n* côte *f*; **~food** *n* fruits *mpl* de mer; **~front** *n* bord *m* de mer; **~going** *adj* (*ship*) de mer; **~gull** *n* mouette *f*

seal [siːl] *n* (*animal*) phoque *m*; (*stamp*) sceau *m*, cachet *m* ♦ *vt* sceller; (*envelope*) coller; (: *with ~*) cacheter; **~ off** *vt* (*forbid entry to*) interdire l'accès de

sea level *n* niveau *m* de la mer

sea lion *n* otarie *f*

seam [siːm] *n* couture *f*; (*of coal*) veine *f*, filon *m*

seaman ['siːmən] (*irreg*) *n* marin *m*

seance ['seɪɒns] *n* séance *f* de spiritisme

seaplane ['siːpleɪn] *n* hydravion *m*

search [sɜːtʃ] *n* (*for person, thing, COMPUT*) recherche(s) *f(pl)*; (*LAW: at sb's home*) perquisition *f* ♦ *vt* fouiller; (*examine*) examiner minutieusement; scruter ♦ *vi*: **to ~ for** chercher; **in ~ of** à la recherche de; **~ through** *vt fus* fouiller; **~ engine** *n* (*COMPUT*) moteur *m* de recherche; **~ing** *adj* pénétrant(e); **~light** *n* projecteur *m*; **~ party** *n* expédition *f* de secours; **~ warrant** *n* mandat *m* de perquisition

sea: **~shore** *n* rivage *m*, plage *f*, bord *m* de (la) mer; **~sick** *adj*: **to be ~sick** avoir le mal de mer; **~side** *n* bord *m* de la mer; **~side resort** *n* station *f* balnéaire

season ['siːzn] *n* saison *f* ♦ *vt* assaisonner, relever; **to be in/out of ~** être/ne pas être de saison; **~al** *adj* (*work*) saisonnier(-ère); **~ed** *adj* (*fig*) expérimenté(e); **~ ticket** *n* carte *f* d'abonnement

seat [siːt] *n* siège *m*; (*in bus, train: place*) place *f*; (*buttocks*) postérieur *m*; (*of trousers*) fond *m* ♦ *vt* faire asseoir, placer;

(have room for) avoir des places assises pour, pouvoir accueillir; ~ **belt** n ceinture f de sécurité

sea: ~ **water** n eau f de mer; ~**weed** n algues fpl; ~**worthy** adj en état de naviguer

sec. abbr = **second(s)**

secluded [sɪˈkluːdɪd] adj retiré(e), à l'écart

seclusion [sɪˈkluːʒən] n solitude f

second[1] [sɪˈkɒnd] (BRIT) vt *(employee)* affecter provisoirement

second[2] [ˈsekənd] adj deuxième, second(e) ♦ adv *(in race etc)* en seconde position ♦ n *(unit of time)* seconde f; *(AUT: ~ gear)* seconde; *(COMM: imperfect)* article m de second choix; *(BRIT: UNIV)* licence f avec mention ♦ vt *(motion)* appuyer; ~**ary** adj secondaire; ~**ary school** n collège m, lycée m; ~-**class** adj de deuxième classe; *(RAIL)* de seconde (classe); *(POST)* au tarif réduit; *(pej)* de qualité inférieure ♦ adv *(RAIL)* en seconde; *(POST)* au tarif réduit; ~**hand** adj d'occasion; de seconde main; ~ **hand** n *(on clock)* trotteuse f; ~**ly** adv deuxièmement; ~**ment** [sɪˈkɒndmənt] (BRIT) n détachement m; ~-**rate** adj de deuxième ordre, de qualité inférieure; ~ **thoughts** npl doutes mpl; **on** ~ **thoughts** or *(US)* **thought** à la réflexion

secrecy [ˈsiːkrəsɪ] n secret m

secret [ˈsiːkrɪt] adj secret(-ète) ♦ n secret m; **in** ~ en secret, secrètement, en cachette

secretary [ˈsekrətərɪ] n secrétaire m/f; *(COMM)* secrétaire général; **S~ of State (for)** *(BRIT: POL)* ministre m (de)

secretive [ˈsiːkrətɪv] adj dissimulé(e)

secretly [ˈsiːkrɪtlɪ] adv en secret, secrètement

sectarian [sekˈteərɪən] adj sectaire

section [ˈsekʃən] n section f; *(of document)* section, article m, paragraphe m; *(cut)* coupe f

sector [ˈsektər] n secteur m

secular [ˈsekjulər] adj profane; laïque; séculier(-ère)

secure [sɪˈkjuər] adj *(free from anxiety)* sans

inquiétude, sécurisé(e); *(firmly fixed)* solide, bien attaché(e) *(or fermé(e) etc)*; *(in safe place)* en lieu sûr, en sûreté ♦ vt *(fix)* fixer, attacher; *(get)* obtenir, se procurer

security [sɪˈkjuərɪtɪ] n sécurité f, mesures fpl de sécurité; *(for loan)* caution f, garantie f; ~ **guard** n garde chargé de la sécurité; *(when transporting money)* convoyeur m de fonds

sedate [sɪˈdeɪt] adj calme; posé(e) ♦ vt *(MED)* donner des sédatifs à

sedative [ˈsedɪtɪv] n calmant m, sédatif m

seduce [sɪˈdjuːs] vt séduire; **seduction** [sɪˈdʌkʃən] n séduction f; **seductive** adj séduisant(e); *(smile)* séducteur(-trice); *(fig: offer)* alléchant(e)

see [siː] *(pt* **saw**, *pp* **seen)** vt voir; *(accompany):* **to** ~ **sb to the door** reconduire *or* raccompagner qn jusqu'à la porte ♦ vi voir ♦ n évêché m; **to** ~ **that** *(ensure)* veiller à ce que +sub, faire en sorte que +sub, s'assurer que; ~ **you soon!** à bientôt!; ~ **about** vt fus s'occuper de; ~ **off** vt accompagner (à la gare *or* à l'aéroport *etc)*; ~ **through** vt mener à bonne fin ♦ vt fus voir clair dans; ~ **to** vt fus s'occuper de, se charger de

seed [siːd] n graine f; *(sperm)* semence f; *(fig)* germe m; *(TENNIS etc)* tête f de série; **to go to** ~ monter en graine; *(fig)* se laisser aller; ~**ling** n jeune plant m, semis m; ~**y** adj *(shabby)* minable, miteux(-euse)

seeing [ˈsiːɪŋ] conj: ~ **(that)** vu que, étant donné que

seek [siːk] *(pt, pp* **sought)** vt chercher, rechercher

seem [siːm] vi sembler, paraître; **there ~s to be ...** il semble qu'il y a ...; on dirait qu'il y a ...; ~**ingly** adv apparemment

seen [siːn] pp of **see**

seep [siːp] vi suinter, filtrer

seesaw [ˈsiːsɔː] n (jeu m de) bascule f

seethe [siːð] vi être en effervescence; **to ~ with anger** bouillir de colère

see-through [ˈsiːθruː] adj transparent(e)

segment [ˈsegmənt] n segment m; *(of orange)* quartier m

segregate ['segrɪgeɪt] vt séparer, isoler
seize [si:z] vt saisir, attraper; (take possession of) s'emparer de; (opportunity) saisir; ~ up vi (TECH) se gripper; ~ (up)on vt fus saisir, sauter sur
seizure ['si:ʒə'] n (MED) crise f, attaque f; (of power) prise f
seldom ['seldəm] adv rarement
select [sɪ'lekt] adj choisi(e), d'élite ♦ vt sélectionner, choisir; ~ion n sélection f, choix m
self [self] (pl selves) n: the ~ le moi inv ♦ prefix auto-; ~-assured adj sûr(e) de soi; ~-catering (BRIT) adj avec cuisine, où l'on peut faire sa cuisine; ~-centred (US self-centered) adj égocentrique; ~-confidence n confiance f en soi; ~-conscious adj timide, qui manque d'assurance; ~-contained (BRIT) adj (flat) avec entrée particulière, indépendant(e); ~-control n maîtrise f de soi; ~-defence (US self-defense) n autodéfense f; (LAW) légitime défense f; ~-discipline n discipline personnelle; ~-employed adj qui travaille à son compte; ~-evident adj: to be ~-evident être évident(e), aller de soi; ~-governing adj autonome; ~-indulgent adj qui ne se refuse rien; ~-interest n intérêt personnel; ~-ish adj égoïste; ~ishness n égoïsme m; ~less adj désintéressé(e); ~-pity n apitoiement m sur soi-même; ~-possessed adj assuré(e); ~-preservation n instinct m de conservation; ~-respect n respect m de soi, amour-propre m; ~-righteous adj suffisant(e); ~-sacrifice n abnégation f; ~-satisfied adj content(e) de soi, suffisant(e); ~-service adj libre-service, self-service; ~-sufficient adj autosuffisant(e); (person: independent) indépendant(e); ~-taught adj (artist, pianist) qui a appris par lui-même
sell [sel] (pt, pp sold) vt vendre ♦ vi se vendre; to ~ at or for 10 F se vendre 10 F; ~ off vt liquider; ~ out vi: to ~ out (of sth) (use up stock) vendre tout son stock (de qch); the tickets are all sold out il

ne reste plus de billets; ~-by date n date f limite de vente; ~er n vendeur(-euse), marchand(e); ~ing price n prix m de vente
Sellotape ® ['seləʊteɪp] (BRIT) n papier m collant, scotch ® m
selves [selvz] npl of self
semblance ['sembləns] n semblant m
semen ['si:mən] n sperme m
semester [sɪ'mestə'] (esp US) n semestre m
semi ['semɪ] prefix semi-, demi-; à demi, à moitié; ~circle n demi-cercle m; ~colon n point-virgule m; ~detached (house) (BRIT) n maison jumelée or jumelle; ~final n demi-finale f
seminar ['semɪnɑ:'] n séminaire m; ~y n (REL: for priests) séminaire m
semiskilled [semɪ'skɪld] adj: ~ worker ouvrier(-ère) spécialisé(e)
semi-skimmed milk [semɪ'skɪmd-] n lait m demi-écrémé
senate ['senɪt] n sénat m; senator n sénateur m
send [send] (pt, pp sent) vt envoyer; ~ away (letter, goods) envoyer, expédier; (unwelcome visitor) renvoyer; ~ away for vt fus commander par correspondance, se faire envoyer; ~ back vt renvoyer; ~ for vt fus envoyer chercher; faire venir; ~ off vt (goods) envoyer, expédier; (BRIT: SPORT: player) expulser or renvoyer du terrain; ~ out vt (invitation) envoyer (par la poste); (light, heat, signal) émettre; ~ up vt faire monter; (BRIT: parody) mettre en boîte, parodier; ~er n expéditeur(-trice); ~-off n: a good ~-off des adieux chaleureux
senior ['si:nɪə'] adj (high-ranking) de haut niveau; (of higher rank): to be ~ to sb être le supérieur de qn ♦ n (older): she is 15 years his ~ elle est son aînée de 15 ans, elle est plus âgée que lui de 15 ans; ~ citizen n personne âgée; ~ity [si:nɪ'ɔrɪtɪ] n (in service) ancienneté f
sensation [sen'seɪʃən] n sensation f; ~al adj qui fait sensation; (marvellous) sensationnel(le)
sense [sens] n sens m; (feeling) sentiment

m; (*meaning*) sens, signification *f*; (*wisdom*) bon sens ♦ *vt* sentir, pressentir; **it makes ~** c'est logique; **~less** *adj* insensé(e), stupide; (*unconscious*) sans connaissance
sensible ['sɛnsɪbl] *adj* sensé(e), raisonnable; sage
sensitive ['sɛnsɪtɪv] *adj* sensible
sensual ['sɛnsjuəl] *adj* sensuel(le)
sensuous ['sɛnsjuəs] *adj* voluptueux(-euse), sensuel(le)
sent [sɛnt] *pt, pp of* **send**
sentence ['sɛntns] *n* (LING) phrase *f*; (LAW: *judgment*) condamnation *f*, sentence *f*; (: *punishment*) peine *f* ♦ *vt*: **to ~ sb to death/to 5 years in prison** condamner qn à mort/à 5 ans de prison
sentiment ['sɛntɪmənt] *n* sentiment *m*; (*opinion*) opinion *f*, avis *m*; **~al** [sɛntɪ'mɛntl] *adj* sentimental(e)
sentry ['sɛntrɪ] *n* sentinelle *f*
separate [*adj* 'sɛprɪt, *vb* 'sɛpəreɪt] *adj* séparé(e), indépendant(e), différent(e) ♦ *vt* séparer; (*make a distinction between*) distinguer ♦ *vi* se séparer; **~ly** *adv* séparément; **~s** *npl* (*clothes*) coordonnés *mpl*; **separation** [sɛpə'reɪʃən] *n* séparation *f*
September [sɛp'tɛmbə*] *n* septembre *m*
septic ['sɛptɪk] *adj* (*wound*) infecté(e); **~ tank** *n* fosse *f* septique
sequel ['si:kwl] *n* conséquence *f*; séquelles *fpl*; (*of story*) suite *f*
sequence ['si:kwəns] *n* ordre *m*, suite *f*; (*film ~*) séquence *f*; (*dance ~*) numéro *m*
sequin ['si:kwɪn] *n* paillette *f*
Serbia ['sɜ:bɪə] *n* Serbie *f*
serene [sɪ'ri:n] *adj* serein(e), calme, paisible
sergeant ['sɑ:dʒənt] *n* sergent *m*; (POLICE) brigadier *m*
serial ['sɪərɪəl] *n* feuilleton *m*; **~ killer** *n* meurtrier *m* tuant en série; **~ number** *n* numéro *m* de série
series ['sɪərɪz] *n inv* série *f*; (PUBLISHING) collection *f*
serious ['sɪərɪəs] *adj* sérieux(-euse); (*illness*) grave; **~ly** *adv* sérieusement; (*hurt*) gravement

sermon ['sɜ:mən] *n* sermon *m*
serrated [sɪ'reɪtɪd] *adj* en dents de scie
servant ['sɜ:vənt] *n* domestique *m/f*; (*fig*) serviteur/servante
serve [sɜ:v] *vt* (*employer etc*) servir, être au service de; (*purpose*) servir à; (*customer, food, meal*) servir; (*subj: train*) desservir; (*apprenticeship*) faire, accomplir; (*prison term*) purger ♦ *vi* servir; (*be useful*): **to ~ as/for/to do** servir de/à/à faire ♦ *n* (TENNIS) service *m*; **it ~s him right** c'est bien fait pour lui; **~ out, ~ up** *vt* (*food*) servir
service ['sɜ:vɪs] *n* service *m*; (AUT: *maintenance*) révision *f* ♦ *vt* (*car, washing machine*) réviser; **the S~s** les forces armées; **to be of ~ to sb** rendre service à qn; **15% ~ included** service 15% compris; **~ not included** service non compris; **~able** *adj* pratique, commode; **~ area** *n* (*on motorway*) aire *f* de services; **~ charge** (BRIT) *n* service *m*; **~man** (*irreg*) *n* militaire *m*; **~ station** *n* station-service *f*
serviette [sɜ:vɪ'ɛt] (BRIT) *n* serviette *f* (de table)
session ['sɛʃən] *n* séance *f*
set [sɛt] (*pt, pp* **set**) *n* série *f*, assortiment *m*; (*of tools etc*) jeu *m*; (RADIO, TV) poste *m*; (TENNIS) set *m*; (*group of people*) cercle *m*, milieu *m*; (THEATRE: *stage*) scène *f*; (: *scenery*) décor *m*; (MATH) ensemble *m*; (HAIRDRESSING) mise *f* en plis ♦ *adj* (*fixed*) fixe, déterminé(e); (*ready*) prêt(e) ♦ *vt* (*place*) poser, placer; (*fix, establish*) fixer; (: *record*) établir; (*adjust*) régler; (*decide: rules etc*) fixer, choisir; (*task*) donner; (*exam*) composer ♦ *vi* (*sun*) se coucher; (*jam, jelly, concrete*) prendre; (*bone*) se ressouder; **to be ~ on doing** être résolu à faire; **to ~ the table** mettre la table; **to ~ (to music)** mettre en musique; **to ~ on fire** mettre le feu à; **to ~ free** libérer; **to ~ sth going** déclencher qch; **to ~ sail** prendre la mer; **~ about** *vt fus* (*task*) entreprendre, se mettre à; **~ aside** *vt* mettre de côté; (*time*) garder; **~ back** *vt* (*in time*): **to ~ back (by)** retarder (de); (*cost*): **to ~ sb back £5** coûter 5 livres à qn; **~ off** *vi* se

mettre en route, partir ♦ vt (bomb) faire exploser; (cause to start) déclencher; (show up well) mettre en valeur, faire valoir; ~ out vi se mettre en route, partir ♦ vt (arrange) disposer; (arguments) présenter, exposer; to ~ out to do entreprendre de faire, avoir pour but or intention de faire; ~ up vt (organization) fonder, créer; ~back n (hitch) revers m, contretemps m; ~ menu n menu m

settee [se'ti:] n canapé m

setting ['setɪŋ] n cadre m; (of jewel) monture f; (position: of controls) réglage m

settle ['setl] vt (argument, matter, account) régler; (problem) résoudre; (MED: calm) calmer ♦ vi (bird, dust etc) se poser; (also: ~ **down**) s'installer, se fixer; (calm down) se calmer; **to ~ for sth** accepter qch, se contenter de qch; **to ~ on sth** opter or se décider pour qch; **~ in** vi s'installer; **~ up** vi: **to ~ up with sb** régler (ce que l'on doit à) qn; **~ment** n (payment) règlement m; (agreement) accord m; (village etc) établissement m; hameau m; **~r** n colon m

setup ['setʌp] n (arrangement) manière f dont les choses sont organisées; (situation) situation f

seven ['sevn] num sept; **~teen** num dix-sept; **~th** num septième; **~ty** num soixante-dix

sever ['sevər] vt couper, trancher; (relations) rompre

several ['sevərl] adj, pron plusieurs m/fpl; **~ of us** plusieurs d'entre nous

severance ['sevərəns] n (of relations) rupture f; **~ pay** n indemnité f de licenciement

severe [sɪ'vɪər] adj (stern) sévère, strict(e); (serious) grave, sérieux(-euse); (plain) sévère, austère; **severity** [sɪ'verɪtɪ] n sévérité f; gravité f; rigueur f

sew [səu] (pt **sewed**, pp **sewn**) vt, vi coudre; **~ up** vt (re)coudre

sewage ['su:ɪdʒ] n vidange(s) f(pl)

sewer ['su:ər] n égout m

sewing ['səuɪŋ] n couture f; (item(s)) ouvrage m; **~ machine** n machine f à coudre

sewn [səun] pp of **sew**

sex [seks] n sexe m; **to have ~ with** avoir des rapports (sexuels) avec; **~ism** n sexisme m; **~ist** adj sexiste; **~ual** ['seksjuəl] adj sexuel(le); **~uality** [seksju'ælɪtɪ] n sexualité f; **~y** adj sexy inv

shabby ['ʃæbɪ] adj miteux(-euse); (behaviour) mesquin(e), méprisable

shack [ʃæk] n cabane f, hutte f

shackles ['ʃæklz] npl chaînes fpl, entraves fpl

shade [ʃeɪd] n ombre f; (for lamp) abat-jour m inv; (of colour) nuance f, ton m ♦ vt abriter du soleil, ombrager; **in the ~** à l'ombre; **a ~ too large/more** un tout petit peu trop grand(e)/plus

shadow ['ʃædəu] n ombre f ♦ vt (follow) filer; **~ cabinet** (BRIT) n (POL) cabinet parallèle formé par l'Opposition; **~y** adj ombragé(e); (dim) vague, indistinct(e)

shady ['ʃeɪdɪ] adj ombragé(e); (fig: dishonest) louche, véreux(-euse)

shaft [ʃɑːft] n (of arrow, spear) hampe f; (AUT, TECH) arbre m; (of mine) puits m; (of lift) cage f; (of light) rayon m, trait m

shaggy ['ʃægɪ] adj hirsute; en broussaille

shake [ʃeɪk] (pt **shook**, pp **shaken**) vt secouer; (bottle, cocktail) agiter; (house, confidence) ébranler ♦ vi trembler; **to ~ one's head** (in refusal) dire or faire non de la tête; (in dismay) secouer la tête; **to ~ hands with sb** serrer la main à qn; **~ off** vt secouer; (pursuer) se débarrasser de; **~ up** vt secouer; **~n** pp of **shake**; **shaky** adj (hand, voice) tremblant(e); (building) branlant(e), peu solide

shall [ʃæl] aux vb: **I ~ go** j'irai; **~ I open the door?** j'ouvre la porte?; **I'll get the coffee, ~ I?** je vais chercher le café, d'accord?

shallow ['ʃæləu] adj peu profond(e); (fig) superficiel(le)

sham [ʃæm] n frime f ♦ vt simuler

shambles ['ʃæmblz] n (muddle) confusion f, pagaïe f, fouillis m

shame [ʃeɪm] n honte f ♦ vt faire honte à;

it is a ~ (that/to do) c'est dommage (que +*sub*/de faire); **what a ~!** quel dommage!; **~ful** *adj* honteux(-euse), scandaleux(-euse); **~less** *adj* éhonté(e), effronté(e)

shampoo [ʃæmˈpuː] *n* shampooing *m* ♦ *vt* faire un shampooing à; **~ and set** *n* shampooing *m* (et) mise *f* en plis

shamrock [ˈʃæmrɔk] *n* trèfle *m* (*emblème de l'Irlande*)

shandy [ˈʃændɪ] *n* bière panachée

shan't [ʃɑːnt] = **shall not**

shanty town [ˈʃæntɪ-] *n* bidonville *m*

shape [ʃeɪp] *n* forme *f* ♦ *vt* façonner, modeler; (*sb's ideas*) former; (*sb's life*) déterminer ♦ *vi* (*also:* **~ up**: *events*) prendre tournure; (: *person*) faire des progrès, s'en sortir; **to take ~** prendre forme *or* tournure; **-d** *suffix*: **heart-~d** en forme de cœur; **~less** *adj* informe, sans forme; **~ly** *adj* bien proportionné(e), beau (belle)

share [ʃɛəʳ] *n* part *f*; (COMM) action *f* ♦ *vt* partager; (*have in common*) avoir en commun; **~ out** *vi* partager; **~holder** *n* actionnaire *m/f*

shark [ʃɑːk] *n* requin *m*

sharp [ʃɑːp] *adj* (*razor, knife*) tranchant(e), bien aiguisé(e); (*point, voice*) aigu(-guë); (*nose, chin*) pointu(e); (*outline, increase*) net(te); (*cold, pain*) vif (vive); (*taste*) piquant(e), âcre; (MUS) dièse; (*person: quick-witted*) vif (vive), éveillé(e); (: *unscrupulous*) malhonnête ♦ *n* (MUS) dièse *m* ♦ *adv* (*precisely*): **at 2 o'clock ~** à 2 heures pile *or* précises; **~en** *vt* aiguiser; (*pencil*) tailler; **~ener** *n* (*also:* **pencil ~ener**) taille-crayon(s) *m inv*; **~-eyed** *adj* à qui rien n'échappe; **~ly** *adv* (*turn, stop*) brusquement; (*stand out*) nettement; (*criticize, retort*) sèchement, vertement

shatter [ˈʃætəʳ] *vt* briser; (*fig: upset*) bouleverser; (: *ruin*) briser, ruiner ♦ *vi* voler en éclats, se briser

shave [ʃeɪv] *vt* raser ♦ *vi* se raser ♦ *n*: **to have a ~** se raser; **~r** *n* (*also:* **electric ~r**) rasoir *m* électrique

shaving [ˈʃeɪvɪŋ] (*action*) rasage *m*; **~s** *npl*

(*of wood etc*) copeaux *mpl*; **~ brush** *n* blaireau *m*; **~ cream** *n* crème *f* à raser; **~ foam** *n* mousse *f* à raser

shawl [ʃɔːl] *n* châle *m*

she [ʃiː] *pron* elle ♦ *prefix*: **~-cat** chatte *f*; **~-elephant** éléphant *m* femelle

sheaf [ʃiːf] (*pl* **sheaves**) *n* gerbe *f*; (*of papers*) liasse *f*

shear [ʃɪəʳ] (*pt* **sheared**, *pp* **shorn**) *vt* (*sheep*) tondre; **~s** *npl* (*for hedge*) cisaille(s) *f(pl)*

sheath [ʃiːθ] *n* gaine *f*, fourreau *m*, étui *m*; (*contraceptive*) préservatif *m*

shed [ʃed] (*pt*, *pp* **shed**) *n* remise *f*, resserre *f* ♦ *vt* perdre; (*tears*) verser, répandre; (*workers*) congédier

she'd [ʃiːd] = **she had; she would**

sheen [ʃiːn] *n* lustre *m*

sheep [ʃiːp] *n inv* mouton *m*; **~dog** *n* chien *m* de berger; **~skin** *n* peau *f* de mouton

sheer [ʃɪəʳ] *adj* (*utter*) pur(e), pur et simple; (*steep*) à pic, abrupt(e); (*almost transparent*) extrêmement fin(e) ♦ *adv* à pic, abruptement

sheet [ʃiːt] *n* (*on bed*) drap *m*; (*of paper*) feuille *f*; (*of glass, metal etc*) feuille, plaque *f*

sheik(h) [ʃeɪk] *n* cheik *m*

shelf [ʃelf] (*pl* **shelves**) *n* étagère *f*, rayon *m*

shell [ʃel] *n* (*on beach*) coquillage *m*; (*of egg, nut etc*) coquille *f*; (*explosive*) obus *m*; (*of building*) carcasse *f* ♦ *vt* (*peas*) écosser; (MIL) bombarder (d'obus)

she'll [ʃiːl] = **she will; she shall**

shellfish [ˈʃelfɪʃ] *n inv* (*crab etc*) crustacé *m*; (*scallop etc*) coquillage *m* ♦ *npl* (*as food*) fruits *mpl* de mer

shell suit *n* survêtement *m* (*en synthétique froissé*)

shelter [ˈʃeltəʳ] *n* abri *m*, refuge *m* ♦ *vt* abriter, protéger; (*give lodging to*) donner asile à ♦ *vi* s'abriter, se mettre à l'abri; **~ed housing** *n* foyers *mpl* (*pour personnes âgées ou handicapées*)

shelve [ʃelv] *vt* (*fig*) mettre en suspens *or*

en sommeil; ~s npl of shelf

shepherd ['ʃepəd] n berger m ♦ vt (guide) guider, escorter; ~'s **pie** (BRIT) n ≈ hachis m Parmentier

sheriff ['ʃerɪf] (US) n shérif m

sherry ['ʃerɪ] n xérès m, sherry m

she's [ʃiːz] = **she is; she has**

Shetland ['ʃetlənd] n (also: **the ~ Islands**) les îles fpl Shetland

shield [ʃiːld] n bouclier m; (protection) écran m de protection ♦ vt: **to ~ (from)** protéger (de or contre)

shift [ʃɪft] n (change) changement m; (work period) période f de travail; (of workers) équipe f, poste m ♦ vt déplacer, changer de place; (remove) enlever ♦ vi changer de place, bouger; ~ **work** n travail m en équipe or par relais or par roulement; ~y adj sournois(e); (eyes) fuyant(e)

shimmer ['ʃɪmər] vi miroiter, chatoyer

shin [ʃɪn] n tibia m

shine [ʃaɪn] (pt, pp **shone**) n éclat m, brillant m ♦ vi briller ♦ vt (torch etc): **to ~ on** braquer sur; (polish: pt, pp ~d) faire briller or reluire

shingle ['ʃɪŋɡl] n (on beach) galets mpl; ~s n (MED) zona m

shiny ['ʃaɪnɪ] adj brillant(e)

ship [ʃɪp] n bateau m; (large) navire m ♦ vt transporter (par mer); (send) expédier (par mer); ~**building** n construction navale; ~**ment** n cargaison f; ~**ping** n (ships) navires mpl; (the industry) industrie navale; (transport) transport m; ~**wreck** n (ship) épave f; (event) naufrage m ♦ vt: **to be ~wrecked** faire naufrage; ~**yard** n chantier naval

shire ['ʃaɪər] (BRIT) n comté m

shirt [ʃɜːt] n (man's) chemise f; (woman's) chemisier m; **in (one's) ~ sleeves** en bras de chemise

shit [ʃɪt] (inf!) n, excl merde f (!)

shiver ['ʃɪvər] n frisson m ♦ vi frissonner

shoal [ʃəʊl] n (of fish) banc m; (fig: also: ~s) masse f, foule f

shock [ʃɒk] n choc m; (ELEC) secousse f; (MED) commotion f, choc ♦ vt (offend) choquer, scandaliser; (upset) bouleverser; ~ **absorber** n amortisseur m; ~**ing** adj (scandalizing) choquant(e), scandaleux(-euse); (appalling) épouvantable

shoddy ['ʃɒdɪ] adj de mauvaise qualité, mal fait(e)

shoe [ʃuː] (pt, pp **shod**) n chaussure f, soulier m; (also: **horseshoe**) fer m à cheval ♦ vt (horse) ferrer; ~**lace** n lacet m (de soulier); ~ **polish** n cirage m; ~ **shop** n magasin m de chaussures; ~**string** n (fig): **on a ~string** avec un budget dérisoire

shone [ʃɒn] pt, pp of **shine**

shook [ʃʊk] pt of **shake**

shoot [ʃuːt] (pt, pp **shot**) n (on branch, seedling) pousse f ♦ vt (game) chasser; tirer; abattre; (person) blesser (or tuer) d'un coup de fusil (or de revolver); (execute) fusiller; (arrow) tirer; (gun) tirer un coup de; (film) tourner ♦ vi (with gun, bow): **to ~ (at)** tirer (sur); (FOOTBALL) shooter, tirer; ~ **down** vt (plane) abattre; ~ **in** vi entrer comme une flèche; ~ **out** vi sortir comme une flèche; ~ **up** vi (fig) monter en flèche; ~**ing** n (shots) coups mpl de feu, fusillade f; (HUNTING) chasse f; ~**ing star** n étoile filante

shop [ʃɒp] n magasin m; (workshop) atelier m ♦ vi (also: **go ~ping**) faire ses courses or ses achats; ~ **assistant** (BRIT) n vendeur(-euse); ~ **floor** (BRIT) n (INDUSTRY: fig) ouvriers mpl; ~**keeper** n commerçant(e); ~**lifting** n vol m à l'étalage; ~**per** n personne f qui fait ses courses, acheteur(-euse); ~**ping** n (goods) achats mpl, provisions fpl; ~**ping bag** n sac m (à provisions); ~**ping centre** (US **shopping center**) n centre commercial; ~-**soiled** adj défraîchi(e), qui a fait la vitrine; ~ **steward** (BRIT) n (INDUSTRY) délégué(e) syndical(e); ~ **window** n vitrine f

shore [ʃɔːr] n (of sea, lake) rivage m, rive f ♦ vt: **to ~ (up)** étayer; **on ~** à terre

shorn [ʃɔːn] pp of **shear**

short [ʃɔːt] adj (not long) court(e); (soon finished) court, bref (brève); (person, step) petit(e); (*curt*) brusque, sec (sèche); (*insufficient*) insuffisant(e); **to be/run ~ of sth** être à court de *or* manquer de qch; **in ~** bref; en bref; **~ of doing ...** à moins de faire ...; **everything ~ of** tout sauf; **it is ~ for** c'est l'abréviation *or* le diminutif de; **to cut ~** (*speech, visit*) abréger, écourter; **to fall ~ of** ne pas être à la hauteur de; **to run ~ of** arriver à court de, venir à manquer de; **to stop ~** s'arrêter net; **to stop ~ of** ne pas aller jusqu'à; **~age** *n* manque *m*, pénurie *f*; **~bread** *n* ≃ sablé *m*; **~-change** *vt* ne pas rendre assez à; **~-circuit** *n* court-circuit *m*; **~coming** *n* défaut *m*; **~(crust) pastry** (*BRIT*) *n* pâte brisée; **~cut** *n* raccourci *m*; **~en** *vt* raccourcir; (*text, visit*) abréger; **~fall** *n* déficit *m*; **~hand** (*BRIT*) *n* sténo(graphie) *f*; **~hand typist** (*BRIT*) *n* sténodactylo *m/f*; **~list** (*BRIT*) *n* (*for job*) liste *f* des candidats sélectionnés; **~ly** *adv* bientôt, sous peu; **~ notice** *n*: **at ~ notice** au dernier moment; **~s** *npl*: **(a pair of) ~s** un short; **~-sighted** *adj* (*BRIT*) myope; (*fig*) qui manque de clairvoyance; **~-staffed** *adj* à court de personnel; **~-stay** *adj* (*car park*) de courte durée; **~ story** *n* nouvelle *f*; **~-tempered** *adj* qui s'emporte facilement; **~-term** *adj* (*effect*) à court terme; **~ wave** *n* (*RADIO*) ondes courtes

shot [ʃɔt] *pt, pp* of **shoot** ♦ *n* coup *m* (de feu); (*try*) coup, essai *m*; (*injection*) piqûre *f*; (*PHOT*) photo *f*; **he's a good/poor ~** il tire bien/mal; **like a ~** comme une flèche; (*very readily*) sans hésiter; **~gun** *n* fusil *m* de chasse

should [ʃʊd] *aux vb*: **I ~ go now** je devrais partir maintenant; **he ~ be there now** il devrait être arrivé maintenant; **I ~ go if I were you** si j'étais vous, j'irais; **I ~ like to** j'aimerais bien, volontiers

shoulder ['ʃəʊldər] *n* épaule *f* ♦ *vt* (*fig*) endosser, se charger de; **~ bag** *n* sac *m* à bandoulière; **~ blade** *n* omoplate *f*

shouldn't ['ʃʊdnt] = **should not**

shout [ʃaʊt] *n* cri *m* ♦ *vt* crier ♦ *vi* (*also: ~ out*) crier, pousser des cris; **~ down** *vt*

huer; **~ing** *n* cris *mpl*

shove [ʃʌv] *vt* pousser; (*inf: put*): **to ~ sth in** fourrer *or* ficher qch dans; **~ off** (*inf*) *vi* ficher le camp

shovel ['ʃʌvl] *n* pelle *f*

show [ʃəʊ] (*pt* **showed**, *pp* **shown**) *n* (*of emotion*) manifestation *f*, démonstration *f*; (*semblance*) semblant *m*, apparence *f*; (*exhibition*) exposition *f*, salon *m*; (*THEATRE, TV*) spectacle *m* ♦ *vt* montrer; (*film*) donner; (*courage etc*) faire preuve de, manifester; (*exhibit*) exposer ♦ *vi* se voir, être visible; **for ~** pour l'effet; **on ~** (*exhibits etc*) exposé(e); **~ in** *vt* (*person*) faire entrer; **~ off** *vi* (*pej*) crâner ♦ *vt* (*display*) faire valoir; **~ out** *vt* (*person*) reconduire (jusqu'à la porte); **~ up** *vi* (*stand out*) ressortir; (*inf: turn up*) se montrer ♦ *vt* (*flaw*) faire ressortir; **~ business** *n* le monde du spectacle; **~down** *n* épreuve *f* de force

shower ['ʃaʊər] *n* (*rain*) averse *f*; (*of stones etc*) pluie *f*, grêle *f*; (*~bath*) douche *f* ♦ *vi* prendre une douche, se doucher ♦ *vt*: **to ~ sb with** (*gifts etc*) combler qn de; **to have** *or* **take a ~** prendre une douche; **~proof** *adj* imperméabilisé(e)

showing ['ʃəʊɪŋ] *n* (*of film*) projection *f*

show jumping *n* concours *m* hippique

shown [ʃəʊn] *pp* of **show**

show: ~-off (*inf*) *n* (*person*) crâneur(-euse), m'as-tu-vu(e); **~piece** *n* (*of exhibition*) trésor *m*; **~room** *n* magasin *m or* salle *f* d'exposition

shrank [ʃræŋk] *pt* of **shrink**

shrapnel ['ʃræpnl] *n* éclats *mpl* d'obus

shred [ʃred] *n* (*gen pl*) lambeau *m*, petit morceau ♦ *vt* mettre en lambeaux, déchirer; (*CULIN: grate*) râper; (*: lettuce etc*) couper en lanières; **~der** *n* (*for vegetables*) râpeur *m*; (*for documents*) déchiqueteuse *f*

shrewd [ʃruːd] *adj* astucieux(-euse), perspicace; (*businessman*) habile

shriek [ʃriːk] *vi* hurler, crier

shrill [ʃrɪl] *adj* perçant(e), aigu(-guë), strident(e)

shrimp [ʃrɪmp] *n* crevette *f*

shrine [ʃraɪn] *n* (*place*) lieu *m* de

pèlerinage

shrink [ʃrɪŋk] (pt **shrank**, pp **shrunk**) vi rétrécir; (fig) se réduire, diminuer; (move: also: ~ **away**) reculer ♦ vt (wool) (faire) rétrécir ♦ n (inf: pej) psychiatre m/f, psy m/f; **to ~ from (doing) sth** reculer devant (la pensée de) faire qch; ~**wrap** vt emballer sous film plastique

shrivel [ˈʃrɪvl] vt (also: ~ **up**) ratatiner, flétrir ♦ vi se ratatiner, se flétrir

shroud [ʃraud] n linceul m ♦ vt: ~**ed in mystery** enveloppé(e) de mystère

Shrove Tuesday [ˈʃrəuv-] n (le) Mardi gras

shrub n arbuste m; ~**bery** n massif m d'arbustes

shrug [ʃrʌg] vt, vi: **to ~ (one's shoulders)** hausser les épaules; ~ **off** vt faire fi de

shrunk [ʃrʌŋk] pp of **shrink**

shudder [ˈʃʌdəʳ] vi frissonner, frémir

shuffle [ˈʃʌfl] vt (cards) battre; **to ~ (one's feet)** traîner les pieds

shun [ʃʌn] vt éviter, fuir

shunt [ʃʌnt] vt (RAIL) aiguiller

shut [ʃʌt] (pt, pp **shut**) vt fermer ♦ vi (se) fermer; ~ **down** vt, vi fermer définitivement; ~ **off** vt couper, arrêter; ~ **up** vi (inf: keep quiet) se taire ♦ vt (close) fermer; (silence) faire taire; ~**ter** n volet m; (PHOT) obturateur m

shuttle [ˈʃʌtl] n navette f; (also: ~ **service**) (service de) navette f; ~**cock** n volant m (de badminton); ~ **diplomacy** n navettes fpl diplomatiques

shy [ʃai] adj timide

Siberia [saiˈbiəriə] n Sibérie f

Sicily [ˈsɪsɪli] n Sicile f

sick [sik] adj (ill) malade; (vomiting): **to be ~** vomir; (humour) noir(e), macabre; **to feel ~** avoir envie de vomir, avoir mal au cœur; **to be ~ of** (fig) en avoir assez de; ~ **bay** n infirmerie f; ~**en** vt écœurer; ~**ening** adj (fig) écœurant(e), dégoûtant(e)

sickle [ˈsɪkl] n faucille f

sick: ~ **leave** n congé m de maladie; ~**ly** adj maladif(-ive), souffreteux(-euse); (causing nausea) écœurant(e); ~**ness** n mala-

die f; (vomiting) vomissement(s) m(pl); ~ **note** n (from parents) mot m d'absence; (from doctor) certificat médical; ~ **pay** n indemnité f de maladie

side [said] n côté m; (of lake, road) bord m; (team) camp m, équipe f ♦ adj (door, entrance) latéral(e) ♦ vi: **to ~ with sb** prendre le parti de qn, se ranger du côté de qn; **by the ~ of** au bord de; ~ **by ~** côte à côte; **from ~ to ~** d'un côté à l'autre; **to take ~s (with)** prendre parti (pour); ~**board** n buffet m; ~**boards** (BRIT), ~**burns** npl (whiskers) pattes fpl; ~ **drum** n tambour plat; ~ **effect** n effet m secondaire; ~**light** n (AUT) veilleuse f; ~**line** n (SPORT) (ligne f de) touche f; (fig) travail m secondaire; ~**long** adj oblique; ~**show** n attraction f; ~**step** vt (fig) éluder; éviter; ~ **street** n (petite) rue transversale; ~**track** vt (fig) faire dévier de son sujet; ~**walk** n (US) trottoir m; ~**ways** adv de côté

siding [ˈsaidɪŋ] n (RAIL) voie f de garage

siege [siːdʒ] n siège m

sieve [sɪv] n tamis m, passoire f

sift [sift] vt (fig: also: ~ **through**) passer en revue; (lit: flour etc) passer au tamis

sigh [sai] n soupir m ♦ vi soupirer, pousser un soupir

sight [sait] n (faculty) vue f; (spectacle) spectacle m; (on gun) mire f ♦ vt apercevoir; **in ~** visible; **out of ~** hors de vue; ~**seeing** n tourisme m; **to go ~seeing** faire du tourisme

sign [sain] n signe m; (with hand etc) signe, geste m; (notice) panneau m, écriteau m ♦ vt signer; ~ **on** vi (as unemployed) s'inscrire au chômage; (for course) s'inscrire ♦ vt (employee) embaucher; ~ **over** vt: **to ~ sth over to sb** céder qch par écrit à qn; ~ **up** vt engager ♦ vi (MIL) s'engager; (for course) s'inscrire

signal [ˈsɪgnl] n signal m ♦ vi (AUT) mettre son clignotant ♦ vt (person) faire signe à; (message) communiquer par signaux; ~**man** (irreg) n (RAIL) aiguilleur m

signature [ˈsɪgnətʃəʳ] n signature f; ~

tune *n* indicatif musical

signet ring ['signət-] *n* chevalière *f*

significance [sig'nifikəns] *n* signification *f*; importance *f*

significant [sig'nifikənt] *adj* significatif(-ive); (*important*) important(e), considérable

sign language *n* langage *m* per signes

signpost *n* poteau indicateur

silence ['sailəns] *n* silence *m* ♦ *vt* faire taire, réduire au silence; ~**r** *n* (*on gun*, BRIT: AUT) silencieux *m*

silent ['sailənt] *adj* silencieux(-euse); (*film*) muet(te); **to remain** ~ garder le silence, ne rien dire; ~ **partner** *n* (COMM) bailleur *m* de fonds, commanditaire *m*

silhouette [silu:'et] *n* silhouette *f*

silicon chip ['silikən-] *n* puce *f* électronique

silk [silk] *n* soie *f* ♦ *cpd* de or en soie; ~**y** *adj* soyeux(-euse)

silly ['sili] *adj* stupide, sot(te), bête

silt [silt] *n* vase *f*; limon *m*

silver ['silvər] *n* argent *m*; (*money*) monnaie *f* (en pièces d'argent); (*also:* ~**ware**) argenterie *f* ♦ *adj* d'argent, en argent; ~ **paper** (BRIT) *n* papier *m* d'argent or d'étain; ~-**plated** *adj* plaqué(e) argent *inv*; ~**smith** *n* orfèvre *m/f*; ~**y** *adj* argenté(e)

similar ['similər] *adj*: ~ (**to**) semblable (à); ~**ly** *adv* de la même façon, de même

simmer ['simər] *vi* cuire à feu doux, mijoter

simple ['simpl] *adj* simple; **simplicity** [sim'plisiti] *n* simplicité *f*; **simply** *adv* (*without fuss*) avec simplicité

simultaneous [siməl'teiniəs] *adj* simultané(e)

sin [sin] *n* péché *m* ♦ *vi* pécher

since [sins] *adv, prep* depuis ♦ *conj* (*time*) depuis que; (*because*) puisque, étant donné que, comme; ~ **then, ever** ~ depuis ce moment-là

sincere [sin'siər] *adj* sincère; ~**ly** *adv* see **yours**; **sincerity** [sin'seriti] *n* sincérité *f*

sinew ['sinju:] *n* tendon *m*

sing [siŋ] (*pt* **sang**, *pp* **sung**) *vt, vi* chanter

Singapore [siŋgə'pɔ:r] *n* Singapour *m*

singe [sindʒ] *vt* brûler légèrement; (*clothes*) roussir

singer ['siŋər] *n* chanteur(-euse)

singing ['siŋiŋ] *n* chant *m*

single ['siŋgl] *adj* seul(e), unique; (*unmarried*) célibataire; (*not double*) simple ♦ *n* (BRIT: *also:* ~ **ticket**) aller *m* (simple); (*record*) 45 tours *m*; ~ **out** *vt* choisir; (*distinguish*) distinguer; ~ **bed** *n* lit *m* d'une personne; ~-**breasted** *adj* droit(e); ~ **file** *n*: **in** ~ **file** en file indienne; ~-**handed** *adv* tout(e) seul(e), sans (aucune) aide; ~-**minded** *adj* résolu(e), tenace; ~ **parent** *n* parent *m* unique; ~ **room** *n* chambre *f* à un lit or pour une personne; ~**s** *n* (TENNIS) simple *m*; ~-**track road** *n* route *f* à voie unique; **singly** *adv* séparément

singular ['siŋgjulər] *adj* singulier(-ère), étrange; (*outstanding*) remarquable; (LING) (au) singulier, du singulier ♦ *n* singulier *m*

sinister ['sinistər] *adj* sinistre

sink [siŋk] (*pt* **sank**, *pp* **sunk**) *n* évier *m* ♦ *vt* (*ship*) (faire) couler, faire sombrer; (*foundations*) creuser ♦ *vi* couler, sombrer; (*ground etc*) s'affaisser; (*also:* ~ **back,** ~ **down**) s'affaisser, se laisser retomber; **to** ~ **sth into** enfoncer qch dans; **my heart sank** j'ai complètement perdu courage; ~ **in** *vi* (*fig*) pénétrer, être compris(e)

sinner ['sinər] *n* pécheur(-eresse)

sinus ['sainəs] *n* sinus *m inv*

sip [sip] *n* gorgée *f* ♦ *vt* boire à petites gorgées

siphon ['saifən] *n* siphon *m*; ~ **off** *vt* siphonner; (*money: illegally*) détourner

sir [sər] *n* monsieur *m*; **S~ John Smith** sir John Smith; **yes** ~ oui, Monsieur

siren ['saiərn] *n* sirène *f*

sirloin ['sə:lɔin] *n* (*also:* ~ **steak**) aloyau *m*

sissy ['sisi] (*inf*) *n* (*coward*) poule mouillée

sister ['sistər] *n* sœur *f*; (*nun*) religieuse *f*, sœur; (BRIT: *nurse*) infirmière *f* en chef; ~-**in-law** *n* belle-sœur *f*

sit [sit] (*pt, pp* **sat**) *vi* s'asseoir; (*be* ~*ting*) être assis(e); (*assembly*) être en séance, siéger; (*for painter*) poser ♦ *vt* (*exam*) passer, se présenter à; ~ **down** *vi* s'asseoir; ~ **in on** *vt fus* assister à; ~ **up** *vi* s'asseoir; (*straight*) se redresser; (*not go to bed*) rester debout, ne pas se coucher

sitcom ['sɪtkɔm] *n abbr* (= *situation comedy*) comédie *f* de situation

site [saɪt] *n* emplacement *m*, site *m*; (*also:* **building ~**) chantier *m* ♦ *vt* placer

sit-in ['sɪtɪn] *n* (*demonstration*) sit-in *m inv*, occupation *f* (de locaux)

sitting ['sɪtɪŋ] *n* (*of assembly etc*) séance *f*; (*in canteen*) service *m*; ~ **room** *n* salon *m*

situated ['sɪtjueɪtɪd] *adj* situé(e)

situation [sɪtju'eɪʃən] *n* situation *f*; **"~s vacant"** (*BRIT*) "offres d'emploi"

six [sɪks] *num* six; ~**teen** *num* seize; ~**th** *num* sixième; ~**ty** *num* soixante

size [saɪz] *n* taille *f*; dimensions *fpl*; (*of clothing*) taille *f*; (*of shoes*) pointure *f*; (*fig*) ampleur *f*; (*glue*) colle *f*; ~ **up** *vt* juger, jauger; ~**able** *adj* assez grand(e); assez important(e)

sizzle ['sɪzl] *vi* grésiller

skate [skeɪt] *n* patin *m*; (*fish: pl inv*) raie *f* ♦ *vi* patiner; ~**board** *n* skateboard *m*, planche *f* à roulettes; ~**boarding** *n* skateboard *m*; ~**r** *n* patineur(-euse); **skating** *n* patinage *m*; **skating rink** *n* patinoire *f*

skeleton ['skelɪtn] *n* squelette *m*; (*outline*) schéma *m*; ~ **staff** *n* effectifs réduits

skeptical ['skeptɪkl] (*US*) *adj* = **sceptical**

sketch [sketʃ] *n* (*drawing*) croquis *m*, esquisse *f*; (*THEATRE*) sketch *m*, saynète *f* ♦ *vt* esquisser, faire un croquis *or* une esquisse de; ~ **book** *n* carnet *m* à dessin; ~**y** *adj* incomplet(-ète), fragmentaire

skewer ['skju:ər] *n* brochette *f*

ski [ski:] *n* ski *m* ♦ *vi* skier, faire du ski; ~ **boot** *n* chaussure *f* de ski

skid [skɪd] *vi* déraper

ski: ~**er** *n* skieur(-euse); ~**ing** *n* ski *m*; ~ **jump** *n* saut *m* à skis

skilful ['skɪlful] (*US* **skillful**) *adj* habile, adroit(e)

ski lift *n* remonte-pente *m inv*

skill [skɪl] *n* habileté *f*, adresse *f*, talent *m*;

(*requiring training: gen pl*) compétences *fpl*; ~**ed** *adj* habile, adroit(e); (*worker*) qualifié(e)

skim [skɪm] *vt* (*milk*) écrémer; (*glide over*) raser, effleurer ♦ *vi*: **to ~ through** (*fig*) parcourir; ~**med milk** *n* lait écrémé

skimp [skɪmp] *vt* (*also:* ~ **on**: *work*) bâcler, faire à la va-vite; (: *cloth etc*) lésiner sur; ~**y** *adj* (*skirt*) étriqué(e)

skin [skɪn] *n* peau *f* ♦ *vt* (*fruit etc*) éplucher; (*animal*) écorcher; ~ **cancer** *n* cancer *m* de la peau; ~-**deep** *adj* superficiel(le); ~-**diving** *n* plongée sous-marine; ~**head** *n* skinhead *m/f*; ~**ny** *adj* maigre, maigrichon(ne); ~**tight** *adj* (*jeans etc*) moulant(e), ajusté(e)

skip [skɪp] *n* petit bond *or* saut *m*; (*BRIT: container*) benne *f* ♦ *vi* gambader, sautiller; (*with rope*) sauter à la corde ♦ *vt* sauter

ski pass *n* forfait-skieur(s) *m*

ski pole *n* bâton *m* de ski

skipper ['skɪpər] *n* capitaine *m*; (*in race*) skipper *m*

skipping rope ['skɪpɪŋ-] (*BRIT*) *n* corde *f* à sauter

skirmish ['skɜ:mɪʃ] *n* escarmouche *f*, accrochage *m*

skirt [skɜ:t] *n* jupe *f* ♦ *vt* longer, contourner; ~**ing board** (*BRIT*) *n* plinthe *f*

ski: ~ **slope** *n* piste *f* de ski; ~ **suit** *n* combinaison *f* (de ski); ~ **tow** *n* remonte-pente *m inv*

skittle ['skɪtl] *n* quille *f*; ~**s** *n* (*game*) (jeu *m* de) quilles *fpl*

skive [skaɪv] (*BRIT: inf*) *vi* tirer au flanc

skull [skʌl] *n* crâne *m*

skunk [skʌŋk] *n* mouffette *f*

sky [skaɪ] *n* ciel *m*; ~**light** *n* lucarne *f*; ~**scraper** *n* gratte-ciel *m inv*

slab [slæb] *n* (*of stone*) dalle *f*; (*of food*) grosse tranche

slack [slæk] *adj* (*loose*) lâche, desserré(e); (*slow*) stagnant(e); (*careless*) peu sérieux(-euse) *or* conscientieux(-euse); ~**s** *npl* (*trousers*) pantalon *m*; ~**en** *vi* ralentir, diminuer ♦ *vt* (*speed*) réduire; (*grip*) relâcher; (clothing) desserrer

slag heap [slæg-] n crassier m

slag off (BRIT: inf) vt dire du mal de

slam [slæm] vt (door) (faire) claquer; (throw) jeter violemment, flanquer (fam); (criticize) démolir ♦ vi claquer

slander ['slɑːndəʳ] n calomnie f; diffamation f

slang [slæŋ] n argot m

slant [slɑːnt] n inclinaison f; (fig) angle m, point m de vue; ~**ed** adj = **slanting**; ~**ing** adj en pente, incliné(e); ~**ing eyes** yeux bridés

slap [slæp] n claque f, gifle f; tape f ♦ vt donner une claque or une gifle or une tape à; (paint) appliquer rapidement ♦ adv (directly) tout droit, en plein; ~**dash** adj fait(e) sans soin or à la va-vite; (person) insouciant(e), négligent(e); ~**stick** n (comedy) grosse farce, style m tarte à la crème; ~**-up** (BRIT) adj: **a ~-up meal** un repas extra or fameux

slash [slæʃ] vt entailler, taillader; (fig: prices) casser

slat [slæt] n latte f, lame f

slate [sleɪt] n ardoise f ♦ vt (fig: criticize) éreinter, démolir

slaughter ['slɔːtəʳ] n carnage m, massacre m ♦ vt (animal) abattre; (people) massacrer; ~**house** n abattoir m

slave [sleɪv] n esclave m/f ♦ vi (also: ~ **away**) trimer, travailler comme un forçat; ~**ry** n esclavage m

slay [sleɪ] (pt **slew**, pp **slain**) vt tuer

sleazy ['sliːzɪ] adj miteux(-euse), minable

sledge [slɛdʒ] n luge f ♦ vi: **to go sledging** faire de la luge

sledgehammer n marteau m de forgeron

sleek [sliːk] adj (hair, fur etc) brillant(e), lisse; (car, boat etc) aux lignes pures or élégantes

sleep [sliːp] (pt, pp **slept**) n sommeil m ♦ vi dormir; (spend night) dormir, coucher; **to go to ~** s'endormir; **~ around** vi coucher à droite et à gauche; **~ in** vi (oversleep) se réveiller trop tard; ~**er** (BRIT) n

(RAIL: train) train-couchettes m; (: berth) couchette f; ~**ing bag** n sac m de couchage; ~**ing car** n (RAIL) wagon-lit m, voiture-lit f; ~**ing partner** (BRIT) n = **silent partner**; ~**ing pill** n somnifère m; ~**less** adj: **a ~less night** une nuit blanche; ~**walker** n somnambule m/f; ~**y** adj qui a sommeil; (fig) endormi(e)

sleet [sliːt] n neige fondue

sleeve [sliːv] n manche f; (of record) pochette f

sleigh [sleɪ] n traîneau m

sleight [slaɪt] n: **~ of hand** tour m de passe-passe

slender ['slɛndəʳ] adj svelte, mince; (fig) faible, ténu(e)

slept [slɛpt] pt, pp of **sleep**

slew [sluː] vi (also: ~ **around**) virer, pivoter ♦ pt of **slay**

slice [slaɪs] n tranche f; (round) rondelle f; (utensil) spatule f, truelle f ♦ vt couper en tranches (or en rondelles)

slick [slɪk] adj (skilful) brillant(e) (en apparence); (salesman) qui a du bagout ♦ n (also: **oil ~**) nappe f de pétrole, marée noire

slide [slaɪd] (pt, pp **slid**) n (in playground) toboggan m; (PHOT) diapositive f; (BRIT: also: **hair ~**) barrette f; (in prices) chute f, baisse f ♦ vt (faire) glisser ♦ vi glisser; **sliding** adj (door) coulissant(e); **sliding scale** n échelle f mobile

slight [slaɪt] adj (slim) mince, menu(e); (frail) frêle; (trivial) faible, insignifiant(e); (small) petit(e), léger(-ère) (before n) ♦ n offense f, affront m; **not in the ~est** pas le moins du monde, pas du tout; ~**ly** adv légèrement, un peu

slim [slɪm] adj mince ♦ vi maigrir; (diet) suivre un régime amaigrissant

slime [slaɪm] n (mud) vase f; (other substance) substance visqueuse

slimming ['slɪmɪŋ] adj (diet, pills) amaigrissant(e); (foodstuff) qui ne fait pas grossir

sling [slɪŋ] (pt, pp **slung**) n (MED) écharpe f; (for baby) porte-bébé m; (weapon) fronde f, lance-pierre m ♦ vt lancer, jeter

slip [slɪp] n faux pas; (mistake) erreur f; étourderie f; bévue f; (underskirt) combinaison f; (of paper) petite feuille, fiche f ♦ vt (slide) glisser ♦ vi glisser; (decline) baisser; (move smoothly): **to ~ into/out of** se glisser or se faufiler dans/hors de; **to ~ sth on/off** enfiler/enlever qch; **to give sb the ~** fausser compagnie à qn; **a ~ of the tongue** un lapsus; **~ away** vi s'esquiver; **~ in** vt glisser ♦ vi (errors) s'y glisser; **~ out** vi sortir; **~ up** vi faire une erreur, gaffer; **~ped disc** n déplacement m de vertèbre

slipper ['slɪpə'] n pantoufle f

slippery ['slɪpərɪ] adj glissant(e)

slip: **~ road** (BRIT) n (to motorway) bretelle f d'accès; **~-up** n bévue f; **~way** n cale f (de construction or de lancement)

slit [slɪt] (pt, pp slit) n fente f; (cut) incision f ♦ vt fendre; couper; inciser

slither ['slɪðə'] vi glisser; (snake) onduler

sliver ['slɪvə'] n (of glass, wood) éclat m; (of cheese etc) petit morceau, fine tranche

slob [slɔb] (inf) n rustaud(e)

slog [slɔg] (BRIT) vi travailler très dur ♦ n gros effort; tâche fastidieuse

slogan ['sləʊgən] n slogan m

slope [sləʊp] n pente f, côte f; (side of mountain) versant m; (slant) inclinaison f ♦ vi: **to ~ down** être or descendre en pente; **to ~ up** monter; **sloping** adj en pente; (writing) penché(e)

sloppy ['slɔpɪ] adj (work) peu soigné(e), bâclé(e); (appearance) négligé(e), débraillé(e)

slot [slɔt] n fente f ♦ vt: **to ~ sth into** encastrer or insérer qch dans

sloth [sləʊθ] n (laziness) paresse f

slouch [slaʊtʃ] vi avoir le dos rond, être voûté(e)

slovenly ['slʌvənlɪ] adj sale, débraillé(e); (work) négligé(e)

slow [sləʊ] adj lent(e); (watch): **to be ~** retarder ♦ adv lentement ♦ vt, vi (also: **~ down, ~ up**) ralentir; **"~"** (road sign) "ralentir"; **~ly** adv lentement; **~ motion** n: **in ~ motion** au ralenti

sludge [slʌdʒ] n boue f

slug [slʌg] n limace f; (bullet) balle f

sluggish ['slʌgɪʃ] adj (person) mou (molle), lent(e); (stream, engine, trading) lent

sluice [slu:s] n (also: **~ gate**) vanne f

slum [slʌm] n (house) taudis m

slump [slʌmp] n baisse soudaine, effondrement m; (ECON) crise f ♦ vi s'effondrer, s'affaisser

slung [slʌŋ] pt, pp of **sling**

slur [slɜː'] n (fig: smear): **~ (on)** atteinte f (à); insinuation f (contre) ♦ vt mal articuler

slush [slʌʃ] n neige fondue

slut [slʌt] (pej) n souillon f

sly [slaɪ] adj (person) rusé(e); (smile, expression, remark) sournois(e)

smack [smæk] n (slap) tape f; (on face) gifle f ♦ vt donner une tape à; (on face) gifler; (on bottom) donner la fessée à ♦ vi: **to ~ of** avoir des relents de, sentir

small [smɔːl] adj petit(e); **~ ads** (BRIT) npl petites annonces; **~ change** n petite or menue monnaie; **~holder** (BRIT) n petit cultivateur; **~ hours** npl: **in the ~ hours** au petit matin; **~pox** n variole f; **~ talk** n menus propos

smart [smɑːt] adj (neat, fashionable) élégant(e), chic inv; (clever) intelligent(e), astucieux(-euse), futé(e); (quick) rapide, vif (vive), prompt(e) ♦ vi faire mal, brûler; (fig) être piqué(e) au vif; **~ card** n carte à puce; **~en up** vi devenir plus élégant(e), se faire beau (belle) ♦ vt rendre plus élégant(e)

smash [smæʃ] n (also: **~-up**) collision f, accident m; (also: **~ hit**) succès foudroyant ♦ vt casser, briser, fracasser; (opponent) écraser; (SPORT: record) pulvériser ♦ vi se briser, se fracasser; s'écraser; **~ing** (inf) adj formidable

smattering ['smætərɪŋ] n: **a ~ of** quelques notions de

smear [smɪə'] n tache f, salissure f; trace f; (MED) frottis m ♦ vt enduire; (make dirty) salir; **~ campaign** n campagne f de diffamation

smell [smɛl] (*pt, pp* **smelt** *or* **smelled**) *n* odeur *f*; (*sense*) odorat *m* ♦ *vt* sentir ♦ *vi* (*food etc*): **to ~ (of)** sentir (de); (*pej*) sentir mauvais; **~y** *adj* qui sent mauvais, malodorant(e)

smile [smaɪl] *n* sourire *m* ♦ *vi* sourire

smirk [smɜːk] *n* petit sourire suffisant *or* affecté

smock [smɔk] *n* blouse *f*

smog [smɔg] *n* brouillard mêlé de fumée, smog *m*

smoke [sməʊk] *n* fumée *f* ♦ *vt, vi* fumer; **~d** *adj* (*bacon, glass*) fumé(e); **~r** *n* (*person*) fumeur(-euse); (*RAIL*) wagon *m* fumeurs; **~ screen** *n* rideau *m* or écran *m* de fumée; (*fig*) paravent *m*; **smoking** *n* tabagisme *m*; **"no smoking"** (*sign*) "défense de fumer"; **to give up smoking** arrêter de fumer; **smoking compartment** (*US* **smoking car**) *n* wagon *m* fumeurs; **smoky** *adj* enfumé(e); (*taste*) fumé(e)

smolder ['sməʊldər] (*US*) *vi* = **smoulder**

smooth [smuːð] *adj* lisse; (*sauce*) onctueux(-euse); (*flavour, whisky*) moelleux(-euse); (*movement*) régulier(-ère), sans à-coups *or* heurts; (*pej: person*) doucereux(-euse), mielleux(-euse) ♦ *vt* (*also:* **~ out**: *skirt, paper*) lisser, défroisser; (: *creases, difficulties*) faire disparaître

smother ['smʌðər] *vt* étouffer

smoulder ['sməʊldər] (*US* **smolder**) *vi* couver

smudge [smʌdʒ] *n* tache *f*, bavure *f* ♦ *vt* salir, maculer

smug [smʌg] *adj* suffisant(e)

smuggle ['smʌgl] *vt* passer en contrebande *or* en fraude; **~r** *n* contrebandier(-ère); **smuggling** *n* contrebande *f*

smutty ['smʌtɪ] *adj* (*fig*) grossier(-ère), obscène

snack [snæk] *n* casse-croûte *m inv*; **~ bar** *n* snack(-bar) *m*

snag [snæg] *n* inconvénient *m*, difficulté *f*

snail [sneɪl] *n* escargot *m*

snake [sneɪk] *n* serpent *m*

snap [snæp] *n* (*sound*) claquement *m*, bruit sec; (*photograph*) photo *f*, instantané *m* ♦ *adj* subit(e); fait(e) sans réfléchir ♦ *vt* (*break*) casser net; (*fingers*) faire claquer ♦ *vi* se casser net *or* avec un bruit sec; (*speak sharply*) parler d'un ton brusque; **to ~ shut** se refermer brusquement; **~ at** *vt fus* (*subj: dog*) essayer de mordre; **~ off** *vi* (*break*) casser net; **~ up** *vt* sauter sur, saisir; **~py** (*inf*) *adj* prompt(e); (*slogan*) qui a du punch; **make it ~py!** grouille-toi!, et que ça saute!; **~shot** *n* photo *f*, instantané *m*

snare [snɛər] *n* piège *m*

snarl [snɑːl] *vi* gronder

snatch [snætʃ] *n* (*small amount*): **~es of** des fragments *mpl* or bribes *fpl* de ♦ *vt* saisir (*d'un geste vif*); (*steal*) voler

sneak [sniːk] *vi*: **to ~ in/out** entrer/sortir furtivement *or* à la dérobée ♦ *n* (*inf: pej: informer*) faux jeton; **to ~ up on sb** s'approcher de qn sans faire de bruit; **~ers** *npl* tennis *mpl*, baskets *mpl*

sneer [snɪər] *vi* ricaner; **to ~ at** traiter avec mépris

sneeze [sniːz] *vi* éternuer

sniff [snɪf] *vi* renifler ♦ *vt* renifler, flairer; (*glue, drugs*) sniffer, respirer

snigger ['snɪgər] *vi* ricaner; pouffer de rire

snip [snɪp] *n* (*cut*) petit coup; (*BRIT: inf: bargain*) (bonne) occasion *or* affaire *f* ♦ *vt* couper

sniper ['snaɪpər] *n* tireur embusqué

snippet ['snɪpɪt] *n* bribe(s) *f(pl)*

snob [snɔb] *n* snob *m/f*; **~bish** *adj* snob *inv*

snooker ['snuːkər] *n* sorte de jeu de billard

snoop [snuːp] *vi*: **to ~ about** fureter

snooze [snuːz] *n* petit somme ♦ *vi* faire un petit somme

snore [snɔːr] *vi* ronfler

snorkel ['snɔːkl] *n* (*of swimmer*) tuba *m*

snort [snɔːt] *vi* grogner; (*horse*) renâcler

snout [snaʊt] *n* museau *m*

snow [snəʊ] *n* neige *f* ♦ *vi* neiger; **~ball** *n* boule *f* de neige; **~bound** *adj* enneigé(e), bloqué(e) par la neige; **~drift** *n* congère *f*; **~drop** *n* perce-neige *m or f*; **~fall** *n* chute *f* de neige; **~flake** *n* flocon *m* de neige; **~man** (*irreg*) *n* bonhomme *m* de neige; **~plough** (*US* **snowplow**) *n* chasse-neige *m inv*; **~shoe** *n* raquette *f* (*pour la neige*); **~storm** *n* tempête *f* de neige

snub [snʌb] *vt* repousser, snober ♦ *n* rebuffade *f*; **~-nosed** *adj* au nez retroussé

snuff [snʌf] *n* tabac *m* à priser

snug [snʌg] *adj* douillet(te), confortable; (*person*) bien au chaud

snuggle ['snʌgl] *vi*: **to ~ up to sb** se serrer *or* se blottir contre qn

---

KEYWORD

---

so [səu] *adv* **1** (*thus, likewise*) ainsi; **if so** si oui; **so do** *or* **have I** moi aussi; **it's 5 o'clock – so it is!** il est 5 heures – en effet! *or* c'est vrai!; **I hope/think so** je l'espère/le crois; **so far** jusqu'ici, jusqu'à maintenant; (*in past*) jusque-là

2 (*in comparisons etc*: *to such a degree*) si, tellement; **so big (that)** si *or* tellement grand (que); **she's not so clever as her brother** elle n'est pas aussi intelligente que son frère

3: **so much**
♦ *adj, adv* tant (de); **I've got so much work** j'ai tant de travail; **I love you so much** je vous aime tant; **so many** tant (de)

4 (*phrases*): **10 or so** à peu près *or* environ 10; **so long!** (*inf*: *goodbye*) au revoir!, à un de ces jours!

♦ *conj* **1** (*expressing purpose*): **so as to do** pour faire, afin de faire; **so (that)** pour que *or* afin que +*sub*

2 (*expressing result*) donc, par conséquent; **so that** si bien que, de (telle) sorte que

---

soak [səuk] *vt* faire tremper; (*drench*) tremper ♦ *vi* tremper; **~ in** *vi* être absorbé(e); **~ up** *vt* absorber; **~ing** *adj* trempé(e)

soap [səup] *n* savon *m*; **~flakes** *npl* paillettes *fpl* de savon; **~ opera** *n* feuilleton télévisé; **~ powder** *n* lessive *f*; **~y** *adj* savonneux(-euse)

soar [sɔːʳ] *vi* monter (en flèche), s'élancer;

(*building*) s'élancer

sob [sɔb] *n* sanglot *m* ♦ *vi* sangloter

sober ['səubəʳ] *adj* qui n'est pas (*or* plus) ivre; (*serious*) sérieux(-euse), sensé(e); (*colour, style*) sobre, discret(-ète); **~ up** *vt* dessoûler (*inf*) ♦ *vi* dessoûler (*inf*)

so-called ['səu'kɔːld] *adj* soi-disant *inv*

soccer ['sɔkəʳ] *n* football *m*

social ['səuʃl] *adj* social(e); (*sociable*) sociable ♦ *n* (petite) fête; **~ club** *n* amicale *f*, foyer *m*; **~ism** *n* socialisme *m*; **~ist** *adj* socialiste ♦ *n* socialiste *m/f*; **~ize** *vi*: **to ~ize (with)** lier connaissance (avec); parler (avec); **~ security** (*BRIT*) *n* aide sociale; **~ work** *n* assistance sociale, travail social; **~ worker** *n* assistant(e) social(e)

society [sə'saɪətɪ] *n* société *f*; (*club*) société, association *f*; (*also*: **high ~**) (haute) société, grand monde

sociology [səusɪ'ɔlədʒɪ] *n* sociologie *f*

sock [sɔk] *n* chaussette *f*

socket ['sɔkɪt] *n* cavité *f*; (*BRIT*: *ELEC*: *also*: **wall ~**) prise *f* de courant

sod [sɔd] *n* (*of earth*) motte *f*; (*BRIT*: *inf!*) con *m* (*!*); salaud *m* (*!*)

soda ['səudə] *n* (*CHEM*) soude *f*; (*also*: **~ water**) eau *f* de Seltz; (*US*: *also*: **~ pop**) soda *m*

sofa ['səufə] *n* sofa *m*, canapé *m*

soft [sɔft] *adj* (*not rough*) doux (douce); (*not hard*) doux; mou (molle); (*not loud*) doux, léger(-ère); (*kind*) doux, gentil(le); **~ drink** *n* boisson non alcoolisée; **~en** *vt* (r)amollir; (*fig*) adoucir; atténuer ♦ *vi* se ramollir; s'adoucir; s'atténuer; **~ly** *adv* doucement; gentiment; **~ness** *n* douceur *f*; **~ware** *n* (*COMPUT*) logiciel *m*, software *m*

soggy ['sɔgɪ] *adj* trempé(e); détrempé(e)

soil [sɔɪl] *n* (*earth*) sol *m*, terre *f* ♦ *vt* salir; (*fig*) souiller

solar ['səuləʳ] *adj* solaire; **~ panel** *n* panneau *m* solaire; **~ power** *n* énergie solaire

sold [səuld] *pt, pp of* sell

solder ['səuldəʳ] *vt* souder (*au fil à souder*) ♦ *n* soudure *f*

soldier ['səʊldʒəʳ] n soldat m, militaire m

sole [səʊl] n (of foot) plante f; (of shoe) semelle f; (fish: pl inv) sole f ♦ adj seul(e), unique

solemn ['sɒləm] adj solennel(le); (person) sérieux(-euse), grave

sole trader n (COMM) chef m d'entreprise individuelle

solicit [sə'lɪsɪt] vt (request) solliciter ♦ vi (prostitute) racoler

solicitor [sə'lɪsɪtəʳ] n (for wills etc) ≈ notaire m; (in court) ≈ avocat m

solid ['sɒlɪd] adj solide; (not hollow) plein(e), compact(e), massif(-ive); (entire): **3 ~ hours** 3 heures entières ♦ n solide m

solidarity [sɒlɪ'dærɪtɪ] n solidarité f

solitary ['sɒlɪtərɪ] adj solitaire; ~ **confinement** n (LAW) isolement m

solo ['səʊləʊ] n solo m ♦ adv (fly) en solitaire; ~**ist** n soliste m/f

soluble ['sɒljʊbl] adj soluble

solution [sə'lu:ʃən] n solution f

solve [sɒlv] vt résoudre

solvent ['sɒlvənt] adj (COMM) solvable ♦ n (CHEM) (dis)solvant m

KEYWORD

some [sʌm] adj 1 (a certain amount or number of): **some tea/water/ice cream** du thé/de l'eau/de la glace; **some children/apples** des enfants/pommes

2 (certain: in contrasts): **some people say that ...** il y a des gens qui disent que ...; **some films were excellent, but most ...** certains films étaient excellents, mais la plupart ...

3 (unspecified): **some woman was asking for you** il y avait une dame qui vous demandait; **he was asking for some book (or other)** il demandait un livre quelconque; **some day** un de ces jours; **some day next week** un jour la semaine prochaine

♦ pron 1 (a certain number) quelques-un(e)s, certain(e)s; **I've got some** (books etc) j'en ai (quelques-uns); **some (of them) have been sold** certains ont été vendus

2 (a certain amount) un peu; **I've got some** (money, milk) j'en ai (un peu)

♦ adv: **some 10 people** quelque 10 personnes, 10 personnes environ

some: ~body ['sʌmbədɪ] pron = **someone**; ~**how** adv d'une façon ou d'une autre; (for some reason) pour une raison ou une autre; ~**one** pron quelqu'un; ~**place** (US) adv = **somewhere**

somersault ['sʌməsɔ:lt] n culbute f, saut périlleux ♦ vi faire la culbute or un saut périlleux; (car) faire un tonneau

some: ~thing pron quelque chose; ~**thing interesting** quelque chose d'intéressant; ~**time** adv (in future) un de ces jours, un jour ou l'autre; (in past): ~**time last month** au cours du mois dernier; ~**times** adv quelquefois, parfois; ~**what** adv quelque peu, un peu; ~**where** adv quelque part

son [sʌn] n fils m

song [sɒŋ] n chanson f; (of bird) chant m

son-in-law n gendre m, beau-fils m

soon [su:n] adv bientôt; (early) tôt; ~ **afterwards** peu après; see also **as**; ~**er** adv (time) plus tôt; (preference): **I would ~er do** j'aimerais autant or je préférerais faire; ~**er or later** tôt ou tard

soot [sʊt] n suie f

soothe [su:ð] vt calmer, apaiser

sophisticated [sə'fɪstɪkeɪtɪd] adj raffiné(e); sophistiqué(e); (machinery) hautement perfectionné(e), très complexe

sophomore ['sɒfəmɔ:ʳ] (US) n étudiant(e) de seconde année

sopping ['sɒpɪŋ] adj (also: ~ **wet**) complètement trempé(e)

soppy ['sɒpɪ] (pej) adj sentimental(e)

soprano [sə'prɑ:nəʊ] n (singer) soprano m/f

sorcerer ['sɔ:sərəʳ] n sorcier m

sore [sɔ:ʳ] adj (painful) douloureux(-euse), sensible ♦ n plaie f; ~**ly** ['sɔ:lɪ] adv (tempted) fortement

sorrow ['sɒrəʊ] n peine f, chagrin m

sorry ['sɔrɪ] *adj* désolé(e); (*condition, excuse*) triste, déplorable; ~! pardon!, excusez-moi!; ~? pardon?; **to feel ~ for sb** plaindre qn

sort [sɔːt] *n* genre *m*, espèce *f*, sorte *f* ♦ *vt* (*also:* ~ **out**) trier; classer; ranger; (: *problems*) résoudre, régler; ~**ing office** ['sɔːtɪŋ-] *n* bureau *m* de tri

SOS *n* S.O.S. *m*

so-so ['səusəu] *adv* comme ci comme ça

sought [sɔːt] *pt, pp of* **seek**

soul [səul] *n* âme *f*; ~**ful** ['səulful] *adj* sentimental(e); (*eyes*) expressif(-ive)

sound [saund] *adj* (*healthy*) en bonne santé, sain(e); (*safe, not damaged*) solide, en bon état; (*reliable, not superficial*) sérieux(-euse), solide; (*sensible*) sensé(e) ♦ *adv*: ~ **asleep** profondément endormi(e) ♦ *n* son *m*; bruit *m*; (GEO) détroit *m*, bras *m* de mer ♦ *vt* (*alarm*) sonner ♦ *vi* sonner, retentir; (*fig: seem*) sembler (être); **to ~ like** ressembler à; ~ **out** *vt* sonder; ~ **barrier** *n* mur *m* du son; ~ **bite** *n* phrase *f* toute faite (*pour être citée dans les médias*); ~ **effects** *npl* bruitage *m*; ~**ly** *adv* (*sleep*) profondément; (*beat*) complètement, à plate couture; ~**proof** *adj* insonorisé(e); ~**track** *n* (*of film*) bande *f* sonore

soup [suːp] *n* soupe *f*, potage *m*; ~ **plate** *n* assiette creuse *or* à soupe; ~**spoon** *n* cuiller *f* à soupe

sour ['sauəʳ] *adj* aigre; **it's ~ grapes** (*fig*) c'est du dépit

source [sɔːs] *n* source *f*

south [sauθ] *n* sud *m* ♦ *adj* sud *inv*, du sud ♦ *adv* au sud, vers le sud; **S~ Africa** *n* Afrique *f* du Sud; **S~ African** *adj* sud-africain(e) ♦ *n* Sud-Africain(e); **S~ America** *n* Amérique *f* du Sud; **S~ American** *adj* sud-américain(e) ♦ *n* Sud-Américain(e); ~-**east** *n* sud-est *m*; ~**erly** ['sʌðəlɪ] *adj* du sud; au sud; ~**ern** ['sʌðən] *adj* (du) sud; méridional(e); **S~ Pole** *n* Pôle *m* Sud; **S~ Wales** *n* sud *m* du Pays de Galles; ~**ward(s)** *adv* vers le sud; ~-**west** *n* sud-ouest *m*

souvenir [suːvəˈnɪəʳ] *n* (*objet*) souvenir *m*

sovereign ['sɔvrɪn] *n* souverain(e)

soviet ['səuvɪət] *adj* soviétique; **the S~ Union** l'Union *f* soviétique

sow[1] [sau] *n* truie *f*

sow[2] [səu] (*pt* **sowed**, *pp* **sown**) *vt* semer

sown [səun] *pp of* **sow**

soya ['sɔɪə] (US **soy**) *n*: ~ **bean** graine *f* de soja; **soy(a) sauce** sauce *f* au soja

spa [spɑː] *n* (*town*) station thermale; (US: *also:* **health ~**) établissement *m* de cure de rajeunissement *etc*

space [speɪs] *n* espace *m*; (*room*) place *f*; espace; (*length of time*) laps *m* de temps ♦ *cpd* spatial(e) ♦ *vt* (*also:* ~ **out**) espacer; ~**craft** *n* engin spatial; ~**man** (*irreg*) *n* astronaute *m*, cosmonaute *m*; ~**ship** *n* = **spacecraft**; **spacing** *n* espacement *m*; **spacious** ['speɪʃəs] *adj* spacieux(-euse), grand(e)

spade [speɪd] *n* (*tool*) bêche *f*, pelle *f*; (*child's*) pelle *f*; ~**s** *npl* (CARDS) pique *m*

Spain [speɪn] *n* Espagne *f*

span [spæn] *n* (*of bird, plane*) envergure *f*; (*of arch*) portée *f*; (*in time*) espace *m* de temps, durée *f* ♦ *vt* enjamber, franchir; (*fig*) couvrir, embrasser

Spaniard ['spænjəd] *n* Espagnol(e)

spaniel ['spænjəl] *n* épagneul *m*

Spanish ['spænɪʃ] *adj* espagnol(e) ♦ *n* (LING) espagnol *m*; **the ~** *npl* les Espagnols *mpl*

spank [spæŋk] *vt* donner une fessée à

spanner ['spænəʳ] (BRIT) *n* clé *f* (de mécanicien)

spare [speəʳ] *adj* de réserve, de rechange; (*surplus*) de *or* en trop, de reste ♦ *n* (*part*) pièce *f* de rechange, pièce détachée ♦ *vt* (*do without*) se passer de; (*afford to give*) donner, accorder; (*refrain from hurting*) épargner; **to ~** (*surplus*) en surplus, de trop; ~ **part** *n* pièce de rechange, pièce détachée; ~ **time** *n* moments *mpl* de loisir, temps *m* libre; ~ **wheel** *n* (AUT) roue *f* de secours; **sparingly** *adv* avec modération

spark [spɑːk] *n* étincelle *f*; ~(**ing**) **plug** *n* bougie *f*

sparkle ['spɑːkl] n scintillement m, éclat m ♦ vi étinceler, scintiller; **sparkling** adj (wine) mousseux(-euse), pétillant(e); (water) pétillant(e); (fig: conversation, performance) étincelant(e), pétillant(e)

sparrow ['spærəʊ] n moineau m

sparse [spɑːs] adj clairsemé(e)

spartan ['spɑːtən] adj (fig) spartiate

spasm ['spæzəm] n (MED) spasme m; **~odic** [spæz'mɒdɪk] adj (fig) intermittent(e)

spastic ['spæstɪk] n handicapé(e) moteur

spat [spæt] pt, pp of **spit**

spate [speɪt] n (fig): **a ~ of** une avalanche or un torrent de

spawn [spɔːn] vi frayer ♦ n frai m

speak [spiːk] (pt **spoke**, pp **spoken**) vt parler; (truth) dire ♦ vi parler; (make a speech) prendre la parole; **to ~ to sb/of** or **about sth** parler à qn/de qch; **~ up!** parle plus fort!; **~er** n (in public) orateur m; (also: **loudspeaker**) haut-parleur m; **the S~er** (BRIT: POL) le président de la chambre des Communes; (US: POL) le président de la chambre des Représentants

spear [spɪər] n lance f ♦ vt transpercer; **~head** vt (attack etc) mener

spec [spek] (inf) n: **on ~** à tout hasard

special ['speʃl] adj spécial(e); **~ist** n spécialiste m/f; **~ity** [speʃɪ'ælɪtɪ] n spécialité f; **~ize** vi: **to ~ize (in)** se spécialiser (dans); **~ly** adv spécialement, particulièrement; **~ty** (esp US) n = **speciality**

species ['spiːʃiːz] n inv espèce f

specific [spə'sɪfɪk] adj précis(e); particulier(-ère); (BOT, CHEM etc) spécifique; **~ally** adv expressément, explicitement; **~ation** [spesɪfɪ'keɪʃən] n (TECH) spécification f; (requirement) stipulation f

specimen ['spesɪmən] n spécimen m, échantillon m; (of blood) prélèvement m

speck [spek] n petite tache, petit point; (particle) grain m

speckled ['spekld] adj tacheté(e), moucheté(e)

specs [speks] (inf) npl lunettes fpl

spectacle ['spektəkl] n spectacle m; **~s** npl (glasses) lunettes fpl; **spectacular** [spek'tækjʊlər] adj spectaculaire

spectator [spek'teɪtər] n spectateur(-trice)

spectrum ['spektrəm] (pl **spectra**) n spectre m

speculation [spekjʊ'leɪʃən] n spéculation f

speech [spiːtʃ] n (faculty) parole f; (talk) discours m, allocution f; (manner of speaking) façon f de parler, langage m; (enunciation) élocution f; **~less** adj muet(te)

speed [spiːd] n vitesse f; (promptness) rapidité f ♦ vi: **to ~ along/past** etc aller/passer etc à toute vitesse or allure; **at full** or **top ~** à toute vitesse or allure; **~ up** vi aller plus vite, accélérer ♦ vt accélérer; **~boat** n vedette f, hors-bord m inv; **~ily** adv rapidement, promptement; **~ing** n (AUT) excès m de vitesse; **~ limit** n limitation f de vitesse, vitesse maximale permise; **~ometer** [spɪ'dɒmɪtər] n compteur m (de vitesse); **~way** n (SPORT: also: **~way racing**) épreuve(s) f(pl) de vitesse de motos; **~y** adj rapide, prompt(e)

spell [spel] (pt, pp **spelt** or **spelled**) n (also: **magic ~**) sortilège m, charme m; (period of time) (courte) période ♦ vt (in writing) écrire, orthographier; (aloud) épeler; (fig) signifier; **to cast a ~ on sb** jeter un sort à qn; **he can't ~** il fait des fautes d'orthographe; **~bound** adj envoûté(e), subjugué(e); **~ing** n orthographe f

spend [spend] (pt, pp **spent**) vt (money) dépenser; (time, life) passer; consacrer; **~thrift** n dépensier(-ère)

sperm [spɜːm] n sperme m

sphere [sfɪər] n sphère f

spice [spaɪs] n épice f; **spicy** adj épicé(e), relevé(e); (fig) piquant(e)

spider ['spaɪdər] n araignée f

spike [spaɪk] n pointe f; (BOT) épi m

spill [spɪl] (pt, pp **spilt** or **spilled**) vt renverser; répandre ♦ vi se répandre; **~ over** vi déborder

spin [spɪn] (pt **spun** or **span**, pp **spun**) n (revolution of wheel) tour m; (AVIAT) (chute f en) vrille f; (trip in car) petit tour, balade f ♦ vt (wool etc) filer; (wheel) faire tourner

♦ vi filer; (turn) tourner, tournoyer

spinach ['spɪnɪtʃ] n épinard m; (as food) épinards

spinal ['spaɪnl] adj vertébral(e), spinal(e); ~ **cord** n moelle épinière

spin doctor n personne employée pour présenter un parti politique sous un jour favorable

spin-dryer [spɪn'draɪər] (BRIT) n essoreuse f

spine [spaɪn] n colonne vertébrale; (thorn) épine f; ~**less** adj (fig) mou (molle)

spinning ['spɪnɪŋ] n (of thread) filature f; ~ **top** n toupie f

spin-off ['spɪnɔf] n avantage inattendu; sous-produit m

spinster ['spɪnstər] n célibataire f; vieille fille (péj)

spiral ['spaɪərl] n spirale f ♦ vi (fig) monter en flèche; ~ **staircase** n escalier m en colimaçon

spire ['spaɪər] n flèche f, aiguille f

spirit ['spɪrɪt] n esprit m; (mood) état m d'esprit; (courage) courage m, énergie f; ~**s** npl (drink) spiritueux mpl, alcool m; **in good** ~**s** de bonne humeur; ~**ed** adj vif (vive), fougueux(-euse), plein(e) d'allant; ~**ual** adj spirituel(le); (religious) religieux(-euse)

spit [spɪt] (pt, pp **spat**) n (for roasting) broche f; (saliva) salive f ♦ vi cracher; (sound) crépiter

spite [spaɪt] n rancune f, dépit m ♦ vt contrarier, vexer; **in ~ of** en dépit de, malgré; ~**ful** adj méchant(e), malveillant(e)

spittle ['spɪtl] n salive f; (of animal) bave f; (spat out) crachat m

splash [splæʃ] n (sound) plouf m; (of colour) tache f ♦ vt éclabousser ♦ vi (also: ~ **about**) barboter, patauger

spleen [spliːn] n (ANAT) rate f

splendid ['splendɪd] adj splendide, superbe, magnifique

splint [splɪnt] n attelle f, éclisse f

splinter ['splɪntər] n (wood) écharde f; (glass) éclat m ♦ vi se briser, se fendre

split [splɪt] (pt, pp **split**) n fente f, déchiru-

re f; (fig: POL) scission f ♦ vt diviser; (work, profits) partager, répartir ♦ vi (divide) se diviser; ~ **up** vi (couple) se séparer, rompre; (meeting) se disperser

spoil [spɔɪl] (pt, pp **spoilt** or **spoiled**) vt (damage) abîmer; (mar) gâcher; (child) gâter; ~**s** npl butin m; (fig: profits) bénéfices npl; ~**sport** n trouble-fête m, rabat-joie m

spoke [spəuk] pt of **speak** ♦ n (of wheel) rayon m

spoken ['spəukn] pp of **speak**

spokesman ['spəuksmən], **spokeswoman** ['spəukswumən] (irreg) n porte-parole m inv

sponge [spʌndʒ] n éponge f; (also: ~ **cake**) ≃ biscuit m de Savoie ♦ vt éponger ♦ vi: **to ~ off** or **on** vivre aux crochets de; ~ **bag** (BRIT) n trousse f de toilette

sponsor ['spɔnsər] n (RADIO, TV, SPORT) sponsor m; (for application) parrain m, marraine f; (BRIT: for fund-raising event) donateur(-trice) ♦ vt sponsoriser; parrainer; faire un don à; ~**ship** n sponsoring m; parrainage m; dons mpl

spontaneous [spɔn'teɪnɪəs] adj spontané(e)

spooky ['spuːkɪ] (inf) adj qui donne la chair de poule

spool [spuːl] n bobine f

spoon [spuːn] n cuiller f; ~-**feed** vt nourrir à la cuiller; (fig) mâcher le travail à; ~**ful** n cuillerée f

sport [spɔːt] n sport m; (person) chic type (fille) ♦ vt arborer; ~**ing** adj sportif(-ive); **to give sb a ~ing chance** donner sa chance à qn; ~ **jacket** (US) n = **sports jacket**; ~**s car** n voiture f de sport; ~**s jacket** (BRIT) n veste f de sport; ~**sman** (irreg) n sportif m; ~**smanship** n esprit sportif, sportivité f; ~**swear** n vêtements mpl de sport; ~**swoman** (irreg) n sportive f; ~**y** adj sportif(-ive)

spot [spɔt] n tache f; (dot: on pattern) pois m; (pimple) bouton m; (place) endroit m, coin m; (RADIO, TV: in programme: for person) numéro m; (: for activity) rubrique f;

(*small amount*): **a ~ of** un peu de ♦ *vt* (*notice*) apercevoir, repérer; **on the ~** sur place, sur les lieux; (*immediately*) sur-le-champ; (*in difficulty*) dans l'embarras; ~ **check** *n* sondage *m*, vérification ponctuelle; ~**less** *adj* immaculé(e); ~**light** *n* projecteur *m*; ~**ted** *adj* (*fabric*) à pois; ~**ty** *adj* (*face, person*) boutonneux(-euse)

spouse [spaʊs] *n* époux (épouse)

spout [spaʊt] *n* (*of jug*) bec *m*; (*of pipe*) orifice *m* ♦ *vi* jaillir

sprain [spreɪn] *n* entorse *f*, foulure *f* ♦ *vt*: **to ~ one's ankle** *etc* se fouler *or* se tordre la cheville *etc*

sprang [spræŋ] *pt of* **spring**

sprawl [sprɔ:l] *vi* s'étaler

spray [spreɪ] *n* jet *m* (en fines gouttelettes); (*from sea*) embruns *mpl*, vaporisateur *m*; (*for garden*) pulvérisateur *m*; (*aerosol*) bombe *f*; (*of flowers*) petit bouquet ♦ *vt* vaporiser, pulvériser; (*crops*) traiter

spread [spred] (*pt, pp* **spread**) *n* (*distribution*) répartition *f*; (*CULIN*) pâte *f* à tartiner; (*inf: meal*) festin *m* ♦ *vt* étendre, étaler; répandre; (*wealth, workload*) distribuer ♦ *vi* (*disease, news*) se propager; (*also:* ~ **out:** *stain*) s'étaler; ~ **out** *vi* (*people*) se disperser; ~**-eagled** *adj* étendu(e) bras et jambes écartés; ~**sheet** *n* (*COMPUT*) tableur *m*

spree [spri:] *n*: **to go on a ~** faire la fête

sprightly [ˈspraɪtlɪ] *adj* alerte

spring [sprɪŋ] (*pt* **sprang**, *pp* **sprung**) *n* (*leap*) bond *m*, saut *m*; (*coiled metal*) ressort *m*; (*season*) printemps *m*; (*of water*) source *f* ♦ *vi* (*leap*) bondir, sauter; **in ~** au printemps; **to ~ from** provenir de; ~ **up** *vi* (*problem*) se présenter, surgir; (*plant, buildings*) surgir de terre; ~**board** *n* tremplin *m*; ~**-clean(ing)** *n* grand nettoyage de printemps; ~**time** *n* printemps *m*

sprinkle [ˈsprɪŋkl] *vt*: **to ~ water** *etc* **on,** ~ **with water** *etc* asperger d'eau *etc*; **to ~ sugar** *etc* **on,** ~ **with sugar** *etc* saupoudrer de sucre *etc*; ~**r** *n* (*for lawn*) arroseur *m*; (*to put out fire*) diffuseur *m* d'extincteur automatique d'incendie

sprint [sprɪnt] *n* sprint *m* ♦ *vi* courir à toute vitesse; (*SPORT*) sprinter; ~**er** *n* sprinteur(-euse)

sprout [spraʊt] *vi* germer, pousser; ~**s** *npl* (*also:* **Brussels ~s**) choux *mpl* de Bruxelles

spruce [spru:s] *n inv* épicéa *m* ♦ *adj* net(te), pimpant(e)

sprung [sprʌŋ] *pp of* **spring**

spun [spʌn] *pt, pp of* **spin**

spur [spəːʳ] *n* éperon *m*; (*fig*) aiguillon *m* ♦ *vt* (*also:* ~ **on**) éperonner; aiguillonner; **on the ~ of the moment** sous l'impulsion du moment

spurious [ˈspjʊərɪəs] *adj* faux (fausse)

spurn [spəːn] *vt* repousser avec mépris

spurt [spəːt] *n* (*of blood*) jaillissement *m*; (*of energy*) regain *m*, sursaut *m* ♦ *vi* jaillir, gicler

spy [spaɪ] *n* espion(ne) ♦ *vi*: **to ~ on** espionner, épier; (*see*) apercevoir; ~**ing** *n* espionnage *m*

sq. *abbr* = **square**

squabble [ˈskwɒbl] *vi* se chamailler

squad [skwɒd] *n* (*MIL, POLICE*) escouade *f*, groupe *m*; (*FOOTBALL*) contingent *m*

squadron [ˈskwɒdrn] *n* (*MIL*) escadron *m*; (*AVIAT, NAUT*) escadrille *f*

squalid [ˈskwɒlɪd] *adj* sordide

squall [skwɔːl] *n* rafale *f*, bourrasque *f*

squalor [ˈskwɒləʳ] *n* conditions *fpl* sordides

squander [ˈskwɒndəʳ] *vt* gaspiller, dilapider

square [skwɛəʳ] *n* carré *m*; (*in town*) place *f* ♦ *adj* carré(e); (*inf: ideas, tastes*) vieux jeu *inv* ♦ *vt* (*arrange*) régler; arranger; (*MATH*) élever au carré ♦ *vi* (*reconcile*) concilier; **all ~** quitte; à égalité; **a ~ meal** un repas convenable; **2 metres ~** (de) 2 mètres sur 2; **2 ~ metres** 2 mètres carrés; ~**ly** *adv* carrément

squash [skwɒʃ] *n* (*BRIT: drink*): **lemon/ orange ~** citronnade *f*/orangeade *f*; (*US: marrow*) courge *f*; (*SPORT*) squash *m* ♦ *vt* écraser

squat [skwɒt] *adj* petit(e) et épais(se), ramassé(e) ♦ *vi* (*also:* ~ **down**) s'accroupir;

~ter n squatter m

squeak [skwi:k] vi grincer, crier; (mouse) pousser un petit cri

squeal [skwi:l] vi pousser un or des cri(s) aigu(s) or perçant(s); (brakes) grincer

squeamish ['skwi:mɪʃ] adj facilement dégoûté(e)

squeeze [skwi:z] n pression f; (ECON) restrictions fpl de crédit ♦ vt presser; (hand, arm) serrer; **~ out** vt exprimer

squelch [skweltʃ] vi faire un bruit de succion

squid [skwɪd] n calmar m

squiggle ['skwɪgl] n gribouillis m

squint [skwɪnt] vi loucher ♦ n: **he has a ~** il louche, il souffre de strabisme

squirm [skwɜ:m] vi se tortiller

squirrel ['skwɪrəl] n écureuil m

squirt [skwɜ:t] vi jaillir, gicler

Sr abbr = **senior**

St abbr = **saint**; **street**

stab [stæb] n (with knife etc) coup m (de couteau etc); (of pain) lancée f; (inf: try): **to have a ~ at (doing) sth** s'essayer à (faire) qch ♦ vt poignarder

stable ['steɪbl] n écurie f ♦ adj stable

stack [stæk] n tas m, pile f ♦ vt (also: **~ up**) empiler, entasser

stadium ['steɪdɪəm] (pl **stadia** or **~s**) n stade m

staff [stɑ:f] n (workforce) personnel m; (BRIT: SCOL) professeurs mpl ♦ vt pourvoir en personnel

stag [stæg] n cerf m

stage [steɪdʒ] n scène f; (platform) estrade f ♦ n (point) étape f, stade m; (profession): **the ~** le théâtre ♦ vt (play) monter, mettre en scène; (demonstration) organiser; **in ~s** par étapes, par degrés; **~coach** n diligence f; **~ manager** n régisseur m

stagger ['stægər] vi chanceler, tituber ♦ vt (person: amaze) stupéfier; (hours, holidays) étaler, échelonner; **~ing** adj (amazing) stupéfiant(e), renversant(e)

stagnate [stæg'neɪt] vi stagner, croupir

stag party n enterrement m de vie de garçon

staid [steɪd] adj posé(e), rassis(e)

stain [steɪn] n tache f; (colouring) colorant m ♦ vt tacher; (wood) teindre; **~ed glass window** n vitrail m; **~less steel** n acier m inoxydable, inox m; **~ remover** n détachant m

stair [steər] n (step) marche f; **~s** npl (flight of steps) escalier m; **~case, ~way** n escalier m

stake [steɪk] n pieu m, poteau m; (BETTING) enjeu m; (COMM: interest) intérêts mpl ♦ vt risquer, jouer; **to be at ~** être en jeu; **to ~ one's claim (to)** revendiquer

stale [steɪl] adj (bread) rassis(e); (food) pas frais (fraîche); (beer) éventé(e); (smell) de renfermé; (air) confiné(e)

stalemate ['steɪlmeɪt] n (CHESS) pat m; (fig) impasse f

stalk [stɔ:k] n tige f ♦ vt traquer ♦ vi: **to ~ out/off** sortir/partir d'un air digne

stall [stɔ:l] n (BRIT: in street, market etc) éventaire m, étal m; (in stable) stalle f ♦ vt (AUT) caler; (delay) retarder ♦ vi (AUT) caler; (fig) essayer de gagner du temps; **~s** npl (BRIT: in cinema, theatre) orchestre m

stallion ['stæljən] n étalon m (cheval)

stamina ['stæmɪnə] n résistance f, endurance f

stammer ['stæmər] n bégaiement m ♦ vi bégayer

stamp [stæmp] n timbre m; (rubber ~) tampon m; (mark, also fig) empreinte f ♦ vi (also: **~ one's foot**) taper du pied ♦ vt (letter) timbrer; (with rubber ~) tamponner; **~ album** n album m de timbres(-poste); **~ collecting** n philatélie f

stampede [stæm'pi:d] n ruée f

stance [stæns] n position f

stand [stænd] n (position) position f; (for taxis) station f (de taxis); (music ~) pupitre m à musique; (COMM) étalage m, stand m; (SPORT: also: **~s**) tribune f ♦ vi être or se tenir (debout); (rise) se lever, se mettre debout; (be placed) se trouver; (remain: offer etc) rester valable; (BRIT: in election) être candidat(e), se présenter ♦ vt (place) mettre, poser; (tolerate, *withstand*) supporter; (*treat, invite to*) offrir, payer; **to make** *or* **take a ~** prendre position; **to ~ at** (*score, value etc*) être de; **to ~ for parliament** (*BRIT*) se présenter aux élections législatives; **~ by** *vi* (*be ready*) se tenir prêt(e) ♦ *vt fus* (*opinion*) s'en tenir à; (*person*) ne pas abandonner, soutenir; **~ down** *vi* (*withdraw*) se retirer; **~ for** *vt fus* (*signify*) représenter, signifier; (*tolerate*) supporter, tolérer; **~ in for** *vt fus* remplacer; **~ out** *vi* (*be prominent*) ressortir; **~ up** *vi* (*rise*) se lever, se mettre debout; **~ up for** *vt fus* défendre; **~ up to** *vt fus* tenir tête à, résister à

standard ['stændəd] *n* (*level*) niveau (voulu); (*norm*) norme *f*, étalon *m*; (*criterion*) critère *m*; (*flag*) étendard *m* ♦ *adj* (*size etc*) ordinaire, normal(e); courant(e); (*text*) de base; **~s** *npl* (*morals*) morale *f*, principes *mpl*; **~ lamp** (*BRIT*) *n* lampadaire *m*; **~ of living** *n* niveau *m* de vie

stand-by ['stændbaɪ] *n* remplaçant(e); **to be on ~-~** se tenir prêt(e) (à intervenir); être de garde; **~-~ ticket** *n* (*AVIAT*) billet *m* stand-by

stand-in ['stændɪn] *n* remplaçant(e)

standing ['stændɪŋ] *adj* debout *inv*; (*permanent*) permanent(e) ♦ *n* réputation *f*, rang *m*, standing *m*; **of many years'** qui dure *or* existe depuis longtemps; **~ joke** *n* vieux sujet de plaisanterie; **~ order** (*BRIT*) *n* (*at bank*) virement *m* automatique, prélèvement *m* bancaire; **~ room** *n* places *fpl* debout

standpoint ['stændpɔɪnt] *n* point *m* de vue

standstill ['stændstɪl] *n*: **at a ~** paralysé(e); **to come to a ~** s'immobiliser, s'arrêter

stank [stæŋk] *pt of* **stink**

staple ['steɪpl] *n* (*for papers*) agrafe *f* ♦ *adj* (*food etc*) de base ♦ *vt* agrafer; **~r** *n* agrafeuse *f*

star [staːʳ] *n* étoile *f*; (*celebrity*) vedette *f* ♦ *vi*: **to ~ (in)** être la vedette (de) ♦ *vt* (*CINEMA etc*) avoir pour vedette; **the ~s** *npl* l'horoscope *m*

starboard ['staːbɔːd] *n* tribord *m*

starch [staːtʃ] *n* amidon *m*; (*in food*) fécule *f*

stardom ['staːdəm] *n* célébrité *f*

stare [steəʳ] *n* regard *m* fixe ♦ *vi*: **to ~ at** regarder fixement

starfish ['staːfɪʃ] *n* étoile *f* de mer

stark [staːk] *adj* (*bleak*) désolé(e), morne ♦ *adj*: **~ naked** complètement nu(e)

starling ['staːlɪŋ] *n* étourneau *m*

starry ['staːrɪ] *adj* étoilé(e); **~-eyed** *adj* (*innocent*) ingénu(e)

start [staːt] *n* commencement *m*, début *m*; (*of race*) départ *m*; (*sudden movement*) sursaut *m*; (*advantage*) avance *f*, avantage *m* ♦ *vt* commencer; (*found*) créer; (*engine*) mettre en marche ♦ *vi* partir, se mettre en route; (*jump*) sursauter; **to ~ doing** *or* **to do sth** se mettre à faire qch; **~ off** *vi* commencer; (*leave*) partir; **~ up** *vi* commencer; (*car*) démarrer ♦ *vt* (*business*) créer; (*car*) mettre en marche; **~er** *n* (*AUT*) démarreur *m*; (*SPORT: official*) starter *m*; (*BRIT: CULIN*) entrée *f*; **~ing point** *n* point *m* de départ

startle ['staːtl] *vt* faire sursauter; donner un choc à; **startling** *adj* (*news*) surprenant(e)

starvation [staːˈveɪʃən] *n* faim *f*, famine *f*

starve [staːv] *vi* mourir de faim; être affamé(e) ♦ *vt* affamer

state [steɪt] *n* état *m*; (*POL*) État *m* ♦ *vt* déclarer, affirmer; **the S~s** *npl* (*America*) les États-Unis *mpl*; **to be in a ~** être dans tous ses états; **~ly** *adj* majestueux(-euse), imposant(e); **~ly home** *n* château *m*; **~ment** *n* déclaration *f*; **~sman** (*irreg*) *n* homme *m* d'État

static ['stætɪk] *n* (*RADIO, TV*) parasites *mpl* ♦ *adj* statique

station ['steɪʃən] *n* gare *f*; (*police ~*) poste *m* de police ♦ *vt* placer, poster

stationary ['steɪʃnərɪ] *adj* à l'arrêt, immobile

stationer ['steɪʃənəʳ] *n* papetier(-ère); **~'s (shop)** *n* papeterie *f*; **~y** *n* papier *m* à lettres, petit matériel de bureau

stationmaster ['steɪʃənmɑːstər] n (RAIL) chef m de gare

station wagon (US) n break m

statistic n statistique f; **~s** [stə'tɪstɪks] n (science) statistique f

statue ['stætjuː] n statue f

status ['steɪtəs] n position f, situation f; (official) statut m; (prestige) prestige m; **~ symbol** n signe extérieur de richesse

statute ['stætjuːt] n loi f, statut m; **statutory** adj statutaire, prévu(e) par un article de loi

staunch [stɔːntʃ] adj sûr(e), loyal(e)

stay [steɪ] n (period of time) séjour m ♦ vi rester; (reside) loger; (spend some time) séjourner; **to ~ put** ne pas bouger; **to ~ with friends** loger chez des amis; **to ~ the night** passer la nuit; **~ behind** vi rester en arrière; **~ in** vi (at home) rester à la maison; **~ on** vi rester; **~ out** vi (of house) ne pas rentrer; **~ up** vi (at night) ne pas se coucher; **~ing power** n endurance f

stead [stɛd] n: **in sb's ~** à la place de qn; **to stand sb in good ~** être très utile à qn

steadfast ['stɛdfɑːst] adj ferme, résolu(e)

steadily ['stɛdɪlɪ] adv (regularly) progressivement; (firmly) fermement; (: walk) d'un pas ferme; (fixedly: look) sans détourner les yeux

steady ['stɛdɪ] adj stable, solide, ferme; (regular) constant(e), régulier(-ère); (person) calme, pondéré(e) ♦ vt stabiliser; (nerves) calmer; **a ~ boyfriend** un petit ami

steak [steɪk] n (beef) bifteck m, steak m; (fish, pork) tranche f

steal [stiːl] (pt **stole**, pp **stolen**) vt voler ♦ vi voler; (move secretly) se faufiler, se déplacer furtivement

stealth [stɛlθ] n: **by ~** furtivement

steam [stiːm] n vapeur f ♦ vt (CULIN) cuire à la vapeur ♦ vi fumer; **~ engine** n locomotive f à vapeur; **~er** n (bateau m à) vapeur m; **~ship** n = **steamer**; **~y** adj embué(e), humide

steel [stiːl] n acier m ♦ adj d'acier;

~works n aciérie f

steep [stiːp] adj raide, escarpé(e); (price) excessif(-ive)

steeple ['stiːpl] n clocher m

steer [stɪər] vt diriger; (boat) gouverner; (person) guider, conduire ♦ vi tenir le gouvernail; **~ing** n (AUT) conduite f; **~ing wheel** n volant m

stem [stɛm] n (of plant) tige f; (of glass) pied m ♦ vt contenir, arrêter, juguler; **~ from** vt fus provenir de, découler de

stench [stɛntʃ] n puanteur f

stencil ['stɛnsl] n stencil m; (pattern used) pochoir m ♦ vt polycopier

stenographer [stɛ'nɔgrəfər] (US) n sténographe m/f

step [stɛp] n pas m; (stair) marche f; (action) mesure f, disposition f ♦ vi: **to ~ forward/back** faire un pas en avant/arrière, avancer/reculer; **~s** npl (BRIT) = **stepladder**; **to be in/out of ~ (with)** (fig) aller dans le sens (de)/être déphasé(e) (par rapport à); **~ down** vi (fig) se retirer, se désister; **~ up** vt augmenter; intensifier; **~brother** n demi-frère m; **~daughter** n belle-fille f; **~father** n beau-père m; **~ladder** (BRIT) n escabeau m; **~mother** n belle-mère f; **~ping stone** n pierre f de gué; (fig) tremplin m; **~sister** n demi-sœur f; **~son** n beau-fils m

stereo ['stɛrɪəʊ] n (sound) stéréo f; (hi-fi) chaîne f stéréo inv ♦ adj (also: **~phonic**) stéréo(phonique)

sterile ['stɛraɪl] adj stérile; **sterilize** ['stɛrɪlaɪz] vt stériliser

sterling ['stɜːlɪŋ] adj (silver) de bon aloi, fin(e) ♦ n (ECON) livres fpl sterling inv; **a pound ~** une livre sterling

stern [stɜːn] adj sévère ♦ n (NAUT) arrière m, poupe f

stew [stjuː] n ragoût m ♦ vt, vi cuire (à la casserole)

steward ['stjuːəd] n (on ship, plane, train) steward m; **~ess** n hôtesse f (de l'air)

stick [stɪk] (pt, pp **stuck**) n bâton m; (walking ~) canne f ♦ vt (glue) coller; (inf: put) mettre, fourrer; (: tolerate) supporter;

(*thrust*): **to ~ sth into** planter *or* enfoncer qch dans ♦ *vi* (*become attached*) rester collé(e) *or* fixé(e); (*be unmoveable: wheels etc*) se bloquer; (*remain*) rester; **~ out** *vi* dépasser, sortir; **~ up** *vi* = **stick out**; **~ up for** *vt fus* défendre; **~er** *n* auto-collant *m*; **~ing plaster** *n* sparadrap *m*, pansement adhésif

stick-up [ˈstɪkʌp] (*inf*) *n* braquage *m*, hold-up *m inv*

sticky [ˈstɪkɪ] *adj* poisseux(-euse); (*label*) adhésif(-ive); (*situation*) délicat(e)

stiff [stɪf] *adj* raide; rigide; dur(e); (*difficult*) difficile, ardu(e); (*cold*) froid(e), distant(e); (*strong, high*) fort(e), élevé(e) ♦ *adv*: **to be bored/scared/frozen ~** s'ennuyer à mort/être mort(e) de peur/froid; **~en** *vi* se raidir; **~ neck** *n* torticolis *m*

stifle [ˈstaɪfl] *vt* étouffer, réprimer

stigma [ˈstɪɡmə] *n* stigmate *m*

stile [staɪl] *n* échalier *m*

stiletto [stɪˈlɛtəu] (*BRIT*) *n* (*also:* **~ heel**) talon *m* aiguille

still [stɪl] *adj* immobile ♦ *adv* (*up to this time*) encore, toujours; (*even*) encore; (*nonetheless*) quand même, tout de même; **~born** *adj* mort-né(e); **~ life** *n* nature morte

stilt [stɪlt] *n* (*for walking on*) échasse *f*; (*pile*) pilotis *m*

stilted [ˈstɪltɪd] *adj* guindé(e), emprunté(e)

stimulate [ˈstɪmjuleɪt] *vt* stimuler

stimuli [ˈstɪmjulaɪ] *npl of* **stimulus**

stimulus [ˈstɪmjuləs] (*pl* **stimuli**) *n* stimulant *m*; (*BIOL, PSYCH*) stimulus *m*

sting [stɪŋ] (*pt, pp* **stung**) *n* piqûre *f*; (*organ*) dard *m* ♦ *vt, vi* piquer

stingy [ˈstɪndʒɪ] *adj* avare, pingre

stink [stɪŋk] (*pt* **stank**, *pp* **stunk**) *n* puanteur *f* ♦ *vi* puer, empester; **~ing** (*inf*) *adj* (*fig*) infect(e), vache; **a ~ing ...** un(e) foutu(e) ...

stint [stɪnt] *n* part *f* de travail ♦ *vi*: **to ~ on** lésiner sur, être chiche de

stir [stəːr] *n* agitation *f*, sensation *f* ♦ *vt* remuer ♦ *vi* remuer, bouger; **~ up** *vt* (*trouble*) fomenter, provoquer

stirrup [ˈstɪrəp] *n* étrier *m*

stitch [stɪtʃ] *n* (*SEWING*) point *m*; (*KNITTING*) maille *f*; (*MED*) point de suture; (*pain*) point de côté ♦ *vt* coudre, piquer; (*MED*) suturer

stoat [stəut] *n* hermine *f* (*avec son pelage d'été*)

stock [stɔk] *n* réserve *f*, provision *f*; (*COMM*) stock *m*; (*AGR*) cheptel *m*, bétail *m*; (*CULIN*) bouillon *m*; (*descent, origin*) souche *f*; (*FINANCE*) valeurs *fpl*, titres *mpl* ♦ *adj* (*fig: reply etc*) classique ♦ *vt* (*have in ~*) avoir, vendre; **~s and shares** valeurs (mobilières), titres; **in/out of ~** en stock *or* en magasin/épuisé(e); **to take ~ of** (*fig*) faire le point de; **~ up** *vi*: **to ~ up (with)** s'approvisionner (en); **~broker** *n* agent *m* de change; **~ cube** *n* bouillon-cube *m*; **~ exchange** *n* Bourse *f*

stocking [ˈstɔkɪŋ] *n* bas *m*

stock: ~ market *n* Bourse *f*, marché financier; **~pile** *n* stock *m*, réserve *f* ♦ *vt* stocker, accumuler; **~taking** (*BRIT*) *n* (*COMM*) inventaire *m*

stocky [ˈstɔkɪ] *adj* trapu(e), râblé(e)

stodgy [ˈstɔdʒɪ] *adj* bourratif(-ive), lourd(e)

stoke [stəuk] *vt* (*fire*) garnir, entretenir; (*boiler*) chauffer

stole [stəul] *pt of* **steal** ♦ *n* étole *f*

stolen [ˈstəuln] *pp of* **steal**

stomach [ˈstʌmək] *n* estomac *m*; (*abdomen*) ventre *m* ♦ *vt* digérer, supporter; **~ache** *n* mal *m* à l'estomac *or* au ventre

stone [stəun] *n* pierre *f*; (*pebble*) caillou *m*, galet *m*; (*in fruit*) noyau *m*; (*MED*) calcul *m*; (*BRIT: weight*) 6,348 kg ♦ *adj* de *or* en pierre ♦ *vt* (*person*) lancer des pierres sur, lapider; **~-cold** *adj* complètement froid(e); **~-deaf** *adj* sourd(e) comme un pot; **~work** *n* maçonnerie *f*

stood [stud] *pt, pp of* **stand**

stool [stuːl] *n* tabouret *m*

stoop [stuːp] *vi* (*also:* **have a ~**) être voûté(e); (*also:* **~ down**: *bend*) se baisser

stop [stɔp] *n* arrêt *m*; halte *f*; (*in punctuation: also:* **full ~**) point *m* ♦ *vt* arrêter, bloquer; (*break off*) interrompre; (*also:* **put a**

~ **to**) mettre fin à ♦ vi s'arrêter; (*rain, noise etc*) cesser, s'arrêter; **to ~ doing sth** cesser *or* arrêter de faire qch; ~ **dead** vi s'arrêter net; ~ **off** vi faire une courte halte; ~ **up** vt (*hole*) boucher; **~gap** n (*person*) bouche-trou m; (*measure*) mesure f intérimaire; **~over** n halte f; (*AVIAT*) escale f; **~page** n (*strike*) arrêt de travail; (*blockage*) obstruction f; **~per** n bouchon m; ~ **press** n nouvelles fpl de dernière heure; **~watch** n chronomètre m

storage ['stɔːrɪdʒ] n entreposage m; ~ **heater** n radiateur m électrique par accumulation

store [stɔːr] n (*stock*) provision f, réserve f; (*depot*) entrepôt m; (*BRIT: large shop*) grand magasin; (*US*) magasin m ♦ vt emmagasiner; (*information*) enregistrer; **~s** npl (*food*) provisions f; **in ~** en réserve; ~ **up** vt mettre en réserve; accumuler; **~room** n réserve f, magasin m

storey ['stɔːrɪ] (*US* **story**) n étage m

stork [stɔːk] n cigogne f

storm [stɔːm] n tempête f; (*thunderstorm*) orage m ♦ vi (*fig*) fulminer ♦ vt prendre d'assaut; **~y** adj orageux(-euse)

story ['stɔːrɪ] n histoire f; récit m; (*US*) = **storey**; **~book** n livre m d'histoires *or* de contes

stout [staut] adj solide; (*fat*) gros(se), corpulent(e) ♦ n bière brune

stove [stəuv] n (*for cooking*) fourneau m; (*: small*) réchaud m; (*for heating*) poêle m

stow [stəu] vt (*also:* ~ **away**) ranger; **~away** n passager(-ère) clandestin(e)

straddle ['strædl] vt enjamber, être à cheval sur

straggle ['strægl] vi être (*or* marcher) en désordre

straight [streɪt] adj droit(e); (*hair*) raide; (*frank*) honnête, franc (franche); (*simple*) simple ♦ adv (tout) droit; (*drink*) sec, sans eau; **to put** *or* **get ~** (*fig*) mettre au clair; ~ **away**, ~ **off** (at once) tout de suite; **~en** vt ajuster; (*bed*) arranger; **~en out** vt (*fig*) débrouiller; **~-faced** adj impassible; **~forward** adj simple; (*honest*) direct(e)

strain [streɪn] n tension f; pression f; (*physical*) effort m; (*mental*) tension (nerveuse); (*breed*) race f ♦ vt (*stretch: resources etc*) mettre à rude épreuve, grever; (*hurt: back etc*) se faire mal à; (*vegetables*) égoutter; **~s** npl (*MUS*) accords mpl, accents mpl; **back ~** tour m de rein; **~ed** adj (*muscle*) froissé(e), (*laugh etc*) forcé(e), contraint(e); (*relations*) tendu(e); **~er** n passoire f

strait [streɪt] n (*GEO*) détroit m; **~s** npl: **to be in dire ~s** avoir de sérieux ennuis (d'argent); **~jacket** n camisole f de force; **~-laced** [streɪt'leɪst] adj collet monté inv

strand [strænd] n (*of thread*) fil m, brin m; (*of rope*) toron m; (*of hair*) mèche f; **~ed** adj en rade, en plan

strange [streɪndʒ] adj (*not known*) inconnu(e); (*odd*) étrange, bizarre; **~ly** adv étrangement, bizarrement; *see also* **enough**; **~r** n inconnu(e); (*from another area*) étranger(-ère)

strangle ['stræŋgl] vt étrangler; **~hold** n (*fig*) emprise totale, mainmise f

strap [stræp] n lanière f, courroie f, sangle f; (*of slip, dress*) bretelle f; **~py** adj (*dress*) à bretelles; (*sandals*) à lanières

strategic [strəˈtiːdʒɪk] adj stratégique; **strategy** ['strætɪdʒɪ] n stratégie f

straw [strɔː] n paille f; **that's the last ~!** ça, c'est le comble!

strawberry ['strɔːbərɪ] n fraise f

stray [streɪ] adj (*animal*) perdu(e), errant(e); (*scattered*) isolé(e) ♦ vi s'égarer; ~ **bullet** n balle perdue

streak [striːk] n bande f, filet m; (*in hair*) raie f ♦ vt zébrer, strier ♦ vi: **to ~ past** passer à toute allure

stream [striːm] n (*brook*) ruisseau m; (*current*) courant m, flot m; (*of people*) défilé ininterrompu, flot f ♦ vt (*SCOL*) répartir par niveau ♦ vi ruisseler; **to ~ in/out** entrer/sortir à flots

streamer ['striːmər] n serpentin m; (*banner*) banderole f

streamlined ['striːmlaɪnd] adj aérodynamique; (*fig*) rationalisé(e)

street [striːt] n rue f; **~car** (*US*) n tramway

_m;_ ~ **lamp** _n_ réverbère _m;_ ~ **plan** _n_ plan _m_ (des rues); ~**wise** (_inf_) _adj_ futé(e), réaliste

strength [streŋθ] _n_ force _f;_ (_of girder, knot etc_) solidité _f;_ ~**en** _vt_ (_muscle etc_) fortifier; (_nation, case etc_) renforcer; (_building, ECON_) consolider

strenuous ['strenjuəs] _adj_ vigoureux(-euse), énergique

stress [stres] _n_ (_force, pressure_) pression _f;_ (_mental strain_) tension (nerveuse), stress _m;_ (_accent_) accent _m_ ♦ _vt_ insister sur, souligner

stretch [stretʃ] _n_ (_of sand etc_) étendue _f_ ♦ _vi_ s'étirer; (_extend_): **to** ~ **to** _or_ **as far as** s'étendre jusqu'à ♦ _vt_ tendre, étirer; (_fig_) pousser (au maximum); ~ **out** _vi_ s'étendre ♦ _vt_ (_arm etc_) allonger, tendre; (_spread_) étendre

stretcher ['stretʃər] _n_ brancard _m_, civière _f_

stretchy ['stretʃi] _adj_ élastique

strewn [stru:n] _adj_: ~ **with** jonché(e) de

stricken ['strɪkən] _adj_ (_person_) très éprouvé(e); (_city, industry etc_) dévasté(e); ~ **with** (_disease etc_) frappé(e) _or_ atteint(e) de

strict [strɪkt] _adj_ strict(e)

stride [straɪd] (_pt_ **strode**, _pp_ **stridden**) _n_ grand pas, enjambée _f_ ♦ _vi_ marcher à grands pas

strife [straɪf] _n_ conflit _m_, dissensions _fpl_

strike [straɪk] (_pt, pp_ **struck**) _n_ grève _f;_ (_of oil etc_) découverte _f;_ (_attack_) raid _m_ ♦ _vt_ frapper; (_oil etc_) trouver, découvrir; (_deal_) conclure ♦ _vi_ faire grève; (_attack_) attaquer; (_clock_) sonner; **on** ~ (_workers_) en grève; **to** ~ **a match** frotter une allumette; ~ **down** _vt_ terrasser; ~ **up** _vt_ (_MUS_) se mettre à jouer; **to** ~ **up a friendship with** se lier d'amitié avec; **to** ~ **up a conversation (with)** engager une conversation (avec); ~**r** _n_ gréviste _m/f;_ (_SPORT_) buteur _m;_ **striking** _adj_ frappant(e), saisissant(e); (_attractive_) éblouissant(e)

string [strɪŋ] (_pt, pp_ **strung**) _n_ ficelle _f;_ (_row: of beads_) rang _m;_ (: _of onions_) chapelet _m;_ (_MUS_) corde _f_ ♦ _vt_: **to** ~ **out** échelonner; **the** ~**s** _npl_ (_MUS_) les instruments _mpl_ à cordes; **to** ~ **together** enchaîner; **to pull** ~**s** (_fig_) faire jouer le piston; ~(**ed**) **instrument** _n_ (_MUS_) instrument _m_ à cordes

stringent ['strɪndʒənt] _adj_ rigoureux(-euse)

strip [strɪp] _n_ bande _f_ ♦ _vt_ (_undress_) déshabiller; (_paint_) décaper ♦ _vi_ se déshabiller; ~ **cartoon** _n_ bande dessinée

stripe [straɪp] _n_ raie _f_, rayure _f;_ (_MIL_) galon _m;_ ~**d** _adj_ rayé(e), à rayures

strip: ~ **lighting** (_BRIT_) _n_ éclairage _m_ au néon _or_ fluorescent; ~**per** _n_ strip-teaseur(-euse) _f;_ ~ **search** _n_ fouille corporelle (_en faisant se déshabiller la personne_) ♦ _vt_: **he was** ~ **searched** on l'a fait se déshabiller et soumis à une fouille corporelle

stripy ['straɪpɪ] _adj_ rayé(e)

strive [straɪv] (_pt_ **strove**, _pp_ **striven**) _vi_: **to** ~ **to do/for sth** s'efforcer de faire/d'obtenir qch

strode [strəud] _pt of_ **stride**

stroke [strəuk] _n_ coup _m;_ (_SWIMMING_) nage _f;_ (_MED_) attaque _f_ ♦ _vt_ caresser; **at a** ~ d'un (seul) coup

stroll [strəul] _n_ petite promenade ♦ _vi_ flâner, se promener nonchalamment; ~**er** (_US_) _n_ (_pushchair_) poussette _f_

strong [strɒŋ] _adj_ fort(e); vigoureux(-euse); (_heart, nerves_) solide; **they are 50** ~ ils sont au nombre de 50; ~**hold** _n_ bastion _m;_ ~**ly** _adv_ fortement, avec force; vigoureusement; solidement; ~**room** _n_ chambre forte

strove [strəuv] _pt of_ **strive**

struck [strʌk] _pt, pp of_ **strike**

structural ['strʌktʃrəl] _adj_ structural(e); (_CONSTR: defect_) de construction; (_damage_) affectant les parties portantes

structure ['strʌktʃər] _n_ structure _f;_ (_building_) construction _f_

struggle ['strʌgl] _n_ lutte _f_ ♦ _vi_ lutter, se battre

strum [strʌm] _vt_ (_guitar_) jouer (en sourdine) de

strung [strʌŋ] _pt, pp of_ **string**

strut [strʌt] n étai m, support m ♦ vi se pavaner

stub [stʌb] n (of cigarette) bout m, mégot m; (of cheque etc) talon m ♦ vt: **to ~ one's toe** se cogner le doigt de pied; **~ out** vt écraser

stubble ['stʌbl] n chaume m; (on chin) barbe f de plusieurs jours

stubborn ['stʌbən] adj têtu(e), obstiné(e), opiniâtre

stuck [stʌk] pt, pp of **stick** ♦ adj (jammed) bloqué(e), coincé(e); **~-up** (inf) adj prétentieux(-euse)

stud [stʌd] n (on boots etc) clou m; (on collar) bouton m de col; (earring) petite boucle d'oreille; (of horses: also: **~ farm**) écurie f, haras m; (also: **~ horse**) étalon m ♦ vt (fig): **~ded with** parsemé(e) or criblé(e) de

student ['stju:dənt] n étudiant(e) ♦ adj estudiantin(e); d'étudiant; **~ driver** (US) n (conducteur-trice) débutant(e)

studio ['stju:dɪəu] n studio m, atelier m; (TV etc) studio

studious ['stju:dɪəs] adj studieux(-euse), appliqué(e); (attention) soutenu(e); **~ly** adv (carefully) soigneusement

study ['stʌdɪ] n étude f; (room) bureau m ♦ vt étudier; (examine) examiner ♦ vi étudier, faire ses études

stuff [stʌf] n chose(s) f(pl); affaires fpl, trucs mpl; (substance) substance f ♦ vt rembourrer; (CULIN) farcir; (inf: push) fourrer; **~ing** n bourre f, rembourrage m; (CULIN) farce f; **~y** adj (room) mal ventilé(e) or aéré(e); (ideas) vieux jeu inv

stumble ['stʌmbl] vi trébucher; **to ~ across** or **on** (fig) tomber sur; **stumbling block** n pierre f d'achoppement

stump [stʌmp] n souche f; (of limb) moignon m ♦ vt: **to be ~ed** sécher, ne pas savoir que répondre

stun [stʌn] vt étourdir; (fig) abasourdir

stung [stʌŋ] pt, pp of **sting**

stunk [stʌŋk] pp of **stink**

stunned [stʌnd] adj sidéré(e)

stunning ['stʌnɪŋ] adj (news etc) stupéfiant(e); (girl etc) éblouissant(e)

stunt [stʌnt] n (in film) cascade f, acrobatie f; (publicity ~) truc m publicitaire ♦ vt retarder, arrêter; **~man** ['stʌntmæn] (irreg) n cascadeur m

stupendous [stju:'pendəs] adj prodigieux(-euse), fantastique

stupid ['stju:pɪd] adj stupide, bête; **~ity** [stju:'pɪdɪtɪ] n stupidité f, bêtise f

sturdy ['stə:dɪ] adj robuste; solide

stutter ['stʌtər] vi bégayer

sty [staɪ] n (for pigs) porcherie f

stye [staɪ] n (MED) orgelet m

style [staɪl] n style m; (distinction) allure f, cachet m, style; **stylish** adj élégant(e), chic inv

stylus ['staɪləs] (pl **styli** or **~es**) n (of record player) pointe f de lecture

suave [swɑ:v] adj doucereux(-euse), onctueux(-euse)

sub... [sʌb] prefix sub..., sous-; **~conscious** adj subconscient(e); **~contract** vt sous-traiter

subdue [səb'dju:] vt subjuguer, soumettre; **~d** adj (light) tamisé(e); (person) qui a perdu de son entrain

subject [n 'sʌbdʒɪkt, vb səb'dʒɛkt] n sujet m; (SCOL) matière f ♦ vt: **to ~ to** soumettre à; exposer à; **to be ~ to** (law) être soumis(e) à; (disease) être sujet(te) à; **~ive** [səb'dʒɛktɪv] adj subjectif(-ive); **~ matter** n (content) contenu m

sublet [sʌb'lɛt] vt sous-louer

submarine [sʌbmə'ri:n] n sous-marin m

submerge [səb'mə:dʒ] vt submerger ♦ vi plonger

submission [səb'mɪʃən] n soumission f; **submissive** adj soumis(e)

submit [səb'mɪt] vt soumettre ♦ vi se soumettre

subnormal [sʌb'nɔ:ml] adj au-dessous de la normale

subordinate [sə'bɔ:dɪnət] adj subalterne ♦ n subordonné(e)

subpoena [səb'pi:nə] n (LAW) citation f, assignation f

subscribe [səb'skraɪb] vi cotiser; **to ~ to**

(*opinion, fund*) souscrire à; (*newspaper*) s'abonner à; être abonné(e) à; **~r** *n* (*to periodical, telephone*) abonné(e); **subscription** [səb'skrɪpʃən] *n* (*to magazine etc*) abonnement *m*

subsequent ['sʌbsɪkwənt] *adj* ultérieur(e), suivant(e); conséctif(-ive); **~ly** *adv* par la suite

subside [səb'saɪd] *vi* (*flood*) baisser; (*wind, feelings*) tomber; **~nce** [səb'saɪdns] *n* affaissement *m*

subsidiary [səb'sɪdɪərɪ] *adj* subsidiaire; accessoire ♦ *n* filiale *f*

subsidize ['sʌbsɪdaɪz] *vt* subventionner; **subsidy** ['sʌbsɪdɪ] *n* subvention *f*

substance ['sʌbstəns] *n* substance *f*

substantial [səb'stænʃl] *adj* substantiel(le); (*fig*) important(e); **~ly** *adv* considérablement; (*in essence*) en grande partie

substantiate [səb'stænʃɪeɪt] *vt* étayer, fournir des preuves à l'appui de

substitute ['sʌbstɪtjuːt] *n* (*person*) remplaçant(e); (*thing*) succédané *m* ♦ *vt*: **to ~ sth/sb for** substituer qch/qn à, remplacer par qch/qn

subterranean [sʌbtə'reɪnɪən] *adj* souterrain(e)

subtitle ['sʌbtaɪtl] *n* (*CINEMA, TV*) sous-titre *m*; **~d** *adj* sous-titré(e)

subtle ['sʌtl] *adj* subtil(e)

subtotal [sʌb'təʊtl] *n* total partiel

subtract [səb'trækt] *vt* soustraire, retrancher; **~ion** *n* soustraction *f*

suburb ['sʌbɜːb] *n* faubourg *m*; **the ~s** *npl* la banlieue; **~an** [sə'bɜːbən] *adj* de banlieue, suburbain(e); **~ia** [sə'bɜːbɪə] *n* la banlieue

subway ['sʌbweɪ] *n* (*US: railway*) métro *m*; (*BRIT: underpass*) passage souterrain

succeed [sək'siːd] *vi* réussir ♦ *vt* succéder à; **to ~ in doing** réussir à faire; **~ing** *adj* (*following*) suivant(e)

success [sək'ses] *n* succès *m*; réussite *f*; **~ful** *adj* (*venture*) couronné(e) de succès; **to be ~ful (in doing)** réussir (à faire); **~fully** *adv* avec succès

succession [sək'seʃən] *n* succession *f*; **3**

days in ~ 3 jours de suite

successive [sək'sesɪv] *adj* successif(-ive); consécutif(-ive)

such [sʌtʃ] *adj* tel (telle); (*of that kind*): **~ a book** un livre de ce genre, un livre pareil, un tel livre; (*so much*): **~ courage** un tel courage ♦ *adv* si; **~ books** des livres de ce genre, des livres pareils, de tels livres; **~ a long trip** un si long voyage; **~ a lot of** tellement *or* tant de; **~ as** (*like*) tel que, comme; **as ~** en tant que tel, à proprement parler; **~-and-~** *adj* tel ou tel

suck [sʌk] *vt* sucer; (*breast, bottle*) téter; **~er** *n* ventouse *f*; (*inf*) poire *f*

suction ['sʌkʃən] *n* succion *f*

sudden ['sʌdn] *adj* soudain(e), subit(e); **all of a ~** soudain, tout à coup; **~ly** *adv* brusquement, tout à coup, soudain

suds [sʌdz] *npl* eau savonneuse

sue [suː] *vt* poursuivre en justice, intenter un procès à

suede [sweɪd] *n* daim *m*

suet ['sʊɪt] *n* graisse *f* de rognon

suffer ['sʌfə*r*] *vt* souffrir, subir; (*bear*) tolérer, supporter ♦ *vi* souffrir; **~er** *n* (*MED*) malade *m/f*; **~ing** *n* souffrance(s) *f(pl)*

sufficient [sə'fɪʃənt] *adj* suffisant(e); **~ money** suffisamment d'argent; **~ly** *adv* suffisamment, assez

suffocate ['sʌfəkeɪt] *vi* suffoquer; étouffer

sugar ['ʃʊgə*r*] *n* sucre *m* ♦ *vt* sucrer; **~ beet** *n* betterave sucrière; **~ cane** *n* canne *f* à sucre

suggest [sə'dʒest] *vt* suggérer, proposer; (*indicate*) dénoter; **~ion** *n* suggestion *f*

suicide ['sʊɪsaɪd] *n* suicide *m*; *see also* **commit**; **~ bomber** *n* kamikaze *m/f*; **~ bombing** *n* attentat suicide *m*

suit [suːt] *n* (*man's*) costume *m*, complet *m*; (*woman's*) tailleur *m*, ensemble *m*; (*LAW*) poursuite(s) *f(pl)*, procès *m*; (*CARDS*) couleur *f* ♦ *vt* aller à; convenir à; (*adapt*): **to ~ sth to** adapter *or* approprier qch à; **well ~ed** (*matched*) faits l'un pour l'autre, très bien assortis; **~able** *adj* qui convient; approprié(e); **~ably** *adv* comme il se doit (*or* se devait *etc*), convenablement

suitcase ['su:tkeɪs] n valise f

suite [swi:t] n (of rooms, also MUS) suite f; (furniture): **bedroom / dining room ~** (ensemble m de) chambre f à coucher/salle f à manger

suitor ['su:tər] n soupirant m, prétendant m

sulfur ['sʌlfər] (US) n = **sulphur**

sulk [sʌlk] vi bouder; **~y** adj boudeur(-euse), maussade

sullen ['sʌlən] adj renfrogné(e), maussade

sulphur ['sʌlfər] (US **sulfur**) n soufre m

sultana [sʌl'tɑ:nə] n (CULIN) raisin (sec) de Smyrne

sultry ['sʌltrɪ] adj étouffant(e)

sum [sʌm] n somme f; (SCOL etc) calcul m; **~ up** vt, vi résumer

summarize ['sʌməraɪz] vt résumer

summary ['sʌmərɪ] n résumé m

summer ['sʌmər] n été m ♦ adj d'été, estival(e); **~house** n (in garden) pavillon m; **~time** n été m; **~ time** n (by clock) heure f d'été

summit ['sʌmɪt] n sommet m

summon ['sʌmən] vt appeler, convoquer; **~ up** vt rassembler, faire appel à; **~s** n citation f, assignation f

sun [sʌn] n soleil m; **in the ~** au soleil; **~bathe** vi prendre un bain de soleil; **~block** n écran m total; **~burn** n coup m de soleil; **~burned**, **~burnt** adj (tanned) bronzé(e)

Sunday ['sʌndɪ] n dimanche m; **~ school** n ≈ catéchisme m

sundial ['sʌndaɪəl] n cadran m solaire

sundown ['sʌndaun] n coucher m du (or de) soleil

sundries ['sʌndrɪz] npl articles divers

sundry ['sʌndrɪ] adj divers(e), différent(e) ♦ n: **all and ~** tout le monde, n'importe qui

sunflower ['sʌnflauər] n tournesol m

sung [sʌŋ] pp of **sing**

sunglasses ['sʌnglɑ:sɪz] npl lunettes fpl de soleil

sunk [sʌŋk] pp of **sink**

sun: ~light n (lumière f du) soleil m; **~lit** adj ensoleillé(e); **~ny** adj ensoleillé(e); **~rise** n lever m du (or de) soleil; **~ roof** n (AUT) toit ouvrant; **~screen** n crème f solaire; **~set** n coucher m du (or de) soleil; **~shade** n (over table) parasol m; **~shine** n (lumière f du) soleil m; **~stroke** n insolation f; **~tan** n bronzage m; **~tan lotion** n lotion f or lait m solaire; **~tan oil** n huile f solaire

super ['su:pər] (inf) adj formidable

superannuation [su:pərænju'eɪʃən] n (contribution) cotisations fpl pour la pension

superb [su:'pə:b] adj superbe, magnifique

supercilious [su:pə'sɪlɪəs] adj hautain(e), dédaigneux(-euse)

superficial [su:pə'fɪʃəl] adj superficiel(le)

superimpose ['su:pərɪm'pəuz] vt superposer

superintendent [su:pərɪn'tendənt] n directeur(-trice); (POLICE) ≈ commissaire m

superior [su'pɪərɪər] adj, n supérieur(e); **~ity** [supɪərɪ'ɔrɪtɪ] n supériorité f

superlative [su'pə:lətɪv] n (LING) superlatif m

superman ['su:pəmæn] (irreg) n surhomme m

supermarket ['su:pəmɑ:kɪt] n supermarché m

supernatural [su:pə'nætʃərəl] adj surnaturel(le)

superpower ['su:pəpauər] n (POL) superpuissance f

supersede [su:pə'si:d] vt remplacer, supplanter

superstitious [su:pə'stɪʃəs] adj superstitieux(-euse)

supervise ['su:pəvaɪz] vt surveiller; diriger; **supervision** [su:pə'vɪʒən] n surveillance f; contrôle m; **supervisor** n surveillant(e); (in shop) chef m de rayon

supper ['sʌpər] n dîner m; (late) souper m

supple ['sʌpl] adj souple

supplement [n 'sʌplɪmənt, vb sʌplɪ'mɛnt] n supplément m ♦ vt compléter; **~ary** [sʌplɪ'mɛntərɪ] adj supplémentaire; **~ary benefit** (BRIT) n allocation f (supplémentaire) d'aide sociale

supplier [sə'plaɪəʳ] n fournisseur m

supply [sə'plaɪ] vt (*provide*) fournir; (*equip*): **to ~ (with)** approvisionner or ravitailler (en); fournir (en) ♦ n provision f, réserve f; (~*ing*) approvisionnement m; **supplies** npl (*food*) vivres mpl; (*MIL*) subsistances fpl; **~ teacher** (*BRIT*) n suppléant(e)

support [sə'pɔːt] n (*moral, financial etc*) soutien m, appui m; (*TECH*) support m, soutien ♦ vt soutenir, supporter; (*financially*) subvenir aux besoins de; (*uphold*) être pour, être partisan de, appuyer; **~er** n (*POL etc*) partisan(e); (*SPORT*) supporter m

suppose [sə'pəuz] vt supposer; imaginer; **to be ~d to do** être censé(e) faire; **~dly** [sə'pəuzɪdlɪ] adv soi-disant; **supposing** conj si, à supposer que +sub

suppress [sə'prɛs] vt (*revolt*) réprimer; (*information*) supprimer; (*yawn*) étouffer; (*feelings*) refouler

supreme [su'priːm] adj suprême

surcharge ['sɜːtʃɑːdʒ] n surcharge f

sure [ʃuəʳ] adj sûr(e); (*definite, convinced*) sûr, certain(e); **~!** (*of course*) bien sûr!; **~ enough** effectivement; **to make ~ of sth** s'assurer de or vérifier qch; **to make ~ that** s'assurer or vérifier que; **~ly** adv sûrement; certainement

surf [sɜːf] n (*waves*) ressac m

surface ['sɜːfɪs] n surface f ♦ vt (*road*) poser un revêtement sur ♦ vi remonter à la surface; faire surface; **~ mail** n courrier m par voie de terre (or maritime)

surfboard ['sɜːfbɔːd] n planche f de surf

surfeit ['sɜːfɪt] n: **a ~ of** un excès de; une indigestion de

surfing ['sɜːfɪŋ] n surf m

surge [sɜːdʒ] n vague f, montée f ♦ vi déferler

surgeon ['sɜːdʒən] n chirurgien m

surgery ['sɜːdʒərɪ] n chirurgie f; (*BRIT: room*) cabinet m (de consultation); (: *also:* **~ hours**) heures fpl de consultation

surgical ['sɜːdʒɪkl] adj chirurgical(e); **~ spirit** (*BRIT*) n alcool m à 90º

surname ['sɜːneɪm] n nom m de famille

surplus ['sɜːpləs] n surplus m, excédent m ♦ adj en surplus, de trop; (*COMM*) excédentaire

surprise [sə'praɪz] n surprise f; (*astonishment*) étonnement m ♦ vt surprendre; (*astonish*) étonner; **surprising** adj surprenant(e), étonnant(e); **surprisingly** adv (*easy, helpful*) étonnamment

surrender [sə'rɛndəʳ] n reddition f, capitulation f ♦ vi se rendre, capituler

surreptitious [sʌrəp'tɪʃəs] adj subreptice, furtif(-ive)

surrogate ['sʌrəgɪt] n substitut m; **~ mother** n mère porteuse or de substitution

surround [sə'raund] vt entourer; (*MIL etc*) encercler; **~ing** adj environnant(e); **~ings** npl environs mpl, alentours mpl

surveillance [sɜː'veɪləns] n surveillance f

survey [n 'sɜːveɪ, vb sɜː'veɪ] n enquête f, étude f; (*in housebuying etc*) inspection f, (rapport m d')expertise f; (*of land*) levé m ♦ vt enquêter sur; inspecter; (*look at*) embrasser du regard; **~or** n (*of house*) expert m; (*of land*) (arpenteur m) géomètre m

survival [sə'vaɪvl] n survie f; (*relic*) vestige m

survive [sə'vaɪv] vi survivre; (*custom etc*) subsister ♦ vt survivre à; **survivor** n survivant(e); (*fig*) battant(e)

susceptible [sə'sɛptəbl] adj: **~ (to)** sensible (à); (*disease*) prédisposé(e) (à)

suspect [adj, n 'sʌspɛkt, vb sə'spɛkt] adj, n suspect(e) ♦ vt soupçonner, suspecter

suspend [səs'pɛnd] vt suspendre; **~ed sentence** n condamnation f avec sursis; **~er belt** n porte-jarretelles m inv; **~ers** npl (*BRIT*) jarretelles fpl; (*US*) bretelles fpl

suspense [səs'pɛns] n attente f, incertitude f; (*in film etc*) suspense m

suspension [səs'pɛnʃən] n suspension f; (*of driving licence*) retrait m provisoire; **~ bridge** n pont suspendu

suspicion [səs'pɪʃən] n soupçon(s) m(pl); **suspicious** adj (*suspecting*) soupçonneux(-euse), méfiant(e); (*causing suspicion*) suspect(e)

sustain [səs'teɪn] *vt* soutenir; (*food etc*) nourrir, donner des forces à; (*suffer*) subir; recevoir; **~able** *adj* (*development, growth etc*) viable; **~ed** *adj* (*effort*) soutenu(e), prolongé(e); **sustenance** ['sʌstɪnəns] *n* nourriture *f*; (*money*) moyens *mpl* de subsistance

swab [swɔb] *n* (MED) tampon *m*

swagger ['swægər] *vi* plastronner

swallow ['swɔləu] *n* (*bird*) hirondelle *f* ♦ *vt* avaler; **~ up** *vt* engloutir

swam [swæm] *pt of* **swim**

swamp [swɔmp] *n* marais *m*, marécage *m* ♦ *vt* submerger

swan [swɔn] *n* cygne *m*

swap [swɔp] *vt*: **to ~ (for)** échanger (contre), troquer (contre)

swarm [swɔːm] *n* essaim *m* ♦ *vi* fourmiller, grouiller

swastika ['swɔstɪkə] *n* croix gammée *f*

swat [swɔt] *vt* écraser

sway [sweɪ] *vi* se balancer, osciller ♦ *vt* (*influence*) influencer

swear [sweər] (*pt* **swore**, *pp* **sworn**) *vt, vi* jurer; **~word** *n* juron *m*, gros mot

sweat [swet] *n* sueur *f*, transpiration *f* ♦ *vi* suer

sweater ['swetər] *n* tricot *m*, pull *m*

sweaty ['swetɪ] *adj* en sueur, moite *or* mouillé(e) de sueur

Swede [swiːd] *n* Suédois(e)

swede [swiːd] (BRIT) *n* rutabaga *m*

Sweden ['swiːdn] *n* Suède *f*; **Swedish** *adj* suédois(e) ♦ *n* (LING) suédois *m*

sweep [swiːp] (*pt, pp* **swept**) *n* (*also:* **chimney ~**) ramoneur *m* ♦ *vt* balayer; (*subj: current*) emporter; **~ away** *vt* balayer; entraîner; emporter; **~ past** *vi* passer majestueusement *or* rapidement; **~ up** *vt, vi* balayer; **~ing** *adj* (*gesture*) large; circulaire; **a ~ing statement** une généralisation hâtive

sweet [swiːt] *n* (*candy*) bonbon *m*; (BRIT: *pudding*) dessert *m* ♦ *adj* doux (douce); (*not savoury*) sucré(e); (*fig: kind*) gentil(le); (*baby*) mignon(ne); **~corn** *n* ['swiːtkɔːn] *n* maïs *m*; **~en** *vt* adoucir; (*with sugar*) su-

crer; **~heart** *n* amoureux(-euse); **~ness** *n* goût sucré; douceur *f*; **~ pea** *n* pois *m* de senteur

swell [swel] (*pt* **swelled**, *pp* **swollen** *or* **swelled**) *n* (*of sea*) houle *f* ♦ *adj* (US: *inf: excellent*) chouette ♦ *vi* grossir, augmenter; (*sound*) s'enfler; (MED) enfler; **~ing** *n* (MED) enflure *f*; (*lump*) grosseur *f*

sweltering ['sweltərɪŋ] *adj* étouffant(e), oppressant(e)

swept [swept] *pt, pp of* **sweep**

swerve [swəːv] *vi* faire une embardée *or* un écart; dévier

swift [swɪft] *n* (*bird*) martinet *m* ♦ *adj* rapide, prompt(e)

swig [swɪɡ] (*inf*) *n* (*drink*) lampée *f*

swill [swɪl] *vt* (*also:* **~ out, ~ down**) laver à grande eau

swim [swɪm] (*pt* **swam**, *pp* **swum**) *n*: **to go for a ~** aller nager *or* se baigner ♦ *vi* nager; (SPORT) faire de la natation; (*head, room*) tourner ♦ *vt* traverser (à la nage); (*a length*) faire (à la nage); **~mer** *n* nageur(-euse); **~ming** *n* natation *f*; **~ming cap** *n* bonnet *m* de bain; **~ming costume** (BRIT) *n* maillot *m* (de bain); **~ming pool** *n* piscine *f*; **~ming trunks** *npl* caleçon *m* *or* slip *m* de bain; **~suit** *n* maillot *m* (de bain)

swindle ['swɪndl] *n* escroquerie *f*

swine [swaɪn] (*inf!*) *n inv* salaud *m* (!)

swing [swɪŋ] (*pt, pp* **swung**) *n* balançoire *f*; (*movement*) balancement *m*, oscillations *fpl*; (*change: in opinion etc*) revirement *m* ♦ *vt* balancer, faire osciller; (*also:* **~ round**) tourner, faire virer ♦ *vi* se balancer, osciller; (*also:* **~ round**) virer, tourner; **to be in full ~** battre son plein; **~ bridge** *n* pont tournant; **~ door** (US **swinging door**) *n* porte battante

swingeing ['swɪndʒɪŋ] (BRIT) *adj* écrasant(e); (*cuts etc*) considérable

swipe [swaɪp] (*inf*) *vt* (*steal*) piquer

swirl [swəːl] *vi* tourbillonner, tournoyer

Swiss [swɪs] *adj* suisse ♦ *n inv* Suisse *m/f*

switch [swɪtʃ] *n* (*for light, radio etc*) bouton *m*; (*change*) changement *m*, revirement *m*

♦ *vt* changer; ~ **off** *vt* éteindre; *(engine)* arrêter; ~ **on** *vt* allumer; *(engine, machine)* mettre en marche; **~board** *n (TEL)* standard *m*

Switzerland ['swɪtsələnd] *n* Suisse *f*

swivel ['swɪvl] *vi (also:* ~ **round)** pivoter, tourner

swollen ['swəulən] *pp of* **swell**

swoon [swu:n] *vi* se pâmer

swoop [swu:p] *n (by police)* descente *f* ♦ *vi (also:* ~ **down)** descendre en piqué, piquer

swop [swɔp] *vt =* **swap**

sword [sɔ:d] *n* épée *f*; **~fish** *n* espadon *m*

swore [swɔ:ʳ] *pt of* **swear**

sworn [swɔ:n] *pp of* **swear** ♦ *adj (statement, evidence)* donné(e) sous serment

swot [swɔt] *vi* bûcher, potasser

swum [swʌm] *pp of* **swim**

swung [swʌŋ] *pt, pp of* **swing**

syllable ['sɪləbl] *n* syllabe *f*

syllabus ['sɪləbəs] *n* programme *m*

symbol ['sɪmbl] *n* symbole *m*

symmetry ['sɪmɪtrɪ] *n* symétrie *f*

sympathetic [sɪmpə'θɛtɪk] *adj* compatissant(e); bienveillant(e), compréhensif(ive); *(likeable)* sympathique; ~ **towards** bien disposé(e) envers

sympathize ['sɪmpəθaɪz] *vi:* **to** ~ **with sb** plaindre qn; *(in grief)* s'associer à la douleur de qn; **to** ~ **with sth** comprendre qch; ~**r** *n (POL)* sympathisant(e)

sympathy ['sɪmpəθɪ] *n (pity)* compassion *f*; **sympathies** *npl (support)* soutien *m*; **left-wing** *etc* **sympathies** penchants *mpl* à gauche *etc*; **in** ~ **with** *(strike)* en or par solidarité avec; **with our deepest** ~ en vous priant d'accepter nos sincères condoléances

symphony ['sɪmfənɪ] *n* symphonie *f*

symptom ['sɪmptəm] *n* symptôme *m*; indice *m*

syndicate ['sɪndɪkɪt] *n* syndicat *m*, coopérative *f*

synopsis [sɪ'nɔpsɪs] *n (pl* **synopses)** *n* résumé *m*

synthetic [sɪn'θɛtɪk] *adj* synthétique

syphon ['saɪfən] *n, vb =* **siphon**

Syria ['sɪrɪə] *n* Syrie *f*

syringe [sɪ'rɪndʒ] *n* seringue *f*

syrup ['sɪrəp] *n* sirop *m*; *(also:* **golden** ~) mélasse raffinée

system ['sɪstəm] *n* système *m*; *(ANAT)* organisme *m*; **~atic** [sɪstə'mætɪk] *adj* systématique; méthodique; ~ **disk** *n (COMPUT)* disque *m* système; **~s analyst** *n* analyste fonctionnel(le)

T, t

ta [tɑ:] *(BRIT: inf)* *excl* merci!

tab [tæb] *n (label)* étiquette *f*; *(on drinks can etc)* languette *f*; **to keep ~s on** *(fig)* surveiller

tabby ['tæbɪ] *n (also:* ~ **cat)** chat(te) tigré(e)

table ['teɪbl] *n* table *f* ♦ *vt (BRIT: motion etc)* présenter; **to lay** *or* **set the** ~ mettre le couvert *or* la table; **~cloth** *n* nappe *f*; ~ **d'hôte** [tɑ:bl'dəut] *adj (meal)* à prix fixe; ~ **lamp** *n* lampe *f* de table; **~mat** *n (for plate)* napperon *m*, set *m*; *(for hot dish)* dessous-de-plat *m inv*; ~ **of contents** *n* table *f* des matières; **~spoon** *n* cuiller *f* de service; *(also:* **~spoonful:** *as measurement)* cuillerée *f* à soupe

tablet ['tæblɪt] *n (MED)* comprimé *m*

table tennis *n* ping-pong ® *m*, tennis *m* de table

table wine *n* vin *m* de table

tabloid ['tæblɔɪd] *n* quotidien *m* populaire

⎯⎯⎯| **tabloid press** |⎯⎯⎯

i *Le terme* **tabloid press** *désigne les journaux populaires de demi-format où l'on trouve beaucoup de photos et qui adoptent un style très concis. Ce type de journaux vise des lecteurs s'intéressant aux faits divers ayant un parfum de scandale; voir* **quality (news)papers.**

tack [tæk] *n (nail)* petit clou ♦ *vt* clouer; *(fig)* direction *f*; *(BRIT: stitch)* faufiler ♦ *vi* tirer un *or* des bord(s)

tackle ['tækl] *n* matériel *m*, équipement *m*; (*for lifting*) appareil *m* de levage; (*RUGBY*) plaquage *m* ♦ *vt* (*difficulty, animal, burglar etc*) s'attaquer à; (*person: challenge*) s'expliquer avec; (*RUGBY*) plaquer

tacky ['tæki] *adj* collant(e); (*pej: of poor quality*) miteux(-euse)

tact [tækt] *n* tact *m*; **~ful** *adj* plein(e) de tact

tactical ['tæktɪkl] *adj* tactique

tactics ['tæktɪks] *npl* tactique *f*

tactless ['tæktlɪs] *adj* qui manque de tact

tadpole ['tædpəul] *n* têtard *m*

tag [tæg] *n* étiquette *f*; **~ along** *vi* suivre

tail [teɪl] *n* queue *f*; (*of shirt*) pan *m* ♦ *vt* (*follow*) suivre, filer; **~s** *npl* habit *m*; **~ away**, **~ off** *vi* (*in size, quality etc*) baisser peu à peu; **~back** (*BRIT*) *n* (*AUT*) bouchon *m*; **~ end** *n* bout *m*, fin *f*; **~gate** *n* (*AUT*) hayon *m* arrière

tailor ['teɪlə*r*] *n* tailleur *m*; **~ing** *n* (*cut*) coupe *f*; **~-made** *adj* fait(e) sur mesure; (*fig*) conçu(e) spécialement

tailwind ['teɪlwɪnd] *n* vent *m* arrière *inv*

tainted ['teɪntɪd] *adj* (*food*) gâté(e); (*water, air*) infecté(e); (*fig*) souillé(e)

take [teɪk] (*pt* **took**, *pp* **taken**) *vt* prendre; (*gain: prize*) remporter; (*require: effort, courage*) demander; (*tolerate*) accepter, supporter; (*hold: passengers etc*) contenir; (*accompany*) emmener, accompagner; (*bring, carry*) apporter, emporter; (*exam*) passer, se présenter à; **to ~ sth from** (*drawer etc*) prendre qch dans; (*person*) prendre qch à; **I ~ it that ...** je suppose que ...; **~ after** *vt fus* ressembler à; **~ apart** *vt* démonter; **~ away** *vt* enlever; (*carry off*) emporter; **~ back** *vt* (*return*) rendre, rapporter; (*one's words*) retirer; **~ down** *vt* (*building*) démolir; (*letter etc*) prendre, écrire; **~ in** *vt* (*deceive*) tromper, rouler; (*understand*) comprendre, saisir; (*include*) comprendre, inclure; (*lodger*) prendre; **~ off** *vi* (*AVIAT*) décoller ♦ *vt* (*go away*) s'en aller; (*remove*) enlever; **~ on** *vt* (*work*) accepter, se charger de; (*employee*) prendre, embaucher;

(*opponent*) accepter de se battre contre; **~ out** *vt* (*invite*) emmener, sortir; (*remove*) enlever; **to ~ sth out of sth** (*drawer, pocket etc*) prendre qch dans qch; **~ over** *vt* (*business*) reprendre ♦ *vi*: **to ~ over from sb** prendre la relève de qn; **~ to** *vt fus* (*person*) se prendre d'amitié pour; (*thing*) prendre goût à; **~ up** *vt* (*activity*) se mettre à; (*dress*) raccourcir; (*occupy: time, space*) prendre, occuper; **to ~ sb up on an offer** accepter la proposition de qn; **~away** (*BRIT*) *adj* (*food*) à emporter ♦ *n* (*shop, restaurant*) café *m* qui vend de plats à emporter; **~off** *n* (*AVIAT*) décollage *m*; **~over** *n* (*COMM*) rachat *m*; **takings** *npl* (*COMM*) recette *f*

talc [tælk] *n* (*also:* **~um powder**) talc *m*

tale [teɪl] *n* (*story*) conte *m*, histoire *f*; (*account*) récit *m*; **to tell ~s** (*fig*) rapporter

talent ['tælnt] *n* talent *m*, don *m*; **~ed** *adj* doué(e), plein(e) de talent

talk [tɔːk] *n* (*a speech*) causerie *f*, exposé *m*; (*conversation*) discussion *f*, entretien *m*; (*gossip*) racontars *mpl* ♦ *vi* parler; **~s** *npl* (*POL etc*) entretiens *mpl*; **to ~ about** parler de; **to ~ sb into/out of doing** persuader qn de faire/ne pas faire; **~ over** *vt* discuter (de); **~ative** *adj* bavard(e); **~ show** *n* causerie (télévisée *or* radiodiffusée)

tall [tɔːl] *adj* (*person*) grand(e); (*building, tree*) haut(e); **to be 6 feet ~** ≃ mesurer 1 mètre 80; **~ story** *n* histoire *f* invraisemblable

tally ['tæli] *n* compte *m* ♦ *vi*: **to ~ (with)** correspondre (à)

talon ['tælən] *n* griffe *f*; (*of eagle*) serre *f*

tame [teɪm] *adj* apprivoisé(e); (*fig: story, style*) insipide

tamper ['tæmpə*r*] *vi*: **to ~ with** toucher à

tampon ['tæmpɔn] *n* tampon *m* (hygiénique *or* périodique)

tan [tæn] *n* (*also:* **suntan**) bronzage *m* ♦ *vt, vi* bronzer ♦ *adj* (*colour*) brun roux *inv*

tang [tæŋ] *n* odeur (*or* saveur) piquante

tangent ['tændʒənt] *n* (*MATH*) tangente *f*; **to go off at a ~** (*fig*) changer de sujet

tangerine [tændʒə'ri:n] *n* mandarine *f*

tangle ['tæŋgl] *n* enchevêtrement *m*; **to get in(to) a ~** s'embrouiller

tank [tæŋk] *n* (*water ~*) réservoir *m*; (*for fish*) aquarium *m*; (*MIL*) char *m* d'assaut, tank *m*

tanker ['tæŋkər] *n* (*ship*) pétrolier *m*, tanker *m*; (*truck*) camion-citerne *m*

tantalizing ['tæntəlaizɪŋ] *adj* (*smell*) extrêmement appétissant(e); (*offer*) terriblement tentant(e)

tantamount ['tæntəmaunt] *adj*: **~ to** qui équivaut à

tantrum ['tæntrəm] *n* accès *m* de colère

tap [tæp] *n* (*on sink etc*) robinet *m*; (*gentle blow*) petite tape ♦ *vt* frapper *or* taper légèrement; (*resources*) exploiter, utiliser; (*telephone*) mettre sur écoute; **on ~** (*fig: resources*) disponible; **~-dancing** *n* claquettes *fpl*

tape [teɪp] *n* ruban *m*; (*also:* **magnetic ~**) bande *f* (magnétique); (*cassette*) cassette *f*; (*sticky*) scotch *m* ♦ *vt* (*record*) enregistrer; (*stick with ~*) coller avec du scotch; **~ deck** *n* platine *f* d'enregistrement; **~ measure** *n* mètre *m* à ruban

taper ['teɪpər] *vi* s'effiler

tape recorder *n* magnétophone *m*

tapestry ['tæpɪstrɪ] *n* tapisserie *f*

tar [tɑ:] *n* goudron *m*

target ['tɑ:gɪt] *n* cible *f*; (*fig*) objectif *m*

tariff ['tærɪf] *n* (*COMM*) tarif *m*; (*taxes*) tarif douanier

tarmac ['tɑ:mæk] *n* (*BRIT: on road*) macadam *m*; (*AVIAT*) piste *f*

tarnish ['tɑ:nɪʃ] *vt* ternir

tarpaulin [tɑ:'pɔ:lɪn] *n* bâche (goudronnée)

tarragon ['tærəgən] *n* estragon *m*

tart [tɑ:t] *n* (*CULIN*) tarte *f*; (*BRIT: inf: prostitute*) putain *f* ♦ *adj* (*flavour*) âpre, aigrelet(te); **~ up** (*BRIT: inf*) *vt* (*object*) retaper; **to ~ o.s. up** se faire beau (belle), s'attifer (*pej*)

tartan ['tɑ:tn] *n* tartan *m* ♦ *adj* écossais(e)

tartar ['tɑ:tər] *n* (*on teeth*) tartre *m*; **~(e) sauce** *n* sauce *f* tartare

task [tɑ:sk] *n* tâche *f*; **to take sb to ~** prendre qn à partie; **~ force** *n* (*MIL, POLICE*) détachement spécial

tassel ['tæsl] *n* gland *m*; pompon *m*

taste [teɪst] *n* goût *m*; (*fig: glimpse, idea*) idée *f*, aperçu *m* ♦ *vt* goûter ♦ *vi*: **~ of** *or* **like** (*fish etc*) avoir le *or* un goût de; **you can ~ the garlic (in it)** on sent bien l'ail; **can I have a ~ of this wine?** puis-je goûter un peu de ce vin?; **in good/bad ~** de bon/mauvais goût; **~ful** *adj* de bon goût; **~less** *adj* (*food*) fade; (*remark*) de mauvais goût; **tasty** *adj* savoureux(-euse), délicieux(-euse)

tatters ['tætəz] *npl*: **in ~** en lambeaux

tattoo [tə'tu:] *n* tatouage *m*; (*spectacle*) parade *f* militaire ♦ *vt* tatouer

tatty ['tætɪ] (*BRIT: inf*) *adj* (*clothes*) frippé(e); (*shop, area*) délabré(e)

taught [tɔ:t] *pt, pp of* **teach**

taunt [tɔ:nt] *n* raillerie *f* ♦ *vt* railler

Taurus ['tɔ:rəs] *n* le Taureau

taut [tɔ:t] *adj* tendu(e)

tax [tæks] *n* (*on goods etc*) taxe *f*; (*on income*) impôts *mpl*, contributions *fpl* ♦ *vt* taxer; imposer; (*fig: patience etc*) mettre à l'épreuve; **~able** *adj* (*income*) imposable; **~ation** [tæk'seɪʃən] *n* taxation *f*; impôts *mpl*, contributions *fpl*; **~ avoidance** *n* dégrèvement fiscal; **~ disc** (*BRIT*) *n* (*AUT*) vignette *f* (automobile); **~ evasion** *n* fraude fiscale; **~-free** *adj* exempt(e) d'impôts

taxi ['tæksɪ] *n* taxi *m* ♦ *vi* (*AVIAT*) rouler (lentement) au sol; **~ driver** *n* chauffeur *m* de taxi; **~ rank** (*BRIT*) *n* station *f* de taxis; **~ stand** *n* = **taxi rank**

tax: ~ payer *n* contribuable *m/f*; **~ relief** *n* dégrèvement fiscal; **~ return** *n* déclaration *f* d'impôts *or* de revenus

TB *n abbr* = **tuberculosis**

tea [ti:] *n* thé *m*; (*BRIT: snack: for children*) goûter *m*; **high ~** collation combinant goûter et dîner; **~ bag** *n* sachet *m* de thé; **~ break** (*BRIT*) *n* pause-thé *f*

teach [ti:tʃ] (*pt, pp* **taught**) *vt*: **to ~ sb sth, ~ sth to sb** apprendre qch à qn; (*in* *school etc*) enseigner qch à qn ♦ *vi* enseigner; **~er** *n* (*in secondary school*) professeur *m*; (*in primary school*) instituteur(-trice); **~ing** *n* enseignement *m*

tea: ~ **cloth** *n* torchon *m*; ~ **cosy** *n* cloche *f* à thé; **~cup** *n* tasse *f* à thé

teak [tiːk] *n* teck *m*

tea leaves *npl* feuilles *fpl* de thé

team [tiːm] *n* équipe *f*; (*of animals*) attelage *m*; **~work** *n* travail *m* d'équipe

teapot ['tiːpɔt] *n* théière *f*

tear¹ [tɛər] (*pt* **tore**, *pp* **torn**) *n* déchirure *f* ♦ *vt* déchirer ♦ *vi* se déchirer; ~ **along** *vi* (*rush*) aller à toute vitesse; ~ **up** *vt* (*sheet of paper etc*) déchirer, mettre en morceaux *or* pièces

tear² [tɪər] *n* larme *f*; **in ~s** en larmes; **~ful** *adj* larmoyant(e); ~ **gas** *n* gaz *m* lacrymogène

tearoom ['tiːruːm] *n* salon *m* de thé

tease [tiːz] *vt* taquiner; (*unkindly*) tourmenter

tea set *n* service *m* à thé

teaspoon ['tiːspuːn] *n* petite cuiller; (*also*: **~ful**: *as measurement*) ≈ cuillerée *f* à café

teat [tiːt] *n* tétine *f*

teatime ['tiːtaɪm] *n* l'heure *f* du thé

tea towel (*BRIT*) *n* torchon *m* (à vaisselle)

technical ['tɛknɪkl] *adj* technique; **~ity** [tɛknɪ'kælɪtɪ] *n* (*detail*) détail *m* technique; (*point of law*) vice *m* de forme; **~ly** *adv* techniquement; (*strictly speaking*) en théorie

technician [tɛk'nɪʃən] *n* technicien(ne)

technique [tɛk'niːk] *n* technique *f*

techno ['tɛknəʊ] *n* (*music*) techno *f*

technological [tɛknə'lɔdʒɪkl] *adj* technologique

technology [tɛk'nɔlədʒɪ] *n* technologie *f*

teddy (bear) ['tɛdɪ(-)] *n* ours *m* en peluche

tedious ['tiːdɪəs] *adj* fastidieux(-euse)

teem [tiːm] *vi*: **to ~ (with)** grouiller (de); **it is ~ing (with rain)** il pleut à torrents

teenage ['tiːneɪdʒ] *adj* (*fashions etc*) pour jeunes, pour adolescents; (*children*) adolescent(e); **~r** *n* adolescent(e)

teens [tiːnz] *npl*: **to be in one's ~** être adolescent(e)

tee-shirt ['tiːʃəːt] *n* = **T-shirt**

teeter ['tiːtər] *vi* chanceler, vaciller

teeth [tiːθ] *npl of* **tooth**

teethe [tiːð] *vi* percer ses dents

teething troubles *npl* (*fig*) difficultés initiales

teetotal ['tiː'təʊtl] *adj* (*person*) qui ne boit jamais d'alcool

tele: **~communications** *npl* télécommunications *fpl*; **~conferencing** *n* téléconférence(s) *f(pl)*; **~gram** *n* télégramme *m*; **~graph** *n* télégraphe *m*; **~graph pole** *n* poteau *m* télégraphique

telephone ['tɛlɪfəʊn] *n* téléphone *m* ♦ *vt* (*person*) téléphoner à; (*message*) téléphoner; **on the ~** au téléphone; **to be on the ~** (*BRIT*: *have a ~*) avoir le téléphone; ~ **booth**, ~ **box** (*BRIT*) *n* cabine *f* téléphonique; ~ **call** *n* coup *m* de téléphone, appel *m* téléphonique; ~ **directory** *n* annuaire *m* (du téléphone); ~ **number** *n* numéro *m* de téléphone; **telephonist** [tə'lɛfənɪst] (*BRIT*) *n* téléphoniste *m/f*

telesales ['tɛlɪseɪlz] *n* télévente *f*

telescope ['tɛlɪskəʊp] *n* télescope *m*

television ['tɛlɪvɪʒən] *n* télévision *f*; **on ~** à la télévision; ~ **set** *n* (poste *f* de) télévision *m*

telex ['tɛlɛks] *n* télex *m*

tell [tɛl] (*pt*, *pp* **told**) *vt* dire; (*relate: story*) raconter; (*distinguish*): **to ~ sth from** distinguer qch de ♦ *vi* (*talk*): **to ~ (of)** parler (de); (*have effect*) se faire sentir, se voir; **to ~ sb to do** dire à qn de faire; ~ **off** *vt* réprimander, gronder; **~er** *n* (*in bank*) caissier(-ère); **~ing** *adj* (*remark, detail*) révélateur(-trice); **~tale** *adj* (*sign*) éloquent(e), révélateur(-trice)

telly ['tɛlɪ] (*BRIT*: *inf*) *n abbr* (= *television*) télé *f*

temp [tɛmp] *n abbr* (= *temporary*) (secrétaire *f*) intérimaire *f*

temper ['tɛmpər] *n* (*nature*) caractère *m*; (*mood*) humeur *f*; (*fit of anger*) colère *f* ♦ *vt* (*moderate*) tempérer, adoucir; **to be**

in a ~ être en colère; **to lose one's ~** se mettre en colère

temperament ['tɛmprəmənt] *n* (*nature*) tempérament *m*; **~al** [tɛmprə'mɛntl] *adj* capricieux(-euse)

temperate ['tɛmprət] *adj* (*climate, country*) tempéré(e)

temperature ['tɛmprətʃəʳ] *n* température *f*; **to have** *or* **run a ~** avoir de la fièvre

temple ['tɛmpl] *n* (*building*) temple *m*; (*ANAT*) tempe *f*

temporary ['tɛmpərərɪ] *adj* temporaire, provisoire; (*job, worker*) temporaire

tempt [tɛmpt] *vt* tenter; **to ~ sb into doing** persuader qn de faire; **~ation** [tɛmp'teɪʃən] *n* tentation *f*; **~ing** *adj* tentant(e)

ten [tɛn] *num* dix

tenacity [tə'næsɪtɪ] *n* ténacité *f*

tenancy ['tɛnənsɪ] *n* location *f*; état *m* de locataire

tenant ['tɛnənt] *n* locataire *m/f*

tend [tɛnd] *vt* s'occuper de ♦ *vi*: **to ~ to do** avoir tendance à faire; **~ency** ['tɛndənsɪ] *n* tendance *f*

tender ['tɛndəʳ] *adj* tendre; (*delicate*) délicat(e); (*sore*) sensible ♦ *n* (*COMM: offer*) soumission *f* ♦ *vt* offrir

tenement ['tɛnəmənt] *n* immeuble *m*

tennis ['tɛnɪs] *n* tennis *m*; **~ ball** *n* balle *f* de tennis; **~ court** *n* (court *m* de) tennis; **~ player** *n* joueur(-euse) de tennis; **~ racket** *n* raquette *f* de tennis; **~ shoes** *npl* (chaussures *fpl* de) tennis *mpl*

tenor ['tɛnəʳ] *n* (*MUS*) ténor *m*

tenpin bowling ['tɛnpɪn-] (*BRIT*) *n* bowling *m* (à dix quilles)

tense [tɛns] *adj* tendu(e) ♦ *n* (*LING*) temps *m*

tension ['tɛnʃən] *n* tension *f*

tent [tɛnt] *n* tente *f*

tentative ['tɛntətɪv] *adj* timide, hésitant(e); (*conclusion*) provisoire

tenterhooks ['tɛntəhuks] *npl*: **on ~** sur des charbons ardents

tenth [tɛnθ] *num* dixième

tent peg *n* piquet *m* de tente

tent pole *n* montant *m* de tente

tenuous ['tɛnjuəs] *adj* ténu(e)

tenure ['tɛnjuəʳ] *n* (*of property*) bail *m*; (*of job*) période *f* de jouissance

tepid ['tɛpɪd] *adj* tiède

term [tə:m] *n* terme *m*; (*SCOL*) trimestre *m* ♦ *vt* appeler; **~s** *npl* (*conditions*) conditions *fpl*; (*COMM*) tarif *m*; **in the short/long ~** à court/long terme; **to come to ~s with** (*problem*) faire face à

terminal ['tə:mɪnl] *adj* (*disease*) dans sa phase terminale; (*patient*) incurable ♦ *n* (*ELEC*) borne *f*; (*for oil, ore etc, COMPUT*) terminal *m*; (*also*: **air ~**) aérogare *f*; (*BRIT: also*: **coach ~**) gare routière; **~ly** *adv*: **to be ~ly ill** être condamné(e)

terminate ['tə:mɪneɪt] *vt* mettre fin à; (*pregnancy*) interrompre

termini ['tə:mɪnaɪ] *npl of* **terminus**

terminus ['tə:mɪnəs] (*pl* **termini**) *n* terminus *m inv*

terrace ['tɛrəs] *n* terrasse *f*; (*BRIT: row of houses*) rangée *f* de maisons (*attenantes*); **the ~s** *npl* (*BRIT: SPORT*) les gradins *mpl*; **~d** *adj* (*garden*) en terrasses

terracotta ['tɛrə'kɔtə] *n* terre cuite

terrain [tɛ'reɪn] *n* terrain *m* (*sol*)

terrible ['tɛrɪbl] *adj* terrible, atroce; (*weather, conditions*) affreux(-euse), épouvantable; **terribly** *adv* terriblement; (*very badly*) affreusement mal

terrier ['tɛrɪəʳ] *n* terrier *m* (*chien*)

terrific [tə'rɪfɪk] *adj* fantastique, incroyable, terrible; (*wonderful*) formidable, sensationnel(le)

terrify ['tɛrɪfaɪ] *vt* terrifier

territory ['tɛrɪtərɪ] *n* territoire *m*

terror ['tɛrəʳ] *n* terreur *f*; **~ism** *n* terrorisme *m*; **~ist** *n* terroriste *m/f*

test [tɛst] *n* (*trial, check*) essai *m*; (*of courage etc*) épreuve *f*; (*MED*) examen *m*; (*CHEM*) analyse *f*; (*SCOL*) interrogation *f*; (*also*: **driving ~**) (examen du) permis *m* de conduire ♦ *vt* essayer; mettre à l'épreuve; examiner; analyser; faire subir une interrogation à

testament ['tɛstəmənt] *n* testament *m*;

the Old/New T~ l'Ancien/le Nouveau Testament

testicle ['testɪkl] *n* testicule *m*

testify ['testɪfaɪ] *vi* (*LAW*) témoigner, déposer; **to ~ to sth** attester qch

testimony ['testɪmənɪ] *n* témoignage *m*; (*proof*): **to be (a) ~ to** être la preuve de

test match *n* (*CRICKET, RUGBY*) match international

test tube *n* éprouvette *f*

tetanus ['tetənəs] *n* tétanos *m*

tether ['teðəʳ] *vt* attacher ♦ *n*: **at the end of one's ~** à bout (de patience)

text [tekst] *n* texte *m*; SMS *m* ♦ *vi* envoyer un SMS ♦ *vt*: **to text sb** envoyer un SMS à qn **~book** *n* manuel *m*

texture ['tekstʃəʳ] *n* texture *f*; (*of skin, paper etc*) grain *m*

Thailand ['taɪlænd] *n* Thaïlande *f*

Thames [temz] *n*: **the ~** la Tamise

than [ðæn, ðən] *conj* que; (*with numerals*): **more ~ 10/once** plus de 10/d'une fois; **I have more/less ~ you** j'en ai plus/moins que toi; **she has more apples ~ pears** elle a plus de pommes que de poires

thank [θæŋk] *vt* remercier, dire merci à; **~s** *npl* (*gratitude*) remerciements *mpl* ♦ *excl* merci!; **~ you (very much)** merci (beaucoup); **~s to** grâce à; **~ God!** Dieu merci!; **~ful** *adj*: **~ful (for)** reconnaissant(e) (de); **~less** *adj* ingrat(e); **T~sgiving (Day)** *n* jour *m* d'action de grâce (*fête américaine*)

⎡ **Thanksgiving Day** ⎤

ⓘ **Thanksgiving Day** *est un jour de congé aux États-Unis, le quatrième jeudi du mois de novembre, commémorant la bonne récolte que les Pélerins venus de Grande-Bretagne ont eue en 1621; traditionnellement, c'est un jour où l'on remerciait Dieu et où l'on organisait un grand festin. Une fête semblable a lieu au Canada le deuxième lundi d'octobre.*

⎡ *KEYWORD* ⎤

that [ðæt] *adj* (*demonstrative: pl those*) ce,

cet +*vowel or h mute*, cette *f*; **that man/ woman/book** cet homme/cette femme/ ce livre; (*not "this"*) cet homme-là/cette femme-là/ce livre-là; **that one** celui-là (celle-là)

♦ *pron* 1 (*demonstrative: pl those*) ce; (*not "this one"*) cela, ça; **who's that?** qui estce?; **what's that?** qu'est-ce que c'est?; **is that you?** c'est toi?; **I prefer this to that** je préfère ceci à cela or ça; **that's what he said** c'est or voilà ce qu'il a dit; **that is (to say)** c'est-à-dire, à savoir

2 (*relative: subject*) qui; (*: object*) que; (*: indirect*) lequel (laquelle), lesquels (lesquelles) *pl*; **the book that I read** le livre que j'ai lu; **the books that are in the library** les livres qui sont dans la bibliothèque; **all that I have** tout ce que j'ai; **the box that I put it in** la boîte dans laquelle je l'ai mis; **the people that I spoke to** les gens auxquels or à qui j'ai parlé

3 (*relative: of time*) où; **the day that he came** le jour où il est venu

♦ *conj* que; **he thought that I was ill** il pensait que j'étais malade

♦ *adv* (*demonstrative*): **I can't work that much** je ne peux pas travailler autant que cela; **I didn't know it was that bad** je ne savais pas que c'était si or aussi mauvais; **it's about that high** c'est à peu près de cette hauteur

thatched [θætʃt] *adj* (*roof*) de chaume; **~ cottage** chaumière *f*

thaw [θɔː] *n* dégel *m* ♦ *vi* (*ice*) fondre; (*food*) dégeler ♦ *vt* (*food: also:* **~ out**) (faire) dégeler

⎡ *KEYWORD* ⎤

the [ðiː, ðə] *def art* 1 (*gen*) le, la *f*, l' +*vowel or h mute*, les *pl*; **the boy/girl/ink** le garçon/la fille/l'encre; **the children** les enfants; **the history of the world** l'histoire du monde; **give it to the postman** donne-le au facteur; **to play the piano/ flute** jouer du piano/de la flûte; **the rich and the poor** les riches et les pauvres

2 (*in titles*): **Elizabeth the First** Elisabeth
première; **Peter the Great** Pierre le Grand
3 (*in comparisons*): **the more he works,
the more he earns** plus il travaille, plus il
gagne de l'argent

theatre ['θɪətər] *n* théâtre *m*; (*also:* **lecture
~**) amphi(théâtre) *m*; (MED: *also:* **operating ~**) salle *f* d'opération; **~-goer** *n* ha-
bitué(e) du théâtre; **theatrical** [θɪ'ætrɪkl]
adj théâtral(e)
theft [θɛft] *n* vol *m* (*larcin*)
their [ðɛər] *adj* leur; (*pl*) leurs; *see also* **my**;
~s *pron* le (la) leur; (*pl*) les leurs; *see also*
mine¹
them [ðɛm, ðəm] *pron* (*direct*) les; (*indirect*)
leur; (*stressed, after prep*) eux (elles); *see
also* **me**
theme [θi:m] *n* thème *m*; **~ park** *n* parc
m (d'attraction) à thème; **~ song** *n* chanson principale
themselves [ðəm'sɛlvz] *pl pron* (*reflexive*)
se; (*emphatic, after prep*) eux-mêmes
(elles-mêmes); *see also* **oneself**
then [ðɛn] *adv* (*at that time*) alors, à ce
moment-là; (*next*) puis, ensuite; (*and also*)
et puis ♦ *conj* (*therefore*) alors, dans ce cas
♦ *adj*: **the ~ president** le président d'alors
or de l'époque; **by ~** (*past*) à ce
moment-là; (*future*) d'ici là; **from ~ on** dès
lors
theology [θɪ'ɔlədʒɪ] *n* théologie *f*
theoretical [θɪə'rɛtɪkl] *adj* théorique
theory ['θɪərɪ] *n* théorie *f*
therapy ['θɛrəpɪ] *n* thérapie *f*

KEYWORD

there [ðɛər] *adv* 1: **there is, there are** il y
a; **there are 3 of them** (*people, things*) il y
en a 3; **there has been an accident** il y
a eu un accident
2 (*referring to place*) là, là-bas; **it's there**
c'est là(-bas); **in/on/up/down there** là-
dedans/là-dessus/là-haut/en bas; **he went
there on Friday** il y est allé vendredi; **I
want that book there** je veux ce livre-là;
there he is! le voilà!

3: **there, there** (*esp to child*) allons, allons!

there: **~abouts** *adv* (*place*) par là, près de
là; (*amount*) environ, à peu près; **~after**
adv par la suite; **~by** *adv* ainsi; **~fore** *adv*
donc, par conséquent; **~'s = there is;
there has**
thermal ['θɜ:ml] *adj* (*springs*) thermal(e);
(*underwear*) en thermolactyl ®; (COMPUT:
paper) thermosensible; (: *printer*) thermi-
que
thermometer [θə'mɔmɪtər] *n* thermomètre *m*
Thermos ® ['θɜ:məs] *n* (*also:* **~ flask**)
thermos ® *m or f inv*
thermostat ['θɜ:məustæt] *n* thermostat *m*
thesaurus [θɪ'sɔ:rəs] *n* dictionnaire *m* des
synonymes
these [ði:z] *pl adj* ces; (*not "those"*): **~
books** ces livres-ci ♦ *pl pron* ceux-ci
(celles-ci)
thesis ['θi:sɪs] (*pl* **theses**) *n* thèse *f*
they [ðeɪ] *pl pron* ils (elles); (*stressed*) eux
(elles); **~ say that ...** (*it is said that*) on dit
que ...; **~'d = they had; they would; ~'ll
= they shall; they will; ~'re = they are;
~'ve = they have**
thick [θɪk] *adj* épais(se); (*stupid*) bête, bor-
né(e) ♦ *n*: **in the ~ of** au beau milieu de,
en plein cœur de; **it's 20 cm ~** il/elle a
20 cm d'épaisseur; **~en** vi s'épaissir ♦ *vt*
(*sauce etc*) épaissir; **~ness** *n* épaisseur *f*;
~set *adj* trapu(e), costaud(e)
thief [θi:f] (*pl* **thieves**) *n* voleur(-euse)
thigh [θaɪ] *n* cuisse *f*
thimble ['θɪmbl] *n* dé *m* (à coudre)
thin [θɪn] *adj* mince; (*skinny*) maigre; (*soup,
sauce*) peu épais(se), clair(e); (*hair, crowd*)
clairsemé(e) ♦ *vt*: **to ~ (down)** (*sauce,
paint*) délayer
thing [θɪŋ] *n* chose *f*; (*object*) objet *m*;
(*contraption*) truc *m*; (*mania*): **to have a ~
about** être obsédé(e) par; **~s** *npl* (*belongings*) affaires *fpl*; **poor ~!** le (la) pauvre!;
the best ~ would be to le mieux serait
de; **how are ~s?** comment ça va?
think [θɪŋk] (*pt, pp* **thought**) *vi* penser, ré-

fléchir; (*believe*) penser ♦ *vt* (*imagine*) imaginer; **what did you ~ of them?** qu'avez-vous pensé d'eux?; **to ~ about sth/sb** penser à qch/qn; **I'll ~ about it** je vais y réfléchir; **to ~ of doing** avoir l'idée de faire; **I ~ so/not** je crois or pense que oui/non; **to ~ well of** avoir une haute opinion de; **~ over** *vt* bien réfléchir à; **~ up** *vt* inventer, trouver; **~ tank** *n* groupe *m* de réflexion

thinly ['θɪnlɪ] *adv* (*cut*) en fines tranches; (*spread*) en une couche mince

third [θəːd] *num* troisième ♦ *n* (*fraction*) tiers *m*; (*AUT*) troisième (vitesse) *f*; (*BRIT: SCOL: degree*) ≈ licence *f* sans mention; **~ly** *adv* troisièmement; **~ party insurance** *n* assurance *f* au tiers; **~-rate** *adj* de qualité médiocre; **the T~ World** *n* le tiers monde

thirst [θəːst] *n* soif *f*; **~y** *adj* (*person*) qui a soif, assoiffé(e); (*work*) qui donne soif; **to be ~y** avoir soif

thirteen [θəː'tiːn] *num* treize

thirty ['θəːtɪ] *num* trente

KEYWORD
---

this [ðɪs] *adj* (*demonstrative: pl* these) ce, cet +*vowel or h* mute, cette *f*; **this man/woman/book** cet homme/cette femme/ce livre; (*not "that"*) cet homme-ci/cette femme-ci/ce livre-ci; **this one** celui-ci (celle-ci)

♦ *pron* (*demonstrative: pl* these) ce; (*not "that one"*) celui-ci (celle-ci), ceci; **who's this?** qui est-ce?; **what's this?** qu'est-ce que c'est?; **I prefer this to that** je préfère ceci à cela; **this is what he said** voici ce qu'il a dit; **this is Mr Brown** (*in introductions*) je vous présente Mr Brown; (*in photo*) c'est Mr Brown; (*on telephone*) ici Mr Brown

♦ *adv* (*demonstrative*): **it was about this big** c'était à peu près de cette grandeur *or* grand comme ça; **I didn't know it was this bad** je ne savais pas que c'était si *or* aussi mauvais

thistle ['θɪsl] *n* chardon *m*

thorn [θɔːn] *n* épine *f*

thorough ['θʌrə] *adj* (*search*) minutieux(-euse); (*knowledge, research*) approfondi(e); (*work, person*) consciencieux(-euse); (*cleaning*) à fond; **~bred** *n* (*horse*) pur-sang *m inv*; **~fare** *n* route *f*; **"no ~fare"** "passage interdit"; **~ly** *adv* minutieusement; en profondeur; à fond; (*very*) tout à fait

those [ðəʊz] *pl adj* ces; (*not "these"*): **~ books** ces livres-là ♦ *pl pron* ceux-là (celles-là)

though [ðəʊ] *conj* bien que +*sub*, quoique +*sub* ♦ *adv* pourtant

thought [θɔːt] *pt, pp of* **think** ♦ *n* pensée *f*; (*idea*) idée *f*; (*opinion*) avis *m*; **~ful** *adj* (*deep in thought*) pensif(-ive); (*serious*) réfléchi(e); (*considerate*) prévenant(e); **~less** *adj* étourdi(e); qui manque de considération

thousand ['θaʊzənd] *num* mille; **two ~** deux mille; **~s of** des milliers de; **~th** *num* millième

thrash [θræʃ] *vt* rouer de coups; donner une correction à; (*defeat*) battre à plate couture; **~ about**, **~ around** *vi* se débattre; **~ out** *vt* débattre de

thread [θrɛd] *n* fil *m*; (*TECH*) pas *m*, filetage *m* ♦ *vt* (*needle*) enfiler; **~bare** *adj* râpé(e), élimé(e)

threat [θrɛt] *n* menace *f*; **~en** *vi* menacer ♦ *vt*: **to ~en sb with sth/to do** menacer qn de qch/de faire

three [θriː] *num* trois; **~-dimensional** *adj* à trois dimensions; **~-piece suit** *n* complet *m* (avec gilet); **~-piece suite** *n* salon *m* comprenant un canapé et deux fauteuils assortis; **~-ply** *adj* (*wool*) trois fils *inv*

threshold ['θrɛʃhəʊld] *n* seuil *m*

threw [θruː] *pt of* **throw**

thrifty ['θrɪftɪ] *adj* économe

thrill [θrɪl] *n* (*excitement*) émotion *f*, sensation forte; (*shudder*) frisson *m* ♦ *vt* (*audience*) électriser; **to be ~ed** (*with gift etc*) être ravi(e); **~er** *n* film *m* (*or* roman *m or* pièce *f*) à suspense; **~ing** *adj* saisissant(e), palpitant(e)

thrive [θraɪv] (*pt, pp* **thrived**) *vi* pousser, se développer; (*business*) prospérer; **he ~s on it** cela lui réussit; **thriving** *adj* (*business, community*) prospère

throat [θrəut] *n* gorge *f*; **to have a sore ~** avoir mal à la gorge

throb [θrɔb] *vi* (*heart*) palpiter; (*engine*) vibrer; **my head is ~bing** j'ai des élancements dans la tête

throes [θrəuz] *npl*: **in the ~ of** au beau milieu de

throne [θrəun] *n* trône *m*

throng [θrɔŋ] *n* foule *f* ♦ *vt* se presser dans

throttle ['θrɔtl] *n* (*AUT*) accélérateur *m* ♦ *vt* étrangler

through [θru:] *prep* à travers; (*time*) pendant, durant; (*by means of*) par, par l'intermédiaire de; (*owing to*) à cause de ♦ *adj* (*ticket, train, passage*) direct(e) ♦ *adv* à travers; **to put sb ~ to sb** (*BRIT: TEL*) passer qn à qn; **to be ~** (*BRIT: TEL*) avoir la communication; (*esp US: have finished*) avoir fini; **to be ~ with sb** (*relationship*) avoir rompu avec qn; **"no ~ road"** (*BRIT*) "impasse"; **~out** *prep* (*place*) partout dans; (*time*) durant tout(e) le (la) ♦ *adv* partout

throw [θrəu] (*pt* **threw**, *pp* **thrown**) *n* jet *m*; (*SPORT*) lancer *m* ♦ *vt* lancer, jeter; (*SPORT*) lancer; (*rider*) désarçonner; (*fig*) décontenancer; **to ~ a party** donner une réception; **~ away** *vt* jeter; **~ off** *vt* se débarrasser de; **~ out** *vt* jeter; (*reject*) rejeter; (*person*) mettre à la porte; **~ up** *vi* vomir; **~away** *adj* à jeter; (*remark*) fait(e) en passant; **~-in** *n* (*SPORT*) remise *f* en jeu

thru [θru:] (*US*) = **through**

thrush [θrʌʃ] *n* (*bird*) grive *f*

thrust [θrʌst] (*pt, pp* **thrust**) *n* (*TECH*) poussée *f* ♦ *vt* pousser brusquement; (*push in*) enfoncer

thud [θʌd] *n* bruit sourd

thug [θʌg] *n* voyou *m*

thumb [θʌm] *n* (*ANAT*) pouce *m* ♦ *vt*: **to ~ a lift** faire de l'auto-stop, arrêter une voi-

ture; **~ through** *vt* (*book*) feuilleter; **~tack** (*US*) *n* punaise *f* (*clou*)

thump [θʌmp] *n* grand coup; (*sound*) bruit sourd ♦ *vt* cogner sur ♦ *vi* cogner, battre fort

thunder ['θʌndər] *n* tonnerre *m* ♦ *vi* tonner; (*train etc*): **to ~ past** passer dans un grondement *or* un bruit de tonnerre; **~bolt** *n* foudre *f*; **~clap** *n* coup *m* de tonnerre; **~storm** *n* orage *m*; **~y** *adj* orageux(-euse)

Thursday ['θə:zdɪ] *n* jeudi *m*

thus [ðʌs] *adv* ainsi

thwart [θwɔ:t] *vt* contrecarrer

thyme [taɪm] *n* thym *m*

tiara [tɪ'ɑ:rə] *n* diadème *m*

tick [tɪk] *n* (*sound: of clock*) tic-tac *m*; (*mark*) coche *f*; (*ZOOL*) tique *f*; (*BRIT: inf*): **in a ~** dans une seconde ♦ *vi* faire tic-tac ♦ *vt* (*item on list*) cocher; **~ off** *vt* (*item on list*) cocher; (*person*) réprimander, attraper; **~ over** *vi* (*engine*) tourner au ralenti; (*fig*) aller *or* marcher doucement

ticket ['tɪkɪt] *n* billet *m*; (*for bus, tube*) ticket *m*; (*in shop: on goods*) étiquette *f*; (*for library*) carte *f*; (*parking ~*) papillon *m*, p.-v. *m*; **~ collector**, **~ inspector** *n* contrôleur(-euse); **~ office** *n* guichet *m*, bureau *m* de vente des billets

tickle ['tɪkl] *vt, vi* chatouiller; **ticklish** *adj* (*person*) chatouilleux(-euse); (*problem*) épineux(-euse)

tidal ['taɪdl] *adj* (*force*) de la marée; (*estuary*) à marée; **~ wave** *n* raz-de-marée *m inv*

tidbit ['tɪdbɪt] (*US*) *n* = **titbit**

tiddlywinks ['tɪdlɪwɪŋks] *n* jeu *m* de puce

tide [taɪd] *n* marée *f*; (*fig: of events*) cours *m* ♦ *vt*: **to ~ sb over** dépanner qn; **high/low ~** marée haute/basse

tidy ['taɪdɪ] *adj* (*room*) bien rangé(e); (*dress, work*) net(te), soigné(e); (*person*) ordonné(e), qui a de l'ordre ♦ *vt* (*also:* **~ up**) ranger

tie [taɪ] *n* (*string etc*) cordon *m*; (*BRIT: also:* **necktie**) cravate *f*; (*fig: link*) lien *m*; (*SPORT: draw*) égalité *f* de points; match nul ♦ vt (parcel) attacher; (ribbon, shoe-laces) nouer ♦ vi (SPORT) faire match nul; finir à égalité de points; **to ~ sth in a bow** faire un nœud à or avec qch; **to ~ a knot in sth** faire un nœud à qch; ~ **down** vt (fig): **to ~ sb down (to)** contraindre qn (à accepter); **to be ~d down** (by relationship) se fixer; ~ **up** vt (parcel) ficeler; (dog, boat) attacher; (prisoner) ligoter; (arrangements) conclure; **to be ~d up** (busy) être pris(e) or occupé(e)

tier [tɪəʳ] n gradin m; (of cake) étage m

tiger ['taɪgəʳ] n tigre m

tight [taɪt] adj (rope) tendu(e), raide; (clothes) étroit(e), très juste; (budget, programme, bend) serré(e); (control) strict(e), sévère; (inf: drunk) ivre, rond(e) ♦ adv (squeeze) très fort; (shut) hermétiquement, bien; ~**en** vt (rope) tendre; (screw) resserrer; (control) renforcer ♦ vi se tendre, se resserrer; ~**fisted** adj avare; ~**ly** adv (grasp) bien, très fort; ~**rope** n corde f raide; ~**s** (BRIT) npl collant m

tile [taɪl] n (on roof) tuile f; (on wall or floor) carreau m; ~**d** adj en tuiles; carrelé(e)

till [tɪl] n caisse (enregistreuse) ♦ vt (land) cultiver ♦ prep, conj = **until**

tiller ['tɪləʳ] n (NAUT) barre f (du gouvernail)

tilt [tɪlt] vt pencher, incliner ♦ vi pencher, être incliné(e)

timber ['tɪmbəʳ] n (material) bois m (de construction); (trees) arbres mpl

time [taɪm] n temps m; (epoch: often pl) époque f, temps; (by clock) heure f; (moment) moment m; (occasion, also MATH) fois f; (MUS) mesure f ♦ vt (race) chronométrer; (programme) minuter; (visit) fixer; (remark etc) choisir le moment de; **a long ~** un long moment, longtemps; **for the ~ being** pour le moment; **4 at a ~** 4 à la fois; **from ~ to ~** de temps en temps; **at ~s** parfois; **in ~** (soon enough) à temps; (after some ~) avec le temps, à la longue; (MUS) en mesure; **in a week's ~** dans une semaine; **in no ~** en un rien de temps; **any ~** n'importe quand; **on ~** à

l'heure; **5 ~s 5** 5 fois 5; **what ~ is it?** quelle heure est-il?; **to have a good ~** bien s'amuser; ~ **bomb** n bombe f à retardement; ~ **lag** (BRIT) n décalage m; (in travel) décalage horaire; ~**less** adj éternel(le); ~**ly** adj opportun(e); ~ **off** n temps m libre; ~**r** n (TECH) minuteur m; (in kitchen) compte-minutes m inv; ~**scale** n délais mpl; ~**share** n maison f/appartement m en multipropriété; ~ **switch** (BRIT) n minuteur m; (for lighting) minuterie f; ~**table** n (RAIL) (indicateur m) horaire m; (SCOL) emploi m du temps; ~ **zone** n fuseau m horaire

timid ['tɪmɪd] adj timide; (easily scared) peureux(-euse)

timing ['taɪmɪŋ] n minutage m; chronométrage m; **the ~ of his resignation** le moment choisi pour sa démission

timpani ['tɪmpənɪ] npl timbales fpl

tin [tɪn] n étain m; (also: ~ **plate**) fer-blanc m; (BRIT: can) boîte f (de conserve); (for storage) boîte f; ~**foil** n papier m d'étain or aluminium

tinge [tɪndʒ] n nuance f ♦ vt: ~**d with** teinté(e) de

tingle ['tɪŋgl] vi picoter; (person) avoir des picotements

tinker ['tɪŋkəʳ] n (gipsy) romanichel m; ~ **with** vt fus bricoler, rafistoler

tinkle ['tɪŋkl] vi tinter

tinned [tɪnd] (BRIT) adj (food) en boîte, en conserve

tin opener (BRIT) n ouvre-boîte(s) m

tinsel ['tɪnsl] n guirlandes fpl de Noël (argentées)

tint [tɪnt] n teinte f; (for hair) shampooing colorant; ~**ed** adj (hair) teint(e); (spectacles, glass) teinté(e)

tiny ['taɪnɪ] adj minuscule

tip [tɪp] n (end) bout m; (gratuity) pourboire m; (BRIT: for rubbish) décharge f; (advice) tuyau m ♦ vt (waiter) donner un pourboire à; (tilt) incliner; (overturn: also: ~ **over**) renverser; (empty: ~ **out**) déverser; ~-**off** n (hint) tuyau m; ~**ped** (BRIT) adj (cigarette) (à bout) filtre inv

tipsy ['tɪpsɪ] (*inf*) *adj* un peu ivre, éméché(e)

tiptoe ['tɪptəu] *n*: **on ~** sur la pointe des pieds

tiptop [tɪp'tɒp] *adj*: **in ~ condition** en excellent état

tire ['taɪər] *n* (*US*) = **tyre** ♦ *vt* fatiguer ♦ *vi* se fatiguer; **~d** *adj* fatigué(e); **to be ~d of** en avoir assez de, être las (lasse) de; **~less** *adj* (*person*) infatigable; (*efforts*) inlassable; **~some** *adj* ennuyeux(-euse); **tiring** *adj* fatigant(e)

tissue ['tɪʃuː] *n* tissu *m*; (*paper handkerchief*) mouchoir *m* en papier, kleenex ® *m*; **~ paper** *n* papier *m* de soie

tit [tɪt] *n* (*bird*) mésange *f*; **to give ~ for tat** rendre la pareille

titbit ['tɪtbɪt] *n* (*food*) friandise *f*; (*news*) potin *m*

title ['taɪtl] *n* titre *m*; **~ deed** *n* (*LAW*) titre (constitutif) de propriété; **~ role** *n* rôle principal

TM *abbr* = **trademark**

---

to [tuː, tə] *prep* **1** (*direction*) à; **to go to France/Portugal/London/school** aller en France/au Portugal/à Londres/à l'école; **to go to Claude's/the doctor's** aller chez Claude/le docteur; **the road to Edinburgh** la route d'Édimbourg

2 (*as far as*) (jusqu')à; **to count to 10** compter jusqu'à 10; **from 40 to 50 people** de 40 à 50 personnes

3 (*with expressions of time*): **a quarter to 5** 5 heures moins le quart; **it's twenty to 3** il est 3 heures moins vingt

4 (*for, of*) de; **the key to the front door** la clé de la porte d'entrée; **a letter to his wife** une lettre (adressée) à sa femme

5 (*expressing indirect object*) à; **to give sth to sb** donner qch à qn; **to talk to sb** parler à qn

6 (*in relation to*) à; **3 goals to 2** 3 (buts) à 2; **30 miles to the gallon** 9,4 litres aux cent (km)

7 (*purpose, result*): **to come to sb's aid** venir au secours de qn, porter secours à qn; **to sentence sb to death** condamner qn à mort; **to my surprise** à ma grande surprise

♦ *with vb* **1** (*simple infinitive*): **to go/eat** aller/manger

2 (*following another vb*): **to want/try/start to do** vouloir/essayer de/commencer à faire

3 (*with vb omitted*): **I don't want to** je ne veux pas

4 (*purpose, result*) pour; **I did it to help you** je l'ai fait pour vous aider

5 (*equivalent to relative clause*): **I have things to do** j'ai des choses à faire; **the main thing is to try** l'important est d'essayer

6 (*after adjective etc*): **ready to go** prêt(e) à partir; **too old/young to ...** trop vieux/jeune pour ...

♦ *adv*: **push/pull the door to** tirez/poussez la porte

---

toad [təud] *n* crapaud *m*

toadstool ['təudstuːl] *n* champignon (vénéneux)

toast [təust] *n* (*CULIN*) pain grillé, toast *m*; (*drink, speech*) toast ♦ *vt* (*CULIN*) faire griller; (*drink to*) porter un toast à; **~er** *n* grille-pain *m inv*

tobacco [tə'bækəu] *n* tabac *m*; **~nist** *n* marchand(e) de tabac; **~nist's (shop)** *n* (bureau *m* de) tabac *m*

toboggan [tə'bɒgən] *n* toboggan *m*; (*child's*) luge *f* ♦ *vi*: **to go ~ing** faire de la luge

today [tə'deɪ] *adv* (*also fig*) aujourd'hui ♦ *n* aujourd'hui *m*

toddler ['tɒdlər] *n* enfant *m/f* qui commence à marcher, bambin *m*

toe [təu] *n* doigt *m* de pied, orteil *m*; (*of shoe*) bout *m* ♦ *vt*: **to ~ the line** (*fig*) obéir, se conformer; **~nail** *n* ongle *m* du pied

toffee ['tɒfɪ] *n* caramel *m*; **~ apple** (*BRIT*) *n* pomme caramélisée

together [tə'geðər] *adv* ensemble; (*at same*

time) en même temps; **~ with** avec

toil [tɔɪl] *n* dur travail, labeur *m* ♦ *vi* peiner

toilet ['tɔɪlət] *n* (*BRIT: lavatory*) toilettes *fpl* ♦ *cpd* (*accessories etc*) de toilette; **~ bag** *n* nécessaire *m* de toilette; **~ paper** *n* papier *m* hygiénique; **~ries** *npl* articles *mpl* de toilette; **~ roll** *n* rouleau *m* de papier hygiénique

token ['təʊkən] *n* (*sign*) marque *f*, témoignage *m*; (*metal disc*) jeton *m* ♦ *adj* (*strike, payment etc*) symbolique; **book/record ~** (*BRIT*) chèque-livre/-disque *m*; **gift ~** bon-cadeau *m*

told [təʊld] *pt, pp of* **tell**

tolerable ['tɒlərəbl] *adj* (*bearable*) tolérable; (*fairly good*) passable

tolerant ['tɒlərnt] *adj*: **~ (of)** tolérant(e) (à l'égard de)

tolerate ['tɒləreɪt] *vt* supporter, tolérer

toll [təʊl] *n* (*tax, charge*) péage *m*; (*of bell*) sonner; **the accident ~ on the roads** le nombre des victimes de la route

tomato [tə'mɑːtəʊ] (*pl* **~es**) *n* tomate *f*

tomb [tuːm] *n* tombe *f*

tomboy ['tɒmbɔɪ] *n* garçon manqué

tombstone ['tuːmstəʊn] *n* pierre tombale

tomcat ['tɒmkæt] *n* matou *m*

tomorrow [tə'mɒrəʊ] *adv* (*also fig*) demain ♦ *n* demain *m*; **the day after ~** après-demain; **~ morning** demain matin

ton [tʌn] *n* tonne *f* (*BRIT = 1016kg; US = 907kg*), (*metric*) tonne (= *1000 kg*); **~s of** (*inf*) des tas de

tone [təʊn] *n* ton *m* ♦ *vi* (*also:* **~ in**) s'harmoniser; **~ down** *vt* (*colour, criticism*) adoucir; (*sound*) baisser; **~ up** *vt* (*muscles*) tonifier; **~-deaf** *adj* qui n'a pas d'oreille

tongs [tɒŋz] *npl* (*for coal*) pincettes *fpl*; (*for hair*) fer *m* à friser

tongue [tʌŋ] *n* langue *f*; **~ in cheek** ironiquement; **~-tied** *adj* (*fig*) muet(te); **~ twister** *n* phrase *f* très difficile à prononcer

tonic ['tɒnɪk] *n* (*MED*) tonique *m*; (*also:* **~ water**) tonic *m*, Schweppes ® *m*

tonight [tə'naɪt] *adv, n* cette nuit; (*this evening*) ce soir

tonsil ['tɒnsl] *n* amygdale *f*; **~litis** [tɒnsɪ'laɪtɪs] *n* angine *f*

too [tuː] *adv* (*excessively*) trop; (*also*) aussi; **~ much** *adv* trop ♦ *adj* trop de; **~ many** trop de; **~ bad!** tant pis!

took [tʊk] *pt of* **take**

tool [tuːl] *n* outil *m*; **~ box** *n* boîte *f* à outils

toot [tuːt] *n* (*of car horn*) coup *m* de klaxon; (*of whistle*) coup de sifflet ♦ *vi* (*with car horn*) klaxonner

tooth [tuːθ] (*pl* **teeth**) *n* (*ANAT, TECH*) dent *f*; **~ache** *n* mal *m* de dents; **~brush** *n* brosse *f* à dents; **~paste** *n* (pâte *f*) dentifrice *m*; **~pick** *n* cure-dent *m*

top [tɒp] *n* (*of mountain, head*) sommet *m*; (*of page, ladder, garment*) haut *m*; (*of box, cupboard, table*) dessus *m*; (*lid: of box, jar*) couvercle *m*; (: *of bottle*) bouchon *m*; (*toy*) toupie *f* ♦ *adj* du haut; (*in rank*) premier(-ère); (*best*) meilleur(e) ♦ *vt* (*exceed*) dépasser; (*be first in*) être en tête de; **on ~ of** sur; (*in addition to*) en plus de; **from ~ to bottom** de fond en comble; **~ up** (*US* **~ off**) *vt* (*bottle*) remplir; (*salary*) compléter; **~ floor** *n* dernier étage; **~ hat** *n* haut-de-forme *m*; **~-heavy** *adj* (*object*) trop lourd(e) du haut

topic ['tɒpɪk] *n* sujet *m*, thème *m*; **~al** *adj* d'actualité

top: **~less** *adj* (*bather etc*) aux seins nus; **~-level** *adj* (*talks*) au plus haut niveau; **~most** *adj* le (la) plus haut(e)

topple ['tɒpl] *vt* renverser, faire tomber ♦ *vi* basculer

top-secret ['tɒp'siːkrɪt] *adj* top secret(-ète)

topsy-turvy ['tɒpsɪ'tɜːvɪ] *adj, adv* sens dessus dessous

torch [tɔːtʃ] *n* torche *f*; (*BRIT: electric*) lampe *f* de poche

tore [tɔːr] *pt of* **tear**[1]

torment [*n* 'tɔːment, *vb* tɔː'ment] *n* tourment *m* ♦ *vt* tourmenter; (*fig: annoy*) harceler

torn [tɔːn] *pp of* **tear**[1]

tornado [tɔː'neɪdəʊ] (*pl* **~es**) *n* tornade *f*

torpedo [tɔː'piːdəʊ] (*pl* **~es**) *n* torpille *f*

torrent ['tɔrnt] *n* torrent *m*; ~**ial** [tɔ'rɛnʃl] *adj* torrentiel(le)

tortoise ['tɔːtəs] *n* tortue *f*; ~**shell** *adj* en écaille

torture ['tɔːtʃə'] *n* torture *f* ♦ *vt* torturer

Tory ['tɔːrɪ] (*BRIT: POL*) *adj, n* tory (*m/f*), conservateur(-trice)

toss [tɔs] *vt* lancer, jeter; (*pancake*) faire sauter; (*head*) rejeter en arrière; **to ~ a coin** jouer à pile ou face; **to ~ up for sth** jouer qch à pile ou face; **to ~ and turn** (*in bed*) se tourner et se retourner

tot [tɔt] *n* (*BRIT: drink*) petit verre; (*child*) bambin *m*

total ['təʊtl] *adj* total(e) ♦ *n* total *m* ♦ *vt* (*add up*) faire le total de, additionner; (*amount to*) s'élever à; ~**ly** *adv* totalement

totter ['tɔtə'] *vi* chanceler

touch [tʌtʃ] *n* contact *m*, toucher *m*; (*sense, also skill: of pianist etc*) toucher ♦ *vt* toucher; (*tamper with*) toucher à; **a ~ of** (*fig*) un petit peu de; **une touche de; to get in ~ with** prendre contact avec; **to lose ~** (*friends*) se perdre de vue; ~ **on** *vt fus* (*topic*) effleurer, aborder; ~ **up** *vt* (*paint*) retoucher; ~**-and-go** *adj* incertain(e); ~**down** *n* atterrissage *m*; (*on sea*) amerrissage *m*; (*US: FOOTBALL*) touché-en-but *m*; ~**ed** *adj* (*moved*) touché(e); ~**ing** *adj* touchant(e), attendrissant(e); ~**line** *n* (*SPORT*) (ligne *f* de) touche *f*; ~**y** *adj* (*person*) susceptible

tough [tʌf] *adj* dur(e); (*resistant*) résistant(e), solide; (*meat*) dur, coriace; (*firm*) inflexible; (*task*) dur, pénible; ~**en** *vt* (*character*) endurcir; (*glass etc*) renforcer

toupee ['tuːpeɪ] *n* postiche *m*

tour ['tuə'] *n* voyage *m*; (*also:* **package ~**) voyage organisé; (*of town, museum*) tour *m*, visite *f*; (*by artist*) tournée *f* ♦ *vt* visiter; ~ **guide** *n* (*person*) guide *m/f*

tourism ['tuərɪzm] *n* tourisme *m*

tourist ['tuərɪst] *n* touriste *m/f* ♦ *cpd* touristique; ~ **office** *n* syndicat *m* d'initiative

tournament ['tuənəmənt] *n* tournoi *m*

tousled ['tauzld] *adj* (*hair*) ébouriffé(e)

tout [taut] *vi*: **to ~ for** essayer de raccro-

cher, racoler ♦ *n* (*also:* **ticket ~**) revendeur *m* de billets

tow [təʊ] *vt* remorquer; (*caravan, trailer*) tracter; **"on ~"** (*BRIT*) or **"in ~"** (*US*) (*AUT*) "véhicule en remorque"

toward(s) [tə'wɔːd(z)] *prep* vers; (*of attitude*) envers, à l'égard de; (*of purpose*) pour

towel ['tauəl] *n* serviette *f* (de toilette); ~**ling** *n* (*fabric*) tissu éponge *m*; ~ **rail** (*US* **towel rack**) *n* porte-serviettes *m inv*

tower ['tauə'] *n* tour *f*; ~ **block** (*BRIT*) *n* tour *f* (d'habitation); ~**ing** *adj* très haut(e), imposant(e)

town [taun] *n* ville *f*; **to go to ~** aller en ville; (*fig*) y mettre le paquet; ~ **centre** *n* centre *m* de la ville, centre-ville *m*; ~ **council** *n* conseil municipal; ~ **hall** *n* ≈ mairie *f*; ~ **plan** *n* plan *m* de ville; ~ **planning** *n* urbanisme *m*

towrope ['təʊrəʊp] *n* (câble *m* de) remorque *f*

tow truck (*US*) *n* dépanneuse *f*

toy [tɔɪ] *n* jouet *m*; ~ **with** *vt fus* jouer avec; (*idea*) caresser

trace [treɪs] *n* trace *f* ♦ *vt* (*draw*) tracer, dessiner; (*follow*) suivre la trace de; (*locate*) retrouver; **tracing paper** *n* papier-calque *m*

track [træk] *n* (*mark*) trace *f*; (*path: gen*) chemin *m*, piste *f*; (*: of bullet etc*) trajectoire *f*; (*: of suspect, animal*) piste *f*; (*RAIL*) voie ferrée, rails *mpl*; (*on tape, SPORT*) piste; (*on record*) plage *f* ♦ *vt* suivre la trace *or* la piste de; **to keep ~ of** suivre; ~ **down** *vt* (*prey*) trouver et capturer; (*sth lost*) finir par retrouver; ~**suit** *n* survêtement *m*

tract [trækt] *n* (*of land*) étendue *f*

traction ['trækʃən] *n* traction *f*; (*MED*): **in ~** en extension

tractor ['træktə'] *n* tracteur *m*

trade [treɪd] *n* commerce *m*; (*skill, job*) métier *m* ♦ *vi* faire du commerce ♦ *vt* (*exchange*): **to ~ sth (for sth)** échanger qch (contre qch); ~ **in** *vt* (*old car etc*) faire reprendre; ~ **fair** *n* foire(-exposition) commerciale; ~**-in price** *n* prix *m* à la reprise; ~**mark** *n* marque *f* de fabrique; ~

name *n* nom *m* de marque; **~r** *n* commerçant(e), négociant(e); **~sman** (*irreg*) *n* (*shopkeeper*) commerçant; **~ union** *n* syndicat *m*; **~ unionist** *n* syndicaliste *m/f*

tradition [trə'dɪʃən] *n* tradition *f*; **~al** *adj* traditionnel(le)

traffic ['træfɪk] *n* trafic *m*; (*cars*) circulation *f* ♦ *vi*: **to ~ in** (*pej: liquor, drugs*) faire le trafic de; **~ calming** *n* ralentissement *m* de la circulation; **~ circle** (*US*) *n* rond-point *m*; **~ jam** *n* embouteillage *m*; **~ lights** *npl* feux *mpl* (de signalisation); **~ warden** *n* contractuel(le)

tragedy ['trædʒədɪ] *n* tragédie *f*

tragic ['trædʒɪk] *adj* tragique

trail [treɪl] *n* (*tracks*) trace *f*, piste *f*; (*path*) chemin *m*, piste; (*of smoke etc*) traînée *f* ♦ *vt* traîner, tirer; (*follow*) suivre ♦ *vi* traîner; (*in game, contest*) être en retard; **~ behind** *vi* traîner, être à la traîne; **~er** *n* (*AUT*) remorque *f*; (*US*) caravane *f*; (*CINEMA*) bande-annonce *f*; **~er truck** (*US*) *n* (camion *m*) semi-remorque *m*

train [treɪn] *n* train *m*; (*in underground*) rame *f*; (*of dress*) traîne *f* ♦ *vt* (*apprentice, doctor etc*) former; (*sportsman*) entraîner; (*dog*) dresser; (*memory*) exercer; (*point: gun etc*): **to ~ sth on** braquer qch sur ♦ *vi* suivre une formation; (*SPORT*) s'entraîner; **one's ~ of thought** le fil de sa pensée; **~ed** *adj* qualifié(e), qui a reçu une formation; (*animal*) dressé(e); **~ee** [treɪ'niː] *n* stagiaire *m/f*; (*in trade*) apprenti(e); **~er** *n* (*SPORT: coach*) entraîneur(-euse) *n* (*: shoe*) chaussure *f* de sport; (*of dogs etc*) dresseur(-euse) *n* **~ing** *n* formation *f*; entraînement *m*; **in ~ing** (*SPORT*) à l'entraînement; (*fit*) en forme; **~ing college** *n* école professionnelle; (*for teachers*) ≈ école normale; **~ing shoes** *npl* chaussures *fpl* de sport

trait [treɪt] *n* trait *m* (de caractère)

traitor ['treɪtər] *n* traître *m*

tram [træm] (*BRIT*) *n* (*also:* **~car**) tram(way) *m*

tramp [træmp] *n* (*person*) vagabond(e), clo-

chard(e); (*inf: pej: woman*): **to be a ~** être coureuse ♦ *vi* marcher d'un pas lourd

trample ['træmpl] *vt*: **to ~ (underfoot)** piétiner

trampoline ['træmpəliːn] *n* trampoline *m*

tranquil ['træŋkwɪl] *adj* tranquille; **~lizer** (*US* **tranquilizer**) *n* (*MED*) tranquillisant *m*

transact [træn'zækt] *vt* (*business*) traiter; **~ion** *n* transaction *f*

transatlantic ['trænzət'læntɪk] *adj* transatlantique

transfer [*n* 'trænsfər, *vb* træns'fəːr] *n* (*gen, also SPORT*) transfert *m*; (*POL: of power*) passation *f*; (*picture, design*) décalcomanie *f*; (*: stick-on*) autocollant *m* ♦ *vt* transférer; passer; **to ~ the charges** (*BRIT: TEL*) téléphoner en P.C.V.; **~ desk** *n* (*AVIAT*) guichet *m* de transit

transform [træns'fɔːm] *vt* transformer

transfusion [træns'fjuːʒən] *n* transfusion *f*

transient ['trænzɪənt] *adj* transitoire, éphémère

transistor [træn'zɪstər] *n* (**~ radio**) transistor *m*

transit ['trænzɪt] *n*: **in ~** en transit

transitive ['trænzɪtɪv] *adj* (*LING*) transitif(-ive)

transit lounge *n* salle *f* de transit

translate [trænz'leɪt] *vt* traduire; **translation** *n* traduction *f*; **translator** *n* traducteur(-trice)

transmission [trænz'mɪʃən] *n* transmission *f*

transmit [trænz'mɪt] *vt* transmettre; (*RADIO, TV*) émettre

transparency [træns'pɛərnsɪ] *n* (*of glass etc*) transparence *f*; (*BRIT: PHOT*) diapositive *f*

transparent [træns'pærnt] *adj* transparent(e)

transpire [træns'paɪər] *vi* (*turn out*): **it ~d that ...** on a appris que ...; (*happen*) arriver

transplant [*vb* træns'plɑːnt, *n* 'trænsplɑːnt] *vt* transplanter; (*seedlings*) repiquer ♦ *n* (*MED*) transplantation *f*

transport [*n* 'trænspɔːt, *vb* træns'pɔːt] *n*

transport *m*; (*car*) moyen *m* de transport, voiture *f* ♦ *vt* transporter; **~ation** ['trænspɔː'teɪʃən] *n* transport *m*; (*means of transportation*) moyen *m* de transport; **~ café** (*BRIT*) *n* ≈ restaurant *m* de routiers

trap [træp] *n* (*snare, trick*) piège *m*; (*carriage*) cabriolet *m* ♦ *vt* prendre au piège; (*confine*) coincer; **~ door** *n* trappe *f*

trapeze [trə'piːz] *n* trapèze *m*

trappings ['træpɪŋz] *npl* ornements *mpl*; attributs *mpl*

trash [træʃ] (*pej*) *n* (*goods*) camelote *f*; (*nonsense*) sottises *fpl*; **~ can** (*US*) *n* poubelle *f*; **~y** (*inf*) *adj* de camelote; (*novel*) de quatre sous

trauma ['trɔːmə] *n* traumatisme *m*; **~tic** [trɔː'mætɪk] *adj* traumatisant(e)

travel ['trævl] *n* voyage(s) *m(pl)* ♦ *vi* voyager; (*news, sound*) circuler, se propager ♦ *vt* (*distance*) parcourir; **~ agency** *n* agence *f* de voyages; **~ agent** *n* agent *m* de voyages; **~ler** (*US* **traveler**) *n* voyageur(-euse); **~ler's cheque** (*US* **traveler's check**) *n* chèque *m* de voyage; **~ling** (*US* **traveling**) *n* voyage(s) *m(pl)*; **~ sickness** *n* mal *m* de la route (*or* de mer *or* de l'air)

trawler ['trɔːlər] *n* chalutier *m*

tray [treɪ] *n* (*for carrying*) plateau *m*; (*on desk*) corbeille *f*

treacherous ['trɛtʃərəs] *adj* (*person, look*) traître(-esse); (*ground, tide*) dont il faut se méfier

treacle ['triːkl] *n* mélasse *f*

tread [trɛd] (*pt* **trod**, *pp* **trodden**) *n* pas *m*; (*sound*) bruit *m* de pas; (*of tyre*) chape *f*, bande *f* de roulement ♦ *vi* marcher; **~ on** *vt fus* marcher sur

treason ['triːzn] *n* trahison *f*

treasure ['trɛʒər] *n* trésor *m* ♦ *vt* (*value*) tenir beaucoup à; **~r** *n* trésorier(-ère); **treasury** *n*: **the Treasury**, (*US*) **the Treasury Department** le ministère des Finances

treat [triːt] *n* petit cadeau, petite surprise ♦ *vt* traiter; **to ~ sb to sth** offrir qch à qn

treatment *n* traitement *m*

treaty ['triːtɪ] *n* traité *m*

treble ['trɛbl] *adj* triple ♦ *vt, vi* tripler; **~ clef** (*MUS*) clé *f* de sol

tree [triː] *n* arbre *m*

trek [trɛk] *n* (*long*) voyage *m*; (*on foot*) (longue) marche, tirée *f*

tremble ['trɛmbl] *vi* trembler

tremendous [trɪ'mɛndəs] *adj* (*enormous*) énorme, fantastique; (*excellent*) formidable

tremor ['trɛmər] *n* tremblement *m*; (*also:* **earth ~**) secousse *f* sismique

trench [trɛntʃ] *n* tranchée *f*

trend [trɛnd] *n* (*tendency*) tendance *f*; (*of events*) cours *m*; (*fashion*) mode *f*; **~y** *adj* (*idea, person*) dans le vent; (*clothes*) dernier cri *inv*

trespass ['trɛspəs] *vi*: **to ~ on** s'introduire sans permission dans; **"no ~ing"** "propriété privée", "défense d'entrer"

trestle ['trɛsl] *n* tréteau *m*

trial ['traɪəl] *n* (*LAW*) procès *m*, jugement *m*; (*test: of machine etc*) essai *m*; **~s** *npl* (*unpleasant experiences*) épreuves *fpl*; **to be on ~** (*LAW*) passer en jugement; **by ~ and error** par tâtonnements; **~ period** *n* période d'essai

triangle ['traɪæŋgl] *n* (*MATH, MUS*) triangle *m*; **triangular** [traɪ'æŋgjulər] *adj* triangulaire

tribe [traɪb] *n* tribu *f*; **~sman** (*irreg*) *n* membre *m* d'une tribu

tribunal [traɪ'bjuːnl] *n* tribunal *m*

tributary ['trɪbjutəri] *n* (*river*) affluent *m*

tribute ['trɪbjuːt] *n* tribut *m*, hommage *m*; **to pay ~ to** rendre hommage à

trick [trɪk] *n* (*magic ~*) tour *m*; (*joke, prank*) tour, farce *f*; (*skill, knack*) astuce *f*, truc *m*; (*CARDS*) levée *f* ♦ *vt* attraper, rouler; **to play a ~ on sb** jouer un tour à qn; **that should do the ~** ça devrait faire l'affaire; **~ery** *n* ruse *f*

trickle ['trɪkl] *n* (*of water etc*) filet *m* ♦ *vi* couler en un filet *or* goutte à goutte

tricky ['trɪkɪ] *adj* difficile, délicat(e)

tricycle ['traɪsɪkl] *n* tricycle *m*

trifle ['traɪfl] *n* bagatelle *f*; (*CULIN*) ≈ diplomate *m* ♦ *adv*: **a ~ long** un peu long;

trifling adj insignifiant(e)

trigger ['trɪgəʳ] n (of gun) gâchette f; ~ **off** vt déclencher

trim [trɪm] adj (house, garden) bien tenu(e); (figure) svelte ♦ n (haircut etc) légère coupe; (on car) garnitures fpl ♦ vt (cut) couper légèrement; (NAUT: a sail) gréer; (decorate): **to ~ (with)** décorer (de); ~**mings** npl (CULIN) garniture f

trinket ['trɪŋkɪt] n bibelot m; (piece of jewellery) colifichet m

trip [trɪp] n voyage m; (excursion) excursion f; (stumble) faux pas ♦ vi faire un faux pas, trébucher; **on a ~** en voyage; ~ **up** vi trébucher ♦ vt faire un croc-en-jambe à

tripe [traɪp] n (CULIN) tripes fpl; (pej: rubbish) idioties fpl

triple ['trɪpl] adj triple; ~**ts** npl triplés(-ées); **triplicate** ['trɪplɪkət] n: **in triplicate** en trois exemplaires

tripod ['traɪpɔd] n trépied m

trite [traɪt] (pej) adj banal(e)

triumph ['traɪʌmf] n triomphe m ♦ vi: **to ~ (over)** triompher (de)

trivia ['trɪvɪə] (pej) npl futilités fpl; ~**l** adj insignifiant(e); (commonplace) banal(e)

trod [trɔd] pt of **tread**; ~**den** pp of **tread**

trolley ['trɔlɪ] n chariot m

trombone [trɔm'bəun] n trombone m

troop [truːp] n bande f, groupe m ♦ vi: ~ **in/out** entrer/sortir en groupe; ~**s** npl (MIL) troupes fpl; (: men) hommes mpl, soldats mpl; ~**ing the colour** (BRIT) n (ceremony) le salut au drapeau

trophy ['trəufɪ] n trophée m

tropic ['trɔpɪk] n tropique m; ~**al** adj tropical(e)

trot [trɔt] n trot m ♦ vi trotter; **on the ~** (BRIT: fig) d'affilée

trouble ['trʌbl] n difficulté(s) f(pl), problème(s) m(pl); (worry) ennuis mpl, soucis mpl; (bother, effort) peine f; (POL) troubles mpl; (MED): **stomach** etc ~ troubles gastriques etc ♦ vt (disturb) déranger, gêner; (worry) inquiéter ♦ vi: **to ~ to do** prendre la peine de faire; ~**s** npl (POL etc) troubles mpl; (personal) ennuis, soucis; **to be in ~**

avoir des ennuis; (ship, climber etc) être en difficulté; **what's the ~?** qu'est-ce qui ne va pas?; ~**d** adj (person) inquiet(-ète); (epoch, life) agité(e); ~**maker** n élément perturbateur, fauteur m de troubles; ~**shooter** n (in conflict) médiateur m; ~**some** adj (child) fatigant(e), difficile; (cough etc) gênant(e)

trough [trɔf] n (also: **drinking ~**) abreuvoir m; (also: **feeding ~**) auge f; (depression) creux m

trousers ['trauzəz] npl pantalon m; **short ~** culottes courtes

trout [traut] n inv truite f

trowel ['trauəl] n truelle f; (garden tool) déplantoir m

truant ['truənt] (BRIT) n: **to play ~** faire l'école buissonnière

truce [truːs] n trêve f

truck [trʌk] n camion m; (RAIL) wagon m à plate-forme; ~ **driver** n camionneur m; ~ **farm** (US) n jardin maraîcher

true [truː] adj vrai(e); (accurate) exact(e); (genuine) vrai, véritable; (faithful) fidèle; **to come ~** se réaliser

truffle ['trʌfl] n truffe f

truly ['truːlɪ] adv vraiment, réellement; (truthfully) sans mentir; see also **yours**

trump [trʌmp] n (also: ~ **card**) atout m

trumpet ['trʌmpɪt] n trompette f

truncheon ['trʌntʃən] (BRIT) n bâton m (d'agent de police); matraque f

trundle ['trʌndl] vt, vi: **to ~ along** rouler lentement (et bruyamment)

trunk [trʌŋk] n (of tree, person) tronc m; (of elephant) trompe f; (case) malle f; (US: AUT) coffre m; ~**s** npl (also: **swimming ~s**) maillot m or slip m de bain

truss [trʌs] vt: **to ~ (up)** ligoter

trust [trʌst] n confiance f; (responsibility) charge f; (LAW) fidéicommis m ♦ vt (rely on) avoir confiance en; (hope) espérer; (entrust): **to ~ sth to sb** confier qch à qn; **to take sth on ~** accepter qch les yeux fermés; ~**ed** adj en qui l'on a confiance; ~**ee** [trʌs'tiː] n (LAW) fidéicommissaire m/f; (of school etc) administrateur(-trice); ~**ful,**

~**ing** *adj* confiant(e); ~**worthy** *adj* digne de confiance

truth [truːθ] *n* vérité *f*; ~**ful** *adj* (*person*) qui dit la vérité; (*answer*) sincère

try [traɪ] *n* essai *m*, tentative *f*; (*RUGBY*) essai ♦ *vt* (*attempt*) essayer, tenter; (*test: sth new: also:* ~ **out**) essayer, tester; (*LAW: person*) juger; (*strain*) éprouver ♦ *vi* essayer; **to have a** ~ essayer; **to** ~ **to do** essayer de faire; (*seek*) chercher à faire; ~ **on** *vt* (*clothes*) essayer; ~**ing** *adj* pénible

T-shirt [ˈtiːʃəːt] *n* tee-shirt *m*

T-square [ˈtiːskwɛəʳ] *n* équerre *f* en T, té *m*

tub [tʌb] *n* cuve *f*; (*for washing clothes*) baquet *m*; (*bath*) baignoire *f*

tubby [ˈtʌbɪ] *adj* rondelet(te)

tube [tjuːb] *n* tube *m*; (*BRIT: underground*) métro *m*; (*for tyre*) chambre *f* à air

tuberculosis [tjubəːkjuˈləʊsɪs] *n* tuberculose *f*

TUC *n abbr* (*BRIT: Trades Union Congress*) *confédération des syndicats britanniques*

tuck [tʌk] *vt* (*put*) mettre; ~ **away** *vt* cacher, ranger; ~ **in** *vt* rentrer; (*child*) border ♦ *vi* (*eat*) manger (de bon appétit); ~ **up** *vt* (*child*) border; ~ **shop** (*BRIT*) *n* boutique *f* à provisions (*dans une école*)

Tuesday [ˈtjuːzdɪ] *n* mardi *m*

tuft [tʌft] *n* touffe *f*

tug [tʌg] *n* (*ship*) remorqueur *m* ♦ *vt* tirer (sur); ~**-of-war** *n* lutte *f* à la corde; (*fig*) lutte acharnée

tuition [tjuːˈɪʃən] *n* (*BRIT*) leçons *fpl*; (: *private* ~) cours particuliers; (*US: school fees*) frais *mpl* de scolarité

tulip [ˈtjuːlɪp] *n* tulipe *f*

tumble [ˈtʌmbl] *n* (*fall*) chute *f*, culbute *f* ♦ *vi* tomber, dégringoler; **to** ~ **to sth** (*inf*) réaliser qch; ~**down** *adj* délabré(e); ~**dryer** (*BRIT*) *n* séchoir *m* à air chaud

tumbler [ˈtʌmbləʳ] *n* (*glass*) verre (droit), gobelet *m*

tummy [ˈtʌmɪ] (*inf*) *n* ventre *m*; ~ **upset** *n* maux *mpl* de ventre

tumour [ˈtjuːməʳ] (*US* **tumor**) *n* tumeur *f*

tuna [ˈtjuːnə] *n inv* (*also:* ~ **fish**) thon *m*

tune [tjuːn] *n* (*melody*) air *m* ♦ *vt* (*MUS*) accorder; (*RADIO, TV, AUT*) régler; **to be in/out of** ~ (*instrument*) être accordé/désaccordé; (*singer*) chanter juste/faux; **to be in/out of** ~ **with** (*fig*) être en accord/désaccord avec; ~ **in** *vi* (*RADIO, TV*): **to** ~ **in (to)** se mettre à l'écoute (de); ~ **up** *vi* (*musician*) accorder son instrument; ~**ful** *adj* mélodieux(-euse); ~**r** *n*: **piano** ~**r** accordeur *m* (de pianos)

tunic [ˈtjuːnɪk] *n* tunique *f*

Tunisia [tjuːˈnɪzɪə] *n* Tunisie *f*

tunnel [ˈtʌnl] *n* tunnel *m*; (*in mine*) galerie *f* ♦ *vi* percer un tunnel

turbulence [ˈtəːbjuləns] *n* (*AVIAT*) turbulence *f*

tureen [təˈriːn] *n* (*for soup*) soupière *f*; (*for vegetables*) légumier *m*

turf [təːf] *n* gazon *m*; (*clod*) motte *f* (de gazon) ♦ *vt* gazonner; ~ **out** (*inf*) *vt* (*person*) jeter dehors

Turk [təːk] *n* Turc (Turque)

Turkey [ˈtəːkɪ] *n* Turquie *f*

turkey [ˈtəːkɪ] *n* dindon *m*, dinde *f*

Turkish [ˈtəːkɪʃ] *adj* turc (turque) ♦ *n* (*LING*) turc *m*

turmoil [ˈtəːmɔɪl] *n* trouble *m*, bouleversement *m*; **in** ~ en émoi, en effervescence

turn [təːn] *n* tour *m*; (*in road*) tournant *m*; (*of mind, events*) tournure *f*; (*performance*) numéro *m*; (*MED*) crise *f*, attaque *f* ♦ *vt* tourner; (*collar, steak*) retourner; (*change*): **to** ~ **sth into** changer qch en ♦ *vi* (*object, wind, milk*) tourner; (*person: look back*) se (re)tourner; (*reverse direction*) faire demi-tour; (*become*) devenir; (*age*) atteindre; **to** ~ **into** se changer en; **a good** ~ un service; **it gave me quite a** ~ ça m'a fait un coup; **"no left** ~**"** (*AUT*) "défense de tourner à gauche"; **it's your** ~ c'est (à) votre tour; **in** ~ à son tour; à tour de rôle; **to take** ~**s (at)** se relayer (pour *or* à); ~ **away** *vi* se détourner ♦ *vt* (*applicants*) refuser; ~ **back** *vi* revenir, faire demi-tour ♦ *vt* (*person, vehicle*) faire faire demi-tour à; (*clock*) reculer; ~ **down** *vt* (*refuse*) rejeter, refuser; (*reduce*) baisser; (*fold*) rabattre; ~ **in** *vi* (*inf: go to bed*) aller se coucher ♦ *vt* (*fold*) rentrer; ~ **off** *vi* (*from road*) tourner ♦ *vt* (*light, radio etc*) éteindre; (*tap*) fermer; (*engine*) arrêter; ~ **on** *vt* (*light, radio etc*) allumer; (*tap*) ouvrir; (*engine*) mettre en marche; ~ **out** *vt* (*light, gas*) éteindre; (*produce*) produire ♦ *vi* (*voters, troops etc*) se présenter; **to ~ out to be ...** s'avérer ..., se révéler ...; ~ **over** *vi* (*person*) se retourner ♦ *vt* (*object*) retourner; (*page*) tourner; ~ **round** *vi* faire demi-tour; (*rotate*) tourner; ~ **up** *vi* (*person*) arriver, se pointer (*inf*); (*lost object*) être retrouvé(e) ♦ *vt* (*collar*) remonter; (*radio, heater*) mettre plus fort; ~**ing** *n* (*in road*) tournant *m*; ~**ing point** *n* (*fig*) tournant *m*, moment décisif

turnip ['tɜːnɪp] *n* navet *m*

turn: ~**out** *n* (*of voters*) taux *m* de participation; ~**over** *n* (COMM: *amount of money*) chiffre *m* d'affaires; (: *of goods*) roulement *m*; (*of staff*) renouvellement *m*, changement *m*; ~**pike** (US) *n* autoroute *f* à péage; ~**stile** *n* tourniquet *m* (*d'entrée*); ~**table** *n* (*on record player*) platine *f*; ~**-up** *n* (BRIT) (*on trousers*) revers *m*

turpentine ['tɜːpəntaɪn] *n* (*also:* **turps**) (*essence f de*) térébenthine *f*

turquoise ['tɜːkwɔɪz] *n* (*stone*) turquoise *f* ♦ *adj* turquoise *inv*

turret ['tʌrɪt] *n* tourelle *f*

turtle ['tɜːtl] *n* tortue marine *or* d'eau douce; ~**neck (sweater)** *n* (BRIT) pullover *m* à col montant; (US) pullover à col roulé

tusk [tʌsk] *n* défense *f*

tutor ['tjuːtə*] *n* (*in college*) directeur(-trice) d'études; (*private teacher*) précepteur(-trice); ~**ial** [tjuː'tɔːrɪəl] *n* (SCOL) (*séance f de*) travaux *mpl* pratiques

tuxedo [tʌk'siːdəu] (US) *n* smoking *m*

TV *n abbr* (= *television*) télé *f*

twang [twæŋ] *n* (*of instrument*) son vibrant; (*of voice*) ton nasillard

tweed [twiːd] *n* tweed *m*

tweezers ['twiːzəz] *npl* pince *f* à épiler

twelfth [twelfθ] *num* douzième

twelve [twelv] *num* douze; **at ~ (o'clock)** à midi; (*midnight*) à minuit

twentieth ['twentɪθ] *num* vingtième

twenty ['twentɪ] *num* vingt

twice [twaɪs] *adv* deux fois; **~ as much** deux fois plus

twiddle ['twɪdl] *vt, vi*: **to ~ (with) sth** tripoter qch; **to ~ one's thumbs** (*fig*) se tourner les pouces

twig [twɪg] *n* brindille *f* ♦ *vi* (*inf*) piger

twilight ['twaɪlaɪt] *n* crépuscule *m*

twin [twɪn] *adj*, *n* jumeau(-elle) ♦ *vt* jumeler; ~**(-bedded) room** *n* chambre *f* à deux lits; ~ **beds** *npl* lits jumeaux

twine [twaɪn] *n* ficelle *f* ♦ *vi* (*plant*) s'enrouler

twinge [twɪndʒ] *n* (*of pain*) élancement *m*; **a ~ of conscience** un certain remords; **a ~ of regret** un pincement au cœur

twinkle ['twɪŋkl] *vi* scintiller; (*eyes*) pétiller

twirl [twɜːl] *vt* faire tournoyer ♦ *vi* tournoyer

twist [twɪst] *n* torsion *f*, tour *m*; (*in road*) virage *m*; (*in wire, flex*) tortillon *m*; (*in story*) coup *m* de théâtre ♦ *vt* tordre; (*weave*) entortiller; (*roll around*) enrouler; (*fig*) déformer ♦ *vi* (*road, river*) serpenter

twit [twɪt] *(inf)* *n* crétin(e)

twitch [twɪtʃ] *n* (*pull*) coup sec, saccade *f*; (*nervous*) tic *m* ♦ *vi* se convulser; avoir un tic

two [tuː] *num* deux; **to put ~ and ~ together** (*fig*) faire le rapprochement; ~**-door** *adj* (AUT) à deux portes; ~**-faced** (*pej*) *adj* (*person*) faux (fausse); ~**fold** *adv*: **to increase ~fold** doubler; ~**-piece (suit)** *n* (*man's*) costume *m* (deux-pièces); (*woman's*) (tailleur *m*) deux-pièces *m inv*; ~**-piece (swimsuit)** *n* (maillot *m* de bain) deux-pièces *m inv*; ~**some** *n* (*people*) couple *m*; ~**-way** *adj* (*traffic*) dans les deux sens

tycoon [taɪ'kuːn] *n*: **(business) ~** gros homme d'affaires

type [taɪp] *n* (*category*) type *m*, genre *m*, espèce *f*; (*model, example*) type *m*, modèle *m*; (TYP) type, caractère *m* ♦ *vt* (*letter etc*) taper (à la machine); ~**-cast** *adj* (*actor*) condamné(e) à toujours jouer le même rôle; **~face** n (TYP) œil m de caractère; **~script** n texte dactylographié; **~writer** n machine f à écrire; **~written** adj dactylographié(e)

typhoid ['taɪfɔɪd] n typhoïde f

typical ['tɪpɪkl] adj typique, caractéristique

typing ['taɪpɪŋ] n dactylo(graphie) f

typist ['taɪpɪst] n dactylo m/f

tyrant ['taɪərnt] n tyran m

tyre ['taɪər] (US **tire**) n pneu m; **~ pressure** n pression f (de gonflage)

U, u

U-bend ['juːbend] n (in pipe) coude m

ubiquitous [juːˈbɪkwɪtəs] adj omniprésent(e)

udder ['ʌdər] n pis m, mamelle f

UFO ['juːfəu] n abbr (= unidentified flying object) OVNI m

Uganda [juːˈɡændə] n Ouganda m

ugh [əːh] excl pouah!

ugly ['ʌɡlɪ] adj laid(e), vilain(e); (situation) inquiétant(e)

UHT abbr (= ultra heat treated): **UHT milk** lait m UHT or longue conservation

UK n abbr = **United Kingdom**

ulcer ['ʌlsər] n ulcère m; (also: **mouth ~**) aphte f

Ulster ['ʌlstər] n Ulster m; (inf: Northern Ireland) Irlande f du Nord

ulterior [ʌlˈtɪərɪər] adj: **~ motive** arrière-pensée f

ultimate ['ʌltɪmət] adj ultime, final(e); (authority) suprême; **~ly** adv (at last) en fin de compte; (fundamentally) finalement

ultrasound ['ʌltrəsaund] n ultrason m

umbilical cord [ʌmˈbɪlɪkl-] n cordon ombilical

umbrella [ʌmˈbrelə] n parapluie m; (for sun) parasol m

umpire ['ʌmpaɪər] n arbitre m

umpteen [ʌmpˈtiːn] adj je ne sais combien de; **~th** adj: **for the ~th time** pour la nième fois

UN n abbr = **United Nations**

unable [ʌnˈeɪbl] adj: **to be ~ to** ne pas pouvoir, être dans l'impossibilité de; (incapable) être incapable de

unacceptable [ʌnəkˈseptəbl] adj (behaviour) inadmissible; (price, proposal) inacceptable

unaccompanied [ʌnəˈkʌmpənɪd] adj (child, lady) non accompagné(e); (song) sans accompagnement

unaccustomed [ʌnəˈkʌstəmd] adj: **to be ~ to sth** ne pas avoir l'habitude de qch

unanimous [juːˈnænɪməs] adj unanime; **~ly** adv à l'unanimité

unarmed [ʌnˈɑːmd] adj (without a weapon) non armé(e); (combat) sans armes

unattached [ʌnəˈtætʃt] adj libre, sans attaches; (part) non attaché(e), indépendant(e)

unattended [ʌnəˈtendɪd] adj (car, child, luggage) sans surveillance

unattractive [ʌnəˈtræktɪv] adj peu attrayant(e); (character) peu sympathique

unauthorized [ʌnˈɔːθəraɪzd] adj non autorisé(e), sans autorisation

unavoidable [ʌnəˈvɔɪdəbl] adj inévitable

unaware [ʌnəˈwɛər] adj: **to be ~ of** ignorer, être inconscient(e) de; **~s** adv à l'improviste, au dépourvu

unbalanced [ʌnˈbælənst] adj déséquilibré(e); (report) peu objectif(-ive)

unbearable [ʌnˈbɛərəbl] adj insupportable

unbeatable [ʌnˈbiːtəbl] adj imbattable

unbeknown(st) [ʌnbɪˈnaʊn(st)] adv: **~ to me/Peter** à mon insu/l'insu de Peter

unbelievable [ʌnbɪˈliːvəbl] adj incroyable

unbend [ʌnˈbend] (irreg) vi se détendre ♦ vt (wire) redresser, détordre

unbiased [ʌnˈbaɪəst] adj impartial(e)

unborn [ʌnˈbɔːn] adj à naître, qui n'est pas encore né(e)

unbreakable [ʌnˈbreɪkəbl] adj incassable

unbroken [ʌnˈbrəukən] adj intact(e); (fig) continu(e), ininterrompu(e)

unbutton [ʌnˈbʌtn] vt déboutonner

uncalled-for [ʌnˈkɔːldfɔːr] adj déplacé(e), injustifié(e)

uncanny [ʌn'kænɪ] *adj* étrange, troublant(e)

unceremonious [ʌnserɪ'məunɪəs] *adj* (*abrupt, rude*) brusque

uncertain [ʌn'sə:tn] *adj* incertain(e); (*hesitant*) hésitant(e); **in no ~ terms** sans équivoque possible; **~ty** *n* incertitude *f*, doute(s) *m(pl)*

uncivilized [ʌn'sɪvɪlaɪzd] *adj* (*gen*) non civilisé(e); (*fig: behaviour etc*) barbare; (*hour*) indu(e)

uncle ['ʌŋkl] *n* oncle *m*

uncomfortable [ʌn'kʌmfətəbl] *adj* inconfortable, peu confortable; (*uneasy*) mal à l'aise, gêné(e); (*situation*) désagréable

uncommon [ʌn'kɔmən] *adj* rare, singulier(-ère), peu commun(e)

uncompromising [ʌn'kɔmprəmaɪzɪŋ] *adj* intransigeant(e), inflexible

unconcerned [ʌnkən'sə:nd] *adj*: **to be ~ (about)** ne pas s'inquiéter (de)

unconditional [ʌnkən'dɪʃənl] *adj* sans conditions

unconscious [ʌn'kɔnʃəs] *adj* sans connaissance, évanoui(e); (*unaware*): **~ of** inconscient(e) de ♦ *n*: **the ~** l'inconscient *m*; **~ly** *adv* inconsciemment

uncontrollable [ʌnkən'trəuləbl] *adj* indiscipliné(e); (*temper, laughter*) irrépressible

unconventional [ʌnkən'venʃənl] *adj* peu conventionnel(le)

uncouth [ʌn'ku:θ] *adj* grossier(-ère), fruste

uncover [ʌn'kʌvər] *vt* découvrir

undecided [ʌndɪ'saɪdɪd] *adj* indécis(e), irrésolu(e)

under ['ʌndər] *prep* sous; (*less than*) (de) moins que; au-dessous de; (*according to*) selon, en vertu de ♦ *adv* au-dessous; en dessous; **~ there** là-dessous; **~ repair** en (cours de) réparation; **~age** *adj* (*person*) qui n'a pas l'âge réglementaire; **~carriage** *n* (*AVIAT*) train *m* d'atterrissage; **~charge** *vt* ne pas faire payer assez à; **~coat** *n* (*paint*) couche *f* de fond; **~cover** *adj* secret(-ète), clandestin(e); **~current** *n* courant *or* sentiment sous-jacent; **~cut** (*irreg*) *vt* vendre moins cher que;

~dog *n* opprimé *m*; **~done** *adj* (*CULIN*) saignant(e); (*pej*) pas assez cuit(e); **~estimate** *vt* sous-estimer; **~fed** *adj* sous-alimenté(e); **~foot** *adv* sous les pieds; **~go** (*irreg*) *vt* subir; (*treatment*) suivre; **~graduate** *n* étudiant(e) (*qui prépare la licence*); **~ground** *n* (*BRIT: railway*) métro *m*; (*POL*) clandestinité *f* ♦ *adj* souterrain(e); (*fig*) clandestin(e) ♦ *adv* dans la clandestinité, clandestinement; **~growth** *n* broussailles *fpl*, sous-bois *m*; **~hand(ed)** *adj* (*fig: behaviour, method etc*) en dessous; **~lie** (*irreg*) *vt* être à la base de; **~line** *vt* souligner; **~mine** *vt* saper, miner; **~neath** *adv* (en) dessous ♦ *prep* sous, au-dessous de; **~paid** *adj* sous-payé(e); **~pants** *npl* caleçon *m*, slip *m*; **~pass** (*BRIT*) *n* passage souterrain; (*on motorway*) passage inférieur; **~privileged** *adj* défavorisé(e), économiquement faible; **~rate** *vt* sous-estimer; **~shirt** (*US*) *n* tricot *m* de corps; **~shorts** (*US*) *npl* caleçon *m*, slip *m*; **~side** *n* dessous *m*; **~skirt** (*BRIT*) *n* jupon *m*

understand [ʌndə'stænd] (*irreg: like stand*) *vt, vi* comprendre; **I ~ that ...** je me suis laissé dire que ...; je crois comprendre que ...; **~able** *adj* compréhensible; **~ing** *adj* compréhensif(-ive) ♦ *n* compréhension *f*; (*agreement*) accord *m*

understatement ['ʌndəsteɪtmənt] *n*: **that's an ~** c'est (bien) peu dire, le terme est faible

understood [ʌndə'stud] *pt, pp of* **understand** ♦ *adj* entendu(e); (*implied*) sous-entendu(e)

understudy ['ʌndəstʌdɪ] *n* doublure *f*

undertake [ʌndə'teɪk] (*irreg*) *vt* entreprendre; se charger de; **to ~ to do sth** s'engager à faire qch

undertaker ['ʌndəteɪkər] *n* entrepreneur *m* des pompes funèbres, croque-mort *m*

undertaking ['ʌndəteɪkɪŋ] *n* entreprise *f*; (*promise*) promesse *f*

under: **~tone** *n*: **in an ~tone** à mi-voix; **~water** *adv* sous l'eau ♦ *adj* sous-marin(e); **~wear** *n* sous-vêtements *mpl*;

(*women's only*) dessous *mpl*; **~world** *n* (*of crime*) milieu *m*, pègre *f*; **~write** *n* (*IN-SURANCE*) assureur *m*

undies ['ʌndɪz] (*inf*) *npl* dessous *mpl*, lingerie *f*

undiplomatic ['ʌndɪplə'mætɪk] *adj* peu diplomatique

undo [ʌn'duː] (*irreg*) *vt* défaire; **~ing** *n* ruine *f*, perte *f*

undoubted [ʌn'dautɪd] *adj* indubitable, certain(e); **~ly** *adv* sans aucun doute

undress [ʌn'drɛs] *vi* se déshabiller

undue [ʌn'djuː] *adj* indu(e), excessif(-ive)

undulating ['ʌndjuleɪtɪŋ] *adj* ondoyant(e), onduleux(-euse)

unduly [ʌn'djuːlɪ] *adv* trop, excessivement

unearth [ʌn'ɜːθ] *vt* déterrer; (*fig*) dénicher

unearthly [ʌn'ɜːθlɪ] *adj* (*hour*) indu(e), impossible

uneasy [ʌn'iːzɪ] *adj* mal à l'aise, gêné(e); (*worried*) inquiet(-ète); (*feeling*) désagréable; (*peace, truce*) fragile

uneconomic(al) ['ʌniːkə'nɔmɪk(l)] *adj* peu économique

uneducated [ʌn'ɛdjukeɪtɪd] *adj* (*person*) sans instruction

unemployed [ʌnɪm'plɔɪd] *adj* sans travail, en or au chômage ♦ *n*: **the ~** les chômeurs *mpl*; **unemployment** *n* chômage *m*

unending [ʌn'ɛndɪŋ] *adj* interminable, sans fin

unerring [ʌn'ɜːrɪŋ] *adj* infaillible, sûr(e)

uneven [ʌn'iːvn] *adj* inégal(e); (*quality, work*) irrégulier(-ère)

unexpected [ʌnɪks'pɛktɪd] *adj* inattendu(e), imprévu(e); **~ly** [ʌnɪks'pɛktɪdlɪ] *adv* (*arrive*) à l'improviste; (*succeed*) contre toute attente

unfailing [ʌn'feɪlɪŋ] *adj* inépuisable; (*remedy*) infaillible

unfair [ʌn'fɛər] *adj*: **~ (to)** injuste (envers)

unfaithful [ʌn'feɪθful] *adj* infidèle

unfamiliar [ʌnfə'mɪlɪər] *adj* étrange, inconnu(e); **to be ~ with** mal connaître

unfashionable [ʌn'fæʃnəbl] *adj* (*clothes*) démodé(e); (*place*) peu chic *inv*

unfasten [ʌn'fɑːsn] *vt* défaire; détacher; (*open*) ouvrir

unfavourable [ʌn'feɪvrəbl] (*US* **unfavorable**) *adj* défavorable

unfeeling [ʌn'fiːlɪŋ] *adj* insensible, dur(e)

unfinished [ʌn'fɪnɪʃt] *adj* inachevé(e)

unfit [ʌn'fɪt] *adj* en mauvaise santé; pas en forme; (*incompetent*): **~ (for)** impropre (à); (*work, service*) inapte (à)

unfold [ʌn'fauld] *vt* déplier ♦ *vi* se dérouler

unforeseen ['ʌnfɔː'siːn] *adj* imprévu(e)

unforgettable [ʌnfə'gɛtəbl] *adj* inoubliable

unfortunate [ʌn'fɔːtʃənət] *adj* malheureux(-euse); (*event, remark*) malencontreux(-euse); **~ly** *adv* malheureusement

unfounded [ʌn'faundɪd] *adj* sans fondement

unfriendly [ʌn'frɛndlɪ] *adj* inamical(e), peu aimable

ungainly [ʌn'geɪnlɪ] *adj* gauche, dégingandé(e)

ungodly [ʌn'gɔdlɪ] *adj* (*hour*) indu(e)

ungrateful [ʌn'greɪtful] *adj* ingrat(e)

unhappiness [ʌn'hæpɪnɪs] *n* tristesse *f*, peine *f*

unhappy [ʌn'hæpɪ] *adj* triste, malheureux(-euse); **~ about** or **with** (*arrangements etc*) mécontent(e) de, peu satisfait(e) de

unharmed [ʌn'hɑːmd] *adj* indemne, sain(e) et sauf (sauve)

UNHCR *n abbr* (= *United Nations High Commission for refugees*) HCR *m*

unhealthy [ʌn'hɛlθɪ] *adj* malsain(e); (*person*) maladif(-ive)

unheard-of [ʌn'hɜːdɔv] *adj* inouï(e), sans précédent

unhurt [ʌn'hɜːt] *adj* indemne

unidentified [ʌnaɪ'dɛntɪfaɪd] *adj* non identifié(e); *see also* **UFO**

uniform ['juːnɪfɔːm] *n* uniforme *m* ♦ *adj* uniforme

uninhabited [ʌnɪn'hæbɪtɪd] *adj* inhabité(e)

unintentional [ʌnɪn'tɛnʃənəl] *adj* involontaire

union ['ju:njən] n union f; (also: **trade ~**) syndicat m ♦ cpd du syndicat, syndical(e); U~ Jack n drapeau du Royaume-Uni

unique [ju:'ni:k] adj unique

UNISON ['ju:nɪsn] n grand syndicat des services publics en Grande-Bretagne

unison ['ju:nɪsn] n: **in ~** (sing) à l'unisson; (say) en chœur

unit ['ju:nɪt] n unité f; (section: of furniture etc) élément m, bloc m; **kitchen ~** élément de cuisine

unite [ju:'naɪt] vt unir ♦ vi s'unir; ~d adj uni(e); unifié(e); (effort) conjugué(e); U~d Kingdom n Royaume-Uni m; U~d Nations (Organization) n (Organisation f des) Nations unies; U~d States (of America) n États-Unis mpl

unit trust (BRIT) n fonds commun de placement

unity ['ju:nɪtɪ] n unité f

universal [ju:nɪ'və:sl] adj universel(le)

universe ['ju:nɪvə:s] n univers m

university [ju:nɪ'və:sɪtɪ] n université f

unjust [ʌn'dʒʌst] adj injuste

unkempt [ʌn'kɛmpt] adj négligé(e), débraillé(e); (hair) mal peigné(e)

unkind [ʌn'kaɪnd] adj peu gentil(le), méchant(e)

unknown [ʌn'nəun] adj inconnu(e)

unlawful [ʌn'lɔ:ful] adj illégal(e)

unleaded ['ʌn'lɛdɪd] adj (petrol, fuel) sans plomb

unleash [ʌn'li:ʃ] vt (fig) déchaîner, déclencher

unless [ʌn'lɛs] conj: **~ he leaves** à moins qu'il ne parte

unlike [ʌn'laɪk] adj dissemblable, différent(e) ♦ prep contrairement à

unlikely [ʌn'laɪklɪ] adj (happening) improbable; (explanation) invraisemblable

unlimited [ʌn'lɪmɪtɪd] adj illimité(e)

unlisted ['ʌn'lɪstɪd] (US) adj (TEL) sur la liste rouge

unload [ʌn'ləud] vt décharger

unlock [ʌn'lɔk] vt ouvrir

unlucky [ʌn'lʌkɪ] adj (person) malchanceux(-euse); (object, number) qui porte malheur; **to be ~** (person) ne pas avoir de chance

unmarried [ʌn'mærɪd] adj célibataire

unmistak(e)able [ʌnmɪs'teɪkəbl] adj indubitable; qu'on ne peut pas ne pas reconnaître

unmitigated [ʌn'mɪtɪgeɪtɪd] adj non mitigé(e), absolu(e), pur(e)

unnatural [ʌn'nætʃrəl] adj non naturel(le); (habit) contre nature

unnecessary [ʌn'nɛsəsərɪ] adj inutile, superflu(e)

unnoticed [ʌn'nəutɪst] adj: **(to go** or **pass) ~** (passer) inaperçu(e)

UNO n abbr = **United Nations Organization**

unobtainable [ʌnəb'teɪnəbl] adj impossible à obtenir

unobtrusive [ʌnəb'tru:sɪv] adj discret(-ète)

unofficial [ʌnə'fɪʃl] adj (news) officieux(-euse); (strike) sauvage

unorthodox [ʌn'ɔ:θədɔks] adj peu orthodoxe; (REL) hétérodoxe

unpack [ʌn'pæk] vi défaire sa valise ♦ vt (suitcase) défaire; (belongings) déballer

unpalatable [ʌn'pælətəbl] adj (meal) mauvais(e); (truth) désagréable (à entendre)

unparalleled [ʌn'pærəleld] adj incomparable, sans égal

unpleasant [ʌn'plɛznt] adj déplaisant(e), désagréable

unplug [ʌn'plʌg] vt débrancher

unpopular [ʌn'pɔpjulər] adj impopulaire

unprecedented [ʌn'prɛsɪdəntɪd] adj sans précédent

unpredictable [ʌnprɪ'dɪktəbl] adj imprévisible

unprofessional [ʌnprə'fɛʃənl] adj: **~ conduct** manquement m aux devoirs de la profession

UNPROFOR n abbr (= United Nations Protection Force) FORPRONU f

unqualified [ʌn'kwɔlɪfaɪd] adj (teacher) non diplômé(e), sans titres; (success, disaster) sans réserve, total(e)

unquestionably [ʌn'kwɛstʃənəblɪ] adv incontestablement

unravel [ʌnˈrævl] _vt_ démêler

unreal [ʌnˈrɪəl] _adj_ irréel(le); (_extraordinary_) incroyable

unrealistic [ˈʌnrɪəˈlɪstɪk] _adj_ irréaliste; peu réaliste

unreasonable [ʌnˈriːznəbl] _adj_ qui n'est pas raisonnable

unrelated [ʌnrɪˈleɪtɪd] _adj_ sans rapport; sans lien de parenté

unreliable [ʌnrɪˈlaɪəbl] _adj_ sur qui (_or_ quoi) on ne peut pas compter, peu fiable

unremitting [ʌnrɪˈmɪtɪŋ] _adj_ inlassable, infatigable, acharné(e)

unreservedly [ʌnrɪˈzɜːvɪdlɪ] _adv_ sans réserve

unrest [ʌnˈrest] _n_ agitation _f_, troubles _mpl_

unroll [ʌnˈrəul] _vt_ dérouler

unruly [ʌnˈruːlɪ] _adj_ indiscipliné(e)

unsafe [ʌnˈseɪf] _adj_ (_in danger_) en danger; (_journey, car_) dangereux(-euse)

unsaid [ʌnˈsed] _adj_: **to leave sth ~** passer qch sous silence

unsatisfactory [ˈʌnsætɪsˈfæktərɪ] _adj_ peu satisfaisant(e)

unsavoury [ʌnˈseɪvərɪ] (_US_ **unsavory**) _adj_ (_fig_) peu recommandable

unscathed [ʌnˈskeɪðd] _adj_ indemne

unscrew [ʌnˈskruː] _vt_ dévisser

unscrupulous [ʌnˈskruːpjuləs] _adj_ sans scrupules

unsettled [ʌnˈsetld] _adj_ perturbé(e); instable

unshaven [ʌnˈʃeɪvn] _adj_ non _or_ mal rasé(e)

unsightly [ʌnˈsaɪtlɪ] _adj_ disgracieux(-euse), laid(e)

unskilled [ʌnˈskɪld] _adj_: **~ worker** manœuvre _m_

unspeakable [ʌnˈspiːkəbl] _adj_ indicible; (_awful_) innommable

unstable [ʌnˈsteɪbl] _adj_ instable

unsteady [ʌnˈstedɪ] _adj_ mal assuré(e), chancelant(e), instable

unstuck [ʌnˈstʌk] _adj_: **to come ~** se décoller; (_plan_) tomber à l'eau

unsuccessful [ʌnsəkˈsesful] _adj_ (_attempt_) infructueux(-euse), vain(e); (_writer, proposal_) qui n'a pas de succès; **to be ~** (_in attempting sth_) ne pas réussir; ne pas avoir de succès; (_application_) ne pas être retenu(e)

unsuitable [ʌnˈsuːtəbl] _adj_ qui ne convient pas, peu approprié(e); inopportun(e)

unsure [ʌnˈʃuər] _adj_ pas sûr(e); **to be ~ of o.s.** manquer de confiance en soi

unsuspecting [ʌnsəsˈpektɪŋ] _adj_ qui ne se doute de rien

unsympathetic [ˈʌnsɪmpəˈθetɪk] _adj_ (_person_) antipathique; (_attitude_) peu compatissant(e)

untapped [ʌnˈtæpt] _adj_ (_resources_) inexploité(e)

unthinkable [ʌnˈθɪŋkəbl] _adj_ impensable, inconcevable

untidy [ʌnˈtaɪdɪ] _adj_ (_room_) en désordre; (_appearance, person_) débraillé(e); (_person: in character_) sans ordre, désordonné

untie [ʌnˈtaɪ] _vt_ (_knot, parcel_) défaire; (_prisoner, dog_) détacher

until [ənˈtɪl] _prep_ jusqu'à; (_after negative_) avant ♦ _conj_ jusqu'à ce que +_sub_; (_in past, after negative_) avant que +_sub_; **~ he comes** jusqu'à ce qu'il vienne, jusqu'à son arrivée; **~ now** jusqu'à présent, jusqu'ici; **~ then** jusque-là

untimely [ʌnˈtaɪmlɪ] _adj_ inopportun(e); (_death_) prématuré(e)

untold [ʌnˈtəuld] _adj_ (_story_) jamais raconté(e); (_wealth_) incalculable; (_joy, suffering_) indescriptible

untoward [ʌntəˈwɔːd] _adj_ fâcheux(-euse), malencontreux(-euse)

unused[1] [ʌnˈjuːzd] _adj_ (_clothes_) neuf (neuve)

unused[2] [ʌnˈjuːst] _adj_: **to be ~ to sth/to doing sth** ne pas avoir l'habitude de qch/de faire qch

unusual [ʌnˈjuːʒuəl] _adj_ insolite, exceptionnel(le), rare

unveil [ʌnˈveɪl] _vt_ dévoiler

unwanted [ʌnˈwɒntɪd] _adj_ (_child, pregnancy_) non désiré(e); (_clothes etc_) à donner

unwelcome [ʌn'wɛlkəm] *adj* importun(e); (*news*) fâcheux(-euse)

unwell [ʌn'wɛl] *adj* souffrant(e); **to feel ~** ne pas se sentir bien

unwieldy [ʌn'wiːldɪ] *adj* (*object*) difficile à manier; (*system*) lourd(e)

unwilling [ʌn'wɪlɪŋ] *adj*: **to be ~ to do** ne pas vouloir faire; **~ly** *adv* à contrecœur, contre son gré

unwind [ʌn'waɪnd] (*irreg*) *vt* dérouler ♦ *vi* (*relax*) se détendre

unwise [ʌn'waɪz] *adj* irréfléchi(e), imprudent(e)

unwitting [ʌn'wɪtɪŋ] *adj* involontaire

unworkable [ʌn'wəːkəbl] *adj* (*plan*) impraticable

unworthy [ʌn'wəːðɪ] *adj* indigne

unwrap [ʌn'ræp] *vt* défaire; ouvrir

unwritten [ʌn'rɪtn] *adj* (*agreement*) tacite

KEYWORD
---

up [ʌp] *prep*: **he went up the stairs/the hill** il a monté l'escalier/la colline; **the cat was up a tree** le chat était dans un arbre; **they live further up the street** ils habitent plus haut dans la rue
♦ *adv* **1** (*upwards, higher*): **up in the sky/the mountains** (là-haut) dans le ciel/les montagnes; **put it a bit higher up** mettez-le un peu plus haut; **up there** là-haut; **up above** au-dessus
2: **to be up** (*out of bed*) être levé(e); (*prices*) avoir augmenté *or* monté
3: **up to** (*as far as*) jusqu'à; **up to now** jusqu'à présent
4: **to be up to** (*depending on*): **it's up to you** c'est à vous de décider; (*equal to*): **he's not up to it** (*job, task etc*) il n'en est pas capable; (*inf: be doing*): **what is he up to?** qu'est-ce qu'il peut bien faire?
♦ *n*: **ups and downs** hauts et bas *mpl*

---

up-and-coming [ʌpənd'kʌmɪŋ] *adj* plein(e) d'avenir *or* de promesses

upbringing ['ʌpbrɪŋɪŋ] *n* éducation *f*

update [ʌp'deɪt] *vt* mettre à jour

upgrade [ʌp'greɪd] *vt* (*house*) moderniser; (*job*) revaloriser; (*employee*) promouvoir

upheaval [ʌp'hiːvl] *n* bouleversement *m*; branle-bas *m*

uphill ['ʌp'hɪl] *adj* qui monte; (*fig: task*) difficile, pénible ♦ *adv* (*face, look*) en amont; **to go ~** monter

uphold [ʌp'həuld] (*irreg*) *vt* (*law, decision*) maintenir

upholstery [ʌp'həulstərɪ] *n* rembourrage *m*; (*cover*) tissu *m* d'ameublement; (*of car*) garniture *f*

upkeep ['ʌpkiːp] *n* entretien *m*

upon [ə'pɔn] *prep* sur

upper ['ʌpər] *adj* supérieur(e); du dessus ♦ *n* (*of shoe*) empeigne *f*; **~-class** *adj* de la haute société, aristocratique; **~ hand** *n*: **to have the ~ hand** avoir le dessus; **~most** *adj* le (la) plus haut(e); **what was ~most in my mind** ce à quoi je pensais surtout; **~ sixth** *n* terminale *f*

upright ['ʌpraɪt] *adj* droit(e); vertical(e); (*fig*) droit, honnête

uprising ['ʌpraɪzɪŋ] *n* soulèvement *m*, insurrection *f*

uproar ['ʌprɔːr] *n* tumulte *m*; (*protests*) tempête *f* de protestations

uproot [ʌp'ruːt] *vt* déraciner

upset [*n* 'ʌpsɛt, *vb, adj* ʌp'sɛt] (*irreg: like* **set**) *n* bouleversement *m*; (*stomach ~*) indigestion *f* ♦ *vt* (*glass etc*) renverser; (*plan*) déranger; (*person: offend*) contrarier; (*: grieve*) faire de la peine à; bouleverser ♦ *adj* contrarié(e); peiné(e); (*stomach*) dérangé(e)

upshot ['ʌpʃɔt] *n* résultat *m*

upside-down ['ʌpsaɪd'daun] *adv* à l'envers; **to turn ~ ~** mettre sens dessus dessous

upstairs [ʌp'stɛəz] *adv* en haut ♦ *adj* (*room*) du dessus, d'en haut ♦ *n*: **the ~** l'étage *m*

upstart ['ʌpstɑːt] (*pej*) *n* parvenu(e)

upstream [ʌp'striːm] *adv* en amont

uptake ['ʌpteɪk] *n*: **to be quick/slow on the ~** comprendre vite/être lent à comprendre

uptight [ʌp'taɪt] (*inf*) *adj* très tendu(e), crispé(e)

up-to-date [ˈʌptəˈdeɪt] *adj* moderne; *(information)* très récent(e)

upturn [ˈʌptəːn] *n (in luck)* retournement *m*; *(COMM: in market)* hausse *f*

upward [ˈʌpwəd] *adj* ascendant(e); vers le haut; **~(s)** *adv* vers le haut; **~(s) of 200** 200 et plus

urban [ˈəːbən] *adj* urbain(e); **~ clearway** *n* rue *f* à stationnement einterdit

urbane [əːˈbeɪn] *adj* urbain(e), courtois(e)

urchin [ˈəːtʃɪn] *n* polisson *m*

urge [əːdʒ] *n* besoin *m*; envie *f*; forte envie, désir *m* ♦ *vt*: **to ~ sb to do** exhorter qn à faire, pousser qn à faire; recommander vivement à qn de faire

urgency [ˈəːdʒənsɪ] *n* urgence *f*; *(of tone)* insistance *f*

urgent [ˈəːdʒənt] *adj* urgent(e); *(tone)* insistant(e), pressant(e)

urinal [ˈjuərɪnl] *n* urinoir *m*

urine [ˈjuərɪn] *n* urine *f*

urn [əːn] *n* urne *f*; *(also:* **tea ~)** fontaine *f* à thé

US *n abbr* = **United States**

us [ʌs] *pron* nous; *see also* **me**

USA *n abbr* = **United States of America**

use [*n* juːs, *vb* juːz] *n* emploi *m*, utilisation *f*; usage *m*; *(~fulness)* utilité *f* ♦ *vt* se servir de, utiliser, employer; **in ~** en usage; **out of ~** hors d'usage; **to be of ~** servir, être utile; **it's no ~** ça ne sert à rien; **she ~d to do it** elle le faisait (autrefois), elle avait coutume de le faire; **~d to:** **to be ~d to** avoir l'habitude de, être habitué(e) à; **~ up** *vt* finir, épuiser; consommer; **~d** [juːzd] *adj (car)* d'occasion; **~ful** [ˈjuːsful] *adj* utile; **~fulness** *n* utilité *f*; **~less** [ˈjuːslɪs] *adj* inutile; *(person: hopeless)* nul(le); **~r** [ˈjuːzəʳ] *n* utilisateur(-trice), usager *m*; **~r-friendly** *adj (computer)* convivial(e), facile d'emploi

usher [ˈʌʃəʳ] *n (at wedding ceremony)* placeur *m*; **~ette** [ʌʃəˈrɛt] *n (in cinema)* ouvreuse *f*

usual [ˈjuːʒuəl] *adj* habituel(le); **as ~** comme d'habitude; **~ly** [ˈjuːʒəlɪ] *adv*

d'habitude, d'ordinaire

utensil [juːˈtɛnsl] *n* ustensile *m*

uterus [ˈjuːtərəs] *n* utérus *m*

utility [juːˈtɪlɪtɪ] *n* utilité *f*; *(also:* **public ~)** service public; **~ room** *n* buanderie *f*

utmost [ˈʌtməust] *adj* extrême, le (la) plus grand(e) ♦ *n*: **to do one's ~** faire tout son possible

utter [ˈʌtəʳ] *adj* total(e), complet(-ète) ♦ *vt* *(words)* prononcer, proférer; *(sounds)* émettre; **~ance** *n* paroles *fpl*; **~ly** *adv* complètement, totalement

U-turn [ˈjuːˈtəːn] *n* demi-tour *m*

V, v

v. *abbr* = **verse**; **versus**; **volt**; *(= vide)* voir

vacancy [ˈveɪkənsɪ] *n (BRIT: job)* poste vacant; *(room)* chambre *f* disponible; **"no vacancies"** "complet"

vacant [ˈveɪkənt] *adj (seat etc)* libre, disponible; *(expression)* distrait(e)

vacate [vəˈkeɪt] *vt* quitter

vacation [vəˈkeɪʃən] *n* vacances *fpl*

vaccinate [ˈvæksɪneɪt] *vt* vacciner

vacuum [ˈvækjum] *n* vide *m*; **~ cleaner** *n* aspirateur *m*; **~-packed** *adj* emballé(e) sous vide

vagina [vəˈdʒaɪnə] *n* vagin *m*

vagrant [ˈveɪɡrənt] *n* vagabond(e)

vague [veɪɡ] *adj* vague, imprécis(e); *(blurred: photo, outline)* flou(e); **~ly** *adv* vaguement

vain [veɪn] *adj (useless)* vain(e); *(conceited)* vaniteux(-euse); **in ~** en vain

valentine [ˈvæləntaɪn] *n (also:* **~ card)** carte *f* de la Saint-Valentin; *(person)* bienaimé(e) *(le jour de la Saint-Valentin)*; **V~'s day** *n* Saint-Valentin *f*

valiant [ˈvælɪənt] *adj* vaillant(e)

valid [ˈvælɪd] *adj* valable; *(document)* valable, valide

valley [ˈvælɪ] *n* vallée *f*

valour [ˈvæləʳ] *(US* **valor)** *n* courage *m*

valuable [ˈvæljuəbl] *adj (jewel)* de valeur; *(time, help)* précieux(-euse); **~s** *npl* objets *mpl* de valeur

valuation [vælju'eɪʃən] *n* (*price*) estimation *f*; (*quality*) appréciation *f*

value ['vælju:] *n* valeur *f* ♦ *vt* (*fix price*) évaluer, expertiser; (*appreciate*) apprécier; ~ **added tax** (*BRIT*) *n* taxe *f* à la valeur ajoutée; ~**d** *adj* (*person*) estimé(e); (*advice*) précieux(-euse)

valve [vælv] *n* (*in machine*) soupape *f*, valve *f*; (*MED*) valve, valvule *f*

van [væn] *n* (*AUT*) camionnette *f*

vandal ['vændl] *n* vandale *m/f*; ~**ism** *n* vandalisme *m*; ~**ize** *vt* saccager

vanguard ['vængɑːd] *n* (*fig*): **in the ~ of** à l'avant-garde de

vanilla [və'nɪlə] *n* vanille *f*

vanish ['vænɪʃ] *vi* disparaître

vanity ['vænɪtɪ] *n* vanité *f*

vantage point ['vɑːntɪdʒ-] *n* bonne position

vapour ['veɪpər] (*US* **vapor**) *n* vapeur *f*; (*on window*) buée *f*

variable ['veərɪəbl] *adj* variable; (*mood*) changeant(e)

variance ['veərɪəns] *n*: **to be at ~ (with)** être en désaccord (avec); (*facts*) être en contradiction (avec)

varicose ['værɪkəus] *adj*: ~ **veins** varices *fpl*

varied ['veərɪd] *adj* varié(e), divers(e)

variety [və'raɪətɪ] *n* variété *f*; (*quantity*) nombre *m*, quantité *f*; ~ **show** *n* (spectacle *m* de) variétés *fpl*

various ['veərɪəs] *adj* divers(e), différent(e); (*several*) divers, plusieurs

varnish ['vɑːnɪʃ] *n* vernis *m* ♦ *vt* vernir

vary ['veərɪ] *vt, vi* varier, changer

vase [vɑːz] *n* vase *m*

Vaseline ® ['væsɪliːn] *n* vaseline *f*

vast [vɑːst] *adj* vaste, immense; (*amount, success*) énorme

VAT [væt] *n* abbr (= value added tax) TVA *f*

vat [væt] *n* cuve *f*

vault [vɔːlt] *n* (*of roof*) voûte *f*; (*tomb*) caveau *m*; (*in bank*) salle *f* des coffres; chambre forte ♦ *vt* (*also*: ~ **over**) sauter (d'un bond)

vaunted ['vɔːntɪd] *adj*: **much-~** tant vanté(e)

VCR *n abbr* = **video cassette recorder**

VD *n abbr* = **venereal disease**

VDU *n abbr* = **visual display unit**

veal [viːl] *n* veau *m*

veer [vɪər] *vi* tourner, virer

vegan ['viːgən] *n* végétalien(ne)

vegeburger ['vedʒɪbəːgər] *n* burger végétarien

vegetable ['vedʒtəbl] *n* légume *m* ♦ *adj* végétal(e)

vegetarian [vedʒɪ'teərɪən] *adj, n* végétarien(ne)

vehement ['viːɪmənt] *adj* violent(e), impétueux(-euse); (*impassioned*) ardent(e)

vehicle ['viːɪkl] *n* véhicule *m*

veil [veɪl] *n* voile *m*

vein [veɪn] *n* veine *f*; (*on leaf*) nervure *f*

velocity [vɪ'lɔsɪtɪ] *n* vitesse *f*

velvet ['velvɪt] *n* velours *m*

vending machine ['vendɪŋ-] *n* distributeur *m* automatique

veneer [və'nɪər] *n* (*on furniture*) placage *m*; (*fig*) vernis *m*

venereal [vɪ'nɪərɪəl] *adj*: ~ **disease** maladie vénérienne

Venetian blind [vɪ'niːʃən-] *n* store vénitien

vengeance ['vendʒəns] *n* vengeance *f*; **with a ~** (*fig*) vraiment, pour de bon

venison ['venɪsn] *n* venaison *f*

venom ['venəm] *n* venin *f*

vent [vent] *n* conduit *m* d'aération; (*in dress, jacket*) fente *f* ♦ *vt* (*fig: one's feelings*) donner libre cours à

ventilator ['ventɪleɪtər] *n* ventilateur *m*

ventriloquist [ven'trɪləkwɪst] *n* ventriloque *m/f*

venture ['ventʃər] *n* entreprise *f* ♦ *vt* risquer, hasarder ♦ *vi* s'aventurer, se risquer

venue ['venjuː] *n* lieu *m*

verb [vəːb] *n* verbe *m*; ~**al** *adj* verbal(e); (*translation*) littéral(e)

verbatim [vəː'beɪtɪm] *adj, adv* mot pour mot

verdict ['vəːdɪkt] *n* verdict *m*

verge [vəːdʒ] *n* (BRIT) bord *m*, bas-côté *m*; **"soft ~s"** (BRIT: AUT) "accotement non stabilisé"; **on the ~ of doing** sur le point de faire; **~ on** *vt fus* approcher de

verify ['vɛrɪfaɪ] *vt* vérifier; (confirm) confirmer

vermin ['vəːmɪn] *npl* animaux *mpl* nuisibles; (insects) vermine *f*

vermouth ['vəːməθ] *n* vermouth *m*

versatile ['vəːsətaɪl] *adj* polyvalent(e)

verse [vəːs] *n* (poetry) vers *mpl*; (stanza) strophe *f*; (in Bible) verset *m*

version ['vəːʃən] *n* version *f*

versus ['vəːsəs] *prep* contre

vertical ['vəːtɪkl] *adj* vertical(e) ♦ *n* verticale *f*

vertigo ['vəːtɪɡəu] *n* vertige *m*

verve [vəːv] *n* brio *m*, enthousiasme *m*

very ['vɛrɪ] *adv* très ♦ *adj*: **the ~ book which** le livre même que; **the ~ last** le tout dernier; **at the ~ least** tout au moins; **~ much** beaucoup

vessel ['vɛsl] *n* (ANAT, NAUT) vaisseau *m*; (container) récipient *m*

vest [vɛst] *n* (BRIT) tricot *m* de corps; (US: waistcoat) gilet *m*

vested interest *n* (COMM) droits acquis

vet [vɛt] *n abbr* (BRIT: veterinary surgeon) vétérinaire *m/f* ♦ *vt* examiner soigneusement

veteran ['vɛtərn] *n* vétéran *m*; (also: **war ~**) ancien combattant

veterinary surgeon ['vɛtrɪnərɪ-] (BRIT), **veterinarian** [vɛtrɪ'nɛərɪən] (US) *n* vétérinaire *m/f*

veto ['viːtəu] (*pl* **~es**) *n* veto *m* ♦ *vt* opposer son veto à

vex [vɛks] *vt* fâcher, contrarier; **~ed** *adj* (question) controversé(e)

via ['vaɪə] *prep* par, via

viable ['vaɪəbl] *adj* viable

vibrate [vaɪ'breɪt] *vi* vibrer

vicar ['vɪkə*r*] *n* pasteur *m* (de l'Église anglicane); **~age** *n* presbytère *m*

vicarious [vɪ'kɛərɪəs] *adj* indirect(e)

vice [vaɪs] *n* (evil) vice *m*; (TECH) étau *m*

vice- [vaɪs] *prefix* vice-

vice squad *n* ≃ brigade mondaine

vice versa ['vaɪsɪ'vəːsə] *adv* vice versa

vicinity [vɪ'sɪnɪtɪ] *n* environs *mpl*, alentours *mpl*

vicious ['vɪʃəs] *adj* (remark) cruel(le), méchant(e); (blow) brutal(e); (dog) méchant(e), dangereux(-euse); (horse) vicieux(-euse); **~ circle** *n* cercle vicieux

victim ['vɪktɪm] *n* victime *f*

victor ['vɪktə*r*] *n* vainqueur *m*

Victorian [vɪk'tɔːrɪən] *adj* victorien(ne)

victory ['vɪktərɪ] *n* victoire *f*

video ['vɪdɪəu] *cpd* vidéo *inv* ♦ *n* (~ film) vidéo *f*; (also: **~ cassette**) vidéocassette *f*; (also: **~ cassette recorder**) magnétoscope *m*; **~ tape** *n* bande *f* vidéo *inv*; (cassette) vidéocassette *f*; **~ wall** *n* mur *m* d'images vidéo

vie [vaɪ] *vi*: **to ~ with** rivaliser avec

Vienna [vɪ'ɛnə] *n* Vienne

Vietnam ['vjɛt'næm] *n* Viêt-Nam *m*, Vietnam *m*; **~ese** [vjɛtnə'miːz] *adj* vietnamien(ne) ♦ *n inv* Vietnamien(ne); (LING) vietnamien *m*

view [vjuː] *n* vue *f*; (opinion) avis *m*, vue ♦ *vt* voir, regarder; (situation) considérer; (house) visiter; **in full ~ of** sous les yeux de; **in ~ of the weather/the fact that** étant donné le temps/que; **in my ~** à mon avis; **~er** *n* (TV) téléspectateur(-trice); **~finder** *n* viseur *m*; **~point** *n* point *m* de vue

vigorous ['vɪɡərəs] *adj* vigoureux(-euse)

vile [vaɪl] *adj* (action) vil(e); (smell, food) abominable; (temper) massacrant(e)

villa ['vɪlə] *n* villa *f*

village ['vɪlɪdʒ] *n* village *m*; **~r** *n* villageois(e)

villain ['vɪlən] *n* (scoundrel) scélérat *m*; (BRIT: criminal) bandit *m*; (in novel etc) traître *m*

vindicate ['vɪndɪkeɪt] *vt* (person) innocenter; (action) justifier

vindictive [vɪn'dɪktɪv] *adj* vindicatif(-ive), rancunier(-ère)

vine [vaɪn] *n* vigne *f*; (climbing plant) plante grimpante

vinegar ['vɪnɪgəʳ] *n* vinaigre *m*

vineyard ['vɪnjɑːd] *n* vignoble *m*

vintage ['vɪntɪdʒ] *n* (*year*) année *f*, millésime *m*; **~ car** *n* voiture *f* d'époque; **~ wine** *n* vin *m* de grand cru

viola [vɪ'əʊlə] *n* (MUS) alto *m*

violate ['vaɪəleɪt] *vt* violer

violence ['vaɪələns] *n* violence *f*

violent ['vaɪələnt] *adj* violent(e)

violet ['vaɪələt] *adj* violet(te) ♦ *n* (*colour*) violet *m*; (*plant*) violette *f*

violin [vaɪə'lɪn] *n* violon *m*; **~ist** [vaɪə'lɪnɪst] *n* violoniste *m/f*

VIP *n abbr* (= *very important person*) V.I.P. *m*

virgin ['vɜːdʒɪn] *n* vierge *f* ♦ *adj* vierge

Virgo ['vɜːgəʊ] *n* la Vierge

virile ['vɪraɪl] *adj* viril(e)

virtually ['vɜːtjuəlɪ] *adv* (*almost*) pratiquement

virtual reality ['vɜːtjuəl-] *n* (COMPUT) réalité virtuelle

virtue ['vɜːtjuː] *n* vertu *f*; (*advantage*) mérite *m*, avantage *m*; **by ~ of** en vertu *or* en raison de; **virtuous** *adj* vertueux(-euse)

virus ['vaɪərəs] *n* (COMPUT) virus *m*

visa ['viːzə] *n* visa *m*

visibility [vɪzɪ'bɪlɪtɪ] *n* visibilité *f*

visible ['vɪzəbl] *adj* visible

vision ['vɪʒən] *n* (*sight*) vue *f*, vision *f*; (*foresight, in dream*) vision

visit ['vɪzɪt] *n* visite *f*; (*stay*) séjour *m* ♦ *vt* (*person*) rendre visite à; (*place*) visiter; **~ing hours** *npl* (*in hospital etc*) heures *fpl* de visite; **~or** *n* visiteur(-euse); (*to one's house*) visite *f*, invité(e); **~or centre** *n* hall *m or* centre *m* d'accueil

visor ['vaɪzəʳ] *n* visière *f*

vista ['vɪstə] *n* vue *f*

visual ['vɪzjuəl] *adj* visuel(le); **~ aid** *n* support visuel; **~ display unit** *n* console *f* de visualisation, visuel *m*; **~ize** *vt* se représenter, s'imaginer; **~ly-impaired** *adj* malvoyant(e)

vital ['vaɪtl] *adj* vital(e); (*person*) plein(e) d'entrain; **~ly** *adv* (*important*) absolument; **~ statistics** *npl* (*fig*) mensurations *fpl*

vitamin ['vɪtəmɪn] *n* vitamine *f*

vivacious [vɪ'veɪʃəs] *adj* animé(e), qui a de la vivacité

vivid ['vɪvɪd] *adj* (*account*) vivant(e); (*light, imagination*) vif (vive); **~ly** *adv* (*describe*) d'une manière vivante; (*remember*) de façon précise

V-neck ['viːnɛk] *n* décolleté *m* en V

vocabulary [vəu'kæbjulərɪ] *n* vocabulaire *m*

vocal ['vəukl] *adj* vocal(e); (*articulate*) qui sait s'exprimer; **~ cords** *npl* cordes vocales

vocation [vəu'keɪʃən] *n* vocation *f*; **~al** *adj* professionnel(le)

vociferous [və'sɪfərəs] *adj* bruyant(e)

vodka ['vɔdkə] *n* vodka *f*

vogue [vəug] *n*: **in ~** en vogue *f*

voice [vɔɪs] *n* voix *f* ♦ *vt* (*opinion*) exprimer, formuler; **~ mail** *n* (*system*) messagerie *f* vocale; (*device*) boîte *f* vocale

void [vɔɪd] *n* vide *m* ♦ *adj* nul(le); **~ of** vide de, dépourvu(e) de

volatile ['vɔlətaɪl] *adj* volatil(e); (*person*) versatile; (*situation*) explosif(-ive)

volcano [vɔl'keɪnəu] (*pl* **~es**) *n* volcan *m*

volition [və'lɪʃən] *n*: **of one's own ~** de son propre gré

volley ['vɔlɪ] *n* (*of gunfire*) salve *f*; (*of stones etc*) grêle *f*, volée *f*; (*of questions*) multitude *f*, série *f*; (TENNIS *etc*) volée *f*; **~ball** *n* volley(-ball) *m*

volt [vəult] *n* volt *m*; **~age** *n* tension *f*, voltage *m*

volume ['vɔljuːm] *n* volume *m*

voluntarily ['vɔləntrɪlɪ] *adv* volontairement

voluntary ['vɔləntərɪ] *adj* volontaire; (*unpaid*) bénévole

volunteer [vɔlən'tɪəʳ] *n* volontaire *m/f* ♦ *vi* (MIL) s'engager comme volontaire; **to ~ to do** se proposer pour faire

vomit ['vɔmɪt] *vt, vi* vomir

vote [vəut] *n* vote *m*, suffrage *m*; (*cast*) voix *f*, vote; (*franchise*) droit *m* de vote ♦ *vt* (*elect*): **to be ~d chairman** *etc* être élu président *etc*; (*propose*): **to ~ that** proposer que ♦ *vi* voter; **~ of thanks** discours

m de remerciement; ~r *n* électeur(-trice);
voting *n* scrutin *m*, vote *m*

voucher ['vautʃər] *n* (*for meal, petrol, gift*)
bon *m*

vouch for ['vautʃ-] *vt fus* se porter garant
de

vow [vau] *n* vœu *m*, serment *m* ♦ *vi* jurer

vowel ['vauəl] *n* voyelle *f*

voyage ['vɔ ɪdʒ] *n* voyage *m* par mer, traversée *f*; (*by spacecraft*) voyage

vulgar ['vʌlgər] *adj* vulgaire

vulnerable ['vʌlnərəbl] *adj* vulnérable

vulture ['vʌltʃər] *n* vautour *m*

W, w

wad [wɔd] *n* (*of cotton wool, paper*) tampon
m; (*of banknotes etc*) liasse *f*

waddle ['wɔdl] *vi* se dandiner

wade [weɪd] *vi*: **to ~ through** marcher
dans, patauger dans; (*fig: book*) s'évertuer
à lire

wafer ['weɪfər] *n* (*CULIN*) gaufrette *f*

waffle ['wɔfl] *n* (*CULIN*) gaufre *f*; (*inf*) ver-
biage *m*, remplissage *m* ♦ *vi* parler pour
ne rien dire, faire du remplissage

waft [wɔft] *vt* porter ♦ *vi* flotter

wag [wæg] *vt* agiter, remuer ♦ *vi* remuer

wage [weɪdʒ] *n* (*also:* **~s**) salaire *m*, paye *f*
♦ *vt*: **to ~ war** faire la guerre; **~ earner** *n*
salarié(e); **~ packet** *n* (enveloppe *f* de)
paye *f*

wager ['weɪdʒər] *n* pari *m*

wag(g)on ['wægən] *n* (*horse-drawn*) chariot
m; (*BRIT: RAIL*) wagon *m* (de marchandises)

wail [weɪl] *vi* gémir; (*siren*) hurler

waist [weɪst] *n* taille *f*; **~coat** (*BRIT*) *n* gilet
m; **~line** *n* (tour *m* de) taille *f*

wait [weɪt] *n* attente *f* ♦ *vi* attendre; **to
keep sb ~ing** faire attendre qn; **to ~ for**
attendre; **I can't ~ to ...** (*fig*) je meurs
d'envie de ...; **~ behind** *vi* rester (à attendre); **~ on** *vt fus* servir; **~er** *n* garçon
m (de café), serveur *m*; **~ing** *n*: **"no
~ing"** (*BRIT: AUT*) "stationnement inter-

dit"; **~ing list** *n* liste *f* d'attente; **~ing
room** *n* salle *f* d'attente; **~ress** *n* serveuse *f*

waive [weɪv] *vt* renoncer à, abandonner

wake [weɪk] (*pt* **woke, waked**, *pp* **woken,
waked**) *vt* (*also:* **~ up**) réveiller ♦ *vi* (*also:*
~ up) se réveiller ♦ *n* (*for dead person*) veillée *f* mortuaire; (*NAUT*) sillage *m*

Wales [weɪlz] *n* pays *m* de Galles; **the
Prince of ~** le prince de Galles

walk [wɔːk] *n* promenade *f*; (*short*) petit
tour; (*gait*) démarche *f*; (*path*) chemin *m*;
(*in park etc*) allée *f* ♦ *vi* marcher; (*for pleasure, exercise*) se promener ♦ *vt* (*distance*)
faire à pied; (*dog*) promener; **10 minutes'
~ from** à 10 minutes à pied de; **from all
~s of life** de toutes conditions sociales; **~
out** *vi* (*audience*) sortir, quitter la salle;
(*workers*) se mettre en grève; **~ out on**
(*inf*) *vt fus* quitter, plaquer; **~er** *n* (*person*)
marcheur(-euse); **~ie-talkie** *n* talkie-
walkie *m*; **~ing** *n* marche *f* à pied; **~ing
shoes** *npl* chaussures *fpl* de marche;
~ing stick *n* canne *f*; **W~man** ® *n*
Walkman ® *m*; **~out** *n* (*of workers*)
grève-surprise *f*; **~over** (*inf*) *n* victoire *f* or
examen *m* etc facile; **~way** *n* promenade
f

wall [wɔːl] *n* mur *m*; (*of tunnel, cave etc*) paroi *m*; **~ed** *adj* (*city*) fortifié(e); (*garden*)
entouré(e) d'un mur, clos(e)

wallet ['wɔlɪt] *n* portefeuille *m*

wallflower ['wɔːlflauər] *n* giroflée *f*; **to be
a ~** (*fig*) faire tapisserie

wallow ['wɔləu] *vi* se vautrer

wallpaper ['wɔːlpeɪpər] *n* papier peint ♦ *vt*
tapisser

walnut ['wɔːlnʌt] *n* noix *f*; (*tree, wood*)
noyer *m*

walrus ['wɔːlrəs] (*pl* **~** or **~es**) *n* morse *m*

waltz [wɔːlts] *n* valse *f* ♦ *vi* valser

wand [wɔnd] *n* (*also:* **magic ~**) baguette *f*
(magique)

wander ['wɔndər] *vi* (*person*) errer;
(*thoughts*) vagabonder, errer ♦ *vt* errer
dans

wane [weɪn] *vi* (*moon*) décroître; (*reputa-*

tion) décliner

wangle ['wæŋgl] (BRIT: inf) vt se débrouiller pour avoir; carotter

want [wɒnt] vt vouloir; (need) avoir besoin de ♦ n: **for ~ of** par manque de, faute de; **~s** npl (needs) besoins mpl; **to ~ to do** vouloir faire; **to ~ sb to do** vouloir que qn fasse; **~ed** adj (criminal) recherché(e) par la police; **"cook ~ed"** "on recherche un cuisinier"; **~ing** adj: **to be found ~ing** ne pas être à la hauteur

war [wɔːʳ] n guerre f; **to make ~ (on)** faire la guerre (à)

ward [wɔːd] n (in hospital) salle f; (POL) canton m; (LAW: child) pupille m/f; **~ off** vt (attack, enemy) repousser, éviter

warden ['wɔːdn] n gardien(ne); (BRIT: of institution) directeur(-trice); (: also: **traffic ~**) contractuel(le); (of youth hostel) père m or mère f aubergiste

warder ['wɔːdəʳ] (BRIT) n gardien m de prison

wardrobe ['wɔːdrəub] n (cupboard) armoire f; (clothes) garde-robe f; (THEATRE) costumes mpl

warehouse ['weəhaus] n entrepôt m

wares [weəz] npl marchandises fpl

warfare ['wɔːfeəʳ] n guerre f

warhead ['wɔːhed] n (MIL) ogive f

warily ['weərɪlɪ] adv avec prudence

warm [wɔːm] adj chaud(e); (thanks, welcome, applause, person) chaleureux(-euse); **it's ~** il fait chaud; **I'm ~** j'ai chaud; **~ up** vi (person, room) se réchauffer; (water) chauffer; (athlete) s'échauffer ♦ vt (food) (faire) réchauffer, (faire) chauffer; (engine) faire chauffer; **~-hearted** adj affectueux(-euse); **~ly** adv chaudement; chaleureusement; **~th** n chaleur f

warn [wɔːn] vt avertir, prévenir; **to ~ sb (not) to do** conseiller à qn de (ne pas) faire; **~ing** n avertissement m; (notice) avis m; (signal) avertisseur m; **~ing light** n avertisseur lumineux; **~ing triangle** n (AUT) triangle m de présignalisation

warp [wɔːp] vi (wood) travailler, se déformer ♦ vt (fig: character) pervertir

warrant ['wɒrnt] n (guarantee) garantie f; (LAW: to arrest) mandat m d'arrêt; (: to search) mandat de perquisition; **~y** n garantie f

warren ['wɒrən] n (of rabbits) terrier m; (fig: of streets etc) dédale m

warrior ['wɒrɪəʳ] n guerrier(-ère)

Warsaw ['wɔːsɔː] n Varsovie

warship ['wɔːʃɪp] n navire m de guerre

wart [wɔːt] n verrue f

wartime ['wɔːtaɪm] n: **in ~** en temps de guerre

wary ['weərɪ] adj prudent(e)

was [wɒz] pt of **be**

wash [wɒʃ] vt laver ♦ vi se laver; (sea): **to ~ over/against sth** inonder/baigner qch ♦ n (clothes) lessive f; (~ing programme) lavage m; (of ship) sillage m; **to have a ~** se laver, faire sa toilette; **to give sth a ~** laver qch; **~ away** vt (stain) enlever au lavage; (subj: river etc) emporter; **~ off** vi partir au lavage; **~ up** vi (BRIT) faire la vaisselle; (US) se débarbouiller; **~able** adj lavable; **~basin** (US **washbowl**) n lavabo m; **~cloth** (US) n gant m de toilette; **~er** n (TECH) rondelle f, joint m; **~ing** n (dirty) linge m; (clean) lessive f; **~ing machine** n machine f à laver; **~ing powder** (BRIT) n lessive f (en poudre); **~ing-up** n vaisselle f; **~ing-up liquid** n produit m pour la vaisselle; **~-out** (inf) n désastre m; **~room** (US) n toilettes fpl

wasn't ['wɒznt] = **was not**

wasp [wɒsp] n guêpe f

wastage ['weɪstɪdʒ] n gaspillage m; (in manufacturing, transport etc) pertes fpl, déchets mpl; **natural ~** départs naturels

waste [weɪst] n gaspillage m; (of time) perte f; (rubbish) déchets mpl; (also: **household ~**) ordures fpl ♦ adj (land, ground: in city) à l'abandon; (leftover): **~ material** déchets mpl ♦ vt gaspiller; (time, opportunity) perdre; **~s** npl (area) étendue f désertique; **~ away** vi dépérir; **~ disposal unit** (BRIT) n broyeur m d'ordures; **~ful** adj gaspilleur(-euse); (process) peu économique; **~ ground** (BRIT) n terrain m vague;

~**paper basket** n corbeille f à papier

watch [wɒtʃ] n montre f; (act of ~ing) surveillance f; guet m; (MIL: guards) garde f; (NAUT: guards, spell of duty) quart m ♦ vt (look at) observer; (: match, programme, TV) regarder; (spy on, guard) surveiller; (be careful of) faire attention à ♦ vi regarder; (keep guard) monter la garde; ~ **out** vi faire attention; ~**dog** n chien m de garde; (fig) gardien(ne); ~**ful** adj attentif(-ive), vigilant(e); ~**maker** n horloger(-ère) f; ~**man** (irreg) n see **night**; ~**strap** n bracelet m de montre

water [ˈwɔːtəʳ] n eau f ♦ vt (plant, garden) arroser ♦ vi (eyes) larmoyer; (mouth): **it makes my mouth ~** j'en ai l'eau à la bouche; **in British ~s** dans les eaux territoriales britanniques; ~ **down** vt (milk) couper d'eau; (fig: story) édulcorer; ~**colour** (US **watercolor**) n aquarelle f; ~**cress** n cresson m (de fontaine); ~**fall** n chute f d'eau; ~ **heater** n chauffe-eau m; ~**ing can** n arrosoir m; ~ **lily** n nénuphar m; ~**line** n (NAUT) ligne f de flottaison; ~**logged** adj (ground) détrempé(e); ~ **main** n canalisation f d'eau; ~**melon** n pastèque f; ~**proof** adj imperméable; ~**shed** n (GEO) ligne f de partage des eaux; (fig) moment m critique, point décisif; ~-**skiing** n ski m nautique; ~**tight** adj étanche; ~**way** n cours m d'eau navigable; ~**works** n (building) station f hydraulique; ~**y** adj (coffee, soup) trop faible; (eyes) humide, larmoyant(e)

watt [wɒt] n watt m

wave [weɪv] n vague f; (of hand) geste m, signe m; (RADIO) onde f; (in hair) ondulation f ♦ vi faire signe de la main; (flag) flotter au vent; (grass) ondoyer ♦ vt (handkerchief) agiter; (stick) brandir; ~**length** n longueur f d'ondes

waver [ˈweɪvəʳ] vi vaciller; (voice) trembler; (person) hésiter

wavy [ˈweɪvɪ] adj (hair, surface) ondulé(e); (line) onduleux(-euse)

wax [wæks] n cire f; (for skis) fart m ♦ vt cirer; (car) lustrer; (skis) farter ♦ vi (moon)

croître; ~**works** npl personnages mpl de cire ♦ n musée m de cire

way [weɪ] n chemin m, voie f; (distance) distance f; (direction) chemin, direction f; (manner) façon f, manière f; (habit) habitude f, façon; **which ~? - this ~** par où? - par ici; **on the ~** (en route) en route; **to be on one's ~** être en route; **to go out of one's ~ to do** (fig) se donner du mal pour faire; **to be in the ~** bloquer le passage; (fig) gêner; **to lose one's ~** perdre son chemin; **under ~** en cours; **in a ~** dans un sens; **in some ~s** à certains égards; **no ~!** (inf) pas question; **by the ~ ...** à propos ...; **"~ in"** (BRIT) "entrée"; **"~ out"** (BRIT) "sortie"; **the ~ back** le chemin du retour; **"give ~"** (BRIT: AUT) "cédez le passage"; ~**lay** (irreg) vt attaquer

wayward [ˈweɪwəd] adj capricieux(-euse), entêté(e)

W.C. n abbr w.c. mpl, waters mpl

we [wiː] pl pron nous

weak [wiːk] adj faible; (health) fragile; (beam etc) peu solide; ~**en** vi faiblir, décliner ♦ vt affaiblir; ~**ling** n (physically) gringalet m; (morally etc) faible m/f; ~**ness** n faiblesse f; (fault) point m faible; **to have a ~ness for** avoir un faible pour

wealth [welθ] n (money, resources) richesse(s) f(pl); (of details) profusion f; ~**y** adj riche

wean [wiːn] vt sevrer

weapon [ˈwepən] n arme f

wear [weəʳ] (pt **wore**, pp **worn**) n (use) usage m; (deterioration through use) usure f; (clothing): **sports/babywear** vêtements mpl de sport/pour bébés ♦ vt (clothes) porter; (put on) mettre; (damage: through use) user ♦ vi (last) faire de l'usage; (rub etc through) s'user; **town/evening ~** tenue f de ville/soirée; ~ **away** vt user, ronger ♦ vi (inscription) s'effacer; ~ **down** vt user; (strength, person) épuiser; ~ **off** vi disparaître; ~ **out** vt user; (person, strength) épuiser; ~ **and tear** n usure f

weary [ˈwɪərɪ] adj (tired) épuisé(e); (dispirited) las (lasse), abattu(e) ♦ vi: **to ~ of** se lasser de

weasel ['wiːzl] n (ZOOL) belette f

weather ['weðə'] n temps m ♦ vt (tempest, crisis) essuyer, réchapper à, survivre à; **under the ~** (fig: ill) mal fichu(e); **~-beaten** adj (person) hâlé(e); (building) dégradé(e) par les intempéries; **~cock** n girouette f; **~ forecast** n prévisions fpl météorologiques, météo f; **~ man** (irreg) (inf) n météorologue m; **~ vane** n = **weathercock**

weave [wiːv] (pt **wove**, pp **woven**) vt (cloth) tisser; (basket) tresser; **~r** n tisserand(e)

web [web] n (of spider) toile f; (on foot) palmure f; (fabric, also fig) tissu m; **the (World Wide) W~** le Web

website ['websaɪt] n (COMPUT) site m Web

wed [wed] (pt, pp **wedded**) vt épouser ♦ vi se marier

we'd [wiːd] = **we had**; **we would**

wedding ['wedɪŋ] n mariage m; **silver/golden ~ (anniversary)** noces fpl d'argent/d'or; **~ day** n jour m du mariage; **~ dress** n robe f de mariée; **~ ring** n alliance f

wedge [wedʒ] n (of wood etc) coin m, cale f; (of cake) part f ♦ vt (pack tightly) enfoncer

Wednesday ['wednzdɪ] n mercredi m

wee [wiː] (SCOTTISH) adj (tout(e)) petit(e)

weed [wiːd] n mauvaise herbe ♦ vt désherber; **~killer** n désherbant m; **~y** adj (man) gringalet

week [wiːk] n semaine f; **a ~ today/on Friday** aujourd'hui/vendredi en huit; **~day** n jour m de semaine; (COMM) jour ouvrable; **~end** n week-end m; **~ly** adv une fois par semaine, chaque semaine ♦ adj hebdomadaire ♦ n hebdomadaire m

weep [wiːp] (pt, pp **wept**) vi (person) pleurer; **~ing willow** n saule pleureur

weigh [weɪ] vt, vi peser; **to ~ anchor** lever l'ancre; **~ down** vt (person, animal) écraser; (fig: with worry) accabler; **~ up** vt examiner

weight [weɪt] n poids m; **to lose/put on ~** maigrir/grossir; **~ing** n (allowance) indemnité f, allocation f; **~lifter** n haltérophile m; **~lifting** n haltérophilie f; **~y** adj lourd(e); (important) de poids, important(e)

weir [wɪə'] n barrage m

weird [wɪəd] adj bizarre

welcome ['welkəm] adj bienvenu(e) ♦ n accueil m ♦ vt accueillir; (also: **bid ~**) souhaiter la bienvenue à; (be glad of) se réjouir de; **thank you - you're ~!** merci - de rien or il n'y a pas de quoi!

welder ['weldə'] n soudeur(-euse)

welfare ['welfeə'] n (well-being) bien-être m; (social aid) assistance sociale; **~ state** n État-providence m

well [wel] n puits m ♦ adv bien ♦ adj: **to be ~** aller bien ♦ excl eh bien!; (relief also) bon!; (resignation) enfin!; **as ~** aussi, également; **as ~ as** en plus de; **~ done!** bravo!; **get ~ soon** remets-toi vite!; **to do ~** bien réussir; (business) prospérer; **~ up** vi monter

we'll [wiːl] = **we will**; **we shall**

well: ~-behaved adj sage, obéissant(e); **~-being** n bien-être m; **~-built** adj (person) bien bâti(e); **~-deserved** adj (bien) mérité(e); **~-dressed** adj bien habillé(e); **~-heeled** (inf) adj (wealthy) nanti(e)

wellingtons ['welɪŋtənz] npl (also: **wellington boots**) bottes fpl de caoutchouc

well: ~-known adj (person) bien connu(e); **~-mannered** adj bien élevé(e); **~-meaning** adj bien intentionné(e); **~-off** adj aisé(e); **~-read** adj cultivé(e); **~-to-do** adj aisé(e); **~-wishers** npl amis mpl et admirateurs mpl; (friends) amis mpl

Welsh [welʃ] adj gallois(e) ♦ n (LING) gallois m; **the ~** npl (people) les Gallois mpl; **~ Assembly** n Parlement m gallois; **~man** (irreg) n Gallois m; **~woman** (irreg) n Galloise f

went [went] pt of **go**

wept [wept] pt, pp of **weep**

were [wəː'] pt of **be**

we're [wɪə'] = **we are**

weren't [wəːnt] = **were not**

west [west] n ouest m ♦ adj ouest inv, de or à l'ouest ♦ adv à or vers l'ouest; **the W~** l'Occident m, l'Ouest; **the W~ Coun-**

try (*BRIT*) ♦ *n* le sud-ouest de l'Angleterre; **~erly** *adj* (*wind*) d'ouest; (*point*) à l'ouest; **~ern** *adj* occidental(e), de *or* à l'ouest ♦ *n* (*CINEMA*) western *m*; **W~ Indian** *adj* antillais(e) ♦ *n* Antillais(e); **W~ Indies** *npl* Antilles *fpl*; **~ward(s)** *adv* vers l'ouest

wet [wɛt] *adj* mouillé(e); (*damp*) humide; (*soaked*) trempé(e); (*rainy*) pluvieux(-euse) ♦ *n* (*BRIT: POL*) modéré *m* du parti conservateur; **to get ~** se mouiller; **"~ paint"** "attention peinture fraîche"; **~ suit** *n* combinaison *f* de plongée

we've [wiːv] = **we have**

whack [wæk] *vt* donner un grand coup à

whale [weɪl] *n* (*ZOOL*) baleine *f*

wharf [wɔːf] (*pl* **wharves**) *n* quai *m*

KEYWORD

what [wɔt] *adj* quel(le); **what size is he?** quelle taille fait-il?; **what colour is it?** de quelle couleur est-ce?; **what books do you need?** quels livres vous faut-il?; **what a mess!** quel désordre!
♦ *pron* **1** (*interrogative*) que, *prep* +quoi; **what are you doing?** que faites-vous?, qu'est-ce que vous faites?; **what is happening?** qu'est-ce qui se passe?, que se passe-t-il?; **what are you talking about?** de quoi parlez-vous?; **what is it called?** comment est-ce que ça s'appelle?; **what about me?** et moi?; **what about doing ...?** et si on faisait ...?
2 (*relative: subject*) ce qui; (*: direct object*) ce que; (*: indirect object*) ce +*prep* +quoi, ce dont; **I saw what you did/was on the table** j'ai vu ce que vous avez fait/ce qui était sur la table; **tell me what you remember** dites-moi ce dont vous vous souvenez
♦ *excl* (*disbelieving*) quoi!, comment!

---

whatever [wɔtˈɛvəʳ] *adj*: **~ book** quel que soit le livre que (*or* qui) +*sub*; n'importe quel livre ♦ *pron*: **do ~ is necessary** faites (tout) ce qui est nécessaire; **~ happens** quoi qu'il arrive; **no reason ~** pas la moindre raison; **nothing ~** rien du tout

whatsoever [wɔtsəʊˈɛvəʳ] *adj* = **whatever**

wheat [wiːt] *n* blé *m*, froment *m*

wheedle [ˈwiːdl] *vt*: **to ~ sb into doing sth** cajoler *or* enjôler qn pour qu'il fasse qch; **to ~ sth out of sb** obtenir qch de qn par des cajoleries

wheel [wiːl] *n* roue *f*; (*also*: **steering ~**) volant *m*; (*NAUT*) gouvernail *m* ♦ *vt* (*pram etc*) pousser ♦ *vi* (*birds*) tournoyer; (*also*: **~ round**: *person*) virevolter; **~barrow** *n* brouette *f*; **~chair** *n* fauteuil roulant; **~ clamp** *n* (*AUT*) sabot *m* (de Denver)

wheeze [wiːz] *vi* respirer bruyamment

KEYWORD

when [wɛn] *adv* quand; **when did he go?** quand est-ce qu'il est parti?
♦ *conj* **1** (*at, during, after the time that*) quand, lorsque; **she was reading when I came in** elle lisait quand *or* lorsque je suis entré
2 (*on, at which*): **on the day when I met him** le jour où je l'ai rencontré
3 (*whereas*) alors que; **I thought I was wrong when in fact I was right** j'ai cru que j'avais tort alors qu'en fait j'avais raison

---

whenever [wɛnˈɛvəʳ] *adv* quand donc ♦ *conj* quand; (*every time that*) chaque fois que

where [wɛəʳ] *adv*, *conj* où; **this is ~** c'est là que; **~abouts** [ˈwɛərəbauts] *adv* où donc ♦ *n*: **nobody knows his ~abouts** personne ne sait où il se trouve; **~as** [wɛərˈæz] *conj* alors que; **~by** *adv* par lequel (*or* laquelle *etc*); **~ver** [wɛərˈɛvəʳ] *adv* où donc ♦ *conj* où que +*sub*; **~withal** [ˈwɛəwiðɔːl] *n* moyens *mpl*

whether [ˈwɛðəʳ] *conj* si; **I don't know ~ to accept or not** je ne sais pas si je dois accepter ou non; **it's doubtful ~** il est peu probable que +*sub*; **~ you go or not** que vous y alliez ou non

which [wɪtʃ] *adj* (*interrogative: direct, indirect*) quel(le); **which picture do you want?** quel tableau voulez-vous?; **which one?** lequel (laquelle)?; **in which case** auquel cas
♦ *pron* **1** (*interrogative*) lequel (laquelle), lesquels (lesquelles) *pl*; **I don't mind which** peu importe lequel; **which (of these) are yours?** lesquels sont à vous?; **tell me which you want** dites-moi lesquels *or* ceux que vous voulez
2 (*relative: subject*) qui; (: *object*) que, *prep* +lequel (laquelle); **the apple which you ate/which is on the table** la pomme que vous avez mangée/qui est sur la table; **the chair on which you are sitting** la chaise sur laquelle vous êtes assis; **the book of which you spoke** le livre dont vous avez parlé; **he knew, which is true/I feared** il le savait, ce qui est vrai/ce que je craignais; **after which** après quoi

whichever [wɪtʃ'ɛvəʳ] *adj*: **take ~ book you prefer** prenez le livre que vous préférez, peu importe lequel; **~ book you take** quel que soit le livre que vous preniez
while [waɪl] *n* moment *m* ♦ *conj* pendant que; (*as long as*) tant que; (*whereas*) alors que; bien que +*sub*; **for a ~** pendant quelque temps; **~ away** *vt* (*time*) (faire) passer
whim [wɪm] *n* caprice *m*
whimper ['wɪmpəʳ] *vi* geindre
whimsical ['wɪmzɪkəl] *adj* (*person*) capricieux(-euse); (*look, story*) étrange
whine [waɪn] *vi* gémir, geindre
whip [wɪp] *n* fouet *m*; (*for riding*) cravache *f*; (*POL: person*) chef de file assurant la discipline dans son groupe parlementaire ♦ *vt* fouetter; (*eggs*) battre; (*move quickly*) enlever/sortir brusquement; **~ped cream** *n* crème fouettée; **~-round** *n* (*BRIT*) collecte *f*
whirl [wə:l] *vi* tourbillonner; (*dancers*) tour-

noyer ♦ *vt* faire tourbillonner; faire tournoyer; **~pool** *n* tourbillon *m*; **~wind** *n* tornade *f*
whirr [wə:ʳ] *vi* (*motor etc*) ronronner; (: *louder*) vrombir
whisk [wɪsk] *n* (*CULIN*) fouet *m* ♦ *vt* fouetter; (*eggs*) battre; **to ~ sb away** *or* **off** emmener qn rapidement
whiskers ['wɪskəz] *npl* (*of animal*) moustaches *fpl*; (*of man*) favoris *mpl*
whisky ['wɪskɪ] (*IRELAND, US* **whiskey**) *n* whisky *m*
whisper ['wɪspəʳ] *vt, vi* chuchoter
whistle ['wɪsl] *n* (*sound*) sifflement *m*; (*object*) sifflet *m* ♦ *vi* siffler
white [waɪt] *adj* blanc (blanche); (*with fear*) blême ♦ *n* blanc *m*; (*person*) blanc (blanche); **~ coffee** (*BRIT*) *n* café *m* au lait, (café) crème *m*; **~-collar worker** *n* employé(e) de bureau; **~ elephant** *n* (*fig*) objet dispendieux et superflu; **~ lie** *n* pieux mensonge; **~ paper** *n* (*POL*) livre blanc; **~wash** *vt* blanchir à la chaux; (*fig*) blanchir ♦ *n* (*paint*) blanc *m* de chaux
whiting ['waɪtɪŋ] *n inv* (*fish*) merlan *m*
Whitsun ['wɪtsn] *n* la Pentecôte
whizz [wɪz] *vi*: **to ~ past** *or* **by** passer à toute vitesse; **~ kid** (*inf*) *n* petit prodige
who [hu:] *pron* qui; **~dunit** [hu:'dʌnɪt] (*inf*) *n* roman policier
whoever [hu:'ɛvəʳ] *pron*: **~ finds it** celui (celle) qui le trouve(, qui que ce soit), quiconque le trouve; **ask ~ you like** demandez à qui vous voulez; **~ he marries** quelle que soit la personne qu'il épouse; **~ told you that?** qui a bien pu vous dire ça?
whole [həul] *adj* (*complete*) entier(-ère), tout(e); (*not broken*) intact(e), complet(-ète) ♦ *n* (*all*): **the ~ of** la totalité de, tout(e) le (la); (*entire unit*) tout *m*; **the ~ of the town** la ville tout entière; **on the ~, as a ~** dans l'ensemble; **~food(s)** *n(pl)* aliments complets; **~hearted** *adj* sans réserve(s); **~meal** (*BRIT*) *adj* (*bread, flour*) complet(-ète); **~sale** *n* (vente *f* en) gros *m* ♦ *adj* (*price*) de gros; (*destruction*)

systématique ♦ *adv* en gros; ~**saler** *n* grossise *m/f*; ~**some** *adj* sain(e); ~**wheat** *adj* = **wholemeal**; **wholly** ['həʊlɪ] *adv* entièrement, tout à fait

KEYWORD

whom [huːm] *pron* **1** (*interrogative*) qui; **whom did you see?** qui avez-vous vu?; **to whom did you give it?** à qui l'avez-vous donné?

2 (*relative*) que, *prep* +qui; **the man whom I saw/to whom I spoke** l'homme que j'ai vu/à qui j'ai parlé

whooping cough ['huːpɪŋ-] *n* coqueluche *f*

whore [hɔːʳ] (*inf: pej*) *n* putain *f*

KEYWORD

whose [huːz] *adj* **1** (*possessive: interrogative*): **whose book is this?** à qui est ce livre?; **whose pencil have you taken?** à qui est le crayon que vous avez pris?, c'est le crayon de qui que vous avez pris?; **whose daughter are you?** de qui êtes-vous la fille?

2 (*possessive: relative*): **the man whose son you rescued** l'homme dont *or* de qui vous avez sauvé le fils; **the girl whose sister you were speaking to** la fille à la sœur de qui *or* de laquelle vous parliez; **the woman whose car was stolen** la femme dont la voiture a été volée

♦ *pron* à qui; **whose is this?** à qui est ceci?; **I know whose it is** je sais à qui c'est

why [waɪ] *adv* pourquoi ♦ *excl* eh bien!, tiens!; **the reason** ~ la raison pour laquelle; **tell me** ~ dites-moi pourquoi; ~ **not?** pourquoi pas?

wicked ['wɪkɪd] *adj* mauvais(e), méchant(e); (*crime*) pervers(e); (*mischievous*) malicieux(-euse)

wicket ['wɪkɪt] *n* (CRICKET) guichet *m*; terrain *m* (*entre les deux guichets*)

wide [waɪd] *adj* large; (*area, knowledge*) vas-te, très étendu(e); (*choice*) grand(e) ♦ *adv*: **to open** ~ ouvrir tout grand; **to shoot** ~ tirer à côté; ~**awake** *adj* bien éveillé(e); ~**ly** *adv* (*differing*) radicalement; (*spaced*) sur une grande étendue; (*believed*) généralement; (*travel*) beaucoup; ~n *vt* élargir ♦ *vi* s'élargir; ~ **open** *adj* grand(e) ouvert(e); ~**spread** *adj* (*belief etc*) très répandu(e)

widow ['wɪdəʊ] *n* veuve *f*; ~**ed** *adj* veuf (veuve); ~**er** *n* veuf *m*

width [wɪdθ] *n* largeur *f*

wield [wiːld] *vt* (*sword*) manier; (*power*) exercer

wife [waɪf] (*pl* **wives**) *n* femme *f*, épouse *f*

wig [wɪg] *n* perruque *f*

wiggle ['wɪgl] *vt* agiter, remuer

wild [waɪld] *adj* sauvage; (*sea*) déchaîné(e); (*idea, life*) fou (folle); (*behaviour*) extravagant(e), déchaîné(e); **to make a** ~ **guess** émettre une hypothèse à tout hasard; ~**erness** ['wɪldənɪs] *n* désert *m*, région *f* sauvage; ~**life** *n* (*animals*) faune *f*; ~**ly** *adv* (*behave*) de manière déchaînée; (*applaud*) frénétiquement; (*hit, guess*) au hasard; (*happy*) follement; ~**s** *npl* (*remote area*) régions *fpl* sauvages

wilful ['wɪlful] (*US* **willful**) *adj* (*person*) obstiné(e); (*action*) délibéré(e)

KEYWORD

will [wɪl] (*vt: pt, pp* **willed**) *aux vb* **1** (*forming future tense*): **I will finish it tomorrow** je le finirai demain; **I will have finished it by tomorrow** je l'aurai fini d'ici demain; **will you do it? - yes I will/no I won't** le ferez-vous? - oui/non

2 (*in conjectures, predictions*): **he will** *or* **he'll be there by now** il doit être arrivé à l'heure qu'il est; **that will be the postman** ça doit être le facteur

3 (*in commands, requests, offers*): **will you be quiet!** voulez-vous bien vous taire!; **will you help me?** est-ce que vous pouvez m'aider?; **will you have a cup of tea?** voulez-vous une tasse de thé?; **I won't put up with it!** je ne le tolérerai pas!

♦ vt: **to will sb to do** souhaiter ardemment que qn fasse; **he's ~ to do it** il est disposé à le faire, il veut bien le faire; ~**ly** adv volontiers; ~**ness** n bonne volonté

willow ['wɪləʊ] n saule m

willpower ['wɪl'paʊəʳ] n volonté f

willy-nilly ['wɪlɪ'nɪlɪ] adv bon gré mal gré

wilt [wɪlt] vi dépérir; (flower) se faner

win [wɪn] (pt, pp **won**) n (in sports etc) victoire f ♦ vt gagner; (prize) remporter; (popularity) acquérir ♦ vi gagner; ~ **over** vt convaincre; ~ **round** (BRIT) vt = **win over**

wince [wɪns] vi tressaillir

winch [wɪntʃ] n treuil m

wind¹ [wɪnd] n (also MED) vent m; (breath) souffle m ♦ vt (take breath) couper le souffle à

wind² [waɪnd] (pt, pp **wound**) vt enrouler; (wrap) envelopper; (clock, toy) remonter ♦ vi (road, river) serpenter; ~ **up** vt (clock) remonter; (debate) terminer, clôturer

windfall ['wɪndfɔːl] n coup m de chance

winding ['waɪndɪŋ] adj (road) sinueux(-euse); (staircase) tournant(e)

wind instrument [wɪnd-] n (MUS) instrument m à vent

windmill ['wɪndmɪl] n moulin m à vent

window ['wɪndəʊ] n fenêtre f; (in car, train, also: ~ pane) vitre f; (in shop etc) vitrine f; ~ **box** n jardinière f; ~ **cleaner** n (person) laveur(-euse) de vitres; ~ **ledge** n rebord m de la fenêtre; ~ **pane** n vitre f, carreau m; ~**-shopping** n: **to go ~-shopping** faire du lèche-vitrines; ~**sill** ['wɪndəʊsɪl] n (inside) appui m de la fenêtre; (outside) rebord m de la fenêtre

windpipe ['wɪndpaɪp] n trachée f

wind power [wɪnd-] n énergie éolienne

windscreen ['wɪndskriːn] n pare-brise m inv; ~ **washer** n lave-glace m inv; ~

wiper n essuie-glace m inv

windshield ['wɪndʃiːld] (US) n = **windscreen**

windswept ['wɪndswept] adj balayé(e) par le vent; (person) ébouriffé(e)

windy ['wɪndɪ] adj venteux(-euse); **it's ~** il y a du vent

wine [waɪn] n vin m; ~ **bar** n bar m à vin; ~ **cellar** n cave f à vin; ~ **glass** n verre m à vin; ~ **list** n carte f des vins; ~ **waiter** n sommelier m

wing [wɪŋ] n aile f; ~**s** npl (THEATRE) coulisses fpl; ~**er** n (SPORT) ailier m

wink [wɪŋk] n clin m d'œil ♦ vi faire un clin d'œil; (blink) cligner des yeux

winner ['wɪnəʳ] n gagnant(e)

winning ['wɪnɪŋ] adj (team) gagnant(e); (goal) décisif(-ive); ~**s** npl gains mpl

winter ['wɪntəʳ] n hiver m; **in ~** en hiver; ~ **sports** npl sports mpl d'hiver; **wintry** adj hivernal(e)

wipe [waɪp] n: **to give sth a ~** donner un coup de torchon/de chiffon/d'éponge à qch ♦ vt essuyer; (erase: tape) effacer; ~ **off** vt enlever; ~ **out** vt (debt) éteindre, amortir; (memory) effacer; (destroy) anéantir; ~ **up** vt essuyer

wire ['waɪəʳ] n fil m (de fer); (ELEC) fil électrique; (TEL) télégramme m ♦ vt (house) faire l'installation électrique de; (also: ~ **up**) brancher; (person: send telegram to) télégraphier à; ~**less** (BRIT) n poste m de radio; **wiring** n installation f électrique; **wiry** adj noueux(-euse), nerveux(-euse); (hair) dru(e)

wisdom ['wɪzdəm] n sagesse f; (of action) prudence f; ~ **tooth** n dent f de sagesse

wise [waɪz] adj sage, prudent(e); (remark) judicieux(-euse) ♦ **...wise** suffix: **timewise** etc en ce qui concerne le temps etc

wish [wɪʃ] n (desire) désir m; (specific desire) souhait m, vœu m ♦ vt souhaiter, désirer, vouloir; **best ~es** (on birthday etc) meilleurs vœux; **with best ~es** (in letter) bien amicalement; **to ~ sb goodbye** dire au revoir à qn; **he ~ed me well** il m'a souhaité bonne chance; **to ~ to do/sb to do**

désirer *or* vouloir faire/que qn fasse; **to ~ for** souhaiter; **~ful** *adj*: **it's ~ful thinking** c'est prendre ses désirs pour des réalités

wistful ['wɪstful] *adj* mélancolique

wit [wɪt] *n* (*gen pl*) intelligence *f*, esprit *m*; (*presence of mind*) présence *f* d'esprit; (*wittiness*) esprit; (*person*) homme/femme d'esprit

witch [wɪtʃ] *n* sorcière *f*; **~craft** *n* sorcellerie *f*

KEYWORD

---

with [wɪð, wɪθ] *prep* **1** (*in the company of*) avec; (*at the home of*) chez; **we stayed with friends** nous avons logé chez des amis; **I'll be with you in a minute** je suis à vous dans un instant

2 (*descriptive*): **a room with a view** une chambre avec vue; **the man with the grey hat/blue eyes** l'homme au chapeau gris/aux yeux bleus

3 (*indicating manner, means, cause*): **with tears in her eyes** les larmes aux yeux; **to walk with a stick** marcher avec une canne; **red with anger** rouge de colère; **to shake with fear** trembler de peur; **to fill sth with water** remplir qch d'eau

4: **I'm with you** (*I understand*) je vous suis; **to be with it** (*inf: up-to-date*) être dans le vent

---

withdraw [wɪθ'drɔː] (*irreg*) *vt* retirer ♦ *vi* se retirer; **~al** *n* retrait *m*; **~al symptoms** *npl* (MED): **to have ~al symptoms** être en état de manque; **~n** *adj* (*person*) renfermé(e)

wither ['wɪðəʳ] *vi* (*plant*) se faner

withhold [wɪθ'həuld] (*irreg*) *vt* (*money*) retenir; **to ~ (from)** (*information*) cacher (à); (*permission*) refuser (à)

within [wɪð'ɪn] *prep* à l'intérieur de ♦ *adv* à l'intérieur; **~ his reach** à sa portée; **~ sight of** en vue de; **~ a kilometre of** à moins d'un kilomètre de; **~ the week** avant la fin de la semaine

without [wɪð'aut] *prep* sans; **~ a coat** sans manteau; **~ speaking** sans parler; **to go ~**

sth se passer de qch

withstand [wɪθ'stænd] (*irreg*) *vt* résister à

witness ['wɪtnɪs] *n* (*person*) témoin *m* ♦ *vt* (*event*) être témoin de; (*document*) attester l'authenticité de; **to bear ~ (to)** (*fig*) attester; **~ box** (*US* **witness stand**) *n* barre *f* des témoins

witty ['wɪtɪ] *adj* spirituel(le), plein(e) d'esprit

wives [waɪvz] *npl of* **wife**

wizard ['wɪzəd] *n* magicien *m*

wk *abbr* = **week**

wobble ['wɔbl] *vi* trembler; (*chair*) branler

woe [wəu] *n* malheur *m*

woke [wəuk] *pt of* **wake**; **~n** *pp of* **wake**

wolf [wulf] (*pl* **wolves**) *n* loup *m*

woman ['wumən] (*pl* **women**) *n* femme *f*; **~ doctor** *n* femme *f* médecin; **~ly** *adj* féminin(e)

womb [wuːm] *n* (ANAT) utérus *m*

women ['wɪmɪn] *npl of* **woman**; **~'s lib** (*inf*) *n* MLF *m*; **W~'s (Liberation) Movement** *n* mouvement *m* de libération de la femme

won [wʌn] *pt, pp of* **win**

wonder ['wʌndəʳ] *n* merveille *f*, miracle *m*; (*feeling*) émerveillement *m* ♦ *vi*: **to ~ whether/why** se demander si/pourquoi; **to ~ at** (*marvel*) s'émerveiller de; **to ~ about** songer à; **it's no ~ (that)** il n'est pas étonnant (que +*sub*); **~ful** *adj* merveilleux(-euse)

won't [wəunt] = **will not**

wood [wud] *n* (*timber, forest*) bois *m*; **~ carving** *n* sculpture *f* en *or* sur bois; **~ed** *adj* boisé(e); **~en** *adj* en bois; (*fig*) raide; inexpressif(-ive); **~pecker** *n* pic *m* (*oiseau*); **~wind** *n* (MUS): **the ~wind** les bois *mpl*; **~work** *n* menuiserie *f*; **~worm** *n* ver *m* du bois

wool [wul] *n* laine *f*; **to pull the ~ over sb's eyes** (*fig*) en faire accroire à qn; **~len** (*US* **woolen**) *adj* de *or* en laine; (*industry*) lainier(-ère); **~lens** *npl* (*clothes*) lainages *mpl*; **~ly** (*US* **wooly**) *adj* laineux(-euse); (*fig: ideas*) confus(e)

word [wəːd] *n* mot *m*; (*promise*) parole *f*;

(news) nouvelles *fpl* ♦ *vt* rédiger, formuler; **in other ~s** en d'autres termes; **to break/keep one's ~** manquer à sa parole/tenir parole; ~ing *n* termes *mpl*; libellé *m*; ~ **processing** *n* traitement *m* de texte; ~ **processor** *n* machine *f* de traitement de texte

wore [wɔːʳ] *pt of* **wear**

work [wəːk] *n* travail *m*; *(ART, LITERATURE)* œuvre *f* ♦ *vi* travailler; *(mechanism)* marcher, fonctionner; *(plan etc)* marcher; *(medicine)* agir ♦ *vt* *(clay, wood etc)* travailler; *(mine etc)* exploiter; *(machine)* faire marcher *or* fonctionner; *(miracles, wonders etc)* faire *or* **to be out of ~** être sans emploi; **to ~ loose** se défaire, se desserrer; ~ **on** *vt fus* travailler à; *(influence)* (essayer d')influencer; ~ **out** *vi* *(plans etc)* marcher ♦ *vt* *(problem)* résoudre; *(plan)* élaborer; **it ~s out at £100** ça fait 100 livres; ~ **up** *vt:* **to get ~ed up** se mettre dans tous ses états; ~**able** *adj* *(solution)* réalisable; ~**aholic** [wəːkəˈhɔlɪk] *n* bourreau *m* de travail; ~**er** *n* travailleur(-euse), ouvrier(-ère); ~ **experience** *n* stage *m*; ~**force** *n* main-d'œuvre *f*; ~**ing class** *n* classe ouvrière; ~**ing-class** *adj* ouvrier(-ère); ~**ing order** *n:* **in ~ing order** en état de marche; ~**man** *(irreg)* *n* ouvrier *m*; ~**manship** *(skill)* *n* métier *m*, habileté *f*; ~**s** *n* *(BRIT: factory)* usine *f* ♦ *npl* *(of clock, machine)* mécanisme *m*; ~ **sheet** *n* *(COMPUT)* feuille *f* de programmation; ~**shop** *n* atelier *m*; ~ **station** *n* poste *m* de travail; ~**-to-rule** *(BRIT)* *n* grève *f* du zèle

world [wəːld] *n* monde *m* ♦ *cpd* *(champion)* du monde; *(power, war)* mondial(e); **to think the ~ of sb** *(fig)* ne jurer que par qn; ~**ly** *adj* de ce monde; *(knowledgeable)* qui a l'expérience du monde; ~**wide** *adj* universel(le); **W~-Wide Web** *n* Web *m*

worm [wəːm] *n* ver *m*

worn [wɔːn] *pp of* **wear** ♦ *adj* usé(e); ~**-out** *adj* *(object)* complètement usé(e); *(person)* épuisé(e)

worried [ˈwʌrɪd] *adj* inquiet(-ète)

worry [ˈwʌrɪ] *n* souci *m* ♦ *vt* inquiéter ♦ *vi* s'inquiéter, se faire du souci

worse [wəːs] *adj* pire, plus mauvais(e) ♦ *adv* plus mal ♦ *n* pire *m*; **a change for the ~** une détérioration; ~**n** *vt, vi* empirer; ~ **off** *adj* moins à l'aise financièrement; *(fig):* **you'll be ~ off this way** ça ira moins bien de cette façon

worship [ˈwəːʃɪp] *n* culte *m* ♦ *vt* *(God)* rendre un culte à; *(person)* adorer; **Your W~** *(BRIT: to mayor)* Monsieur le maire; (: *to judge)* Monsieur le juge

worst [wəːst] *adj* le (la) pire, le (la) plus mauvais(e) ♦ *adv* le plus mal ♦ *n* pire *m*; **at ~** au pis aller

worth [wəːθ] *n* valeur *f* ♦ *adj:* **to be ~** valoir; **it's ~ it** cela en vaut la peine, ça vaut la peine; **it is ~ one's while (to do)** on gagne (à faire); ~**less** *adj* qui ne vaut rien; ~**while** *adj* *(activity, cause)* utile, louable

worthy [wəːðɪ] *adj* *(person)* digne; *(motive)* louable; ~ **of** digne de

---
KEYWORD
---

would [wʊd] *aux vb* **1** *(conditional tense):* **if you asked him he would do it** si vous le lui demandiez, il le ferait; **if you had asked him he would have done it** si vous le lui aviez demandé, il l'aurait fait

2 *(in offers, invitations, requests):* **would you like a biscuit?** voulez-vous un biscuit?; **would you close the door please?** voulez-vous fermer la porte, s'il vous plaît?

3 *(in indirect speech):* **I said I would do it** j'ai dit que je le ferais

4 *(emphatic):* **it WOULD have to snow today!** naturellement il neige aujourd'hui! *or* il fallait qu'il neige aujourd'hui!

5 *(insistence):* **she wouldn't do it** elle n'a pas voulu *or* elle a refusé de le faire

6 *(conjecture):* **it would have been midnight** il devait être minuit

7 *(indicating habit):* **he would go there on Mondays** il y allait le lundi

---

would-be [ˈwʊdbiː] *(pej)* *adj* soi-disant

wouldn't ['wudnt] = **would not**
wound[1] [wu:nd] *n* blessure *f* ♦ *vt* blesser
wound[2] [waund] *pt, pp* of **wind**[2]
wove [wəuv] *pt* of **weave**; **~n** *pp* of **weave**
wrap [ræp] *vt* (*also:* **~ up**) envelopper, emballer; (*wind*) enrouler; **~per** *n* (BRIT: *of book*) couverture *f*; (*on chocolate*) emballage *m*, papier *m*; **~ping paper** *n* papier *m* d'emballage; (*for gift*) papier cadeau
wreak [ri:k] *vt*: **to ~ havoc (on)** avoir un effet désastreux (sur)
wreath [ri:θ] (*pl* **~s**) *n* couronne *f*
wreck [rɛk] *n* (*ship*) épave *f*; (*vehicle*) véhicule accidenté; (*pej: person*) loque humaine ♦ *vt* démolir; (*fig*) briser, ruiner; **~age** *n* débris *mpl*; (*of building*) décombres *mpl*; (*of ship*) épave *f*
wren [rɛn] *n* (ZOOL) roitelet *m*
wrench [rɛntʃ] *n* (TECH) clé *f* (à écrous); (*tug*) violent mouvement de torsion; (*fig*) déchirement *m* ♦ *vt* tirer violemment sur, tordre; **to ~ sth from** arracher qch à *or* de
wrestle ['rɛsl] *vi*: **to ~ (with sb)** lutter (avec qn); **~r** *n* lutteur(-euse); **wrestling** *n* lutte *f*; (*also:* **all-in wrestling**) catch *m*, lutte *f* libre
wretched ['rɛtʃɪd] *adj* misérable; (*inf*) maudit(e)
wriggle ['rɪgl] *vi* (*also:* **~ about**) se tortiller
wring [rɪŋ] (*pt, pp* **wrung**) *vt* tordre; (*wet clothes*) essorer; (*fig*): **to ~ sth out of sb** arracher qch à qn
wrinkle ['rɪŋkl] *n* (*on skin*) ride *f*; (*on paper etc*) pli *m* ♦ *vt* plisser ♦ *vi* se plisser; **~d** *adj* (*skin, face*) ridé(e)
wrist [rɪst] *n* poignet *m*; **~watch** *n* montre-bracelet *f*
writ [rɪt] *n* acte *m* judiciaire
write [raɪt] (*pt* **wrote**, *pp* **written**) *vt, vi* écrire; (*prescription*) rédiger; **~ down** *vt* noter; (*put in writing*) mettre par écrit; **~ off** *vt* (*debt*) passer aux profits et pertes; (*project*) mettre une croix sur; **~ out** *vt* écrire; **~ up** *vt* rédiger; **~-off** *n* perte totale; **~r** *n* auteur *m*, écrivain *m*
writhe [raɪð] *vi* se tordre

writing ['raɪtɪŋ] *n* écriture *f*; (*of author*) œuvres *fpl*; **in ~** par écrit; **~ paper** *n* papier *m* à lettres
wrong [rɒŋ] *adj* (*incorrect*) faux (fausse); (*morally*) mauvais(e); (*wicked*) mal; (*unfair*) injuste ♦ *adv* mal ♦ *n* tort *m* ♦ *vt* faire du tort à, léser; **you are ~ to do it** tu as tort de le faire; **you are ~ about that, you've got it ~** tu te trompes; **what's ~?** qu'est-ce qui ne va pas?; **you've got the ~ number** vous vous êtes trompé de numéro; **to go ~** (*person*) se tromper; (*plan*) mal tourner; (*machine*) tomber en panne; **to be in the ~** avoir tort; **~ful** *adj* injustifié(e); **~ly** *adv* mal, incorrectement; **~ side** *n* (*of material*) envers *m*
wrote [rəut] *pt* of **write**
wrought iron [rə:t] *n* fer forgé
wrung [rʌŋ] *pt, pp* of **wring**
wt. *abbr* = **weight**
WWW *n abbr* (= World Wide Web): **the ~** le Web

X, x

Xmas ['ɛksməs] *n abbr* = **Christmas**
X-ray ['ɛksreɪ] *n* (*ray*) rayon *m* X; (*photo*) radio(graphie) *f*
xylophone ['zaɪləfəun] *n* xylophone *m*

Y, y

yacht [jɒt] *n* yacht *m*; voilier *m*; **~ing** *n* yachting *m*, navigation *f* de plaisance; **~sman** (*irreg*) *n* plaisancier *m*
Yank [jæŋk], **Yankee** ['jæŋkɪ] (*pej*) *n* Amerloque *m/f*
yap [jæp] *vi* (*dog*) japper
yard [jɑːd] *n* (*of house etc*) cour *f*; (*measure*) yard *m* (= 91,4 cm); **~stick** *n* (*fig*) mesure *f*, critères *mpl*
yarn [jɑːn] *n* fil *m*; (*tale*) longue histoire
yawn [jɔːn] *n* bâillement *m* ♦ *vi* bâiller; **~ing** *adj* (*gap*) béant(e)
yd. *abbr* = **yard(s)**

yeah [jɛə] (*inf*) *adv* ouais

year [jɪəʳ] *n* an *m*, année *f*; **to be 8 ~s old** avoir 8 ans; **an eight-~-old child** un enfant de huit ans; **~ly** *adj* annuel(le) ♦ *adv* annuellement

yearn [jəːn] *vi*: **to ~ for sth** aspirer à qch, languir après qch

yeast [jiːst] *n* levure *f*

yell [jɛl] *vi* hurler

yellow [ˈjɛləu] *adj* jaune

yelp [jɛlp] *vi* japper; glapir

yes [jɛs] *adv* oui; (*answering negative question*) si ♦ *n* oui *m*; **to say/answer ~** dire/répondre oui

yesterday [ˈjɛstədɪ] *adv* hier ♦ *n* hier *m*; **~ morning/evening** hier matin/soir; **all day ~** toute la journée d'hier

yet [jɛt] *adv* encore; déjà ♦ *conj* pourtant, néanmoins; **it is not finished ~** ce n'est pas encore fini *or* toujours pas fini; **the best ~** le meilleur jusqu'ici *or* jusque-là; **as ~** jusqu'ici, encore

yew [juː] *n* if *m*

yield [jiːld] *n* production *f*, rendement *m*; rapport *m* ♦ *vt* produire, rendre, rapporter; (*surrender*) céder ♦ *vi* céder; (*US: AUT*) céder la priorité

YMCA *n abbr* (= *Young Men's Christian Association*) YMCA *m*

yob [jɔb] (*BRIT: inf*) *n* loubar(d) *m*

yoghourt [ˈjəugət] *n* yaourt *m*

yog(h)urt [ˈjəugət] *n* = **yoghourt**

yoke [jəuk] *n* joug *m*

yolk [jəuk] *n* jaune *m* (d'œuf)

---

you [juː] *pron* **1** (*subject*) tu; (*polite form*) vous; (*plural*) vous; **you French enjoy your food** vous autres Français, vous aimez bien manger; **you and I will go** toi et moi *or* vous et moi, nous irons

2 (*object: direct, indirect*) te, t' +*vowel*, vous; **I know you** je te *or* vous connais; **I gave it to you** je vous l'ai donné, je te l'ai donné

3 (*stressed*) toi; vous; **I told YOU to do it** c'est à toi *or* vous que j'ai dit de le faire

4 (*after prep, in comparisons*) toi; vous; **it's for you** c'est pour toi *or* vous; **she's younger than you** elle est plus jeune que toi *or* vous

5 (*impersonal: one*) on; **fresh air does you good** l'air frais fait du bien; **you never know** on ne sait jamais

---

you'd [juːd] = **you had**; **you would**

you'll [juːl] = **you will**; **you shall**

young [jʌŋ] *adj* jeune ♦ *npl* (*of animal*) petits *mpl*; (*people*): **the ~** les jeunes, la jeunesse; **~er** [ˈjʌŋɡəʳ] *adj* (*brother etc*) cadet(te); **~ster** *n* jeune *m* (garçon *m*); (*child*) enfant *m/f*

your [jɔːʳ] *adj* ton (ta), tes *pl*; (*polite form, pl*) votre, vos *pl*; *see also* **my**

you're [juəʳ] = **you are**

yours [jɔːz] *pron* le (la) tien(ne), les tiens (tiennes); (*polite form, pl*) le (la) vôtre, les vôtres; **~ sincerely/faithfully/truly** veuillez agréer l'expression de mes sentiments les meilleurs; *see also* **mine**[1]

yourself [jɔːˈsɛlf] *pron* (*reflexive*) te; (: *polite form*) vous; (*after prep*) toi; vous; (*emphatic*) toi-même; vous-même; *see also* **oneself**; **yourselves** *pl pron* vous; (*emphatic*) vous-mêmes

youth [juːθ] *n* jeunesse *f*; (*young man: pl* ~s) jeune homme *m*; **~ club** *n* centre *m* de jeunes; **~ful** *adj* jeune; (*enthusiasm*) de jeunesse, juvénile; **~ hostel** *n* auberge *f* de jeunesse

you've [juːv] = **you have**

YTS *n abbr* (*BRIT: Youth Training Scheme*) ≃ TUC *m*

Yugoslav [ˈjuːgəuslɑːv] *adj* yougoslave ♦ *n* Yougoslave *m/f*

Yugoslavia [ˈjuːgəuˈslɑːviə] *n* Yougoslavie *f*

yuppie [ˈjʌpɪ] (*inf*) *n* yuppie *m/f*

YWCA *n abbr* (= *Young Women's Christian Association*) YWCA *m*

Z, z

zany ['zeɪnɪ] *adj* farfelu(e), loufoque

zap [zæp] *vt* (*COMPUT*) effacer

zeal [ziːl] *n* zèle *m*, ferveur *f*; empressement *m*

zebra ['ziːbrə] *n* zèbre *m*; ~ **crossing** (*BRIT*) *n* passage clouté *or* pour piétons

zero ['zɪərəu] *n* zéro *m*

zest [zɛst] *n* entrain *m*, élan *m*; (*of orange*) zeste *m*

zigzag ['zɪgzæg] *n* zigzag *m*

Zimbabwe [zɪm'bɑːbwɪ] *n* Zimbabwe *m*

Zimmer frame ['zɪmə-] *n* déambulateur *m*

zinc [zɪŋk] *n* zinc *m*

zip [zɪp] *n* fermeture *f* éclair ® ♦ *vt* (*also:* ~ **up**) fermer avec une fermeture éclair ®; ~ **code** (*US*) *n* code postal; ~**per** (*US*) *n* = **zip**

zit [zɪt] (*inf*) *n* bouton *m*

zodiac ['zəudɪæk] *n* zodiaque *m*

zone [zəun] *n* zone *f*

zoo [zuː] *n* zoo *m*

zoom [zuːm] *vi*: **to ~ past** passer en trombe; ~ **lens** *n* zoom *m*

zucchini [zuː'kiːnɪ] (*US*) *n(pl)* courgette(s) *f(pl)*

LE DICTIONNAIRE ET LA GRAMMAIRE

Bien qu'un dictionnaire ne puisse jamais remplacer une grammaire détaillée, il fournit néanmoins un grand nombre de renseignements grammaticaux. Le Robert & Collins Mini présente les indications grammaticales de la façon suivante:

Les catégories grammaticales

Elles sont données en italique immédiatement après la transcription phonétique des entrées. La liste des abréviations se trouve pages xi et xii.

Les changements de catégorie grammaticale au sein d'un article – par exemple, d'adjectif à adverbe, ou de nom à verbe intransitif à verbe transitif – sont indiqués au moyen de losanges – comme pour le mot français "large" et l'anglais "act".

Les adverbes

La règle générale pour former les adverbes en anglais est d'ajouter "-ly" à l'adjectif ou à sa racine. Ainsi:

bad > badly

gentle > gently

La terminaison en "-ly" est souvent l'équivalent du français "-ment":

slowly – lentement

slyly – sournoisement

Il faut toutefois faire attention car certains mots en "-ly" sont des adjectifs et non des adverbes. Par exemple: "friendly", "likely", "ugly", "silly". Ces mots ne peuvent pas être utilisés en tant qu'adverbes. Il faut donc bien vérifier la catégorie grammaticale du mot que vous voulez utiliser.

Les adverbes figurent soit dans les articles des adjectifs correspondants s'ils suivent ces adjectifs dans l'ordre alphabétique ("fortunately"), soit comme entrées à part entière s'ils précèdent alphabétiquement l'adjectif ("happily"). Si leur usage est moins fréquent, ils n'apparaissent pas du tout. Vous pouvez cependant les traduire facilement en français d'après la traduction de l'adjectif correspondant.

Le pluriel des noms en anglais

Normalement, on forme le pluriel des noms anglais en ajoutant un "-s" au singulier.

cat > cats

Le pluriel des noms qui finissent en "-o" est formé en ajoutant "-es" au singulier.

Tous les pluriels irréguliers sont donnés entre parenthèses et en caractères gras immédiatement après la transcription phonétique (v. "tomato").

Certains noms ont un pluriel irrégulier, comme "knife" et "man" en regard. Ces pluriels irréguliers apparaissent également en tant qu'entrées à part entière dans le texte et renvoient au singulier (v. "knives" et "men").

Les verbes irréguliers

Les verbes irréguliers sont clairement signalés dans ce dictionnaire: les formes du prétérit (*pt*) et du participe passé (*pp*) sont données en caractères gras entre parenthèses immédiatement après la transcription phonétique de l'entrée. Voir les verbes "to teach" et "to swim".

Par ailleurs les formes du prétérit et du participe passé des verbes irréguliers apparaissent elles-mêmes comme des entrées à part entière dans le dictionnaire et renvoient à l'infinitif du verbe. Voir "taught", "swam" et "swum".

De plus, vous avez la possibilité de vous référer rapidement à la liste des verbes irréguliers anglais pages 587 et 588 vers la fin de votre dictionnaire.

Enfin, pour ce qui est des verbes réguliers, vous remarquerez que leur prétérit et leur participe passé ne sont pas donnés. Ceci est dû au fait que ces formes ne présentent aucun problème puisqu'on ajoute toujours "-ed" à l'infinitif pour les obtenir (ou bien "-d" si l'infinitif se termine par la voyelle "-e").

		prétérit		**participe passé**
exemples:	to help	–	helped	–	helped
	to love	–	loved	–	loved

THE DICTIONARY AND GRAMMAR

While it is true that a dictionary can never be a substitute for a detailed grammar it nevertheless provides a great deal of grammatical information. If you know how to extract this information you will be able to use French more accurately both in speech and in writing.

The Collins French Dictionary presents grammatical information as follows.

Parts of speech

Parts of speech are given in italics immediately after the phonetic spellings of headwords. Abbreviated forms are used. Abbreviations can be checked on pages xi and xii.

Changes in parts of speech within an entry – for example, from adjective to adverb to noun, or from noun to intransitive verb to transitive verb – are indicated by means of lozenges - ♦ - as with the French 'large' and the English 'act'.

Genders of French nouns

The gender of each noun in the French-English section of the dictionary is indicated in the following way:

nm = nom masculin

nf = nom féminin

You will occasionally see *nm/f* beside an entry. This indicates that a noun – 'concierge', for example – can be either masculine or feminine.

Feminine and *irregular* plural forms of nouns are shown, as with 'chercheur' and 'cheval': the ending which follows the entry is substituted, so that 'chercheur' becomes 'chercheuse' in the feminine, and 'cheval' becomes 'chevaux' in the plural.

In the English-French section of the dictionary, the gender immediately follows the noun translation, as with 'grass'. Where a noun can be either masculine or feminine, this is shown by '*m/f*' if the form of the noun does not change, or by the bracketed feminine ending if it does change, as with 'graduate'.

So many things depend on your knowing the correct gender of a French noun – whether you use 'il' or 'elle' to translate 'it'; the way you spell and pronounce certain adjectives; the changes you make to past participles, etc. If you are in any doubt as to the gender of a noun, it is always best to check it in your dictionary.

Adjectives

Adjectives are given in both their masculine and feminine forms, where these are different. The usual rule is to add an '-e' to the masculine form to make an adjective feminine, as with 'noir'.

In the English-French section, an adjective's feminine form or ending appears immediately after it in brackets, as with 'soft'.

Some adjectives have identical masculine and feminine forms. Where this occurs, there is no 'e' beside the basic masculine form.

Many French adjectives, however, do not follow the regular pattern. Where an adjective has an irregular feminine or plural form, this information is clearly provided in your dictionary, usually with the irregular form being given in full. Consider the entries for 'net' and 'sec'.

Adverbs

The normal 'rule' for forming adverbs in French is to add '-ment' to the feminine form of the adjective. Thus:

> lent > lente > lentement

The '-ment' ending is often the equivalent of the English '-ly':

> lentement   – slowly
> sournoisement – slyly

Adjectives ending in '-ant' and '-ent' are slightly different:

> courant   >   couramment
> prudent   >   prudemment

In your dictionary some adverbs appear as a separate entry; others appear as subentries of adjective headwords; while others do not feature in the dictionary at all. Compare 'heureusement', 'froidement' and 'sournoisement'.

Where an adverb does not appear, this is usually because it is not a particularly common one. However, you should be able to work out a translation from the adjective once you have found that in the dictionary.

Information about verbs

A major problem facing language learners is that the form of a verb will change according to the subject and/or the tense being used. A typical French verb can take many different forms – too many to list in a dictionary entry.

Yet, although verbs are listed in your dictionary in their infinitive forms only, this does not mean that the dictionary is of limited value when it comes to handling the verb system of the French language. On the contrary, it contains much valuable information.

First of all, your dictionary will help you with the meanings of unfamiliar verbs. If you came across the word 'remplit' in a text and looked it up in your dictionary you wouldn't find it. You must deduce that it is part of a verb and look for the infinitive form. Thus you will see that 'remplit' is a form of the verb 'remplir'. You now have the basic meaning of the word you are concerned with – something to do with the English verb 'fill' – and this should be enough to help you understand the text you are reading.

It is usually an easy task to make the connection between the form of a verb and the infinitive. For example, 'remplissent', 'remplira', 'remplissons' and 'rempli' are all recognisable as parts of the infinitive 'remplir'. However, sometimes it is less obvious – for example, 'voyons', 'verrai' and 'vu' are all parts of 'voir'. The only real solution to this problem is to learn the various forms of the main French regular and irregular verbs.

And this is the second source of help offered by your dictionary. The verb tables on pages 585 to 586 of the Collins French Dictionary provide a summary of some of the main forms of the main tenses of regular and irregular verbs. Consider the verb 'voir' below where the following information is given:

1	voyant	– Present Participle
2	vu	– Past Participle
3	vois, voyons, voient	– Present Tense forms
4	voyais	– 1st Person Singular of the Imperfect Tense
5	verrai	– 1st Person Singular of the Future Tense
7	voie	– 1st Person Singular of the Present Subjunctive

The regular '-er' verb 'parler' is presented in greater detail. The main tenses and the different endings are given in full. This information can be transferred and applied to all verbs in the list. In addition, the main parts of the most common irregular verbs are listed in the body of the dictionary.

PARLER

1 parlant
2 parlé
3 parle, parles, parle, parlons, parlez, parlent
4 parlais, parlais, parlait, parlions, parliez, parlaient
5 parlerai, parleras, parlera, parlerons, parlerez, parleront
6 parlerais, parlerais, parlerait, parlerions, parleriez, parleraient
7 parle, parles, parle, parlions, parliez, parlent *impératif* parle!, parlez!

In order to make maximum use of the information contained in these pages, a good working knowledge of the various rules affecting French verbs is required. You will acquire this in the course of your French studies and your Collins dictionary will serve as a useful 'aide-mémoire'. If you happen to forget how to form the second person singular form of the Future Tense of 'voir' there will be no need to panic — your dictionary contains the information!

FRENCH VERB FORMS

1 Participe présent *2* Participe passé *3* Présent *4* Imparfait *5* Futur *6* Conditionnel *7* Subjonctif présent

acquérir *1* acquérant *2* acquis *3* acquiers, acquérons, acquièrent *4* acquérais *5* acquerrai *7* acquière

ALLER *1* allant *2* allé *3* vais, vas, va, allons, allez, vont *4* allais *5* irai *6* irais *7* aille

asseoir *1* asseyant *2* assis *3* assieds, asseyons, asseyez, asseyent *4* asseyais *5* assiérai *7* asseye

atteindre *1* atteignant *2* atteint *3* atteins, atteignons *4* atteignais *7* atteigne

AVOIR *1* ayant *2* eu *3* ai, as, a, avons, avez, ont *4* avais *5* aurai *6* aurais *7* aie, aies, ait, ayons, ayez, aient

battre *1* battant *2* battu *3* bats, bat, battons *4* battais *7* batte

boire *1* buvant *2* bu *3* bois, buvons, boivent *4* buvais *7* boive

bouillir *1* bouillant *2* bouilli *3* bous, bouillons *4* bouillais *7* bouille

conclure *1* concluant *2* conclu *3* conclus, concluons *4* concluais *7* conclue

conduire *1* conduisant *2* conduit *3* conduis, conduisons *4* conduisais *7* conduise

connaître *1* connaissant *2* connu *3* connais, connaît, connaissons *4* connaissais *7* connaisse

coudre *1* cousant *2* cousu *3* couds, cousons, cousez, cousent *4* cousais *7* couse

courir *1* courant *2* couru *3* cours, courons *4* courais *5* courrai *7* coure

couvrir *1* couvrant *2* couvert *3* couvre, couvrons *4* couvrais *7* couvre

craindre *1* craignant *2* craint *3* crains, craignons *4* craignais *7* craigne

croire *1* croyant *2* cru *3* crois, croyons, croient *4* croyais *7* croie

croître *1* croissant *2* crû, crue, crus, crues *3* crois, croissons *4* croissais *7* croisse

cueillir *1* cueillant *2* cueilli *3* cueille, cueillons *4* cueillais *5* cueillerai *7* cueille

devoir *1* devant *2* dû, due, dus, dues *3* dois, devons, doivent *4* devais *5* devrai *7* doive

dire *1* disant *2* dit *3* dis, disons, dites, disent *4* disais *7* dise

dormir *1* dormant *2* dormi *3* dors, dormons *4* dormais *7* dorme

écrire *1* écrivant *2* écrit *3* écris, écrivons *4* écrivais *7* écrive

ÊTRE *1* étant *2* été *3* suis, es, est, sommes, êtes, sont *4* étais *5* serai *6* serais *7* sois, sois, soit, soyons, soyez, soient

FAIRE *1* faisant *2* fait *3* fais, fais, fait, faisons, faites, font *4* faisais *5* ferai *6* ferais *7* fasse

falloir *2* fallu *3* faut *4* fallait *5* faudra *7* faille

FINIR *1* finissant *2* fini *3* finis, finis, finit, finissons, finissez, finissent *4* finissais *5* finirai *6* finirais *7* finisse

fuir *1* fuyant *2* fui *3* fuis, fuyons, fuient *4* fuyais *7* fuie

joindre *1* joignant *2* joint *3* joins, joignons *4* joignais *7* joigne

lire *1* lisant *2* lu *3* lis, lisons *4* lisais *7* lise

luire *1* luisant *2* lui *3* luis, luisons *4* luisais *7* luise

maudire *1* maudissant *2* maudit *3* maudis, maudissons *4* maudissait *7* maudisse

mentir *1* mentant *2* menti *3* mens, mentons *4* mentais *7* mente

mettre *1* mettant *2* mis *3* mets, mettons *4* mettais *7* mette

mourir *1* mourant *2* mort *3* meurs, mourons, meurent *4* mourais *5* mourrai *7* meure

naître *1* naissant *2* né *3* nais, naît, naissons *4* naissais *7* naisse

offrir *1* offrant *2* offert *3* offre, offrons *4* offrais *7* offre

PARLER *1* parlant *2* parlé *3* parle, parles, parle, parlons, parlez, parlent *4* parlais, parlais, parlait, parlions, parliez, parlaient *5* parlerai, parleras, parlera, parlerons, parlerez, parleront *6* parlerais, parlerais, parlerait, parlerions, parleriez, parleraient *7* parle, parles, parle, parlions, parliez, parlent *impératif* parle, parlez

partir *1* partant *2* parti *3* pars, partons *4* partais *7* parte

plaire *1* plaisant *2* plu *3* plais, plaît, plaisons *4* plaisais *7* plaise

pleuvoir *1* pleuvant *2* plu *3* pleut, pleuvent *4* pleuvait *5* pleuvra *7* pleuve

pourvoir *1* pourvoyant *2* pourvu *3* pourvois, pourvoyons, pourvoient *4* pourvoyais *7* pourvoie

pouvoir *1* pouvant *2* pu *3* peux, peut, pouvons, peuvent *4* pouvais *5* pourrai *7* puisse

prendre *1* prenant *2* pris *3* prends, prenons, prennent *4* prenais *7* prenne

prévoir *comme voir* *5* prévoirai

RECEVOIR *1* recevant *2* reçu *3* reçois, reçois,

reçoit, recevons, recevez, reçoivent *4* recevais *5* recevrai *6* recevrais *7* reçoive

RENDRE *1* rendant *2* rendu *3* rends, rends, rend, rendons, rendez, rendent *4* rendais *5* rendrai *6* rendrais *7* rende

résoudre *1* résolvant *2* résolu *3* résous, résout, résolvons *4* résolvais *7* résolve

rire *1* riant *2* ri *3* ris, rions *4* riais *7* rie

savoir *1* sachant *2* su *3* sais, savons, savent *4* savais *5* saurai *7* sache *impératif* sache, sachons, sachez

servir *1* servant *2* servi *3* sers, servons *4* servais *7* serve

sortir *1* sortant *2* sorti *3* sors, sortons *4* sortais *7* sorte

souffrir *1* souffrant *2* souffert *3* souffre, souffrons *4* souffrais *7* souffre

suffire *1* suffisant *2* suffi *3* suffis, suffisons *4* suffisais *7* suffise

suivre *1* suivant *2* suivi *3* suis, suivons *4* suivais *7* suive

taire *1* taisant *2* tu *3* tais, taisons *4* taisais *7* taise

tenir *1* tenant *2* tenu *3* tiens, tenons, tiennent *4* tenais *5* tiendrai *7* tienne

vaincre *1* vainquant *2* vaincu *3* vaincs, vainc, vainquons *4* vainquais *7* vainque

valoir *1* valant *2* valu *3* vaux, vaut, valons *4* valais *5* vaudrai *7* vaille

venir *1* venant *2* venu *3* viens, venons, viennent *4* venais *5* viendrai *7* vienne

vivre *1* vivant *2* vécu *3* vis, vivons *4* vivais *7* vive

voir *1* voyant *2* vu *3* vois, voyons, voient *4* voyais *5* verrai *7* voie

vouloir *1* voulant *2* voulu *3* veux, veut, voulons, veulent *4* voulais *5* voudrai *7* veuille *impératif* veuillez

LE VERBE ANGLAIS

present	pt	pp
arise	arose	arisen
awake	awoke	awoken
be (am, is, are; being)	was, were	been
bear	bore	born(e)
beat	beat	beaten
become	became	become
begin	began	begun
behold	beheld	beheld
bend	bent	bent
beseech	besought	besought
beset	beset	beset
bet	bet, betted	bet, betted
bid	bid, bade	bid, bidden
bind	bound	bound
bite	bit	bitten
bleed	bled	bled
blow	blew	blown
break	broke	broken
breed	bred	bred
bring	brought	brought
build	built	built
burn	burnt, burned	burnt, burned
burst	burst	burst
buy	bought	bought
can	could	(been able)
cast	cast	cast
catch	caught	caught
choose	chose	chosen
cling	clung	clung
come	came	come
cost	cost	cost
creep	crept	crept
cut	cut	cut
deal	dealt	dealt
dig	dug	dug
do (3rd person: he/she/it does)	did	done
draw	drew	drawn
dream	dreamed, dreamt	dreamed, dreamt
drink	drank	drunk
drive	drove	driven
dwell	dwelt	dwelt
eat	ate	eaten

present	pt	pp
fall	fell	fallen
feed	fed	fed
feel	felt	felt
fight	fought	fought
find	found	found
flee	fled	fled
fling	flung	flung
fly (flies)	flew	flown
forbid	forbade	forbidden
forecast	forecast	forecast
forego	forewent	foregone
foresee	foresaw	foreseen
foretell	foretold	foretold
forget	forgot	forgotten
forgive	forgave	forgiven
forsake	forsook	forsaken
freeze	froze	frozen
get	got	got, (US) gotten
give	gave	given
go (goes)	went	gone
grind	ground	ground
grow	grew	grown
hang	hung, hanged	hung, hanged
have (has; having)	had	had
hear	heard	heard
hide	hid	hidden
hit	hit	hit
hold	held	held
hurt	hurt	hurt
keep	kept	kept
kneel	knelt, kneeled	knelt, kneeled
know	knew	known
lay	laid	laid
lead	led	led
lean	leant, leaned	leant, leaned
leap	leapt, leaped	leapt, leaped
learn	learnt, learned	learnt, learned
leave	left	left
lend	lent	lent
let	let	let

present	pt	pp	present	pt	pp
lie (lying)	lay	lain	speed	sped, speeded	sped, speeded
light	lit, lighted	lit, lighted			
lose	lost	lost	spell	spelt, spelled	spelt, spelled
make	made	made			
may	might	—	spend	spent	spent
mean	meant	meant	spill	spilt, spilled	spilt, spilled
meet	met	met			
mistake	mistook	mistaken	spin	spun	spun
mow	mowed	mown, mowed	spit	spat	spat
must	(had to)	(had to)	split	split	split
pay	paid	paid	spoil	spoiled, spoilt	spoiled, spoilt
put	put	put			
quit	quit, quitted	quit, quitted	spread	spread	spread
			spring	sprang	sprung
read	read	read	stand	stood	stood
rid	rid	rid	steal	stole	stolen
ride	rode	ridden	stick	stuck	stuck
ring	rang	rung	sting	stung	stung
rise	rose	risen	stink	stank	stunk
run	ran	run	stride	strode	stridden
saw	sawed	sawn	strike	struck	struck, stricken
say	said	said			
see	saw	seen	strive	strove	striven
seek	sought	sought	swear	swore	sworn
sell	sold	sold	sweep	swept	swept
send	sent	sent	swell	swelled	swollen, swelled
set	set	set			
shake	shook	shaken	swim	swam	swum
shall	should	—	swing	swung	swung
shear	sheared	shorn, sheared	take	took	taken
shed	shed	shed	teach	taught	taught
shine	shone	shone	tear	tore	torn
shoot	shot	shot	tell	told	told
show	showed	shown	think	thought	thought
shrink	shrank	shrunk	throw	threw	thrown
shut	shut	shut	thrust	thrust	thrust
sing	sang	sung	tread	trod	trodden
sink	sank	sunk	wake	woke	woken
sit	sat	sat	waylay	waylaid	waylaid
slay	slew	slain	wear	wore	worn
sleep	slept	slept	weave	wove, weaved	woven, weaved
slide	slid	slid			
sling	slung	slung	wed	wedded, wed	wedded, wed
slit	slit	slit			
smell	smelt, smelled	smelt, smelled	weep	wept	wept
			win	won	won
sow	sowed	sown, sowed	wind	wound	wound
speak	spoke	spoken	wring	wrung	wrung
			write	wrote	written

LES NOMBRES

NUMBERS

un(une)	1	one
deux	2	two
trois	3	three
quatre	4	four
cinq	5	five
six	6	six
sept	7	seven
huit	8	eight
neuf	9	nine
dix	10	ten
onze	11	eleven
douze	12	twelve
treize	13	thirteen
quatorze	14	fourteen
quinze	15	fifteen
seize	16	sixteen
dix-sept	17	seventeen
dix-huit	18	eighteen
dix-neuf	19	nineteen
vingt	20	twenty
vingt et un(une)	21	twenty-one
vingt-deux	22	twenty-two
trente	30	thirty
quarante	40	forty
cinquante	50	fifty
soixante	60	sixty
soixante-dix	70	seventy
soixante et onze	71	seventy-one
soixante-douze	72	seventy-two
quatre-vingts	80	eighty
quatre-vingt-un(-une)	81	eighty-one
quatre-vingt-dix	90	ninety
quatre-vingt-onze	91	ninety-one
cent	100	a hundred
cent un(une)	101	a hundred and one
trois cents	300	three hundred
trois cent un(une)	301	three hundred and one
mille	1 000	a thousand
un million	1 000 000	a million

premier (première), 1er	first, 1st
deuxième, 2e *or* 2ème	second, 2nd
troisième, 3e *or* 3ème	third, 3rd
quatrième	fourth, 4th
cinquième	fifth, 5th
sixième	sixth, 6th
septième	seventh

LES NOMBRES

huitième
neuvième
dixième
onzième
douzième
treizième
quatorzième
quinzième
seizième
dix-septième
dix-huitième
dix-neuvième
vingtième
vingt-et-unième
vingt-deuxième
trentième
centième
cent-unième
millième

Les Fractions etc

un demi
un tiers
deux tiers
un quart
un cinquième
zéro virgule cinq, 0,5
trois virgule quatre, 3,4
dix pour cent
cent pour cent

Exemples

il habite au dix
c'est au chapitre sept
à la page sept
il habite au septième (étage)
il est arrivé (le) septième
une part d'un septième
échelle au vingt-cinq millième

NUMBERS

eighth
ninth
tenth
eleventh
twelfth
thirteenth
fourteenth
fifteenth
sixteenth
seventeenth
eighteenth
nineteenth
twentieth
twenty-first
twenty-second
thirtieth
hundredth
hundred-and-first
thousandth

Fractions etc

a half
a third
two thirds
a quarter
a fifth
(nought) point five, 0.5
three point four, 3.4
ten per cent
a hundred per cent

Examples

he lives at number 10
it's in chapter 7
on page 7
he lives on the 7th floor
he came in 7th
a share of one seventh
scale one to twenty-five
thousand

L'HEURE

THE TIME

quelle heure est-il?	*what time is it?*
il est ...	*it's ...*
minuit	midnight
une heure (du matin)	one o'clock (in the morning), one (a.m.)
une heure cinq	five past one
une heure dix	ten past one
une heure et quart	a quarter past one, one fifteen
une heure vingt-cinq	twenty-five past one, one twenty-five
une heure et demie, une heure trente	half past one, one thirty
une heure trente-cinq, deux heures moins vingt-cinq	twenty-five to two, one thirty-five
deux heures moins vingt, une heure quarante	twenty to two, one forty
deux heures moins le quart, une heure quarante-cinq	a quarter to two, one forty-five
deux heures moins dix, une heure cinquante	ten to two, one fifty
midi	twelve o'clock, midday, noon
deux heures (de l'après-midi)	two o'clock (in the afternoon), two (p.m.)
sept heures (du soir)	seven o'clock (in the evening), seven (p.m.)
à quelle heure?	*at what time?*
à minuit	at midnight
à sept heures	at seven o'clock
dans vingt minutes	in twenty minutes
il y a quinze minutes	fifteen minutes ago